Contemporary American Literature

Contemporary American Literature

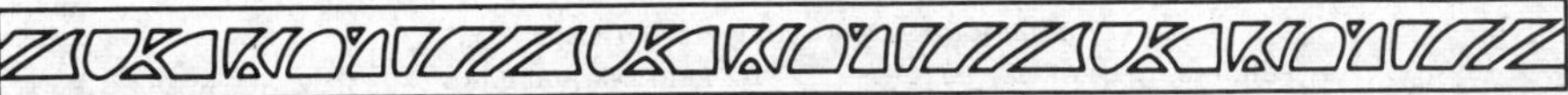

Edited by

George Perkins
PROFESSOR OF ENGLISH
EASTERN MICHIGAN UNIVERSITY

and

Barbara Perkins
MANAGING EDITOR
THE JOURNAL OF NARRATIVE TECHNIQUE
EASTERN MICHIGAN UNIVERSITY

FIRST EDITION
987654321

PUBLISHED IN THE UNITED STATES BY RANDOM HOUSE, INC., AND SIMULTANEOUSLY IN CANADA BY RANDOM HOUSE OF CANADA LIMITED, TORONTO.

LIBRARY OF CONGRESS CATALOGING IN PUBLICATION DATA

CONTEMPORARY AMERICAN LITERATURE.

BIBLIOGRAPHY.
INCLUDES INDEX.
1. AMERICAN LITERATURE—20TH CENTURY.
I. PERKINS, GEORGE B., 1930– II. PERKINS, BARBARA, 1933–
PS535.5.C66 1987 810'.8'0054 87-13051
ISBN 0-394-35432-X

MANUFACTURED IN THE UNITED STATES OF AMERICA

PAINTING ON COVER BY JANE FREILICHER. SUMMER VIEW (OIL ON CANVAS), 1979

COVER DESIGN: LORRAINE HOHMAN

JOHN BARTH "Lost in the Funhouse" from *Lost in the Funhouse,* by John Barth. Copyright © 1967 by Atlantic Monthly Company. Reprinted by permission of Doubleday & Company, Inc.

DONALD BARTHELME "How I Write My Songs," Copyright © 1978 by Donald Barthelme. First published in *The New Yorker.* Reprinted by permission of International Creative Management.

ANN BEATTIE "Shifting" from *Secrets and Surprises,* by Ann Beattie. Copyright © 1976, 1977, 1978 by Ann Beattie. Reprinted by permission of Random House, Inc.

SAUL BELLOW "Looking for Mr. Green" from *Mosby's Memoirs,* by Saul Bellow. Copyright 1951 by Saul Bellow. Copyright renewed © 1979 by Saul Bellow. Reprinted by permission of Viking Penguin, Inc.

JOHN BERRYMAN "The Ball Poem" and "The Moon and the Night and the Men" from *Short Poems,* by John Berryman. Copyright © 1948 by John Berryman. Reprinted by permission of Farrar, Straus and Giroux, Inc. "Dream Songs" 1, 4, 14, 29, 76, 145, 153, 384, 385 from *The Dream Songs,* by John Berryman. Copyright © 1965, 1966, 1967, 1968, 1969 by John Berryman. Reprinted by permission of Farrar, Straus and Giroux, Inc.

ELIZABETH BISHOP "The Fish," "At the Fishhouses," "Questions of Travel," "The Armadillo," "Sestina," "Crusoe in England," "The Moose," "Poem," "One Art," and "North Haven" from *The Complete Poems 1927–1979,* by Elizabeth Bishop. Copyright © 1947, 1956, 1971, 1972, 1976, 1979 by Elizabeth Bishop. "At the Fishhouses," "Questions of Travel," "The Armadillo," "Crusoe in England," "The Moose," "Poem," and "One Art" originally appeared in *The New Yorker.* Reprinted by permission of Farrar, Straus and Giroux, Inc.

ROBERT BLY "Driving to Town Late to Mail a Letter," "Driving toward the Lac Qui Parle River," "In a Train," and "Watering the Horse" from *Silence in the Snowy Fields* (Wesleyan University Press, 1962). Copyright © 1962 by Robert Bly and reprinted with his permission. "Fishing on a Lake at Night" from *This Tree Will Be Here for a Thousand Years* (Harper & Row, Publishers, 1981). Copyright © 1981 by Robert Bly and reprinted with his permission. "Looking at New Fallen Snow from a Train" from *The Light Around the Body* by Robert Bly. Copyright © 1966 by Robert Bly. Reprinted by permission of Harper & Row, Publishers, Inc. "The Executive's Death" from *Selected Poems,* by Robert Bly. Copyright © 1960 by Robert Bly. Reprinted by permission of Harper & Row, Publishers, Inc. "Snowbanks North of the House" by Robert Bly Copyright © 1975 by World Poetry, Incorporated, from the book *The Man in the Black Coat Turns.* Reprinted by permission of Doubleday & Company, Inc.

GWENDOLYN BROOKS "a song in the front yard," "The Lovers of the Poor," and "We Real Cool" from *Selected Poems,* by Gwendolyn Brooks. Copyright © 1944, 1945, 1949, 1959, 1960, 1963 by Gwendolyn Brooks Blakely. Reprinted by permission of the author. "Horses Graze" from *Beckonings,* by Gwendolyn Brooks. Copyright © 1975 by Gwendolyn Brooks. Reprinted by permission of Broadside Press.

RAYMOND CARVER "A Small Good Thing" and "Cathedral" from *Cathedral,* by Raymond Carver. Copyright © 1981, 1982, 1983 by Raymond Carver. Reprinted by permission of Alfred A. Knopf, Inc.

JOHN CHEEVER "The Enormous Radio" and "The Swimmer" from *The Stories of John Cheever.* Copyright © 1978 by John Cheever. Reprinted by permission of Alfred A. Knopf, Inc.

AMY CLAMPITT "The Kingfisher," copyright © 1983 by Amy Clampitt; "The Woodlot," copyright © 1982 by Amy Clampitt; reprinted from *The Kingfisher,* by Amy Clampitt, by permission of Alfred A. Knopf, Inc. "The Reedbeds of Hackensack" and "Time" from *What the Light Was Like,* by Amy Clampitt. Copyright © 1985 by Amy Clampitt. Reprinted by permission of Alfred A. Knopf, Inc.

ROBERT COOVER "The Gingerbread House" from *Pricksongs & Descants,* by Robert Coover. Copyright © 1969 by Robert Coover. Reprinted by permission of the publisher, E. P. Dutton, a division of New American Library.

ROBERT CREELEY "For Fear," "I Know a Man," and "The Rain" from *For Love: Poems 1950–1960.* Copyright © 1962 Robert Creeley. Reprinted with the permission of Charles Scribner's Sons. "I Keep to Myself Such Measures . . . ," "One Way," and "The Rhythm" from *The Collected Poems of Robert Creeley,* © 1983 The Regents of the University of California. Reprinted by permission of the publisher, University of California Press.

JAMES DICKEY "Cherrylog Road," copyright © 1963 by James Dickey. Reprinted from *Helmets* by permission of Wesleyan University Press. This poem first appeared in *The New Yorker.* "The Hospital Window," copyright © 1962 by James Dickey. Reprinted from *Drowning with Others* by permission of Wesleyan University Press. This poem first appeared in *Poetry.* "The Lifeguard," copyright © 1961 by James Dickey. Reprinted from *Drowning with Others* by permission of Wesleyan University Press. This poem first appeared in *The New Yorker.* "The Shark's Parlor," copyright © 1965 by James Dickey. Reprinted from *Buckdancer's Choice* by permission of Wesleyan University Press. This poem first appeared in *The New Yorker.*

E. L. DOCTOROW "The Writer in the Family" from *The Lives of Poets,* by E. L. Doctorow. Copyright © 1984 by E. L. Doctorow. Reprinted by permission of Random House, Inc.

RITA DOVE "Champagne" and "Ö" are reprinted from *The Yellow House on the Corner* by permission of Carnegie-Mellon University Press. Copyright © 1980 by Rita Dove. "Dusting" and "Roast Possum" are reprinted from *Thomas and Beulah* by permission of Carnegie-Mellon University Press. Copyright © 1983 by Rita Dove.

NORMAN DUBIE "Danse Macabre" and "Lamentations" are reprinted from *The Springhouse: Poems,* by Norman Dubie, by permission of W. W. Norton & Company, Inc. Copyright © 1986 by Norman Dubie. "Elizabeth's War with the Christmas Bear: 1601" and "The Fox Who Watched for the Midnight Sun" are reprinted from *Selected and New Poems,* by Norman Dubie, by permission of W. W. Norton & Company, Inc. Copyright © 1983 by Norman Dubie. "Norway" first appeared in *The New Yorker,* copyright © 1977 by The New Yorker Magazine, Inc., and is reprinted by permission of the author.

RALPH ELLISON "King of the Bingo Game." Reprinted by permission of William Morris Agency, Inc., on behalf of the author; copyright © 1944 by Ralph Ellison.

ROBERT FRANCIS "Apple Peeler" and "Pitcher," copyrights © 1953 by Robert Francis. "Cold," copyright © 1954 by Robert Francis. "Epitaph" and "Three Darks Come Down Together," copyrights © 1959 by Robert Francis. "The Orb Weaver," copyright © 1946 by Robert Francis. All above reprinted from *The Orb Weaver* by permission of Wesleyan University Press. "Hide-and-Seek" and "Like Ghosts of Eagles" from *Robert Francis Collected Poems, 1936–1976* (Amherst: University of Massachusetts Press, 1976), copyright © 1946, 1973 by Robert Francis.

WILLIAM GADDIS From *Carpenter's Gothic,* by William Gaddis. Copyright © William Gaddis, 1985. Reprinted by permission of Viking Penguin, Inc.

ISABELLA GARDNER "In the Museum," "Letter from Slough Pond," "Part of the Darkness," and "Summers Ago," copyright © 1980 by Isabella Gardner. Reprinted from *That Was Then: New and Selected Poems,* by Isabella Gardner, with the permission of BOA Editions, Ltd.

JOHN GARDNER "Redemption," copyright © 1977 by John Gardner. Reprinted from *The Art of Living and Other Stories,* by John Gardner, by permission of Alfred A. Knopf, Inc.

ALLEN GINSBERG "America," copyright © 1956, 1959 by Allen Ginsberg; "A Supermarket in California," "Howl," and "Sunflower Sutra," copyrights © 1955 by Allen Ginsberg; "Fourth Floor, Dawn, Up All Night Writing Letters," copyright © 1980 by Allen Ginsberg; all reprinted from *Collected Poems: 1947–1980,* by Allen Ginsberg, by permission of Harper & Row, Publishers, Inc.

LOUISE GLÜCK "Brooding Likeness," copyright © 1985 by Louise Glück. From *The Triumph of Achilles* by Louise Glück, published by The Ecco Press in 1985. "Lamentations," "Palais des Arts," and "The Garden," copyright © 1980 by Louise Glück. From *Descending Figure* by Louise Glück, published by The Ecco Press in 1980. "Poem" and "The School Children," copyright © 1975 by Louise Glück. From *The House on Marshland* by Louise Glück, published by The Ecco Press in 1975. All reprinted by permission.

GAIL GODWIN "Dream Children." Copyright © 1976 by Gail Godwin. Reprinted from *Dream Children,* by Gail Godwin, by permission of Alfred A. Knopf, Inc.

ALBERT GOLDBARTH "A History of Civilization" and "The Form and Function of the Novel" are reprinted from *Original Light,* copyright © 1973, 1974, 1976, 1980, 1981, 1983 by Albert Goldbarth, with the permission of Ontario Review Press. "Poem Whose Last Sentence Is 17 Syllables," "Reading In," and "The Elements" are reprinted from *Arts & Sciences,* copyright © 1983, 1984, 1985, 1986 by Albert Goldbarth, with the permission of Ontario Review Press.

PHILIP LEVINE "Heaven," copyright © 1966 by Philip Levine. Reprinted from *Not This Pig* by permission of Wesleyan University Press. "One for the Rose," "They Feed They Lion," and "You Can Have It" from *Selected Poems* by Philip Levine. Copyright © 1984 Philip Levine. Reprinted with the permission of Atheneum Publishers, Inc.

ROBERT LOWELL "After the Surprising Conversion," "Colloquy in Black Rock," and "In Memory of Arthur Winslow" from *Lord Weary's Castle* by Robert Lowell. Copyright 1946, 1974 by Robert Lowell. Reprinted by permission of Harcourt Brace Jovanovich, Inc. "Epilogue" and "Flight" from *Day by Day* by Robert Lowell. Copyright © 1975, 1976, 1977 by Robert Lowell. Reprinted by permission of Farrar, Straus and Giroux, Inc. "For the Union Dead," "History," "Home after Three Months Away," "Man and Wife," "Memories of West Street and Lepke," "Obit," "Reading Myself," "Robert Frost," "Sailing Home from Rapallo," "Skunk Hour," "The March 1," "The Mouth of the Hudson," "The Neo-Classical Urn," "To Speak of Woe That Is in Marriage," "Waking in the Blue," and "Watchmaker God" from *Selected Poems,* by Robert Lowell. Copyright © 1944, 1946, 1947, 1950, 1951, 1956, 1959, 1960, 1961, 1962, 1963, 1964, 1965, 1966, 1967, 1968, 1969, 1970, 1973, 1976 by Robert Lowell. Copyright renewed © 1972, 1974, 1975 by Robert Lowell. Reprinted by permission of Farrar, Straus and Giroux, Inc. "Her Dead Brother," copyright 1947, 1975 by Robert Lowell. Reprinted from his volume *The Mills of the Kavanaughs* by permission of Harcourt Brace Jovanovich, Inc.

NORMAN MAILER "The Man Who Studied Yoga" from *Advertisements for Myself,* by Norman Mailer. © 1959 by Norman Mailer. Reprinted by permission of the author and the author's agents, Scott Meredith Literary Agency, Inc., 845 Third Avenue, New York, New York 10022.

BERNARD MALAMUD "The Mourners" from *The Magic Barrel,* by Bernard Malamud. Copyright 1955, copyright renewed © 1983 by Bernard Malamud. Reprinted by permission of Farrar, Straus and Giroux, Inc.

BOBBIE ANN MASON "Third Monday" from *Shiloh and Other Stories,* by Bobbie Ann Mason. Originally appeared in *The New Yorker.* Copyright © 1982 by Bobbie Ann Mason. Reprinted by permission of Harper & Row, Publishers, Inc.

JAMES MERRILL "A Timepiece" from *The Country of a Thousand Years of Peace and Other Poems* by James Merrill. Copyright © 1970 James Merrill. "Charles on Fire," "Days of 1964," "Lost in Translation," "Matinees," "The Broken Home," "The Octopus," and "Yánnina" from *The First Nine: Poems 1946–1979,* by James Merrill. Copyright © 1982 James Merrill. "Samos" from *The Changing Light at Sandover,* by James Merrill. Copyright © 1982 James Merrill. All reprinted with the permission of Atheneum Publishers, Inc.

W. S. MERWIN "A Door" from *Writing to an Unfinished Accompaniment,* by W. S. Merwin. Copyright © 1973 W. S. Merwin. "For the Anniversary of My Death" and "The Last One" from *The Lice,* by W. S. Merwin. Copyright © 1967 W. S. Merwin. "Grandmother and Grandson" and "The Drunk in the Furnace" from *The First Four Books of Poems,* by W. S. Merwin. Copyright © 1975 W. S. Merwin. "The Fields" from *Opening the Hand,* by W. S. Merwin. Copyright © 1983 W. S. Merwin. "Vision" and "Trees" from *The Compass Flower,* by W. S. Merwin. Copyright © 1977 W. S. Merwin. All reprinted with the permission of Atheneum Publishers, Inc.

ARTHUR MILLER "Death of a Salesman," copyright 1949, copyright renewed © 1977 by Arthur Miller. Reprinted by permission of Viking Penguin, Inc.

TONI MORRISON "1922" from *Sula,* by Toni Morrison. Copyright © 1973 by Toni Morrison. Reprinted by permission of Alfred A. Knopf, Inc.

VLADIMIR NABOKOV "First Love" from *Speak, Memory,* by Vladimir Nabokov. Copyright 1947, 1948, 1949, 1950, 1951 by Vladimir Nabokov. © 1960, 1966 by Vladimir Nabokov. Reprinted by permission of Véra Nabokov.

HOWARD NEMEROV "Figures of Thought," "The Goose Fish," "The Sanctuary," "The Vacuum," "The Western Approaches," and "Thirtieth Anniversary Report of the Class of '41" from *The Collected Poems of Howard Nemerov* (University of Chicago Press, 1977). © 1977 by Howard Nemerov.

JOYCE CAROL OATES "The Seasons" from *Raven's Wing,* by Joyce Carol Oates. Copyright © 1986 by The Ontario Review, Inc. Reprinted by permission of the publisher, E. P. Dutton, a division of NAL Penguin, Inc.

TIM O'BRIEN "Night March" from *Going After Cacciato,* by Tim O'Brien. Copyright © 1978 by Tim O'Brien. Reprinted by permission of Delacorte Press/Seymour Lawrence.

FLANNERY O'CONNOR "Good Country People" from *A Good Man Is Hard to Find and Other Stories,* by Flannery O'Connor. Copyright 1955 by Flannery O'Connor; renewed 1983 by Regina O'Connor. Reprinted by permission of Harcourt Brace Jovanovich, Inc.

FRANK O'HARA "A Step Away from Them," "Steps," and "The Day Lady Died" from *Lunch Poems,* by Frank O'Hara. Copyright © 1964 by Frank O'Hara. Reprinted by permission of City Lights Books. "A True Account of Talking to the Sun at Fire Island," "Ave Maria," "To My Dead Father," and "Why I am Not a Painter" from *The Collected Poems of Frank O'Hara,* edited by Donald Allen. Copyright © 1971 by Maureen Granville-Smith, Administratrix of the Estate of Frank O'Hara. Reprinted by permission of Alfred A. Knopf, Inc. "To the Film Industry in Crisis," copyright © 1957 by Frank O'Hara. Reprinted by permission of Maureen Granville-Smith and Grove Press.

CHARLES OLSON "I, Maximus of Gloucester, to You," "Maximus to Gloucester, Letter 27 (withheld)," and "The Songs of Maximus: Song 3" from *The Maximus Poems,* by Charles Olson. © 1983 The Regents of the University of California. Reprinted by permission of the publisher, University of California Press.

CYNTHIA OZICK "The Shawl," copyright © 1980 by Cynthia Ozick. Reprinted by permission of Cynthia Ozick and her agents Raines & Raines, 71 Park Avenue, New York, New York 10016. First published in *The New Yorker.*

JAYNE ANNE PHILLIPS "The Heavenly Animal" from *Black Tickets,* by Jayne Anne Phillips. Copyright © 1979 by Jayne Anne Phillips. Reprinted by permission of Delacorte Press/Seymour Lawrence.

ROBERT PINSKY "Dying" and "The Figured Wheel," copyright © 1984 by Robert Pinsky, from *History of My Heart,* by Robert Pinsky, published by The Ecco Press in 1984. Reprinted by permission. "Memorial" and "Local Politics" from *An Explanation of America,* by Robert Pinsky. Copyright © 1979 by Princeton University Press. ("Memorial" first appeared in *The Nation;* "Local Politics" first appeared in *Poetry.*) Reprinted with the permission of Princeton University Press.

SYLVIA PLATH "Blackberrying," copyright © 1962 by Ted Hughes; "Black Rook in Rainy Weather," copyright © 1960 by the Estate of Sylvia Plath; "Daddy," "Death & Co.," "Lady Lazarus," "Mystic," "The Applicant," and "The Arrival of the Bee Box," copyright © 1963 by Ted Hughes; "Morning Song" and "The Rival," copyright © 1961 by Ted Hughes; "Sheep in Fog," copyright © 1965 by the Estate of Sylvia Plath. All reprinted from *The Collected Poems of Sylvia Plath,* edited by Ted Hughes, by permission of Harper & Row, Publishers, Inc. "The Colossus," copyright © 1961 by Sylvia Plath. Reprinted from *The Colossus and Other Poems,* by Sylvia Plath, by permission of Alfred A. Knopf, Inc.

STANLEY PLUMLY "Out-of-the-Body Travel" and "For Esther," copyright © 1974, 1975, 1976 by Stanley Plumly, from *Out-of-the-Body Travel,* by Stanley Plumly, published by The Ecco Press in 1977. "My Mother's Feet," "Snowing, Sometimes," and "Waders and Swimmers," copyright © 1983 by Stanley Plumly, from *Summer Celestial,* by Stanley Plumly, published by The Ecco Press in 1983. All reprinted by permission.

THOMAS PYNCHON "Entropy" from *Slow Learner: Early Stories,* by Thomas Pynchon. Copyright © 1960 by Thomas Pynchon. First appeared in *The Kenyon Review.* Reprinted by permission of Little, Brown and Company.

DAVID RABE "Sticks and Bones," copyright © 1969, 1972, 1973, 1987 by David Rabe. Reprinted by permission of Viking Penguin, Inc. Caution: Professionals and amateurs are hereby warned that "Sticks and Bones," being fully protected under the copyright laws of the United States of America, the British Commonwealth, including the Dominion of Canada, and all other countries of the International Copyright Union and the Universal Copyright Convention, is subject to royalty. All rights, including professional, amateur, motion picture, recitation, lecturing, public reading, radio and television broadcasting, and the rights of translation into foreign languages, are strictly reserved. Particular emphasis is laid on the question of readings, permission for which must be secured from the author's agent in writing. The stock and amateur acting rights of "Sticks and Bones" are controlled exclusively by Samuel French, Inc., 45 West 25th Street, New York,

New York 10010, without whose permission in writing no performance of it may be made. Inquiries concerning all other rights should be addressed to Ellen Neuwald Agency, Inc., 905 West End Avenue, New York, New York 10025.

ADRIENNE RICH "Aunt Jennifer's Tigers," "Diving into the Wreck," "Face to Face," "For the Dead," "For the Record," "Integrity," "Necessities of Life," "The Diamond Cutters," "The Middle-aged," "The Trees," and "Upper Broadway" are reprinted from *The Fact of a Doorframe: Poems Selected and New, 1950–1984,* by Adrienne Rich, by permission of W. W. Norton and Company, Inc. Copyright © 1984 by Adrienne Rich. Copyright © 1975, 1978 by W. W. Norton & Company, Inc. Copyright © 1981 by Adrienne Rich.

THEODORE ROETHKE "Elegy for Jane," copyright 1950 by Theodore Roethke; "I Knew a Woman," copyright 1954 by Theodore Roethke; "In a Dark Time," copyright © 1960 by Beatrice Roethke as Administratrix of the Estate of Theodore Roethke; "Meditations of an Old Woman: Fourth Meditation," copyright © 1958 by Theodore Roethke; "My Papa's Waltz," copyright 1942 by Hearst Magazines, Inc.; "Night Crow," copyright 1944 by Saturday Review Association; "Open House," copyright 1941 by Theodore Roethke; "The Far Field," copyright © 1962 by Beatrice Roethke as Administratrix of the Estate of Theodore Roethke; "The Pike" and "Wish for a Young Wife," copyright © 1963 by Beatrice Roethke as Administratrix of the Estate of Theodore Roethke; "The Waking," copyright 1953 by Theodore Roethke. All reprinted from *The Collected Poems of Theodore Roethke* by permission of Doubleday & Company, Inc.

PHILIP ROTH "The Conversion of the Jews" from *Goodbye Columbus,* by Philip Roth. Copyright © 1959 by Philip Roth. Reprinted by permission of Houghton Mifflin Company.

ANNE SEXTON "All My Pretty Ones," "Letter Written on a Ferry While Crossing Long Island Sound," "The Truth the Dead Know," and "With Mercy for the Greedy" from *All My Pretty Ones,* by Anne Sexton. Copyright © 1962 by Anne Sexton. "Her Kind" and "The Farmer's Wife" from *To Bedlam and Part Way Back,* by Anne Sexton. Copyright © 1960 by Anne Sexton. "January 1st" from *Words for Dr. Y,* by Anne Sexton. Copyright © 1978 by Linda Gray Sexton and Loring Conant, Jr., Executors of the Will of Anne Sexton. All reprinted by permission of Houghton Mifflin Company.

SAM SHEPARD "True West," appearing in the collection *Seven Plays,* by Sam Shepard. Copyright © 1981 by Sam Shepard. Reprinted by permission of Bantam Books, Inc. All rights reserved.

LESLIE MARMON SILKO "Yellow Woman" from *Storyteller,* copyright © 1973 by Leslie Marmon Silko. Reprinted by permission of the author.

CHARLES SIMIC "A Wall," "Bestiary for the Fingers of My Right Hand," "Charon's Cosmology," "Euclid Avenue," "Fear," "Fork," "My Weariness of Epic Proportions," and "Prodigy" are reprinted from *Selected Poems 1963–1983* by Charles Simic, copyright © 1971, 1974, 1977, 1980, 1982 by Charles Simic, by permission of George Braziller, Inc., New York.

LOUIS SIMPSON "American Poetry," copyright © 1963 by Louis Simpson. Reprinted from *At the End of the Open Road,* by Louis Simpson, by permission of Wesleyan University Press. "Carentan O Carentan," copyright © 1949 by Louis Simpson, and "To the Western World," copyright © 1957, reprinted from *A Dream of Governors,* by Louis Simpson, by permission of Wesleyan University Press. "Why Do You Write about Russia?" from *Caviare at the Funeral,* by Louis Simpson, copyright © 1980 by Louis Simpson. Reprinted with the permission of the publisher, Franklin Watts, Inc.

ISAAC BASHEVIS SINGER "Gimpel the Fool" from *A Treasury of Yiddish Stories,* edited by Irving Howe and Eliezer Greenberg. Copyright © 1953, 1954 by The Viking Press, Inc. Copyright renewed © 1982 by Irving Howe and Eva Greenberg. Reprinted by permission of Viking Penguin, Inc.

DAVE SMITH "Cumberland Station" and "On a Field Trip at Fredericksburg" from *Cumberland Station* (University of Illinois Press, 1976). © 1975 Dave Smith. Originally appeared in *The New Yorker.* "Elegy in an Abandoned Boatyard" from *Dream Flights* (University of Illinois Press, 1981). © 1980 Dave Smith. Originally appeared in *The New Yorker.* "Night Fishing for Blues" from *Cumberland Station,* copyright © 1971, 1973, 1974, 1975, 1976 by Dave Smith, originally appeared in *Shenandoah.* All reprinted by permission of the author and the publisher, University of Illinois Press. "The Chesapeake and Ohio Canal," copyright © 1985 by Dave Smith, and "In the House of the Judge," copyright © 1982 by Dave Smith (originally appeared in *The New*

Yorker) are reprinted from *The Roundhouse Voices,* by Dave Smith, by permission of Harper & Row, Publishers, Inc. "The Roundhouse Voices" from *Goshawk, Antelope* (University of Illinois Press, 1979). © 1979 Dave Smith. Originally appeared in *The New Yorker.*

W. D. SNODGRASS "April Inventory" and "Heart's Needle 6" from *Heart's Needle,* by W. D. Snodgrass. Copyright © 1959 by William Snodgrass. Reprinted by permission of Alfred A. Knopf, Inc. "The Examination" from *After Experience,* copyright © 1958, 1959, 1960, 1961, 1962, 1963, 1964, 1965, 1966, 1967, 1968 by W. D. Snodgrass. Reprinted by permission of the author.

GARY SNYDER "Axe Handles" from *Axe Handles,* copyright © 1983 by Gary Snyder. Published by North Point Press and reprinted by permission. All rights reserved. "Hay for the Horses," "Riprap," and "The Late Snow & Lumber Strike of the Summer of Fifty-four," copyright © 1966 by Gary Snyder and reprinted by permission of the author. "Not Leaving the House" from *Regarding Wave,* by Gary Snyder, copyright © 1970 by Gary Snyder; "this poem is for bear" from *Myths and Texts,* by Gary Snyder, copyright © 1960, 1978 by Gary Snyder; and "Vapor Trails" from *The Back Country,* by Gary Snyder, copyright © 1959 by Gary Snyder, are reprinted by permission of New Directions Publishing Company.

WILLIAM STAFFORD "Before the Big Storm," copyright 1951 by William Stafford; "Judgments," copyright © 1964 by William Stafford; "One Home," copyright © 1960 by William Stafford; and "Traveling through the Dark," copyright © 1960 by William Stafford, are reprinted from *Stories That Could Be True: New and Collected Poems,* by William Stafford, by permission of Harper & Row, Publishers, Inc. "The Farm on the Great Plains," copyright © 1960 by William Stafford. Reprinted from *The Rescued Year,* by William Stafford, by permission of Harper & Row, Publishers, Inc. "Things That Happen Where There Aren't Any People," copyright © 1980 by William Stafford. Reprinted from *Things That Happen Where There Aren't Any People,* by William Stafford, with the permission of BOA Editions, Ltd.

MARK STRAND "Always," copyright © 1983 by Mark Strand. Reprinted by permission of the author. "A Morning," "Keeping Things Whole," "My Mother on an Evening in Late Summer," "Nights in Hackett's Cove," "Shooting Whales," "The Coming of Light," "The Prediction," and "Where Are the Waters of Childhood?" from *Selected Poems,* by Mark Strand, copyright © 1980 Mark Strand. Reprinted with the permission of Atheneum Publishers, Inc.

ELIZABETH TALLENT "Ice" from *In Constant Flight,* by Elizabeth Tallent. Copyright © 1983 by Elizabeth Tallent. Reprinted by permission of Alfred A. Knopf, Inc.

PETER TAYLOR "Porte Cochere" from *The Old Forest and Other Stories,* by Peter Taylor. Copyright © 1944, 1945, 1947, 1949, 1951, 1958, 1959, 1979, 1981, 1985 by Peter Taylor. Reprinted by permission of Doubleday & Company, Inc.

ANNE TYLER "Average Waves in Unprotected Waters," copyright © 1977 by Anne Tyler. Originally published in *The New Yorker.* Reprinted by permission of Russell & Volkening, Inc., as agents for the author.

JOHN UPDIKE "A & P," copyright © 1962 by John Updike. Reprinted from *Pigeon Feathers and Other Stories,* by John Updike, by permission of Alfred A. Knopf, Inc. "Separating," copyright © 1975 by John Updike. Reprinted from *Problems and Other Stories,* by John Updike, by permission of Alfred A. Knopf, Inc.

KURT VONNEGUT "Report on the Barnhouse Effect" from *Welcome to the Monkey House,* by Kurt Vonnegut, Jr. Copyright © 1950 by Kurt Vonnegut, Jr. Originally published in *Collier's.* Reprinted by permission of Delacorte Press/Seymour Lawrence.

ALICE WALKER "Everyday Use," copyright © 1973 by Alice Walker. Reprinted from her volume *In Love and Trouble* by permission of Harcourt Brace Jovanovich, Inc.

ROBERT PENN WARREN "Blow, West Wind," "Founding Fathers, Early-Nineteenth-Century Style, Southeast U.S.A.," "History Among the Rocks," "Masts at Dawn," and "Mortal Limit" from *New and Selected Poems 1923–1985,* by Robert Penn Warren. Copyright © 1985 by Robert Penn Warren. Reprinted by permission of Random House, Inc.

EUDORA WELTY "Livvie," copyright 1942, 1970 by Eudora Welty. Reprinted from her volume *The Wide Net and Other Stories* by permission of Harcourt Brace Jovanovich, Inc. "Why I Live at the P.O.," copyright 1941, 1969 by Eudora Welty. Reprinted from her volume *A Curtain of Green and Other Stories* by permission of Harcourt Brace Jovanovich, Inc.

Preface

Contemporary American Literature is both an anthology and a history. As an anthology, it presents selections from about a hundred writers judged to represent the best of their time. As a history, it presents overviews of the periods from 1945 to the 1960's and from the 1960's to the present, supplementing these with introductions to the work of each writer that serve in part to suggest connections between writers and the intellectual and social currents of their times. As both anthology and history, this work fills a need long apparent to students of American literature. The standard textbook treatments of American literature have for several decades divided their contents on the watershed years of the Civil War. But 120 years have passed since then, and much more has been published in the decades after World War II than in earlier post–Civil War years. Editors of anthologies who have strained, generally in their fat second volumes, to encompass all of American literature since 1865 have discovered that the task becomes more nearly impossible with each succeeding edition. Meanwhile, teachers of classes in contemporary American literature have had to make do with the tail ends of huge anthologies, or else compile their own representative selections as best they can from numerous separate paperbacks.

In compiling this volume, we have taken as our model *The American Tradition in Literature*. We have chosen writers primarily for their literary value as found in the best fiction, poetry, and drama, considering other forms of literature—essays, letters, criticism, history, sociology, current affairs, and the literature of the popular press—to be generally not to our purpose. To writers we consider more important than others we have tried to give more space, but for all whom we include we have tried to provide a solid, representative sample of their work. Other considerations have also guided us, however. Writers whose best work is in the novel have proven a challenge that we have tried to meet by selecting from their good short fiction and directing attention to their novels in headnotes; attempting to avoid the presentation of excerpts, we have only rarely selected passages from novels, and then almost always passages that the writer had earlier printed in self-contained form. Considerations of history, of trends in American writing, and of literary influence have prompted our inclusion of some writers. Finally, because we have wanted to emphasize our literature as a continual process of development, we have included some younger writers not yet fully established, choosing from among many with fine claims for attention in the future.

Our aim has been to define the canon of American literature for the period. We have been guided as far as possible by the consensus of current critical thought, making every effort to suppress our own idiosyncratic opinions and resist the sometimes powerful but equally idiosyncratic arguments of others in favor of or against this work, this writer, or that school of writers. For perhaps half the writers in this volume, the consensus seems already firm, although continually under discussion, as may be observed in the contents of the second volume of *The American Tradition in Literature* (1985) and similar textbooks. Building on the achievement of that volume, we have taken and revised some of our author introductions from it; some of the selections also are duplicated from that volume, but all have been reconsidered in the context of this new work.

We have divided the decades since 1945 into two periods, each with its own general introduction: "American Literature from 1945 to the 1960's" and "American Literature in the 1960's and After." Within the section devoted to each period, we have created subsections devoted to fiction, drama, and poetry, finding this a more useful division than a strictly chronological progression of authors without consideration of their primary genres. Within each subsection, our arrangement is generally chronological, but we have sometimes forsaken the chronology of birth in order to present authors in an order dictated by the years of their greatest activity or influence. Since individual writers do not, of course, begin or cease to write by period dates imposed by critics and historians, some naturally override the bounds suggested by our divisions: some we have placed in the first period continue their work well into the second, and some we have placed in the second began in the first. Still, we have found the division useful, as the general introductions should make clear. Similarly, some of our writers began their careers before 1945; most noteworthy of these is William Carlos Williams. Williams, however, we have felt merited inclusion because of the impact of his later work and the tremendous rise of his influence within our period.

For each author, we have included a biographical, critical, and bibliographical introduction. A general bibliography at the end of the book provides sources of information beyond those included in the author headnotes. Our texts are those that in our opinion provide the best reading; sources that seem not to be obvious are given in headnotes or footnotes. Omissions of text are indicated by asterisks. Significant dates follow each selection: first publication in a book by the author is given in the right margin, preceded in some instances by the date of first serial publication; date of composition, if known and significant, appears in the left margin.

This book is the result of a long effort supported by many people and institutions. Steven Pensinger, Executive Editor at Random House, was quick to see the need and materially and spiritually encouraging. Cynthia Ward provided helpful guidance as developmental editor. Nancy Brooks maintained her fine tradition of excellent editorial work. Eastern Michigan University gave early support in the form of a research grant. The libraries of Eastern Michigan University and the University of Michigan supplied trustworthy texts.

We owe much to scholars who have helped define the canon of recent American literature. Their books are listed in our bibliographies, which also list guides to their work in scholarly journals. Many others have assisted directly, sometimes by their comments on the inclusions in the latter part of recent editions of *The American Tradition in Literature,* sometimes by comments that have helped us see recent literature more clearly in the context of our country's earlier tradition, and sometimes by responses to specific queries on plans for the present book. We wish to express our thanks particularly to the following: Alfred Bendixen, Barnard College;

Louis J. Budd, Duke University; Frank R. Cunningham, University of South Dakota; Robert DeMott, Ohio University; Richard F. Dietrich, University of South Florida; John Ditsky, University of Windsor; Thomas R. Edwards, Rutgers University; Clayton Eshleman, Eastern Michigan University; Kelley Griffith, University of North Carolina at Greensboro; William Harmon, University of North Carolina at Chapel Hill; William P. Kelly, Queens College; Hugh Luke, University of Nebraska; Sanford E. Marovitz, Kent State University; Geoffrey Rans, University of Western Ontario; John M. Reilly, State University of New York at Albany; Louis D. Rubin, Jr., University of North Carolina at Chapel Hill; Roger Sale, University of Washington; Joseph Schwartz, Marquette University; John Slatin, University of Texas, Austin; Werner Sollors, Harvard University; W. J. Stuckey, Purdue University; Linda Wagner-Martin, Michigan State University; T. D. Young, Vanderbilt University; and Robert Lee Zimmerman, Florida Southern College.

GEORGE PERKINS
BARBARA PERKINS

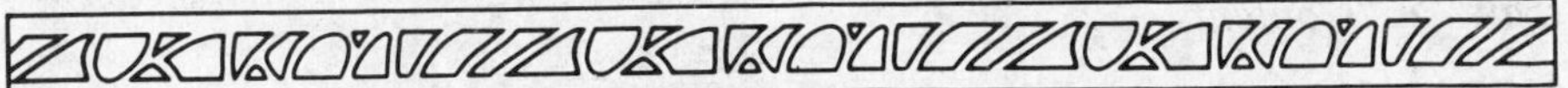

Contents

Contemporary American Literature

American Literature from 1945 to the 1960's

When Americans resumed their peacetime lives at the end of World War II, the majority began by picking up the traditions of the past. The year 1945 had brought an end not only to a war fought on a massive scale both in Europe and Asia, but also to two and a half decades of economic and social turmoil, as World War I was followed first by the frenzied 1920's—with prohibition, voting rights for women, speakeasies, economic boom and collapse—and then by the Great Depression of the 1930's—with the dust bowl, soup lines, the New Deal, and a war in Spain that tested ideologies, weapons, and modes of propaganda for the bigger war to follow. In 1945 it seemed that not just the Second World War but an era had come to a close. A world witness to extraordinary expansion of the technological means to kill between 1914 and 1945, culminating in the atomic horror of Hiroshima and Nagasaki, seemed unlikely to engage soon again in mass destruction. In the new prosperity of peace, war workers turned to the production of Buicks, Fords, Plymouths, and Studebakers on assembly lines converted from the production of tanks and bombers. Soldiers and their sweethearts at home or their war-brides from abroad married and settled down. On Long Island, New York, the mass-produced houses of Levittown met a demand that had been accumulating throughout the depression and war years, and served as models for planned suburban communities down to the present. Many returning veterans, their educational expenses paid by the G.I. Bill, swelled the ranks of college students, changing forever by their presence a university milieu that had previously belonged to the privileged few. An education, a family, a good job, a house, and a car—these ingredients of the American dream, the concrete embodiments of the "life, liberty, and the pursuit of happiness" asserted in the Declaration of Independence as all men's rights, had for many been held too long in abeyance.

In literature, the years immediately after 1945 produced strong evidence of the strength of the American conservative tradition—honor displayed toward established forms and values—through the continued dominance of authors, books, and forms already accepted as important in the two decades prior to the end of the war. Less visible at first was evidence of the American revolutionary tradition—independence asserted through subversion of accepted forms and values—but this, too, was soon to produce its memorable literature.

BACKGROUNDS: THE SHADOWS OF GIANTS

A young American writing fiction between 1945 and 1955 was inevitably in the shadow of great writers, mostly men, who were still alive and still productive, but whose best work, for the most part, was behind them. William Faulkner was at the height of his fame, much more widely acclaimed after the publication of *The Portable Faulkner* in 1946 than he had been during the time, considerably earlier, when he had first published *The Sound and the Fury* (1929), *As I Lay Dying* (1930), and many of his other best fictions. Ernest Hemingway was a public figure, sport-fishing in the Caribbean, big-game hunting in Montana, surviving airplane crashes in Africa, publishing distinguished fiction in mass market magazines (*The Old Man and the Sea* appeared first in *Life,* in 1952), and still remembered through *A Farewell to Arms* (1929) and *For Whom the Bell Tolls* (1940), even after this most recent conflict, as one of the best war writers of all time. Both Hemingway and Faulkner were awarded Nobel Prizes for literature in the first decade after the war; in the United States, with the distribution of cheap, mass-market paperback books through neighborhood drugstores and newsstands a relatively new phenomenon, both were everywhere available to readers without the funds, or hesitant to spend them, for new novels in hard covers. Other long-established writers of fiction, still alive, still active, and only slightly less eminent, included Katherine Anne Porter, whose stories and short novels—*Flowering Judas* (1930), *Noon Wine* (1937), and *Pale Horse, Pale Rider* (1939)—had established her reputation, and who was still to publish one of the fine novels of the 1960's, *Ship of Fools* (1962); John Steinbeck, whose *The Grapes of Wrath* (1939) had gained almost immediate acceptance as a classic, and whose post-war work such as *East of Eden* (1952), though generally weaker, was immensely popular; John Dos Passos, whose trilogy *U.S.A.* (1930–1936) remains a landmark fiction of its time, and who used its methods as late as 1961 in *Midcentury;* and James T. Farrell, whose *Studs Lonigan* trilogy (1932–1935) remains a late and fine example of American naturalism. Living in Paris, and less active in the post-war period but still an important stimulus to the writing of American blacks, was Richard Wright, author of *Native Son* (1938) and *Black Boy* (1945).

For aspiring poets, the situation was similar, as major poets from the past, also mostly men, occupied positions of a seemingly unassailable eminence. Unrivaled in his combined authority as poet, critic, editor, and dramatist, T. S. Eliot was a London sage who even in the title he had chosen for his most influential essay, "Tradition and the Individual Talent," seemed to suggest mysteries daunting to the uninitiated or undereducated. Catapulted to international fame with the publication of *The Waste Land* in 1922, Eliot had as recently as 1943 completed his final masterwork, *Four Quartets.* Ezra Pound, along with Eliot largely responsible for the spirit of Modernism that dominated poetry in English between the wars, languished in an insane ward in St. Elizabeth's Hospital, Washington, D.C., for a dozen years after the war, under threat of trial for treason for his wartime efforts on behalf of Mussolini's fascism. Pound's poetry, nevertheless, remained an inspiration to younger writers, a number of whom paid him homage in pilgrimages to the hospital. Meanwhile, the appearance of *The Pisan Cantos* (1948) and other sections of his lifelong masterwork kept his poetic accomplishment and his theories of poetry continually in the public eye.

Celebrated alternatives to the learned, allusive, discontinuous styles of Eliot and Pound existed most prominently in the work of Robert Frost and W. H. Auden. Frost had long since gained fame for a powerful narrative and a lyric voice that successfully stretched colloquial New England speech patterns along a traditional iambic line, often with rhyme. A mastery first displayed in *A Boy's Will* (1913) and *North of Boston* (1914) remained as strong as ever in late poems, like "Directive" from *Steeple Bush* (1947), some of which were now overlaid with admonition as age passed on its wisdom to the young. Auden, much younger, had earned fame in England before the war, but had come to New York in 1939, carrying with him a reputation as a poet unmatched in his mastery of varied traditional forms. Until 1972, the year before his death, he remained a strong presence in America with a succession of books, giving to historians and sociologists a label for the post-war period with one of his titles, *The Age of Anxiety* (1948).

Less eminent, but established and still active, were Carl Sandburg, whose *Complete Poems* appeared in 1950; H. D. (Hilda Doolittle), remembered mostly for her early imagistic poems, with her wartime and post-war work yet to be appreciated; Robinson Jeffers, celebrated in the 1920's for a series of starkly naturalistic narrative poems and briefly in the limelight once again for his reworking of *Medea* (1946), which starred Judith Anderson in a famed Broadway production; Conrad Aiken, who published a *Collected Poems* in 1953 (and a much later *Collected Poems* in 1971); Archibald MacLeish, who won Pulitzer Prizes for poetry with *Collected Poems* (1952) and for drama with *J.B.: A Play in Verse* (1958); E. E. Cummings, celebrated for the fractured syntax and typographical experimentation in work collected for the post-war generation in *Poems 1923–1954* (1954); Marianne Moore, emerging from an earlier reputation for poetic strangeness as seen in her syllabic verse and anti-poetic subject matter when her *Collected Poems* of 1951 swept three major literary prizes, the Bollingen, the National Book Award, and the Pulitzer; John Crowe Ransom, prominent exponent of the New Criticism, whose *Selected Poems* appeared in 1945; Allen Tate, like Ransom a southerner and a strong voice for traditionalism in poetic practice as in life, whose *Poems 1922–1947* appeared in 1948; and Langston Hughes, spokesman for black attitudes and aspirations from *The Weary Blues* (1926) through and beyond *Montage of a Dream Deferred* (1951).

Among major poets of the first half of the twentieth century, Wallace Stevens and William Carlos Williams stand apart as writers who had accomplished much of their best work by 1945, but whose reputations had yet far to go before they would reach the heights readers and critics later assigned to them. Both carried on lifelong careers apart from poetry, Stevens as an insurance executive and Williams as a physician. The genius of Stevens, first evident in *Harmonium* (1923), was confirmed in *Ideas of Order* (1935) and subsequent volumes, culminating in *Collected Poems* (1954). His reputation among critics and his influence on younger poets has continued to grow in the decades since. Williams, however, was the poet who in the 1950's and after was to replace T. S. Eliot as the twentieth-century poet most admired and most emulated by younger writers serious about their craft. An early friend of Pound, he self-published his first book, *Poems* (1909), some years before books by Frost, Eliot, and Stevens had found their way into print, and he maintained a voluminous production of poems, essays, and fiction for forty years without extending his reputation much beyond his circle of friends and acquaintances. Aware that he was writing against the grain of the times, he maintained his faith, he says in his *Autobiography* (1951), that the world would one day turn his way (he had announced as early as 1932, in a letter to Kay Boyle, that "Eliot is finally and definitely dead—and his troop along with him"). Circumstances after the war, including the publication of his masterful *Paterson* (five books, and fragments of a sixth, 1946–1963), finally combined to thrust his work to the forefront of the period.

American drama as a native creation featuring plays strong enough to stand beside the best works from Europe had before 1945 depended largely on the writing of Eugene O'Neill. By 1945, he was in ill health, but plays written in the 1930's and not then produced continued to appear in the post-war period, including *The Iceman Cometh* (1946) and, three years after his death, his masterpiece, *Long Day's Journey into Night* (1956). Other strong dramatists with earlier reputations and continuing production included Maxwell Anderson, whose *Elizabeth the Queen* (1930) had established a high standard for American poetic drama and whose late *The Bad Seed* (1955) still ranks among the best of his approximately forty plays; Thornton Wilder, author of the frequently revived *Our Town* (1938) and *The Skin of Our Teeth* (1942), as well as *The Matchmaker* (1954); and Lillian Hellman, author of *The Little Foxes* (1939) and *Toys in the Attic* (1960).

THE NEW PROSE WRITERS: EXTENSIONS OF THE REALISTIC TRADITION

After hostilities ended in 1945, the war provided material for novelists, most of whom began by treating it in conventional works of direct report. Among these writers, Norman Mailer earned the earliest and, to date, the most enduring fame. Writing directly of combat in his first novel, he turned afterwards to other subjects and methods, and sustained for the next four decades a highly visible place before the public eye for both his writing and his personal life. A Harvard graduate, student of engineering and writing, he used his war experiences in the Pacific as the basis for *The Naked and the Dead* (1948), a wide-ranging narrative of physical and philosophical conflict. Although his next few novels did little to advance his reputation, they did not obscure the fact that his was a large talent, rooted in an intensely personal vision, and that his own best subject was himself—and the conflicts he perceived with other persons and with society. In *Advertisements for Myself* (1959), a collection of prose and verse, he boldly asserted the value of personality—at least his personality—providing early sanction to a self-centeredness so widespread in America by the 1970's that social observers began to speak of the "me generation." "The sour truth," he wrote in this book, "is that I am imprisoned with a perception which will settle for nothing less than making a revolution in the consciousness of our time." Early results of this vision were the satiric *An American Dream* (1965) and *Why Are We in Vietnam?* (1967), personal reactions to the tense American years in which they were written. Later, he inserted himself as a central actor, referred to in the third person as "Mailer," into books of reportage chronicling major public events of our time; of these, the finest is *Armies of the Night* (1968), significantly subtitled *History as a Novel, The Novel as History,* an account of the 1967 Peace March on the Pentagon, with himself and Robert Lowell in edgy cooperation and conflict at the middle of the events.

Like Mailer, John Horne Burns reported the war seen directly, in his case in North Africa and Italy, in *The Gallery* (1947). John Hersey reported on the Allied occupation of Sicily in *A Bell for Adano* (1944), and told in documentary fashion of the 1943 uprising in the Warsaw ghetto in *The Wall* (1950). An older writer, James Gould Cozzens, focused on the problems of the air force at home in *Guard of Honor* (1948). Irwin Shaw's *The Young Lions* (1948) followed an American Jew and a Gentile as soldiers in Germany. Against this background of American views of the conflict, John Hawkes, his studies interrupted by wartime ambulance driving in Italy and Germany, returned to Harvard, where as a student he began *The Cannibal* (1949), a surrealistic view of devastation as seen by the Germans. Other accounts of the war followed, some much later. From Hemingway came the weak, but for him psychologically significant, *Across the River and into the Trees* (1950), and then, in the posthumous *Islands in the Stream* (1970), some passages on submarine hunting in the Caribbean. James Jones's hugely successful *From Here to Eternity* (1951) examined the peacetime army in Hawaii in the period just before the attack on Pearl

Harbor. Later, in *The Thin Red Line* (1962), Jones followed the action on Guadalcanal through 1942–1943, and with *Whistle* (1978), completed by another writer, his work became a trilogy as he explored the difficulties encountered by war wounded attempting to adjust to civilian life. In *The Caine Mutiny* (1951) Herman Wouk analyzed a mutiny on an American destroyer during a storm in the Pacific through the perspective of a trial raising issues about authority, paranoia, and loyalty.

For a few writers, even initial reactions were long in developing. Joseph Heller, who served in the army air force in World War II, finally brought the madly comic vision of *Catch-22* (1961) before the public, coincidentally in the same year that the first American support troops arrived in Vietnam. In an increasingly frustrating time for Americans, *Catch-22* provided the nation with a catch-phrase for circular futility, giving impetus also to the mounting strain of black humor in American novels of the next decade. The decision of Heller's hero, Yossarian, to desert the army and seek refuge in Sweden prefigured similar decisions of huge numbers of young men during the Vietnam conflict. For Kurt Vonnegut, Jr., seeds planted in World War II took still longer to grow and mature. Witness to the firebombing of Dresden, he established a reputation with a number of other books long before he was able to bring his memories and imagination together in the bleakly pessimistic *Slaughterhouse-Five* (1969). And nearly three decades after the war, Thomas Pynchon, eight years old in 1945 (and having to that extent an advantage over Stephen Crane, author of the best Civil War novel and not yet born in 1865), created in *Gravity's Rainbow* (1973) a monumental account of a wartime London under threat of annihilation by German bombs and rockets.

Many of the most impressive careers that began to be evident in the years immediately after the war, however, belonged to novelists and short story writers who used the war as material very little or not at all. Some had not experienced the war directly. Others had experienced it and chose not to write about it. Most joined to create between 1945 and 1965 a prose literature strongly characterized by its continuation of the American realistic and naturalistic tradition, as writers examined lives close to their own, creating works that more often than not made no attempt to extend or even to approach the limits of experimentation of such earlier Modernists as Joyce and Faulkner.

Write about what you know—that was the lesson most evident in the work of those writers most admired in these years, Fitzgerald, Faulkner, Hemingway, Wolfe, Steinbeck—and most explicit in their comments about the art of writing. When newer writers did just that in this period, they developed a literature marked by a new regionalism and a new ethnicity, testimony to a United States in which differences were beginning to be seen once again as important, just as they had in the years after the Civil War that witnessed the rise of "local color."

One result was an extraordinary growth in the strength of southern writing, which, with a few distinguished exceptions, had been disproportionately weak in prior times. Within a few years after 1945, however, it became disproportionately strong, with the rising fame of Faulkner leading the way. Post-war Americans were still haunted by the nostalgic view of the past presented by Margaret Mitchell in *Gone with the Wind* (1936) and by Hollywood's lavish movie version, with Clark Gable and Vivien Leigh, when the sudden fame of Tennessee Williams's *The Glass Menagerie* (1945) and *A Streetcar Named Desire* (1947), first on stage and then in the movies, thrust into the public mind another enduring vision of a region twisted by nostalgia for the irrecoverable. Other versions of the South had already achieved wide notice in the work of the Southern Agrarians or Fugitives (mostly poets, led by John

Crowe Ransom and Allen Tate) and in the fiction of Katherine Anne Porter. Among these earlier southerners, most of whom remained active well into the post-war years, Robert Penn Warren, originally a poet and a Fugitive, soon emerged as one of our foremost novelists. Especially strong is his third novel, *All the King's Men* (1946), a study of a corrupt politician modeled upon Louisiana's Huey Long. After following that success with a series of novels set mostly in Kentucky and Tennessee, he turned again more fully to verse, developing one of the distinctive poetic voices of the 1970's and 1980's. Eudora Welty, who had published some of her fine stories in *A Curtain of Green* (1941) and *The Wide Net* (1943), continued her work in a series of novels and short story collections throughout the post-war years, *The Collected Stories* (1980) appearing when she was past seventy. Much less active as a critic than the scholarly Warren, Welty nevertheless in invoking notions of "time, "blood," and "heritage" in her essay "Some Notes on Time in Fiction" seemed to speak for most southern writers as they appeal to the almost talismanic power of memory: "Remembering is done through the blood, it is a bequeathment, it takes account of what happens before a man is born as if he were there taking part. * * * it is a spiritual heritage."

Younger than Warren and Welty, Carson McCullers achieved fame for *The Heart Is a Lonely Hunter* (1940) and *Reflections in a Golden Eye* (1941) and continued a strong literary presence with *The Member of the Wedding* (1946) and *The Ballad of the Sad Café* (1951). The same age as McCullers, Peter Taylor began his career with the stories of *A Long Fourth* (1948) and has continued it through *The Old Forest and Other Stories* (1985). A few years younger, Truman Capote achieved early fame with an exotic novel, *Other Voices, Other Rooms* (1948), a collection of stories, *A Tree of Night* (1949), and another novel, *The Grass Harp* (1951), before turning away from the South in his later work. Flannery O'Connor, a writer of Capote's generation who died in her thirties, viewed through the lens of a deep Catholic commitment a world surprisingly grotesque and violent, especially in the short story collections *A Good Man Is Hard to Find* (1955) and *Everything That Rises Must Converge* (1965). William Styron first won praise for a Virginia family novel, *Lie Down in Darkness* (1951); among his other substantial works is his historical novel of a slave rebellion, *The Confessions of Nat Turner* (1967). Of the same generation as McCullers and Taylor, Walker Percy came to fiction later, with his acclaimed first novel, *The Moviegoer* (1961).

Each of the writers of the post-war South—Williams on the stage, the others mostly through fiction—creates a strong sense of place, grounded in experience and close observation: St. Louis or New Orleans for Williams; Louisiana, Kentucky, or Tennessee for Warren; Mississippi for Welty; Georgia for McCullers and O'Connor; Tennessee for Taylor; Louisiana and Mississippi for Capote and Percy; Virginia for Styron. Many are masters of short forms, with several doing their best work in a length midway between short story and fully developed novel. Together they portray an area found primarily within a triangle enclosed by lines drawn between Richmond, St. Louis, and New Orleans, providing for it a depth of observation and analysis unmatched in their time by writers from other regions.

Parallel with the post-war rise of southern fiction was the rise of American Jewish fiction, which was also in part a rise in fiction centered in New York City or in other large urban areas. Dreiser had brought the American city into literature. Fitzgerald had rejected it, at the end of *The Great Gatsby,* sending Nick Carraway back to his small-town Midwest. Hemingway and Faulkner had never embraced it. Steinbeck went into the city only for comedy. Now came Saul Bellow, later, like Hemingway, Faulkner, and Steinbeck, a

Nobel Prize winner, centering his work in cities and in American Jewishness.

Bellow began with a wartime novel, *Dangling Man* (1944), the diary of a man who has quit work and is waiting to be drafted. By the time of his third novel, *The Adventures of Augie March* (1953), in which a Chicago boy tells of his wanderings through America, it became clear that in Bellow's vision the rural world of Huckleberry Finn and Nick Adams had become decidedly urban, Jewish, and comic. Later novels are set sometimes in Chicago, sometimes in New York, as the heroes, suffering from crises of spirit, attempt to escape from or fulfill needs shaped by family, community, and material pressures that are particular to them because they are Jews and Americans, general to all of us because we are human. Haunted by a sense of personal failure, as in *Seize the Day* (1956) and *Herzog* (1964), but survivors, like the former Nazi concentration camp inmate of *Mr. Sammler's Planet* (1969), they are driven by a need expressed in the repeated "I want, I want" of *Henderson the Rain King* (1959). Neurotically critical of wives, children, friends, and associates, and of the country they live in, they are also humorously and unsparingly critical of themselves. Most achieve in the end an uneasy truce with an imperfect existence.

Not all Jewish writers, of course, have centered their writing in their ethnic or religious background, any more than all southern writers have continued to write of the South. Indeed, more than the writers of the South, they have inhabited places with varied cultural heritages, the distinctive social, ethnic, and religious communities of the northern city. Their work, therefore, tends to range between fictions reflective of the urban experience in general and, within that generality, the Jewish experience in particular. Besides Bellow, these writers include Norman Mailer and Joseph Heller, discussed above in the context of war literature, and Arthur Miller, who with Tennessee Williams is one of the two major playwrights of the period. Miller's Willy Loman in *Death of a Salesman* (1949), largely without indications of an ethnic background, sees his American dream of a house, a garden, and a happy family literally and figuratively shadowed by the encroachments of the city. In *Focus* (1945), a novel, Miller dealt directly with anti-Semitism.

Others who, like Bellow, have mined significant amounts of material from their Jewish heritage include Isaac Bashevis Singer, Bernard Malamud, and Philip Roth. Singer, an immigrant in 1935, began writing in Yiddish for a New York readership. With the publication of *The Family Moskat* (1950) in English he became a major American writer, though he has continued to write first in Yiddish (later supervising translations into English) and to find most of his subjects in his native Poland. Malamud, a native New Yorker, sprinkles Yiddish in his work, emphasizing both cultural heritage and contemporary mannerisms. In *The Assistant* (1957), a Gentile becomes a Jew. In *A New Life* (1961), an eastern intellectual finds himself misplaced in a small college in the Pacific Northwest. *The Tenants* (1971) deals with conflict between blacks and Jews in New York. Philip Roth, from New Jersey, began his career with Jews confronting Jews in the stories of *Goodbye, Columbus* (1959) and has gone from that fine beginning to a series of strikingly different novels, always imaginative and frequently witty. Most famous is *Portnoy's Complaint* (1969), whose hero thinks of himself as "the son in a Jewish joke—*only it ain't no joke!*"

The rise of post-war Jewish literature had been preceded by a rise of Jewish consciousness in the period from 1918 to 1945. In this it resembled the literature of the post-war South: both were second-generation phenomena. Just as the Southern Agrarians had given a philosophical justification for a life rooted in the past and had lamented the shift within the twentieth-century away from rural values, so the Jewish intellectuals of the 1920's and 1930's confronted the need of their people, mostly recent immigrants, to make a new way of life in a land that was for them mostly urban and industrial. In the South, there were William Faulkner, Katherine Anne Porter, and the Fugitives as forerunners of the literature to come. In the North, though often more interesting as historical documents than as literature, there were strong treatments of Jewishness in such books as Abraham Cahan's *The Rise of David Levinsky* (1917), Michael Gold's *Jews without Money* (1930), Henry Roth's *Call It Sleep* (1934), and Jerome Weidman's *I Can Get It for You Wholesale* (1937). The Agrarian South had its generative and supportive journals in *The Fugitive* and *The Southern Review;* for the cosmopolitan North there were *The Partisan Review* and the more Jewish *Commentary.* In the background, too, for post-war Jews, was the horror of the Holocaust of Nazi Germany. The impetus was great to record, explain, and justify both ancient traditions and a new life.

Insofar as the literature of American Jews from 1945 to the 1960's was primarily a literature of cities and suburbs, it was part of a larger phenomenon, as many writers, regardless of ethnic or religious background, found their material especially in the urban Northeast, in the cities themselves, or in towns not far removed from these centers. One of the best of these was John O'Hara, who began his long career in the 1930's and continued it through the 1960's, examining the high and low life especially of a small city in Pennsylvania, and of Philadelphia and New York, in such novels as *Ten North Frederick* (1955) and *From the Terrace* (1958) and in a remarkable number of tight, colloquial stories collected in *The Cape Cod Lighter* (1962) and other volumes. Another, James T. Farrell, remembered first for his *Studs Lonigan* trilogy in the 1930's, continued prolific with novels and stories of Chicago and New York into the 1970's. Still another, John Cheever, belongs primarily to the post-war period, establishing a reputation with *The Enormous Radio and Other Stories* (1953). A chronicler of wealthy suburbia, Cheever in time established himself as one of the finest short story writers of the period, with *The Stories of John Cheever* (1978) standing as a monument to his own talent and to the influence on the fiction of recent decades of *The New Yorker* magazine, where most of them were first published. For J. D. Salinger, a mixed Jewish and Irish Catholic heritage and a New York City upbringing provided material out of which he wove one of the landmark fictions of his time, *The Catcher in the Rye* (1951), a boy's adventures in New York on the way to mental breakdown after he leaves an expensive prep school in Pennsylvania. A world with similar boundaries is also explored in Salinger's *Nine Stories* (1953), *Franny and Zooey* (1961), and *Raise High the Roof Beam, Carpenters and Seymour: An Introduction* (1963). For Jack Kerouac, fiction was largely a way to examine the conflicts resulting from growing up French Canadian and Catholic during the Depression in Lowell, Massachusetts, a mill town, and evolving into a leading spokesman for the Beat Generation during wartime years spent mainly in Manhattan, with periods in the merchant marine. His most important novel, *On the Road* (1957), ranges far from New York, across the country to California and into Mexico. For Mary McCarthy, the world examined, with wit and satire, was mostly that of the eastern intellectual: in Manhattan in *The Company She Keeps* (1942), in a women's liberal arts college in *The Groves of Academe* (1952), in the lives in the 1930's of eight Vassar alumnae in *The Group* (1963). In Nelson Algren's best work, *The Man with the Golden Arm* (1949), the city is not New York, but Chicago.

Related to the rise both of southern and urban fiction was the sudden appearance of Ralph Ellison and James Baldwin, writers who thrust the literature of American blacks much more firmly into the American consciousness than it had been even in the days of the Harlem Renaissance of the 1920's. Insofar as they dealt primarily with race and race relationships in their work, they had, like southern and Jewish writers, a number of forerunners in decades immediately preceding, including Langston Hughes and Richard Wright. Nothing except individual genius, however, seemed to explain fully the power of *Invisible Man* (1952), one of the great novels of its time. Following his hero from a racially humiliating southern beginning through an education at a Negro college, Ellison brings him finally to searing experiences in New York City that drive him literally underground. James Baldwin's *Go Tell It on the Mountain* (1953), an autobiographical novel about growing up in Harlem, inaugurated the career of one of the literary giants of our time, a fine novelist and short story writer and, in works like *Notes of a Native Son* (1955) and *The Fire Next Time* (1963), an extraordinary essayist and polemicist. Other black writers of the period included Chester Himes, whose *If He Hollers Let Him Go* (1945) pictures racial prejudice in a California defense plant, and Ann Petry, who deals with race in Connecticut and New York in novels like *The Street* (1946) and *Country Life* (1947) and in short stories collected in *Miss Muriel* (1971). Writers whose works are mostly later include John A. Williams and William Melvin Kelly. On the stage, Lorraine Hansberry's *A Raisin in the Sun* (1959) powerfully expressed the post-war aspirations toward equality and social dignity of middle-class blacks in Chicago. Among blacks of the period who chose not to write much of race, Frank Yerby achieved considerable success for a series of historical romances, including *The Foxes of Harrow* (1946).

Outside of the South and Northeast (and Chicago as a second New York), fiction from 1945 to 1965 was less common and generally less successful. This was in part because writers (like Mary McCarthy, born in Seattle but educated at Vassar) tended to gravitate toward New York as a publishing center and write about what they saw there. There were impressive exceptions, however. In *The Dollmaker* (1954), Harriette Arnow skillfully portrayed the lives of displaced Kentuckians living in Detroit for the World War II jobs to be found there. A. B. Guthrie, Jr., moved a century into the past to portray the West, from Kentucky to Oregon, in *The Big Sky* (1947) and *The Way West* (1949). Walter Van Tilburg Clark, famous first for a novel about a Nevada lynching, *The Ox-Bow Incident* (1940), followed that with a symbolic struggle to survive in the High Sierra as brothers hunt a mountain lion in *The Track of the Cat* (1949). Later, Douglas Woolf displayed considerable humor and insight in *Fade Out* (1959), chronicling the cross-country adventures of two men who escape lingering disintegration in an old-age home to find new life in an Arizona ghost town. In the Pacific Northwest, Ken Kesey followed with the hugely popular *One Flew Over the Cuckoo's Nest* (1962), about life in a mental hospital, and the even more impressive *Sometimes a Great Notion* (1964), about a family and a lumbering feud in Oregon. In Woolf and Kesey, although the effort was in part documentation, there were also strong evidences of the turn toward alienation and black humor important elsewhere also by the later part of the period. A more sustained effort has been that of the Nebraska writer Wright Morris. Although his many works, from 1942 into the 1980's, range as far afield as Los Angeles, Mexico, Chicago, and Philadelphia, he returns to his beginnings in some of the best, like *Ceremony in Lone Tree* (1960). As recently as *Plains Song: For Female Voices* (1980) he was still concerned with the heritage of generations on the plains.

THE BEAT GENERATION

The Beat Generation owed much of its influence to the mass media response to the notoriety of Allen Ginsberg's *Howl* (1956) and Jack Kerouac's *On the Road*

(1957). A flood of radio and TV interviews, picture essays in *Life,* and somber attempts at definition in magazines ranging from *Esquire* to *Saturday Review* gave "Beat" the status of a national condition. In time, "beatniks" and "hippies" became stock characters, symbols of rebellion to the young and figures of fun in comic strips and political cartoons down to the present, where they have become "aging hippies," whose children in turn are rebelling against their parents by wearing suits and ties and prom dresses.

The original Beat Generation was earlier than its fame, however, and by the middle 1980's they were more nearly the grandparents than the parents of contemporary youth. Offspring of the Depression, the first beats came together amid the disruptions of war-time Manhattan and nurtured their post-war disillusion there. Alienated from mainstream society, distrustful of American traditions and values, they sought an alternative way of life and fostered an alternative literature. For all the publicity later accorded them, few were more than modestly successful as writers, but those few exerted an immense influence on others of their time and on the literature of succeeding years.

Jack Kerouac was central. He is generally credited with originating the term "beat," which for him was associated with the concepts "beaten down," "upbeat," and "beatific." Unifying these senses was a posture of removal from the world, an attitude of distinction and separateness summarized by Kerouac in a 1948 conversation as later remembered by his friend John Clellon Holmes, himself the author of the Beat novel *Go* (1952):

> It's a sort of furtiveness. * * * Like we were a generation of furtives. You know, with an inner knowledge there's no use flaunting on that level, the level of the "public," a kind of beatness * * * and a weariness with all the forms, all the conventions of the world * * *. So I guess you might say we're a *beat* generation.

However defined, the Beat life for Kerouac and his friends of the 1940's and 1950's was marked by excessive drinking, drug abuse, frenetic heterosexual and homosexual activity, violence—and attempts to create a literature reflective of this side of America. Problems with publication became legendary, as did also the continual struggle to find literary forms suited to the new content. For William S. Burroughs, the oldest of the group, there was initially the difficulty of his relation to his socially prominent family, with the result that his first and autobiographical novel, *Junkie* (1953), was published under the pseudonym "William Lee." Kerouac's wrestlings with form were symbolized when at one point he submitted to his publisher a manuscript of *On the Road* typed in three frenetic weeks on a continuous roll of paper. Ginsberg's *Howl* created a sensation that in the end helped sell the book as it was attacked for being obscene, attempts were made to censor it, and Ginsberg assisted the notoriety by appearing naked at a poetry reading in California.

To the extent that they were beaten down, the Beats spoke for members of society weary of economic, social, and personal failure, dispirited by war and its aftermath, distrustful of the suburban dream of America. To the extent that they were upbeat, they spoke for the hipsters who got along, who made it in their own way, who, in the words of an expression popular in a later generation, did "their own thing." To the extent that they were beatific, they were holy angels, attuned to a vision of universal peace and love, chastising unbelievers and encouraging the faithful with their inspired works of prose and verse.

Besides Kerouac, Burroughs, and Ginsberg, they included a few writers at home on the West Coast, helping to make San Francisco rival to New York as a center for the new ideas. Lawrence Ferlinghetti, proprietor of the City Lights Bookstore, published Ginsberg's *Howl* and later poems and the work of other *avant-garde* writers, and wrote one of the influential poetry collections of the time, *A Coney Island of the Mind* (1958). The poet Gary Snyder was especially important to the beatific claims of the Beats, helping then and later to make Zen Buddhism a significant part of American alternative culture.

Never a cohesive movement except insofar as friends shared experiences and viewpoints, the Beats had affinities with many individuals and groups. As recorders of the underside of life in New York and San Francisco, they were part of the larger phenomenon of post-war urban literature, as seen especially in works like George Mandel's *Flee the Angry Strangers* (1952), depicting the drug world in Greenwich Village, Chandler Brossard's *The Bold Saboteurs* (1953), a memorable evocation of a youth spent in delinquency, and John Rechy's *City of Night* (1963). Their impetus toward new literary forms and their celebrations of personal idiosyncracies allied them to the Black Mountain poets and to the experimentations of later prose writers who were influenced especially by the spontaneous writing and collage constructions of Kerouac and Burroughs.

EXPERIMENTAL PROSE

Contemporaneous with the Beats and with the traditionalists of the years 1945 to the 1960's were a relatively few writers distinguished for their experiments with fictional form and content. Generally, this was not a period for bold and successful experimentation in American writing. It looked to many, writers and readers alike, as though Modernists like Joyce, Woolf, Kafka, and Faulkner had pushed the limits of fiction about as far as they could be fruitfully extended, and most of the newer writers—Singer, Warren, Welty, Cheever, Ellison, Bellow, Baldwin, and others—worked well within those limits. Because fiction, however, as something created, is inevitably always something new (the novel suggesting newness even by its name), and because short stories and novels are more shapeless than traditional poems, experimentation is always present as a possibility.

A part of the Beats' rejection of the values of their time was a rejection of the accepted modes and methods of its literature. Hence Kerouac, for example, agonized over the linear presentation of material printed line by line, page by page; believing *On the Road* too "horizontal" in structure because too close to the chronological order in which things happened, he tried to arrange the same material "vertically" in *Visions of Cody* (1972) in mimicry of the way memory cuts across time. Like others of the immediate post-war generation, he looked to the spontaneity and improvisations of jazz as a model for prose. Both Kerouac and Burroughs (and, in poetry, Ginsberg) sought a "factualism" partly rendered through intimate personal report—some years before the "nonfiction novel" and "confessional poetry" became fashionable concepts. For Burroughs, cut-and-paste, a procedure borrowed directly from graphic art, became a technique for the haphazard disjunctions of his literary montages. None of this was new in theory, however, no matter how strange the effects: spontaneity had served as a tool for insight in American prose and poetry at least since Emerson; disordered time was one of the hallmarks of the earlier moderns, especially apparent in Faulkner; and the value of the personal had been preached by Fitzgerald and Hemingway. Fundamental to all of these writers was the sense that the real world is important, that temporal experience holds clues to eternal truths, that literature must cut through illusions to reveal vital facts.

Other post-war experimentalists worked from different and, for American literature, newer premises. For them, the world of fact was less intriguing than the world of illusion. Fiction is a game, a mechanical construction parallel with life but not necessarily directly reflective of it. The realist's mirror reflects life directly. In the mirrors of the literary magician, however, illusion piles upon illusion as the images return upon themselves to reflect at the end nothing more substantial than the very inventions with which the work began. The lady has not been sawed in half, but if she were . . . This is a literature of parody and irony in which *is* becomes replaced by *what if* and *should be*. It is always in danger of sinking to the purely escapist or ploddingly derivative, as more often than not in the self-reflections of formula fiction, where the new Western or detective story or space fantasy reflects nothing more exciting than the conventions of earlier works in the same genre (which is exciting enough for the addict). Self-reflective fictions in the hands of masters, however, have become one of the more interesting literary developments of our time.

In American literature, the old master is Vladimir Nabokov, a Russian immigrant whose long career had begun years before the war in novels written in Germany in the Russian language. Writing in English in the United States, he began to develop a reputation in the 1940's and gained fame and wealth with the huge success of *Lolita* after its 1958 publication in the United States (fear of censorship at home had led to its earlier publication in Paris in 1955). Earlier novels written originally in Russian such as *Laughter in the Dark* (English version 1938) or *The Gift* (English version 1963) are fine introductions to his work, as is *Pnin* (1957), with its immigrant view of American colleges. Major late works, intensely self-reflective, are *Pale Fire* (1962) and *Ada* (1969).

Other writers similarly self-reflective, their fictions more true to interior logic than to external norms of reality, are John Hawkes, William Gaddis, Thomas Pynchon, and Donald Barthelme. From Hawkes's first novel, *The Cannibal* (1949), set in a surrealistic wartime Germany, he has been interested in nightmarish, sexual, and violent Freudian visions perceived through minds troubled by the thin line between the actual and the potential. Gaddis earned a special place in the minds of critics for *The Recognitions* (1955), a sprawling novel in which layer upon layer of narrative leave the reader in doubt as to precisely what should be recognized in a tale in which forgery in art serves as metaphor for illusion in fiction. Pynchon and Barthelme came later. After the success of *V.* (1963), Pynchon emerged as one of the most critically discussed novelists of recent decades, a model for many younger writers. With *Come Back, Dr. Caligari* (1964), Barthelme established himself as a master of enigmatic short forms akin to the fables of the Argentinian Jorge Luis Borges, whose work was just then becoming popular in the United States. By the mid-1960's the impetus toward self-reflective fiction had become a force responsible for some of the most impressive literature of ensuing decades.

POETRY: THE ACADEMIC TRADITION

By 1945 the Modernist poetry that Pound, Eliot, and other American poets had helped create in the years around the First World War had developed its own tradition. Most of the older poets still active after the end of World War II—among them, Eliot, Pound, Frost, MacLeish, Cummings, Ransom, Tate—wrote in forms either directly traditional in meter and rhyme or consciously manipulative of traditional forms (so that Eliot, for example, played with tetrameter couplets and quatrains within his looser lines and Cummings disguised his traditional meters and rhymes beneath a surface of idiosyncratic typography). Most wrote an intellectual poetry, highly allusive, strong in metaphor and symbol, carefully crafted to produce a lyric and thematic intensity sometimes more rewarding to careful reading and thorough analysis than it was immediately accessible. In colleges and universities the New Criticism was in vogue, as Cleanth Brooks and Robert Penn Warren, in their textbook *Understanding Poetry* (1938), taught a whole generation of students, and their instructors, the rewards of close reading.

Most of the younger poets celebrated in the early years after 1945 followed this academic tradition, writing in the shadow of their elders Modernist poetry of a kind admired in the schools, extending the tradition or bending it to their personalities as far as they were able. Most were well educated, thoroughly immersed in Modernist poetry and in the poetic traditions that undergirded it. Most supported themselves by teaching in colleges or universities, creating in time a cycle of poetry, critical approval, and more poetry that came to be resented by other poets, many of them outside the mainstream of American poetic and academic life, who were not interested in poetry in the high Modernist mode then fashionable.

Foremost among the post-war academic poets was Robert Lowell. First interested in poetry at St. Mark's School, where his poetic ambitions were influenced by Richard Eberhart, Lowell attended Harvard briefly before transferring to Kenyon, where he studied with John Crowe Ransom and roomed with Randall Jarrell. In 1944 he published his first volume, *Land of Unlikeness.* By the time of his second collection, *Lord Weary's Castle* (1946), which Jarrell reviewed in *The Nation,* he was poised for the Pulitzer Prize, Guggenheim Fellowship, Poetry Consultantship to the Library of Congress, and other forms of acclaim that immediately followed. *The Mills of the Kavanaughs* (1951) confirmed his reputation as a complex poet, skilled in traditional forms, obsessed and tormented by his family history and New England heritage. A teacher of poets at the University of Iowa, Boston University, Harvard, and other places, he passed on his vision directly to others. That vision, however, changed dramatically during and after the 1950's from causes that included a series of personal crises and Lowell's growing response to the poetic spell of William Carlos Williams.

Impressed especially with Williams's *Paterson,* Lowell turned from the tight forms and public material of his earlier books to looser lines embodying a more personal voice in *Life Studies* (1959), thereby providing a tremendous boost to the "confessional" poetry of the next decade. Writing to Williams while at work on that volume, he expressed his sense of advantages to be gained by compromise between strict and open meters:

> I wouldn't like ever to completely give up meter; it's a wonderful opposition to wrench against and revise with. Yet now that I've joined you in unscanned verse, I am struck by how often the old classics get boxed up in their machinery, the sonority of the iambic pentameter line, the apparatus of logic and conceit and even set subjects. Still, the muscle is there in the classics * * *. We would always rather read a good old sonneteer, such as Raleigh or Sidney, than some merely competent modern fellow who is on the right track. The excellent speak to the excellent.

Later, Lowell mixed poems in tight forms with others much more open, standing forth in a series of volumes from *Imitations* (1961) and *For the Union Dead* (1964) through *Day by Day* (1977) as a fine example to younger poets of success won through willingness to adopt a variety of poetic approaches.

Other significant poets who were mostly cast in a similar academic mold include Randall Jarrell, Elizabeth Bishop, Richard Wilbur, Howard Nemerov, Louis Simpson, and John Berryman. Randall Jarrell, a master of traditional forms, was skilled in dramatic monologues of empty and alienated characters. As the title of one of his best books, *Losses* (1948), suggests, his people often grieve for something gone that they once possessed. Jarrell was also a fine critic, his *Poetry and the Age* (1953) one of the most influential books of its time. Elizabeth Bishop wrote poems highly evocative of the places she lived, including Nova Scotia, Maine, and Brazil, in *North and South* (1946), *Questions of Travel* (1965), and other books. Richard Wilbur wrote urbane poems exploiting traditional forms in a succession of volumes beginning with *The Beautiful Changes* (1947). Howard Nemerov's witty poems, frequently in blank verse, first appeared in

The Image and the Law (1947). Louis Simpson drew significantly on images of the war in traditional poems in his first two books; by the time of his third, *A Dream of Governors* (1959) he was beginning the experimentation characteristic of his later work and of the period in which it has been written. John Berryman, though he had published earlier, first attained wide notice for *Homage to Mistress Bradstreet* (1956), a book that in the manner of Lowell's earlier work dealt with New England history. *The Dream Songs* (1969), his most significant work, which had begun to appear in book form in 1964, was important in hastening the widespread acceptance into academia of non-metered poems of highly personal content.

Poets from a different mold included Theodore Roethke, Robert Penn Warren, Isabella Gardner, and Robert Francis. Just as Lowell and the other poets mentioned immediately above belonged clearly to the East (Simpson, however, going to California to teach in 1959), Theodore Roethke, whose roots were in Michigan, came in time to influence the poetry of an entire region, the Pacific Northwest. A teacher of poets at the University of Washington from 1947 through 1963, he helped through his poetry and his personality to spread the idea (earlier Williams's) that verse should be local in subject and voice. Skilled in traditional and open forms, after publishing his first volume, *Open House,* in 1941, he followed with two post-war volumes before printing the influential collection *The Waking: Poems 1933–1953* in 1953. Warren's strong southern voice in poetry, as seen in *Selected Poems 1923–1943* (1944) and subsequent volumes, was in this period obscured by his fame as a novelist; his importance as a poet began to be clearer in the 1960's and after. Isabella Gardner, a professional actress from a prominent Massachusetts family, published her first book, *Birthdays from the Ocean* (1955), when she was forty and then only two others before her fourth and last during her lifetime, *That Was Then: New and Selected Poems* (1980). Another New Englander, Robert Francis, living privately and unconnected with universities, gained little notice with three books between 1936 and 1944; after a period of no success at all, he began to emerge from obscurity after *The Orb Weaver* (1960).

Among American blacks, Langston Hughes, who had established his reputation long before, continued a strong presence with *Montage of a Dream Deferred* (1951), one of the landmark post-war books, and other volumes. Newly emerging poets included Gwendolyn Brooks, whose *A Street in Bronzeville* (1945) launched an important career that turned from expressions of a deep-seated racial pride to a more militant anger after the late 1960's; and Robert Hayden, a poet who desired to rise above race and whose books, though he began to publish in 1940, remained little noticed until his *Selected Poems* (1966).

POETRY: THE ANTI-ACADEMICS

Between 1945 and the mid-1960's the ancient split between classic and romantic poetry—between intellectual, traditional, and communal values and emotional, inspirational, and personal values—produced two distinct streams in American poetry. Simply put, the classic or academic stream derived from T. S. Eliot and the dominant poets of the English and American tradition, but the romantic or anti-academic stream derived from William Carlos Williams and a few earlier rebels from the tradition, especially Walt Whitman. The academic stream of poetry was the poetry of the universities and the major quarterlies, canonized in the writings of the New Critics. The experiments of the Modernists had been carefully assimilated into the tradition, and for the most part the younger academic poets, at least until the late 1950's, diverged from the methods and materials of the past no further than had their immediate predecessors in poetry between the wars. Many members of this new generation—including Lowell, Jarrell, Wilbur, Nemerov, Simpson, Berryman, Roethke, Warren, Hayden, and, later, Brooks and Bishop—were professors of poetry in universities; meanwhile, those institutions were significantly expanding their influence after the war, as higher education became for the first time broadly available to the masses.

There were challenges, however, to the idea that poetry belongs to universities and depends on a tradition rigorously taught and thoroughly understood. The anti-academics were sometimes virulent in their attacks upon the establishment, as in Allen Ginsberg's 1959 defense of *Howl* (1956):

> A word on Academies; poetry has been attacked by an ignorant & frightened bunch of bores who don't understand how it's made, & the trouble with these creeps is they wouldn't know Poetry if it came up and buggered them in broad daylight.

Like Ginsberg, poets outside the universities were sometimes identified with the Beat Generation, and all shared with that group a sense of the failure of received values, a distrust of the intellect, and a desire to enlarge experience through avenues of emotion and intuition, sometimes broadened with drugs and oriental mysticism. Like Ginsberg, most suffered through years of failure and neglect. Dropping out of traditional colleges or scornful of what they found there, they discovered the teaching positions that supported the academic poets mostly closed to them, publication in major literary journals largely unavailable, established book publishers uninterested in their kind of poetry. Donald Allen's hugely successful *The New American Poetry: 1945–1960* (1960) gave many their first significant readership; by that time, however, they had been provided a ready climate of discussion even within the universities by the widespread recognition of William Carlos Williams as a major poet, the notoriety of Ginsberg's *Howl,* and the turn toward personal and unscanned verse in the late 1950's work of Lowell and other celebrated poets of the establishment.

Of those most frequently considered Beat poets, Ginsberg first appeared on the East Coast, Lawrence Ferlinghetti and Gary Snyder on the West. Ginsberg was a young follower of the older Beats in New York City in the 1940's, earning a reputation for personal strangeness and a place as a character in early Beat novels before, at age thirty, he finally achieved fame with *Howl,* published by Ferlinghetti in San Francisco. Ferlinghetti, born in New York and with a doctorate from the Sorbonne, gave weight to the anti-academic movement in the 1950's in San Francisco by establishing his City Lights Bookstore and publishing house there, and by encouraging what he called "street poetry":

> For it amounts to getting the poet out of the inner esthetic sanctum where he has too long been contemplating his complicated navel. It amounts to getting poetry back into the street where it once was, out of the classroom, out of the speech department, and—in fact—off the printed page. The printed word has made poetry so silent.

Encouraged by Ferlinghetti and others, poetry became a staple of the coffee houses of the period, often accompanied by jazz. Spoken, colloquial rhythms, backed by musical ones, became more important than traditional meters, as the movement fed also off the increasing popularity of folk songs. To this scene, Gary Snyder, a student of oriental languages at Berkeley, brought a sensitivity to the environment, an interest in primitivism (especially as found in Native American culture), and a knowledge of Zen Buddhism, as his books *Riprap* (1959) and *Myths and Texts* (1960) proved widely influential.

In North Carolina, Black Mountain College emerged as a center for anti-academic poetry during the years from 1951 to 1956 when Charles Olson was rector. In the late 1940's Olson began to publish experimental verse in little magazines.

Advancing ideas especially of Pound and Williams, in 1950 he published "Projective Verse," an essay immensely influential on younger poets in its call for open poems shaped by personal breathing patterns. At Black Mountain, Olson supported Robert Creeley's *Black Mountain Review* (1954–1957) and attracted as students or faculty a number of experimental poets, including Creeley, Robert Duncan, and Edward Dorn. Olson's most important poetic work, *The Maximus Poems,* appearing in pieces from 1953 onward, was incomplete at his death.

Among poets associated with Olson at Black Mountain, Robert Creeley and Robert Duncan have achieved the greatest notice. Leaving Harvard without graduating in 1947, Creeley pursued his poetic career in France and Majorca, publishing his poems with little presses, including his own, before securing a major publisher and a wider readership with *For Love, Poems 1950–1960* (1960). Briefly at Black Mountain, Creeley was also an associate of the Beats, many of whom he met in 1956 in San Francisco. Somewhat older than Creeley, Duncan edited little magazines in Berkeley in the 1930's and 1940's and lived on Majorca briefly before coming to Black Mountain in 1956. After he had published half a dozen books with small presses, including Creeley's Divers Press on Majorca, his work began to be more generally available in *Selected Poems* (1959), from Ferlinghetti's City Lights Press; major New York publication soon followed.

Outside of the San Francisco–North Carolina axis connecting Beat and Black Mountain poets, experimental poetry and other verse outside the universities during the post-war period was harder to classify. The English poet Denise Levertov came to the United States in 1948 and soon transformed herself into an American poet on the model of William Carlos Williams, publishing her early American poems in Cid Corman's *Origin,* an outlet also for the Black Mountain poets. "I think of Robert Duncan and Robert Creeley as the chief poets among my contemporaries," she wrote in Allen's *New American Poetry* in 1960. By the time of *With Eyes at the Back of Our Heads* (1959) she had developed a strong personal style that has served her well in later books in which she has written sometimes on personal, sometimes on public themes as a participant in the anti-war movement of the 1960's. Living abroad much of the time, W. S. Merwin earned a reputation particularly for his translations, as in *The Poem of the Cid* (1959), though he also wrote original verse, mostly traditional. With *The Drunk in the Furnace* (1960), he moved with the times toward looser lines and in subsequent books his work became more surrealistic. In New York City, Frank O'Hara and John Ashbery occupied the center of a group sometimes called the New York School; much of their best work and their major influence, however, came after the mid-1960's. In the Midwest, Robert Bly began his influential journal *The Fifties* in 1958; the best of his poetry, too, came later.

THE NEW DRAMA

Younger dramatists after 1945, like prose writers and poets, had to compete with strong new works from an established older generation, including Eugene O'Neill, Maxwell Anderson, Thornton Wilder, and Lillian Hellman. Broadway was thriving, however, and almost immediately two new playwrights, Tennessee Williams and Arthur Miller, emerged to rank with the best America has yet produced. To the extent that the fiction writers of the South and Northeast from 1945 to the 1960's illuminated American life by realistic reports of the way people live, Williams and Miller complemented their efforts with compelling testimony to the life-shaping power of dreams.

After some early failures, Tennessee Williams achieved stunning success with the Broadway production of *The Glass Menagerie* (1945). For the next fifteen years he was a dominant figure in the theater—and in the movies, where films of his plays made him one of the wealthiest writers of his time. Among his huge successes were *A Streetcar Named Desire* (1947), *Cat on a Hot Tin Roof* (1955), and *The Night of the Iguana* (1961), all heavily laden with sex, symbolism, and a Gothic extravagance that connects him in spirit with many of the southern writers of fiction of the period. One of the most prolific American playwrights, he is interesting even in experimental plays that proved largely unacceptable to audiences, such as the expressionistic *Camino Real* (1953).

Less prolific than Williams during this period, Arthur Miller also created some of its masterpieces, including one of the best of all American plays, *Death of a Salesman* (1949), a family drama set in a New York and Boston far removed in spirit from the St. Louis of *The Glass Menagerie* and the New Orleans of *A Streetcar Named Desire*, but sharing with those plays an overwhelming sense of the power of illusion—even within the most gritty and commercial confines of Northeast cities. Before *Salesman*, Miller had achieved success with *All My Sons* (1947), about a World War II manufacturer of defective aircraft parts. In *The Crucible* (1953) he found in the Salem witchcraft trials material for a parable on unjust persecution similar to that of the contemporary McCarthy hearings on Communism.

Other new playwrights of the period were generally less powerful than Williams and Miller. In the early years, only William Inge rivaled them for sustained achievement, with *Come Back, Little Sheba* (1950), *Picnic* (1953), *Bus Stop* (1955), and *The Dark at the Top of the Stairs* (1957) ranking among the finest plays of the decade. Robert Anderson's *Tea and Sympathy* (1953) achieved notoriety for its discussion of confused prep school sexuality. Later, the theater was vitalized by the appearance of Edward Albee at a time when Williams and Miller had produced much of their major work. His work, however, belongs to the 1960's and after.

Fiction

VLADIMIR NABOKOV
(1899–1977)

In the late 1950's, three decades after the publication in Russian of his first novel, *Mashen'ka* (1926; translated as *Mary,* 1970), Vladimir Nabokov began to be widely recognized as the possessor of a major literary talent. *Lolita* (Paris, 1955; New York, 1958) catapulted him to fame and financial independence. At sixty he was a celebrity, by seventy acclaimed as one of the finest stylists in English, one of the greatest novelists of his time. At an age when other writers had long since ceased to write or had turned to pale imitations of their younger selves, Nabokov continued to produce works of increasing depth and complexity. At the same time he collaborated with his son and other translators in making available in English the novels that he had originally written in Russian and published in Berlin and Paris in the 1920's and 1930's.

Much of his story, up until his immigration to the United States in 1940, is told in the remarkable autobiography *Speak, Memory* (1952; revised 1966; earlier titled *Conclusive Evidence,* 1951). He was born in St. Petersburg, Russia, and enjoyed the privileges of a wealthy aristocrat until forced to emigrate in 1919 as a result of the revolution. After four years at Trinity College, Cambridge, he settled in Berlin, where he lived until 1937, supplementing his income from writing by giving lessons in English, French, and tennis. In 1937 he moved to Paris, in 1940 to the United States, where he supported himself by a variety of academic positions, culminating in his eleven years as professor of Russian literature at Cornell (1948–1959). After 1959 he lived in Switzerland, devoting himself full-time to his writing.

A novelist of dazzling stylistic audacity, complex plot structures, multi-layered meanings, and, with it all, a puckish sense of humor, Nabokov is not a writer who can be mastered with ease, though not all his works are difficult. Among his earlier novels, *Laughter in the Dark* (1938; a revised version of *Camera Obscura,* 1933) might well serve as an introduction to the themes and techniques of the later ones. Among those written in English, *Pnin* (1957) remains the most amusing, the most accessible. Neither approaches the complexity of *Lolita, Pale Fire* (1962), or *Ada or Ardor: A Family Chronicle* (1969). A critic, poet, playwright, translator, short story writer, composer of chess problems, and student of lepidoptera, as well as a novelist, he was a man of monumental accomplishment.

Novels written originally in Russian include *Mary,* 1926, 1970; *King, Queen, Knave,* 1928, 1968; *The Defense,* 1930, 1964; *Glory,* 1932, 1971; *Camera Obscura,* 1933, 1937 (*Laughter in the Dark,* 1938); *Despair,* 1936, 1937, 1966; *Invitation to a Beheading,* 1938, 1959; and *The Gift,* 1952, 1963. *The Enchanter,* a novella originally written in Russian in 1939, was published in English in 1986. Novels written in English are *The Real Life of Sebastian Knight,* 1941; *Bend Sinister,* 1947; *Lolita,* 1955; *Pnin,* 1957; *Pale Fire,* 1962; *Ada * * *,* 1969; *Transparent Things,* 1972; and *Look at the Harlequins!,* 1974. Short story collections include *Nine Stories,* 1947; *Nabokov's Dozen,* 1958; *Nabokov's Quartet,* 1966; *A Russian Beauty and Other Stories,* 1973; *Tyrants Destroyed and Other Stories,* 1975; and *Details of a Sunset and Other Stories,* 1976. A play is *The*

Waltz Invention, 1966. Collections of verse are *Poems,* 1959; and *Poems and Problems,* 1971. A critical study is *Nikolai Gogol,* 1944. The most ambitious of several translations is Aleksandr Pushkin, *Eugene Onegin,* 4 vols., 1964. A memoir is *Speak, Memory: An Autobiography Revisited,* 1966 (earlier version *Conclusive Evidence,* 1951; *Speak, Memory,* 1952). *Strong Opinions,* a collection of essays and interviews, appeared in 1973. *Lectures on Literature,* with an introduction by John Updike, appeared in 1980. *Lectures on Russian Literature,* edited by Fredson Bowers, appeared in 1981. Selections from the works include Page Stegner, ed., *Nabokov's Congeries,* 1968; and *The Portable Nabokov,* 1971. Simon Karlinsky edited *The Nabokov–Wilson Letters: Correspondence Between Vladimir Nabokov and Edmund Wilson, 1940–1971,* 1979.

Biographies include Andrew Field, *VN: The Life and Art of Vladimir Nabokov,* 1986, and Field, *Nabokov, His Life in Part,* 1977. Critical studies include Page Stegner, *The Art of Vladimir Nabokov: Escape into Aesthetics,* 1966; Andrew Field, *Nabokov: His Life in Art,* 1967; L. S. Dembo, ed., *Nabokov: The Man and His Work,* 1967; Carl R. Proffer, *Keys to Lolita,* 1968; Alfred Appel, Jr., and Charles Newman, eds., *Nabokov: Criticism, Reminiscences,* * * *, 1970; Alfred Appel, Jr., ed., *The Annotated Lolita,* 1970; W. Woodlin Rowe, *Nabokov's Deceptive World,* 1971; Alfred Appel, Jr., *Nabokov's Dark Cinema,* 1974; Alex de Jonge, *The Real Life of Vladimir Nabokov,* 1976; Ellen Pifer, *Nabokov and the Novel,* 1980; Laurie Clancy, *The Novels of Vladimir Nabokov,* 1985; and David Rampton, *Vladimir Nabokov: A Critical Study of the Novels,* 1985.

[First Love][1]

1

In the early years of this century, a travel agency on Nevski Avenue displayed a three-foot-long model of an oak-brown international sleeping car. In delicate verisimilitude it completely outranked the painted tin of my clockwork trains. Unfortunately it was not for sale. One could make out the blue upholstery inside, the embossed leather lining of the compartment walls, their polished panels, inset mirrors, tulip-shaped reading lamps, and other maddening details. Spacious windows alternated with narrow ones, single or geminate, and some of these were of frosted glass. In a few of the compartments, the beds had been made.

The then great and glamorous Nord-Express (it was never the same after World War One when its elegant brown became a nouveau-riche blue), consisting solely of such international cars and running but twice a week, connected St. Petersburg with Paris. I would have said: directly with Paris, had passengers not been obliged to change from one train to a superficially similar one at the Russo-German frontier (Verzhbolovo-Eydtkuhnen), where the ample and lazy Russian sixty-and-a-half-inch gauge was replaced by the fifty-six-and-a-half-inch standard of Europe and coal succeeded birch logs.

In the far end of my mind I can unravel, I think, at least five such journeys to Paris, with the Riviera or Biarritz as their ultimate destination. In 1909, the year I now single out, our party consisted of eleven people and one dachshund. Wearing gloves and a traveling cap, my father sat reading a book in the compartment he shared with our tutor. My brother and I were separated from them by a washroom. My mother and her maid Natasha occupied a compartment adjacent to ours. Next came my two small sisters, their English governess, Miss Lavington, and a Russian nurse. The odd one of our party, my father's valet, Osip (whom a decade later, the pedantic Bolsheviks were to shoot, because he appropriated our bicycles instead of turning them over to the nation), had a stranger for companion.

Historically and artistically, the year had started with a political cartoon in *Punch:*[2] goddess England bending over goddess Italy, on whose head one of Messina's bricks has landed—probably, the worst picture *any* earthquake has ever inspired. In April

1. Chapter 7 of Nabokov's autobiography, *Speak, Memory,* published also as a short story under the title given above. The source of the present text is the revised edition of 1966.
2. British humor magazine.

of that year, Peary had reached the North Pole. In May, Shalyapin[3] had sung in Paris. In June, bothered by rumors of new and better Zeppelins, the United States War Department had told reporters of plans for an aerial Navy. In July, Blériot had flown from Calais to Dover (with a little additional loop when he lost his bearings). It was late August now. The firs and marshes of Northwestern Russia sped by, and on the following day gave way to German pinewoods and heather.

At a collapsible table, my mother and I played a card game called *durachki*. Although it was still broad daylight, our cards, a glass and, on a different plane, the locks of a suitcase were reflected in the window. Through forest and field, and in sudden ravines, and among scuttling cottages, those discarnate gamblers kept steadily playing on for steadily sparkling stakes. It was a long, very long game: on this gray winter morning, in the looking glass of my bright hotel room, I see shining the same, the very same, locks of that now seventy-year-old valise, a highish, heavyish *nécessaire de voyage*[4] of pigskin, with "H.N." elaborately interwoven in thick silver under a similar coronet, which had been bought in 1897 for my mother's wedding trip to Florence. In 1917 it transported from St. Petersburg to the Crimea and then to London a handful of jewels. Around 1930, it lost to a pawnbroker its expensive receptacles of crystal and silver leaving empty the cunningly contrived leathern holders on the inside of the lid. But that loss has been amply recouped during the thirty years it then traveled with me—from Prague to Paris, from St. Nazaire to New York and through the mirrors of more than two hundred motel rooms and rented houses, in forty-six states. The fact that of our Russian heritage the hardiest survivor proved to be a traveling bag is both logical and emblematic.

"*Ne budet-li, tï ved' ustal* [Haven't you had enough, aren't you tired]?" my mother would ask, and then would be lost in thought as she slowly shuffled the cards. The door of the compartment was open and I could see the corridor window, where the wires—six thin black wires—were doing their best to slant up, to ascend skywards, despite the lightning blows dealt them by one telegraph pole after another; but just as all six, in a triumphant swoop of pathetic elation, were about to reach the top of the window, a particularly vicious blow would bring them down, as low as they had ever been, and they would have to start all over again.

When, on such journeys as these, the train changed its pace to a dignified amble and all but grazed housefronts and shop signs, as we passed through some big German town, I used to feel a twofold excitement, which terminal stations could not provide. I saw a city, with its toylike trams, linden trees and brick walls, enter the compartment, hobnob with the mirrors, and fill to the brim the windows on the corridor side. This informal contact between train and city was one part of the thrill. The other was putting myself in the place of some passer-by who, I imagined, was moved as I would be moved myself to see the long, romantic, auburn cars, with their intervestibular connecting curtains as black as bat wings and their metal lettering copper-bright in the low sun, unhurriedly negotiate an iron bridge across an everyday thoroughfare and then turn, with all windows suddenly ablaze, around a last block of houses.

There were drawbacks to those optical amalgamations. The wide-windowed dining car, a vista of chaste bottles of mineral water, miter-folded napkins, and dummy chocolate bars (whose wrappers—Cailler, Kohler, and so forth—enclosed nothing

3. Feodor Chaliapin (1873–1938), Russian opera star.

4. Travel necessity.

but wood), would be perceived at first as a cool haven beyond a consecution of reeling blue corridors; but as the meal progressed toward its fatal last course, and more and more dreadfully one equilibrist with a full tray would back against our table to let another equilibrist pass with another full tray, I would keep catching the car in the act of being recklessly sheathed, lurching waiters and all, in the landscape, while the landscape itself went through a complex system of motion, the daytime moon stubbornly keeping abreast of one's plate, the distant meadows opening fanwise, the near trees sweeping up on invisible swings toward the track, a parallel rail line all at once committing suicide by anastomosis,[5] a bank of nictitating[6] grass rising, rising, rising, until the little witness of mixed velocities was made to disgorge his portion of *omelette aux confitures de fraises.*[7]

It was at night, however, that the *Compagnie Internationale des Wagons-Lits et des Grands Express Européens*[8] lived up to the magic of its name. From my bed under my brother's bunk (Was he asleep? Was he there at all?), in the semidarkness of our compartment, I watched things, and parts of things, and shadows, and sections of shadows cautiously moving about and getting nowhere. The woodwork gently creaked and crackled. Near the door that led to the toilet, a dim garment on a peg and, higher up, the tassel of the blue, bivalved nightlight swung rhythmically. It was hard to correlate those halting approaches, that hooded stealth, with the headlong rush of the outside night, which I knew *was* rushing by, spark-streaked, illegible.

I would put myself to sleep by the simple act of identifying myself with the engine driver. A sense of drowsy well-being invaded my veins as soon as I had everything nicely arranged—the carefree passengers in their rooms enjoying the ride I was giving them, smoking, exchanging knowing smiles, nodding, dozing; the waiters and cooks and train guards (whom I had to place somewhere) carousing in the diner; and myself, goggled and begrimed, peering out of the engine cab at the tapering track, at the ruby or emerald point in the black distance. And then, in my sleep, I would see something totally different—a glass marble rolling under a grand piano or a toy engine lying on its side with its wheels still working gamely.

A change in the speed of the train sometimes interrupted the current of my sleep. Slow lights were stalking by; each, in passing, investigated the same chink, and then a luminous compass measured the shadows. Presently, the train stopped with a long-drawn Westinghousian sigh. Something (my brother's spectacles, as it proved next day) fell from above. It was marvelously exciting to move to the foot of one's bed, with part of the bedclothes following, in order to undo cautiously the catch of the window shade, which could be made to slide only halfway up, impeded as it was by the edge of the upper berth.

Like moons around Jupiter, pale moths revolved about a lone lamp. A dismembered newspaper stirred on a bench. Somewhere on the train one could hear muffled voices, somebody's comfortable cough. There was nothing particularly interesting in the portion of station platform before me, and still I could not tear myself away from it until it departed of its own accord.

Next morning, wet fields with misshapen willows along the radius of a ditch or

5. Here, an optical illusion in which the rail lines seem to merge.
6. Winking: another illusion caused by the train's motion.
7. Omelet with strawberry jam.
8. International Company of Sleeping Cars and Grand European Express.

a row of poplars afar, traversed by a horizontal band of milky-white mist, told one that the train was spinning through Belgium. It reached Paris at 4 P.M., and even if the stay was only an overnight one, I had always time to purchase something—say, a little brass *Tour Eiffel,* rather roughly coated with silver paint—before we boarded, at noon on the following day, the Sud-Express[9] which, on its way to Madrid, dropped us around 10 P.M., at the La Négresse station of Biarritz, a few miles from the Spanish frontier.

2

Biarritz still retained its quiddity in those days. Dusty blackberry bushes and weedy *terrains à vendre*[1] bordered the road that led to our villa. The Carlton was still being built. Some thirty-six years had to elapse before Brigadier General Samuel McCroskey would occupy the royal suite of the Hôtel du Palais, which stands on the site of a former palace, where in the sixties, that incredibly agile medium, Daniel Home,[2] is said to have been caught stroking with his bare foot (in imitation of a ghost hand) the kind, trustful face of Empress Eugénie.[3] On the promenade near the Casino, an elderly flower girl, with carbon eyebrows and a painted smile, nimbly slipped the plump torus of a carnation into the buttonhole of an intercepted stroller whose left jowl accentuated its royal fold as he glanced down sideways at the coy insertion of the flower.

The rich-hued Oak Eggars[4] questing amid the brush were quite unlike ours (which did not breed on oak, anyway), and here the Speckled Woods haunted not woods, but hedges and had tawny, not pale-yellowish, spots. Cleopatra, a tropical-looking, lemon-and-orange Brimstone, languorously flopping about in gardens, had been a sensation in 1907 and was still a pleasure to net.

Along the back line of the *plage,*[5] various seaside chairs and stools supported the parents of straw-hatted children who were playing in front on the sand. I could be seen on my knees trying to set a found comb aflame by means of a magnifying glass. Men sported white trousers that to the eye of today would look as if they had comically shrunk in the washing; ladies wore, that particular season, light coats with silk-faced lapels, hats with big crowns and wide brims, dense embroidered white veils, frill-fronted blouses, frills at their wrists, frills on their parasols. The breeze salted one's lips. At a tremendous pace a stray Clouded Yellow came dashing across the palpitating *plage.*

Additional movement and sound were provided by venders hawking *cacahuètes,*[6] sugared violets, pistachio ice cream of a heavenly green, cachou pellets,[7] and huge convex pieces of dry, gritty, waferlike stuff that came from a red barrel. With a distinctness that no later superpositions have dimmed, I see that waffleman stomp along through deep mealy sand, with the heavy cask on his bent back. When called, he would sling it off his shoulder by a twist of its strap, bang it down on the sand in a Tower of Pisa position, wipe his face with his sleeve, and proceed to manipulate a kind of arrow-and-dial arrangement with numbers on the lid of the cask. The arrow rasped and whirred around. Luck was supposed to fix the size of a sou's worth of wafer. The bigger the piece, the more I was sorry for him.

9. Southern Express.
1. Plots of land for sale.
2. (1833–1886), Scottish-American spiritualist.
3. (1826–1920), consort of Napoleon III.
4. Like the following names, a kind of butterfly.
5. Beach.
6. Peanuts.
7. Breath lozenges.

The process of bathing took place on another part of the beach. Professional bathers, burly Basques in black bathing suits, were there to help ladies and children enjoy the terrors of the surf. Such a *baigneur* would place the *client* with his back to the incoming wave and hold him by the hand as the rising, rotating mass of foamy, green water violently descended from behind, knocking one off one's feet with a mighty wallop. After a dozen of these tumbles, the *baigneur,* glistening like a seal, would lead his panting, shivering, moistly snuffling charge landward, to the flat foreshore, where an unforgettable old woman with gray hairs on her chin promptly chose a bathing robe from several hanging on a clothesline. In the security of a little cabin, one would be helped by yet another attendant to peel off one's soggy, sand-heavy bathing suit. It would plop onto the boards, and, still shivering, one would step out of it and trample on its bluish, diffuse stripes. The cabin smelled of pine. The attendant, a hunchback with beaming wrinkles, brought a basin of steaming-hot water, in which one immersed one's feet. From him I learned, and have preserved ever since in a glass cell of my memory, that "butterfly" in the Basque language is *misericoletea*—or at least it sounded so (among the seven words I have found in dictionaries the closest approach is *micheletea*).

3

On the browner and wetter part of the *plage,* that part which at low tide yielded the best mud for castles, I found myself digging, one day, side by side with a little French girl called Colette.

She would be ten in November, I had been ten in April. Attention was drawn to a jagged bit of violet mussel shell upon which she had stepped with the bare sole of her narrow long-toed foot. No, I was not English. Her greenish eyes seemed flecked with the overflow of the freckles that covered her sharp-featured face. She wore what might now be termed a playsuit, consisting of a blue jersey with rolled-up sleeves and blue knitted shorts. I had taken her at first for a boy and then had been puzzled by the bracelet on her thin wrist and the corkscrew brown curls dangling from under her sailor cap.

She spoke in birdlike bursts of rapid twitter, mixing governess English and Parisian French. Two years before, on the same *plage,* I had been much attached to Zina, the lovely, sun-tanned, bad-tempered little daughter of a Serbian naturopath —she had, I remember (absurdly, for she and I were only eight at the time), a *grain de beauté*[8] on her apricot skin just below the heart, and there was a horrible collection of chamber pots, full and half-full, and one with surface bubbles, on the floor of the hall in her family's boardinghouse lodgings which I visited early one morning to be given by her as she was being dressed, a dead hummingbird moth found by the cat. But when I met Colette, I knew at once that this was the real thing. Colette seemed to me so much stranger than all my other chance playmates at Biarritz! I somehow acquired the feeling that she was less happy than I, less loved. A bruise on her delicate, downy forearm gave rise to awful conjectures. "He pinches as bad as my mummy," she said, speaking of a crab. I evolved various schemes to save her from her parents, who were *"des bourgeois de Paris"*[9] as I heard somebody tell my mother with a slight shrug. I interpreted the disdain in my own fashion, as I knew that those people had come all the way from Paris in their blue-and-yellow

8. Beauty mark.

9. Middle-class Parisians.

limousine (a fashionable adventure in those days) but had drably sent Colette with her dog and governess by an ordinary coachtrain. The dog was a female fox terrier with bells on her collar and a most waggly behind. From sheer exuberance, she would lap up salt water out of Colette's toy pail. I remember the sail, the sunset and the lighthouse pictured on that pail, but I cannot recall the dog's name, and this bothers me.

During the two months of our stay at Biarritz, my passion for Colette all but surpassed my passion for Cleopatra. Since my parents were not keen to meet hers, I saw her only on the beach; but I thought of her constantly. If I noticed she had been crying, I felt a surge of helpless anguish that brought tears to my own eyes. I could not destroy the mosquitoes that had left their bites on her frail neck, but I could, and did, have a successful fistfight with a red-haired boy who had been rude to her. She used to give me warm handfuls of hard candy. One day, as we were bending together over a starfish, and Colette's ringlets were tickling my ear, she suddenly turned toward me and kissed me on the cheek. So great was my emotion that all I could think of saying was, "You little monkey."

I had a gold coin that I assumed would pay for our elopement. Where did I want to take her? Spain? America? The mountains above Pau? *"Là-bas, là-bas, dans la montagne,"*[1] as I had heard Carmen sing at the opera. One strange night, I lay awake, listening to the recurrent thud of the ocean and planning our flight. The ocean seemed to rise and grope in the darkness and then heavily fall on its face.

Of our actual getaway, I have little to report. My memory retains a glimpse of her obediently putting on rope-soled canvas shoes, on the lee side of a flapping tent, while I stuffed a folding butterfly net into a brown-paper bag. The next glimpse is of our evading pursuit by entering a pitch-dark *cinéma* near the Casino (which, of course, was absolutely out of bounds). There we sat, holding hands across the dog, which now and then gently jingled in Colette's lap, and were shown a jerky, drizzly, but highly exciting bullfight at San Sebastián. My final glimpse is of myself being led along the promenade by Linderovski. His long legs move with a kind of ominous briskness and I can see the muscles of his grimly set jaw working under the tight skin. My bespectacled brother, aged nine, whom he happens to hold with his other hand, keeps trotting out forward to peer at me with awed curiosity, like a little owl.

Among the trivial souvenirs acquired at Biarritz before leaving, my favorite was not the small bull of black stone and not the sonorous seashell but something which now seems almost symbolic—a meerschaum penholder with a tiny peephole of crystal in its ornamental part. One held it quite close to one's eye, screwing up the other, and when one had got rid of the shimmer of one's own lashes, a miraculous photographic view of the bay and of the line of cliffs ending in a lighthouse could be seen inside.

And now a delightful thing happens. The process of recreating that penholder and the microcosm in its eyelet stimulates my memory to a last effort. I try again to recall the name of Colette's dog—and, triumphantly, along those remote beaches, over the glossy evening sands of the past, where each footprint slowly fills up with sunset water, here it comes, here it comes, echoing and vibrating: Floss, Floss, Floss!

Colette was back in Paris by the time we stopped there for a day before continuing our homeward journey; and there, in a fawn park under a cold blue sky, I saw her

1. Over there, over there, in the mountains.

(by arrangement between our mentors, I believe) for the last time. She carried a hoop and a short stick to drive it with, and everything about her was extremely proper and stylish in an autumnal, Parisian, *tenue-de-ville-pour-fillettes*[2] way. She took from her governess and slipped into my brother's hand a farewell present, a box of sugar-coated almonds, meant, I knew, solely for me; and instantly she was off, tap-tapping her glinting hoop through light and shade, around and around a fountain choked with dead leaves, near which I stood. The leaves mingle in my memory with the leather of her shoes and gloves, and there was, I remember, some detail in her attire (perhaps a ribbon on her Scottish cap, or the pattern of her stockings) that reminded me then of the rainbow spiral in a glass marble. I still seem to be holding that wisp of iridescence, not knowing exactly where to fit it, while she runs with her hoop ever faster around me and finally dissolves among the slender shadows cast on the graveled path by the interlaced arches of its low looped fence.

1948, 1951

ISAAC BASHEVIS SINGER
(1904–)

Writing in Yiddish all his life, except for a period in his youth when he composed in Hebrew, Isaac Bashevis Singer has revitalized a dying language and demonstrated the transcendent importance of the writer's cultural heritage in supplying his deepest imaginative resources.

Singer was born a few miles from Warsaw, in the Polish village of Leoncin. His father was a rabbi, his mother the daughter of a rabbi. Later, his older brother, Israel Joshua Singer, for a while much better known as a novelist, was to describe the village of their youth in *Of a World That Is No More* (1946). For Isaac, the Leoncin period ended in 1908, when his father became an ecclesiastical judge in Warsaw, a time later described in Singer's autobiographical *In My Father's Court* (1966). Four years as a teenager in the village of Bilgoray gave him the setting, though not the time period, for his first novel, *Satan in Goray* (Yiddish, 1935; English, 1955), an account of warfare with the Ukrainians and ensuing civil strife in seventeenth-century Poland. A brief enrollment in a rabbinical seminary in Warsaw was followed by twelve more years in that city, proofreading for a Yiddish literary journal and composing his early fiction, before he immigrated to the United States in 1935.

Singer's arrival in New York effectively put an end to his serious writing accomplishment for most of the next decade. "When I came to this country," he has said, "I lived through a terrible disappointment. I felt then—more than I believe now—that Yiddish had no future in this country." He had no desire to write in another language and felt cut off from his cultural roots. As a journalist for the *Jewish Daily Forward* in New York, he could accomplish little creative work during either the Depression or the early 1940's. Finally turning to fiction again in the darkness of World War II, he began *The Family Moskat,* impelled by a desire to record a vanished world: "I said to myself, 'Warsaw has just now been destroyed. No one will ever see the Warsaw I knew. Let me just write about it. Let this Warsaw not disappear forever.' " *The Family Moskat,* after serial publication in Yiddish in the *Forward* (1945–1948), was published in book form

2. City clothes for little girls.

in 1950 both in Yiddish and in English, winning an enthusiastic reception. Revitalized by this success, Singer became in the decades after 1950 one of the most prolific of first-rank American authors, writing in Yiddish, but closely supervising the translations into English to ensure that each work would retain as much as possible the flavor of the original. His reputation spread world-wide and in 1978 he was awarded the Nobel Prize for literature.

Singer's world, especially in his novels, is generally Poland before 1939. *The Family Moskat* traces three generations of Polish Jews from before the First World War to the brink of the Second. *The Manor* (1967) and *The Estate* (1970) are related chronicles dealing with czarist domination in the nineteenth century. *The Magician of Lublin* (1960) presents an early twentieth-century world of magic, religious questioning, and marital infidelity. *The Slave* (1962) is the story of a Jew enslaved by Polish peasants in the seventeenth century. In his short stories, he ranges as far afield as New York and Tel Aviv, but only to return again and again to his beloved Poland. *The Collected Stories* appeared in 1982.

In some respects an old-fashioned writer, Singer is distrustful of such twentieth-century techniques as stream of consciousness. He prefers the deceptively simple magic of the old-time storyteller to the sophisticated sleight of hand practiced by many of his contemporaries. Literature is in his understanding primarily an entertainment for the reader, a delightful puzzle for the writer, as both attempt to come together to understand an infinitely variable humanity in an inscrutable universe.

Besides those named above, Singer's works of adult fiction to date include *Gimpel the Fool and Other Stories,* 1957; *The Spinoza of Market Street and Other Stories,* 1961; *Short Friday and Other Stories,* 1964; *The Séance and Other Stories,* 1968; *A Friend of Kafka and Other Stories,* 1970; *Enemies: A Love Story,* 1972; *A Crown of Feathers and Other Stories,* 1973; *Passions and Other Stories,* 1975; *Shosha,* 1978; *Old Love,* 1979; *The Penitent,* 1983; and *The Image and Other Stories,* 1985. *Selected Short Stories* was published in 1966. Singer has also published many works of juvenile literature. *Lost in America,* 1981; and *Love and Exile: The Early Years,* 1985, are memoirs.

Biographical and critical studies include Irving H. Buchen, *Isaac Bashevis Singer and the Eternal Past,* 1968; Marcia Allentuck, ed., *The Achievement of Isaac Bashevis Singer,* 1970; Irving Malin, ed., *Critical Views of Isaac Bashevis Singer,* 1969; Irving Malin, *Isaac Bashevis Singer,* 1972; Paul Kresh, *Isaac Bashevis Singer: The Magician of West 86th Street,* 1979; and Edward Alexander, *Isaac Bashevis Singer,* 1980. Clive Sinclair, *The Brothers Singer,* 1983, is a biographical study of I. B. Singer and of his older brother Israel Joshua, also a novelist.

Gimpel the Fool[1]

I

I am Gimpel the fool. I don't think myself a fool. On the contrary. But that's what folks call me. They gave me the name while I was still in school. I had seven names in all: imbecile, donkey, flax-head, dope, glump, ninny, and fool. The last name stuck. What did my foolishness consist of? I was easy to take in. They said, "Gimpel, you know the rabbi's wife has been brought to childbed?" So I skipped school. Well, it turned out to be a lie. How was I supposed to know? She hadn't had a big belly. But I never looked at her belly. Was that really so foolish? The gang laughed and hee-hawed, stomped and danced and chanted a good-night prayer. And instead of the raisins they give when a woman's lying in, they stuffed my hand full of goat turds. I was no weakling. If I slapped someone he'd see all the way to Cracow. But I'm really not a slugger by nature. I think to myself: Let it pass. So they take advantage of me.

1. Translated by Saul Bellow.

I was coming home from school and heard a dog barking. I'm not afraid of dogs, but of course I never want to start up with them. One of them may be mad, and if he bites there's not a Tartar in the world who can help you. So I made tracks. Then I looked around and saw the whole market place wild with laughter. It was no dog at all but Wolf-Leib the Thief. How was I supposed to know it was he? It sounded like a howling bitch.

When the pranksters and leg-pullers found that I was easy to fool, every one of them tried his luck with me. "Gimpel, the Czar is coming to Frampol; Gimpel, the moon fell down in Turbeen; Gimpel, little Hodel Furpiece found a treasure behind the bathhouse." And I like a golem[2] believed everyone. In the first place, everything is possible, as it is written in the Wisdom of the Fathers, I've forgotten just how. Second, I had to believe when the whole town came down on me! If I ever dared to say, "Ah, you're kidding!" there was trouble. People got angry. "What do you mean! You want to call everyone a liar?" What was I to do? I believed them, and I hope at least that did them some good.

I was an orphan. My grandfather who brought me up was already bent toward the grave. So they turned me over to a baker, and what a time they gave me there! Every woman or girl who came to bake a batch of noodles had to fool me at least once. "Gimpel, there's a fair in heaven; Gimpel, the rabbi gave birth to a calf in the seventh month; Gimpel, a cow flew over the roof and laid brass eggs." A student from the yeshiva[3] came once to buy a roll, and he said, "You, Gimpel, while you stand here scraping with your baker's shovel the Messiah has come. The dead have arisen." "What do you mean?" I said. "I heard no one blowing the ram's horn!" He said, "Are you deaf?" And all began to cry, "We heard it, we heard!" Then in came Rietze the Candle-dipper and called out in her hoarse voice, "Gimpel, your father and mother have stood up from the grave. They're looking for you."

To tell the truth, I knew very well that nothing of the sort had happened, but all the same, as folks were talking, I threw on my wool vest and went out. Maybe something had happened. What did I stand to lose by looking? Well, what a cat music went up! And then I took a vow to believe nothing more. But that was no go either. They confused me so that I didn't know the big end from the small.

I went to the rabbi to get some advice. He said, "It is written, better to be a fool all your days than for one hour to be evil. You are not a fool. They are the fools. For he who causes his neighbor to feel shame loses Paradise himself." Nevertheless the rabbi's daughter took me in. As I left the rabbinical court she said, "Have you kissed the wall yet?" I said, "No; what for?" She answered, "It's the law; you've got to do it after every visit." Well, there didn't seem to be any harm in it. And she burst out laughing. It was a fine trick. She put one over on me, all right.

I wanted to go off to another town, but then everyone got busy matchmaking, and they were after me so they nearly tore my coat tails off. They talked at me and talked until I got water on the ear. She was no chaste maiden, but they told me she was virgin pure. She had a limp, and they said it was deliberate, from coyness. She had a bastard, and they told me the child was her little brother. I cried, "You're wasting your time. I'll never marry that whore." But they said indignantly, "What a way to talk! Aren't you ashamed of yourself? We can take you to the rabbi and have you fined for giving her a bad name." I saw then that I wouldn't escape them

2. In Jewish folklore an artificial person supernaturally given life, a robot.

3. A school for studying the Talmud, or one combining religious and secular studies.

so easily and I thought: They're set on making me their butt. But when you're married the husband's the master, and if that's all right with her it's agreeable to me too. Besides, you can't pass through life unscathed, nor expect to.

I went to her clay house, which was built on the sand, and the whole gang, hollering and chorusing, came after me. They acted like bear-baiters. When we came to the well they stopped all the same. They were afraid to start anything with Elka. Her mouth would open as if it were on a hinge, and she had a fierce tongue. I entered the house. Lines were strung from wall to wall and clothes were drying. Barefoot she stood by the tub, doing the wash. She was dressed in a worn hand-me-down gown of plush. She had her hair put up in braids and pinned across her head. It took my breath away, almost, the reek of it all.

Evidently she knew who I was. She took a look at me and said, "Look who's here! He's come, the drip. Grab a seat."

I told her all; I denied nothing. "Tell me the truth," I said, "are you really a virgin, and is that mischievous Yechiel actually your little brother? Don't be deceitful with me, for I'm an orphan."

"I'm an orphan myself," she answered, "and whoever tries to twist you up, may the end of his nose take a twist. But don't let them think they can take advantage of me. I want a dowry of fifty guilders, and let them take up a collection besides. Otherwise they can kiss my you-know-what." She was very plainspoken. I said, "It's the bride and not the groom who gives a dowry." Then she said, "Don't bargain with me. Either a flat 'yes' or a flat 'no'—Go back where you came from."

I thought: No bread will ever be baked from *this* dough. But ours is not a poor town. They consented to everything and proceeded with the wedding. It so happened that there was a dysentery epidemic at the time. The ceremony was held at the cemetery gates, near the little corpse-washing hut. The fellows got drunk. While the marriage contract was being drawn up I heard the most pious high rabbi ask, "Is the bride a widow or a divorced woman?" And the sexton's wife answered for her, "Both a widow and divorced." It was a black moment for me. But what was I to do, run away from under the marriage canopy?

There was singing and dancing. An old granny danced opposite me, hugging a braided white *chalah.*[4] The master of revels made a "God 'a mercy" in memory of the bride's parents. The schoolboys threw burrs, as on Tishe b'Av[5] fast day. There were a lot of gifts after the sermon: a noodle board, a kneading trough, a bucket, brooms, ladles, household articles galore. Then I took a look and saw two strapping young men carrying a crib. "What do we need this for?" I asked. So they said, "Don't rack your brains about it. It's all right, it'll come in handy." I realized I was going to be rooked. Take it another way though, what did I stand to lose? I reflected: I'll see what comes of it. A whole town can't go altogether crazy.

II

At night I came where my wife lay, but she wouldn't let me in. "Say, look here, is this what they married us for?" I said. And she said, "My monthly has come." "But yesterday they took you to the ritual bath, and that's afterward, isn't it supposed to be?" "Today isn't yesterday," said she, "and yesterday's not today. You can beat it if you don't like it." In short, I waited.

4. Bread for the Sabbath.

5. A day of mourning commemorating the destruction of the Temple, A.D. 70.

Nor four months later she was in childbed. The townsfolk hid their laughter with their knuckles. But what could I do? She suffered intolerable pains and clawed at the walls. "Gimpel," she cried, "I'm going. Forgive me!" The house filled with women. They were boiling pans of water. The screams rose to the welkin.

The thing to do was to go to the House of Prayer to repeat Psalms, and that was what I did.

The townsfolk liked that, all right. I stood in a corner saying Psalms and prayers, and they shook their heads at me. "Pray, pray!" they told me. "Prayer never made any woman pregnant." One of the congregation put a straw to my mouth and said, "Hay for the cows." There was something to that too, by God!

She gave birth to a boy. Friday at the synagogue the sexton stood up before the Ark, pounded on the reading table, and announced, "The wealthy Reb Gimpel invites the congregation to a feast in honor of the birth of a son." The whole House of Prayer rang with laughter. My face was flaming. But there was nothing I could do. After all, I *was* the one responsible for the circumcision honors and rituals.

Half the town came running. You couldn't wedge another soul in. Women brought peppered chick-peas, and there was a keg of beer from the tavern. I ate and drank as much as anyone, and they all congratulated me. Then there was a circumcision, and I named the boy after my father, may he rest in peace. When all were gone and I was left with my wife alone, she thrust her head through the bed-curtain and called me to her.

"Gimpel," said she, "why are you silent? Has your ship gone and sunk?"

"What shall I say?" I answered. "A fine thing you've done to me! If my mother had known of it she'd have died a second time."

She said, "Are you crazy, or what?"

"How can you make such a fool," I said, "of one who should be the lord and master?"

"What's the matter with you?" she said. "What have you taken it into your head to imagine?"

I saw that I must speak bluntly and openly. "Do you think this is the way to use an orphan?" I said. "You have borne a bastard."

She answered, "Drive this foolishness out of your head. The child is yours."

"How can he be mine?" I argued. "He was born seventeen weeks after the wedding."

She told me then that he was premature. I said, "Isn't he a little too premature?" She said, she had had a grandmother who carried just as short a time and she resembled this grandmother of hers as one drop of water does another. She swore to it with such oaths that you would have believed a peasant at the fair if he had used them. To tell the plain truth, I didn't believe her; but when I talked it over next day with the schoolmaster he told me that the very same thing had happened to Adam and Eve. Two they went up to bed, and four they descended.

"There isn't a woman in the world who is not the granddaughter of Eve," he said.

That was how it was; they argued me dumb. But then, who really knows how such things are?

I began to forget my sorrow. I loved the child madly, and he loved me too. As soon as he saw me he'd wave his little hands and want me to pick him up, and when he was colicky I was the only one who could pacify him. I bought him a little bone teething ring and a little gilded cap. He was forever catching the evil eye from someone, and then I had to run to get one of those abracadabras for him that would get him out of it. I worked like an ox. You know how expenses go up when there's an infant in the house. I don't want to lie about it; I didn't dislike Elka either, for that matter. She swore at me and cursed, and I couldn't get enough of her. What strength she had! One of her looks could rob you of the power of speech. And her orations! Pitch and sulphur, that's what they were full of, and yet somehow also full of charm. I adored her every word. She gave me bloody wounds though.

In the evening I brought her a white loaf as well as a dark one, and also poppyseed rolls I baked myself. I thieved because of her and swiped everything I could lay hands on: macaroons, raisins, almonds, cakes. I hope I may be forgiven for stealing from the Saturday pots the women left to warm in the baker's oven. I would take out scraps of meat, a chunk of pudding, a chicken leg or head, a piece of tripe, whatever I could nip quickly. She ate and became fat and handsome.

I had to sleep away from home all during the week, at the bakery. On Friday nights when I got home she always made an excuse of some sort. Either she had heartburn, or a stitch in the side, or hiccups, or headaches. You know what women's excuses are. I had a bitter time of it. It was rough. To add to it, this little brother of hers, the bastard, was growing bigger. He'd put lumps on me, and when I wanted to hit back she'd open her mouth and curse so powerfully I saw a green haze floating before my eyes. Ten times a day she threatened to divorce me. Another man in my place would have taken French leave and disappeared. But I'm the type that bears it and says nothing. What's one to do? Shoulders are from God, and burdens too.

One night there was a calamity in the bakery; the oven burst, and we almost had a fire. There was nothing to do but go home, so I went home. Let me, I thought, also taste the joy of sleeping in bed in mid-week. I didn't want to wake the sleeping mite and tiptoed into the house. Coming in, it seemed to me that I heard not the snoring of one but, as it were, a double snore, one a thin enough snore and the other like the snoring of a slaughtered ox. Oh, I didn't like that! I didn't like it at all. I went up to the bed, and things suddenly turned black. Next to Elka lay a man's form. Another in my place would have made an uproar, and enough noise to rouse the whole town, but the thought occurred to me that I might wake the child. A little thing like that—why frighten a little swallow, I thought. All right then, I went back to the bakery and stretched out on a sack of flour and till morning I never shut an eye. I shivered as if I had had malaria. "Enough of being a donkey," I said to myself. "Gimpel isn't going to be a sucker all his life. There's a limit even to the foolishness of a fool like Gimpel."

In the morning I went to the rabbi to get advice, and it made a great commotion in the town. They sent the beadle for Elka right away. She came, carrying the child. And what do you think she did? She denied it, denied everything, bone and stone! "He's out of his head," she said. "I know nothing of dreams or divinations." They yelled at her, warned her, hammered on the table, but she stuck to her guns: it was a false accusation, she said.

The butchers and the horse-traders took her part. One of the lads from the slaughterhouse came by and said to me, "We've got our eye on you, you're a marked man." Meanwhile the child started to bear down and soiled itself. In the rabbinical court there was an Ark of the Covenant, and they couldn't allow that, so they sent Elka away.

I said to the rabbi, "What shall I do?"

"You must divorce her at once," said he.

"And what if she refuses?" I asked.

He said, "You must serve the divorce. That's all you'll have to do."

I said, "Well, all right, Rabbi. Let me think about it."

"There's nothing to think about," said he. "You mustn't remain under the same roof with her."

"And if I want to see the child?" I asked.

"Let her go, the harlot," said he, "and her brood of bastards with her."

The verdict he gave was that I mustn't even cross her threshold—never again, as long as I should live.

During the day it didn't bother me so much. I thought: It was bound to happen, the abscess had to burst. But at night when I stretched out upon the sacks I felt it all very bitterly. A longing took me, for her and for the child. I wanted to be angry, but that's my misfortune exactly, I don't have it in me to be really angry. In the first place—this was how my thoughts went—there's bound to be a slip sometimes. You can't live without errors. Probably that lad who was with her led her on and gave her presents and what not, and women are often long on hair and short on sense, and so he got around her. And then since she denies it so, maybe I was only seeing things? Hallucinations do happen. You see a figure or a mannikin or something, but when you come up closer it's nothing, there's not a thing there. And if that's so, I'm doing her an injustice. And when I got so far in my thoughts I started to weep. I sobbed so that I wet the flour where I lay. In the morning I went to the rabbi and told him that I had made a mistake. The rabbi wrote on with his quill, and he said that if that were so he would have to reconsider the whole case. Until he had finished I wasn't to go near my wife, but I might send her bread and money by messenger.

III

Nine months passed before all the rabbis could come to an agreement. Letters went back and forth. I hadn't realized that there could be so much erudition about a matter like this.

Meanwhile Elka gave birth to still another child, a girl this time. On the Sabbath I went to the synagogue and invoked a blessing on her. They called me up to the Torah, and I named the child for my mother-in-law—may she rest in peace. The louts and loudmouths of the town who came into the bakery gave me a going over. All Frampol refreshed its spirits because of my trouble and grief. However, I resolved that I would always believe what I was told. What's the good of *not* believing? Today it's your wife you don't believe; tomorrow it's God Himself you won't take stock in.

By an apprentice who was her neighbor I sent her daily a corn or a wheat loaf, or a piece of pastry, rolls or bagels, or, when I got the chance, a slab of pudding, a slice of honeycake, or wedding strudel—whatever came my way. The apprentice was a goodhearted lad, and more than once he added something on his own. He had formerly annoyed me a lot, plucking my nose and digging me in the ribs, but when he started to be a visitor to my house he became kind and friendly. "Hey, you, Gimpel," he said to me, "you have a very decent little wife and two fine kids. You don't deserve them."

"But the things people say about her," I said.

"Well, they have long tongues," he said, "and nothing to do with them but babble. Ignore it as you ignore the cold of last winter."

One day the rabbi sent for me and said, "Are you certain, Gimpel, that you were wrong about your wife?"

I said, "I'm certain."

"Why, but look here! You yourself saw it."

"It must have been a shadow," I said.

"The shadow of what?"

"Just of one of the beams, I think."

"You can go home then. You owe thanks to the Yanover rabbi. He found an obscure reference in Maimonides that favored you."

I seized the rabbi's hand and kissed it.

I wanted to run home immediately. It's no small thing to be separated for so long a time from wife and child. Then I reflected: I'd better go back to work now, and go home in the evening. I said nothing to anyone, although as far as my heart was concerned it was like one of the Holy Days. The women teased and twitted me as they did every day, but my thought was: Go on, with your loose talk. The truth is out, like the oil upon the water. Maimonides says it's right, and therefore it is right!

At night, when I had covered the dough to let it rise, I took my share of bread and a little sack of flour and started homeward. The moon was full and the stars were glistening, something to terrify the soul. I hurried onward, and before me darted a long shadow. It was winter, and a fresh snow had fallen. I had a mind to sing, but it was growing late and I didn't want to wake the householders. Then I felt like whistling, but I remembered that you don't whistle at night because it brings the demons out. So I was silent and walked as fast as I could.

Dogs in the Christian yards barked at me when I passed, but I thought: Bark your teeth out! What are you but mere dogs? Whereas I am a man, the husband of a fine wife, the father of promising children.

As I approached the house my heart started to pound as though it were the heart of a criminal. I felt no fear, but my heart went thump! thump! Well, no drawing back. I quietly lifted the latch and went in. Elka was asleep. I looked at the infant's cradle. The shutter was closed, but the moon forced its way through the cracks. I saw the newborn child's face and loved it as soon as I saw it—immediately—each tiny bone.

Then I came nearer to the bed. And what did I see but the apprentice lying there beside Elka. The moon went out all at once. I was utterly black, and I trembled. My teeth chattered. The bread fell from my hands, and my wife waked and said, "Who is that, ah?"

I muttered, "It's me."

"Gimpel?" she asked. "How come you're here? I thought it was forbidden."

"The rabbi said," I answered and shook as with a fever.

"Listen to me, Gimpel," she said, "go out to the shed and see if the goat's all right. It seems she's been sick." I have forgotten to say that we had a goat. When I heard she was unwell I went into the yard. The nannygoat was a good little creature. I had a nearly human feeling for her.

With hesitant steps I went up to the shed and opened the door. The goat stood there on her four feet. I felt her everywhere, drew her by the horns, examined her udders, and found nothing wrong. She had probably eaten too much bark. "Good night, little goat," I said. "Keep well." And the little beast answered with a "Maa" as though to thank me for the good will.

I went back. The apprentice had vanished.

"Where," I asked, "is the lad?"

"What lad?" my wife answered.

"What do you mean?" I said. "The apprentice. You were sleeping with him."

"The things I have dreamed this night and the night before," she said, "may they come true and lay you low, body and soul! An evil spirit has taken root in you and dazzles your sight." She screamed out, "You hateful creature! You moon calf! You spook! You uncouth man! Get out, or I'll scream all Frampol out of bed!"

Before I could move, her brother sprang out from behind the oven and struck me a blow on the back of the head. I thought he had broken my neck. I felt that something about me was deeply wrong, and I said, "Don't make a scandal. All that's needed now is that people should accuse me of raising spooks and *dybbuks*."[6] For that was what she had meant. "No one will touch bread of my baking."

In short, I somehow calmed her.

"Well," she said, "that's enough. Lie down, and be shattered by wheels."

Next morning I called the apprentice aside. "Listen here, brother!" I said. And so on and so forth. "What do you say?" He stared at me as though I had dropped from the roof or something.

"I swear," he said, "you'd better go to an herb doctor or some healer. I'm afraid you have a screw loose, but I'll hush it up for you." And that's how the thing stood.

To make a long story short, I lived twenty years with my wife. She bore me six children, four daughters and two sons. All kinds of things happened, but I neither saw nor heard. I believed, and that's all. The rabbi recently said to me, "Belief in itself is beneficial. It is written that a good man lives by his faith."

Suddenly my wife took sick. It began with a trifle, a little growth upon the breast. But she evidently was not destined to live long; she had no years. I spent a fortune on her. I have forgotten to say that by this time I had a bakery of my own and in Frampol was considered to be something of a rich man. Daily the healer came, and every witch doctor in the neighborhood was brought. They decided to use leeches, and after that to try cupping. They even called a doctor from Lublin, but it was too late. Before she died she called me to her bed and said, "Forgive me, Gimpel."

I said, "What is there to forgive? You have been a good and faithful wife."

"Woe, Gimpel!" she said. "It was ugly how I deceived you all these years. I want to go clean to my Maker, and so I have to tell you that the children are not yours."

If I had been clouted on the head with a piece of wood it couldn't have bewildered me more.

"Whose are they?" I asked.

"I don't know," she said. "There were a lot . . . but they're not yours." And as she spoke she tossed her head to the side, her eyes turned glassy, and it was all up with Elka. On her whitened lips there remained a smile.

I imagined that, dead as she was, she was saying, "I deceived Gimpel. That was the meaning of my brief life."

IV

One night, when the period of mourning was done, as I lay dreaming on the flour sacks, there came the Spirit of Evil himself and said to me, "Gimpel, why do you sleep?"

I said, "What should I be doing? Eating *kreplach?*"[7]

6. Spirits of the dead who enter the bodies of the living.

7. A case of noodle dough filled with ground or chopped meat.

"The whole world deceives you," he said, "and you ought to deceive the world in your turn."

"How can I deceive all the world?" I asked him.

He answered, "You might accumulate a bucket of urine every day and at night pour it into the dough. Let the sages of Frampol eat filth."

"What about the judgment in the world to come?" I said.

"There is no world to come," he said. "They've sold you a bill of goods and talked you into believing you carried a cat in your belly. What nonsense!"

"Well then," I said, "and is there a God?"

He answered, "There is no God either."

"What," I said, "*is* there, then?"

"A thick mire."

He stood before my eyes with a goatish beard and horn, long-toothed, and with a tail. Hearing such words, I wanted to snatch him by the tail, but I tumbled from the flour sacks and nearly broke a rib. Then it happened that I had to answer the call of nature, and, passing, I saw the risen dough, which seemed to say to me, "Do it!" In brief, I let myself be persuaded.

At dawn the apprentice came. We kneaded the bread, scattered caraway seeds on it, and set it to bake. Then the apprentice went away, and I was left sitting in the little trench by the oven, on a pile of rags. Well, Gimpel, I thought, you've revenged yourself on them for all the shame they've put on you. Outside the frost glittered, but it was warm beside the oven. The flames heated my face. I bent my head and fell into a doze.

I saw in a dream, at once, Elka in her shroud. She called to me, "What have you done, Gimpel?"

I said to her, "It's all your fault," and started to cry.

"You fool!" she said. "You fool! Because I was false is everything false too? I never deceived anyone but myself. I'm paying for it all, Gimpel. They spare you nothing here."

I looked at her face. It was black; I was startled and waked, and remained sitting dumb. I sensed that everything hung in the balance. A false step now and I'd lose Eternal Life. But God gave me His help. I seized the long shovel and took out the loaves, carried them into the yard, and started to dig a hole in the frozen earth.

My apprentice came back as I was doing it. "What are you doing boss?" he said, and grew pale as a corpse.

"I know what I'm doing," I said, and I buried it all before his very eyes.

Then I went home, took my hoard from its hiding place, and divided it among the children. "I saw your mother tonight," I said. "She's turning black, poor thing."

They were so astounded they couldn't speak a word.

"Be well," I said, "and forget that such a one as Gimpel ever existed." I put on my short coat, a pair of boots, took the bag that held my prayer shawl in one hand, my stock in the other, and kissed the *mezzuzah.*[8] When people saw me in the street they were greatly surprised.

"Where are you going?" they said.

I answered, "Into the world." And so I departed from Frampol.

I wandered over the land, and good people did not neglect me. After many years

8. A parchment scroll inscribed with texts from Deuteronomy and with the name of God, enclosed in a case and attached to a doorpost.

I became old and white; I heard a great deal, many lies and falsehoods, but the longer I lived the more I understood that there were really no lies. Whatever doesn't really happen is dreamed at night. It happens to one if it doesn't happen to another, tomorrow if not today, or a century hence if not next year. What difference can it make? Often I heard tales of which I said, "Now this is a thing that cannot happen." But before a year had elapsed I heard that it actually had come to pass somewhere.

Going from place to place, eating at strange tables, it often happens that I spin yarns—improbable things that could never have happened—about devils, magicians, windmills, and the like. The children run after me, calling, "Grandfather, tell us a story." Sometimes they ask for particular stories, and I try to please them. A fat young boy once said to me, "Grandfather, it's the same story you told us before." The little rogue, he was right.

So it is with dreams too. It is many years since I left Frampol, but as soon as I shut my eyes I am there again. And whom do you think I see? Elka. She is standing by the washtub, as at our first encounter, but her face is shining and her eyes are as radiant as the eyes of a saint, and she speaks outlandish words to me, strange things. When I wake I have forgotten it all. But while the dream lasts I am comforted. She answers all my queries, and what comes out is that all is right. I weep and implore, "Let me be with you." And she consoles me and tells me to be patient. The time is nearer than it is far. Sometimes she strokes and kisses me and weeps upon my face. When I awaken I feel her lips and taste the salt of her tears.

No doubt the world is entirely an imaginary world, but it is only once removed from the true world. At the door of the hovel where I lie, there stands the plank on which the dead are taken away. The gravedigger Jew has his spade ready. The grave waits and the worms are hungry; the shrouds are prepared—I carry them in my beggar's sack. Another *shnorrer*[9] is waiting to inherit my bed of straw. When the time comes I will go joyfully. Whatever may be there, it will be real, without complication, without ridicule, without deception. God be praised: there even Gimpel cannot be deceived.

1953, 1957

EUDORA WELTY

(1909–)

"It seems plain," Eudora Welty once wrote, "that the art that speaks most clearly, explicitly, directly, and passionately from its place of origin will remain the longest understood." From the beginning hers has been an art informed by saturation; behind each finely wrought sentence there lies a sense of absorption from depths that are not readily plumbed by writers less familiar with their material. She knows her region thoroughly and conveys its surface with the skill of a trained photographer; shimmering beneath that surface, however, there are almost always the deeper waters where objective reality merges with symbol and myth. There is a sense in which the opening sentence of *The Wide Net and Other Stories* (1943) may be taken as an appropriate epigraph for all her work: "Whatever happened, it happened in extraordinary times, in a season of dreams * * *."

9. Beggar.

Eudora Welty was born in Jackson, Mississippi, and has spent most of her life there, living since age six in the same house. Her ancestors were country people, with an American heritage predating the Revolution. That her parents were not from the deep South, but from West Virginia and Ohio, has suggested to some critics a reason for the sensitive mixture of objectivity and compassion with which she views the southern scene. Educated at Mississippi State College for Women and at the University of Wisconsin, she did graduate work at the School of Business of Columbia University. In the 1930's she found employment in a variety of advertising, publicity, and newspaper positions in Mississippi, while she took the photographs that resulted in a show in New York in 1936, and wrote the stories that, initially at least, she thought inferior to the photographs. In 1936 she began publishing in magazines the stories that were first collected in *A Curtain of Green and Other Stories* (1941). Honored with a Guggenheim Fellowship, grants from the Rockefeller Foundation and the National Institute of Arts and Letters, and honorary degrees from institutions such as Smith College and the University of Wisconsin, she has continued for forty years to be a significant figure in American literature.

"People ask me about Faulkner," she once said. "It's a big fact. Like living near a mountain." Given their long residence in the same state and their shared Mississippi materials, the comparison is almost inevitable and it is enforced by the comic sensibility that seems so Faulknerian in a long work like *Losing Battles* (1970). Like Faulkner, she is not a protest writer nor an advocate of causes, and like him, though never so spectacularly, she has always been an experimenter in the modes of fictional presentation. Finally, however, she remains her own woman. As such, she has written some of the finest stories of her generation.

The Collected Stories of Eudora Welty was published in 1980. Besides *A Curtain of Green* and *The Wide Net,* individual volumes of short stories are *The Golden Apples,* 1949; and *The Bride of Innisfallen and Other Stories,* 1955. Novels are *The Robber Bridegroom,* 1942; *Delta Wedding,* 1946; *The Ponder Heart,* 1954; *Losing Battles,* 1970; and *The Optimist's Daughter,* 1972. Welty's criticism appears in *Place in Fiction,* 1957; *Three Papers on Fiction,* published by Smith College in 1962; and *The Eye of the Story: Selected Essays and Reviews,* 1978. *One Time, One Place,* 1971, is a collection of her photographs from the 1930's. *One Writer's Beginnings,* 1984, is autobiographical. Peggy Whitman Prenshaw edited *Conversations with Eudora Welty,* 1985.

Ruth M. Vande Kieft edited *Thirteen Stories,* 1965, and wrote a critical account, *Eudora Welty,* 1962. Also useful are Alfred Appel, Jr., *A Season of Dreams: The Fiction of Eudora Welty,* 1965; J. A. Bryant, Jr.'s brief *Eudora Welty,* 1968; Michael Kreyling, *Eudora Welty's Achievement of Order,* 1980; Peggy Whitman Prenshaw, ed., *Eudora Welty: Critical Essays,* 1979 (portions reprinted as *Eudora Welty: Thirteen Essays,* 1983); and Albert J. Devlin, *Eudora Welty's Chronicle: A Story of Mississippi Life,* 1983.

Why I Live at the P.O.[1]

I was getting along fine with Mama, Papa-Daddy and Uncle Rondo until my sister Stella-Rondo just separated from her husband and came back home again. Mr. Whitaker! Of course I went with Mr. Whitaker first, when he first appeared here in China Grove, taking "Pose Yourself" photos, and Stella-Rondo broke us up. Told him I was one-sided. Bigger on one side than the other, which is a deliberate, calculated falsehood: I'm the same. Stella-Rondo is exactly twelve months to the day younger than I am and for that reason she's spoiled.

She's always had anything in the world she wanted and then she'd throw it away. Papa-Daddy gave her this gorgeous Add-a-Pearl necklace when she was eight years old and she threw it away playing baseball when she was nine, with only two pearls.

1. First collected in *A Curtain of Green and Other Stories* (1941). The source of the present text is *The Collected Stories of Eudora Welty* (1980).

So as soon as she got married and moved away from home the first thing she did was separate! From Mr. Whitaker! This photographer with the popeyes she said she trusted. Came home from one of those towns up in Illinois and to our complete surprise brought this child of two.

Mama said she like to made her drop dead for a second. "Here you had this marvelous blonde child and never so much as wrote your mother a word about it," says Mama. "I'm thoroughly ashamed of you." But of course she wasn't.

Stella-Rondo just calmly takes off this *hat,* I wish you could see it. She says, "Why, Mama, Shirley-T.'s adopted, I can prove it."

"How?" says Mama, but all I says was, "H'm!" There I was over the hot stove, trying to stretch two chickens over five people and a completely unexpected child into the bargain, without one moment's notice.

"What do you mean—'H'm!'?" says Stella-Rondo, and Mama says, "I heard that, Sister."

I said that oh, I didn't mean a thing, only that whoever Shirley-T. was, she was the spit-image of Papa-Daddy if he'd cut off his beard, which of course he'd never do in the world. Papa-Daddy's Mama's papa and sulks.

Stella-Rondo got furious! She said, "Sister, I don't need to tell you you got a lot of nerve and always did have and I'll thank you to make no future reference to my adopted child whatsoever."

"Very well," I said. "Very well, very well. Of course I noticed at once she looks like Mr. Whitaker's side too. That frown. She looks like a cross between Mr. Whitaker and Papa-Daddy."

"Well, all I can say is she isn't."

"She looks exactly like Shirley Temple to me," says Mama, but Shirley-T. just ran away from her.

So the first thing Stella-Rondo did at the table was turn Papa-Daddy against me.

"Papa-Daddy," she says. He was trying to cut up his meat. "Papa-Daddy!" I was taken completely by surprise. Papa-Daddy is about a million years old and's got this long-long beard. "Papa-Daddy, Sister says she fails to understand why you don't cut off your beard."

So Papa-Daddy l-a-y-s down his knife and fork! He's real rich. Mama says he is, he says he isn't. So he says, "Have I heard correctly? You don't understand why I don't cut off my beard?"

"Why," I says, "Papa-Daddy, of course I understand, I did not say any such of a thing, the idea!"

He says, "Hussy!"

I says, "Papa-Daddy, you know I wouldn't any more want you to cut off your beard than the man in the moon. It was the farthest thing from my mind! Stella-Rondo sat there and made that up while she was eating breast of chicken."

But he says, "So the postmistress fails to understand why I don't cut off my beard. Which job I got you through my influence with the government. 'Bird's nest'—is that what you call it?"

Not that it isn't the next to smallest P.O. in the entire state of Mississippi.

I says, "Oh, Papa-Daddy," I says, "I didn't say any such of a thing, I never dreamed it was a bird's nest, I have always been grateful though this is the next to smallest P.O. in the state of Mississippi, and I do not enjoy being referred to as a hussy by my own grandfather."

But Stella-Rondo says, "Yes, you did say it too. Anybody in the world could of heard you, that had ears."

"Stop right there," says Mama, looking at *me.*

So I pulled my napkin straight back through the napkin ring and left the table.

As soon as I was out of the room Mama says, "Call her back, or she'll starve to death," but Papa-Daddy says, "This is the beard I started growing on the Coast when I was fifteen years old." He would of gone on till nightfall if Shirley-T. hadn't lost the Milky Way she ate in Cairo.

So Papa-Daddy says, "I am going out and lie in the hammock, and you can all sit here and remember my words: I'll never cut off my beard as long as I live, even one inch, and I don't appreciate it in you at all." Passed right by me in the hall and went straight out and got in the hammock.

It would be a holiday. It wasn't five minutes before Uncle Rondo suddenly appeared in the hall in one of Stella-Rondo's flesh-colored kimonos, all cut on the bias, like something Mr. Whitaker probably thought was gorgeous.

"Uncle Rondo!" I says. "I didn't know who that was! Where are you going?"

"Sister," he says, "get out of my way, I'm poisoned."

"If you're poisoned stay away from Papa-Daddy," I says. "Keep out of the hammock. Papa-Daddy will certainly beat you on the head if you come within forty miles of him. He thinks I deliberately said he ought to cut off his beard after he got me the P.O., and I've told him and told him and told him, and he acts like he just don't hear me. Papa-Daddy must of gone stone deaf."

"He picked a fine day to do it then," says Uncle Rondo, and before you could say "Jack Robinson" flew out in the yard.

What he'd really done, he'd drunk another bottle of that prescription. He does it every single Fourth of July as sure as shooting, and it's horribly expensive. Then he falls over in the hammock and snores. So he insisted on zigzagging right on out to the hammock, looking like a half-wit.

Papa-Daddy woke up with this horrible yell and right there without moving an inch he tried to turn Uncle Rondo against me. I heard every word he said. Oh, he told Uncle Rondo I didn't learn to read till I was eight years old and he didn't see how in the world I ever got the mail put up at the P.O., much less read it all, and he said if Uncle Rondo could only fathom the lengths he had gone to to get me that job! And he said on the other hand he thought Stella-Rondo had a brilliant mind and deserved credit for getting out of town. All the time he was just lying there swinging as pretty as you please and looping out his beard, and poor Uncle Rondo was *pleading* with him to slow down the hammock, it was making him as dizzy as a witch to watch it. But that's what Papa-Daddy likes about a hammock. So Uncle Rondo was too dizzy to get turned against me for the time being. He's Mama's only brother and is a good case of a one-track mind. Ask anybody. A certified pharmacist.

Just then I heard Stella-Rondo raising the upstairs window. While she was married she got this peculiar idea that it's cooler with the windows shut and locked. So she has to raise the window before she can make a soul hear her outdoors.

So she raises the window and says, *"Oh!"* You would have thought she was mortally wounded.

Uncle Rondo and Papa-Daddy didn't even look up, but kept right on with what they were doing. I had to laugh.

I flew up the stairs and threw the door open! I says, "What in the wide world's the matter, Stella-Rondo? You mortally wounded?"

"No," she says, "I am not mortally wounded but I wish you would do me the favor of looking out that window there and telling me what you see."

So I shade my eyes and look out the window.

"I see the front yard," I says.

"Don't you see any human beings?" she says.

"I see Uncle Rondo trying to run Papa-Daddy out of the hammock," I says. "Nothing more. Naturally, it's so suffocating-hot in the house, with all the windows shut and locked, everybody who cares to stay in their right mind will have to go out and get in the hammock before the Fourth of July is over."

"Don't you notice anything different about Uncle Rondo?" asks Stella-Rondo.

"Why, no, except he's got on some terrible-looking flesh-colored contraption I wouldn't be found dead in, is all I can see," I says.

"Never mind, you won't be found dead in it, because it happens to be part of my trousseau, and Mr. Whitaker took several dozen photographs of me in it," says Stella-Rondo. "What on earth could Uncle Rondo *mean* by wearing part of my trousseau out in the broad open daylight without saying so much as 'Kiss my foot,' *knowing* I only got home this morning after my separation and hung my negligee up on the bathroom door, just as nervous as I could be?"

"I'm sure I don't know, and what do you expect me to do about it?" I says. "Jump out the window?"

"No, I expect nothing of the kind. I simply declare that Uncle Rondo looks like a fool in it, that's all," she says. "It makes me sick to my stomach."

"Well, he looks as good as he can," I says. "As good as anybody in reason could." I stood up for Uncle Rondo, please remember. And I said to Stella-Rondo, "I think I would do well not to criticize so freely if I were you and came home with a two-year-old child I had never said a word about, and no explanation whatever about my separation."

"I asked you the instant I entered this house not to refer one more time to my adopted child, and you gave me your word of honor you would not," was all Stella-Rondo would say, and started pulling out every one of her eyebrows with some cheap Kress tweezers.

So I merely slammed the door behind me and went down and made some green-tomato pickle. Somebody had to do it. Of course Mama had turned both the Negroes loose; she always said no earthly power could hold one anyway on the Fourth of July, so she wouldn't even try. It turned out that Jaypan fell in the lake and came within a very narrow limit of drowning.

So Mama trots in. Lifts up the lid and says, "H'm! Not very good for your Uncle Rondo in his precarious condition, I must say. Or poor little adopted Shirley-T. Shame on you!"

That made me tired. I says, "Well, Stella-Rondo had better thank her lucky stars it was her instead of me came trotting in with that very peculiar-looking child. Now if it had been me that trotted in from Illinois and brought a peculiar-looking child of two, I shudder to think of the reception I'd of got, much less controlled the diet of an entire family."

"But you must remember, Sister, that you were never married to Mr. Whitaker in the first place and didn't go up to Illinois to live," says Mama, shaking a spoon in my face. "If you had I would of been just as overjoyed to see you and your little adopted girl as I was to see Stella-Rondo, when you wound up with your separation and came on back home."

"You would not," I says.

"Don't contradict me, I would," says Mama.

But I said she couldn't convince me though she talked till she was blue in the face. Then I said, "Besides, you know as well as I do that that child is not adopted."

"She most certainly is adopted," says Mama, stiff as a poker.

I says, "Why, Mama, Stella-Rondo had her just as sure as anything in this world, and just too stuck up to admit it."

"Why, Sister," said Mama. "Here I thought we were going to have a pleasant Fourth of July, and you start right out not believing a word your own baby sister tells you!"

"Just like Cousin Annie Flo. Went to her grave denying the facts of life," I remind Mama.

"I told you if you ever mentioned Annie Flo's name I'd slap your face," says Mama, and slaps my face.

"All right, you wait and see," I says.

"I," says Mama, *"I* prefer to take my children's word for anything when it's humanly possible." You ought to see Mama, she weighs two hundred pounds and has real tiny feet.

Just then something perfectly horrible occurred to me.

"Mama," I says, "can that child talk?" I simply had to whisper! "Mama, I wonder if that child can be—you know—in any way? Do you realize," I says, "that she hasn't spoken one single, solitary word to a human being up to this minute? This is the way she looks," I says, and I looked like this.

Well, Mama and I just stood there and stared at each other. It was horrible!

"I remember well that Joe Whitaker frequently drank like a fish," says Mama. "I believed to my soul he drank *chemicals.*" And without another word she marches to the foot of the stairs and calls Stella-Rondo.

"Stella-Rondo? O-o-o-o-o! Stella-Rondo!"

"What?" says Stella-Rondo from upstairs. Not even the grace to get up off the bed.

"Can that child of yours talk?" asks Mama.

Stella-Rondo says, "Can she what?"

"Talk! Talk!" says Mama. "Burdyburdyburdyburdy!"

So Stella-Rondo yells back, "Who says she can't talk?"

"Sister says so," says Mama.

"You didn't have to tell me, I know whose word of honor don't mean a thing in this house," says Stella-Rondo.

And in a minute the loudest Yankee voice I ever heard in my life yells out, "OE'm Pop-OE the Sailor-r-r-r Ma-a-an!" and then somebody jumps up and down in the upstairs hall. In another second the house would of fallen down.

"Not only talks, she can tap-dance!" calls Stella-Rondo. "Which is more than some people I won't name can do."

"Why, the little precious darling thing!" Mama says, so surprised. "Just as smart as she can be!" Starts talking baby talk right there. Then she turns on me. "Sister, you ought to be thoroughly ashamed! Run upstairs this instant and apologize to Stella-Rondo and Shirley-T."

"Apologize for what?" I says. "I merely wondered if the child was normal, that's all. Now that she's proved she is, why, I have nothing further to say."

But Mama just turned on her heel and flew out, furious. She ran right upstairs and hugged the baby. She believed it was adopted. Stella-Rondo hadn't done a thing but turn her against me from upstairs while I stood there helpless over the hot stove. So that made Mama, Papa-Daddy and the baby all on Stella-Rondo's side.

Next, Uncle Rondo.

I must say that Uncle Rondo has been marvelous to me at various times in the past and I was completely unprepared to be made to jump out of my skin, the way it turned out. Once Stella-Rondo did something perfectly horrible to him—broke a chain letter from Flanders Field—and he took the radio back he had given her and gave it to me. Stella-Rondo was furious! For six months we all had to call her Stella instead of Stella-Rondo, or she wouldn't answer. I always thought Uncle Rondo had all the brains of the entire family. Another time he sent me to Mammoth Cave, with all expenses paid.

But this would be the day he was drinking that prescription, the Fourth of July.

So at supper Stella-Rondo speaks up and says she thinks Uncle Rondo ought to try to eat a little something. So finally Uncle Rondo said he would try a little cold biscuits and ketchup, but that was all. So *she* brought it to him.

"Do you think it wise to disport with ketchup in Stella-Rondo's flesh-colored kimono?" I says. Trying to be considerate! If Stella-Rondo couldn't watch out for her trousseau, somebody had to.

"Any objections?" asks Uncle Rondo, just about to pour out all the ketchup.

"Don't mind what she says, Uncle Rondo," says Stella-Rondo. "Sister has been devoting this solid afternoon to sneering out my bedroom window at the way you look."

"What's that?" says Uncle Rondo. Uncle Rondo has got the most terrible temper in the world. Anything is liable to make him tear the house down if it comes at the wrong time.

So Stella-Rondo says, "Sister says, 'Uncle Rondo certainly does look like a fool in that pink kimono!' "

Do you remember who it was really said that?

Uncle Rondo spills out all the ketchup and jumps out of his chair and tears off the kimono and throws it down on the dirty floor and puts his foot on it. It had to be sent all the way to Jackson to the cleaners and re-pleated.

"So that's your opinion of your Uncle Rondo, is it?" he says. "I look like a fool, do I? Well, that's the last straw. A whole day in this house with nothing to do, and then to hear you come out with a remark like that behind my back!"

"I didn't say any such of a thing, Uncle Rondo," I says, "and I'm not saying who did, either. Why, I think you look all right. Just try to take care of yourself and not talk and eat at the same time," I says. "I think you better go lie down."

"Lie down my foot," says Uncle Rondo. I ought to of known by that he was fixing to do something perfectly horrible.

So he didn't do anything that night in the precarious state he was in—just played Casino with Mama and Stella-Rondo and Shirley-T. and gave Shirley-T. a nickel with a head on both sides. It tickled her nearly to death, and she called him "Papa." But at 6:30 A.M. the next morning, he threw a whole five-cent package of some unsold one-inch firecrackers from the store as hard as he could into my bedroom and they every one went off. Not one bad one in the string. Anybody else, there'd be one that wouldn't go off.

Well, I'm just terribly susceptible to noise of any kind, the doctor has always told me I was the most sensitive person he had ever seen in his whole life, and I was simply prostrated. I couldn't eat! People tell me they heard it as far as the cemetery, and old Aunt Jep Patterson, that had been holding her own so good, thought it was Judgment Day and she was going to meet her whole family. It's usually so quiet here.

And I'll tell you it didn't take me any longer than a minute to make up my mind what to do. There I was with the whole entire house on Stella-Rondo's side and turned against me. If I have anything at all I have pride.

So I just decided I'd go straight down to the P.O. There's plenty of room there in the back, I says to myself.

Well! I made no bones about letting the family catch on to what I was up to. I didn't try to conceal it.

The first thing they knew, I marched in where they were all playing Old Maid and pulled the electric oscillating fan out by the plug, and everything got real hot. Next I snatched the pillow I'd done the needlepoint on right off the davenport from behind Papa-Daddy. He went "Ugh!" I beat Stella-Rondo up the stairs and finally found my charm bracelet in her bureau drawer under a picture of Nelson Eddy.

"So that's the way the land lies," says Uncle Rondo. There he was, piecing on the ham. "Well, Sister, I'll be glad to donate my army cot if you got any place to set it up, providing you'll leave right this minute and let me get some peace." Uncle Rondo was in France.

"Thank you kindly for the cot and 'peace' is hardly the word I would select if I had to resort to firecrackers at 6:30 A.M. in a young girl's bedroom," I says back to him. "And as to where I intend to go, you seem to forget my position as postmistress of China Grove, Mississippi," I says. "I've always got the P.O."

Well, that made them all sit up and take notice.

I went out front and started digging up some four-o'clocks to plant around the P.O.

"Ah-ah-ah!" says Mama, raising the window. "Those happen to be my four-o'clocks. Everything planted in that star is mine. I've never known you to make anything grow in your life."

"Very well," I says. "But I take the fern. Even you, Mama, can't stand there and deny that I'm the one watered that fern. And I happen to know where I can send in a box top and get a packet of one thousand mixed seeds, no two the same kind, free."

"Oh, where?" Mama wants to know.

But I says, "Too late. You 'tend to your house, and I'll 'tend to mine. You hear things like that all the time if you know how to listen to the radio. Perfectly marvelous offers. Get anything you want free."

So I hope to tell you I marched in and got that radio, and they could of all bit a nail in two, especially Stella-Rondo, that it used to belong to, and she well knew she couldn't get it back, I'd sue for it like a shot. And I very politely took the sewing-machine motor I helped pay the most on to give Mama for Christmas back in 1929, and a good big calendar, with the first-aid remedies on it. The thermometer and the Hawaiian ukulele certainly were rightfully mine, and I stood on the step-ladder and got all my watermelon-rind preserves and every fruit and vegetable I'd put up, every jar. Then I began to pull the tacks out of the bluebird wall vases on the archway to the dining room.

"Who told you you could have those, Miss Priss?" says Mama, fanning as hard as she could.

"I bought 'em and I'll keep track of 'em," I says. "I'll tack 'em up one on each side the post-office window, and you can see 'em when you come to ask me for your mail, if you're so dead to see 'em."

"Not I! I'll never darken the door to that post office again if I live to be a hundred," Mama says. "Ungrateful child! After all the money we spent on you at the Normal."

"Me either," says Stella-Rondo. "You can just let my mail lie there and *rot,* for all I care. I'll never come and relieve you of a single, solitary piece."

"I should worry," I says. "And who you think's going to sit down and write you all those big fat letters and postcards, by the way? Mr. Whitaker? Just because he was the only man ever dropped down in China Grove and you got him—unfairly—is he going to sit down and write you a lengthy correspondence after you come home giving no rhyme nor reason whatsoever for your separation and no explanation for the presence of that child? I may not have your brilliant mind, but I fail to see it."

So Mama says, "Sister, I've told you a thousand times that Stella-Rondo simply got homesick, and this child is far too big to be hers," and she says, "Now, why don't you all just sit down and play Casino?"

Then Shirley-T. sticks out her tongue at me in this perfectly horrible way. She has no more manners than the man in the moon. I told her she was going to cross her eyes like that some day and they'd stick.

"It's too late to stop me now," I says. "You should have tried that yesterday. I'm going to the P.O. and the only way you can possibly see me is to visit me there."

So Papa-Daddy says, "You'll never catch me setting foot in that post office, even if I should take a notion into my head to write a letter some place." He says, "I won't have you reachin' out of that little old window with a pair of shears and cuttin' off any beard of mine. I'm too smart for you!"

"We all are," says Stella-Rondo.

But I said, "If you're so smart, where's Mr. Whitaker?"

So then Uncle Rondo says, "I'll thank you from now on to stop reading all the orders I get on postcards and telling everybody in China Grove what you think is the matter with them," but I says, "I draw my own conclusions and will continue in the future to draw them." I says, "If people want to write their inmost secrets on penny postcards, there's nothing in the wide world you can do about it, Uncle Rondo."

"And if you think we'll ever *write* another postcard you're sadly mistaken," says Mama.

"Cutting off your nose to spite your face then," I says. "But if you're all determined to have no more to do with the U.S. mail, think of this: What will Stella-Rondo do now, if she wants to tell Mr. Whitaker to come after her?"

"Wah!" says Stella-Rondo. I knew she'd cry. She had a conniption fit right there in the kitchen.

"It will be interesting to see how long she holds out," I says. "And now—I am leaving."

"Good-bye," says Uncle Rondo.

"Oh, I declare," says Mama, "to think that a family of mine should quarrel on the Fourth of July, or the day after, over Stella-Rondo leaving old Mr. Whitaker and having the sweetest little adopted child! It looks like we'd all be glad!"

"Wah!" says Stella-Rondo, and has a fresh conniption fit.

"*He* left *her*—you mark my words," I says. "That's Mr. Whitaker. I know Mr. Whitaker. After all, I knew him first. I said from the beginning he'd up and leave her. I foretold every single thing that's happened."

"Where did he go?" asks Mama.

"Probably to the North Pole, if he knows what's good for him," I says.

But Stella-Rondo just bawled and wouldn't say another word. She flew to her room and slammed the door.

"Now look what you've gone and done, Sister," says Mama. "You go apologize."

"I haven't got time, I'm leaving," I says.

"Well, what are you waiting around for?" asks Uncle Rondo.

So I just picked up the kitchen clock and marched off, without saying "Kiss my foot" or anything, and never did tell Stella-Rondo good-bye.

There was a girl going along on a little wagon right in front.

"Girl," I says, "come help me haul these things down the hill, I'm going to live in the post office."

Took her nine trips in her express wagon. Uncle Rondo came out on the porch and threw her a nickel.

And that's the last I've laid eyes on any of my family or my family laid eyes on me for five solid days and nights. Stella-Rondo may be telling the most horrible tales in the world about Mr. Whitaker, but I haven't heard them. As I tell everybody, I draw my own conclusions.

But oh, I like it here. It's ideal, as I've been saying. You see, I've got everything cater-cornered, the way I like it. Hear the radio? All the war news. Radio, sewing machine, book ends, ironing board and that great big piano lamp—peace, that's what I like. Butter-bean vines planted all along the front where the strings are.

Of course, there's not much mail. My family are naturally the main people in China Grove, and if they prefer to vanish from the face of the earth, for all the mail they get or the mail they write, why, I'm not going to open my mouth. Some of the folks here in town are taking up for me and some turned against me. I know which is which. There are always people who will quit buying stamps just to get on the right side of Papa-Daddy.

But here I am, and here I'll stay. I want the world to know I'm happy.

And if Stella-Rondo should come to me this minute, on bended knees, and *attempt* to explain the incidents of her life with Mr. Whitaker, I'd simply put my fingers in both my ears and refuse to listen.

1941

Livvie[2]

Solomon carried Livvie twenty-one miles away from her home when he married her. He carried her away up on the Old Natchez Trace into the deep country to live in his house. She was sixteen—only a girl, then. Once people said he thought nobody would ever come along there. He told her himself that it had been a long time, and a day she did not know about, since that road was a traveled road with *people* coming and going. He was good to her, but he kept her in the house. She had not thought that she could not get back. Where she came from, people said an old man did not want anybody in the world to ever find his wife, for fear they would steal her back from him. Solomon asked her before he took her, would she be happy?—very dignified, for he was a colored man that owned his land and had it written down in the courthouse; and she said, "Yes, sir," since he was an old man and she was young and just listened and answered. He asked her, if she was choosing winter, would she pine for spring, and she said, "No indeed." Whatever she said, always, was because he was an old man . . . while nine years went by. All the time, he got older, and he got so old he gave out. At last he slept the whole day in bed, and she was young still.

It was a nice house, inside and outside both. In the first place, it had three rooms. The front room was papered in holly paper, with green palmettos from the swamp spaced at careful intervals over the walls. There was fresh newspaper cut with fancy borders on the mantel-shelf, on which were propped photographs of old or very young men printed in faint yellow—Solomon's people. Solomon had a houseful of furniture. There was a double settee, a tall scrolled rocker and an organ in the front room, all around a three-legged table with a pink marble top, on which was set a lamp with three gold feet, besides a jelly glass with pretty hen feathers in it. Behind the front room, the other room had the bright iron bed with the polished knobs like a throne, in which Solomon slept all day. There were snow-white curtains of wiry lace at the window, and a lace bedspread belonged on the bed. But what old Solomon slept so sound under was a big feather-stitched piece-quilt in the pattern "Trip Around the World," which had twenty-one different colors, four hundred and forty pieces, and a thousand yards of thread, and that was what Solomon's mother made in her life and old age. There was a table holding the Bible, and a trunk with a key. On the wall were two calendars, and a diploma from somewhere in Solomon's family, and under that, Livvie's one possession was nailed, a picture of the little white baby of the family she worked for, back in Natchez before she was married. Going through that room and on to the kitchen, there was a big wood stove and a big round table always with a wet top and with the knives and forks in one jelly glass and the spoons in another, and a cut-glass vinegar bottle between, and going out from those, many shallow dishes of pickled peaches, fig preserves, watermelon pickles and blackberry jam always sitting there. The churn sat in the sun, the doors of the safe were always both shut, and there were four baited mousetraps in the kitchen, one in every corner.

The outside of Solomon's house looked nice. It was not painted, but across the porch was an even balance. On each side there was one easy chair with high springs,

2. First collected in *The Wide Net and Other Stories* (1943). The source of the present text is *The Collected Stories of Eudora Welty* (1980).

looking out, and a fern basket hanging over it from the ceiling, and a dishpan of zinnia seedlings growing at its foot on the floor. By the door was a plow-wheel, just a pretty iron circle, nailed up on one wall, and a square mirror on the other, a turquoise-blue comb stuck up in the frame, with the wash stand beneath it. On the door was a wooden knob with a pearl in the end, and Solomon's black hat hung on that, if he was in the house.

Out front was a clean dirt yard with every vestige of grass patiently uprooted and the ground scarred in deep whorls from the strike of Livvie's broom. Rose bushes with tiny blood-red roses blooming every month grew in threes on either side of the steps. On one side was a peach tree, on the other a pomegranate. Then coming around up the path from the deep cut of the Natchez Trace below was a line of bare crape-myrtle trees with every branch of them ending in a colored bottle, green or blue. There was no word that fell from Solomon's lips to say what they were for, but Livvie knew that there could be a spell put in trees, and she was familiar from the time she was born with the way bottle trees kept evil spirits from coming into the house—by luring them inside the colored bottles, where they cannot get out again. Solomon had made the bottle trees with his own hands over the nine years, in labor amounting to about a tree a year, and without a sign that he had any uneasiness in his heart, for he took as much pride in his precautions against spirits coming in the house as he took in the house, and sometimes in the sun the bottle trees looked prettier than the house did.

It was a nice house. It was in a place where the days would go by and surprise anyone that they were over. The lamplight and the firelight would shine out the door after dark, over the still and breathing country, lighting the roses and the bottle trees, and all was quiet there.

But there was nobody, nobody at all, not even a white person. And if there had been anybody, Solomon would not have let Livvie look at them, just as he would not let her look at a field hand, or a field hand look at her. There was no house near, except for the cabins of the tenants that were forbidden to her, and there was no house as far as she had been, stealing away down the still, deep Trace. She felt as if she waded a river when she went, for the dead leaves on the ground reached as high as her knees, and when she was all scratched and bleeding she said it was not like a road that went anywhere. One day, climbing up the high bank, she had found a graveyard without a church, with ribbon-grass growing about the foot of an angel (she had climbed up because she thought she saw angel wings), and in the sun, trees shining like burning flames through the great caterpillar nets which enclosed them. Scarey thistles stood looking like the prophets in the Bible in Solomon's house. Indian paint brushes grew over her head, and the mourning dove made the only sound in the world. Oh, for a stirring of the leaves, and a breaking of the nets! But not by a ghost, prayed Livvie, jumping down the bank. After Solomon took to his bed, she never went out, except one more time.

Livvie knew she made a nice girl to wait on anybody. She fixed things to eat on a tray like a surprise. She could keep from singing when she ironed, and to sit by a bed and fan away the flies, she could be so still she could not hear herself breathe. She could clean up the house and never drop a thing, and wash the dishes without a sound, and she would step outside to churn, for churning sounded too sad to her, like sobbing, and if it made her homesick and not Solomon, she did not think of that.

But Solomon scarcely opened his eyes to see her, and scarcely tasted his food. He was not sick or paralyzed or in any pain that he mentioned, but he was surely wearing out in the body, and no matter what nice hot thing Livvie would bring him to taste, he would only look at it now, as if he were past seeing how he could add anything more to himself. Before she could beg him, he would go fast asleep. She could not surprise him any more, if he would not taste, and she was afraid that he was never in the world going to taste another thing she brought him—and so how could he last?

But one morning it was breakfast time and she cooked his eggs and grits, carried them in on a tray, and called his name. He was sound asleep. He lay in a dignified way with his watch beside him, on his back in the middle of the bed. One hand drew the quilt up high, though it was the first day of spring. Through the white lace curtains a little puffy wind was blowing as if it came from round cheeks. All night the frogs had sung out in the swamp, like a commotion in the room, and he had not stirred, though she lay wide awake and saying "Shh, frogs!" for fear he would mind them.

He looked as if he would like to sleep a little longer, and so she put back the tray and waited. When she tiptoed and stayed so quiet, she surrounded herself with a little reverie, and sometimes it seemed to her when she was so stealthy that the quiet she kept was for a sleeping baby, and that she had a baby and was its mother. When she stood at Solomon's bed and looked down at him, she would be thinking, "He sleeps so well," and she would hate to wake him up. And in some other way, too, she was afraid to wake him up because even in his sleep he seemed to be such a strict man.

Of course, nailed to the wall over the bed—only she would forget who it was—there was a picture of him when he was young. Then he had a fan of hair over his forehead like a king's crown. Now his hair lay down on his head, the spring had gone out of it. Solomon had a lightish face, with eyebrows scattered but rugged, the way privet grows, strong eyes, with second sight, a strict mouth, and a little gold smile. This was the way he looked in his clothes, but in bed in the daytime he looked a different and smaller man, even when he was wide awake, and holding the Bible. He looked like somebody kin to himself. And then sometimes when he lay in sleep and she stood fanning the flies away, and the light came in, his face was like new, so smooth and clear that it was like a glass of jelly held to the window, and she could almost look through his forehead and see what he thought.

She fanned him and at length he opened his eyes and spoke her name, but he would not taste the nice eggs she had kept warm under a pan.

Back in the kitchen she ate heartily, his breakfast and hers, and looked out the open door at what went on. The whole day, and the whole night before, she had felt the stir of spring close to her. It was as present in the house as a young man would be. The moon was in the last quarter and outside they were turning the sod and planting peas and beans. Up and down the red fields, over which smoke from the brush-burning hung showing like a little skirt of sky, a white horse and a white mule pulled the plow. At intervals hoarse shouts came through the air and roused her as if she dozed neglectfully in the shade, and they were telling her, "Jump up!" She could see how over each ribbon of field were moving men and girls, on foot and mounted on mules, with hats set on their heads and bright with tall hoes and forks as if they carried streamers on them and were going to some place on a journey—and how as if at a signal now and then they would all start at once shouting, hollering, cajoling, calling and answering back, running, being leaped on and breaking away, flinging to earth with a shout and lying motionless in the trance of twelve o'clock. The old women came out of the cabins and brought them the food they had ready for them, and then all worked together, spread evenly out. The little children came too, like a bouncing stream overflowing the fields, and set upon the men, the women, the dogs, the rushing birds, and the wave-like rows of earth, their little voices almost too high to be heard. In the middle distance like some white and gold towers were the haystacks, with black cows coming around to eat their edges. High above everything, the wheel of fields, house, and cabins, and the deep road surrounding like a moat to keep them in, was the turning sky, blue with long, far-flung white mare's-tail clouds, serene and still as high flames. And sound asleep while all this went around him that was his, Solomon was like a little still spot in the middle.

Even in the house the earth was sweet to breathe. Solomon had never let Livvie go any farther than the chicken house and the well. But what if she would walk now into the heart of the fields and take a hoe and work until she fell stretched out and drenched with her efforts, like other girls, and laid her cheek against the laid-open earth, and shamed the old man with her humbleness and delight? To shame him! A cruel wish could come in uninvited and so fast while she looked out the back door. She washed the dishes and scrubbed the table. She could hear the cries of the little lambs. Her mother, that she had not seen since her wedding day, had said one time, "I rather a man be anything, than a woman be mean."

So all morning she kept tasting the chicken broth on the stove, and when it was right she poured off a nice cupful. She carried it in to Solomon, and there he lay having a dream. Now what did he dream about? For she saw him sigh gently as if not to disturb some whole thing he held round in his mind, like a fresh egg. So even an old man dreamed about something pretty. Did he dream of her, while his eyes were shut and sunken, and his small hand with the wedding ring curled close in sleep around the quilt? He might be dreaming of what time it was, for even through his sleep he kept track of it like a clock, and knew how much of it went by, and waked up knowing where the hands were even before he consulted the silver watch that he never let go. He would sleep with the watch in his palm, and even holding it to his cheek like a child that loves a plaything. Or he might dream of journeys and travels on a steamboat to Natchez. Yet she thought he dreamed of her; but even while she scrutinized him, the rods of the foot of the bed seemed to rise up like a rail fence between them, and she could see that people never could be sure of anything as long as one of them was asleep and the other awake. To look at him dreaming of her when he might be going to die frightened her a little, as if he might carry her with him that way, and she wanted to run out of the room. She took hold of the bed and held on, and Solomon opened his eyes and called her name, but he did not want anything. He would not taste the good broth.

Just a little after that, as she was taking up the ashes in the front room for the last time in the year, she heard a sound. It was somebody coming. She pulled the curtains together and looked through the slit.

Coming up the path under the bottle trees was a white lady. At first she looked young, but then she looked old. Marvelous to see, a little car stood steaming like a kettle out in the field-track—it had come without a road.

Livvie stood listening to the long, repeated knockings at the door, and after a while she opened it just a little. The lady came in through the crack, though she was more than middle-sized and wore a big hat.

"My name is Miss Baby Marie," she said.

Livvie gazed respectfully at the lady and at the little suitcase she was holding close to her by the handle until the proper moment. The lady's eyes were running over the room, from palmetto to palmetto, but she was saying, "I live at home . . . out from Natchez . . . and get out and show these pretty cosmetic things to the white people and the colored people both . . . all around . . . years and years. . . . Both shades of powder and rouge . . . It's the kind of work a girl can do and not go clear 'way from home. . . ." And the harder she looked, the more she talked. Suddenly she turned up her nose and said, "It is not Christian or sanitary to put feathers in a vase," and then she took a gold key out of the front of her dress and began unlocking the locks on her suitcase. Her face drew the light, the way it was covered with intense white and red, with a little patty-cake of white between the wrinkles by her upper lip. Little red tassels of hair bobbed under the rusty wires of her picture-hat, as with an air of triumph and secrecy she now drew open her little suitcase and brought out bottle after bottle and jar after jar, which she put down on the table, the mantel-piece, the settee, and the organ.

"Did you ever see so many cosmetics in your life?" cried Miss Baby Marie.

"No'm," Livvie tried to say, but the cat had her tongue.

"Have you ever applied cosmetics?" asked Miss Baby Marie next.

"No'm," Livvie tried to say.

"Then look!" she said, and pulling out the last thing of all, "Try this!" she said. And in her hand was unclenched a golden lipstick which popped open like magic. A fragrance came out of it like incense, and Livvie cried out suddenly, "Chinaberry flowers!"

Her hand took the lipstick, and in an instant she was carried away in the air through the spring, and looking down with a half-drowsy smile from a purple cloud she saw from above a chinaberry tree, dark and smooth and neatly leaved, neat as a guinea hen in the dooryard, and there was her home that she had left. On one side of the tree was her mama holding up her heavy apron, and she could see it was loaded with ripe figs, and on the other side was her papa holding a fish-pole over the pond, and she could see it transparently, the little clear fishes swimming up to the brim.

"Oh, no, not chinaberry flowers—secret ingredients," said Miss Baby Marie. "My cosmetics have secret ingredients—not chinaberry flowers."

"It's purple," Livvie breathed, and Miss Baby Marie said, "Use it freely. Rub it on."

Livvie tiptoed out to the wash stand on the front porch and before the mirror put the paint on her mouth. In the wavery surface her face danced before her like a flame. Miss Baby Marie followed her out, took a look at what she had done, and said, "That's it."

Livvie tried to say "Thank you" without moving her parted lips where the paint lay so new.

By now Miss Baby Marie stood behind Livvie and looked in the mirror over her shoulder, twisting up the tassels of her hair. "The lipstick I can let you have for only two dollars," she said, close to her neck.

"Lady, but I don't have no money, never did have," said Livvie.

"Oh, but you don't pay the first time. I make another trip, that's the way I do. I come back again—later."

"Oh," said Livvie, pretending she understood everything so as to please the lady.

"But if you don't take it now, this may be the last time I'll call at your house," said Miss Baby Marie sharply. "It's far away from anywhere, I'll tell you that. You don't live close to anywhere."

"Yes'm. My husband, he keep the *money,*" said Livvie, trembling. "He is strict as he can be. He don't know *you* walk in here—Miss Baby Marie!"

"Where is he?"

"Right now, he in yonder sound asleep, an old man. I wouldn't ever ask him for anything."

Miss Baby Marie took back the lipstick and packed it up. She gathered up the jars for both black and white and got them all inside the suitcase, with the same little fuss of triumph with which she had brought them out. She started away.

"Good-bye," she said, making herself look grand from the back, but at the last minute she turned around in the door. Her old hat wobbled as she whispered, "Let me see your husband."

Livvie obediently went on tiptoe and opened the door to the other room. Miss Baby Marie came behind her and rose on her toes and looked in.

"My, what a little tiny old, old man!" she whispered, clasping her hands and shaking her head over them. "What a beautiful quilt! What a tiny old, old man!"

"He can sleep like that all day," whispered Livvie proudly.

They looked at him awhile so fast asleep, and then all at once they looked at each other. Somehow that was as if they had a secret, for he had never stirred. Livvie then politely, but all at once, closed the door.

"Well! I'd certainly like to leave you with a lipstick!" said Miss Baby Marie vivaciously. She smiled in the door.

"Lady, but I told you I don't have no money, and never did have."

"And never will?" In the air and all around, like a bright halo around the white lady's nodding head, it was a true spring day.

"Would you take eggs, lady?" asked Livvie softly.

"No, I have plenty of eggs—plenty," said Miss Baby Marie.

"I still don't have no money," said Livvie, and Miss Baby Marie took her suitcase and went on somewhere else.

Livvie stood watching her go, and all the time she felt her heart beating in her left side. She touched the place with her hand. It seemed as if her heart beat and her whole face flamed from the pulsing color of her lips. She went to sit by Solomon and when he opened his eyes he could not see a change in her. "He's fixin' to die," she said inside. That was the secret. That was when she went out of the house for a little breath of air.

She went down the path and down the Natchez Trace a way, and she did not know how far she had gone, but it was not far, when she saw a sight. It was a man, looking like a vision—she standing on one side of the Old Natchez Trace and he standing on the other.

As soon as this man caught sight of her, he began to look himself over. Starting at the bottom with his pointed shoes, he began to look up, lifting his peg-top pants the higher to see fully his bright socks. His coat long and wide and leaf-green he opened like doors to see his high-up tawny pants and his pants he smoothed downward from the points of his collar, and he wore a luminous baby-pink satin shirt. At the end, he reached gently above his wide platter-shaped round hat, the color of a plum, and one finger touched at the feather, emerald green, blowing in the spring winds.

No matter how she looked, she could never look so fine as he did, and she was not sorry for that, she was pleased.

He took three jumps, one down and two up, and was by her side.

"My name is Cash," he said.

He had a guinea pig in his pocket. They began to walk along. She stared on and on at him, as if he were doing some daring spectacular thing, instead of just walking beside her. It was not simply the city way he was dressed that made her look at him and see hope in its insolence looking back. It was not only the way he moved along kicking the flowers as if he could break through everything in the way and destroy anything in the world, that made her eyes grow bright. It might be, if he had not appeared *that day* she would never have looked so closely at him, but the time people come makes a difference.

They walked through the still leaves of the Natchez Trace, the light and the shade falling through trees about them, the white irises shining like candles on the banks and the new ferns shining like green stars up in the oak branches. They came out at Solomon's house, bottle trees and all. Livvie stopped and hung her head.

Cash began whistling a little tune. She did not know what it was, but she had heard it before from a distance, and she had a revelation. Cash was a field hand. He was a transformed field hand. Cash belonged to Solomon. But he had stepped out of his overalls into this. There in front of Solomon's house he laughed. He had a round head, a round face, all of him was young, and he flung his head up, rolled it against the mare's-tail sky in his round hat, and he could laugh just to see Solomon's house sitting there. Livvie looked at it, and there was Solomon's black hat hanging on the peg on the front door, the blackest thing in the world.

"I been to Natchez," Cash said, wagging his head around against the sky. "*I* taken a trip, I ready for Easter!"

How was it possible to look so fine before the harvest? Cash must have stolen the money, stolen it from Solomon. He stood in the path and lifted his spread hand high and brought it down again and again in his laughter. He kicked up his heels. A little chill went through her. It was as if Cash was bringing that strong hand down to beat a drum or to rain blows upon a man, such an abandon and menace were in his laugh. Frowning, she went closer to him and his swinging arm drew her in at once and the fright was crushed from her body, as a little match-flame might be smothered out by what it lighted. She gathered the folds of his coat behind him and fastened her red lips to his mouth, and she was dazzled at herself then, the way he had been dazzled at himself to begin with.

In that instant she felt something that could not be told—that Solomon's death was at hand, that he was the same to her as if he were dead now. She cried out, and uttering little cries turned and ran for the house.

At once Cash was coming, following after, he was running behind her. He came close, and half-way up the path he laughed and passed her. He even picked up a stone and sailed it into the bottle trees. She put her hands over her head, and sounds clattered through the bottle trees like cries of outrage. Cash stamped and plunged zigzag up the front steps and in at the door.

When she got there, he had stuck his hands in his pockets and was turning slowly about in the front room. The little guinea pig peeped out. Around Cash, the pinned-up palmettos looked as if a lazy green monkey had walked up and down and around the walls leaving green prints of his hands and feet.

She got through the room and his hands were still in his pockets, and she fell upon the closed door to the other room and pushed it open. She ran to Solomon's bed, calling "Solomon! Solomon!" The little shape of the old man never moved at all, wrapped under the quilt as if it were winter still.

"Solomon!" She pulled the quilt away, but there was another one under that, and she fell on her knees beside him. He made no sound except a sigh, and then she could hear in the silence the light springy steps of Cash walking and walking in the front room, and the ticking of Solomon's silver watch, which came from the bed. Old Solomon was far away in his sleep, his face looked small, relentless, and devout, as if he were walking somewhere where she could imagine the snow falling.

Then there was a noise like a hoof pawing the floor, and the door gave a creak, and Cash appeared beside her. When she looked up, Cash's face was so black it was bright, and so bright and bare of pity that it looked sweet to her. She stood up and held up her head. Cash was so powerful that his presence gave her strength even when she did not need any.

Under their eyes Solomon slept. People's faces tell of things and places not known to the one who looks at them while they sleep, and while Solomon slept under the eyes of Livvie and Cash his face told them like a mythical story that all his life he had built, little scrap by little scrap, respect. A beetle could not have been more laborious or more ingenious in the task of its destiny. When Solomon was young, as he was in his picture overhead, it was the infinite thing with him, and he could see no end to the respect he would contrive and keep in a house. He had built a lonely house, the way he would make a cage, but it grew to be the same with him as a great monumental pyramid and sometimes in his absorption of getting it erected he was like the builder-slaves of Egypt who forgot or never knew the origin and meaning of the thing to which they gave all the strength of their bodies and used up all their days. Livvie and Cash could see that as a man might rest from a life-labor he lay in his bed, and they could hear how, wrapped in his quilt, he sighed to himself comfortably in sleep, while in his dreams he might have been an ant, a beetle, a bird, an Egyptian, assembling and carrying on his back and building with his hands, or he might have been an old man of India or a swaddled baby, about to smile and brush all away.

Then without warning old Solomon's eyes flew wide open under the hedge-like brows. He was wide awake.

And instantly Cash raised his quick arm. A radiant sweat stood on his temples. But he did not bring his arm down—it stayed in the air, as if something might have taken hold.

It was not Livvie—she did not move. As if something said "Wait," she stood waiting. Even while her eyes burned under motionless lids, her lips parted in a stiff grimace, and with her arms stiff at her sides she stood above the prone old man and the panting young one, erect and apart.

Movement when it came came in Solomon's face. It was an old and strict face, a frail face, but behind it, like a covered light, came an animation that could play hide and seek, that would dart and escape, had always escaped. The mystery flickered in him, and invited from his eyes. It was that very mystery that Cash with his quick arm would have to strike, and that Livvie could not weep for. But Cash only stood holding his arm in the air, when the gentlest flick of his great strength, almost a puff of his breath, would have been enough, if he had known how to give it, to send the old man over the obstruction that kept him away from death.

"Young ones can't wait," said Solomon.

Livvie shuddered violently, and then in a gush of tears she stooped for a glass of water and handed it to him, but he did not see her.

"So here come the young man Livvie wait for. Was no prevention. No prevention. Now I lay eyes on young man and it come to be somebody I know all the time, and been knowing since he were born in a cotton patch, and watched grow up year to year, Cash McCord, growed to size, growed up to come in my house in the end—ragged and barefoot."

Solomon gave a cough of distaste. Then he shut his eyes vigorously, and his lips began to move like a chanter's.

"When Livvie married, her husband were already somebody. He had paid great cost for his land. He spread sycamore leaves over the ground from wagon to door, day he brought her home, so her foot would not have to touch ground. He carried her through his door. Then he growed old and could not lift her, and she were still young."

Livvie's sobs followed his words like a soft melody repeating each thing as he stated it. His lips moved for a little without sound, or she cried too fervently, and unheard he might have been telling his whole life, and then he said, "God forgive Solomon for sins great and small. God forgive Solomon for carrying away too young girl for wife and keeping her away from her people and from all the young people would clamor for her back."

Then he lifted up his right hand toward Livvie where she stood by the bed and offered her his silver watch. He dangled it before her eyes, and she hushed crying; her tears stopped. For a moment the watch could be heard ticking as it always did, precisely in his proud hand. She lifted it away. Then he took hold of the quilt; then he was dead.

Livvie left Solomon dead and went out of the room. Stealthily, nearly without noise, Cash went beside her. He was like a shadow, but his shiny shoes moved over the floor in spangles, and the green downy feather shone like a light in his hat. As they reached the front room, he seized her deftly as a long black cat and dragged her hanging by the waist round and round him, while he turned in a circle, his face bent down to hers. The first moment, she kept one arm and its hand stiff and still, the one that held Solomon's watch. Then the fingers softly let go, all of her was limp, and the watch fell somewhere on the floor. It ticked away in the still room, and all at once there began outside the full song of a bird.

They moved around and around the room and into the brightness of the open door, then he stopped and shook her once. She rested in silence in his trembling arms, unprotesting as a bird on a nest. Outside the redbirds were flying and criss-crossing, the sun was in all the bottles on the prisoned trees, and the young peach was shining in the middle of them with the bursting light of spring.

1943

JOHN CHEEVER
(1912–1982)

John Cheever, born and raised in Quincy, Massachusetts, decided by twelve that he wanted to be a writer and stuck by that decision with uncommon single-mindedness over the years. At eighteen, he published his first story, "Expelled," in *The New Republic,* basing it upon his own recent expulsion from Thayer Academy in South Braintree, Massachusetts. In between, he had witnessed the family tensions associated with the failure of his father's shoe factory and the separation of his parents. His father, descendant of a line of New England sea captains, had left the family and attempted suicide. His mother had opened a gift shop, asserting her independence and assisting the family to survive. Helped financially by his older brother, Fred, "the strongest love of my life," and encouraged by Malcolm Cowley and others of the New York literary establishment, Cheever settled down in a room on the lower West Side of Manhattan to begin his long career.

Married in 1941, Cheever served for the next four years in the army, meanwhile continuing to write and publishing the first of his collections, *The Way Some People Live: A Book of Stories* (1943). The next book, *The Enormous Radio and Other Stories* (1953), earned him a reputation, reconfirmed with each succeeding collection, as one of the most accomplished short fiction writers of his generation. *The Housebreaker of Shady Hill and Other Stories* (1958) focuses on the personal problems masked by the surface affluence and serenity of American suburbia. *Some People, Places, and Things That Will Not Appear in My Next Novel* (1961), *The Brigadier and the Golf Widow* (1964), and *The World of Apples* (1973) range more widely in theme and location, including, along with the usual contemporary American settings, some fine stories that take place in Italy. *The Stories of John Cheever* (1978), a retrospective collection, establishes a mastery of delicate renderings of family tensions and individual spiritual crises that has seldom been surpassed.

Cheever's novels, though accomplished, have been less universally admired. *The Wapshot Chronicle* (1957) and *The Wapshot Scandal* (1964) are loosely organized chronicles of a family in some details much like Cheever's own. *Bullet Park* (1969) is a dark rendition of evil in the Eden of suburbia. *Falconer* (1977) is a tight, much admired examination of fratricide, prison, and homosexuality, based in part upon Cheever's lifelong relationship to his brother, in part upon the underside of his own character as it had surfaced in severe bouts with alcoholism, in part upon his observations as a teacher of writing in Sing Sing state prison, not far from his home in Ossining, New York. In *Oh What a Paradise It Seems* (1982), a novelette, an elderly man is caught up in a confusing new love and in a community effort to save a threatened pond from industrial contamination.

Cheever's writing has always been so close to his experience that it is tempting to view it as thinly disguised autobiography. Aware of this, he has been careful to remind readers of the unfathomable depths of art. "It seems to me," he has said, "that any confusion between autobiography and fiction debases fiction. The role autobiography plays in fiction is precisely the role that reality plays in a dream. As you dream your ship, you perhaps know the boat, but you're going towards a coast that is quite strange; you're wearing strange clothes, the language that is being spoken around you is a language you don't understand, but the woman on your left is your wife. It seems to me that this not capricious but quite mysterious union of fact and imagination one also finds in fiction."

The Stories of John Cheever, 1978, includes, with four previously uncollected stories, the contents of *The Enormous Radio, The Housebreaker of Shady Hill, Some People * * *, The Brigadier and the Golf Widow,* and *The World of Apples,* but does not include the stories of *The Way Some People Live.* A number of stories remain uncollected. Novels are named above.

Cheever's daughter, Susan Cheever, wrote *Home Before Dark,* 1984, a biography. Critical studies are Samuel Coale, *John Cheever,* 1977; Lynn Waldeland, *John Cheever,* 1979; R. G. Collins, ed., *Critical Essays on John Cheever,* 1982; and George W. Hunt, *John Cheever: The Company of Love,* 1983.

The Enormous Radio[1]

Jim and Irene Westcott were the kind of people who seem to strike that satisfactory average of income, endeavor, and respectability that is reached by the statistical reports in college alumni bulletins. They were the parents of two young children, they had been married nine years, they lived on the twelfth floor of an apartment house near Sutton Place, they went to the theatre on an average of 10.3 times a year, and they hoped someday to live in Westchester. Irene Westcott was a pleasant, rather plain girl with soft brown hair and a wide, fine forehead upon which nothing at all had been written, and in the cold weather she wore a coat of fitch skins dyed to resemble mink. You could not say that Jim Westcott looked younger than he was, but you could at least say of him that he seemed to feel younger. He wore his graying hair cut very short, he dressed in the kind of clothes his class had worn at Andover, and his manner was earnest, vehement, and intentionally naïve. The Westcotts differed from their friends, their classmates, and their neighbors only in an interest they shared in serious music. They went to a great many concerts—although they seldom mentioned this to anyone—and they spent a good deal of time listening to music on the radio.

Their radio was an old instrument, sensitive, unpredictable, and beyond repair. Neither of them understood the mechanics of radio—or of any of the other appliances that surrounded them—and when the instrument faltered, Jim would strike the side of the cabinet with his hand. This sometimes helped. One Sunday afternoon, in the middle of a Schubert quartet, the music faded away altogether. Jim struck the cabinet repeatedly, but there was no response; the Schubert was lost to them forever. He promised to buy Irene a new radio, and on Monday when he came home from work he told her that he had got one. He refused to describe it, and said it would be a surprise for her when it came.

The radio was delivered at the kitchen door the following afternoon, and with the assistance of her maid and the handyman Irene uncrated it and brought it into the living room. She was struck at once with the physical ugliness of the large gumwood cabinet. Irene was proud of her living room, she had chosen its furnishings and colors as carefully as she chose her clothes, and now it seemed to her that the new radio stood among her intimate possessions like an aggressive intruder. She was confounded by the number of dials and switches on the instrument panel, and she studied them thoroughly before she put the plug into a wall socket and turned the radio on. The dials flooded with a malevolent green light, and in the distance she heard the music of a piano quintet. The quintet was in the distance for only an instant; it bore down upon her with a speed greater than light and filled the

1. First collected in *The Enormous Radio and Other Stories* (1953). The source of the present text is *The Stories of John Cheever* (1978).

apartment with the noise of music amplified so mightily that it knocked a china ornament from a table to the floor. She rushed to the instrument and reduced the volume. The violent forces that were snared in the ugly gumwood cabinet made her uneasy. Her children came home from school then, and she took them to the Park. It was not until later in the afternoon that she was able to return to the radio.

The maid had given the children their suppers and was supervising their baths when Irene turned on the radio, reduced the volume, and sat down to listen to a Mozart quintet that she knew and enjoyed. The music came through clearly. The new instrument had a much purer tone, she thought, than the old one. She decided that tone was most important and that she could conceal the cabinet behind a sofa. But as soon as she had made her peace with the radio, the interference began. A crackling sound like the noise of a burning powder fuse began to accompany the singing of the strings. Beyond the music, there was a rustling that reminded Irene unpleasantly of the sea, and as the quintet progressed, these noises were joined by many others. She tried all the dials and switches but nothing dimmed the interference, and she sat down, disappointed and bewildered, and tried to trace the flight of the melody. The elevator shaft in her building ran beside the living-room wall, and it was the noise of the elevator that gave her a clue to the character of the static. The rattling of the elevator cables and the opening and closing of the elevator doors were reproduced in her loudspeaker, and, realizing that the radio was sensitive to electrical currents of all sorts, she began to discern through the Mozart the ringing of telephone bells, the dialing of phones, and the lamentation of a vacuum cleaner. By listening more carefully, she was able to distinguish doorbells, elevator bells, electric razors, and Waring mixers, whose sounds had been picked up from the apartments that surrounded hers and transmitted through her loudspeaker. The powerful and ugly instrument, with its mistaken sensitivity to discord, was more than she could hope to master, so she turned the thing off and went into the nursery to see her children.

When Jim Westcott came home that night, he went to the radio confidently and worked the controls. He had the same sort of experience Irene had had. A man was speaking on the station Jim had chosen, and his voice swung instantly from the distance into a force so powerful that it shook the apartment. Jim turned the volume control and reduced the voice. Then, a minute or two later, the interference began. The ringing of telephones and doorbells set in, joined by the rasp of the elevator doors and the whir of cooking appliances. The character of the noise had changed since Irene had tried the radio earlier; the last of the electric razors was being unplugged, the vacuum cleaners had all been returned to their closets, and the static reflected that change in pace that overtakes the city after the sun goes down. He fiddled with the knobs but couldn't get rid of the noises, so he turned the radio off and told Irene that in the morning he'd call the people who had sold it to him and give them hell.

The following afternoon, when Irene returned to the apartment from a luncheon date, the maid told her that a man had come and fixed the radio. Irene went into the living room before she took off her hat or her furs and tried the instrument. From the loudspeaker came a recording of the "Missouri Waltz." It reminded her of the thin, scratchy music from an old-fashioned phonograph that she sometimes heard across the lake where she spent her summers. She waited until the waltz had finished, expecting an explanation of the recording, but there was none. The music was followed by silence, and then the plaintive and scratchy record was repeated. She turned the dial and got a satisfactory burst of Caucasian music—the thump of bare feet in the dust and the rattle of coin jewelry—but in the background she could hear the ringing of bells and a confusion of voices. Her children came home from school then, and she turned off the radio and went to the nursery.

When Jim came home that night, he was tired, and he took a bath and changed his clothes. Then he joined Irene in the living room. He had just turned on the radio when the maid announced dinner, so he left it on, and he and Irene went to the table.

Jim was too tired to make even a pretense of sociability, and there was nothing about the dinner to hold Irene's interest, so her attention wandered from the food to the deposits of silver polish on the candlesticks and from there to the music in the other room. She listened for a few minutes to a Chopin prelude and then was surprised to hear a man's voice break in. "For Christ's sake, Kathy," he said, "do you always have to play the piano when I get home?" The music stopped abruptly. "It's the only chance I have," a woman said. "I'm at the office all day." "So am I," the man said. He added something obscene about an upright piano, and slammed a door. The passionate and melancholy music began again.

"Did you hear that?" Irene asked.

"What?" Jim was eating his dessert.

"The radio. A man said something while the music was still going on—something dirty."

"It's probably a play."

"I don't think it *is* a play," Irene said.

They left the table and took their coffee into the living room. Irene asked Jim to try another station. He turned the knob. "Have you seen my garters?" a man asked. "Button me up," a woman said. "Have you seen my garters?" the man said again. "Just button me up and I'll find your garters," the woman said. Jim shifted to another station. "I wish you wouldn't leave apple cores in the ashtrays," a man said. "I hate the smell."

"This is strange," Jim said.

"Isn't it?" Irene said.

Jim turned the knob again. " 'On the coast of Coromandel where the early pumpkins blow,' " a woman with a pronounced English accent said, " 'in the middle of the woods lived the Yonghy-Bonghy-Bò. Two old chairs, and half a candle, one old jug without a handle . . .' "

"My God!" Irene cried. "That's the Sweeneys' nurse."

" 'These were all his worldly goods,' " the British voice continued.

"Turn that thing off," Irene said. "Maybe they can hear *us.*" Jim switched the radio off. "That was Miss Armstrong, the Sweeneys' nurse," Irene said. "She must be reading to the little girl. They live in 17-B. I've talked with Miss Armstrong in the Park. I know her voice very well. We must be getting other people's apartments."

"That's impossible," Jim said.

"Well, that was the Sweeneys' nurse," Irene said hotly. "I know her voice. I know it very well. I'm wondering if they can hear us."

Jim turned the switch. First from a distance and then nearer, nearer, as if borne on the wind, came the pure accents of the Sweeneys' nurse again: " '*Lady Jingly!*

Lady Jingly!' " she said, " '*sitting where the pumpkins blow, will you come and be my wife?* said the Yonghy-Bonghy-Bò . . .' "

Jim went over to the radio and said "Hello" loudly into the speaker.

" '*I am tired of living singly,*' " the nurse went on, " '*on this coast so wild and shingly, I'm a-weary of my life; if you'll come and be my wife, quite serene would be my life* . . .' "

"I guess she can't hear us," Irene said. "Try something else."

Jim turned to another station, and the living room was filled with the uproar of a cocktail party that had overshot its mark. Someone was playing the piano and singing the "Whiffenpoof Song," and the voices that surrounded the piano were vehement and happy. "Eat some more sandwiches," a woman shrieked. There were screams of laughter and a dish of some sort crashed to the floor.

"Those must be the Fullers, in 11-E," Irene said. "I knew they were giving a party this afternoon. I saw her in the liquor store. Isn't this too divine? Try something else. See if you can get those people in 18-C."

The Westcotts overheard that evening a monologue on salmon fishing in Canada, a bridge game, running comments on home movies of what had apparently been a fortnight at Sea Island, and a bitter family quarrel about an overdraft at the bank. They turned off their radio at midnight and went to bed, weak with laughter. Sometime in the night, their son began to call for a glass of water and Irene got one and took it to his room. It was very early. All the lights in the neighborhood were extinguished, and from the boy's window she could see the empty street. She went into the living room and tried the radio. There was some faint coughing, a moan, and then a man spoke. "Are you all right, darling?" he asked. "Yes," a woman said wearily. "Yes, I'm all right, I guess," and then she added with great feeling, "But, you know, Charlie, I don't feel like myself any more. Sometimes there are about fifteen or twenty minutes in the week when I feel like myself. I don't like to go to another doctor, because the doctor's bills are so awful already, but I just don't feel like myself, Charlie. I just never feel like myself." They were not young, Irene thought. She guessed from the timbre of their voices that they were middle-aged. The restrained melancholy of the dialogue and the draft from the bedroom window made her shiver, and she went back to bed.

The following morning, Irene cooked breakfast for the family—the maid didn't come up from her room in the basement until ten—braided her daughter's hair, and waited at the door until her children and her husband had been carried away in the elevator. Then she went into the living room and tried the radio. "I don't want to go to school," a child screamed. "I hate school. I won't go to school. I hate school." "You will go to school," an enraged woman said. "We paid eight hundred dollars to get you into that school and you'll go if it kills you." The next number on the dial produced the worn record of the "Missouri Waltz." Irene shifted the control and invaded the privacy of several breakfast tables. She overheard demonstrations of indigestion, carnal love, abysmal vanity, faith, and despair. Irene's life was nearly as simple and sheltered as it appeared to be, and the forthright and sometimes brutal language that came from the loudspeaker that morning astonished and troubled her. She continued to listen until her maid came in. Then she turned off the radio quickly, since this insight, she realized, was a furtive one.

Irene had a luncheon date with a friend that day, and she left her apartment at a little after twelve. There were a number of women in the elevator when it stopped at her floor. She stared at their handsome and impassive faces, their furs, and the cloth flowers in their hats. Which one of them had been to Sea Island? she wondered. Which one had overdrawn her bank account? The elevator stopped at the tenth floor and a woman with a pair of Skye terriers joined them. Her hair was rigged high on her head and she wore a mink cape. She was humming the "Missouri Waltz."

Irene had two Martinis at lunch, and she looked searchingly at her friend and wondered what her secrets were. They had intended to go shopping after lunch, but Irene excused herself and went home. She told the maid that she was not to be disturbed; then she went into the living room, closed the doors, and switched on the radio. She heard, in the course of the afternoon, the halting conversation of a woman entertaining her aunt, the hysterical conclusion of a luncheon party, and a hostess briefing her maid about some cocktail guests. "Don't give the best Scotch to anyone who hasn't white hair," the hostess said. "See if you can get rid of that liver paste before you pass those hot things, and could you lend me five dollars? I want to tip the elevator man."

As the afternoon waned, the conversations increased in intensity. From where Irene sat, she could see the open sky above the East River. There were hundreds of clouds in the sky, as though the south wind had broken the winter into pieces and were blowing it north, and on her radio she could hear the arrival of cocktail guests and the return of children and businessmen from their schools and offices. "I found a good-sized diamond on the bathroom floor this morning," a woman said. "It must have fallen out of that bracelet Mrs. Dunston was wearing last night." "We'll sell it," a man said. "Take it down to the jeweler on Madison Avenue and sell it. Mrs. Dunston won't know the difference, and we could use a couple of hundred bucks . . ." " 'Oranges and lemons, say the bells of St. Clement's,' " the Sweeneys' nurse sang. " 'Halfpence and farthings, say the bells of St. Martin's. When will you pay me? say the bells at old Bailey . . .' " "It's not a hat," a woman cried, and at her back roared a cocktail party. "It's not a hat, it's a love affair. That's what Walter Florell said. He said it's not a hat, it's a love affair," and then, in a lower voice, the same woman added, "Talk to somebody, for Christ's sake, honey, talk to somebody. If she catches you standing here not talking to anybody, she'll take us off her invitation list, and I love these parties."

The Westcotts were going out for dinner that night, and when Jim came home, Irene was dressing. She seemed sad and vague, and he brought her a drink. They were dining with friends in the neighborhood, and they walked to where they were going. The sky was broad and filled with light. It was one of those splendid spring evenings that excite memory and desire, and the air that touched their hands and faces felt very soft. A Salvation Army band was on the corner playing "Jesus Is Sweeter." Irene drew on her husband's arm and held him there for a minute, to hear the music. "They're really such nice people, aren't they?" she said. "They have such nice faces. Actually, they're so much nicer than a lot of the people we know." She took a bill from her purse and walked over and dropped it into the tambourine. There was in her face, when she returned to her husband, a look of radiant melancholy that he was not familiar with. And her conduct at the dinner party that night seemed strange to him, too. She interrupted her hostess rudely and stared at the people across the table from her with an intensity for which she would have punished her children.

It was still mild when they walked home from the party, and Irene looked up at the spring stars. " 'How far that little candle throws its beams,' " she exclaimed. " 'So shines a good deed in a naughty world.' " She waited that night until Jim had fallen asleep, and then went into the living room and turned on the radio.

Jim came home at about six the next night. Emma, the maid, let him in, and he had taken off his hat and was taking off his coat when Irene ran into the hall. Her face was shining with tears and her hair was disordered. "Go up to 16-C, Jim!" she screamed. "Don't take off your coat. Go up to 16-C. Mr. Osborn's beating his wife. They've been quarreling since four o'clock, and now he's hitting her. Go up there and stop him."

From the radio in the living room, Jim heard screams, obscenities, and thuds. "You know you don't have to listen to this sort of thing," he said. He strode into the living room and turned the switch. "It's indecent," he said. "It's like looking in windows. You know you don't have to listen to this sort of thing. You can turn it off."

"Oh, it's so horrible, it's so dreadful," Irene was sobbing. "I've been listening all day, and it's so depressing."

"Well, if it's so depressing, why do you listen to it? I bought this damned radio to give you some pleasure," he said. "I paid a great deal of money for it. I thought it might make you happy. I wanted to make you happy."

"Don't, don't, don't, don't quarrel with me," she moaned, and laid her head on his shoulder. "All the others have been quarreling all day. Everybody's been quarreling. They're all worried about money. Mrs. Hutchinson's mother is dying of cancer in Florida and they don't have enough money to send her to the Mayo Clinic. At least, Mr. Hutchinson says they don't have enough money. And some woman in this building is having an affair with the handyman—with that hideous handyman. It's too disgusting. And Mrs. Melville has heart trouble and Mr. Hendricks is going to lose his job in April and Mrs. Hendricks is horrid about the whole thing and that girl who plays the 'Missouri Waltz' is a whore, a common whore, and the elevator man has tuberculosis and Mr. Osborn has been beating Mrs. Osborn." She wailed, she trembled with grief and checked the stream of tears down her face with the heel of her palm.

"Well, why do you have to listen?" Jim asked again. "Why do you have to listen to this stuff if it makes you so miserable?"

"Oh, don't, don't, don't," she cried. "Life is too terrible, too sordid and awful. But we've never been like that, have we, darling? Have we? I mean, we've always been good and decent and loving to one another, haven't we? And we have two children, two beautiful children. Our lives aren't sordid, are they, darling? Are they?" She flung her arms around his neck and drew his face down to hers. "We're happy, aren't we, darling? We are happy, aren't we?"

"Of course we're happy," he said tiredly. He began to surrender his resentment. "Of course we're happy. I'll have that damned radio fixed or taken away tomorrow." He stroked her soft hair. "My poor girl," he said.

"You love me, don't you?" she asked. "And we're not hypercritical or worried about money or dishonest, are we?"

"No, darling," he said.

A man came in the morning and fixed the radio. Irene turned it on cautiously and was happy to hear a California-wine commercial and a recording of Beethoven's

Ninth Symphony, including Schiller's "Ode to Joy." She kept the radio on all day and nothing untoward came from the speaker.

A Spanish suite was being played when Jim came home. "Is everything all right?" he asked. His face was pale, she thought. They had some cocktails and went in to dinner to the "Anvil Chorus" from *Il Trovatore.* This was followed by Debussy's "La Mer."

"I paid the bill for the radio today," Jim said. "It cost four hundred dollars. I hope you'll get some enjoyment out of it."

"Oh, I'm sure I will," Irene said.

"Four hundred dollars is a good deal more than I can afford," he went on. "I wanted to get something that you'd enjoy. It's the last extravagance we'll be able to indulge in this year. I see that you haven't paid your clothing bills yet. I saw them on your dressing table." He looked directly at her. "Why did you tell me you'd paid them? Why did you lie to me?"

"I just didn't want you to worry, Jim," she said. She drank some water. "I'll be able to pay my bills out of this month's allowance. There were the slipcovers last month, and that party."

"You've got to learn to handle the money I give you a little more intelligently, Irene," he said. "You've got to understand that we won't have as much money this year as we had last. I had a very sobering talk with Mitchell today. No one is buying anything. We're spending all our time promoting new issues, and you know how long that takes. I'm not getting any younger, you know. I'm thirty-seven. My hair will be gray next year. I haven't done as well as I'd hoped to do. And I don't suppose things will get any better."

"Yes, dear," she said.

"We've got to start cutting down," Jim said. "We've got to think of the children. To be perfectly frank with you, I worry about money a great deal. I'm not at all sure of the future. No one is. If anything should happen to me, there's the insurance, but that wouldn't go very far today. I've worked awfully hard to give you and the children a comfortable life," he said bitterly. "I don't like to see all of my energies, all of my youth, wasted in fur coats and radios and slipcovers and—"

"Please, Jim," she said. "Please. They'll hear us."

"*Who'll hear us?* Emma can't hear us."

"The radio."

"Oh, I'm sick!" he shouted. "I'm sick to death of your apprehensiveness. The radio can't hear us. Nobody can hear us. And what if they can hear us? Who cares?"

Irene got up from the table and went into the living room. Jim went to the door and shouted at her from there. "Why are you so Christly all of a sudden? What's turned you overnight into a convent girl? You stole your mother's jewelry before they probated her will. You never gave your sister a cent of that money that was intended for her—not even when she needed it. You made Grace Howland's life miserable, and where was all your piety and your virtue when you went to that abortionist? I'll never forget how cool you were. You packed your bag and went off to have that child murdered as if you were going to Nassau. If you'd had any reasons, if you'd had any good reasons—"

Irene stood for a minute before the hideous cabinet, disgraced and sickened, but she held her hand on the switch before she extinguished the music and the voices, hoping that the instrument might speak to her kindly, that she might hear the Sweeneys' nurse. Jim continued to shout at her from the door. The voice on the radio was suave and noncommittal. "An early-morning railroad disaster in Tokyo," the loudspeaker said, "killed twenty-nine people. A fire in a Catholic hospital near Buffalo for the care of blind children was extinguished early this morning by nuns. The temperature is forty-seven. The humidity is eighty-nine."

1953

The Swimmer[2]

It was one of those midsummer Sundays when everyone sits around saying, "I *drank* too much last night." You might have heard it whispered by the parishioners leaving church, heard it from the lips of the priest himself, struggling with his cassock in the *vestiarium,* heard it from the golf links and the tennis courts, heard it from the wildlife preserve where the leader of the Audubon group was suffering from a terrible hangover. "I *drank* too much," said Donald Westerhazy. "We all *drank* too much," said Lucinda Merrill. "It must have been the wine," said Helen Westerhazy. "I *drank* too much of that claret."

This was at the edge of the Westerhazys' pool. The pool, fed by an artesian well with a high iron content, was a pale shade of green. It was a fine day. In the west there was a massive stand of cumulus cloud so like a city seen from a distance—from the bow of an approaching ship—that it might have had a name. Lisbon. Hackensack. The sun was hot. Neddy Merrill sat by the green water, one hand in it, one around a glass of gin. He was a slender man—he seemed to have the especial slenderness of youth—and while he was far from young he had slid down his banister that morning and given the bronze backside of Aphrodite on the hall table a smack, as he jogged toward the smell of coffee in his dining room. He might have been compared to a summer's day, particularly the last hours of one, and while he lacked a tennis racket or a sail bag the impression was definitely one of youth, sport, and clement weather. He had been swimming and now he was breathing deeply, stertorously as if he could gulp into his lungs the components of that moment, the heat of the sun, the intenseness of his pleasure. It all seemed to flow into his chest. His own house stood in Bullet Park, eight miles to the south, where his four beautiful daughters would have had their lunch and might be playing tennis. Then it occurred to him that by taking a dogleg to the southwest he could reach his home by water.

His life was not confining and the delight he took in this observation could not be explained by its suggestion of escape. He seemed to see, with a cartographer's eye, that string of swimming pools, that quasi-subterranean stream that curved across the county. He had made a discovery, a contribution to modern geography; he would name the stream Lucinda after his wife. He was not a practical joker nor was he a fool but he was determinedly original and had a vague and modest idea of himself as a legendary figure. The day was beautiful and it seemed to him that a long swim might enlarge and celebrate its beauty.

He took off a sweater that was hung over his shoulders and dove in. He had an inexplicable contempt for men who did not hurl themselves into pools. He swam a choppy crawl, breathing either with every stroke or every fourth stroke and counting somewhere well in the back of his mind the one-two one-two of a flutter

2. "The Swimmer" was first collected in *The Brigadier and the Golf Widow* (1964). The source of the present text is *The Stories of John Cheever* (1978).

kick. It was not a serviceable stroke for long distances but the domestication of swimming had saddled the sport with some customs and in his part of the world a crawl was customary. To be embraced and sustained by the light green water was less a pleasure, it seemed, than the resumption of a natural condition, and he would have liked to swim without trunks, but this was not possible, considering his project. He hoisted himself up on the far curb—he never used the ladder—and started across the lawn. When Lucinda asked where he was going he said he was going to swim home.

The only maps and charts he had to go by were remembered or imaginary but these were clear enough. First there were the Grahams, the Hammers, the Lears, the Howlands, and the Crosscups. He would cross Ditmar Street to the Bunkers and come, after a short portage, to the Levys, the Welchers, and the public pool in Lancaster. Then there were the Hallorans, the Sachses, the Biswangers, Shirley Adams, the Gilmartins, and the Clydes. The day was lovely, and that he lived in a world so generously supplied with water seemed like a clemency, a beneficence. His heart was high and he ran across the grass. Making his way home by an uncommon route gave him the feeling that he was a pilgrim, an explorer, a man with a destiny, and he knew that he would find friends all along the way; friends would line the banks of the Lucinda River.

He went through a hedge that separated the Westerhazys' land from the Grahams', walked under some flowering apple trees, passed the shed that housed their pump and filter, and came out at the Grahams' pool. "Why, Neddy," Mrs. Graham said, "what a marvelous surprise. I've been trying to get you on the phone all morning. Here, let me get you a drink." He saw then, like any explorer, that the hospitable customs and traditions of the natives would have to be handled with diplomacy if he was ever going to reach his destination. He did not want to mystify or seem rude to the Grahams nor did he have the time to linger there. He swam the length of their pool and joined them in the sun and was rescued, a few minutes later, by the arrival of two carloads of friends from Connecticut. During the uproarious reunions he was able to slip away. He went down by the front of the Grahams' house, stepped over a thorny hedge, and crossed a vacant lot to the Hammers'. Mrs. Hammer, looking up from her roses, saw him swim by although she wasn't quite sure who it was. The Lears heard him splashing past the open windows of their living room. The Howlands and the Crosscups were away. After leaving the Howlands' he crossed Ditmar Street and started for the Bunkers', where he could hear, even at that distance, the noise of a party.

The water refracted the sound of voices and laughter and seemed to suspend it in midair. The Bunkers' pool was on a rise and he climbed some stairs to a terrace where twenty-five or thirty men and women were drinking. The only person in the water was Rusty Towers, who floated there on a rubber raft. Oh, how bonny and lush were the banks of the Lucinda River! Prosperous men and women gathered by the sapphire-colored waters while caterer's men in white coats passed them cold gin. Overhead a red de Haviland trainer was circling around and around and around in the sky with something like the glee of a child in a swing. Ned felt a passing affection for the scene, a tenderness for the gathering, as if it was something he might touch. In the distance he heard thunder. As soon as Enid Bunker saw him she began to scream: "Oh, look who's here! What a marvelous surprise! When Lucinda said that you couldn't come I thought I'd *die.*" She made her way to him through the crowd, and when they had finished kissing she led him to the bar, a progress that was slowed by the fact that he stopped to kiss eight or ten other women and shake the hands of as many men. A smiling bartender he had seen at a hundred parties gave him a gin and tonic and he stood by the bar for a moment, anxious not to get stuck in any conversation that would delay his voyage. When he seemed about to be surrounded he dove in and swam close to the side to avoid colliding with Rusty's raft. At the far end of the pool he bypassed the Tomlinsons with a broad smile and jogged up the garden path. The gravel cut his feet but this was the only unpleasantness. The party was confined to the pool, and as he went toward the house he heard the brilliant, watery sound of voices fade, heard the noise of a radio from the Bunkers' kitchen, where someone was listening to a ball game. Sunday afternoon. He made his way through the parked cars and down the grassy border of their driveway to Alewives Lane. He did not want to be seen on the road in his bathing trunks but there was no traffic and he made the short distance to the Levys' driveway, marked with a PRIVATE PROPERTY sign and a green tube for *The New York Times.* All the doors and windows of the big house were open but there were no signs of life; not even a dog barked. He went around the side of the house to the pool and saw that the Levys had only recently left. Glasses and bottles and dishes of nuts were on a table at the deep end, where there was a bathhouse or gazebo, hung with Japanese lanterns. After swimming the pool he got himself a glass and poured a drink. It was his fourth or fifth drink and he had swum nearly half the length of the Lucinda River. He felt tired, clean, and pleased at that moment to be alone; pleased with everything.

It would storm. The stand of cumulus cloud—that city—had risen and darkened, and while he sat there he heard the percussiveness of thunder again. The de Haviland trainer was still circling overhead and it seemed to Ned that he could almost hear the pilot laugh with pleasure in the afternoon; but when there was another peal of thunder he took off for home. A train whistle blew and he wondered what time it had gotten to be. Four? Five? He thought of the provincial station at that hour, where a waiter, his tuxedo concealed by a raincoat, a dwarf with some flowers wrapped in newspaper, and a woman who had been crying would be waiting for the local. It was suddenly growing dark; it was that moment when the pin-headed birds seem to organize their song into some acute and knowledgeable recognition of the storm's approach. Then there was a fine noise of rushing water from the crown of an oak at his back, as if a spigot there had been turned. Then the noise of fountains came from the crowns of all the tall trees. Why did he love storms, what was the meaning of his excitement when the door sprang open and the rain wind fled rudely up the stairs, why had the simple task of shutting the windows of an old house seemed fitting and urgent, why did the first watery notes of a storm wind have for him the unmistakable sound of good news, cheer, glad tidings? Then there was an explosion, a smell of cordite, and rain lashed the Japanese lanterns that Mrs. Levy had bought in Kyoto the year before last, or was it the year before that?

He stayed in the Levys' gazebo until the storm had passed. The rain had cooled the air and he shivered. The force of the wind had stripped a maple of its red and yellow leaves and scattered them over the grass and the water. Since it was midsummer the tree must be blighted, and yet he felt a peculiar sadness at this sign of autumn. He braced his shoulders, emptied his glass, and started for the Welchers' pool. This meant crossing the Lindleys' riding ring and he was surprised to find it overgrown with grass and all the jumps dismantled. He wondered if the Lindleys had sold their horses or gone away for the summer and put them out to board. He seemed to remember having heard something about the Lindleys and their horses but the memory was unclear. On he went, barefoot through the wet grass, to the Welchers', where he found their pool was dry.

This breach in his chain of water disappointed him absurdly, and he felt like some explorer who seeks a torrential headwater and finds a dead stream. He was disappointed and mystified. It was common enough to go away for the summer but no one ever drained his pool. The Welchers had definitely gone away. The pool furniture was folded, stacked, and covered with a tarpaulin. The bathhouse was locked. All the windows of the house were shut, and when he went around to the driveway in front he saw a FOR SALE sign nailed to a tree. When had he last heard from the Welchers—when, that is, had he and Lucinda last regretted an invitation to dine with them? It seemed only a week or so ago. Was his memory failing or had he so disciplined it in the repression of unpleasant facts that he had damaged his sense of the truth? Then in the distance he heard the sound of a tennis game. This cheered him, cleared away all his apprehensions and let him regard the overcast sky and the cold air with indifference. This was the day that Neddy Merrill swam across the county. That was the day! He started off then for his most difficult portage.

Had you gone for a Sunday afternoon ride that day you might have seen him, close to naked, standing on the shoulders of Route 424, waiting for a chance to cross. You might have wondered if he was the victim of foul play, had his car broken down, or was he merely a fool. Standing barefoot in the deposits of the highway—beer cans, rags, and blowout patches—exposed to all kinds of ridicule, he seemed pitiful. He had known when he started that this was a part of his journey—it had been on his maps—but confronted with the lines of traffic, worming through the summery light, he found himself unprepared. He was laughed at, jeered at, a beer can was thrown at him, and he had no dignity or humor to bring to the situation. He could have gone back, back to the Westerhazys', where Lucinda would still be sitting in the sun. He had signed nothing, vowed nothing, pledged nothing, not even to himself. Why, believing as he did, that all human obduracy was susceptible to common sense, was he unable to turn back? Why was he determined to complete his journey even if it meant putting his life in danger? At what point had this prank, this joke, this piece of horseplay become serious? He could not go back, he could not even recall with any clearness the green water at the Westerhazys', the sense of inhaling the day's components, the friendly and relaxed voices saying that they had *drunk* too much. In the space of an hour, more or less, he had covered a distance that made his return impossible.

An old man, tooling down the highway at fifteen miles an hour, let him get to the middle of the road, where there was a grass divider. Here he was exposed to the ridicule of the northbound traffic, but after ten or fifteen minutes he was able to cross. From here he had only a short walk to the Recreation Center at the edge of the village of Lancaster, where there were some handball courts and a public pool.

The effect of the water on voices, the illusion of brilliance and suspense, was the same here as it had been at the Bunkers' but the sounds here were louder, harsher, and more shrill, and as soon as he entered the crowded enclosure he was confronted with regimentation. "ALL SWIMMERS MUST TAKE A SHOWER BEFORE USING THE POOL.

ALL SWIMMERS MUST USE THE FOOTBATH. ALL SWIMMERS MUST WEAR THEIR IDENTIFICATION DISKS." He took a shower, washed his feet in a cloudy and bitter solution, and made his way to the edge of the water. It stank of chlorine and looked to him like a sink. A pair of lifeguards in a pair of towers blew police whistles at what seemed to be regular intervals and abused the swimmers through a public address system. Neddy remembered the sapphire water at the Bunkers' with longing and thought that he might contaminate himself—damage his own prosperousness and charm—by swimming in this murk, but he reminded himself that he was an explorer, a pilgrim, and that this was merely a stagnant bend in the Lucinda River. He dove, scowling with distaste, into the chlorine and had to swim with his head above water to avoid collisions, but even so he was bumped into, splashed, and jostled. When he got to the shallow end both lifeguards were shouting at him: "Hey, you, you without the identification disk, get outa the water." He did, but they had no way of pursuing him and he went through the reek of suntan oil and chlorine out through the hurricane fence and passed the handball courts. By crossing the road he entered the wooded part of the Halloran estate. The woods were not cleared and the footing was treacherous and difficult until he reached the lawn and the clipped beech hedge that encircled their pool.

The Hallorans were friends, an elderly couple of enormous wealth who seemed to bask in the suspicion that they might be Communists. They were zealous reformers but they were not Communists, and yet when they were accused, as they sometimes were, of subversion, it seemed to gratify and excite them. Their beech hedge was yellow and he guessed this had been blighted like the Levys' maple. He called hullo, hullo, to warn the Hallorans of his approach, to palliate his invasion of their privacy. The Hallorans, for reasons that had never been explained to him, did not wear bathing suits. No explanations were in order, really. Their nakedness was a detail in their uncompromising zeal for reform and he stepped politely out of his trunks before he went through the opening in the hedge.

Mrs. Halloran, a stout woman with white hair and a serene face, was reading the *Times*. Mr. Halloran was taking beech leaves out of the water with a scoop. They seemed not surprised or displeased to see him. Their pool was perhaps the oldest in the county, a fieldstone rectangle, fed by a brook. It had no filter or pump and its waters were the opaque gold of the stream.

"I'm swimming across the county," Ned said.

"Why, I didn't know one could," exclaimed Mrs. Halloran.

"Well, I've made it from the Westerhazys'," Ned said. "That must be about four miles."

He left his trunks at the deep end, walked to the shallow end, and swam this stretch. As he was pulling himself out of the water he heard Mrs. Halloran say, "We've been *terribly* sorry to hear about all your misfortunes, Neddy."

"My misfortunes?" Ned asked. "I don't know what you mean."

"Why, we heard that you'd sold the house and that your poor children . . ."

"I don't recall having sold the house," Ned said, "and the girls are at home."

"Yes," Mrs. Halloran sighed. "Yes . . ." Her voice filled the air with an unseasonable melancholy and Ned spoke briskly. "Thank you for the swim."

"Well, have a nice trip," said Mrs. Halloran.

Beyond the hedge he pulled on his trunks and fastened them. They were loose and he wondered if, during the space of an afternoon, he could have lost some weight. He was cold and he was tired and the naked Hallorans and their dark water had depressed him. The swim was too much for his strength but how could he have guessed this, sliding down the banister that morning and sitting in the Westerhazys' sun? His arms were lame. His legs felt rubbery and ached at the joints. The worst of it was the cold in his bones and the feeling that he might never be warm again. Leaves were falling down around him and he smelled wood smoke on the wind. Who would be burning wood at this time of year?

He needed a drink. Whiskey would warm him, pick him up, carry him through the last of his journey, refresh his feeling that it was original and valorous to swim across the county. Channel swimmers took brandy. He needed a stimulant. He crossed the lawn in front of the Hallorans' house and went down a little path to where they had built a house for their only daughter, Helen, and her husband, Eric Sachs. The Sachses' pool was small and he found Helen and her husband there.

"Oh, *Neddy,*" Helen said. "Did you lunch at Mother's?"

"Not *really,*" Ned said. "I *did* stop to see your parents." This seemed to be explanation enough. "I'm terribly sorry to break in on you like this but I've taken a chill and I wonder if you'd give me a drink."

"Why, I'd *love* to," Helen said, "but there hasn't been anything in this house to drink since Eric's operation. That was three years ago."

Was he losing his memory, had his gift for concealing painful facts let him forget that he had sold his house, that his children were in trouble, and that his friend had been ill? His eyes slipped from Eric's face to his abdomen, where he saw three pale, sutured scars, two of them at least a foot long. Gone was his navel, and what, Neddy thought, would the roving hand, bed-checking one's gifts at 3 A.M., make of a belly with no navel, no link to birth, this breach in the succession?

"I'm sure you can get a drink at the Biswangers'," Helen said. "They're having an enormous do. You can hear it from here. Listen!"

She raised her head and from across the road, the lawns, the gardens, the woods, the fields, he heard again the brilliant noise of voices over water. "Well, I'll get wet," he said, still feeling that he had no freedom of choice about his means of travel. He dove into the Sachses' cold water and, gasping, close to drowning, made his way from one end of the pool to the other. "Lucinda and I want *terribly* to see you," he said over his shoulder, his face set toward the Biswangers'. "We're sorry it's been so long and we'll call you *very* soon."

He crossed some fields to the Biswangers' and the sounds of revelry there. They would be honored to give him a drink, they would be happy to give him a drink. The Biswangers invited him and Lucinda for dinner four times a year, six weeks in advance. They were always rebuffed and yet they continued to send out their invitations, unwilling to comprehend the rigid and undemocratic realities of their society. They were the sort of people who discussed the price of things at cocktails, exchanged market tips during dinner, and after dinner told dirty stories to mixed company. They did not belong to Neddy's set—they were not even on Lucinda's Christmas-card list. He went toward their pool with feelings of indifference, charity, and some unease, since it seemed to be getting dark and these were the longest days of the year. The party when he joined it was noisy and large. Grace Biswanger was the kind of hostess who asked the optometrist, the veterinarian, the real-estate dealer, and the dentist. No one was swimming and the twilight, reflected on the water of the pool, had a wintry gleam. There was a bar and he started for this. When

Grace Biswanger saw him she came toward him, not affectionately as he had every right to expect, but bellicosely.

"Why, this party has everything," she said loudly, "including a gate crasher."

She could not deal him a social blow—there was no question about this and he did not flinch. "As a gate crasher," he asked politely, "do I rate a drink?"

"Suit yourself," she said. "You don't seem to pay much attention to invitations."

She turned her back on him and joined some guests, and he went to the bar and ordered a whiskey. The bartender served him but he served him rudely. His was a world in which the caterer's men kept the social score, and to be rebuffed by a part-time barkeep meant that he had suffered some loss of social esteem. Or perhaps the man was new and uninformed. Then he heard Grace at his back say: "They went for broke overnight—nothing but income—and he showed up drunk one Sunday and asked us to loan him five thousand dollars. . . ." She was always talking about money. It was worse than eating your peas off a knife. He dove into the pool, swam its length and went away.

The next pool on his list, the last but two, belonged to his old mistress, Shirley Adams. If he had suffered any injuries at the Biswangers' they would be cured here. Love—sexual roughhouse in fact—was the supreme elixir, the pain killer, the brightly colored pill that would put the spring back into his step, the joy of life in his heart. They had had an affair last week, last month, last year. He couldn't remember. It was he who had broken it off, his was the upper hand, and he stepped through the gate of the wall that surrounded her pool with nothing so considered as self-confidence. It seemed in a way to be his pool, as the lover, particularly the illicit lover, enjoys the possessions of his mistress with an authority unknown to holy matrimony. She was there, her hair the color of brass, but her figure, at the edge of the lighted, cerulean water, excited in him no profound memories. It had been, he thought, a lighthearted affair, although she had wept when he broke it off. She seemed confused to see him and he wondered if she was still wounded. Would she, God forbid, weep again?

"What do you want?" she asked.

"I'm swimming across the county."

"Good Christ. Will you ever grow up?"

"What's the matter?"

"If you've come here for money," she said, "I won't give you another cent."

"You could give me a drink."

"I could but I won't. I'm not alone."

"Well, I'm on my way."

He dove in and swam the pool, but when he tried to haul himself up onto the curb he found that the strength in his arms and shoulders had gone, and he paddled to the ladder and climbed out. Looking over his shoulder he saw, in the lighted bathhouse, a young man. Going out onto the dark lawn he smelled chrysanthemums or marigolds—some stubborn autumnal fragrance—on the night air, strong as gas. Looking overhead he saw that the stars had come out, but why should he seem to see Andromeda, Cepheus, and Cassiopeia? What had become of the constellations of midsummer? He began to cry.

It was probably the first time in his adult life that he had ever cried, certainly the first time in his life that he had ever felt so miserable, cold, tired, and bewildered. He could not understand the rudeness of the caterer's barkeep or the rudeness of a mistress who had come to him on her knees and showered his trousers with tears. He had swum too long, he had been immersed too long, and his nose and his throat were sore from the water. What he needed then was a drink, some company, and some clean, dry clothes, and while he could have cut directly across the road to his home he went on to the Gilmartins' pool. Here, for the first time in his life, he did not dive but went down the steps into the icy water and swam a hobbled sidestroke that he might have learned as a youth. He staggered with fatigue on his way to the Clydes' and paddled the length of their pool, stopping again and again with his hand on the curb to rest. He climbed up the ladder and wondered if he had the strength to get home. He had done what he wanted, he had swum the county, but he was so stupefied with exhaustion that his triumph seemed vague. Stooped, holding on to the gateposts for support, he turned up the driveway of his own house.

The place was dark. Was it so late that they had all gone to bed? Had Lucinda stayed at the Westerhazys' for supper? Had the girls joined her there or gone someplace else? Hadn't they agreed, as they usually did on Sunday, to regret all their invitations and stay at home? He tried the garage doors to see what cars were in but the doors were locked and rust came off the handles onto his hands. Going toward the house, he saw that the force of the thunderstorm had knocked one of the rain gutters loose. It hung down over the front door like an umbrella rib, but it could be fixed in the morning. The house was locked, and he thought that the stupid cook or the stupid maid must have locked the place up until he remembered that it had been some time since they had employed a maid or a cook. He shouted, pounded on the door, tried to force it with his shoulder, and then, looking in at the windows, saw that the place was empty.

1964

RALPH ELLISON
(1914–)

In a poll conducted in 1965 by *Book Week* a group of critics selected Ralph Ellison's novel *Invisible Man* (1952) as the most distinguished work of fiction to appear in the post-World War II period. That poll may be taken as a tribute not only to the power of the novel but to the continuing literary reputation of a man who, past fifty, had published only one other volume, a collection of essays called *Shadow and Act* (1964). Yet, Ellison did not come late to writing. Rather, he is a slow, painstaking author, who, after some success with short stories in his twenties, directed his attention to the completion of *Invisible Man,* which was published when he was thirty-eight. Excerpts from a second novel began to appear in magazines in 1960 and continued to appear throughout the following years as the novel slowly progressed toward completion. Meanwhile, Ellison taught and lectured and remained a formidable literary presence.

Christened Ralph Waldo Ellison, he was born in Oklahoma City, Oklahoma, and educated at Tuskegee Institute. An early interest in music, especially jazz and blues, remains as an influence in his work. After supporting himself by a variety of jobs, including service in the merchant marine, he began teaching in 1958 at Bard College and has taught since then at Rutgers and New York University. He has also served on the editorial board of *American*

Scholar and as a trustee of the John F. Kennedy Center for the Performing Arts and has been the recipient of numerous awards and honorary degrees.

The effect of *Invisible Man* is due in large measure to the successful amalgamation of so many diverse elements in its structure. It is a folk novel, strong in the rhythms of jazz and blues, powerful in its projection of the dual consciousness of the American black. It is also a highly literary, and literate, novel, its epigraphs taken from Melville and T. S. Eliot, its prose polished, its episodes constructed with a care reminiscent of the practice of the greatest American and English novelists. In addition to *Invisible Man,* Ellison's fictive skill has been apparent in a number of short stories, as yet uncollected, one of which is printed below.

Robert G. O'Meally, *The Craft of Ralph Ellison,* 1980, is a full-scale study. John M. Reilly edited *Twentieth Century Interpretations of Invisible Man,* 1970. Ronald Gottesman edited *Studies in Invisible Man,* 1971. John Hersey edited *Ralph Ellison: A Collection of Critical Essays,* 1974.

King of the Bingo Game[1]

The woman in front of him was eating roasted peanuts that smelled so good that he could barely contain his hunger. He could not even sleep and wished they'd hurry and begin the bingo game. There, on his right, two fellows were drinking wine out of a bottle wrapped in a paper bag, and he could hear soft gurgling in the dark. His stomach gave a low, gnawing growl. "If this was down South," he thought, "all I'd have to do is lean over and say, 'Lady, gimme a few of those peanuts, please ma'am,' and she'd pass me the bag and never think nothing of it." Or he could ask the fellows for a drink in the same way. Folks down South stuck together that way; they didn't even have to know you. But up here it was different. Ask somebody for something, and they'd think you were crazy. Well, I ain't crazy. I'm just broke, 'cause I got no birth certificate to get a job, and Laura 'bout to die 'cause we got no money for a doctor. But I ain't crazy. And yet a pinpoint of doubt was focused in his mind as he glanced toward the screen and saw the hero stealthily entering a dark room and sending the beam of a flashlight along a wall of bookcases. This is where he finds the trapdoor, he remembered. The man would pass abruptly through the wall and find the girl tied to a bed, her legs and arms spread wide, and her clothing torn to rags. He laughed softly to himself. He had seen the picture three times, and this was one of the best scenes.

On his right the fellow whispered wide-eyed to his companion, "Man, look a-yonder!"

"Damn!"

"Wouldn't I like to have her tied up like that . . ."

"Hey! That fool's letting her loose!"

"Aw, man, he loves her."

"Love or no love!"

The man moved impatiently beside him, and he tried to involve himself in the scene. But Laura was on his mind. Tiring quickly of watching the picture he looked back to where the white beam filtered from the projection room above the balcony. It started small and grew large, specks of dust dancing in its whiteness as it reached the screen. It was strange how the beam always landed right on the screen and didn't mess up and fall somewhere else. But they had it all fixed. Everything was fixed. Now

1. First published in *Tomorrow,* November, 1944, "King of the Bingo Game" has not been collected in a volume by Ellison.

suppose when they showed that girl with her dress torn the girl started taking off the rest of her clothes, and when the guy came in he didn't untie her but kept her there and went to taking off his own clothes? *That* would be something to see. If a picture got out of hand like that those guys up there would go nuts. Yeah, and there'd be so many folks in here you couldn't find a seat for nine months! A strange sensation played over his skin. He shuddered. Yesterday he'd seen a bedbug on a woman's neck as they walked out into the bright street. But exploring his thigh through a hole in his pocket he found only goose pimples and old scars.

The bottle gurgled again. He closed his eyes. Now a dreamy music was accompanying the film and train whistles were sounding in the distance, and he was a boy again walking along a railroad trestle down South, and seeing the train coming, and running back as fast as he could go, and hearing the whistle blowing, and getting off the trestle to solid ground just in time, with the earth trembling beneath his feet, and feeling relieved as he ran down the cinder-strewn embankment onto the highway, and looking back and seeing with terror that the train had left the track and was following him right down the middle of the street, and all the white people laughing as he ran screaming . . .

"Wake up there, buddy! What the hell do you mean hollering like that? Can't you see we trying to enjoy this here picture?"

He stared at the man with gratitude.

"I'm sorry, old man," he said. "I musta been dreaming."

"Well, here, have a drink. And don't be making no noise like that, damn!"

His hands trembled as he tilted his head. It was not wine, but whiskey. Cold rye whiskey. He took a deep swoller, decided it was better not to take another, and handed the bottle back to its owner.

"Thanks, old man," he said.

Now he felt the cold whiskey breaking a warm path straight through the middle of him, growing hotter and sharper as it moved. He had not eaten all day, and it made him light-headed. The smell of the peanuts stabbed him like a knife, and he got up and found a seat in the middle aisle. But no sooner did he sit than he saw a row of intense-faced young girls, and got up again, thinking, "You chicks musta been Lindy-hopping somewhere." He found a seat several rows ahead as the lights came on, and he saw the screen disappear behind a heavy red and gold curtain; then the curtain rising, and the man with the microphone and a uniformed attendant coming on the stage.

He felt for his bingo cards, smiling. The guy at the door wouldn't like it if he knew about his having *five* cards. Well, not everyone played the bingo game; and even with five cards he didn't have much of a chance. For Laura, though, he had to have faith. He studied the cards, each with its different numerals, punching the free center hole in each and spreading them neatly across his lap; and when the lights faded he sat slouched in his seat so that he could look from his cards to the bingo wheel with but a quick shifting of his eyes.

Ahead, at the end of the darkness, the man with the microphone was pressing a button attached to a long cord and spinning the bingo wheel and calling out the number each time the wheel came to rest. And each time the voice rang out his finger raced over the cards for the number. With five cards he had to move fast. He became nervous; there were too many cards, and the man went too fast with his grating voice. Perhaps he should just select one and throw the others away. But he was afraid. He became warm. Wonder how much Laura's doctor would cost?

Damn that, watch the cards! And with despair he heard the man call three in a row which he missed on all five cards. This way he'd never win . . .

When he saw the row of holes punched across the third card, he sat paralyzed and heard the man call three more numbers before he stumbled forward, screaming.

"Bingo! Bingo!"

"Let that fool up there," someone called.

"Get up there, man!"

He stumbled down the aisle and up the steps to the stage into a light so sharp and bright that for a moment it blinded him, and he felt that he had moved into the spell of some strange, mysterious power. Yet it was as familiar as the sun, and he knew it was the perfectly familiar bingo.

The man with the microphone was saying something to the audience as he held out his card. A cold light flashed from the man's finger as the card left his hand. His knees trembled. The man stepped closer, checking the card against the numbers chalked on the board. Suppose he had made a mistake? The pomade on the man's hair made him feel faint, and he backed away. But the man was checking the card over the microphone now, and he had to stay. He stood tense, listening.

"Under the O, forty-four," the man chanted. "Under the I, seven. Under the G, three. Under the B, ninety-six. Under the N, thirteen!"

His breath came easier as the man smiled at the audience.

"Yessir, ladies and gentlemen, he's one of the chosen people!"

The audience rippled with laughter and applause.

"Step right up to the front of the stage."

He moved slowly forward, wishing that the light was not so bright.

"To win to-night's jackpot of $36.90 the wheel must stop between the double zero, understand?"

He nodded, knowing the ritual from the many days and nights he had watched the winners march across the stage to press the button that controlled the spinning wheel and receive the prizes. And now he followed the instructions as though he'd crossed the slippery stage a million prize-winning times.

The man was making some kind of a joke, and he nodded vacantly. So tense had he become that he felt a sudden desire to cry and shook it away. He felt vaguely that his whole life was determined by the bingo wheel; not only that which would happen now that he was at last before it, but all that had gone before, since his birth, and his mother's birth and the birth of his father. It had always been there, even though he had not been aware of it, handing out the unlucky cards and numbers of his days. The feeling persisted, and he started quickly away. I better get down from here before I make a fool of myself, he thought.

"Here, boy," the man called. "You haven't started yet."

Someone laughed as he went hesitantly back.

"Are you all reet?"

He grinned at the man's jive talk, but no words would come, and he knew it was not a convincing grin. For suddenly he knew that he stood on the slippery brink of some terrible embarrassment.

"Where are you from, boy?" the man asked.

"Down South."

"He's from down South, ladies and gentlemen," the man said. "Where from? Speak right into the mike."

"Rocky Mont," he said. "Rock' Mont, North Car'lina."

"So you decided to come down off that mountain to the U. S.," the man laughed. He felt that the man was making a fool of him, but then something cold was placed in his hand, and the lights were no longer behind him.

Standing before the wheel he felt alone, but that was somehow right, and he remembered his plan. He would give the wheel a short quick twirl. Just a touch of the button. He had watched it many times, and always it came close to double zero when it was short and quick. He steeled himself; the fear had left, and he felt a profound sense of promise, as though he were about to be repaid for all the things he'd suffered all his life. Trembling, he pressed the button. There was a whirl of lights, and in a second he realized with finality that though he wanted to, he could not stop. It was as though he held a high-powered line in his naked hand. His nerves tightened. As the wheel increased its speed it seemed to draw him more and more into its power, as though it held his fate; and with it came a deep need to submit, to whirl, to lose himself in its swirl of color. He could not stop it now. So let it be.

The button rested snugly in his palm where the man had placed it. And now he became aware of the man beside him, advising him through the microphone, while behind the shadowy audience hummed with noisy voices. He shifted his feet. There was still that feeling of helplessness within him, making part of him desire to turn back, even now that the jackpot was right in his hand. He squeezed the button until his fist ached. Then, like the sudden shriek of a subway whistle, a doubt tore through his head. Suppose he did not spin the wheel long enough? What could he do, and how could he tell? And then he knew, even as he wondered, that as long as he pressed the button, he could control the jackpot. He and only he could determine whether or not it was to be his. Not even the man with the microphone could do anything about it now. He felt drunk. Then, as though he had come down from a high hill into a valley of people, he heard the audience yelling.

"Come down from there, you jerk!"

"Let somebody else have a chance . . ."

"Ole Jack thinks he done found the end of the rainbow . . ."

The last voice was not unfriendly, and he turned and smiled dreamily into the yelling mouths. Then he turned his back squarely on them.

"Don't take too long, boy," a voice said.

He nodded. They were yelling behind him. Those folks did not understand what had happened to him. They had been playing the bingo game day in and night out for years, trying to win rent money or hamburger change. But not one of those wise guys had discovered this wonderful thing. He watched the wheel whirling past the numbers and experienced a burst of exaltation: This is God! This is the really truly God! He said it aloud, "This is God!"

He said it with such absolute conviction that he feared he would fall fainting into the footlights. But the crowd yelled so loud that they could not hear. Those fools, he thought. I'm here trying to tell them the most wonderful secret in the world, and they're yelling like they gone crazy. A hand fell upon his shoulder.

"You'll have to make a choice now, boy. You've taken too long."

He brushed the hand violently away.

"Leave me alone, man. I know what I'm doing!"

The man looked surprised and held on to the microphone for support. And because he did not wish to hurt the man's feelings he smiled, realizing with a sudden pang that there was no way of explaining to the man just why he had to stand there pressing the button forever.

"Come here," he called tiredly.

The man approached, rolling the heavy microphone across the stage.

"Anybody can play this bingo game, right?" he said.

"Sure, but . . ."

He smiled, feeling inclined to be patient with this slick looking white man with his blue shirt and his sharp gabardine suit.

"That's what I thought," he said. "Anybody can win the jackpot as long as they get the lucky number, right?"

"That's the rule, but after all . . ."

"That's what I thought," he said. "And the big prize goes to the man who knows how to win it?"

The man nodded speechlessly.

"Well then, go on over there and watch me win like I want to. I ain't going to hurt nobody," he said, "and I'll show you how to win. I mean to show the whole world how it's got to be done."

And because he understood, he smiled again to let the man know that he held nothing against him for being white and impatient. Then he refused to see the man any longer and stood pressing the button, the voices of the crowd reaching him like sounds in distant streets. Let them yell. All the Negroes down there were just ashamed because he was black like them. He smiled inwardly, knowing how it was. Most of the time he was ashamed of what Negroes did himself. Well, let them be ashamed for something this time. Like him. He was like a long thin black wire that was being stretched and wound upon the bingo wheel; wound until he wanted to scream; wound, but this time himself controlling the winding and the sadness and the shame, and because he did, Laura would be all right. Suddenly the lights flickered. He staggered backwards. Had something gone wrong? All this noise. Didn't they know that although he controlled the wheel, it also controlled him, and unless he pressed the button forever and forever and ever it would stop, leaving him high and dry, dry and high on this hard high slippery hill and Laura dead? There was only one chance; he had to do whatever the wheel demanded. And gripping the button in despair, he discovered with surprise that it imparted a nervous energy. His spine tingled. He felt a certain power.

Now he faced the raging crowd with defiance, its screams penetrating his eardrums like trumpets shrieking from a juke-box. The vague faces glowing in the bingo lights gave him a sense of himself that he had never known before. He was running the show, by God! They had to react to him, for he was their luck. This is *me,* he thought. Let the bastards yell. Then someone was laughing inside him, and he realized that somehow he had forgotten his own name. It was a sad, lost feeling to lose your name, and a crazy thing to do. That name had been given him by the white man who had owned his grandfather a long lost time ago down South. But maybe those wise guys knew his name.

"Who am I?" he screamed.

"Hurry up and bingo, you jerk!"

They didn't know either, he thought sadly. They didn't even know their own names, they were all poor nameless bastards. Well, he didn't need that old name; he was reborn. For as long as he pressed the button he was The-man-who-pressed-the-button-who-held-the-prize-who-was-the-King-of-Bingo. That was the way it was, and he'd have to press the button even if nobody understood, even though Laura did not understand.

"Live!" he shouted.

The audience quieted like the dying of a huge fan.

"Live, Laura, baby. I got holt of it now, sugar. Live!"

He screamed it, tears streaming down his face. "I got nobody but YOU!"

The screams tore from his very guts. He felt as though the rush of blood to his head would burst out in baseball seams of small red droplets, like a head beaten by police clubs. Bending over he saw a trickle of blood splashing the toe of his shoe. With his free hand he searched his head. It was his nose. God, suppose something has gone wrong? He felt that the whole audience had somehow entered him and was stamping its feet in his stomach and he was unable to throw them out. They wanted the prize, that was it. They wanted the secret for themselves. But they'd never get it; he would keep the bingo wheel whirling forever, and Laura would be safe in the wheel. But would she? It had to be, because if she were not safe the wheel would cease to turn; it could not go on. He had to get away, *vomit* all, and his mind formed an image of himself running with Laura in his arms down the tracks of the subway just ahead of an A train, running desperately *vomit* with people screaming for him to come out but knowing no way of leaving the tracks because to stop would bring the train crushing down upon him and to attempt to leave across the other tracks would mean to run into a hot third rail as high as his waist which threw blue sparks that blinded his eyes until he could hardly see.

He heard singing and the audience was clapping its hands.

> Shoot the liquor to him, Jim, boy!
> Clap-clap-clap
> Well a-calla the cop
> He's blowing his top!
> Shoot the liquor to him, Jim, boy!

Bitter anger grew within him at the singing. They think I'm crazy. Well let 'em laugh. I'll do what I got to do.

He was standing in an attitude of intense listening when he saw that they were watching something on the stage behind him. He felt weak. But when he turned he saw no one. If only his thumb did not ache so. Now they were applauding. And for a moment he thought that the wheel had stopped. But that was impossible, his thumb still pressed the button. Then he saw them. Two men in uniform beckoned from the end of the stage. They were coming toward him, walking in step, slowly, like a tap-dance team returning for a third encore. But their shoulders shot forward, and he backed away, looking wildly about. There was nothing to fight them with. He had only the long black cord which led to a plug somewhere back stage, and he couldn't use that because it operated the bingo wheel. He backed slowly, fixing the men with his eyes as his lips stretched over his teeth in a tight, fixed grin; moved toward the end of the stage and realizing that he couldn't go much further, for suddenly the cord became taut and he couldn't afford to break the cord. But he had to do something. The audience was howling. Suddenly he stopped dead, seeing the men halt, their legs lifted as in an interrupted step of a slow-motion dance. There was nothing to do but run in the other direction and he dashed forward, slipping and sliding. The men fell back, surprised. He struck out violently going past.

"Grab him!"

He ran, but all too quickly the cord tightened, resistingly, and he turned and ran back again. This time he slipped them, and discovered by running in a circle before the wheel he could keep the cord from tightening. But this way he had to flail his arms to keep the men away. Why couldn't they leave a man alone? He ran, circling.

"Ring down the curtain," someone yelled. But they couldn't do that. If they did the wheel flashing from the projection room would be cut off. But they had him before he could tell them so, trying to pry open his fist, and he was wrestling and trying to bring his knees into the fight and holding on to the button, for it was his life. And now he was down, seeing a foot coming down, crushing his wrist cruelly, down, as he saw the wheel whirling serenely above.

"I can't give it up," he screamed. Then quietly, in a confidential tone, "Boys, I really can't give it up."

It landed hard against his head. And in the blank moment they had it away from him, completely now. He fought them trying to pull him up from the stage as he watched the wheel spin slowly to a stop. Without surprise he saw it rest at double-zero.

"You see," he pointed bitterly.

"Sure, boy, sure, it's O. K.," one of the men said smiling.

And seeing the man bow his head to someone he could not see, he felt very, very happy; he would receive what all the winners received.

But as he warmed in the justice of the man's tight smile he did not see the man's slow wink, nor see the bow-legged man behind him step clear of the swiftly descending curtain and set himself for a blow. He only felt the dull pain exploding in his skull, and he knew even as it slipped out of him that his luck had run out on the stage.

[1944]

BERNARD MALAMUD
(1914–1986)

The recognition of the polarity of tragedy and comedy inherent in human suffering characterized Bernard Malamud's writing from his first novel, *The Natural* (1952), to *God's Grace* (1982) and was brilliantly displayed in the short stories collected in *The Stories of Bernard Malamud* (1983). Concerned with the essential pathos in the human condition, he frequently found his most congenial subject to be the bereft, bewildered, and wandering Jew. There is a universality in his work, however, that raises him above the plane of the local colorist or racial writer. If his protagonist is an insignificant, exasperating, and pathetic old Jew lost in the maelstrom of New York, as in the story below, he is also the focal point of the spiritual force inherent in an ancient race. Malamud makes strategic use of the tensions between comedy and terror, corrosive failure and qualified success, absurdity and high courage so accentuated in the Jewish experience but shared by all people of feeling and reflection.

Born in Brooklyn in 1914, in the spring before the outbreak of the First World War, he shared the dislocations of that generation, his adolescence affected if not afflicted by the Great Depression. He attended public school in New York City and received his B.A. in 1936 from the College of the City of New York. He survived and profited from the wearing experience of teaching evening high school classes in New York for nine years, from 1940 to 1949. He received his M.A. from Columbia in 1942 and afterwards taught at Oregon State University and at Bennington College in Vermont, with leaves of absence to lecture at Harvard. His second novel, *The Assistant* (1957), is an acknowledged masterpiece, and his first collection of short stories, *The Magic Barrel* (1958), from which this story is taken, won the National Book Award.

In his review of that collection, R. C. Blackman characterized Malamud's writing in terms that are equally applicable to his later fiction: "unified by a tone of resigned and humorous wisdom and unsentimental cultural compassion. * * * The responsibility of being, first of all, a man, and then a Jew, involves all these characters. * * * Depth, but not darkness; for even hopelessness, in Mr. Malamud's hands, is infused with a kind of New World vitality."

Malamud's novels are *The Natural,* 1952; *The Assistant,* 1957; *A New Life,* 1961; *The Fixer,* 1966; *Pictures of Fidelman,* 1969; *The Tenants,* 1971; *Dubin's Lives,* 1979; and *God's Grace,* 1982. Individual volumes of short stories are *The Magic Barrel,* 1958; *Idiots First,* 1963; and *Rembrandt's Hat,* 1973. Philip Rahv edited *A Malamud Reader,* 1967.

Critical studies are Sidney Richman, *Bernard Malamud,* 1967; Leslie and Joyce Field, eds., *Bernard Malamud and the Critics,* 1970; Sandy Cohen, *Bernard Malamud and the Trial by Love,* 1974; L. and J. Field, eds., *Bernard Malamud: A Collection of Critical Essays,* 1975; Richard Astro and Jackson Benson, eds., *The Fiction of Bernard Malamud,* 1977; and Jeffrey Helterman, *Understanding Bernard Malamud,* 1985.

The Mourners

Kessler, formerly an egg candler, lived alone on social security. Though past sixty-five, he might have found well-paying work with more than one butter and egg wholesaler, for he sorted and graded with speed and accuracy, but he was a quarrelsome type and considered a trouble maker, so the wholesalers did without him. Therefore, after a time he retired, living with few wants on his old-age pension. Kessler inhabited a small cheap flat on the top floor of a decrepit tenement on the East Side. Perhaps because he lived above so many stairs, no one bothered to visit him. He was much alone, as he had been most of his life. At one time he'd had a family, but unable to stand his wife or children, always in his way, he had after some years walked out on them. He never saw them thereafter, because he never sought them, and they did not seek him. Thirty years had passed. He had no idea where they were, nor did he think much about it.

In the tenement, although he had lived there ten years, he was more or less unknown. The tenants on both sides of his flat on the fifth floor, an Italian family of three middle-aged sons and their wizened mother, and a sullen, childless German couple named Hoffman, never said hello to him, nor did he greet any of them on the way up or down the narrow wooden stairs. Others of the house recognized Kessler when they passed him in the street, but they thought he lived elsewhere on the block. Ignace, the small, bent-back janitor, knew him best, for they had several times played two-handed pinochle; but Ignace, usually the loser because he lacked skill at cards, had stopped going up after a time. He complained to his wife that he couldn't stand the stink there, that the filthy flat with its junky furniture made him sick. The janitor had spread the word about Kessler to the others on the floor, and they shunned him as a dirty old man. Kessler understood this but had contempt for them all.

One day Ignace and Kessler began a quarrel over the way the egg candler piled oily bags overflowing with garbage into the dumb-waiter, instead of using a pail. One word shot off another, and they were soon calling each other savage names, when Kessler slammed the door in the janitor's face. Ignace ran down five flights of stairs and loudly cursed out the old man to his impassive wife. It happened that Gruber, the landlord, a fat man with a consistently worried face, who wore yards of baggy clothes, was in the building, making a check of plumbing repairs, and to him the enraged Ignace related the trouble he was having with Kessler. He described, holding his nose, the smell in Kessler's flat, and called him the dirtiest person he had ever seen. Gruber knew his janitor was exaggerating, but he felt burdened by financial worries which shot his blood pressure up to astonishing heights, so he settled it quickly by saying, "Give him notice." None of the tenants in the house had held a written lease since the war, and Gruber felt confident, in case somebody asked questions, that he could easily justify his dismissal of Kessler as an undesirable tenant. It had occurred to him that Ignace could then slap a cheap coat of paint on the walls and the flat would be let to someone for five dollars more than the old man was paying.

That night after supper, Ignace victoriously ascended the stairs and knocked on Kessler's door. The egg candler opened it, and seeing who stood there, immediately slammed it shut. Ignace shouted through the door. "Mr. Gruber says to give notice. We don't want you around here. Your dirt stinks the whole house." There was silence, but Ignace waited, relishing what he had said. Although after five minutes he still heard no sound, the janitor stayed there, picturing the old Jew trembling behind the locked door. He spoke again. "You got two weeks' notice till the first, then you better move out or Mr. Gruber and myself will throw you out." Ignace watched as the door slowly opened. To his surprise he found himself frightened at the old man's appearance. He looked, in the act of opening the door, like a corpse adjusting his coffin lid. But if he appeared dead, his voice was alive. It rose terrifyingly harsh from his throat, and he sprayed curses over all the years of Ignace's life. His eyes were reddened, his cheeks sunken, and his wisp of beard moved agitatedly. He seemed to be losing weight as he shouted. The janitor no longer had any heart for the matter, but he could not bear so many insults all at once so he cried out, "You dirty old bum, you better get out and don't make so much trouble." To this the enraged Kessler swore they would first have to kill him and drag him out dead.

On the morning of the first of December, Ignace found in his letter box a soiled folded paper containing Kessler's twenty-five dollars. He showed it to Gruber that evening when the landlord came to collect the rent money. Gruber, after a minute of absently contemplating the money, frowned disgustedly.

"I thought I told you to give notice."

"Yes, Mr. Gruber," Ignace agreed. "I gave him."

"That's a helluva chuzpah,"[1] said Gruber. "Gimme the keys."

Ignace brought the ring of pass keys, and Gruber, breathing heavily, began the lumbering climb up the long avenue of stairs. Although he rested on each landing, the fatigue of climbing, and his profuse flowing perspiration, heightened his irritation.

1. Yiddish: impudence, bravado.

Arriving at the top floor he banged his fist on Kessler's door. "Gruber, the landlord. Open up here."

There was no answer, no movement within, so Gruber inserted the key into the lock and twisted. Kessler had barricaded the door with a chest and some chairs. Gruber had to put his shoulder to the door and shove before he could step into the hallway of the badly-lit two and a half room flat. The old man, his face drained of blood, was standing in the kitchen doorway.

"I warned you to scram outa here," Gruber said loudly. "Move out or I'll telephone the city marshal."

"Mr. Gruber—" began Kessler.

"Don't bother me with your lousy excuses, just beat it." He gazed around. "It looks like a junk shop and it smells like a toilet. It'll take me a month to clean up here."

"This smell is only cabbage that I am cooking for my supper. Wait, I'll open a window and it will go away."

"When you go away, it'll go away." Gruber took out his bulky wallet, counted out twelve dollars, added fifty cents, and plunked the money on top of the chest. "You got two more weeks till the fifteenth, then you gotta be out or I will get a dispossess. Don't talk back talk. Get outa here and go somewhere that they don't know you and maybe you'll get a place."

"No, Mr. Gruber," Kessler cried passionately. "I didn't do nothing, and I will stay here."

"Don't monkey with my blood pressure," said Gruber. "If you're not out by the fifteenth, I will personally throw you on your bony ass."

Then he left and walked heavily down the stairs.

The fifteenth came and Ignace found the twelve fifty in his letter box. He telephoned Gruber and told him.

"I'll get a dispossess," Gruber shouted. He instructed the janitor to write out a note saying to Kessler that his money was refused and to stick it under his door. This Ignace did. Kessler returned the money to the letter box, but again Ignace wrote a note and slipped it, with the money, under the old man's door.

After another day Kessler received a copy of his eviction notice. It said to appear in court on Friday at 10 A.M. to show cause why he should not be evicted for continued neglect and destruction of rental property. The official notice filled Kessler with great fright because he had never in his life been to court. He did not appear on the day he had been ordered to.

That same afternoon the marshal appeared with two brawny assistants. Ignace opened Kessler's lock for them and as they pushed their way into the flat, the janitor hastily ran down the stairs to hide in the cellar. Despite Kessler's wailing and carrying on, the two assistants methodically removed his meager furniture and set it out on the sidewalk. After that they got Kessler out, though they had to break open the bathroom door because the old man had locked himself in there. He shouted, struggled, pleaded with his neighbors to help him, but they looked on in a silent group outside the door. The two assistants, holding the old man tightly by the arms and skinny legs, carried him, kicking and moaning, down the stairs. They sat him in the street on a chair amid his junk. Upstairs, the marshal bolted the door with a lock Ignace had supplied, signed a paper which he handed to the janitor's wife, and then drove off in an automobile with his assistants.

Kessler sat on a split chair on the sidewalk. It was raining and the rain soon turned to sleet, but he still sat there. People passing by skirted the pile of his belongings. They stared at Kessler and he stared at nothing. He wore no hat or coat, and the snow fell on him, making him look like a piece of his dispossessed goods. Soon the wizened Italian woman from the top floor returned to the house with two of her sons, each carrying a loaded shopping bag. When she recognized Kessler sitting amid his furniture, she began to shriek. She shrieked in Italian at Kessler although he paid no attention to her. She stood on the stoop, shrunken, gesticulating with thin arms, her loose mouth working angrily. Her sons tried to calm her, but still she shrieked. Several of the neighbors came down to see who was making the racket. Finally, the two sons, unable to think what else to do, set down their shopping bags, lifted Kessler out of the chair, and carried him up the stairs. Hoffman, Kessler's other neighbor, working with a small triangular file, cut open the padlock, and Kessler was carried into the flat from which he had been evicted. Ignace screeched at everybody, calling them filthy names, but the three men went downstairs and hauled up Kessler's chairs, his broken table, chest, and ancient metal bed. They piled all the furniture into the bedroom. Kessler sat on the edge of the bed and wept. After a while, after the old Italian woman had sent in a soup plate full of hot macaroni seasoned with tomato sauce and grated cheese, they left.

Ignace phoned Gruber. The landlord was eating and the food turned to lumps in his throat. "I'll throw them all out, the bastards," he yelled. He put on his hat, got into his car and drove through the slush to the tenement. All the time he was thinking of his worries: high repair costs; it was hard to keep the place together; maybe the building would someday collapse. He had read of such things. All of a sudden the front of the building parted from the rest and fell like a breaking wave into the street. Gruber cursed the old man for taking him from his supper. When he got to the house he snatched Ignace's keys and ascended the sagging stairs. Ignace tried to follow, but Gruber told him to stay the hell in his hole. When the landlord was not looking, Ignace crept up after him.

Gruber turned the key and let himself into Kessler's dark flat. He pulled the light chain and found the old man sitting limply on the side of the bed. On the floor at his feet lay a plate of stiffened macaroni.

"What do you think you're doing here?" Gruber thundered.

The old man sat motionless.

"Don't you know it's against the law? This is trespassing and you're breaking the law. Answer me."

Kessler remained mute.

Gruber mopped his brow with a large yellowed handkerchief.

"Listen, my friend, you're gonna make lots of trouble for yourself. If they catch you in here you might go to the workhouse. I'm only trying to advise you."

To his surprise Kessler looked at him with wet, brimming eyes.

"What did I did to you?" he bitterly wept. "Who throws out of his house a man that he lived there ten years and pays every month on time his rent? What did I do, tell me? Who hurts a man without a reason? Are you a Hitler or a Jew?" He was hitting his chest with his fist.

Gruber removed his hat. He listened carefully, at first at a loss what to say, but then answered: "Listen, Kessler, it's not personal. I own this house and it's falling apart. My bills are sky high. If the tenants don't take care they have to go. You don't take care and you fight with my janitor, so you have to go. Leave in the morning, and I won't say another word. But if you don't leave the flat, you'll get the heave-ho again. I'll call the marshal."

"Mr. Gruber," said Kessler, "I won't go. Kill me if you want it, but I won't go."

Ignace hurried away from the door as Gruber left in anger. The next morning, after a restless night of worries, the landlord set out to drive to the city marshal's office. On the way he stopped at a candy store for a pack of cigarettes, and there decided once more to speak to Kessler. A thought had occurred to him: he would offer to get the old man into a public home.

He drove to the tenement and knocked on Ignace's door.

"Is the old gink still up there?"

"I don't know if so, Mr. Gruber." The janitor was ill at ease.

"What do you mean you don't know?"

"I didn't see him go out. Before, I looked in his keyhole but nothing moves."

"So why didn't you open the door with your key?"

"I was afraid," Ignace answered nervously.

"What are you afraid?"

Ignace wouldn't say.

A fright went through Gruber but he didn't show it. He grabbed the keys and walked ponderously up the stairs, hurrying every so often.

No one answered his knock. As he unlocked the door he broke into heavy sweat.

But the old man was there, alive, sitting without shoes on the bedroom floor.

"Listen, Kessler," said the landlord, relieved although his head pounded. "I got an idea that, if you do it the way I say, your troubles are over."

He explained his proposal to Kessler, but the egg candler was not listening. His eyes were downcast, and his body swayed slowly sideways. As the landlord talked on, the old man was thinking of what had whirled through his mind as he had sat out on the sidewalk in the falling snow. He had thought through his miserable life, remembering how, as a young man, he had abandoned his family, walking out on his wife and three innocent children, without even in some way attempting to provide for them; without, in all the intervening years—so God help him—once trying to discover if they were alive or dead. How, in so short a life, could a man do so much wrong? This thought smote him to the heart and he recalled the past without end and moaned and tore at his flesh with his fingernails.

Gruber was frightened at the extent of Kessler's suffering. Maybe I should let him stay, he thought. Then as he watched the old man, he realized he was bunched up there on the floor engaged in an act of mourning. There he sat, white from fasting, rocking back and forth, his beard dwindled to a shade of itself.

Something wrong here—Gruber tried to imagine what and found it all oppressive. He felt he ought to run out, get away, but then saw himself fall and go tumbling down the five flights of stairs; he groaned at the broken picture of himself lying at the bottom. Only he was still there in Kessler's bedroom, listening to the old man praying. Somebody's dead, Gruber muttered. He figured Kessler had got bad news, yet instinctively knew he hadn't. Then it struck him with a terrible force that the mourner was mourning him: it was *he* who was dead.

The landlord was agonized. Sweating brutally, he felt an enormous constricted weight in him that slowly forced itself up, until his head was at the point of bursting. For a full minute he awaited a stroke; but the feeling painfully passed, leaving him miserable.

When after a while, he gazed around the room, it was clean, drenched in daylight and fragrance. Gruber then suffered unbearable remorse for the way he had treated the old man.

At last he could stand it no longer. With a cry of shame he tore the sheet off Kessler's bed, and wrapping it around his bulk, sank heavily to the floor and became a mourner.

1958

SAUL BELLOW
(1915–)

Saul Bellow is a product not of the compact cities of the eastern seaboard, nor yet of the open spaces of the plains and small towns of the Midwest, but rather of the urban sprawl of Chicago. He is, in his own words, "a Chicagoan, out and out." Among post-World War II American novels his are the ones that best present the problems of the modern urban man in search of his identity. His heroes are rootless, or rooted to a past that no longer seems relevant to the present. Surrounded by friends and acquaintances who adjust, who learn to conform, they seek to be individuals in a world that appears to have little room for individuality. Convinced of the need for freedom, they do not know where to seek it except on paths that lead often to loneliness and despair. Yet there is also an affirmation in their lives. Hemmed in on all sides by society, they continue to assert the worth and dignity of the individual human spirit.

The son of Russian Jews who had settled in Canada in 1913, Bellow was born in Lachine, Quebec, in 1915. As a child he was familiar with Hebrew, Yiddish, and French, as well as English. After the family moved to Chicago in 1924 he was educated "after a fashion" in the public schools and attended the University of Chicago before graduating from Northwestern in 1937. He began graduate school at the University of Wisconsin, but did not stay long, and since that time has supported himself mainly by teaching and writing. Since 1962, he has been a professor at the University of Chicago. In 1976 he was awarded the Nobel Prize for literature.

Dangling Man (1944) and *The Victim* (1947) were tightly constructed, traditional novels that earned the author some critical praise, but with the appearance of the sprawling, picaresque *The Adventures of Augie March* (1953) it became apparent that Bellow possessed a talent of major proportions. *Henderson the Rain King* (1959), in some ways Bellow's most engaging fiction, seemed self-indulgently romantic to some of his critics, but both *Herzog* (1964) and *Mr. Sammler's Planet* (1970) received general acclaim. *Humboldt's Gift* (1975), a novel based upon the author's early relationship to the poet Delmore Schwartz, has also been highly praised. *The Dean's December* (1982), Bellow's first novel after receiving the Nobel Prize, is a masterful study of dissolution within an American academic community, in the urban street life of Chicago, and under an oppressive Communist regime in Bucharest, Rumania. Unlike many of his contemporaries, Bellow has appeared to grow with each new book, while his concern for individuality in an age of conformity has remained essentially the same.

Primarily a novelist, Bellow has also had plays produced in New York, London, and Glasgow and has written a handful of memorable short stories and novellas, the best of which are collected in *Seize the*

Day (1956), *Mosby's Memoirs and Other Stories* (1968) and *Him with His Foot in His Mouth and Other Stories* (1984).

Bellow's major fiction is named above. A play is *The Last Analysis,* 1965. *To Jerusalem and Back,* 1976, tells of a visit to Israel. Gabriel Josipovici edited *The Portable Bellow,* 1974. Biographical and critical studies include Tony Tanner, *Saul Bellow,* 1965; Irving Malin, ed., *Saul Bellow and the Critics,* 1967; Keith M. Opdahl, *The Novels of Saul Bellow: An Introduction,* 1967; Irving Malin, *Saul Bellow's Fiction,* 1969; Brigitte Scheer-Schäzler, *Saul Bellow,* 1972; Sarah Blacher Cohen, *Saul Bellow's Enigmatic Laughter,* 1974; M. Gilbert Porter, *Whence the Power? The Artistry and Humanity of Saul Bellow,* 1974; John J. Clayton, *Saul Bellow: In Defense of Man,* second ed., 1979; Mark Harris, *Saul Bellow: Drumlin Woodchuck,* 1980; Malcolm Bradbury, *Saul Bellow,* 1982; Jeanne Braham, *A Sort of Columbus: The American Voyages of Saul Bellow's Fiction,* 1984; Daniel Fuchs, *Saul Bellow: Vision and Revision,* 1984; Judie Newman, *Saul Bellow and History,* 1984; and Jonathan Wilson, *On Bellow's Planet: Readings from the Dark Side,* 1985.

Looking for Mr. Green

Whatsoever thy hand findeth to do, do it with thy might. . . .[1]

Hard work? No, it wasn't really so hard. He wasn't used to walking and stair-climbing, but the physical difficulty of his new job was not what George Grebe felt most. He was delivering relief checks in the Negro district, and although he was a native Chicagoan this was not a part of the city he knew much about—it needed a depression to introduce him to it. No, it wasn't literally hard work, not as reckoned in foot-pounds, but yet he was beginning to feel the strain of it, to grow aware of its peculiar difficulty. He could find the streets and numbers, but the clients were not where they were supposed to be, and he felt like a hunter inexperienced in the camouflage of his game. It was an unfavorable day, too—fall, and cold, dark weather, windy. But, anyway, instead of shells in his deep trenchcoat pocket he had the cardboard of checks, punctured for the spindles of the file, the holes reminding him of the holes in player-piano paper. And he didn't look much like a hunter, either; his was a city figure entirely, belted up in this Irish conspirator's coat. He was slender without being tall, stiff in the back, his legs looking shabby in a pair of old tweed pants gone through and fringy at the cuffs. With this stiffness, he kept his head forward, so that his face was red from the sharpness of the weather; and it was an indoors sort of face with gray eyes that persisted in some kind of thought and yet seemed to avoid definiteness of conclusion. He wore sideburns that surprised you somewhat by the tough curl of the blond hair and the effect of assertion in their length. He was not so mild as he looked, nor so youthful; and nevertheless there was no effort on his part to seem what he was not. He was an educated man; he was a bachelor; he was in some ways simple; without lushing, he liked a drink; his luck had not been good. Nothing was deliberately hidden.

He felt that his luck was better than usual today. When he had reported for work that morning he had expected to be shut up in the relief office at a clerk's job, for he had been hired downtown as a clerk, and he was glad to have, instead, the freedom of the streets and welcomed, at least at first, the vigor of the cold and even the blowing of the hard wind. But on the other hand he was not getting on with the distribution of the checks. It was true that it was a city job; nobody expected you to push too hard at a city job. His supervisor, that young Mr. Raynor, had practically told him that. Still, he wanted to do well at it. For one thing, when he

1. Ecclesiastes ix: 10. The verse concludes, "for there is no work, nor device, nor knowledge, nor wisdom, in the grave, whither thou goest."

knew how quickly he could deliver a batch of checks, he would know also how much time he could expect to clip for himself. And then, too, the clients would be waiting for their money. That was not the most important consideration, though it certainly mattered to him. No, but he wanted to do well, simply for doing-well's sake, to acquit himself decently of a job because he so rarely had a job to do that required just this sort of energy. Of this peculiar energy he now had a superabundance; once it had started to flow, it flowed all too heavily. And, for the time being anyway, he was balked. He could not find Mr. Green.

So he stood in his big-skirted trenchcoat with a large envelope in his hand and papers showing from his pocket, wondering why people should be so hard to locate who were too feeble or sick to come to the station to collect their own checks. But Raynor had told him that tracking them down was not easy at first and had offered him some advice on how to proceed. "If you can see the postman, he's your first man to ask, and your best bet. If you can't connect with him, try the stores and tradespeople around. Then the janitor and the neighbors. But you'll find the closer you come to your man the less people will tell you. They don't want to tell you anything."

"Because I'm a stranger."

"Because you're white. We ought to have a Negro doing this, but we don't at the moment, and of course you've got to eat, too, and this is public employment. Jobs have to be made. Oh, that holds for me too. Mind you, I'm not letting myself out. I've got three years of seniority on you, that's all. And a law degree. Otherwise, you might be back of the desk and I might be going out into the field this cold day. The same dough pays us both and for the same, exact, identical reason. What's my law degree got to do with it? But you have to pass out these checks, Mr. Grebe, and it'll help if you're stubborn, so I hope you are."

"Yes, I'm fairly stubborn."

Raynor sketched hard with an eraser in the old dirt of his desk, left-handed, and said, "Sure, what else can you answer to such a question. Anyhow, the trouble you're going to have is that they don't like to give information about anybody. They think you're a plain-clothes dick or an installment collector, or summons-server or something like that. Till you've been seen around the neighborhood for a few months and people know you're only from the relief."

It was dark, ground-freezing, pre-Thanksgiving weather; the wind played hob with the smoke, rushing it down, and Grebe missed his gloves, which he had left in Raynor's office. And no one would admit knowing Green. It was past three o'clock and the postman had made his last delivery. The nearest grocer, himself a Negro, had never heard the name Tulliver Green, or said he hadn't. Grebe was inclined to think that it was true, that he had in the end convinced the man that he wanted only to deliver a check. But he wasn't sure. He needed experience in interpreting looks and signs and, even more, the will not to be put off or denied and even the force to bully if need be. If the grocer did know, he had got rid of him easily. But since most of his trade was with reliefers, why should he prevent the delivery of a check? Maybe Green, or Mrs. Green, if there was a Mrs. Green, patronized another grocer. And was there a Mrs. Green? It was one of Grebe's great handicaps that he hadn't looked at any of the case records. Raynor should have let him read files for a few hours. But he apparently saw no need for that, probably considering the job unimportant. Why prepare systematically to deliver a few checks?

But now it was time to look for the janitor. Grebe took in the building in the wind and gloom of the late November day—trampled, frost-hardened lots on one side; on the other, an automobile junk yard and then the infinite work of Elevated frames, weak-looking, gaping with rubbish fires; two sets of leaning brick porches three stories high and a flight of cement stairs to the cellar. Descending, he entered the underground passage, where he tried the doors until one opened and he found himself in the furnace room. There someone rose toward him and approached, scraping on the coal grit and bending under the canvas-jacketed pipes.

"Are you the janitor?"

"What do you want?"

"I'm looking for a man who's supposed to be living here. Green."

"What Green?"

"Oh, you maybe have more than one Green?" said Grebe with new, pleasant hope. "This is Tulliver Green."

"I don't think I c'n help you, mister. I don't know any."

"A crippled man."

The janitor stood bent before him. Could it be that he was crippled? Oh, God! what if he was. Grebe's gray eyes sought with excited difficulty to see. But no, he was only very short and stooped. A head awakened from meditation, a strong-haired beard, low, wide shoulders. A staleness of sweat and coal rose from his black shirt and the burlap sack he wore as an apron.

"Crippled how?"

Grebe thought and then answered with the light voice of unmixed candor, "I don't know. I've never seen him." This was damaging, but his only other choice was to make a lying guess, and he was not up to it. "I'm delivering checks for the relief to shut-in cases. If he weren't crippled he'd come to collect himself. That's why I said crippled. Bedridden, chair-ridden—is there anybody like that?"

This sort of frankness was one of Grebe's oldest talents, going back to childhood. But it gained him nothing here.

"No suh. I've got four buildin's same as this that I take care of. I don' know all the tenants, leave alone the tenants' tenants. The rooms turn over so fast, people movin' in and out every day. I can't tell you."

The janitor opened his grimy lips but Grebe did not hear him in the piping of the valves and the consuming pull of air to flame in the body of the furnace. He knew, however, what he had said.

"Well, all the same, thanks. Sorry I bothered you. I'll prowl around upstairs again and see if I can turn up someone who knows him."

Once more in the cold air and early darkness he made the short circle from the cellarway to the entrance crowded between the brickwork pillars and began to climb to the third floor. Pieces of plaster ground under his feet; strips of brass tape from which the carpeting had been torn away marked old boundaries at the sides. In the passage, the cold reached him worse than in the street; it touched him to the bone. The hall toilets ran like springs. He thought grimly as he heard the wind burning around the building with a sound like that of the furnace, that this was a great piece of constructed shelter. Then he struck a match in the gloom and searched for names and numbers among the writings and scribbles on the walls. He saw WHOODY-DOODY GO TO JESUS, and zigzags, caricatures, sexual scrawls, and curses. So the sealed rooms of pyramids were also decorated, and the caves of human dawn.

The information on his card was, TULLIVER GREEN—APT 3D. There were no names, however, and no numbers. His shoulders drawn up, tears of cold in his eyes, breathing vapor, he went the length of the corridor and told himself that if he had been lucky enough to have the temperament for it he would bang on one of the doors and bawl out "Tulliver Green!" until he got results. But it wasn't in him to make an uproar and he continued to burn matches, passing the light over the walls. At the rear, in a corner off the hall, he discovered a door he had not seen before and he thought it best to investigate. It sounded empty when he knocked, but a young Negress answered, hardly more than a girl. She opened only a bit, to guard the warmth of the room.

"Yes suh?"

"I'm from the district relief station on Prairie Avenue. I'm looking for a man named Tulliver Green to give him his check. Do you know him?"

No, she didn't; but he thought she had not understood anything of what he had said. She had a dream-bound, dream-blind face, very soft and black, shut off. She wore a man's jacket and pulled the ends together at her throat. Her hair was parted in three directions, at the sides and transversely, standing up at the front in a dull puff.

"Is there somebody around here who might know?"

"I jus' taken this room las' week."

He observed that she shivered, but even her shiver was somnambulistic and there was no sharp consciousness of cold in the big smooth eyes of her handsome face.

"All right, miss, thank you. Thanks," he said, and went to try another place.

Here he was admitted. He was grateful, for the room was warm. It was full of people, and they were silent as he entered—ten people, or a dozen, perhaps more, sitting on benches like a parliament. There was no light, properly speaking, but a tempered darkness that the window gave, and everyone seemed to him enormous, the men padded out in heavy work clothes and winter coats, and the women huge, too, in their sweaters, hats, and old furs. And, besides, bed and bedding, a black cooking range, a piano piled towering to the ceiling with papers, a dining-room table of the old style of prosperous Chicago. Among these people Grebe, with his cold-heightened fresh color and his smaller stature, entered like a schoolboy. Even though he was met with smiles and good will, he knew, before a single word was spoken, that all the currents ran against him and that he would make no headway. Nevertheless he began. "Does anybody here know how I can deliver a check to Mr. Tulliver Green?"

"Green?" It was the man that had let him in who answered. He was in short sleeves, in a checkered shirt, and had a queer, high head, profusely overgrown and long as a shako;[2] the veins entered it strongly from his forehead. "I never heard mention of him. Is this where he live?"

"This is the address they gave me at the station. He's a sick man, and he'll need his check. Can't anybody tell me where to find him?"

He stood his ground and waited for a reply, his crimson wool scarf wound about his neck and drooping outside his trenchcoat, pockets weighted with the block of checks and official forms. They must have realized that he was not a college boy employed afternoons by a bill collector, trying foxily to pass for a relief clerk,

2. A high military cap, often with a plume.

recognized that he was an older man who knew himself what need was, who had had more than an average seasoning in hardship. It was evident enough if you looked at the marks under his eyes and at the sides of his mouth.

"Anybody know this sick man?"

"No suh." On all sides he saw heads shaken and smiles of denial. No one knew. And maybe it was true, he considered, standing silent in the earthen, musky human gloom of the place as the rumble continued. But he could never really be sure.

"What's the matter with this man?" said shako-head.

"I've never seen him. All I can tell you is that he can't come in person for his money. It's my first day in this district."

"Maybe they given you the wrong number?"

"I don't believe so. But where else can I ask about him?" He felt that this persistence amused them deeply, and in a way he shared their amusement that he should stand up so tenaciously to them. Though smaller, though slight, he was his own man, he retracted nothing about himself, and he looked back at them, gray-eyed, with amusement and also with a sort of courage. On the bench some man spoke in his throat, the words impossible to catch, and a woman answered with a wild, shrieking laugh, which was quickly cut off.

"Well, so nobody will tell me?"

"Ain't nobody who knows."

"At least, if he lives here, he pays rent to someone. Who manages the building?"

"Greatham Company. That's on Thirty-ninth Street."

Grebe wrote it in his pad. But, in the street again, a sheet of wind-driven paper clinging to his leg while he deliberated what direction to take next, it seemed a feeble lead to follow. Probably this Green didn't rent a flat, but a room. Sometimes there were as many as twenty people in an apartment; the real-estate agent would know only the lessee. And not even the agent could tell you who the renters were. In some places the beds were even used in shifts, watchmen or jitney drivers or short-order cooks in night joints turning out after a day's sleep and surrendering their beds to a sister, a nephew, or perhaps a stranger, just off the bus. There were large numbers of newcomers in this terrific, blight-bitten portion of the city between Cottage Grove and Ashland, wandering from house to house and room to room. When you saw them, how could you know them? They didn't carry bundles on their backs or look picturesque. You only saw a man, a Negro, walking in the street or riding in the car, like everyone else, with his thumb closed on a transfer. And therefore how were you supposed to tell? Grebe thought the Greatham agent would only laugh at his question.

But how much it would have simplified the job to be able to say that Green was old, or blind, or consumptive. An hour in the files, taking a few notes, and he needn't have been at such a disadvantage. When Raynor gave him the block of checks he asked, "How much should I know about these people?" Then Raynor had looked as though he were preparing to accuse him of trying to make the job more important than it was. He smiled, because by then they were on fine terms, but nevertheless he had been getting ready to say something like that when the confusion began in the station over Staika and her children.

Grebe had waited a long time for this job. It came to him through the pull of an old schoolmate in the Corporation Counsel's office, never a close friend, but suddenly sympathetic and interested—pleased to show, moreover, how well he had done, how strongly he was coming on even in these miserable times. Well, he was coming through strongly, along with the Democratic administration itself. Grebe had gone to see him in City Hall, and they had had a counter lunch or beers at least once a month for a year, and finally it had been possible to swing the job. He didn't mind being assigned the lowest clerical grade, nor even being a messenger, though Raynor thought he did.

This Raynor was an original sort of guy and Grebe had taken to him immediately. As was proper on the first day, Grebe had come early, but he waited long, for Raynor was late. At last he darted into his cubicle of an office as though he had just jumped from one of those hurtling huge red Indian Avenue cars. His thin, rough face was wind-stung and he was grinning and saying something breathlessly to himself. In his hat, a small fedora, and his coat, the velvet collar a neat fit about his neck, and his silk muffler that set off the nervous twist of his chin, he swayed and turned himself in his swivel chair, feet leaving the ground; so that he pranced a little as he sat. Meanwhile he took Grebe's measure out of his eyes, eyes of an unusual vertical length and slightly sardonic. So the two men sat for a while, saying nothing, while the supervisor raised his hat from his miscombed hair and put it in his lap. His cold-darkened hands were not clean. A steel beam passed through the little make-shift room, from which machine belts once had hung. The building was an old factory.

"I'm younger than you; I hope you won't find it hard taking orders from me," said Raynor. "But I don't make them up, either. You're how old, about?"

"Thirty-five."

"And you thought you'd be inside doing paper work. But it so happens I have to send you out."

"I don't mind."

"And it's mostly a Negro load we have in this district."

"So I thought it would be."

"Fine. You'll get along. *C'est un bon boulot.*[3] Do you know French?"

"Some."

"I thought you'd be a university man."

"Have you been in France?" said Grebe.

"No, that's the French of the Berlitz School. I've been at it for more than a year, just as I'm sure people have been, all over the world, office boys in China and braves in Tanganyika. In fact, I damn well know it. Such is the attractive power of civilization. It's overrated, but what do you want? *Que voulez-vous?*[4] I get *Le Rire*[5] and all the spicy papers, just like in Tanganyika. It must be mystifying, out there. But my reason is that I'm aiming at the diplomatic service. I have a cousin who's a courier, and the way he describes it is awfully attractive. He rides in the *wagon-lits*[6] and reads books. While we— What did you do before?"

"I sold."

"Where?"

"Canned meat at Stop and Shop. In the basement."

"And before that?"

"Window shades, at Goldblatt's."

"Steady work?"

3. It's a good job.
4. What do you want?
5. *Laughter,* a magazine.
6. Sleeping cars on a train.

"No, Thursdays and Saturdays. I also sold shoes."

"You've been a shoe-dog too. Well. And prior to that? Here it is in your folder." He opened the record. "Saint Olaf's College, instructor in classical languages. Fellow, University of Chicago, 1926–27. I've had Latin, too. Let's trade quotations —'*Dum spiro spero.*' "[7]

" '*Da dextram misero.*' "[8]

" '*Alea jacta est.*' "[9]

" '*Excelsior.*' "[1]

Raynor shouted with laughter, and other workers came to look at him over the partition. Grebe also laughed, feeling pleased and easy. The luxury of fun on a nervous morning.

When they were done and no one was watching or listening, Raynor said rather seriously, "What made you study Latin in the first place? Was it for the priesthood?"

"No."

"Just for the hell of it? For the culture? Oh, the things people think they can pull!" He made his cry hilarious and tragic. "I ran my pants off so I could study for the bar, and I've passed the bar, so I get twelve dollars a week more than you as a bonus for having seen life straight and whole. I'll tell you, as a man of culture, that even though nothing looks to be real, and everything stands for something else, and that thing for another thing, and that thing for a still further one—there ain't any comparison between twenty-five and thirty-seven dollars a week, regardless of the last reality. Don't you think that was clear to your Greeks? They were a thoughtful people, but they didn't part with their slaves."

This was a great deal more than Grebe had looked for in his first interview with his supervisor. He was too shy to show all the astonishment he felt. He laughed a little, aroused, and brushed at the sunbeam that covered his head with its dust. "Do you think my mistake was so terrible?"

"Damn right it was terrible, and you know it now that you've had the whip of hard times laid on your back. You should have been preparing yourself for trouble. Your people must have been well off to send you to the university. Stop me, if I'm stepping on your toes. Did your mother pamper you? Did your father give in to you? Were you brought up tenderly, with permission to go and find out what were the last things that everything else stands for while everybody else labored in the fallen world of appearances?"

"Well, no, it wasn't exactly like that." Grebe smiled. *The fallen world of appearances!* no less. But now it was his turn to deliver a surprise. "We weren't rich. My father was the last genuine English butler in Chicago—"

"Are you kidding?"

"Why should I be?"

"In a livery?"

"In livery. Up on the Gold Coast."

"And he wanted you to be educated like a gentleman?"

"He did not. He sent me to the Armour Institute to study chemical engineering. But when he died I changed schools."

He stopped himself, and considered how quickly Raynor had reached him. In no time he had your valise on the table and all your stuff unpacked. And afterward, in

7. Where there's life [breath] there's hope.
8. Give your right hand to those who suffer.
9. The die is cast.
1. Onward and upward.

the streets, he was still reviewing how far he might have gone, and how much he might have been led to tell if they had not been interrupted by Mrs. Staika's great noise.

But just then a young woman, one of Raynor's workers, ran into the cubicle exclaiming, "Haven't you heard all the fuss?"

"We haven't heard anything."

"It's Staika, giving out with all her might. The reporters are coming. She said she phoned the papers, and you know she did."

"But what is she up to?" said Raynor.

"She brought her wash and she's ironing it here, with our current, because the relief won't pay her electric bill. She has her ironing board set up by the admitting desk, and her kids are with her, all six. They never are in school more than once a week. She's always dragging them around with her because of her reputation."

"I don't want to miss any of this," said Raynor, jumping up. Grebe, as he followed with the secretary, said, "Who is this Staika?"

"They call her the 'Blood Mother of Federal Street.' She's a professional donor at the hospitals. I think they pay ten dollars a pint. Of course it's no joke, but she makes a very big thing out of it and she and the kids are in the papers all the time."

A small crowd, staff and clients divided by a plywood barrier, stood in the narrow space of the entrance, and Staika was shouting in a gruff, mannish voice, plunging the iron on the board and slamming it on the metal rest.

"My father and mother came in a steerage, and I was born in our house, Robey by Huron. I'm no dirty immigrant. I'm a U.S. citizen. My husband is a gassed veteran from France with lungs weaker'n paper, that hardly can he go to the toilet by himself. These six children of mine, I have to buy the shoes for their feet with my own blood. Even a lousy little white Communion necktie, that's a couple of drops of blood; a little piece of mosquito veil for my Vadja so she won't be ashamed in church for the other girls, they take my blood for it by Goldblatt. That's how I keep goin'. A fine thing if I had to depend on the relief. And there's plenty of people on the rolls—fakes! There's nothin' *they* can't get, that can go and wrap bacon at Swift and Armour any time. They're lookin' for them by the Yards. They never have to be out of work. Only they rather lay in their lousy beds and eat the public's money." She was not afraid, in a predominantly Negro station, to shout this way about Negroes.

Grebe and Raynor worked themselves forward to get a closer view of the woman. She was flaming with anger and with pleasure at herself, broad and huge, a golden-headed woman who wore a cotton cap laced with pink ribbon. She was barelegged and had on black gym shoes, her Hoover apron was open and her great breasts, not much restrained by a man's undershirt, hampered her arms as she worked at the kid's dress on the ironing board. And the children, silent and white, with a kind of locked obstinacy, in sheepskins and lumberjackets, stood behind her. She had captured the station, and the pleasure this gave her was enormous. Yet her grievances were true grievances. She was telling the truth. But she behaved like a liar. The look of her small eyes was hidden, and while she raged she also seemed to be spinning and planning.

"They send me out college case workers in silk pants to talk me out of what I got comin'. Are they better'n me? Who told them? Fire them. Let 'em go and get married, and then you won't have to cut electric from people's budget."

The chief supervisor, Mr. Ewing, couldn't silence her and he stood with folded arms at the head of his staff, bald, bald-headed, saying to his subordinates like the ex-school principal he was, "Pretty soon she'll be tired and go."

"No she won't," said Raynor to Grebe. "She'll get what she wants. She knows more about the relief even then Ewing. She's been on the rolls for years, and she always gets what she wants because she puts on a noisy show. Ewing knows it. He'll give in soon. He's only saving face. If he gets bad publicity, the Commissioner'll have him on the carpet, downtown. She's got him submerged; she'll submerge everybody in time, and that includes nations and governments."

Grebe replied with his characteristic smile, disagreeing completely. Who would take Staika's orders, and what changes could her yelling ever bring about?

No, what Grebe saw in her, the power that made people listen, was that her cry expressed the war of flesh and blood, perhaps turned a little crazy and certainly ugly, on this place and this condition. And at first, when he went out, the spirit of Staika somehow presided over the whole district for him, and it took color from her; he saw her color, in the spotty curb fires, and the fires under the El, the straight alley of flamy gloom. Later, too, when he went into a tavern for a shot of rye, the sweat of beer, association with West Side Polish streets, made him think of her again.

He wiped the corners of his mouth with his muffler, his handkerchief being inconvenient to reach for, and went out again to get on with the delivery of his checks. The air bit cold and hard and a few flakes of snow formed near him. A train struck by and left a quiver in the frames and a bristling icy hiss over the rails.

Crossing the street, he descended a flight of board steps into a basement grocery, setting off a little bell. It was a dark, long store and it caught you with its stinks of smoked meat, soap, dried peaches, and fish. There was a fire wrinkling and flapping in the little stove, and the proprietor was waiting, an Italian with a long, hollow face and stubborn bristles. He kept his hands warm under his apron.

No, he didn't know Green. You knew people but not names. The same man might not have the same name twice. The police didn't know, either, and mostly didn't care. When somebody was shot or knifed they took the body away and didn't look for the murderer. In the first place, nobody would tell them anything. So they made up a name for the coroner and called it quits. And in the second place, they didn't give a goddamn anyhow. But they couldn't get to the bottom of a thing even if they wanted to. Nobody would get to know even a tenth of what went on among these people. They stabbed and stole, they did every crime and abomination you ever heard of, men and men, women and women, parents and children, worse than the animals. They carried on their own way, and the horrors passed off like a smoke. There was never anything like it in the history of the whole world.

It was a long speech, deepening with every word in its fantasy and passion and becoming increasingly senseless and terrible: a swarm amassed by suggestion and invention, a huge, hugging, despairing knot, a human wheel of heads, legs, bellies, arms, rolling through his shop.

Grebe felt that he must interrupt him. He said sharply, "What are you talking about! All I asked was whether you knew this man."

"That isn't even the half of it. I been here six years. You probably don't want to believe this. But suppose it's true?"

"All the same," said Grebe, "there must be a way to find a person."

The Italian's close-spaced eyes had been queerly concentrated, as were his muscles, while he leaned across the counter trying to convince Grebe. Now he gave up the effort and sat down on his stool. "Oh—I suppose. Once in a while. But I been telling you, even the cops don't get anywhere."

"They're always after somebody. It's not the same thing."

"Well, keep trying if you want. I can't help you."

But he didn't keep trying. He had no more time to spend on Green. He slipped Green's check to the back of the block. The next name on the list was FIELD, WINSTON.

He found the back-yard bungalow without the least trouble; it shared a lot with another house, a few feet of yard between. Grebe knew these two-shack arrangements. They had been built in vast numbers in the days before the swamps were filled and the streets raised, and they were all the same—a boardwalk along the fence, well under street level, three or four ball-headed posts for clotheslines, greening wood, dead shingles, and a long, long flight of stairs to the rear door.

A twelve-year-old boy let him into the kitchen, and there the old man was, sitting by the table in a wheel chair.

"Oh, it's d' Government man," he said to the boy when Grebe drew out his checks. "Go bring me my box of papers." He cleared a space on the table.

"Oh, you don't have to go to all that trouble," said Grebe. But Field laid out his papers: Social Security card, relief certification, letters from the state hospital in Manteno, and a naval discharge dated San Diego, 1920.

"That's plenty," Grebe said. "Just sign."

"You got to know who I am," the old man said. "You're from the Government. It's not your check, it's a Government check and you got no business to hand it over till everything is proved."

He loved the ceremony of it, and Grebe made no more objections. Field emptied his box and finished out the circle of cards and letters.

"There's everything I done and been. Just the death certificate and they can close book on me." He said this with a certain happy pride and magnificence. Still he did not sign; he merely held the little pen upright on the golden-green corduroy of his thigh. Grebe did not hurry him. He felt the old man's hunger for conversation.

"I got to get better coal," he said. "I send my little gran'son to the yard with my order and they fill his wagon with screening. The stove ain't made for it. It fall through the grate. The order says Franklin County egg-size coal."

"I'll report it and see what can be done."

"Nothing can be done, I expect. You know and I know. There ain't no little ways to make things better, and the only big thing is money. That's the only sunbeams, money. Nothing is black where it shines, and the only place you see black is where it ain't shining. What we colored have to have is our own rich. There ain't no other way."

Grebe sat, his reddened forehead bridged levelly by his close-cut hair and his cheeks lowered in the wings of his collar—the caked fire shone hard within the isinglass-and-iron frames but the room was not comfortable—sat and listened while the old man unfolded his scheme. This was to create one Negro millionaire a month by subscription. One clever, good-hearted young fellow elected every month would sign a contract to use the money to start a business employing Negroes. This would be advertised by chain letters and word of mouth, and every Negro wage earner would contribute a dollar a month. Within five years there would be sixty millionaires.

"That'll fetch respect," he said with a throat-stopped sound that came out like a foreign syllable. "You got to take and organize all the money that gets thrown away on the policy wheel and horse race. As long as they can take it away from you, they got no respect for you. Money, that's d' sun of human kind!" Field was a Negro of mixed blood, perhaps Cherokee, or Natchez; his skin was reddish. And he sounded, speaking about a golden sun in this dark room, and looked, shaggy and slab-headed, with the mingled blood of his face and broad lips, the little pen still upright in his hand, like one of the underground kings of mythology, old judge Minos[2] himself.

And now he accepted the check and signed. Not to soil the slip, he held it down with his knuckles. The table budged and creaked, the center of the gloomy, heathen midden of the kitchen covered with bread, meat, and cans, and the scramble of papers.

"Don't you think my scheme'd work?"

"It's worth thinking about. Something ought to be done, I agree."

"It'll work if people will do it. That's all. That's the only thing, any time. When they understand it in the same way, all of them."

"That's true," said Grebe, rising. His glance met the old man's.

"I know you got to go," he said. "Well, God bless you, boy, you ain't been sly with me. I can tell it in a minute."

He went back through the buried yard. Someone nursed a candle in a shed, where a man unloaded kindling wood from a sprawl-wheeled baby buggy and two voices carried on a high conversation. As he came up the sheltered passage he heard the hard boost of the wind in the branches and against the house fronts, and then, reaching the sidewalk, he saw the needle-eye red of cable towers in the open icy height hundreds of feet above the river and the factories—those keen points. From here, his view was obstructed all the way to the South Branch and its timber banks, and the cranes beside the water. Rebuilt after the Great Fire, this part of the city was, not fifty years later, in ruins again, factories boarded up, buildings deserted or fallen, gaps of prairie between. But it wasn't desolation that this made you feel, but rather a faltering of organization that set free a huge energy, an escaped, unattached, unregulated power from the giant raw place. Not only must people feel it but, it seemed to Grebe, they were compelled to match it. In their very bodies. He no less than others, he realized. Say that his parents had been servants in their time, whereas he was not supposed to be one. He thought that they had never done any service like this, which no one visible asked for, and probably flesh and blood could not even perform. Nor could anyone show why it should be performed; or see where the performance would lead. That did not mean that he wanted to be released from it, he realized with a grimly pensive face. On the contrary. He had something to do. To be compelled to feel this energy and yet have no task to do—that was horrible; that was suffering; he knew what that was. It was now quitting time. Six o'clock. He could go home if he liked, to his room, that is, to wash in hot water, to pour a drink, lie down on his quilt, read the paper, eat some liver paste on crackers before going out to dinner. But to think of this actually made him feel a little sick, as though he had swallowed hard air. He had six checks left, and he was determined to deliver at least one of these: Mr. Green's check.

So he started again. He had four or five dark blocks to go, past open lots,

2. Legendary king of Crete, after death a judge in the underworld.

condemned houses, old foundations, closed schools, black churches, mounds, and he reflected that there must be many people alive who had once seen the neighborhood rebuilt and new. Now there was a second layer of ruins; centuries of history accomplished through human massing. Numbers had given the place forced growth; enormous numbers had also broken it down. Objects once so new, so concrete that it could have occurred to anyone they stood for other things, had crumbled. Therefore, reflected Grebe, the secret of them was out. It was that they stood for themselves by agreement, and were natural and not unnatural by agreement, and when the things themselves collapsed the agreement became visible. What was it, otherwise, that kept cities from looking peculiar? Rome, that was almost permanent, did not give rise to thoughts like these. And was it abidingly real? But in Chicago, where the cycles were so fast and the familiar died out, and again rose changed, and died again in thirty years, you saw the common agreement or covenant, and you were forced to think about appearances and realities. (He remembered Raynor and he smiled. Raynor was a clever boy.) Once you had grasped this, a great many things became intelligible. For instance, why Mr. Field should conceive such a scheme. Of course, if people were to agree to create a millionaire, a real millionaire would come into existence. And if you wanted to know how Mr. Field was inspired to think of this, why, he had within sight of his kitchen window the chart, the very bones of a successful scheme—the El with its blue and green confetti of signals. People consented to pay dimes and ride the crash-box cars, and so it was a success. Yet how absurd it looked; how little reality there was to start with. And yet Yerkes, the great financier who built it, had known that he could get people to agree to do it. Viewed as itself, what a scheme of a scheme it seemed, how close to an appearance. Then why wonder at Mr. Field's idea? He had grasped a principle. And then Grebe remembered, too, that Mr. Yerkes had established the Yerkes Observatory and endowed it with millions. Now how did the notion come to him in his New York museum of a palace or his Aegean-bound yacht to give money to astronomers? Was he awed by the success of his bizarre enterprise and therefore ready to spend money to find out where in the universe being and seeming were identical? Yes, he wanted to know what abides; and whether flesh is Bible grass;[3] and he offered money to be burned in the fire of suns. Okay, then, Grebe thought further, these things exist because people consent to exist with them—we have got so far—and also there is a reality which doesn't depend on consent but within which consent is a game. But what about need, the need that keeps so many vast thousands in position? You tell me that, you *private* little gentleman and *decent* soul—he used these words against himself scornfully. Why is the consent given to misery? And why so painfully ugly? Because there is *something* that is dismal and permanently ugly? Here he sighed and gave it up, and thought it was enough for the present moment that he had a real check in his pocket for a Mr. Green who must be real beyond question. If only his neighbors didn't think they had to conceal him.

This time he stopped at the second floor. He struck a match and found a door. Presently a man answered his knock and Grebe had the check ready and showed it even before he began. "Does Tulliver Green live here? I'm from the relief."

The man narrowed the opening and spoke to someone at his back.

"Does he live here?"

3. *Cf.* Isaiah xl: 6, "All flesh is grass," and Psalms ciii: 15, "As for man, his days are as grass: as a flower of the field, so he flourisheth."

"Uh-uh. No."

"Or anywhere in this building? He's a sick man and he can't come for his dough." He exhibited the check in the light, which was smoky—the air smelled of charred lard—and the man held off the brim of his cap to study it.

"Uh-uh. Never seen the name."

"There's nobody around here that uses crutches?"

He seemed to think, but it was Grebe's impression that he was simply waiting for a decent interval to pass.

"No, suh. Nobody I ever see."

"I've been looking for this man all afternoon"—Grebe spoke out with sudden force—"and I'm going to have to carry this check back to the station. It seems strange not to be able to find a person to *give* him something when you're looking for him for a good reason. I suppose if I had bad news for him I'd find him quick enough."

There was a responsive motion in the other man's face. "That's right, I reckon."

"It almost doesn't do any good to have a name if you can't be found by it. It doesn't stand for anything. He might as well not have any," he went on, smiling. It was as much of a concession as he could make to his desire to laugh.

"Well, now, there's a little old knot-back man I see once in a while. He might be the one you lookin' for. Downstairs."

"Where? Right side or left? Which door?"

"I don't know which. Thin-face little knot-back with a stick."

But no one answered at any of the doors on the first floor. He went to the end of the corridor, searching by matchlight, and found only a stairless exit to the yard, a drop of about six feet. But there was a bungalow near the alley, an old house like Mr. Field's. To jump was unsafe. He ran from the front door, through the underground passage and into the yard. The place was occupied. There was a light through the curtains, upstairs. The name on the ticket under the broken, scoop-shaped mailbox was Green! He exultantly rang the bell and pressed against the locked door. Then the lock clicked faintly and a long staircase opened before him. Someone was slowly coming down—a woman. He had the impression in the weak light that she was shaping her hair as she came, making herself presentable, for he saw her arms raised. But it was for support that they were raised; she was feeling her way downward, down the wall, stumbling. Next he wondered about the pressure of her feet on the treads; she did not seem to be wearing shoes. And it was a freezing stairway. His ring had got her out of bed, perhaps, and she had forgotten to put them on. And then he saw that she was not only shoeless but naked; she was entirely naked, climbing down while she talked to herself, a heavy woman, naked and drunk. She blundered into him. The contact of her breasts, though they touched only his coat, made him go back against the door with a blind shock. See what he had tracked down, in his hunting game!

The woman was saying to herself, furious with insult, "So I cain't ———k, huh? I'll show that son-of-a-bitch kin I, cain't I."

What should he do now? Grebe asked himself. Why, he should go. He should turn away and go. He couldn't talk to this woman. He couldn't keep her standing naked in the cold. But when he tried he found himself unable to turn away.

He said, "Is this where Mr. Green lives?"

But she was still talking to herself and did not hear him.

"Is this Mr. Green's house?"

At last she turned her furious drunken glance on him. "What do you want?"

Again her eyes wandered from him; there was a dot of blood in their enraged brilliance. He wondered why she didn't feel the cold.

"I'm from the relief."

"Awright, what?"

"I've got a check for Tulliver Green."

This time she heard him and put out her hand.

"No, no, for *Mr.* Green. He's got to sign," he said. How was he going to get Green's signature tonight!

"I'll take it. He cain't."

He desperately shook his head, thinking of Mr. Field's precautions about identification. "I can't let you have it. It's for him. Are you Mrs. Green?"

"Maybe I is, and maybe I ain't. Who want to know?"

"Is he upstairs?"

"Awright. Take it up yourself, you goddamn fool."

Sure, he was a goddamn fool. Of course he could not go up because Green would probably be drunk and naked, too. And perhaps he would appear on the landing soon. He looked eagerly upward. Under the light was a high narrow brown wall. Empty! It remained empty!

"Hell with you, then!" he heard her cry. To deliver a check for coal and clothes, he was keeping her in the cold. She did not feel it, but his face was burning with frost and self-ridicule. He backed away from her.

"I'll come tomorrow, tell him."

"Ah, hell with you. Don' never come. What you doin' here in the nighttime? Don' come back." She yelled so that he saw the breadth of her tongue. She stood astride in the long cold box of the hall and held on to the banister and the wall. The bungalow itself was shaped something like a box, a clumsy, high box pointing into the freezing air with its sharp, wintry lights.

"If you are Mrs. Green, I'll give you the check," he said, changing his mind.

"Give here, then." She took it, took the pen offered with it in her left hand, and tried to sign the receipt on the wall. He looked around, almost as though to see whether his madness was being observed, and came near believing that someone was standing on a mountain of used tires in the auto-junking shop next door.

"But are you Mrs. Green?" he now thought to ask. But she was already climbing the stairs with the check, and it was too late, if he had made an error, if he was now in trouble, to undo the thing. But he wasn't going to worry about it. Though she might not be Mrs. Green, he was convinced that Mr. Green was upstairs. Whoever she was, the woman stood for Green, whom he was not to see this time. Well, you silly bastard, he said to himself, so you think you found him. So what? Maybe you really did find him—what of it? But it was important that there was a real Mr. Green whom they could not keep him from reaching because he seemed to come as an emissary from hostile appearances. And though the self-ridicule was slow to diminish, and his face still blazed with it, he had, nevertheless, a feeling of elation, too. "For after all," he said, "he *could* be found!"

1968

PETER TAYLOR
(1917–)

Born in Trenton, Tennessee, in 1917, the youngest of four children, Peter Taylor lived in a rural environment only for his first seven years, but the values and customs of the agrarian South are the bedrock of his fiction. He dedicated his collected stories to his mother, whom he called "* * * the best teller of tales I know * * * from whose lips I first heard many of the stories in this book." Until he was fifteen, the family lived in Nashville and then St. Louis, where his father was the president of an insurance company. Young Taylor attended St. Louis Country Day School until 1932, when the family moved to Memphis. He graduated from Memphis Central High School in 1935.

In 1936, Taylor began his college career, taking courses from Allen Tate at Southwestern at Memphis. Enrolling that fall at Vanderbilt, he studied with John Crowe Ransom and met Randall Jarrell, a fellow student and one of several poets with whom he was to maintain close and long friendships. In 1937, he dropped out of college to sell real estate, managing also that year to publish his first stories in *River.* The following year, he enrolled as a sophomore at Kenyon, where Ransom had gone to teach, and shared a room with Robert Lowell, a transfer from Harvard. Taylor and Lowell went on to graduate school together at Louisiana State University, and Lowell was best man at Taylor's wedding.

Graduating from Kenyon in 1940, Taylor studied briefly with Robert Penn Warren and Cleanth Brooks at Louisiana State University and published poetry and fiction in the *Kenyon Review* and the *Southern Review.* The next few years he was in the army; after his discharge as a sergeant, he began teaching English in 1946 at the Woman's College of the University of North Carolina. Since then he has taught at Indiana University, the University of Chicago, Kenyon College, Ohio State University, Harvard, and the University of Virginia.

Taylor's first collection of stories, *The Long Fourth,* appeared in 1948. Although he had been taught by Ransom and Tate, the romantic ideas articulated by these Nashville Agrarians appear in only one of his early stories, "The Party." The man who hosts the party of the title has returned to till an inherited farm, to which he invites friends who chose a city life as a test of his wife's enthusiasm for rural living; Taylor omitted this story from his *Collected Stories* (1969). More typically, Taylor's protagonists leave a rural background to settle successfully in one of the cities of Tennessee or Missouri, often bringing with them distant relations who join the household, or members of lower-class families who act as servants, thus preserving the social structure of the hometown. They learn to make a truce with the past and tradition, not to revolt against change.

Many of his stories are first-person narrations, often told by a child or a young adult observing events not fully understood. The narrator of "The Scoutmaster," for instance, describes events that took place when he was ten. The central incident dramatizes the older generation's discomfort in dealing with changed moral values and their longing for a simpler time when, as the Scoutmaster—Uncle Jake—describes it, "a race of noble gentlemen and gracious ladies inhabited the land of the South."

The typical pace of a Taylor story is leisurely; descriptions are realistic; actions are described but not analyzed—the author does not intrude with interpretation. He is a self-confident craftsman who often extends his short stories to create fine miniature novels; of these, the title piece of

The Old Forest and Other Stories (1985) is a masterpiece of its kind.

Taylor's two novels, *A Woman of Means* (1950) and the Pulitzer Prize winning *A Summons to Memphis* (1986) treat similar material at greater length than his stories.

Most of Taylor's stories are gathered in *The Collected Stories of Peter Taylor,* 1977; and *The Old Forest and Other Stories,* 1986. Earlier collections are *A Long Fourth and Other Stories,* 1948; *The Widows of Thornton* (1954); *Happy Families Are All Alike: A Collection of Stories* (1959); *Miss Leonora When Last Seen and Fifteen Other Stories* (1963); and *In the Miro District* (1977). Novels to date are named above. Published drama includes *Tennessee Day in St. Louis: A Comedy,* 1957; and *Presences: Seven Dramatic Pieces,* 1973.

An early study is Albert J. Griffith, *Peter Taylor,* 1970; a more recent brief assessment appears in the *Dictionary of Literary Biography Yearbook, 1981,* 1982.

Porte Cochere

Clifford and Ben Jr. always came for Old Ben's birthday. Clifford came all the way from Dallas. Ben Jr. came only from Cincinnati. They usually stayed in Nashville through the following weekend, or came the weekend before and stayed through the birthday. Old Ben, who was seventy-six and nearly blind—the cataracts had been removed twice since he was seventy—could hear them now on the side porch, their voices louder than the others', Clifford's the loudest and strongest of all. "Clifford's the real man amongst them," he said to himself, hating to say it but needing to say it. There was no knowing what went on in the heads of the other children, but there were certain things Clifford did know and understand. Clifford, being a lawyer, knew something about history—about Tennessee history he knew, for instance, the difference between Chucky Jack Sevier and Judge John Overton and could debate with you the question of whether or not Andy Jackson had played the part of the coward when he and Chucky Jack met in the wilderness that time. Old Ben kept listening for Cliff's voice above the others. All of his grown-up children were down on the octagonal side porch, which was beyond the porte cochere and which, under its red tile roof, looked like a pagoda stuck out there on the side lawn. Old Ben was in his study.

His study was directly above the porte cochere, or what his wife, in her day, had called the porte cochere—he called it the drive-under and the children used to call it the portcullis—but the study was not a part of the second floor; it opened off the landing halfway up the stairs. Under his south window was the red roof of the porch. He sat by the open window, wearing his dark glasses, his watery old eyes focused vaguely on the peak of the roof. He had napped a little since dinner but had not removed his suit coat or even unbuttoned his linen vest. During most of the afternoon, he had been awake and had heard his five children talking down there on the porch—Cliff and Ben Jr. had arrived only that morning—talking on and on in such loud voices that his good right ear could catch individual words and sometimes whole sentences.

Midday dinner had been a considerable ordeal for Old Ben. Nell's interminable chatter had been particularly taxing and obnoxious. Afterward, he had hurried to his study for his prescribed nap and had spent a good part of the afternoon dreading the expedition to the Country Club for supper that had been planned for that evening. Now it was almost time to begin getting ready for that expedition, and simultaneously with the thought of it and with the movement of his hand toward his watch pocket he became aware that Clifford was taking his leave of the group on the side porch. Ah yes, at dinnertime Clifford had said he had a letter to write before supper—to his wife. Yet here it was six and he had dawdled away the afternoon palavering with the others down there on the porch. Old Ben could recognize Cliff's leave-taking and the teasing voices of the others, and then he heard Cliff's footsteps at the bottom of the stairs. In a moment he would go sailing by Old Ben's door, without a thought for anyone but himself. Old Ben's lower lip trembled. Wasn't there some business matter he could take up with Cliff? Or some personal matter? And now Cliff's footsteps on the stairs—heavy footsteps, like his own. Suddenly, though, the footsteps halted, and Clifford went downstairs again. His father heard him go across the hall and into the living room, where the carpet silenced his footsteps; he was getting writing paper from the desk there. Old Ben hastily pulled the cord that closed the draperies across the south window, leaving only the vague light from the east window in the room. No, sir, he would not advertise his presence when Cliff passed on the landing.

With the draperies drawn, the light in the room had a strange quality—strange because Old Ben seldom drew the draperies at night. For one moment, he felt that his eyes or his glasses were playing him some new trick. Then he dropped his head on the chairback, for the strange quality now seemed strangely familiar, and no longer strange—only familiar. It was like the light in the cellar where, long ago, he used to go fetch Mason jars for his great-aunt Nell Partee. Aunt Nell would send for him all the way across town to come fetch her Mason jars, and even when he was ten or twelve, she made him whistle the whole time he was down in the cellar, to make certain he didn't drink her wine. Aunt Nell, dead and gone. Was this something for Clifford's attention? Where Aunt Nell's shacky house had been, the Trust Company now stood—a near-skyscraper. Her cellar, he supposed, had been in the space now occupied by the basement barbershop—not quite so deep or so large as the shop, its area without boundaries now, suspended in the center of the barbershop, where the ceiling fan revolved. Would this be of interest to Cliff, who would soon ascend the stairs with his own train of thoughts and would pass the open door to the study without a word or a glance? And whatever Cliff was thinking about—his law, his gold, or his wife and children—would be of no real interest to Old Ben. But did not Clifford know that merely the sound of his voice gave his father hope, that his attention gave him comfort? What would old age be without children? Desolation, desolation. But what would old age be with children who chose to ignore the small demands that he would make upon them, that he had ever made upon them? A nameless torment! And with his thoughts Old Ben Brantley's white head rocked on his shoulders and his smoked glasses went so crooked on his nose that he had to frown them back into position.

But now Clifford was hurrying up the stairs again. He was on the landing outside the open study door. It was almost despite himself that the old man cleared his throat and said hoarsely, "The news will be on in five minutes, if you want to listen to it." Then as though he might have sounded too cordial (he would not be reduced to toadying to his own boy), "But if you don't want to, don't say you do." Had Cliff seen his glasses slip down his nose? Cliff, no less than the others, would be capable of laughing at him in his infirmity.

"I wouldn't be likely to, would I, Papa?" Cliff had stopped at the doorway and was stifling a yawn as he spoke, half covering his face with the envelope and the folded sheet of paper. Old Ben nodded his head to indicate that he had heard what

Cliff had said, but also, to himself, he was nodding that yes, this was the way he had raised his children to talk to him.

"Just the hourly newscast," Old Ben said indifferently. "But it don't matter."

"Naw, can't make it, Papa. I got to go and write Sue Alice. The stupid woman staying with her while I'm away bores her pretty much." As he spoke, he looked directly into the dark lenses of his father's glasses, and for a brief second he rested his left hand on the doorjamb. His manner was self-possessed and casual, but Old Ben felt that he didn't need good sight to detect his poor son's ill-concealed haste to be off and away. Cliff had, in fact, turned back to the stairs when his father stopped him with a question, spoken without expression and almost under his breath.

"Why did you come at all? Why did you even bother to come if you weren't going to bring Sue Alice and the grandchildren? Did you think I wanted to see you without them?"

Clifford stopped with one foot on the first step of the second flight. "By God, Papa!" He turned on the ball of the other foot and reappeared in the doorway. "Ever travel with two small kids?" The motion of his body as he turned back from the steps had been swift and sure, calculated to put him exactly facing his father. "And in hot weather like we're having in Texas?"

Despite the undeniable thickness in Clifford's hips and the thin spot on the back of his head, his general appearance was still youthful; about this particular turning on the stairs there had been something decidedly athletic. Imperceptibly, behind the dark glasses, Old Ben lifted his eyebrows in admiration. Clifford was the only boy he had who had ever made any team at the University or done any hunting worth speaking of. For a moment, his eyes rested gently on Cliff's white summer shoes, set wide apart in the doorway. Then, jerking his head up, as though he had just heard Cliff's last words, he began, "Two small *kids?* (Why don't you use the word *brats?* It's more elegant.) I have traveled considerably with five—from here to the mountain and back every summer for fifteen years, from my thirty-first to my forty-sixth year."

"I remember," Cliff said stoically. Then, after a moment, "But now I'm going up to my room and write Sue Alice."

"Then go on up! Who's holding you?" He reached for his smoking stand and switched on the radio. It was a big cabinet radio with a dark mahogany finish, a piece from the late twenties, like all the other furniture in the room, and the mechanism was slow to warm up.

Clifford took several steps toward his father. "Papa, we're due to leave for the Club in thirty minutes—less than that now—and I intend to scratch off a note to my wife." He held up the writing paper, as though to prove his intention.

"No concern of mine! No concern of mine! To begin with, I, personally, am not going to the Club or anywhere else for supper."

Clifford came even closer. "You may go to the Club or not, as you like, Papa. But unless I misunderstand, there is not a servant on the place, and we are all going."

"That is, you are going after you scratch off a note to your wife."

"Papa, Ben Jr. and I have each come well over five hundred miles—"

"Not to see me, Clifford."

"Don't be so damned childish, Papa." Cliff was turning away again. Old Ben held his watch in his hand, and he glanced down at it quickly.

"I'm not getting childish, am I, Clifford?"

This time, Clifford's turning back was not accomplished in one graceful motion but by a sudden jerking and twisting of his shoulder and leg muscles. Behind the spectacles, Old Ben's eyes narrowed and twitched. His fingers were folded over the face of the watch. Clifford spoke very deliberately. "I didn't say *getting* childish, Papa. When ever in your life have you been anything but that? There's not a senile bone in your brain. It's your children that have got old, and you've stayed young —and not in any good sense, Papa, only in a bad one! You play sly games with us still or you quarrel with us. What the hell do you want of us, Papa? I've thought about it a lot. Why haven't you ever asked for what it is you want? Or are *we* all blind and it's really obvious? You've never given but one piece of advice to us, and that's to be direct and talk up to you like men—as equals. And we've done that, all right, and listened to your wrangling, but somehow it has never satisfied you! What is it?"

"Go on up to your letter-writing; go write your spouse," said Old Ben.

The room had been getting darker while they talked. Old Ben slipped his watch back into his vest pocket nervously, then slipped it out again, constantly running his fingers over the gold case, as though it were a piece of money.

"Thanks for your permission, sir." Clifford took a step backward. During his long speech he had advanced all the way across the room until he was directly in front of his father.

"My permission?" Old Ben said. "Let us not forget one fact, Clifford. No child of mine has ever had to ask my permission to do anything whatsoever he took a mind to do. You have all been free as the air, to come and go in this house. . . . You still are!"

Clifford smiled. "Free to come and go, with you perched here on the landing registering every footstep on the stairs and every car that passed underneath. I used to turn off the ignition and coast through the drive-under, and then think how foolish it was, since there was no back stairway. No back stairway in a house this size!" He paused a moment, running his eyes over the furniture and the other familiar objects in the shadowy room. "And how like the old times this was, Papa —your listening in here in the dark when I came up! By God, Papa, I wouldn't have thought when I was growing up that I'd ever come back and fuss with you once I was grown. But here I am, and, Papa—"

Old Ben pushed himself up from the chair. He put his watch in the vest pocket and buttoned his suit coat with an air of satisfaction. "I'm going along to the Club for supper," he said, "since there's to be no-un here to serve me." As he spoke, he heard the clock chiming the half hour downstairs. And Ben Jr. was shouting to Old Ben and Clifford from the foot of the stairs, "Get a move on up there."

Clifford went out on the landing and called down the steps. "Wait till I change my shirt. I believe Papa's all ready."

"No letter written?" Ben Jr. asked.

Clifford was hurrying up the second flight with the blank paper. "Nope, no letter this day of Our Lord."

Old Ben heard Ben Jr. say, "What did I tell you?" and heard the others laughing. He stood an instant by his chair without putting on a light. Then he reached out his hand for one of the walking canes in the umbrella stand by the radio. His hand lighting on the carved head of a certain oak stick, he felt the head with trembling fingers and quickly released it, and quickly, in three strides, without the help of any cane, he crossed the room to the south window. For several moments, he stood motionless at the window, his huge, soft hands held tensely at his sides, his long body erect, his almost freakishly large head at a slight angle, while he seemed to peer between the open draperies and through the pane of the upper sash, out into the twilight of the wide, shady park that stretched from his great yellow-brick house to the pike. Old Ben's eyes, behind the smoked lenses, were closed, and he was visualizing the ceiling fan in the barbershop. Presently, opening his eyes, he reflected, almost with a smile, that his aunt's cellar was not the only Nashville cellar that had disappeared. Many a cellar! His father's cellar, round like a dungeon; it had been a cistern in the very earliest days, before Old Ben's time, and when he was a boy, he would go around and around the brick walls and then come back with a hollow sound, as though the cistern were still half full of water. One time, ah—Old Ben drew back from the window with a grimace—one time he had been so sure there was water below! In fright at the very thought of the water, he had clasped a rung of the ladder tightly with one hand and swung the lantern out, expecting certainly to see the light reflected in the depths below. But the lantern had struck the framework that supported the circular shelves and gone whirling and flaming to the brick floor, which Ben had never before seen. Crashing on the floor, it sent up yellow flames that momentarily lit the old cistern to its very top, and when Ben looked upward, he saw the furious face of his father with the flames casting jagged shadows on the long, black beard and high, white forehead. "Come out of there before you burn out my cellar and my whole damn house to the ground!" He had climbed upward toward his father, wishing the flames might engulf him before he came within reach of those arms. But as his father jerked him up onto the back porch, he saw that the flames had already died out. The whole cellar was pitch-black dark again, and the boy Ben stood with his face against the white-washed brick wall while his father went to the carriage house to find the old plow line. Presently, he heard his father step up on the porch again. He braced himself for the first blow, but instead there was only the deafening command from his father: "Attention!" Ben whirled about and stood erect, with his chin in the air, his eyes on the ceiling. "Where have you hidden my plow lines?" "I don't know, sir." And then the old man, with his coattails somehow clinging close to his buttocks and thighs, so that his whole powerful form was outlined—his black figure against the white brick and the door—stepped over to the doorway, reached around to the cane stand in the hall, and drew out the oak stick that had his own bearded face carved upon the head. "About face!" he commanded. The boy drew back his toe and made a quick, military turn. The old man dealt him three sharp blows across the upper part of his back. . . . Tears had run down young Ben Brantley's cheeks, even streaking down his neck under his open collar and soaking the neckline binding of his woolen underwear, but he had uttered not a sound. When his father went into the house, Ben remained for a long while standing with his face to the wall. At last, he quietly left the porch and walked through the yard beneath the big shade trees, stopping casually to watch a gray squirrel and then to listen to Aunt Sally Ann's soft nigger voice whispering to him out the kitchen window. He did not answer or turn around but walked on to the latticed summerhouse, between the house and the kitchen garden. There he had lain down on a bench, looked back at the house through the latticework, and said to himself that when he got to be a grown man, he would go away to another country, where there would be no maple trees and no oak trees, no elms, not even sycamores or poplars; where there would be no squirrels and no niggers, no houses that resembled this one; and, most of all, where there would be no children and no fathers.

In the hall, now, Old Ben could hear, very faintly, Ben Jr.'s voice and Laura Nell's and Katie's and Lawrence's. He stepped to the door and looked down the dark flight of steps at his four younger children. They stood in a circle directly beneath the overhead light, which one of them had just switched on. Their faces were all turned upward in the direction of the open doorway where he was standing, yet he knew in reason that they could not see him there. They were talking about him! Through his dark lenses, their figures were indistinct, their faces were blurs, and it was hard for him to distinguish their lowered voices one from another. But they were talking about him! And from upstairs he could hear Clifford's footsteps. Clifford, with his letter to Sue Alice unwritten, was thinking about him! Never once in his life had he punished or restrained them in any way! He had given them a freedom unknown to children in the land of his childhood, yet from the time they could utter a word they had despised him and denied his right to any affection or gratitude. Suddenly, stepping out onto the landing, he screamed down the stairs to them, "I've a right to some gratitude!"

They were silent and motionless for a moment. Then he could hear them speaking in lowered voices again, and moving slowly toward the stairs. At the same moment he heard Clifford's footsteps in the upstairs hall. Presently, a light went on up there, and he could dimly see Clifford at the head of the stairs. The four children were advancing up the first flight, and Clifford was coming down from upstairs. Old Ben opened his mouth to call to them, "I'm not afraid of you!" But his voice had left him, and in his momentary fright, in his fear that his wrathful, merciless children might do him harm, he suddenly pitied them. He pitied them for all they had suffered at his hands. And while he stood there, afraid, he realized, or perhaps recalled, how he had tortured and plagued them in all the ways that his resentment of their very good fortune had taught him to do. He even remembered the day when it had occurred to him to build his study above the drive-under and off the stairs, so that he could keep tab on them. He had declared that he wanted his house to be as different from his father's house as a house could be, and so it was! And now he stood in the half-darkness, afraid that he was a man about to be taken by his children and at the same time pitying them, until one of them, ascending the steps switched on the light above the landing.

In the sudden brightness, Old Ben felt that his senses had returned to him. Quickly, he stepped back into the study, closed the door, and locked it. As the lock clicked, he heard Clifford say, "Papa!" Then he heard them all talking at once, and while they talked, he stumbled through the dark study to the umbrella stand. He pulled out the stick with his father's face carved on the head, and in the darkness, while he heard his children's voices, he stumbled about the room beating the upholstered chairs with the stick and calling the names of children under his breath.

1985

JACK KEROUAC
(1922–1969)

Jean Louis Kerouac was born of French-Canadian parents in the textile mill town of Lowell, Massachusetts, and educated through fifth grade in parochial schools where French was the language of instruction and English taught as a second language. As a high school junior he played football well enough to be offered scholarships to the Horace Mann School in New York City for his senior year (1939–1940) and to Columbia College the next. At Columbia, however, he stayed just one year and part of a second, leaving in the fall of 1941, without completing the football season, to begin his career as a wanderer, outcast, and chronicler of the Beat Generation. In fall 1942 he returned to Columbia and football, but only to quit again before the term was over. For a while after the war, in 1948–1949, he studied the American novel and creative writing at the New School for Social Research, but the most important part of his education after age twenty came from reading, friends, experiences—and his endless effort to write.

During World War II, Kerouac served in the merchant marine in the North Atlantic, enlisted in the navy only to be quickly discharged for "indifferent character," served in the merchant marine again for a voyage to England, but then, on yet another merchant marine trip he jumped ship, effectively ending that career. On shore, he worked at odd jobs, drank heavily, turned to drugs, was supported for a while by the woman he lived with, and was jailed in 1944 as accessory to a stabbing murder by one of his friends. Meanwhile, in the early 1940's he met the literary friends who most supported and shaped his writing, the younger Allen Ginsberg and the older William S. Burroughs. Not until the next decade did any of the three publish a book as they lived the Beat life and evolved its artistic aims and methods.

"And now to make up for the botch of my days I think I can create a great universe and of course I can," Kerouac was to write in *Visions of Cody* (1972). In his first book, *The Town and the City* (1950), he recorded in autobiographical fiction the emotional distance between Lowell and New York. For the fame that he sought, however, he had to await the publication of *On the Road* (1957), for many the quintessential Beat novel, recording a period of frenetic shuttling from coast to coast, with an occasional dip into Mexico, high on alcohol, drugs, and sex. *On the Road* received much of its energy from Dean Moriarty, whom Kerouac saw as an anti-hero of mythic proportions, a character he based on his friend Neal Cassady, who was also the model for Cody Pomeray of *Visions of Cody*.

Among Kerouac's later fictions, *The Dharma Bums* (1958) has been popular for its treatment of the relationship between the Beats and Zen Buddhism, *The Subterraneans* (1958) for its interracial theme. *Tristessa* (1960), *Big Sur* (1962), and *Desolation Angels* (1965) are further chronicles of the Beats, while *Doctor Sax* (1959), *Maggie Cassidy* (1959), *Visions of Gerard* (1963), and *Vanity of Duluoz* (1968) draw heavily on Kerouac's youth in Lowell.

By the time of *On the Road,* Kerouac was convinced his art could succeed only if it came as directly as possible from experience. He spoke of "factualism" and thought of some of his books as "confessions." In order to get close to the understanding of the moment, he advocated a "spontaneous prose," akin to jazz, fixed on the objects of memory or present experience, writing "without consciousness" in a pure flow of expression. But because understandings change, he wrote and rewrote, telling the same stories, reliving the same experiences, engaged, as he expressed it in *Visions of Cody*, in a "struggle in the dark with the enormity of my soul, trying desperately to be a great rememberer redeeming life from darkness * * *."

Besides those named above, Kerouac's books include *Book of Dreams*, 1960, a recounting of his dreams; *Satori in Paris*, 1966, on travels in France; and *Pic*, 1971, a story of a black jazz musician, posthumously published. *Visions of Cody* was published in part in 1960, in complete form in 1972.

Biographical and critical studies include Ann Charters, *Kerouac: A Biography*, 1973; Robert A. Hipkiss, *Jack Kerouac: Prophet of the New Romanticism*, 1976; Barry Gifford and Lawrence Lee, *Jack's Book: An Oral Biography*, 1978; Tim Hunt, *Kerouac's Crooked Road*, 1981; Gerald Nicosia, *Memory Babe: A Critical Biography of Jack Kerouac*, 1983; Chris Challis, *Quest for Kerouac*, 1984; Tom Clark, *Jack Kerouac*, 1985; and Regina Weinrich, *The Spontaneous Poetics of Jack Kerouac*, 1986.

From On the Road

Part Three

1

In the spring of 1949 I had a few dollars saved from my GI education checks and I went to Denver, thinking of settling down there. I saw myself in Middle America, a patriarch. I was lonesome. Nobody was there—no Babe Rawlins, Ray Rawlins, Tim Gray, Betty Gray, Roland Major, Dean Moriarty, Carlo Marx, Ed Dunkel, Roy Johnson, Tommy Snark, nobody. I wandered around Curtis Street and Larimer Street, worked awhile in the wholesale fruit market where I almost got hired in 1947—the hardest job of my life; at one point the Japanese kids and I had to move a whole boxcar a hundred feet down the rail by hand with a jack-gadget that made it move a quarter-inch with each yank. I lugged watermelon crates over the ice floor of reefers into the blazing sun, sneezing. In God's name and under the stars, what for?

At dusk I walked. I felt like a speck on the surface of the sad red earth. I passed the Windsor Hotel, where Dean Moriarty had lived with his father in the depression thirties, and as of yore I looked everywhere for the sad and fabled tinsmith of my mind. Either you find someone who looks like your father in places like Montana or you look for a friend's father where he is no more.

At lilac evening I walked with every muscle aching among the lights of 27th and Welton in the Denver colored section, wishing I were a Negro, feeling that the best the white world had offered was not enough ecstasy for me, not enough life, joy, kicks, darkness, music, not enough night. I stopped at a little shack where a man sold hot red chili in paper containers; I bought some and ate it, strolling in the dark mysterious streets. I wished I were a Denver Mexican, or even a poor overworked Jap, anything but what I was so drearily, a "white man" disillusioned. All my life I'd had white ambitions; that was why I'd abandoned a good woman like Terry in the San Joaquin Valley. I passed the dark porches of Mexican and Negro homes; soft voices were there, occasionally the dusky knee of some mysterious sensual gal; and dark faces of the men behind rose arbors. Little children sat like sages in ancient rocking chairs. A gang of colored women came by, and one of the young ones detached herself from motherlike elders and came to me fast—"Hello Joe!"—and suddenly saw it wasn't Joe, and ran back, blushing. I wished I were Joe. I was only myself, Sal Paradise, sad, strolling in this violent dark, this unbearably sweet night, wishing I could exchange worlds with the happy, true-hearted, ecstatic Negroes of

America. The raggedy neighborhoods reminded me of Dean and Marylou, who knew these streets so well from childhood. How I wished I could find them.

Down at 23rd and Welton a softball game was going on under floodlights which also illuminated the gas tank. A great eager crowd roared at every play. The strange young heroes of all kinds, white, colored, Mexican, pure Indian, were on the field, performing with heart-breaking seriousness. Just sandlot kids in uniform. Never in my life as an athlete had I ever permitted myself to perform like this in front of families and girl friends and kids of the neighborhood, at night, under lights; always it had been college, big-time, sober-faced; no boyish, human joy like this. Now it was too late. Near me sat an old Negro who apparently watched the games every night. Next to him was an old white bum; then a Mexican family, then some girls, some boys—all humanity, the lot. Oh, the sadness of the lights that night! The young pitcher looked just like Dean. A pretty blonde in the seats looked just like Marylou. It was the Denver Night; all I did was die.

Down in Denver, down in Denver
All I did was die

Across the street Negro families sat on their front steps, talking and looking up at the starry night through the trees and just relaxing in the softness and sometimes watching the game. Many cars passed in the street meanwhile, and stopped at the corner when the light turned red. There was excitement and the air was filled with the vibration of really joyous life that knows nothing of disappointment and "white sorrows" and all that. The old Negro man had a can of beer in his coat pocket, which he proceeded to open; and the old white man enviously eyed the can and groped in his pocket to see if *he* could buy a can too. How I died! I walked away from there.

I went to see a rich girl I knew. In the morning she pulled a hundred-dollar bill out of her silk stocking and said, "You've been talking of a trip to Frisco; that being the case, take this and go and have your fun." So all my problems were solved and I got a travel-bureau car for eleven dollars' gas-fare to Frisco and zoomed over the land.

Two fellows were driving this car; they said they were pimps. Two other fellows were passengers with me. We sat tight and bent our minds to the goal. We went over Berthoud Pass, down to the great plateau, Tabernash, Troublesome, Kremmling; down Rabbit Ears Pass to Steamboat Springs, and out; fifty miles of dusty detour; then Craig and the Great American Desert. As we crossed the Colorado-Utah border I saw God in the sky in the form of huge gold sunburning clouds above the desert that seemed to point a finger at me and say, "Pass here and go on, you're on the road to heaven." Ah well, alackaday, I was more interested in some old rotted covered wagons and pool tables sitting in the Nevada desert near a Coca-Cola stand and where there were huts with the weatherbeaten signs still flapping in the haunted shrouded desert wind, saying, "Rattlesnake Bill lived here" or "Brokenmouth Annie holed up here for years." Yes, zoom! In Salt Lake City the pimps checked on their girls and we drove on. Before I knew it, once again I was seeing the fabled city of San Francisco stretched on the bay in the middle of the night. I ran immediately to Dean. He had a little house now. I was burning to know what was on his mind and what would happen now, for there was nothing behind me any more, all my bridges were gone and I didn't give a damn about anything at all. I knocked on his door at two o'clock in the morning.

2

He came to the door stark naked and it might have been the President knocking for all he cared. He received the world in the raw. "Sal!" he said with genuine awe. "I didn't think you'd actually do it. You've finally come to *me.*"

"Yep," I said. "Everything fell apart in me. How are things with you?"

"Not so good, not so good. But we've got a million things to talk about. Sal, the time has *fi-nally* come for us to talk and get with it." We agreed it was about time and went in. My arrival was somewhat like the coming of the strange most evil angel in the home of the snow-white fleece, as Dean and I began talking excitedly in the kitchen downstairs, which brought forth sobs from upstairs. Everything I said to Dean was answered with a wild, whispering, shuddering *"Yes!"* Camille knew what was going to happen. Apparently Dean had been quiet for a few months; now the angel had arrived and he was going mad again. "What's the matter with her?" I whispered.

He said, "She's getting worse and worse, man, she cries and makes tantrums, won't let me out to see Slim Gaillard, gets mad every time I'm late, then when I stay home she won't talk to me and says I'm an utter beast." He ran upstairs to soothe her. I heard Camille yell, *"You're a liar, you're a liar, you're a liar!"* I took the opportunity to examine the very wonderful house they had. It was a two-story crooked, rickety wooden cottage in the middle of tenements, right on top of Russian Hill with a view of the bay; it had four rooms, three upstairs and one immense sort of basement kitchen downstairs. The kitchen door opened onto a grassy court where washlines were. In back of the kitchen was a storage room where Dean's old shoes still were caked an inch thick with Texas mud from the night the Hudson got stuck on the Brazos River. Of course the Hudson was gone; Dean hadn't been able to make further payments on it. He had no car at all now. Their second baby was accidentally coming. It was horrible to hear Camille sobbing so. We couldn't stand it and went out to buy beer and brought it back to the kitchen. Camille finally went to sleep or spent the night staring blankly at the dark. I had no idea what was really wrong, except perhaps Dean had driven her mad after all.

After my last leaving of Frisco he had gone crazy over Marylou again and spent months haunting her apartment on Divisadero, where every night she had a different sailor in and he peeked down through her mail-slot and could see her bed. There he saw Marylou sprawled in the mornings with a boy. He trailed her around town. He wanted absolute proof that she was a whore. He loved her, he sweated over her. Finally he got hold of some bad green, as it's called in the trade—green, uncured marijuana—quite by mistake, and smoked too much of it.

"The first day," he said, "I lay rigid as a board in bed and couldn't move or say a word; I just looked straight up with my eyes open wide. I could hear buzzing in my head and saw all kinds of wonderful technicolor visions and felt wonderful. The second day everything came to me, EVERYTHING I'd ever done or known or read or heard of or conjectured came back to me and rearranged itself in my mind in a brand-new logical way and because I could think of nothing else in the interior concerns of holding and catering to the amazement and gratitude I felt, I kept saying, 'Yes, yes, yes, yes.' Not loud. Just 'yes,' real quiet, and these green tea visions lasted until the third day. I had understood everything by then, my whole life was decided, I knew I loved Marylou, I knew I had to find my father wherever he is and save him, I knew you were my buddy et cetera, I knew how great Carlo is. I knew a thousand things about everybody everywhere. Then the third day I began having a terrible series of waking nightmares, and they were so absolutely horrible and grisly and green that I just lay there doubled up with my hands around my knees, saying, 'Oh, oh, oh, ah, oh . . .' The neighbors heard me and sent for a doctor. Camille was away with the baby, visiting her folks. The whole neighborhood was concerned. They came in and found me lying on the bed with my arms stretched out forever. Sal, I ran to Marylou with some of that tea. And do you know that the same thing happened to that dumb little box?—the same visions, the same logic, the same final decision about everything, the view of all truths in one painful lump leading to nightmares and pain—ack! Then I knew I loved her so much I wanted to kill her. I ran home and beat my head on the wall. I ran to Ed Dunkel; he's back in Frisco with Galatea; I asked him about a guy we know has a gun, I went to the guy, I got the gun, I ran to Marylou, I looked down the mail-slot, she was sleeping with a guy, had to retreat and hesitate, came back in an hour, I barged in, she was alone—and I gave her the gun and told her to kill me. She held the gun in her hand the longest time. I asked her for a sweet dead pact. She didn't want. I said one of us had to die. She said no. I beat my head on the wall. Man, I was out of my mind. She'll tell you, she talked me out of it."

"Then what happened?"

"That was months ago—after you left. She finally married a used-car dealer, dumb bastit has promised to kill me if he finds me, if necessary I shall have to defend myself and kill him and I'll go to San Quentin, 'cause, Sal, one more rap of *any* kind and I go to San Quentin for life—that's the end of me. Bad hand and all." He showed me his hand. I hadn't noticed in the excitement that he had suffered a terrible accident to his hand. "I hit Marylou on the brow on February twenty-sixth at six o'clock in the evening—in fact six-ten, because I remember I had to make my hotshot freight in an hour and twenty minutes—the last time we met and the last time we decided everything, and now listen to this: my thumb only deflected off her brow and she didn't even have a bruise and in fact laughed, but my thumb broke above the wrist and a horrible doctor made a setting of the bones that was difficult and took three separate castings, twenty-three combined hours of sitting on hard benches waiting, et cetera, and the final cast had a traction pin stuck through the tip of my thumb, so in April when they took off the cast the pin infected my bone and I developed osteomyelitis which has become chronic, and after an operation which failed and a month in a cast the result was the amputation of a wee bare piece off the tip-ass end."

He unwrapped the bandages and showed me. The flesh, about half an inch, was missing under the nail.

"It got from worse to worse. I had to support Camille and Amy and had to work as fast as I could at Firestone as mold man, curing recapped tires and later hauling big hunnerd-fifty-pound tires from the floor to the top of the cars—could only use my good hand and kept banging the bad—broke it again, had it reset again, and it's getting all infected and swoled again. So now I take care of baby while Camille works. You see? Heeby-jeebies, I'm classification three-A, jazz-hounded Moriarty has a sore butt, his wife gives him daily injections of penicillin for his thumb, which produces hives, for he's allergic. He must take sixty thousand units of Fleming's juice within a month. He must take one tablet every four hours for this month to combat allergy produced from his juice. He must take codeine aspirin to relieve the pain in his thumb. He must have surgery on his leg for an inflamed cyst. He must rise next Monday at six A.M. to get his teeth cleaned. He must see a foot doctor twice a week for treatment. He must take cough syrup each night. He must blow and snort constantly to clear his nose, which has collapsed just under the bridge where an operation some years ago weakened it. He lost his thumb on his throwing arm. Greatest seventy-yard passer in the history of New Mexico State Reformatory. And yet—and yet, I've never felt better and finer and happier with the world and to see little lovely children playing in the sun and I am so glad to see you, my fine gone wonderful Sal, and I know, I *know* everything will be all right. You'll see her tomorrow, my terrific darling beautiful daughter can now stand alone for thirty seconds at a time, she weighs twenty-two pounds, is twenty-nine inches long. I've just figured out she is thirty-one-and-a-quarter-per-cent English, twenty-seven-and-a-half-per-cent Irish, twenty-five-per-cent German, eight-and-three-quarters-per-cent Dutch, seven-and-a-half-per-cent Scotch, one-hundred-per-cent wonderful." He fondly congratulated me for the book I had finished, which was now accepted by the publishers. "We know life, Sal, we're growing older, each of us, little by little, and are coming to know things. What you tell me about your life I understand well, I've always dug your feelings, and now in fact you're ready to hook up with a real great girl if you can only find her and cultivate her and make her mind your soul as I have tried so hard with these damned women of mine. Shit! shit! shit!" he yelled.

And in the morning Camille threw both of us out, baggage and all. It began when we called Roy Johnson, old Denver Roy, and had him come over for beer, while Dean minded the baby and did the dishes and the wash in the backyard but did a sloppy job of it in his excitement. Johnson agreed to drive us to Mill City to look for Remi Boncoeur. Camille came in from work at the doctor's office and gave us all the sad look of a harassed woman's life. I tried to show this haunted woman that I had no mean intentions concerning her home life by saying hello to her and talking as warmly as I could, but she knew it was a con and maybe one I'd learned from Dean, and only gave a brief smile. In the morning there was a terrible scene: she lay on the bed sobbing, and in the midst of this I suddenly had the need to go to the bathroom, and the only way I could get there was through her room. "Dean, Dean," I cried, "where's the nearest bar?"

"Bar?" he said, surprised; he was washing his hands in the kitchen sink downstairs. He thought I wanted to get drunk. I told him my dilemma and he said, "Go right ahead, she does that all the time." No, I couldn't do that. I rushed out to look for a bar; I walked uphill and downhill in a vicinity of four blocks on Russian Hill and found nothing but laundromats, cleaners, soda fountains, beauty parlors. I came back to the crooked little house. They were yelling at each other as I slipped through with a feeble smile and locked myself in the bathroom. A few moments later Camille was throwing Dean's things on the living-room floor and telling him to pack. To my amazement I saw a full-length oil painting of Galatea Dunkel over the sofa. I suddenly realized that all these women were spending months of loneliness and womanliness together, chatting about the madness of the men. I heard Dean's maniacal giggle across the house, together with the wails of his baby. The next thing I knew he was gliding around the house like Groucho Marx, with his broken thumb wrapped in a huge white bandage sticking up like a beacon that stands motionless above the frenzy of the waves. Once again I saw his pitiful huge battered trunk with socks and dirty underwear sticking out; he bent over it, throwing in everything he could find. Then he got his suitcase, the beatest suitcase in the USA. It was made of paper with designs on it to make it look like leather, and hinges of some kind pasted on. A great rip ran down the top; Dean lashed on a rope. Then he grabbed his seabag and threw things into that. I got my bag, stuffed it, and as Camille lay in bed saying, "Liar! Liar! Liar!" we leaped out of the house and struggled down the street to the nearest cable car—a mass of men and suitcases with that enormous bandaged thumb sticking up in the air.

That thumb became the symbol of Dean's final development. He no longer cared about anything (as before) but now he also *cared about everything in principle;* that is to say, it was all the same to him and he belonged to the world and there was nothing he could do about it. He stopped me in the middle of the street.

"Now, man, I know you're probably real bugged; you just got to town and we get thrown out the first day and you're wondering what I've done to deserve this and so on—together with all horrible appurtenances—hee-hee-hee!—but look at me. Please, Sal, look at me."

I looked at him. He was wearing a T-shirt, torn pants hanging down his belly, tattered shoes; he had not shaved, his hair was wild and bushy, his eyes bloodshot, and that tremendous bandaged thumb stood supported in midair at heart-level (he had to hold it up that way), and on his face was the goofiest grin I ever saw. He stumbled around in a circle and looked everywhere.

"What do my eyeballs see? Ah—the blue sky. Long-fellow!" He swayed and blinked. He rubbed his eyes. "Together with windows—have you ever dug windows? Now let's talk about windows. I have seen some really crazy windows that made faces at me, and some of them had shades drawn and so they winked." Out of his seabag he fished a copy of Eugene Sue's *Mysteries of Paris* and, adjusting the front of his T-shirt, began reading on the street corner with a pedantic air. "Now really, Sal, let's dig everything as we go along . . ." He forgot about that in an instant and looked around blankly. I was glad I had come, he needed me now.

"Why did Camille throw you out? What are you going to do?"

"Eh?" he said. "Eh? Eh?" We racked our brains for where to go and what to do. I realized it was up to me. Poor, poor Dean—the devil himself had never fallen farther; in idiocy, with infected thumb, surrounded by the battered suitcases of his motherless feverish life across America and back numberless times, an undone bird. "Let's walk to New York," he said, "and as we do so let's take stock of everything along the way—yass." I took out my money and counted it; I showed it to him.

"I have here," I said, "the sum of eighty-three dollars and change, and if you come with me let's go to New York—and after that let's go to Italy."

"Italy?" he said. His eyes lit up. "Italy, yass—how shall we get there, dear Sal?"

I pondered this. "I'll make some money, I'll get a thousand dollars from the publishers. We'll go dig all the crazy women in Rome, Paris, all those places; we'll sit at sidewalk cafés; we'll live in whorehouses. Why not go to Italy?"

"Why yass," said Dean, and then realized I was serious and looked at me out of the corner of his eye for the first time, for I'd never committed myself before with regard to his burdensome existence, and that look was the look of a man weighing his chances at the last moment before the bet. There were triumph and insolence in his eyes, a devilish look, and he never took his eyes off mine for a long time. I looked back at him and blushed.

I said, "What's the matter?" I felt wretched when I asked it. He made no answer but continued looking at me with the same wary insolent side-eye.

I tried to remember everything he'd done in his life and if there wasn't something back there to make him suspicious of something now. Resolutely and firmly I repeated what I said—"Come to New York with me; I've got the money." I looked at him; my eyes were watering with embarrassment and tears. Still he stared at me. Now his eyes were blank and looking through me. It was probably the pivotal point of our friendship when he realized I had actually spent some hours thinking about him and his troubles, and he was trying to place that in his tremendously involved and tormented mental categories. Something clicked in both of us. In me it was suddenly concern for a man who was years younger than I, five years, and whose fate was wound with mine across the passage of the recent years; in him it was a matter that I can ascertain only from what he did afterward. He became extremely joyful and said everything was settled. "What was that look?" I asked. He was pained to hear me say that. He frowned. It was rarely that Dean frowned. We both felt perplexed and uncertain of something. We were standing on top of a hill on a beautiful sunny day in San Francisco; our shadows fell across the sidewalk. Out of the tenement next to Camille's house filed eleven Greek men and women who instantly lined themselves up on the sunny pavement while another backed up across the narrow street and smiled at them over a camera. We gaped at these ancient people who were having a wedding party for one of their daughters, probably the thousandth in an unbroken dark generation of smiling in the sun. They were well dressed, and they were strange. Dean and I might have been in Cyprus for all of that. Gulls flew overhead in the sparkling air.

"Well," said Dean in a very shy and sweet voice, "shall we go?"

"Yes," I said, "let's go to Italy." And so we picked up our bags, he the trunk with his one good arm and I the rest, and staggered to the cable-car stop; in a moment rolled down the hill with our legs dangling to the sidewalk from the jiggling shelf, two broken-down heroes of the Western night.

3

First thing, we went to a bar down on Market Street and decided everything—that we would stick together and be buddies till we died. Dean was very quiet and preoccupied, looking at the old bums in the saloon that reminded him of his father. "I think he's in Denver—this time we must absolutely find him, he may be in County Jail, he may be around Larimer Street again, but he's to be found. Agreed?"

Yes, it was agreed; we were going to do everything we'd never done and had been too silly to do in the past. Then we promised ourselves two days of kicks in San Francisco before starting off, and of course the agreement was to go by travel bureau in share-the-gas cars and save as much money as possible. Dean claimed he no longer needed Marylou though he still loved her. We both agreed he would make out in New York.

Dean put on his pin-stripe suit with a sports shirt, we stashed our gear in a Greyhound bus locker for ten cents, and we took off to meet Roy Johnson who was going to be our chauffeur for two-day Frisco kicks. Roy agreed over the phone to do so. He arrived at the corner of Market and Third shortly thereafter and picked us up. Roy was now living in Frisco, working as a clerk and married to a pretty little blonde called Dorothy. Dean confided that her nose was too long—this was his big point of contention about her, for some strange reason—but her nose wasn't too long at all. Roy Johnson is a thin, dark, handsome kid with a pin-sharp face and combed hair that he keeps shoving back from the sides of his head. He had an extremely earnest approach and a big smile. Evidently his wife, Dorothy, had wrangled with him over the chauffeuring idea—and, determined to make a stand as the man of the house (they lived in a little room), he nevertheless stuck by his promise to us, but with consequences; his mental dilemma resolved itself in a bitter silence. He drove Dean and me all over Frisco at all hours of day and night and never said a word; all he did was go through red lights and make sharp turns on two wheels, and this was telling us the shifts to which we'd put him. He was midway between the challenge of his new wife and the challenge of his old Denver poolhall gang leader. Dean was pleased, and of course unperturbed by the driving. We paid absolutely no attention to Roy and sat in the back and yakked.

The next thing was to go to Mill City to see if we could find Remi Boncoeur. I noticed with some wonder that the old ship *Admiral Freebee* was no longer in the bay; and then of course Remi was no longer in the second-to-last compartment of the shack in the canyon. A beautiful colored girl opened the door instead; Dean and I talked to her a great deal. Roy Johnson waited in the car, reading Eugene Sue's *Mysteries of Paris.* I took one last look at Mill City and knew there was no sense trying to dig up the involved past; instead we decided to go see Galatea Dunkel about sleeping accommodations. Ed had left her again, was in Denver, and damned if she still didn't plot to get him back. We found her sitting crosslegged on the Oriental-type rug of her four-room tenement flat on upper Mission with a deck of fortune cards. Good girl. I saw sad signs that Ed Dunkel had lived here awhile and then left out of stupors and disinclinations only.

"He'll come back," said Galatea. "That guy can't take care of himself without me." She gave a furious look at Dean and Roy Johnson. "It was Tommy Snark who did it this time. All the time before he came Ed was perfectly happy and worked and we went out and had wonderful times. Dean, you know that. Then they'd sit in the bathroom for hours, Ed in the bathtub and Snarky on the seat, and talk and talk and talk—such silly things."

Dean laughed. For years he had been chief prophet of that gang and now they were learning his technique. Tommy Snark had grown a beard and his big sorrowful blue eyes had come looking for Ed Dunkel in Frisco; what happened (actually and no lie), Tommy had his small finger amputated in a Denver mishap and collected a good sum of money. For no reason under the sun they decided to give Galatea the slip and go to Portland, Maine, where apparently Snark had an aunt. So they were now either in Denver, going through, or already in Portland.

"When Tom's money runs out Ed'll be back," said Galatea, looking at her cards. "Damn fool—he doesn't know anything and never did. All he has to do is know that I love him."

Galatea looked like the daughter of the Greeks with the sunny camera as she sat there on the rug, her long hair streaming to the floor, plying the fortune-telling cards. I got to like her. We even decided to go out that night and hear jazz, and Dean would take a six-foot blonde who lived down the street, Marie.

That night Galatea, Dean, and I went to get Marie. This girl had a basement apartment, a little daughter, and an old car that barely ran and which Dean and I had to push down the street as the girls jammed at the starter. We went to Galatea's, and there everybody sat around—Marie, her daughter, Galatea, Roy Johnson, Dorothy his wife—all sullen in the overstuffed furniture as I stood in a corner, neutral in Frisco problems, and Dean stood in the middle of the room with his balloon-thumb in the air breast-high, giggling. "Gawd damn," he said, "we're all losing our fingers—hawr-hawr-hawr."

"Dean, why do you act so foolish?" said Galatea. "Camille called and said you left her. Don't you realize you have a daughter?"

"He didn't leave her, she kicked him out!" I said, breaking my neutrality. They all gave me dirty looks; Dean grinned. "And with that thumb, what do you expect the poor guy to do?" I added. They all looked at me; particularly Dorothy Johnson lowered a mean gaze on me. It wasn't anything but a sewing circle, and the center of it was the culprit, Dean—responsible, perhaps, for everything that was wrong. I looked out the window at the buzzing night-street of Mission; I wanted to get going and hear the great jazz of Frisco—and remember, this was only my second night in town.

"I think Marylou was very, very wise leaving you, Dean," said Galatea. "For years now you haven't had any sense of responsibility for anyone. You've done so many awful things I don't know what to say to you."

And in fact that was the point, and they all sat around looking at Dean with lowered and hating eyes, and he stood on the carpet in the middle of them and giggled—he just giggled. He made a little dance. His bandage was getting dirtier all the time; it began to flop and unroll. I suddenly realized that Dean, by virtue of his enormous series of sins, was becoming the Idiot, the Imbecile, the Saint of the lot.

"You have absolutely no regard for anybody but yourself and your damned kicks. All you think about is what's hanging between your legs and how much money or fun you can get out of people and then you just throw them aside. Not only that but you're silly about it. It never occurs to you that life is serious and there are people trying to make something decent out of it instead of just goofing all the time."

That's what Dean was, the HOLY GOOF.

"Camille is crying her heart out tonight, but don't think for a minute she wants you back, she said she never wanted to see you again and she said it was to be final this time. Yet you stand here and make silly faces, and I don't think there's a care in your heart."

This was not true; I knew better and I could have told them all. I didn't see any sense in trying it. I longed to go and put my arm around Dean and say, Now look here, all of you, remember just one thing: this guy has his troubles too, and another thing, he never complains and he's given all of you a damned good time just being himself, and if that isn't enough for you then send him to the firing squad, that's apparently what you're itching to do anyway . . .

Nevertheless Galatea Dunkel was the only one in the gang who wasn't afraid of Dean and could sit there calmly, with her face hanging out, telling him off in front of everybody. There were earlier days in Denver when Dean had everybody sit in the dark with the girls and just talked, and talked, and talked, with a voice that was once hypnotic and strange and was said to make the girls come across by sheer force of persuasion and the content of what he said. This was when he was fifteen, sixteen. Now his disciples were married and the wives of his disciples had him on the carpet for the sexuality and the life he had helped bring into being. I listened further.

"Now you're going East with Sal," Galatea said, "and what do you think you're going to accomplish by that? Camille has to stay home and mind the baby now you're gone—how can she keep her job?—and she never wants to see you again and I don't blame her. If you see Ed along the road you tell him to come back to me or I'll kill him."

Just as flat as that. It was the saddest night. I felt as if I was with strange brothers and sisters in a pitiful dream. Then a complete silence fell over everybody; where once Dean would have talked his way out, he now fell silent himself, but standing in front of everybody, ragged and broken and idiotic, right under the lightbulbs, his bony mad face covered with sweat and throbbing veins, saying, "Yes, yes, yes," as though tremendous revelations were pouring into him all the time now, and I am convinced they were, and the others suspected as much and were frightened. He was BEAT—the root, the soul of Beatific. What was he knowing? He tried all in his power to tell me what he was knowing, and they envied that about me, my position at his side, defending him and drinking him in as they once tried to do. Then they looked at me. What was I, a stranger, doing on the West Coast this fair night? I recoiled from the thought.

"We're going to Italy," I said. I washed my hands of the whole matter. Then, too, there was a strange sense of maternal satisfaction in the air, for the girls were really looking at Dean the way a mother looks at the dearest and most errant child, and he with his sad thumb and all his revelations knew it well, and that was why he was able, in tick-tocking silence, to walk out of the apartment without a word, to wait for us downstairs as soon as we'd made up our minds about *time.* This was what we sensed about the ghost on the sidewalk. I looked out the window. He was alone in the doorway, digging the street. Bitterness, recriminations, advice, morality, sadness—everything was behind him, and ahead of him was the ragged and ecstatic joy of pure being.

"Come on, Galatea, Marie, let's go hit the jazz joints and forget it. Dean will be dead someday. Then what can you say to him?"

"The sooner he's dead the better," said Galatea, and she spoke officially for almost everyone in the room.

"Very well, then," I said, "but now he's alive and I'll bet you want to know what he does next and that's because he's got the secret that we're all busting to find and it's splitting his head wide open and if he goes mad don't worry, it won't be your fault but the fault of God."

They objected to this; they said I really didn't know Dean; they said he was the worst scoundrel that ever lived and I'd find out someday to my regret. I was amused to hear them protest so much. Roy Johnson rose to the defense of the ladies and said he knew Dean better than anybody, and all Dean was, was just a very interesting and even amusing con-man. I went out to find Dean and we had a brief talk about it.

"Ah, man, don't worry, everything is perfect and fine." He was rubbing his belly and licking his lips.

1957

KURT VONNEGUT

(1922–)

Kurt Vonnegut's hometown of Indianapolis was filled with buildings designed by his father and grandfather and, in the early years, life in his large extended family was comfortable and affluent. The family fortune was lost in the Depression, however, and, unlike his older brother and sister, Kurt attended public school. A chemistry major at Cornell, he dropped out in his senior year, was drafted into the infantry, captured at the Battle of the Bulge, and endured the 1945 firebombing of Dresden in a bunker constructed in the basement of a slaughterhouse.

After graduate work in anthropology at the University of Chicago, he worked as a police reporter and as a publicist for General Electric before quitting to become a free-lance writer. Between 1950 and 1963, he wrote fifty stories for popular magazines, generally uncritical of middle-class virtues. In his first novel, *Player Piano* (1952), he adopted a science-fiction format to approach key issues of the 1950's—conformity and mechanization—using conventional narrative techniques, flat characters, and a third-person perspective. It excited little critical note.

In the late 1950's when *Collier's, The Saturday Evening Post,* and other customers of his stories ceased publication, Vonnegut turned to the pulp market with *The Sirens of Titan* (1959), a space-exploration fantasy, which he followed with *Mother Night* (1961), a paperback in which he first drew on his war experiences and adopted what has come to be his characteristic style: short sentences and paragraphs gathered in very short chapters—45 in 200 pages. Vonnegut later said *Mother Night* was the only novel for which he knew the moral: "We are what we pretend to be, so we must be careful what we pretend to be." An American playwright, living in Germany during World War II, makes German propaganda broadcasts, filled with Nazi hate but containing messages for the Allies. Later he is tried as a war criminal. Written as a confession by an unreliable narrator with a fondness for black humor, this is the first in a series of novels in which a character ponders the role of an artist in the modern world.

Subsequent novels address a variety of contemporary problems. In *Cat's Cradle* (1963), the first Vonnegut novel to receive critical attention, the narrator discovers a religion built on untruth, and watches as the world comes to a frozen end, the legacy of the atomic age. *God Bless You, Mr. Rosewater* (1965) is a fable of a millionaire's thwarted attempt to disperse his money to the unloved in small towns. In *Breakfast of Champions* (1973), a Job-like character is tested by life in a text where line drawings supplement Vonnegut's usual short units and jokes. In *Slapstick* (1976), an energy-exhausted United States has reverted to a more primitive stage of civilization. The narrator, a hundred-year-old former president, has developed a utopian scheme for bringing a measure of health to society. *Jailbird* (1979) also deals with possibilities for revitalizing the "American dream," this time by redistribution of wealth. *Deadeye Dick* (1982) is a very pessimistic book in which moral issues are treated fleetingly by characters passive in the face of degeneration. In *Galapagos* (1985), contemporary celebrities are fated to repopulate the earth after disasters have all but wiped out humanity.

Slaughterhouse-Five (1970) remains Vonnegut's most famous work. Its main character, Billy Pilgrim, who survived the Dresden bombing, alternates between his suburban home in upstate New York and the planet Tralfamadore, where he and a former movie sex queen are on display in the zoo. Vonnegut's aim might be described in words the narrator uses to explain Tralfamadorian novels: "There isn't any particular relationship between all the messages, except that the author has chosen them carefully, so that, when seen all at once, they produce an image of life that is beautiful and surprising and deep."

Vonnegut has been very popular with general readers, perhaps because his overriding message is that good and evil turn out the same in the end, and that life goes on despite tragedy and heroics. As he says in a headnote to his play *Happy Birthday, Wanda June* (1971), "I felt and still feel that everybody is right, no matter what he says * * * And I gave a name * * * to a mathematical point where all opinions, no matter how contradictory, harmonized. I call it a *chronosynclastic infundibulum.* I live in one."

Novels to date are named above. Short fiction is collected in *Canary in a Cathouse,* 1961, and *Welcome to the Monkey House,* 1969. Essays appear in *Wampeters, Foma and Granfaloons,* 1975; and *Palm Sunday,* 1982. A children's book, *Sun Moon Star,* 1980, was written with Ivan Chermayeff.

Studies include Jerome Klinkowitz and John Somer, eds., *The Vonnegut Statement: Original Essays on the Life and Work of Kurt Vonnegut,* 1973; Richard Giannone, *Vonnegut: A Preface to His Novels,* 1975; Stanley Schatt, *Kurt Vonnegut, Jr.,* 1976; and Jerome Klinkowitz, *Kurt Vonnegut,* 1982.

Report on the Barnhouse Effect

Let me begin by saying that I don't know any more about where Professor Arthur Barnhouse is hiding than anyone else does. Save for one short, enigmatic message left in my mailbox on Christmas Eve, I have not heard from him since his disappearance a year and a half ago.

What's more, readers of this article will be disappointed if they expect to learn how *they* can bring about the so-called "Barnhouse Effect." If I were able and willing to give away that secret, I would certainly be something more important than a psychology instructor.

I have been urged to write this report because I did research under the professor's direction and because I was the first to learn of his astonishing discovery. But while I was his student I was never entrusted with knowledge of how the mental forces could be released and directed. He was unwilling to trust anyone with that information.

I would like to point out that the term "Barnhouse Effect" is a creation of the popular press, and was never used by Professor Barnhouse. The name he chose for the phenomenon was *"dynamopsychism,"* or *force of the mind.*

I cannot believe that there is a civilized person yet to be convinced that such a force exists, what with its destructive effects on display in every national capital. I think humanity has always had an inkling that this sort of force does exist. It has been common knowledge that some people are luckier than others with inanimate objects like dice. What Professor Barnhouse did was to show that such "luck" was a measurable force, which in his case could be enormous.

By my calculations, the professor was about fifty-five times more powerful than a Nagasaki-type atomic bomb at the time he went into hiding. He was not bluffing when, on the eve of "Operation Brainstorm," he told General Honus Barker: "Sitting here at the dinner table, I'm pretty sure I can flatten anything on earth—from Joe Louis to the Great Wall of China."

There is an understandable tendency to look upon Professor Barnhouse as a supernatural visitation. The First Church of Barnhouse in Los Angeles has a congregation numbering in the thousands. He is godlike in neither appearance nor intellect. The man who disarms the world is single, shorter than the average American male, stout, and averse to exercise. His I.Q. is 143, which is good but certainly not sensational. He is quite mortal, about to celebrate his fortieth birthday, and in good health. If he is alone now, the isolation won't bother him too much. He was quiet and shy when I knew him, and seemed to find more companionship in books and music than in his associations at the college.

Neither he nor his powers fall outside the sphere of Nature. His dynamopsychic radiations are subject to many known physical laws that apply in the field of radio. Hardly a person has not now heard the snarl of "Barnhouse static" on his home receiver. The radiations are affected by sunspots and variations in the ionosphere.

However, they differ from ordinary broadcast waves in several important ways. Their total energy can be brought to bear on any single point the professor chooses, and that energy is undiminished by distance. As a weapon, then, dynamopsychism has an impressive advantage over bacteria and atomic bombs, beyond the fact that it costs nothing to use: it enables the professor to single out critical individuals and objects instead of slaughtering whole populations in the process of maintaining international equilibrium.

As General Honus Barker told the House Military Affairs Committee: "Until someone finds Barnhouse, there is no defense against the Barnhouse Effect." Efforts to "jam" or block the radiations have failed. Premier Slezak could have saved himself the fantastic expense of his "Barnhouseproof" shelter. Despite the shelter's twelve-foot-thick lead armor, the premier has been floored twice while in it.

There is talk of screening the population for men potentially as powerful dynamopsychically as the professor. Senator Warren Foust demanded funds for this purpose last month, with the passionate declaration: "He who rules the Barnhouse Effect rules the world!" Commissar Kropotnik said much the same thing, so another costly armaments race, with a new twist, has begun.

This race at least has its comical aspects. The world's best gamblers are being coddled by governments like so many nuclear physicists. There may be several hundred persons with dynamopsychic talent on earth, myself included. But, without knowledge of the professor's technique, they can never be anything but dice-table despots. With the secret, it would probably take them ten years to become dangerous weapons. It took the professor that long. He who rules the Barnhouse Effect is Barnhouse and will be for some time.

Popularly, the "Age of Barnhouse" is said to have begun a year and a half ago, on the day of Operation Brainstorm. That was when dynamopsychism became significant politically. Actually, the phenomenon was discovered in May, 1942, shortly after the professor turned down a direct commission in the Army and enlisted as an artillery private. Like X-rays and vulcanized rubber, dynamopsychism was discovered by accident.

From time to time Private Barnhouse was invited to take part in games of chance by his barrack mates. He knew nothing about the games, and usually begged off. But one evening, out of social grace, he agreed to shoot craps. It was terrible or wonderful that he played, depending upon whether or not you like the world as it now is.

"Shoot sevens, Pop," someone said.

So "Pop" shot sevens—ten in a row to bankrupt the barracks. He retired to his bunk and, as a mathematical exercise, calculated the odds against his feat on the back of a laundry slip. His chances of doing it, he found, were one in almost ten million! Bewildered, he borrowed a pair of dice from the man in the bunk next to his. He tried to roll sevens again, but got only the usual assortment of numbers. He lay back for a moment, then resumed his toying with the dice. He rolled ten more sevens in a row.

He might have dismissed the phenomenon with a low whistle. But the professor instead mulled over the circumstances surrounding his two lucky streaks. There was one single factor in common: on both occasions, *the same thought train had flashed through his mind just before he threw the dice.* It was that thought train which aligned the professor's brain cells into what has since become the most powerful weapon on earth.

The soldier in the next bunk gave dynamopsychism its first token of respect. In an understatement certain to bring wry smiles to the faces of the world's dejected demagogues, the soldier said, "You're hotter'n a two-dollar pistol, Pop." Professor Barnhouse was all of that. The dice that did his bidding weighed but a few grams, so the forces involved were minute; but the unmistakable fact that there were such forces was earth-shaking.

Professional caution kept him from revealing his discovery immediately. He wanted more facts and a body of theory to go with them. Later, when the atomic bomb was dropped on Hiroshima, it was fear that made him hold his peace. At no time were his experiments, as Premier Slezak called them, "a bourgeois plot to shackle the true democracies of the world." The professor didn't know where they were leading.

In time, he came to recognize another startling feature of dynamopsychism: *its strength increased with use.* Within six months, he was able to govern dice thrown by men the length of a barracks distant. By the time of his discharge in 1945, he could knock bricks loose from chimneys three miles away.

Charges that Professor Barnhouse could have won the last war in a minute, but did not care to do so, are perfectly senseless. When the war ended, he had the range and power of a 37-millimeter cannon, perhaps—certainly no more. His dynamopsychic powers graduated from the small-arms class only after his discharge and return to Wyandotte College.

I enrolled in the Wyandotte Graduate School two years after the professor had rejoined the faculty. By chance, he was assigned as my thesis adviser. I was unhappy about the assignment, for the professor was, in the eyes of both colleagues and students, a somewhat ridiculous figure. He missed classes or had lapses of memory during lectures. When I arrived, in fact, his shortcomings had passed from the ridiculous to the intolerable.

"We're assigning you to Barnhouse as a sort of temporary thing," the dean of social studies told me. He looked apologetic and perplexed. "Brilliant man, Barnhouse, I guess. Difficult to know since his return, perhaps, but his work before the war brought a great deal of credit to our little school."

When I reported to the professor's laboratory for the first time, what I saw was more distressing than the gossip. Every surface in the room was covered with dust; books and apparatus had not been disturbed for months. The professor sat napping at his desk when I entered. The only signs of recent activity were three overflowing ashtrays, a pair of scissors, and a morning paper with several items clipped from its front page.

As he raised his head to look at me, I saw that his eyes were clouded with fatigue. "Hi," he said, "just can't seem to get my sleeping done at night." He lighted a cigarette, his hands trembling slightly. "You the young man I'm supposed to help with a thesis?"

"Yes, sir," I said. In minutes he converted my misgivings to alarm.

"You an overseas veteran?" he asked.

"Yes, sir."

"Not much left over there, is there?" He frowned. "Enjoy the last war?"

"No, sir."

"Look like another war to you?"

"Kind of, sir."

"What can be done about it?"

I shrugged. "Looks pretty hopeless."

He peered at me intently. "Know anything about international law, the U.N., and all that?"

"Only what I pick up from the papers."

"Same here," he sighed. He showed me a fat scrapbook packed with newspaper clippings. "Never used to pay any attention to international politics. Now I study them the way I used to study rats in mazes. Everybody tells me the same thing—'Looks hopeless.'"

"Nothing short of a miracle—" I began.

"Believe in magic?" he asked sharply. The professor fished two dice from his vest pocket. "I will try to roll twos," he said. He rolled twos three times in a row. "One chance in about 47,000 of that happening. There's a miracle for you." He beamed for an instant, then brought the interview to an end, remarking that he had a class which had begun ten minutes ago.

He was not quick to take me into his confidence, and he said no more about his trick with the dice. I assumed they were loaded, and forgot about them. He set me the task of watching male rats cross electrified metal strips to get to food or female rats—an experiment that had been done to everyone's satisfaction in the nineteen-thirties. As though the pointlessness of my work were not bad enough, the professor annoyed me further with irrelevant questions. His favorites were: "Think we should have dropped the atomic bomb on Hiroshima?" and "Think every new piece of scientific information is a good thing for humanity?"

However, I did not feel put upon for long. "Give those poor animals a holiday," he said one morning, after I had been with him only a month. "I wish you'd help me look into a more interesting problem—namely, my sanity."

I returned the rats to their cages.

"What you must do is simple," he said, speaking softly. "Watch the inkwell on my desk. If you see nothing happen to it, say so, and I'll go quietly—relieved, I might add—to the nearest sanitarium."

I nodded uncertainly.

He locked the laboratory door and drew the blinds, so that we were in twilight for a moment. "I'm odd, I know," he said. "It's fear of myself that's made me odd."

"I've found you somewhat eccentric, perhaps, but certainly not—"

"If nothing happens to that inkwell, 'crazy as a bedbug' is the only description of me that will do," he interrupted, turning on the overhead lights. His eyes narrowed. "To give you an idea of how crazy, I'll tell you what's been running through my mind when I should have been sleeping. I think maybe I can save the world. I think maybe I can make every nation a *have* nation, and do away with war for good. I think maybe I can clear roads through jungles, irrigate deserts, build dams overnight."

"Yes, sir."

"Watch the inkwell!"

Dutifully and fearfully I watched. A high-pitched humming seemed to come from the inkwell; then it began to vibrate alarmingly, and finally to bound about the top of the desk, making two noisy circuits. It stopped, hummed again, glowed red, then popped in splinters with a blue-green flash.

Perhaps my hair stood on end. The professor laughed gently. "Magnets?" I managed to say at last.

"Wish to heaven it were magnets," he murmured. It was then that he told me of dynamopsychism. He knew only that there was such a force; he could not explain it. "It's me and me alone—and it's awful."

"I'd say it was amazing and wonderful!" I cried.

"If all I could do was make inkwells dance, I'd be tickled silly with the whole business." He shrugged disconsolately. "But I'm no toy, my boy. If you like, we can drive around the neighborhood, and I'll show you what I mean." He told me about pulverized boulders, shattered oaks, and abandoned farm buildings demolished within a fifty-mile radius of the campus. "Did every bit of it sitting right here, just thinking—not even thinking hard."

He scratched his head nervously. "I have never dared to concentrate as hard as I can for fear of the damage I might do. I'm to the point where a mere whim is a blockbuster." There was a depressing pause. "Up until a few days ago, I've thought it best to keep my secret for fear of what use it might be put to," he continued. "Now I realize that I haven't any more right to it than a man has a right to own an atomic bomb."

He fumbled through a heap of papers. "This says about all that needs to be said, I think." He handed me a draft of a letter to the Secretary of State.

Dear Sir:

I have discovered a new force which costs nothing to use, and which is probably more important than atomic energy. I should like to see it used most effectively in the cause of peace, and am, therefore, requesting your advice as to how this might best be done.

Yours truly,
A. Barnhouse.

"I have no idea what will happen next," said the professor.

There followed three months of perpetual nightmare, wherein the nation's political and military great came at all hours to watch the professor's tricks.

We were quartered in an old mansion near Charlottesville, Virginia, to which we had been whisked five days after the letter was mailed. Surrounded by barbed wire and twenty guards, we were labeled "Project Wishing Well," and were classified as Top Secret.

For companionship we had General Honus Barker and the State Department's William K. Cuthrell. For the professor's talk of peace-through-plenty they had indulgent smiles and much discourse on practical measures and realistic thinking. So treated, the professor, who had at first been almost meek, progressed in a matter of weeks toward stubbornness.

He had agreed to reveal the thought train by means of which he aligned his mind into a dynamopsychic transmitter. But, under Cuthrell's and Barker's nagging to do so, he began to hedge. At first he declared that the information could be passed on simply by word of mouth. Later he said that it would have to be written up in a long report. Finally, at dinner one night, just after General Barker had read the secret orders for Operation Brainstorm, the professor announced, "The report may take as long as five years to write." He looked fiercely at the general. "Maybe twenty."

The dismay occasioned by this flat announcement was offset somewhat by the exciting anticipation of Operation Brainstorm. The general was in a holiday mood. "The target ships are on their way to the Caroline Islands at this very moment," he declared ecstatically. "One hundred and twenty of them! At the same time, ten V-2s are being readied for firing in New Mexico, and fifty radiocontrolled jet bombers are being equipped for a mock attack on the Aleutians. Just think of it!" Happily he reviewed his orders. "At exactly 1100 hours next Wednesday, I will give you the order to *concentrate;* and you, professor, will think as hard as you can about sinking the target ships, destroying the V-2s before they hit the ground, and knocking down the bombers before they reach the Aleutians! Think you can handle it?"

The professor turned gray and closed his eyes. "As I told you before, my friend, I don't know what I can do." He added bitterly, "As for this Operation Brainstorm, I was never consulted about it, and it strikes me as childish and insanely expensive."

General Barker bridled. "Sir," he said, "your field is psychology, and I wouldn't presume to give you advice in that field. Mine is national defense. I have had thirty years of experience and success, Professor, and I'll ask you not to criticize my judgment."

The professor appealed to Mr. Cuthrell. "Look," he pleaded, "isn't it war and military matters we're all trying to get rid of? Wouldn't it be a whole lot more significant and lots cheaper for me to try moving cloud masses into drought areas, and things like that? I admit I know next to nothing about international politics, but it seems reasonable to suppose that nobody would want to fight wars if there were enough of everything to go around. Mr. Cuthrell, I'd like to try running generators where there isn't any coal or water power, irrigating deserts, and so on. Why, you could figure out what each country needs to make the most of its resources, and I could give it to them without costing American taxpayers a penny."

"Eternal vigilance is the price of freedom," said the general heavily.

Mr. Cuthrell threw the general a look of mild distaste. "Unfortunately, the general is right in his own way," he said. "I wish to heaven the world were ready for ideals like yours, but it simply isn't. We aren't surrounded by brothers, but by enemies. It isn't a lack of food or resources that has us on the brink of war—it's a struggle for power. Who's going to be in charge of the world, our kind of people or theirs?"

The professor nodded in reluctant agreement and arose from the table. "I beg your pardon, gentlemen. You are, after all, better qualified to judge what is best for the country. I'll do whatever you say." He turned to me. "Don't forget to wind the restricted clock and put the confidential cat out," he said gloomily, and ascended the stairs to his bedroom.

For reasons of national security, Operation Brainstorm was carried on without the knowledge of the American citizenry which was paying the bill. The observers, technicians, and military men involved in the activity knew that a test was under way—a test of what, they had no idea. Only thirty-seven key men, myself included, knew what was afoot.

In Virginia, the day for Operation Brainstorm was unseasonably cool. Inside, a log fire crackled in the fireplace, and the flames were reflected in the polished metal cabinets that lined the living room. All that remained of the room's lovely old furniture was a Victorian love seat, set squarely in the center of the floor, facing three television receivers. One long bench had been brought in for the ten of us privileged to watch. The television screens showed, from left to right, the stretch of desert which was the rocket target, the guinea-pig fleet, and a section of the Aleutian sky through which the radio-controlled bomber formation would roar.

Ninety minutes before H-hour the radios announced that the rockets were ready, that the observation ships had backed away to what was thought to be a safe distance, and that the bombers were on their way. The small Virginia audience lined up on the bench in order of rank, smoked a great deal, and said little. Professor Barnhouse was in his bedroom. General Barker bustled about the house like a woman preparing Thanksgiving dinner for twenty.

At ten minutes before H-hour the general came in, shepherding the professor before him. The professor was comfortably attired in sneakers, gray flannels, a blue sweater, and a white shirt open at the neck. The two of them sat side by side on the love seat. The general was rigid and perspiring; the professor was cheerful. He looked at each of the screens, lighted a cigarette and settled back.

"Bombers sighted!" cried the Aleutian observers.

"Rockets away!" barked the New Mexico radio operator.

All of us looked quickly at the big electric clock over the mantel, while the professor, a half-smile on his face, continued to watch the television sets. In hollow tones, the general counted away the seconds remaining. "Five . . . four . . . three . . . two . . . one . . . *Concentrate!*"

Professor Barnhouse closed his eyes, pursed his lips, and stroked his temples. He held the position for a minute. The television images were scrambled, and the radio signals were drowned in the din of Barnhouse static. The professor sighed, opened his eyes, and smiled confidently.

"Did you give it everything you had?" asked the general dubiously.

"I was wide open," the professor replied.

The television images pulled themselves together, and mingled cries of amazement came over the radios tuned to the observers. The Aleutian sky was streaked with the smoke trails of bombers screaming down in flames. Simultaneously, there appeared high over the rocket target a cluster of white puffs, followed by faint thunder.

General Barker shook his head happily. "By George!" he crowed. "Well, sir, by George, by George, by George!"

"Look!" shouted the admiral seated next to me. "The fleet—it wasn't touched!"

"The guns seem to be drooping," said Mr. Cuthrell.

We left the bench and clustered about the television sets to examine the damage more closely. What Mr. Cuthrell had said was true. The ships' guns curved downward, their muzzles resting on the steel decks. We in Virginia were making such a hullabaloo that it was impossible to hear the radio reports. We were so engrossed, in fact, that we didn't miss the professor until two short snarls of Barnhouse static shocked us into sudden silence. The radios went dead.

We looked around apprehensively. The professor was gone. A harassed guard threw open the front door from the outside to yell that the professor had escaped. He brandished his pistol in the direction of the gates, which hung open, limp and twisted. In the distance, a speeding government station wagon topped a ridge and dropped from sight into the valley beyond. The air was filled with choking smoke, for every vehicle on the grounds was ablaze. Pursuit was impossible.

"What in God's name got into him?" bellowed the general.

Mr. Cuthrell, who had rushed out onto the front porch, now slouched back into the room, reading a penciled note as he came. He thrust the note into my hands. "The good man left this billet-doux under the door knocker. Perhaps our young friend will be kind enough to read it to you gentlemen, while I take a restful walk through the woods."

"Gentlemen," I read aloud, *"As the first superweapon with a conscience, I am removing myself from your national defense stockpile. Setting a new precedent in the behavior of ordnance, I have humane reasons for going off. A. Barnhouse."*

Since that day, of course, the professor has been systematically destroying the world's armaments, until there is now little with which to equip an army other than rocks and sharp sticks. His activities haven't exactly resulted in peace, but have, rather, precipitated a bloodless and entertaining sort of war that might be called the "War of the Tattletales." Every nation is flooded with enemy agents whose sole mission is to locate military equipment, which is promptly wrecked when it is brought to the professor's attention in the press.

Just as every day brings news of more armaments pulverized by dynamopsychism, so has it brought rumors of the professor's whereabouts. During last week alone, three publications carried articles proving variously that he was hiding in an Inca ruin in the Andes, in the sewers of Paris, and in the unexplored lower chambers of Carlsbad Caverns. Knowing the man, I am inclined to regard such hiding places as unnecessarily romantic and uncomfortable. While there are numerous persons eager to kill him, there must be millions who would care for him and hide him. I like to think that he is in the home of such a person.

One thing is certain: at this writing, Professor Barnhouse is not dead. Barnhouse static jammed broadcasts not ten minutes ago. In the eighteen months since his disappearance, he has been reported dead some half-dozen times. Each report has stemmed from the death of an unidentified man resembling the professor, during a period free of the static. The first three reports were followed at once by renewed talk of rearmament and recourse to war. The saber-rattlers have learned how imprudent premature celebrations of the professor's demise can be.

Many a stouthearted patriot has found himself prone in the tangled bunting and timbers of a smashed reviewing stand, seconds after having announced that the arch-tyranny of Barnhouse was at an end. But those who would make war if they could, in every country in the world, wait in sullen silence for what must come—the passing of Professor Barnhouse.

To ask how much longer the professor will live is to ask how much longer we must wait for the blessings of another world war. He is of short-lived stock: his mother lived to be fifty-three, his father to be forty-nine; and the life-spans of his grandparents on both sides were of the same order. He might be expected to live, then, for perhaps fifteen years more, if he can remain hidden from his enemies. When one considers the number and vigor of these enemies, however, fifteen years seems an extraordinary length of time, which might better be revised to fifteen days, hours, or minutes.

The professor knows that he cannot live much longer. I say this because of the message left in my mailbox on Christmas Eve. Unsigned, typewritten on a soiled scrap of paper, the note consisted of ten sentences. The first nine of these, each a bewildering tangle of psychological jargon and references to obscure texts, made no sense to me at first reading. The tenth, unlike the rest, was simply constructed and contained no large words—but its irrational content made it the most puzzling and bizarre sentence of all. I nearly threw the note away, thinking it a colleague's warped notion of a practical joke. For some reason, though, I added it to the clutter on top of my desk, which included, among other mementos, the professor's dice.

It took me several weeks to realize that the message really meant something, that the first nine sentences, when unsnarled, could be taken as instructions. The tenth still told me nothing. It was only last night that I discovered how it fitted in with the rest. The sentence appeared in my thoughts last night, while I was toying absently with the professor's dice.

I promised to have this report on its way to the publishers today. In view of what has happened, I am obliged to break that promise, or release the report incomplete. The delay will not be a long one, for one of the few blessings accorded a bachelor like myself is the ability to move quickly from one abode to another, or from one way of life to another. What property I want to take with me can be packed in a few hours. Fortunately, I am not without substantial private means, which may take as long as a week to realize in liquid and anonymous form. When this is done, I shall mail the report.

I have just returned from a visit to my doctor, who tells me my health is excellent. I am young, and, with any luck at all, I shall live to a ripe old age indeed, for my family on both sides is noted for longevity.

Briefly, I propose to vanish.

Sooner or later, Professor Barnhouse must die. But long before then I shall be ready. So, to the saber-rattlers of today—and even, I hope, of tomorrow—I say: Be advised. Barnhouse will die. But not the Barnhouse Effect.

Last night, I tried once more to follow the oblique instructions on the scrap of paper. I took the professor's dice, and then, with the last, nightmarish sentence flitting through my mind, I rolled fifty consecutive sevens.

Good-by.

1969

NORMAN MAILER
(1923–)

The publication of *The Naked and the Dead* (1948) brought Norman Mailer fame at twenty-five. It was widely acclaimed as the best novel to come out of World War II, its author seen by many as the finest young writer of his time. Mailer had been born in Long Branch, New Jersey, in 1923, and raised in Brooklyn, New York, graduating from Boys' High School in 1939. At Harvard he had concentrated in aeronautical engineering, graduating with honors in 1943. As an undergraduate he had also published three short stories in the *Harvard Advocate* and one of them had won the annual *Story* magazine prize in 1941. Two years in the army in the Pacific had given him the material for *The Naked and the Dead* and the G.I. Bill provided him with the means for study at the Sorbonne while he awaited its publication. He seemed eminently prepared for a major literary career.

For years he appeared to most critics to have failed in fulfilling his early promise. *Barbary Shore* (1951), *The Deer Park* (1955), *An American Dream* (1965), and *Why Are We in Vietnam?* (1967) all lacked the firm sense of a reality based on accurate and objective observation that contributed greatly to the success of *The Naked and the Dead.* The prose was looser, the characterization exaggerated and at times surrealistic, the vision subjective and apocalyptic. In the meantime, as these novels appeared, Mailer's energies seemed more and more concentrated in other directions. He was an editor of *Dissent* (publishing there the influential essay "The White Negro" in 1957) and co-founder of *The Village Voice.* He wrote columns for *Esquire,* was a participant in the 1967 march on the Pentagon, became a filmmaker, and ran for mayor of New York City.

From the beginning, however, Mailer has clearly taken himself with total seriousness as a writer. Like Hemingway, whom he resembles in other respects as well, he wants to rank not simply with the best of his contemporaries, but with the best writers of all times and places. Increasingly, he has seen his route to lie not within the bounds of the traditional realistic novel, but in the exploitation of a personality at odds with the current social and political absurdities. With other writers of the 1960's he became a practitioner of the "new journalism" that combined authorial involvement with the traditional role of objective reporter, and his success in this genre began to win back the critics. *The Armies of the Night: History as a Novel, The Novel as History* (1968), an autobiographical report of the Pentagon march, is one of the best of his books. With the publication of *Miami and the Siege of Chicago* (1969), *Of a Fire on the Moon* (1970), *The Prisoner of Sex* (1971), and *St. George and the Godfather* (1972) in the years immediately following, it appeared as though he had abandoned the novel, at least temporarily. In *The Executioner's Song* (1979), however, he demonstrated again his impressive command of novelistic techniques in a documentary account of the life of convicted murderer Gary Gilmore. With *Ancient Evenings* (1983), Mailer returned to straight fiction in a huge novel, set in ancient Egypt, that received a mixed response from reviewers. Taken together, these works clearly established the continuing importance of his voice.

A recent novel is *Tough Guys Don't Dance,* 1984. Mailer's other novels are named above. Non-fiction, in addition to titles above, includes *Advertisements for Myself,* 1959; *The Presidential Papers,* 1963; *Cannibals and Christians,* 1966; *The Bullfight,* 1967; *Existential Errands* (a selection from earlier works), 1972; *Maidstone: A Mystery,* 1971; *Marilyn,* 1973; *Genius and Lust: A Journey Through the Major Writings of Henry*

Miller, 1976; and *Pieces and Pontifications,* 1982. Verse is collected in *Deaths for the Ladies and Other Disasters,* 1962.

Biographical material may be found in Hilary Mills, *Mailer: A Biography,* 1982; and Peter Manso, *Mailer: His Life and Times,* 1985. Critical studies include Donald Kaufmann, *Norman Mailer: The Countdown (The First Twenty Years),* 1969; B. H. Leeds, *The Structured Vision of Norman Mailer,* 1969; Robert F. Lucid, ed., *Norman Mailer: The Man and His Work,* 1971; Richard Poirier, *Norman Mailer,* 1972; Jean Radford, *Norman Mailer: A Critical Study,* 1974; Robert Solotaroff, *Down Mailer's Way,* 1974; Laura Adams, *Existential Battles: The Growth of Norman Mailer,* 1975; Philip Bufithis, *Norman Mailer,* 1978; Robert J. Begiebing, *Acts of Regeneration: Allegory and Archetype in the Works of Norman Mailer,* 1980; Jennifer Bailey, *Norman Mailer: Quick-Change Artist,* 1980; and Andrew Gordon, *An American Dreamer: A Psychological Study of the Fiction of Norman Mailer,* 1980.

The Man Who Studied Yoga

1

I would introduce myself if it were not useless. The name I had last night will not be the same as the name I have tonight. For the moment, then, let me say that I am thinking of Sam Slovoda. Obligatorily, I study him, Sam Slovoda who is neither ordinary nor extraordinary, who is not young nor yet old, not tall nor short. He is sleeping, and it is fit to describe him now, for like most humans he prefers sleeping to not sleeping. He is a mild pleasant-looking man who has just turned forty. If the crown of his head reveals a little bald spot, he has nourished in compensation the vanity of a mustache. He has generally when he is awake an agreeable manner, at least with strangers; he appears friendly, tolerant, and genial. The fact is that like most of us, he is full of envy, full of spite, a gossip, a man who is pleased to find others are as unhappy as he, and yet—this is the worst to be said—he is a decent man. He is better than most. He would prefer to see a more equitable world, he scorns prejudice and privilege, he tries to hurt no one, he wishes to be liked. I will go even further. He has one serious virtue—he is not fond of himself, he wishes he were better. He would like to free himself of envy, of the annoying necessity to talk about his friends, he would like to love people more; specifically, he would like to love his wife more, and to love his two daughters without the tormenting if nonetheless irremediable vexation that they closet his life in the dusty web of domestic responsibilities and drudging for money.

How often he tells himself with contempt that he has the cruelty of a kind weak man.

May I state that I do not dislike Sam Slovoda; it is just that I am disappointed in him. He has tried too many things and never with a whole heart. He has wanted to be a serious novelist and now merely indulges the ambition; he wished to be of consequence in the world, and has ended, temporarily perhaps, as an overworked writer of continuity for comic magazines; when he was young he tried to be a bohemian and instead acquired a wife and family. Of his appetite for a variety of new experience I may say that it is matched only by his fear of new people and novel situations.

I will give an instance. Yesterday, Sam was walking along the street and a bum approached him for money. Sam did not see the man until too late; lost in some inconsequential thought, he looked up only in time to see a huge wretch of a fellow with a red twisted face and an outstretched hand. Sam is like so many; each time a derelict asks for a dime, he feels a coward if he pays the money, and is ashamed of himself if he doesn't. This once, Sam happened to think, I will not be bullied, and hurried past. But the bum was not to be lost so easily. "Have a heart, Jack," he called after in a whisky voice, "I need a drink bad." Sam stopped, Sam began to laugh. "Just so it isn't for coffee, here's a quarter," he said, and he laughed, and the bum laughed. "You're a man's man," the bum said. Sam went away pleased with himself, thinking about such things as the community which existed between all people. It was cheap of Sam. He should know better. He should know he was merely relieved the situation had turned out so well. Although he thinks he is sorry for bums, Sam really hates them. Who knows what violence they can offer?

At this time, there is a powerful interest in Sam's life, but many would ridicule it. He is in the process of being psychoanalyzed. Myself, I do not jeer. It has created the most unusual situation between Sam and me. I could go into details but they are perhaps premature. It would be better to watch Sam awaken.

His wife, Eleanor, has been up for an hour, and she has shut the window and neglected to turn off the radiator. The room is stifling. Sam groans in a stupor which is neither sleep nor refreshment, opens one eye, yawns, groans again, and lies twisted, strangled and trussed in pajamas which are too large for him. How painful it is for him to rise. Last night there was a party, and this morning, Sunday morning, he is awakening with a hangover. Invariably, he is depressed in the morning, and it is no different today. He finds himself in the flat and familiar dispirit of nearly all days.

It is snowing outside. Sam finally lurches to the window, and opens it for air. With the oxygen of a winter morning clearing his brain, he looks down six stories into the giant quadrangle of the Queens housing development in which he lives, staring morosely at the inch of slush which covers the monotonous artificial park that separates his apartment building from an identical structure not two hundred feet away. The walks are black where the snow has melted, and in the children's playground, all but deserted, one swing oscillates back and forth, pushed by an irritable little boy who plays by himself among the empty benches, swaddled in galoshes, muffler, and overcoat. The snow falls sluggishly, a wet snow which probably will turn to rain. The little boy in the playground gives one last disgusted shove to the swing and trudges away gloomily, his overshoes leaving a small animal track behind him. Back of Sam, in the four-room apartment he knows like a blind man, there is only the sound of Eleanor making breakfast.

Well, thinks Sam, depression in the morning is a stage of his analysis, Dr. Sergius has said.

This is the way Sam often phrases his thoughts. It is not altogether his fault. Most of the people he knows think that way and talk that way, and Sam is not the strongest of men. His language is doomed to the fashion of the moment. I have heard him remark mildly, almost apologetically, about his daughters: "My relation with them still suffers because I haven't worked through all my feminine identifications." The saddest thing is that the sentence has meaning to Sam even if it will not have meaning to you. A great many ruminations, discoveries, and memories contribute their connotation to Sam. It has the significance of a cherished line of poetry to him.

Although Eleanor is not being analyzed, she talks in a similar way. I have heard her remark in company, "Oh, you know Sam, he not only thinks I'm his mother, he blames me for being born." Like most women, Eleanor can be depended upon to employ the idiom of her husband.

What amuses me is that Sam is critical of the way others speak. At the party last night he was talking to a Hollywood writer, a young man with a great deal of energy and enthusiasm. The young man spoke something like this: "You see, boychick, I can spike any script with yaks, but the thing I can't do is heartbreak. My wife says she's gonna give me heartbreak. The trouble is I've had a real solid-type life. I mean I've had my ups and downs like all of humanity, but there's never been a shriek in my life. I don't know how to write shrieks."

On the trip home, Sam had said to Eleanor, "It was disgraceful. A writer should have some respect for language."

Eleanor answered with a burlesque of Sam's indignation. "Listen, I'm a real artist-type. Culture is for comic-strip writers."

Generally, I find Eleanor attractive. In the ten years they have been married she has grown plump, and her dark hair which once was long is now cropped in a mannish cut of the prevailing mode. But, this is quibbling. She still possesses her best quality, a healthy exuberance which glows in her dark eyes and beams in her smile. She has beautiful teeth. She seems aware of her body and pleased with it. Sam tells himself he would do well to realize how much he needs her. Since he has been in analysis he has come to discover that he remains with Eleanor for more essential reasons than mere responsibility. Even if there were no children, he would probably cleave to her.

Unhappily, it is more complicated than that. She is always—to use their phrase—competing with him. At those times when I do not like Eleanor, I am irritated by her lack of honesty. She is too sharp-tongued, and she does not often give Sam what he needs most, a steady flow of uncritical encouragement to counteract the harshness with which he views himself. Like so many who are articulate on the subject, Eleanor will tell you that she resents being a woman. As Sam is disappointed in life, so is Eleanor. She feels Sam has cheated her from a proper development of her potentialities and talent, even as Sam feels cheated. I call her dishonest because she is not so ready as Sam to put the blame on herself.

Sam, of course, can say all this himself. It is just that he experiences it in a somewhat different way. Like most men who have been married for ten years, Eleanor is not quite real to him. Last night at the party, there were perhaps half a dozen people whom he met for the first time, and he talked animatedly with them, sensing their reactions, feeling their responses, aware of the life in them, as they were aware of the life in him. Eleanor, however, exists in his nerves. She is a rather vague embodiment, he thinks of her as "she" most of the time, someone to conceal things from. Invariably, he feels uneasy with her. It is too bad. No matter how inevitable, I am always sorry when love melts into that pomade of affection, resentment, boredom and occasional compassion which is the best we may expect of a man and woman who have lived together a long time. So often, it is worse, so often no more than hatred.

They are eating breakfast now, and Eleanor is chatting about the party. She is pretending to be jealous about a young girl in a strapless evening gown, and indeed, she does not have to pretend altogether. Sam, with liquor inside him, had been leaning over the girl; obviously he had coveted her. Yet, this morning, when Eleanor begins to talk about her, Sam tries to be puzzled.

"Which girl was it now?" he asks a second time.

"Oh, you know, the hysteric," Eleanor says, "the one who was parading her bazooms in your face." Eleanor has ways of impressing certain notions upon Sam. "She's Charlie's new girl."

"I didn't know that," Sam mutters. "He didn't seem to be near her all evening."

Eleanor spreads marmalade over her toast and takes a bite with evident enjoyment. "Apparently, they're all involved. Charles was funny about it. He said he's come to the conclusion that the great affairs of history are between hysterical women and detached men."

"Charles hates women," Sam says smugly. "If you notice, almost everything he says about them is a discharge of aggression." Sam has the best of reasons for not liking Charles. It takes more than ordinary character for a middle-aged husband to approve of a friend who moves easily from woman to woman.

"At least Charles discharges his aggression," Eleanor remarks.

"He's almost a classic example of the Don Juan complex. You notice how masochistic his women are?"

"I know a man or two who's just as masochistic."

Sam sips his coffee. "What made you say the girl was an hysteric?"

Eleanor shrugs. "She's an actress. And I could see she was a tease."

"You can't jump to conclusions," Sam lectures. "I had the impression she was a compulsive. Don't forget you've got to distinguish between the outer defenses, and the more deeply rooted conflicts."

I must confess that this conversation bores me. As a sample it is representative of the way Sam and Eleanor talk to each other. In Sam's defense I can say nothing; he has always been too partial to jargon.

I am often struck by how eager we are to reveal all sorts of supposedly ugly secrets about ourselves. We can explain the hatred we feel for our parents, we are rather pleased with the perversions to which we are prone. We seem determinedly proud to be superior to ourselves. No motive is too terrible for our inspection. Let someone hint, however, that we have bad table manners and we fly into a rage. Sam will agree to anything you may say about him, provided it is sufficiently serious—he will be the first to agree he has fantasies of murdering his wife. But tell him that he is afraid of waiters, or imply to Eleanor that she is a nag, and they will be quite annoyed.

Sam has noticed this himself. There are times when he can hear the jargon in his voice, and it offends him. Yet, he seems powerless to change his habits.

An example: He is sitting in an armchair now, brooding upon his breakfast, while Eleanor does the dishes. The two daughters are not home; they have gone to visit their grandmother for the weekend. Sam had encouraged the visit. He had looked forward to the liberty Eleanor and himself would enjoy. For the past few weeks the children had seemed to make the most impossible demands upon his attention. Yet now they are gone and he misses them, he even misses their noise. Sam, however, cannot accept the notion that many people are dissatisfied with the present, and either dream of the past or anticipate the future. Sam must call this "ambivalence over possessions." Once he even felt obliged to ask his analyst, Dr. Sergius, if ambivalence over possessions did not characterize him almost perfectly, and Sergius whom I always picture with the flat precision of a coin's head—bald skull and horn-rimmed glasses—answered in his German accent, "But, my dear Mr. Slovoda, as I have told you, it would make me happiest if you did not include in your reading, these psychoanalytical text-works."

At such rebukes, Sam can only wince. It is so right, he tells himself, he is exactly the sort of ambitious fool who uses big words when small ones would do.

2

While Sam sits in the armchair, gray winter light is entering the windows, snow falls outside. He sits alone in a modern seat, staring at the gray, green, and beige décor of their living room. Eleanor was a painter before they were married, and she has arranged this room. It is very pleasant, but like many husbands, Sam resents it, resents the reproductions of modern painters upon the wall, the slender coffee table, a free-form poised like a spider on wire legs, its feet set onto a straw rug. In the corner, most odious of all, is the playmate of his children, a hippopotamus of a television-radio-and-phonograph cabinet with the blind monstrous snout of the video tube.

Eleanor has set the Sunday paper near his hand. Soon, Sam intends to go to work. For a year, he has been giving a day once or twice a month to a bit of thought and a little writing on a novel he hopes to begin sometime. Last night, he told himself he would work today. But he has little enthusiasm now. He is tired, he is too depressed. Writing for the comic strips seems to exhaust his imagination.

Sam reads the paper as if he were peeling an enormous banana. Flap after flap of newsprint is stripped away and cast upon the straw rug until only the Magazine Section is left. Sam glances through it with restless irritability. A biography of a political figure runs its flatulent prose into the giant crossword puzzle at the back. An account of a picturesque corner of the city becomes lost in statistics and exhortations on juvenile delinquency, finally to emerge with photographs about the new style of living which desert architecture provides. Sam looks at a wall of windows in rotogravure with a yucca tree framing the pool.

There is an article about a workingman. His wife and his family are described, his apartment, his salary and his budget. Sam reads a description of what the worker has every evening for dinner, and how he spends each night of the week. The essay makes its point; the typical American workingman must watch his pennies, but he is nonetheless secure and serene. He would not exchange his life for another.

Sam is indignant. A year ago he had written a similar article in an attempt to earn some extra money. Subtly, or so he thought, he had suggested that the average workingman was raddled with insecurity. Naturally, the article had been rejected.

Sam throws the Magazine Section away. Moments of such anger torment him frequently. Despite himself, Sam is enraged at editorial dishonesty, at the smooth strifeless world which such articles present. How angry he is—how angry and how helpless. "It is the actions of men and not their sentiments which make history," he thinks to himself, and smiles wryly. In his living room he would go out to tilt the windmills of a vast, powerful, and hypocritical society; in his week of work he labors in an editorial cubicle to create spaceships, violent death, women with golden tresses and wanton breasts, men who act with their fists and speak with patriotic slogans.

I know what Sam feels. As he sits in the armchair, the Sunday papers are strewn around him, carrying their war news, their murders, their parleys, their entertainments, mummery of a real world which no one can grasp. It is terribly frustrating. One does not know where to begin.

Today, Sam considers himself half a fool for having been a radical. There is no longer much consolation in the thought that the majority of men who succeed in a corrupt and acquisitive society are themselves obligatorily corrupt, and one's failure is therefore the price of one's idealism. Sam cannot recapture the pleasurable bitterness which resides in the notion that one has suffered for one's principles. Sergius is too hard on him for that.

They have done a lot of work on the subject. Sergius feels that Sam's concern with world affairs has always been spurious. For example, they have uncovered in analysis that Sam wrote his article about the worker in such a way as to make certain it would be refused. Sam, after all, hates editors; to have such a piece accepted would mean he is no better than they, that he is a mediocrity. So long as he fails he is not obliged to measure himself. Sam, therefore, is being unrealistic. He rejects the world with his intellect, and this enables him not to face the more direct realities of his present life.

Sam will argue with Sergius but it is very difficult. He will say, "Perhaps you sneer at radicals because it is more comfortable to ignore such ideas. Once you became interested it might introduce certain unpleasant changes in your life."

"Why," says Sergius, "do you feel it so necessary to assume that I am a bourgeois interested only in my comfort?"

"How can I discuss these things," says Sam, "if you insist that my opinions are the expression of neurotic needs, and your opinions are merely dispassionate medical advice?"

"You are so anxious to defeat me in an argument," Sergius will reply. "Would you admit it is painful to relinquish the sense of importance which intellectual discussion provides you?"

I believe Sergius has his effect. Sam often has thoughts these days which would have been repellent to him years ago. For instance, at the moment, Sam is thinking it might be better to live the life of a worker, a simple life, to be completely absorbed with such necessities as food and money. Then one could believe that to be happy it was necessary only to have more money, more goods, less worries. It would be nice, Sam thinks wistfully, to believe that the source of one's unhappiness comes not from oneself, but from the fault of the boss, or the world, or bad luck.

Sam has these casual daydreams frequently. He likes to think about other lives he might have led, and he envies the most astonishing variety of occupations. It is easy enough to see why he should wish for the life of an executive with the power and sense of command it may offer, but virtually from the same impulse Sam will wish himself a bohemian living in an unheated loft, his life a catch-as-catch-can from day to day. Once, after reading an article, Sam even wished himself a priest. For about ten minutes it seemed beautiful to him to surrender his life to God. Such fancies are common, I know. It is just that I, far better than Sam, know how serious he really is, how fanciful, how elaborate, his imagination can be.

The phone is ringing. Sam can hear Eleanor shouting at him to answer. He picks up the receiver with a start. It is Marvin Rossman who is an old friend, and Marvin has an unusual request. They talk for several minutes, and Sam squirms a little in his seat. As he is about to hang up, he laughs. "Why, no, Marvin, it gives me a sense of adventure," he says.

Eleanor has come into the room toward the end of this conversation. "What is it all about?" she asks.

Sam is obviously a bit agitated. Whenever he attempts to be most casual, Eleanor can well suspect him. "It seems," he says slowly, "that Marvin has acquired a pornographic movie."

"From whom?" Eleanor asks.

"He said something about an old boy friend of Louise's."

Eleanor laughs. "I can't imagine Louise having an old boy friend with a dirty movie."

"Well, people are full of surprises," Sam says mildly.

"Look here," says Eleanor suddenly. "Why did he call us?"

"It was about our projector."

"They want to use it?" Eleanor asks.

"That's right." Sam hesitates. "I invited them over."

"Did it ever occur to you I might want to spend my Sunday some other way?" Eleanor asks crossly.

"We're not doing anything," Sam mumbles. Like most men, he feels obliged to act quite nonchalantly about pornography. "I'll tell you, I am sort of curious about the film. I've never seen one, you know."

"Try anything once, is that it?"

"Something of the sort." Sam is trying to conceal his excitement. The truth is that in common with most of us, he is fascinated by pornography. It is a minor preoccupation, but more from lack of opportunity than anything else. Once or twice, Sam has bought the sets of nude photographs which are sold in marginal bookstores, and with guilty excitement has hidden them in the apartment.

"Oh, this is silly," Eleanor says. "You were going to work today."

"I'm just not in the mood."

"I'll have to feed them," Eleanor complains. "Do we have enough liquor?"

"We can get beer." Sam pauses. "Alan Sperber and his wife are coming too."

"Sam, you're a child."

"Look, Eleanor," says Sam, controlling his voice, "if it's too much trouble, I can take the projector over there."

"I ought to make you do that."

"Am I such an idiot that I must consult you before I invite friends to the house?"

Eleanor has the intuition that Sam, if he allowed himself, could well drown in pornography. She is quite annoyed at him, but she would never dream of allowing Sam to take the projector over to Marvin Rossman's where he could view the movie without her—that seems indefinably dangerous. Besides she would like to see it, too. The mother in Eleanor is certain it cannot hurt her.

"All right, Sam," she says, "but you are a child."

More exactly, an adolescent, Sam decides. Ever since Marvin phoned, Sam has felt the nervous glee of an adolescent locking himself in the bathroom. Anal fixation, Sam thinks automatically.

While Eleanor goes down to buy beer and cold cuts in a delicatessen, Sam gets out the projector and begins to clean it. He is far from methodical in this. He knows the machine is all right, he has shown movies of Eleanor and his daughters only a few weeks ago, but from the moment Eleanor left the apartment, Sam has been consumed by an anxiety that the projection bulb is burned out. Once he has examined it, he begins to fret about the motor. He wonders if it needs oiling, he blunders through a drawer of household tools looking for an oilcan. It is ridiculous. Sam knows that what he is trying to keep out of his mind are the reactions Sergius will have. Sergius will want to "work through" all of Sam's reasons for seeing the movie. Well, Sam tells himself, he knows in advance what will be discovered:

detachment, not wanting to accept Eleanor as a sexual partner, evasion of responsibility, etc. etc. The devil with Sergius. Sam has never seen a dirty movie, and he certainly wants to.

He feels obliged to laugh at himself. He could not be more nervous, he knows, if he were about to make love to a woman he had never touched before. It is really disgraceful.

When Eleanor comes back, Sam hovers about her. He is uncomfortable with her silence. "I suppose they'll be here soon," Sam says.

"Probably."

Sam does not know if he is angry at Eleanor or apprehensive that she is angry at him. Much to his surprise he catches her by the waist and hears himself saying, "You know, maybe tonight when they're gone . . . I mean, we do have the apartment to ourselves." Eleanor moves neither toward him nor away from him. "Darling, it's not because of the movie," Sam goes on, "I swear. Don't you think maybe we could . . ."

"Maybe," says Eleanor.

3

The company has arrived, and it may be well to say a word or two about them. Marvin Rossman who has brought the film is a dentist, although it might be more accurate to describe him as a frustrated doctor. Rossman is full of statistics and items of odd information about the malpractice of physicians, and he will tell these things in his habitually gloomy voice, a voice so slow, so sad, that it almost conceals the humor of his remarks. Or, perhaps, that is what creates his humor. In his spare time, he is a sculptor, and if Eleanor may be trusted, he is not without talent. I often picture him working in the studio loft he has rented, his tall bony frame the image of dejection. He will pat a piece of clay to the armature, he will rub it sadly with his thumb, he will shrug, he does not believe that anything of merit could come from him. When he talked to Sam over the phone, he was pessimistic about the film they were to see. "It can't be any good," he said in his melancholy voice. "I know it'll be a disappointment." Like Sam, he has a mustache, but Rossman's will droop at the corners.

Alan Sperber who has come with Rossman is the subject of some curiosity for the Slovodas. He is not precisely womanish; in fact, he is a large plump man, but his voice is too soft, his manners too precise. He is genial, yet he is finicky; waspish, yet bland; he is fond of telling long rather affected stories, he is always prepared with a new one, but to general conversation he contributes little. As a lawyer, he seems miscast. One cannot imagine him inspiring a client to confidence. He is the sort of heavy florid man who seems boyish at forty, and the bow ties and gray flannel suits he wears do not make him appear more mature.

Roslyn Sperber, his wife, used to be a schoolteacher, and she is a quiet nervous woman who talks a great deal when she is drunk. She is normally quite pleasant, and has only one habit which is annoying to any degree. It is a little flaw, but social life is not unlike marriage in that habit determines far more than vice or virtue. This mannerism which has become so offensive to the friends of the Sperbers is Roslyn's social pretension. Perhaps I should say intellectual pretension. She entertains people as if she were conducting a salon, and in her birdlike voice is forever forcing her guests to accept still another intellectual canapé. "You must hear Sam's view of the world market," she will say, or "Has Louise told you her statistics on divorce?" It is quite pathetic for she is so eager to please. I have seen her eyes fill with tears at a sharp word from Alan.

Marvin Rossman's wife, Louise, is a touch grim and definite in her opinions. She is a social welfare worker, and will declare herself with force whenever conversation impinges on those matters where she is expert. She is quite opposed to psychoanalysis, and will say without quarter, "It's all very well for people in the upper-middle area"—she is referring to the upper middle class—"but, it takes more than a couch to solve the problems of . . ." and she will list narcotics, juvenile delinquency, psychosis, relief distribution, slum housing, and other descriptions of our period. She recites these categories with an odd anticipation. One would guess she was ordering a meal.

Sam is fond of Marvin but he cannot abide Louise. "You'd think she discovered poverty," he will complain to Eleanor.

The Slovodas do feel superior to the Rossmans and the Sperbers. If pressed, they could not offer the most convincing explanation why. I suppose what it comes down to is that Sam and Eleanor do not think of themselves as really belonging to a class, and they feel that the Sperbers and Rossmans are petit-bourgeois. I find it hard to explain their attitude. Their company feels as much discomfort and will apologize as often as the Slovodas for the money they have, and the money they hope to earn. They are all of them equally concerned with progressive education and the methods of raising children to be well adjusted—indeed, they are discussing that now—they consider themselves relatively free of sexual taboo, or put more properly, Sam and Eleanor are no less possessive than the others. The Slovodas' culture is not more profound; I should be hard put to say that Sam is more widely read, more seriously informed, than Marvin or Alan, or for that matter, Louise. Probably, it comes to this: Sam, in his heart, thinks himself a rebel, and there are few rebels who do not claim an original mind. Eleanor has been a bohemian and considers herself more sophisticated than her friends who merely went to college and got married. Louise Rossman could express it most soundly. "Artists, writers, and people of the creative layer have in their occupational ideology the belief that they are classless."

One thing I might remark about the company. They are all being the most unconscionable hypocrites. They have rushed across half the city of New York to see a pornographic film, and they are not at all interested in each other at the moment. The women are giggling like tickled children at remarks which cannot possibly be so funny. Yet, they are all determined to talk for a respectable period of time. No less, it must be serious talk. Roslyn has said once, "I feel so funny at the thought of seeing such a movie," and the others have passed her statement by.

At the moment, Sam is talking about value. I might note that Sam loves conversation and thrives when he can expound an idea.

"What are our values today?" he asks. "It's really fantastic when you stop to think of it. Take any bright talented kid who's getting out of college now."

"My kid brother, for example," Marvin interposes morosely. He passes his bony hand over his sad mustache, and somehow the remark has become amusing, much as if Marvin had said, "Oh, yes, you have reminded me of the trials, the worries, and the cares which my fabulous younger brother heaps upon me."

"All right, take him," Sam says. "What does he want to be?"

"He doesn't want to be anything," says Marvin.

"That's my point," Sam says excitedly. "Rather than work at certain occupations, the best of these kids would rather do nothing at all."

"Alan has a cousin," Roslyn says, "who swears he'll wash dishes before he becomes a businessman."

"I wish that were true," Eleanor interrupts. "It seems to me everybody is conforming more and more these days."

They argue about this. Sam and Eleanor claim the country is suffering from hysteria; Alan Sperber disagrees and says it's merely a reflection of the headlines; Louise says no adequate criteria exist to measure hysteria; Marvin says he doesn't know anything at all.

"More solid liberal gains are being made in this period," says Alan, "than you would believe. Consider the Negro—"

"Is the Negro any less maladjusted?" Eleanor shouts with passion.

Sam maneuvers the conversation back to his thesis. "The values of the young today, and by the young, I mean the cream of the kids, the ones with ideas, are a reaction of indifference to the culture crisis. It really is despair. All they know is what they don't want to do."

"That is easier," Alan says genially.

"It's not altogether unhealthy," Sam says. "It's a corrective for smugness and the false value of the past, but it has created new false value." He thinks it worth emphasizing. "False value seems always to beget further false value."

"Define your terms," says Louise, the scientist.

"No, look," Sam says, "there's no revolt, there's no acceptance. Kids today don't want to get married, and—"

Eleanor interrupts. "Why should a girl rush to get married? She loses all chance for developing herself."

Sam shrugs. They are all talking at once. "Kids don't want to get married," he repeats, "and they don't want not to get married. They merely drift."

"It's a problem we'll all have to face with our own kids in ten years," Alan says, "although I think you make too much of it, Sam."

"My daughter," Marvin states. "She's embarrassed I'm a dentist. Even more embarrassed than I am." They laugh.

Sam tells a story about his youngest, Carol Ann. It seems he had a fight with her, and she went to her room. Sam followed, he called through the door.

"No answer," Sam says. "I called her again, 'Carol Ann.' I was a little worried you understand, because she seemed so upset, so I said to her, 'Carol-Ann, you know I love you.' What do you think she answered?"

"What?" asks Roslyn.

"She said, 'Daddie, why are you so anxious?' "

They all laugh again. There are murmurs about what a clever thing it was to say. In the silence which follows, Roslyn leans forward and says quickly in her high voice, "You must get Alan to tell you his wonderful story about the man who studied yogi."

"Yoga," Alan corrects. "It's too long to tell."

The company prevails on him.

"Well," says Alan, in his genial courtroom voice, "it concerns a friend of mine named Cassius O'Shaugnessy."

"You don't mean Jerry O'Shaugnessy, do you?" asks Sam.

Alan does not know Jerry O'Shaugnessy. "No, no, this is Cassius O'Shaugnessy," he says. "He's really quite an extraordinary fellow." Alan sits plumply in his chair, fingering his bow tie. They are all used to his stories, which are told in a formal style and exhibit the attempt to recapture a certain note of urbanity, wit, and *élan* which Alan has probably copied from someone else. Sam and Eleanor respect his ability to tell these stories, but they resent the fact that he talks *at* them.

"You'd think we were a jury of his inferiors," Eleanor has said. "I hate being talked down to." What she resents is Alan's quiet implication that his antecedents, his social position, in total his life outside the room is superior to the life within. Eleanor now takes the promise from Alan's story by remarking, "Yes, and let's see the movie when Alan has finished."

"Sssh," Roslyn says.

"Cassius was at college a good while before me," says Alan, "but I knew him while I was an undergraduate. He would drop in and visit from time to time. An absolutely extraordinary fellow. The most amazing career. You see, he's done about everything."

"I love the way Alan tells it," Roslyn pipes nervously.

"Cassius was in France with Dos Passos and Cummings,[1] he was even arrested with e.e. After the war, he was one of the founders of the Dadaist school,[2] and for a while I understand he was Fitzgerald's[3] guide to the gold of the Côte D'Azur. He knew everybody, he did everything. Do you realize that before the twenties had ended, Cassius had managed his father's business and then entered a monastery? It is said he influenced T. S. Eliot."

"Today, we'd call Cassius a psychopath," Marvin observes.

"Cassius called himself a great dilettante," Alan answers, "although perhaps the nineteenth-century Russian conception of the great sinner would be more appropriate? What do you say if I tell you this was only the beginning of his career?"

"What's the point?" Louise asks.

"Not yet," says Alan, holding up a hand. His manner seems to say that if his audience cannot appreciate the story, he does not feel obliged to continue. "Cassius studied Marx in the monastery. He broke his vows, quit the Church, and became a Communist. All through the thirties he was a figure in the Party, going to Moscow, involved in all the Party struggles. He left only during the Moscow trials."

Alan's manner while he relates such stories is somewhat effeminate. He talks with little caresses of his hand, he mentions names and places with a lingering ease as if to suggest that his audience and he are aware, above all, of nuance. The story as Alan tells it is drawn overlong. Suffice it that the man about whom he is talking, Cassius O'Shaughnessy, becomes a Trotskyist, becomes an anarchist, is a pacifist during the second World War, and suffers it from a prison cell.

"I may say," Alan goes on, "that I worked for his defense, and was successful in getting him acquitted. Imagine my dolor when I learned that he had turned his back on his anarchist friends and was living with gangsters."

"This is weird," Eleanor says.

"Weird, it is," Alan agrees. "Cassius got into some scrape, and disappeared. What

1. John Dos Passos (1896–1970) and E. E. Cummings (1894–1963), American writers, both drove ambulances in World War I. Cummings's *The Enormous Room* (1922) describes his experiences in a French detention camp.
2. A nihilist artistic movement from 1916 to 1924.
3. F. Scott Fitzgerald (1896–1940), American short story writer and novelist.

could you do with him? I learned only recently that he had gone to India and was studying yoga. In fact, I learned it from Cassius himself. I asked him of his experiences at Brahnaputh-thar, and he told me the following story."

Now Alan's voice alters, he assumes the part of Cassius and speaks in a tone weary of experience, wise and sad in its knowledge. " 'I was sitting on my haunches contemplating my navel,' Cassius said to me, 'when of a sudden I discovered my navel under a different aspect. It seemed to me that if I were to give a counterclockwise twist, my navel would unscrew.' "

Alan looks up, he surveys his audience which is now rapt and uneasy, not certain as yet whether a joke is to come. Alan's thumb and forefinger pluck at the middle of his ample belly, his feet are crossed upon the carpet in symbolic suggestion of Cassius upon his haunches.

" 'Taking a deep breath, I turned, and the abysses of Vishtarni loomed beneath. My navel had begun to unscrew. I knew I was about to accept the reward of three years of contemplation. So,' said Cassius, 'I turned again, and my navel unscrewed a little more. I turned and I turned,' " Alan's fingers now revolving upon his belly, " 'and after a period I knew that with one more turn my navel would unscrew itself forever. At the edge of revelation, I took one sweet breath, and turned my navel free.' "

Alan looks up at his audience.

" 'Damn,' said Cassius, 'if my ass didn't fall off.' "

4

The story has left the audience in an exasperated mood. It has been a most untypical story for Alan to tell, a little out of place, not offensive exactly, but irritating and inconsequential. Sam is the only one to laugh with more than bewildered courtesy, and his mirth seems excessive to everyone but Alan, and of course, Roslyn, who feels as if she has been the producer. I suppose what it reduces to, is a lack of taste. Perhaps that is why Alan is not the lawyer one would expect. He does not have that appreciation—as necessary in his trade as for an actor—of what is desired at any moment, of that which will encourage as opposed to that which does not encourage a stimulating but smooth progression of logic and sentiment. Only a fool would tell so long a story when everyone is awaiting the movie.

Now, they are preparing. The men shift armchairs to correspond with the couch, the projector is set up, the screen is unfolded. Sam attempts to talk while he is threading the film, but no one listens. They seem to realize suddenly that a frightful demand has been placed upon them. One does not study pornography in a living room with a beer glass in one's hand, and friends at the elbow. It is the most unsatisfactory of compromises; one can draw neither the benefits of solitary contemplation nor of social exchange. There is, at bottom, the same exasperated fright which one experiences in turning the shower tap and receiving cold water when the flesh has been prepared for heat. Perhaps that is why they are laughing so much now that the movie is begun.

A title, *The Evil Act,* twitches on the screen, shot with scars, holes, and the dust lines of age. A man and woman are sitting on a couch, they are having coffee. They chat. What they say is conveyed by printed words upon an ornately flowered card, interjected between glimpses of their casual gestures, a cup to the mouth, a smile, a cigarette being lit. The man's name, it seems, is Frankie Idell; he is talking to his wife, Magnolia. Frankie is dark, he is sinister, he confides in Magnolia, his dark counterpart, with a grimace of his brows, black from make-up pencil.

This is what the titles read:

FRANKIE: She will be here soon.
MAGNOLIA: This time the little vixen will not escape.
FRANKIE: No, my dear, this time we are prepared.
(He looks at his watch.)
FRANKIE: Listen, she knocks!

There is a shot of a tall blond woman knocking on the door. She is probably over thirty, but by her short dress and ribboned hat it is suggested that she is a girl of fifteen.

FRANKIE: Come in, Eleanor.

As may be expected, the audience laughs hysterically at this. It is so wonderful a coincidence. "How I remember Frankie," says Eleanor Slovoda, and Roslyn Sperber is the only one not amused. In the midst of the others' laughter, she says in a worried tone, obviously adrift upon her own concerns, "Do you think we'll have to stop the film in the middle to let the bulb cool off?" The others hoot, they giggle, they are weak from the combination of their own remarks and the action of the plot.

Frankie and Magnolia have sat down on either side of the heroine, Eleanor. A moment passes. Suddenly, stiffly, they attack. Magnolia from her side kisses Eleanor, and Frankie commits an indecent caress.

ELEANOR: How dare you? Stop!
MAGNOLIA: Scream, my little one. It will do you no good. The walls are soundproofed.
FRANKIE: We've fixed a way to make you come across.
ELEANOR: This is hideous. I am hitherto undefiled. Do not touch me!

The captions fade away. A new title takes their place. It says, *But There Is No Escape From The Determined Pair.* On the fade-in, we discover Eleanor in the most distressing situation. Her hands are tied to loops running from the ceiling, and she can only writhe in helpless perturbation before the deliberate and progressive advances of Frankie and Magnolia. Slowly they humiliate her, with relish they probe her.

The audience laughs no longer. A hush has come upon them. Eyes unblinking they devour the images upon Sam Slovoda's screen.

Eleanor is without clothing. As the last piece is pulled away, Frankie and Magnolia circle about her in a grotesque of pantomime, a leering of lips, limbs in a distortion of desire. Eleanor faints. Adroitly, Magnolia cuts her bonds. We see Frankie carrying her inert body.

Now, Eleanor is trussed to a bed, and the husband and wife are tormenting her with feathers. Bodies curl upon the bed in postures so complicated, in combinations so advanced, that the audience leans forward, Sperbers, Rossmans, and Slovodas, as if tempted to embrace the moving images. The hands trace abstract circles upon the screen, passes and recoveries upon a white background so illumined that hollows and swells, limb to belly and mouth to undescribables, tip of a nipple, orb of a navel, swim in giant magnification, flow and slide in a lurching yawing fall, blotting out the camera eye.

A little murmur, all unconscious, passes from their lips. The audience sways, each now finally lost in himself, communing hungrily with shadows, violated or violating, fantasy triumphant.

At picture's end, Eleanor the virgin whore is released from the bed. She kisses Frankie, she kisses Magnolia. "You dears," she says, "let's do it again." The projector lamp burns empty light, the machine keeps turning, the tag of film goes *slap-tap, slap-tap, slap-tap, slap-tap, slap-tap, slap-tap.*

"Sam, turn it off," says Eleanor.

But when the room lights are on, they cannot look at one another. "Can we see it again?" someone mutters. So, again, Eleanor knocks on the door, is tied, defiled, ravished, and made rapturous. They watch it soberly now, the room hot with the heat of their bodies, the darkness a balm for orgiastic vision. To the Deer Park, Sam is thinking, to the Deer Park of Louis XV were brought the most beautiful maidens of France, and there they stayed, dressed in fabulous silks, perfumed and wigged, the mole drawn upon their cheek, ladies of pleasure awaiting the pleasure of the king. So Louis had stripped an empire, bankrupt a treasury, prepared a deluge, while in his garden on summer evenings the maidens performed their pageants, eighteenth-century tableau of the evil act, beauteous instruments of one man's desire, lewd translation of a king's power. That century men sought wealth so they might use its fruits; this epoch men lusted for power in order to amass more power, a compounding of power into pyramids of abstraction whose yield are cannon and wire enclosure, pillars of statistics to the men who are the kings of this century and do no more in power's leisure time than go to church, claim to love their wives, and eat vegetables.

Is it possible, Sam wonders, that each of them here, two Rossmans, two Sperbers, two Slovodas, will cast off their clothes when the movie is done and perform the orgy which tickles at the heart of their desire? They will not, he knows, they will make jokes when the projector is put away, they will gorge the plate of delicatessen Eleanor provides, and swallow more beer, he among them. He will be the first to make jokes.

Sam is right. The movie has made him extraordinarily alive to the limits of them all. While they sit with red faces, eyes bugged, glutting sandwiches of ham, salami, and tongue, he begins the teasing.

"Roslyn," he calls out, "is the bulb cooled off yet?"

She cannot answer him. She chokes on beer, her face glazes, she is helpless with self-protecting laughter.

"Why are you so anxious, Daddie?" Eleanor says quickly.

They begin to discuss the film. As intelligent people they must dominate it. Someone wonders about the actors in the piece, and discussion begins afresh. "I fail to see," says Louise, "why they should be hard to classify. Pornography is a job to the criminal and prostitute element."

"No, you won't find an ordinary prostitute doing this," Sam insists. "It requires a particular kind of personality."

"They have to be exhibitionists," says Eleanor.

"It's all economic," Louise maintains.

"I wonder what those girls felt?" Roslyn asks. "I feel sorry for them."

"I'd like to be the cameraman," says Alan.

"I'd like to be Frankie," says Marvin sadly.

There is a limit to how long such a conversation may continue. The jokes lapse into silence. They are all busy eating. When they begin to talk again, it is of other things. Each dollop of food sops the agitation which the movie has spilled. They gossip about the party the night before, they discuss which single men were interested in which women, who got drunk, who got sick, who said the wrong thing, who went home with someone else's date. When this is exhausted, one of them mentions a play the others have not seen. Soon they are talking about books, a concert, a one-man show by an artist who is a friend. Dependably, conversation will voyage its orbit. While the men talk of politics, the women are discussing fashions, progressive schools, and recipes they have attempted. Sam is uncomfortable with the division; he knows Eleanor will resent it, he knows she will complain later of the insularity of men and the basic contempt they feel for women's intelligence.

"But you collaborated," Sam will argue. "No one forced you to be with the women."

"Was I to leave them alone?" Eleanor will answer.

"Well, why do the women always have to go off by themselves?"

"Because the men aren't interested in what we have to say."

Sam sighs. He has been talking with interest, but really he is bored. These are nice pleasant people, he thinks, but they are ordinary people, exactly the sort he has spent so many years with, making little jokes, little gossip, living little everyday events, a close circle where everyone mothers the other by his presence. The womb of middle-class life, Sam decides heavily. He is in a bad mood indeed. Everything is laden with dissatisfaction.

Alan has joined the women. He delights in preparing odd dishes when friends visit the Sperbers, and he is describing to Eleanor how he makes blueberry pancakes. Marvin draws closer to Sam.

"I wanted to tell you," he says, "Alan's story reminded me. I saw Jerry O'Shaugnessy the other day."

"Where was he?"

Marvin is hesitant. "It was a shock, Sam. He's on the Bowery. I guess he's become a wino."

"He always drank a lot," says Sam.

"Yeah." Marvin cracks his bony knuckles. "What a stinking time this is, Sam."

"It's probably like the years after 1905 in Russia," Sam says.

"No revolutionary party will come out of this."

"No," Sam says, "nothing will come."

He is thinking of Jerry O'Shaugnessy. What did he look like? what did he say? Sam asks Marvin, and clucks his tongue at the dispiriting answer. It is a shock to him. He draws closer to Marvin, he feels a bond. They have, after all, been through some years together. In the thirties they have been in the Communist Party, they have quit together, they are both weary of politics today, still radicals out of habit, but without enthusiasm and without a cause. "Jerry was a hero to me," Sam says.

"To all of us," says Marvin.

The fabulous Jerry O'Shaugnessy, thinks Sam. In the old days, in the Party, they had made a legend of him. All of them with their middle-class origins and their desire to know a worker-hero.

I may say that I was never as fond of Jerry O'Shaugnessy as was Sam. I thought him a showman and too pleased with himself. Sam, however, with his timidity, his desire to travel, to have adventure and know many women, was obliged to adore O'Shaugnessy. At least he was enraptured with his career.

Poor Jerry who ends as a bum. He has been everything else. He has been a trapper in Alaska, a chauffeur for gangsters, an officer in the Foreign Legion, a labor organizer. His nose was broken, there were scars on his chin. When he would talk about his years at sea or his experiences in Spain, the stenographers and garment workers, the radio writers and unemployed actors would listen to his speeches as if he were the prophet of new romance, and their blood would be charged with the magic of revolutionary vision. A man with tremendous charm. In those days it had been easy to confuse his love for himself with his love for all underprivileged workingmen.

"I thought he was still in the Party," Sam says.

"No," says Marvin, "I remember they kicked him out a couple of years ago. He was supposed to have piddled some funds, that's what they say."

"I wish he'd taken the treasury," Sam remarks bitterly. "The Party used him for years."

Marvin shrugs. "They used each other." His mustache droops. "Let me tell you about Sonderson. You know he's still in the Party. The most progressive dentist in New York." They laugh.

While Marvin tells the story, Sam is thinking of other things. Since he has quit Party work, he has studied a great deal. He can tell you about prison camps and the secret police, political murders, the Moscow trials, the exploitation of Soviet labor, the privileges of the bureaucracy; it is all painful to him. He is straddled between the loss of a country he has never seen, and his repudiation of the country in which he lives. "Doesn't the Party seem a horror now?" he bursts out.

Marvin nods. They are trying to comprehend the distance between Party members they have known, people by turn pathetic, likable, or annoying—people not unlike themselves—and in contrast the immensity of historic logic which deploys along statistics of the dead.

"It's all schizoid," Sam says. "Modern life is schizoid."

Marvin agrees. They have agreed on this many times, bored with the petulance of their small voices, yet needing the comfort of such complaints. Marvin asks Sam if he has given up his novel, and Sam says, "Temporarily." He cannot find a form, he explains. He does not want to write a realistic novel, because reality is no longer realistic. "I don't know what it is," says Sam. "To tell you the truth, I think I'm kidding myself. I'll never finish this book. I just like to entertain the idea I'll do something good some day." They sit there in friendly depression. Conversation has cooled. Alan and the women are no longer talking.

"Marvin," asks Louise, "what time is it?"

They are ready to go. Sam must say directly what he had hoped to approach by suggestion. "I was wondering," he whispers to Rossman, "would you mind if I held onto the film for a day or two?"

Marvin looks at him. "Oh, why of course, Sam," he says in his morose voice. "I know how it is." He pats Sam on the shoulder as if, symbolically, to convey the exchange of ownership. They are fellow conspirators.

"If you ever want to borrow the projector," Sam suggests.

"Nah," says Marvin, "I don't know that it would make much difference."

5

It has been, when all is said, a most annoying day. As Sam and Eleanor tidy the apartment, emptying ash trays and washing the few dishes, they are fond neither of themselves nor each other. "What a waste today has been," Eleanor remarks, and Sam can only agree. He has done no writing, he has not been outdoors, and still it is late in the evening, and he has talked too much, eaten too much, is nervous from the movie they have seen. He knows that he will watch it again with Eleanor before they go to sleep; she has given her assent to that. But as is so often the case with Sam these days, he cannot await their embrace with any sure anticipation. Eleanor may be in the mood or Eleanor may not; there is no way he can control the issue. It is depressing; Sam knows that he circles about Eleanor at such times with the guilty maneuvers of a sad hound. Resent her as he must, be furious with himself as he will, there is not very much he can do about it. Often, after they have made love, they will lie beside each other in silence, each offended, each certain the other is to blame. At such times, memory tickles them with a cruel feather. Not always has it been like this. When they were first married, and indeed for the six months they lived together before marriage, everything was quite different. Their affair was very exciting to them; each told the other with some hyperbole but no real mistruth that no one in the past had ever been comparable as lover.

I suppose I am a romantic. I always feel that this is the best time in people's lives. There is, after all, so little we accomplish, and that short period when we are beloved and triumph as lovers is sweet with power. Rarely are we concerned then with our lack of importance; we are too important. In Sam's case, disillusion means even more. Like so many young men, he entertained the secret conceit that he was an extraordinary lover. One cannot really believe this without supporting at the same time the equally secret conviction that one is fundamentally inept. It is—no matter what Sergius would say—a more dramatic and therefore more attractive view of oneself than the sober notion which Sam now accepts with grudging wisdom, that the man as lover is dependent upon the bounty of the woman. As I say, he accepts the notion, it is one of the lineaments of maturity, but there is a part of him which, no matter how harried by analysis, cannot relinquish the antagonism he feels that Eleanor has respected his private talent so poorly, and has not allowed him to confer its benefits upon more women. I mock Sam, but he would mock himself on this. It hardly matters; mockery cannot accomplish everything, and Sam seethes with that most private and tender pain: even worse than being unattractive to the world is to be unattractive to one's mate; or, what is the same and describes Sam's case more accurately, never to know in advance when he shall be undesirable to Eleanor.

I make perhaps too much of the subject, but that is only because it is so important to Sam. Relations between Eleanor and him are not really that bad—I know other couples who have much less or nothing at all. But comparisons are poor comfort to Sam; his standards are so high. So are Eleanor's. I am convinced the most unfortunate people are those who would make an art of love. It sours other effort. Of all artists, they are certainly the most wretched.

Shall I furnish a model? Sam and Eleanor are on the couch and the projector, adjusted to its slowest speed, is retracing the elaborate pantomime of the three principals. If one could allow these shadows a life . . . but indeed such life has been given them. Sam and Eleanor are no more than an itch, a smart, a threshold of satisfaction; the important share of themselves has steeped itself in Frankie-, Magnolia-, and Eleanor-of-the-film. Indeed the variations are beyond telling. It is the most outrageous orgy performed by five ghosts.

Self-critical Sam! He makes love in front of a movie, and one cannot say that it is unsatisfactory any more than one can say it is pleasant. It is dirty, downright porno dirty, it is a lewd slop-brush slapped through the middle of domestic exasperations and breakfast eggs. It is so dirty that only half of Sam—he is quite divisible into fractions—can be exercised at all. The part that is his brain worries along like a cuckolded burgher. He is taking the pulse of his anxiety. Will he last long enough to satisfy Eleanor? Will the children come back tonight? He cannot help it. In the midst of the circus, he is suddenly convinced the children will walk through the door. "Why are you so anxious, Daddie?"

So it goes. Sam the lover is conscious of exertion. One moment he is Frankie Idell, destroyer of virgins—take that! you whore!—the next, body moving, hands caressing, he is no more than some lines from a psychoanalytical text. He is thinking about the sensitivity of his scrotum. He has read that this is a portent of femininity in a male. How strong is his latent homosexuality worries Sam, thrusting stiffly, warm sweat running cold. Does he identify with Eleanor-of-the-film?

Technically, the climax is satisfactory. They lie together in the dark, the film ended, the projector humming its lonely revolutions in the quiet room. Sam gets up to turn it off; he comes back and kisses Eleanor upon the mouth. Apparently, she has enjoyed herself more than he; she is tender and fondles the tip of his nose.

"You know, Sam," she says from her space beside him, "I think I saw this picture before."

"When?"

"Oh, you know when. That time."

Sam thinks dully that women are always most loving when they can reminisce about infidelity.

"That time!" he repeats.

"I think so."

Racing forward from memory like the approaching star which begins as a point on the mind and swells to explode the eyeball with its odious image, Sam remembers, and is weak in the dark. It is ten years, eleven perhaps, before they were married, yet after they were lovers. Eleanor has told him, but she has always been vague about details. There had been two men it seemed, and another girl, and all had been drunk. They had seen movie after movie. With reluctant fascination, Sam can conceive the rest. How it had pained him, how excited him. It is years now since he has remembered, but he remembers. In the darkness he wonders at the unreasonableness of jealous pain. That night was impossible to imagine any longer—therefore it is more real; Eleanor his plump wife who presses a pigeon's shape against her housecoat, forgotten heroine of black orgies. It had been meaningless, Eleanor claimed; it was Sam she loved, and the other had been no more than a fancy of which she wished to rid herself. Would it be the same today, thinks Sam, or had Eleanor been loved by Frankie, by Frankie of the other movies, by Frankie of the two men she never saw again on that night so long ago?

The pleasure I get from this pain, Sam thinks furiously.

It is not altogether perverse. If Eleanor causes him pain, it means after all that she is alive for him. I have often observed that the reality of a person depends upon his ability to hurt us; Eleanor as the vague accusing embodiment of the wife is different, altogether different, from Eleanor who lies warmly in Sam's bed, an attractive Eleanor who may wound his flesh. Thus, brother to the pleasure of pain, is the sweeter pleasure which follows pain. Sam, tired, lies in Eleanor's arms, and they talk with the cozy trade words of old professionals, agreeing that they will not make love again before a movie, that it was exciting but also not without detachment, that all in all it has been good but not quite right, that she had loved this action he had done, and was uncertain about another. It is their old familiar critique, a sign that they are intimate and well disposed. They do not talk about the act when it has failed to fire; then they go silently to sleep. But now, Eleanor's enjoyment having mollified Sam's sense of no enjoyment, they talk with the apologetics and encomiums of familiar mates. Eleanor falls asleep, and Sam falls almost asleep, curling next to her warm body, his hand over her round belly with the satisfaction of a sculptor. He is drowsy, and he thinks drowsily that these few moments of creature-pleasure, this brief compassion he can feel for the body that trusts itself to sleep beside him, his comfort in its warmth, is perhaps all the meaning he may ask for his life. That out of disappointment, frustration, and the passage of dreary years come these few moments when he is close to her, and their years together possess a connotation more rewarding than the sum of all which has gone into them.

But then he thinks of the novel he wants to write, and he is wide-awake again. Like the sleeping pill which fails to work and leaves one warped in an exaggeration of the ills which sought the drug, Sam passes through the promise of sex-emptied sleep, and is left with nervous loins, swollen jealousy of an act ten years dead, and sweating irritable resentment of the woman's body which hinders his limbs. He has wasted the day, he tells himself, he has wasted the day as he has wasted so many days of his life, and tomorrow in the office he will be no more than his ten fingers typing plot and words for Bramba the Venusian and Lee-Lee Deeds, Hollywood Star, while that huge work with which he has cheated himself, holding it before him as a covenant of his worth, that enormous novel which would lift him at a bound from the impasse in which he stifles, whose dozens of characters would develop a vision of life in bountiful complexity, lies foundered, rotting on a beach of purposeless effort. Notes here, pages there, it sprawls through a formless wreck of incidental ideas and half-episodes, utterly without shape. He has not even a hero for it.

One could not have a hero today, Sam thinks, a man of action and contemplation, capable of sin, large enough for good, a man immense. There is only a modern hero damned by no more than the ugliness of wishes whose satisfaction he will never know. One needs a man who could walk the stage, someone who—no matter who, not himself. Someone, Sam thinks, who reasonably could not exist.

The novelist, thinks Sam, perspiring beneath blankets, must live in paranoia and seek to be one with the world; he must be terrified of experience and hungry for it; he must think himself nothing and believe he is superior to all. The feminine in his nature cries for proof he is a man; he dreams of power and is without capacity to gain it; he loves himself above all and therefore despises all that he is.

He is that, thinks Sam, he is part of the perfect prescription, and yet he is not a novelist. He lacks energy and belief. It is left for him to write an article some day about the temperament of the ideal novelist.

In the darkness, memories rise, yeast-swells of apprehension. Out of bohemian days so long ago, comes the friend of Eleanor, a girl who had been sick and was committed to an institution. They visited her, Sam and Eleanor, they took the suburban train and sat on the lawn of the asylum grounds while patients circled about intoning a private litany, or shuddering in boob-blundering fright from an insect that crossed their skin. The friend had been silent. She had smiled, she had answered their questions with the fewest words, and had returned again to her study of sunlight and blue sky. As they were about to leave, the girl had taken Sam aside. "They violate me," she said in a whisper. "Every night when the doors are locked, they come to my room and they make the movie. I am the heroine and am subjected to all variety of sexual viciousness. Tell them to leave me alone so I may enter the convent." And while she talked, in a horror of her body, one arm scrubbed the other. Poor tortured friend. They had seen her again, and she babbled, her face had coarsened into an idiot leer.

Sam sweats. There is so little he knows, and so much to know. Youth of the depression with its economic terms, what can he know of madness or religion? They are both so alien to him. He is the mongrel, Sam thinks, brought up without religion from a mother half Protestant and half Catholic, and a father half Catholic and half Jew. He is the quarter-Jew, and yet he is a Jew, or so he feels himself, knowing nothing of Gospel, tabernacle, or Mass, the Jew through accident, through state of mind. What . . . whatever did he know of penance? self-sacrifice? mortification of the flesh? the love of his fellow man? Am I concerned with my relation to God? ponders Sam, and smiles sourly in the darkness. No, that has never concerned him, he thinks, not for better nor for worse. "They are making the movie," says the girl into the ear of memory, "and so I cannot enter the convent."

How hideous was the mental hospital. A concentration camp, decides Sam. Perhaps it would be the world some day, or was that only his projection of feelings of hopelessness? "Do not try to solve the problems of the world," he hears from Sergius, and pounds a lumpy pillow.

However could he organize his novel? What form to give it? It is so complex. Too loose, thinks Sam, too scattered. Will he ever fall asleep? Wearily, limbs tense, his stomach too keen, he plays again the game of putting himself to sleep. "I do not feel my toes," Sam says to himself, "my toes are dead, my calves are asleep, my calves are sleeping . . ."

In the middle from wakefulness to slumber, in the torpor which floats beneath blankets, I give an idea to Sam. "Destroy time, and chaos may be ordered," I say to him.

"Destroy time, and chaos may be ordered," he repeats after me, and in desperation to seek his coma, mutters back, "I do not feel my nose, my nose is numb, my eyes are heavy, my eyes are heavy."

So Sam enters the universe of sleep, a man who seeks to live in such a way as to avoid pain, and succeeds merely in avoiding pleasure. What a dreary compromise is life!

1959

JAMES BALDWIN
(1924–)

"I do not think, if one is a writer," James Baldwin has written, "that one escapes it by trying to become something else." From the beginning he has been painfully aware of his identity as a black man from Harlem and almost from the time that he was old enough to possess ambitions he seems to have desired to become a writer. Because he was in some ways the most spectacularly successful of the black writers of the 1950's and 1960's and because his own rise coincided with the rise of the black freedom movement, there has always existed some pressure to speak for black political and social goals. His civil rights activity, however, has been secondary to his work as a writer. Seldom a spokesman for a particular cause, he has nevertheless recorded, out of the stresses of his personal situation, a memorable sense of what it means to be black and American in the second half of the twentieth century. In *The Fire Next Time* (1963) and in *No Name in the Street* (1972) he has thrown out a direct challenge to Americans. His other works present the personal vision that lies behind the challenge. His subject has been himself.

Baldwin's early years formed the basis for his first novel, *Go Tell It on the Mountain* (1953). Born in Harlem in 1924, he was raised by his mother and his foster father, a minister. While he was in high school he did some preaching, but he also continued the writing that he had begun as a child and for which he was regularly praised by his teachers. When he was eighteen he left home. World War II provided him with a job in New Jersey, where he lived and worked with friends from high school, but New Jersey provided him also with some searing racial encounters. Before long he was living in Greenwich Village, supporting himself in any way he could, determined to become a writer. In 1948 he left the United States for Paris and for the next eight years he made his home in France. In 1957 he returned to New York and in subsequent years he traveled in the South and became active in civil rights, but he continued to see his principal role as that of a writer.

All of Baldwin's novels contain powerful passages and superior writing, but none does full justice to his talent. Usually the subject is the racial situation in the United States, but in *Giovanni's Room* (1955), for which he had difficulty finding a publisher, the subject is homosexuality, the setting is France, and race is not an issue. In *Another Country* (1962), *Tell Me How Long the Train's Been Gone* (1968), *If Beale Street Could Talk* (1974), and *Just Above My Head* (1979), he returned to the themes that dominate his work. His search for a satisfactory fictional mode of presentation has also led to the production of some memorable short stories and the plays *Blues for Mister Charley* (1964) and *The Amen Corner* (1965).

His own search for personal identity plays an important role in his fiction and also forms the basis for the non-fictional prose that ranks with his finest work. The essays collected in *Notes of a Native Son* (1955) and *Nobody Knows My Name* (1961) stand with the best that his generation has produced.

Baldwin's novels and plays are named above. A collection of short stories is *Going to Meet the Man,* 1965. Essays are collected in *The Price of the Ticket: Collected Non-Fiction 1948–1985,* 1985. Other non-fiction titles, besides those named above, are *Nothing Personal* (with Richard Avedon), 1964; *A Rap on Race* (with Margaret Mead), 1971; *The Devil Finds Work,* 1976; and *The Evidence of Things Not Seen,* 1985. A biographical study is Fern M. Eckman, *The Furious Passage of James Baldwin,* 1966. Critical studies include Kenneth Kinnamon, ed., *James Baldwin: A Collection of Critical Essays,* 1974; Therman B. O'Daniel, ed., *James Baldwin: A Critical Evaluation,* 1977; Louis H. Pratt, *James Baldwin,* 1978; and Carolyn W. Sylvander, *James Baldwin,* 1980.

Sonny's Blues[1]

I read about it in the paper, in the subway, on my way to work. I read it, and I couldn't believe it, and I read it again. Then perhaps I just stared at it, at the newsprint spelling out his name, spelling out the story. I stared at it in the swinging lights of the subway car, and in the faces and bodies of the people, and in my own face, trapped in the darkness which roared outside.

It was not to be believed and I kept telling myself that, as I walked from the subway station to the high school. And at the same time I couldn't doubt it. I was scared, scared for Sonny. He became real to me again. A great block of ice got settled in my belly and kept melting there slowly all day long, while I taught my classes algebra. It was a special kind of ice. It kept melting, sending trickles of ice water all up and down my veins, but it never got less. Sometimes it hardened and seemed to expand until I felt my guts were going to come spilling out or that I was going to choke or scream. This would always be at a moment when I was remembering some specific thing Sonny had once said or done.

When he was about as old as the boys in my classes his face had been bright and open, there was a lot of copper in it; and he'd had wonderfully direct brown eyes, and great gentleness and privacy. I wondered what he looked like now. He had been picked up, the evening before, in a raid on an apartment downtown, for peddling and using heroin.

I couldn't believe it: but what I mean by that is that I couldn't find any room for it anywhere inside me. I had kept it outside me for a long time. I hadn't wanted to know. I had had suspicions, but I didn't name them, I kept putting them away. I told myself that Sonny was wild, but he wasn't crazy. And he'd always been a good boy, he hadn't ever turned hard or evil or disrespectful, the way kids can, so quick, so quick, especially in Harlem. I didn't want to believe that I'd ever see my brother going down, coming to nothing, all that light in his face gone out, in the condition I'd already seen so many others. Yet it had happened and here I was, talking about algebra to a lot of boys who might, every one of them for all I knew, be popping off needles every time they went to the head. Maybe it did more for them than algebra could.

I was sure that the first time Sonny had ever had horse,[2] he couldn't have been much older than these boys were now. These boys, now, were living as we'd been living then, they were growing up with a rush and their heads bumped abruptly against the low ceiling of their actual possibilities. They were filled with rage. All they really knew were two darknesses, the darkness of their lives, which was now closing in on them, and the darkness of the movies, which had blinded them to that other darkness, and in which they now, vindictively, dreamed, at once more together than they were at any other time, and more alone.

When the last bell rang, the last class ended, I let out my breath. It seemed I'd been holding it for all that time. My clothes were wet—I may have looked as though I'd been sitting in a steam bath, all dressed up, all afternoon. I sat alone in the classroom a long time. I listened to the boys outside, downstairs, shouting and cursing and laughing. Their laughter struck me for perhaps the first time. It was not

1. First published in *Partisan Review,* Summer, 1957, "Sonny's Blues" was collected in *Going to Meet the Man,* 1965, the source of the present text.
2. Heroin.

the joyous laughter which—God knows why—one associates with children. It was mocking and insular, its intent was to denigrate. It was disenchanted, and in this, also, lay the authority of their curses. Perhaps I was listening to them because I was thinking about my brother and in them I heard my brother. And myself.

One boy was whistling a tune, at once very complicated and very simple, it seemed to be pouring out of him as though he were a bird, and it sounded very cool and moving through all that harsh, bright air, only just holding its own through all those other sounds.

I stood up and walked over to the window and looked down into the courtyard. It was the beginning of the spring and the sap was rising in the boys. A teacher passed through them every now and again, quickly, as though he or she couldn't wait to get out of that courtyard, to get those boys out of their sight and off their minds. I started collecting my stuff. I thought I'd better get home and talk to Isabel.

The courtyard was almost deserted by the time I got downstairs. I saw this boy standing in the shadow of a doorway, looking just like Sonny. I almost called his name. Then I saw that it wasn't Sonny, but somebody we used to know, a boy from around our block. He'd been Sonny's friend. He'd never been mine, having been too young for me, and, anyway, I'd never liked him. And now, even though he was a grown-up man, he still hung around that block, still spent hours on the street corners, was always high and raggy. I used to run into him from time to time and he'd often work around to asking me for a quarter or fifty cents. He always had some real good excuse, too, and I always gave it to him, I don't know why.

But now, abruptly, I hated him. I couldn't stand the way he looked at me, partly like a dog, partly like a cunning child. I wanted to ask him what the hell he was doing in the school courtyard.

He sort of shuffled over to me, and he said, "I see you got the papers. So you already know about it."

"You mean about Sonny? Yes, I already know about it. How come they didn't get you?"

He grinned. It made him repulsive and it also brought to mind what he'd looked like as a kid. "I wasn't there. I stay away from them people."

"Good for you." I offered him a cigarette and I watched him through the smoke. "You come all the way down here just to tell me about Sonny?"

"That's right." He was sort of shaking his head and his eyes looked strange, as though they were about to cross. The bright sun deadened his damp dark brown skin and it made his eyes look yellow and showed up the dirt in his kinked hair. He smelled funky. I moved a little away from him and I said, "Well, thanks. But I already know about it and I got to get home."

"I'll walk you a little ways," he said. We started walking. There were a couple of kids still loitering in the courtyard and one of them said goodnight to me and looked strangely at the boy beside me.

"What're you going to do?" he asked me. "I mean, about Sonny?"

"Look. I haven't seen Sonny for over a year, I'm not sure I'm going to do anything. Anyway, what the hell *can* I do?"

"That's right," he said quickly, "ain't nothing you can do. Can't much help old Sonny no more, I guess."

It was what I was thinking and so it seemed to me he had no right to say it.

"I'm surprised at Sonny, though," he went on—he had a funny way of talking, he looked straight ahead as though he were talking to himself—"I thought Sonny was a smart boy, I thought he was too smart to get hung."

"I guess he thought so too," I said sharply, "and that's how he got hung. And how about you? You're pretty goddamn smart, I bet."

Then he looked directly at me, just for a minute. "I ain't smart," he said. "If I was smart, I'd have reached for a pistol a long time ago."

"Look. Don't tell *me* your sad story, if it was up to me, I'd give you one." Then I felt guilty—guilty, probably, for never having supposed that the poor bastard *had* a story of his own, much less a sad one, and I asked, quickly, "What's going to happen to him now?"

He didn't answer this. He was off by himself some place. "Funny thing," he said, and from his tone we might have been discussing the quickest way to get to Brooklyn, "when I saw the papers this morning, the first thing I asked myself was if I had anything to do with it. I felt sort of responsible."

I began to listen more carefully. The subway station was on the corner, just before us, and I stopped. He stopped, too. We were in front of a bar and he ducked slightly, peering in, but whoever he was looking for didn't seem to be there. The juke box was blasting away with something black and bouncy and I half watched the barmaid as she danced her way from the juke box to her place behind the bar. And I watched her face as she laughingly responded to something someone said to her, still keeping time to the music. When she smiled one saw the little girl, one sensed the doomed, still-struggling woman beneath the battered face of the semi-whore.

"I never *give* Sonny nothing," the boy said finally, "but a long time ago I come to school high and Sonny asked me how it felt." He paused, I couldn't bear to watch him, I watched the barmaid, and I listened to the music which seemed to be causing the pavement to shake. "I told him it felt great." The music stopped, the barmaid paused and watched the juke box until the music began again. "It did."

All this was carrying me some place I didn't want to go. I certainly didn't want to know how it felt. It filled everything, the people, the houses, the music, the dark, quicksilver barmaid, with menace; and this menace was their reality.

"What's going to happen to him now?" I asked again.

"They'll send him away some place and they'll try to cure him." He shook his head. "Maybe he'll even think he's kicked the habit. Then they'll let him loose"—he gestured, throwing his cigarette into the gutter. "That's all."

"What do you mean, that's *all?*"

But I knew what he meant.

"I *mean,* that's *all.*" He turned his head and looked at me, pulling down the corners of his mouth. "Don't you know what I mean?" he asked, softly.

"How the hell *would* I know what you mean?" I almost whispered it, I don't know why.

"That's right," he said to the air, "how would *he* know what I mean?" He turned toward me again, patient and calm, and yet I somehow felt him shaking, shaking as though he were going to fall apart. I felt that ice in my guts again, the dread I'd felt all afternoon; and again I watched the barmaid, moving about the bar, washing glasses, and singing. "Listen. They'll let him out and then it'll just start all over again. That's what I mean."

"You mean—they'll let him out. And then he'll just start working his way back in again. You mean he'll never kick the habit. Is that what you mean?"

"That's right," he said, cheerfully. "*You* see what I mean."

"Tell me," I said at last, "why does he want to die? He must want to die, he's killing himself, why does he want to die?"

He looked at me in surprise. He licked his lips. "He don't want to die. He wants to live. Don't nobody want to die, ever."

Then I wanted to ask him—too many things. He could not have answered, or if he had, I could not have borne the answers. I started walking. "Well, I guess it's none of my business."

"It's going to be rough on old Sonny," he said. We reached the subway station. "This is your station?" he asked. I nodded. I took one step down. "Damn!" he said, suddenly. I looked up at him. He grinned again. "Damn it if I didn't leave all my money home. You ain't got a dollar on you, have you? Just for a couple of days, is all."

All at once something inside gave and threatened to come pouring out of me. I didn't hate him any more. I felt that in another moment I'd start crying like a child.

"Sure," I said. "Don't sweat." I looked in my wallet and didn't have a dollar, I only had a five. "Here," I said. "That hold you?"

He didn't look at it—he didn't want to look at it. A terrible, closed look came over his face, as though he were keeping the number on the bill a secret from him and me. "Thanks," he said, and now he was dying to see me go. "Don't worry about Sonny. Maybe I'll write him or something."

"Sure," I said. "You do that. So long."

"Be seeing you," he said. I went on down the steps.

And I didn't write Sonny or send him anything for a long time. When I finally did, it was just after my little girl died, he wrote me back a letter which made me feel like a bastard.

Here's what he said:

Dear brother,

You don't know how much I needed to hear from you. I wanted to write you many a time but I dug how much I must have hurt you and so I didn't write. But now I feel like a man who's been trying to climb up out of some deep, real deep and funky hole and just saw the sun up there, outside. I got to get outside.

I can't tell you much about how I got here. I mean I don't know how to tell you. I guess I was afraid of something or I was trying to escape from something and you know I have never been very strong in the head (smile). I'm glad Mama and Daddy are dead and can't see what's happened to their son and I swear if I'd known what I was doing I would never have hurt you so, you and a lot of other fine people who were nice to me and who believed in me.

I don't want you to think it had anything to do with me being a musician. It's more than that. Or maybe less than that. I can't get anything straight in my head down here and I try not to think about what's going to happen to me when I get outside again. Sometime I think I'm going to flip and *never* get outside and sometime I think I'll come straight back. I tell you one thing, though, I'd rather blow my brains out than go through this again. But that's what they all say, so they tell me. If I tell you when I'm coming to New York and if you could meet me, I sure would appreciate it. Give my love to Isabel and the kids and I was sure sorry to hear about little Gracie. I wish I could be like Mama and say the Lord's will be done, but I don't know it seems to me that trouble is the one thing that never does get stopped and I don't know what good it does to blame it on the Lord. But maybe it does some good if you believe it.

Your brother,
Sonny

Then I kept in constant touch with him and I sent him whatever I could and I went to meet him when he came back to New York. When I saw him many things I thought I had forgotten came flooding back to me. This was because I had begun, finally, to wonder about Sonny, about the life that Sonny lived inside. This life, whatever it was, had made him older and thinner and it had deepened the distant stillness in which he had always moved. He looked very unlike my baby brother. Yet, when he smiled, when we shook hands, the baby brother I'd never known looked out from the depths of his private life, like an animal waiting to be coaxed into the light.

"How you been keeping?" he asked me.

"All right. And you?"

"Just fine." He was smiling all over his face. "It's good to see you again."

"It's good to see you."

The seven years' difference in our ages lay between us like a chasm: I wondered if these years would ever operate between us as a bridge. I was remembering, and it made it hard to catch my breath, that I had been there when he was born; and I had heard the first words he had ever spoken. When he started to walk, he walked from our mother straight to me. I caught him just before he fell when he took the first steps he ever took in this world.

"How's Isabel?"

"Just fine. She's dying to see you."

"And the boys?"

"They're fine, too. They're anxious to see their uncle."

"Oh, come on. You know they don't remember me."

"Are you kidding? Of course they remember you."

He grinned again. We got into a taxi. We had a lot to say to each other, far too much to know how to begin.

As the taxi began to move, I asked, "You still want to go to India?"

He laughed. "You still remember that. Hell, no. This place is Indian enough for me."

"It used to belong to them," I said.

And he laughed again. "They damn sure knew what they were doing when they got rid of it."

Years ago, when he was around fourteen, he'd been all hipped on the idea of going to India. He read books about people sitting on rocks, naked, in all kinds of weather, but mostly bad, naturally, and walking barefoot through hot coals and arriving at wisdom. I used to say that it sounded to me as though they were getting away from wisdom as fast as they could. I think he sort of looked down on me for that.

"Do you mind," he asked, "if we have the driver drive alongside the park? On the west side—I haven't seen the city in so long."

"Of course not," I said. I was afraid that I might sound as though I were humoring him, but I hoped he wouldn't take it that way.

So we drove along, between the green of the park and the stony, lifeless elegance of hotels and apartment buildings, toward the vivid, killing streets of our childhood. These streets hadn't changed, though housing projects jutted up out of them now like rocks in the middle of a boiling sea. Most of the houses in which we had grown up had vanished, as had the stores from which we had stolen, the basements in which we had first tried sex, the rooftops from which we had hurled tin cans and bricks. But houses exactly like the houses of our past yet dominated the landscape, boys exactly like the boys we once had been found themselves smothering in these houses, came down into the streets for light and air and found themselves encircled by disaster. Some escaped the trap, most didn't. Those who got out always left something of themselves behind, as some animals amputate a leg and leave it in the trap. It might be said, perhaps, that I had escaped, after all, I was a school teacher; or that Sonny had, he hadn't lived in Harlem for years. Yet, as the cab moved uptown through streets which seemed, with a rush, to darken with dark people, and as I covertly studied Sonny's face, it came to me that what we both were seeking through our separate cab windows was that part of ourselves which had been left behind. It's always at the hour of trouble and confrontation that the missing member aches.

We hit 110th Street and started rolling up Lenox Avenue. And I'd known this avenue all my life, but it seemed to me again, as it had seemed on the day I'd first heard about Sonny's trouble, filled with a hidden menace which was its very breath of life.

"We almost there," said Sonny.

"Almost." We were both too nervous to say anything more.

We live in a housing project. It hasn't been up long. A few days after it was up it seemed uninhabitably new, now, of course, it's already rundown. It looks like a parody of the good, clean, faceless life—God knows the people who live in it do their best to make it a parody. The beat-looking grass lying around isn't enough to make their lives green, the hedges will never hold out the streets, and they know it. The big windows fool no one, they aren't big enough to make space out of no space. They don't bother with the windows, they watch the TV screen instead. The playground is most popular with the children who don't play at jacks, or skip rope, or roller skate, or swing, and they can be found in it after dark. We moved in partly because it's not too far from where I teach, and partly for the kids; but it's really just like the houses in which Sonny and I grew up. The same things happen, they'll have the same things to remember. The moment Sonny and I started into the house I had the feeling that I was simply bringing him back into the danger he had almost died trying to escape.

Sonny has never been talkative. So I don't know why I was sure he'd be dying to talk to me when supper was over the first night. Everything went fine, the oldest boy remembered him, and the youngest boy liked him, and Sonny had remembered to bring something for each of them; and Isabel, who is really much nicer than I am, more open and giving, had gone to a lot of trouble about dinner and was genuinely glad to see him. And she's always been able to tease Sonny in a way that I haven't. It was nice to see her face so vivid again and to hear her laugh and watch her make Sonny laugh. She wasn't, or, anyway, she didn't seem to be, at all uneasy or embarrassed. She chatted as though there were no subject which had to be avoided and she got Sonny past his first, faint stiffness. And thank God she was there, for I was filled with that icy dread again. Everything I did seemed awkward to me, and everything I said sounded freighted with hidden meaning. I was trying to remember everything I'd heard about dope addiction and I couldn't help watching Sonny for signs. I wasn't doing it out of malice. I was trying to find out something about my brother. I was dying to hear him tell me he was safe.

"Safe!" my father grunted, whenever Mama suggested trying to move to a neighborhood which might be safer for children. "Safe, hell! Ain't no place safe for kids, nor nobody."

He always went on like this, but he wasn't, ever, really as bad as he sounded, not even on weekends, when he got drunk. As a matter of fact, he was always on the lookout for "something a little better," but he died before he found it. He died suddenly, during a drunken weekend in the middle of the war, when Sonny was fifteen. He and Sonny hadn't ever got on too well. And this was partly because Sonny was the apple of his father's eye. It was because he loved Sonny so much and was frightened for him, that he was always fighting with him. It doesn't do any good to fight with Sonny. Sonny just moves back, inside himself, where he can't be reached. But the principal reason that they never hit it off is that they were so much alike. Daddy was big and rough and loud-talking, just the opposite of Sonny, but they both had—that same privacy.

Mama tried to tell me something about this, just after Daddy died. I was home on leave from the army.

This was the last time I ever saw my mother alive. Just the same, this picture gets all mixed up in my mind with pictures I had of her when she was younger. The way I always see her is the way she used to be on a Sunday afternoon, say, when the old folks were talking after the big Sunday dinner. I always see her wearing pale blue. She'd be sitting on the sofa. And my father would be sitting in the easy chair, not far from her. And the living room would be full of church folks and relatives. There they sit, in chairs all around the living room, and the night is creeping up outside, but nobody knows it yet. You can see the darkness growing against the windowpanes and you hear the street noises every now and again, or maybe the jangling beat of a tambourine from one of the churches close by, but it's real quiet in the room. For a moment nobody's talking, but every face looks darkening, like the sky outside. And my mother rocks a little from the waist, and my father's eyes are closed. Everyone is looking at something a child can't see. For a minute they've forgotten the children. Maybe a kid is lying on the rug, half asleep. Maybe somebody's got a kid in his lap and is absent-mindedly stroking the kid's head. Maybe there's a kid, quiet and big-eyed, curled up in a big chair in the corner. The silence, the darkness coming, and the darkness in the faces frightens the child obscurely. He hopes that the hand which strokes his forehead will never stop—will never die. He hopes that there will never come a time when the old folks won't be sitting around the living room, talking about where they've come from, and what they've seen, and what's happened to them and their kinfolk.

But something deep and watchful in the child knows that this is bound to end, is already ending. In a moment someone will get up and turn on the light. Then the old folks will remember the children and they won't talk any more that day. And when light fills the room, the child is filled with darkness. He knows that every time this happens he's moved just a little closer to that darkness outside. The darkness outside is what the old folks have been talking about. It's what they've come from. It's what they endure. The child knows that they won't talk any more because if he knows too much about what's happened to *them*, he'll know too much too soon, about what's going to happen to *him*.

The last time I talked to my mother, I remember I was restless. I wanted to get out and see Isabel. We weren't married then and we had a lot to straighten out between us.

There Mama sat, in black, by the window. She was humming an old church song, *Lord, you brought me from a long ways off.* Sonny was out somewhere. Mama kept watching the streets.

"I don't know," she said, "if I'll ever see you again, after you go off from here. But I hope you'll remember the things I tried to teach you."

"Don't talk like that," I said, and smiled. "You'll be here a long time yet."

She smiled, too, but she said nothing. She was quiet for a long time. And I said, "Mama, don't you worry about nothing. I'll be writing all the time, and you be getting the checks. . . ."

"I want to talk to you about your brother," she said, suddenly. "If anything happens to me he ain't going to have nobody to look out for him."

"Mama," I said, "ain't nothing going to happen to you *or* Sonny. Sonny's all right. He's a good boy and he's got good sense."

"It ain't a question of his being a good boy," Mama said, "nor of his having good sense. It ain't only the bad ones, nor yet the dumb ones that gets sucked under." She stopped, looking at me. "Your Daddy once had a brother," she said, and she smiled in a way that made me feel she was in pain. "You didn't never know that, did you?"

"No," I said, "I never knew that," and I watched her face.

"Oh, yes," she said, "your Daddy had a brother." She looked out of the window again. "I know you never saw your Daddy cry. But *I* did—many a time, through all these years."

I asked her, "What happened to his brother? How come nobody's ever talked about him?"

This was the first time I ever saw my mother look old.

"His brother got killed," she said, "when he was just a little younger than you are now. I knew him. He was a fine boy. He was maybe a little full of the devil, but he didn't mean nobody no harm."

Then she stopped and the room was silent, exactly as it had sometimes been on those Sunday afternoons. Mama kept looking out into the streets.

"He used to have a job in the mill," she said, "and, like all young folks, he just liked to perform on Saturday nights. Saturday nights, him and your father would drift around to different places, go to dances and things like that, or just sit around with people they knew, and your father's brother would sing, he had a fine voice, and play along with himself on his guitar. Well, this particular Saturday night, him and your father was coming home from some place, and they were both a little drunk and there was a moon that night, it was bright like day. Your father's brother was feeling kind of good, and he was whistling to himself, and he had his guitar slung over his shoulder. They was coming down a hill and beneath them was a road that turned off from the highway. Well, your father's brother, being always kind of frisky, decided to run down this hill, and he did, with that guitar banging and clanging behind him, and he ran across the road, and he was making water behind a tree. And your father was sort of amused at him and he was still coming down the hill, kind of slow. Then he heard a car motor and that same minute his brother stepped from behind the tree, into the road, in the moonlight. And he started to cross the road. And your father started to run down the hill, he says he don't know why. This car was full of white men. They was all drunk, and when they seen your father's brother they let out a great whoop and holler and they aimed the car straight at him. They was having fun, they just wanted to scare him, the way they do sometimes, you know. But they was drunk. And I guess the boy, being drunk, too, and scared, kind of lost his head. By the time he jumped it was too late. Your father says he heard his brother scream when the car rolled over him, and he heard the wood of that guitar when it give, and he heard them strings go flying, and he heard them white men shouting, and the car kept on a-going and it ain't stopped till this day. And, time your father got down the hill, his brother weren't nothing but blood and pulp."

Tears were gleaming on my mother's face. There wasn't anything I could say.

"He never mentioned it," she said, "because I never let him mention it before you children. Your Daddy was like a crazy man that night and for many a night thereafter. He says he never in his life seen anything as dark as that road after the lights of that car had gone away. Weren't nothing, weren't nobody on that road, just your Daddy and his brother and that busted guitar. Oh, yes. Your Daddy never did really get right again. Till the day he died he weren't sure but that every white man he saw was the man that killed his brother."

She stopped and took out her handkerchief and dried her eyes and looked at me.

"I ain't telling you all this," she said, "to make you scared or bitter or to make you hate nobody. I'm telling you this because you got a brother. And the world ain't changed."

I guess I didn't want to believe this. I guess she saw this in my face. She turned away from me, toward the window again, searching those streets.

"But I praise my Redeemer," she said at last, "that He called your Daddy home before me. I ain't saying it to throw no flowers at myself, but, I declare, it keeps me from feeling too cast down to know I helped your father get safely through this world. Your father always acted like he was the roughest, strongest man on earth. And everybody took him to be like that. But if he hadn't had *me* there—to see his tears!"

She was crying again. Still, I couldn't move. I said, "Lord, Lord, Mama, I didn't know it was like that."

"Oh, honey," she said, "there's a lot that you don't know. But you are going to find it out." She stood up from the window and came over to me. "You got to hold on to your brother," she said, "and don't let him fall, no matter what it looks like is happening to him and no matter how evil you gets with him. You going to be evil with him many a time. But don't you forget what I told you, you hear?"

"I won't forget," I said. "Don't you worry, I won't forget. I won't let nothing happen to Sonny."

My mother smiled as though she were amused at something she saw in my face. Then, "You may not be able to stop nothing from happening. But you got to let him know you's *there.*"

Two days later I was married, and then I was gone. And I had a lot of things on my mind and I pretty well forgot my promise to Mama until I got shipped home on a special furlough for her funeral.

And, after the funeral, with just Sonny and me alone in the empty kitchen, I tried to find out something about him.

"What do you want to do?" I asked him.

"I'm going to be a musician," he said.

For he had graduated, in the time I had been away, from dancing to the juke box to finding out who was playing what, and what they were doing with it, and he had bought himself a set of drums.

"You mean, you want to be a drummer?" I somehow had the feeling that being a drummer might be all right for other people but not for my brother Sonny.

"I don't think," he said, looking at me very gravely, "that I'll ever be a good drummer. But I think I can play a piano."

I frowned. I'd never played the role of the older brother quite so seriously before, had scarcely ever, in fact, *asked* Sonny a damn thing. I sensed myself in the presence of something I didn't really know how to handle, didn't understand. So I made my frown a little deeper as I asked: "What kind of musician do you want to be?"

He grinned. "How many kinds do you think there are?"

"Be *serious,*" I said.

He laughed, throwing his head back, and then looked at me. "I *am* serious."

"Well, then, for Christ's sake, stop kidding around and answer a serious question. I mean, do you want to be a concert pianist, you want to play classical music and all that, or—or what?" Long before I finished he was laughing again. "For Christ's *sake,* Sonny!"

He sobered, but with difficulty. "I'm sorry. But you sound so—*scared!*" and he was off again.

"Well, you may think it's funny now, baby, but it's not going to be so funny when you have to make your living at it, let me tell you *that.*" I was furious because I knew he was laughing at me and I didn't know why.

"No," he said, very sober now, and afraid, perhaps, that he'd hurt me, "I don't want to be a classical pianist. That isn't what interests me. I mean"—he paused, looking hard at me, as though his eyes would help me to understand, and then gestured helplessly, as though perhaps his hand would help—"I mean, I'll have a lot of studying to do, and I'll have to study *everything,* but, I mean, I want to play *with*—jazz musicians." He stopped. "I want to play jazz," he said.

Well, the word had never before sounded as heavy, as real, as it sounded that afternoon in Sonny's mouth. I just looked at him and I was probably frowning a real frown by this time. I simply couldn't see why on earth he'd want to spend his time hanging around nightclubs, clowning around on bandstands, while people pushed each other around a dance floor. It seemed—beneath him, somehow. I had never thought about it before, had never been forced to, but I suppose I had always put jazz musicians in a class with what Daddy called "good-time people."

"Are you *serious?*"

"Hell, *yes*, I'm serious."

He looked more helpless than ever, and annoyed, and deeply hurt.

I suggested, helpfully: "You mean—like Louis Armstrong?"

His face closed as though I'd struck him. "No. I'm not talking about none of that old-time, down home crap."

"Well, look, Sonny, I'm sorry, don't get mad. I just don't altogether get it, that's all. Name somebody—you know, a jazz musician you admire."

"Bird."

"Who?"

"Bird! Charlie Parker! Don't they teach you nothing in the goddamn army?"

I lit a cigarette. I was surprised and then a little amused to discover that I was trembling. "I've been out of touch," I said. "You'll have to be patient with me. Now. Who's this Parker character?"

"He's just one of the greatest jazz musicians alive," said Sonny, sullenly, his hands in his pockets, his back to me. "Maybe *the* greatest," he added, bitterly, "that's probably why *you* never heard of him."

"All right," I said, "I'm ignorant. I'm sorry. I'll go out and buy all the cat's records right away, all right?"

"It don't," said Sonny, with dignity, "make any difference to me. I don't care what you listen to. Don't do me no favors."

I was beginning to realize that I'd never seen him so upset before. With another part of my mind I was thinking that this would probably turn out to be one of those things kids go through and that I shouldn't make it seem important by pushing it too hard. Still, I didn't think it would do any harm to ask: "Doesn't all this take a lot of time? Can you make a living at it?"

He turned back to me and half leaned, half sat, on the kitchen table. "Everything takes time," he said, "and—well, yes, sure, I can make a living at it. But what I don't seem to be able to make you understand is that it's the only thing I want to do."

"Well, Sonny," I said, gently, "you know people can't always do exactly what they *want* to do—"

"*No*, I don't know that," said Sonny, surprising me. "I think people *ought* to do what they want to do, what else are they alive for?"

"You getting to be a big boy," I said desperately, "it's time you started thinking about your future."

"I'm thinking about my future," said Sonny, grimly. "I think about it all the time."

I gave up. I decided, if he didn't change his mind, that we could always talk about it later. "In the meantime," I said, "you got to finish school." We had already decided that he'd have to move in with Isabel and her folks. I knew this wasn't the ideal arrangement because Isabel's folks are inclined to be dicty and they hadn't especially wanted Isabel to marry me. But I didn't know what else to do. "And we have to get you fixed up at Isabel's."

There was a long silence. He moved from the kitchen table to the window. "That's a terrible idea. You know it yourself."

"Do you have a *better* idea?"

He just walked up and down the kitchen for a minute. He was as tall as I was. He had started to shave. I suddenly had the feeling that I didn't know him at all.

He stopped at the kitchen table and picked up my cigarettes. Looking at me with a kind of mocking, amused defiance, he put one between his lips. "You mind?"

"You smoking already?"

He lit the cigarette and nodded, watching me through the smoke. "I just wanted to see if I'd have the courage to smoke in front of you." He grinned and blew a great cloud of smoke to the ceiling. "It was easy." He looked at my face. "Come on, now. I bet you was smoking at my age, tell the truth."

I didn't say anything but the truth was on my face, and he laughed. But now there was something very strained in his laugh. "Sure. And I bet that ain't all you was doing."

He was frightening me a little. "Cut the crap," I said. "We already decided that you was going to go and live at Isabel's. Now what's got into you all of a sudden?"

"*You* decided it," he pointed out. "*I* didn't decide nothing." He stopped in front of me, leaning against the stove, arms loosely folded. "Look, brother. I don't want to stay in Harlem no more, I really don't." He was very earnest. He looked at me, then over toward the kitchen window. There was something in his eyes I'd never seen before, some thoughtfulness, some worry all his own. He rubbed the muscle of one arm. "It's time I was getting out of here."

"Where do you want to *go,* Sonny?"

"I want to join the army. Or the navy, I don't care. If I say I'm old enough, they'll believe me."

Then I got mad. It was because I was so scared. "You must be crazy. You goddamn fool, what the hell do you want to go and join the *army* for?"

"I just told you. To get out of Harlem."

"Sonny, you haven't even finished *school.* And if you really want to be a musician, how do you expect to study if you're in the *army?*"

He looked at me, trapped, and in anguish. "There's ways. I might be able to work out some kind of deal. Anyway, I'll have the G.I. Bill when I come out."

"*If* you come out." We stared at each other. "Sonny, please. Be reasonable. I know the setup is far from perfect. But we got to do the best we can."

"I ain't learning nothing in school," he said. "Even when I go." He turned away from me and opened the window and threw his cigarette out into the narrow alley. I watched his back. "At least, I ain't learning nothing you'd want me to learn." He slammed the window so hard I thought the glass would fly out, and turned back to me. "And I'm sick of the stink of these garbage cans!"

"Sonny," I said, "I know how you feel. But if you don't finish school now, you're going to be sorry later that you didn't." I grabbed him by the shoulders. "And you only got another year. It ain't so bad. And I'll come back and I swear I'll help you do *whatever* you want to do. Just try to put up with it till I come back. Will you please do that? For me?"

He didn't answer and he wouldn't look at me.

"Sonny. You hear me?"

He pulled away. "I hear you. But you never hear anything *I* say."

I didn't know what to say to that. He looked out of the window and then back at me. "OK," he said, and sighed. "I'll try."

Then I said, trying to cheer him up a little, "They got a piano at Isabel's. You can practice on it."

And as a matter of fact, it did cheer him up for a minute. "That's right," he said to himself. "I forgot that." His face relaxed a little. But the worry, the thoughtfulness, played on it still, the way shadows play on a face which is staring into the fire.

But I thought I'd never hear the end of that piano. At first, Isabel would write me, saying how nice it was that Sonny was so serious about his music and how, as soon as he came in from school, or wherever he had been when he was supposed to be at school, he went straight to that piano and stayed there until suppertime. And, after supper, he went back to that piano and stayed there until everybody went to bed. He was at the piano all day Saturday and all day Sunday. Then he bought a record player and started playing records. He'd play one record over and over again, all day long sometimes, and he'd improvise along with it on the piano. Or he'd play one section of the record, one chord, one change, one progression, then he'd do it on the piano. Then back to the record. Then back to the piano.

Well, I really don't know how they stood it. Isabel finally confessed that it wasn't like living with a person at all, it was like living with sound. And the sound didn't make any sense to her, didn't make any sense to any of them—naturally. They began, in a way, to be afflicted by this presence that was living in their home. It was as though Sonny were some sort of god, or monster. He moved in an atmosphere which wasn't like theirs at all. They fed him and he ate, he washed himself, he walked in and out of their door; he certainly wasn't nasty or unpleasant or rude, Sonny isn't any of those things; but it was as though he were all wrapped up in some cloud, some fire, some vision all his own; and there wasn't any way to reach him.

At the same time, he wasn't really a man yet, he was still a child, and they had to watch out for him in all kinds of ways. They certainly couldn't throw him out. Neither did they dare to make a great scene about that piano because even they dimly sensed, as I sensed, from so many thousands of miles away, that Sonny was at that piano playing for his life.

But he hadn't been going to school. One day a letter came from the school board and Isabel's mother got it—there had, apparently, been other letters but Sonny had torn them up. This day, when Sonny came in, Isabel's mother showed him the letter and asked where he'd been spending his time. And she finally got it out of him that he'd been down in Greenwich Village, with musicians and other characters, in a white girl's apartment. And this scared her and she started to scream at him and what came up, once she began—though she denies it to this day—was what sacrifices they were making to give Sonny a decent home and how little he appreciated it.

Sonny didn't play the piano that day. By evening, Isabel's mother had calmed down but then there was the old man to deal with, and Isabel herself. Isabel says she did her best to be calm but she broke down and started crying. She says she just watched Sonny's face. She could tell, by watching him, what was happening with him. And what was happening was that they penetrated his cloud, they had reached him. Even if their fingers had been a thousand times more gentle than human fingers ever are, he could hardly help feeling that they had stripped him naked and were spitting on that nakedness. For he also had to see that his presence, that music, which was life or death to him, had been torture for them and that they had endured it, not at all for his sake, but only for mine. And Sonny couldn't take that. He can take it a little better today than he could then but he's still not very good at it and, frankly, I don't know anybody who is.

The silence of the next few days must have been louder than the sound of all the music ever played since time began. One morning, before she went to work, Isabel was in his room for something and she suddenly realized that all of his records were gone. And she knew for certain that he was gone. And he was. He went as far as the navy would carry him. He finally sent me a postcard from some place in Greece and that was the first I knew that Sonny was still alive. I didn't see him any more until we were both back in New York and the war had long been over.

He was a man by then, of course, but I wasn't willing to see it. He came by the house from time to time, but we fought almost every time we met. I didn't like the way he carried himself, loose and dreamlike all the time, and I didn't like his friends, and his music seemed to be merely an excuse for the life he led. It sounded just that weird and disordered.

Then we had a fight, a pretty awful fight, and I didn't see him for months. By and by I looked him up, where he was living, in a furnished room in the Village, and I tried to make it up. But there were lots of other people in the room and Sonny just lay on his bed, and he wouldn't come downstairs with me, and he treated these other people as though they were his family and I weren't. So I got mad and then he got mad, and then I told him that he might just as well be dead as live the way he was living. Then he stood up and he told me not to worry about him any more in life, that he *was* dead as far as I was concerned. Then he pushed me to the door and the other people looked on as though nothing were happening, and he slammed the door behind me. I stood in the hallway, staring at the door. I heard somebody laugh in the room and then the tears came to my eyes. I started down the steps, whistling to keep from crying, I kept whistling to myself, *You going to need me, baby, one of these cold, rainy days.*

I read about Sonny's trouble in the spring. Little Grace died in the fall. She was a beautiful little girl. But she only lived a little over two years. She died of polio and she suffered. She had a slight fever for a couple of days, but it didn't seem like anything and we just kept her in bed. And we would certainly have called the doctor, but the fever dropped, she seemed to be all right. So we thought it had just been a cold. Then, one day, she was up, playing, Isabel was in the kitchen fixing lunch for the two boys when they'd come in from school, and she heard Grace fall down in the living room. When you have a lot of children you don't always start running when one of them falls, unless they start screaming or something. And, this time, Grace was quiet. Yet, Isabel says that when she heard that *thump* and then that silence, something happened in her to make her afraid. And she ran to the living room and there was little Grace on the floor, all twisted up, and the reason she hadn't screamed was that she couldn't get her breath. And when she did scream, it was the worst sound, Isabel says, that she'd ever heard in all her life, and she still hears it sometimes in her dreams. Isabel will sometimes wake me up with a low, moaning, strangled sound and I have to be quick to awaken her and hold her to me and where Isabel is weeping against me seems a mortal wound.

I think I may have written Sonny the very day that little Grace was buried. I was sitting in the living room in the dark, by myself, and I suddenly thought of Sonny. My trouble made his real.

One Saturday afternoon, when Sonny had been living with us, or, anyway, been in our house, for nearly two weeks, I found myself wandering aimlessly about the living room, drinking from a can of beer, and trying to work up the courage to search Sonny's room. He was out, he was usually out whenever I was home, and Isabel had taken the children to see their grandparents. Suddenly I was standing still in front of the living room window, watching Seventh Avenue. The idea of searching Sonny's room made me still. I scarcely dared to admit to myself what I'd be searching for. I didn't know what I'd do if I found it. Or if I didn't.

On the sidewalk across from me, near the entrance to a barbecue joint, some people were holding an old-fashioned revival meeting. The barbecue cook, wearing a dirty white apron, his conked hair reddish and metallic in the pale sun, and a cigarette between his lips, stood in the doorway, watching them. Kids and older people paused in their errands and stood there, along with some older men and a couple of very tough-looking women who watched everything that happened on the avenue, as though they owned it, or were maybe owned by it. Well, they were watching this, too. The revival was being carried on by three sisters in black, and a brother. All they had were their voices and their Bibles and a tambourine. The brother was testifying and while he testified two of the sisters stood together, seeming to say, amen, and the third sister walked around with the tambourine outstretched and a couple of people dropped coins into it. Then the brother's testimony ended and the sister who had been taking up the collection dumped the coins into her palm and transferred them to the pocket of her long black robe. Then she raised both hands, striking the tambourine against the air, and then against one hand, and she started to sing. And the two other sisters and the brother joined in.

It was strange, suddenly, to watch, though I had been seeing these street meetings all my life. So, of course, had everybody else down there. Yet, they paused and watched and listened and I stood still at the window. *"Tis the old ship of Zion,"* they sang, and the sister with the tambourine kept a steady, jangling beat, *"it has rescued many a thousand!"* Not a soul under the sound of their voices was hearing this song for the first time, not one of them had been rescued. Nor had they seen much in the way of rescue work being done around them. Neither did they especially believe in the holiness of the three sisters and the brother, they knew too much about them, knew where they lived, and how. The woman with the tambourine, whose voice dominated the air, whose face was bright with joy, was divided by very little from the woman who stood watching her, a cigarette between her heavy, chapped lips, her hair a cuckoo's nest, her face scarred and swollen from many beatings, and her black eyes glittering like coal. Perhaps they both knew this, which was why, when, as rarely, they addressed each other, they addressed each other as Sister. As the singing filled the air the watching, listening faces underwent a change, the eyes focusing on something within; the music seemed to soothe a poison out of them; and time seemed, nearly, to fall away from the sullen, belligerent, battered faces, as though they were fleeing back to their first condition, while dreaming of their last. The barbecue cook half shook his head and smiled, and dropped his cigarette and disappeared into his joint. A man fumbled in his pockets for change and stood holding it in his hand impatiently, as though he had just remembered a pressing appointment further up the avenue. He looked furious. Then I saw Sonny, standing on the edge of the crowd. He was carrying a wide, flat notebook with a green cover, and it made him look, from where I was standing, almost like a schoolboy. The coppery sun brought out the copper in his skin, he was very faintly smiling, standing very still. Then the singing stopped, the tambourine turned into a collection plate again. The furious man dropped in his coins and vanished, so did a couple of the women, and Sonny dropped some change in the plate, looking directly at the woman with a little smile. He started across the avenue, toward the house. He has a slow, loping walk, something like the way Harlem hipsters walk, only he's imposed on this his own half-beat. I had never really noticed it before.

I stayed at the window, both relieved and apprehensive. As Sonny disappeared from my sight, they began singing again. And they were still singing when his key turned in the lock.

"Hey," he said.

"Hey, yourself. You want some beer?"

"No. Well, maybe." But he came up to the window and stood beside me, looking out. "What a warm voice," he said.

They were singing *If I could only hear my mother pray again!*

"Yes," I said, "and she can sure beat that tambourine."

"But what a terrible song," he said, and laughed. He dropped his notebook on the sofa and disappeared into the kitchen. "Where's Isabel and the kids?"

"I think they went to see their grandparents. You hungry?"

"No." He came back into the living room with his can of beer. "You want to come some place with me tonight?"

I sensed, I don't know how, that I couldn't possibly say no. "Sure. Where?"

He sat down on the sofa and picked up his notebook and started leafing through it. "I'm going to sit in with some fellows in a joint in the Village."

"You mean, you're going to play, tonight?"

"That's right." He took a swallow of his beer and moved back to the window. He gave me a sidelong look. "If you can stand it."

"I'll try," I said.

He smiled to himself and we both watched as the meeting across the way broke up. The three sisters and the brother, heads bowed, were singing *God be with you till we meet again.* The faces around them were very quiet. Then the song ended. The small crowd dispersed. We watched the three women and the lone man walk slowly up the avenue.

"When she was singing before," said Sonny, abruptly, "her voice reminded me for a minute of what heroin feels like sometimes—when it's in your veins. It makes you feel sort of warm and cool at the same time. And distant. And—and sure." He sipped his beer, very deliberately not looking at me. I watched his face. "It makes you feel—in control. Sometimes you've got to have that feeling."

"Do you?" I sat down slowly in the easy chair.

"Sometimes." He went to the sofa and picked up his notebook again. "Some people do."

"In order," I asked, "to play?" And my voice was very ugly, full of contempt and anger.

"Well"—he looked at me with great, troubled eyes, as though, in fact, he hoped his eyes would tell me things he could never otherwise say—"they *think* so. And *if* they think so—!"

"And what do *you* think?" I asked.

He sat on the sofa and put his can of beer on the floor. "I don't know," he said, and I couldn't be sure if he were answering my question or pursuing his thoughts. His face didn't tell me. "It's not so much to *play.* It's to *stand* it, to be able to make it at all. On any level." He frowned and smiled: "In order to keep from shaking to pieces."

"But these friends of yours," I said, "they seem to shake themselves to pieces pretty goddamn fast."

"Maybe." He played with the notebook. And something told me that I should curb my tongue, that Sonny was doing his best to talk, that I should listen. "But of course you only know the ones that've gone to pieces. Some don't—or at least they haven't *yet* and that's just about all *any* of us can say." He paused. "And then there are some who just live, really, in hell, and they know it and they see what's happening and they go right on. I don't know." He sighed, dropped the notebook, folded his arms. "Some guys, you can tell from the way they play, they on something *all* the time. And you can see that, well, it makes something real for them. But of course," he picked up his beer from the floor and sipped it and put the can down again, "they *want* to, too, you've got to see that. Even some of them that say they don't—*some,* not all."

"And what about you?" I asked—I couldn't help it. "What about you? Do *you* want to?"

He stood up and walked to the window and remained silent for a long time. Then he sighed. "Me," he said. Then: "While I was downstairs before, on my way here, listening to that woman sing, it struck me all of a sudden how much suffering she must have had to go through—to sing like that. It's *repulsive* to think you have to suffer that much."

I said: "But there's no way not to suffer—is there, Sonny?"

"I believe not," he said and smiled, "but that's never stopped anyone from trying." He looked at me. "Has it?" I realized, with this mocking look, that there stood between us, forever, beyond the power of time or forgiveness, the fact that I had held silence—so long!—when he had needed human speech to help him. He turned back to the window. "No, there's no way not to suffer. But you try all kinds of ways to keep from drowning in it, to keep on top of it, and to make it seem—well, like *you.* Like you did something, all right, and now you're suffering for it. You know?" I said nothing. "Well you know," he said, impatiently, "why *do* people suffer? Maybe it's better to do something to give it a reason, *any* reason."

"But we just agreed," I said, "that there's no way not to suffer. Isn't it better, then, just to—take it?"

"But nobody just takes it," Sonny cried, "that's what I'm telling you! *Everybody* tries not to. You're just hung up on the *way* some people try—it's not *your* way!"

The hair on my face began to itch, my face felt wet. "That's not true," I said, "that's not true. I don't give a damn what other people do, I don't even care how they suffer. I just care how *you* suffer." And he looked at me. "Please believe me," I said, "I don't want to see you—die—trying not to suffer."

"I won't," he said, flatly, "die trying not to suffer. At least, not any faster than anybody else."

"But there's no need," I said, trying to laugh, "is there? in killing yourself."

I wanted to say more, but I couldn't. I wanted to talk about will power and how life could be—well, beautiful. I wanted to say that it was all within; but was it? or, rather, wasn't that exactly the trouble? And I wanted to promise that I would never fail him again. But it would all have sounded—empty words and lies.

So I made the promise to myself and prayed that I would keep it.

"It's terrible sometimes, inside," he said, "that's what's the trouble. You walk these streets, black and funky and cold, and there's not really a living ass to talk to, and there's nothing shaking, and there's no way of getting it out—that storm inside. You can't talk it and you can't make love with it, and when you finally try to get with it and play it, you realize *nobody's* listening. So *you've* got to listen. You got to find a way to listen."

And then he walked away from the window and sat on the sofa again, as though all the wind had suddenly been knocked out of him. "Sometimes you'll do *anything* to play, even cut your mother's throat." He laughed and looked at me. "Or your brother's." Then he sobered. "Or your own." Then: "Don't worry. I'm all right now and I think I'll *be* all right. But I can't forget—where I've been. I don't mean just the physical place I've been, I mean where I've *been.* And *what* I've been."

"What have you been, Sonny?" I asked.

He smiled—but sat sideways on the sofa, his elbow resting on the back, his fingers playing with his mouth and chin, not looking at me. "I've been something I didn't recognize, didn't know I could be. Didn't know anybody could be." He stopped, looking inward, looking helplessly young, looking old. "I'm not talking about it now because I feel *guilty* or anything like that—maybe it would be better if I did, I don't know. Anyway, I can't really talk about it. Not to you, not to anybody," and now he turned and faced me. "Sometimes, you know, and it was actually when I was most *out* of the world, I felt that I was in it, that I was *with* it, really, and I could play or I didn't really have to *play,* it just came out of me, it was there. And I don't know how I played, thinking about it now, but I know I did awful things, those times, sometimes, to people. Or it wasn't that I *did* anything to them—it was that they weren't real." He picked up the beer can; it was empty; he rolled it between his palms: "And other times—well, I needed a fix, I needed to find a place to lean, I needed to clear a space to *listen*—and I couldn't find it, and I—went crazy, I did terrible things to *me,* I was terrible *for* me." He began pressing the beer can between his hands, I watched the metal begin to give. It glittered, as he played with it, like a knife, and I was afraid he would cut himself, but I said nothing. "Oh well. I can never tell you. I was all by myself at the bottom of something, stinking and sweating and crying and shaking, and I smelled it, you know? *my* stink, and I thought I'd die if I couldn't get away from it and yet, all the same, I knew that everything I was doing was just locking me in with it. And I didn't know," he paused, still flattening the beer can, "I didn't know, I still *don't* know, something kept telling me that maybe it was good to smell your own stink, but I didn't think that *that* was what I'd been trying to do—and—who can stand it?" and he abruptly dropped the ruined beer can, looking at me with a small, still smile, and then rose, walking to the window as though it were the lodestone rock. I watched his face, he watched the avenue. "I couldn't tell you when Mama died—but the reason I wanted to leave Harlem so bad was to get away from drugs. And then, when I ran away, that's what I was running from—really. When I came back, nothing had changed, *I* hadn't changed, I was just—older." And he stopped, drumming with his fingers on the windowpane. The sun had vanished, soon darkness would fall. I watched his face. "It can come again," he said, almost as though speaking to himself. Then he turned to me. "It can come again," he repeated. "I just want you to know that."

"All right," I said, at last. "So it can come again, All right."

He smiled, but the smile was sorrowful. "I had to try to tell you," he said.

"Yes," I said. "I understand that."

"You're my brother," he said, looking straight at me, and not smiling at all.

"Yes," I repeated, "yes. I understand that."

He turned back to the window, looking out. "All that hatred down there," he said, "all that hatred and misery and love. It's a wonder it doesn't blow the avenue apart."

We went to the only nightclub on a short, dark street, downtown. We squeezed through the narrow, chattering, jam-packed bar to the entrance of the big room, where the bandstand was. And we stood there for a moment, for the lights were very dim in this room and we couldn't see. Then, "Hello, boy," said a voice and an enormous black man, much older than Sonny or myself, erupted out of all that atmospheric lighting and put an arm around Sonny's shoulder. "I been sitting right here," he said, "waiting for you."

He had a big voice, too, and heads in the darkness turned toward us.

Sonny grinned and pulled a little away, and said, "Creole, this is my brother. I told you about him."

Creole shook my hand. "I'm glad to meet you, son," he said, and it was clear that he was glad to meet me *there,* for Sonny's sake. And he smiled, "You got a real musician in *your* family," and he took his arm from Sonny's shoulder and slapped him, lightly, affectionately, with the back of his hand.

"Well. Now I've heard it all," said a voice behind us. This was another musician, and a friend of Sonny's, a coal-black, cheerful-looking man, built close to the ground. He immediately began confiding to me, at the top of his lungs, the most terrible things about Sonny, his teeth gleaming like a lighthouse and his laugh coming up out of him like the beginning of an earthquake. And it turned out that everyone at the bar knew Sonny, or almost everyone; some were musicians, working there, or nearby, or not working, some were simply hangers-on, and some were there to hear Sonny play. I was introduced to all of them and they were all very polite to me. Yet, it was clear that, for them, I was only Sonny's brother. Here, I was in Sonny's world. Or, rather: his kingdom. Here, it was not even a question that his veins bore royal blood.

They were going to play soon and Creole installed me, by myself, at a table in a dark corner. Then I watched them, Creole, and the little black man, and Sonny, and the others, while they horsed around, standing just below the bandstand. The light from the bandstand spilled just a little short of them and, watching them laughing and gesturing and moving about, I had the feeling that they, nevertheless, were being most careful not to step into that circle of light too suddenly: that if they moved into the light too suddenly, without thinking, they would perish in flame. Then, while I watched, one of them, the small, black man, moved into the light and crossed the bandstand and started fooling around with his drums. Then—being funny and being, also, extremely ceremonious—Creole took Sonny by the arm and led him to the piano. A woman's voice called Sonny's name and a few hands started clapping. And Sonny, also being funny and being ceremonious, and so touched, I think, that he could have cried, but neither hiding it nor showing it, riding it like a man, grinned, and put both hands to his heart and bowed from the waist.

Creole then went to the bass fiddle and a lean, very bright-skinned brown man jumped up on the bandstand and picked up his horn. So there they were, and the atmosphere on the bandstand and in the room began to change and tighten. Someone stepped up to the microphone and announced them. Then there were all kinds of murmurs. Some people at the bar shushed others. The waitress ran around, frantically getting in the last orders, guys and chicks got closer to each other, and the lights on the bandstand, on the quartet, turned to a kind of indigo. Then they all looked different there. Creole looked about him for the last time, as though he were making certain that all his chickens were in the coop, and then he—jumped and struck the fiddle. And there they were.

All I know about music is that not many people ever really hear it. And even then, on the rare occasions when something opens within, and the music enters, what we mainly hear, or hear corroborated, are personal, private, vanishing evocations. But the man who creates the music is hearing something else, is dealing with the roar rising from the void and imposing order on it as it hits the air. What is evoked in him, then, is of another order, more terrible because it has no words, and triumphant, too, for that same reason. And his triumph, when he triumphs, is ours. I just watched Sonny's face. His face was troubled, he was working hard, but he wasn't with it. And I had the feeling that, in a way, everyone on the bandstand was waiting for him, both waiting for him and pushing him along. But as I began to watch Creole, I realized that it was Creole who held them all back. He had them on a short rein. Up there, keeping the beat with his whole body, wailing on the fiddle, with his eyes half closed, he was listening to everything, but he was listening to Sonny. He was having a dialogue with Sonny. He wanted Sonny to leave the shoreline and strike out for the deep water. He was Sonny's witness that deep water and drowning were not the same thing—he had been there, and he knew. And he wanted Sonny to know. He was waiting for Sonny to do the things on the keys which would let Creole know that Sonny was in the water.

And, while Creole listened, Sonny moved, deep within, exactly like someone in torment. I had never before thought of how awful the relationship must be between the musician and his instrument. He has to fill it, this instrument, with the breath of life, his own. He has to make it do what he wants it to do. And a piano is just a piano. It's made out of so much wood and wires and little hammers and big ones, and ivory. While there's only so much you can do with it, the only way to find this out is to try; to try and make it do everything.

And Sonny hadn't been near a piano for over a year. And he wasn't on much better terms with his life, not the life that stretched before him now. He and the piano stammered, started one way, got scared, stopped; started another way, panicked, marked time, started again; then seemed to have found a direction, panicked again, got stuck. And the face I saw on Sonny I'd never seen before. Everything had been burned out of it, and, at the same time, things usually hidden were being burned in, by the fire and fury of the battle which was occurring in him up there.

Yet, watching Creole's face as they neared the end of the first set, I had the feeling that something had happened, something I hadn't heard. Then they finished, there was scattered applause, and then, without an instant's warning, Creole started into something else, it was almost sardonic, it was *Am I Blue.* And, as though he commanded, Sonny began to play. Something began to happen. And Creole let out the reins. The dry, low, black man said something awful on the drums, Creole answered, and the drums talked back. Then the horn insisted, sweet and high, slightly detached perhaps, and Creole listened, commenting now and then, dry, and driving, beautiful and calm and old. Then they all came together again, and Sonny was part of the family again. I could tell this from his face. He seemed to have found, right there beneath his fingers, a damn brand-new piano. It seemed that he couldn't get over it. Then, for awhile, just being happy with Sonny, they seemed to be agreeing with him that brand-new pianos certainly were a gas.

Then Creole stepped forward to remind them that what they were playing was the blues. He hit something in all of them, he hit something in me, myself, and the music tightened and deepened, apprehension began to beat the air. Creole began to tell us what the blues were all about. They were not about anything very new. He and his boys up there were keeping it new, at the risk of ruin, destruction, madness, and death, in order to find new ways to make us listen. For, while the tale of how we suffer, and how we are delighted, and how we may triumph is never new, it always must be heard. There isn't any other tale to tell, it's the only light we've got in all this darkness.

And this tale, according to that face, that body, those strong hands on those strings, has another aspect in every country, and a new depth in every generation. Listen, Creole seemed to be saying, listen. Now these are Sonny's blues. He made the little black man on the drums know it, and the bright, brown man on the horn. Creole wasn't trying any longer to get Sonny in the water. He was wishing him Godspeed. Then he stepped back, very slowly, filling the air with the immense suggestion that Sonny speak for himself.

Then they all gathered around Sonny and Sonny played. Every now and again one of them seemed to say, amen. Sonny's fingers filled the air with life, his life. But that life contained so many others. And Sonny went all the way back, he really began with the spare, flat statement of the opening phrase of the song. Then he began to make it his. It was very beautiful because it wasn't hurried and it was no longer a lament. I seemed to hear with what burning he had made it his, with what burning we had yet to make it ours, how we could cease lamenting. Freedom lurked around us and I understood, at last, that he could help us to be free if we would listen, that he would never be free until we did. Yet, there was no battle in his face now. I heard what he had gone through, and would continue to go through until he came to rest in earth. He had made it his: that long line, of which we knew only Mama and Daddy. And he was giving it back, as everything must be given back, so that, passing through death, it can live forever. I saw my mother's face again, and felt, for the first time, how the stones of the road she had walked on must have bruised her feet. I saw the moonlit road where my father's brother died. And it brought something else back to me, and carried me past it, I saw my little girl again and felt Isabel's tears again, and I felt my own tears begin to rise. And I was yet aware that this was only a moment, that the world waited outside, as hungry as a tiger, and that trouble stretched above us, longer than the sky.

Then it was over. Creole and Sonny let out their breath, both soaking wet, and grinning. There was a lot of applause and some of it was real. In the dark, the girl came by and I asked her to take drinks to the bandstand. There was a long pause, while they talked up there in the indigo light and after awhile I saw the girl put a Scotch and milk on top of the piano for Sonny. He didn't seem to notice it, but just before they started playing again, he sipped from it and looked toward me, and nodded. Then he put it back on top of the piano. For me, then, as they began to play again, it glowed and shook above my brother's head like the very cup of trembling.

1957, 1965

FLANNERY O'CONNOR
(1925–1964)

Flannery O'Connor had a realistic intelligence, an ironic and unsentimental approach to literary creativity. There is a simplicity in her novels and short stories, a basic acceptance of the human situation, that illuminates and justifies her choice of subject matter. She admitted to a preference for the vulgar and the grotesque, but her sympathetic detachment presents her characters in an appealing and unforgettable light.

A native Georgian, she was born in Savannah, March 25, 1925, and spent her youth in Milledgeville, where she died at the age of thirty-nine. Her creative ability was in evidence during her college years; she began to publish before she received her M.A. in 1947, and she had a number of subsequent grants for creative writing.

She was a serious craftsman who acknowledged and exploited her southern Catholic background, yet she was genuinely concerned with the enigmatic, subconscious levels of experience. She had the gift of countering the mystical with reality. As she said, "The fiction writer presents mystery through manners, grace through nature, but when he finishes, there always has to be left over that sense of Mystery which cannot be accounted for by any human formula." The story below appears in the volume *A Good Man Is Hard to Find* (1955).

The novels are *Wise Blood,* 1952, and *The Violent Bear It Away,* 1960. Volumes of stories are *A Good Man Is Hard to Find,* 1955, and *Everything That Rises Must Converge,* 1965. *The Complete Stories* was published in 1971. *Mystery and Manners: Occasional Prose,* 1969, was edited by Sally and Robert Fitzgerald. Sally Fitzgerald edited a collection of letters, *The Habit of Being,* 1979. Charles Stephens edited *The Correspondence of Flannery O'Connor and the Brainard Cheneys,* 1986.

Critical studies include Melvin J. Friedman and Lewis A. Lawson, eds., *The Added Dimension: The Art and Mind of Flannery O'Connor,* 1966; Carter W. Martin, *The True Country: Themes in the Fiction of Flannery O'Connor,* 1969; Josephine Hendin, *The World of Flannery O'Connor,* 1970; David Eggenschwiler, *The Christian Humanism of Flannery O'Connor,* 1972; Sister Kathleen Feeley, *Flannery O'Connor: Voice of the Peacock,* 1972; Miles Orvell, *Invisible Parade: The Fiction of Flannery O'Connor,* 1972; Dorothy Walters, *Flannery O'Connor,* 1973; Preston M. Browning, *Flannery O'Connor,* 1974; Dorothy Tuck McFarland, *Flannery O'Connor,* 1976; John R. May, *The Pruning Word: The Parables of Flannery O'Connor,* 1976; Robert Coles, *Flannery O'Connor's South,* 1980; Carol Shloss, *Flannery O'Connor's Dark Comedies,* 1980; Marshall Gentry, *Flannery O'Connor's Religion of the Grotesque,* 1986; and Edward Kessler, *Flannery O'Connor and the Language of Apocalypse,* 1986.

Good Country People

Besides the neutral expression that she wore when she was alone, Mrs. Freeman had two others, forward and reverse, that she used for all her human dealings. Her forward expression was steady and driving like the advance of a heavy truck. Her eyes never swerved to left or right but turned as the story turned as if they followed a yellow line down the center of it. She seldom used the other expression because it was not often necessary for her to retract a statement, but when she did, her face came to a complete stop, there was an almost imperceptible movement of her black eyes, during which they seemed to be receding, and then the observer would see that Mrs. Freeman, though she might stand there as real as several grain sacks thrown on top of each other, was no longer there in spirit. As for getting anything across to her when this was the case, Mrs. Hopewell had given it up. She might talk her head off. Mrs. Freeman could never be brought to admit herself wrong on any point. She would stand there and if she could be brought to say anything, it was something like, "Well, I wouldn't of said it was and I wouldn't of said it wasn't," or letting her gaze range over the top kitchen shelf where there was an assortment of dusty bottles, she might remark, "I see you ain't ate many of them figs you put up last summer."

They carried on their most important business in the kitchen at breakfast. Every morning Mrs. Hopewell got up at seven o'clock and lit her gas heater and Joy's. Joy was her daughter, a large blonde girl who had an artificial leg. Mrs. Hopewell thought of her as a child though she was thirty-two years old and highly educated. Joy would get up while her mother was eating and lumber into the bathroom and slam the door, and before long, Mrs. Freeman would arrive at the back door. Joy would hear her mother call, "Come on in," and then they would talk for a while in low voices that were indistinguishable in the bathroom. By the time Joy came in, they had usually finished the weather report and were on one or the other of Mrs. Freeman's daughters, Glynese or Carramae. Joy called them Glycerin and Caramel. Glynese, a redhead, was eighteen and had many admirers; Carramae, a blonde, was only fifteen but already married and pregnant. She could not keep anything on her stomach. Every morning Mrs. Freeman told Mrs. Hopewell how many times she had vomited since the last report.

Mrs. Hopewell liked to tell people that Glynese and Carramae were two of the finest girls she knew and that Mrs. Freeman was a *lady* and that she was never ashamed to take her anywhere or introduce her to anybody they might meet. Then she would tell how she had happened to hire the Freemans in the first place and how they were a godsend to her and how she had had them four years. The reason for her keeping them so long was that they were not trash. They were good country people. She had telephoned the man whose name they had given as a reference and he had told her that Mr. Freeman was a good farmer but that his wife was the nosiest woman ever to walk the earth. "She's got to be into everything," the man said. "If she don't get there before the dust settles, you can bet she's dead, that's all. She'll want to know all your business. I can stand him real good," he had said, "but me nor my wife neither could have stood that woman one more minute on this place." That had put Mrs. Hopewell off for a few days.

She had hired them in the end because there were no other applicants but she had made up her mind beforehand exactly how she would handle the woman. Since she was the type who had to be into everything, then, Mrs. Hopewell had decided, she would not only let her be into everything, she would *see to it* that she was into everything—she would give her the responsibility of everything, she would put her in charge. Mrs. Hopewell had no bad qualities of her own but she was able to use other people's in such a constructive way that she never felt the lack. She had hired the Freemans and she had kept them four years.

Nothing is perfect. This was one of Mrs. Hopewell's favorite sayings. Another was: that is life! And still another, the most important, was: well, other people have their opinions too. She would make these statements, usually at the table, in a tone of gentle insistence as if no one held them but her, and the large hulking Joy, whose constant outrage had obliterated every expression from her face, would stare just a little to the side of her, her eyes icy blue, with the look of someone who has achieved blindness by an act of will and means to keep it.

When Mrs. Hopewell said to Mrs. Freeman that life was like that, Mrs. Freeman would say, "I always said so myself." Nothing had been arrived at by anyone that had not first been arrived at by her. She was quicker than Mr. Freeman. When Mrs.

Hopewell said to her after they had been on the place a while, "You know, you're the wheel behind the wheel," and winked, Mrs. Freeman had said, "I know it. I've always been quick. It's some that are quicker than others."

"Everybody is different," Mrs. Hopewell said.

"Yes, most people is," Mrs. Freeman said.

"It takes all kinds to make the world."

"I always said it did myself."

The girl was used to this kind of dialogue for breakfast and more of it for dinner; sometimes they had it for supper too. When they had no guest they ate in the kitchen because that was easier. Mrs. Freeman always managed to arrive at some point during the meal and to watch them finish it. She would stand in the doorway if it were summer but in the winter she would stand with one elbow on top of the refrigerator and look down on them, or she would stand by the gas heater, lifting the back of her skirt slightly. Occasionally she would stand against the wall and roll her head from side to side. At no time was she in any hurry to leave. All this was very trying on Mrs. Hopewell but she was a woman of great patience. She realized that nothing is perfect and that in the Freemans she had good country people and that if, in this day and age, you get good country people, you had better hang onto them.

She had had plenty of experience with trash. Before the Freemans she had averaged one tenant family a year. The wives of these farmers were not the kind you would want to be around you for very long. Mrs. Hopewell, who had divorced her husband long ago, needed someone to walk over the fields with her; and when Joy had to be impressed for these services, her remarks were usually so ugly and her face so glum that Mrs. Hopewell would say, "If you can't come pleasantly, I don't want you at all," to which the girl, standing square and rigid-shouldered with her neck thrust slightly forward, would reply, "If you want me, here I am—LIKE I AM."

Mrs. Hopewell excused this attitude because of the leg (which had been shot off in a hunting accident when Joy was ten). It was hard for Mrs. Hopewell to realize that her child was thirty-two now and that for more than twenty years she had had only one leg. She thought of her still as a child because it tore her heart to think instead of the poor stout girl in her thirties who had never danced a step or had any *normal* good times. Her name was really Joy but as soon as she was twenty-one and away from home, she had had it legally changed. Mrs. Hopewell was certain that she had thought and thought until she had hit upon the ugliest name in any language. Then she had gone and had the beautiful name, Joy, changed without telling her mother until after she had done it. Her legal name was Hulga.

When Mrs. Hopewell thought the name, Hulga, she thought of the broad blank hull of a battleship. She would not use it. She continued to call her Joy to which the girl responded but in a purely mechanical way.

Hulga had learned to tolerate Mrs. Freeman who saved her from taking walks with her mother. Even Glynese and Carramae were useful when they occupied attention that might otherwise have been directed at her. At first she had thought she could not stand Mrs. Freeman for she had found that it was not possible to be rude to her. Mrs. Freeman would take on strange resentments and for days together she would be sullen but the source of her displeasure was always obscure; a direct attack, a positive leer, blatant ugliness to her face—these never touched her. And without warning one day, she began calling her Hulga.

She did not call her that in front of Mrs. Hopewell who would have been incensed but when she and the girl happened to be out of the house together, she would say something and add the name Hulga to the end of it, and the big spectacled Joy-Hulga would scowl and redden as if her privacy had been intruded upon. She considered the name her personal affair. She had arrived at it first purely on the basis of its ugly sound and then the full genius of its fitness had struck her. She had a vision of the name working like the ugly sweating Vulcan[1] who stayed in the furnace and to whom, presumably, the goddess had to come when called. She saw it as the name of her highest creative act. One of her major triumphs was that her mother had not been able to turn her dust into Joy, but the greater one was that she had been able to turn it herself into Hulga. However, Mrs. Freeman's relish for using the name only irritated her. It was as if Mrs. Freeman's beady steel-pointed eyes had penetrated far enough behind her face to reach some secret fact. Something about her seemed to fascinate Mrs. Freeman and then one day Hulga realized that it was the artificial leg. Mrs. Freeman had a special fondness for the details of secret infections, hidden deformities, assaults upon children. Of diseases, she preferred the lingering or incurable. Hulga had heard Mrs. Hopewell give her the details of the hunting accident, how the leg had been literally blasted off, how she had never lost consciousness. Mrs. Freeman could listen to it any time as if it had happened an hour ago.

When Hulga stumped into the kitchen in the morning (she could walk without making the awful noise but she made it—Mrs. Hopewell was certain—because it was ugly-sounding), she glanced at them and did not speak. Mrs. Hopewell would be in her red kimono with her hair tied around her head in rags. She would be sitting at the table, finishing her breakfast and Mrs. Freeman would be hanging by her elbow outward from the refrigerator, looking down at the table. Hulga always put her eggs on the stove to boil and then stood over them with her arms folded, and Mrs. Hopewell would look at her—a kind of indirect gaze divided between her and Mrs. Freeman—and would think that if she would only keep herself up a little, she wouldn't be so bad looking. There was nothing wrong with her face that a pleasant expression wouldn't help. Mrs. Hopewell said that people who looked on the bright side of things would be beautiful even if they were not.

Whenever she looked at Joy this way, she could not help but feel that it would have been better if the child had not taken the Ph.D. It had certainly not brought her out any and now that she had it, there was no more excuse for her to go to school again. Mrs. Hopewell thought it was nice for girls to go to school to have a good time but Joy had "gone through." Anyhow, she would not have been strong enough to go again. The doctors had told Mrs. Hopewell that with the best of care, Joy might see forty-five. She had a weak heart. Joy had made it plain that if it had not been for this condition, she would be far from these red hills and good country people. She would be in a university lecturing to people who knew what she was talking about. And Mrs. Hopewell could very well picture her there, looking like a scarecrow and lecturing to more of the same. Here she went about all day in a six-year-old skirt and a yellow sweat shirt with a faded cowboy on a horse embossed

1. In Roman mythology, the lame blacksmith to the gods and husband of Venus, goddess of love.

on it. She thought this was funny; Mrs. Hopewell thought it was idiotic and showed simply that she was still a child. She was brilliant but she didn't have a grain of sense. It seemed to Mrs. Hopewell that every year she grew less like other people and more like herself—bloated, rude, and squint-eyed. And she said such strange things! To her own mother she had said—without warning, without excuse, standing up in the middle of a meal with her face purple and her mouth half full—"Woman! do you ever look inside? Do you ever look inside and see what you are *not?* God!" she had cried sinking down again and staring at her plate, "Malebranche was right: we are not our own light. We are not our own light!" Mrs. Hopewell had no idea to this day what brought that on. She had only made the remark, hoping Joy would take it in, that a smile never hurt anyone.

The girl had taken the Ph.D. in philosophy and this left Mrs. Hopewell at a complete loss. You could say, "My daughter is a nurse," or "My daughter is a school teacher," or even, "My daughter is a chemical engineer." You could not say, "My daughter is a philosopher." That was something that had ended with the Greeks and Romans. All day Joy sat on her neck in a deep chair, reading. Sometimes she went for walks but she didn't like dogs or cats or birds or flowers or nature or nice young men. She looked at nice young men as if she could smell their stupidity.

One day Mrs. Hopewell had picked up one of the books the girl had just put down and opening it at random, she read, "Science, on the other hand, has to assert its soberness and seriousness afresh and declare that it is concerned solely with what-is. Nothing—how can it be for science anything but a horror and a phantasm? If science is right, then one thing stands firm: science wishes to know nothing of nothing. Such is after all the strictly scientific approach to Nothing. We know it by wishing to know nothing of Nothing." These words had been underlined with a blue pencil and they worked on Mrs. Hopewell like some evil incantation in gibberish. She shut the book quickly and went out of the room as if she were having a chill.

This morning when the girl came in, Mrs. Freeman was on Carramae. "She thrown up four times after supper," she said, "and was up twict in the night after three o'clock. Yesterday she didn't do nothing but ramble in the bureau drawer. All she did. Stand up there and see what she could run up on."

"She's got to eat," Mrs. Hopewell muttered, sipping her coffee, while she watched Joy's back at the stove. She was wondering what the child had said to the Bible salesman. She could not imagine what kind of a conversation she could possibly have had with him.

He was a tall gaunt hatless youth who had called yesterday to sell them a Bible. He had appeared at the door, carrying a large black suitcase that weighted him so heavily on one side that he had to brace himself against the door facing. He seemed on the point of collapse but he said in a cheerful voice, "Good morning, Mrs. Cedars!" and set the suitcase down on the mat. He was not a bad-looking young man though he had on a bright blue suit and yellow socks that were not pulled up far enough. He had prominent face bones and a streak of sticky-looking brown hair falling across his forehead.

"I'm Mrs. Hopewell," she said.

"Oh!" he said, pretending to look puzzled but with his eyes sparkling, "I saw it said 'The Cedars,' on the mailbox so I thought you was Mrs. Cedars!" and he burst out in a pleasant laugh. He picked up the satchel and under cover of a pant, he fell forward into her hall. It was rather as if the suitcase had moved first, jerking him after it. "Mrs. Hopewell!" he said and grabbed her hand. "I hope you are well!" and he laughed again and then all at once his face sobered completely. He paused and gave her a straight earnest look and said, "Lady, I've come to speak of serious things."

"Well, come in," she muttered, none too pleased because her dinner was almost ready. He came into the parlor and sat down on the edge of a straight chair and put the suitcase between his feet and glanced around the room as if he were sizing her up by it. Her silver gleamed on the two sideboards; she decided he had never been in a room as elegant as this.

"Mrs. Hopewell," he began, using her name in a way that sounded almost intimate, "I know you believe in Chrustian service."

"Well yes," she murmured.

"I know," he said and paused, looking very wise with his head cocked on one side, "that you're a good woman. Friends have told me."

Mrs. Hopewell never liked to be taken for a fool. "What are you selling?" she asked.

"Bibles," the young man said and his eye raced around the room before he added, "I see you have no family Bible in your parlor, I see that is the one lack you got!"

Mrs. Hopewell could not say, "My daughter is an atheist and won't let me keep the Bible in the parlor." She said, stiffening slightly, "I keep my Bible by my bedside." This was not the truth. It was in the attic somewhere.

"Lady," he said, "the word of God ought to be in the parlor."

"Well, I think that's a matter of taste," she began. "I think . . ."

"Lady," he said, "for a Chrustian, the word of God ought to be in every room in the house besides in his heart. I know you're a Chrustian because I can see it in every line of your face."

She stood up and said, "Well, young man, I don't want to buy a Bible and I smell my dinner burning."

He didn't get up. He began to twist his hands and looking down at them, he said softly, "Well lady, I'll tell you the truth—not many people want to buy one nowadays and besides, I know I'm real simple. I don't know how to say a thing but to say it. I'm just a country boy." He glanced up into her unfriendly face. "People like you don't like to fool with country people like me!"

"Why!" she cried, "good country people are the salt of the earth! Besides, we all have different ways of doing, it takes all kinds to make the world go 'round. That's life!"

"You said a mouthful," he said.

"Why, I think there aren't enough good country people in the world!" she said, stirred. "I think that's what's wrong with it!"

His face had brightened. "I didn't inraduce myself," he said. "I'm Manley Pointer from out in the country around Willohobie, not even from a place, just from near a place."

"You wait a minute," she said. "I have to see about my dinner." She went out to the kitchen and found Joy standing near the door where she had been listening.

"Get rid of the salt of the earth," she said, "and let's eat."

Mrs. Hopewell gave her a pained look and turned the heat down under the vegetables. "*I* can't be rude to anybody," she murmured and went back into the parlor.

He had opened the suitcase and was sitting with a Bible on each knee.

"You might as well put those up," she told him. "I don't want one."

"I appreciate your honesty," he said. "You don't see any more real honest people unless you go way out in the country."

"I know," she said, "real genuine folks!" Through the crack in the door she heard a groan.

"I guess a lot of boys come telling you they're working their way through college," he said, "but I'm not going to tell you that. Somehow," he said, "I don't want to go to college. I want to devote my life to Chrustian service. See," he said, lowering his voice, "I got this heart condition. I may not live long. When you know it's something wrong with you and you may not live long, well then, lady . . ." He paused, with his mouth open, and stared at her.

He and Joy had the same condition! She knew that her eyes were filling with tears but she collected herself quickly and murmured, "Won't you stay for dinner? We'd love to have you!" and was sorry the instant she heard herself say it.

"Yes mam," he said in an abashed voice, "I would sher love to do that!"

Joy had given him one look on being introduced to him and then throughout the meal had not glanced at him again. He had addressed several remarks to her, which she had pretended not to hear. Mrs. Hopewell could not understand deliberate rudeness, although she lived with it, and she felt she had always to overflow with hospitality to make up for Joy's lack of courtesy. She urged him to talk about himself and he did. He said he was the seventh child of twelve and that his father had been crushed under a tree when he himself was eight year old. He had been crushed very badly, in fact, almost cut in two and was practically not recognizable. His mother had got along the best she could by hard working and she had always seen that her children went to Sunday School and that they read the Bible every evening. He was now nineteen year old and he had been selling Bibles for four months. In that time he had sold seventy-seven Bibles and had the promise of two more sales. He wanted to become a missionary because he thought that was the way you could do most for people. "He who losest his life shall find it," he said simply and he was so sincere, so genuine and earnest that Mrs. Hopewell would not for the world have smiled. He prevented his peas from sliding onto the table by blocking them with a piece of bread which he later cleaned his plate with. She could see Joy observing sidewise how he handled his knife and fork and she saw too that every few minutes, the boy would dart a keen appraising glance at the girl as if he were trying to attract her attention.

After dinner Joy cleared the dishes off the table and disappeared and Mrs. Hopewell was left to talk with him. He told her again about his childhood and his father's accident and about various things that had happened to him. Every five minutes or so she would stifle a yawn. He sat for two hours until finally she told him she must go because she had an appointment in town. He packed his Bibles and thanked her and prepared to leave, but in the doorway he stopped and wrung her hand and said that not on any of his trips had he met a lady as nice as her and he asked if he could come again. She had said she would always be happy to see him.

Joy had been standing in the road, apparently looking at something in the distance, when he came down the steps toward her, bent to the side with his heavy valise. He stopped where she was standing and confronted her directly. Mrs. Hopewell could not hear what he said but she trembled to think what Joy would say to him. She could see that after a minute Joy said something and that then the boy began to speak again, making an excited gesture with his free hand. After a minute Joy said something else at which the boy began to speak once more. Then to her amazement, Mrs. Hopewell saw the two of them walk off together, toward the gate. Joy had walked all the way to the gate with him and Mrs. Hopewell could not imagine what they had said to each other, and she had not yet dared to ask.

Mrs. Freeman was insisting upon her attention. She had moved from the refrigerator to the heater so that Mrs. Hopewell had to turn and face her in order to seem to be listening. "Glynese gone out with Harvey Hill again last night," she said. "She had this sty."

"Hill," Mrs. Hopewell said absently, "is that the one who works in the garage?"

"Nome, he's the one that goes to chiropracter school," Mrs. Freeman said. "She had this sty. Been had it two days. So she says when he brought her in the other night he says, 'Lemme get rid of that sty for you,' and she says, 'How?' and he says, 'You just lay yourself down acrost the seat of that car and I'll show you.' So she done it and he popped her neck. Kept on a-popping it several times until she made him quit. This morning," Mrs. Freeman said, "she ain't got no sty. She ain't got no traces of a sty."

"I never heard of that before," Mrs. Hopewell said.

"He ast her to marry him before the Ordinary," Mrs. Freeman went on, "and she told him she wasn't going to be married in no *office*."

"Well, Glynese is a fine girl," Mrs. Hopewell said. "Glynese and Carramae are both fine girls."

"Carramae said when her and Lyman was married Lyman said it sure felt sacred to him. She said he said he wouldn't take five hundred dollars for being married by a preacher."

"How much would he take?" the girl asked from the stove.

"He said he wouldn't take five hundred dollars," Mrs. Freeman repeated.

"Well we all have work to do," Mrs. Hopewell said.

"Lyman said it just felt more sacred to him," Mrs. Freeman said. "The doctor wants Carramae to eat prunes. Says instead of medicine. Says them cramps is coming from pressure. You know where I think it is?"

"She'll be better in a few weeks," Mrs. Hopewell said.

"In the tube," Mrs. Freeman said. "Else she wouldn't be as sick as she is."

Hulga had cracked her two eggs into a saucer and was bringing them to the table along with a cup of coffee that she had filled too full. She sat down carefully and began to eat, meaning to keep Mrs. Freeman there by questions if for any reason she showed an inclination to leave. She could perceive her mother's eye on her. The first round-about question would be about the Bible salesman and she did not wish to bring it on. "How did he pop her neck?" she asked.

Mrs. Freeman went into a description of how he had popped her neck. She said he owned a '55 Mercury but that Glynese said she would rather marry a man with only a '36 Plymouth who would be married by a preacher. The girl asked what if he had a '32 Plymouth and Mrs. Freeman said what Glynese had said was a '36 Plymouth.

Mrs. Hopewell said there were not many girls with Glynese's common sense. She said what she admired in those girls was their common sense. She said that reminded her that they had had a nice visitor yesterday, a young man selling Bibles. "Lord," she said, "he bored me to death but he was so sincere and genuine I couldn't be rude to him. He was just good country people, you know," she said, "—just the salt of the earth."

"I seen him walk up," Mrs. Freeman said, "and then later—I seen him walk off," and Hulga could feel the slight shift in her voice, the slight insinuation, that he had not walked off alone, had he? Her face remained expressionless but the color rose into her neck and she seemed to swallow it down with the next spoonful of egg. Mrs. Freeman was looking at her as if they had a secret together.

"Well, it takes all kinds of people to make the world go 'round," Mrs. Hopewell said. "It's very good we aren't all alike."

"Some people are more alike than others," Mrs. Freeman said.

Hulga got up and stumped, with about twice the noise that was necessary, into her room and locked the door. She was to meet the Bible salesman at ten o'clock at the gate. She had thought about it half the night. She had started thinking of it as a great joke and then she had begun to see profound implications in it. She had lain in bed imagining dialogues for them that were insane on the surface but that reached below to depths that no Bible salesman would be aware of. Their conversation yesterday had been of this kind.

He had stopped in front of her and had simply stood there. His face was bony and sweaty and bright, with a little pointed nose in the center of it, and his look was different from what it had been at the dinner table. He was gazing at her with open curiosity, with fascination, like a child watching a new fantastic animal at the zoo, and he was breathing as if he had run a great distance to reach her. His gaze seemed somehow familiar but she could not think where she had been regarded with it before. For almost a minute he didn't say anything. Then on what seemed an insuck of breath, he whispered, "You ever ate a chicken that was two days old?"

The girl looked at him stonily. He might have just put this question up for consideration at the meeting of a philosophical association. "Yes," she presently replied as if she had considered it from all angles.

"It must have been mighty small!" he said triumphantly and shook all over with little nervous giggles, getting very red in the face, and subsiding finally into his gaze of complete admiration, while the girl's expression remained exactly the same.

"How old are you?" he asked softly.

She waited some time before she answered. Then in a flat voice she said, "Seventeen."

His smiles came in succession like waves breaking on the surface of a little lake. "I see you got a wooden leg," he said. "I think you're real brave. I think you're real sweet."

The girl stood blank and solid and silent.

"Walk to the gate with me," he said. "You're a brave sweet little thing and I liked you the minute I seen you walk in the door."

Hulga began to move forward.

"What's your name?" he asked, smiling down on the top of her head.

"Hulga," she said.

"Hulga," he murmured, "Hulga. Hulga. I never heard of anybody name Hulga before. You're shy, aren't you, Hulga?" he asked.

She nodded, watching his large red hand on the handle of the giant valise.

"I like girls that wear glasses," he said. "I think a lot. I'm not like these people that a serious thought don't ever enter their heads. It's because I may die."

"I may die too," she said suddenly and looked up at him. His eyes were very small and brown, glittering feverishly.

"Listen," he said, "don't you think some people was meant to meet on account of what all they got in common and all? Like they both think serious thoughts and all?" He shifted the valise to his other hand so that the hand nearest her was free. He caught hold of her elbow and shook it a little. "I don't work on Saturday," he said. "I like to walk in the woods and see what Mother Nature is wearing. O'er the hills and far away. Pic-nics and things. Couldn't we go on a pic-nic tomorrow? Say yes, Hulga," he said and gave her a dying look as if he felt his insides about to drop out of him. He had even seemed to sway slightly toward her.

During the night she had imagined that she seduced him. She imagined that the two of them walked on the place until they came to the storage barn beyond the two back fields and there, she imagined, that things came to such a pass that she very easily seduced him and that then, of course, she had to reckon with his remorse. True genius can get an idea across even to an inferior mind. She imagined that she took his remorse in hand and changed it into a deeper understanding of life. She took all his shame away and turned it into something useful.

She set off for the gate at exactly ten o'clock, escaping without drawing Mrs. Hopewell's attention. She didn't take anything to eat, forgetting that food is usually taken on a picnic. She wore a pair of slacks and a dirty white shirt, and as an afterthought, she had put some Vapex on the collar of it since she did not own any perfume. When she reached the gate no one was there.

She looked up and down the empty highway and had the furious feeling that she had been tricked, that he had only meant to make her walk to the gate after the idea of him. Then suddenly he stood up, very tall, from behind a bush on the opposite embankment. Smiling, he lifted his hat which was new and wide-brimmed. He had not worn it yesterday and she wondered if he had bought it for the occasion. It was toast-colored with a red and white band around it and was slightly too large for him. He stepped from behind the bush still carrying the black valise. He had on the same suit and the same yellow socks sucked down in his shoes from walking. He crossed the highway and said, "I knew you'd come!"

The girl wondered acidly how he had known this. She pointed to the valise and asked, "Why did you bring your Bibles?"

He took her elbow, smiling down on her as if he could not stop. "You can never tell when you'll need the word of God, Hulga," he said. She had a moment in which she doubted that this was actually happening and then they began to climb the embankment. They went down into the pasture toward the woods. The boy walked lightly by her side, bouncing on his toes. The valise did not seem to be heavy today; he even swung it. They crossed half the pasture without saying anything and then, putting his hand easily on the small of her back, he asked softly, "Where does your wooden leg join on?"

She turned an ugly red and glared at him and for an instant the boy looked abashed. "I didn't mean you no harm," he said. "I only meant you're so brave and all. I guess God takes care of you."

"No," she said, looking forward and walking fast, "I don't even believe in God."

At this he stopped and whistled. "No!" he exclaimed as if he were too astonished to say anything else.

She walked on and in a second he was bouncing at her side, fanning with his hat. "That's very unusual for a girl," he remarked, watching her out of the corner of his eye. When they reached the edge of the wood, he put his hand on her back again and drew her against him without a word and kissed her heavily.

The kiss, which had more pressure than feeling behind it, produced that extra surge of adrenalin in the girl that enables one to carry a packed trunk out of a burning house, but in her, the power went at once to the brain. Even before he released her, her mind, clear and detached and ironic anyway, was regarding him from a great distance, with amusement but with pity. She had never been kissed before and she was pleased to discover that it was an unexceptional experience and all a matter of the mind's control. Some people might enjoy drain water if they were told it was vodka. When the boy, looking expectant but uncertain, pushed her gently away, she turned and walked on, saying nothing as if such business, for her, were common enough.

He came along panting at her side, trying to help her when he saw a root that she might trip over. He caught and held back the long swaying blades of thorn vine until she had passed beyond them. She led the way and he came breathing heavily behind her. Then they came out on a sunlit hillside, sloping softly into another one a little smaller. Beyond, they could see the rusted top of the old barn where the extra hay was stored.

The hill was sprinkled with small pink weeds. "Then you ain't saved?" he asked suddenly, stopping.

The girl smiled. It was the first time she had smiled at him at all. "In my economy," she said, "I'm saved and you are damned but I told you I didn't believe in God."

Nothing seemed to destroy the boy's look of admiration. He gazed at her now as if the fantastic animal at the zoo had put its paw through the bars and given him a loving poke. She thought he looked as if he wanted to kiss her again and she walked on before he had the chance.

"Ain't there somewheres we can sit down sometime?" he murmured, his voice softening toward the end of the sentence.

"In that barn," she said.

They made for it rapidly as if it might slide away like a train. It was a large two-story barn, cool and dark inside. The boy pointed up the ladder that led into the loft and said, "It's too bad we can't go up there."

"Why can't we?" she asked.

"Yer leg," he said reverently.

The girl gave him a contemptuous look and putting both hands on the ladder, she climbed it while he stood below, apparently awestruck. She pulled herself expertly through the opening and then looked down at him and said, "Well, come on if you're coming," and he began to climb the ladder, awkwardly bringing the suitcase with him.

"We won't need the Bible," she observed.

"You never can tell," he said, panting. After he had got into the loft, he was a few seconds catching his breath. She had sat down in a pile of straw. A wide sheath of sunlight, filled with dust particles, slanted over her. She lay back against a bale, her face turned away, looking out the front opening of the barn where hay was thrown from a wagon into the loft. The two pink-speckled hillsides lay back against a dark ridge of woods. The sky was cloudless and cold blue. The boy dropped down by her side and put one arm under her and the other over her and began methodically kissing her face, making little noises like a fish. He did not remove his hat but it was pushed far enough back not to interfere. When her glasses got in his way, he took them off of her and slipped them into his pocket.

The girl at first did not return any of the kisses but presently she began to and after she had put several on his cheek, she reached his lips and remained there, kissing him again and again as if she were trying to draw all the breath out of him. His breath was clear and sweet like a child's and the kisses were sticky like a child's. He mumbled about loving her and about knowing when he first seen her that he loved her, but the mumbling was like the sleepy fretting of a child being put to sleep by his mother. Her mind, throughout this, never stopped or lost itself for a second to her feelings. "You ain't said you loved me none," he whispered finally, pulling back from her. "You got to say that."

She looked away from him off into the hollow sky and then down at a black ridge and then down farther into what appeared to be two green swelling lakes. She didn't realize he had taken her glasses but this landscape could not seem exceptional to her for she seldom paid any close attention to her surroundings.

"You got to say it," he repeated. "You got to say you love me."

She was always careful how she committed herself. "In a sense," she began, "if you use the word loosely, you might say that. But it's not a word I use. I don't have illusions. I'm one of those people who see *through* to nothing."

The boy was frowning. "You got to say it. I said it and you got to say it," he said.

The girl looked at him almost tenderly. "You poor baby," she murmured. "It's just as well you don't understand," and she pulled him by the neck, face-down, against her. "We are all damned," she said, "but some of us have taken off our blindfolds and see that there's nothing to see. It's a kind of salvation."

The boy's astonished eyes looked blankly through the ends of her hair. "Okay," he almost whined, "but do you love me or don'tcher?"

"Yes," she said and added, "in a sense. But I must tell you something. There mustn't be anything dishonest between us." She lifted his head and looked him in the eye. "I am thirty years old," she said. "I have a number of degrees."

The boy's look was irritated but dogged. "I don't care," he said. "I don't care a thing about what all you done. I just want to know if you love me or don'tcher?" and he caught her to him and wildly planted her face with kisses until she said, "Yes, yes."

"Okay then," he said, letting her go. "Prove it."

She smiled, looking dreamily out on the shifty landscape. She had seduced him without even making up her mind to try. "How?" she asked, feeling that he should be delayed a little.

He leaned over and put his lips to her ear. "Show me where your wooden leg joins on," he whispered.

The girl uttered a sharp little cry and her face instantly drained of color. The obscenity of the suggestion was not what shocked her. As a child she had sometimes been subject to feelings of shame but education had removed the last traces of that as a good surgeon scrapes for cancer; she would no more have felt it over what he was asking than she would have believed in his Bible. But she was as sensitive about the artificial leg as a peacock about his tail. No one ever touched it but her. She took care of it as someone else would his soul, in private and almost with her own eyes turned away. "No," she said.

"I known it," he muttered, sitting up. "You're just playing me for a sucker."

"Oh no no!" she cried. "It joins on at the knee. Only at the knee. Why do you want to see it?"

The boy gave her a long penetrating look. "Because," he said, "it's what makes you different. You ain't like anybody else."

She sat staring at him. There was nothing about her face or her round freezing-blue eyes to indicate that this had moved her; but she felt as if her heart had stopped and left her mind to pump her blood. She decided that for the first time in her life she was face to face with real innocence. This boy, with an instinct that came from beyond wisdom, had touched the truth about her. When after a minute, she said in a hoarse high voice, "All right," it was like surrendering to him completely. It was like losing her own life and finding it again, miraculously, in his.

Very gently he began to roll the slack leg up. The artificial limb, in a white sock and brown flat shoe, was bound in a heavy material like canvas and ended in an ugly jointure where it was attached to the stump. The boy's face and his voice were entirely reverent as he uncovered it and said, "Now show me how to take it off and on."

She took it off for him and put it back on again and then he took it off himself, handling it as tenderly as if it were a real one. "See!" he said with a delighted child's face. "Now I can do it myself!"

"Put it back on," she said. She was thinking that she would run away with him and that every night he would take the leg off and every morning put it back on again. "Put it back on," she said.

"Not yet," he murmured, setting it on its foot out of her reach. "Leave it off for a while. You got me instead."

She gave a little cry of alarm but he pushed her down and began to kiss her again. Without the leg she felt entirely dependent on him. Her brain seemed to have stopped thinking altogether and to be about some other function that it was not very good at. Different expressions raced back and forth over her face. Every now and then the boy, his eyes like two steel spikes, would glance behind him where the leg stood. Finally she pushed him off and said, "Put it back on me now."

"Wait," he said. He leaned the other way and pulled the valise toward him and opened it. It had a pale blue spotted lining and there were only two Bibles in it. He took one of these out and opened the cover of it. It was hollow and contained a pocket flask of whiskey, a pack of cards, and a small blue box with printing on it. He laid these out in front of her one at a time in an evenly-spaced row, like one presenting offerings at the shrine of a goddess. He put the blue box in her hand. THIS PRODUCT TO BE USED ONLY FOR THE PREVENTION OF DISEASE, she read, and dropped it. The boy was unscrewing the top of the flask. He stopped and pointed, with a smile, to the deck of cards. It was not an ordinary deck but one with an obscene picture on the back of each card. "Take a swig," he said, offering her the bottle first. He held it in front of her, but like one mesmerized, she did not move.

Her voice when she spoke had an almost pleading sound. "Aren't you," she murmured, "aren't you just good country people?"

The boy cocked his head. He looked as if he were just beginning to understand that she might be trying to insult him. "Yeah," he said, curling his lip slightly, "but it ain't held me back none. I'm as good as you any day in the week."

"Give me my leg," she said.

He pushed it farther away with his foot. "Come on now, let's begin to have us a good time," he said coaxingly. "We ain't got to know one another good yet."

"Give me my leg!" she screamed and tried to lunge for it but he pushed her down easily.

"What's the matter with you all of a sudden?" he asked, frowning as he screwed the top on the flask and put it quickly back inside the Bible. "You just a while ago said you didn't believe in nothing. I thought you was some girl!"

Her face was almost purple. "You're a Christian!" she hissed. "You're a fine Christian! You're just like them all—say one thing and do another. You're a perfect Christian, you're . . ."

The boy's mouth was set angrily. "I hope you don't think," he said in a lofty indignant tone, "that I believe in that crap! I may sell Bibles but I know which end is up and I wasn't born yesterday and I know where I'm going!"

"Give me my leg!" she screeched. He jumped up so quickly that she barely saw him sweep the cards and the blue box back into the Bible and throw the Bible into the valise. She saw him grab the leg and then she saw it for an instant slanted forlornly across the inside of the suitcase with a Bible at either side of its opposite ends. He slammed the lid shut and snatched up the valise and swung it down the hole and then stepped through himself.

When all of him had passed but his head, he turned and regarded her with a look that no longer had any admiration in it. "I've gotten a lot of interesting things," he said. "One time I got a woman's glass eye this way. And you needn't to think you'll catch me because Pointer ain't really my name. I use a different name at every house I call at and don't stay nowhere long. And I'll tell you another thing, Hulga," he said, using the name as if he didn't think much of it, "you ain't so smart. I been believing in nothing ever since I was born!" and then the toast-colored hat disappeared down the hole and the girl was left, sitting on the straw in the dusty sunlight. When she turned her churning face toward the opening, she saw his blue figure struggling successfully over the green speckled lake.

Mrs. Hopewell and Mrs. Freeman, who were in the back pasture, digging up onions, saw him emerge a little later from the woods and head across the meadow toward the highway. "Why, that looks like that nice dull young man that tried to sell me a Bible yesterday," Mrs. Hopewell said, squinting. "He must have been selling them to the Negroes back in there. He was so simple," she said, "but I guess the world would be better off if we were all that simple."

Mrs. Freeman's gaze drove forward and just touched him before he disappeared under the hill. Then she returned her attention to the evil-smelling onion shoot she was lifting from the ground. "Some can't be that simple," she said. "I know I never could."

1955

JOHN HAWKES
(1925–)

John Hawkes was born in Stamford, Connecticut, in 1925, in a world of country estates soon falling to ruin in the economic depression of the 1930's. An asthmatic childhood in Old Greenwich gave way to a brief stay in New York City before his mother took him, when he was ten, to Juneau, Alaska, to join his father, who hoped to find there the riches no longer within reach in Connecticut. "Those were years," Hawkes has written, "of being hemmed in and oppressed by grim mountains, black waters smelling of dead fish, eighty-mile-an-hour winds." In 1940, the threat of Japanese invasion of the Aleutian Islands sent the mother and boy back to New York, where Hawkes attended Trinity School on 91st Street, learned to fence, and heard boys bragging of "a game of kicking a dead baby in a gunny sack along a side street off Amsterdam Avenue." After a further retreat, to escape the possibility of German bombing of New York City, Hawkes spent a year and a half in Pawling, New York. He graduated from Pawling High School in 1943.

Admitted to Harvard that year, but soon failing, he left for the army only to receive a quick discharge because of his asthma. His experience of the war came as a volunteer ambulance driver with the American Field Service in Italy and Germany in 1944 and 1945. He had begun to write poetry in high school and had privately published a collection, *Fiasco Hall,* at Harvard in 1943. In the summer of 1947, however, he turned to prose fiction in his off hours while working as a guide at Fort Peck, Montana. Back at Harvard that fall, newly married, he began *The Cannibal* (1950), a nightmarish novel of a devastated Germany, seen from a German perspective. For the next several years he remained at Harvard, working after graduation for six years with Harvard University Press and then teaching English for three more years before accepting an assistant professorship in 1958 at Brown University, where he has taught, with leaves, ever since.

Hawkes's third novel, *The Lime Twig* (1961), consolidated his position as an American exotic, a prose stylist concerned less with telling a story than with juxtaposing brilliant images in parodic presentations of life and literature as demented dreams, riddled with sex and violence, guilt and anxiety. "I'm not interested in reflection or representation," he has said. "The writing of each fiction is a taking of a psychic journey; the fictions, themselves, are a form of journey." In *The Lime Twig* the setting is a post-war British racetrack world; its sources were as varied as the horses of Hawkes's Connecticut childhood, Mary Poppins books, British soldiers Hawkes had known in Europe, and Graham Greene's *Brighton Rock.* So, too, with his other fictions: Hawkes begins with a scene or character rooted in a small way in his experience or reading. He then works outward, following ripples of imagination that surround the central idea with strange relationships, erotic fantasies, and death. For *Second Skin* (1964), a brief stay on Vinalhaven, off the coast of Maine, and a year spent on Grenada provided imaginative background for a tale of incestuous attraction and suicide. Similarly, time spent in Vence, on the Cote d'Azur, led to the tangled marital relations, in a mythical Mediterranean setting, of *The Blood Oranges* (1971).

"After *The Blood Oranges,*" Hawkes has written, "travel and foreign countries were for me inseparable from writing." The next novel, *Death, Sleep & the Traveler* (1974), is set on shipboard. *Travesty* (1976) is the monologue of a suicidal murderer, set in France. *The Passion Artist*

(1979) centers on a prison for women in a city in central Europe. In *Virginie, Her Two Lives* (1982) the eleven-year-old narrator, a precocious sexual initiate, recounts the tangled, incestuous relationships leading to her deaths in eighteenth-century and twentieth-century France. In *Adventures in the Alaskan Skin Trade* (1985) Hawkes returns to the Alaska of his youth, narrating from the persona of the female proprietor of a house of prostitution.

Humors of Blood & Skin: A John Hawkes Reader, 1984, includes short fiction and selections from most of the novels, accompanied by commentary by the author. An earlier collection, *Lunar Landscapes: Stories and Short Novels 1949–1963,* 1969, includes *The Goose on the Grave* and *The Owl,* first published together in 1954, as well as other short pieces. An early novel not named above is *The Beetle Leg,* 1954. A recent short novel is *Innocence in Extremis,* 1985. *The Innocent Party,* 1966, collects four short plays.

Studies include Donald J. Grenier, *Comic Terror: The Novels of John Hawkes,* 1973; Patrick O'Donnell, *John Hawkes,* 1982; and Donald J. Grenier, *Understanding John Hawkes,* 1985.

The Universal Fears

Monday morning, bright as the birds, and there he stood for the first time among the twenty-seven girls who, if he had only known, were already playing the silence game. He looked at them, they looked at him, he never thought of getting a good grip on the pointer laid out lengthwise on that bare desk. Twenty-seven teen-age girls—homeless, bad-off, unloved, semi-literate, and each one of their poor unattractive faces was a condemnation of him, of all such schools for delinquent girls, of the dockyards lying round them like a seacoast of iron cranes, of the sunlight knifing through the grilles on the windows. They weren't faces to make you smile. Their sexual definition was vague and bleak. Hostile. But even then, in their first institutional moment together, he knew he didn't offer them any better from their point of view—only another fat man in the mid-fifties whose maleness meant nothing more than pants and jacket and belted belly and thin hair blacked with a cheap dye and brushed flat to the skull. Nothing in the new teacher to sigh about. So it was tit for tat, for them the desolation of more of the same, for him the deflation of the first glance that destroyed the possibility of finding just one keen lovely face to make the whole dreary thing worthwhile. Or a body promising a good shape to come. Or one set of sensual lips. Or one sign of adult responsiveness in any of those small eyes. But there was nothing, except the thought that perhaps their very sullenness might actually provide the most provocative landscape for the discovery of the special chemistry of pain that belongs to girls. Still he was already sweating in the armpits and going dry in the mouth.

"Right, girls," he said, "let's come to order."

In a shabby display of friendliness, accessibility, confidence, he slid from behind the desk and stood leaning the backs of his upper thighs against the front edge of it. Through the south window came the sounds of whistles and windlasses, from closer came the sounds of unloading coal. It made him think of a prison within a prison. No doubt the docks were considered the most suitable context for a school, so-called, for girls like these. Yes, the smells of brine and tar and buckets of oil that rode faintly in on the knifing light were only complementary to the stench of the room, to the soap, the thick shellac, the breath of the girls, the smell of their hair. It was a man's world for an apparently sexless lot of girls, and there was only one exotic aroma to be caught on that tide: the flowery wash of the sweet bay rum that clung to the thick embarrassed person of their old teacher new on the job.

"Right, girls," he said, returning warm glance for hostile stare, tic-like winks for the smoky and steady appraisal of small eyes, "right now, let's start with a few names. . . ."

And there they sat, unmoving, silent, ranked at three wooden benches of nine girls each, and all of their faces, whether large or small, thin or broad, dark or light, were blank as paper. Apparently they had made a pact before he entered the room to breathe in unison, so that now wherever he looked—first row on the left, first on the right—he was only too aware of the deliberate and ugly harmony of flat chests or full that were rising and falling slowly, casually, but always together.

Challenging the prof? Had they really agreed among themselves to be uncooperative? To give him a few bad minutes on the first day? Poor things, he thought, and crossed his fatty ankles, rested one flat hand on the uphill side of the belly, and then once more he looked them over at random, bearing down on a pair of shoulders like broken sticks, two thin lips bruised from chewing, a head of loose brown hair and another with a thin mane snarled in elastic bands, and some eyes without lashes, the closed books, claw marks evident on a sallow cheek.

"Girl on the end, there," he said all at once, stopping and swinging his attention back to the long black hair, the boy's shirt buttoned to the throat, the slanted eyes that never moved, "what's your name? Or you," he said, nodding at one of the younger ones, "what's yours?" He smiled, he waited, he shifted his glance from girl to girl, he began to make small but comforting gestures with the hand already resting on what he called his middle mound.

And then they attacked. The nearest bench was going over and coming his way like the side of a house undergoing demolition, and then the entire room was erupting not in noise but in the massed and silent motion of girls determined to drive their teacher out of the door, out of the school, and away, away, if they did not destroy him first right there on the floor. They leaped, they swung round the ends, tightlipped they toppled against each other and rushed at him. He managed to raise his two hands to the defensive position, fingers fanned out in sheer disbelief and terror, but the cry with which he had thought to stop them merely stuck in his throat, while for an instant longer he stood there pushing air with his trembling outthrust hands. The girls tripped, charged from both sides of the room, swarmed over the fallen benches in the middle, dove with undeniable intent to seize and incapacitate his person.

The pointer, yes, the pointer, it flashed to his mind, invisibly it hovered within his reach, burned like a long thin weapon with which he might have struck them, stabbed them, beaten them, fended them off. But of course the pointer was behind him and he dared not turn, dared not drop the guard of his now frenzied hands. In an instant he saw it all—the moving girls between himself and the door, the impenetrable web of iron battened to each one of the dusty windows, and he knew there was no way out, no help. A shoe flew past his ear, a full-fifty tin of cigarettes hit the high ceiling above his head and exploded, rained down on him in his paralysis and the girls in their charge. No pointer, no handy instrument for self-defense, no assistance coming from anywhere.

And then the sound came on, adding to that turbulent pantomime the shrieks of their anger, so that what until this instant had been impending violence brimming in a bowl of unnatural silence, now became imminent brutality in a conventional context of the audionics of wrath. His own cry was stifled, his head was filled with the fury of that small mob.

"Annette . . . !"
"Deborah . . . !"
"Fuck off . . ."
"Now . . . now . . ."
"Kill him . . . !"

Despite their superior numbers they were not able to smother him in the first rush, and despite his own disbelief and fear he did not go down beneath them without a fight. Quite the contrary, because the first to reach him was of medium height, about fourteen, with her ribs showing through her jersey and a cheap bracelet twirling on her ankle. And before she could strike a blow he caught her in the crook of his left arm and locked her against his trembling belly and squeezed the life from her eyes, the breath from her lungs, the hate from her undersized constricted heart. He felt her warmth, her limpness, her terror. Then he relaxed the pressure of his arm and as the slight girl sank to his feet, he drove a doubled fist into the pimpled face of a young thick-lipped assailant whose auburn hair had been milked of its fire in long days and nights of dockyard rain. The nose broke, the mouth dissolved, his fist was ringed with blood and faded hair.

"You fucking old bastard," said a voice off his left shoulder, and then down he went with a knee in his ribs, arms around his neck and belly, a shod foot in the small of his back. For one more moment, while black seas washed over the deck and the clouds burst, the pit yawned, the molten light of the sun drained down as from a pink collapsing sack in the sky, he managed to keep to his all-fours. And it was exactly in this position that he opened his eyes, looked up, but only in time to receive full in the mouth the mighty downward blow of the small sharp fist of the slant-eyed girl whose name he had first requested. The black hair, the boy's gray workshirt buttoned tight around the neck, a look of steady intensity in the brown eyes, and the legs apart, the body bent slightly down, the elbow cocked, and then the aim, the frown, the little fist landing with unexpected force on the loose torn vulnerable mouth—yes, it was the same girl, no doubt of it.

Blood on the floor. Mouth full of broken china. A loud kick driven squarely between the buttocks. And still through the forests of pain he noted the little brassy zipper of someone's fly, a sock like striped candy, a flat bare stomach gouged by an old scar, bright red droplets making a random pattern on the open pages of an outmoded Form One Math. He tried to shake a straddling bony tormentor off his bruised back, bore another shock to the head, another punch in the side, and then he went soft, dropped, rolled over, tried to shield his face with his shoulder, cupped both hurt hands over the last of the male features hiding down there between his legs.

They piled on. He saw the sudden blade of a knife. They dragged each other off, they screamed. He groaned. He tried to worm his heavy beaten way toward the door. He tried to defend himself with hip, with elbow. And beneath that struggling mass of girls he began to feel his fat and wounded body slowing down, stopping, becoming only a still wet shadow on the rough and splintered wood of the classroom floor. And now and then through the shrieking he heard the distant voices.

"Cathy . . ."
"Eleanora . . ."
"Get his fucking globes . . ."
"Get the globes . . ."

They pushed, they pulled, they tugged, and then with his eyes squeezed shut he knew suddenly that they were beginning to work together in some terrible accord that depended on childish unspoken intelligence, cruel cooperation. He heard the hissing of the birds, he felt their hands. They turned him over—face up, belly up —and sat on his still-breathing carcass. One of them tore loose his necktie of cream-colored and magenta silk while simultaneously his only white shirt, fabric bleached and weakened by the innumerable Sunday washings he had given it in his small lavatory sink, split in a long clean easy tear from his neck to navel. They flung his already mangled spectacles against the blackboard. They removed one shoe, one sock, and yanked the shabby jacket off his right shoulder and bounced up and down on his sagging knees, dug fingernails into the exposed white bareness of his right breast. Momentarily his left eye came unstuck and through the film of his tears he noted that the ringleader was the girl with the auburn hair and broken nose. She was riding his thighs, her sleeves were rolled, her thick lower lip was caught between her teeth in a parody of schoolgirl concentration, despite her injury and the blood on her face. It occurred to him that her pale hair deserved the sun. But then he felt a jolt in the middle, a jolt at the hips, and of course he had known all along that it was his pants they were after, pants and underpants. Then she had them halfway down, and he smelled her cheap scent, heard their gasping laughter, and felt the point of the clasp knife pierce his groin.

"He's fucking fat, he is . . ."

"The old suck . . ."

In his welter of pain and humiliation he writhed but did not cry out, writhed but made no final effort to heave them off, to stop the knife. What was the use? And wasn't he aware at last that all his poor street girls were actually bent to an operation of love not murder? Mutilated, demeaned, room a shambles and teacher overcome, still he knew in his fluid and sinking consciousness that all his young maenads[1] were trying only to feast on love.

"Off him! Off him!" came the loud and menacing voice from the doorway while he, who no longer wanted saving, commenced a long low moan.

"Get away from him at once, you little bitches . . . !"

There he was, lying precisely as the victim lies, helplessly inseparable from the sprawled and bloodied shape the victim makes in the middle of the avenue at the foot of the trembling omnibus. He was blind. He could not move, could not speak. But in customary fashion he had the distinct impression of his mangled self as noted, say, from the doorway where the director stood. Yes, it was all perfectly clear. He was quite capable of surveying what the director surveyed—the naked foot, the abandoned knife, the blood like a pattern spread beneath the body, the soft dismembered carcass fouling the torn shirt and crumpled pants. The remnants of significant male anatomy were still in hiding, dazed, anesthetized, but the pinched white hairy groin, still bleeding, was calling itself to his passive consciousness while beckoning the director to a long proud glance of disapproval, scorn, distaste.

Gongs rang, the ambulance came and went, he lay alone on the floor. Had the girls fled? Or were they simply backed against those dusty walls with legs crossed and thumbs hooked in leather belts, casually defying the man in the doorway? Or silent, sullen, knowing the worst was yet to come for them, perhaps they were simply

1. Frenzied worshiper of Bacchus.

trying to right the benches, repair the room. In any case he was too bruised to regret the hands that did not reach for him, the white ambulance that would forever pass him by.

"Sovrowsky, Coletta, Rivers, Fiume," said the director from his point of authority at the door. "Pick him up. Fix his pants. Follow me. You bitches."

In the otherwise empty room off the director's office was an old leather couch, there not merely for the girls' cramps but, more important, for the director's rest, a fact which he knew intuitively and immediately the moment he came awake and felt beneath him the pinched and puffy leather surface of the listing couch. And now the couch was bearing him down the dirty tide and he was conscious enough of adding new blood to fading stains.

Somebody was matter-of-factly brushing the cut above his eye with the flaming tip of a long and treacherous needle. And this same person, he discovered in the next moment, was pouring a hot and humiliating syrup into the wounds in his groin.

"Look at him," murmured the thin young woman, and made another stroke, another daub at the eye, "look at him, he's coming round."

Seeing the old emergency kit opened and breathing off ammonia on the young woman's knees pressed close together, and furthermore, seeing the tape and scissors in the young woman's bony hands and hearing the tape, seeing the long bite of the scissors, it was then that he did indeed come round, as his helpful young colleague had said, and rolled one gelatinous quarter-turn to the edge of the couch and vomited fully and heavily into the sluggish tide down which he still felt himself sailing, awake or not. His vomit missed the thin black-stockinged legs and narrow flat-heeled shoes of the young teacher seated beside him.

"I warned you," the director was saying, "I told you they were dangerous. I told you they beat your predecessor nearly to death. How do you think we had your opening? And now it's not at all clear you can handle the job. You might have been killed. . . ."

"Next time they'll kill him, rightly enough," said the young woman, raising her brows and speaking through the cheap tin nasal funnel of her narrow mouth and laying on another foot-long strip of tape.

Slowly, lying half on his belly, sinking in the vast hurt of his depthless belly, he managed to lift his head and raise his eyes for one long dismal stare at the impassive face of the director.

"I can handle the job," he whispered, just as vomiting started up again from the pit of his life. From somewhere in the depths of the building he heard the rising screams of the girl with the thick lips, auburn hair, and broken nose.

He was most seriously injured, as it turned out, not in the groin or flanks or belly, but in the head. And the amateurish and careless ministrations of the cadaverous young female teacher were insufficient, as even the director recognized. So they recovered his cream and magenta tie, which he stuffed into his jacket pocket, helped to replace the missing shoe and sock, draped his shoulders in an old and hairy blanket, and together steadied him down to his own small ancient automobile in which the young female teacher drove him to the hospital. There he submitted himself to something under two hours of waiting and three at least of professional care, noting in the midst of fresh pain and the smells of antiseptic how the young teacher stood by to see the handiwork of her own first aid destroyed, the long strips of tape pulled off brusquely with the help of cotton swabs and a bottle of cold alcohol, and the head rather than chest or groin wrapped in endless footage of soft gauze and new strips of official tape. He felt the muffling of the ears, the thickening sensation of the gauze going round the top of his head and down his swollen cheeks, was aware of the care taken to leave stark minimal openings for the eyes, the nose, the battered mouth.

"Well," muttered the medical student entrusted with this operation of sculpting and binding the head in its helmet and face-mask of white bandages, "somebody did a job on you, all right."

No sooner had he entered the flat than his little dog Murphy, or Murph for short, glanced at the enormous white hive of antiseptic bandages and then scampered behind the conveniently open downstairs door of the china cabinet, making a thin and steady cry of uncommonly high pitch. He had frightened his own poor little dog, he with his great white head, and now he heard Murph clawing at the lower inside rear wall of the china cabinet and, leaning just inside his own doorway, became freshly nauseous, freshly weak.

"Come out, Murph," he tried to say, "it's me." But within its portable padded cell of bandage, his muffled voice was as wordless as Murphy's. From within the cabinet came the slow circular sounds of Murphy's claws, still accompanied by the steady shrill music of the little animal's panic, so that within the yet larger context of his own personal shock, he knew at once that he must devote himself to convincing the little dog that the man inside the bandages was familiar and unchanged. It could take days.

"Murphy," he meant to say, "shut your eyes, smell my hands, trust me, Murph." But even to his own steady ear the appeal sounded only like a faint wind trapped in the mouth of a mute.

It was dusk, his insulated and mummified head was floating, throbbing, while the rest of him, the masses of beaten and lacerated flesh beneath the disheveled clothes, cried out for sleep and small soft hands to press against him and slowly eliminate, by tender touch, these unfamiliar aches, these heavy pains. He wanted to lie forever on his iron bed, to sit swathed and protected in his broken-down padded chair with Murph on his lap. But the night was inimical, approaching, descending, filling space everywhere, and the flat no longer felt his own. The chair would be as hard as the bed, as unfamiliar, and even Murphy's latest hectic guilt-ridden trail of constraint and relief appeared to have been laid down by somebody else's uncontrollable household pet. Why did the window of his flat give onto the same dockyard scene, though further away and at a different angle, as the window of the schoolroom in which he had all but died? Why didn't he switch on a light, prepare his usual tea, put water in Murphy's bowl? A few minutes later, on hands and knees and with his heavy white head ready to sink to the floor, he suddenly realized that injury attacks identity, which was why, he now knew, that assault was a crime.

He did his clean-up job on hands and knees, he made no further effort to entice his dog from the china cabinet, he found himself wondering why the young teacher had allowed him to climb to the waiting and faintly kennelish-smelling flat alone. When he had dropped the last of poor little bewhiskered Murphy's fallen fruit into a paper sack now puffy with air and unavoidable waste, and in pain and darkness had sealed the sack and disposed of it in the tin pail beneath the sink, he slowly dragged himself to the side of the iron bed and then, more slowly still, hauled himself up and over. Shoes and all. Jacket and torn shirt and pants and all. Nausea and all. And lay on his side. And for the first time allowed the fingers of one hand to settle gently on the bandages that bound his head, and slowly and gently to touch, poke, caress, explore. Then at last, and with the same hand, he groped and drew to his chin the old yellow comforter that still exhaled the delicate scent of his dead mother.

**Teacher Assaulted at
Training School for Girls**

Mr. Walter Jones, newly appointed to the staff of St. Dunster's Training School for Girls, received emergency treatment today at St. Dunster's Hospital for multiple bruises which, as Mr. Jones admitted and Dr. Smyth-Jones, director of the school, confirmed, were inflicted by the young female students in Mr. Jones's first class at the school. Mr. Jones's predecessor, Mr. William Smyth, was so severely injured by these same students November last that he has been forced into early and permanent retirement. Dr. Smyth-Jones expressed regret for both incidents, but indicated that Mr. Jones's place on the staff would be awaiting him upon his full and, it is to be hoped, early recovery. "The public," he commented, "little appreciates the obstacles faced by educators at a school such as St. Dunster's. After all, within the system for the rehabilitation of criminally inclined female minors, St. Dunster's has been singled out to receive only the most intractable of girls. Occasional injury to our staff and to the girls themselves is clearly unavoidable."

With both hands on the wheel and Murph on his lap and a large soft-brimmed felt hat covering a good half of the offending white head, in this condition and full into the sun he slowly and cautiously drove the tortuous cobbled route toward Rose and Thyme, that brutally distended low-pitted slab of tenements into which his father, Old Jack, as he was known by all, had long since cut his filthy niche. The sun on the roof of the small old coffin of a car was warm, the narrow and dusty interior was filled with the hovering aroma of fresh petrol, and Murph, with his nose raised just to the level of the glass on the driver's side, was bobbing and squirming gently to the rhythm first of the footbrake and then the clutch. As for himself, and aside from the welcome heat of the little dog and the ice and glitter of the new day, it gave him special pleasure to be driving cautiously along with a lighted cigarette protruding from the mouth-slit in the bandages and, now and again, his entire head turning to give some timorous old woman the whole shock full in the face. He was only too conscious that he could move, that he could drive the car, that he filled the roaring but slowly moving vehicle with his bulk and age, that Murph's tiny pointed salt-and-pepper ears rose just above the edge of the window, and then was only too conscious, suddenly, of the forgotten girls.

Why, he asked himself, had he forgotten the girls? Why had he forced from his mind so simply, so unintentionally, the very girls whose entry into his life had been so briefly welcome, so briefly violent? Would he give up? Would he see them again? But why had he applied for that job in the first place? Surely he had not been going his own way, finally, after what his nimble old Dad called the juicy rough. All this pain and confusion for easy sex? Not a bit of it.

And then, making a difficult turn and drawing up behind a narrow flat-bedded lorry loaded down with stone and chugging, crawling, suddenly he saw it all, saw himself standing in Old Jack's doorway with Murph in his arms, saw his nimble Dad spring back, small and sallow face already contorted into the familiar look of alarm, and duck and turn, and from somewhere in the uncharted litter of that filthy room whip out his trench knife and standing there against the peeling wall with his knees knocking and weapon high and face contorted into that expression of fear and grievous pride common to most of those who lived in the ruin and desolation of Rose and Thyme. Then he heard the silent voices as the little old man threw down the trench knife and wiped his little beak and small square toothless mouth down the length of his bare arm.

It's you, is it?

Just me, Dad. Come to visit.

You might know better than to be stalking up here like some telly monster with that head of yours and that dead dog in your arms.

Murph's all right, Jack. Aren't you, Murph?

It's that school, that fucking school. My own son beaten near to death by a bunch of girls and written up in the papers. I read it, the whole sad story. And then stalking up here like a murderous monster.

They're very strong girls. And there were a lot of them. Twenty-seven actually.

Why were you there? Tell me why, eh? Oh, the Good Samaritan. . . .

Yes, the Good Samaritan.

Or were you really after a little juicy rough?

Mere sex? Not a bit of it. Of course I wouldn't rule out possibilities, but there's more than that.

Juicy rough. Walter, juicy rough. Don't lie.

I believe I want to know how those girls exist without romance. Or do they?

Use the glove, Walter! Let me give you the old fur glove. It does a lovely job. You can borrow it. . . .

"Yes," he heard himself musing aloud from within the bundle of antiseptic stuffing that was his head, and pressing first the brake and then the accelerator, "yes, I want to be at the bottom where those girls are. Without romance."

At a faster pace now and passing the lorry, he headed the little blue car once more in the direction from which he and Murphy had started out in the first place. Occasionally it was preferable to meet Old Jack not in the flesh but in the mind, he told himself, and this very moment was a case in point.

"No," said the young female teacher in the otherwise empty corridor, "it's you! And still in bandages."

"On the stroke of eight," he heard himself saying through the mouth-slit, which he had enlarged progressively with his fingers. "I'm always punctual."

"But you're not ready to come back. Just look at you."

"Ready enough. They couldn't keep me away."

"Wait," she said then, her voice jumping at him and her face full of alarm, "don't go in there . . . !"

"Must," he said, and shook her off, reached out, opened the door.

The same room. The same grilled and dusty windows. The same machinery in spidery operation in the vista beyond. Yes, it might have been his first day, his first morning, except that he recognized them and picked them out one by one from the silent rows—the narrow slant-eyed face, the girl with tuberculosis of the bone, the auburn-haired ringleader who had held the knife. Yes, all the same, except that the ringleader was wearing a large piece of sticking plaster across her nose. Even a name or two came back to him and for an instant these names evoked the shadowy partial poem of the forgotten rest. But named or unnamed their eyes were on him, as before, and though they could not know it, he was smiling in the same old suit and flaming tie and dusty pointed shoes. Yes, they knew who he was, and he in turn knew all about their silence game and actually was counting on the ugliness, the surprise, of the fully bandaged head to put them off, to serve as a measure of what they had done and all he had forgiven even before they had struck, to serve them as the first sign of courage and trust.

"Now, girls," he said in a voice they could not hear, "if you'll take out pencils and paper and listen attentively, we'll just begin." Across the room the pointer was lying on the old familiar desk like a sword in the light.

1984

Drama

TENNESSEE WILLIAMS

(1911–1983)

Thomas Lanier Williams was born in Columbus, Mississippi, and lived in Nashville, Tennessee, and in various towns in Mississippi before his family settled in St. Louis in 1918. The atmosphere of his early years was that of the various Episcopal rectories where he, his mother, and his sister Rose lived with his clergyman grandfather prior to the move to St. Louis to join the father, a sales manager for a shoe company. If his early life was unsettled, it was at least sheltered; the years in St. Louis were marked by family problems, by Rose's gradual withdrawal into her own inner world, and by Williams's abortive attempts to launch his literary career. At sixteen he won a prize in a national writing contest and at seventeen he saw his first short story in print in *Weird Tales.* After three years at the University of Missouri, however, he was forced to leave school to spend three years in the "living death" of a shoe factory. Briefly a student at Washington University, he finally secured his A.B. from the University of Iowa in 1938. By this time he had seen his plays in local productions in Memphis, in Webster Groves, Missouri, and in St. Louis, and two years later *Battle of Angels* (1940) opened in Boston under the auspices of the Theatre Guild, but failed to make it to New York.

The arrival of *The Glass Menagerie* in New York in 1945 was a major theatrical event. It signaled the emergence from obscurity of a playwright whose talent, together with that of Arthur Miller, was to dominate the American theater for the next two decades. More prolific than Miller, and a prodigious rewriter of his earlier efforts, Williams for years averaged at least one play on Broadway every two years. With rare exceptions, his plays have been huge successes on both critical and commercial terms; not since the heyday of Eugene O'Neill has an American playwright written so much, so successfully, so well. Frequently the best of his efforts have become major Hollywood films, with Williams demonstrating his versatility by his work on the film scripts.

The success of the film versions of so many of his plays underscores the fluidity of his stage management. Rarely is the action in a Williams play confined to one moment of time or one corner of physical space throughout a scene of any great duration. Rather the dialogue of the characters dwells continually on another time or another place. Intrusions from without—street cries, songs heard in the distance, the arrival of unexpected guests—serve as reminders of action past, and yet to come. More than some other playwrights (and in this respect following the strong lead of O'Neill), Williams makes use of the technical possibilities of the twentieth-century stage. Sets dissolve, walls fade away, lights bring one part of the stage into the foreground, while the rest recedes in darkness. A novelist, short story writer, and poet, as well as a playwright, Williams was at his best when writing for the theater, but he did not allow himself to be hampered by any of its conventions or by the expectations of his audience.

"I write from my own tensions," Williams once said. "For me, this is a form of therapy." His work has a quality of obsession about it. Much of it is clearly, in origin, autobiographical, but whether the core of observed fact is large, as it is in *The Glass Menagerie,* or considerably smaller, as it appears to be in *A Streetcar Named Desire* (1947) or *Suddenly Last Summer* (1958), that core is relatively unimportant when measured against the drive toward metaphor and symbol that characterizes the work as a whole. At times, as in its indifferent reaction to *Camino Real* (1953), the theater-going public has not been completely willing to accept Williams's frequent disregard for the usual conventions of theatrical verisimilitude. On the whole, however, it has accepted from him a language that is often poetic in its intensity, situations more marked by distortions than faithfulness to actuality, and characters and themes that appear to strike at the truth through the sidelong routes of dream, myth, and nightmare.

The major plays, with dates of first production, include *Battle of Angels,* 1940; *The Glass Menagerie,* 1944; *Summer and Smoke,* 1947; *A Streetcar Named Desire,* 1947; *The Rose Tattoo,* 1951; *Camino Real,* 1953; *Cat on a Hot Tin Roof,* 1955; *Orpheus Descending,* 1957; *Suddenly Last Summer,* 1958; *Sweet Bird of Youth,* 1959; *Period of Adjustment,* 1959; *The Night of the Iguana,* 1961; and *The Milk Train Doesn't Stop Here Anymore,* 1962. The standard collection is *The Theatre of Tennessee Williams,* 7 vols., 1971–1981. Short plays are collected in *27 Wagons Full of Cotton and Other One-Act Plays,* 1946 (revised, 1953); and *Dragon Country: A Book of Plays,* 1970. *Stopped Rocking and Other Screenplays,* 1984, is introduced by Richard Gilman. A novel is *The Roman Spring of Mrs. Stone,* 1950. Short-story collections are *One Arm and Other Stories,* 1948; *Hard Candy: A Book of Stories,* 1954; *The Knightly Quest,* 1967 (revised, 1968); *Eight Mortal Ladies Possessed,* 1974; *Moise and The World of Reason,* 1975; and *Collected Stories,* 1985. Verse is *In the Winter of Cities,* 1956 (revised, 1964); and *Androgyne, Mon Amour,* 1977. *Where I Live: Selected Essays,* 1978, was edited by Christine R. Day and Bob Woods. *Tennessee Williams' Letters to Donald Windham, 1940–1965,* 1977, was edited by Donald Windham.

Biographical and critical studies include Signi Falk, *Tennessee Williams,* 1961; Nancy M. Tischler, *Tennessee Williams: Rebellious Puritan,* 1961; Edwina D. Williams, *Remember Me to Tom,* 1963; Gilbert Maxwell, *Tennessee Williams and Friends: An Informal Biography,* 1965; Esther M. Jackson, *The Broken World of Tennessee Williams,* 1966; and Dakin Williams, *Tennessee Williams: An Intimate Biography,* 1983. Mike Steen edited *A Look at Tennessee Williams,* 1969. Stephen S. Stanton edited *Tennessee Williams: A Collection of Critical Essays,* 1977. See also Richard F. Leavitt, *The World of Tennessee Williams,* 1978; and *Dictionary of Literary Biography: Documentary Series,* Volume 4, 1984.

The Glass Menagerie[1]

Nobody, not even the rain, has such small hands.

—E. E. CUMMINGS

SCENE: *An Alley in St. Louis*

Part I. Preparation for a Gentleman Caller.
Part II. The Gentleman calls.

Time: Now and the Past.

THE CHARACTERS

AMANDA WINGFIELD (*the mother*)

A little woman of great but confused vitality clinging frantically to another time and place. Her characterization must be carefully created, not copied from type. She is not paranoiac, but her life is paranoia. There is much to admire in Amanda, and

1. The source of the present text is *The Theatre of Tennessee Williams,* 5 vols., 1971–1976.

as much to love and pity as there is to laugh at. Certainly she has endurance and a kind of heroism, and though her foolishness makes her unwittingly cruel at times, there is tenderness in her slight person.

LAURA WINGFIELD (*her daughter*)

Amanda, having failed to establish contact with reality, continues to live vitally in her illusions, but Laura's situation is even graver. A childhood illness has left her crippled, one leg slightly shorter than the other, and held in a brace. This defect need not be more than suggested on the stage. Stemming from this, Laura's separation increases till she is like a piece of her own glass collection, too exquisitely fragile to move from the shelf.

TOM WINGFIELD (*her son*)

And the narrator of the play. A poet with a job in a warehouse. His nature is not remorseless, but to escape from a trap he has to act without pity.

JIM O'CONNOR (*the gentleman caller*)

A nice, ordinary, young man.

Scene I

The Wingfield apartment is in the rear of the building, one of those vast hive-like conglomerations of cellular living-units that flower as warty growths in overcrowded urban centers of lower middle-class population and are symptomatic of the impulse of this largest and fundamentally enslaved section of American society to avoid fluidity and differentiation and to exist and function as one interfused mass of automatism.

The apartment faces an alley and is entered by a fire escape, a structure whose name is a touch of accidental poetic truth, for all of these huge buildings are always burning with the slow and implacable fires of human desperation. The fire escape is part of what we see—that is, the landing of it and steps descending from it.

The scene is memory and is therefore nonrealistic. Memory takes a lot of poetic license. It omits some details; others are exaggerated, according to the emotional value of the articles it touches, for memory is seated predominantly in the heart. The interior is therefore rather dim and poetic.

At the rise of the curtain, the audience is faced with the dark, grim rear wall of the Wingfield tenement. This building is flanked on both sides by dark, narrow alleys which run into murky canyons of tangled clotheslines, garbage cans, and the sinister latticework of neighboring fire escapes. It is up and down these side alleys that exterior entrances and exits are made during the play. At the end of Tom's opening commentary, the dark tenement wall slowly becomes transparent and reveals the interior of the ground-floor Wingfield apartment.

Nearest the audience is the living room, which also serves as a sleeping room for Laura, the sofa unfolding to make her bed. Just beyond, separated from the living room by a wide arch or second proscenium with transparent faded portieres (or second curtain), is the dining room. In an old-fashioned whatnot in the living room are seen scores of transparent glass animals. A blown-up photograph of the father hangs on the wall of the living room, to the left of the archway. It is the face of a very handsome young man in a doughboy's First World War cap. He is gallantly smiling, ineluctably smiling, as if to say "I will be smiling forever."

Also hanging on the wall, near the photograph, are a typewriter keyboard chart and a Gregg shorthand diagram. An upright typewriter on a small table stands beneath the charts.

The audience hears and sees the opening scene in the dining room through both the transparent fourth wall of the building and the transparent gauze portieres of the dining-room arch. It is during this revealing scene that the fourth wall slowly ascends, out of sight. This transparent exterior wall is not brought down again until the very end of the play, during Tom's final speech.

The narrator is an undisguised convention of the play. He takes whatever license with dramatic convention is convenient to his purposes.

Tom enters, dressed as a merchant sailor, and strolls across to the fire escape. There he stops and lights a cigarette. He addresses the audience.

TOM. Yes, I have tricks in my pocket, I have things up my sleeve. But I am the opposite of a stage magician. He gives you illusion that has the appearance of truth. I give you truth in the pleasant disguise of illusion.

To begin with, I turn back time. I reverse it to that quaint period, the thirties, when the huge middle class of America was matriculating in a school for the blind. Their eyes had failed them, or they had failed their eyes, and so they were having their fingers pressed forcibly down on the fiery Braille alphabet of a dissolving economy. In Spain there was revolution. Here there was only shouting and confusion. In Spain there was Guernica. Here there were disturbances of labor, sometimes pretty violent, in otherwise peaceful cities such as Chicago, Cleveland, Saint Louis . . . This is the social background of the play.

[*Music begins to play.*]

The play is memory. Being a memory play, it is dimly lighted, it is sentimental, it is not realistic. In memory everything seems to happen to music. That explains the fiddle in the wings. I am the narrator of the play, and also a character in it. The other characters are my mother, Amanda, my sister, Laura, and a gentleman caller who appears in the final scenes. He is the most realistic character in the play, being an emissary from a world of reality that we were somehow set apart from. But since I have a poet's weakness for symbols, I am using this character also as a symbol; he is the long-delayed but always expected something that we live for.

There is a fifth character in the play who doesn't appear except in this larger-than-life-size photograph over the mantel. This is our father who left us a long time ago. He was a telephone man who fell in love with long distances; he gave up his job with the telephone company and skipped the light fantastic out of town . . . The last we heard of him was a picture postcard from Mazatlan, on the Pacific coast of Mexico, containing a message of two words: "Hello—Goodbye!" and no address. I think the rest of the play will explain itself. . . .

[*Amanda's voice becomes audible through the portieres.*]

[*Legend on screen:* "Où sont les neiges."[2]]

[*Tom divides the portieres and enters the dining room. Amanda and Laura are seated at a drop-leaf table. Eating is indicated by gestures without food or utensils. Amanda faces the audience. Tom and Laura are seated in profile. The interior has lit up softly and through the scrim*[3] *we see Amanda and Laura seated at the table.*]

2. A partial quotation of the refrain, "Mais où sont les neiges d'antan?" ("But where are the snows of yesteryear?") from the "Ballade des dames du temps jadis" ("Ballade of the Ladies of Bygone Times") by François Villon (1431–?).

3. A gauze curtain, often painted, opaque when lit from the front and transparent when backlit.

AMANDA. [*Calling.*] Tom?

TOM. Yes, Mother.

AMANDA. We can't say grace until you come to the table!

TOM. Coming, Mother. [*He bows slightly and withdraws, reappearing a few moments later in his place at the table.*]

AMANDA. [*To her son.*] Honey, don't *push* with your *fingers.* If you have to push with something, the thing to push with is a crust of bread. And chew—chew! Animals have secretions in their stomachs which enable them to digest food without mastication, but human beings are supposed to chew their food before they swallow it down. Eat food leisurely, son, and really enjoy it. A well-cooked meal has lots of delicious flavors that have to be held in the mouth for appreciation. So chew your food and give your salivary glands a chance to function!

[*Tom deliberately lays his imaginary fork down and pushes his chair back from the table.*]

TOM. I haven't enjoyed one bite of this dinner because of your constant directions on how to eat it. It's you that make me rush through meals with your hawklike attention to every bite I take. Sickening—spoils my appetite—all this discussion of —animals' secretion—salivary glands—mastication!

AMANDA. [*Lightly.*] Temperament like a Metropolitan star!

[*Tom rises and walks toward the living room.*]

You're not excused from the table.

TOM. I'm getting a cigarette.

AMANDA. You smoke too much.

[*Laura rises.*]

LAURA. I'll bring in the blanc mange.

[*Tom remains standing with his cigarette by the portieres.*]

AMANDA. [*Rising.*] No, sister, no, sister—you be the lady this time and I'll be the darky.

LAURA. I'm already up.

AMANDA. Resume your seat, little sister—I want you to stay fresh and pretty—for gentlemen callers!

LAURA. [*Sitting down.*] I'm not expecting any gentlemen callers.

AMANDA. [*Crossing out to the kitchenette, airily.*] Sometimes they come when they are least expected! Why, I remember one Sunday afternoon in Blue Mountain—

[*She enters the kitchenette.*]

TOM. I know what's coming!

LAURA. Yes. But let her tell it.

TOM. Again?

LAURA. She loves to tell it.

[*Amanda returns with a bowl of dessert.*]

AMANDA. One Sunday afternoon in Blue Mountain—your mother received—*seventeen!*—gentlemen callers! Why, sometimes there weren't chairs enough to accommodate them all. We had to send the nigger over to bring in folding chairs from the parish house.

TOM. [*Remaining at the portieres.*] How did you entertain those gentlemen callers?

AMANDA. I understood the art of conversation!

TOM. I bet you could talk.

AMANDA. Girls in those days *knew* how to talk, I can tell you.

TOM. Yes?

[*Image on screen:* Amanda as a girl on a porch, greeting callers.]

AMANDA. They knew how to entertain their gentlemen callers. It wasn't enough for a girl to be possessed of a pretty face and a graceful figure—although I wasn't slighted in either respect. She also needed to have a nimble wit and a tongue to meet all occasions.

TOM. What did you talk about?

AMANDA. Things of importance going on in the world! Never anything coarse or common or vulgar.

[*She addresses Tom as though he were seated in the vacant chair at the table though he remains by the portieres. He plays this scene as though reading from a script.*]

My callers were gentlemen—all! Among my callers were some of the most prominent young planters of the Mississippi Delta—planters and sons of planters!

[*Tom motions for music and a spot of light on Amanda. Her eyes lift, her face glows, her voice becomes rich and elegiac.*]

[*Screen legend:* "Où sont les neiges d'antan?"]

There was young Champ Laughlin who later became vice-president of the Delta Planters Bank. Hadley Stevenson who was drowned in Moon Lake and left his widow one hundred and fifty thousand in Government bonds. There were the Cutrere brothers, Wesley and Bates. Bates was one of my bright particular beaux! He got in a quarrel with that wild Wainwright boy. They shot it out on the floor of Moon Lake Casino. Bates was shot through the stomach. Died in the ambulance on his way to Memphis. His widow was also well provided-for, came into eight or ten thousand acres, that's all. She married him on the rebound—never loved her—carried my picture on him the night he died! And there was that boy that every girl in the Delta had set her cap for! That beautiful, brilliant young Fitzhugh boy from Greene County!

TOM. What did he leave his widow?

AMANDA. He never married! Gracious, you talk as though all of my old admirers had turned up their toes to the daisies!

TOM. Isn't this the first you've mentioned that still survives?

AMANDA. That Fitzhugh boy went North and made a fortune—came to be known as the Wolf of Wall Street! He had the Midas touch, whatever he touched turned to gold! And I could have been Mrs. Duncan J. Fitzhugh, mind you! But—I picked your *father!*

LAURA. [*Rising.*] Mother, let me clear the table.

AMANDA. No, dear, you go in front and study your typewriter chart. Or practice your shorthand a little. Stay fresh and pretty!—It's almost time for our gentlemen callers to start arriving. [*She flounces girlishly toward the kitchenette.*] How many do you suppose we're going to entertain this afternoon?

[*Tom throws down the paper and jumps up with a groan.*]

LAURA. [*Alone in the dining room.*] I don't believe we're going to receive any, Mother.

AMANDA. [*Reappearing, airily.*] What? No one—not one? You must be joking!

[*Laura nervously echoes her laugh. She slips in a fugitive manner through the half-open portieres and draws them gently behind her. A shaft of very clear light is thrown on her face against the faded tapestry of the curtains. Faintly the music of "The Glass Menagerie" is heard as she continues, lightly.*]

Not one gentleman caller? It can't be true! There must be a flood, there must have been a tornado!

LAURA. It isn't a flood, it's not a tornado, Mother. I'm just not popular like you were in Blue Mountain. . . .

[*Tom utters another groan. Laura glances at him with a faint, apologetic smile. Her voice catches a little.*]

Mother's afraid I'm going to be an old maid.

[*The scene dims out with the "Glass Menagerie" music.*]

Scene II

On the dark stage the screen is lighted with the image of blue roses. Gradually Laura's figure becomes apparent and the screen goes out. The music subsides.

Laura is seated in the delicate ivory chair at the small claw-foot table. She wears a dress of soft violet material for a kimono—her hair is tied back from her forehead with a ribbon. She is washing and polishing her collection of glass. Amanda appears on the fire escape steps. At the sound of her ascent, Laura catches her breath, thrusts the bowl of ornaments away, and seats herself stiffly before the diagram of the typewriter keyboard as though it held her spellbound. Something has happened to Amanda. It is written in her face as she climbs to the landing: a look that is grim and hopeless and a little absurd. She has on one of those cheap or imitation velvety-looking cloth coats with imitation fur collar. Her hat is five or six years old, one of those dreadful cloche hats that were worn in the late Twenties, and she is clutching an enormous black patent-leather pocketbook with nickel clasps and initials. This is her full-dress outfit, the one she usually wears to the D.A.R. Before entering she looks through the door. She purses her lips, opens her eyes very wide, rolls them upward and shakes her head. Then she slowly lets herself in the door. Seeing her mother's expression Laura touches her lips with a nervous gesture.

LAURA. Hello, Mother, I was— [*She makes a nervous gesture toward the chart on the wall. Amanda leans against the shut door and stares at Laura with a martyred look.*]

AMANDA. Deception? Deception? [*She slowly removes her hat and gloves, continuing the sweet suffering stare. She lets the hat and gloves fall on the floor—a bit of acting.*]

LAURA. [*Shakily.*] How was the D.A.R. meeting?

[*Amanda slowly opens her purse and removes a dainty white handkerchief which she shakes out delicately and delicately touches to her lips and nostrils.*]

Didn't you go to the D.A.R. meeting, Mother?

AMANDA. [*Faintly, almost inaudibly.*] —No.—No. [*Then more forcibly.*] I did not have the strength—to go to the D.A.R. In fact, I did not have the courage! I wanted to find a hole in the ground and hide myself in it forever! [*She crosses slowly to the wall and removes the diagram of the typewriter keyboard. She holds it in front of her for a second, staring at it sweetly and sorrowfully—then bites her lips and tears it in two pieces.*]

LAURA. [*Faintly.*] Why did you do that, Mother?

[*Amanda repeats the same procedure with the chart of the Gregg Alphabet.*]
Why are you—

AMANDA. Why? Why? How old are you, Laura?

LAURA. Mother, you know my age.

AMANDA. I thought that you were an adult; it seems that I was mistaken. [*She crosses slowly to the sofa and sinks down and stares at Laura.*]

LAURA. Please don't stare at me, Mother.

[*Amanda closes her eyes and lowers her head. There is a ten-second pause.*]

AMANDA. What are we going to do, what is going to become of us, what is the future?

[*There is another pause.*]

LAURA. Has something happened, Mother?

[*Amanda draws a long breath, takes out the handkerchief again, goes through the dabbing process.*]
Mother, has—something happened?

AMANDA. I'll be all right in a minute, I'm just bewildered— [*She hesitates.*] —by life. . . .

LAURA. Mother, I wish that you would tell me what's happened!

AMANDA. As you know, I was supposed to be inducted into my office at the D.A.R. this afternoon.

[*Screen image:* A swarm of typewriters.]
But I stopped off at Rubicam's Business College to speak to your teachers about your having a cold and ask them what progress they thought you were making down there.

LAURA. Oh. . . .

AMANDA. I went to the typing instructor and introduced myself as your mother. She didn't know who you were. "Wingfield," she said, "We don't have any such student enrolled at the school!" I assured her she did, that you had been going to classes since early in January. "I wonder," she said, "If you could be talking about that terribly shy little girl who dropped out of school after only a few days' attendance?" "No," I said, "Laura, my daughter, has been going to school every day for the past six weeks!" "Excuse me," she said. She took the attendance book out and there was your name, unmistakably printed, and all the dates you were absent until they decided that you had dropped out of school. I still said, "No, there must have been some mistake! There must have been some mix-up in the records!" And she said, "No—I remember her perfectly now. Her hands shook so that she couldn't hit the right keys! The first time we gave a speed test, she broke down completely—was sick at the stomach and almost had to be carried into the wash room! After that morning she never showed up any more. We phoned the house but never got any answer"—While I was working at Famous–Barr, I suppose, demonstrating those—

[*She indicates a brassiere with her hands.*]
Oh! I felt so weak I could barely keep on my feet! I had to sit down while they got me a glass of water! Fifty dollars' tuition, all of our plans—my hopes and ambitions for you—just gone up the spout, just gone up the spout like that.

[*Laura draws a long breath and gets awkwardly to her feet. She crosses to the Victrola and winds it up.*]
What are you doing?

LAURA. Oh! [*She releases the handle and returns to her seat.*]

AMANDA. Laura, where have you been going when you've gone out pretending that you were going to business college?

LAURA. I've just been going out walking.

AMANDA. That's not true.

LAURA. It is. I just went walking.

AMANDA. Walking? Walking? In winter? Deliberately courting pneumonia in that light coat? Where did you walk to, Laura?

LAURA. All sorts of places—mostly in the park.

AMANDA. Even after you'd started catching that cold?

LAURA. It was the lesser of two evils, Mother.

[*Screen image:* Winter scene in a park.]

I couldn't go back there. I—threw up—on the floor!

AMANDA. From half past seven till after five every day you mean to tell me you walked around in the park, because you wanted to make me think that you were still going to Rubicam's Business College?

LAURA. It wasn't as bad as it sounds. I went inside places to get warmed up.

AMANDA. Inside where?

LAURA. I went in the art museum and the bird houses at the Zoo. I visited the penguins every day! Sometimes I did without lunch and went to the movies. Lately I've been spending most of my afternoons in the Jewel Box, that big glass house where they raise the tropical flowers.

AMANDA. You did all this to deceive me, just for deception? [*Laura looks down.*] Why?

LAURA. Mother, when you're disappointed, you get that awful suffering look on your face, like the picture of Jesus' mother in the museum!

AMANDA. Hush!

LAURA. I couldn't face it.

[*There is a pause. A whisper of strings is heard. Legend on screen:* "The Crust of Humility."]

AMANDA. [*Hopelessly fingering the huge pocketbook.*] So what are we going to do the rest of our lives? Stay home and watch the parades go by? Amuse ourselves with the glass menagerie, darling? Eternally play those worn-out phonograph records your father left as a painful reminder of him? We won't have a business career—we've given that up because it gave us nervous indigestion! [*She laughs wearily.*] What is there left but dependency all our lives? I know so well what becomes of unmarried women who aren't prepared to occupy a position. I've seen such pitiful cases in the South—barely tolerated spinsters living upon the grudging patronage of sister's husband or brother's wife!—stuck away in some little mousetrap of a room—encouraged by one in-law to visit another—little birdlike women without any nest—eating the crust of humility all their life!

Is that the future that we've mapped out for ourselves? I swear it's the only alternative I can think of! [*She pauses.*] It isn't a very pleasant alternative, is it? [*She pauses again.*] Of course—some girls *do marry.*

[*Laura twists her hands nervously.*]

Haven't you ever liked some boy?

LAURA. Yes. I liked one once. [*She rises.*] I came across his picture a while ago.

AMANDA. [*With some interest.*] He gave you his picture?

LAURA. No, it's in the yearbook.

AMANDA. [*Disappointed.*] Oh—a high school boy.

[*Screen image:* Jim as the high school hero bearing a silver cup.]

LAURA. Yes. His name was Jim. [*She lifts the heavy annual from the claw-foot table.*] Here he is in *The Pirates of Penzance.*

AMANDA. [*Absently.*] The what?

LAURA. The operetta the senior class put on. He had a wonderful voice and we sat across the aisle from each other Mondays, Wednesdays and Fridays in the Aud. Here he is with the silver cup for debating! See his grin?

AMANDA. [*Absently.*] He must have had a jolly disposition.

LAURA. He used to call me—Blue Roses.

[*Screen image:* Blue roses.]

AMANDA. Why did he call you such a name as that?

LAURA. When I had that attack of pleurosis—he asked me what was the matter when I came back. I said pleurosis—he thought that I said Blue Roses! So that's what he always called me after that. Whenever he saw me, he'd holler, "Hello, Blue Roses!" I didn't care for the girl that he went out with. Emily Meisenbach. Emily was the best-dressed girl at Soldan. She never struck me, though, as being sincere . . . It says in the Personal Section—they're engaged. That's—six years ago! They must be married by now.

AMANDA. Girls that aren't cut out for business careers usually wind up married to some nice man. [*She gets up with a spark of revival.*] Sister, that's what you'll do!

[*Laura utters a startled, doubtful laugh. She reaches quickly for a piece of glass.*]

LAURA. But, Mother

AMANDA. Yes? [*She goes over to the photograph.*]

LAURA. [*In a tone of frightened apology.*] I'm—crippled!

AMANDA. Nonsense! Laura, I've told you never, never to use that word. Why, you're not crippled, you just have a little defect—hardly noticeable, even! When people have some slight disadvantage like that, they cultivate other things to make up for it—develop charm—and vivacity—and—*charm!* That's all you have to do! [*She turns again to the photograph.*] One thing your father had *plenty of*—was *charm!*

[*The scene fades out with music.*]

Scene III

Legend on screen: "After the fiasco—"
Tom speaks from the fire escape landing.

TOM. After the fiasco at Rubicam's Business College, the idea of getting a gentleman caller for Laura began to play a more and more important part in Mother's calculations. It became an obsession. Like some archetype of the universal unconscious, the image of the gentleman caller haunted our small apartment. . . .

[*Screen image:* A young man at the door of a house with flowers.]

An evening at home rarely passed without some allusion to this image, this specter, this hope. . . . Even when he wasn't mentioned, his presence hung in Mother's preoccupied look and in my sister's frightened, apologetic manner—hung like a sentence passed upon the Wingfields!

Mother was a woman of action as well as words. She began to take logical steps in the planned direction. Late that winter and in the early spring—realizing that extra money would be needed to properly feather the nest and plume the bird—she conducted a vigorous campaign on the telephone, roping in subscribers to one of those magazines for matrons called *The Homemaker's Companion,* the type of journal that features the serialized sublimations of ladies of letters who think in terms of delicate cuplike breasts, slim, tapering waists, rich, creamy thighs, eyes like wood smoke in autumn, fingers that soothe and caress like strains of music, bodies as powerful as Etruscan sculpture.

[*Screen image:* The cover of a glamor magazine.]

[*Amanda enters with the telephone on a long extension cord. She is spotlighted in the dim stage.*]

AMANDA. Ida Scott? This is Amanda Wingfield! We *missed* you at the D.A.R. last Monday! I said to myself: She's probably suffering with that sinus condition! How is that sinus condition?

Horrors! Heaven have mercy!—You're a Christian martyr, yes, that's what you are, a Christian martyr!

Well, I just now happened to notice that your subscription to the *Companion's* about to expire! Yes, it expires with the next issue, honey!—just when that wonderful new serial by Bessie Mae Hopper is getting off to such an exciting start. Oh, honey, it's something that you can't miss! You remember how *Gone with the Wind* took everybody by storm? You simply couldn't go out if you hadn't read it. All everybody *talked* was Scarlett O'Hara. Well, this is a book that critics already compare to *Gone with the Wind.* It's the *Gone with the Wind* of the post-World-War generation! —What?—Burning?—Oh, honey, don't let them burn, go take a look in the oven and I'll hold the wire! Heavens—I think she's hung up!

[*The scene dims out.*]

[*Legend on screen:* "You think I'm in love with Continental Shoemakers?"]

[*Before the lights come up again, the violent voices of Tom and Amanda are heard. They are quarreling behind the portieres. In front of them stands Laura with clenched hands and panicky expression. A clear pool of light on her figure throughout this scene.*]

TOM. What in Christ's name am I—

AMANDA. [*Shrilly.*] Don't you use that—

TOM. —supposed to do?

AMANDA. —expression! Not in my—

TOM. Ohhh!

AMANDA. —presence! Have you gone out of your senses?

TOM. I have, that's true, *driven* out!

AMANDA. What is the matter with you, you—big—big—IDIOT!

TOM. Look!—I've got *no thing,* no single thing—

AMANDA. Lower your voice!

TOM. —in my life here that I can call my OWN! Everything is—

AMANDA. Stop that shouting!

TOM. Yesterday you confiscated my books! You had the nerve to—

AMANDA. I took that horrible novel back to the library—yes! That hideous book by that insane Mr. Lawrence.

[*Tom laughs wildly.*]

I cannot control the output of diseased minds or people who cater to them—

[*Tom laughs still more wildly.*]

BUT I WON'T ALLOW SUCH FILTH BROUGHT INTO MY HOUSE! No, no, no, no, no!

TOM. House, house! Who pays rent on it, who makes a slave of himself to—

AMANDA. [*Fairly screeching.*] Don't you DARE to—

TOM. No, no, *I* mustn't say things! *I've* got to just—

AMANDA. Let me tell you—

TOM. I don't want to hear any more!

[*He tears the portieres open. The dining-room area is lit with a turgid smoky red glow. Now we see Amanda; her hair is in metal curlers and she is wearing a very old bathrobe, much too large for her slight figure, a relic of the faithless Mr. Wingfield. The upright typewriter now stands on the drop-leaf table, along with a wild disarray of manuscripts. The quarrel was probably precipitated by Amanda's interruption of Tom's creative labor. A chair lies overthrown on the floor. Their gesticulating shadows are cast on the ceiling by the fiery glow.*]

AMANDA. You *will* hear more, you—

TOM. No, I won't hear more, I'm going out!

AMANDA. You come right back in—

TOM. Out, out, out! Because I'm—

AMANDA. Come back here, Tom Wingfield! I'm not through talking to you!

TOM. Oh, go—

LAURA. [*Desperately.*] —Tom!

AMANDA. You're going to listen, and no more insolence from you! I'm at the end of my patience!

[*He comes back toward her.*]

TOM. What do you think I'm at? Aren't I supposed to have any patience to reach the end of, Mother? I know, I know. It seems unimportant to you, what I'm *doing*—what I *want* to do—having a little *difference* between them! You don't think that—

AMANDA. I think you've been doing things that you're ashamed of. That's why you act like this. I don't believe that you go every night to the movies. Nobody goes to the movies night after night. Nobody in their right mind goes to the movies as often as you pretend to. People don't go to the movies at nearly midnight, and movies don't let out at two A.M. Come in stumbling. Muttering to yourself like a maniac! You get three hours' sleep and then go to work. Oh, I can picture the way you're doing down there. Moping, doping, because you're in no condition!

TOM. [*Wildly.*] No, I'm in no condition!

AMANDA. What right have you got to jeopardize your job? Jeopardize the security of us all? How do you think we'd manage if you were—

TOM. Listen! You think I'm crazy about the *warehouse?* [*He bends fiercely toward her slight figure.*] You think I'm in love with the Continental Shoemakers? You think I want to spend fifty-five *years* down there in that—*celotex interior!* with—*fluorescent—tubes!* Look! I'd rather somebody picked up a crowbar and battered out my brains—than go back mornings! I *go!* Every time you come in yelling that Goddamn *"Rise and Shine!" "Rise and Shine!"* I say to myself, "How *lucky dead* people are!" But I get up. I *go!* For sixty-five dollars a month I give up all that I dream of doing and being *ever!* And you say self—*self's* all I ever think of. Why, listen, if self is what I thought of, Mother, I'd be where he is—GONE! [*He points to his father's picture.*] As far as the system of transportation reaches! [*He starts past her. She grabs his arm.*] Don't grab at me, Mother!

AMANDA. Where are you going?

TOM. I'm going to the *movies!*

AMANDA. I don't believe that lie!

[*Tom crouches toward her, overtowering her tiny figure. She backs away, gasping.*]

TOM. I'm going to opium dens! Yes, opium dens, dens of vice and criminals' hangouts, Mother. I've joined the Hogan Gang, I'm a hired assassin, I carry a tommy gun in a violin case! I run a string of cat houses in the Valley! They call me Killer, Killer Wingfield, I'm leading a double-life, a simple, honest warehouse worker by day, by night a dynamic *czar* of the *underworld, Mother.* I go to gambling casinos, I spin away fortunes on the roulette table! I wear a patch over one eye and a false mustache, sometimes I put on green whiskers. On those occasions they call me—*El Diablo!* Oh, I could tell you many things to make you sleepless! My enemies plan to dynamite this place. They're going to blow us all sky-high some night! I'll be glad, very happy, and so will you! You'll go up, up on a broomstick, over Blue Mountain with seventeen gentlemen callers! You ugly—babbling old—*witch. . . .* [*He goes through a series of violent, clumsy movements, seizing his overcoat, lunging to the door, pulling it fiercely open. The women watch him, aghast. His arm catches in the sleeve of the coat as he struggles to pull it on. For a moment he is pinioned by the bulky garment. With an outraged groan he tears the coat off again, splitting the shoulder of it, and hurls it across the room. It strikes against the shelf of Laura's glass collection, and there is a tinkle of shattering glass. Laura cries out as if wounded.*]

[*Music.*]

[*Screen legend:* "The Glass Menagerie."]

LAURA. [*Shrilly.*] *My glass!*— menagerie. . . . [*She covers her face and turns away.*]

[*But Amanda is still stunned and stupefied by the "ugly witch" so that she barely notices this occurrence. Now she recovers her speech.*]

AMANDA. [*In an awful voice.*] I won't speak to you—until you apologize!

[*She crosses through the portieres and draws them together behind her. Tom is left with Laura. Laura clings weakly to the mantel with her face averted. Tom stares at her stupidly for a moment. Then he crosses to the shelf. He drops awkwardly on his knees to collect the fallen glass, glancing at Laura as if he would speak but couldn't.*]

[*"The Glass Menagerie" music steals in as the scene dims out.*]

Scene IV

The interior of the apartment is dark. There is a faint light in the alley. A deep-voiced bell in a church is tolling the hour of five.

Tom appears at the top of the alley. After each solemn boom of the bell in the tower, he shakes a little noisemaker or rattle as if to express the tiny spasm of man in contrast to the sustained power and dignity of the Almighty. This and the unsteadiness of his advance make it evident that he has been drinking. As he climbs the few steps to the fire escape landing light steals up inside. Laura appears in the front room in a nightdress. She notices that Tom's bed is empty. Tom fishes in his pockets for his door key, removing a motley assortment of articles in the search, including a shower of movie ticket stubs and an empty bottle. At last he finds the key, but just as he is about to insert it, it slips from his fingers. He strikes a match and crouches below the door.

TOM. [*Bitterly.*] One crack—and it falls through!

[LAURA *opens the door.*]

LAURA. Tom! Tom, what are you doing?

TOM. Looking for a door key.

LAURA. Where have you been all this time?

TOM. I have been to the movies.

LAURA. All this time at the movies?

TOM. There was a very long program. There was a Garbo picture and a Mickey Mouse and a travelogue and a newsreel and a preview of coming attractions. And there was an organ solo and a collection for the Milk Fund—simultaneously—which ended up in a terrible fight between a fat lady and an usher!

LAURA. [*Innocently.*] Did you have to stay through everything?

TOM. Of course! And, oh, I forgot! There was a big stage show! The headliner on this stage show was Malvolio the Magician. He performed wonderful tricks, many of them, such as pouring water back and forth between pitchers. First it turned to wine and then it turned to beer and then it turned to whisky. I know it was whisky it finally turned into because he needed somebody to come up out of the audience to help him, and I came up—both shows! It was Kentucky Straight Bourbon. A very generous fellow, he gave souvenirs. [*He pulls from his back pocket a shimmering rainbow-colored scarf.*] He gave me this. This is his magic scarf. You can have it, Laura. You wave it over a canary cage and you get a bowl of goldfish. You wave it over the goldfish bowl and they fly away canaries. . . . But the wonderfullest trick of all was the coffin trick. We nailed him into a coffin and he got out of the coffin without removing one nail. [*He has come inside.*] There is a trick that would come in handy for me—get me out of this two-by-four situation! [*He flops onto the bed and starts removing his shoes.*]

LAURA. Tom—shhh!

TOM. What're you shushing me for?

LAURA. You'll wake up Mother.

TOM. Goody, goody! Pay 'er back for all those "Rise an' Shines." [*He lies down, groaning.*] You know it don't take much intelligence to get yourself into a nailed-up coffin, Laura. But who in hell ever got himself out of one without removing one nail?

[*As if in answer, the father's grinning photograph lights up. The scene dims out.*]

[*Immediately following, the church bell is heard striking six. At the sixth stroke the alarm clock goes off in Amanda's room, and after a few moments we hear her calling: "Rise and Shine! Rise and Shine! Laura, go tell your brother to rise and shine!"*]

TOM. [*Sitting up slowly.*] I'll rise—but I won't shine.

[*The light increases.*]

AMANDA. Laura, tell your brother his coffee is ready.

[*Laura slips into the front room.*]

LAURA. Tom!—It's nearly seven. Don't make Mother nervous.

[*He stares at her stupidly.*]

[*Beseechingly.*] Tom, speak to Mother this morning. Make up with her, apologize, speak to her!

TOM. She won't to me. It's her that started not speaking.

LAURA. If you just say you're sorry she'll start speaking.

TOM. Her not speaking—is that such a tragedy?

LAURA. Please—please!

AMANDA. [*Calling from the kitchenette.*] Laura, are you going to do what I asked you to do, or do I have to get dressed and go out myself?

LAURA. Going, going—soon as I get on my coat!

[*She pulls on a shapeless felt hat with a nervous, jerky movement, pleadingly glancing at Tom. She rushes awkwardly for her coat. The coat is one of Amanda's, inaccurately made-over, the sleeves too short for Laura.*]

Butter and what else?

AMANDA. [*Entering from the kitchenette.*] Just butter. Tell them to charge it.

LAURA. Mother, they make such faces when I do that.

AMANDA. Sticks and stones can break our bones, but the expression on Mr. Garfinkel's face won't harm us! Tell your brother his coffee is getting cold.

LAURA. [*At the door.*] Do what I asked you, will you, will you, Tom?

[*He looks sullenly away.*]

AMANDA. Laura, go now or just don't go at all!

LAURA. [*Rushing out.*] Going—going!

[*A second later she cries out. Tom springs up and crosses to the door. Tom opens the door.*]

TOM. Laura?

LAURA. I'm all right. I slipped, but I'm all right.

AMANDA. [*Peering anxiously after her.*] If anyone breaks a leg on those fire-escape steps, the landlord ought to be sued for every cent he possesses! [*She shuts the door. Now she remembers she isn't speaking to Tom and returns to the other room.*]

[*As Tom comes listlessly for his coffee, she turns her back to him and stands rigidly facing the window on the gloomy gray vault of the areaway. Its light on her face with its aged but childish features is cruelly sharp, satirical as a Daumier print.*]

[*The music of "Ave Maria," is heard softly.*]

[*Tom glances sheepishly but sullenly at her averted figure and slumps at the table. The coffee is scalding hot; he sips it and gasps and spits it back in the cup. At his gasp, Amanda catches her breath and half turns. Then she catches herself and turns back to the window. Tom blows on his coffee, glancing sidewise at his mother. She clears her throat. Tom clears his. He starts to rise, sinks back down again, scratches his head, clears his throat again. Amanda coughs. Tom raises his cup in both hands to blow on it, his eyes staring over the rim of it at his mother for several moments. Then he slowly sets the cup down and awkwardly and hesitantly rises from the chair.*]

TOM. [*Hoarsely.*] Mother. I—I apologize, Mother.

[*Amanda draws a quick, shuddering breath. Her face works grotesquely. She breaks into childlike tears.*]

I'm sorry for what I said, for everything that I said, I didn't mean it.

AMANDA. [*Sobbingly.*] My devotion has made me a witch and so I make myself hateful to my children!

TOM. *No,* you *don't.*

AMANDA. I worry so much, don't sleep, it makes me nervous!

TOM. [*Gently.*] I understand that.

AMANDA. I've had to put up a solitary battle all these years. But you're my right-hand bower! Don't fall down, don't fail!

TOM. [*Gently.*] I try, Mother.

AMANDA. [*With great enthusiasm.*] Try and you will *succeed!* [*The notion makes her breathless.*] Why, you—you're just *full* of natural endowments! Both of my children—they're *unusual* children! Don't you think I know it? I'm so—*proud!* Happy and—feel I've—so much to be thankful for but—promise me one thing, son!

TOM. What, Mother?

AMANDA. Promise, son, you'll—never be a drunkard!

TOM. [*Turns to her grinning.*] I will never be a drunkard, Mother.

AMANDA. That's what frightened me so, that you'd be drinking! Eat a bowl of Purina!

TOM. Just coffee, Mother.

AMANDA. Shredded wheat biscuit?

TOM. No. No, Mother, just coffee.

AMANDA. You can't put in a day's work on an empty stomach. You've got ten minutes—don't gulp! Drinking too-hot liquids makes cancer of the stomach. . . . Put cream in.

TOM. No, thank you.

AMANDA. To cool it.

TOM. No! No, thank you, I want it black.

AMANDA. I know, but it's not good for you. We have to do all that we can do to build ourselves up. In these trying times we live in, all that we have to cling to is —each other. . . . That's why it's so important to— Tom, I— I sent out your sister so I could discuss something with you. If you hadn't spoken I would have spoken to you. [*She sits down.*]

TOM. [*Gently.*] What is it, Mother, that you want to discuss?

AMANDA. *Laura!*

[*Tom puts his cup down slowly.*]

[*Legend on screen.* "Laura." *Music: "The Glass Menagerie."*]

TOM. —Oh.—Laura . . .

AMANDA. [*Touching his sleeve.*] You know how Laura is. So quiet but—still water runs deep! She notices things and I think she—broods about them.

[*Tom looks up.*]

A few days ago I came in and she was crying.

TOM. What about?

AMANDA. You.

TOM. Me?

AMANDA. She has an idea that you're not happy here.

TOM. What gave her that idea?

AMANDA. What gives her any idea? However, you do act strangely. I—I'm not criticizing, understand *that!* I know your ambitions do not lie in the warehouse, that like everybody in the whole wide world—you've had to—make sacrifices, but—Tom —Tom—life's not easy, it calls for—Spartan endurance! There's so many things in my heart that I cannot describe to you! I've never told you but I—*loved* your father. . . .

TOM. [*Gently.*] I know that, Mother.

AMANDA. And you—when I see you taking after his ways! Staying out late—and —well, you *had* been drinking the night you were in that—terrifying condition! Laura says that you hate the apartment and that you go out nights to get away from it! Is that true, Tom?

TOM. No. You say there's so much in your heart that you can't describe to me. That's true of me, too. There's so much in my heart that I can't describe to *you!* So let's respect each other's—

AMANDA. But, why—*why,* Tom—are you always so *restless?* Where do you *go* to, nights?

TOM. I—go to the movies.

AMANDA. Why do you go to the movies so much, Tom?

TOM. I go to the movies because—I like adventure. Adventure is something I don't have much of at work, so I go to the movies.

AMANDA. But, Tom, you go to the movies *entirely* too *much!*

TOM. I like a lot of adventure.

[*Amanda looks baffled, then hurt. As the familiar inquisition resumes, Tom becomes hard and impatient again. Amanda slips back into her querulous attitude toward him.*]

[*Image on screen:* A sailing vessel with Jolly Roger.]

AMANDA. Most young men find adventure in their careers.

TOM. Then most young men are not employed in a warehouse.

AMANDA. The world is full of young men employed in warehouses and offices and factories.

TOM. Do all of them find adventure in their careers?

AMANDA. They do or they do without it! Not everybody has a craze for adventure.

TOM. Man is by instinct a lover, a hunter, a fighter, and none of those instincts are given much play at the warehouse!

AMANDA. Man is by instinct! Don't quote instinct to me! Instinct is something that people have got away from! It belongs to animals! Christian adults don't want it!

TOM. What do Christian adults want, then, Mother?

AMANDA. Superior things! Things of the mind and the spirit! Only animals have to satisfy instincts! Surely your aims are somewhat higher than theirs! Than monkeys—pigs—

TOM. I reckon they're not.

AMANDA. You're joking. However, that isn't what I wanted to discuss.

TOM. [*Rising.*] I haven't much time.

AMANDA. [*Pushing his shoulders.*] Sit down.

TOM. You want me to punch in red at the warehouse, Mother?

AMANDA. You have five minutes. I want to talk about Laura.

[*Screen legend:* "Plans and Provisions."]

TOM. All right! What about Laura?

AMANDA. We have to be making some plans and provisions for her. She's older than you, two years, and nothing has happened. She just drifts along doing nothing. It frightens me terribly how she just drifts along.

TOM. I guess she's the type that people call home girls.

AMANDA. There's no such type, and if there is, it's a pity! That is unless the home is hers, with a husband!

TOM. What?

AMANDA. Oh, I can see the handwriting on the wall as plain as I see the nose in front of my face! It's terrifying! More and more you remind me of your father! He was out all hours without explanation!—Then *left! Goodbye!* And me with the bag to hold. I saw that letter you got from the Merchant Marine. I know what you're dreaming of. I'm not standing here blindfolded. [*She pauses.*] Very well, then. Then *do* it! But not till there's somebody to take your place.

TOM. What do you mean?

AMANDA. I mean that as soon as Laura has got somebody to take care of her, married, a home of her own, independent—why, then you'll be free to go wherever you please, on land, on sea, whichever way the wind blows you! But until that time you've got to look out for your sister. I don't say me because I'm old and don't matter! I say for your sister because she's young and dependent.

I put her in business college—a dismal failure! Frightened her so it made her sick at the stomach. I took her over to the Young People's League at the church. Another fiasco. She spoke to nobody, nobody spoke to her. Now all she does is fool with those pieces of glass and play those worn-out records. What kind of a life is that for a girl to lead?

TOM. What can I do about it?

AMANDA. Overcome selfishness! Self, self, self is all that you think of!

[*Tom springs up and crosses to get his coat. It is ugly and bulky. He pulls on a cap with earmuffs.*]

Where is your muffler? Put your wool muffler on!

[*He snatches it angrily from the closet, tosses it around his neck and pulls both ends tight.*]

Tom! I haven't said what I had in mind to ask you.

TOM. I'm too late to—

AMANDA. [*Catching his arm—very importunately; then shyly.*] Down at the warehouse, aren't there some—nice young men?

TOM. No!

AMANDA. There *must* be—*some* . . .

TOM. Mother—[*He gestures.*]

AMANDA. Find out one that's clean-living—doesn't drink and ask him out for sister!

TOM. What?

AMANDA. For *sister!* To *meet!* Get *acquainted!*

TOM. [*Stamping to the door.*] Oh, my *go-osh!*

AMANDA. Will you?

[*He opens the door. She says, imploringly.*]

Will you?

[*He starts down the fire escape.*]

Will you? *Will* you, dear?

TOM. [*Calling back.*] *Yes!*

[*Amanda closes the door hesitantly and with a troubled but faintly hopeful expression.*]

[*Screen image:* The cover of a glamor magazine.]

[*The spotlight picks up Amanda at the phone.*]

AMANDA. Ella Cartwright? This is Amanda Wingfield! How are you, honey? How is that kidney condition?

[*There is a five-second pause.*]

Horrors!

[*There is another pause.*]

You're a Christian martyr, yes, honey, that's what you are, a Christian martyr! Well, I just now happened to notice in my little red book that your subscription to the *Companion* has just run out! I knew that you wouldn't want to miss out on the wonderful serial starting in this new issue. It's by Bessie Mae Hopper, the first thing she's written since *Honeymoon for Three.* Wasn't that a strange and interesting story? Well, this one is even lovelier, I believe. It has a sophisticated, society background. It's all about the horsey set on Long Island!

[*The light fades out.*]

Scene V

Legend on the screen: "Annunciation."
Music is heard as the light slowly comes on.

It is early dusk of a spring evening. Supper has just been finished in the Wingfield apartment. Amanda and Laura, in light-colored dresses, are removing dishes from the table in the dining room, which is shadowy, their movements formalized almost as a dance or ritual, their moving forms as pale and silent as moths. Tom, in white shirt and trousers, rises from the table and crosses toward the fire escape.

AMANDA. [*As he passes her.*] Son, will you do me a favor?

TOM. What?

AMANDA. Comb your hair! You look so pretty when your hair is combed!

[*Tom slouches on the sofa with the evening paper. Its enormous headline reads: "Franco Triumphs."*]

There is only one respect in which I would like you to emulate your father.

TOM. What respect is that?

AMANDA. The care he always took of his appearance. He never allowed himself to look untidy.

[*He throws down the paper and crosses to the fire escape.*]

Where are you going?

TOM. I'm going out to smoke.

AMANDA. You smoke too much. A pack a day at fifteen cents a pack. How much would that amount to in a month? Thirty times fifteen is how much, Tom? Figure it out and you will be astounded at what you could save. Enough to give you a night-school course in accounting at Washington U.! Just think what a wonderful thing that would be for you, son!

[*Tom is unmoved by the thought.*]

TOM. I'd rather smoke. [*He steps out on the landing, letting the screen door slam.*]

AMANDA. [*Sharply.*] I know! That's the tragedy of it. . . . [*Alone, she turns to look at her husband's picture.*]

[*Dance music: "The World Is Waiting for the Sunrise!"*]

TOM. [*To the audience.*] Across the alley from us was the Paradise Dance Hall. On evenings in spring the windows and doors were open and the music came outdoors. Sometimes the lights were turned out except for a large glass sphere that hung from the ceiling. It would turn slowly about and filter the dusk with delicate rainbow colors. Then the orchestra played a waltz or a tango, something that had a slow and sensuous rhythm. Couples would come outside, to the relative privacy of the alley. You could see them kissing behind ash pits and telephone poles. This was the compensation for lives that passed like mine, without any change or adventure. Adventure and change were imminent in this year. They were waiting around the corner for all these kids. Suspended in the mist over Berchtesgaden, caught in the folds of Chamberlain's umbrella. In Spain there was Guernica! But here there was only hot swing music and liquor, dance halls, bars, and movies, and sex that hung in the gloom like a chandelier and flooded the world with brief, deceptive rainbows. . . . All the world was waiting for bombardments!

[*Amanda turns from the picture and comes outside.*]

AMANDA. [*Sighing.*] A fire escape landing's a poor excuse for a porch. [*She spreads a newspaper on a step and sits down, gracefully and demurely as if she were settling into a swing on a Mississippi veranda.*] What are you looking at?

TOM. The moon.

AMANDA. Is there a moon this evening?

TOM. It's rising over Garfinkel's Delicatessen.

AMANDA. So it is! A little silver slipper of a moon. Have you made a wish on it yet?

TOM. Um-hum.

AMANDA. What did you wish for?

TOM. That's a secret.

AMANDA. A secret, huh? Well, I won't tell mine either. I will be just as mysterious as you.

TOM. I bet I can guess what yours is.

AMANDA. Is my head so transparent?

TOM. You're not a sphinx.

AMANDA. No, I don't have secrets. I'll tell you what I wished for on the moon. Success and happiness for my precious children! I wish for that whenever there's a moon, and when there isn't a moon, I wish for it, too.

TOM. I thought perhaps you wished for a gentleman caller.

AMANDA. Why do you say that?

TOM. Don't you remember asking me to fetch one?

AMANDA. I remember suggesting that it would be nice for your sister if you brought home some nice young man from the warehouse. I think that I've made that suggestion more than once.

TOM. Yes, you have made it repeatedly.

AMANDA. Well?

TOM. We are going to have one.

AMANDA. *What?*

TOM. A gentleman caller!

[*The annunciation is celebrated with music.*]

[*Amanda rises.*]

[*Image on screen:* A caller with a bouquet.]

AMANDA. You mean you have asked some nice young man to come over?

TOM. Yep. I've asked him to dinner.

AMANDA. You really did?

TOM. I did!

AMANDA. You did, and did he—*accept?*

TOM. He did!

AMANDA. Well, well—well, well! That's—lovely!

TOM. I thought that you would be pleased.

AMANDA. It's definite then?

TOM. Very definite.

AMANDA. Soon?

TOM. Very soon.

AMANDA. For heaven's sake, stop putting on and tell me some things, will you?

TOM. What things do you want me to tell you?

AMANDA. *Naturally* I would like to know when he's *coming!*

TOM. He's coming tomorrow.

AMANDA. *Tomorrow?*

TOM. Yep. Tomorrow.

AMANDA. But, Tom!

TOM. Yes, Mother?

AMANDA. Tomorrow gives me no time!

TOM. Time for what?

AMANDA. Preparations! Why didn't you phone me at once, as soon as you asked him, the minute that he accepted? Then, don't you see, I could have been getting ready!

TOM. You don't have to make any fuss.

AMANDA. Oh, Tom, Tom, Tom, of course I have to make a fuss! I want things nice, not sloppy! Not thrown together. I'll certainly have to do some fast thinking, won't I?

TOM. I don't see why you have to think at all.

AMANDA. You just don't know. We can't have a gentleman caller in a pigsty! All my wedding silver has to be polished, the monogrammed table linen ought to be laundered! The windows have to be washed and fresh curtains put up. And how about clothes? We have to *wear* something, don't we?

TOM. Mother, this boy is no one to make a fuss over!

AMANDA. Do you realize he's the first young man we've introduced to your sister? It's terrible, dreadful, disgraceful that poor little sister has never received a single gentleman caller! Tom, come inside! [*She opens the screen door.*]

TOM. What for?

AMANDA. I want to ask you some things.

TOM. If you're going to make such a fuss, I'll call it off, I'll tell him not to come!

AMANDA. You certainly won't do anything of the kind. Nothing offends people worse than broken engagements. It simply means I'll have to work like a Turk! We won't be brilliant, but we will pass inspection. Come on inside.

[*Tom follows her inside, groaning.*]

Sit down.

TOM. Any particular place you would like me to sit?

AMANDA. Thank heavens I've got that new sofa! I'm also making payments on a floor lamp I'll have sent out! And put the chintz covers on, they'll brighten things up! Of course I'd hoped to have these walls re-papered. . . . What is the young man's name?

TOM. His name is O'Connor.

AMANDA. That, of course, means fish—tomorrow is Friday! I'll have that salmon loaf—with Durkee's dressing! What does he do? He works at the warehouse?

TOM. Of course! How else would I—

AMANDA. Tom, he—doesn't drink?

TOM. Why do you ask me that?

AMANDA. Your father *did!*

TOM. Don't get started on that!

AMANDA. He *does* drink, then?

TOM. Not that I know of!

AMANDA. Make sure, be certain! The last thing I want for my daughter's a boy who drinks!

TOM. Aren't you being a little bit premature? Mr. O'Connor has not yet appeared on the scene!

AMANDA. But will tomorrow. To meet your sister, and what do I know about his character? Nothing! Old maids are better off than wives of drunkards!

TOM. Oh, my God!

AMANDA. Be still!

TOM. [*Leaning forward to whisper.*] Lots of fellows meet girls whom they don't marry!

AMANDA. Oh, talk sensibly, Tom—and don't be sarcastic! [*She has gotten a hairbrush.*]

TOM. What are you doing?

AMANDA. I'm brushing that cowlick down! [*She attacks his hair with the brush.*] What is this young man's position at the warehouse?

TOM. [*Submitting grimly to the brush and the interrogation.*] This young man's position is that of a shipping clerk, Mother.

AMANDA. Sounds to me like a fairly responsible job, the sort of job *you* would be in if you had more *get-up.* What is his salary? Have you any idea?

TOM. I would judge it to be approximately eighty-five dollars a month.

AMANDA. Well—not princely, but—

TOM. Twenty more than I make.

AMANDA. Yes, how well I know! But for a family man, eighty-five dollars a month is not much more than you can just get by on. . . .

TOM. Yes, but Mr. O'Connor is not a family man.

AMANDA. He might be, mightn't he? Some time in the future?

TOM. I see. Plans and provisions.

AMANDA. You are the only young man that I know of who ignores the fact that the future becomes the present, the present the past, and the past turns into everlasting regret if you don't plan for it!

TOM. I will think that over and see what I can make of it.

AMANDA. Don't be supercilious with your mother! Tell me some more about this —what do you call him?

TOM. James D. O'Connor. The D. is for Delaney.

AMANDA. Irish on *both* sides! *Gracious!* And doesn't drink?

TOM. Shall I call him up and ask him right this minute?

AMANDA. The only way to find out about those things is to make discreet inquiries at the proper moment. When I was a girl in Blue Mountain and it was suspected that a young man drank, the girl whose attentions he had been receiving, if any girl *was,* would sometimes speak to the minister of his church, or rather her father would if her father was living, and sort of feel him out on the young man's character. That is the way such things are discreetly handled to keep a young woman from making a tragic mistake!

TOM. Then how did you happen to make a tragic mistake?

AMANDA. That innocent look of your father's had everyone fooled! He *smiled*—

the world was *enchanted!* No girl can do worse than put herself at the mercy of a handsome appearance! I hope that Mr. O'Connor is not too good-looking.

TOM. No, he's not too good-looking. He's covered with freckles and hasn't too much of a nose.

AMANDA. He's not right-down homely, though?

TOM. Not right-down homely. Just medium homely, I'd say.

AMANDA. Character's what to look for in a man.

TOM. That's what I've always said, Mother.

AMANDA. You've never said anything of the kind and I suspect you would never give it a thought.

TOM. Don't be suspicious of me.

AMANDA. At least I hope he's the type that's up and coming.

TOM. I think he really goes in for self-improvement.

AMANDA. What reason have you to think so?

TOM. He goes to night school.

AMANDA. [*Beaming.*] Splendid! What does he do, I mean study?

TOM. Radio engineering and public speaking!

AMANDA. Then he has visions of being advanced in the world! Any young man who studies public speaking is aiming to have an executive job some day! And radio engineering? A thing for the future! Both of these facts are very illuminating. Those are the sort of things that a mother should know concerning any young man who comes to call on her daughter. Seriously or—not.

TOM. One little warning. He doesn't know about Laura. I didn't let on that we had dark ulterior motives. I just said, why don't you come and have dinner with us? He said okay and that was the whole conversation.

AMANDA. I bet it was! You're eloquent as an oyster. However, he'll know about Laura when he gets here. When he sees how lovely and sweet and pretty she is, he'll thank his lucky stars he was asked to dinner.

TOM. Mother, you mustn't expect too much of Laura.

AMANDA. What do you mean?

TOM. Laura seems all those things to you and me because she's ours and we love her. We don't even notice she's crippled any more.

AMANDA. Don't say crippled! You know that I never allow that word to be used!

TOM. But face facts, Mother. She is and—that's not all—

AMANDA. What do you mean "not all"?

TOM. Laura is very different from other girls.

AMANDA. I think the difference is all to her advantage.

TOM. Not quite all—in the eyes of others—strangers—she's terribly shy and lives in a world of her own and those things make her seem a little peculiar to people outside the house.

AMANDA. Don't say peculiar.

TOM. Face the facts. She is.

[*The dance hall music changes to a tango that has a minor and somewhat ominous tone.*]

AMANDA. In what way is she peculiar—may I ask?

TOM. [*Gently.*] She lives in a world of her own—a world of little glass ornaments, Mother. . . .

[*He gets up. Amanda remains holding the brush, looking at him, troubled.*]

She plays old phonograph records and—that's about all— [*He glances at himself in the mirror and crosses to the door.*]

AMANDA. [*Sharply.*] Where are you going?

TOM. I'm going to the movies. [*He goes out the screen door.*]

AMANDA. Not to the movies, every night to the movies! [*She follows quickly to the screen door.*] I don't believe you always go to the movies!

[*He is gone. Amanda looks worriedly after him for a moment. Then vitality and optimism return and she turns from the door, crossing to the portieres.*]

Laura! Laura!

[*Laura answers from the kitchenette.*]

LAURA. Yes, Mother.

AMANDA. Let those dishes go and come in front!

[*Laura appears with a dish towel. Amanda speaks to her gaily.*]

Laura, come here and make a wish on the moon!

[*Screen image:* The Moon.]

LAURA. [*Entering.*] Moon—moon?

AMANDA. A little silver slipper of a moon. Look over your left shoulder, Laura, and make a wish!

[*Laura looks faintly puzzled as if called out of sleep. Amanda seizes her shoulders and turns her at an angle by the door.*]

Now! Now, darling, *wish!*

LAURA. What shall I wish for, Mother?

AMANDA. [*Her voice trembling and her eyes suddenly filling with tears.*] Happiness! Good fortune!

[*The sound of the violin rises and the stage dims out.*]

Scene VI

The light comes up on the fire escape landing. Tom is leaning against the grill, smoking.

[*Screen image:* The high school hero.]

TOM. And so the following evening I brought Jim home to dinner. I had known Jim slightly in high school. In high school Jim was a hero. He had tremendous Irish good nature and vitality with the scrubbed and polished look of white chinaware. He seemed to move in a continual spotlight. He was a star in basketball, captain of the debating club, president of the senior class and the glee club and he sang the male lead in the annual light operas. He was always running or bounding, never just walking. He seemed always at the point of defeating the law of gravity. He was shooting with such velocity through his adolescence that you would logically expect him to arrive at nothing short of the White House by the time he was thirty. But Jim apparently ran into more interference after his graduation from Soldan. His speed had definitely slowed. Six years after he left high school he was holding a job that wasn't much better than mine.

[*Screen image:* The Clerk.]

He was the only one at the warehouse with whom I was on friendly terms. I was valuable to him as someone who could remember his former glory, who had seen him win basketball games and the silver cup in debating. He knew of my secret practice of retiring to a cabinet of the washroom to work on poems when business was slack in the warehouse. He called me Shakespeare. And while the other boys in the warehouse regarded me with suspicious hostility, Jim took a humorous attitude toward me. Gradually his attitude affected the others, their hostility wore off and they also began to smile at me as people smile at an oddly fashioned dog who trots across their path at some distance.

I knew that Jim and Laura had known each other at Soldan, and I had heard Laura speak admiringly of his voice. I didn't know if Jim remembered her or not. In high school Laura had been as unobtrusive as Jim had been astonishing. If he did remember Laura, it was not as my sister, for when I asked him to dinner, he grinned and said, "You know, Shakespeare, I never thought of you as having folks!"

He was about to discover that I did. . . .

[*Legend on screen:* "The accent of a coming foot."]

[*The light dims out on Tom and comes up in the Wingfield living room—a delicate lemony light. It is about five on a Friday evening of late spring which comes "scattering poems in the sky."*]

[*Amanda has worked like a Turk in preparation for the gentleman caller. The results are astonishing. The new floor lamp with its rose silk shade is in place, a colored paper lantern conceals the broken light fixture in the ceiling, new billowing white curtains are at the windows, chintz covers are on the chairs and sofa, a pair of new sofa pillows make their initial appearance. Open boxes and tissue paper are scattered on the floor.*]

[*Laura stands in the middle of the room with lifted arms while Amanda crouches before her, adjusting the hem of a new dress, devout and ritualistic. The dress is colored and designed by memory. The arrangement of Laura's hair is changed; it is softer and more becoming. A fragile, unearthly prettiness has come out in Laura: she is like a piece of translucent glass touched by light, given a momentary radiance, not actual, not lasting.*]

AMANDA. [*Impatiently.*] Why are you trembling?

LAURA. Mother, you've made me so nervous!

AMANDA. How have I made you nervous?

LAURA. By all this fuss! You make it seem so important!

AMANDA. I don't understand you, Laura. You couldn't be satisfied with just sitting home, and yet whenever I try to arrange something for you, you seem to resist it. [*She gets up.*] Now take a look at yourself. No, wait! Wait just a moment—I have an idea!

LAURA. What is it now?

[*Amanda produces two powder puffs which she wraps in handkerchiefs and stuffs in Laura's bosom.*]

LAURA. Mother, what are you doing?

AMANDA. They call them "Gay Deceivers"!

LAURA. I won't wear them!

AMANDA. You will!

LAURA. Why should I?

AMANDA. Because, to be painfully honest, your chest is flat.

LAURA. You make it seem like we were setting a trap.

AMANDA. All pretty girls are a trap, a pretty trap, and men expect them to be.

[*Legend on screen:* "A pretty trap."]

Now look at yourself, young lady. This is the prettiest you will ever be! [*She stands back to admire Laura.*] I've got to fix myself now! You're going to be surprised by your mother's appearance!

[*Amanda crosses through the portieres, humming gaily. Laura moves slowly to the long mirror and stares solemnly at herself. A wind blows the white curtains inward in a slow, graceful motion and with a faint, sorrowful sighing.*]

AMANDA. [*From somewhere behind the portieres.*] It isn't dark enough yet.

[*Laura turns slowly before the mirror with a troubled look.*]

[*Legend on screen:* "This is my sister: Celebrate her with strings!" *Music plays.*]

AMANDA. [*Laughing, still not visible.*] I'm going to show you something. I'm going to make a spectacular appearance!

LAURA. What is it, Mother?

AMANDA. Possess your soul in patience—you will see! Something I've resurrected from that old trunk! Styles haven't changed so terribly much after all. . . . [*She parts the portieres.*] Now just look at your mother! [*She wears a girlish frock of yellowed voile with a blue silk sash. She carries a bunch of jonquils—the legend of her youth is nearly revived. Now she speaks feverishly.*] This is the dress in which I led the cotillion. Won the cakewalk twice at Sunset Hill, wore one Spring to the Governor's Ball in Jackson! See how I sashayed around the ballroom, Laura? [*She raises her skirt and does a mincing step around the room.*] I wore it on Sundays for my gentlemen callers! I had it on the day I met your father. . . . I had malaria fever all that Spring. The change of climate from East Tennessee to the Delta—weakened resistance. I had a little temperature all the time—not enough to be serious—just enough to make me restless and giddy! Invitations poured in—parties all over the Delta! "Stay in bed," said Mother, "you have a fever!"—but I just wouldn't. I took quinine but kept on going, going! Evenings, dances! Afternoons, long, long rides! Picnics—lovely! So lovely, that country in May—all lacy with dogwood, literally flooded with jonquils! That was the spring I had the craze for jonquils. Jonquils became an absolute obsession. Mother said, "Honey, there's no more room for jonquils." And still I kept on bringing in more jonquils. Whenever, wherever I saw them, I'd say, "Stop! Stop! I see jonquils!" I made the young men help me gather the jonquils! It was a joke, Amanda and her jonquils. Finally there were no more vases to hold them, every available space was filled with jonquils. No vases to hold them? All right, I'll hold them myself! And then I—[*She stops in front of the picture. Music plays.*] met your father! Malaria fever and jonquils and then—this—boy. . . . [*She switches on the rose-colored lamp.*]I hope they get here before it starts to rain. [*She crosses the room and places the jonquils in a bowl on the table.*] I gave your brother a little extra change so he and Mr. O'Connor could take the service car home.

LAURA. [*With an altered look.*] What did you say his name was?

AMANDA. O'Connor.

LAURA. What is his first name?

AMANDA. I don't remember. Oh, yes, I do. It was—Jim!

[*Laura sways slightly and catches hold of a chair.*]

[*Legend on screen:* "Not Jim!"]

LAURA. [*Faintly.*] Not—Jim!

AMANDA. Yes, that was it, it was Jim! I've never known a Jim that wasn't nice!

[*The music becomes ominous.*]

LAURA. Are you sure his name is Jim O'Connor?

AMANDA. Yes. Why?

LAURA. Is he the one that Tom used to know in high school?

AMANDA. He didn't say so. I think he just got to know him at the warehouse.

LAURA. There was a Jim O'Connor we both knew in high school—[*Then, with effort.*] If that is the one that Tom is bringing to dinner—you'll have to excuse me, I won't come to the table.

AMANDA. What sort of nonsense is this?

LAURA. You asked me once if I ever liked a boy. Don't you remember I showed you this boy's picture?

AMANDA. You mean the boy you showed me in the yearbook?

LAURA. Yes, that boy.

AMANDA. Laura, Laura, were you in love with that boy?

LAURA. I don't know, Mother. All I know is I couldn't sit at the table if it was him!

AMANDA. It won't be him! It isn't the least bit likely. But whether it is or not, you will come to the table. You will not be excused.

LAURA. I'll have to be, Mother.

AMANDA. I don't intend to humor your silliness, Laura. I've had too much from you and your brother, both! So just sit down and compose yourself till they come. Tom has forgotten his key so you'll have to let them in, when they arrive.

LAURA. [*Panicky.*] Oh, Mother—*you* answer the door!

AMANDA. [*Lightly.*] I'll be busy in the kitchen—busy!

LAURA. Oh, Mother, please answer the door, don't make me do it!

AMANDA. [*Crossing into the kitchenette.*] I've got to fix the dressing for the salmon. Fuss, fuss—silliness!—over a gentleman caller!

[*The door swings shut. Laura is left alone.*]

[*Legend on screen:* "Terror!"]

[*She utters a low moan and turns off the lamp—sits stiffly on the edge of the sofa, knotting her fingers together.*]

[*Legend on screen:* "The Opening of a Door!"]

[*Tom and Jim appear on the fire escape steps and climb to the landing. Hearing their approach, Laura rises with a panicky gesture. She retreats to the portieres. The doorbell rings. Laura catches her breath and touches her throat. Low drums sound.*]

AMANDA. [*Calling.*] Laura, sweetheart! The door!

[*Laura stares at it without moving.*]

JIM. I think we just beat the rain.

TOM. Uh-huh. [*He rings again, nervously. Jim whistles and fishes for a cigarette.*]

AMANDA. [*Very, very gaily.*] Laura, that is your brother and Mr. O'Connor! Will you let them in, darling?

[*Laura crosses toward the kitchenette door.*]

LAURA. [*Breathlessly.*] Mother—you go to the door!

[*Amanda steps out of the kitchenette and stares furiously at Laura. She points imperiously at the door.*]

LAURA. Please, please!

AMANDA. [*In a fierce whisper.*] What is the matter with you, you silly thing?

LAURA. [*Desperately.*] Please, you answer it, *please!*

AMANDA. I told you I wasn't going to humor you, Laura. Why have you chosen this moment to lose your mind?

LAURA. Please, please, please, you go!

AMANDA. You'll have to go to the door because I can't!

LAURA. [*Despairingly.*] I can't either!

AMANDA. *Why?*

LAURA. I'm *sick!*

AMANDA. I'm sick, too—of your nonsense! Why can't you and your brother be normal people? Fantastic whims and behavior!

[*Tom gives a long ring.*]

Preposterous goings on! Can you give me one reason— [*She calls out lyrically.*] *Coming! Just one second!*—why you should be afraid to open a door? Now you answer it, Laura!

LAURA. Oh, oh, oh . . . [*She returns through the portieres, darts to the Victrola, winds it frantically and turns it on.*]

AMANDA. Laura Wingfield, you march right to that door!

LAURA. *Yes—yes, Mother!*

[*A faraway, scratchy rendition of "Dardanella" softens the air and gives her strength to move through it. She slips to the door and draws it cautiously open. Tom enters with the caller, Jim O'Connor.*]

TOM. Laura, this is Jim. Jim, this is my sister, Laura.

JIM. [*Stepping inside.*] I didn't know that Shakespeare had a sister!

LAURA. [*Retreating, stiff and trembling, from the door.*] How—how do you do?

JIM. [*Heartily, extending his hand.*] Okay!

[*Laura touches it hesitantly with hers.*]

JIM. Your hand's *cold*, Laura!

LAURA. Yes, well—I've been playing the Victrola. . . .

JIM. Must have been playing classical music on it! You ought to play a little hot swing music to warm you up!

LAURA. Excuse me—I haven't finished playing the Victrola . . .

[*She turns awkwardly and hurries into the front room. She pauses a second by the Victrola. Then she catches her breath and darts through the portieres like a frightened deer.*]

JIM. [*Grinning.*] What was the matter?

TOM. Oh—with Laura? Laura is—terribly shy.

JIM. Shy, huh? It's unusual to meet a shy girl nowadays. I don't believe you ever mentioned you had a sister.

TOM. Well, now you know. I have one. Here is the *Post Dispatch.* You want a piece of it?

JIM. Uh-huh.

TOM. What piece? The comics?

JIM. Sports! [*He glances at it.*] Ole Dizzy Dean is on his bad behavior.

TOM. [*Uninterested.*] Yeah? [*He lights a cigarette and goes over to the fire-escape door.*]

JIM. Where are *you* going?

TOM. I'm going out on the terrace.

JIM. [*Going after him.*] You know, Shakespeare—I'm going to sell you a bill of goods!

TOM. What goods?

JIM. A course I'm taking.

TOM. Huh?

JIM. In public speaking! You and me, we're not the warehouse type.

TOM. Thanks—that's good news. But what has public speaking got to do with it?

JIM. It fits you for—executive positions!

TOM. Awww.

JIM. I tell you it's done a helluva lot for me.

[*Image on screen:* Executive at his desk.]

TOM. In what respect?

JIM. In every! Ask yourself what is the difference between you an' me and men in the office down front? Brains?—No!—Ability?—No! Then what? Just one little thing—

TOM. What is that one little thing?

JIM. Primarily it amounts to—social poise! Being able to square up to people and hold your own on any social level!

AMANDA. [*From the kitchenette.*] Tom?

TOM. Yes, Mother?

AMANDA. Is that you and Mr. O'Connor?

TOM. Yes, Mother.

AMANDA. Well, you just make yourselves comfortable in there.

TOM. Yes, Mother.

AMANDA. Ask Mr. O'Connor if he would like to wash his hands.

JIM. Aw, no—no—thank you—I took care of that at the warehouse. Tom—

TOM. Yes?

JIM. Mr. Mendoza was speaking to me about you.

TOM. Favorably?

JIM. What do you think?

TOM. Well—

JIM. You're going to be out of a job if you don't wake up.

TOM. I am waking up—

JIM. You show no signs.

TOM. The signs are interior.

[*Image on screen:* The sailing vessel with the Jolly Roger again.]

TOM. I'm planning to change. [*He leans over the fire-escape rail, speaking with quiet exhilaration. The incandescent marquees and signs of the first-run movie houses light his face from across the alley. He looks like a voyager.*] I'm right at the point of committing myself to a future that doesn't include the warehouse and Mr. Mendoza or even a night-school course in public speaking.

JIM. What are you gassing about?

TOM. I'm tired of the movies.

JIM. Movies!

TOM. Yes, movies! Look at them— [*A wave toward the marvels of Grand Avenue.*] All of those glamorous people—having adventures—hogging it all, gobbling the whole thing up! You know what happens? People go to the *movies* instead of *moving!* Hollywood characters are supposed to have all the adventures for everybody in America, while everybody in America sits in a dark room and watches them have them! Yes, until there's a war. That's when adventure becomes available to the masses! *Everyone's* dish, not only Gable's! Then the people in the dark room come out of the dark room to have some adventures themselves—goody, goody! It's our turn now, to go to the South Sea Island—to make a safari—to be exotic, far-off! But I'm not patient. I don't want to wait till then. I'm tired of the *movies* and I am *about* to *move!*

JIM. [*Incredulously.*] Move?

TOM. Yes.

JIM. When?

TOM. Soon!

JIM. Where? Where?

[*The music seems to answer the question, while Tom thinks it over. He searches in his pockets.*]

TOM. I'm starting to boil inside. I know I seem dreamy, but inside—well, I'm boiling! Whenever I pick up a shoe, I shudder a little thinking how short life is and what I am doing! Whatever that means, I know it doesn't mean shoes—except as something to wear on a traveler's feet! [*He finds what he has been searching for in his pockets and holds out a paper to Jim.*] Look—

JIM. What?

TOM. I'm a member.

JIM. [*Reading.*] The Union of Merchant Seamen.

TOM. I paid my dues this month, instead of the light bill.

JIM. You will regret it when they turn the lights off.

TOM. I won't be here.

JIM. How about your mother?

TOM. I'm like my father. The bastard son of a bastard! Did you notice how he's grinning in his picture in there? And he's been absent going on sixteen years!

JIM. You're just talking, you drip. How does your mother feel about it?

TOM. Shhh! Here comes Mother! Mother is not acquainted with my plans!

AMANDA. [*Coming through the portieres.*] Where are you all?

TOM. On the terrace, Mother.

[*They start inside. She advances to them. Tom is distinctly shocked at her appearance. Even Jim blinks a little. He is making his first contact with girlish Southern vivacity and in spite of the night-school course in public speaking is somewhat thrown off the beam by the unexpected outlay of social charm. Certain responses are attempted by Jim but are swept aside by Amanda's gay laughter and chatter. Tom is embarrassed but after the first shock Jim reacts very warmly. He grins and chuckles, is altogether won over.*]

[*Image on screen:* Amanda as a girl.]

AMANDA. [*Coyly smiling, shaking her girlish ringlets.*] Well, well, well, so this is Mr. O'Connor. Introductions entirely unnecessary. I've heard so much about you from my boy. I finally said to him, Tom—good gracious!—why don't you bring this paragon to supper? I'd like to meet this nice young man at the warehouse!—instead of just hearing him sing your praises so much! I don't know why my son is so stand-offish—that's not Southern behavior!

Let's sit down and—I think we could stand a little more air in here! Tom, leave the door open. I felt a nice fresh breeze a moment ago. Where has it gone to? Mmm, so warm already! And not quite summer, even. We're going to burn up when summer really gets started. However, we're having—we're having a very light supper. I think light things are better fo' this time of year. The same as light clothes are. Light clothes an' light food are what warm weather calls fo'. You know our blood gets so thick during th' winter—it takes a while fo' us to *adjust* ou'selves!—when the season changes . . . It's come so quick this year. I wasn't prepared. All of a sudden—heavens! Already summer! I ran to the trunk an' pulled out this light dress—terribly old! Historical almost! But feels so good—so good an' co-ol, y' know. . . .

TOM. Mother—

AMANDA. Yes, honey?

TOM. How about—supper?

AMANDA. Honey, you go ask Sister if supper is ready! You know Sister is in full charge of supper! Tell her you hungry boys are waiting for it. [*To Jim.*] Have you met Laura?

JIM. She—

AMANDA. Let you in? Oh, good, you've met already! It's rare for a girl as sweet an' pretty as Laura to be domestic! But Laura is, thank heavens, not only pretty but also very domestic. I'm not at all. I never was a bit. I never could make a thing but angel-food cake. Well, in the South we had so many servants. Gone, gone, gone. All vestige of gracious living! Gone completely! I wasn't prepared for what the future brought me. All of my gentlemen callers were sons of planters and so of course I assumed that I would be married to one and raise my family on a large piece of land with plenty of servants. But man proposes—and woman accepts the proposal! To vary that old, old saying a little bit—I married no planter! I married a man who worked for the telephone company! That gallantly smiling gentleman over there! [*She points to the picture.*] A telephone man who—fell in love with long-distance! Now he travels and I don't even know where! But what am I going on for about my—tribulations? Tell me yours—I hope you don't have any! Tom?

TOM. [*Returning.*] Yes, Mother?

AMANDA. Is supper nearly ready?

TOM. It looks to me like supper is on the table.

AMANDA. Let me look— [*She rises prettily and looks through the portieres.*] Oh, lovely! But where is Sister?

TOM. Laura is not feeling well and she says that she thinks she'd better not come to the table.

AMANDA. What? Nonsense! Laura? Oh, Laura!

LAURA. [*From the kitchenette, faintly.*] Yes, Mother.

AMANDA. You really must come to the table. We won't be seated until you come to the table! Come in, Mr. O'Connor. You sit over there, and I'll. . . . Laura? Laura Wingfield! You're keeping us waiting, honey! We can't say grace until you come to the table!

[*The kitchenette door is pushed weakly open and Laura comes in. She is obviously quite faint, her lips trembling, her eyes wide and staring. She moves unsteadily toward the table.*]

[*Screen legend:* "Terror!"]

[*Outside a summer storm is coming on abruptly. The white curtains billow inward at the windows and there is a sorrowful murmur from the deep blue dusk.*]

[*Laura suddenly stumbles; she catches at a chair with a faint moan.*]

TOM. Laura!

AMANDA. Laura!

[*There is a clap of thunder.*]

[*Screen legend:* "Ah!"]

[*Despairingly.*] Why, Laura, you *are* ill, darling! Tom, help your sister into the living room, dear! Sit in the living room, Laura—rest on the sofa. Well! [*To Jim as Tom helps his sister to the sofa in the living room.*] Standing over the hot stove made her ill! I told her that it was just too warm this evening, but—

[*Tom comes back to the table.*]

Is Laura all right now?

TOM. Yes.

AMANDA. What *is* that? Rain? A nice cool rain has come up! [*She gives Jim a frightened look.*] I think we may—have grace—now . . .

[*Tom looks at her stupidly.*] Tom, honey—you say grace!

TOM. Oh . . . "For these and all thy mercies—"

[*They bow their heads, Amanda stealing a nervous glance at Jim. In the living room Laura, stretched on the sofa, clenches her hand to her lips, to hold back a shuddering sob.*]

God's Holy Name be praised—

[*The scene dims out.*]

Scene VII

It is half an hour later. Dinner is just being finished in the dining room, Laura is still huddled upon the sofa, her feet drawn under her, her head resting on a pale blue pillow, her eyes wide and mysteriously watchful. The new floor lamp with its shade of rose-colored silk gives a soft, becoming light to her face, bringing out the fragile, unearthly prettiness which usually escapes attention. From outside there is a steady murmur of rain, but it is slackening and soon stops; the air outside becomes pale and luminous as the moon breaks through the clouds. A moment after the curtain rises, the lights in both rooms flicker and go out.

JIM. Hey, there, Mr. Light Bulb!

[*Amanda laughs nervously.*]

[*Legend on screen:* "Suspension of a public service."]

AMANDA. Where was Moses when the lights went out? Ha-ha. Do you know the answer to that one, Mr. O'Connor?

JIM. No, Ma'am, what's the answer?

AMANDA. In the dark!

[*Jim laughs appreciatively.*]

Everybody sit still. I'll light the candles. Isn't it lucky we have them on the table? Where's a match? Which of you gentlemen can provide a match?

JIM. Here.

AMANDA. Thank you, Sir.

JIM. Not at all, Ma'am!

AMANDA. [*As she lights the candles.*] I guess the fuse has burnt out. Mr. O'Connor, can you tell a burnt-out fuse? I know I can't and Tom is a total loss when it comes to mechanics.

[*They rise from the table and go into the kitchenette, from where their voices are heard.*]

Oh, be careful you don't bump into something. We don't want our gentleman caller to break his neck. Now wouldn't that be a fine howdy-do?

JIM. Ha-ha! Where is the fuse-box?

AMANDA. Right here next to the stove. Can you see anything?

JIM. Just a minute.

AMANDA. Isn't electricity a mysterious thing? Wasn't it Benjamin Franklin who tied a key to a kite? We live in such a mysterious universe, don't we? Some people say that science clears up all the mysteries for us. In my opinion it only creates more! Have you found it yet?

JIM. No, Ma'am. All these fuses look okay to me.

AMANDA. Tom!

TOM. Yes, Mother?

AMANDA. That light bill I gave you several days ago. The one I told you we got the notices about?

[*Legend on screen:* "Ha!"]

TOM. Oh—yeah.

AMANDA. You didn't neglect to pay it by any chance?

TOM. Why, I—

AMANDA. Didn't! I might have known it!

JIM. Shakespeare probably wrote a poem on that light bill, Mrs. Wingfield.

AMANDA. I might have known better than to trust him with it! There's such a high price for negligence in this world!

JIM. Maybe the poem will win a ten-dollar prize.

AMANDA. We'll just have to spend the remainder of the evening in the nineteenth century, before Mr. Edison made the Mazda lamp!

JIM. Candlelight is my favorite kind of light.

AMANDA. That shows you're romantic! But that's no excuse for Tom. Well, we got through dinner. Very considerate of them to let us get through dinner before they plunged us into everlasting darkness, wasn't it, Mr. O'Connor?

JIM. Ha-ha!

AMANDA. Tom, as a penalty for your carelessness you can help me with the dishes.

JIM. Let me give you a hand.

AMANDA. Indeed you will not!

JIM. I ought to be good for something.

AMANDA. Good for something? [*Her tone is rhapsodic.*] *You?* Why, Mr. O'Connor, nobody, *nobody's* given me this much entertainment in years—as you have!

JIM. Aw, now, Mrs. Wingfield!

AMANDA. I'm not exaggerating, not one bit! But Sister is all by her lonesome. You go keep her company in the parlor! I'll give you this lovely old candelabrum that used to be on the altar at the Church of the Heavenly Rest. It was melted a little out of shape when the church burnt down. Lightning struck it one spring. Gypsy Jones was holding a revival at the time and he intimated that the church was destroyed because the Episcopalians gave card parties.

JIM. Ha-ha.

AMANDA. And how about you coaxing Sister to drink a little wine? I think it would be good for her! Can you carry both at once?

JIM. Sure. I'm Superman!

AMANDA. Now, Thomas, get into this apron!

[Jim comes into the dining room, carrying the candelabrum, its candles lighted, in one hand and a glass of wine in the other. The door of the kitchenette swings closed on Amanda's gay laughter; the flickering light approaches the portieres. Laura sits up nervously as Jim enters. She can hardly speak from the almost intolerable strain of being alone with a stranger.]

[*Screen legend:* "I don't suppose you remember me at all!"]

[At first, before Jim's warmth overcomes her paralyzing shyness, Laura's voice is thin and breathless, as though she had just run up a steep flight of stairs. Jim's attitude is gently humorous. While the incident is apparently unimportant, it is to Laura the climax of her secret life.]

JIM. Hello there, Laura.

LAURA. [*Faintly.*] Hello.

[She clears her throat.]

JIM. How are you feeling now? Better?

LAURA. Yes. Yes, thank you.

JIM. This is for you. A little dandelion wine. [*He extends the glass toward her with extravagant gallantry.*]

LAURA. Thank you.

JIM. Drink it—but don't get drunk!

[He laughs heartily. Laura takes the glass uncertainly; she laughs shyly.]

Where shall I set the candles?

LAURA. Oh—oh, anywhere . . .

JIM. How about here on the floor? Any objections?

LAURA. No.

JIM. I'll spread a newspaper under to catch the drippings. I like to sit on the floor. Mind if I do?

LAURA. Oh, no.

JIM. Give me a pillow?

LAURA. What?

JIM. A pillow!

LAURA. Oh . . . [*She hands him one quickly.*]

JIM. How about you? Don't you like to sit on the floor?

LAURA. Oh—yes.

JIM. Why don't you, then?

LAURA. I—will.

JIM. Take a pillow!

[Laura does. She sits on the floor on the other side of the candelabrum. Jim crosses his legs and smiles engagingly at her.]

I can't hardly see you sitting way over there.

LAURA. I can—see you.

JIM. I know, but that's not fair, I'm in the limelight.

[Laura moves her pillow closer.]

Good! Now I can see you! Comfortable?

LAURA. Yes.

JIM. So am I. Comfortable as a cow! Will you have some gum?

LAURA. No, thank you.

JIM. I think that I will indulge, with your permission. [*He musingly unwraps a stick of gum and holds it up.*] Think of the fortune made by the guy that invented the first piece of chewing gum. Amazing, huh? The Wrigley Building is one of the sights of Chicago—I saw it when I went up to the Century of Progress. Did you take in the Century of Progress?

LAURA. No, I didn't.

JIM. Well, it was quite a wonderful exposition. What impressed me most was the Hall of Science. Gives you an idea of what the future will be in America, even more wonderful than the present time is! [*There is a pause. Jim smiles at her.*] Your brother tells me you're shy. Is that right, Laura?

LAURA. I—don't know.

JIM. I judge you to be an old-fashioned type of girl. Well, I think that's a pretty good type to be. Hope you don't think I'm being too personal—do you?

LAURA. [*Hastily, out of embarrassment.*] I believe I *will* take a piece of gum, if you—don't mind. [*Clearing her throat.*] Mr. O'Connor, have you—kept up with your singing?

JIM. Singing? Me?

LAURA. Yes. I remember what a beautiful voice you had.

JIM. When did you hear me sing?

[*Laura does not answer, and in the long pause which follows a man's voice is heard singing offstage.*]

VOICE:

O blow, ye winds, heigh-ho,
A-roving I will go!
I'm off to my love
With a boxing glove—
Ten thousand miles away!

JIM. You say you've heard me sing?

LAURA. Oh, yes! Yes, very often . . . I—don't suppose—you remember me—at all?

JIM. [*Smiling doubtfully.*] You know I have an idea I've seen you before. I had that idea soon as you opened the door. It seemed almost like I was about to remember your name. But the name that I started to call you—wasn't a name! And so I stopped myself before I said it.

LAURA. Wasn't it—Blue Roses?

JIM. [*Springing up, grinning.*] Blue Roses! My gosh, yes—Blue Roses! That's what I had on my tongue when you opened the door! Isn't it funny what tricks your memory plays? I didn't connect you with high school somehow or other. But that's where it was; it was high school. I didn't even know you were Shakespeare's sister! Gosh, I'm sorry.

LAURA. I didn't expect you to. You—barely knew me!

JIM. But we did have a speaking acquaintance, huh?

LAURA. Yes, we—spoke to each other.

JIM. When did you recognize me?

LAURA. Oh, right away!

JIM. Soon as I came in the door?

LAURA. When I heard your name I thought it was probably you. I knew that Tom used to know you a little in high school. So when you came in the door—well, then I was—sure.

JIM. Why didn't you *say* something, then?

LAURA. [*Breathlessly.*] I didn't know what to say, I was—too surprised!

JIM. For goodness' sakes! You know, this sure is funny!

LAURA. Yes! Yes, isn't it, though . . .

JIM. Didn't we have a class in something together?

LAURA. Yes, we did.

JIM. What class was that?

LAURA. It was—singing—chorus!

JIM. Aw!

LAURA. I sat across the aisle from you in the Aud.

JIM. Aw.

LAURA. Mondays, Wednesdays, and Fridays.

JIM. Now I remember—you always came in late.

LAURA. Yes, it was so hard for me, getting upstairs. I had that brace on my leg—it clumped so loud!

JIM. I never heard any clumping.

LAURA. [*Wincing at the recollection.*] To me it sounded like—thunder!

JIM. Well, well, well, I never even noticed.

LAURA. And everybody was seated before I came in. I had to walk in front of all those people. My seat was in the back row. I had to go clumping all the way up the aisle with everyone watching!

JIM. You shouldn't have been self-conscious.

LAURA. I know, but I was. It was always such a relief when the singing started.

JIM. Aw, yes, I've placed you now! I used to call you Blue Roses. How was it that I got started calling you that?

LAURA. I was out of school a little while with pleurosis. When I came back you asked me what was the matter. I said I had pleurosis—you thought I said *Blue Roses.* That's what you always called me after that!

JIM. I hope you didn't mind.

LAURA. Oh, no—I liked it. You see, I wasn't acquainted with many—people. . . .

JIM. As I remember you sort of stuck by yourself.

LAURA. I—I—never have had much luck at—making friends.

JIM. I don't see why you wouldn't.

LAURA. Well, I—started out badly.

JIM. You mean being—

LAURA. Yes, it sort of—stood between me—

JIM. You shouldn't have let it!

LAURA. I know, but it did, and—

JIM. You were shy with people!

LAURA. I tried not to be but never could—

JIM. Overcome it?

LAURA. No, I—I never could!

JIM. I guess being shy is something you have to work out of kind of gradually.

LAURA. [*Sorrowfully.*] Yes—I guess it—

JIM. Takes time!

LAURA. Yes—

JIM. People are not so dreadful when you know them. That's what you have to remember! And everybody has problems, not just you, but practically everybody has got some problems. You think of yourself as having the only problems, as being the only one who is disappointed. But just look around you and you will see lots of people as disappointed as you are. For instance, I hoped when I was going to high school that I would be further along at this time, six years later, than I am now. You remember that wonderful write-up I had in *The Torch?*

LAURA. Yes! [*She rises and crosses to the table.*]

JIM. It said I was bound to succeed in anything I went into!

[*Laura returns with the high school yearbook.*]

Holy Jeez! *The Torch!*

[*He accepts it reverently. They smile across the book with mutual wonder. Laura crouches beside him and they begin to turn the pages. Laura's shyness is dissolving in his warmth.*]

LAURA. Here you are in *The Pirates of Penzance!*

JIM. [*Wistfully.*] I sang the baritone lead in that operetta.

LAURA. [*Raptly.*] So—*beautifully!*

JIM. [*Protesting.*] Aw—

LAURA. Yes, yes—beautifully—beautifully!

JIM. You heard me?

LAURA. All three times!

JIM. No!

LAURA. Yes!

JIM. All three performances?

LAURA. [*Looking down.*] Yes.

JIM. Why?

LAURA. I—wanted to ask you to—autograph my program. [*She takes the program from the back of the yearbook and shows it to him.*]

JIM. Why didn't you ask me to?

LAURA. You were always surrounded by your own friends so much that I never had a chance to.

JIM. You should have just—

LAURA. Well, I—thought you might think I was—

JIM. Thought I might think you was—what?

LAURA. Oh—

JIM. [*With reflective relish.*] I was beleaguered by females in those days.

LAURA. You were terribly popular!

JIM. Yeah—

LAURA. You had such a—friendly way—

JIM. I was spoiled in high school.

LAURA. Everybody—liked you!

JIM. Including you?

LAURA. I—yes, I—did, too— [*She gently closes the book in her lap.*]

JIM. Well, well, well! Give me that program, Laura.

[*She hands it to him. He signs it with a flourish.*]

There you are—better late than never!

LAURA. Oh, I—what a—surprise!

JIM. My signature isn't worth very much right now. But some day—maybe—it will increase in value! Being disappointed is one thing and being discouraged is something else. I am disappointed but I am not discouraged. I'm twenty-three years old. How old are you?

LAURA. I'll be twenty-four in June.

JIM. That's not old age!

LAURA. No, but—

JIM. You finished high school?

LAURA. [*With difficulty.*] I didn't go back.

JIM. You mean you dropped out?

LAURA. I made bad grades in my final examinations. [*She rises and replaces the book and the program on the table. Her voice is strained.*] How is—Emily Meisenbach getting along?

JIM. Oh, that kraut-head!

LAURA. Why do you call her that?

JIM. That's what she was.

LAURA. You're not still—going with her?

JIM. I never see her.

LAURA. It said in the "Personal" section that you were—engaged!

JIM. I know, but I wasn't impressed by that—propaganda!

LAURA. It wasn't—the truth?

JIM. Only in Emily's optimistic opinion!

LAURA. Oh—

[*Legend:* "What have you done since high school?"]

[*Jim lights a cigarette and leans indolently back on his elbows smiling at Laura with a warmth and charm which lights her inwardly with altar candles. She remains by the table, picks up a piece from the glass menagerie collection, and turns it in her hands to cover her tumult.*]

JIM. [*After several reflective puffs on his cigarette.*] What have you done since high school?

[*She seems not to hear him.*]

Huh?

[*Laura looks up.*]

I said what have you done since high school, Laura?

LAURA. Nothing much.

JIM. You must have been doing something these six long years.

LAURA. Yes.

JIM. Well, then, such as what?

LAURA. I took a business course at business college—

JIM. How did that work out?

LAURA. Well, not very—well—I had to drop out, it gave me—indigestion—

[*Jim laughs gently.*]

JIM. What are you doing now?

LAURA. I don't do anything—much. Oh, please don't think I sit around doing nothing! My glass collection takes up a good deal of time. Glass is something you have to take good care of.

JIM. What did you say—about glass?

LAURA. Collection I said—I have one— [*She clears her throat and turns away again, acutely shy.*]

JIM. [*Abruptly.*] You know what I judge to be the trouble with you? Inferiority complex! Know what that is? That's what they call it when someone low-rates himself! I understand it because I had it, too. Although my case was not so aggravated as yours seems to be. I had it until I took up public speaking, developed my voice, and learned that I had an aptitude for science. Before that time I never thought of myself as being outstanding in any way whatsoever! Now I've never made a regular study of it, but I have a friend who says I can analyze people better than doctors that make a profession of it. I don't claim that to be necessarily true, but I can sure guess a person's psychology, Laura! [*He takes out his gum.*] Excuse me, Laura. I always take it out when the flavor is gone. I'll use this scrap of paper to wrap it in. I know how it is to get it stuck on a shoe. [*He wraps the gum in paper and puts it in his pocket.*] Yep—that's what I judge to be your principal trouble. A lack of confidence in yourself as a person. You don't have the proper amount of faith in yourself. I'm basing that fact on a number of your remarks and also on certain observations I've made. For instance that clumping you thought was so awful in high school. You say that you even dreaded to walk into class. You see what you did? You dropped out of school, you gave up an education because of a clump, which as far as I know was practically non-existent! A little physical defect is what you have. Hardly noticeable even! Magnified thousands of times by imagination! You know what my strong advice to you is? Think of yourself as *superior* in some way!

LAURA. In what way would I think?

JIM. Why, man alive, Laura! Just look about you a little. What do you see? A world full of common people! All of 'em born and all of 'em going to die! Which of them has one-tenth of your good points! Or mine! Or anyone else's, as far as that goes —gosh! Everybody excels in some one thing. Some in many! [*He unconsciously glances at himself in the mirror.*] All you've got to do is discover in *what!* Take me, for instance. [*He adjusts his tie at the mirror.*] My interest happens to lie in electro-dynamics. I'm taking a course in radio engineering at night school, Laura, on top of a fairly responsible job at the warehouse. I'm taking that course and studying public speaking.

LAURA. Ohhhh.

JIM. Because I believe in the future of television! [*Turning his back to her.*] I wish to be ready to go up right along with it. Therefore I'm planning to get in on the ground floor. In fact I've already made the right connections and all that remains is for the industry itself to get under way! Full steam— [*His eyes are starry.*] *Knowledge*—Zzzzzp! *Money*—Zzzzzzp!—*Power!* That's the cycle democracy is built on!

[*His attitude is convincingly dynamic. Laura stares at him, even her shyness eclipsed in her absolute wonder. He suddenly grins.*]

I guess you think I think a lot of myself!

LAURA. No—o-o-o, I—

JIM. Now how about you? Isn't there something you take more interest in than anything else?

LAURA. Well, I do—as I said—have my—glass collection—

[*A peal of girlish laughter rings from the kitchenette.*]

JIM. I'm not right sure I know what you're talking about. What kind of glass is it?

LAURA. Little articles of it, they're ornaments mostly! Most of them are little animals made out of glass, the tiniest little animals in the world. Mother calls them a glass menagerie! Here's an example of one, if you'd like to see it! This one is one of the oldest. It's nearly thirteen.

[*Music:* "The Glass Menagerie."]

[*He stretches out his hand.*]

Oh, be careful—if you breathe, it breaks!

JIM. I'd better not take it. I'm pretty clumsy with things.

LAURA. Go on, I trust you with him! [*She places the piece in his palm.*] There now—you're holding him gently! Hold him over the light, he loves the light! You see how the light shines through him?

JIM. It sure does shine!

LAURA. I shouldn't be partial, but he is my favorite one.

JIM. What kind of a thing is this one supposed to be?

LAURA. Haven't you noticed the single horn on his forehead?

JIM. A unicorn, huh?

LAURA. Mmmm-hmmm!

JIM. Unicorns—aren't they extinct in the modern world?

LAURA. I know!

JIM. Poor little fellow, he must feel sort of lonesome.

LAURA. [*Smiling.*] Well, if he does, he doesn't complain about it. He stays on a shelf with some horses that don't have horns and all of them seem to get along nicely together.

JIM. How do you know?

LAURA. [*Lightly.*] I haven't heard any arguments among them!

JIM. [*Grinning.*] No arguments, huh? Well, that's a pretty good sign! Where shall I set him?

LAURA. Put him on the table. They all like a change of scenery once in a while!

JIM. Well, well, well, well— [*He places the glass piece on the table, then raises his arms and stretches.*] Look how big my shadow is when I stretch!

LAURA. Oh, oh, yes—it stretches across the ceiling!

JIM. [*Crossing to the door.*] I think it's stopped raining. [*He opens the fire-escape door and the background music changes to a dance tune.*] Where does the music come from?

LAURA. From the Paradise Dance Hall across the alley.

JIM. How about cutting the rug a little, Miss Wingfield?

LAURA. Oh, I—

JIM. Or is your program filled up? Let me have a look at it. [*He grasps an imaginary card.*] Why, every dance is taken! I'll just have to scratch some out.

[*Waltz music:* "La Golondrina."]

Ahhh, a waltz! [*He executes some sweeping turns by himself, then holds his arms toward Laura.*]

LAURA. [*Breathlessly.*] I—can't dance!

JIM. There you go, that inferiority stuff!

LAURA. I've never danced in my life!

JIM. Come on, try!

LAURA. Oh, but I'd step on you!

JIM. I'm not made out of glass.

LAURA. How—how—how do we start?

JIM. Just leave it to me. You hold your arms out a little.

LAURA. Like this?

JIM. [*Taking her in his arms.*] A little bit higher. Right. Now don't tighten up, that's the main thing about it—relax.

LAURA. [*Laughing breathlessly.*] It's hard not to.

JIM. Okay.

LAURA. I'm afraid you can't budge me.

JIM. What do you bet I can't? [*He swings her into motion.*]

LAURA. Goodness, yes, you can!

JIM. Let yourself go, now, Laura, just let yourself go.

LAURA. I'm—

JIM. Come on!

LAURA. —trying!

JIM. Not so stiff—easy does it!

LAURA. I know but I'm—

JIM. Loosen th' backbone! There now, that's a lot better.

LAURA. Am I?

JIM. Lots, lots better! [*He moves her about the room in a clumsy waltz.*]

LAURA. Oh, my!

JIM. Ha-ha!

LAURA. Oh, my goodness!

JIM. Ha-ha-ha!

[*They suddenly bump into the table, and the glass piece on it falls to the floor. Jim stops the dance.*]

What did we hit on?

LAURA. Table.

JIM. Did something fall off it? I think—

LAURA. Yes.

JIM. I hope that it wasn't the little glass horse with the horn!

LAURA. Yes. [*She stoops to pick it up.*]

JIM. Aw, aw, aw. Is it broken?

LAURA. Now it is just like all the other horses.

JIM. It's lost its—

LAURA. Horn! It doesn't matter. Maybe it's a blessing in disguise.

JIM. You'll never forgive me. I bet that that was your favorite piece of glass.

LAURA. I don't have favorites much. It's no tragedy, Freckles. Glass breaks so easily. No matter how careful you are. The traffic jars the shelves and things fall off them.

JIM. Still I'm awfully sorry that I was the cause.

LAURA. [*Smiling.*] I'll just imagine he had an operation. The horn was removed to make him feel less—freakish!

[*They both laugh.*]

Now he will feel more at home with the other horses, the ones that don't have horns. . . .

JIM. Ha-ha, that's very funny! [*Suddenly he is serious.*] I'm glad to see that you have a sense of humor. You know—you're—well—very different! Surprisingly different from anyone else I know! [*His voice becomes soft and hesitant with a genuine feeling.*] Do you mind me telling you that?

[*Laura is abashed beyond speech.*]

I mean it in a nice way—

[*Laura nods shyly, looking away.*]

You make me feel sort of—I don't know how to put it! I'm usually pretty good at expressing things, but—this is something that I don't know how to say!

[*Laura touches her throat and clears it—turns the broken unicorn in her hands. His voice becomes softer.*]

Has anyone ever told you that you were pretty?

[*There is a pause, and the music rises slightly. Laura looks up slowly, with wonder, and shakes her head.*]

Well, you are! In a very different way from anyone else. And all the nicer because of the difference, too.

[*His voice becomes low and husky. Laura turns away, nearly faint with the novelty of her emotions.*]

I wish that you were my sister. I'd teach you to have some confidence in yourself. The different people are not like other people, but being different is nothing to be ashamed of. Because other people are not such wonderful people. They're one hundred times one thousand. You're one times one! They walk all over the earth. You just stay here. They're common as—weeds, but—you—well, you're—*Blue Roses!*

[*Image on screen:* Blue Roses.]

[*The music changes.*]

LAURA. But blue is wrong for—roses. . . .

JIM. It's right for you! You're—pretty!

LAURA. In what respect am I pretty?

JIM. In all respects—believe me! Your eyes—your hair—are pretty! Your hands are pretty! [*He catches hold of her hand.*] You think I'm making this up because I'm invited to dinner and have to be nice. Oh, I could do that! I could put on an act for you, Laura, and say lots of things without being very sincere. But this time I am. I'm talking to you sincerely. I happened to notice you had this inferiority complex that keeps you from feeling comfortable with people. Somebody needs to build your confidence up and make you proud instead of shy and turning away and —blushing. Somebody—ought to—*kiss* you, Laura!

[*His hand slips slowly up her arm to her shoulder as the music swells tumultuously. He suddenly turns her about and kisses her on the lips. When he releases her, Laura sinks on the sofa with a bright, dazed look. Jim backs away and fishes in his pocket for a cigarette.*]

[*Legend on screen:* "A souvenir."]

Stumblejohn!

[*He lights the cigarette, avoiding her look. There is a peal of girlish laughter from Amanda in the kitchenette. Laura slowly raises and opens her hand. It still contains the little broken glass animal. She looks at it with a tender, bewildered expression.*]

Stumblejohn! I shouldn't have done that—that was way off the beam. You don't smoke, do you?

[*She looks up, smiling, not hearing the question. He sits beside her rather gingerly. She looks at him speechlessly—waiting. He coughs decorously and moves a little farther aside as he considers the situation and senses her feelings, dimly, with perturbation. He speaks gently.*]

Would you—care for a—mint?

[*She doesn't seem to hear him but her look grows brighter even.*]

Peppermint? Life Saver? My pocket's a regular drugstore—wherever I go. . . . [*He pops a mint in his mouth. Then he gulps and decides to make a clean breast of it. He speaks slowly and gingerly.*] Laura, you know, if I had a sister like you, I'd do the same thing as Tom. I'd bring out fellows and—introduce her to them. The right type of boys—of a type to—appreciate her. Only—well—he made a mistake about me. Maybe I've got no call to be saying this. That may not have been the idea in having me over. But what if it was? There's nothing wrong about that. The only trouble is that in my case—I'm not in a situation to—do the right thing. I can't take down your number and say I'll phone. I can't call up next week and—ask for a date. I thought I had better explain the situation in case you—misunderstood it and—I hurt your feelings. . . .

[*There is a pause. Slowly, very slowly, Laura's look changes, her eyes returning slowly from his to the glass figure in her palm. Amanda utters another gay laugh in the kitchenette.*]

LAURA. [*Faintly.*] You—won't—call again?

JIM. No, Laura, I can't. [*He rises from the sofa.*] As I was just explaining, I've—got strings on me, Laura, I've—been going steady! I go out all the time with a girl named Betty. She's a home-girl like you, and Catholic, and Irish, and in a great many ways we—get along fine. I met her last summer on a moonlight boat trip up the river to Alton, on the *Majestic.* Well—right away from the start it was—love!

[*Legend:* Love!]

[*Laura sways slightly forward and grips the arm of the sofa. He fails to notice, now enrapt in his own comfortable being.*]

Being in love has made a new man of me!

[*Leaning stiffly forward, clutching the arm of the sofa, Laura struggles visibly with her storm. But Jim is oblivious; she is a long way off.*]

The power of love is really pretty tremendous! Love is something that—changes the whole world, Laura!

[*The storm abates a little and Laura leans back. He notices her again.*]

It happened that Betty's aunt took sick, she got a wire and had to go to Centralia. So Tom—when he asked me to dinner—I naturally just accepted the invitation, not knowing that you—that he—that I— [*He stops awkwardly.*] Huh—I'm a stumblejohn!

[*He flops back on the sofa. The holy candles on the altar of Laura's face have been snuffed out. There is a look of almost infinite desolation. Jim glances at her uneasily.*]

I wish that you would—say something.

[*She bites her lip which was trembling and then bravely smiles. She opens her hand again on the broken glass figure. Then she gently takes his hand and raises it level with her own. She carefully places the unicorn in the palm of his hand, then pushes his fingers closed upon it.*]

What are you—doing that for? You want me to have him? Laura?

[*She nods.*]

What for?

LAURA. A—souvenir. . . .

[*She rises unsteadily and crouches beside the Victrola to wind it up.*]

[*Legend on screen:* "Things have a way of turning out so badly!" *Or image:* "Gentleman caller waving goodbye—gaily."]

[*At this moment Amanda rushes brightly back into the living room. She bears a pitcher of fruit punch in an old-fashioned cut-glass pitcher, and a plate of macaroons. The plate has a gold border and poppies painted on it.*]

AMANDA. Well, well, well! Isn't the air delightful after the shower? I've made you children a little liquid refreshment.

[*She turns gaily to Jim.*] Jim, do you know that song about lemonade?

"Lemonade, lemonade
Made in the shade and stirred with a spade—
Good enough for any old maid!"

JIM. [*Uneasily.*] Ha-ha! No—I never heard it.

AMANDA. Why, Laura! You look so serious!

JIM. We were having a serious conversation.

AMANDA. Good! Now you're better acquainted!

JIM. [*Uncertainly.*] Ha-ha! Yes.

AMANDA. You modern young people are much more serious-minded than my generation. I was so gay as a girl!

JIM. You haven't changed, Mrs. Wingfield.

AMANDA. Tonight I'm rejuvenated! The gaiety of the occasion, Mr. O'Connor! [*She tosses her head with a peal of laughter, spilling some lemonade.*] Oooo! I'm baptizing myself!

JIM. Here—let me—

AMANDA. [*Setting the pitcher down.*] There now. I discovered we had some maraschino cherries. I dumped them in, juice and all!

JIM. You shouldn't have gone to that trouble, Mrs. Wingfield.

AMANDA. Trouble, trouble? Why it was loads of fun! Didn't you hear me cutting up in the kitchen? I bet your ears were burning! I told Tom how outdone with him I was for keeping you to himself so long a time! He should have brought you over much, much sooner! Well, now that you've found your way, I want you to be a very frequent caller! Not just occasional but all the time. Oh, we're going to have a lot of gay times together! I see them coming! Mmm, just breathe that air! So fresh, and the moon's so pretty! I'll skip back out—I know where my place is when young folks are having a—serious conversation!

JIM. Oh, don't go out, Mrs. Wingfield. The fact of the matter is I've got to be going.

AMANDA. Going, now? You're joking! Why, it's only the shank of the evening, Mr. O'Connor!

JIM. Well, you know how it is.

AMANDA. You mean you're a young workingman and have to keep workingmen's hours. We'll let you off early tonight. But only on the condition that next time you stay later. What's the best night for you? Isn't Saturday night the best night for you workingmen?

JIM. I have a couple of time-clocks to punch, Mrs. Wingfield. One at morning, another one at night!

AMANDA. My, but you *are* ambitious! You work at night, too?

JIM. No, Ma'am, not work but—Betty!

[*He crosses deliberately to pick up his hat. The band at the Paradise Dance Hall goes into a tender waltz.*]

AMANDA. Betty? Betty? Who's—Betty!

[*There is an ominous cracking sound in the sky.*]

JIM. Oh, just a girl. The girl I go steady with!

[*He smiles charmingly. The sky falls.*]

[*Legend:* "The Sky Falls."]

AMANDA. [*A long-drawn exhalation.*] Ohhhh . . . Is it a serious romance, Mr. O'Connor?

JIM. We're going to be married the second Sunday in June.

AMANDA. Ohhhh—how nice! Tom didn't mention that you were engaged to be married.

JIM. The cat's not out of the bag at the warehouse yet. You know how they are. They call you Romeo and stuff like that. [*He stops at the oval mirror to put on his hat. He carefully shapes the brim and the crown to give a discreetly dashing effect.*] It's been a wonderful evening, Mrs. Wingfield. I guess this is what they mean by Southern hospitality.

AMANDA. It really wasn't anything at all.

JIM. I hope it don't seem like I'm rushing off. But I promised Betty I'd pick her up at the Wabash depot, an' by the time I get my jalopy down there her train'll be in. Some women are pretty upset if you keep 'em waiting.

AMANDA. Yes, I know—the tyranny of women! [*She extends her hand.*] Goodbye, Mr. O'Connor. I wish you luck—and happiness—and success! All three of them, and so does Laura! Don't you, Laura?

LAURA. Yes!

JIM. [*Taking Laura's hand.*] Goodbye, Laura. I'm certainly going to treasure that souvenir. And don't you forget the good advice I gave you. [*He raises his voice to a cheery shout.*] So long, Shakespeare! Thanks again, ladies. Good night!

[*He grins and ducks jauntily out. Still bravely grimacing, Amanda closes the door on the gentleman caller. Then she turns back to the room with a puzzled expression. She and Laura don't dare to face each other. Laura crouches beside the Victrola to wind it.*]

AMANDA. [*Faintly.*] Things have a way of turning out so badly. I don't believe that I would play the Victrola. Well, well—well! Our gentleman caller was engaged to be married! [*She raises her voice.*] Tom!

TOM. [*From the kitchenette.*] Yes, Mother?

AMANDA. Come in here a minute. I want to tell you something awfully funny.

TOM. [*Entering with a macaroon and a glass of the lemonade.*] Has the gentleman caller gotten away already?

AMANDA. The gentleman caller has made an early departure. What a wonderful joke you played on us!

TOM. How do you mean?

AMANDA. You didn't mention that he was engaged to be married.

TOM. Jim? Engaged?

AMANDA. That's what he just informed us.

TOM. I'll be jiggered! I didn't know about that.

AMANDA. That seems very peculiar.

TOM. What's peculiar about it?

AMANDA. Didn't you call him your best friend down at the warehouse?

TOM. He is, but how did I know?

AMANDA. It seems extremely peculiar that you wouldn't know your best friend was going to be married!

TOM. The warehouse is where I work, not where I know things about people!

AMANDA. You don't know things anywhere! You live in a dream; you manufacture illusions!

[*He crosses to the door.*]

Where are you going?

TOM. I'm going to the movies.

AMANDA. That's right, now that you've had us make such fools of ourselves. The effort, the preparations, all the expense! The new floor lamp, the rug, the clothes for Laura! All for what? To entertain some other girl's fiancé! Go to the movies, go! Don't think about us, a mother deserted, an unmarried sister who's crippled and has no job! Don't let anything interfere with your selfish pleasure! Just go, go, go—to the movies!

TOM. All right, I will! The more you shout about my selfishness to me the quicker I'll go, and I won't go to the movies!

AMANDA. Go, then! Go to the moon—you selfish dreamer!

[*Tom smashes his glass on the floor. He plunges out on the fire escape, slamming the door. Laura screams in fright. The dance-hall music becomes louder. Tom stands on the fire escape, gripping the rail. The moon breaks through the storm clouds, illuminating his face.*]

[*Legend on screen:* "And so goodbye . . ."]

[*Tom's closing speech is timed with what is happening inside the house. We see, as though through soundproof glass, that Amanda appears to be making a comforting speech to Laura, who is huddled upon the sofa. Now that we cannot hear the mother's speech, her silliness is gone and she has dignity and tragic beauty. Laura's hair hides her face until, at the end of the speech, she lifts her head to smile at her mother. Amanda's gestures are slow and graceful, almost dancelike, as she comforts her daughter. At the end of her speech she glances a moment at the father's picture—then withdraws through the portieres. At the close of Tom's speech, Laura blows out the candles, ending the play.*]

TOM. I didn't go to the moon, I went much further—for time is the longest distance between two places. Not long after that I was fired for writing a poem on the lid of a shoe-box. I left Saint Louis. I descended the steps of this fire escape for a last time and followed, from then on, in my father's footsteps, attempting to find in motion what was lost in space. I traveled around a great deal. The cities swept about me like dead leaves, leaves that were brightly colored but torn away from the branches. I would have stopped, but I was pursued by something. It always came upon me unawares, taking me altogether by surprise. Perhaps it was a familiar bit of music. Perhaps it was only a piece of transparent glass. Perhaps I am walking along a street at night, in some strange city, before I have found companions. I pass the lighted window of a shop where perfume is sold. The window is filled with pieces of colored glass, tiny transparent bottles in delicate colors, like bits of a shattered rainbow. Then all at once my sister touches my shoulder. I turn around and look into her eyes. Oh, Laura, Laura, I tried to leave you behind me, but I am more faithful than I intended to be! I reach for a cigarette, I cross the street, I run into the movies or a bar, I buy a drink, I speak to the nearest stranger—anything that can blow your candles out!

[*Laura bends over the candles.*]

For nowadays the world is lit by lightning! Blow out your candles, Laura—and so goodbye. . . .

[*She blows the candles out.*]

1945

ARTHUR MILLER

(1915–)

Arthur Miller was born and raised to age thirteen in a Jewish household on the upper East Side of Manhattan, attending school in Harlem. His ancestry was German and his home life middle class, with his father a manufacturer of ladies' coats and his mother a teacher. In 1928 the family moved to Brooklyn, experiencing there the hard times of the Depression. Miller graduated from high school in 1932, but since he had been more interested in athletics than studies his grades were too poor for admission to college. After a series of jobs, he settled down to a daily grind in an automobile parts warehouse. Later, in the one-act play *A Memory of Two Mondays* (1955), he evoked this period in loving detail, providing a fine introduction to the milieu that produced his determination to write. Finally accepted to the University of Michigan in 1934, he began writing in earnest, won two undergraduate Hopwood Awards for his plays, and met Mary Slattery, who later became the first of his three wives. Graduating in 1938, he went to New York, wrote briefly for the Federal Theatre Project, and was soon employed at the Brooklyn Navy Yard while writing plays for radio.

Miller's first Broadway play, *The Man Who Had All the Luck* (1944), failed after four performances, but three years later he was back with a substantial success in *All My Sons* (1947), a drama based on guilt arising from a shipment of faulty airplane parts in World War II. This play and *Death of a Salesman* (1949), which came next, established Miller as a master of family dramas carrying strong social implications, an interest confirmed in his next production, an adaptation of Ibsen's *An Enemy of the People* (1951). In *The Crucible* (1953) Miller continued his social analysis, finding in the witchcraft trials of colonial Massachusetts an analogue for the increasingly restrictive environment of cold war America.

After *The Crucible,* Miller's work seemed for some years less successful, his life more troubled. In ironic confirmation of ideas expressed in *The Crucible,* he was accused of leftwing sympathies, denied a passport to the Belgian opening of the play, and brought under the scrutiny of the House Committee on Un-American Activities. In 1956, his first marriage ending in divorce, he married Marilyn Monroe, from whom he was divorced in 1961. Within this period, his major work was limited to *A View from the Bridge* and *A Memory of Two Mondays,* first produced and published together in 1955, a *Collected Plays* (1957), and the screenplay for the film *The Misfits* (1961). In 1962 he married the photographer Inge Morath, with whom he later collaborated in producing several books of photographs and essays. *After the Fall* and *Incident at Vichy,* both produced in 1964, brought him back to Broadway after a long absence and reaffirmed his major status among American playwrights. Later plays, including *The Price* (1968), *The Creation of the World and Other Business* (1972), *The Archbishop's Ceiling* (1976), and *The American Clock* (1980) demonstrated his continuing concern with a theater of ideas.

Miller's plays are often autobiographical and almost always steeped in social consciousness. His one novel, *Focus* (1945), the story of a Gentile whose life is shaken by a confrontation with anti-Semitism, though flawed as art, nevertheless highlights Miller's abiding sense of the individual's need to come to terms with his personal responsibilities as he confronts the world's injustice. In an essay titled "Our Guilt for the World's Evil," he has written of our primary need as humans "to discover our own relationship to evil, its reflection of ourselves." Because such discoveries are inner, he frequently structures his plays to reveal psychological crises through expressionistic techniques that undercut the surface realism. The resulting thematic underlining gives an ordinary life like Willy Loman's an emblematic significance that places his creator among the enduring masters of twentieth-century theater.

Miller's major plays are named above. Two new one-act plays were produced in 1987 as *Danger: Memory! Arthur Miller's Collected Plays* was published in two volumes, 1957 and 1981. A collection of stories is *I Don't Need You Any More,* 1967. *Situation Normal,* 1944, is a non-fiction account of a tour of wartime army camps. Harold Clurman edited *The Portable Arthur Miller,* 1971. Books in collaboration with Inge Morath include *In Russia,* 1969; *In the Country,* 1977; and *Chinese Encounters,* 1979. Robert A. Martin edited *The Theater Essays of Arthur Miller,* 1978.

Biographical and critical studies include Dennis Welland, *Arthur Miller,* 1961; Robert G. Hogan, *Arthur Miller,* 1964; Sheila Huftel, *Arthur Miller: The Burning Glass,* 1965; Edward Murray, *Arthur Miller: Dramatist,* 1967; Benjamin Nelson, *Arthur Miller: Portrait of a Playwright,* 1970; Ronald Hayman, *Arthur Miller,* 1970; Dennis Welland, *Arthur Miller: A Study of His Plays,* 1979; and Leonard Moss, *Arthur Miller,* rev. ed., 1980.

Death of a Salesman[1]

Certain Private Conversations in Two Acts and a Requiem

THE CHARACTERS

WILLY LOMAN	UNCLE BEN
LINDA	HOWARD WAGNER
BIFF	JENNY
HAPPY	STANLEY
BERNARD	MISS FORSYTHE
THE WOMAN	LETTA
CHARLEY	

The action takes place in Willy Loman's house and yard and in various places he visits in the New York and Boston of today.

Act One

A melody is heard, played upon a flute. It is small and fine, telling of grass and trees and the horizon. The curtain rises.

Before us is the Salesman's house. We are aware of towering, angular shapes behind it, surrounding it on all sides. Only the blue light of the sky falls upon the house and forestage; the surrounding area shows an angry glow of orange. As more light appears, we see a solid vault of apartment houses around the small, fragile-seeming home. An air of the dream clings to the place, a dream rising out of reality. The kitchen at center seems actual enough, for there is a kitchen table with three chairs, and a refrigerator. But no other fixtures are seen. At the back of the kitchen there is a draped entrance, which leads to the living-room. To the right of the kitchen, on a level raised two feet, is a bedroom furnished only with a brass bedstead and a straight chair. On a shelf over the bed a silver athletic trophy stands. A window opens onto the apartment house at the side.

1. The source of the present text is *Arthur Miller's Collected Plays,* 1957. This play in its printed form is designed for the reading public only. All dramatic rights in it are fully protected by copyright, and no public or private performance—professional or amateur—may be given without the written permission of the author and the payment of royalty. As the courts have also ruled that the public reading of a play constitutes a public performance, no such reading may be given except under the conditions stated above. Communication should be addressed to the author's representative, International Creative Management, Inc., 40 West 57th Street, New York, N.Y. 10019.

Behind the kitchen, on a level raised six and a half feet, is the boys' bedroom, at present barely visible. Two beds are dimly seen, and at the back of the room a dormer window. (This bedroom is above the unseen living-room.) At the left a stairway curves up to it from the kitchen.

The entire setting is wholly or, in some places, partially transparent. The roof-line of the house is one-dimensional; under and over it we see the apartment buildings. Before the house lies an apron, curving beyond the forestage into the orchestra. This forward area serves as the back yard as well as the locale of all Willy's imaginings and of his city scenes. Whenever the action is in the present the actors observe the imaginary wall-lines, entering the house only through its door at the left. But in the scenes of the past these boundaries are broken, and characters enter or leave a room by stepping "through" a wall onto the forestage.

From the right, Willy Loman, the Salesman, enters, carrying two large sample cases. The flute plays on. He hears but is not aware of it. He is past sixty years of age, dressed quietly. Even as he crosses the stage to the doorway of the house, his exhaustion is apparent. He unlocks the door, comes into the kitchen, and thankfully lets his burden down, feeling the soreness of his palms. A word-sigh escapes his lips —it might be "Oh, boy, oh, boy." He closes the door, then carries his cases out into the living-room, through the draped kitchen doorway.

Linda, his wife, has stirred in her bed at the right. She gets out and puts on a robe, listening. Most often jovial, she has developed an iron repression of her exceptions to Willy's behavior—she more than loves him, she admires him, as though his mercurial nature, his temper, his massive dreams and little cruelties, served her only as sharp reminders of the turbulent longings within him, longings which she shares but lacks the temperament to utter and follow to their end.

LINDA, *hearing Willy outside the bedroom, calls with some trepidation:* Willy!

WILLY: It's all right. I came back.

LINDA: Why? What happened? *Slight pause.* Did something happen, Willy?

WILLY: No, nothing happened.

LINDA: You didn't smash the car, did you?

WILLY, *with casual irritation:* I said nothing happened. Didn't you hear me?

LINDA: Don't you feel well?

WILLY: I'm tired to the death. *The flute has faded away. He sits on the bed beside her, a little numb.* I couldn't make it. I just couldn't make it, Linda.

LINDA, *very carefully, delicately:* Where were you all day? You look terrible.

WILLY: I got as far as a little above Yonkers. I stopped for a cup of coffee. Maybe it was the coffee.

LINDA: What?

WILLY, *after a pause:* I suddenly couldn't drive any more. The car kept going off onto the shoulder, y'know?

LINDA, *helpfully:* Oh. Maybe it was the steering again. I don't think Angelo knows the Studebaker.

WILLY: No, it's me, it's me. Suddenly I realize I'm goin' sixty miles an hour and I don't remember the last five minutes. I'm—I can't seem to—keep my mind to it.

LINDA: Maybe it's your glasses. You never went for your new glasses.

WILLY: No, I see everything. I came back ten miles an hour. It took me nearly four hours from Yonkers.

LINDA, *resigned:* Well, you'll just have to take a rest, Willy, you can't continue this way.

WILLY: I just got back from Florida.

LINDA: But you didn't rest your mind. Your mind is overactive, and the mind is what counts, dear.

WILLY: I'll start out in the morning. Maybe I'll feel better in the morning. *She is taking off his shoes.* These goddam arch supports are killing me.

LINDA: Take an aspirin. Should I get you an aspirin? It'll soothe you.

WILLY, *with wonder:* I was driving along, you understand? And I was fine. I was even observing the scenery. You can imagine, me looking at scenery, on the road every week of my life. But it's so beautiful up there, Linda, the trees are so thick, and the sun is warm. I opened the windshield and just let the warm air bathe over me. And then all of a sudden I'm goin' off the road! I'm tellin' ya, I absolutely forgot I was driving. If I'd've gone the other way over the white line I might've killed somebody. So I went on again—and five minutes later I'm dreamin' again, and I nearly—*He presses two fingers against his eyes.* I have such thoughts, I have such strange thoughts.

LINDA: Willy, dear. Talk to them again. There's no reason why you can't work in New York.

WILLY: They don't need me in New York. I'm the New England man. I'm vital in New England.

LINDA: But you're sixty years old. They can't expect you to keep traveling every week.

WILLY: I'll have to send a wire to Portland. I'm supposed to see Brown and Morrison tomorrow morning at ten o'clock to show the line. Goddammit, I could sell them! *He starts putting on his jacket.*

LINDA, *taking the jacket from him:* Why don't you go down to the place tomorrow and tell Howard you've simply got to work in New York? You're too accommodating, dear.

WILLY: If old man Wagner was alive I'd a been in charge of New York now! That man was a prince, he was a masterful man. But that boy of his, that Howard, he don't appreciate. When I went north the first time, the Wagner Company didn't know where New England was!

LINDA: Why don't you tell those things to Howard, dear?

WILLY, *encouraged:* I will, I definitely will. Is there any cheese?

LINDA: I'll make you a sandwich.

WILLY: No, go to sleep. I'll take some milk. I'll be up right away. The boys in?

LINDA: They're sleeping. Happy took Biff on a date tonight.

WILLY, *interested:* That so?

LINDA: It was so nice to see them shaving together, one behind the other, in the bathroom. And going out together. You notice? The whole house smells of shaving lotion.

WILLY: Figure it out. Work a lifetime to pay off a house. You finally own it, and there's nobody to live in it.

LINDA: Well, dear, life is a casting off. It's always that way.

WILLY: No, no, some people—some people accomplish something. Did Biff say anything after I went this morning?

LINDA: You shouldn't have criticized him, Willy, especially after he just got off the train. You mustn't lose your temper with him.

WILLY: When the hell did I lose my temper? I simply asked him if he was making any money. Is that a criticism?

LINDA: But, dear, how could he make any money?

WILLY, *worried and angered:* There's such an undercurrent in him. He became a moody man. Did he apologize when I left this morning?

LINDA: He was crestfallen, Willy. You know how he admires you. I think if he finds himself, then you'll both be happier and not fight any more.

WILLY: How can he find himself on a farm? Is that a life? A farmhand? In the beginning, when he was young, I thought, well, a young man, it's good for him to tramp around, take a lot of different jobs. But it's more than ten years now and he has yet to make thirty-five dollars a week!

LINDA: He's finding himself, Willy.

WILLY: Not finding yourself at the age of thirty-four is a disgrace!

LINDA: Shh!

WILLY: The trouble is he's lazy, goddammit!

LINDA: Willy, please!

WILLY: Biff is a lazy bum!

LINDA: They're sleeping. Get something to eat. Go on down.

WILLY: Why did he come home? I would like to know what brought him home.

LINDA: I don't know. I think he's still lost, Willy. I think he's very lost.

WILLY: Biff Loman is lost. In the greatest country in the world a young man with such—personal attractiveness, gets lost. And such a hard worker. There's one thing about Biff—he's not lazy.

LINDA: Never.

WILLY, *with pity and resolve:* I'll see him in the morning; I'll have a nice talk with him. I'll get him a job selling. He could be big in no time. My God! Remember how they used to follow him around in high school? When he smiled at one of them their faces lit up. When he walked down the street . . . *He loses himself in reminiscences.*

LINDA, *trying to bring him out of it:* Willy, dear, I got a new kind of American-type cheese today. It's whipped.

WILLY: Why do you get American when I like Swiss?

LINDA: I just thought you'd like a change—

WILLY: I don't want a change! I want Swiss cheese. Why am I always being contradicted?

LINDA, *with a covering laugh:* I thought it would be a surprise.

WILLY: Why don't you open a window in here, for God's sake?

LINDA, *with infinite patience:* They're all open, dear.

WILLY: The way they boxed us in here. Bricks and windows, windows and bricks.

LINDA: We should've bought the land next door.

WILLY: The street is lined with cars. There's not a breath of fresh air in the neighborhood. The grass don't grow any more, you can't raise a carrot in the back yard. They should've had a law against apartment houses. Remember those two beautiful elm trees out there? When I and Biff hung the swing between them?

LINDA: Yeah, like being a million miles from the city.

WILLY: They should've arrested the builder for cutting those down. They massacred the neighborhood. *Lost:* More and more I think of those days, Linda. This time of year it was lilac and wisteria. And then the peonies would come out, and the daffodils. What fragrance in this room!

LINDA: Well, after all, people had to move somewhere.

WILLY: No, there's more people now.

LINDA: I don't think there's more people. I think—

WILLY: There's more people! That's what ruining this country! Population is getting out of control. The competition is maddening! Smell the stink from that apartment house! And another one on the other side . . . How can they whip cheese?

On Willy's last line, Biff and Happy raise themselves up in their beds, listening.

LINDA: Go down, try it. And be quiet.

WILLY, *turning to Linda, guiltily:* You're not worried about me, are you, sweetheart?

BIFF: What's the matter?

HAPPY: Listen!

LINDA: You've got too much on the ball to worry about.

WILLY: You're my foundation and my support, Linda.

LINDA: Just try to relax, dear. You make mountains out of molehills.

WILLY: I won't fight with him any more. If he wants to go back to Texas, let him go.

LINDA: He'll find his way.

WILLY: Sure. Certain men just don't get started till later in life. Like Thomas Edison, I think. Or B. F. Goodrich. One of them was deaf. *He starts for the bedroom doorway.* I'll put my money on Biff.

LINDA: And Willy—if it's warm Sunday we'll drive in the country. And we'll open the windshield, and take lunch.

WILLY: No, the windshields don't open on the new cars.

LINDA: But you opened it today.

WILLY: Me? I didn't. *He stops.* Now isn't that peculiar! Isn't that a remarkable —*He breaks off in amazement and fright as the flute is heard distantly.*

LINDA: What, darling?

WILLY: That is the most remarkable thing.

LINDA: What, dear?

WILLY: I was thinking of the Chevvy. *Slight pause.* Nineteen twenty-eight . . . when I had that red Chevvy—*Breaks off.* That funny? I coulda sworn I was driving that Chevvy today.

LINDA: Well, that's nothing. Something must've reminded you.

WILLY: Remarkable. Ts. Remember those days? The way Biff used to simonize that car? The dealer refused to believe there was eighty thousand miles on it. *He shakes his head.* Heh! *To Linda:* Close your eyes, I'll be right up. *He walks out of the bedroom.*

HAPPY, *to Biff:* Jesus, maybe he smashed up the car again!

LINDA, *calling after Willy:* Be careful on the stairs, dear! The cheese is on the middle shelf! *She turns, goes over to the bed, takes his jacket, and goes out of the bedroom.*

Light has risen on the boys' room. Unseen, Willy is heard talking to himself, "Eighty thousand miles," and a little laugh. Biff gets out of bed, comes downstage a bit, and stands attentively. Biff is two years older than his brother Happy, well built, but in these days bears a worn air and seems less self-assured. He has succeeded less, and his dreams are stronger and less acceptable than Happy's. Happy is tall, powerfully made. Sexuality is like a visible color on him, or a scent that many women have discovered. He, like his brother, is lost, but in a different way, for he has never allowed himself to turn his face toward defeat and is thus more confused and hard-skinned, although seemingly more content.

HAPPY, *getting out of bed:* He's going to get his license taken away if he keeps that up. I'm getting nervous about him, y'know, Biff?

BIFF: His eyes are going.

HAPPY: No, I've driven with him. He sees all right. He just doesn't keep his mind on it. I drove into the city with him last week. He stops at a green light and then it turns red and he goes. *He laughs.*

BIFF: Maybe he's color-blind.

HAPPY: Pop? Why he's got the finest eye for color in the business. You know that.

BIFF, *sitting down on his bed:* I'm going to sleep.

HAPPY: You're not still sour on Dad, are you, Biff?

BIFF: He's all right, I guess.

WILLY, *underneath them, in the living-room:* Yes, sir, eighty thousand miles—eighty-two thousand!

BIFF: You smoking?

HAPPY, *holding out a pack of cigarettes:* Want one?

BIFF, *taking a cigarette:* I can never sleep when I smell it.

WILLY: What a simonizing job, heh!

HAPPY, *with deep sentiment:* Funny, Biff, y'know? Us sleeping in here again? The old beds. *He pats his bed affectionately.* All the talk that went across those two beds, huh? Our whole lives.

BIFF: Yeah. Lotta dreams and plans.

HAPPY, *with a deep and masculine laugh:* About five hundred women would like to know what was said in this room.

They share a soft laugh.

BIFF: Remember that big Betsy something—what the hell was her name—over on Bushwick Avenue?

HAPPY, *combing his hair:* With the collie dog!

BIFF: That's the one. I got you in there, remember?

HAPPY: Yeah, that was my first time—I think. Boy, there was a pig! *They laugh, almost crudely.* You taught me everything I know about women. Don't forget that.

BIFF: I bet you forgot how bashful you used to be. Especially with girls.

HAPPY: Oh, I still am, Biff.

BIFF: Oh, go on.

HAPPY: I just control it, that's all. I think I got less bashful and you got more so. What happened, Biff? Where's the old humor, the old confidence? *He shakes Biff's knee. Biff gets up and moves restlessly about the room.* What's the matter?

BIFF: Why does Dad mock me all the time?

HAPPY: He's not mocking you, he—

BIFF: Everything I say there's a twist of mockery on his face. I can't get near him.

HAPPY: He just wants you to make good, that's all. I wanted to talk to you about Dad for a long time, Biff. Something's—happening to him. He—talks to himself.

BIFF: I noticed that this morning. But he always mumbled.

HAPPY: But not so noticeable. It got so embarrassing I sent him to Florida. And you know something? Most of the time he's talking to you.

BIFF: What's he say about me?

HAPPY: I can't make it out.

BIFF: What's he say about me?

HAPPY: I think the fact that you're not settled, that you're still kind of up in the air . . .

BIFF: There's one or two other things depressing him, Happy.

HAPPY: What do you mean?

BIFF: Never mind. Just don't lay it all to me.

HAPPY: But I think if you just got started—I mean—is there any future for you out there?

BIFF: I tell ya, Hap, I don't know what the future is. I don't know—what I'm supposed to want.

HAPPY: What do you mean?

BIFF: Well, I spent six or seven years after high school trying to work myself up. Shipping clerk, salesman, business of one kind or another. And it's a measly manner of existence. To get on that subway on the hot mornings in summer. To devote your whole life to keeping stock, or making phone calls, or selling or buying. To suffer fifty weeks of the year for the sake of a two-week vacation, when all you really desire is to be outdoors, with your shirt off. And always to have to get ahead of the next fella. And still—that's how you build a future.

HAPPY: Well, you really enjoy it on a farm? Are you content out there?

BIFF, *with rising agitation:* Hap, I've had twenty or thirty different kinds of jobs since I left home before the war, and it always turns out the same. I just realized it lately. In Nebraska when I herded cattle, and the Dakotas, and Arizona, and now in Texas. It's why I came home now, I guess, because I realized it. This farm I work on, it's spring there now, see? And they've got about fifteen new colts. There's nothing more inspiring or—beautiful than the sight of a mare and a new colt. And it's cool there now, see? Texas is cool now, and it's spring. And whenever spring comes to where I am, I suddenly get the feeling, my God, I'm not gettin' anywhere! What the hell am I doing, playing around with horses, twenty-eight dollars a week! I'm thirty-four years old, I oughta be makin' my future. That's when I come running home. And now, I get here, and I don't know what to do with myself. *After a pause:* I've always made a point of not wasting my life, and everytime I come back here I know that all I've done is to waste my life.

HAPPY: You're a poet, you know that, Biff? You're a—you're an idealist!

BIFF: No, I'm mixed up very bad. Maybe I oughta get married. Maybe I oughta get stuck into something. Maybe that's my trouble. I'm like a boy. I'm not married, I'm not in business, I just—I'm like a boy. Are you content, Hap? You're a success, aren't you? Are you content?

HAPPY: Hell, no!

BIFF: Why? You're making money, aren't you?

HAPPY, *moving about with energy, expressiveness:* All I can do now is wait for the merchandise manager to die. And suppose I get to be merchandise manager? He's a good friend of mine, and he just built a terrific estate on Long Island. And he lived there about two months and sold it, and now he's building another one. He can't enjoy it once it's finished. And I know that's just what I would do. I don't know what the hell I'm workin' for. Sometimes I sit in my apartment—all alone. And I think of the rent I'm paying. And it's crazy. But then, it's what I always wanted. My own apartment, a car, and plenty of women. And still, goddammit, I'm lonely.

BIFF, *with enthusiasm:* Listen, why don't you come out West with me?

HAPPY: You and I, heh?

BIFF: Sure, maybe we could buy a ranch. Raise cattle, use our muscles. Men built like we are should be working out in the open.

HAPPY, *avidly:* The Loman Brothers, heh?

BIFF, *with vast affection:* Sure, we'd be known all over the counties!

HAPPY, *enthralled:* That's what I dream about, Biff. Sometimes I want to just rip my clothes off in the middle of the store and outbox that goddam merchandise manager. I mean I can outbox, outrun, and outlift anybody in that store, and I have to take orders from those common, petty sons-of-bitches till I can't stand it any more.

BIFF: I'm tellin' you, kid, if you were with me I'd be happy out there.

HAPPY, *enthused:* See, Biff, everybody around me is so false that I'm constantly lowering my ideals . . .

BIFF: Baby, together we'd stand up for one another, we'd have someone to trust.

HAPPY: If I were around you—

BIFF: Hap, the trouble is we weren't brought up to grub for money. I don't know how to do it.

HAPPY: Neither can I!

BIFF: Then let's go!

HAPPY: The only thing is—what can you make out there?

BIFF: But look at your friend. Builds an estate and then hasn't the peace of mind to live in it.

HAPPY: Yeah, but when he walks into the store the waves part in front of him. That's fifty-two thousand dollars a year coming through the revolving door, and I got more in my pinky finger than he's got in his head.

BIFF: Yeah, but you just said—

HAPPY: I gotta show some of those pompous, self-important executives over there that Hap Loman can make the grade. I want to walk into the store the way he walks in. Then I'll go with you, Biff. We'll be together yet, I swear. But take those two we had tonight. Now weren't they gorgeous creatures?

BIFF: Yeah, yeah, most gorgeous I've had in years.

HAPPY: I get that any time I want, Biff. Whenever I feel disgusted. The only trouble is, it gets like bowling or something. I just keep knockin' them over and it doesn't mean anything. You still run around a lot?

BIFF: Naa. I'd like to find a girl—steady, somebody with substance.

HAPPY: That's what I long for.

BIFF: Go on! You'd never come home.

HAPPY: I would! Somebody with character, with resistance! Like Mom, y'know? You're gonna call me a bastard when I tell you this. That girl Charlotte I was with tonight is engaged to be married in five weeks. *He tries on his new hat.*

BIFF: No kiddin'!

HAPPY: Sure, the guy's in line for the vice-presidency of the store. I don't know what gets into me, maybe I just have an overdeveloped sense of competition or something, but I went and ruined her, and furthermore I can't get rid of her. And he's the third executive I've done that to. Isn't that a crummy characteristic? And to top it all, I go to their weddings! *Indignantly, but laughing:* Like I'm not supposed to take bribes. Manufacturers offer me a hundred-dollar bill now and then to throw an order their way. You know how honest I am, but it's like this girl, see. I hate myself for it. Because I don't want the girl, and, still, I take it and—I love it!

BIFF: Let's go to sleep.

HAPPY: I guess we didn't settle anything, heh?

BIFF: I just got one idea that I think I'm going to try.

HAPPY: What's that?

BIFF: Remember Bill Oliver?

HAPPY: Sure, Oliver is very big now. You want to work for him again?

BIFF: No, but when I quit he said something to me. He put his arm on my shoulder, and he said, "Biff, if you ever need anything, come to me."

HAPPY: I remember that. That sounds good.

BIFF: I think I'll go to see him. If I could get ten thousand or even seven or eight thousand dollars I could buy a beautiful ranch.

HAPPY: I bet he'd back you. 'Cause he thought highly of you, Biff. I mean, they all do. You're well liked, Biff. That's why I say to come back here, and we both have the apartment. And I'm tellin' you, Biff, any babe you want . . .

BIFF: No, with a ranch I could do the work I like and still be something. I just wonder though. I wonder if Oliver still thinks I stole that carton of basketballs.

HAPPY: Oh, he probably forgot that long ago. It's almost ten years. You're too sensitive. Anyway, he didn't really fire you.

BIFF: Well, I think he was going to. I think that's why I quit. I was never sure whether he knew or not. I know he thought the world of me, though. I was the only one he'd let lock up the place.

WILLY, *below:* You gonna wash the engine, Biff?

HAPPY: Shh!

Biff looks at Happy, who is gazing down, listening. Willy is mumbling in the parlor.

HAPPY: You hear that?

They listen. Willy laughs warmly.

BIFF, *growing angry:* Doesn't he know Mom can hear that?

WILLY: Don't get your sweater dirty, Biff!

A look of pain crosses Biff's face.

HAPPY: Isn't that terrible? Don't leave again, will you? You'll find a job here. You gotta stick around. I don't know what to do about him, it's getting embarrassing.

WILLY: What a simonizing job!

BIFF: Mom's hearing that!

WILLY: No kiddin', Biff, you got a date? Wonderful!

HAPPY: Go on to sleep. But talk to him in the morning, will you?

BIFF, *reluctantly getting into bed:* With her in the house, Brother!

HAPPY, *getting into bed:* I wish you'd have a good talk with him.

The light on their room begins to fade.

BIFF, *to himself in bed:* That selfish, stupid . . .

HAPPY: Sh . . . Sleep, Biff.

Their light is out. Well before they have finished speaking, Willy's form is dimly seen below in the darkened kitchen. He opens the refrigerator, searches in there, and takes out a bottle of milk. The apartment houses are fading out, and the entire house and surroundings become covered with leaves. Music insinuates itself as the leaves appear.

WILLY: Just wanna be careful with those girls, Biff, that's all. Don't make any promises. No promises of any kind. Because a girl, y'know, they always believe what you tell 'em, and you're very young, Biff, you're too young to be talking seriously to girls.

Light rises on the kitchen. Willy, talking, shuts the refrigerator door and comes downstage to the kitchen table. He pours milk into a glass. He is totally immersed in himself, smiling faintly.

WILLY: Too young entirely, Biff. You want to watch your schooling first. Then when you're all set, there'll be plenty of girls for a boy like you. *He smiles broadly at a kitchen chair.* That so? The girls pay for you? *He laughs.* Boy, you must really be makin' a hit.

Willy is gradually addressing—physically—a point offstage, speaking through the wall of the kitchen, and his voice has been rising in volume to that of a normal conversation.

WILLY: I been wondering why you polish the car so careful. Ha! Don't leave the hubcaps, boys. Get the chamois to the hubcaps. Happy, use newspaper on the windows, it's the easiest thing. Show him how to do it, Biff! You see, Happy? Pad it up, use it like a pad. That's it, that's it, good work. You're doin' all right, Hap. *He pauses, then nods in approbation for a few seconds, then looks upward.* Biff, first thing we gotta do when we get time is clip that big branch over the house. Afraid it's gonna fall in a storm and hit the roof. Tell you what. We get a rope and sling her around, and then we climb up there with a couple of saws and take her down. Soon as you finish the car, boys, I wanna see ya. I got a surprise for you, boys.

BIFF, *offstage:* Whatta ya got, Dad?

WILLY: No, you finish first. Never leave a job till you're finished—remember that. *Looking toward the "big trees":* Biff, up in Albany I saw a beautiful hammock. I think I'll buy it next trip, and we'll hang it right between those two elms. Wouldn't that be something? Just swingin' there under those branches. Boy, that would be . . .

Young Biff and Young Happy appear from the direction Willy was addressing. Happy carries rags and a pail of water. Biff, wearing a sweater with a block "S," carries a football.

BIFF, *pointing in the direction of the car offstage:* How's that, Pop, professional?

WILLY: Terrific. Terrific job, boys. Good work, Biff.

HAPPY: Where's the surprise, Pop?

WILLY: In the back seat of the car.

HAPPY: Boy! *He runs off.*

BIFF: What is it, Dad? Tell me, what'd you buy?

WILLY, *laughing, cuffs him:* Never mind, something I want you to have.

BIFF, *turns and starts off:* What is it, Hap?

HAPPY, *offstage:* It's a punching bag!

BIFF: Oh, Pop!

WILLY: It's got Gene Tunney's signature on it!

Happy runs onstage with a punching bag.

BIFF: Gee, how'd you know we wanted a punching bag?

WILLY: Well, it's the finest thing for the timing.

HAPPY, *lies down on his back and pedals with his feet:* I'm losing weight, you notice, Pop?

WILLY, *to Happy:* Jumping rope is good too.

BIFF: Did you see the new football I got?

WILLY, *examining the ball:* Where'd you get a new ball?

BIFF: The coach told me to practice my passing.

WILLY: That so? And he gave you the ball, heh?

BIFF: Well, I borrowed it from the locker room. *He laughs confidentially.*

WILLY, *laughing with him at the theft:* I want you to return that.

HAPPY: I told you he wouldn't like it!

BIFF, *angrily:* Well, I'm bringing it back!

WILLY, *stopping the incipient argument, to Happy:* Sure, he's gotta practice with a regulation ball, doesn't he? *To Biff:* Coach'll probably congratulate you on your initiative!

BIFF: Oh, he keeps congratulating my initiative all the time, Pop.

WILLY: That's because he likes you. If somebody else took that ball there'd be an uproar. So what's the report, boys, what's the report?

BIFF: Where'd you go this time, Dad? Gee we were lonesome for you.

WILLY, *pleased, puts an arm around each boy and they come down to the apron:* Lonesome, heh?

BIFF: Missed you every minute.

WILLY: Don't say? Tell you a secret, boys. Don't breathe it to a soul. Someday I'll have my own business, and I'll never have to leave home any more.

HAPPY: Like Uncle Charley, heh?

WILLY: Bigger than Uncle Charley! Because Charley is not—liked. He's liked, but he's not—well liked.

BIFF: Where'd you go this time, Dad?

WILLY: Well, I got on the road, and I went north to Providence. Met the Mayor.

BIFF: The Mayor of Providence!

WILLY: He was sitting in the hotel lobby.

BIFF: What'd he say?

WILLY: He said, "Morning!" And I said, "You got a fine city here, Mayor." And then he had coffee with me. And then I went to Waterbury. Waterbury is a fine city. Big clock city, the famous Waterbury clock. Sold a nice bill there. And then Boston—Boston is the cradle of the Revolution. A fine city. And a couple of other towns in Mass., and on to Portland and Bangor and straight home!

BIFF: Gee, I'd love to go with you sometime, Dad.

WILLY: Soon as summer comes.

HAPPY: Promise?

WILLY: You and Hap and I, and I'll show you all the towns. America is full of beautiful towns and fine, upstanding people. And they know me, boys, they know me up and down New England. The finest people. And when I bring you fellas up, there'll be open sesame for all of us, 'cause one thing, boys: I have friends. I can park my car in any street in New England, and the cops protect it like their own. This summer, heh?

BIFF and HAPPY, *together:* Yeah! You bet!

WILLY: We'll take our bathing suits.

HAPPY: We'll carry your bags, Pop!

WILLY: Oh, won't that be something! Me comin' into the Boston stores with you boys carryin' my bags. What a sensation!

Biff is prancing around, practicing passing the ball.

WILLY: You nervous, Biff, about the game?

BIFF: Not if you're gonna be there.

WILLY: What do they say about you in school, now that they made you captain?

HAPPY: There's a crowd of girls behind him everytime the classes change.

BIFF, *taking Willy's hand:* This Saturday, Pop, this Saturday—just for you, I'm going to break through for a touchdown.

HAPPY: You're supposed to pass.

BIFF: I'm takin' one play for Pop. You watch me, Pop, and when I take off my helmet, that means I'm breakin' out. Then you watch me crash through that line!

WILLY, *kisses Biff:* Oh, wait'll I tell this in Boston!

Bernard enters in knickers. He is younger than Biff, earnest and loyal, a worried boy.

BERNARD: Biff, where are you? You're supposed to study with me today.

WILLY: Hey, looka Bernard. What're you lookin' so anemic about, Bernard?

BERNARD: He's gotta study, Uncle Willy. He's got Regents[2] next week.

HAPPY, *tauntingly, spinning Bernard around:* Let's box, Bernard!

BERNARD: Biff! *He gets away from Happy.* Listen, Biff, I heard Mr. Birnbaum say that if you don't start studyin' math he's gonna flunk you, and you won't graduate. I heard him!

WILLY: You better study with him, Biff. Go ahead now.

BERNARD: I heard him!

BIFF: Oh, Pop, you didn't see my sneakers! *He holds up a foot for Willy to look at.*

WILLY: Hey, that's a beautiful job of printing!

BERNARD, *wiping his glasses:* Just because he printed University of Virginia on his sneakers doesn't mean they've got to graduate him, Uncle Willy!

WILLY, *angrily:* What're you talking about? With scholarships to three universities they're gonna flunk him?

BERNARD: But I heard Mr. Birnbaum say—

WILLY: Don't be a pest, Bernard! *To his boys:* What an anemic!

BERNARD: Okay, I'm waiting for you in my house, Biff.

Bernard goes off. The Lomans laugh.

WILLY: Bernard is not well liked, is he?

BIFF: He's liked, but he's not well liked.

HAPPY: That's right, Pop.

WILLY: That's just what I mean. Bernard can get the best marks in school, y'understand, but when he gets out in the business world, y'understand, you are going to be five times ahead of him. That's why I thank Almighty God you're both built like Adonises.[3] Because the man who makes an appearance in the business world, the man who creates personal interest, is the man who gets ahead. Be liked and you will never want. You take me, for instance. I never have to wait in line to see a buyer. "Willy Loman is here!" That's all they have to know, and I go right through.

BIFF: Did you knock them dead, Pop?

2. In New York, a statewide high school proficiency examination.

3. In Greek myth, Adonis, a handsome mortal, was loved by Aphrodite, goddess of love and beauty.

WILLY: Knocked 'em cold in Providence, slaughtered 'em in Boston.

HAPPY, *on his back, pedaling again:* I'm losing weight, you notice, Pop?

Linda enters, as of old, a ribbon in her hair, carrying a basket of washing.

LINDA, *with youthful energy:* Hello, dear!

WILLY: Sweetheart!

LINDA: How'd the Chevvy run?

WILLY: Chevrolet, Linda, is the greatest car ever built. *To the boys:* Since when do you let your mother carry wash up the stairs?

BIFF: Grab hold there, boy!

HAPPY: Where to, Mom?

LINDA: Hang them up on the line. And you better go down to your friends, Biff. The cellar is full of boys. They don't know what to do with themselves.

BIFF: Ah, when Pop comes home they can wait!

WILLY, *laughs appreciatively:* You better go down and tell them what to do, Biff.

BIFF: I think I'll have them sweep out the furnace room.

WILLY: Good work, Biff.

BIFF, *goes through wall-line of kitchen to doorway at back and calls down:* Fellas! Everybody sweep out the furnace room! I'll be right down!

VOICES: All right! Okay, Biff.

BIFF: George and Sam and Frank, come out back! We're hangin' up the wash! Come on, Hap, on the double! *He and Happy carry out the basket.*

LINDA: The way they obey him!

WILLY: Well, that's training, the training. I'm tellin' you, I was sellin' thousands and thousands, but I had to come home.

LINDA: Oh, the whole block'll be at that game. Did you sell anything?

WILLY: I did five hundred gross in Providence and seven hundred gross in Boston.

LINDA: No! Wait a minute, I've got a pencil. *She pulls pencil and paper out of her apron pocket.* That makes your commission . . . Two hundred—my God! Two hundred and twelve dollars!

WILLY: Well, I didn't figure it yet, but . . .

LINDA: How much did you do?

WILLY: Well, I—I did—about a hundred and eighty gross in Providence. Well, no—it came to—roughly two hundred gross on the whole trip.

LINDA, *without hesitation:* Two hundred gross. That's . . . *She figures.*

WILLY: The trouble was that three of the stores were half closed for inventory in Boston. Otherwise I woulda broke records.

LINDA: Well, it makes seventy dollars and some pennies. That's very good.

WILLY: What do we owe?

LINDA: Well, on the first there's sixteen dollars on the refrigerator—

WILLY: Why sixteen?

LINDA: Well, the fan belt broke, so it was a dollar eighty.

WILLY: But it's brand new.

LINDA: Well, the man said that's the way it is. Till they work themselves in, y'know.

They move through the wall-line into the kitchen.

WILLY: I hope we didn't get stuck on that machine.

LINDA: They got the biggest ads of any of them!

WILLY: I know, it's a fine machine. What else?

LINDA: Well, there's nine-sixty for the washing machine. And for the vacuum cleaner there's three and a half due on the fifteenth. Then the roof, you got twenty-one dollars remaining.

WILLY: It don't leak, does it?

LINDA: No, they did a wonderful job. Then you owe Frank for the carburetor.

WILLY: I'm not going to pay that man! That goddam Chevrolet, they ought to prohibit the manufacture of that car!

LINDA: Well, you owe him three and a half. And odds and ends, comes to around a hundred and twenty dollars by the fifteenth.

WILLY: A hundred and twenty dollars! My God, if business don't pick up I don't know what I'm gonna do!

LINDA: Well, next week you'll do better.

WILLY: Oh, I'll knock 'em dead next week. I'll go to Hartford. I'm very well liked in Hartford. You know, the trouble is, Linda, people don't seem to take to me.

They move onto the forestage.

LINDA: Oh, don't be foolish.

WILLY: I know it when I walk in. They seem to laugh at me.

LINDA: Why? Why would they laugh at you? Don't talk that way, Willy.

Willy moves to the edge of the stage. Linda goes into the kitchen and starts to darn stockings.

WILLY: I don't know the reason for it, but they just pass me by. I'm not noticed.

LINDA: But you're doing wonderful, dear. You're making seventy to a hundred dollars a week.

WILLY: But I gotta be at it ten, twelve hours a day. Other men—I don't know—they do it easier. I don't know why—I can't stop myself—I talk too much. A man oughta come in with a few words. One thing about Charley. He's a man of few words, and they respect him.

LINDA: You don't talk too much, you're just lively.

WILLY, *smiling:* Well, I figure, what the hell, life is short, a couple of jokes. *To himself:* I joke too much! *The smile goes.*

LINDA: Why? You're—

WILLY: I'm fat. I'm very—foolish to look at, Linda. I didn't tell you, but Christmas time I happened to be calling on F. H. Stewarts, and a salesman I know, as I was going in to see the buyer I heard him say something about—walrus. And I—I cracked him right across the face. I won't take that. I simply will not take that. But they do laugh at me. I know that.

LINDA: Darling . . .

WILLY: I gotta overcome it. I know I gotta overcome it. I'm not dressing to advantage, maybe.

LINDA: Willy, darling, you're the handsomest man in the world—

WILLY: Oh, no, Linda.

LINDA: To me you are. *Slight pause.* The handsomest.

From the darkness is heard the laughter of a woman. Willy doesn't turn to it, but it continues through Linda's lines.

LINDA: And the boys, Willy. Few men are idolized by their children the way you are.

Music is heard as behind a scrim,[4] *to the left of the house, The Woman, dimly seen, is dressing.*

WILLY, *with great feeling:* You're the best there is, Linda, you're a pal, you know that? On the road—on the road I want to grab you sometimes and just kiss the life outa you.

The laughter is loud now, and he moves into a brightening area at the left, where The Woman has come from behind the scrim and is standing, putting on her hat, looking into a "mirror" and laughing.

WILLY: 'Cause I get so lonely—especially when business is bad and there's nobody to talk to. I get the feeling that I'll never sell anything again, that I won't make a living for you, or a business, a business for the boys. *He talks through The Woman's subsiding laughter. The Woman primps at the "mirror."* There's so much I want to make for—

THE WOMAN: Me? You didn't make me, Willy. I picked you.

WILLY, *pleased:* You picked me?

THE WOMAN, *who is quite proper-looking, Willy's age:* I did. I've been sitting at that desk watching all the salesmen go by, day in, day out. But you've got such a sense of humor, and we do have such a good time together, don't we?

WILLY: Sure, sure. *He takes her in his arms.* Why do you have to go now?

THE WOMAN: It's two o'clock . . .

WILLY: No, come on in! *He pulls her.*

THE WOMAN: . . . my sisters'll be scandalized. When'll you be back?

WILLY: Oh, two weeks about. Will you come up again?

THE WOMAN: Sure thing. You do make me laugh. It's good for me. *She squeezes his arm, kisses him.* And I think you're a wonderful man.

WILLY: You picked me, heh?

THE WOMAN: Sure. Because you're so sweet. And such a kidder.

WILLY: Well, I'll see you next time I'm in Boston.

THE WOMAN: I'll put you right through to the buyers.

WILLY, *slapping her bottom:* Right. Well, bottoms up!

THE WOMAN *slaps him gently and laughs:* You just kill me, Willy. *He suddenly grabs her and kisses her roughly.* You kill me. And thanks for the stockings. I love a lot of stockings. Well, good night.

WILLY: Good night. And keep your pores open!

THE WOMAN: Oh, Willy!

The Woman bursts out laughing, and Linda's laughter blends in. The Woman disappears into the dark. Now the area at the kitchen table brightens. Linda is sitting where she was at the kitchen table, but now is mending a pair of her silk stockings.

LINDA: You are, Willy. The handsomest man. You've got no reason to feel that—

WILLY, *coming out of The Woman's dimming area and going over to Linda:* I'll make it all up to you, Linda, I'll—

LINDA: There's nothing to make up, dear. You're doing fine, better than—

WILLY, *noticing her mending:* What's that?

LINDA: Just mending my stockings. They're so expensive—

4. A painted gauze cloth that is either opaque or transparent, depending on how it is illuminated.

WILLY, *angrily, taking them from her:* I won't have you mending stockings in this house! Now throw them out!

Linda puts the stockings in her pocket.

BERNARD, *entering on the run:* Where is he? If he doesn't study!

WILLY, *moving to the forestage, with great agitation:* You'll give him the answers!

BERNARD: I do, but I can't on a Regents! That's a state exam! They're liable to arrest me!

WILLY: Where is he? I'll whip him, I'll whip him!

LINDA: And he'd better give back that football, Willy, it's not nice.

WILLY: Biff! Where is he? Why is he taking everything?

LINDA: He's too rough with the girls, Willy. All the mothers are afraid of him!

WILLY: I'll whip him!

BERNARD: He's driving the car without a license!

The Woman's laugh is heard.

WILLY: Shut up!

LINDA: All the mothers—

WILLY: Shut up!

BERNARD, *backing quietly away and out:* Mr. Birnbaum says he's stuck up.

WILLY: Get outa here!

BERNARD: If he doesn't buckle down he'll flunk math! *He goes off.*

LINDA: He's right, Willy, you've gotta—

WILLY, *exploding at her:* There's nothing the matter with him! You want him to be a worm like Bernard? He's got spirit, personality . . .

As he speaks, Linda, almost in tears, exits into the living-room. Willy is alone in the kitchen, wilting and staring. The leaves are gone. It is night again, and the apartment houses look down from behind.

WILLY: Loaded with it. Loaded! What is he stealing? He's giving it back, isn't he? Why is he stealing? What did I tell him? I never in my life told him anything but decent things.

Happy in pajamas has come down the stairs; Willy suddenly becomes aware of Happy's presence.

HAPPY: Let's go now, come on.

WILLY, *sitting down at the kitchen table:* Huh! Why did she have to wax the floors herself? Everytime she waxes the floors she keels over. She knows that!

HAPPY: Shh! Take it easy. What brought you back tonight?

WILLY: I got an awful scare. Nearly hit a kid in Yonkers. God! Why didn't I go to Alaska with my brother Ben that time! Ben! That man was a genius, that man was success incarnate! What a mistake! He begged me to go.

HAPPY: Well, there's no use in—

WILLY: You guys! There was a man started with the clothes on his back and ended up with diamond mines!

HAPPY: Boy, someday I'd like to know how he did it.

WILLY: What's the mystery? The man knew what he wanted and went out and got it! Walked into a jungle, and comes out, the age of twenty-one, and he's rich! The world is an oyster, but you don't crack it open on a mattress!

HAPPY: Pop, I told you I'm gonna retire you for life.

WILLY: You'll retire me for life on seventy goddam dollars a week? And your women and your car and your apartment, and you'll retire me for life! Christ's sake,

I couldn't get past Yonkers today! Where are you guys, where are you? The woods are burning! I can't drive a car!

Charley has appeared in the doorway. He is a large man, slow of speech, laconic, immovable. In all he says, despite what he says, there is pity, and, now, trepidation. He has a robe over pajamas, slippers on his feet. He enters the kitchen.

CHARLEY: Everything all right?

HAPPY: Yeah, Charley, everything's . . .

WILLY: What's the matter?

CHARLEY: I heard some noise. I thought something happened. Can't we do something about the walls? You sneeze in here, and in my house hats blow off.

HAPPY: Let's go to bed, Dad. Come on.

Charley signals to Happy to go.

WILLY: You go ahead, I'm not tired at the moment.

HAPPY, *to Willy:* Take it easy, huh? *He exits.*

WILLY: What're you doin' up?

CHARLEY, *sitting down at the kitchen table opposite Willy:* Couldn't sleep good. I had a heartburn.

WILLY: Well, you don't know how to eat.

CHARLEY: I eat with my mouth.

WILLY: No, you're ignorant. You gotta know about vitamins and things like that.

CHARLEY: Come on, let's shoot. Tire you out a little.

WILLY, *hesitantly:* All right. You got cards?

CHARLEY, *taking a deck from his pocket:* Yeah, I got them. Someplace. What is it with those vitamins?

WILLY, *dealing:* They build up your bones. Chemistry.

CHARLEY: Yeah, but there's no bones in a heartburn.

WILLY: What are you talkin' about? Do you know the first thing about it?

CHARLEY: Don't get insulted.

WILLY: Don't talk about something you don't know anything about.

They are playing. Pause.

CHARLEY: What're you doin' home?

WILLY: A little trouble with the car.

CHARLEY: Oh. *Pause.* I'd like to take a trip to California.

WILLY: Don't say.

CHARLEY: You want a job?

WILLY: I got a job, I told you that. *After a slight pause:* What the hell are you offering me a job for?

CHARLEY: Don't get insulted.

WILLY: Don't insult me.

CHARLEY: I don't see no sense in it. You don't have to go on this way.

WILLY: I got a good job. *Slight pause.* What do you keep comin' in here for?

CHARLEY: You want me to go?

WILLY, *after a pause, withering:* I can't understand it. He's going back to Texas again. What the hell is that?

CHARLEY: Let him go.

WILLY: I got nothin' to give him, Charley, I'm clean, I'm clean.

CHARLEY: He won't starve. None a them starve. Forget about him.

WILLY: Then what have I got to remember?

CHARLEY: You take it too hard. To hell with it. When a deposit bottle is broken you don't get your nickel back.

WILLY: That's easy enough for you to say.

CHARLEY: That ain't easy for me to say.

WILLY: Did you see the ceiling I put up in the living-room?

CHARLEY: Yeah, that's a piece of work. To put up a ceiling is a mystery to me. How do you do it?

WILLY: What's the difference?

CHARLEY: Well, talk about it.

WILLY: You gonna put up a ceiling?

CHARLEY: How could I put up a ceiling?

WILLY: Then what the hell are you bothering me for?

CHARLEY: You're insulted again.

WILLY: A man who can't handle tools is not a man. You're disgusting.

CHARLEY: Don't call me disgusting, Willy.

Uncle Ben, carrying a valise and an umbrella, enters the forestage from around the right corner of the house. He is a stolid man, in his sixties, with a mustache and an authoritative air. He is utterly certain of his destiny, and there is an aura of far places about him. He enters exactly as Willy speaks.

WILLY: I'm getting awfully tired, Ben.

Ben's music is heard. Ben looks around at everything.

CHARLEY: Good, keep playing; you'll sleep better. Did you call me Ben?

Ben looks at his watch.

WILLY: That's funny. For a second there you reminded me of my brother Ben.

BEN: I only have a few minutes. *He strolls, inspecting the place. Willy and Charley continue playing.*

CHARLEY: You never heard from him again, heh? Since that time?

WILLY: Didn't Linda tell you? Couple of weeks ago we got a letter from his wife in Africa. He died.

CHARLEY: That so.

BEN, *chuckling:* So this is Brooklyn, eh?

CHARLEY: Maybe you're in for some of his money.

WILLY: Naa, he had seven sons. There's just one opportunity I had with that man . . .

BEN: I must take a train, William. There are several properties I'm looking at in Alaska.

WILLY: Sure, sure! If I'd gone with him to Alaska that time, everything would've been totally different.

CHARLEY: Go on, you'd froze to death up there.

WILLY: What're you talking about?

BEN: Opportunity is tremendous in Alaska, William. Surprised you're not up there.

WILLY: Sure, tremendous.

CHARLEY: Heh?

WILLY: There was the only man I ever met who knew the answers.

CHARLEY: Who?

BEN: How are you all?

WILLY, *taking a pot, smiling:* Fine, fine.

CHARLEY: Pretty sharp tonight.

BEN: Is Mother living with you?

WILLY: No, she died a long time ago.

CHARLEY: Who?

BEN: That's too bad. Fine specimen of a lady, Mother.

WILLY, *to Charley:* Heh?

BEN: I'd hoped to see the old girl.

CHARLEY: Who died?

BEN: Heard anything from Father, have you?

WILLY, *unnerved:* What do you mean, who died?

CHARLEY, *taking a pot:* What're you talkin' about?

BEN, *looking at his watch:* William, it's half-past eight!

WILLY, *as though to dispel his confusion he angrily stops Charley's hand:* That's my build!

CHARLEY: I put the ace—

WILLY: If you don't know how to play the game I'm not gonna throw my money away on you!

CHARLEY, *rising:* It was my ace, for God's sake!

WILLY: I'm through, I'm through!

BEN: When did Mother die?

WILLY: Long ago. Since the beginning you never knew how to play cards.

CHARLEY, *picks up the cards and goes to the door:* All right! Next time I'll bring a deck with five aces.

WILLY: I don't play that kind of game!

CHARLEY, *turning to him:* You ought to be ashamed of yourself!

WILLY: Yeah?

CHARLEY: Yeah! *He goes out.*

WILLY, *slamming the door after him:* Ignoramus!

BEN, *as Willy comes toward him through the wall-line of the kitchen:* So you're William.

WILLY, *shaking Ben's hand:* Ben! I've been waiting for you so long! What's the answer? How did you do it?

BEN: Oh, there's a story in that.

Linda enters the forestage, as of old, carrying the wash basket.

LINDA: Is this Ben?

BEN, *gallantly:* How do you do, my dear.

LINDA: Where've you been all these years? Willy's always wondered why you—

WILLY, *pulling Ben away from her impatiently:* Where is Dad? Didn't you follow him? How did you get started?

BEN: Well, I don't know how much you remember.

WILLY: Well, I was just a baby, of course, only three or four years old—

BEN: Three years and eleven months.

WILLY: What a memory, Ben!

BEN: I have many enterprises, William, and I have never kept books.

WILLY: I remember I was sitting under the wagon in—was it Nebraska?

BEN: It was South Dakota, and I gave you a bunch of wild flowers.

WILLY: I remember you walking away down some open road.

BEN, *laughing:* I was going to find Father in Alaska.

Ben is symbolic of success.

WILLY: Where is he?

BEN: At that age I had a very faulty view of geography, William. I discovered after a few days that I was heading due south, so instead of Alaska, I ended up in Africa.

LINDA: Africa!

WILLY: The Gold Coast!

BEN: Principally diamond mines.

LINDA: Diamond mines!

BEN: Yes, my dear. But I've only a few minutes—

WILLY: No! Boys! Boys! *Young Biff and Happy appear.* Listen to this. This is your Uncle Ben, a great man! Tell my boys, Ben!

BEN: Why, boys, when I was seventeen I walked into the jungle, and when I was twenty-one I walked out. *He laughs.* And by God I was rich.

WILLY, *to the boys:* You see what I been talking about? The greatest things can happen!

BEN, *glancing at his watch:* I have an appointment in Ketchikan Tuesday week.

WILLY: No, Ben! Please tell about Dad. I want my boys to hear. I want them to know the kind of stock they spring from. All I remember is a man with a big beard, and I was in Mamma's lap, sitting around a fire, and some kind of high music.

BEN: His flute. He played the flute.

WILLY: Sure, the flute, that's right!

New music is heard, a high, rollicking tune.

BEN: Father was a very great and a very wild-hearted man. We would start in Boston, and he'd toss the whole family into the wagon, and then he'd drive the team right across the country; through Ohio, and Indiana, Michigan, Illinois, and all the Western states. And we'd stop in the towns and sell the flutes that he'd made on the way. Great inventor, Father. With one gadget he made more in a week than a man like you could make in a lifetime.

WILLY: That's just the way I'm bringing them up, Ben—rugged, well liked, all-around.

BEN: Yeah? *To Biff:* Hit that, boy—hard as you can. *He pounds his stomach.*

BIFF: Oh, no, sir!

BEN, *taking boxing stance:* Come on, get to me! *He laughs.*

WILLY: Go to it, Biff! Go ahead, show him!

BIFF: Okay! *He cocks his fists and starts in.*

LINDA, *to Willy:* Why must he fight, dear?

BEN, *sparring with Biff:* Good boy! Good boy!

WILLY: How's that, Ben, heh?

HAPPY: Give him the left, Biff!

LINDA: Why are you fighting?

BEN: Good boy! *Suddenly comes in, trips Biff, and stands over him, the point of his umbrella poised over Biff's eye.*

LINDA: Look out, Biff!

BIFF: Gee!

BEN, *patting Biff's knee:* Never fight fair with a stranger, boy. You'll never get out of the jungle that way. *Taking Linda's hand and bowing:* It was an honor and a pleasure to meet you, Linda.

LINDA, *withdrawing her hand coldly, frightened:* Have a nice—trip.

BEN, *to Willy:* And good luck with your—what do you do?

WILLY: Selling.

BEN: Yes. Well . . . *He raises his hand in farewell to all.*

WILLY: No, Ben, I don't want you to think . . . *He takes Ben's arm to show him.* It's Brooklyn, I know, but we hunt too.

BEN: Really, now.

WILLY: Oh, sure, there's snakes and rabbits and—that's why I moved out here. Why, Biff can fell any one of these trees in no time! Boys! Go right over to where they're building the apartment house and get some sand. We're gonna rebuild the entire front stoop right now! Watch this, Ben!

BIFF: Yes, sir! On the double, Hap!

HAPPY, *as he and Biff run off:* I lost weight, Pop, you notice?

Charley enters in knickers, even before the boys are gone.

CHARLEY: Listen, if they steal any more from that building the watchman'll put the cops on them!

LINDA, *to Willy:* Don't let Biff . . .

Ben laughs lustily.

WILLY: You shoulda seen the lumber they brought home last week. At least a dozen six-by-tens worth all kinds a money.

CHARLEY: Listen, if that watchman—

WILLY: I gave them hell, understand. But I got a couple of fearless characters there.

CHARLEY: Willy, the jails are full of fearless characters.

BEN, *clapping Willy on the back, with a laugh at Charley:* And the stock exchange, friend!

WILLY, *joining in Ben's laughter:* Where are the rest of your pants?

CHARLEY: My wife bought them.

WILLY: Now all you need is a golf club and you can go upstairs and go to sleep. *To Ben:* Great athlete! Between him and his son Bernard they can't hammer a nail!

BERNARD, *rushing in:* The watchman's chasing Biff!

WILLY, *angrily:* Shut up! He's not stealing anything!

LINDA, *alarmed, hurrying off left:* Where is he? Biff, dear! *She exits.*

WILLY, *moving toward the left, away from Ben:* There's nothing wrong. What's the matter with you?

BEN: Nervy boy. Good!

WILLY, *laughing:* Oh, nerves of iron, that Biff!

CHARLEY: Don't know what it is. My New England man comes back and he's bleedin', they murdered him up there.

WILLY: It's contacts, Charley, I got important contacts!

CHARLEY, *sarcastically:* Glad to hear it, Willy. Come in later, we'll shoot a little casino. I'll take some of your Portland money. *He laughs at Willy and exits.*

WILLY, *turning to Ben:* Business is bad, it's murderous. But not for me, of course.

BEN: I'll stop by on my way back to Africa.

WILLY, *longingly:* Can't you stay a few days? You're just what I need, Ben, because I—I have a fine position here, but I—well, Dad left when I was such a baby and I never had a chance to talk to him and I still feel—kind of temporary about myself.

BEN: I'll be late for my train.

They are at opposite ends of the stage.

WILLY: Ben, my boys—can't we talk? They'd go into the jaws of hell for me, see, but I—

BEN: William, you're being first-rate with your boys. Outstanding, manly chaps!

WILLY, *hanging on to his words:* Oh, Ben, that's good to hear! Because sometimes I'm afraid that I'm not teaching them the right kind of—Ben, how should I teach them?

BEN, *giving great weight to each word, and with a certain vicious audacity:* William, when I walked into the jungle, I was seventeen. When I walked out I was twenty-one. And, by God, I was rich! *He goes off into darkness around the right corner of the house.*

WILLY: . . . was rich! That's just the spirit I want to imbue them with! To walk into a jungle! I was right! I was right! I was right!

Ben is gone, but Willy is still speaking to him as Linda, in nightgown and robe, enters the kitchen, glances around for Willy, then goes to the door of the house, looks out and sees him. Comes down to his left. He looks at her.

LINDA: Willy, dear? Willy?

WILLY: I was right!

LINDA: Did you have some cheese? *He can't answer.* It's very late, darling. Come to bed, heh?

WILLY, *looking straight up:* Gotta break your neck to see a star in this yard.

LINDA: You coming in?

WILLY: Whatever happened to that diamond watch fob? Remember? When Ben came from Africa that time? Didn't he give me a watch fob with a diamond in it?

LINDA: You pawned it, dear. Twelve, thirteen years ago. For Biff's radio correspondence course.

WILLY: Gee, that was a beautiful thing. I'll take a walk.

LINDA: But you're in your slippers.

WILLY, *starting to go around the house at the left:* I was right! I was! *Half to Linda, as he goes, shaking his head:* What a man! There was a man worth talking to. I was right!

LINDA, *calling after Willy:* But in your slippers, Willy!

Willy is almost gone when Biff, in his pajamas, comes down the stairs and enters the kitchen.

BIFF: What is he doing out there?

LINDA: Sh!

BIFF: God Almighty, Mom, how long has he been doing this?

LINDA: Don't, he'll hear you.

BIFF: What the hell is the matter with him?

LINDA: It'll pass by morning.

BIFF: Shouldn't we do anything?

LINDA: Oh, my dear, you should do a lot of things, but there's nothing to do, so go to sleep.

Happy comes down the stair and sits on the steps.

HAPPY: I never heard him so loud, Mom.

LINDA: Well, come around more often; you'll hear him. *She sits down at the table and mends the lining of Willy's jacket.*

BIFF: Why didn't you ever write me about this, Mom?

LINDA: How would I write to you? For over three months you had no address.

BIFF: I was on the move. But you know I thought of you all the time. You know that, don't you, pal?

LINDA: I know, dear, I know. But he likes to have a letter. Just to know that there's still a possibility for better things.

BIFF: He's not like this all the time, is he?

LINDA: It's when you come home he's always the worst.

BIFF: When I come home?

LINDA: When you write you're coming, he's all smiles, and talks about the future, and—he's just wonderful. And then the closer you seem to come, the more shaky he gets, and then, by the time you get here, he's arguing, and he seems angry at you. I think it's just that maybe he can't bring himself to—to open up to you. Why are you so hateful to each other? Why is that?

BIFF, *evasively:* I'm not hateful, Mom.

LINDA: But you no sooner come in the door than you're fighting!

BIFF: I don't know why. I mean to change. I'm tryin', Mom, you understand?

LINDA: Are you home to stay now?

BIFF: I don't know. I want to look around, see what's doin'.

LINDA: Biff, you can't look around all your life, can you?

BIFF: I just can't take hold, Mom. I can't take hold of some kind of a life.

LINDA: Biff, a man is not a bird, to come and go with the springtime.

BIFF: Your hair . . . *He touches her hair.* Your hair got so gray.

LINDA: Oh, it's been gray since you were in high school. I just stopped dyeing it, that's all.

BIFF: Dye it again, will ya? I don't want my pal looking old. *He smiles.*

LINDA: You're such a boy! You think you can go away for a year and . . . You've got to get it into your head now that one day you'll knock on this door and there'll be strange people here—

BIFF: What are you talking about? You're not even sixty, Mom.

LINDA: But what about your father?

BIFF, *lamely:* Well, I meant him too.

HAPPY: He admires Pop.

LINDA: Biff, dear, if you don't have any feeling for him, then you can't have any feeling for me.

BIFF: Sure I can, Mom.

LINDA: No. You can't just come to see me, because I love him. *With a threat, but only a threat, of tears:* He's the dearest man in the world to me, and I won't have anyone making him feel unwanted and low and blue. You've got to make up your mind now, darling, there's no leeway any more. Either he's your father and you pay him that respect, or else you're not to come here. I know he's not easy to get along with—nobody knows that better than me—but . . .

WILLY, *from the left, with a laugh:* Hey, hey, Biffo!

BIFF, *starting to go out after Willy:* What the hell is the matter with him? *Happy stops him.*

LINDA: Don't—don't go near him!

BIFF: Stop making excuses for him! He always, always wiped the floor with you. Never had an ounce of respect for you.

HAPPY: He's always had respect for—

BIFF: What the hell do you know about it?

HAPPY, *surlily:* Just don't call him crazy!

BIFF: He's got no character—Charley wouldn't do this. Not in his own house—spewing out that vomit from his mind.

HAPPY: Charley never had to cope with what he's got to.

BIFF: People are worse off than Willy Loman. Believe me, I've seen them!

LINDA: Then make Charley your father, Biff. You can't do that, can you? I don't say he's a great man. Willy Loman never made a lot of money. His name was never in the paper. He's not the finest character that ever lived. But he's a human being, and a terrible thing is happening to him. So attention must be paid. He's not to be allowed to fall into his grave like an old dog. Attention, attention must be finally paid to such a person. You called him crazy—

BIFF: I didn't mean—

LINDA: No, a lot of people think he's lost his—balance. But you don't have to be very smart to know what his trouble is. The man is exhausted.

HAPPY: Sure!

LINDA: A small man can be just as exhausted as a great man. He works for a company thirty-six years this March, opens up unheard-of territories to their trademark, and now in his old age they take his salary away.

HAPPY, *indignantly:* I didn't know that, Mom.

LINDA: You never asked, my dear! Now that you get your spending money someplace else you don't trouble your mind with him.

HAPPY: But I gave you money last—

LINDA: Christmas time, fifty dollars! To fix the hot water it cost ninety-seven fifty! For five weeks he's been on straight commission, like a beginner, an unknown!

BIFF: Those ungrateful bastards!

LINDA: Are they any worse than his sons? When he brought them business, when he was young, they were glad to see him. But now his old friends, the old buyers that loved him so and always found some order to hand him in a pinch—they're all dead, retired. He used to be able to make six, seven calls a day in Boston. Now he takes his valises out of the car and puts them back and takes them out again and he's exhausted. Instead of walking he talks now. He drives seven hundred miles, and when he gets there no one knows him any more, no one welcomes him. And what goes through a man's mind, driving seven hundred miles home without having earned a cent? Why shouldn't he talk to himself? Why? When he has to go to Charley and borrow fifty dollars a week and pretend to me that it's his pay? How long can that go on? How long? You see what I'm sitting here and waiting for? And you tell me he has no character? The man who never worked a day but for your benefit? When does he get the medal for that? Is this his reward—to turn around at the age of sixty-three and find his sons, who he loved better than his life, one a philandering bum—

HAPPY: Mom!

LINDA: That's all you are, my baby! *To Biff:* And you! What happened to the love you had for him? You were such pals! How you used to talk to him on the phone every night! How lonely he was till he could come home to you!

BIFF: All right, Mom. I'll live here in my room, and I'll get a job. I'll keep away from him, that's all.

LINDA: No, Biff. You can't stay here and fight all the time.

BIFF: He threw me out of this house, remember that.

LINDA: Why did he do that? I never knew why.

BIFF: Because I know he's a fake and he doesn't like anybody around who knows!

LINDA: Why a fake? In what way? What do you mean?

BIFF: Just don't lay it all at my feet. It's between me and him—that's all I have to say. I'll chip in from now on. He'll settle for half my pay check. He'll be all right. I'm going to bed. *He starts for the stairs.*

LINDA: He won't be all right.

BIFF, *turning on the stairs, furiously:* I hate this city and I'll stay here. Now what do you want?

LINDA: He's dying, Biff.

Happy turns quickly to her, shocked.

BIFF, *after a pause:* Why is he dying?

LINDA: He's been trying to kill himself.

BIFF, *with great horror:* How?

LINDA: I live from day to day.

BIFF: What're you talking about?

LINDA: Remember I wrote you that he smashed up the car again? In February?

BIFF: Well?

LINDA: The insurance inspector came. He said that they have evidence. That all these accidents in the last year—weren't—weren't—accidents.

HAPPY: How can they tell that? That's a lie.

LINDA: It seems there's a woman . . . *She takes a breath as*

{ BIFF, *sharply but contained:* What woman?
{ LINDA, *simultaneously:* . . . and this woman . . .

LINDA: What?

BIFF: Nothing. Go ahead.

LINDA: What did you say?

BIFF: Nothing. I just said what woman?

HAPPY: What about her?

LINDA: Well, it seems she was walking down the road and saw his car. She says that he wasn't driving fast at all, and that he didn't skid. She says he came to that little bridge, and then deliberately smashed into the railing, and it was only the shallowness of the water that saved him.

BIFF: Oh, no, he probably just fell asleep again.

LINDA: I don't think he fell asleep.

BIFF: Why not?

LINDA: Last month . . . *With great difficulty:* Oh, boys, it's so hard to say a thing like this! He's just a big stupid man to you, but I tell you there's more good in him than in many other people. *She chokes, wipes her eyes.* I was looking for a fuse. The lights blew out, and I went down the cellar. And behind the fuse box—it happened to fall out—was a length of rubber pipe—just short.

HAPPY: No kidding?

LINDA: There's a little attachment on the end of it. I knew right away. And sure enough, on the bottom of the water heater there's a new little nipple on the gas pipe.

HAPPY, *angrily:* That—jerk.

BIFF: Did you have it taken off?

LINDA: I'm—I'm ashamed to. How can I mention it to him? Every day I go down and take away that little rubber pipe. But, when he comes home, I put it back where it was. How can I insult him that way? I don't know what to do. I live from day to day, boys. I tell you, I know every thought in his mind. It sounds so old-fashioned and silly, but I tell you he put his whole life into you and you've turned your backs on him. *She is bent over in the chair, weeping, her face in her hands.* Biff, I swear to God! Biff, his life is in your hands!

HAPPY, *to Biff:* How do you like that damned fool!

BIFF, *kissing her:* All right, pal, all right. It's all settled now. I've been remiss. I know that, Mom. But now I'll stay, and I swear to you, I'll apply myself. *Kneeling in front of her, in a fever of self-reproach:* It's just—you see, Mom, I don't fit in business. Not that I won't try. I'll try, and I'll make good.

HAPPY: Sure you will. The trouble with you in business was you never tried to please people.

BIFF: I know, I—

HAPPY: Like when you worked for Harrison's. Bob Harrison said you were tops, and then you go and do some damn fool thing like whistling whole songs in the elevator like a comedian.

BIFF, *against Happy:* So what? I like to whistle sometimes.

HAPPY: You don't raise a guy to a responsible job who whistles in the elevator!

LINDA: Well, don't argue about it now.

HAPPY: Like when you'd go off and swim in the middle of the day instead of taking the line around.

BIFF, *his resentment rising:* Well, don't you run off? You take off sometimes, don't you? On a nice summer day?

HAPPY: Yeah, but I cover myself!

LINDA: Boys!

HAPPY: If I'm going to take a fade the boss can call any number where I'm supposed to be and they'll swear to him that I just left. I'll tell you something that I hate to say, Biff, but in the business world some of them think you're crazy.

BIFF, *angered:* Screw the business world!

HAPPY: All right, screw it! Great, but cover yourself!

LINDA: Hap, Hap!

BIFF: I don't care what they think! They've laughed at Dad for years, and you know why? Because we don't belong in this nuthouse of a city! We should be mixing cement on some open plain, or—or carpenters. A carpenter is allowed to whistle!

Willy walks in from the entrance of the house, at left.

WILLY: Even your grandfather was better than a carpenter. *Pause. They watch him.* You never grew up. Bernard does not whistle in the elevator, I assure you.

BIFF, *as though to laugh Willy out of it:* Yeah, but you do, Pop.

WILLY: I never in my life whistled in an elevator! And who in the business world thinks I'm crazy?

BIFF: I didn't mean it like that, Pop. Now don't make a whole thing out of it, will ya?

WILLY: Go back to the West! Be a carpenter, a cowboy, enjoy yourself!

LINDA: Willy, he was just saying—

WILLY: I heard what he said!

HAPPY, *trying to quiet Willy:* Hey, Pop, come on now . . .

WILLY, *continuing over Happy's line:* They laugh at me, heh? Go to Filene's, go to the Hub, go to Slattery's, Boston. Call out the name Willy Loman and see what happens! Big shot!

BIFF: All right, Pop.

WILLY: Big!

BIFF: All right!

WILLY: Why do you always insult me?

BIFF: I didn't say a word. *To Linda:* Did I say a word?

LINDA: He didn't say anything, Willy.

WILLY, *going to the doorway of the living-room:* All right, good night, good night.

LINDA: Willy, dear, he just decided . . .

WILLY, *to Biff:* If you get tired hanging around tomorrow, paint the ceiling I put up in the living-room.

BIFF: I'm leaving early tomorrow.

HAPPY: He's going to see Bill Oliver, Pop.

WILLY, *interestedly:* Oliver? For what?

BIFF, *with reserve, but trying, trying:* He always said he'd stake me. I'd like to go into business, so maybe I can take him up on it.

LINDA: Isn't that wonderful?

WILLY: Don't interrupt. What's wonderful about it? There's fifty men in the City of New York who'd stake him. *To Biff:* Sporting goods?

BIFF: I guess so. I know something about it and—

WILLY: He knows something about it! You know sporting goods better than Spalding, for God's sake! How much is he giving you?

BIFF: I don't know, I didn't even see him yet, but—

WILLY: Then what're you talkin' about?

BIFF, *getting angry:* Well, all I said was I'm gonna see him, that's all!

WILLY, *turning away:* Ah, you're counting your chickens again.

BIFF, *starting left for the stairs:* Oh, Jesus, I'm going to sleep!

WILLY, *calling after him:* Don't curse in this house!

BIFF, *turning:* Since when did you get so clean?

HAPPY, *trying to stop them:* Wait a . . .

WILLY: Don't use that language to me! I won't have it!

HAPPY, *grabbing Biff, shouts:* Wait a minute! I got an idea. I got a feasible idea. Come here, Biff, let's talk this over now, let's talk some sense here. When I was down in Florida last time, I thought of a great idea to sell sporting goods. It just came back to me. You and I, Biff—we have a line, the Loman Line. We train a couple of weeks, and put on a couple of exhibitions, see?

WILLY: That's an idea!

HAPPY: Wait! We form two basketball teams, see? Two water-polo teams. We play each other. It's a million dollars' worth of publicity. Two brothers, see? The Loman Brothers. Displays in the Royal Palms—all the hotels. And banners over the ring and the basketball court: "Loman Brothers." Baby, we could sell sporting goods!

WILLY: That is a one-million-dollar idea!

LINDA: Marvelous!

BIFF: I'm in great shape as far as that's concerned.

HAPPY: And the beauty of it is, Biff, it wouldn't be like a business. We'd be out playin' ball again . . .

BIFF, *enthused:* Yeah, that's . . .

WILLY: Million-dollar . . .

HAPPY: And you wouldn't get fed up with it, Biff. It'd be the family again. There'd be the old honor, and comradeship, and if you wanted to go off for a swim or somethin'—well, you'd do it! Without some smart cooky gettin' up ahead of you!

WILLY: Lick the world! You guys together could absolutely lick the civilized world.

BIFF: I'll see Oliver tomorrow. Hap, if we could work that out . . .

LINDA: Maybe things are beginning to—

WILLY, *wildly enthused, to Linda:* Stop interrupting! *To Biff:* But don't wear sport jacket and slacks when you see Oliver.

BIFF: No, I'll—

WILLY: A business suit, and talk as little as possible, and don't crack any jokes.

BIFF: He did like me. Always liked me.

LINDA: He loved you!

WILLY, *to Linda:* Will you stop! *To Biff:* Walk in very serious. You are not applying for a boy's job. Money is to pass. Be quiet, fine, and serious. Everybody likes a kidder, but nobody lends him money.

HAPPY: I'll try to get some myself, Biff. I'm sure I can.

WILLY: I see great things for you kids, I think your troubles are over. But remember, start big and you'll end big. Ask for fifteen. How much you gonna ask for?

BIFF: Gee, I don't know—

WILLY: And don't say "Gee." "Gee" is a boy's word. A man walking in for fifteen thousand dollars does not say "Gee!"

BIFF: Ten, I think, would be top though.

WILLY: Don't be so modest. You always started too low. Walk in with a big laugh. Don't look worried. Start off with a couple of your good stories to lighten things up. It's not what you say, it's how you say it—because personality always wins the day.

LINDA: Oliver always thought the highest of him—

WILLY: Will you let me talk?

BIFF: Don't yell at her, Pop, will ya?

WILLY, *angrily:* I was talking, wasn't I?

BIFF: I don't like you yelling at her all the time, and I'm tellin' you, that's all.

WILLY: What're you, takin' over this house?

LINDA: Willy—

WILLY, *turning on her:* Don't take his side all the time, goddammit!

BIFF, *furiously:* Stop yelling at her!

WILLY, *suddenly pulling on his cheek, beaten down, guilt ridden:* Give my best to Bill Oliver—he may remember me. *He exits through the living-room doorway.*

LINDA, *her voice subdued:* What'd you have to start that for? *Biff turns away.* You see how sweet he was as soon as you talked hopefully? *She goes over to Biff.* Come up and say good night to him. Don't let him go to bed that way.

HAPPY: Come on, Biff, let's buck him up.

LINDA: Please, dear. Just say good night. It takes so little to make him happy. Come. *She goes through the living-room doorway, calling upstairs from within the living-room:* Your pajamas are hanging in the bathroom, Willy!

HAPPY, *looking toward where Linda went out:* What a woman! They broke the mold when they made her. You know that, Biff?

BIFF: He's off salary. My God, working on commission!

HAPPY: Well, let's face it: he's no hot-shot selling man. Except that sometimes, you have to admit, he's a sweet personality.

BIFF, *deciding:* Lend me ten bucks, will ya? I want to buy some new ties.

HAPPY: I'll take you to a place I know. Beautiful stuff. Wear one of my striped shirts tomorrow.

BIFF: She got gray. Mom got awful old. Gee, I'm gonna go in to Oliver tomorrow and knock him for a—

HAPPY: Come on up. Tell that to Dad. Let's give him a whirl. Come on.

BIFF, *steamed up:* You know, with ten thousand bucks, boy!

HAPPY, *as they go into the living-room:* That's the talk, Biff, that's the first time I've heard the old confidence out of you! *From within the living-room, fading off:* You're gonna live with me, kid, and any babe you want just say the word . . . *The last lines are hardly heard. They are mounting the stairs to their parents' bedroom.*

LINDA, *entering her bedroom and addressing Willy, who is in the bathroom. She is straightening the bed for him:* Can you do anything about the shower? It drips.

WILLY, *from the bathroom:* All of a sudden everything falls to pieces! Goddam plumbing, oughta be sued, those people. I hardly finished putting it in and the thing . . . *His words rumble off.*

LINDA: I'm just wondering if Oliver will remember him. You think he might?

WILLY, *coming out of the bathroom in his pajamas:* Remember him? What's the matter with you, you crazy? If he'd've stayed with Oliver he'd be on top by now! Wait'll Oliver gets a look at him. You don't know the average caliber any more. The average young man today—*he is getting into bed*—is got a caliber of zero. Greatest thing in the world for him was to bum around.

Biff and Happy enter the bedroom. Slight pause.

WILLY, *stops short, looking at Biff:* Glad to hear it, boy.

HAPPY: He wanted to say good night to you, sport.

WILLY, *to Biff:* Yeah. Knock him dead, boy. What'd you want to tell me?

BIFF: Just take it easy, Pop. Good night. *He turns to go.*

WILLY, *unable to resist:* And if anything falls off the desk while you're talking to him—like a package or something—don't you pick it up. They have office boys for that.

LINDA: I'll make a big breakfast—

WILLY: Will you let me finish? *To Biff:* Tell him you were in the business in the West. Not farm work.

BIFF: All right, Dad.

LINDA: I think everything—

WILLY, *going right through her speech:* And don't undersell yourself. No less than fifteen thousand dollars.

BIFF, *unable to bear him:* Okay. Good night, Mom. *He starts moving.*

WILLY: Because you got a greatness in you, Biff, remember that. You got all kinds a greatness . . . *He lies back, exhausted. Biff walks out.*

LINDA, *calling after Biff:* Sleep well, darling!

HAPPY: I'm gonna get married, Mom. I wanted to tell you.

LINDA: Go to sleep, dear.

HAPPY, *going:* I just wanted to tell you.

WILLY: Keep up the good work. *Happy exits.* God . . . remember that Ebbets Field game? The championship of the city?

LINDA: Just rest. Should I sing to you?

WILLY: Yeah. Sing to me. *Linda hums a soft lullaby.* When that team came out —he was the tallest, remember?

LINDA: Oh, yes. And in gold.

Biff enters the darkened kitchen, takes a cigarette, and leaves the house. He comes downstage into a golden pool of light. He smokes, staring at the night.

WILLY: Like a young god. Hercules—something like that. And the sun, the sun all around him. Remember how he waved to me? Right up from the field, with the representatives of three colleges standing by? And the buyers I brought, and the cheers when he came out—Loman, Loman, Loman! God Almighty, he'll be great yet. A star like that, magnificent, can never really fade away!

The light on Willy is fading. The gas heater begins to glow through the kitchen wall, near the stairs, a blue flame beneath red coils.

LINDA, *timidly:* Willy, dear, what has he got against you?

WILLY: I'm so tired. Don't talk any more.

Biff slowly returns to the kitchen. He stops, stares toward the heater.

LINDA: Will you ask Howard to let you work in New York?

WILLY: First thing in the morning. Everything'll be all right.

Biff reaches behind the heater and draws out a length of rubber tubing. He is horrified and turns his head toward Willy's room, still dimly lit, from which the strains of Linda's desperate but monotonous humming rise.

WILLY, *staring through the window into the moonlight:* Gee, look at the moon moving between the buildings!

Biff wraps the tubing around his hand and quickly goes up the stairs.

CURTAIN

Act Two

Music is heard, gay and bright. The curtain rises as the music fades away. Willy, in shirt sleeves, is sitting at the kitchen table, sipping coffee, his hat in his lap. Linda is filling his cup when she can.

WILLY: Wonderful coffee. Meal in itself.

LINDA: Can I make you some eggs?

WILLY: No. Take a breath.

LINDA: You look so rested, dear.

WILLY: I slept like a dead one. First time in months. Imagine, sleeping till ten on a Tuesday morning. Boys left nice and early, heh?

LINDA: They were out of here by eight o'clock.

WILLY: Good work!

LINDA: It was so thrilling to see them leaving together. I can't get over the shaving lotion in this house!

WILLY, *smiling:* Mmm—

LINDA: Biff was very changed this morning. His whole attitude seemed to be hopeful. He couldn't wait to get downtown to see Oliver.

WILLY: He's heading for a change. There's no question, there simply are certain men that take longer to get—solidified. How did he dress?

LINDA: His blue suit. He's so handsome in that suit. He could be a—anything in that suit!

Willy gets up from the table. Linda holds his jacket for him.

WILLY: There's no question, no question at all. Gee, on the way home tonight I'd like to buy some seeds.

LINDA, *laughing:* That'd be wonderful. But not enough sun gets back there. Nothing'll grow any more.

WILLY: You wait, kid, before it's all over we're gonna get a little place out in the country, and I'll raise some vegetables, a couple of chickens . . .

LINDA: You'll do it yet, dear.

Willy walks out of his jacket. Linda follows him.

WILLY: And they'll get married, and come for a weekend. I'd build a little guest house. 'Cause I got so many fine tools, all I'd need would be a little lumber and some peace of mind.

LINDA, *joyfully:* I sewed the lining . . .

WILLY: I could build two guest houses, so they'd both come. Did he decide how much he's going to ask Oliver for?

LINDA, *getting him into the jacket:* He didn't mention it, but I imagine ten or fifteen thousand. You going to talk to Howard today?

WILLY: Yeah. I'll put it to him straight and simple. He'll just have to take me off the road.

LINDA: And Willy, don't forget to ask for a little advance, because we've got the insurance premium. It's the grace period now.

WILLY: That's a hundred . . . ?

LINDA: A hundred and eight, sixty-eight. Because we're a little short again.

WILLY: Why are we short?

LINDA: Well, you had the motor job on the car . . .

WILLY: That goddam Studebaker!

LINDA: And you got one more payment on the refrigerator . . .

WILLY: But it just broke again!

LINDA: Well, it's old, dear.

WILLY: I told you we should've bought a well-advertised machine. Charley bought a General Electric and it's twenty years old and it's still good, that son-of-a-bitch.

LINDA: But, Willy—

WILLY: Whoever heard of a Hastings refrigerator? Once in my life I would like to own something outright before it's broken! I'm always in a race with the junkyard! I just finished paying for the car and it's on its last legs. The refrigerator consumes belts like a goddam maniac. They time those things. They time them so when you finally paid for them, they're used up.

LINDA, *buttoning up his jacket as he unbuttons it:* All told, about two hundred dollars would carry us, dear. But that includes the last payment on the mortgage. After this payment, Willy, the house belongs to us.

WILLY: It's twenty-five years!

LINDA: Biff was nine years old when we bought it.

WILLY: Well, that's a great thing. To weather a twenty-five year mortgage is—

LINDA: It's an accomplishment.

WILLY: All the cement, the lumber, the reconstruction I put in this house! There ain't a crack to be found in it any more.

LINDA: Well, it served its purpose.

WILLY: What purpose? Some stranger'll come along, move in, and that's that. If only Biff would take this house, and raise a family . . . *He starts to go.* Good-by, I'm late.

LINDA, *suddenly remembering:* Oh, I forgot! You're supposed to meet them for dinner.

WILLY: Me?

LINDA: At Frank's Chop House on Forty-eighth near Sixth Avenue.

WILLY: Is that so! How about you?

LINDA: No, just the three of you. They're gonna blow you to a big meal!

WILLY: Don't say! Who thought of that?

LINDA: Biff came to me this morning, Willy, and he said, "Tell Dad, we want to blow him to a big meal." Be there six o'clock. You and your two boys are going to have dinner.

WILLY: Gee whiz! That's really somethin'. I'm gonna knock Howard for a loop, kid. I'll get an advance, and I'll come home with a New York job. Goddammit, now I'm gonna do it!

LINDA: Oh, that's the spirit, Willy!

WILLY: I will never get behind a wheel the rest of my life!

LINDA: It's changing, Willy, I can feel it changing!

WILLY: Beyond a question. G'by, I'm late. *He starts to go again.*

LINDA, *calling after him as she runs to the kitchen table for a handkerchief:* You got your glasses?

WILLY, *feels for them, then comes back in:* Yeah, yeah, got my glasses.

LINDA, *giving him the handkerchief:* And a handkerchief.

WILLY: Yeah, handkerchief.

LINDA: And your saccharine?

WILLY: Yeah, my saccharine.

LINDA: Be careful on the subway stairs.

She kisses him, and a silk stocking is seen hanging from her hand. Willy notices it.

WILLY: Will you stop mending stockings? At least while I'm in the house. It gets me nervous. I can't tell you. Please.

Linda hides the stocking in her hand as she follows Willy across the forestage in front of the house.

LINDA: Remember, Frank's Chop House.

WILLY, *passing the apron:* Maybe beets would grow out there.

LINDA, *laughing:* But you tried so many times.

WILLY: Yeah. Well, don't work hard today. *He disappears around the right corner of the house.*

LINDA: Be careful!

As Willy vanishes, Linda waves to him. Suddenly the phone rings. She runs across the stage and into the kitchen and lifts it.

LINDA: Hello? Oh, Biff! I'm so glad you called, I just . . . Yes, sure, I just told him. Yes, he'll be there for dinner at six o'clock, I didn't forget. Listen, I was just dying to tell you. You know that little rubber pipe I told you about? That he connected to the gas heater? I finally decided to go down the cellar this morning and take it away and destroy it. But it's gone! Imagine! He took it away himself, it isn't there! *She listens.* When? Oh, then you took it. Oh—nothing, it's just that I'd hoped he'd taken it away himself. Oh, I'm not worried, darling, because this morning he left in such high spirits, it was like the old days! I'm not afraid any more. Did Mr. Oliver see you? . . . Well, you wait there then. And make a nice impression on him, darling. Just don't perspire too much before you see him. And have a nice time with Dad.

He may have big news too! . . . That's right, a New York job. And be sweet to him tonight, dear. Be loving to him. Because he's only a little boat looking for a harbor. *She is trembling with sorrow and joy.* Oh, that's wonderful, Biff, you'll save his life. Thanks, darling. Just put your arm around him when he comes into the restaurant. Give him a smile. That's the boy . . . Good-by, dear. . . . You got your comb? . . . That's fine. Good-by, Biff dear.

In the middle of her speech, Howard Wagner, thirty-six, wheels on a small typewriter table on which is a wire-recording machine and proceeds to plug it in. This is on the left forestage. Light slowly fades on Linda as it rises on Howard. Howard is intent on threading the machine and only glances over his shoulder as Willy appears.

WILLY: Pst! Pst!

HOWARD: Hello, Willy, come in.

WILLY: Like to have a little talk with you, Howard.

HOWARD: Sorry to keep you waiting. I'll be with you in a minute.

WILLY: What's that, Howard?

HOWARD: Didn't you ever see one of these? Wire recorder.

WILLY: Oh. Can we talk a minute?

HOWARD: Records things. Just got delivery yesterday. Been driving me crazy, the most terrific machine I ever saw in my life. I was up all night with it.

WILLY: What do you do with it?

HOWARD: I bought it for dictation, but you can do anything with it. Listen to this. I had it home last night. Listen to what I picked up. The first one is my daughter. Get this. *He flicks the switch and "Roll out the Barrel" is heard being whistled.* Listen to that kid whistle.

WILLY: That is lifelike, isn't it?

HOWARD: Seven years old. Get that tone.

WILLY: Ts, ts. Like to ask a little favor if you . . .

The whistling breaks off, and the voice of Howard's daughter is heard.

HIS DAUGHTER: "Now you, Daddy."

HOWARD: She's crazy for me! *Again the same song is whistled.* That's me! Ha! *He winks.*

WILLY: You're very good!

The whistling breaks off again. The machine runs silent for a moment.

HOWARD: Sh! Get this now, this is my son.

HIS SON: "The capital of Alabama is Montgomery; the capital of Arizona is Phoenix; the capital of Arkansas is Little Rock; the capital of California is Sacramento . . ." *and on, and on.*

HOWARD, *holding up five fingers:* Five years old, Willy!

WILLY: He'll make an announcer some day!

HIS SON, *continuing:* "The capital . . ."

HOWARD: Get that—alphabetical order! *The machine breaks off suddenly.* Wait a minute. The maid kicked the plug out.

WILLY: It certainly is a—

HOWARD: Sh, for God's sake!

HIS SON: "It's nine o'clock, Bulova watch time. So I have to go to sleep."

WILLY: That really is—

HOWARD: Wait a minute! The next is my wife.

They wait.

HOWARD'S VOICE: "Go on, say something." *Pause.* "Well, you gonna talk?"

HIS WIFE: "I can't think of anything."

HOWARD'S VOICE: "Well, talk—it's turning."

HIS WIFE, *shyly, beaten:* "Hello." *Silence.* "Oh, Howard, I can't talk into this . . ."

HOWARD, *snapping the machine off:* That was my wife.

WILLY: That is a wonderful machine. Can we—

HOWARD: I tell you, Willy, I'm gonna take my camera, and my bandsaw, and all my hobbies, and out they go. This is the most fascinating relaxation I ever found.

WILLY: I think I'll get one myself.

HOWARD: Sure, they're only a hundred and a half. You can't do without it. Supposing you wanna hear Jack Benny, see? But you can't be at home at that hour. So you tell the maid to turn the radio on when Jack Benny comes on, and this automatically goes on with the radio . . .

WILLY: And when you come home you . . .

HOWARD: You can come home twelve o'clock, one o'clock, any time you like, and you get yourself a Coke and sit yourself down, throw the switch, and there's Jack Benny's program in the middle of the night!

WILLY: I'm definitely going to get one. Because lots of time I'm on the road, and I think to myself, what I must be missing on the radio!

HOWARD: Don't you have a radio in the car?

WILLY: Well, yeah, but who ever thinks of turning it on?

HOWARD: Say, aren't you supposed to be in Boston?

WILLY: That's what I want to talk to you about, Howard. You got a minute? *He draws a chair in from the wing.*

HOWARD: What happened? What're you doing here?

WILLY: Well . . .

HOWARD: You didn't crack up again, did you?

WILLY: Oh, no. No . . .

HOWARD: Geez, you had me worried there for a minute. What's the trouble?

WILLY: Well, tell you the truth, Howard. I've come to the decision that I'd rather not travel any more.

HOWARD: Not travel! Well, what'll you do?

WILLY: Remember, Christmas time, when you had the party here? You said you'd try to think of some spot for me here in town.

HOWARD: With us?

WILLY: Well, sure.

HOWARD: Oh, yeah, yeah. I remember. Well, I couldn't think of anything for you, Willy.

WILLY: I tell ya, Howard. The kids are all grown up, y'know. I don't need much any more. If I could take home—well, sixty-five dollars a week. I could swing it.

HOWARD: Yeah, but Willy, see I—

WILLY: I tell ya why, Howard. Speaking frankly and between the two of us, y'know—I'm just a little tired.

HOWARD: Oh, I could understand that, Willy. But you're a road man, Willy, and we do a road business. We've only got a half-dozen salesmen on the floor here.

WILLY: God knows, Howard, I never asked a favor of any man. But I was with the firm when your father used to carry you in here in his arms.

HOWARD: I know that, Willy, but—

WILLY: Your father came to me the day you were born and asked me what I thought of the name of Howard, may he rest in peace.

HOWARD: I appreciate that, Willy, but there just is no spot here for you. If I had a spot I'd slam you right in, but I just don't have a single solitary spot.

He looks for his lighter. Willy has picked it up and gives it to him. Pause.

WILLY, *with increasing anger:* Howard, all I need to set my table is fifty dollars a week.

HOWARD: But where am I going to put you, kid?

WILLY: Look, it isn't a question of whether I can sell merchandise, is it?

HOWARD: No, but it's a business, kid, and everybody's gotta pull his own weight.

WILLY, *desperately:* Just let me tell you a story, Howard—

HOWARD: 'Cause you gotta admit, business is business.

WILLY, *angrily:* Business is definitely business, but just listen for a minute. You don't understand this. When I was a boy—eighteen, nineteen—I was already on the road. And there was a question in my mind as to whether selling had a future for me. Because in those days I had a yearning to go to Alaska. See, there were three gold strikes in one month in Alaska, and I felt like going out. Just for the ride, you might say.

HOWARD, *barely interested:* Don't say.

WILLY: Oh, yeah, my father lived many years in Alaska. He was an adventurous man. We've got quite a little streak of self-reliance in our family. I thought I'd go out with my older brother and try to locate him, and maybe settle in the North with the old man. And I was almost decided to go, when I met a salesman in the Parker House. His name was Dave Singleman. And he was eighty-four years old, and he'd drummed merchandise in thirty-one states. And old Dave, he'd go up to his room, y'understand, put on his green velvet slippers—I'll never forget—and pick up his phone and call the buyers, and without ever leaving his room, at the age of eighty-four, he made his living. And when I saw that, I realized that selling was the greatest career a man could want. 'Cause what could be more satisfying than to be able to go, at the age of eighty-four, into twenty or thirty different cities, and pick up a phone, and be remembered and loved and helped by so many different people? Do you know? When he died—and by the way he died the death of a salesman, in his green velvet slippers in the smoker of the New York, New Haven, and Hartford, going into Boston—when he died, hundreds of salesmen and buyers were at his funeral. Things were sad on a lotta trains for months after that. *He stands up. Howard has not looked at him.* In those days there was personality in it, Howard. There was respect, and comradeship, and gratitude, in it. Today, it's all cut and dried, and there's no chance for bringing friendship to bear—or personality. You see what I mean? They don't know me any more.

HOWARD, *moving away, toward the right:* That's just the thing, Willy.

WILLY: If I had forty dollars a week—that's all I'd need. Forty dollars, Howard.

HOWARD: Kid, I can't take blood from a stone, I—

WILLY, *desperation is on him now:* Howard, the year Al Smith[5] was nominated, your father came to me and—

HOWARD, *starting to go off:* I've got to see some people, kid.

5. Alfred E. Smith (1873–1944), Democratic candidate for president in 1928.

WILLY, *stopping him:* I'm talking about your father! There were promises made across this desk! You mustn't tell me you've got people to see—I put thirty-four years into this firm, Howard, and now I can't pay my insurance! You can't eat the orange and throw the peel away—a man is not a piece of fruit! *After a pause:* Now pay attention. Your father—in 1928 I had a big year. I averaged a hundred and seventy dollars a week in commissions.

HOWARD, *impatiently:* Now, Willy, you never averaged—

WILLY, *banging his hand on the desk:* I averaged a hundred and seventy dollars a week in the year of 1928! And your father came to me—or rather, I was in the office here—it was right over this desk—and he put his hand on my shoulder—

HOWARD, *getting up:* You'll have to excuse me, Willy, I gotta see some people. Pull yourself together. *Going out:* I'll be back in a little while.

On Howard's exit, the light on his chair grows very bright and strange.

WILLY: Pull myself together! What the hell did I say to him? My God, I was yelling at him! How could I? *Willy breaks off, staring at the light, which occupies the chair, animating it. He approaches this chair, standing across the desk from it.* Frank, Frank, don't you remember what you told me that time? How you put your hand on my shoulder, and Frank . . . *He leans on the desk and as he speaks the dead man's name he accidentally switches on the recorder, and instantly*

HOWARD'S SON: ". . . of New York is Albany. The capital of Ohio is Cincinnati, the capital of Rhode Island is . . ." *The recitation continues.*

WILLY, *leaping away with fright, shouting:* Ha! Howard! Howard! Howard!

HOWARD, *rushing in:* What happened?

WILLY, *pointing at the machine, which continues nasally, childishly, with the capital cities:* Shut it off! Shut it off!

HOWARD, *pulling the plug out:* Look, Willy . . .

WILLY, *pressing his hands to his eyes:* I gotta get myself some coffee. I'll get some coffee . . .

Willy starts to walk out. Howard stops him.

HOWARD, *rolling up the cord:* Willy, look . . .

WILLY: I'll go to Boston.

HOWARD: Willy, you can't go to Boston for us.

WILLY: Why can't I go?

HOWARD: I don't want you to represent us. I've been meaning to tell you for a long time now.

WILLY: Howard, are you firing me?

HOWARD: I think you need a good long rest, Willy.

WILLY: Howard—

HOWARD: And when you feel better, come back, and we'll see if we can work something out.

WILLY: But I gotta earn money, Howard. I'm in no position to—

HOWARD: Where are your sons? Why don't your sons give you a hand?

WILLY: They're working on a very big deal.

HOWARD: This is no time for false pride, Willy. You go to your sons and you tell them that you're tired. You've got two great boys haven't you?

WILLY: Oh, no question, no question, but in the meantime . . .

HOWARD: Then that's that, heh?

WILLY: All right, I'll go to Boston tomorrow.

HOWARD: No, no.

WILLY: I can't throw myself on my sons. I'm not a cripple!

HOWARD: Look, kid, I'm busy this morning.

WILLY, *grasping Howard's arm:* Howard, you've got to let me go to Boston!

HOWARD, *hard, keeping himself under control:* I've got a line of people to see this morning. Sit down, take five minutes, and pull yourself together, and then go home, will ya? I need the office, Willy. *He starts to go, turns, remembering the recorder, starts to push off the table holding the recorder.* Oh, yeah. Whenever you can this week, stop by and drop off the samples. You'll feel better, Willy, and then come back and we'll talk. Pull yourself together, kid, there's people outside.

Howard exits, pushing the table off left. Willy stares into space, exhausted. Now the music is heard—Ben's music—first distantly, then closer, closer. As Willy speaks, Ben enters from the right. He carries valise and umbrella.

WILLY: Oh, Ben, how did you do it? What is the answer? Did you wind up the Alaska deal already?

BEN: Doesn't take much time if you know what you're doing. Just a short business trip. Boarding ship in an hour. Wanted to say good-by.

WILLY: Ben, I've got to talk to you.

BEN, *glancing at his watch:* Haven't the time, William.

WILLY, *crossing the apron to Ben:* Ben, nothing's working out. I don't know what to do.

BEN: Now, look here, William. I've bought timberland in Alaska and I need a man to look after things for me.

WILLY: God, timberland! Me and my boys in those grand outdoors!

BEN: You've a new continent at your doorstep, William. Get out of these cities, they're full of talk and time payments and courts of law. Screw on your fists and you can fight for a fortune up there.

WILLY: Yes, yes! Linda, Linda!

Linda enters as of old, with the wash.

LINDA: Oh, you're back?

BEN: I haven't much time.

WILLY: No, wait! Linda, he's got a proposition for me in Alaska.

LINDA: But you've got—*To Ben:* He's got a beautiful job here.

WILLY: But in Alaska, kid, I could—

LINDA: You're doing well enough, Willy!

BEN, *to Linda:* Enough for what, my dear?

LINDA, *frightened of Ben and angry at him:* Don't say those things to him! Enough to be happy right here, right now. *To Willy, while Ben laughs:* Why must everybody conquer the world? You're well liked, and the boys love you, and someday—*To Ben* —why, old man Wagner told him just the other day that if he keeps it up he'll be a member of the firm, didn't he, Willy?

WILLY: Sure, sure. I am building something with this firm, Ben, and if a man is building something he must be on the right track, mustn't he?

BEN: What are you building? Lay your hand on it. Where is it?

WILLY, *hesitantly:* That's true, Linda, there's nothing.

LINDA: Why? *To Ben:* There's a man eighty-four years old—

WILLY: That's right, Ben, that's right. When I look at that man I say, what is there to worry about?

BEN: Bah!

WILLY: It's true, Ben. All he has to do is go into any city, pick up the phone, and he's making his living and you know why?

BEN, *picking up his valise:* I've got to go.

WILLY, *holding Ben back:* Look at this boy!

Biff, in his high school sweater, enters carrying suitcase. Happy carries Biff's shoulder guards, gold helmet, and football pants.

WILLY: Without a penny to his name, three great universities are begging for him, and from there the sky's the limit, because it's not what you do, Ben. It's who you know and the smile on your face! It's contacts, Ben, contacts! The whole wealth of Alaska passes over the lunch table at the Commodore Hotel, and that's the wonder, the wonder of this country, that a man can end with diamonds here on the basis of being liked! *He turns to Biff.* And that's why when you get out on that field today it's important. Because thousands of people will be rooting for you and loving you. *To Ben, who has again begun to leave:* And Ben! when he walks into a business office his name will sound out like a bell and all the doors will open to him! I've seen it, Ben, I've seen it a thousand times! You can't feel it with your hand like timber, but it's there!

BEN: Good-by, William.

WILLY: Ben, am I right? Don't you think I'm right? I value your advice.

BEN: There's a new continent at your doorstep, William. You could walk out rich. Rich! *He is gone.*

WILLY: We'll do it here, Ben! You hear me? We're gonna do it here!

Young Bernard rushes in. The gay music of the Boys is heard.

BERNARD: Oh, gee, I was afraid you left already!

WILLY: Why? What time is it?

BERNARD: It's half-past one!

WILLY: Well, come on, everybody! Ebbets Field next stop! Where's the pennants? *He rushes through the wall-line of the kitchen and out into the living-room.*

LINDA, *to Biff:* Did you pack fresh underwear?

BIFF, *who has been limbering up:* I want to go!

BERNARD: Biff, I'm carrying your helmet, ain't I?

HAPPY: No, I'm carrying the helmet.

BERNARD: Oh, Biff, you promised me.

HAPPY: I'm carrying the helmet.

BERNARD: How am I going to get in the locker room?

LINDA: Let him carry the shoulder guards. *She puts her coat and hat on in the kitchen.*

BERNARD: Can I, Biff? 'Cause I told everybody I'm going to be in the locker room.

HAPPY: In Ebbets Field it's the clubhouse.

BERNARD: I meant the clubhouse, Biff!

HAPPY: Biff!

BIFF, *grandly, after a slight pause:* Let him carry the shoulder guards.

HAPPY, *as he gives Bernard the shoulder guards:* Stay close to us now.

Willy rushes in with the pennants.

WILLY, *handing them out:* Everybody wave when Biff comes out on the field. *Happy and Bernard run off.* You set now, boy?

The music has died away.

BIFF: Ready to go, Pop. Every muscle is ready.

WILLY, *at the edge of the apron:* You realize what this means?

BIFF: That's right, Pop.

WILLY *feeling Biff's muscles:* You're comin' home this afternoon captain of the All-Scholastic Championship Team of the City of New York.

BIFF: I got it, Pop. And remember, pal, when I take off my helmet, that touchdown is for you.

WILLY: Let's go! *He is starting out, with his arm around Biff, when Charley enters, as of old, in knickers.* I got no room for you, Charley.

CHARLEY: Room? For what?

WILLY: In the car.

CHARLEY: You goin' for a ride? I wanted to shoot some casino.

WILLY, *furiously:* Casino! *Incredulously:* Don't you realize what today is?

LINDA: Oh, he knows, Willy. He's just kidding you.

WILLY: That's nothing to kid about!

CHARLEY: No, Linda, what's goin' on?

LINDA: He's playing in Ebbets Field.

CHARLEY: Baseball in this weather?

WILLY: Don't talk to him. Come on, come on! *He is pushing them out.*

CHARLEY: Wait a minute, didn't you hear the news?

WILLY: What?

CHARLEY: Don't you listen to the radio? Ebbets Field just blew up.

WILLY: You go to hell! *Charley laughs. Pushing them out:* Come on, come on! We're late.

CHARLEY, *as they go:* Knock a homer, Biff, knock a homer!

WILLY, *the last to leave, turning to Charley:* I don't think that was funny, Charley. This is the greatest day of his life.

CHARLEY: Willy, when are you going to grow up?

WILLY: Yeah, heh? When this game is over, Charley, you'll be laughing out of the other side of your face. They'll be calling him another Red Grange.[6] Twenty-five thousand a year.

CHARLEY, *kidding:* Is that so?

WILLY: Yeah, that's so.

CHARLEY: Well, then, I'm sorry, Willy. But tell me something.

WILLY: What?

CHARLEY: Who is Red Grange?

WILLY: Put up your hands. Goddam you, put up your hands!

Charley, chuckling, shakes his head and walks away, around the left corner of the stage. Willy follows him. The music rises to a mocking frenzy.

WILLY: Who the hell do you think you are, better than everybody else? You don't know everything, you big, ignorant, stupid . . . Put up your hands!

Light rises, on the right side of the forestage, on a small table in the reception room of Charley's office. Traffic sounds are heard. Bernard, now mature, sits whistling to himself. A pair of tennis rackets and an overnight bag are on the floor beside him.

WILLY, *offstage:* What are you walking away for? Don't walk away! If you're going

6. Harold Edward Grange, All-American football player at the University of Illinois, 1923–1925.

to say something say it to my face! I know you laugh at me behind my back. You'll laugh out of the other side of your goddam face after this game. Touchdown! Touchdown! Eighty thousand people! Touchdown! Right between the goal posts.

Bernard is a quiet, earnest, but self-assured young man. Willy's voice is coming from right upstage now. Bernard lowers his feet off the table and listens. Jenny, his father's secretary, enters.

JENNY, *distressed:* Say, Bernard, will you go out in the hall?

BERNARD: What is that noise? Who is it?

JENNY: Mr. Loman. He just got off the elevator.

BERNARD, *getting up:* Who's he arguing with?

JENNY: Nobody. There's nobody with him. I can't deal with him any more, and your father gets all upset everytime he comes. I've got a lot of typing to do, and your father's waiting to sign it. Will you see him?

WILLY, *entering:* Touchdown! Touch— *He sees Jenny.* Jenny, Jenny, good to see you. How're ya? Workin'? Or still honest?

JENNY: Fine. How've you been feeling?

WILLY: Not much any more, Jenny. Ha, ha! *He is surprised to see the rackets.*

BERNARD: Hello, Uncle Willy.

WILLY, *almost shocked:* Bernard! Well, look who's here! *He comes quickly, guiltily, to Bernard and warmly shakes his hand.*

BERNARD: How are you? Good to see you.

WILLY: What are you doing here?

BERNARD: Oh, just stopped by to see Pop. Get off my feet till my train leaves. I'm going to Washington in a few minutes.

WILLY: Is he in?

BERNARD: Yes, he's in his office with the accountant. Sit down.

WILLY, *sitting down:* What're you going to do in Washington?

BERNARD: Oh, just a case I've got there, Willy.

WILLY: That so? *Indicating the rackets:* You going to play tennis there?

BERNARD: I'm staying with a friend who's got a court.

WILLY: Don't say. His own tennis court. Must be fine people, I bet.

BERNARD: They are, very nice. Dad tells me Biff's in town.

WILLY, *with a big smile:* Yeah, Biff's in. Working on a very big deal, Bernard.

BERNARD: What's Biff doing?

WILLY: Well, he's been doing very big things in the West. But he decided to establish himself here. Very big. We're having dinner. Did I hear your wife had a boy?

BERNARD: That's right. Our second.

WILLY: Two boys! What do you know!

BERNARD: What kind of a deal has Biff got?

WILLY: Well, Bill Oliver—very big sporting-goods man—he wants Biff very badly. Called him in from the West. Long distance, carte blanche, special deliveries. Your friends have their own private tennis court?

BERNARD: You still with the old firm, Willy?

WILLY, *after a pause:* I'm—I'm overjoyed to see how you made the grade, Bernard, overjoyed. It's an encouraging thing to see a young man really—really—Looks very good for Biff—very—*He breaks off, then:* Bernard—*He is so full of emotion, he breaks off again.*

BERNARD: What is it, Willy?

WILLY, *small and alone:* What—what's the secret?

BERNARD: What secret?

WILLY: How—how did you? Why didn't he ever catch on?

BERNARD: I wouldn't know that, Willy.

WILLY, *confidentially, desperately:* You were his friend, his boyhood friend. There's something I don't understand about it. His life ended after that Ebbets Field game. From the age of seventeen nothing good ever happened to him.

BERNARD: He never trained himself for anything.

WILLY: But he did, he did. After high school he took so many correspondence courses. Radio mechanics; television; God knows what, and never made the slightest mark.

BERNARD, *taking off his glasses:* Willy, do you want to talk candidly?

WILLY, *rising, faces Bernard:* I regard you as a very brilliant man, Bernard. I value your advice.

BERNARD: Oh, the hell with the advice, Willy. I couldn't advise you. There's just one thing I've always wanted to ask you. When he was supposed to graduate, and the math teacher flunked him—

WILLY: Oh, that son-of-a-bitch ruined his life.

BERNARD: Yeah, but, Willy, all he had to do was go to summer school and make up that subject.

WILLY: That's right, that's right.

BERNARD: Did you tell him not to go to summer school?

WILLY: Me? I begged him to go. I ordered him to go!

BERNARD: Then why wouldn't he go?

WILLY: Why? Why! Bernard, that question has been trailing me like a ghost for the last fifteen years. He flunked the subject, and laid down and died like a hammer hit him!

BERNARD: Take it easy, kid.

WILLY: Let me talk to you—I got nobody to talk to. Bernard, Bernard, was it my fault? Y'see? It keeps going around in my mind, maybe I did something to him. I got nothing to give him.

BERNARD: Don't take it so hard.

WILLY: Why did he lay down? What is the story there? You were his friend!

BERNARD: Willy, I remember, it was June, and our grades came out. And he'd flunked math.

WILLY: That son-of-a-bitch!

BERNARD: No, it wasn't right then. Biff just got very angry, I remember, and he was ready to enroll in summer school.

WILLY, *surprised:* He was?

BERNARD: He wasn't beaten by it at all. But then, Willy, he disappeared from the block for almost a month. And I got the idea that he'd gone up to New England to see you. Did he have a talk with you then?

Willy stares in silence.

BERNARD: Willy?

WILLY, *with a strong edge of resentment in his voice:* Yeah, he came to Boston. What about it?

BERNARD: Well, just that when he came back—I'll never forget this, it always mystifies me. Because I'd thought so well of Biff, even though he'd always taken advantage of me. I loved him, Willy, y'know? And he came back after that month and took his sneakers—remember those sneakers with "University of Virginia" printed on them? He was so proud of those, wore them every day. And he took them down in the cellar, and burned them up in the furnace. We had a fist fight. It lasted at least half an hour. Just the two of us, punching each other down the cellar, and crying right through it. I've often thought of how strange it was that I knew he'd given up his life. What happened in Boston, Willy?

Willy looks at him as at an intruder.

BERNARD: I just bring it up because you asked me.

WILLY, *angrily:* Nothing. What do you mean, "What happened?" What's that got to do with anything?

BERNARD: Well, don't get sore.

WILLY: What are you trying to do, blame it on me? If a boy lays down is that my fault?

BERNARD: Now, Willy, don't get—

WILLY: Well, don't—don't talk to me that way! What does that mean, "What happened?"

Charley enters. He is in his vest, and he carries a bottle of bourbon.

CHARLEY: Hey, you're going to miss that train. *He waves the bottle.*

BERNARD: Yeah, I'm going. *He takes the bottle.* Thanks, Pop. *He picks up his rackets and bag.* Good-by, Willy, and don't worry about it. You know, "If at first you don't succeed . . ."

WILLY: Yes, I believe in that.

BERNARD: But sometimes, Willy, it's better for a man just to walk away.

WILLY: Walk away?

BERNARD: That's right.

WILLY: But if you can't walk away?

BERNARD, *after a slight pause:* I guess that's when it's tough. *Extending his hand:* Good-by, Willy.

WILLY, *shaking Bernard's hand:* Good-by, boy.

CHARLEY, *an arm on Bernard's shoulder:* How do you like this kid? Gonna argue a case in front of the Supreme Court.

BERNARD, *protesting:* Pop!

WILLY, *genuinely shocked, pained, and happy:* No! The Supreme Court!

BERNARD: I gotta run. 'By, Dad!

CHARLEY: Knock 'em dead, Bernard!

Bernard goes off.

WILLY, *as Charley takes out his wallet:* The Supreme Court! And he didn't even mention it!

CHARLEY, *counting out money on the desk:* He don't have to—he's gonna do it.

WILLY: And you never told him what to do, did you? You never took any interest in him.

CHARLEY: My salvation is that I never took any interest in anything. There's some money—fifty dollars. I got an accountant inside.

WILLY: Charley, look . . . *With difficulty:* I got my insurance to pay. If you can manage it—I need a hundred and ten dollars.

Charley doesn't reply for a moment; merely stops moving.

WILLY: I'd draw it from my bank but Linda would know, and I . . .

CHARLEY: Sit down, Willy.

WILLY, *moving toward the chair:* I'm keeping an account of everything, remember. I'll pay every penny back. *He sits.*

CHARLEY: Now listen to me, Willy.

WILLY: I want you to know I appreciate . . .

CHARLEY, *sitting down on the table:* Willy, what're you doin'? What the hell is goin' on in your head?

WILLY: Why? I'm simply . . .

CHARLEY: I offered you a job. You can make fifty dollars a week. And I won't send you on the road.

WILLY: I've got a job.

CHARLEY: Without pay? What kind of a job is a job without pay? *He rises.* Now, look, kid, enough is enough. I'm no genius but I know when I'm being insulted.

WILLY: Insulted!

CHARLEY: Why don't you want to work for me?

WILLY: What's the matter with you? I've got a job.

CHARLEY: Then what're you walkin' in here every week for?

WILLY, *getting up:* Well, if you don't want me to walk in here—

CHARLEY: I am offering you a job.

WILLY: I don't want your goddam job!

CHARLEY: When the hell are you going to grow up?

WILLY, *furiously:* You big ignoramus, if you say that to me again I'll rap you one! I don't care how big you are! *He's ready to fight.*

Pause.

CHARLEY, *kindly, going to him:* How much do you need, Willy?

WILLY: Charley, I'm strapped, I'm strapped. I don't know what to do. I was just fired.

CHARLEY: Howard fired you?

WILLY: That snotnose. Imagine that? I named him. I named him Howard.

CHARLEY: Willy, when're you gonna realize that them things don't mean anything? You named him Howard, but you can't sell that. The only thing you got in this world is what you can sell. And the funny thing is that you're a salesman, and you don't know that.

WILLY: I've always tried to think otherwise, I guess. I always felt that if a man was impressive, and well liked, that nothing—

CHARLEY: Why must everybody like you? Who liked J. P. Morgan?[7] Was he impressive? In a Turkish bath he'd look like a butcher. But with his pockets on he was very well liked. Now listen, Willy, I know you don't like me, and nobody can say I'm in love with you, but I'll give you a job because—just for the hell of it, put it that way. Now what do you say?

WILLY: I—I just can't work for you, Charley.

CHARLEY: What're you, jealous of me?

WILLY: I can't work for you, that's all, don't ask me why.

CHARLEY, *angered, takes out more bills:* You been jealous of me all your life, you damned fool! Here, pay your insurance. *He puts the money in Willy's hand.*

7. J. P. Morgan, famous financier, died in 1943.

WILLY: I'm keeping strict accounts.

CHARLEY: I've got some work to do. Take care of yourself. And pay your insurance.

WILLY, *moving to the right:* Funny, y'know? After all the highways, and the trains, and the appointments, and the years, you end up worth more dead than alive.

CHARLEY: Willy, nobody's worth nothin' dead. *After a slight pause:* Did you hear what I said?

Willy stands still, dreaming.

CHARLEY: Willy!

WILLY: Apologize to Bernard for me when you see him. I didn't mean to argue with him. He's a fine boy. They're all fine boys, and they'll end up big—all of them. Someday they'll all play tennis together. Wish me luck, Charley. He saw Bill Oliver today.

CHARLEY: Good luck.

WILLY, *on the verge of tears:* Charley, you're the only friend I got. Isn't that a remarkable thing? *He goes out.*

CHARLEY: Jesus!

Charley stares after him a moment and follows. All light blacks out. Suddenly raucous music is heard, and a red glow rises behind the screen at right. Stanley, a young waiter, appears, carrying a table, followed by Happy, who is carrying two chairs.

STANLEY, *putting the table down:* That's all right, Mr. Loman, I can handle it myself. *He turns and takes the chairs from Happy and places them at the table.*

HAPPY, *glancing around:* Oh, this is better.

STANLEY: Sure, in the front there you're in the middle of all kinds a noise. Whenever you got a party, Mr. Loman, you just tell me and I'll put you back here. Y'know, there's a lotta people they don't like it private, because when they go out they like to see a lotta action around them because they're sick and tired to stay in the house by theirself. But I know you, you ain't from Hackensack. You know what I mean?

HAPPY, *sitting down:* So how's it coming, Stanley?

STANLEY: Ah, it's a dog's life. I only wish during the war they'd a took me in the Army. I coulda been dead by now.

HAPPY: My brother's back, Stanley.

STANLEY: Oh, he come back, heh? From the Far West.

HAPPY: Yeah, big cattle man, my brother, so treat him right. And my father's coming too.

STANLEY: Oh, your father too!

HAPPY: You got a couple of nice lobsters?

STANLEY: Hundred per cent, big.

HAPPY: I want them with the claws.

STANLEY: Don't worry, I don't give you no mice. *Happy laughs.* How about some wine? It'll put a head on the meal.

HAPPY: No. You remember, Stanley, that recipe I brought you from overseas? With the champagne in it?

STANLEY: Oh, yeah, sure. I still got it tacked up yet in the kitchen. But that'll have to cost a buck apiece anyways.

HAPPY: That's all right.

STANLEY: What'd you, hit a number or somethin'?

HAPPY: No, it's a little celebration. My brother is—I think he pulled off a big deal today. I think we're going into business together.

STANLEY: Great! That's the best for you. Because a family business, you know what I mean?—that's the best.

HAPPY: That's what I think.

STANLEY: 'Cause what's the difference? Somebody steals? It's in the family. Know what I mean? *Sotto voce:*[8] Like this bartender here. The boss is goin' crazy what kinda leak he's got in the cash register. You put it in but it don't come out.

HAPPY, *raising his head:* Sh!

STANLEY: What?

HAPPY: You notice I wasn't lookin' right or left, was I?

STANLEY: No.

HAPPY: And my eyes are closed.

STANLEY: So what's the—?

HAPPY: Strudel's comin'.

STANLEY, *catching on, looks around:* Ah, no, there's no—

He breaks off as a furred, lavishly dressed girl enters and sits at the next table. Both follow her with their eyes.

STANLEY: Geez, how'd ya know?

HAPPY: I got radar or something. *Staring directly at her profile:* Ooooooo . . . Stanley.

STANLEY: I think that's for you, Mr. Loman.

HAPPY: Look at that mouth. Oh, God. And the binoculars.

STANLEY: Geez, you got a life, Mr. Loman.

HAPPY: Wait on her.

STANLEY, *going to the Girl's table:* Would you like a menu, ma'am?

GIRL: I'm expecting someone, but I'd like a—

HAPPY: Why don't you bring her—excuse me, miss, do you mind? I sell champagne, and I'd like you to try my brand. Bring her a champagne, Stanley.

GIRL: That's awfully nice of you.

HAPPY: Don't mention it. It's all company money. *He laughs.*

GIRL: That's a charming product to be selling, isn't it?

HAPPY: Oh, gets to be like everything else. Selling is selling, y'know.

GIRL: I suppose.

HAPPY: You don't happen to sell, do you?

GIRL: No, I don't sell.

HAPPY: Would you object to a compliment from a stranger? You ought to be on a magazine cover.

GIRL, *looking at him a little archly:* I have been.

Stanley comes in with a glass of champagne.

HAPPY: What'd I say before, Stanley? You see? She's a cover girl.

STANLEY: Oh, I could see, I could see.

HAPPY, *to the Girl:* What magazine?

GIRL: Oh, a lot of them. *She takes the drink.* Thank you.

HAPPY: You know what they say in France, don't you? "Champagne is the drink of the complexion"—Hya, Biff!

8. Speaking in an undertone.

Biff has entered and sits with Happy.

BIFF: Hello, kid. Sorry I'm late.

HAPPY: I just got here. Uh, Miss—?

GIRL: Forsythe.

HAPPY: Miss Forsythe, this is my brother.

BIFF: Is Dad here?

HAPPY: His name is Biff. You might've heard of him. Great football player.

GIRL: Really? What team?

HAPPY: Are you familiar with football?

GIRL: No, I'm afraid I'm not.

HAPPY: Biff is quarterback with the New York Giants.

GIRL: Well, that is nice, isn't it? *She drinks.*

HAPPY: Good health.

GIRL: I'm happy to meet you.

HAPPY: That's my name. Hap. It's really Harold, but at West Point they called me Happy.

GIRL, *now really impressed:* Oh, I see. How do you do? *She turns her profile.*

BIFF: Isn't Dad coming?

HAPPY: You want her?

BIFF: Oh, I could never make that.

HAPPY: I remember the time that idea would never come into your head. Where's the old confidence, Biff?

BIFF: I just saw Oliver—

HAPPY: Wait a minute. I've got to see that old confidence again. Do you want her? She's on call.

BIFF: Oh, no. *He turns to look at the Girl.*

HAPPY: I'm telling you. *Watch this. Turning to the Girl:* Honey? *She turns to him.* Are you busy?

GIRL: Well, I am . . . but I could make a phone call.

HAPPY: Do that, will you, honey? And see if you can get a friend. We'll be here for a while. Biff is one of the greatest football players in the country.

GIRL, *standing up:* Well, I'm certainly happy to meet you.

HAPPY: Come back soon.

GIRL: I'll try.

HAPPY: Don't try, honey, try hard.

The Girl exits. Stanley follows, shaking his head in bewildered admiration.

HAPPY: Isn't that a shame now? A beautiful girl like that? That's why I can't get married. There's not a good woman in a thousand. New York is loaded with them, kid!

BIFF: Hap, look—

HAPPY: I told you she was on call!

BIFF, *strangely unnerved:* Cut it out, will ya? I want to say something to you.

HAPPY: Did you see Oliver?

BIFF: I saw him all right. Now look, I want to tell Dad a couple of things and I want you to help me.

HAPPY: What? Is he going to back you?

BIFF: Are you crazy? You're out of your goddam head, you know that?

HAPPY: Why? What happened?

BIFF, *breathlessly:* I did a terrible thing today, Hap. It's been the strangest day I ever went through. I'm all numb, I swear.

HAPPY: You mean he wouldn't see you?

BIFF: Well, I waited six hours for him, see? All day. Kept sending my name in. Even tried to date his secretary so she'd get me to him, but no soap.

HAPPY: Because you're not showin' the old confidence, Biff. He remembered you, didn't he?

BIFF, *stopping Happy with a gesture:* Finally, about five o'clock, he comes out. Didn't remember who I was or anything. I felt like such an idiot, Hap.

HAPPY: Did you tell him my Florida idea?

BIFF: He walked away. I saw him for one minute. I got so mad I could've torn the walls down! How the hell did I ever get the idea I was a salesman there? I even believed myself that I'd been a salesman for him! And then he gave me one look and—I realized what a ridiculous lie my whole life has been! We've been talking in a dream for fifteen years. I was a shipping clerk.

HAPPY: What'd you do?

BIFF, *with great tension and wonder:* Well, he left, see. And the secretary went out. I was all alone in the waiting-room. I don't know what came over me, Hap. The next thing I know I'm in his office—paneled walls, everything. I can't explain it. I —Hap, I took his fountain pen.

HAPPY: Geez, did he catch you?

BIFF: I ran out. I ran down all eleven flights. I ran and ran and ran.

HAPPY: That was an awful dumb—what'd you do that for?

BIFF, *agonized:* I don't know, I just—wanted to take something, I don't know. You gotta help me, Hap, I'm gonna tell Pop.

HAPPY: You crazy? What for?

BIFF: Hap, he's got to understand that I'm not the man somebody lends that kind of money to. He thinks I've been spiting him all these years and it's eating him up.

HAPPY: That's just it. You tell him something nice.

BIFF: I can't.

HAPPY: Say you got a lunch date with Oliver tomorrow.

BIFF: So what do I do tomorrow?

HAPPY: You leave the house tomorrow and come back at night and say Oliver is thinking it over. And he thinks it over for a couple of weeks, and gradually it fades away and nobody's the worse.

BIFF: But it'll go on forever!

HAPPY: Dad is never so happy as when he's looking forward to something!

Willy enters.

HAPPY: Hello, scout!

WILLY: Gee, I haven't been here in years!

Stanley has followed Willy in and sets a chair for him. Stanley starts off but Happy stops him.

HAPPY: Stanley!

Stanley stands by, waiting for an order.

BIFF, *going to Willy with guilt, as to an invalid:* Sit down, Pop. You want a drink?

WILLY: Sure, I don't mind.

BIFF: Let's get a load on.

WILLY: You look worried.

BIFF: N-no. *To Stanley:* Scotch all around. Make it doubles.

STANLEY: Doubles, right. *He goes.*

WILLY: You had a couple already, didn't you?

BIFF: Just a couple, yeah.

WILLY: Well, what happened, boy? *Nodding affirmatively, with a smile:* Everything go all right?

BIFF, *takes a breath, then reaches out and grasps Willy's hand:* Pal . . . *He is smiling bravely, and Willy is smiling too.* I had an experience today.

HAPPY: Terrific, Pop.

WILLY: That so? What happened?

BIFF, *high, slightly alcoholic, above the earth:* I'm going to tell you everything from first to last. It's been a strange day. *Silence. He looks around, composes himself as best he can, but his breath keeps breaking the rhythm of his voice.* I had to wait quite a while for him, and—

WILLY: Oliver?

BIFF: Yeah, Oliver. All day, as a matter of cold fact. And a lot of—instances—facts, Pop, facts about my life came back to me. Who was it, Pop? Who ever said I was a salesman with Oliver?

WILLY: Well, you were.

BIFF: No, Dad, I was a shipping clerk.

WILLY: But you were practically—

BIFF, *with determination:* Dad, I don't know who said it first, but I was never a salesman for Bill Oliver.

WILLY: What're you talking about?

BIFF: Let's hold on to the facts tonight, Pop. We're not going to get anywhere bullin' around. I was a shipping clerk.

WILLY, *angrily:* All right, now listen to me—

BIFF: Why don't you let me finish?

WILLY: I'm not interested in stories about the past or any crap of that kind because the woods are burning, boys, you understand? There's a big blaze going on all around. I was fired today.

BIFF, *shocked:* How could you be?

WILLY: I was fired, and I'm looking for a little good news to tell your mother, because the woman has waited and the woman has suffered. The gist of it is that I haven't got a story left in my head, Biff. So don't give me a lecture about facts and aspects. I am not interested. Now what've you got to say to me?

Stanley enters with three drinks. They wait until he leaves.

WILLY: Did you see Oliver?

BIFF: Jesus, Dad!

WILLY: You mean you didn't go up there?

HAPPY: Sure he went up there.

BIFF: I did. I—saw him. How could they fire you?

WILLY, *on the edge of his chair:* What kind of a welcome did he give you?

BIFF: He won't even let you work on commission?

WILLY: I'm out! *Driving:* So tell me, he gave you a warm welcome?

HAPPY: Sure, Pop, sure!

BIFF, *driven:* Well, it was kind of—

WILLY: I was wondering if he'd remember you. *To Happy:* Imagine, man doesn't see him for ten, twelve years and gives him that kind of a welcome!

HAPPY: Damn right!

BIFF, *trying to return to the offensive:* Pop, look—

WILLY: You know why he remembered you, don't you? Because you impressed him in those days.

BIFF: Let's talk quietly and get this down to the facts, huh?

WILLY, *as though Biff had been interrupting:* Well, what happened? It's great news, Biff. Did he take you into his office or'd you talk in the waiting-room?

BIFF: Well, he came in, see, and—

WILLY, *with a big smile:* What'd he say? Betcha he threw his arm around you.

BIFF: Well, he kinda—

WILLY: He's a fine man. *To Happy:* Very hard man to see, y'know.

HAPPY, *agreeing:* Oh, I know.

WILLY, *to Biff:* Is that where you had the drinks?

BIFF: Yeah, he gave me a couple of—no, no!

HAPPY, *cutting in:* He told him my Florida idea.

WILLY: Don't interrupt. *To Biff:* How'd he react to the Florida idea?

BIFF: Dad, will you give me a minute to explain?

WILLY: I've been waiting for you to explain since I sat down here! What happened? He took you into his office and what?

BIFF: Well—I talked. And—and he listened, see.

WILLY: Famous for the way he listens, y'know. What was his answer?

BIFF: His answer was— *He breaks off, suddenly angry.* Dad, you're not letting me tell you what I want to tell you!

WILLY, *accusing, angered:* You didn't see him, did you?

BIFF: I did see him!

WILLY: What'd you insult him or something? You insulted him, didn't you?

BIFF: Listen, will you let me out of it, will you just let me out of it!

HAPPY: What the hell!

WILLY: Tell me what happened!

BIFF, *to Happy:* I can't talk to him!

A single trumpet note jars the ear. The light of green leaves stains the house, which holds the air of night and a dream. Young Bernard enters and knocks on the door of the house.

YOUNG BERNARD, *frantically:* Mrs. Loman, Mrs. Loman!

HAPPY: Tell him what happened!

BIFF, *to Happy:* Shut up and leave me alone!

WILLY: No, no! You had to go and flunk math!

BIFF: What math? What're you talking about?

YOUNG BERNARD: Mrs. Loman, Mrs. Loman!

Linda appears in the house, as of old.

WILLY, *wildly:* Math, math, math!

BIFF: Take it easy, Pop!

YOUNG BERNARD: Mrs. Loman!

WILLY, *furiously:* If you hadn't flunked you'd've been set by now!

BIFF: Now, look, I'm gonna tell you what happened, and you're going to listen to me.

YOUNG BERNARD: Mrs. Loman!

BIFF: I waited six hours—

HAPPY: What the hell are you saying?

BIFF: I kept sending in my name but he wouldn't see me. So finally he . . . *He continues unheard as light fades low on the restaurant.*

YOUNG BERNARD: Biff flunked math!

LINDA: No!

YOUNG BERNARD: Birnbaum flunked him! They won't graduate him!

LINDA: But they have to. He's gotta go to the university. Where is he? Biff! Biff!

YOUNG BERNARD: No, he left. He went to Grand Central.

LINDA: Grand— You mean he went to Boston!

YOUNG BERNARD: Is Uncle Willy in Boston?

LINDA: Oh, maybe Willy can talk to the teacher. Oh, the poor, poor boy!

Light on house area snaps out.

BIFF, *at the table, now audible, holding up a gold fountain pen:* . . . so I'm washed up with Oliver, you understand? Are you listening to me?

WILLY, *at a loss:* Yeah, sure. If you hadn't flunked—

BIFF: Flunked what? What're you talking about?

WILLY: Don't blame everything on me! I didn't flunk math—you did! What pen?

HAPPY: That was awful dumb, Biff, a pen like that is worth—

WILLY, *seeing the pen for the first time:* You took Oliver's pen?

BIFF, *weakening:* Dad, I just explained it to you.

WILLY: You stole Bill Oliver's fountain pen!

BIFF: I didn't exactly steal it! That's just what I've been explaining to you!

HAPPY: He had it in his hand and just then Oliver walked in, so he got nervous and stuck it in his pocket!

WILLY: My God, Biff!

BIFF: I never intended to do it, Dad!

OPERATOR'S VOICE: Standish Arms, good evening!

WILLY, *shouting:* I'm not in my room!

BIFF, *frightened:* Dad, what's the matter? *He and Happy stand up.*

OPERATOR: Ringing Mr. Loman for you!

WILLY: I'm not there, stop it!

BIFF, *horrified, gets down on one knee before Willy:* Dad, I'll make good, I'll make good. *Willy tries to get to his feet. Biff holds him down.* Sit down now.

WILLY: No, you're no good, you're no good for anything.

BIFF: I am, Dad, I'll find something else, you understand? Now don't worry about anything. *He holds up Willy's face:* Talk to me, Dad.

OPERATOR: Mr. Loman does not answer. Shall I page him?

WILLY, *attempting to stand, as though to rush and silence the Operator:* No, no, no!

HAPPY: He'll strike something, Pop.

WILLY: No, no . . .

BIFF, *desperately, standing over Willy:* Pop, listen! Listen to me! I'm telling you something good. Oliver talked to his partner about the Florida idea. You listening? He—he talked to his partner, and he came to me . . . I'm going to be all right, you hear? Dad, listen to me, he said it was just a question of the amount!

WILLY: Then you . . . got it?

HAPPY: He's gonna be terrific, Pop!

WILLY, *trying to stand:* Then you got it, haven't you? You got it! You got it!

BIFF, *agonized, holds Willy down:* No, no. Look, Pop. I'm supposed to have lunch with them tomorrow. I'm just telling you this so you'll know that I can still make an impression, Pop. And I'll make good somewhere, but I can't go tomorrow, see?

WILLY: Why not? You simply—

BIFF: But the pen, Pop!

WILLY: You give it to him and tell him it was an oversight!

HAPPY: Sure, have lunch tomorrow!

BIFF: I can't say that—

WILLY: You were doing a crossword puzzle and accidentally used his pen!

BIFF: Listen, kid, I took those balls years ago, now I walk in with his fountain pen? That clinches it, don't you see? I can't face him like that! I'll try elsewhere.

PAGE'S VOICE: Paging Mr. Loman!

WILLY: Don't you want to be anything?

BIFF: Pop, how can I go back?

WILLY: You don't want to be anything, is that what's behind it?

BIFF, *now angry at Willy for not crediting his sympathy:* Don't take it that way! You think it was easy walking into that office after what I'd done to him? A team of horses couldn't have dragged me back to Bill Oliver!

WILLY: Then why'd you go?

BIFF: Why did I go? Why did I go! Look at you! Look at what's become of you!

Off left, The Woman laughs.

WILLY: Biff, you're going to go to that lunch tomorrow, or—

BIFF: I can't go. I've got no appointment!

HAPPY: Biff, for . . . !

WILLY: Are you spiting me?

BIFF: Don't take it that way! Goddammit!

WILLY, *strikes Biff and falters away from the table:* You rotten little louse! Are you spiting me?

THE WOMAN: Someone's at the door, Willy!

BIFF: I'm no good, can't you see what I am?

HAPPY, *separating them:* Hey, you're in a restaurant! Now cut it out, both of you! *The girls enter.* Hello, girls, sit down.

The Woman laughs, off left.

MISS FORSYTHE: I guess we might as well. This is Letta.

THE WOMAN: Willy, are you going to wake up?

BIFF, *ignoring Willy:* How're ya, miss, sit down. What do you drink?

MISS FORSYTHE: Letta might not be able to stay long.

LETTA: I gotta get up very early tomorrow. I got jury duty. I'm so excited! Were you fellows ever on a jury?

BIFF: No, but I been in front of them! *The girls laugh.* This is my father.

LETTA: Isn't he cute? Sit down with us, Pop.

HAPPY: Sit him down, Biff!

BIFF, *going to him:* Come on, slugger, drink us under the table. To hell with it! Come on, sit down, pal.

On Biff's last insistence, Willy is about to sit.

THE WOMAN, *now urgently:* Willy, are you going to answer the door!

The Woman's call pulls Willy back. He starts right, befuddled.

BIFF: Hey, where are you going?

WILLY: Open the door.

BIFF: The door?

WILLY: The washroom . . . the door . . . where's the door?

BIFF, *leading Willy to the left:* Just go straight down.

Willy moves left.

THE WOMAN: Willy, Willy, are you going to get up, get up, get up, get up?

Willy moves left.

LETTA: I think it's sweet you bring your daddy along.

MISS FORSYTHE: Oh, he isn't really your father!

BIFF, *at left, turning to her resentfully:* Miss Forsythe, you've just seen a prince walk by. A fine, troubled prince. A hardworking, unappreciated prince. A pal, you understand? A good companion. Always for his boys.

LETTA: That's so sweet.

HAPPY: Well, girls, what's the program? We're wasting time. Come on, Biff. Gather round. Where would you like to go?

BIFF: Why don't you do something for him?

HAPPY: Me!

BIFF: Don't you give a damn for him, Hap?

HAPPY: What're you talking about? I'm the one who—

BIFF: I sense it, you don't give a good goddam about him. *He takes the rolled-up hose from his pocket and puts it on the table in front of Happy.* Look what I found in the cellar, for Christ's sake. How can you bear to let it go on?

HAPPY: Me? Who goes away? Who runs off and—

BIFF: Yeah, but he doesn't mean anything to you. You could help him—I can't! Don't you understand what I'm talking about? He's going to kill himself, don't you know that?

HAPPY: Don't I know it! Me!

BIFF: Hap, help him! Jesus . . . help him . . . Help me, help me, I can't bear to look at his face! *Ready to weep, he hurries out, up right.*

HAPPY, *staring after him:* Where are you going?

MISS FORSYTHE: What's he so mad about?

HAPPY: Come on, girls, we'll catch up with him.

MISS FORSYTHE, *as Happy pushes her out:* Say, I don't like that temper of his!

HAPPY: He's just a little overstrung, he'll be all right!

WILLY, *off left, as The Woman laughs:* Don't answer! Don't answer!

LETTA: Don't you want to tell your father—

HAPPY: No, that's not my father. He's just a guy. Come on, we'll catch Biff, and, honey, we're going to paint this town! Stanley, where's the check! Hey, Stanley!

They exit. Stanley looks toward left.

STANLEY, *calling to Happy indignantly:* Mr. Loman! Mr. Loman!

Stanley picks up a chair and follows them off. Knocking is heard off left. The Woman enters, laughing. Willy follows her. She is in a black slip; he is buttoning his shirt. Raw, sensuous music accompanies their speech.

WILLY: Will you stop laughing? Will you stop?

THE WOMAN: Aren't you going to answer the door? He'll wake the whole hotel.

WILLY: I'm not expecting anybody.

THE WOMAN: Whyn't you have another drink, honey, and stop being so damn self-centered?

WILLY: I'm so lonely.

THE WOMAN: You know you ruined me, Willy? From now on, whenever you come to the office, I'll see that you go right through to the buyers. No waiting at my desk any more, Willy. You ruined me.

WILLY: That's nice of you to say that.

THE WOMAN: Gee, you are self-centered! Why so sad? You are the saddest, self-centeredest soul I ever did see-saw. *She laughs. He kisses her.* Come on inside, drummer boy. It's silly to be dressing in the middle of the night. *As knocking is heard:* Aren't you going to answer the door?

WILLY: They're knocking on the wrong door.

THE WOMAN: But I felt the knocking. And he heard us talking in here. Maybe the hotel's on fire!

WILLY, *his terror rising:* It's a mistake.

THE WOMAN: Then tell him to go away!

WILLY: There's nobody there.

THE WOMAN: It's getting on my nerves, Willy. There's somebody standing out there and it's getting on my nerves!

WILLY, *pushing her away from him:* All right, stay in the bathroom here, and don't come out. I think there's a law in Massachusetts about it, so don't come out. It may be that new room clerk. He looked very mean. So don't come out. It's a mistake, there's no fire.

The knocking is heard again. He takes a few steps away from her, and she vanishes into the wing. The light follows him, and now he is facing Young Biff, who carries a suitcase. Biff steps toward him. The music is gone.

BIFF: Why didn't you answer?

WILLY: Biff! What are you doing in Boston?

BIFF: Why didn't you answer? I've been knocking for five minutes, I called you on the phone—

WILLY: I just heard you. I was in the bathroom and had the door shut. Did anything happen home?

BIFF: Dad—I let you down.

WILLY: What do you mean?

BIFF: Dad . . .

WILLY: Biffo, what's this about? *Putting his arm around Biff:* Come on, let's go downstairs and get you a malted.

BIFF: Dad, I flunked math.

WILLY: Not for the term?

BIFF: The term. I haven't got enough credits to graduate.

WILLY: You mean to say Bernard wouldn't give you the answers?

BIFF: He did, he tried, but I only got a sixty-one.

WILLY: And they wouldn't give you four points?

BIFF: Birnbaum refused absolutely. I begged him, Pop, but he won't give me those points. You gotta talk to him before they close the school. Because if he saw the kind of man you are, and you just talked to him in your way, I'm sure he'd come through for me. The class came right before practice, see, and I didn't go enough. Would you talk to him? He'd like you, Pop. You know the way you could talk.

WILLY: You're on. We'll drive right back.

BIFF: Oh, Dad, good work! I'm sure he'll change it for you!

WILLY: Go downstairs and tell the clerk I'm checkin' out. Go right down.

BIFF: Yes, sir! See, the reason he hates me, Pop—one day he was late for class so I got up at the blackboard and imitated him. I crossed my eyes and talked with a lithp.

WILLY, *laughing:* You did? The kids like it?

BIFF: They nearly died laughing!

WILLY: Yeah? What'd you do?

BIFF: The thquare root of thixthy twee is . . . *Willy bursts out laughing; Biff joins him.* And in the middle of it he walked in!

Willy laughs and The Woman joins in offstage.

WILLY, *without hesitation:* Hurry downstairs and—

BIFF: Somebody in there?

WILLY: No, that was next door.

The Woman laughs offstage.

BIFF: Somebody got in your bathroom!

WILLY: No, it's the next room, there's a party—

THE WOMAN, *enters, laughing. She lisps this:* Can I come in? There's something in the bathtub, Willy, and it's moving!

Willy looks at Biff, who is staring open-mouthed and horrified at The Woman.

WILLY: Ah—you better go back to your room. They must be finished painting by now. They're painting her room so I let her take a shower here. Go back, go back . . . *He pushes her.*

THE WOMAN, *resisting:* But I've got to get dressed, Willy, I can't—

WILLY: Get out of here! Go back, go back . . . *Suddenly striving for the ordinary:* This is Miss Francis, Biff, she's a buyer. They're painting her room. Go back, Miss Francis, go back . . .

THE WOMAN: But my clothes, I can't go out naked in the hall!

WILLY, *pushing her offstage:* Get outa here! Go back, go back!

Biff slowly sits down on his suitcase as the argument continues offstage.

THE WOMAN: Where's my stockings? You promised me stockings, Willy!

WILLY: I have no stockings here!

THE WOMAN: You had two boxes of size nine sheers for me, and I want them!

WILLY: Here, for God's sake, will you get outa here!

THE WOMAN, *enters holding a box of stockings:* I just hope there's nobody in the hall. That's all I hope. *To Biff:* Are you football or baseball?

BIFF: Football.

THE WOMAN, *angry, humiliated:* That's me too. G'night. *She snatches her clothes from Willy, and walks out.*

WILLY, *after a pause:* Well, better get going. I want to get to the school first thing in the morning. Get my suits out of the closet. I'll get my valise. *Biff doesn't move.* What's the matter? *Biff remains motionless, tears falling.* She's a buyer. Buys for J. H. Simmons. She lives down the hall—they're painting. You don't imagine—*He breaks off. After a pause:* Now listen, pal, she's just a buyer. She sees merchandise in her room and they have to keep it looking just so . . . *Pause. Assuming command:* All right, get my suits. *Biff doesn't move.* Now stop crying and do as I say. I gave you an order. Biff, I gave you an order! Is that what you do when I give you an order? How dare you cry! *Putting his arm around Biff:* Now look, Biff, when you grow up you'll understand about these things. You mustn't—you mustn't overemphasize a thing like this. I'll see Birnbaum first thing in the morning.

BIFF: Never mind.

WILLY, *getting down beside Biff:* Never mind! He's going to give you those points. I'll see to it.

BIFF: He wouldn't listen to you.

WILLY: He certainly will listen to me. You need those points for the U. of Virginia.

BIFF: I'm not going there.

WILLY: Heh? If I can't get him to change that mark you'll make it up in summer school. You've got all summer to—

BIFF, *his weeping breaking from him:* Dad . . .

WILLY, *infected by it:* Oh, my boy . . .

BIFF: Dad . . .

WILLY: She's nothing to me, Biff. I was lonely, I was terribly lonely.

BIFF: You—you gave her Mama's stockings! *His tears break through and he rises to go.*

WILLY, *grabbing for Biff:* I gave you an order!

BIFF: Don't touch me, you—liar!

WILLY: Apologize for that!

BIFF: You fake! You phony little fake! You fake! *Overcome, he turns quickly and weeping fully goes out with his suitcase. Willy is left on the floor on his knees.*

WILLY: I gave you an order! Biff, come back here or I'll beat you! Come back here! I'll whip you!

Stanley comes quickly in from the right and stands in front of Willy.

WILLY, *shouts at Stanley:* I gave you an order . . .

STANLEY: Hey, let's pick it up, pick it up, Mr. Loman. *He helps Willy to his feet.* Your boys left with the chippies. They said they'll see you at home.

A second waiter watches some distance away.

WILLY: But we were supposed to have dinner together.

Music is heard, Willy's theme.

STANLEY: Can you make it?

WILLY: I'll—sure, I can make it. *Suddenly concerned about his clothes:* Do I—I look all right?

STANLEY: Sure, you look all right. *He flicks a speck off Willy's lapel.*

WILLY: Here—here's a dollar.

STANLEY: Oh, your son paid me. It's all right.

WILLY, *putting it in Stanley's hand:* No, take it. You're a good boy.

STANLEY: Oh, no, you don't have to . . .

WILLY: Here—here's some more, I don't need it any more. *After a slight pause:* Tell me—is there a seed store in the neighborhood?

STANLEY: Seeds? You mean like to plant?

As Willy turns, Stanley slips the money back into his jacket pocket.

WILLY: Yes. Carrots, peas . . .

STANLEY: Well, there's hardware stores on Sixth Avenue, but it may be too late now.

WILLY, *anxiously:* Oh, I'd better hurry. I've got to get some seeds. *He starts off to the right.* I've got to get some seeds, right away. Nothing's planted. I don't have a thing in the ground.

Willy hurries out as the light goes down. Stanley moves over to the right after him, watches him off. The other waiter has been staring at Willy.

STANLEY, *to the waiter:* Well, whatta you looking at?

The waiter picks up the chairs and moves off right. Stanley takes the table and follows him. The light fades on this area. There is a long pause, the sound of the flute coming over. The light gradually rises on the kitchen, which is empty. Happy appears at the door of the house, followed by Biff. Happy is carrying a large bunch of long-stemmed roses. He enters the kitchen, looks around for Linda. Not seeing her, he turns to Biff, who is just outside the house door, and makes a gesture with his hands, indicating "Not here, I guess." He looks into the living-room and freezes. Inside, Linda, unseen, is seated, Willy's coat on her lap. She rises ominously and quietly and moves toward Happy, who backs up into the kitchen, afraid.

HAPPY: Hey, what're you doing up? *Linda says nothing but moves toward him implacably.* Where's Pop? *He keeps backing to the right, and now Linda is in full view in the doorway to the living-room.* Is he sleeping?

LINDA: Where were you?

HAPPY, *trying to laugh it off:* We met two girls, Mom, very fine types. Here, we brought you some flowers. *Offering them to her:* Put them in your room, Ma.

She knocks them to the floor at Biff's feet. He has now come inside and closed the door behind him. She stares at Biff, silent.

HAPPY: Now what'd you do that for? Mom, I want you to have some flowers—

LINDA, *cutting Happy off, violently to Biff:* Don't you care whether he lives or dies?

HAPPY, *going to the stairs:* Come upstairs, Biff.

BIFF, *with a flare of disgust, to Happy:* Go away from me! *To Linda:* What do you mean, lives or dies? Nobody's dying around here, pal.

LINDA: Get out of my sight! Get out of here!

BIFF: I wanna see the boss.

LINDA: You're not going near him!

BIFF: Where is he? *He moves into the living-room and Linda follows.*

LINDA, *shouting after Biff:* You invite him for dinner. He looks forward to it all day—*Biff appears in his parents' bedroom, looks around, and exits*—and then you desert him there. There's no stranger you'd do that to!

HAPPY: Why? He had a swell time with us. Listen, when I—*Linda comes back into the kitchen*—desert him I hope I don't outlive the day!

LINDA: Get out of here!

HAPPY: Now look, Mom . . .

LINDA: Did you have to go to women tonight? You and your lousy rotten whores!

Biff re-enters the kitchen.

HAPPY: Mom, all we did was follow Biff around trying to cheer him up! *To Biff:* Boy, what a night you gave me!

LINDA: Get out of here, both of you, and don't come back! I don't want you tormenting him any more. Go on now, get your things together! *To Biff:* You can sleep in his apartment. *She starts to pick up the flowers and stops herself.* Pick up this stuff, I'm not your maid any more. Pick it up, you bum, you!

Happy turns his back to her in refusal. Biff slowly moves over and gets down on his knees, picking up the flowers.

LINDA: You're a pair of animals! Not one, not another living soul would have had the cruelty to walk out on that man in a restaurant!

BIFF, *not looking at her:* Is that what he said?

LINDA: He didn't have to say anything. He was so humiliated he nearly limped when he came in.

HAPPY: But, Mom, he had a great time with us—

BIFF, *cutting him off violently:* Shut up!

Without another word, Happy goes upstairs.

LINDA: You! You didn't even go in to see if he was all right!

BIFF, *still on the floor in front of Linda, the flowers in his hand; with self-loathing:* No. Didn't. Didn't do a damned thing. How do you like that, heh? Left him babbling in a toilet.

LINDA: You louse. You . . .

BIFF: Now you hit it on the nose! *He gets up, throws the flowers in the wastebasket.* The scum of the earth, and you're looking at him!

LINDA: Get out of here!

BIFF: I gotta talk to the boss, Mom. Where is he?

LINDA: You're not going near him. Get out of this house!

BIFF, *with absolute assurance, determination:* No. We're gonna have an abrupt conversation, him and me.

LINDA: You're not talking to him!

Hammering is heard from outside the house, off right. Biff turns toward the noise.

LINDA, *suddenly pleading:* Will you please leave him alone?

BIFF: What's he doing out there?

LINDA: He's planting the garden!

BIFF, *quietly:* Now? Oh, my God!

Biff moves outside, Linda following. The light dies down on them and comes up on the center of the apron as Willy walks into it. He is carrying a flashlight, a hoe, and a handful of seed packets. He raps the top of the hoe sharply to fix it firmly, and then moves to the left, measuring off the distance with his foot. He holds the flashlight to look at the seed packets, reading off the instructions. He is in the blue of night.

WILLY: Carrots . . . quarter-inch apart. Rows . . . one-foot rows. *He measures it off.* One foot. *He puts down a package and measures off.* Beets. *He puts down another package and measures again.* Lettuce. *He reads the package, puts it down.* One foot—*He breaks off as Ben appears at the right and moves slowly down to him.* What a proposition, ts, ts. Terrific, terrific. 'Cause she's suffered, Ben, the woman has suffered. You understand me? A man can't go out the way he came in, Ben, a man has got to add up to something. You can't, you can't— *Ben moves toward him as though to interrupt.* You gotta consider, now. Don't answer so quick. Remember, it's a guaranteed twenty-thousand-dollar proposition. Now look, Ben, I want you to go through the ins and outs of this thing with me. I've got nobody to talk to, Ben, and the woman has suffered, you hear me?

BEN, *standing still, considering:* What's the proposition?

WILLY: It's twenty thousand dollars on the barrelhead. Guaranteed, gilt-edged, you understand?

BEN: You don't want to make a fool of yourself. They might not honor the policy.

WILLY: How can they dare refuse? Didn't I work like a coolie to meet every premium on the nose? And now they don't pay off! Impossible!

BEN: It's called a cowardly thing, William.

WILLY: Why? Does it take more guts to stand here the rest of my life ringing up a zero?

BEN, *yielding:* That's a point, William. *He moves, thinking, turns.* And twenty thousand—that *is* something one can feel with the hand, it is there.

WILLY, *now assured, with rising power:* Oh, Ben, that's the whole beauty of it! I see it like a diamond, shining in the dark, hard and rough, that I can pick up and touch in my hand. Not like—like an appointment! This would not be another damned-fool appointment, Ben, and it changes all the aspects. Because he thinks I'm nothing, see, and so he spites me. But the funeral— *Straightening up:* Ben, that funeral will be massive! They'll come from Maine, Massachusetts, Vermont, New Hampshire! All the old-timers with the strange license plates—that boy will be thunder-struck, Ben, because he never realized—I am known! Rhode Island, New York, New Jersey—I am known, Ben, and he'll see it with his eyes once and for all. He'll see what I am, Ben! He's in for a shock, that boy!

BEN, *coming down to the edge of the garden:* He'll call you a coward.

WILLY, *suddenly fearful:* No, that would be terrible.

BEN: Yes. And a damned fool.

WILLY: No, no, he mustn't, I won't have that! *He is broken and desperate.*

BEN: He'll hate you, William.

The gay music of the Boys is heard.

WILLY: Oh, Ben, how do we get back to all the great times? Used to be so full of light, and comradeship, the sleigh-riding in winter, and the ruddiness on his cheeks. And always some kind of good news coming up, always something nice coming up ahead. And never even let me carry the valises in the house, and simonizing, simonizing that little red car! Why, why can't I give him something and not have him hate me?

BEN: Let me think about it. *He glances at his watch.* I still have a little time. Remarkable proposition, but you've got to be sure you're not making a fool of yourself.

Ben drifts off upstage and goes out of sight. Biff comes down from the left.

WILLY, *suddenly conscious of Biff, turns and looks up at him, then begins picking up the packages of seeds in confusion:* Where the hell is that seed? *Indignantly:* You can't see nothing out here! They boxed in the whole goddam neighborhood!

BIFF: There are people all around here. Don't you realize that?

WILLY: I'm busy. Don't bother me.

BIFF, *taking the hoe from Willy:* I'm saying good-by to you, Pop. *Willy looks at him, silent, unable to move.* I'm not coming back any more.

WILLY: You're not going to see Oliver tomorrow?

BIFF: I've got no appointment, Dad.

WILLY: He put his arm around you, and you've got no appointment?

BIFF: Pop, get this now, will you? Everytime I've left it's been a fight that sent me out of here. Today I realized something about myself and I tried to explain it to you and I—I think I'm just not smart enough to make any sense out of it for you. To hell with whose fault it is or anything like that. *He takes Willy's arm.* Let's just wrap it up, heh? Come on in, we'll tell Mom. *He gently tries to pull Willy to left.*

WILLY, *frozen, immobile, with guilt in his voice:* No, I don't want to see her.

BIFF: Come on! *He pulls again, and Willy tries to pull away.*

WILLY, *highly nervous:* No, no, I don't want to see her.

BIFF, *tries to look into Willy's face, as if to find the answer there:* Why don't you want to see her?

WILLY, *more harshly now:* Don't bother me, will you?

BIFF: What do you mean, you don't want to see her? You don't want them calling you yellow, do you? This isn't your fault; it's me, I'm a bum. Now come inside! *Willy strains to get away.* Did you hear what I said to you?

Willy pulls away and quickly goes by himself into the house. Biff follows.

LINDA, *to Willy:* Did you plant, dear?

BIFF, *at the door, to Linda:* All right, we had it out. I'm going and I'm not writing any more.

LINDA, *going to Willy in the kitchen:* I think that's the best way, dear. 'Cause there's no use drawing it out, you'll just never get along.

Willy doesn't respond.

BIFF: People ask where I am and what I'm doing, you don't know, and you don't care. That way it'll be off your mind and you can start brightening up again. All right? That clears it, doesn't it? *Willy is silent, and Biff goes to him.* You gonna wish me luck, scout? *He extends his hand.* What do you say?

LINDA: Shake his hand, Willy.

WILLY, *turning to her, seething with hurt:* There's no necessity to mention the pen at all, y'know.

BIFF, *gently:* I've got no appointment, Dad.

WILLY, *erupting fiercely:* He put his arm around . . . ?

BIFF: Dad, you're never going to see what I am, so what's the use of arguing? If I strike oil I'll send you a check. Meantime forget I'm alive.

WILLY, *to Linda:* Spite, see?

BIFF: Shake hands, Dad.

WILLY: Not my hand.

BIFF: I was hoping not to go this way.

WILLY: Well, this is the way you're going. Good-by.

Biff looks at him a moment, then turns sharply and goes to the stairs.

WILLY, *stops him with:* May you rot in hell if you leave this house!

BIFF, *turning:* Exactly what is it that you want from me?

WILLY: I want you to know, on the train, in the mountains, in the valleys, wherever you go, that you cut down your life for spite!

BIFF: No, no.

WILLY: Spite, spite, is the word of your undoing! And when you're down and out, remember what did it. When you're rotting somewhere beside the railroad tracks, remember, and don't you dare blame it on me!

BIFF: I'm not blaming it on you!

WILLY: I won't take the rap for this, you hear?

Happy comes down the stairs and stands on the bottom step, watching.

BIFF: That's just what I'm telling you!

WILLY, *sinking into a chair at the table, with full accusation:* You're trying to put a knife in me—don't think I don't know what you're doing!

BIFF: All right, phony! Then let's lay it on the line. *He whips the rubber tube out of his pocket and puts it on the table.*

HAPPY: You crazy—

LINDA: Biff! *She moves to grab the hose, but Biff holds it down with his hand.*

BIFF: Leave it there! Don't move it!

WILLY, *not looking at it:* What is that?

BIFF: You know goddam well what that is.

WILLY, *caged, wanting to escape:* I never saw that.

BIFF: You saw it. The mice didn't bring it into the cellar! What is this supposed to do, make a hero out of you? This supposed to make me sorry for you?

WILLY: Never heard of it.

BIFF: There'll be no pity for you, you hear it? No pity!

WILLY, *to Linda:* You hear the spite!

BIFF: No, you're going to hear the truth—what you are and what I am!

LINDA: Stop it!

WILLY: Spite!

HAPPY, *coming down toward Biff:* You cut it now!

BIFF, *to Happy:* The man don't know who we are! The man is gonna know! *To Willy:* We never told the truth for ten minutes in this house!

HAPPY: We always told the truth!

BIFF, *turning on him:* You big blow, are you the assistant buyer? You're one of the two assistants to the assistant, aren't you?

HAPPY: Well, I'm practically—

BIFF: You're practically full of it! We all are! And I'm through with it. *To Willy:* Now hear this, Willy, this is me.

WILLY: I know you!

BIFF: You know why I had no address for three months? I stole a suit in Kansas City and I was in jail. *To Linda, who is sobbing:* Stop crying. I'm through with it.

Linda turns away from them, her hands covering her face.

WILLY: I suppose that's my fault!

BIFF: I stole myself out of every good job since high school!

WILLY: And whose fault is that?

BIFF: And I never got anywhere because you blew me so full of hot air I could never stand taking orders from anybody! That's whose fault it is!

WILLY: I hear that!

LINDA: Don't, Biff!

BIFF: It's goddam time you heard that! I had to be boss big shot in two weeks, and I'm through with it!

WILLY: Then hang yourself! For spite, hang yourself!

BIFF: No! Nobody's hanging himself, Willy! I ran down eleven flights with a pen in my hand today. And suddenly I stopped, you hear me? And in the middle of that office building, do you hear this? I stopped in the middle of that building and I saw —the sky. I saw the things that I love in this world. The work and the food and time to sit and smoke. And I looked at the pen and said to myself, what the hell am I grabbing this for? Why am I trying to become what I don't want to be? What am I doing in an office, making a contemptuous, begging fool of myself, when all I want is out there, waiting for me the minute I say I know who I am! Why can't I say that, Willy? *He tries to make Willy face him, but Willy pulls away and moves to the left.*

WILLY, *with hatred, threateningly:* The door of your life is wide open!

BIFF: Pop! I'm a dime a dozen, and so are you!

WILLY, *turning on him now in an uncontrolled outburst:* I am not a dime a dozen! I am Willy Loman, and you are Biff Loman!

Biff starts for Willy, but is blocked by Happy. In his fury, Biff seems on the verge of attacking his father.

BIFF: I am not a leader of men, Willy, and neither are you. You were never anything but a hard-working drummer who landed in the ash can like all the rest of them! I'm one dollar an hour, Willy! I tried seven states and couldn't raise it. A buck an hour! Do you gather my meaning? I'm not bringing home any prizes any more, and you're going to stop waiting for me to bring them home!

WILLY, *directly to Biff:* You vengeful, spiteful mutt!

Biff breaks from Happy. Willy, in fright, starts up the stairs. Biff grabs him.

BIFF, *at the peak of his fury:* Pop, I'm nothing! I'm nothing, Pop. Can't you understand that? There's no spite in it any more. I'm just what I am, that's all.

Biff's fury has spent itself, and he breaks down, sobbing, holding on to Willy, who dumbly fumbles for Biff's face.

WILLY, *astonished:* What're you doing? What're you doing? *To Linda:* Why is he crying?

BIFF, *crying, broken:* Will you let me go, for Christ's sake? Will you take that phony dream and burn it before something happens? *Struggling to contain himself, he pulls away and moves to the stairs.* I'll go in the morning. Put him—put him to bed. *Exhausted, Biff moves up the stairs to his room.*

WILLY, *after a long pause, astonished, elevated:* Isn't that—isn't that remarkable? Biff—he likes me!

LINDA: He loves you, Willy!

HAPPY, *deeply moved:* Always did, Pop.

WILLY: Oh, Biff! *Staring wildly:* He cried! Cried to me. *He is choking with his love, and now cries out his promise:* That boy—that boy is going to be magnificent!

Ben appears in the light just outside the kitchen.

BEN: Yes, outstanding, with twenty thousand behind him.

LINDA, *sensing the racing of his mind, fearfully, carefully:* Now come to bed, Willy. It's all settled now.

WILLY, *finding it difficult not to rush out of the house:* Yes, we'll sleep. Come on. Go to sleep, Hap.

BEN: And it does take a great kind of a man to crack the jungle.

In accents of dread, Ben's idyllic music starts up.

HAPPY, *his arm around Linda:* I'm getting married, Pop, don't forget it. I'm changing everything. I'm gonna run that department before the year is up. You'll see, Mom. *He kisses her.*

BEN: The jungle is dark but full of diamonds, Willy.

Willy turns, moves, listening to Ben.

LINDA: Be good. You're both good boys, just act that way, that's all.

HAPPY: 'Night, Pop. *He goes upstairs.*

LINDA, *to Willy:* Come, dear.

BEN, *with greater force:* One must go in to fetch a diamond out.

WILLY, *to Linda, as he moves slowly along the edge of the kitchen, toward the door:* I just want to get settled down, Linda. Let me sit alone for a little.

LINDA, *almost uttering her fear:* I want you upstairs.

WILLY, *taking her in his arms:* In a few minutes, Linda. I couldn't sleep right now. Go on, you look awful tired. *He kisses her.*

BEN: Not like an appointment at all. A diamond is rough and hard to the touch.

WILLY: Go on now. I'll be right up.

LINDA: I think this is the only way, Willy.

WILLY: Sure, it's the best thing.

BEN: Best thing!

WILLY: The only way. Everything is gonna be—go on, kid, get to bed. You look so tired.

LINDA: Come right up.

WILLY: Two minutes.

Linda goes into the living-room, then reappears in her bedroom. Willy moves just outside the kitchen door.

WILLY: Loves me. *Wonderingly:* Always loved me. Isn't that a remarkable thing? Ben, he'll worship me for it!

BEN, *with promise:* It's dark there, but full of diamonds.

WILLY: Can you imagine that magnificence with twenty thousand dollars in his pocket?

LINDA, *calling from her room:* Willy! Come up!

WILLY, *calling into the kitchen:* Yes! Yes. Coming! It's very smart, you realize that, don't you, sweetheart? Even Ben sees it. I gotta go, baby. 'By! 'By! *Going over to Ben, almost dancing:* Imagine? When the mail comes he'll be ahead of Bernard again!

BEN: A perfect proposition all around.

WILLY: Did you see how he cried to me? Oh, if I could kiss him, Ben!

BEN: Time, William, time!

WILLY: Oh, Ben, I always knew one way or another we were gonna make it, Biff and I!

BEN, *looking at his watch:* The boat. We'll be late. *He moves slowly off into the darkness.*

WILLY, *elegiacally, turning to the house:* Now when you kick off, boy, I want a seventy-yard boot, and get right down the field under the ball, and when you hit, hit low and hit hard, because it's important, boy. *He swings around and faces the audience.* There's all kinds of important people in the stands, and the first thing you know . . . *Suddenly realizing he is alone:* Ben! Ben, where do I . . . ? *He makes a sudden movement of search.* Ben, how do I . . . ?

LINDA, *calling:* Willy, you coming up?

WILLY, *uttering a gasp of fear, whirling about as if to quiet her.* Sh! *He turns around as if to find his way; sounds, faces, voices, seem to be swarming in upon him and he flicks at them, crying.* Sh! Sh! *Suddenly music, faint and high, stops him. It rises in intensity, almost to an unbearable scream. He goes up and down on his toes, and rushes off around the house.* Shhh!

LINDA: Willy?

There is no answer. Linda waits. Biff gets up off his bed. He is still in his clothes. Happy sits up. Biff stands listening.

LINDA, *with real fear:* Willy, answer me! Willy!

There is the sound of a car starting and moving away at full speed.

LINDA: No!

BIFF, *rushing down the stairs:* Pop!

As the car speeds off, the music crashes down in a frenzy of sound, which becomes the soft pulsation of a single cello string. Biff slowly returns to his bedroom. He and Happy gravely don their jackets. Linda slowly walks out of her room. The music has developed into a dead march. The leaves of day are appearing over everything.

Charley and Bernard, somberly dressed, appear and knock on the kitchen door. Biff and Happy slowly descend the stairs to the kitchen as Charley and Bernard enter. All stop a moment when Linda, in clothes of mourning, bearing a little bunch of roses, comes through the draped doorway into the kitchen. She goes to Charley and takes his arm. Now all move toward the audience, through the wall-line of the kitchen. At the limit of the apron, Linda lays down the flowers, kneels, and sits back on her heels. All stare down at the grave.

Requiem

CHARLEY: It's getting dark, Linda.

Linda doesn't react. She stares at the grave.

BIFF: How about it, Mom? Better get some rest, heh? They'll be closing the gate soon.

Linda makes no move. Pause.

HAPPY, *deeply angered:* He had no right to do that. There was no necessity for it. We would've helped him.

CHARLEY, *grunting:* Hmmm.

BIFF: Come along, Mom.

LINDA: Why didn't anybody come?

CHARLEY: It was a very nice funeral.

LINDA: But where are all the people he knew? Maybe they blame him.

CHARLEY: Naa. It's a rough world, Linda. They wouldn't blame him.

LINDA: I can't understand it. At this time especially. First time in thirty five years we were just about free and clear. He only needed a little salary. He was even finished with the dentist.

CHARLEY: No man only needs a little salary.

LINDA: I can't understand it.

BIFF: There were a lot of nice days. When he'd come home from a trip; or on Sundays, making the stoop; finishing the cellar; putting on the new porch; when he built the extra bathroom; and put up the garage. You know something, Charley, there's more of him in that front stoop than in all the sales he ever made.

CHARLEY: Yeah. He was a happy man with a batch of cement.

LINDA: He was so wonderful with his hands.

BIFF: He had the wrong dreams. All, all, wrong.

HAPPY, *almost ready to fight Biff:* Don't say that!

BIFF: He never knew who he was.

CHARLEY, *stopping Happy's movement and reply. To Biff:* Nobody dast blame this man. You don't understand: Willy was a salesman. And for a salesman, there is no rock bottom to the life. He don't put a bolt to a nut, he don't tell you the law or give you medicine. He's a man way out there in the blue, riding on a smile and a shoeshine. And when they start not smiling back—that's an earthquake. And then you get yourself a couple of spots on your hat, and you're finished. Nobody dast blame this man. A salesman is got to dream, boy. It comes with the territory.

BIFF: Charley, the man didn't know who he was.

HAPPY, *infuriated:* Don't say that!

BIFF: Why don't you come with me, Happy?

HAPPY: I'm not licked that easily. I'm staying right in this city, and I'm gonna beat this racket! *He looks at Biff, his chin set.* The Loman Brothers!

BIFF: I know who I am, kid.

HAPPY: All right, boy. I'm gonna show you and everybody else that Willy Loman did not die in vain. He had a good dream. It's the only dream you can have—to come out number-one man. He fought it out here, and this is where I'm gonna win it for him.

BIFF, *with a hopeless glance at Happy, bends toward his mother:* Let's go, Mom.

LINDA: I'll be with you in a minute. Go on, Charley. *He hesitates.* I want to, just for a minute. I never had a chance to say good-by.

Charley moves away, followed by Happy. Biff remains a slight distance up and left of Linda. She sits there, summoning herself. The flute begins, not far away, playing behind her speech.

LINDA: Forgive me, dear. I can't cry. I don't know what it is, but I can't cry. I don't understand it. Why did you ever do that? Help me, Willy, I can't cry. It seems to me that you're just on another trip. I keep expecting you. Willy, dear, I can't cry. Why did you do it? I search and search and I search, and I can't understand it, Willy. I made the last payment on the house today. Today, dear. And there'll be nobody home. *A sob rises in her throat.* We're free and clear. *Sobbing more fully, released:* We're free. *Biff comes slowly toward her.* We're free . . . We're free . . .

Biff lifts her to her feet and moves out up right with her in his arms. Linda sobs quietly. Bernard and Charley come together and follow them, followed by Happy. Only the music of the flute is left on the darkening stage as over the house the hard towers of the apartment buildings rise into sharp focus.

CURTAIN

1949

Poetry

WILLIAM CARLOS WILLIAMS (1883–1963)

The physician as man of letters, whether Rabelais or Dr. Oliver Wendell Holmes, has characteristically shown a special knowledge of humanity, a diagnostic reserve toward its frailty or strength, and enough humor to preserve his sanity. These characteristics all appeared strongly in the work of Dr. William Carlos Williams. He displayed a probing and clinical realism, as one taught by science to seek beauty and truth in the vulgar or the common as much as in the uncommon. Wallace Stevens once called his friend's materials "anti-poetic": Dr. Williams writes of "the plums that were in the icebox"; of "a red wheelbarrow * * * beside the white chickens"; of weeds on the sour land "by the contagious hospital." Like Stevens he is a poet of ideas, but he did not share Stevens's interest in metaphysics. Instead he sought his signs of permanence in the local and concrete.

Williams's early interest in painting and the influence of two of his friends, the artists Charles Sheeler and Charles Demuth, is reflected in his sharp and graphic figures and in his feeling for form, texture, and color. Just as his material experiences and their metaphors were rooted in the common American soil, so also the language of Williams's poems—vocabulary, "measures," and rhythm, were inherent in the natural and common American speech. "The American idiom," he wrote, "is the language we use in the United States, * * * the language which governed Walt Whitman in his choice of words. * * * Measure in verse is inescapable. * * * To the fixed foot of the ancient line, including the Elizabethan, we must have a reply: it is the variable foot which we are beginning to discover after Whitman's advent." By "the variable foot," Williams meant a "measure" or foot not regulated by the number of syllables or by their distinction as "long" or "short." English formal poetry had been committed to syllable counting since the fourteenth century. The Old English meter had been accentual, not syllabic; popular balladry had remained accentual and so had the common English and American speech, but only Whitman had taken the hint for poetry before Williams.

William Carlos Williams was born in Rutherford, New Jersey, on September 17, 1883. After attending preparatory schools in New York and in Switzerland, he began his medical training at the University of Pennsylvania. There he gave serious attention to his poems and found another poet and friend in Pound, a student in the graduate school. After his graduation in 1906, followed by two years' internship in New York City, Williams went to Leipzig for work in pediatrics. He renewed his friendship with Pound, then in London and a leader among the young experimental poets of imagism and other *avant-garde* writing. Although Pound included work by Williams in the first imagist anthology, the young physician was an individualist always.

Williams soon returned to his birthplace, Rutherford, where in 1910 he began his engrossing medical practice and, in spite of its exactions, produced more than twenty-five volumes of fiction and poetry. In many of his poems, and in the prose essays that often appeared in the same volumes, he kept up a running fire of commentary on his age, its foibles, and its art. He won his *alma mater's* laurels for medical practice while deriving from that practice the knowledge of people and of a community history and life that inspired the best of his poems, his stories and sketches of life along the Passaic, and his epic *Paterson,* in five books, 1946–1958 (fragments of a sixth book were posthumously published in 1963). *Paterson,* perhaps Williams's major accomplishment, shows the hand of the gifted writer, a knowledge of life at once humane and disciplined, disillusioned, witty, and yet compassionate. The work incorporates the history, the characters, and the myths of Paterson from its Indian origins to its industrial present. The lively *Autobiography* (1951) shows the surprising range of his association with the *avant-garde* of American letters, especially during the critical period from 1910 to 1930. Williams received the *Dial* Award for Services to American Literature in 1926, the Guarantors Prize awarded by *Poetry: A Magazine of Verse* in 1931, the Loines Award in 1948, and the National Book Award for *Paterson* in 1949. *Journey to Love* (1955)—see "The Ivy Crown" and "The Sparrow" (below)—and *Paterson V* (1958) show an actual advance, after several years of declining health, in power and formal invention, including the "three-stress line." His acceptance of life, too often before muted, now speaks almost joyfully, as in the opening of *Paterson V,* "In old age / the mind / casts off / rebelliously / an eagle / from its crag." He died on March 4, 1963.

The Collected Poems of William Carlos Williams, Volume One: 1909–1939, edited by A. Walton Litz and Christopher MacGowan, 1987, supersedes earlier collections. A second volume will follow. Other useful collections include *Collected Later Poetry of William Carlos Williams,* 1950; *The Desert Music and Other Poems,* 1954; *Journey to Love,* 1955; and *Pictures from Brueghel,* 1962. *Paterson* (Books I–V, with fragments of VI), was published in 1963. *The Farmers' Daughters: The Collected Stories* was published in 1961. Earlier short story collections include *The Knife of the Times,* 1932; *Life Along the Passaic River,* 1938; *Make Light of It,* 1950. His novels are *A Voyage to Pagany,* 1928; *White Mule,* 1937; *In the Money,* 1940; and *The Build-Up,* 1952. Collections of his essays are *The Great American Novel,* 1923; *In the American Grain,* 1925, reissued 1940; and *Selected Essays of William Carlos Williams,* 1954. *Many Loves,* a play, was produced in 1958. *The Selected Letters of William Carlos Williams,* 1957, was edited by J. C. Thirlwall. *Imaginations: Collected Early Prose,* 1970, was edited by Webster Schott. *Something to Say: William Carlos Williams on Younger Poets,* 1985, was edited by James E. Breslin.

The Autobiography of William Carlos Williams appeared in 1951. Williams dictated his recollections of many of his books in bibliographical order in *I Wanted to Write a Poem,* edited by Edith Heal, 1958. Emily M. Wallace compiled *A Bibliography of William Carlos Williams,* 1968.

The first complete biography is Paul Mariani, *William Carlos Williams: A New World Naked,* 1981. Critical studies include Vivienne Koch, *William Carlos Williams,* 1950; Linda W. Wagner, *The Poems of William Carlos Williams,* 1964, and *The Prose of William Carlos Williams,* 1970; James Guimond, *The Art of William Carlos Williams,* 1968; Sherman Paul, *The Music of Survival: A Biography of a Poem by William Carlos Williams,* 1968; Thomas R. Whitaker, *William Carlos Williams,* 1968; Bram Dijkstra, *The Hieroglyphics of a New Speech: Cubism, Stieglitz, and the Early Poetry of William Carlos Williams,* 1969; James E. Breslin, *William Carlos Williams: An American Artist,* 1970; Joel Conarroe, *William Carlos Williams' Paterson,* 1970; Benjamin Sankey, *A Companion to William Carlos Williams's Paterson,* 1971; Mike Weaver, *William Carlos Williams: The American Background,* 1971; Robert Coles, *William Carlos Williams: The Knack of Survival in America,* 1975; Louis Simpson, *Three on the Tower: The Lives and Works of Ezra Pound, T. S. Eliot, and William Carlos Williams,* 1975; Reed Whittemore, *William Carlos Williams: Poet from New Jersey,* 1975; Rod Townley, *The Early Poetry of William Carlos Williams,* 1976; Margaret Glynne Lloyd, *William Carlos Williams's Paterson: A Critical Reappraisal,* 1980; Charles Doyle, *William Carlos Williams and the American Poem,* 1982; and Bernard Duffey, *A Poetry of Presence: The Writing of William Carlos Williams,* 1986. Charles Doyle edited *William Carlos Williams: The Critical Heritage,* 1980.

To Mark Anthony in Heaven

This quiet morning light
reflected, how many times
from grass and trees and clouds
enters my north room
touching the walls with
grass and clouds and trees.
Anthony,
trees and grass and clouds.
Why did you follow
that beloved body
with your ships at Actium?[1]
I hope it was because
you knew her inch by inch
from slanting feet upward
to the roots of her hair
and down again and that
you saw her
above the battle's fury—
clouds and trees and grass—

For then you are
listening in heaven.

1913

Portrait of a Lady

Your thighs are appletrees
whose blossoms touch the sky.
Which sky? The sky
where Watteau[2] hung a lady's
slipper. Your knees
are a southern breeze—or
a gust of snow. Agh! what
sort of man was Fragonard?[3]
—as if that answered
anything. Ah, yes—below
the knees, since the tune
drops that way, it is
one of those white summer days,
the tall grass of your ankles
flickers upon the shore—
Which shore?—
the sand clings to my lips—

1. This refers to the story that Cleopatra betrayed her lover Anthony by withdrawing her navy from the crucial battle of Actium (31 B.C.); that in Alexandria she drove Anthony to suicide by pretending to be dead; and that her suicide resulted from these events.
2. Jean Antoine Watteau (1684–1721), French painter celebrated for romantic, idealized outdoor scenes. See Fragonard, below.
3. Jean Honoré Fragonard (1732–1806), French court painter of scenes of love and gallantry. His familiar painting, "The Swing," with a girl who has just kicked her shoe in air, is suggestive. Ascribing this gay jest to Watteau may have been intentional, since Fragonard did paint scenes regarded as salacious.

Which shore?
Agh, petals maybe. How
should I know?
Which shore? Which shore?
I said petals from an appletree.

1915

Tract

I will teach you my townspeople
how to perform a funeral—
for you have it over a troop
of artists—
unless one should scour the world—
you have the ground sense necessary.

See! the hearse leads.
I begin with a design for a hearse.
For Christ's sake not black
nor white either—and not polished!
Let it be weathered—like a farm wagon—
with gilt wheels (this could be
applied fresh at small expense)
or no wheels at all:
a rough dray to drag over the ground.

Knock the glass out!
My God—glass, my townspeople!
For what purpose? Is it for the dead
to look out or for us to see
how well he is housed or to see
the flowers or the lack of them—
or what?
To keep the rain and snow from him?
He will have a heavier rain soon:
pebbles and dirt and what not.
Let there be no glass—
and no upholstery! phew!
and no little brass rollers
and small easy wheels on the bottom—
my townspeople what are you thinking of!

A rough plain hearse then
with gilt wheels and no top at all.
On this the coffin lies
by its own weight.

No wreaths please—
especially no hot-house flowers.
Some common memento is better,
something he prized and is known by:
his old clothes—a few books perhaps—

God knows what! You realize
how we are about these things,
my townspeople—
something will be found—anything—
even flowers if he had come to that.
So much for the hearse.

For heaven's sake though see to the driver!
Take off the silk hat! In fact
that's no place at all for him
up there unceremoniously
dragging our friend out of his own dignity!
Bring him down—bring him down!
Low and inconspicuous! I'd not have him ride
on the wagon at all—damn him—
the undertaker's understrapper!
Let him hold the reins
and walk at the side
and inconspicuously too!

Then briefly as to yourselves:
Walk behind—as they do in France,
seventh class, or if you ride
Hell take curtains! Go with some show
of inconvenience; sit openly—
to the weather as to grief.
Or do you think you can shut grief in?
What—from us? We who have perhaps
nothing to lose? Share with us
share with us—it will be money
in your pockets.
Go now
I think you are ready.

1917

The Young Housewife

At ten A.M. the young housewife
moves about in negligée behind
the wooden walls of her husband's house.
I pass solitary in my car.

Then again she comes to the curb
to call the ice-man, fish-man, and stands
shy, uncorseted, tucking in
stray ends of hair, and I compare her
to a fallen leaf.

The noiseless wheels of my car
rush with a crackling sound over
dried leaves as I bow and pass smiling.

1917

Queen Anne's Lace

Her body is not so white as
anemone petals nor so smooth—nor
so remote a thing. It is a field
of the wild carrot taking
the field by force; the grass
does not raise above it.
Here is no question of whiteness,
white as can be, with a purple mole[4]
at the center of each flower.
Each flower is a hand's span
of her whiteness. Wherever
his hand has lain there is
a tiny purple blemish. Each part
is a blossom under his touch
to which the fibres of her being
stem one by one, each to its end,
until the whole field is a
white desire, empty, a single stem,
a cluster, flower by flower,
a pious wish to whiteness gone over—
or nothing.

1921

Spring and All

By the road to the contagious hospital
under the surge of the blue
mottled clouds driven from the
northeast—a cold wind. Beyond, the
waste of broad, muddy fields
brown with dried weeds, standing and fallen

patches of standing water
the scattering of tall trees

All along the road the reddish
purplish, forked, upstanding, twiggy
stuff of bushes and small trees
with dead, brown leaves under them
leafless vines—

Lifeless in appearance, sluggish
dazed spring approaches—

They enter the new world naked,
cold, uncertain of all
save that they enter. All about them
the cold, familiar wind—

4. A single purple blossom in the center of the flower Queen Anne's lace, or wild carrot. Actually, the "flower" is an umbel composed of a multitude of tiny blossoms, all white except this one, and all joined downward to the top of the main stalk by an intricate system of tiny stems (*cf.* ll. 15–16).

Now the grass, tomorrow
the stiff curl of wildcarrot leaf
One by one objects are defined—
It quickens: clarity, outline of leaf

But now the stark dignity of
entrance—Still, the profound change
has come upon them: rooted, they
grip down and begin to awaken

1923

The Red Wheelbarrow

so much depends
upon

a red wheel
barrow

glazed with rain
water

beside the white
chickens.

1923

This Is Just to Say

I have eaten
the plums
that were in
the icebox

and which
you were probably
saving
for breakfast

Forgive me
they were delicious
so sweet
and so cold

1934

The Yachts

contend in a sea which the land partly encloses
shielding them from the too-heavy blows
of an ungoverned ocean which when it chooses

tortures the biggest hulls, the best man knows
to pit against its beatings, and sinks them pitilessly.
Mothlike in mists, scintillant in the minute

brilliance of cloudless days, with broad bellying sails
they glide to the wind tossing green water
from their sharp prows while over them the crew crawls

ant-like, solicitously grooming them, releasing,
making fast as they turn, lean far over and having
caught the wind again, side by side, head for the mark.

In a well guarded arena of open water surrounded by
lesser and greater craft which, sycophant, lumbering
and flittering follow them, they appear youthful, rare

as the light of a happy eye, live with the grace
of all that in the mind is fleckless, free and
naturally to be desired. Now the sea which holds them

is moody, lapping their glossy sides, as if feeling
for some slightest flaw but fails completely.
Today no race. Then the wind comes again. The yachts

move, jockeying for a start, the signal is set and they
are off. Now the waves strike at them but they are too
well made, they slip through, though they take in canvas.

Arms with hands grasping seek to clutch at the prows.
Bodies thrown recklessly in the way are cut aside.
It is a sea of faces about them in agony, in despair

until the horror of the race dawns staggering the mind;
the whole sea become an entanglement of watery bodies
lost to the world bearing what they cannot hold. Broken,

beaten, desolate, reaching from the dead to be taken up
they cry out, failing, failing! their cries rising
in waves still as the skillful yachts pass over.

1935

A Sort of a Song

Let the snake wait under
his weed
and the writing
be of words, slow and quick, sharp
to strike, quiet to wait,
sleepless.

—through metaphor to reconcile
the people and the stones.
Compose. (No ideas
but in things) Invent!

Saxifrage[5] is my flower that splits
the rocks.

1944

The Dance[6]

In Brueghel's great picture, The Kermess,
the dancers go round, they go round and
around, the squeal and the blare and the
tweedle of bagpipes, a bugle and fiddles
tipping their bellies (round as the thick-
sided glasses whose wash they impound)
their hips and their bellies off balance
to turn them. Kicking and rolling about
the Fair Grounds, swinging their butts, those
shanks must be sound to bear up under such
rollicking measures, prance as they dance
in Brueghel's great picture, The Kermess.

1944

Raleigh Was Right[7]

We cannot go to the country
for the country will bring us no peace
What can the small violets tell us
that grow on furry stems in
the long grass among lance shaped leaves?

Though you praise us
and call to mind the poets
who sung of our loveliness
it was long ago!
long ago! when country people
would plough and sow with
flowering minds and pockets at ease—
if ever this were true.

Not now. Love itself a flower
with roots in a parched ground.
Empty pockets make empty heads.
Cure it if you can but
do not believe that we can live
today in the country
for the country will bring us no peace.

1944

5. By derivation, "rock-breaker"; the saxifrage is a family of plants that characteristically grow in the clefts of rocks.
6. Pieter Brueghel (active 1551, died 1569), Flemish artist especially known for paintings of peasant life and the countryside. He was a favorite of Williams, who named one of his volumes *Pictures from Brueghel.* "The Kermess" is most exactly reproduced in the poet's words. Kermess has come to mean "fair" or "dance." It was originally in the Low Countries an outdoor festival celebrating the local saint's day.
7. Compare Christopher Marlowe's famous poem, "The Passionate Shepherd to His Love" ("Come live with me and be my love") and Sir Walter Raleigh's amusing rejoinder, "The Nymph's Reply to the Shepherd," which Williams skillfully represents in language wry, modern, and original.

From Paterson, Book II

Sunday in the Park[8]

Outside
outside myself
there is a world,
he rumbled, subject to my incursions
—a world
(to me) at rest,
which I approach
concretely—

The scene's the Park
upon the rock,
female to the city

—upon whose body Paterson instructs his thoughts
(concretely)

—late spring,
a Sunday afternoon!

—and goes by the footpath to the cliff (counting:
the proof)

himself among the others,
—treads there the same stones
on which their feet slip as they climb,
paced by their dogs!

laughing, calling to each other—

Wait for me!

. . the ugly legs of the young girls,
pistons too powerful for delicacy!
the men's arms, red, used to heat and cold,
to toss quartered beeves and

Yah! Yah! Yah! Yah!

8. This poem marks the author's literary command of the vulgate American, and in its meter it demonstrates his mastery of the musical phrasing and cadence of what he called the "variable foot." *Paterson* is in the long tradition of the "comic" epic: the heroic is rejected in favor of the common, modern, and urban interpretation of the history and myth of a city and the common speech of the people. In publishing Book III (1949) Williams was able to prepare a descriptive analysis of the four volumes, in which he emphasized the questions of language and the city suggested above. As for the modern mind and the city, his epigraph—quoted from Santayana, *The Last Puritan*—gives the meaning: "cities are a second body for the human mind, a second organism, more rational, permanent, and decorative * * *; a work of natural yet moral art, where the soul sets up her trophies." The narrator of *Paterson,* "Dr. Paterson," the poet's *alter ego,* incorporates the Paterson myths centered on its "mountain," its river (the Passaic) with its falls and final plunge to the sea. This Williams makes explicit: "Paterson is a man (since I am a man) who dives from cliffs and the edges of waterfalls, to his death—finally. But for all that he is a woman * * * who *is* the cliff and the waterfall * * * But he escapes in the end * * * As he dies the rocks fission gradually into wild flowers the better to express their sorrow, a language that would have liberated them * * * had they but known it in time to prevent catastrophe. The brunt of the four books of *Paterson* * * * is a search for the redeeming language by which a man's premature death * * * might have been prevented." (See *Paterson V* comment, end of the biographical note on Williams.)

—over-riding
the risks:
pouring down!
For the flower of a day!

Arrived breathless, after a hard climb he,
looks back (beautiful but expensive!) to
the pearl-grey towers! Re-turns
and starts, possessive, through the trees,

— that love,
that is not, is not in those terms
to which I'm still the positive
in spite of all;
the ground dry, — passive-possessive

Walking —

Thickets gather about groups of squat sand-pine,
all but from bare rock

—a scattering of man-high cedars (sharp cones),
antlered sumac

—roots, for the most part, writhing
upon the surface
(so close are we to ruin every
day!)
searching the punk-dry rot

Walking —

The body is tilted slightly forward from the basic standing
position and the weight thrown on the ball of the foot,
while the other thigh is lifted and the leg and opposite
arm are swung forward (fig. 6B). Various muscles, aided

Despite my having said that I'd never write to you again, I do so now because I find, with the passing of time, that the outcome of my failure with you has been the complete damming up of all my creative capacities in a particularly disastrous manner such as I have never before experienced.

For a great many weeks now (whenever I've tried to write poetry) every thought I've had, even every feeling, has been struck off some surface crust of myself which began gathering when I first sensed that you were ignoring the real contents of my last letters to you, and which finally congealed into some impenetrable substance when you asked me to quit corresponding with you altogether without even an explanation.

That kind of blockage, exiling one's self from one's self—have you ever experienced it? I dare say you have, at moments; and if so, you can well understand what a serious psychological injury it amounts to when turned into a permanent day-to-day condition.[9]

9. One of Williams's innovations in *Paterson* is the inclusion of prose taken directly from newspapers, books, or, as in this passage, from the letters of friends and acquaintances. This excerpt is one of several from the letters of a woman identified in *Paterson* as "C.," actually the poet Marcia Nardi, whose *Poems* was published by Alan Swallow in 1956.

How do I love you? These!

(He hears! Voices . indeterminate! Sees them
moving, in groups, by twos and fours — filtering
off by way of the many bypaths.)

I asked him, What do you do?

He smiled patiently, The typical American question.
In Europe they would ask, What are you doing? Or,
What are you doing now?

What do I do? I listen, to the water falling. (No
sound of it here but with the wind!) This is my entire
occupation.

No fairer day ever dawned anywhere than May 2, 1880, when the German Singing Societies of Paterson met on Garret Mountain, as they did many years before on the first Sunday in May.

However the meeting of 1880 proved a fatal day, when William Dalzell, who owned a piece of property near the scene of the festivities, shot John Joseph Van Houten. Dalzell claimed that the visitors had in previous years walked over his garden and was determined that this year he would stop them from crossing any part of his grounds.

Immediately after the shot the quiet group of singers was turned into an infuriated mob who would take Dalzell into their own hands. The mob then proceeded to burn the barn into which Dalzell had retreated from the angry group.

Dalzell fired at the approaching mob from a window in the barn and one of the bullets struck a little girl in the cheek. . . . Some of the Paterson Police rushed Dalzell out of the barn [to] the house of John Ferguson some half furlong away.

The crowd now numbered some ten thousand,

"a great beast!"

for many had come from the city to join the conflict. The case looked serious, for the Police were greatly outnumbered. The crowd then tried to burn the Ferguson house and Dalzell went to the house of John McGuckin. While in this house it was that Sergeant John McBride suggested that it might be well to send for William McNulty, Dean of Saint Joseph's Catholic Church.

In a moment the Dean set on a plan. He proceeded to the scene in a hack. Taking Dalzell by the arm, in full view of the infuriated mob, he led the man to the hack and seating himself by his side, ordered the driver to proceed. The crowd hesitated, bewildered between the bravery of the Dean and

Signs everywhere of birds nesting, while
in the air, slow, a crow zigzags
with heavy wings before the wasp-thrusts
of smaller birds circling about him
that dive from above stabbing for his eyes

Walking—

he leaves the path, finds hard going
across-field, stubble and matted brambles
seeming a pasture—but no pasture
—old furrows, to say labor sweated or

had sweated here
                                                  a flame,
spent.

        The file-sharp grass

When! from before his feet, half tripping,
picking a way, there starts   .
        a flight of empurpled wings!
—invisibly created (their
jackets dust-grey) from the dust kindled
to sudden ardor!

        They fly away, churring! until
their strength spent they plunge
to the coarse cover again and disappear
—but leave, livening the mind, a flashing
of wings and a churring song   .

AND a grasshopper of red basalt, boot-long,
tumbles from the core of his mind,
a rubble-bank disintegrating beneath a
tropic downpour

Chapultepec! grasshopper hill!

—a matt stone solicitously instructed
to bear away some rumor
of the living presence that has preceded
it, out-precedented its breath   .

These wings do not unfold for flight—
no need!
the weight (to the hand) finding
a counter-weight or counter buoyancy
by the mind's wings   .

He is afraid! What then?

Before his feet, at each step, the flight
is renewed. A burst of wings, a quick
churring sound   :

        couriers to the ceremonial of love!

—aflame in flight!
        —aflame only in flight!

                No flesh but the caress!

He is led forward by their announcing wings.

* * *

1948

The Ivy Crown

The whole process is a lie,
unless,
crowned by excess,
it break forcefully,
one way or another,
from its confinement—
or find a deeper well.
Antony and Cleopatra
were right;
they have shown
the way. I love you
or I do not live
at all.

Daffodil time
is past. This is
summer, summer!
the heart says,
and not even the full of it.
No doubts
are permitted—
though they will come
and may
before our time
overwhelm us.
We are only mortal
but being mortal
can defy our fate.
We may
by an outside chance
even win! We do not
look to see
jonquils and violets
come again
but there are,
still,
the roses!

Romance has no part in it.
The business of love is
cruelty *which,*
by our wills,
we transform
to live together.
It has its seasons,
for and against,
whatever the heart
fumbles in the dark
to assert
toward the end of May.
Just as the nature of briars
is to tear flesh,
I have proceeded

through them.
Keep
the briars out,
they say.
You cannot live
and keep free of
briars.

Children pick flowers.
Let them.
Though having them
in hand
they have no further use for them
but leave them crumpled
at the curb's edge.

At our age the imagination
across the sorry facts
lifts us
to make roses
stand before thorns.
Sure
love is cruel
and selfish
and totally obtuse—
at least, blinded by the light,
young love is.
But we are older,
I to love
and you to be loved,
we have,
no matter how,
by our wills survived
to keep
the jeweled prize
always
at our finger tips.

We will it so
and so it is
past all accident.

1955

The Sparrow

(To My Father)

This sparrow
who comes to sit at my window
is a poetic truth
more than a natural one.
His voice,
his movements,

his habits—
how he loves to
flutter his wings
in the dust—
all attest it;
granted, he does it
to rid himself of lice
but the relief he feels
makes him
cry out lustily—
which is a trait
more related to music
than otherwise.
Wherever he finds himself
in early spring,
on back streets
or beside palaces,
he carries on
unaffectedly
his amours.
It begins in the egg,
his sex genders it:
What is more pretentiously
useless
or about which
we more pride ourselves?
It leads as often as not
to our undoing.
The cockerel, the crow
with their challenging voices
cannot surpass
the insistence
of his cheep!
Once
at El Paso
toward evening,
I saw—and heard!—
ten thousand sparrows
who had come in from
the desert
to roost. They filled the trees
of a small park. Men fled
(with ears ringing!)
from their droppings,
leaving the premises
to the alligators
who inhabit
the fountain. His image
is familiar
as that of the aristocratic
unicorn, a pity
there are not more oats eaten
nowadays
to make living easier

for him.
At that,
his small size,
keen eyes,
serviceable beak
and general truculence
assure his survival—
to say nothing
of his innumerable
brood.
Even the Japanese
know him
and have painted him
sympathetically,
with profound insight
into his minor
characteristics.
Nothing even remotely
subtle
about his lovemaking.
He crouches
before the female,
drags his wings,
waltzing,
throws back his head
and simply—
yells! The din
is terrific.
The way he swipes his bill
across a plank
to clean it,
is decisive.
So with everything
he does. His coppery
eyebrows
give him the air
of being always
a winner—and yet
I saw once,
the female of his species
clinging determinedly
to the edge of
a water pipe,
catch him
by his crown-feathers
to hold him
silent,
subdued,
hanging above the city streets
until
she was through with him.
What was the use
of that?
She hung there

herself,
        puzzled at her success.
                I laughed heartily.
Practical to the end,
        it is the poem
                of his existence
that triumphed
        finally;
                a wisp of feathers
flattened to the pavement,
        wings spread symmetrically
                as if in flight,
the head gone,
        the black escutcheon of the breast
                undecipherable,
an effigy of a sparrow,
        a dried wafer only,
                left to say
and it says it
        without offense,
                beautifully;
This was I,
        a sparrow.
                I did my best;
farewell.

1955

ROBERT FRANCIS
(1901–1987)

Born in Upland, Pennsylvania, and educated at Harvard—where he earned a B.A. in 1923 and an Ed.M. in 1926—Robert Francis has lived for sixty years in Amherst, Massachusetts, developing there as a poet somewhat in the shadows of Emily Dickinson and Robert Frost. Like Dickinson, he has earned a reputation as a recluse; like Frost, he has written carefully crafted nature poems. But there is more to him than either comparison would suggest.

He came slowly to the mastery of his craft, dedicating himself to poetry with a single-mindedness and patience matched by few of his contemporaries. After Harvard, he came to Amherst to teach in high school, but quit after only one year. Living as best he could—he gave violin lessons, but stopped that in his forties—he nursed his talent largely in isolation. In 1936, he published his first book of verse, *Stand with Me Here.* Two others followed in the next eight years, but after 1944 he found it difficult to achieve publication, and he passed through his forties and fifties largely unknown. During that period of self-examination, he decided that "for better or worse, I was a poet and there was really nothing else for me to do but go on being a poet * * *. It was too late to change even if I had wanted to. Poetry was my most central, intense and inwardly rewarding experience." *The Orb Weaver* (1960) revived his reputation, and includes some of his best work. Since then, he has continued a flow of books of verse and prose into his eighties. In 1984 the Academy of American Poets gave him its award for distinguished poetic achievement.

An autobiography, *The Trouble with Francis* (1971), details his struggle with neglect. Among the works that represent him best he lists a little-noticed novella, *We Fly Away* (1948).

Collected Poems, 1936–1976, 1976, includes verse to that date. Earlier titles, in addition to those named above, are *Valhalla and Other Poems,* 1938; *The Sound I Listened For,* 1944; *The Face against the Glass,* 1950; *Come Out into the Sun: Poems New and Selected,* 1965; and *Like Ghosts of Eagles,* 1974. A more recent collection is *Butter Hill and Other Poems,* 1984. Miscellaneous prose is collected in *The Satirical Rogue on Poetry,* 1968; *Pot Shots at Poetry,* 1980; *The Satirical Rogue on All Fronts,* 1984; and *Travelling in Amherst: A Poet's Journal,* 1986. A memoir is *Frost: A Time to Talk,* 1972.

The Orb Weaver

Here is the spinner, the orb weaver,
Devised of jet, embossed with sulphur,
Hanging among the fruits of summer,

Hour after hour serenely sullen,
Ripening as September ripens,
Plumping like a grape or melon.

And in its winding-sheet the grasshopper.

The art, the craftsmanship, the cunning,
The patience, the self-control, the waiting,
The sudden dart and the needled poison.

I have no quarrel with the spider
But with the mind or mood that made her
To thrive in nature and in man's nature.

1960

Pitcher

His art is eccentricity, his aim
How not to hit the mark he seems to aim at,

His passion how to avoid the obvious,
His technique how to vary the avoidance.

The others throw to be comprehended. He
Throws to be a moment misunderstood.

Yet not too much. Not errant, arrant, wild,
But every seeming aberration willed.

Not to, yet still, still to communicate
Making the batter understand too late.

1960

Apple Peeler

Why the unbroken spiral, Virtuoso,
Like a trick sonnet in one long, versatile sentence?

Is it a pastime merely, this perfection,
For an old man, sharp knife, long night, long winter?

Or do your careful fingers move at the stir
Of unadmitted immemorial magic?

Solitaire. The ticking clock. The apple
Turning, turning as the round earth turns.

1960

Cold

Cold and the colors of cold: mineral, shell,
And burning blue. The sky is on fire with blue
And wind keeps ringing, ringing the fire bell.

I am caught up into a chill as high
As creaking glaciers and powder-plumed peaks
And the absolutes of interstellar sky.

Abstract, impersonal, metaphysical, pure,
This dazzling art derides me. How should warm breath
Dare to exist—exist, exult, endure?

Hums in my ear the old Ur-father of freeze
And burn, that pre-post-Christian Fellow before
And after all myths and demonologies.

Under the glaring and sardonic sun,
Behind the icicles and double glass
I huddle, hoard, hold out, hold on, hold on.

1960

Three Darks Come Down Together

Three darks come down together,
Three darks close in around me:
Day dark, year dark, dark weather.

They whisper and conspire,
They search me and they sound me
Hugging my private fire.

Day done, year done, storm blowing,
Three darknesses impound me
With dark of white snow snowing.

Three darks gang up to end me,
To browbeat and dumbfound me.
Three future lights defend me.

1960

Epitaph

Believer he and unbeliever both
For less than both would have been less than truth.

His creed was godliness and godlessness.
His credit had been cramped with any less.

Freedom he loved and order he embraced.
Fifty extremists called him Janus-faced.
Though cool centrality was his desire,
He drew the zealot fire and counter-fire.

Baffled by what he deeply understood,
He found life evil and he found life good.
Lover he was, unlonely, yet alone—
Esteemed, belittled, nicknamed, and unknown.

1960

Hide-and-Seek

Here where the dead lie hidden
Too well ever to speak,
Three children unforbidden
Are playing hide-and-seek.

What if for such a hiding
These stones were not designed?
The dead are far from chiding;
The living need not mind.

Too soon the stones that hid them
Anonymously in play
Will learn their names and bid them
Come back to hide to stay.

1974

Like Ghosts of Eagles

The Indians have mostly gone
but not before they named the rivers
the rivers flow on
and the names of the rivers flow with them
  Susquehanna Shenandoah

The rivers are now polluted plundered
but not the names of the rivers
cool and inviolate as ever
pure as on the morning of creation
  Tennessee Tombigbee

If the rivers themselves should ever perish
I think the names will somehow somewhere hover
like ghosts of eagles
those mighty whisperers
  Missouri Mississippi.

1974

ROBERT PENN WARREN
(1905–)

One of the most versatile men of letters in the United States in the twentieth century, Robert Penn Warren has successfully combined the roles of scholar, critic, teacher, and creative artist on a scale in some ways reminiscent of the nineteenth-century careers of Henry Wadsworth Longfellow and James Russell Lowell. Until recently best known as a novelist, he has published as many volumes of verse as he has novels, and both together are outnumbered by the many critical works and textbooks he has written or edited (often in collaboration with others).

Born in 1905 in Guthrie, Kentucky, on the Tennessee border, Warren began his serious interest in writing at Vanderbilt, where he studied freshman English under John Crowe Ransom and soon became associated with Ransom, Allen Tate, and Donald Davidson in the influential group known as the Fugitives. After taking an M.A. at Berkeley, he studied at Yale and then spent two years at Oxford as a Rhodes Scholar. Returning to the United States in 1930, he began at Southwestern College in Memphis the long and distinguished academic career that took him to Vanderbilt, Louisiana State, the University of Minnesota, and Yale.

Most of Warren's fiction and poetry has its roots in the American South, an area which he did not leave permanently until 1942, when the influential journal that he had co-founded and edited, *Southern Review,* lost its backing and ceased to publish. His first novel, *Night Rider* (1939), deals with the tobacco wars of the Kentucky of his childhood. *All the King's Men* (1946) develops from the career of the Louisiana politician Huey Long. *World Enough and Time* (1950) is based on a nineteenth-century seduction and murder that had earlier been treated in such works as William Gilmore Simms's *Beauchampe: or, The Kentucky Tragedy* (1842). *Brother to Dragons: A Tale in Verse and Voices* (1953) grows out of the ax murder of a slave by a nephew of Thomas Jefferson. Other works are similarly placed in Kentucky and Tennessee from the early nineteenth century to the 1960's.

It is a mistake, however, to consider Warren as essentially a regional writer. Local history is only the starting place for his imagination, and his overriding concern is frequently thematic and structural. A highly intellectual writer, Warren continually impresses the reader with the sense of a mind at work shaping the material in the ways best suited to enforce its meanings.

In addition to those works mentioned above, novels include *At Heaven's Gate,* 1943; *Band of Angels,* 1955; *The Cave* (1959); *Flood* (1964); and *Meet Me in the Green Glen,* 1971. Warren's *New and Selected Poems, 1923–1985* appeared in 1985. Additional volumes of verse include *Thirty-Six Poems,* 1935; *Eleven Poems on the Same Theme,* 1942; *Selected Poems, 1923–1943,* 1944; *Promises: Poems, 1954–1956,* 1957; *You, Emperors and Others: Poems, 1957–1960,* 1960; *Selected Poems: New and Old, 1923–1966,* 1966; *Incarnations: Poems, 1966–1968,* 1968; *Audubon: A Vision,* 1969; and *Selected Poems, 1923–1975,* 1976. *Blackberry Winter* was published separately in 1946 and collected in *The Circus in the Attic and Other Stories,* 1947. Non-fictional prose includes *John Brown: The Making of a Martyr,* 1929; *I'll Take My Stand: The South and the Agrarian Tradition* (with others), 1930; *Segregation: The Inner Conflict in the South,* 1956; *Remember the Alamo!,* 1958; *Selected Essays,* 1958; *The Gods of Mount Olympus,* 1959; *The Legacy of the Civil War * * *,* 1961; *Who Speaks for the Negro?,* 1965; *Homage to Theodore Dreiser,* 1971; and *Jefferson Davis Gets His Citizenship Back,* 1980. Influential textbooks include *Understanding Poetry,* 1938; and *Understanding Fiction,* 1943 (both with Cleanth Brooks). *American Literature: The Makers and the Making* (with Cleanth Brooks and R. W. B. Lewis), 2 vols., appeared in 1973. Floyd C. Watkins and John T. Hiers edited *Robert Penn Warren Talking: Interviews 1950–1978,* 1980.

Critical studies include John M. Bradbury, *The Fugitives: A Critical Account,* 1958; Louise Cowan, *The Fugitive Group: A Literary History,* 1959; Leonard Casper, *Robert Penn Warren: The Dark and Bloody Ground,* 1960; Charles H. Bohner, *Robert Penn Warren,* 1964 (revised, 1981); John L. Stewart, *The Burden of Time: The Fugitives and Agrarians,* 1965; J. L. Longley, Jr., ed., *Robert Penn Warren: A Collection of Critical Essays,* 1965; Victor Strandberg, *A Colder Fire: The Poetry of Robert Penn Warren,* 1965; J. L. Longley, Jr., *Robert Penn Warren,* 1969; Barnett Guttenberg, *Web of Being: The Novels of Robert Penn Warren,* 1975; Victor H. Strandberg, *The Poetic Vision of Robert Penn Warren,* 1977; Richard Gray, ed., *Robert Penn Warren: A Collection of Critical Essays,* 1980; James H. Justus, *The Achievement of Robert Penn Warren,* 1981; and Floyd C. Watkins, *Then and Now: The Personal Past in the Poetry of Robert Penn Warren,* 1982; William Bradford Clark, ed., *Critical Essays on Robert Penn Warren,* 1982; and Calvin Bedient, *In the Heart's Last Kingdom: Robert Penn Warren's Major Poetry,* 1986.

History Among the Rocks[1]

There are many ways to die
Here among the rocks in any weather:
Wind, down the eastern gap, will lie
Level along the snow, beating the cedar,
And lull the drowsy head that it blows over
To startle a cold and crystalline dream forever.

The hound's black paw will print the grass in May,
And sycamores rise down a dark ravine,
Where a creek in flood, sucking the rock and clay,
Will tumble the laurel, the sycamore away.
Think how a body, naked and lean
And white as the splintered sycamore, would go
Tumbling and turning, hushed in the end,
With hair afloat in waters that gently bend
To ocean where the blind tides flow.

Under the shadow of ripe wheat,
By flat limestone, will coil the copperhead,
Fanged as the sunlight, hearing the reaper's feet.
But there are other ways, the lean men said:
In these autumn orchards once young men lay dead—
Gray coats, blue coats. Young men on the mountainside
Clambered, fought. Heels muddied the rocky spring.
Their reason is hard to guess, remembering
Blood on their black mustaches in moonlight.
Their reason is hard to guess and a long time past:
The apple falls, falling in the quiet night.

1935

Founding Fathers, Early-Nineteenth-Century Style, Southeast U.S.A.

They were human, they suffered, wore long black coat and gold watch chain.
They stare from daguerreotype with severe reprehension,
Or from genuine oil, and you'd never guess any pain
In those merciless eyes that now remark our own time's sad declension.

Some composed declarations, remembering Jefferson's language.
Knew pose of the patriot, left hand in crook of the spine or
With finger to table, while right invokes the Lord's just rage.
There was always a grandpa, or cousin at least, who had been a real Signer.

1. The third of four poems in the sequence "Kentucky Mountain Farm."

Some were given to study, read Greek in the forest, and these
Longed for an epic to do their own deeds right honor;
Were Nestor by pigpen, in some tavern brawl played Achilles.
In the ring of Sam Houston they found, when he died, one word engraved: *Honor.*

Their children were broadcast, like millet seed flung in a wind-flare.
Wives died, were dropped like old shirts in some corner of country.
Said, "Mister," in bed, the child-bride; hadn't known what to find there;
Wept all the next morning for shame; took pleasure in silk; wore the keys to the pantry.

"Will die in these ditches if need be," wrote Bowie, at the Alamo.
And did, he whose left foot, soft-catting, came forward, and breath hissed:
Head back, gray eyes narrow, thumb flat along knife-blade, blade low.
"Great gentleman," said Henry Clay, "and a patriot." Portrait by Benjamin West.

Or take those, the nameless, of whom no portraits remain,
No locket or seal ring, though somewhere, broken and rusted,
In attic or earth, the long Decherd, stock rotten, has lain;
Or the mold-yellow Bible, God's Word, in which, in their strength, they also trusted.

Some wrestled the angel, and took a fall by the corncrib.
Fought the brute, stomp-and-gouge, but knew they were doomed in that glory.
All night, in sweat, groaned; fell at last with spit red and a cracked rib.
How sweet then the tears! Thus gentled, they roved the dark land with the old story.

Some prospered, had black men and acres, and silver on table,
But remembered the owl call, the smell of burnt bear fat on dusk-air.
Loved family and friends, and stood it as long as able—
"But money and women, too much is ruination, am Arkansas-bound." So went there.

One of mine was a land shark, or so the book with scant praise
Denominates him. "A man large and shapeless,
Like a sack of potatoes set on a saddle," it says,
"Little learning but shrewd, not well trusted." Rides thus out of history, neck fat and napeless.

One fought Shiloh and such, got cranky, would fiddle all night.
The boys nagged for Texas. "God damn it, there's nothing, God damn it,
In Texas"—but took wagons, went, and to prove he was right,
Stayed a year and a day—"hell, nothing in Texas"—had proved it, came back to black vomit,

And died, and they died, and are dead, and now their voices
Come thin, like the last cricket in frost-dark, in grass lost,
With nothing to tell us for our complexity of choices,
But beg us only one word to justify their own life-cost.

So let us bend ear to them in this hour of lateness,
And what they are trying to say, try to understand,
And try to forgive them their defects, even their greatness,
For we are their children in the light of humanness, and under the shadow of God's closing hand.

1957

Masts at Dawn

Past second cock-crow yacht masts in the harbor go slowly white.

No light in the east yet, but the stars show a certain fatigue.
They withdraw into a new distance, have discovered our unworthiness. It is long since

The owl, in the dark eucalyptus, dire and melodious, last called, and

Long since the moon sank and the English
Finished fornicating in their ketches. In the evening there was a strong swell.

Red died the sun, but at dark wind rose easterly, white sea nagged the black harbor
headland.

When there is a strong swell, you may, if you surrender to it, experience
A sense, in the act, of mystic unity with that rhythm. Your peace is the sea's will.

But now no motion, the bay-face is glossy in darkness, like

An old window pane flat on black ground by the wall, near the ash heap. It neither
Receives nor gives light. Now is the hour when the sea

Sinks into meditation. It doubts its own mission. The drowned cat
That on the evening swell had kept nudging the piles of the pier and had seemed

To want to climb out and lick itself dry, now floats free. On that surface a slight convexity
only, it is like

An eyelid, in darkness, closed. You must learn to accept the kiss of fate, for

The masts go white slow, as light, like dew, from darkness
Condensed on them, on oiled wood, on metal. Dew whitens in darkness.

I lie in my bed and think how, in darkness, the masts go white.

The sound of the engine of the first fishing dory dies seaward. Soon
In the inland glen wakes the dawn-dove. We must try

To love so well the world that we may believe, in the end, in God.

1968

Blow, West Wind

I know, I know—though the evidence
Is lost, and the last who might speak are dead.
Blow, west wind, blow, and the evidence, O,

Is lost, and wind shakes the cedar, and O,
I know how the kestrel hung over Wyoming,
Breast reddened in sunset, and O, the cedar

Shakes, and I know how cold
Was the sweat on my father's mouth, dead.
Blow, west wind, blow, shake the cedar, I know

How once I, a boy, crouching at creekside,
Watched, in the sunlight, a handful of water
Drip, drip, from my hand. The drops—they were bright!

But you believe nothing, with the evidence lost.

1975

Mortal Limit

I saw the hawk ride updraft in the sunset over Wyoming.
It rose from coniferous darkness, past gray jags
Of mercilessness, past whiteness, into the gloaming
Of dream-spectral light above the last purity of snow-snags.

There—west—were the Tetons. Snow-peaks would soon be
In dark profile to break constellations. Beyond what height
Hangs now the black speck? Beyond what range will gold eyes see
New ranges rise to mark a last scrawl of light?

Or, having tasted that atmosphere's thinness, does it
Hang motionless in dying vision before
It knows it will accept the mortal limit,
And swing into the great circular downwardness that will restore

The breath of earth? Of rock? Of rot? Of other such
Items, and the darkness of whatever dream we clutch?

1985

THEODORE ROETHKE
(1908–1963)

Roethke is distinguished among his most gifted contemporaries in having defined independently his own universe and the language appropriate for his discussion of it. Since the Second World War, American literature, even poetry, has reflected rapid changes in its sense of lost values and in negative moods of defeat, from cynicism to despair. By contrast, Roethke rediscovered the roots of life imbedded eternally in nature. Finding himself in torturing conflict with the ingrained values of an obsolete culture, he came by painful stages back to the aboriginal sources of being—in the inert rock, in the root of a dahlia, in the flesh of man. Experience of the family greenhouse does not guarantee such discoveries: there were questions to be asked, knowledge to be attained, and some mysterious trauma to be overcome. This was evident in his early poems in which the metaphysical tension expresses itself in metaphoric luxuriance and fractured syntax. His short life was devoted to the constant discipline of his powers and to the increasing clarity and success in this expression.

He was born in 1908 in Saginaw, Michigan, where his father and his uncle had a successful business as florists. He studied locally, took the A.B. (1929) and M.A. (1936) at the University of Michigan, did further work at Harvard, and taught in several colleges—Lafayette, Pennsylvania State, and Bennington—while learning his craft as writer. He was slow at first: his first volume of poems was collected in 1941, his thirty-third year, his second in 1948. In all, eight volumes appeared before his death. He received his first Guggenheim award in 1946, his second in 1950; he also won the Pulitzer Prize, Bollingen Prize, and the National Book Award. From 1947 he taught at the University of Washington at Seattle.

"I believe that to go forward as a spiritual man, it is necessary to go back," he wrote to John Ciardi in the "Open Letter" of 1950. And again he said, in retrospect, "some of these pieces * * * begin in the mire, as if man is no more than a shape writhing from the old rock." Of growing up in Michigan he declared, "sometimes one gets the feeling that not even the animals have been there before, but the marsh, the mire, the Void is always there. * * * It is America." His view of existence discards paleontology; all the life on the earth is still continuously present, as Eliot, one of his mentors, discovered of "time." So, in 1951, he wrote, "Once upon a tree / I came across a time / * * * What's the time, papaseed? / Everything has been twice. / My father was a fish." Ideas such as these remind one of Whitman, as does his rhythm, and Roethke gratefully acknowledged the influence. However, his conviction of continuity was strengthened by recent science where Whitman had to depend on an intuition originating, perhaps, in childhood. But this gift Roethke also declared: "approach these poems as a child would, naïvely, with your whole being awake, your faculties loose and alert * * *." Of his rhythms he wrote, as Lowes wrote of Whitman, "Listen to them, for they are written to be heard, with the themes often coming alternately, as in music."

It was all well and good to begin with what Kenneth Burke discerned as his "vegetal radicalism," with what a boy could learn of "being" by standing in the root cellar of the greenhouse listening to the "breathing" of roots stored for the winter. Being is proved, but what is the possibility of "becoming"? Vegetal "torpidity without cognition or coition" is not human enough. "Am I but nothing leaning toward a thing?" Early in his writing Roethke's image of the father represented continuity, the hope of becoming; but then suddenly that father "was all whitey bones." A "lost son" must wonder, ask, reply: "I'm somebody else now / * * * Have I come to always? / Not yet. / * * * Maybe God has a house. / But not here." Something of this is in "My Papa's Waltz," but the father is also the florist, coming into the hothouse early in the morning like the new light, crying "Ordnung!" ("order"); again the father is the gardener who would "stand all night watering roses, his fat blue in rubber boots."

The evidence that Roethke's death interrupted him in midcareer is to be found in the affirmative spirit, the new amplitude of thought and form, in such late poems as "The Dying Man" and "Meditations of an Old Woman." The most significant development was that these latest poems and some posthumously published have mature faith, beyond the need of proof, the least condition on which this probing poet would have been content to accept death.

The Collected Poems of Theodore Roethke was published in 1966. Individual titles are: *Open House,* 1941; *The Lost Son and Other Poems,* 1948; *Praise to the End,* 1951; *The Waking: Poems, 1933–1953,* 1953; *Words for the Wind: The Collected Verse of Theodore Roethke,* 1958, 1961; *I Am! Says the Lamb,* 1961; *Sequence, Sometimes Metaphysical, Poems,* 1963; *The Far Field,* 1964. A collection of Roethke's critical writings, *On the Poet and His Craft: Selected Prose of Theodore Roethke,* edited by Ralph J. Mills, Jr., 1965, is the source of the self-criticism quoted in the headnote above, but see also John Ciardi, *Mid-Century American Poets,* 1950, in which first appeared the poet's "Open Letter," a remarkably objective self-analysis. *Selected Letters of Theodore Roethke,* 1968, was edited by Ralph J. Mills, Jr. *Straw for the Fire: From the Notebooks of Theodore Roethke,* 1972, was edited by David Wagoner.

A biography is Allan Seager, *The Glass House:*

The Life of Theodore Roethke, 1968. Critical studies include a brief survey by Ralph J. Mills, Jr., *Theodore Roethke,* 1963; and Karl Malkoff, *Theodore Roethke: An Introduction to the Poetry,* 1966. A collection of critical commentary is Arnold Stein, ed., *Theodore Roethke: Essays on the Poetry,* 1965. William J. Martz, ed., *The Achievement of Theodore Roethke,* 1966, includes an introduction and a selection of the poetry. Recent studies are Rosemary Sullivan, *Theodore Roethke: The Garden Master,* 1975; Jenijoy La Belle, *The Echoing Wood of Theodore Roethke,* 1977; Jay Parini, *Theodore Roethke: An American Romantic,* 1979; George Wolff, *Theodore Roethke,* 1981; Norman Chaney, *Theodore Roethke, The Poetics of Wonder,* 1981; and Lynn Ross-Bryant, *Theodore Roethke, Poetry of the Earth, Poet of the Spirit,* 1981.

Open House

My secrets cry aloud.
I have no need for tongue.
My heart keeps open house,
My doors are widely swung.
An epic of the eyes
My love, with no disguise.

My truths are all foreknown,
This anguish self-revealed.
I'm naked to the bone,
With nakedness my shield.
Myself is what I wear:
I keep the spirit spare.

The anger will endure,
The deed will speak the truth
In language strict and pure.
I stop the lying mouth:
Rage warps my clearest cry
To witless agony.

1941

My Papa's Waltz

The whiskey on your breath
Could make a small boy dizzy;
But I hung on like death:
Such waltzing was not easy.

We romped until the pans
Slid from the kitchen shelf;
My mother's countenance
Could not unfrown itself.

The hand that held my wrist
Was battered on one knuckle;
At every step you missed
My right ear scraped a buckle.

You beat time on my head
With a palm caked hard by dirt,
Then waltzed me off to bed
Still clinging to your shirt.

1948

Night Crow

When I saw that clumsy crow
Flap from a wasted tree,
A shape in the mind rose up:
Over the gulfs of dream
Flew a tremendous bird
Further and further away
Into a moonless black,
Deep in the brain, far back.

1948

Elegy for Jane

My Student, Thrown by a Horse

I remember the neckcurls, limp and damp as tendrils;
And her quick look, a sidelong pickerel[1] smile;
And how, once startled into talk, the light syllables leaped for her,
And she balanced in the delight of her thought,
A wren, happy, tail into the wind,
Her song trembling the twigs and small branches.
The shade sang with her;
The leaves, their whispers turned to kissing;
And the mold sang in the bleached valleys under the rose.

Oh, when she was sad, she cast herself down into such a pure depth,
Even a father could not find her:
Scraping her cheek against straw;
Stirring the clearest water.

My sparrow, you are not here,
Waiting like a fern, making a spiny shadow.
The sides of wet stones cannot console me,
Nor the moss, wound with the last light.

If only I could nudge you from this sleep,
My maimed darling, my skittery pigeon.
Over this damp grave I speak the words of my love:
I, with no rights in this matter,
Neither father nor lover.

1953

The Waking

I wake to sleep, and take my waking slow.
I feel my fate in what I cannot fear.
I learn by going where I have to go.

We think by feeling. What is there to know?
I hear my being dance from ear to ear.
I wake to sleep, and take my waking slow.

1. The jaws in the long, narrow head of the pickerel fish suggest a smile.

Of those so close beside me, which are you?
God bless the Ground! I shall walk softly there,
And learn by going where I have to go.

Light takes the Tree; but who can tell us how?
The lowly worm climbs up a winding stair;
I wake to sleep, and take my waking slow.

Great Nature has another thing to do
To you and me; so take the lively air,
And, lovely, learn by going where to go.

This shaking keeps me steady. I should know.
What falls away is always. And is near.
I wake to sleep, and take my waking slow.
I learn by going where I have to go.

1953

I Knew a Woman

I knew a woman, lovely in her bones,
When small birds sighed, she would sigh back at them;
Ah, when she moved, she moved more ways than one:
The shapes a bright container can contain!
Of her choice virtues only gods should speak,
Or English poets who grew up on Greek
(I'd have them sing in chorus, cheek to cheek).

How well her wishes went! She stroked my chin,
She taught me Turn, and Counter-turn, and Stand;
She taught me Touch, that undulant white skin;
I nibbled meekly from her proffered hand;
She was the sickle; I, poor I, the rake,
Coming behind her for her pretty sake
(But what prodigious mowing we did make).

Love likes a gander, and adores a goose:
Her full lips pursed, the errant note to seize;
She played it quick, she played it light and loose;
My eyes, they dazzled at her flowing knees;
Her several parts could keep a pure repose,
Or one hip quiver with a mobile nose
(She moved in circles, and those circles moved).

Let seed be grass, and grass turn into hay:
I'm martyr to a motion not my own;
What's freedom for? To know eternity.
I swear she cast a shadow white as stone.
But who would count eternity in days?
These old bones live to learn her wanton ways:
(I measure time by how a body sways).

1958

Meditations of an Old Woman: Fourth Meditation[2]

1

I was always one for being alone,
Seeking in my own way, eternal purpose;
At the edge of the field waiting for the pure moment;
Standing, silent, on sandy beaches or walking along green embankments;
Knowing the sinuousness of small waters:
As a chip or shell, floating lazily with a slow current,
A drop of the night rain still in me,
A bit of water caught in a wrinkled crevice,
A pool riding and shining with the river,
Dipping up and down in the ripples,
Tilting back the sunlight.

Was it yesterday I stretched out the thin bones of my innocence?
O the songs we hide, singing only to ourselves!
Once I could touch my shadow, and be happy;
In the white kingdoms, I was light as a seed,
Drifting with the blossoms,
A pensive petal.

But a time comes when the vague life of the mouth no longer suffices;
The dead make more impossible demands from their silence,
The soul stands, lonely in its choice,
Waiting, itself a slow thing,
In the changing body.

> The river moves, wrinkled by midges,
> A light wind stirs in the pine needles.
> The shape of a lark rises from a stone;
> But there is no song.

2

What is it to be a woman?
To be contained, to be a vessel?
To prefer a window to a door?
A pool to a river?
To become lost in a love,
Yet remain only half aware of the intransient glory?
To be a mouth, a meal of meat?
To gaze at a face with the fixed eyes of a spaniel?

I think of the self-involved:
The ritualists of mirror, the lonely drinkers,

2. "Meditations of an Old Woman," five poems, first appeared as a whole in *Words for the Wind* in 1958. The "Meditations" took their source in Roethke's memories of his mother's aging, but his own search for meaning—for "becoming"—inevitably entered their thought; almost the last lines are, "I'm wet with another life. / Yea, I have gone and stayed." Here he was embarking on a new phase in which, as he freely said, both the ideas and the rhythms were influenced by Whitman.

The minions[3] of benzedrine and paraldehyde,[4]
And those who submerge themselves deliberately in trivia,
Women who become their possessions,
Shapes stiffening into metal,
Match-makers, arrangers of picnics—
What do their lives mean,
And the lives of their children?—
The young, brow-beaten early into a baleful silence,
Frozen by a father's lip, a mother's failure to answer.
Have they seen, ever, the sharp bones of the poor?
Or known, once, the soul's authentic hunger,
Those cat-like immaculate creatures
For whom the world works?

What do they need?
O more than a roaring boy,
For the sleek captains of intuition cannot reach them;
They feel neither the tearing iron
Nor the sound of another footstep—
How I wish them awake!
May the high flower of the hay climb into their hearts;
May they lean into light and live;
May they sleep in robes of green, among the ancient ferns;
May their eyes gleam with the first dawn;
May the sun gild them a worm;
May they be taken by the true burning;
May they flame into being!—

I see them as figures walking in a greeny garden,
Their gait formal and elaborate, their hair a glory,
The gentle and beautiful still-to-be-born;
The descendants of the playful tree-shrew that survived the archaic killers,
The fang and the claw, the club and the knout, the irrational edict,
The fury of the hate-driven zealot, the meanness of the human weasel;
Who turned a corner in time, when at last he grew a thumb;
A prince of small beginnings, enduring the slow stretches of change,
Who spoke first in the coarse short-hand of the subliminal depths,
Made from his terror and dismay a grave philosophical language;
A lion of flame, pressed to the point of love,
Yet moves gently among the birds.

3

Younglings, the small fish keep heading into the current.
What's become of care? This lake breathes like a rose.
Beguile me, change. What have I fallen from?
I drink my tears in a place where all light comes.
I'm in love with the dead! My whole forehead's a noise!
On a dark day I walk straight toward the rain.
Who else sweats light from a stone?
By singing we defend;
The husk lives on, ardent as a seed;
My back creaks with the dawn.

3. Servile followers.

4. Drugs: a stimulant; a sedative.

Is my body speaking? I breathe what I am:
The first and last of all things.
Near the graves of the great dead,
Even the stones speak.

1958

The Far Field

1

I dream of journeys repeatedly:
Of flying like a bat deep into a narrowing tunnel,
Of driving alone, without luggage, out a long peninsula,
The road lined with snow-laden second growth,
A fine dry snow ticking the windshield,
Alternate snow and sleet, no on-coming traffic,
And no lights behind, in the blurred side-mirror,
The road changing from glazed tarface to a rubble of stone,
Ending at last in a hopeless sand-rut,
Where the car stalls,
Churning in a snowdrift
Until the headlights darken.

2

At the field's end, in the corner missed by the mower,
Where the turf drops off into a grass-hidden culvert,
Haunt of the cat-bird, nesting-place of the field-mouse,
Not too far away from the ever-changing flower-dump,
Among the tin cans, tires, rusted pipes, broken machinery,—
One learned of the eternal;
And in the shrunken face of a dead rat, eaten by rain and ground-beetles
(I found it lying among the rubble of an old coal bin)
And the tom-cat, caught near the pheasant-run,
Its entrails strewn over the half-grown flowers,
Blasted to death by the night watchman.

I suffered for birds, for young rabbits caught in the mower,
My grief was not excessive.
For to come upon warblers in early May
Was to forget time and death:
How they filled the oriole's elm, a twittering restless cloud, all one morning,
And I watched and watched till my eyes blurred from the bird shapes,—
Cape May, Blackburnian, Cerulean,—
Moving, elusive as fish, fearless,
Hanging, bunched like young fruit, bending the end branches,
Still for a moment,
Then pitching away in half-flight,
Lighter than finches,
While the wrens bickered and sang in the half-green hedgerows,
And the flicker drummed from his dead tree in the chicken-yard.

—Or to lie naked in sand,
In the silted shallows of a slow river,

Fingering a shell,
Thinking:
Once I was something like this, mindless,
Or perhaps with another mind, less peculiar;
Or to sink down to the hips in a mossy quagmire;
Or, with skinny knees, to sit astride a wet log,
Believing:
I'll return again,
As a snake or a raucous bird,
Or, with luck, as a lion.

I learned not to fear infinity,
The far field, the windy cliffs of forever,
The dying of time in the white light of tomorrow,
The wheel turning away from itself,
The sprawl of the wave,
The on-coming water.

3

The river turns on itself,
The tree retreats into its own shadow.
I feel a weightless change, a moving forward
As of water quickening before a narrowing channel
When banks converge, and the wide river whitens;
Or when two rivers combine, the blue glacial torrent
And the yellowish-green from the mountainy upland,—
At first a swift rippling between rocks,
Then a long running over flat stones
Before descending to the alluvial plain,
To the clay banks, and the wild grapes hanging from the elmtrees.
The slightly trembling water
Dropping a fine yellow silt where the sun stays;
And the crabs bask near the edge,
The weedy edge, alive with small snakes and bloodsuckers,—
I have come to a still, but not a deep center,
A point outside the glittering current;
My eyes stare at the bottom of a river,
At the irregular stones, iridescent sandgrains,
My mind moves in more than one place,
In a country half-land, half-water.

I am renewed by death, thought of my death,
The dry scent of a dying garden in September,
The wind fanning the ash of a low fire.
What I love is near at hand,
Always, in earth and air.

4

The lost self changes,
Turning toward the sea,
A sea-shape turning around,—
An old man with his feet before the fire,
In robes of green, in garments of adieu.

A man faced with his own immensity
Wakes all the waves, all their loose wandering fire.
The murmur of the absolute, the why
Of being born fails on his naked ears.
His spirit moves like monumental wind
That gentles on a sunny blue plateau.
He is the end of things, the final man.

All finite things reveal infinitude:
The mountain with its singular bright shade
Like the blue shine on freshly frozen snow,
The after-light upon ice-burdened pines;
Odor of basswood on a mountain-slope,
A scent beloved of bees;
Silence of water above a sunken tree:
The pure serene of memory in one man,—
A ripple widening from a single stone
Winding around the waters of the world.

1964

Wish for a Young Wife

My lizard, my lively writher,
May your limbs never wither,
May the eyes in your face
Survive the green ice
Of envy's mean gaze;
May you live out your life
Without hate, without grief,
And your hair ever blaze,
In the sun, in the sun,
When I am undone,
When I am no one.

1964

The Pike

The river turns,
Leaving a place for the eye to rest,
A furred, a rocky pool,
A bottom of water.

The crabs tilt and eat, leisurely,
And the small fish lie, without shadow, motionless,
Or drift lazily in and out of the weeds.
The bottom-stones shimmer back their irregular striations,
And the half-sunken branch bends away from the gazer's eye.

A scene for the self to abjure!—
And I lean, almost into the water,
My eye always beyond the surface reflection;
I lean, and love these manifold shapes,

Until, out from a dark cove,
From beyond the end of a mossy log,
With one sinuous ripple, then a rush,
A thrashing-up of the whole pool,
The pike strikes.

1964

In a Dark Time

In a dark time, the eye begins to see,
I meet my shadow in the deepening shade;
I hear my echo in the echoing wood—
A lord of nature weeping to a tree.
I live between the heron and the wren,
Beasts of the hill and serpents of the den.

What's madness but nobility of soul
At odds with circumstance? The day's on fire!
I know the purity of pure despair,
My shadow pinned against a sweating wall.
That place among the rocks—is it a cave,
Or winding path? The edge is what I have.

A steady storm of correspondences!
A night flowing with birds, a ragged moon,
And in broad day the midnight come again!
A man goes far to find out what he is—
Death of the self in a long, tearless night,
All natural shapes blazing unnatural light.

Dark, dark my light, and darker my desire.
My soul, like some heat-maddened summer fly,
Keeps buzzing at the sill. Which I is *I*?
A fallen man, I climb out of my fear.
The mind enters itself, and God the mind,
And one is One, free in the tearing wind.

1964

CHARLES OLSON

(1910–1970)

In 1950, when Charles Olson published his essay "Projective Verse" in *Poetry New York,* the time seemed ripe to many for a pronounced swing of American poetry in a new direction. William Carlos Williams was so impressed that he included a large portion of it in his *Autobiography* (1951). A decade later, Donald Allen included the essay in his influential anthology *The New American Poetry: 1945–1960* (1960), along with more pages for Olson's poetry than he allotted to any other poet. The 1950's had flashed and flickered with experimentation, some directly influenced by Olson and some fanned by the same winds of change that blew around him.

Olson himself had by 1960 not finished his major work, *The Maximus Poems,* and he was not to complete it in the decade remaining to him. Conceived as a rival to Ezra Pound's *Cantos,* Hart Crane's *The Bridge,* and Williams's *Paterson,* it remains an incoherent whole, with interesting passages, much less powerful than those earlier works he sought to equal or surpass, but Olson's influence on the poetry of others was great.

Born and raised in Worcester, Massachusetts, with summers spent in Gloucester, Olson attended Wesleyan University in Connecticut, graduating in 1932 and staying another year for an M.A. degree, writing his thesis on Melville. He taught English briefly at Clark University before entering the new Ph.D. program in American studies at Harvard in 1936. After leaving Harvard in 1939 with a Guggenheim Fellowship to continue his study of Melville, he soon turned to political activity, working in the next few years for the American Civil Liberties Union, the Office of War Information, and the Democratic party. About 1945, his career took another sharp turn. Refusing further political appointments, he turned to creative literature, falling soon under the influence of Ezra Pound, whom he visited at the Washington mental hospital where he was confined after the war. In 1947 he published a quirky, subjective study of Melville, *Call Me Ishmael.* In 1950, after his experimental poetry had begun to appear in little magazines, he published the essay "Projective Verse."

The program set forth in "Projective Verse" supported the anti-academic movement in American poetry of the 1950's that saw poetry as stagnant in the universities, while young poets rebelled by turning to Williams rather than Eliot for inspiration. Olson exhorted poets to compose "OPEN" poems, quoted Robert Creeley that "FORM IS NEVER MORE THAN AN EXTENSION OF CONTENT," insisted that "ONE PERCEPTION MUST IMMEDIATELY AND DIRECTLY LEAD TO A FURTHER PERCEPTION," and argued that poetry must be written by ear to the sound of the human voice and composed in lines determined by the poet's breathing patterns. The typewriter should be used to score the work, "its space precisions" allowing the poet to "indicate exactly the breath, the pauses, the suspensions even of syllables, the juxtapositions even of parts of phrases, which he intends."

For the remainder of his life, Olson was an ardent poet, teacher, correspondent, and encourager of other poets. From 1951 until the college's dissolution in 1956 he served as rector of Black Mountain College in North Carolina, greatly influencing such other Black Mountain poets as Robert Duncan, Creeley, and Edward Dorn. After 1957, he lived mostly in Gloucester, scene of *The Maximus Poems,* leaving from 1963 to 1965 to teach at the State University of New York at Buffalo and in 1969, just before his death, to teach at the University of Connecticut.

In *The Maximus Poems,* published in parts from 1953 through 1968, with other parts left in manuscript, Olson attempted to use Gloucester much as Williams had used Paterson, as a focal point for large truths to be seen in the small.

The Maximus Poems, 1983, edited by George F. Butterick and published by the University of California, supersedes earlier forms of that work. *Archeologist of Morning,* 1970, collects poems outside the Maximus group. *Selected Writings,* 1966, was edited by Robert Creeley. George F. Butterick edited *Additional Prose: A Bibliography of America, Proprioception, and Other Notes and Essays,* 1974, and *Muthologos: The Collected Lectures and Interviews,* 1976. *The Post Office: A Memoir of His Father* appeared in 1975 and *The Fiery Hunt and Other Plays* in 1977. Letters are collected in *Mayan Letters,* 1953; *Pleistocene Man: Letters from Olson to John Clarke during October, 1965,* 1968; and *Letters for "Origin," 1950–1956,* 1969.

Studies include Ann Charters, *Olson/Melville: A Study in Affinity,* 1968; George F. Butterick, *A Guide to the Maximus Poems,* 1978; Robert Von Hallberg, *Charles Olson: The Scholar's Art,* 1978; Sherman Paul, *Olson's Push: Origin, Black Mountain, and Recent American Poetry,* 1978; and Paul Christensen, *Charles Olson: Call Him Ishmael,* 1978.

I, Maximus of Gloucester, to You[1]

Off-shore, by islands hidden in the blood
jewels & miracles, I, Maximus
a metal hot from boiling water, tell you
what is a lance, who obeys the figures of
the present dance

1

the thing you're after
may lie around the bend
of the nest (second, time slain, the bird! the bird!

And there! (strong) thrust, the mast! flight
(of the bird
o kylix, o
Antony of Padua
sweep low, o bless

the roofs, the old ones, the gentle steep ones
on whose ridge-poles the gulls sit, from which they depart,

And the flake-racks

of my city!

2

love is form, and cannot be without
important substance (the weight
say, 58 carats each one of us, perforce
our goldsmith's scale

feather to feather added
(and what is mineral, what
is curling hair, the string
you carry in your nervous beak, these

make bulk, these, in the end, are
the sum

(o my lady of good voyage
in whose arm, whose left arm rests
no boy but a carefully carved wood, a painted face, a schooner!
a delicate mast, as bow-sprit for

forwarding

3

the underpart is, though stemmed, uncertain
is, as sex is, as moneys are, facts!

1. This and other poems of Olson were sometimes changed in different printings. The present text of this and the poems printed below is that of the 1983 Butterick edition.

facts, to be dealt with, as the sea is, the demand
that they be played by, that they only can be, that they must
be played by, said he, coldly, the
ear!

By ear, he sd.
But that which matters, that which insists, that which will last,
that! o my people, where shall you find it, how, where, where shall you listen
when all is become billboards, when, all, even silence, is spray-gunned?

when even our bird, my roofs,
cannot be heard

when even you, when sound itself is neoned in?

when, on the hill, over the water
where she who used to sing,
when the water glowed,
black, gold, the tide
outward, at evening

when bells came like boats
over the oil-slicks, milkweed
hulls

And a man slumped,
attentionless,
against pink shingles

o sea city)

4

one loves only form,
and form only comes
into existence when
the thing is born

                    born of yourself, born
                    of hay and cotton struts,
                    of street-pickings, wharves, weeds
                    you carry in, my bird

                                        of a bone of a fish
                                        of a straw, or will
                                        of a color, of a bell
                                        of yourself, torn

5

love is not easy
but how shall you know,
New England, now
that pejorocracy is here, how
that street-cars, o Oregon, twitter

in the afternoon, offend
a black-gold loin?

how shall you strike,
o swordsman, the blue-red back
when, last night, your aim
was mu-sick, mu-sick, mu-sick
And not the cribbage game?

(o Gloucester-man,
weave
your birds and fingers
new, your roof-tops,
clean shit upon racks
sunned on
American
braid
with others like you, such
extricable surface
as faun and oral,
satyr lesbos vase

o kill kill kill kill kill
those
who advertise you
out)

6

in! in! the bow-sprit, bird, the beak
in, the bend is, in, goes in, the form
that which you make, what holds, which is
the law of object, strut after strut, what you are, what you must be, what
the force can throw up, can, right now hereinafter erect,
the mast, the mast, the tender
mast!

The nest, I say, to you, I Maximus, say
under the hand, as I see it, over the waters
from this place where I am, where I hear,
can still hear

from where I carry you a feather
as though, sharp, I picked up,
in the afternoon delivered you
a jewel,
it flashing more than a wing,
than any old romantic thing,
than memory, than place,
than anything other than that which you carry

than that which is,
call it a nest, around the head of, call it
the next second

than that which you
can do!

1950 1983

Maximus to Gloucester, Letter 27 [*withheld*]

I come back to the geography of it,
the land falling off to the left
where my father shot his scabby golf
and the rest of us played baseball
into the summer darkness until no flies
could be seen and we came home
to our various piazzas where the women
buzzed

To the left the land fell to the city,
to the right, it fell to the sea

I was so young my first memory
is of a tent spread to feed lobsters
to Rexall conventioneers, and my father,
a man for kicks, came out of the tent roaring
with a bread-knife in his teeth to take care of
a druggist they'd told him had made a pass at
my mother, she laughing, so sure, as round
as her face, Hines pink and apple,
under one of those frame hats women then

This, is no bare incoming
of novel abstract form, this

is no welter or the forms
of those events, this,

Greeks, is the stopping
of the battle

It is the imposing
of all those antecedent predecessions, the precessions

of me, the generation of those facts
which are my words, it is coming

from all that I no longer am, yet am,
the slow westward motion of

more than I am

There is no strict personal order

for my inheritance.

No Greek will be able

to discriminate my body.

An American

is a complex of occasions,

themselves a geometry

of spatial nature.

I have this sense,

that I am one

with my skin

Plus this—plus this:

that forever the geography

which leans in

on me I compell

backwards I compell Gloucester

to yield, to

change

Polis

is this

1983

The Songs of Maximus: Song 3

This morning of the small snow
I count the blessings, the leak in the faucet
which makes of the sink time, the drop
of the water on water as sweet
as the Seth Thomas
in the old kitchen
my father stood in his drawers to wind (always
he forgot the 30th day, as I don't want to remember
the rent
a house these days
so much somebody else's,
especially,
Congoleum's

Or the plumbing,
that it doesn't work, this I like, have even used paper clips

as well as string to hold the ball up And flush it
with my hand
But that the car doesn't, that no moving thing moves
without that song I'd void my ear of, the musickracket
of all ownership . . .
Holes
in my shoes, that's all right, my fly
gaping, me out
at the elbows, the blessing
that difficulties are once more

"In the midst of plenty, walk
as close to
bare
In the face of sweetness,
piss
In the time of goodness,
go side, go
smashing, beat them, go as
(as near as you can

tear
In the land of plenty, have
nothing to do with it
take the way of
the lowest,
including
your legs, go
contrary, go

sing

1983

ELIZABETH BISHOP
(1911–1979)

Elizabeth Bishop's subject matter is suggested in the titles of two of her books: *North & South* (1946) and *Questions of Travel* (1965). From the beginning she has had a reputation as an exotic among American poets, shaping her poems out of her experiences and observations in lands widely separated both geographically and spiritually from the New England soil on which she was raised. Yet, there is a spare New England quality to her verse, too. Her diction is precise, her images sharp and clear.

Born in Massachusetts, she grew up in Nova Scotia and New England. Sick much of the time as a child, she read a lot and was writing poetry by the time she was eight. Educated at Walnut Hill School in Natick, Massachusetts, and at Vassar College, she spent two years in Europe shortly after graduation and then returned to the United States to live in Key West, Florida. Throughout most of the 1950's and 1960's she lived in Brazil. Later, she divided her time between that country and Cambridge, Massachusetts, where she taught part-time at Harvard.

Randall Jarrell once wrote that "instead

of crying, with justice, 'This is a world in which no one can get along,' Miss Bishop's poems show that it is barely but perfectly possible—has been, that is, for her." Her precision of statement seems often to be allied to her emotional control. In this respect and in her wit she displays a similarity to her long-time friend, Marianne Moore. Like Miss Moore, too, she quietly went her own way as a poet; it was a way that earned her numerous awards and citations, including a Guggenheim Fellowship, a position as Consultant in Poetry at the Library of Congress, an award from the American Academy of Arts and Letters, and a Pulitzer Prize. More important, it produced some poems that seem destined to last.

The Complete Poems: 1927–1979, 1983, supersedes the earlier *Complete Poems,* 1969. Other volumes of poems besides those listed above are *Poems North & South—A Cold Spring,* 1955; *Selected Poems,* 1967; and *Geography III,* 1976. Robert Giroux edited *The Collected Prose,* 1984. Miss Bishop's translations include *Diary of Helena Morley,* 1957, and many poems in *An Anthology of Twentieth-Century Brazilian Poetry,* 1973, which she edited with Emanuel Brasil. A critical study is Anne Stevenson, *Elizabeth Bishop,* 1966. *Elizabeth Bishop and Her Art* was edited by Lloyd Schwartz and Sybil P. Estess, 1983.

The Fish

I caught a tremendous fish
and held him beside the boat
half out of water, with my hook
fast in a corner of his mouth.
He didn't fight.
He hadn't fought at all.
He hung a grunting weight,
battered and venerable
and homely. Here and there
his brown skin hung in strips
like ancient wallpaper,
and its pattern of darker brown
was like wallpaper:
shapes like full-blown roses
stained and lost through age.
He was speckled with barnacles,
fine rosettes of lime,
and infested
with tiny white sea-lice,
and underneath two or three
rags of green weed hung down.
While his gills were breathing in
the terrible oxygen
—the frightening gills,
fresh and crisp with blood,
that can cut so badly—
I thought of the coarse white flesh
packed in like feathers,
the big bones and the little bones,
the dramatic reds and blacks
of his shiny entrails,
and the pink swim-bladder
like a big peony.
I looked into his eyes
which were far larger than mine

but shallower, and yellowed,
the irises backed and packed
with tarnished tinfoil
seen through the lenses
of old scratched isinglass.
They shifted a little, but not
to return my stare.
—It was more like the tipping
of an object toward the light.
I admired his sullen face,
the mechanism of his jaw,
and then I saw
that from his lower lip
—if you could call it a lip—
grim, wet, and weaponlike,
hung five old pieces of fish-line,
or four and a wire leader
with the swivel still attached,
with all their five big hooks
grown firmly in his mouth.
A green line, frayed at the end
where he broke it, two heavier lines,
and a fine black thread
still crimped from the strain and snap
when it broke and he got away.
Like medals with their ribbons
frayed and wavering,
a five-haired beard of wisdom
trailing from his aching jaw.
I stared and stared
and victory filled up
the little rented boat,
from the pool of bilge
where oil had spread a rainbow
around the rusted engine
to the bailer rusted orange,
the sun-cracked thwarts,
the oarlocks on their strings,
the gunnels—until everything
was rainbow, rainbow, rainbow!
And I let the fish go.

1946

At the Fishhouses

Although it is a cold evening,
down by one of the fishhouses
an old man sits netting,
his net, in the gloaming almost invisible,
a dark purple-brown,
and his shuttle worn and polished.
The air smells so strong of codfish
it makes one's nose run and one's eyes water.

The five fishhouses have steeply peaked roofs
and narrow, cleated gangplanks slant up
to storerooms in the gables
for the wheelbarrows to be pushed up and down on.
All is silver: the heavy surface of the sea,
swelling slowly as if considering spilling over,
is opaque, but the silver of the benches,
the lobster pots, and masts, scattered
among the wild jagged rocks,
is of an apparent translucence
like the small old buildings with an emerald moss
growing on their shoreward walls.
The big fish tubs are completely lined
with layers of beautiful herring scales
and the wheelbarrows are similarly plastered
with creamy iridescent coats of mail,
with small iridescent flies crawling on them.
Up on the little slope behind the houses,
set in the sparse bright sprinkle of grass,
is an ancient wooden capstan,
cracked, with two long bleached handles
and some melancholy stains, like dried blood,
where the ironwork has rusted.
The old man accepts a Lucky Strike.
He was a friend of my grandfather.
We talk of the decline in the population
and of codfish and herring
while he waits for a herring boat to come in.
There are sequins on his vest and on his thumb.
He has scraped the scales, the principal beauty,
from unnumbered fish with that black old knife,
the blade of which is almost worn away.

Down at the water's edge, at the place
where they haul up the boats, up the long ramp
descending into the water, thin silver
tree trunks are laid horizontally
across the gray stones, down and down
at intervals of four or five feet.

Cold dark deep and absolutely clear,
element bearable to no mortal,
to fish and to seals . . . One seal particularly
I have seen here evening after evening.
He was curious about me. He was interested in music;
like me a believer in total immersion,
so I used to sing him Baptist hymns.
I also sang "A Mighty Fortress Is Our God."
He stood up in the water and regarded me
steadily, moving his head a little.
Then he would disappear, then suddenly emerge
almost in the same spot, with a sort of shrug
as if it were against his better judgment.
Cold dark deep and absolutely clear,
the clear gray icy water . . . Back, behind us,

the dignified tall firs begin.
Bluish, associating with their shadows,
a million Christmas trees stand
waiting for Christmas. The water seems suspended
above the rounded gray and blue-gray stones.
I have seen it over and over, the same sea, the same,
slightly, indifferently swinging above the stones,
icily free above the stones,
above the stones and then the world.
If you should dip your hand in,
your wrist would ache immediately,
your bones would begin to ache and your hand would burn
as if the water were a transmutation of fire
that feeds on stones and burns with a dark gray flame.
If you tasted it, it would first taste bitter,
then briny, then surely burn your tongue.
It is like what we imagine knowledge to be:
dark, salt, clear, moving, utterly free,
drawn from the cold hard mouth
of the world, derived from the rocky breasts
forever, flowing and drawn, and since
our knowledge is historical, flowing, and flown.

1955

Questions of Travel

There are too many waterfalls here; the crowded streams
hurry too rapidly down to the sea,
and the pressure of so many clouds on the mountaintops
makes them spill over the sides in soft slow-motion,
turning to waterfalls under our very eyes.
—For if those streaks, those mile-long, shiny, tearstains,
aren't waterfalls yet,
in a quick age or so, as ages go here,
they probably will be.
But if the streams and clouds keep travelling, travelling,
the mountains look like the hulls of capsized ships,
slime-hung and barnacled.

Think of the long trip home.
Should we have stayed at home and thought of here?
Where should we be today?
Is it right to be watching strangers in a play
in this strangest of theatres?
What childishness is it that while there's a breath of life
in our bodies, we are determined to rush
to see the sun the other way around?
The tiniest green hummingbird in the world?
To stare at some inexplicable old stonework,
inexplicable and impenetrable,
at any view,
instantly seen and always, always delightful?
Oh, must we dream our dreams

and have them, too?
And have we room
for one more folded sunset, still quite warm?

But surely it would have been a pity
not to have seen the trees along this road,
really exaggerated in their beauty,
not to have seen them gesturing
like noble pantomimists, robed in pink.
—Not to have had to stop for gas and heard
the sad, two-noted, wooden tune
of disparate wooden clogs
carelessly clacking over
a grease-stained filling-station floor.
(In another country the clogs would all be tested.
Each pair there would have identical pitch.)
—A pity not to have heard
the other, less primitive music of the fat brown bird
who sings above the broken gasoline pump
in a bamboo church of Jesuit baroque:
three towers, five silver crosses.
—Yes, a pity not to have pondered,
blurr'dly and inconclusively,
on what connection can exist for centuries
between the crudest wooden footwear
and, careful and finicky,
the whittled fantasies of wooden cages.
—Never to have studied history in
the weak calligraphy of songbirds' cages.
—And never to have had to listen to rain
so much like politicians' speeches:
two hours of unrelenting oratory
and then a sudden golden silence
in which the traveller takes a notebook, writes:

"Is it lack of imagination that makes us come
to imagined places, not just stay at home?
Or could Pascal have been not entirely right
about just sitting quietly in one's room?

Continent, city, country, society:
the choice is never wide and never free.
And here, or there . . . No. Should we have stayed at home,
wherever that may be?"

1965

The Armadillo

For Robert Lowell

This is the time of year
when almost every night
the frail, illegal fire balloons appear.
Climbing the mountain height,

rising toward a saint
still honored in these parts,
the paper chambers flush and fill with light
that comes and goes, like hearts.

Once up against the sky it's hard
to tell them from the stars—
planets, that is—the tinted ones:
Venus going down, or Mars,

or the pale green one. With a wind,
they flare and falter, wobble and toss;
but if it's still they steer between
the kite sticks of the Southern Cross,

receding, dwindling, solemnly
and steadily forsaking us,
or, in the downdraft from a peak,
suddenly turning dangerous.

Last night another big one fell.
It splattered like an egg of fire
against the cliff behind the house.
The flame ran down. We saw the pair

of owls who nest there flying up
and up, their whirling black-and-white
stained bright pink underneath, until
they shrieked up out of sight.

The ancient owls' nest must have burned.
Hastily, all alone,
a glistening armadillo left the scene,
rose-flecked, head down, tail down,

and then a baby rabbit jumped out,
short-eared, to our surprise.
So soft!—a handful of intangible ash
with fixed, ignited eyes.

Too pretty, dreamlike mimicry!
O falling fire and piercing cry
and panic, and a weak mailed fist
clenched ignorant against the sky!

1965

Sestina

September rain falls on the house.
In the failing light, the old grandmother
sits in the kitchen with the child
beside the Little Marvel Stove,
reading the jokes from the almanac,
laughing and talking to hide her tears.

She thinks that her equinoctial tears
and the rain that beats on the roof of the house
were both foretold by the almanac,
but only known to a grandmother.
The iron kettle sings on the stove.
She cuts some bread and says to the child,

It's time for tea now; but the child
is watching the teakettle's small hard tears
dance like mad on the hot black stove,
the way the rain must dance on the house.
Tidying up, the old grandmother
hangs up the clever almanac

on its string. Birdlike, the almanac
hovers half open above the child,
hovers above the old grandmother
and her teacup full of dark brown tears.
She shivers and says she thinks the house
feels chilly, and puts more wood in the stove.

It was to be, says the Marvel Stove.
I know what I know, says the almanac.
With crayons the child draws a rigid house
and a winding pathway. Then the child
puts in a man with buttons like tears
and shows it proudly to the grandmother.

But secretly, while the grandmother
busies herself about the stove,
the little moons fall down like tears
from between the pages of the almanac
into the flower bed the child
has carefully placed in the front of the house.

Time to plant tears, says the almanac.
The grandmother sings to the marvellous stove
and the child draws another inscrutable house.

1965

Crusoe in England

A new volcano has erupted,
the papers say, and last week I was reading
where some ship saw an island being born:
at first a breath of steam, ten miles away;
and then a black fleck—basalt, probably—
rose in the mate's binoculars
and caught on the horizon like a fly.
They named it. But my poor old island's still
un-rediscovered, un-renamable.
None of the books has ever got it right.

Well, I had fifty-two
miserable, small volcanoes I could climb
with a few slithery strides—
volcanoes dead as ash heaps.
I used to sit on the edge of the highest one
and count the others standing up,
naked and leaden, with their heads blown off.
I'd think that if they were the size
I thought volcanoes should be, then I had
become a giant;
and if I had become a giant,
I couldn't bear to think what size
the goats and turtles were,
or the gulls, or the overlapping rollers
—a glittering hexagon of rollers
closing and closing in, but never quite,
glittering and glittering, though the sky
was mostly overcast.

My island seemed to be
a sort of cloud-dump. All the hemisphere's
left-over clouds arrived and hung
above the craters—their parched throats
were hot to touch.
Was that why it rained so much?
And why sometimes the whole place hissed?
The turtles lumbered by, high-domed,
hissing like teakettles.
(And I'd have given years, or taken a few,
for any sort of kettle, of course.)
The folds of lava, running out to sea,
would hiss. I'd turn. And then they'd prove
to be more turtles.
The beaches were all lava, variegated,
black, red, and white, and gray;
the marbled colors made a fine display.
And I had waterspouts. Oh,
half a dozen at a time, far out,
they'd come and go, advancing and retreating,
their heads in cloud, their feet in moving patches
of scuffed-up white.
Glass chimneys, flexible, attenuated,
sacerdotal beings of glass . . . I watched
the water spiral up in them like smoke.
Beautiful, yes, but not much company.

I often gave way to self-pity.
"Do I deserve this? I suppose I must.
I wouldn't be here otherwise. Was there
a moment when I actually chose this?
I don't remember, but there could have been."
What's wrong about self-pity, anyway?
With my legs dangling down familiarly
over a crater's edge, I told myself

"Pity should begin at home." So the more
pity I felt, the more I felt at home.

The sun set in the sea; the same odd sun
rose from the sea,
and there was one of it and one of me.
The island had one kind of everything:
one tree snail, a bright violet-blue
with a thin shell, crept over everything,
over the one variety of tree,
a sooty, scrub affair.
Snail shells lay under these in drifts
and, at a distance,
you'd swear that they were beds of irises.
There was one kind of berry, a dark red.
I tried it, one by one, and hours apart.
Sub-acid, and not bad, no ill effects;
and so I made home-brew. I'd drink
the awful, fizzy, stinging stuff
that went straight to my head
and play my home-made flute
(I think it had the weirdest scale on earth)
and, dizzy, whoop and dance among the goats.
Home-made, home-made! But aren't we all?
I felt a deep affection for
the smallest of my island industries.
No, not exactly, since the smallest was
a miserable philosophy.

Because I didn't know enough.
Why didn't I know enough of something?
Greek drama or astronomy? The books
I'd read were full of blanks;
the poems—well, I tried
reciting to my iris-beds,
"They flash upon that inward eye,
which is the bliss . . ."[1] The bliss of what?
One of the first things that I did
when I got back was look it up.

The island smelled of goat and guano.
The goats were white, so were the gulls,
and both too tame, or else they thought
I was a goat, too, or a gull.
Baa, baa, baa and *shriek, shriek, shriek,*
baa . . . shriek . . . baa . . . I still can't shake
them from my ears; they're hurting now.
The questioning shrieks, the equivocal replies
over a ground of hissing rain
and hissing, ambulating turtles
got on my nerves.

1. William Wordsworth (1770–1850), "Daffodils." The completed line reads, "Which is the bliss of solitude." Defoe's novel *Robinson Crusoe* was published in 1719.

When all the gulls flew up at once, they sounded
like a big tree in a strong wind, its leaves.
I'd shut my eyes and think about a tree,
an oak, say, with real shade, somewhere.
I'd heard of cattle getting island-sick.
I thought the goats were.
One billy-goat would stand on the volcano
I'd christened *Mont d'Espoir*[2] or *Mount Despair*
(I'd time enough to play with names),
and bleat and bleat, and sniff the air.
I'd grab his beard and look at him.
His pupils, horizontal, narrowed up
and expressed nothing, or a little malice.
I got so tired of the very colors!
One day I dyed a baby goat bright red
with my red berries, just to see
something a little different.
And then his mother wouldn't recognize him.

Dreams were the worst. Of course I dreamed of food
and love, but they were pleasant rather
than otherwise. But then I'd dream of things
like slitting a baby's throat, mistaking it
for a baby goat. I'd have
nightmares of other islands
stretching away from mine, infinities
of islands, islands spawning islands,
like frogs' eggs turning into polliwogs
of islands, knowing that I had to live
on each and every one, eventually,
for ages, registering their flora,
their fauna, their geography.

Just when I thought I couldn't stand it
another minute longer, Friday came.
(Accounts of that have everything all wrong.)
Friday was nice.
Friday was nice, and we were friends.
If only he had been a woman!
I wanted to propagate my kind,
and so did he, I think, poor boy.
He'd pet the baby goats sometimes,
and race with them, or carry one around.
—Pretty to watch; he had a pretty body.

And then one day they came and took us off.

Now I live here, another island,
that doesn't seem like one, but who decides?
My blood was full of them; my brain
bred islands. But that archipelago
has petered out. I'm old.
I'm bored, too, drinking my real tea,

2. Mount Hope, the French pronunciation suggesting the punning English version that follows.

surrounded by uninteresting lumber.
The knife there on the shelf—
it reeked of meaning, like a crucifix.
It lived. How many years did I
beg it, implore it, not to break?
I knew each nick and scratch by heart,
the bluish blade, the broken tip,
the lines of wood-grain on the handle . . .
Now it won't look at me at all.
The living soul has dribbled away.
My eyes rest on it and pass on.

The local museum's asked me to
leave everything to them:
the flute, the knife, the shrivelled shoes,
my shedding goatskin trousers
(moths have got in the fur),
the parasol that took me such a time
remembering the way the ribs should go.
It still will work but, folded up,
looks like a plucked and skinny fowl.
How can anyone want such things?
—And Friday, my dear Friday, died of measles
seventeen years ago come March.

1976

The Moose

For Grace Bulmer Bowers

From narrow provinces
of fish and bread and tea,
home of the long tides
where the bay leaves the sea
twice a day and takes
the herrings long rides,

where if the river
enters or retreats
in a wall of brown foam
depends on if it meets
the bay coming in,
the bay not at home;

where, silted red,
sometimes the sun sets
facing a red sea,
and others, veins the flats'
lavender, rich mud
in burning rivulets;

on red, gravelly roads,
down rows of sugar maples,
past clapboard farmhouses
and neat, clapboard churches,

bleached, ridged as clamshells,
past twin silver birches,

through late afternoon
a bus journeys west,
the windshield flashing pink,
pink glancing off of metal,
brushing the dented flank
of blue, beat-up enamel;

down hollows, up rises,
and waits, patient, while
a lone traveller gives
kisses and embraces
to seven relatives
and a collie supervises.

Goodbye to the elms,
to the farm, to the dog.
The bus starts. The light
grows richer; the fog,
shifting, salty, thin,
comes closing in.

Its cold, round crystals
form and slide and settle
in the white hens' feathers,
in gray glazed cabbages,
on the cabbage roses
and lupins like apostles;

the sweet peas cling
to their wet white string
on the whitewashed fences;
bumblebees creep
inside the foxgloves,
and evening commences.

One stop at Bass River.
Then the Economies—
Lower, Middle, Upper;
Five Islands, Five Houses,
where a woman shakes a tablecloth
out after supper.

A pale flickering. Gone.
The Tantramar marshes
and the smell of salt hay.
An iron bridge trembles
and a loose plank rattles
but doesn't give way.

On the left, a red light
swims through the dark:
a ship's port lantern.
Two rubber boots show,
illuminated, solemn.
A dog gives one bark.

A woman climbs in
with two market bags,
brisk, freckled, elderly.
"A grand night. Yes, sir,
all the way to Boston."
She regards us amicably.

Moonlight as we enter
the New Brunswick woods,
hairy, scratchy, splintery;
moonlight and mist
caught in them like lamb's wool
on bushes in a pasture.

The passengers lie back.
Snores. Some long sighs.
A dreamy divagation
begins in the night,
a gentle, auditory,
slow hallucination. . . .

In the creakings and noises,
an old conversation
—not concerning us,
but recognizable, somewhere,
back in the bus:
Grandparents' voices

uninterruptedly
talking, in Eternity:
names being mentioned,
things cleared up finally;
what he said, what she said,
who got pensioned;

deaths, deaths and sicknesses;
the year he remarried;
the year (something) happened.
She died in childbirth.
That was the son lost
when the schooner foundered.

He took to drink. Yes.
She went to the bad.
When Amos began to pray
even in the store and
finally the family had
to put him away.

"Yes . . ." that peculiar
affirmative. "Yes . . ."
A sharp, indrawn breath,
half groan, half acceptance,
that means "Life's like that.
We know *it* (also death)."

Talking the way they talked
in the old featherbed,
peacefully, on and on,
dim lamplight in the hall,
down in the kitchen, the dog
tucked in her shawl.

Now, it's all right now
even to fall asleep
just as on all those nights.
—Suddenly the bus driver
stops with a jolt,
turns off his lights.

A moose has come out of
the impenetrable wood
and stands there, looms, rather,
in the middle of the road.
It approaches; it sniffs at
the bus's hot hood.

Towering, antlerless,
high as a church,
homely as a house
(or, safe as houses).
A man's voice assures us
"Perfectly harmless. . . ."

Some of the passengers
exclaim in whispers,
childishly, softly,
"Sure are big creatures."
"It's awful plain."
"Look! It's a she!"

Taking her time,
she looks the bus over,
grand, otherworldly.
Why, why do we feel
(we all feel) this sweet
sensation of joy?

"Curious creatures,"
says our quiet driver,
rolling his *r*'s.
"Look at that, would you."
Then he shifts gears.
For a moment longer,

by craning backward,
the moose can be seen
on the moonlit macadam;
then there's a dim
smell of moose, an acrid
smell of gasoline.

1976

Poem

About the size of an old-style dollar bill,
American or Canadian,
mostly the same whites, gray greens, and steel grays
—this little painting (a sketch for a larger one?)
has never earned any money in its life.
Useless and free, it has spent seventy years
as a minor family relic
handed along collaterally to owners
who looked at it sometimes, or didn't bother to.

It must be Nova Scotia; only there
does one see gabled wooden houses
painted that awful shade of brown.
The other houses, the bits that show, are white.
Elm trees, low hills, a thin church steeple
—that gray-blue wisp—or is it? In the foreground
a water meadow with some tiny cows,
two brushstrokes each, but confidently cows;
two minuscule white geese in the blue water,
back-to-back, feeding, and a slanting stick.
Up closer, a wild iris, white and yellow,
fresh-squiggled from the tube.
The air is fresh and cold; cold early spring
clear as gray glass; a half inch of blue sky
below the steel-gray storm clouds.
(They were the artist's specialty.)
A specklike bird is flying to the left.
Or is it a flyspeck looking like a bird?

Heavens, I recognize the place, I know it!
It's behind—I can almost remember the farmer's name.
His barn backed on that meadow. There it is,
titanium white, one dab. The hint of steeple,
filaments of brush-hairs, barely there,
must be the Presbyterian church.
Would that be Miss Gillespie's house?
Those particular geese and cows
are naturally before my time.

A sketch done in an hour, "in one breath,"
once taken from a trunk and handed over.
Would you like this? I'll probably never
have room to hang these things again.
Your Uncle George, no, mine, my Uncle George,
he'd be your great-uncle, left them all with Mother
when he went back to England.
You know, he was quite famous, an R.A. . . .

I never knew him. We both knew this place,
apparently, this literal small backwater,
looked at it long enough to memorize it,
our years apart. How strange. And it's still loved,
or its memory is (it must have changed a lot).

Our visions coincided—"visions" is
too serious a word—our looks, two looks:
art "copying from life" and life itself,
life and the memory of it so compressed
they've turned into each other. Which is which?
Life and the memory of it cramped,
dim, on a piece of Bristol board,
dim, but how live, how touching in detail
—the little that we get for free,
the little of our earthly trust. Not much.
About the sizc of our abidance
along with theirs: the munching cows,
the iris, crisp and shivering, the water
still standing from spring freshets,
the yet-to-be-dismantled elms, the geese.

1976

One Art

The art of losing isn't hard to master;
so many things seem filled with the intent
to be lost that their loss is no disaster.

Lose something every day. Accept the fluster
of lost door keys, the hour badly spent.
The art of losing isn't hard to master.

Then practice losing farther, losing faster:
places, and names, and where it was you meant
to travel. None of these will bring disaster.

I lost my mother's watch. And look! my last, or
next-to-last, of three loved houses went.
The art of losing isn't hard to master.

I lost two cities, lovely ones. And, vaster,
some realms I owned, two rivers, a continent.
I miss them, but it wasn't a disaster.

—Even losing you (the joking voice, a gesture
I love) I shan't have lied. It's evident
the art of losing's not too hard to master
though it may look like (*Write* it!) like disaster.

1976

North Haven

In memoriam: Robert Lowell

I can make out the rigging of a schooner
a mile off; I can count
the new cones on the spruce. It is so still
the pale bay wears a milky skin, the sky
no clouds, except for one long, carded horse's-tail.

The islands haven't shifted since last summer,
even if I like to pretend they have
—drifting, in a dreamy sort of way,
a little north, a little south or sidewise,
and that they're free within the blue frontiers of bay.

This month, our favorite one is full of flowers:
Buttercups, Red Clover, Purple Vetch,
Hawkweed still burning, Daisies pied, Eyebright,
the Fragrant Bedstraw's incandescent stars,
and more, returned, to paint the meadows with delight.

The Goldfinches are back, or others like them,
and the White-throated Sparrow's five-note song,
pleading and pleading, brings tears to the eyes.
Nature repeats herself, or almost does:
repeat, repeat, repeat; revise, revise, revise.

Years ago, you told me it was here
(in 1932?) you first "discovered *girls*"
and learned to sail, and learned to kiss.
You had "such fun," you said, that classic summer.
("Fun"—it always seemed to leave you at a loss . . .)

You left North Haven, anchored in its rock,
afloat in mystic blue . . . And now—you've left
for good. You can't derange, or re-arrange,
your poems again. (But the Sparrows can their song.)
The words won't change again. Sad friend, you cannot change.

1978 1983

ROBERT HAYDEN
(1913–1980)

Born in Detroit, Robert Hayden learned to read before entering school, developed the habit, and soon turned to books as an escape from straitened circumstances. Of George Eliot's *Romola,* Hawthorne's *Marble Faun,* and Bulwer-Lytton's *Last Days of Pompeii,* he wrote, "I loved those books, partly because they took me out of the environment I lived in * * *." Poetry became his first love. Besides traditional English poets, as a young man he admired such contemporary Americans as Sandburg, Millay, and Wylie, and he early discovered the work of Countee Cullen and other writers of the Harlem Renaissance. Graduating from high school in the Depression, he attended Detroit City College (now Wayne State University), and worked on the Federal Writers' Project in Detroit. In 1940 he published his first book of poems, *Heart-Shape in the Dust.*

After a brief stay in New York, where he met Countee Cullen, Hayden returned to Michigan to enroll as a graduate student at the University of Michigan in 1941. There he studied with W. H. Auden, who greatly influenced his work. After receiving his M.A. in 1944, Hayden remained two more years at Michigan before taking a professorial position at Fisk University. In Tennessee, he and his family experienced a more virulent segregation than they had been prepared for by life in the North, but nevertheless he remained at Fisk for over twenty years, publishing two books in Nashville and seeing yet another, *A Ballad of Remembrance* (1962), published in London by a small press. With *Selected Poems* (1966), he finally achieved New York publication and a measure of celebrity. Two years later he went back to the University of Michigan as a professor of English, a position he held until his death. Meanwhile, his many honors culminated with his two years as Poetry Consultant to the Library of Congress, 1976–1978.

A member of the Baha'i faith from his early years at the University of Michigan, Hayden believed in the essential unity of all people, all religions, all races. Hence he was sometimes criticized for his refusal to write polemic poetry and for his desire to be judged as a poet in English, not as a black man who happened to be a writer. This did not mean that he was blind to his surroundings, but only that the black experience and idiom of his poetry came to him as materials close at hand, part of the experience of any human in his circumstances. "I don't believe that races are important," he wrote; "I'm very suspicious of any form of ethnicity or nationalism; I think that these things are very crippling and very divisive * * *. I have the feeling that by holding on to these beliefs and giving them expression in my work * * * I'm doing something to prepare, maybe, for a new time, for a new world."

Hayden's poetry is distinguished by a clear, colloquial voice that speaks evenly of pain and pleasure. Often the contrast is between an unsatisfactory present and a better world "where none is lonely, none hunted, alien," as he writes in "Frederick Douglass," where Aunt Jemima ceases to be a freak because no longer required to enact "someone's notion" of herself—a world that can recognize the striving for beauty even in "The Tattooed Man," for after all "all art is pain / suffered and outlived."

Besides those named above, Hayden's collections of verse include *The Lion and the Archer* (with Myron O'Higgins), 1948; *Figures of Time: Poems,* 1955; *Words in the Mourning Time,* 1970; *The Night-Blooming Cereus,* 1972, *Angle of Ascent: New and Selected Poems,* 1975; and *American Journal,* 1978 (expanded edition, 1980). Frederick Glaysher edited *The Collected Prose of Robert Hayden,* 1984.

A brief appraisal appears in *Dictionary of Literary Biography,* Volume 5: *American Poets Since World War II,* 1980.

Aunt Jemima of the Ocean Waves

I

Enacting someone's notion of themselves
(and me), The One And Only Aunt Jemima
and Kokimo The Dixie Dancing Fool
do a bally for the freak show.

I watch a moment, then move on,
pondering the logic that makes of them
(and me) confederates
of The Spider Girl, The Snake-skinned Man. . . .

Poor devils have to live somehow.

I cross the boardwalk to the beach,
lie in the sand and gaze beyond
the clutter at the sea.

II

Trouble you for a light?
I turn as Aunt Jemima settles down
beside me, her blue-rinsed hair
without the red bandanna now.

I hold the lighter to her cigarette.
Much obliged. Unmindful (perhaps)
of my embarrassment, she looks
at me and smiles: You sure

do favor a friend I used to have.
Guess that's why I bothered you
for a light. So much like him that I—
She pauses, watching white horses rush

to the shore. Way them big old waves
come slamming whooping in,
sometimes it's like they mean to smash
this no-good world to hell.

Well, it could happen. A book I read—
Crossed that very ocean years ago.
London, Paris, Rome,
Constantinople too—I've seen them all.

Back when they billed me everywhere
as the Sepia High Stepper.
Crowned heads applauded me.
Years before your time. Years and years.

I wore me plenty diamonds then,
and counts or dukes or whatever they were
would fill my dressing room
with the costliest flowers. But of course

there was this one you resemble so.
Get me? The sweetest gentleman.
Dead before his time. Killed in the war
to save the world for another war.

High-stepping days for me
were over after that. Still I'm not one
to let grief idle me for long.
I went out with a mental act—

mind-reading—Mysteria From
The Mystic East—veils and beads
and telling suckers how to get
stolen rings and sweethearts back.

One night he was standing by my bed,
seen him plain as I see you,
and warned me without a single word:
Baby, quit playing with spiritual stuff.

So here I am, so here I am,
fake mammy to God's mistakes.
And that's the beauty part,
I mean, ain't that the beauty part.

She laughs, but I do not, knowing what
her laughter shields. And mocks.
I light another cigarette for her.
She smokes, not saying any more.

Scream of children in the surf,
adagios of sun and flashing foam,
the sexual glitter, oppressive fun. . . .
An antique etching comes to mind:

"The Sable Venus" naked on
a baroque Cellini shell—voluptuous
imago floating in the wake
of slave-ships on fantastic seas.

Jemima sighs, Reckon I'd best
be getting back. I help her up.
Don't you take no wooden nickels, hear?
Tin dimes neither. So long, pal.

1970

Frederick Douglass

When it is finally ours, this freedom, this liberty, this beautiful
and terrible thing, needful to man as air,
usable as earth; when it belongs at last to all,
when it is truly instinct, brain matter, diastole, systole,
reflex action; when it is finally won; when it is more
than the gaudy mumbo jumbo of politicians:
this man, this Douglass, this former slave, this Negro
beaten to his knees, exiled, visioning a world
where none is lonely, none hunted, alien,
this man, superb in love and logic, this man
shall be remembered. Oh, not with statues' rhetoric,
not with legends and poems and wreaths of bronze alone,
but with the lives grown out of his life, the lives
fleshing his dream of the beautiful, needful thing.

1975

Those Winter Sundays

Sundays too my father got up early
and put his clothes on in the blueblack cold,
then with cracked hands that ached
from labor in the weekday weather made
banked fires blaze. No one ever thanked him.

I'd wake and hear the cold splintering, breaking.
When the rooms were warm, he'd call,
and slowly I would rise and dress,
fearing the chronic angers of that house,

Speaking indifferently to him,
who had driven out the cold
and polished my good shoes as well.
What did I know, what did I know
of love's austere and lonely offices?

1975

Night, Death, Mississippi

I

A quavering cry. Screech-owl?
Or one of them?
The old man in his reek
and gauntness laughs—

One of them, I bet—
and turns out the kitchen lamp,
limping to the porch to listen
in the windowless night.

Be there with Boy and the rest
if I was well again.
Time was. Time was.
White robes like moonlight

In the sweetgum dark.
Unbucked that one then
and him squealing bloody Jesus
as we cut it off.

Time was. A cry?
A cry all right.
He hawks and spits,
fevered as by groinfire.

Have us a bottle,
Boy and me—
he's earned him a bottle—
when he gets home.

II

Then we beat them, he said,
beat them till our arms was tired
and the big old chains
messy and red.

O Jesus burning on the lily cross

Christ, it was better
than hunting bear
which don't know why
you want him dead.

O night, rawhead and bloodybones night

You kids fetch Paw
some water now so's he
can wash that blood
off him, she said.

O night betrayed by darkness not its own

1975

RANDALL JARRELL
(1914–1965)

Randall Jarrell was born in Nashville, Tennessee, but spent most of his early years in Long Beach and in Hollywood, California. When he was eleven his parents separated and he stayed briefly with his paternal grandparents before joining his mother in Nashville. Prepared in high school for a business career, he attended Vanderbilt University, where he came under the influence of John Crowe Ransom. At Vanderbilt, where he returned after graduation to earn an M.A., and at Kenyon, where he followed Ransom and taught in the English department, he wrote the early poems and reviews that appeared in the *American Review, Southern Review,* and *Kenyon Review.* Among his friends and associates in these years were Robert Penn Warren, Allen Tate, Peter Taylor, and Robert Lowell. Later academic appointments took him to the University of Texas and, for most of the last eighteen years of his life, to the Woman's College of the University of North Carolina, in Greensboro.

A meticulous craftsman, Jarrell worked squarely within the tradition of English metrical verse. An admirer of Robert Frost, he shared something of Frost's ability to stretch the sound of a human voice across a metrical line without doing violence to either the line or the conversational quality of the voice. Yet the speaking voice in most instances is not his own. Although he owed much of his fame in the middle of his career to such World War II flight poems as "Eighth Air Force," "The Death of the Ball Turret Gunner," and "Losses," he had washed out of flight training and spent most of the war on the ground in Illinois and Arizona. Late in life he dispensed with his habitual reserve in order to write two strikingly autobiographic poems, "The Lost World" and "Thinking of the Lost World," but generally speaking he is not a poet who makes capital out of his direct personal experiences.

Modesty was one of his virtues. "I have tried to make my poems plain," he wrote, "and most of them are plain enough; but I wish that they were more difficult because I had known more." Yet for all their plainness, his poems are often deeply resonant; the intelligence that lay behind them was one of the keenest possessed by any of the poets of his generation. Recipient of two Guggenheim Fellowships, poetry editor or critic at various times for *The Nation, Partisan Review,* and *Yale Review,* and Consultant in Poetry at the Library of Congress, he was not only a fine poet, but an excellent critic. A career that had been marked by a continuing capacity for growth was suddenly cut short in 1965 when he was struck and killed by an automobile.

Individual volumes of poetry include *Five Young American Poets,* 1940 (with others); *Blood for a Stranger,* 1942; *Little Friend, Little Friend,* 1945; *Losses,* 1948; *The Seven-League Crutches,* 1951; *Selected Poems,* 1955; *The Woman at the Washington Zoo,* 1960; and *The Lost World,* 1965. *Selected Poems,* 1955, has been superseded by *The Complete Poems,* 1969. A comic academic novel is *Pictures from an Institution,* 1954. Criticism is collected in *Poetry and the Age,* 1953; *A Sad Heart at the Supermarket,* 1962; *The Third Book of Criticism,* 1971; and *Kipling, Auden & Co.: Essays and Reviews 1935–1964,* 1980. See also *Jerome: The Biography of a Poem,* 1972; and Mary Jarrell, ed., *Randall Jarrell's Letters,* 1986. Charles M. Adams compiled *Randall Jarrell: A Bibliography,* 1958. Robert Lowell, Peter Taylor, and Robert Penn Warren edited a volume of reminiscences, *Randall Jarrell: 1914–1965,* 1967. Suzanne Ferguson, *The Poetry of Randall Jarrell,* 1971, is thorough and intelligent. See also Sister Bernetta Quinn, *Randall Jarrell,* 1981; Suzanne Ferguson, ed., *Critical Essays on Randall Jarrell,* 1983; and Stuart Wright, *Randall Jarrell: A Descriptive Bibliography,* 1984.

The Death of the Ball Turret Gunner

From my mother's sleep I fell into the State,
And I hunched in its belly till my wet fur froze.
Six miles from earth, loosed from its dream of life,
I woke to black flak and the nightmare fighters.
When I died they washed me out of the turret with a hose.

1945

Losses

It was not dying: everybody died.
It was not dying: we had died before
In the routine crashes—and our fields
Called up the papers, wrote home to our folks,
And the rates rose, all because of us.
We died on the wrong page of the almanac,
Scattered on mountains fifty miles away;
Diving on haystacks, fighting with a friend,
We blazed up on the lines we never saw.
We died like aunts or pets or foreigners.
(When we left high school nothing else had died
For us to figure we had died like.)

In our new planes, with our new crews, we bombed
The ranges by the desert or the shore,
Fired at towed targets, waited for our scores—
And turned into replacements and woke up
One morning, over England, operational.
It wasn't different: but if we died
It was not an accident but a mistake
(But an easy one for anyone to make).
We read our mail and counted up our missions—
In bombers named for girls, we burned
The cities we had learned about in school—
Till our lives wore out; our bodies lay among
The people we had killed and never seen.
When we lasted long enough they gave us medals;

When we died they said, "Our casualties were low."
They said, "Here are the maps"; we burned the cities.

It was not dying—no, not ever dying;
But the night I died I dreamed that I was dead,
And the cities said to me: "Why are you dying?
We are satisfied, if you are; but why did I die?"

1945

The Woman at the Washington Zoo

The saris go by me from the embassies.

Cloth from the moon. Cloth from another planet.
They look back at the leopard like the leopard.

And I. . . .
this print of mine, that has kept its color
Alive through so many cleanings; this dull null
Navy I wear to work, and wear from work, and so
To my bed, so to my grave, with no
Complaints, no comment: neither from my chief,
The Deputy Chief Assistant, nor his chief—
Only I complain. . . . this serviceable
Body that no sunlight dyes, no hand suffuses
But, dome-shadowed, withering among columns,
Wavy beneath fountains—small, far-off, shining
In the eyes of animals, these beings trapped
As I am trapped but not, themselves, the trap,
Aging, but without knowledge of their age,
Kept safe here, knowing not of death, for death—
Oh, bars of my own body, open, open!

The world goes by my cage and never sees me.
And there come not to me, as come to these,
The wild beasts, sparrows pecking the llamas' grain,
Pigeons settling on the bears' bread, buzzards
Tearing the meat the flies have clouded. . . .
Vulture,
When you come for the white rat that the foxes left,
Take off the red helmet of your head, the black
Wings that have shadowed me, and step to me as man:
The wild brother at whose feet the white wolves fawn,
To whose hand of power the great lioness
Stalks, purring. . . .
You know what I was,
You see what I am: change me, change me!

1960

Next Day

Moving from Cheer to Joy, from Joy to All,
I take a box
And add it to my wild rice, my Cornish game hens.

The slacked or shorted, basketed, identical
Food-gathering flocks
Are selves I overlook. Wisdom, said William James,

Is learning what to overlook. And I am wise
If that is wisdom.
Yet somehow, as I buy All from these shelves
And the boy takes it to my station wagon,
What I've become
Troubles me even if I shut my eyes.

When I was young and miserable and pretty
And poor, I'd wish
What all girls wish: to have a husband,
A house and children. Now that I'm old, my wish
Is womanish:
That the boy putting groceries in my car

See me. It bewilders me he doesn't see me.
For so many years
I was good enough to eat: the world looked at me
And its mouth watered. How often they have undressed me,
The eyes of strangers!
And, holding their flesh within my flesh, their vile

Imaginings within my imagining,
I too have taken
The chance of life. Now the boy pats my dog
And we start home. Now I am good.
The last mistaken,
Ecstatic, accidental bliss, the blind

Happiness that, bursting, leaves upon the palm
Some soap and water—
It was so long ago, back in some Gay
Twenties, Nineties, I don't know . . . Today I miss
My lovely daughter
Away at school, my sons away at school,

My husband away at work—I wish for them.
The dog, the maid,
And I go through the sure unvarying days
At home in them. As I look at my life,
I am afraid
Only that it will change, as I am changing:

I am afraid, this morning, of my face.
It looks at me
From the rear-view mirror, with the eyes I hate,
The smile I hate. Its plain, lined look
Of gray discovery
Repeats to me: "You're old." That's all, I'm old.

And yet I'm afraid, as I was at the funeral
I went to yesterday.

My friend's cold made-up face, granite among its flowers,
Her undressed, operated-on, dressed body
Were my face and body.
As I think of her I hear her telling me

How young I seem; I *am* exceptional;
I think of all I have.
But really no one is exceptional,
No one has anything, I'm anybody,
I stand beside my grave
Confused with my life, that is commonplace and solitary.

1965

The Player Piano

I ate pancakes one night in a Pancake House
Run by a lady my age. She was gay.
When I told her that I came from Pasadena
She laughed and said, "I lived in Pasadena
When Fatty Arbuckle drove the El Molino bus."

I felt that I had met someone from home.
No, not Pasadena, Fatty Arbuckle.
Who's that? Oh, something that we had in common
Like—like—the false armistice. Piano rolls.
She told me her house was the first Pancake House

East of the Mississippi, and I showed her
A picture of my grandson. Going home—
Home to the hotel—I began to hum,
"Smile a while, I bid you sad adieu,
When the clouds roll back I'll come to you."

Let's brush our hair before we go to bed,
I say to the old friend who lives in my mirror.
I remember how I'd brush my mother's hair
Before she bobbed it. How long has it been
Since I hit my funnybone? had a scab on my knee?

Here are Mother and Father in a photograph,
Father's holding me. . . . They both look so *young.*
I'm so much older than they are. Look at them,
Two babies with their baby. I don't blame you,
You weren't old enough to know any better;

If I could I'd go back, sit down by you both,
And sign our true armistice: you weren't to blame.
I shut my eyes and there's our living room.
The piano's playing something by Chopin,
And Mother and Father and their little girl

Listen. Look, the keys go down by themselves!
I go over, hold my hands out, play I play—

If only, somehow, I had learned to live!
The three of us sit watching, as my waltz
Plays itself out a half-inch from my fingers.

1965

The Lost Children

Two little girls, one fair, one dark,
One alive, one dead, are running hand in hand
Through a sunny house. The two are dressed
In red and white gingham, with puffed sleeves and sashes.
They run away from me . . . But I am happy;
When I wake I feel no sadness, only delight.
I've seen them again, and I am comforted
That, somewhere, they still are.

It is strange
To carry inside you someone else's body;
To know it before it's born;
To see at last that it's a boy or girl, and perfect;
To bathe it and dress it; to watch it
Nurse at your breast, till you almost know it
Better than you know yourself—better than it knows itself.
You own it as you made it.
You are the authority upon it.

But as the child learns
To take care of herself, you know her less.
Her accidents, adventures are her own,
You lose track of them. Still, you know more
About her than anyone *except* her.

Little by little the child in her dies.
You say, "I have lost a child, but gained a friend."
You feel yourself gradually discarded.
She argues with you or ignores you
Or is kind to you. She who begged to follow you
Anywhere, just so long as it was you,
Finds follow the leader no more fun.
She makes few demands; you are grateful for the few.

The young person who writes once a week
Is the authority upon herself.
She sits in my living room and shows her husband
My albums of her as a child. He enjoys them
And makes fun of them. I look too
And I realize the girl in the matching blue
Mother-and-daughter dress, the fair one carrying
The tin lunch box with the half-pint thermos bottle
Or training her pet duck to go down the slide
Is lost just as the dark one, who is dead, is lost.
But the world in which the two wear their flared coats
And the hats that match, exists so uncannily
That, after I've seen its pictures for an hour,

I believe in it: the bandage coming loose
One has in the picture of the other's birthday,
The castles they are building, at the beach for asthma.
I look at them and all the old sure knowledge
Floods over me, when I put the album down
I keep saying inside: "I *did* know those children.
I braided those braids. I was driving the car
The day that she stepped in the can of grease
We were taking to the butcher for our ration points.
I *know* those children. I know all about them.
Where are they?"

I stare at her and try to see some sign
Of the child she was. I can't believe there isn't any.
I tell her foolishly, pointing at the picture,
That I keep wondering where she is.
She tells me, "Here I am."
Yes, and the other
Isn't dead, but has everlasting life . . .

The girl from next door, the borrowed child,
Said to me the other day, "You like children so much,
Don't you want to have some of your own?"
I couldn't believe that she could say it.
I thought: "Surely you can look at me and see them."

When I see them in my dreams I feel such joy.
If I could dream of them every night!

When I think of my dream of the little girls
It's as if we were playing hide-and-seek.
The dark one
Looks at me longingly, and disappears;
The fair one stays in sight, just out of reach
No matter where I reach. I am tired
As a mother who's played all day, some rainy day.
I don't want to play it any more, I don't want to,
But the child keeps on playing, so I play.

1965

JOHN BERRYMAN

(1914–1972)

John Berryman is above all a poet dedicated to bringing formal order out of chaos. As such, he is quintessentially a poet of the twentieth century. His failures are the failures of his time, writ large, his successes the personal triumphs of an individual at odds with his environment, and there is always a precarious balance between the two. A scant three years after a critic had written that Berryman had "come to poetic terms with * * * the wreck of the modern world * * * and the wreck of his personal self in that world" he jumped to his death from a bridge in Minneapolis.

He was born John Smith in McAlester,

Oklahoma, the son of a schoolteacher and a well-to-do banker. The family moved to Florida when he was ten, and there, after threatening to swim out to sea with his son, drowning them both, his father shot himself outside John's window. His mother moved to New York and remarried, Berryman taking on the name of his foster father. He attended South Kent School in Connecticut and graduated from Columbia University and Clare College, Oxford. Not long after his return to the United States he began his teaching career and was published, with Randall Jarrell and others, in *Five Young American Poets* (1940). His *Poems* (1942) came two years later, but it was not until *Homage to Mistress Bradstreet* (1956) that he developed the combination of formal structure and fractured syntax that is characteristic of the style of so many of his best poems. In the meantime, he taught at Harvard, Princeton, and the University of Minnesota and developed a reputation as a poet who had never quite fulfilled his promise. Marital problems, heavy drinking, and years spent in and out of analysis formed the chief indications in his personal life of the tensions that he attempted to resolve in his poems.

In his biographical study *Stephen Crane* (1950) his sharp insights into the work of Crane were marred by his inability to organize his thoughts into a totally satisfactory whole. In *Homage to Mistress Bradstreet*, *Berryman's Sonnets* (1967), and *The Dream Songs* (1969), too, he strives for a total coherence that he seldom achieves, but the volumes include such brilliant passages of poetry that, taken together, they had the effect of thrusting Berryman late in life into the front rank of the poets of his time. As he aged he revealed more and more of the origins of his personal anguish. A love affair of twenty years earlier formed the basis for the *Sonnets*, written apparently years before their publication. Into *The Dream Songs* he put a decade and a half of work centering on a figure, "not the poet, not me," who shares a good many of the biographical details and philosophical outlook of the writer. He ended *Love & Fame* (1970) with a section titled "Eleven Addresses to the Lord" that harked back to the strict Roman Catholicism of his childhood and he continued his self-examination in *Delusions, Etc.* (1972). To the end the events of the modern world and of his presence in that world appeared to him so painfully absurd that a direct confrontation could lead to insanity. Nevertheless, he found it possible to achieve some glimpse of wholeness through the fragmented obliqueness of his poetry.

In addition to the titles named above, Berryman published verse in *The Dispossessed,* 1948; *His Thoughts Made Pockets and the Plane Buckt,* 1958; *77 Dream Songs,* 1964 (included later in *The Dream Songs*); *Short Poems,* 1967; and *His Toy, His Dream, His Rest,* 1968 (included in *The Dream Songs*). A posthumous novel, published with an introduction by Saul Bellow, is *Recovery,* 1973. John Haffenden edited a posthumous book of verse, *Henry's Fate and Other Poems, 1967–1972,* 1977. *The Freedom of the Poet,* 1976, is a miscellany of short fiction and essays.

John Haffenden wrote *The Life of John Berryman,* 1982. Eileen Simpson's *Poets in Their Youth: A Memoir,* 1982, covers Berryman, Blackmur, Schwartz, Lowell, and others. Other biographical and critical studies include Joel Conarroe, *John Berryman,* 1977; and John Haffenden, *John Berryman: A Critical Commentary,* 1980.

The Ball Poem

What is the boy now, who has lost his ball,
What, what is he to do? I saw it go
Merrily bouncing, down the street, and then
Merrily over—there it is in the water!
No use to say 'O there are other balls':
An ultimate shaking grief fixes the boy
As he stands rigid, trembling, staring down

All his young days into the harbour where
His ball went. I would not intrude on him,
A dime, another ball, is worthless. Now
He senses first responsibility
In a world of possessions. People will take balls,
Balls will be lost always, little boy.
And no one buys a ball back. Money is external.
He is learning, well behind his desperate eyes,
The epistemology of loss, how to stand up
Knowing what every man must one day know
And most know many days, how to stand up
And gradually light returns to the street,
A whistle blows, the ball is out of sight,
Soon part of me will explore the deep and dark
Floor of the harbour . . I am everywhere,
I suffer and move, my mind and my heart move
With all that move me, under the water
Or whistling, I am not a little boy.

1948

The Moon and the Night and the Men

On the night of the Belgian surrender the moon rose
Late, a delayed moon, and a violent moon
For the English or the American beholder;
The French beholder. It was a cold night,
People put on their wraps, the troops were cold
No doubt, despite the calendar, no doubt
Numbers of refugees coughed, and the sight
Or sound of some killed others. A cold night.

On Outer Drive there was an accident:
A stupid well-intentioned man turned sharp
Right and abruptly he became an angel
Fingering an unfamiliar harp,
Or screamed in hell, or was nothing at all.
Do not imagine this is unimportant.
He was a part of the night, part of the land,
Part of the bitter and exhausted ground
Out of which memory grows.

Michael and I
Stared at each other over chess, and spoke
As little as possible, and drank and played.
The chessmen caught in the European eye,
Neither of us I think had a free look
Although the game was fair. The move one made
It was difficult at last to keep one's mind on.
'Hurt and unhappy' said the man in London.
We said to each other, The time is coming near
When none shall have books or music, none his dear,
And only a fool will speak aloud his mind.

History is approaching a speechless end,
As Henry Adams[1] said. Adams was right.

All this occurred on the night when Leopold[2]
Fulfilled the treachery four years before
Begun—or was he well-intentioned, more
Roadmaker to hell than king? At any rate,
The moon came up late and the night was cold,
Many men died—although we know the fate
Of none, nor of anyone, and the war
Goes on, and the moon in the breast of man is cold.

1948

The Dream Songs

1

Huffy Henry hid the day,
unappeasable Henry sulked.
I see his point,—a trying to put things over.
It was the thought that they thought
they could *do* it made Henry wicked & away.
But he should have come out and talked.

All the world like a woolen lover
once did seem on Henry's side.
Then came a departure.
Thereafter nothing fell out as it might or ought.
I don't see how Henry, pried
open for all the world to see, survived.

What he has now to say is a long
wonder the world can bear & be.
Once in a sycamore I was glad
all at the top, and I sang.
Hard on the land wears the strong sea
and empty grows every bed.

1964

4

Filling her compact & delicious body
with chicken páprika, she glanced at me
twice.
Fainting with interest, I hungered back
and only the fact of her husband & four other people
kept me from springing on her

or falling at her little feet and crying
'You are the hottest one for years of night
Henry's dazed eyes

1. The American historian (1838–1918).

2. Leopold III, Belgian king (1934–1951), exiled after the war, in 1945.

have enjoyed, Brilliance.' I advanced upon
(despairing) my spumoni.—Sir Bones: is stuffed,
de world, wif feeding girls.

—Black hair, complexion Latin, jewelled eyes
downcast . . . The slob beside her feasts . . . What wonders is
she sitting on, over there?
The restaurant buzzes. She might as well be on Mars.
Where did it all go wrong? There ought to be a law against Henry.
—Mr. Bones: there is.

1964

14

Life, friends, is boring. We must not say so.
After all, the sky flashes, the great sea yearns,
we ourselves flash and yearn,
and moreover my mother told me as a boy
(repeatingly) 'Ever to confess you're bored
means you have no

Inner Resources.' I conclude now I have no
inner resources, because I am heavy bored.
Peoples bore me,
literature bores me, especially great literature,
Henry bores me, with his plights & gripes
as bad as achilles,[3]

who loves people and valiant art, which bores me.
And the tranquil hills, & gin, look like a drag
and somehow a dog
has taken itself & its tail considerably away
into mountains or sea or sky, leaving
behind: me, wag.

1964

29

There sat down, once, a thing on Henry's heart
so heavy, if he had a hundred years
& more, & weeping, sleepless, in all them time
Henry could not make good.
Starts again always in Henry's ears
the little cough somewhere, an odour, a chime.

And there is another thing he has in mind
like a grave Sienese face a thousand years
would fail to blur the still profiled reproach of Ghastly,
with open eyes, he attends, blind.
All the bells say: too late. This is not for tears;
thinking.

3. Achilles, in Homer's *Iliad,* is often a sulky and pathetic figure when not engaged in battle.

But never did Henry, as he thought he did,
end anyone and hacks her body up
and hide the pieces, where they may be found.
He knows: he went over everyone, & nobody's missing.
Often he reckons, in the dawn, them up.
Nobody is ever missing.

1964

76

Henry's Confession

Nothin very bad happen to me lately.
How you explain that?—I explain that, Mr Bones,[4]
terms o' your bafflin odd sobriety.
Sober as man can get, no girls, no telephones,
what could happen bad to Mr Bones?
—*If* life is a handkerchief sandwich,

in a modesty of death I join my father
who dared so long agone leave me.
A bullet on a concrete stoop
close by a smothering southern sea
spreadeagled on an island, by my knee.
—You is from hunger, Mr Bones,

I offers you this handkerchief, now set
your left foot by my right foot,
shoulder to shoulder, all that jazz,
arm in arm, by the beautiful sea,
hum a little, Mr Bones.
—I saw nobody coming, so I went instead.

1964

145

Also I love him: me he's done no wrong
for going on forty years—forgiveness time—
I touch now his despair,
he felt as bad as Whitman on his tower
but he did not swim out with me or my brother
as he threatened—

a powerful swimmer, to take one of us along
as company in the defeat sublime,
freezing my helpless mother:
he only, very early in the morning,
rose with his gun and went outdoors by my window
and did what was needed.

I cannot read that wretched mind, so strong
& so undone. I've always tried. I—I'm

4. A traditional name for a minstrel show entertainer.

trying to forgive
whose frantic passage, when he could not live
an instant longer, in the summer dawn
left Henry to live on.

1968

153

I'm cross with god who has wrecked this generation.
First he seized Ted, then Richard, Randall, and now Delmore.[5]
In between he gorged on Sylvia Plath.
That was a first rate haul. He left alive
fools I could number like a kitchen knife
but Lowell he did not touch.

Somewhere the enterprise continues, not—
yellow the sun lies on the baby's blouse—
in Henry's staggered thought.
I suppose the word would be, we must submit.
Later.
I hang, and I will not be part of it.

A friend of Henry's contrasted God's career
with Mozart's, leaving Henry with nothing to say
but praise for a word so apt.
We suffer on, a day, a day, a day.
And never again can come, like a man slapped,
news like this

1968

384

The marker slants, flowerless, day's almost done,
I stand above my father's grave with rage,
often, often before
I've made this awful pilgrimage to one
who cannot visit me, who tore his page
out: I come back for more,

I spit upon this dreadful banker's grave
who shot his heart out in a Florida dawn
O ho alas alas
When will indifference come, I moan & rave
I'd like to scrabble till I got right down
away down under the grass

and ax the casket open ha to see
just how he's taking it, which he sought so hard
we'll tear apart
the mouldering grave clothes ha & then Henry

5. Theodore Roethke, R. P. Blackmur, Randall Jarrell, and Delmore Schwartz, all poets and friends of Berryman who predeceased him.

will heft the ax once more, his final card,
and fell it on the start.

1968

385

My daughter's heavier. Light leaves are flying.
Everywhere in enormous numbers turkeys will be dying
and other birds, all their wings.
They never greatly flew. Did they wish to?
I should know. Off away somewhere once I knew
such things.

Or good Ralph Hodgson[6] back then did, or does.
The man is dead whom Eliot praised. My praise
follows and flows too late.
Fall is grievy, brisk. Tears behind the eyes
almost fall. Fall comes to us as a prize
to rouse us toward our fate.

My house is made of wood and it's made well,
unlike us. My house is older than Henry;
that's fairly old.
If there were a middle ground between things and the soul
or if the sky resembled more the sea,
I wouldn't have to scold
                    my heavy daughter.

1968

ISABELLA GARDNER
(1915–1981)

Isabella Gardner was born in Newton, Massachusetts, into a prominent family that included Isabella Stewart Gardner, a great-aunt who was a patroness of the arts remembered now for her gift of her personal museum to the city of Boston, and Robert Lowell, the poet, a cousin. Educated in a private school, she married at twenty-three but soon turned to the stage, studying acting at the Leighton Rollins School on Long Island and at the Embassy School of Acting in London. After the failure of her first marriage, she married three more times, the last time, in 1959, to Allen Tate, the poet; divorce followed, in 1966. Meanwhile, she had left the stage in 1943, and in the early 1950's served as an associate editor of *Poetry* under Karl Shapiro. Her verse appeared first in *Birthdays from the Ocean* (1955), which Wallace Stevens called "the freshest truest book of poetry that I had read for a long time." Two more books followed to similar praise from a variety of poets within the next decade: *The Looking Glass* (1961) and *West of Childhood: Poems 1950–1965* (1965). Major recognition and awards, however, escaped her, and she did not publish another vol-

6. Ralph Hodgson (1871–1962), English poet. Two of his best-known poems are "Eve" and "Time, You Old Gipsy Man."

ume until *That Was Then: New and Selected Poems,* in 1980, the year before her death.

In the 1950's and 1960's, hers was an isolated voice as the celebrated poetry of the time embraced the open forms of the Beats and Black Mountain poets and the confessional verse of Snodgrass, Lowell, and Plath. Within her lines there is a careful attention to sound patterns reminiscent of Dylan Thomas or Edith Sitwell (to whom she dedicated one of her finest poems). She is fond of slant rhymes and, like Marianne Moore, breaks words on syllables to force a rhyme at line end. Troubled in her life, she chose not to write of her problems; her poems are personal insofar as they address children or a husband, but they speak of small moments, not large and private matters.

Isabella Gardner: *The Complete Poems,* 1985, was edited by Roland Flint. Individual volumes are named above.

In the Museum

Small and emptied woman you lie here a thousand years dead
your hands on your diminished loins flat in this final bed
teeth jutting from your unwound head your spiced bones black and dried,
who knew you and kissed you and kept you and wept when you died;
died you young had you grace? Risus sardonicus replied.
Then quick I seized my husband's hand while he stared at his bride.

1955

Letter from Slough Pond

Here where you left me alone
the soft wind sighs through my wishbone
the sun is lapping at my flesh
I couple with the ripples of the fresh
pond water I am rolled by the roiling sea.
Love, in our wide bed, do you lie lonely?
The spoon of longing stirs my marrow
and I thank God this bed is narrow.

1961

Part of the Darkness

I had thought of the bear in his lair as fiercely free, feasting on honey and wildwood fruits;

I had imagined a forest lunge, regretting the circus shuffle and the zoo's prescribed pursuits.

Last summer I took books and children to Wisconsin's Great North woods. We drove

one night through miles of pines and rainy darkness to a garbage grove

that burgeoned broken crates and bulging paper bags and emptied cans of beer,

to watch for native bears, who local guides had told us, scavenged there.

After parking behind three other cars (leaving our headlights on but dim)

We stumbled over soggy moss to join the families blinking on the rim

of mounded refuse bounded east north and west by the forest.

The parents hushed and warned their pushing children each of whom struggled to stand nearest

the arena, and presently part of the darkness humped away from the foliage and lumbered bear-shaped

toward the heaping spoilage. It trundled into the litter while we gaped,

and for an instant it gaped too, bear-faced, but not a tooth was bared. It grovelled

carefully while tin cans clattered and tense tourists tittered. Pains-takingly it nosed and ravelled

rinds and husks and parings, the used and the refused; bear-skinned and doggedly explored

the second-hand remains while headlights glared and flashlights stared and shamed bored

children booed, wishing aloud that it would trudge away so they might read its tracks.

They hoped to find an as yet unclassified spoor, certain that no authentic bear would turn his back

upon the delicacies of his own domain to flounder where mere housewives' leavings rot.

I also was reluctant to concede that there is no wild honey in the forest and no forest in the bear.

Bereaved, we started home, leaving that animal there.

1961

Summers Ago

For Edith Sitwell

The Ferryman fairied us out to sea
Gold gold gold sang the apple-tree

Children I told you I tell you our sun was a hail of gold!
I say that sun stoned, that sun stormed our tranquil, our blue bay
bellsweet saltfresh water (bluer than tongue-can-tell, daughter)
and dazed us, darlings, and dazzled us, I say that sun crazed
(that sun clove) our serene as ceramic selves and our noon glazed cove,
and children all that grew wild by the wonderful water shot tall
as tomorrow, reeds suddenly shockingly green had sprouted like sorrow
and crimson explosions of roses arose in that flurry of Danaean glory
while at night we did swoon ah we swanned to a silverer moonlight than listen or lute,
we trysted in gondolas blown from glass and kissed in fluted Venetian bliss.

Sister and brother I your mother
Once was a girl in skirling weather

Though summer and swan must alter, falter,
I waltzed on the water once, son and daughter.

1961

GWENDOLYN BROOKS
(1917–)

Born in Topeka, Kansas, but raised on Chicago's South Side, Gwendolyn Brooks was encouraged from childhood to be "the *lady* Paul Laurence Dunbar." By eleven she was keeping a notebook, by thirteen reading *Writer's Digest,* and by sixteen had met James Weldon Johnson and Langston Hughes. After graduation from Englewood High School, she received an associate's degree from Wilson Junior College in Chicago in 1936. Married in 1939, she devoted much of her time to her family for the next few years, but continued writing poetry, learning much in a class taught at the South Side Community Art Center by Inez Stark, a member of the board of Chicago's *Poetry.* Winning a Midwestern Writers' Conference Award in 1943 led to the notice of publishers and to her first book, *A Street in Bronzeville* (1945). Two Guggenheim Fellowships followed, and then *Annie Allen* (1949), which brought her the first Pulitzer Prize for poetry awarded to a black writer. *The Bean Eaters* (1960) confirmed her reputation.

From the first, Brooks's focus was on the black urban poor of Chicago's South Side. *A Street in Bronzeville* includes also a section on World War II, black troops and white, mentioning the "congenital iniquities" that show up in later books in contrasts between ghetto and suburbs. In one of the poems of *The Bean Eaters,* tragedy ensues when a black family moves to a white neighborhood. Apart from her subject matter, Brooks's poetry was in these decades squarely within the tradition that shaped most of the other critically acclaimed poetry of the time. Besides the earlier black writers who stood as models, she was influenced by such poets as Emerson, Dickinson, Frost, and Eliot, and was fond of traditional forms, or variations on them, especially sonnets and ballads.

Brooks's later poetry has taken a different turn, more socially conscious and less structured. At a writers' conference at Fisk University in spring 1967 she discovered that "suddenly there was a New Black to meet." Young and militant, the "New Blacks" were more interested in LeRoi Jones (soon to become Imamu Amiri Baraka) with his "Up against the wall, white man!" attitude than they were in a "lady poet" of fifty. Subsequent events, including the riots of that summer and the assassination of Martin Luther King the following year confirmed the sense of crisis of the conference. With *In the Mecca* (1968), Brooks's reflection of social problems became more urgent; since then she has left her New York publisher to issue most of her books from Dudley Randall's Broadside Press in Detroit, beginning with the recognition of contemporary reality in *Riot* (1969). Of her later poetry, she has said that she writes for "not just the blacks who go to college but also those who have their customary habitat in taverns and the street. * * * anything I write is going to issue from a concern with and interest in blackness and its progress."

Books of verse in addition to those named above include *Selected Poems,* 1963; *Family Pictures,* 1970; *Aloneness,* 1971; *Beckonings,* 1975; and *To Disembark,* 1981. *The World of Gwendolyn Brooks,* 1971, collects poems from earlier books. *Report from Part One,* 1972, is an autobiography, and *Maud Martha,* 1953, an autobiographical novel.

Studies include Harry B. Shaw, *Gwendolyn Brooks,* 1980; and D. H. Melhem, *Gwendolyn Brooks: Poetry and the Heroic Voice,* 1987.

a song in the front yard

I've stayed in the front yard all my life.
I want a peek at the back
Where it's rough and untended and hungry weed grows.
A girl gets sick of a rose.

I want to go in the back yard now
And maybe down the alley,
To where the charity children play.
I want a good time today.

They do some wonderful things.
They have some wonderful fun.
My mother sneers, but I say it's fine
How they don't have to go in at quarter to nine.
My mother, she tells me that Johnnie Mae
Will grow up to be a bad woman.
That George'll be taken to Jail soon or late
(On account of last winter he sold our back gate.)

But I say it's fine. Honest, I do.
And I'd like to be a bad woman, too,
And wear the brave stockings of night-black lace
And strut down the streets with paint on my face.

1945

We Real Cool

The pool players.
Seven at the Golden Shovel.

We real cool. We
Left school. We

Lurk late. We
Strike straight. We

Sing sin. We
Thin gin. We

Jazz June. We
Die soon.

1960

The Lovers of the Poor

arrive. The Ladies from the Ladies' Betterment League
Arrive in the afternoon, the late light slanting
In diluted gold bars across the boulevard brag
Of proud, seamed faces with mercy and murder hinting
Here, there, interrupting, all deep and debonair,

The pink paint on the innocence of fear;
Walk in a gingerly manner up the hall.
Cutting with knives served by their softest care,
Served by their love, so barbarously fair.
Whose mothers taught: You'd better not be cruel!
You had better not throw stones upon the wrens!
Herein they kiss and coddle and assault
Anew and dearly in the innocence
With which they baffle nature. Who are full,
Sleek, tender-clad, fit, fiftyish, a-glow, all
Sweetly abortive, hinting at fat fruit,
Judge it high time that fiftyish fingers felt
Beneath the lovelier planes of enterprise.
To resurrect. To moisten with milky chill.
To be a random hitching post or plush.
To be, for wet eyes, random and handy hem.

Their guild is giving money to the poor.
The worthy poor. The very very worthy
And beautiful poor. Perhaps just not too swarthy?
Perhaps just not too dirty nor too dim
Nor—passionate. In truth, what they could wish
Is—something less than derelict or dull.
Not staunch enough to stab, though, gaze for gaze!
God shield them sharply from the beggar-bold!
The noxious needy ones whose battle's bald
Nonetheless for being voiceless, hits one down.

But it's all so bad! and entirely too much for them.
The stench; the urine, cabbage, and dead beans,
Dead porridges of assorted dusty grains,
The old smoke, *heavy* diapers, and, they're told,
Something called chitterlings. The darkness. Drawn
Darkness, or dirty light. The soil that stirs.
The soil that looks the soil of centuries.
And for that matter the *general* oldness. Old
Wood. Old marble. Old tile. Old old old.
Not homekind Oldness! Not Lake Forest, Glencoe.
Nothing is sturdy, nothing is majestic,
There is no quiet drama, no rubbed glaze, no
Unkillable infirmity of such
A tasteful turn as lately they have left,
Glencoe, Lake Forest, and to which their cars
Must presently restore them. When they're done
With dullards and distortions of this fistic
Patience of the poor and put-upon.

They've never seen such a make-do-ness as
Newspaper rugs before! In this, this "flat,"
Their hostess is gathering up the oozed, the rich
Rugs of the morning (tattered! the bespattered . . .),
Readies to spread clean rugs for afternoon.
Here is a scene for you. The Ladies look,
In horror, behind a substantial citizeness
Whose trains clank out across her swollen heart.
Who, arms akimbo, almost fills a door.
All tumbling children, quilts dragged to the floor
And tortured thereover, potato peelings, soft-

Eyed kitten, hunched-up, haggard, to-be-hurt.
        Their League is allotting largesse to the Lost.
But to put their clean, their pretty money, to put
Their money collected from delicate rose-fingers
Tipped with their hundred flawless rose-nails seems . . .
        They own Spode, Lowestoft, candelabra,
Mantels, and hostess gowns, and sunburst clocks,
Turtle soup, Chippendale, red satin "hangings,"
Aubussons and Hattie Carnegie. They Winter
In Palm Beach; cross the Water in June; attend,
When suitable, the nice Art Institute;
Buy the right books in the best bindings; saunter
On Michigan, Easter mornings, in sun or wind.
Oh Squalor! This sick four-story hulk, this fibre
With fissures everywhere! Why, what are bringings
Of loathe-love largesse? What shall peril hungers
So old old, what shall flatter the desolate?
Tin can, blocked fire escape and chitterling
And swaggering seeking youth and the puzzled wreckage
Of the middle passage, and urine and stale shames
And, again, the porridges of the underslung
And children children children. Heavens! That
Was a rat, surely, off there, in the shadows? Long
And long-tailed? Gray? The Ladies from the Ladies'
Betterment League agree it will be better
To achieve the outer air that rights and steadies,
To hie to a house that does not holler, to ring
Bells elsetime, better presently to cater
To no more Possibilities, to get
Away. Perhaps the money can be posted.
Perhaps they two may choose another Slum!
Some serious sooty half-unhappy home!—
Where loathe-love likelier may be invested.
        Keeping their scented bodies in the center
Of the hall as they walk down the hysterical hall,
They allow their lovely skirts to graze no wall,
Are off at what they manage of a canter,
And, resuming all the clues of what they were,
Try to avoid inhaling the laden air.

1960

Horses Graze

Cows graze.
Horses graze.
They
eat
eat
eat.
Their graceful heads
are bowed
bowed
bowed

in majestic oblivion.
They are nobly oblivious
to your follies,
your inflation,
the knocks and nettles of administration.
They
eat
eat
eat.
And at the crest of their brute satisfaction,
with wonderful gentleness, in affirmation,
they lift their clean calm eyes and they lie down
and love the world.
They speak with their companions.
They do not wish that they were otherwhere.
Perhaps they know that creature feet may press
only a few earth inches at a time,
that earth is anywhere earth,
that an eye may see,
wherever it may be,
the Immediate arc, alone, of life, of love.
In Sweden,
China,
Afrika,
in India or Maine
the animals are sane;
they know and know and know
there's ground below
and sky
up high.

1975

ROBERT LOWELL

(1917–1977)

Robert Lowell's poetry has won serious critical attention and has been received with enthusiasm since the appearance of his first volume in 1944. Lowell's originality and power have greatly influenced contemporary poets and have given to his own varied works the probability of enduring merit.

Born in Boston in 1917, he was given his father's name, Robert Traill Spence Lowell, representing an inheritance of family tradition distinguished and old in New England history. His mother was a Winslow. The poet transformed his youthful embarrassment at family tradition into a literary resource: he developed a psychological interest in family situations which infuses a number of his best poems, and he allowed his tragic sense and his comic spirit to rummage in his own family attics.

After nearly two years at Harvard University Lowell completed his formal education at Kenyon College (1940), where his poetry was encouraged by John Crowe Ransom, poet-teacher, and by others, especially Randall Jarrell. Having twice been refused for enlistment, he was later drafted, declared himself a conscientious objector, and served a jail sentence. He published *Land of Unlikeness,* his first volume (1944), in a limited edition. Two years later *Lord Weary's Castle* won the Pulitzer Prize (1947). Lowell was awarded a Guggenheim Fellowship in 1947–1948, the Guinness Award, and the National Book Award in 1959.

Not long after his graduation from Kenyon, he had been converted to Catholicism, and as Allen Tate had foreseen, Lowell became "consciously a Catholic poet"; however, he retained an earlier interest in the religious philosophy and works of learned Puritans. In Lowell the two became reconciled. This religious motivation gave his style a determined boldness, supported by complexly disciplined language, symbol, and idea.

Randall Jarrell's review of *Lord Weary's Castle* in *The Nation* (1946) gains interest because Lowell approved it, in lieu of writing his own introduction, for publication with a selection of his poems in John Ciardi's *Mid-Century American Poets.* Jarrell commented that these "poems understand the world as a sort of conflict of opposites." One force is the "inertia of the complacent self, the satisfied persistence in evil that is damnation * * * turned inward, incestuous, that blinds or binds." The opposing force "is the realm of freedom, of the Grace that has replaced the Law, of the perfect Liberator." The poems "normally move into liberation"; and in some cases "even death is seen as a liberation."

Lowell shared with Pound and other more recent poets the inclination to imitate or reconstruct poems in other languages and of other times. *Imitations* (1961) collects his versions of writings by such diverse hands as Homer, Rilke, and Pasternak. In a review, Edmund Wilson reminded his readers that while this book "consists of variations on themes provided by those other poets," it "is really an original sequence by Robert Lowell of Boston." *Imitations,* which won the Bollingen translation prize in 1962, is another search into a heritage—that of a poet's classical and European fellow-explorers.

Meanwhile, in 1959, very much under the influence of William Carlos Williams, he published *Life Studies,* the book that with Snodgrass's *Heart's Needle,* also published in 1959, inaugurated the vogue for the kind of poem called "confessional" in the 1960's, including major works by Anne Sexton, Sylvia Plath, and John Berryman. "It is hard not to think of *Life Studies* as a series of personal confidences, rather shameful, that one is honor bound not to reveal," wrote M. L. Rosenthal, but he concluded that "it is also a beautifully articulated poetic sequence." Clearly, Lowell studied, throughout his poetic life, all the materials available. In *For the Union Dead* (1964) Lowell began to return into our world and to New England, as in "Jonathan Edwards in Western Massachusetts," where he comes to the realization that "hope lives in doubt. / Faith is trying to do without / faith."

Drama and "imitation" were first brought together in *Phaedra* (1961), his version of Racine's *Phèdre,* and in 1964 the American Place Theatre produced, to critical acclaim, three short plays under the title *The Old Glory.* The first play (not produced, but included in the published text) combines Hawthorne's "Endicott and the Red Cross" and "The Maypole of Merrymount"; the second is based upon "My Kinsman, Major Molineux"; Melville's story "Benito Cereno" inspired the last. In his preface to the published version, the critic Robert Brustein stated that "Mr. Lowell feels the past working in his very bones. And it is his subtle achievement not only to have evoked this past, but also to have superimposed the present on it."

In *Near the Ocean* (1967) five long poems, written in deceptively simple couplets, concern his life at that time as it is mingled in memory and the past. That life was in a house on the Maine coast willed to the poet by Harriet Winslow. The "imitations" included in this volume are taken from Horace, Juvenal, and Dante.

Lowell's later work culminated in 1973 with the publication of three volumes of largely personal content. *History* is a gathering into their final form of the *Notebook* poems that began to appear in 1969 in *Notebook 1967–68. For Lizzie and Harriet* contains those *Notebook* poems that focus on the poet's second marriage. *The Dolphin* celebrates a new love in the stanza of the *Notebook* poems.

Lowell's *Selected Poems,* revised edition, 1977, should be supplemented by *Day by Day,* 1977, his last volume. Earlier volumes are *Land of Unlikeness,* 1944; *Lord Weary's Castle,* 1946; *The Mills of the Kavanaughs,* 1951; *Poems: 1938–1949,* 1950, which includes the two volumes above, except the title poem, "The Mills of the Kavanaughs"; and *Life Studies,* 1959, which won the National Book Award. *Imitations,* 1961, is a book of "translations." Newer poems are collected in *For the Union Dead,* 1964; *Selected Poems,* 1965; *Near the Ocean,* 1967; *Voyage, and Other Versions of Poems by Baudelaire,* 1968; *Notebook 1967–68,* 1969; *Notebooks, Revised and Expanded,* 1970; *History,* 1973; *For Lizzie and Harriet,* 1973; and *The Dolphin,* 1973. His plays are *Phaedra* (translation), 1961; *The Old Glory* (produced, 1964), 1965, revised, 1968; a version of *Prometheus Bound,* 1969; and *The Oresteia of Aeschylus,* 1979. Robert Giroux edited *Collected Prose,* 1987.

The first complete biography is Ian Hamilton's *Robert Lowell: A Biography,* 1982. Other studies include Jerome Mazzaro, *The Poetic Themes of Robert Lowell,* 1965; Thomas Parkinson, ed., *Robert Lowell: A Collection of Critical Essays,* 1968; Philip Cooper, *The Autobiographical Myth of Robert Lowell,* 1970; Patrick Cosgrave, *The Public Poetry of Robert Lowell,* 1972; Michael London and Robert Boyers, eds., *Robert Lowell: A Portrait of the Artist in His Time,* 1970; Marjorie J. Perloff, *The Poetic Art of Robert Lowell,* 1973; Alan Williamson, *Pity the Monsters: The Political Vision of Robert Lowell,* 1974; Steven Gould Axelrod, *Robert Lowell: Life and Art,* 1978; Vereen M. Bell, *Robert Lowell, Nihilist as Hero,* 1983; Mark Rudman, *Robert Lowell: An Introduction to the Poetry,* 1983; and Steven Axelrod and Helen Deese, eds., *Robert Lowell: Essays on the Poetry,* 1987. See also C. David Heyman, *American Aristocracy: The Lives and Times of James Russell, Amy, and Robert Lowell,* 1980.

Colloquy in Black Rock[1]

Here the jack-hammer jabs into the ocean;
My heart, you race and stagger and demand
More blood-gangs for your nigger-brass percussions,
Till I, the stunned machine of your devotion,
Clanging upon this cymbal of a hand,
Am rattled screw and footloose. All discussions

End in the mud-flat detritus of death.
My heart, beat faster, faster. In Black Mud
Hungarian workmen give their blood
For the martyre Stephen, who was stoned to death.

Black Mud, a name to conjure with: O mud
For watermelons gutted to the crust,
Mud for the mole-tide harbor, mud for mouse,
Mud for the armored Diesel fishing tubs that thud
A year and a day to wind and tide; the dust
Is on this skipping heart that shakes my house,

House of our Savior who was hanged till death.
My heart, beat faster, faster. In Black Mud
Stephen the martyre was broken down to blood:
Our ransom is the rubble of his death.

Christ walks on the black water. In Black Mud
Darts the kingfisher. On Corpus Christi, heart,

1. Written in 1944 in Black Rock, Connecticut, where Lowell lived after his release from imprisonment in Danbury as a conscientious objector. As Stephen Gould Axelrod has suggested, the poem perhaps echoes the Pentecostal concerns of Eliot's "Little Gidding," especially the "dove descending" in flame in part IV.

Over the drum-beat of St. Stephen's choir
I hear him, *Stupor Mundi,*[2] and the mud
Flies from his hunching wings and beak—my heart,
The blue kingfisher dives on you in fire.

1945, 1946

In Memory of Arthur Winslow[3]

I. *Death from Cancer*

This Easter, Arthur Winslow,[4] less than dead,
Your people set you up in Phillips' House
To settle off your wrestling with the crab[5]—
The claws drop flesh upon your yachting blouse
Until longshoreman Charon[6] come and stab
Through your adjusted bed
And crush the crab. On Boston Basin, shells
Hit water by the Union Boat Club wharf:
You ponder why the coxes[7] squeakings dwarf
The *resurrexit dominus*[8] of all the bells.

Grandfather Winslow, look, the swanboats coast
That island in the Public Gardens, where
The bread-stuffed ducks are brooding, where with tub
And strainer the mid-Sunday Irish scare
The sun-struck shallows for the dusky chub[9]
This Easter, and the ghost
Of risen Jesus walks the waves to run[1]
Arthur upon a trumpeting black swan
Beyond Charles River to the Acheron[2]
Where the wide waters and their voyager are one.

II. *Dunbarton*

The stones are yellow and the grass is gray
Past Concord by the rotten lake and hill
Where crutch and trumpet meet the limousine
And half-forgotten Starks and Winslows[3] fill
The granite plot and the dwarf pines are green
From watching for the day
When the great year of the little yeomen[4] come

2. The wonder of the world.
3. First collected in *Lord Weary's Castle* (1946) and included in the collection of 1950.
4. In an autobiographical sketch, "91 Revere Street" (*Life Studies,* pp. 11–46), Lowell describes with affection Grandfather Winslow, his mother's father, a financial adventurer, Boston Brahmin, and family autocrat, proud of his descent from the Stark family of Dunbarton, New Hampshire, as well as the colonial Massachusetts Winslows (both mentioned in the following poem).
5. "Cancer" is the Latin for "crab."
6. In Greek mythology, Charon ferried the souls of the dead across the Styx.
7. "Coxes" ("coxswains"), steersmen of racing shells or ship's boats.
8. "The Lord is risen"; the liturgical message of Easter.
9. A humble variety of carp, on Easter recalling that the fish became a Christian symbol because of miracles associated with fish and fishermen.
1. See the miracle of Jesus walking on the sea, Matthew xiv: 25.
2. The Charles, a river of Boston; Acheron, according to Greek mythology, a shade-haunted river in Hades.
3. For the Starks of Dunbarton, New Hampshire, and the Winslows of Massachusetts, see Section I, note 4.
4. British "yeomen," that is, freeholders of land and commoners of the highest level, made up the majority in colonial New England.

Bringing its landed Promise[5] and the faith
That made the Pilgrim Makers take a lathe
And point their wooden steeples lest the Word[6] be dumb.

O fearful witnesses, your day is done:
The minister from Boston waves your shades,
Like children, out of sight and out of mind.
The first selectman of Dunbarton spreads
Wreaths of New Hampshire pine cones on the lined
Casket where the cold sun
Is melting. But, at last, the end is reached;
We start our cars. The preacher's mouthings still
Deafen my poor relations on the hill:
Their sunken landmarks echo what our fathers preached.[7]

III. *Five Years Later*

This Easter, Arthur Winslow, five years gone
I came to mourn you, not to praise the craft
That netted you a million dollars, late
Hosing out gold in Colorado's waste,[8]
Then lost it all in Boston real estate.
Now from the train, at dawn
Leaving Columbus in Ohio, shell
On shell of our stark culture strikes the sun
To fill my head with all our fathers won
When Cotton Mather wrestled with the fiends from hell.[9]

You must have hankered for our family's craft:
The block-house Edward made, the Governor,[1]
At Marshfield, and the slight coin-silver spoons
The Sheriff beat to shame the gaunt Revere,[2]
And General Stark's[3] coarse bas-relief in bronze
Set on your granite shaft
In rough Dunbarton; for what else could bring
You, Arthur, to the veined and alien West
But devil's notions that your gold at least
Could give back life to men who whipped or backed the King?

IV. *A Prayer for My Grandfather to Our Lady*[4]

Mother, for these three hundred years or more
Neither our clippers nor our slavers reached
The haven of your peace in this Bay State:

5. *I.e.,* the Promised Land of the redeemed on "the day" of Judgment.
6. The Bible (Acts iv: 31) or Messiah (John i: 1, 14).
7. *I.e.,* Bible texts carved on the tombstones.
8. In placer mining the gold is washed out of superficial deposits with high-pressure hoses.
9. Industrial buildings, representing material wealth, are compared with the salvation preached by Cotton Mather (1663–1728), archetype of Puritan divines.
1. Edward Winslow, their ancestor, a *Mayflower* Pilgrim (1622), described in his journal the earliest events in Plymouth and was three times elected governor. *Cf.* "our family's craft," l. 51.
2. Paul Revere, the midnight rider of the Battle of Lexington, was a gifted silversmith and engraver.
3. General John Stark (1728–1822), another ancestor, famous New Hampshire soldier of the Revolution.
4. The poem has proceeded from Arthur Winslow's death and burial, to memories of his material life, and finally to the stage of penitence. The two stanzas of this section are differentiated by the quotation marks enclosing the second and by the two Lazaruses—*cf.* notes 5 and 7 below.

Neither my father nor his father. Beached
On these dry flats of fishy real estate,
O Mother, I implore
Your scorched, blue thunderbreasts of love to pour
Buckets of blessings on my burning head
Until I rise like Lazarus from the dead:[5]
Lavabis nos et super nivem dealbabor.[6]

"On Copley Square,[7] I saw you hold the door
To Trinity, the costly Church, and saw
The painted Paradise of harps and lutes
Sink like Atlantis[8] in the Devil's jaw
And knock the Devil's teeth out by the roots;
But when I strike for shore
I find no painted idols to adore:
Hell is burned out, heaven's harp-strings are slack.
Mother, run to the chalice, and bring back
Blood on your finger-tips for Lazarus who was poor."[9]

1946

After the Surprising Conversions[1]

September twenty-second, Sir:[2] today
I answer. In the latter part of May,
Hard on our Lord's Ascension, it began
To be more sensible.[3] A gentleman
Of more than common understanding, strict
In morals, pious in behavior, kicked
Against our goad. A man of some renown,
An useful, honored person in the town,[4]
He came of melancholy parents; prone
To secret spells, for years they kept alone—
His uncle, I believe, was killed of it:
Good people, but of too much or little wit.
I preached one Sabbath on a text from Kings;
He showed concernment for his soul. Some things

5. Jesus raised Lazarus from the dead (*cf.* John xi: 11–43).

6. "You shall wash us and I shall be made whiter than snow." *Dealbabor* was erroneously printed *delabor* in the 1950 collection.

7. A very old Boston square, once a center of social refinement.

8. Fabulous island civilization presumed to have sunk beneath the ocean.

9. This "Lazarus who was poor" is the beggar in Jesus' parable of the selfish rich man (*cf.* Luke xvi: 19–31). Compare with "Lazarus" in l. 69.

1. First collected in *Lord Weary's Castle* (1949) and reprinted in *Poems: 1938–1949* (1950). The following notes, perhaps unusually full, are intended to show the poet using the words and the substance of a document to create a work of art, a new thing.

2. The source of this poem is a letter written by Jonathan Edwards on May 30, 1735 ("A Narrative of Surprising Conversions," Jonathan Edwards, *Works,* 1808). Edwards's sermon in 1734 inspired the "Great Awakening," a revival in his Northampton parish, whence revivalism spread to the surrounding Massachusetts towns. This letter to Benjamin Colman, Boston clergyman, in response to his request for information, was later amplified for publication by an account of further remarkable experiences, one of which forms the inspiration for the present poem. The "Great Awakening" continued to influence the development of Protestant denominations in the colonies until about 1750.

3. "Sensible": archaic for "evident." This line in full (Edwards's supplementary letter, May, 1735) reads: "it began to be very sensible that the spirit of God was gradually withdrawing from us." The following reported misfortunes were taken for proof of this.

4. In reporting this man's suicide to Colman, Edwards calls him "My Uncle Hawley." Joseph Hawley, who married Edwards's aunt, Rebekah, was the leading merchant of pioneer days in Northampton.

In his experience were hopeful. He
Would sit and watch the wind knocking a tree
And praise this countryside our Lord has made.
Once when a poor man's heifer died, he laid
A shilling on the doorsill; though a thirst
For loving shook him like a snake, he durst
Not entertain much hope of his estate
In heaven. Once we saw him sitting late
Behind his attic window by a light
That guttered on his Bible; through that night
He meditated terror, and he seemed
Beyond advice or reason, for he dreamed
That he was called to trumpet Judgment Day
To Concord. In the latter part of May
He cut his throat.[5] And though the coroner
Judged him delirious, soon a noisome stir
Palsied our village. At Jehovah's nod
Satan seemed more let loose amongst us: God
Abandoned us to Satan,[6] and he pressed
Us hard, until we thought we could not rest
Till we had done with life. Content was gone.
All the good work was quashed. We were undone.
The breath of God had carried out a planned
And sensible withdrawal from this land;
The multitude, once unconcerned with doubt,
Once neither callous, curious nor devout,
Jumped at broad noon, as though some peddler groaned
At it in its familiar twang: "My friend,
Cut your own throat. Cut your own throat. Now! Now!"
September twenty-second, Sir, the bough
Cracks with the unpicked apples, and at dawn
The small-mouth bass breaks water, gorged with spawn.

1946

Her Dead Brother[7]

I

The Lion of St. Mark's upon the glass
Shield in my window reddens, as the night

5. "He cut his throat" on June 1, 1735. Edwards wrote: "My Uncle Hawley, the last Sabbath morning, laid violent hands on himself, by cutting his own throat. He had been for a considerable time greatly concerned about the condition of his soul; by the ordering of Providence he was suffered to fall into a deep melancholy, a distemper that the family are very prone to; the devil took the advantage and drove him into despairing thoughts: he was kept very much awake at nights, so that he had very little sleep for two months * * *. He was in a great measure beyond receiving advice, or being reasoned with. The Coroner's Inquest judged him delirious."

6. The remainder of the poem reflects this abstruse doctrine. Perry Miller, in *Jonathan Edwards,* comments on this, *passim:* over "three hundred people were converted" at Northampton "during the year" (1734–35); but after Hawley's suicide one heard voices crying, as Edwards reports, "cut your own throat! Now! Now!" (*cf.* the poem, l. 43); and the initial revival at Northampton was over. Edwards expressed current doctrine in asserting, "The devil took advantage * * * he seems to be in a great rage at this * * * breaking forth of the works of God. I hope it is because he knows that he has but a short time." Edwards knew, as Miller observes, that "the divine spirit has a tempo, a rise and a fall," and will rise again to redeem, as the poem says, "the unpicked apples and at dawn / The small-mouthed bass."

7. In *The Mills of the Kavanaughs* (1951) but also included in the collection published earlier, *Poems: 1938–1949* (1950).

Enchants the swinging dories to its terrors,
And dulls your distant wind-stung eyes; alas,
Your portrait, coiled in German-silver hawsers, mirrors
The sunset as a dragon. Enough light
Remains to see you through your varnish. Giving
Your life has brought you closer to your friends;
Yes, it has brought you home. All's well that ends:[8]
Achilles dead is greater than the living;

My mind holds you as I would have you live,
A wintering dragon. Summer was too short
When we went picnicking with telescopes
And crocking leather handbooks to that fort
Above the lank and heroned Sheepscot, where its slopes
Are clutched by hemlocks—spotting birds. I give
You back that idyll, Brother. Was it more?
Remember riding, scotching with your spur
That four-foot milk-snake in a juniper?
Father shellacked it to the ice-house door.

Then you were grown; I left you on your own.
We will forget that August twenty-third,
When Mother motored with the maids to Stowe,
And the pale summer shades were drawn—so low
No one could see us; no, nor catch your hissing word,
As false as Cressid![9] Let our deaths atone:
The fingers on your sword-knot are alive,
And Hope, that fouls my brightness with its grace,
Will anchor in the narrows of your face.
My husband's Packard crunches up the drive.

II

(THREE MONTHS LATER)

The ice is out: the tidal current swims
Its blocks against the launches as they pitch
Under the cruisers of my Brother's fleet.
The gas, uncoiling from my oven burners, dims
The face above this bottled *Water Witch*,
The knockabout my Brother fouled and left to eat
Its heart out by the Boston light. My Brother,
I've saved you in the ice-house of my mind—
The ice is out. . . . Our fingers lock behind
The tiller. We are heeling in the smother,

Our sails, balloon and leg-o'mutton, tell
The colors of the rainbow; but they flap,
As the wind fails, and cannot fetch the bell. . . .
His stick is tapping on the millwheel-step,
He lights a match, another and another—

8. *Cf.* the title *All's Well That Ends Well,* a comedy by Shakespeare.

9. Cressida's desertion of her lover, the Trojan hero Troilus, and her amours with the victorious Greek commanders have made her the byword for infidelity; the story has been retold by Boccaccio, Chaucer, and Shakespeare.

The Lord is dark, and holy is His name;
By my own hands, into His hands! My burners
Sing like a kettle, and its nickel mirrors
Your squadron by the Stygian Landing. Brother,
The harbor! The torpedoed cruisers flame,

The motor-launches with their searchlights bristle
About the targets. You are black. You shout,
And cup your broken sword-hand. Yes, your whistle
Across the crackling water: *Quick, the ice is out. . . .*
The wind dies in our canvas; we were running dead
Before the wind, but now our sail is part
Of death. O Brother, a New England town is death
And incest—and I saw it whole. I said,
Life is a thing I own. Brother, my heart
Races for sea-room—we are out of breath.

1950

Sailing Home from Rapallo

[*February 1954*]

Your nurse could only speak Italian,
but after twenty minutes I could imagine your final week,
and tears ran down my cheeks. . . .

When I embarked from Italy with my Mother's body,
the whole shoreline of the *Golfo di Genova*
was breaking into fiery flower.
The crazy yellow and azure sea-sleds
blasting like jack-hammers across
the *spumante*-bubbling wake of our liner,
recalled the clashing colors of my Ford.
Mother traveled first-class in the hold;
her *Risorgimento* black and gold casket
was like Napoleon's at the *Invalides*. . . .

While the passengers were tanning
on the Mediterranean in deck-chairs,
our family cemetery in Dunbarton
lay under the White Mountains
in the sub-zero weather.
The graveyard's soil was changing to stone—
so many of its deaths had been midwinter.
Dour and dark against the blinding snowdrifts,
its black brook and fir trunks were as smooth as masts.
A fence of iron spear-hafts
black-bordered its mostly Colonial grave-slates.
The only "unhistoric" soul to come here
was Father, now buried beneath his recent
unweathered pink-veined slice of marble.
Even the Latin of his Lowell motto:
Occasionem cognosce,
seemed too businesslike and pushing here,

where the burning cold illuminated
the hewn inscriptions of Mother's relatives:
twenty or thirty Winslows and Starks.
Frost had given their names a diamond edge. . . .

In the grandiloquent lettering on Mother's coffin,
Lowell had been misspelled *LOVEL.*
The corpse
was wrapped like *panettone* in Italian tinfoil.

1959

Waking in the Blue

The night attendant, a B.U. sophomore,
rouses from the mare's-nest of his drowsy head
propped on *The Meaning of Meaning.* [1]
He catwalks down our corridor.
Azure day
makes my agonized blue window bleaker.
Crows maunder on the petrified fairway.
Absence! My heart grows tense
as though a harpoon were sparring for the kill.
(This is the house for the "mentally ill.")

What use is my sense of humor?
I grin at Stanley, now sunk in his sixties,
once a Harvard all-American fullback
(if such were possible!),
still hoarding the build of a boy in his twenties,
as he soaks, a ramrod
with the muscle of a seal
in his long tub,
vaguely urinous from the Victorian plumbing.
A kingly granite profile in a crimson golf cap,
worn all day, all night,
he thinks only of his figure,
of slimming on sherbet and ginger ale—
more cut off from words than a seal.

This is the way day breaks in Bowditch Hall at McLean's;[2]
the hooded night lights bring out "Bobbie,"
Porcellian '29,
a replica of Louis XVI
without the wig—
redolent and roly-poly as a sperm whale,
as he swashbuckles about in his birthday suit
and horses at chairs.

These victorious figures of bravado ossified young.

1. A book published in 1923 by I. A. Richards and C. K. Ogden, students of language and communication.
2. McLean Hospital in Waltham, Massachusetts, where Lowell wrote the first draft of this poem in a locked ward while undergoing psychiatric treatment.

In between the limits of day,
hours and hours go by under the crew haircuts
and slightly too little nonsensical bachelor twinkle
of the Roman Catholic attendants.
(There are no Mayflower
screwballs in the Catholic Church.)

After a hearty New England breakfast,
I weigh two hundred pounds
this morning. Cock of the walk,
I strut in my turtle-necked French sailor's jersey
before the metal shaving mirrors,
and see the shaky future grow familiar
in the pinched, indigenous faces
of these thoroughbred mental cases,
twice my age and half my weight.
We are all old-timers,
each of us holds a locked razor.

1959

Home after Three Months Away

Gone now the baby's nurse,
a lioness who ruled the roost
and made the Mother cry.
She used to tie
gobbets of porkrind in bowknots of gauze—
three months they hung like soggy toast
on our eight foot magnolia tree,
and helped the English sparrows
weather a Boston winter.

Three months, three months!
Is Richard now himself again?
Dimpled with exaltation,
my daughter holds her levee in the tub.
Our noses rub,
each of us pats a stringy lock of hair—
they tell me nothing's gone.
Though I am forty-one,
not forty now, the time I put away
was child's-play. After thirteen weeks
my child still dabs her cheeks
to start me shaving. When
we dress her in her sky-blue corduroy,
she changes to a boy,
and floats my shaving brush
and washcloth in the flush. . . .
Dearest, I cannot loiter here
in lather like a polar bear.

Recuperating, I neither spin nor toil.
Three stories down below,

a choreman tends our coffin's length of soil,
and seven horizontal tulips blow.

Just twelve months ago,
these flowers were pedigreed
imported Dutchmen; now no one need
distinguish them from weed.
Bushed by the late spring snow,
they cannot meet
another year's snowballing enervation.

I keep no rank nor station.
Cured, I am frizzled, stale and small.

1959

Memories of West Street and Lepke

Only teaching on Tuesdays, book-worming
in pajamas fresh from the washer each morning,
I hog a whole house on Boston's
"hardly passionate Marlborough Street,"[3]
where even the man
scavenging filth in the back alley trash cans,
has two children, a beach wagon, a helpmate,
and is a "young Republican."
I have a nine months' daughter,
young enough to be my granddaughter.
Like the sun she rises in her flame-flamingo infants' wear.

These are the tranquillized *Fifties,*
and I am forty. Ought I to regret my seedtime?
I was a fire-breathing Catholic C.O.,[4]
and made my manic statement,
telling off the state and president, and then
sat waiting sentence in the bull pen
beside a Negro boy with curlicues
of marijuana in his hair.

Given a year,
I walked on the roof of the West Street Jail,[5] a short
enclosure like my school soccer court,
and saw the Hudson River once a day
through sooty clothesline entanglements
and bleaching khaki tenements.
Strolling, I yammered metaphysics with Abramowitz,
a jaundice-yellow ("it's really tan")
and fly-weight pacifist,

3. A quotation attributed to William James, who is said to have used it to illustrate understatement in his Harvard classes.

4. Conscientious objector.

5. In New York City, where Lowell was briefly incarcerated before being sent to the Federal Correctional Center at Danbury, Connecticut, to serve his sentence. According to another inmate, as reported by Ian Hamilton, "Lowell was in a cell next to Lepke * * * and Lepke says to him: 'I'm in for killing. What are you in for?' 'Oh, I'm in for refusing to kill.' And Lepke burst out laughing. It was kind of ironic."

so vegetarian,
he wore rope shoes and preferred fallen fruit.
He tried to convert Bioff and Brown,
the Hollywood pimps, to his diet.
Hairy, muscular, suburban,
wearing chocolate double-breasted suits,
they blew their tops and beat him black and blue.

I was so out of things, I'd never heard
of the Jehovah's Witnesses.
"Are you a C.O.?" I asked a fellow jailbird.
"No," he answered, "I'm a J.W."
He taught me the "hospital tuck,"
and pointed out the T-shirted back
of *Murder Incorporated's* Czar Lepke,
there piling towels on a rack,
or dawdling off to his little segregated cell full
of things forbidden the common man:
a portable radio, a dresser, two toy American
flags tied together with a ribbon of Easter palm.
Flabby, bald, lobotomized,
he drifted in a sheepish calm,
where no agonizing reappraisal
jarred his concentration on the electric chair—
hanging like an oasis in his air
of lost connections. . . .

1959

Man and Wife

Tamed by *Miltown,* we lie on Mother's bed;
the rising sun in war paint dyes us red;
in broad daylight her gilded bed-posts shine,
abandoned, almost Dionysian.
At last the trees are green on Marlborough Street,
blossoms on our magnolia ignite
the morning with their murderous five days' white.
All night I've held your hand,
as if you had
a fourth time faced the kingdom of the mad—
its hackneyed speech, its homicidal eye—
and dragged me home alive. . . . Oh my *Petite,*
clearest of all God's creatures, still all air and nerve:
you were in your twenties, and I,
once hand on glass
and heart in mouth,
outdrank the Rahvs in the heat
of Greenwich Village, fainting at your feet—
too boiled and shy
and poker-faced to make a pass,
while the shrill verve
of your invective scorched the traditional South.

Now twelve years later, you turn your back.
Sleepless, you hold
your pillow to your hollows like a child;
your old-fashioned tirade—
loving, rapid, merciless—
breaks like the Atlantic Ocean on my head.

1959

"To Speak of Woe That Is in Marriage"[6]

It is the future generation that presses into being by means of these exuberant feelings and supersensible soap bubbles of ours.

—SCHOPENHAUER

"The hot night makes us keep our bedroom windows open.
Our magnolia blossoms. Life begins to happen.
My hopped up husband drops his home disputes,
and hits the streets to cruise for prostitutes,
free-lancing out along the razor's edge.
This screwball might kill his wife, then take the pledge.
Oh the monotonous meanness of his lust. . . .
It's the injustice . . . he is so unjust—
whiskey-blind, swaggering home at five.
My only thought is how to keep alive.
What makes him tick? Each night now I tie
ten dollars and his car key to my thigh. . . .
Gored by the climacteric of his want,
he stalls above me like an elephant."

1959

Skunk Hour

(*For Elizabeth Bishop*)

Nautilus Island's hermit
heiress still lives through winter in her Spartan cottage;
her sheep still graze above the sea.
Her son's a bishop. Her farmer
is first selectman in our village;
she's in her dotage.

Thirsting for
the hierarchic privacy
of Queen Victoria's century,
she buys up all
the eyesores facing her shore,
and lets them fall.

The season's ill—
we've lost our summer millionaire,
who seemed to leap from an L. L. Bean
catalogue. His nine-knot yawl

6. Geoffrey Chaucer, "The Wife of Bath's Prologue," l. 3.

was auctioned off to lobstermen.
A red fox stain covers Blue Hill.

And now our fairy
decorator brightens his shop for fall;
his fishnet's filled with orange cork,
orange, his cobbler's bench and awl;
there is no money in his work,
he'd rather marry.

One dark night,
my Tudor Ford climbed the hill's skull;
I watched for love-cars. Lights turned down,
they lay together, hull to hull,
where the graveyard shelves on the town. . . .
My mind's not right.

A car radio bleats,
"Love, O careless Love. . . ." I hear
my ill-spirit sob in each blood cell,
as if my hand were at its throat. . . .
I myself am hell;
nobody's here—

only skunks, that search
in the moonlight for a bite to eat.
They march on their soles up Main Street:
white stripes, moonstruck eyes' red fire
under the chalk-dry and spar spire
of the Trinitarian Church.

I stand on top
of our back steps and breathe the rich air—
a mother skunk with her column of kittens swills the garbage pail.
She jabs her wedge-head in a cup
of sour cream, drops her ostrich tail,
and will not scare.

1959

The Mouth of the Hudson

(*For Esther Brooks*)

A single man stands like a bird-watcher,
and scuffles the pepper and salt snow
from a discarded, gray
Westinghouse Electric cable drum.
He cannot discover America by counting
the chains of condemned freight-trains
from thirty states. They jolt and jar
and junk in the siding below him.
He has trouble with his balance.
His eyes drop,
and he drifts with the wild ice

ticking seaward down the Hudson,
like the blank sides of a jig-saw puzzle.

The ice ticks seaward like a clock.
A Negro toasts
Wheat-seeds over the coke-fumes
of a punctured barrel.
Chemical air
sweeps in from New Jersey,
and smells of coffee.

Across the river,
ledges of suburban factories tan
in the sulphur-yellow sun
of the unforgivable landscape.

1964

The Neo-Classical Urn

I rub my head and find a turtle shell
stuck on a pole,
each hair electrical
with charges, and the juice alive
with ferment. Bubbles drive
the motor, always purposeful . . .
Poor head!
How its skinny shell once hummed,
as I sprinted down the colonnade
of bleaching pines, cylindrical
clipped trunks without a twig between them. Rest!
I could not rest. At full run on the curve,
I left the cast stone statue of a nymph,
her soaring armpits and her one bare breast,
gray from the rain and graying in the shade,
as on, on, in sun, the pathway now a dyke,
I swerved between two water bogs,
two seins of moss, and stooped to snatch
the painted turtles on dead logs.
In that season of joy,
my turtle catch
was thirty-three,
dropped splashing in our garden urn,
like money in the bank,
the plop and splash
of turtle on turtle,
fed raw gobs of hash . . .

Oh neo-classical white urn, Oh nymph,
Oh lute! The boy was pitiless who strummed
their elegy,
for as the month wore on,
the turtles rose,
and popped up dead on the stale scummed
surface—limp wrinkled heads and legs withdrawn
in pain. What pain? A turtle's nothing. No

grace, no cerebration, less free will
than the mosquito I must kill—
nothings! Turtles! I rub my skull,
that turtle shell,
and breathe their dying smell,
still watch their crippled last survivors pass,
and hobble humpbacked through the grizzled grass.

1964

For the Union Dead[7]

"Relinquunt Omnia Servare Rem Publicam."[8]

The old South Boston Aquarium stands
in a Sahara of snow now. Its broken windows are boarded.
The bronze weathervane cod has lost half its scales.
The airy tanks are dry.

Once my nose crawled like a snail on the glass;
my hand tingled
to burst the bubbles
drifting from the noses of the cowed, compliant fish.

My hand draws back. I often sigh still
for the dark downward and vegetating kingdom
of the fish and reptile. One morning last March,
I pressed against the new barbed and galvanized

fence on the Boston Common. Behind their cage,
yellow dinosaur steamshovels were grunting
as they cropped up tons of mush and grass
to gouge their underworld garage.

Parking spaces luxuriate like civic
sandpiles in the heart of Boston.
A girdle of orange, Puritan-pumpkin colored girders
braces the tingling Statehouse,

shaking over the excavations, as it faces Colonel Shaw[9]
and his bell-cheeked Negro infantry
on St. Gaudens' shaking Civil War relief,
propped by a plank splint against the garage's earthquake.

Two months after marching through Boston,
half the regiment was dead;
at the dedication,
William James could almost hear the bronze Negroes breathe.

7. First collected in an enlarged *Life Studies,* 1960, printed last in the volume and entitled, "Colonel Shaw and the Massachusetts' 54th." In reprints it continued in the last position but bore the present title. Finally it became the title poem of *For the Union Dead,* 1964. All texts are otherwise identical.
8. They gave all to serve the State.

9. Colonel Robert Gould Shaw (1837–1863) commanded the first enlisted black regiment, the Massachusetts 54th; he was killed in the attack on Fort Wagner, July 18, 1863, and buried in the grave with his men. Augustus Saint-Gaudens's monument to Shaw stands opposite the State House on Boston Common.

Their monument sticks like a fishbone
in the city's throat.
Its Colonel is as lean
as a compass-needle.

He has an angry wrenlike vigilance,
a greyhound's gentle tautness;
he seems to wince at pleasure,
and suffocate for privacy.

He is out of bounds now. He rejoices in man's lovely,
peculiar power to choose life and die—
when he leads his black soldiers to death,
he cannot bend his back.

On a thousand small town New England greens,
the old white churches hold their air
of sparse, sincere rebellion; frayed flags
quilt the graveyards of the Grand Army of the Republic.

The stone statues of the abstract Union Soldier
grow slimmer and younger each year—
wasp-waisted, they doze over muskets
and muse through their sideburns . . .

Shaw's father wanted no monument
except the ditch,
where his son's body was thrown
and lost with his "niggers."

The ditch is nearer.
There are no statues for the last war here;
on Boylston Street, a commercial photograph
shows Hiroshima boiling

over a Mosler Safe,[1] the "Rock of Ages"
that survived the blast. Space is nearer.
When I crouch to my television set,
the drained faces of Negro school-children rise like balloons.

Colonel Shaw
is riding on his bubble,
he waits
for the blessèd break.

The Aquarium is gone. Everywhere,
giant finned cars nose forward like fish;
a savage servility
slides by on grease.

1960

1. A safe that escaped destruction in the bombing of Hiroshima was photographed; the picture was used by the company to advertise the durability of its products.

History

History has to live with what was here,
clutching and close to fumbling all we had—
it is so dull and gruesome how we die,
unlike writing, life never finishes.
Abel was finished; death is not remote,
a flash-in-the-pan electrifies the skeptic,
his cows crowding like skulls against high-voltage wire,
his baby crying all night like a new machine.
As in our Bibles, white-faced, predatory,
the beautiful, mist-drunken hunter's moon ascends—
a child could give it a face: two holes, two holes,
my eyes, my mouth, between them a skull's no-nose—
O there's a terrifying innocence in my face
drenched with the silver salvage of the mornfrost.

1973

Watchmaker God

Say life is the one-way trip, the one-way flight,
say this without hysterical undertones—
then you could say you stood in the cold light of science,
seeing as you are seen, espoused to fact.
Strange, life is both the fire and fuel; and we,
the animals and objects, must be here
without striking a spark of evidence
that anything that ever stopped living
ever falls back to living when life stops.
There's a pale romance to the watchmaker God
of Descartes and Paley; He drafted and installed
us in the Apparatus. He loved to tinker;
but having perfected what He had to do,
stood off shrouded in his loneliness.

1973

Robert Frost

Robert Frost at midnight, the audience gone
to vapor, the great act laid on the shelf in mothballs,
his voice is musical and raw—he writes in the flyleaf:
For Robert from Robert, his friend in the art.
"Sometimes I feel too full of myself," I say.
And he, misunderstanding, "When I am low,
I stray away. My son wasn't your kind. The night
we told him Merrill Moore would come to treat him,
he said, 'I'll kill him first.' One of my daughters thought things,
thought every male she met was out to make her;
the way she dressed, she couldn't make a whorehouse."
And I, "Sometimes I'm so happy I can't stand myself."

And he, "When I am too full of joy, I think
how little good my health did anyone near me."

1973

The March 1[2]

[*For Dwight MacDonald*]

Under the too white marmoreal Lincoln Memorial,
the too tall marmoreal Washington Obelisk,
gazing into the too long reflecting pool,
the reddish trees, the withering autumn sky,
the remorseless, amplified harangues for peace—
lovely to lock arms, to march absurdly locked
(unlocking to keep my wet glasses from slipping)
to see the cigarette match quaking in my fingers,
then to step off like green Union Army recruits
for the first Bull Run, sped by photographers,
the notables, the girls . . . fear, glory, chaos, rout . . .
our green army staggered out on the miles-long green fields,
met by the other army, the Martian, the ape, the hero,
his new-fangled rifle, his green new steel helmet.

1973

Reading Myself

Like thousands, I took just pride and more than just,
struck matches that brought my blood to a boil;
I memorized the tricks to set the river on fire—
somehow never wrote something to go back to.
Can I suppose I am finished with wax flowers
and have earned my grass on the minor slopes of Parnassus. . . .
No honeycomb is built without a bee
adding circle to circle, cell to cell,
the wax and honey of a mausoleum—
this round dome proves its maker is alive;
the corpse of the insect lives embalmed in honey,
prays that its perishable work live long
enough for the sweet-tooth bear to desecrate—
this open book . . . my open coffin.

1973

Obit

Our love will not come back on fortune's wheel—

in the end it gets us, though a man know what he'd have:
old cars, old money, old undebased pre-Lyndon
silver, no copper rubbing through . . . old wives;

2. One of two poems in *History* that record Lowell's emotions as a participant in the Peace March of October, 1967. Norman Mailer's *The Armies of the Night* (1968) gives a complete account with some emphasis on Lowell's participation. Dwight MacDonald (1906–1982) was also present.

I could live such a too long time with mine.
In the end, every hypochondriac is his own prophet.
Before the final coming to rest, comes the rest
of all transcendence in a mode of being, hushing
all becoming. I'm for and with myself in my otherness,
in the eternal return of earth's fairer children,
the lily, the rose, the sun on brick at dusk,
the loved, the lover, and their fear of life,
their unconquered flux, insensate oneness, painful "It was. . . ."
After loving you so much, can I forget
you for eternity, and have no other choice?

1973

Flight

If I cannot love myself, can you?
I am better company depressed. . . .
I bring myself here, almost my best friend,
a writer still free to work at home all week,
reading revisions to his gulping wife.
Born twenty years later, I might have been prepared
to alternate with cooking, and wash the baby—
I am a vacation-father . . . no plum—
flown in to New York. . . . I see the rising prospect,
the scaffold glitters, the concrete walls are white,
flying like Feininger's skyscraper yachts,
geometrical romance in the river mouth,
conical foolscap dancing in the sky . . .
the runway growing wintry and distinct.

1973

Epilogue

Those blessèd structures, plot and rhyme—
why are they no help to me now
I want to make
something imagined, not recalled?
I hear the noise of my own voice:
The painter's vision is not a lens,
it trembles to caress the light.
But sometimes everything I write
with the threadbare art of my eye
seems a snapshot,
lurid, rapid, garish, grouped,
heightened from life,
yet paralyzed by fact.
All's misalliance.
Yet why not say what happened?
Pray for the grace of accuracy
Vermeer gave to the sun's illumination
stealing like the tide across a map
to his girl solid with yearning.

We are poor passing facts,
warned by that to give
each figure in the photograph
his living name.

1977

HOWARD NEMEROV
(1920–)

Born in New York in 1920, Howard Nemerov took his baccalaureate at Harvard and served as faculty member at Hollins, the University of Minnesota, Bennington, and Brandeis before becoming professor of English at Washington University in St. Louis in 1969. As a practicing man of letters he has published several novels, numerous short stories, and critical articles and books. From 1946 to 1952, he was associate editor of *Furioso,* one of the sprightliest "little magazines" of literature. In 1963–1964 he held appointment as Consultant in Poetry at the Library of Congress. Among the awards he has won are the Theodore Roethke Award and a Guggenheim Fellowship. In 1976 he was elected to membership in the American Academy of Arts and Letters.

His first collection of poems appeared in 1947, announcing a style and distinction which has only become the more mature with successive volumes. Nemerov belongs to the tradition of Williams, Stevens, Eberhart, and Wilbur, who free poetry from trammels of convention while bringing about a more usable relationship of form, function, and idea, which generally prunes the excesses of emotion and strengthens the authority of wit.

Collected Poems was published in 1977. More recent collections are *Last Things / First Light,* 1984; and *Inside the Onion,* 1984. Earlier titles are *The Image and the Law,* 1947; *Guide to the Ruins,* 1950; *The Salt Garden,* 1955; *Mirrors and Windows,* 1958; *New and Selected Poems* (a general collection), 1960; *The Next Room of the Dream,* 1962; *The Blue Swallows,* 1967; *The Winter Lightning: Selected Poems,* 1968; *Gnomes and Occasions: Poems,* 1972; and *The Western Approaches: Poems 1973–1975,* 1975. A mixture of prose and verse is *Journal of the Fictive Life,* 1965. Short stories are collected in *Stories, Fables, and Other Diversions,* 1971. Essay collections are *Reflexions on Poetry and Poetics,* 1972; *Figures of Thought: Speculations on the Meaning of Poetry and Other Essays,* 1978; and *New and Selected Essays,* 1985. Bowie Duncan edited *The Critical Reception of Howard Nemerov: A Selection of Essays and a Bibliography,* 1971. See also Julia A. Bartholomay, *The Shield of Perseus: The Vision and Imagination of Howard Nemerov,* 1972; and Ross Labrie, *Howard Nemerov,* 1980.

The Sanctuary

Over the ground of slate and light gravel,
Clear water, so shallow that one can see
The numerous springs moving their mouths of sand;
And the dark trout are clearly to be seen,
Swimming this water which is color of air
So that the fish appear suspended nowhere and
In nothing. With a delicate bend and reflex
Of their tails the trout slowly glide
From the shadowy side into the light, so clear,
And back again into the shadows; slow
And so definite, like thoughts emerging
Into a clear place in the mind, then going back,
Exchanging shape for shade. Now and again

One fish slides into the center of the pool
And hangs between the surface and the slate
For several minutes without moving, like
A silence in a dream; and when I stand
At such a time, observing this, my life
Seems to have been suddenly moved a great
Distance away on every side, as though
The quietest thought of all stood in the pale
Watery light alone, and was no more
My own than the speckled trout I stare upon
All but unseeing. Even at such times
The mind goes on transposing and revising
The elements of its long allegory
In which the anagoge is always death;
And while this vision blurs with empty tears,
I visit, in the cold pool of the skull,
A sanctuary where the slender trout
Feed on my drowned eyes. . . . Until this trout
Pokes through the fabric of the surface to
Snap up a fly. As if a man's own eyes
Raised welts upon the mirror whence they stared,
I find this world again in focus, and
This fish, a shadow dammed in artifice,
Swims to the furthest shadows out of sight
Though not, in time's ruining stream, out of mind.

1955

The Goose Fish

On the long shore, lit by the moon
To show them properly alone,
Two lovers suddenly embraced
So that their shadows were as one.
The ordinary night was graced
For them by the swift tide of blood
That silently they took at flood,
And for a little time they prized
  Themselves emparadised.

Then, as if shaken by stage-fright
Beneath the hard moon's bony light,
They stood together on the sand
Embarrassed in each other's sight
But still conspiring hand in hand,
Until they saw, there underfoot,
As though the world had found them out,
The goose fish turning up, though dead,
  His hugely grinning head.

There in the china light he lay,
Most ancient and corrupt and grey.
They hesitated at his smile,
Wondering what it seemed to say
To lovers who a little while
Before had thought to understand,

By violence upon the sand,
The only way that could be known
  To make a world their own.

It was a wide and moony grin
Together peaceful and obscene;
They knew not what he would express,
So finished a comedian
He might mean failure or success,
But took it for an emblem of
Their sudden, new and guilty love
To be observed by, when they kissed,
  That rigid optimist.

So he became their patriarch,
Dreadfully mild in the half-dark.
His throat that the sand seemed to choke,
His picket teeth, these left their mark
But never did explain the joke
That so amused him, lying there
While the moon went down to disappear
Along the still and tilted track
  That bears the zodiac.

1955

The Vacuum

The house is so quiet now
The vacuum cleaner sulks in the corner closet,
Its bag limp as a stopped lung, its mouth
Grinning into the floor, maybe at my
Slovenly life, my dog-dead youth.

I've lived this way long enough,
But when my old woman died her soul
Went into that vacuum cleaner, and I can't bear
To see the bag swell like a belly, eating the dust
And the woolen mice, and begin to howl

Because there is old filth everywhere
She used to crawl, in the corner and under the stair.
I know now how life is cheap as dirt,
And still the hungry, angry heart
Hangs on and howls, biting at air.

1955

Thirtieth Anniversary Report of the Class of '41

We who survived the war and took to wife
And sired the kids and made the decent living,
And piecemeal furnished forth the finished life
Not by grand theft so much as petty thieving—

Who had the routine middle-aged affair
And made our beds and had to lie in them
This way or that because the beds were there,
And turned our bile and choler in for phlegm—

Who saw grandparents, parents, to the vault
And wives and selves grow wrinkled, grey and fat
And children through their acne and revolt
And told the analyst about all that—

Are done with it. What is there to discuss?
There's nothing left for us to say of us.

1973

The Western Approaches

As long as we look forward, all seems free,
Uncertain, subject to the Laws of Chance,
Though strange that chance should lie subject to laws,
But looking back on life it is as if
Our Book of Changes never let us change.

Stories already told a time ago
Were waiting for us down the road, our lives
But filled them out; and dreams about the past
Show us the world is post meridian
With little future left to dream about.

Old stories none but scholars seem to tell
Among us any more, they hide the ways,
Old tales less comprehensible than life
Whence nonetheless we know the things we do
And do the things they say the fathers did.

When I was young I flew past Skerryvore
Where the Nine Maidens still grind Hamlet's meal,
The salt and granite grain of bitter earth,
But knew it not for twenty years and more.
My chances past their changes now, I know

How a long life grows ghostly towards the close
As any man dissolves in Everyman
Of whom the story, as it always did, begins
In a far country, once upon a time,
There lived a certain man and he had three sons . . .

1975

Figures of Thought

To lay the logarithmic spiral on
Sea-shell and leaf alike, and see it fit,
To watch the same idea work itself out
In the fighter pilot's steepening, tightening turn
Onto his target, setting up the kill,

And in the flight of certain wall-eyed bugs
Who cannot see to fly straight into death
But have to cast their sidelong glance at it
And come but cranking to the candle's flame—

How secret that is, and how privileged
One feels to find the same necessity
Ciphered in forms diverse and otherwise
Without kinship—that is the beautiful
In Nature as in art, not obvious,
Not inaccessible, but just between.

It may diminish some our dry delight
To wonder if everything we are and do
Lies subject to some little law like that;
Hidden in nature, but not deeply so.

1975

RICHARD WILBUR
(1921–)

Among the poets of the mid-century generation Richard Wilbur is the youngest. In 1947 he published his first volume at the age of twenty-six. *The Beautiful Changes* promptly won the approval of competent criticism, and in a succession of seven volumes Wilbur met with continued enthusiasm. Upon the publication of the third volume, in 1956, he received three national awards, including the 1957 Pulitzer Prize and the National Book Award for Poetry.

Richard Wilbur was born in New York City in 1921, graduated from Amherst in 1942, and served overseas in the infantry. In 1947, the year of his first book, he took his M.A. at Harvard, where he remained as a Fellow, then as assistant professor, until 1955 when he joined the faculty at Wellesley College. In 1957 he became professor of English at Wesleyan University.

The poetry of Wilbur, although it is not obscure, engages the strict attention of the serious reader; he is the poet thinking, and the reader finds himself excitedly involved. Wilbur's imagination recalls Frost's praise of synecdoche as instrument of revelation. In "The Death of a Toad," for example, a part is substituted for the whole so significantly that a meaning beyond the immediate image is demanded. In other poems a series of metaphors, perhaps individually baffling, will suddenly fuse. Wilbur's imagination is engagingly fresh, resourceful, and witty.

Wilbur thinks of a poem not as a vehicle of "communication" but as an object created, having its own life and its unique and individual identity. "Poems," he says, "are not addressed to anybody in particular * * *. The poem is an effort to express a knowledge imperfectly felt, to articulate relationships not quite seen, to make or discover some pattern in the world. It is a conflict with disorder, not a message from one person to another." And works of art in general "are not coerced into being by rational principles, but spring from the imagination, a condition of spontaneous psychic unity."

Wilbur has expressed the belief that "strictness of form" is an advantage. "The strength of the genie," he says, "comes of his being confined in a bottle"; but while his formal craftsmanship declares the advantage of having ancestors, its resemblance to forebears is only broadly familial in appearance. Wilbur's concern for structure coincides with his evident response to sensory impressions and the arts that embody them—especially painting, music, and the dance.

Wilbur has also emphasized the importance "of that part of the meaning of a poem which is carried by the sound"; he heightens meaning by daring originality of language, often by ambiguity, as when he writes that a bird's nest blown from the tree "down forty *fell* feet"; "fell" acts both as verb and adjective. As a pun for light verse "A Simile for Her Smile" does pretty well. Similar talents were required for his translation of Molière's comic *Misanthrope* (1955) and other plays and his collaboration on lyrics for the Lillian Hellman-Leonard Bernstein operatic *Candide* (performed, 1956).

Richard Wilbur's poetry to date is published in *The Beautiful Changes,* 1947; *Ceremony and Other Poems,* 1950; *A Bestiary* (illustrated by Alexander Calder), 1955; *Things of This World,* 1956; *Poems 1943–1956,* 1957; *Advice to a Prophet,* 1961; *The Poems of Richard Wilbur,* 1963; *Walking to Sleep: New Poems and Translations,* 1969; *Seed Leaves: Homage to R. F.,* 1974; and *The Mind-Reader: New Poems,* 1976. Besides *The Misanthrope,* Wilbur has translated or adapted Molière's *Tartuffe,* 1963; *School for Wives,* 1971; and *The Learned Ladies,* 1978. *Responses: Prose Pieces 1948–1976* appeared in 1976. A brief analytic essay by the poet, entitled "The Genie in the Bottle," appeared in *Mid-Century American Poets,* edited by John Ciardi, 1950, pp. 1–7; the unacknowledged quotations above are from this essay. A full-length study is by Donald L. Hill, *Richard Wilbur,* 1968. John P. Field compiled *Richard Wilbur: A Bibliographical Checklist,* 1971; and Wendy Salinger edited *Richard Wilbur's Creation,* 1983.

The Beautiful Changes

One wading a Fall meadow finds on all sides
The Queen Anne's Lace lying like lilies
On water; it glides
So from the walker, it turns
Dry grass to a lake, as the slightest shade of you
Valleys my mind in fabulous blue Lucernes.[1]

The beautiful changes as a forest is changed
By a chameleon's tuning his skin to it;
As a mantis, arranged
On a green leaf, grows
Into it,[2] makes the leaf leafier, and proves
Any greenness is deeper than anyone knows.

Your hands hold roses always in a way that says
They are not only yours; the beautiful changes
In such kind ways,
Wishing ever to sunder
Things and things' selves for a second finding, to lose
For a moment all that it touches back to wonder.

1947

Praise in Summer

Obscurely yet most surely called to praise,
As sometimes summer calls us all, I said

1. Without capitalization, lucernes are the European blue alfalfa, but here, also, Lake Lucerne.

2. The praying mantis is protectively shaped and colored to resemble a twig with leaves.

The hills are heavens full of branching ways
Where star-nosed moles fly overhead the dead;
I said the trees are mines in air, I said
See how the sparrow burrows in the sky!
And then I wondered why this mad *instead*
Perverts our praise to uncreation, why
Such savor's in this wrenching things awry.
Does sense so stale that it must needs derange
The world to know it? To a praiseful eye
Should it not be enough of fresh and strange
That trees grow green, and moles can course in clay,
And sparrows sweep the ceiling of our day?

1947

The Death of a Toad

A toad the power mower caught,
Chewed and clipped of a leg, with a hobbling hop has got
To the garden verge, and sanctuaried him
Under the cineraria leaves, in the shade
Of the ashen heartshaped leaves, in a dim,
Low, and a final glade.

The rare original heartsblood goes,
Spends on the earthen hide, in the folds and wizenings, flows
In the gutters of the banked and staring eyes. He lies
As still as if he would return to stone,
And soundlessly attending, dies
Toward some deep monotone,

Toward misted and ebullient seas
And cooling shores, toward lost Amphibia's emperies.
Day dwindles, drowning, and at length is gone
In the wide and antique eyes, which still appear
To watch, across the castrate lawn,
The haggard daylight steer.

1950

Mind

Mind in its purest play is like some bat
That beats about in caverns all alone,
Contriving by a kind of senseless wit
Not to conclude against a wall of stone.

It has no need to falter or explore;
Darkly it knows what obstacles are there,
And so may weave and flitter, dip and soar
In perfect courses through the blackest air.

And has this simile a like perfection?
The mind is like a bat. Precisely. Save

That in the very happiest intellection
A graceful error may correct the cave.

1956

Advice to a Prophet

When you come, as you soon must, to the streets of our city,
Mad-eyed from stating the obvious,
Not proclaiming our fall but begging us
In God's name to have self-pity,

Spare us all word of the weapons, their force and range,
The long numbers that rocket the mind;
Our slow, unreckoning hearts will be left behind,
Unable to fear what is too strange.

Nor shall you scare us with talk of the death of the race.
How should we dream of this place without us?—
The sun mere fire, the leaves untroubled about us,
A stone look on the stone's face?

Speak of the world's own change. Though we cannot conceive
Of an undreamt thing, we know to our cost
How the dreamt cloud crumbles, the vines are blackened by frost,
How the view alters. We could believe,

If you told us so, that the white-tailed deer will slip
Into perfect shade, grown perfectly shy,
The lark avoid the reaches of our eye,
The jack-pine lose its knuckled grip

On the cold ledge, and every torrent burn
As Xanthus[3] once, its gliding trout
Stunned in a twinkling. What should we be without
The dolphin's arc, the dove's return,

These things in which we have seen ourselves and spoken?
Ask us, prophet, how we shall call
Our natures forth when that live tongue is all
Dispelled, that glass obscured or broken

In which we have said the rose of our love and the clean
Horse of our courage, in which beheld
The singing locust of the soul unshelled,
And all we mean or wish to mean.

Ask us, ask us whether with the worldless rose
Our hearts shall fail us; come demanding
Whether there shall be lofty or long standing
When the bronze annals of the oak-tree close.

1961

3. Ancient city in Lycia (now Turkey). According to legend the inhabitants in two wars burned their city, the second time with such a blaze that the Xanthus River was afire with debris.

Running

I. *1933*

(North Caldwell, New Jersey)

What were we playing? Was it prisoner's base?
I ran with whacking keds[4]
Down the cart-road past Rickard's place,
And where it dropped beside the tractor-sheds

Leapt out into the air above a blurred
Terrain, through jolted light,
Took two hard lopes, and at the third
Spanked off a hummock-side exactly right,

And made the turn, and with delighted strain
Sprinted across the flat
By the bull-pen, and up the lane.
Thinking of happiness, I think of that.

II. *Patriots' Day*[5]

(Wellesley, Massachusetts)

Restless that noble day, appeased by soft
Drinks and tobacco, littering the grass
While the flag snapped and brightened far aloft,
We waited for the marathon to pass,

We fathers and our little sons, let out
Of school and office to be put to shame.
Now from the street-side someone raised a shout,
And into view the first small runners came.

Dark in the glare, they seemed to thresh in place
Like preening flies upon a window-sill,
Yet gained and grew, and at a cruel pace
Swept by us on their way to Heartbreak Hill—

Legs driving, fists at port, clenched faces, men,
And in amongst them, stamping on the sun,
Our champion Kelley, who would win again,
Rocked in his will, at rest within his run.

III. *Dodwells Road*

(Cummington, Massachusetts)

I jog up out of the woods
To the crown of the road, and slow to a swagger there,
The wind harsh and cool to my throat,
A good ache in my rib-cage.

4. A brand of athletic shoe.
5. April 19, traditionally the day for the running of the Boston Athletic Association Marathon from Hopkinton to Boston. The route passes through Wellesley.

Loud burden of streams at run-off,
And the sun's rocket frazzled in blown tree-heads:
Still I am part of that great going,
Though I stroll now, and am watchful.

Where the road turns and debouches,
The land sinks westward into exhausted pasture.
From fields which yield to aspen now
And pine at last will shadow,

Boy-shouts reach me, and barking.
What is the thing which men will not surrender?
It is what they have never had, I think,
Or missed in its true season,

So that their thoughts turn in
At the same roadhouse nightly, the same cloister,
The wild mouth of the same brave river
Never now to be charted.

You, whoever you are,
If you want to walk with me you must step lively.
I run, too, when the mood offers,
Though the god of that has left me.

But why in the hell spoil it?
I make a clean gift of my young running
To the two boys who break into view,
Hurdling the rocks and racing,

Their dog dodging before them
This way and that, his yaps flushing a pheasant
Who lifts now from the blustery grass
Flying full tilt already.

1969

The Writer

In her room at the prow of the house
Where light breaks, and the windows are tossed with linden,
My daughter is writing a story.

I pause in the stairwell, hearing
From her shut door a commotion of typewriter-keys
Like a chain hauled over a gunwale.

Young as she is, the stuff
Of her life is a great cargo, and some of it heavy:
I wish her a lucky passage.

But now it is she who pauses,
As if to reject my thought and its easy figure.
A stillness greatens, in which

The whole house seems to be thinking,
And then she is at it again with a bunched clamor
Of strokes, and again is silent.

I remember the dazed starling
Which was trapped in that very room, two years ago;
How we stole in, lifted a sash

And retreated, not to affright it;
And how for a helpless hour, through the crack of the door,
We watched the sleek, wild, dark

And iridescent creature
Batter against the brilliance, drop like a glove
To the hard floor, or the desk-top,

And wait then, humped and bloody,
For the wits to try it again; and how our spirits
Rose when, suddenly sure,

It lifted off from a chair-back,
Beating a smooth course for the right window
And clearing the sill of the world.

It is always a matter, my darling,
Of life or death, as I had forgotten. I wish
What I wished you before, but harder.

1976

Cottage Street, 1953

Framed in her phoenix fire-screen, Edna Ward
Bends to the tray of Canton, pouring tea
For frightened Mrs. Plath; then, turning toward
The pale, slumped daughter, and my wife, and me,

Asks if we would prefer it weak or strong.
Will we have milk or lemon, she enquires?
The visit seems already strained and long.
Each in his turn, we tell her our desires.

It is my office to exemplify
The published poet in his happiness,
Thus cheering Sylvia, who has wished to die;
But half-ashamed, and impotent to bless,

I am a stupid life-guard who has found,
Swept to his shallows by the tide, a girl
Who, far from shore, has been immensely drowned,
And stares through water now with eyes of pearl.

How large is her refusal; and how slight
The genteel chat whereby we recommend

Life, of a summer afternoon, despite
The brewing dusk which hints that it may end.

And Edna Ward shall die in fifteen years,
After her eight-and-eighty summers of
Such grace and courage as permit no tears,
The thin hand reaching out, the last word *love,*

Outliving Sylvia who, condemned to live,
Shall study for a decade, as she must,
To state at last her brilliant negative
In poems free and helpless and unjust.

1976

April 5, 1974

The air was soft, the ground still cold.
In the dull pasture where I strolled
Was something I could not believe.
Dead grass appeared to slide and heave,
Though still too frozen-flat to stir,
And rocks to twitch, and all to blur.
What was this rippling of the land?
Was matter getting out of hand
And making free with natural law?
I stopped and blinked, and then I saw
A fact as eerie as a dream.
There was a subtle flood of steam
Moving upon the face of things.
It came from standing pools and springs
And what of snow was still around;
It came of winter's giving ground
So that the freeze was coming out,
As when a set mind, blessed by doubt,
Relaxes into mother-wit.
Flowers, I said, will come of it.

1976

WILLIAM STAFFORD
(1914–)

William Stafford emerged late as a poet. Of the same generation as Delmore Schwartz, Karl Shapiro, Randall Jarrell, and John Berryman, all of whom established reputations in the 1940's, he did not publish his first book of poems, *West of Your City,* until 1960. Prior to that time he had acquired a small following through publication in periodicals and anthologies and he had won some minor literary prizes, but the bulk of his reputation stems from the series of slim volumes produced in the decade when he turned fifty. His voice is quiet, even in tone, modestly self-assured, the voice of a man who has thought long and carefully about what he has to say, a man who does not waste words.

His poetry, as he has said, "is much like talk, with some enhancement." Assuming that poetry is inherent in language, he believes that the poet can best discover the poetry that exists in the sounds he hears about him if he commits himself to no preconceived notions of form. Meter and rhyme are no more to be sought than they are to be avoided: "Relying on forms or rules is always possible—is always one of the possible directions to take. But it is also possible that the everlasting process which led to discovery of forms and rules in the first place will continue to be worthy."

His subject matter reflects a life spent mostly in the open spaces of Kansas, Iowa, and Oregon. Nature bulks large. Personal relationships are important, and long remembered. Born and raised in Hutchinson, Kansas, he graduated from the University of Kansas and some years later took his M.A. there. His service as a conscientious objector in World War II was followed by his later association with the pacifist Fellowship of Reconciliation. Possessor of a Ph.D. from the University of Iowa, he taught for many years in the English department of Lewis and Clark College in Oregon.

Stories That Could Be True: New and Collected Poems was published in 1978. Earlier titles include *West of Your City,* 1960; *Traveling Through the Dark,* 1962; *The Rescued Year,* 1966; *Eleven Untitled Poems,* 1968; *Allegiances,* 1970; *Someday, Maybe,* 1973; *That Other Alone,* 1973; *In the Clock of Reason,* 1973; and *Going Places,* 1974. *A Glass Face in the Rain* appeared in 1982. *Segues: A Correspondence in Poetry,* 1983, contains poems by Stafford and Marvin Bell. Stafford edited *The Achievement of Brother Antoninus,* 1967. A prose account of his experience as a conscientious objector is *Down in My Heart,* 1947. Criticism is *Writing the Australian Crawl: Views on the Writer's Vocation,* 1978; and *You Must Revise Your Life,* 1986. Studies include Jonathan Holden, *The Mark to Turn: A Reading of William Stafford's Poetry,* 1976; and George Lensing and Ronald Moran, *Four Poets of the Emotive Imagination: Robert Bly, James Wright, Louis Simpson and William Stafford,* 1976.

Traveling through the Dark

Traveling through the dark I found a deer
dead on the edge of the Wilson River road.
It is usually best to roll them into the canyon:
that road is narrow; to swerve might make more dead.

By glow of the tail-light I stumbled back of the car
and stood by the heap, a doe, a recent killing;
she had stiffened already, almost cold.
I dragged her off; she was large in the belly.

My fingers touching her side brought me the reason—
her side was warm; her fawn lay there waiting,
alive, still, never to be born.
Beside that mountain road I hesitated.

The car aimed ahead its lowered parking lights;
under the hood purred the steady engine.
I stood in the glare of the warm exhaust turning red;
around our group I could hear the wilderness listen.

I thought hard for us all—my only swerving—,
then pushed her over the edge into the river.

1962

Before the Big Storm

You are famous in my mind.
When anyone mentions your name
all the boxes marked "1930's"
fall off the shelves;
and the orators on the Fourth of July
all begin shouting again.
The audience of our high school commencement
begin to look out of the windows at the big storm.

And I think of you in our play—
oh, helpless and lonely!—crying,
and your father is dead again.
He was drunk; he fell.

When they mention your name,
our houses out there in the wind
creak again in the storm;
and I lean from our play, wherever I am,
to you, quiet at the edge of that town:
"All the world is blowing away."
"It is almost daylight."
"Are you warm?"

1962

Judgments

I accuse—
  Ellen: you have become forty years old,
  and successful, tall, well-groomed,
  gracious, thoughtful, a secretary.
  Ellen, I accuse.

George—
  You know how to help others;
  you manage a school. You never
  let fear or pride or faltering plans
  break your control.
  George, I accuse.

I accuse—
  Tom: you have found a role;
  now you meet all kinds of people
  and let them find the truth of your
  eminence; you need not push.
  Oh, Tom, I do accuse.

Remember—
  The gawky, hardly to survive students
  we were: not one of us going to succeed,
  all of us abjectly aware of how cold,

unmanageable the real world was?
I remember. And that fear was true.
And is true.

Last I accuse—
Myself: my terrible poise, knowing
even this, knowing that then we
sprawled in the world
and were ourselves part of it; now
we hold it firmly away with gracious
gestures (like this of mine!) we've achieved.

I see it all too well—
And I am accused, and I accuse.

1966

One Home

Mine was a Midwest home—you can keep your world.
Plain black hats rode the thoughts that made our code.
We sang hymns in the house; the roof was near God.

The light bulb that hung in the pantry made a wan light,
but we could read by it the names of preserves—
outside, the buffalo grass, and the wind in the night.

A wildcat sprang at Grandpa on the Fourth of July
when he was cutting plum bushes for fuel,
before Indians pulled the West over the edge of the sky.

To anyone who looked at us we said, "My friend";
liking the cut of a thought, we could say, "Hello."
(But plain black hats rode the thoughts that made our code.)

The sun was over our town; it was like a blade.
Kicking cottonwood leaves we ran toward storms.
Wherever we looked the land would hold us up.

1966

The Farm on the Great Plains

A telephone line goes cold;
birds tread it wherever it goes.
A farm back of a great plain
tugs an end of the line.

I call that farm every year,
ringing it, listening, still;
no one is home at the farm,
the line gives only a hum.

Some year I will ring the line
on a night at last the right one,
and with an eye tapered for braille
from the phone on the wall

I will see the tenant who waits—
the last one left at the place;
through the dark my braille eye
will lovingly touch his face.

"Hello, is Mother at home?"
No one is home today.
"But Father—he should be there."
No one—no one is here.

"But you—are you the one . . . ?"
Then the line will be gone
because both ends will be home:
no space, no birds, no farm.

My self will be the plain,
wise as winter is gray,
pure as cold posts go
pacing toward what I know.

1966

Things That Happen Where There Aren't Any People

It's cold on Lakeside Road
with no one traveling. At its turn
on the hill an old sign sags and
finally goes down. The traveler rain
walks back and forth over its victim
flat on the mud.

You don't have to have any people when
sunlight stands on the rocks or gloom
comes following the great dragged clouds
over a huddle of hills. Plenty of
things happen in deserted places, maybe
dust counting millions of its little worlds
or the slow arrival of deep dark.

And out there in the country a rock has been
waiting to be mentioned for thousands of years.
Every day its shadow leans, crouches,
then walks away eastward in one measured stride
exactly right for its way of being. To reach
for that rock we have the same reasons
that explorers always have for their journeys:
because it is far, because there aren't any people.

1980

JAMES DICKEY
(1923–)

Poet, critic, and novelist, James Dickey must be counted among the most impressive of the American writers who came into prominence in the decade of the 1960's. In the eleven years from 1960 to 1970 he published seven volumes of verse, three volumes of literary criticism, a book of *Self-Interviews* (1970), and a novel. Some critics found him severely limited in his essentially visceral subject matter and prosaic style, but others perceived a mythic quality in the material and a kinetic energy in the style that heralded the presence of a major talent.

Dickey dates his real interest in poetry from his air force service in the South Pacific in World War II. He had come to that war from a birth and childhood in Atlanta, Georgia, where his father was a lawyer. High school in Atlanta and a year at Clemson College, where he excelled in football and track, had done little to convince him that poetry could have any meaningful relation to experience, though he had become fond of the poetry of Byron and Shelley. In the air force he took to reading modern poets; when he returned he graduated Phi Beta Kappa from Vanderbilt (1949), took an M.A. there (1950), and began to teach at Rice. Recalled to service in the Korean War, he returned to teaching again briefly before turning to advertising writing in New York and Atlanta. In the meantime his poems had begun to appear in the *Sewanee Review* and *Poetry: A Magazine of Verse.* His first book, *Into the Stone* (1960), brought him the recognition that allowed him to end his frustratingly dual existence as businessman and poet. Since that time he has been most often a teaching poet, with appointments at Reed College, San Fernando Valley State College, the University of Wisconsin, and the University of South Carolina. He received the National Book Award for *Buckdancer's Choice* (1965) and for two years was Consultant in Poetry to the Library of Congress (1967–1969).

Dickey's novel *Deliverance* (1970) is an extraordinary tour de force, marking him as one of the very few American poets who have been able to create sustained imaginative prose of a high order of distinction. The emphasis is on sheer physical sensation, as it is often in the poems as well, and although it is possible to question the clarity of the ideas, it is difficult to deny the book's sensual impact. In the stark clarity of his images, both here and in his verse, he touches at times the roots of human experience. His criticism, too, in *Babel to Byzantium* (1968) and later books has earned him praise.

Behind all that he attempts there lies a strong will to succeed. "The great joy in my life," he says, "is to do something that I love but have no particular aptitude for and become at least reasonably good at it." This joy extends not only to his literary activities, but to marksmanship with a bow and arrow, to playing the guitar, and to acting in movies (he played the sheriff in the film version of *Deliverance*). Concerning his poetry, he believes much of its strength is the result of the route by which he approached it: "I've always had the feeling that nobody really understands poetry but me because I came to it of my own free will and by a very devious and sometimes painful route; I feel that it's something I've earned."

Much of Dickey's verse has been collected in *Poems 1957–1967,* 1968, and *The Central Motion: Poems, 1968–1979,* 1986. Individual verse titles include *Into the Stone and Other Poems,* 1960; *Drowning with Others,* 1962; *Helmets,* 1964; *Two Poems of the Air,* 1964; *Buckdancer's Choice,* 1965; *The Eye-Beaters, Blood, Victory, Madness, Buckhead and Mercy,* 1970; *The Zodiac,* 1976; and *The Strength of the Fields,* 1980. A recent novel is *Alnilam,* 1987. A miscellany is *Night Hurdling: Poems, Essays, Conversations, Commencements, and Afterwords,* 1983. Critical volumes are

The Suspect in Poetry, 1964; *Babel to Byzantium,* 1968; *The Self as Agent,* 1970; and *Sorties,* 1971. Biographical details appear in *Self-Interviews,* edited by Barbara and James Reiss, 1970. A study is Neal Bowers, *James Dickey, the Poet as Pitchman,* 1985. Eileen Glancy edited *James Dickey: The Critic as Poet, An Annotated Bibliography with An Introductory Essay,* 1971.

The Hospital Window

I have just come down from my father.
Higher and higher he lies
Above me in a blue light
Shed by a tinted window.
I drop through six white floors
And then step out onto pavement.

Still feeling my father ascend,
I start to cross the firm street,
My shoulder blades shining with all
The glass the huge building can raise.
Now I must turn round and face it,
And know his one pane from the others.

Each window possesses the sun
As though it burned there on a wick.
I wave, like a man catching fire.
All the deep-dyed windowpanes flash,
And, behind them, all the white rooms
They turn to the color of Heaven.

Ceremoniously, gravely, and weakly,
Dozens of pale hands are waving
Back, from inside their flames.
Yet one pure pane among these
Is the bright, erased blankness of nothing.
I know that my father is there,

In the shape of his death still living.
The traffic increases around me
Like a madness called down on my head.
The horns blast at me like shotguns,
And drivers lean out, driven crazy—
But now my propped-up father

Lifts his arm out of stillness at last.
The light from the window strikes me
And I turn as blue as a soul,
As the moment when I was born.
I am not afraid for my father—
Look! He is grinning; he is not

Afraid for my life, either,
As the wild engines stand at my knees
Shredding their gears and roaring,
And I hold each car in its place
For miles, inciting its horn
To blow down the walls of the world

That the dying may float without fear
In the bold blue gaze of my father.
Slowly I move to the sidewalk
With my pin-tingling hand half dead
At the end of my bloodless arm.
I carry it off in amazement,

High, still higher, still waving,
My recognized face fully mortal,
Yet not; not at all, in the pale,
Drained, otherworldly, stricken,
Created hue of stained glass.
I have just come down from my father.

1962

The Lifeguard

In a stable of boats I lie still,
From all sleeping children hidden.
The leap of a fish from its shadow
Makes the whole lake instantly tremble.
With my foot on the water, I feel
The moon outside

Take on the utmost of its power.
I rise and go out through the boats.
I set my broad sole upon silver,
On the skin of the sky, on the moonlight,
Stepping outward from earth onto water
In quest of the miracle

This village of children believed
That I could perform as I dived
For one who had sunk from my sight.
I saw his cropped haircut go under.
I leapt, and my steep body flashed
Once, in the sun.

Dark drew all the light from my eyes.
Like a man who explores his death
By the pull of his slow-moving shoulders,
I hung head down in the cold,
Wide-eyed, contained, and alone
Among the weeds,

And my fingertips turned into stone
From clutching immovable blackness.
Time after time I leapt upward
Exploding in breath, and fell back
From the change in the children's faces
At my defeat.

Beneath them I swam to the boathouse
With only my life in my arms
To wait for the lake to shine back

At the risen moon with such power
That my steps on the light of the ripples
Might be sustained.

Beneath me is nothing but brightness
Like the ghost of a snowfield in summer.
As I moved toward the center of the lake,
Which is also the center of the moon,
I am thinking of how I may be
The savior of one

Who has already died in my care.
The dark trees fade from around me.
The moon's dust hovers together.
I call softly out, and the child's
Voice answers through blinding water.
Patiently, slowly,

He rises, dilating to break
The surface of stone with his forehead.
He is one I do not remember
Having ever seen in his life.
The ground I stand on is trembling
Upon his smile.

I wash the black mud from my hands.
On a light given off by the grave
I kneel in the quick of the moon
At the heart of a distant forest
And hold in my arms a child
Of water, water, water.

1962

Cherrylog Road

Off Highway 106
At Cherrylog Road I entered
The '34 Ford without wheels,
Smothered in kudzu,[1]
With a seat pulled out to run
Corn whiskey down from the hills,

And then from the other side
Crept into an Essex
With a rumble seat of red leather
And then out again, aboard
A blue Chevrolet, releasing
The rust from its other color,

Reared up on three building blocks.
None had the same body heat;
I changed with them inward, toward

1. A vine of rapid, luxurious growth.

The weedy heart of the junkyard,
For I knew that Doris Holbrook
Would escape from her father at noon

And would come from the farm
To seek parts owned by the sun
Among the abandoned chassis,
Sitting in each in turn
As I did, leaning forward
As in a wild stock-car race

In the parking lot of the dead.
Time after time, I climbed in
And out the other side, like
An envoy or movie star
Met at the station by crickets.
A radiator cap raised its head,

Become a real toad or a kingsnake
As I neared the hub of the yard,
Passing through many states,
Many lives, to reach
Some grandmother's long Pierce-Arrow
Sending platters of blindness forth

From its nickel hubcaps
And spilling its tender upholstery
On sleepy roaches,
The glass panel in between
Lady and colored driver
Not all the way broken out,

The back-seat phone
Still on its hook.
I got in as though to exclaim,
"Let us go to the orphan asylum,
John; I have some old toys
For children who say their prayers."

I popped with sweat as I thought
I heard Doris Holbrook scrape
Like a mouse in the southern-state sun
That was eating the paint in blisters
From a hundred car tops and hoods.
She was tapping like code,

Loosening the screws,
Carrying off headlights,
Sparkplugs, bumpers,
Cracked mirrors and gear-knobs,
Getting ready, already,
To go back with something to show

Other than her lips' new trembling
I would hold to me soon, soon,

Where I sat in the ripped back seat
Talking over the interphone,
Praying for Doris Holbrook
To come from her father's farm

And to get back there
With no trace of me on her face
To be seen by her red-haired father
Who would change, in the squalling barn,
Her back's pale skin with a strop,
Then lay for me

In a bootlegger's roasting car
With a string-triggered 12-gauge shotgun
To blast the breath from the air.
Not cut by the jagged windshields,
Through the acres of wrecks she came
With a wrench in her hand,

Through dust where the blacksnake dies
Of boredom, and the beetle knows
The compost has no more life.
Someone outside would have seen
The oldest car's door inexplicably
Close from within:

I held her and held her and held her,
Convoyed at terrific speed
By the stalled, dreaming traffic around us,
So the blacksnake, stiff
With inaction, curved back
Into life, and hunted the mouse

With deadly overexcitement,
The beetles reclaimed their field
As we clung, glued together,
With the hooks of the seat springs
Working through to catch us red-handed
Amidst the gray breathless batting

That burst from the seat at our backs.
We left by separate doors
Into the changed, other bodies
Of cars, she down Cherrylog Road
And I to my motorcycle
Parked like the soul of the junkyard

Restored, a bicycle fleshed
With power, and tore off
Up Highway 106, continually
Drunk on the wind in my mouth,
Wringing the handlebar for speed,
Wild to be wreckage forever.

1964

The Shark's Parlor

Memory: I can take my head and strike it on a wall   on Cumberland Island
Where the night tide came crawling under the stairs   came up the first
Two or three steps   and the cottage stood on poles all night
With the sea sprawled under it   as we dreamed of the great fin circling
Under the bedroom floor. In daylight there was my first brassy taste of beer
And Payton Ford and I came back from the Glynn County slaughterhouse
With a bucket of entrails and blood. We tied one end of a hawser
To a spindling porch pillar and rowed straight out of the house
Three hundred yards into the vast front yard of windless blue water
The rope outslithering its coil   the two-gallon jug stoppered and sealed
With wax   and a ten-foot chain leader   a drop-forged shark hook nestling.
We cast our blood on the waters   the land blood easily passing
For sea blood   and we sat in it for a moment with the stain spreading
Out from the boat   sat in a new radiance   in the pond of blood in the sea
Waiting for fins   waiting to spill our guts also in the glowing water.
We dumped the bucket, and baited the hook with a run-over collie pup. The jug
Bobbed, trying to shake off the sun as a dog would shake off the sea.
We rowed to the house   feeling the same water lift the boat a new way,
All the time seeing where we lived rise and dip with the oars.
We tied up and sat down in rocking chairs, one eye or the other responding
To the blue-eye wink of the jug. Payton got us a beer and we sat

All morning sat there with blood on our minds   the red mark out
In the harbor slowly failing us   then   the house groaned   the rope
Sprang out of the water   splinters flew   we leapt from our chairs
And grabbed the rope   hauled   did nothing   the house coming subtly
Apart   all around us   underfoot   boards beginning to sparkle like sand
With the glinting of the bright hidden parts of ten-year-old nails
Pulling out   the tarred poles we slept propped-up on   leaning to sea
As in land wind   crabs scuttling from under the floor   as we took turns about
Two more porch pillars   and looked out and saw   something   a fish-flash
An almighty fin in trouble   a moiling of secret forces   a false start
Of water   a round wave growing: in the whole of Cumberland Sound the one ripple.
Payton took off without a word   I could not hold him either

But clung to the rope anyway: it was the whole house bending
Its nails that held whatever it was   coming in a little and like a fool
I took up the slack on my wrist. The rope drew gently   jerked   I lifted
Clean off the porch and hit the water   the same water it was in
I felt in blue blazing terror at the bottom of the stairs and scrambled
Back up looking desperately into the human house as deeply as I could
Stopping my gaze before it went out the wire screen of the back door
Stopped it on the thistled rattan   the rugs I lay on and read
On my mother's sewing basket with next winter's socks spilling from it
The flimsy vacation furniture   a bucktoothed picture of myself.
Payton came back with three men from a filling station   and glanced at me
Dripping water   inexplicable   then we all grabbed hold like a tug-of-war.

We were gaining a little   from us a cry went up   from everywhere
People came running. Behind us the house filled with men and boys.
On the third step from the sea I took my place   looking down the rope
Going into the ocean, humming and shaking off drops. A houseful

Of people put their backs into it   going up the steps from me
Into the living room   through the kitchen   down the back stairs
Up and over a hill of sand   across a dust road   and onto a raised field
Of dunes   we were gaining   the rope in my hands began to be wet
With deeper water   all other haulers retreated through the house
But Payton and I on the stairs   drawing hand over hand on our blood
Drawing into existence by the nose   a huge body   becoming
A hammerhead   rolling in beery shallows   and I began to let up
But the rope still strained behind me   the town had gone
Pulling-mad in our house: far away in a field of sand they struggled
They had turned their backs on the sea   bent double   some on their knees
The rope over their shoulders like a bag of gold   they strove for the ideal
Esso station across the scorched meadow   with the distant fish coming up
The front stairs   the sagging boards   still coming in   up   taking
Another step   toward the empty house   where the rope stood straining
By itself through the rooms   in the middle of the air. "Pass the word,"
Payton said, and I screamed it: "Let up, good God, let up!"   to no one there.
The shark flopped on the porch, grating with salt-sand   driving back in
The nails he had pulled out   coughing chunks of his formless blood.
The screen door banged and tore off   he scrambled on his tail   slid
Curved   did a thing from another world   and was out of his element and in
Our vacation paradise   cutting all four legs from under the dinner table
With one deep-water move   he unwove the rugs in a moment   throwing pints
Of blood over everything we owned   knocked the buck teeth out of my picture
His odd head full of crushed jelly-glass splinters and radio tubes thrashing
Among the pages of fan magazines   all the movie stars drenched in sea-blood
Each time we thought he was dead   he struggled back and smashed
One more thing   in all coming back to die   three or four more times after death.
At last we got him out   log-rolling him   greasing his sandpaper skin
With lard to slide him   pulling on his chained lips as the tide came
Tumbled him down the steps as the first night wave went under the floor.
He drifted off   head back   belly white as the moon. What could I do but buy
That house   for the one black mark still there   against death   a forehead-
toucher in the room he circles beneath   and has been invited to wreck?
Blood hard as iron on the wall   black with time   still bloodlike
Can be touched whenever the brow is drunk enough: all changes: Memory:
Something like three-dimensional dancing in the limbs   with age
Feeling more in two worlds than one   in all worlds the growing encounters.

1965

DENISE LEVERTOV

(1923–   )

Child of a Welshwoman and an Anglican clergyman converted from Judaism, Denise Levertov was born in London in 1923 and has lived in the United States since 1948. She received no formal education, but there was "a houseful of books and everyone in the family engaged in some literary activity." In 1947 she married an American author, Mitchell Goodman, and through him became interested in the American experimental poetry. She was especially influenced by the verse of Wallace Stevens and William Carlos Williams, and by the Black Mountain poets Charles Olson, Robert Duncan, and Robert Creeley, and is now a poet of careful, incisive imagery and ironic wit. Her belief in the essential unity of content and form, as expressed in her essay "Organic Form," often results in verse of impressive inner harmony. This noteworthy directness of statement and her symbolic originality are the principal factors of her characteristic style and her attraction to unusual subjects suitable to her way of seeing things. Perhaps her "difference" inheres in a tendency to substitute for verbal images what might be called symbolic action, as in the poems below.

In the 1960's Levertov joined with her husband in active opposition to the Vietnam War. From *The Sorrow Dance* (1967) on, politics, the women's movement, and third world concerns are intermixed with more personal matter. A recipient of numerous awards, she was from 1975 to 1979 a professor of English at Tufts University.

Volumes of poetry are *The Double Image,* 1946; *Here and Now,* 1957; *With Eyes at the Back of Our Heads,* 1959; *The Jacob's Ladder,* 1961; *O Taste and See,* 1964; *The Sorrow Dance,* 1967; *Embroideries,* 1969; *Relearning the Alphabet,* 1970; *To Stay Alive,* 1971; *Footprints: Poems,* 1972; *The Freeing of the Dust,* 1975; *Life in the Forest,* 1978; and *Oblique Prayers,* 1984. Essays are collected in *The Poet in the World,* 1973. Critical studies are Linda W. Wagner, *Denise Levertov,* 1967; and Linda W. Wagner, ed., *Denise Levertov: In Her Own Province,* 1979.

The Third Dimension

Who'd believe me if
I said, 'They took and

split me open from
scalp to crotch, and

still I'm alive, and
walk around pleased with

the sun and all
the world's bounty.' Honesty

isn't so simple:
a simple honesty is

nothing but a lie.
Don't the trees

hide the wind between
their leaves and

speak in whispers?
The third dimension

hides itself.
If the roadmen

crack stones, the
stones are stones:

but love
cracked me open

and I'm
alive to

tell the tale—but not
honestly:

the words
change it. Let it be—

here in the sweet sun
—a fiction, while I

breathe and
change pace.

1957

To the Snake

Green Snake, when I hung you round my neck
and stroked your cold, pulsing throat
as you hissed to me, glinting
arrowy gold scales, and I felt
the weight of you on my shoulders,
and the whispering silver of your dryness
sounded close at my ears—

Green Snake—I swore to my companions that certainly
you were harmless! But truly
I had no certainty, and no hope, only desiring
to hold you, for that joy,
which left
a long wake of pleasure, as the leaves moved
and you faded into the pattern
of grass and shadows, and I returned
smiling and haunted, to a dark morning.

1959

The Room

With a mirror
I could see the sky.

With two mirrors or three
justly placed, I could see
the sun bowing to the evening chimneys.

Moonrise—the moon itself might appear
in a fourth mirror placed high
and close to the open window.

With enough mirrors within
and even without the room, a cantilever

supporting them, mountains
and oceans might be manifest.

I understand perfectly
that I could encounter my own eyes
too often—I take account
of the danger—.
                    If the mirrors
are large enough, and arranged
with bravura, I can look
beyond my own glance.

With one mirror
how many stars could I see?

I don't want to escape, only to see
the enactment of rites.

1959

The Willows of Massachusetts

Animal willows of November
in pelt of gold enduring when all else
has let go all ornament
and stands naked in the cold.
Cold shine of sun on swamp water,
cold caress of slant beam on bough,
gray light on brown bark.
Willows—last to relinquish a leaf,
curious, patient, lion-headed, tense
with energy, watching
the serene cold through a curtain
of tarnished strands.

1967

From Olga Poems

(*Olga Levertoff, 1914–1964*)[1]

i

By the gas-fire, kneeling
to undress,
scorching luxuriously, raking
her nails over olive sides, the red
waistband ring—

(And the little sister
beady-eyed in the bed—
or drowsy, was I? My head
a camera—)

1. The poet's sister.

Sixteen. Her breasts
round, round, and
dark-nippled—

who now these two months long
is bones and tatters of flesh in earth.

ii

The high pitch of
nagging insistence, lines
creased into raised brows—

Ridden, ridden—
the skin around the nails
nibbled sore—

You wanted
to shout the world to its senses,
did you?—to browbeat

the poor into joy's
socialist republic—
What rage

and human shame swept you
when you were nine and saw
the Ley Street houses,

grasping their meaning as *slum.*
Where I, reaching that age,
teased you, admiring

architectural probity, circa
eighteen-fifty, and noted
pride in the whitened doorsteps.

Black one, black one,
there was a white
candle in your heart.

vi

Your eyes were the brown gold of pebbles under water.
I never crossed the bridge over the Roding, dividing
the open field of the present from the mysteries,
the wraiths and shifts of time-sense Wanstead Park held suspended,
without remembering your eyes. Even when we were estranged
and my own eyes smarted in pain and anger at the thought of you.
And by other streams in other countries; anywhere where the light
reaches down through shallows to gold gravel. Olga's
brown eyes. One rainy summer, down in the New Forest,
when we could hardly breathe for ennui and the low sky,
you turned savagely to the piano and sightread
straight through all the Beethoven sonatas, day after day—
weeks, it seemed to me. I would turn the pages some of the time,

go out to ride my bike, return—you were enduring in the
falls and rapids of the music, the arpeggios rang out, the rectory
trembled, our parents seemed effaced.
I think of your eyes in that photo, six years before I was born,
the fear in them. What did you do with your fear,
later? Through the years of humiliation,
of paranoia and blackmail and near-starvation, losing
the love of those you loved, one after another,
parents, lovers, children, idolized friends, what kept
compassion's candle alight in you, that lit you
clear into another chapter (but the same book) 'a clearing
in the selva oscura,[2]
a house whose door
swings open, a hand beckons
in welcome'?
                    I cross
so many brooks in the world, there is so much light
dancing on so many stones, so many questions my eyes
smart to ask of your eyes, gold brown eyes,
the lashes short but the lids
arched as if carved out of olivewood, eyes with some vision
of festive goodness in back of their hard, or veiled, or shining,
unknowable gaze . . .

MAY–AUGUST, 1964 1967

Living

The fire in leaf and grass
so green it seems
each summer the last summer.

The wind blowing, the leaves
shivering in the sun,
each day the last day.

A red salamander
so cold and so
easy to catch, dreamily

moves his delicate feet
and long tail. I hold
my hand open for him to go.

Each minute the last minute.

1967

Intrusion

After I had cut off my hands
and grown new ones

2. The "dark wood" in Dante's opening lines in the *Inferno,* but also the title of a poem by Louis MacNeice (1907–1963) that Levertov has said was "much beloved by my sister." The quoted lines are "an adaptation" from MacNeice.

something my former hands had longed for
came and asked to be rocked.

After my plucked out eyes
had withered, and new ones grown

something my former eyes had wept for
came asking to be pitied.

AUGUST, 1969

1972

Wedding-Ring

My wedding-ring lies in a basket
as if at the bottom of a well.
Nothing will come to fish it back up
and onto my finger again.
It lies
among keys to abandoned houses,
nails waiting to be needed and hammered
into some wall,
telephone numbers with no names attached,
idle paperclips.
It can't be given away
for fear of bringing ill-luck.
It can't be sold
for the marriage was good in its own
time, though that time is gone.
Could some artificer
beat into it bright stones, transform it
into a dazzling circlet no one could take
for solemn betrothal or to make promises
living will not let them keep? Change it
into a simple gift I could give in friendship?

1978

The 90th Year

High in the jacaranda shines the gilded thread
of a small bird's curlicue of song—too high
for her to see or hear.
I've learned
not to say, these last years,
"O, look!—O listen, Mother!"
as I used to.
(It was she
who taught me to look;
to name the flowers when I was still close to the ground,
my face level with theirs;
or to watch the sublime metamorphoses
unfold and unfold
over the walled back gardens of our street . . .

It had not been given her
to know the flesh as good in itself,

as the flesh of a fruit is good. To her
the human body has been a husk,
a shell in which souls were prisoned.
Yet, from within it, with how much gazing
her life has paid tribute to the world's body!
How tears of pleasure
would choke her, when a perfect voice,
deep or high, clove to its note unfaltering!)

She has swept the crackling seedpots,
the litter of mauve blossoms, off the cement path,
tipped them into the rubbish bucket.
She's made her bed, washed up the breakfast dishes,
wiped the hotplate. I've taken the butter and milkjug
back to the fridge next door—but it's not my place,
visiting here, to usurp the tasks
that weave the day's pattern.
Now she is leaning forward in her chair,
            by the lamp lit in the daylight,
rereading *War and Peace.*
                        When I look up
from her wellworn copy of *The Divine Milieu*,[3]
which she wants me to read, I see her hand
loose on the black stem of the magnifying glass,
she is dozing.
"I am so tired," she has written to me, "of appreciating
the gift of life."

1978

LOUIS SIMPSON

(1923–)

Louis Simpson was born in Kingston, Jamaica, to a father of Scottish descent and a mother whose forebears were Russian Jews who had earlier immigrated to the United States. He was brought up and educated through secondary school in Kingston before moving to New York in 1940 to enroll in Columbia University. Entering the army in 1943, he served with the 101st Airborne Division in the Normandy invasion and the subsequent push into Germany, was wounded and cited for valor, and mustered out in 1945. A subsequent breakdown he called "delayed battle fatigue" hospitalized him with amnesia and depression, but he was soon back at Columbia. He graduated in 1948, in the same class as Allen Ginsberg, whose career had been similarly interrupted.

Shortly after graduation, Simpson privately published his first book in Paris, *The Arrivistes: Poems 1940–1949* (1949), containing "Carentan O Carentan"; like Randall Jarrell, Simpson showed early that the horrors of the war could produce strong and moving verse, and the war continued to serve him as major subject matter through his next two books, *Good News of Death and Other Poems* (1955) and *A Dream of Governors* (1959). Meanwhile, he had returned to Columbia for an M.A. (1950), worked as an editor for the pub-

3. *War and Peace* is by Leo Tolstoi (1829–1910), *The Divine Milieu* by Pierre Teilhard de Chardin (1881–1955).

lisher Bobbs-Merrill from 1950 through 1955, taught at Columbia and at the New School for Social Research in the late 1950's, and completed a Ph.D. in comparative literature at Columbia in 1959. Since then, he has taught at the University of California, Berkeley (1959–1967), and since 1967 at the State University of New York at Stony Brook.

Simpson's early verse is traditionally metered and rhymed. In *A Dream of Governors,* he began to experiment with the free form, colloquial style that characterizes his work in *At the End of the Open Road* (1963) and subsequent volumes. Increasingly, too, he has turned in his subject matter to an engagement with America: a questioning of the values of the suburbs, an involvement with his personal place as an immigrant with a Jewish heritage, a concern with social and political issues from Vietnam onwards.

People Live Here: Selected Poems 1949–1983, 1983, supersedes the earlier *Selected Poems,* 1965. Other books of verse, in addition to those named above, are *Adventures of the Letter I,* 1971; *Searching for the Ox,* 1976; *Armidale,* 1980; *Caviare at the Funeral,* 1980; and *The Best Hour of the Night,* 1983. *Riverside Drive,* 1962, is a novel and *North of Jamaica,* 1972, an autobiography. Simpson's critical books include *Three on a Tower: the Lives and Works of Ezra Pound, T. S. Eliot and William Carlos Williams,* 1975; *A Revolution in Taste: Studies of Dylan Thomas, Allen Ginsberg, Sylvia Plath and Robert Lowell,* 1978; *A Company of Poets,* 1981; and *The Character of the Poet,* 1986.

Ronald Moran, *Louis Simpson,* 1972, is a full-length study. William Roberson compiled *Louis Simpson: A Reference Guide,* 1982.

Carentan O Carentan[1]

Trees in the old days used to stand
And shape a shady lane
Where lovers wandered hand in hand
Who came from Carentan.

This was the shining green canal
Where we came two by two
Walking at combat-interval.
Such trees we never knew.

The day was early June, the ground
Was soft and bright with dew.
Far away the guns did sound,
But here the sky was blue.

The sky was blue, but there a smoke
Hung still above the sea
Where the ships together spoke
To towns we could not see.

Could you have seen us through a glass
You would have said a walk
Of farmers out to turn the grass,
Each with his own hay-fork.

The watchers in their leopard suits
Waited till it was time,
And aimed between the belt and boot
And let the barrel climb.

1. A French port town where a severe battle was fought June 8–12, 1944, a few days after D-Day.

I must lie down at once, there is
A hammer at my knee.
And call it death or cowardice,
Don't count again on me.

Everything's all right, Mother,
Everyone gets the same
At one time or another.
It's all in the game.

I never strolled, nor ever shall,
Down such a leafy lane.
I never drank in a canal,
Nor ever shall again.

There is a whistling in the leaves
And it is not the wind,
The twigs are falling from the knives
That cut men to the ground.

Tell me, Master-Sergeant,
The way to turn and shoot.
But the Sergeant's silent
That taught me how to do it.

O Captain, show us quickly
Our place upon the map.
But the Captain's sickly
And taking a long nap.

Lieutenant, what's my duty,
My place in the platoon?
He too's a sleeping beauty,
Charmed by that strange tune.

Carentan O Carentan
Before we met with you
We never yet had lost a man
Or known what death could do.

1949

To the Western World

A siren sang, and Europe turned away
From the high castle and the shepherd's crook.
Three caravels went sailing to Cathay
On the strange ocean, and the captains shook
Their banners out across the Mexique Bay.

And in our early days we did the same.
Remembering our fathers in their wreck
We crossed the sea from Palos where they came
And saw, enormous to the little deck,
A shore in silence waiting for a name.

The treasures of Cathay were never found.
In this America, this wilderness
Where the axe echoes with a lonely sound,
The generations labor to possess
And grave by grave we civilize the ground.

1959

American Poetry

Whatever it is, it must have
A stomach that can digest
Rubber, coal, uranium, moons, poems.

Like the shark, it contains a shoe.
It must swim for miles through the desert
Uttering cries that are almost human.

1963

Why Do You Write about Russia?

When I was a child
my mother told stories about the country
she came from. Wolves were howling,
snow fell, the drunken Cossack
shouted in the snow.

Rats prowled the floor of the cellar
where the children slept.
Once, after an illness, she was sent
to Odessa, on the sea. There were battleships
painted white, and ladies and gentlemen
walking the esplanade . . . white naval uniforms
and parasols.

These stories were told
against a background of tropical night . . .
a sea breeze stirring the flowers
that open at dusk, smelling like perfume.
The voice that spoke of freezing cold
itself was warm and infinitely comforting.

So it is with poetry: whatever numbing horrors
it may speak of, the voice itself
tells of love and infinite wonder.

Later, when I came to New York,
I used to go to my grandmother's
in Brooklyn. The names of stations
return in their order like a charm:
Franklin, Nostrand, Kingston.
And members of the family gather:
the three sisters, the one brother,

one of the cousins from Washington,
and myself . . . a "student at Columbia."
But what am I really?

For when my grandmother says, "Eat!
People who work with their heads have to eat more" . . .
Work? Does it deserve a name
so full of seriousness and high purpose?
Gazing across Amsterdam Avenue
at the windows opposite, letting my mind
wander where it will, from the page
to Malaya, or some street in Paris . . .
Drifting smoke. The end will be as fatal
as an opium-eater's dream.

The view has changed—to evergreens,
a hedge, and my neighbor's roof.
This too is like a dream, the way we live
with our cars and power-mowers . . .
a life that shuns emotion
and the violence that goes with it,
the object being to live quietly
and bring up children to be happy.

Yes, but what are you going to tell them
of what lies ahead?
That the better life seems
the more it goes sour? The child no longer
a child, his happiness all of a sudden
behind him. And he in turn
expected to bring up his children
to be happy . . .

What then do I want?

A life in which there are depths
beyond happiness. As one of my friends,
Grigoryev, says, "Two things
constantly cry out in creation,
the sea and man's soul."

Reaching from where we are
to where we came from . . . *Thalassa!*
a view of the sea.

I sit listening to the rasp
of a power-saw, the puttering of a motorboat.
The whole meaningless life around me
affirming a positive attitude . . .

When a hat appears, a black felt hat,
gliding along the hedge . . .

then a long, black overcoat
that falls beneath the knee.

He produces a big, purple handkerchief,
brushes off a chair, and sits.

"It's hot," he says, "but I like to walk,
that way you get to see the world.
And so, what are you reading now?"

Chekhov, I tell him.

"Of course. But have you read Leskov?
There are sentences that will stay in your mind
a whole lifetime.
For instance, in the 'Lady Macbeth,'
when the woman says to her lover,
'You couldn't be nearly as desirous
as you say you are, for I heard you singing' . . .
he answers, 'What about gnats?
They sing all their lives, but it's not for joy.' "
So my imaginary friend tells stories
of the same far place the soul comes from.

When I think about Russia
it's not that area of the earth's surface
with Leningrad to the West and Siberia
to the East—I don't know anything
about the continental mass.

It's a sound, such as you hear
in a sea breaking along a shore.

My people came from Russia,
bringing with them nothing
but that sound.

1980

ROBERT CREELEY

(1926–)

Robert Creeley was born in Arlington, Massachusetts, where his father was a physician. The loss of his father when Creeley was four, and of his left eye a little earlier, he has said, "mark for me two conditions I have unequivocally as content." Raised by his mother, a public health nurse, in rural West Acton, not far from the Concord of Emerson and Thoreau, he retreated often to the woods: "* * * all the kinds of dilemma that I would feel sometimes would be resolved by going out into the woods, and equally that immanence, that spill of life all around, * * * the shyness, the particularity of things." After high school on a scholarship at Holderness School in Plymouth, New Hampshire, he entered Harvard in 1943, leaving in the next year to drive an ambulance for the American Field Service in India. Back at Harvard, he soon married and began commuting on the ferry from Provincetown, living on his wife's income and trying to write. In 1947 he left Harvard without graduating.

For most of the next decade, the Creeleys pursued his career as a poet, first in Littleton, New Hampshire, then in France and on Majorca. He corresponded with Charles Olson, helped Cid Corman establish the influential little magazine *Origin,* and operated a small press on Majorca, where he began to publish *The Black Mountain Review* in 1954. The journal lasted only until 1957, but was one of the most influential of its time. Meanwhile, Creeley's marriage, his first, broke up, he taught briefly at Black Mountain College, and left for New Mexico and California. In the following years, he has lived in Guatemala and taught at a number of colleges, including the universities of New Mexico and British Columbia, and the State University of New York at Buffalo.

Although his best poetry achieves a chiseled and almost classic simplicity from his short lines and frequent four-line stanzas, Creeley occupies a central place in the anti-academic movement of the 1950's. Associated with other Black Mountain poets like Olson, Robert Duncan, Edward Dorn, and Denise Levertov, he was also an associate of Allen Ginsberg, Jack Kerouac, Gary Snyder, and other Beat writers whom he met in 1956 in San Francisco just as that movement was about to get national attention with the publication of *Howl* (1956) and *On the Road* (1957). Like Olson, he looked to Pound and Williams as the fathers of the new poetry, distrusting the legacy of Eliot and the strictures of the New Criticism. Inspired by the rhythms of jazz, and by the abstract expressionist and minimalist movements in graphic arts, he has distrusted symbols and metaphors and sought a language in which each word will represent itself only, the thing at that moment present in the poet's mind and transmitted to the printed page. Art, as Williams had said, must be local, and for Creeley "The LOCAL is NOT a place but a place in a given man—what part of it he has been compelled or else brought by love to give witness to in his own mind."

Creeley's early books were published by small presses, including his own Divers Press on Majorca. With *For Love, Poems 1950–1960,* published by Scribners in 1960, he began to receive a wider readership. *The Island,* a novel, followed in 1963. A later poetry collection is *Words* (1967). For many critics the poems of *Pieces* (1968) seemed too slight for serious attention. *A Day Book* (1972) is half prose journal, half poetry.

The Collected Poems of Robert Creeley, 1945–75 was published in 1982. A more recent volume of verse is *Memory Gardens,* 1986. *The Collected Prose of Robert Creeley,* 1984, includes *The Island,* the stories of *The Gold Diggers,* 1954, and other fiction. Earlier poetry collections include *Selected Poems,* 1976; and *The Charm: Early and Uncollected Poems,* 1969. Individual titles by small presses are many. Donald Allen edited *A Quick Graph: Collected Notes & Essays,* 1970; *Contexts of Poetry: Interviews 1961–1971,* 1973; and *Was That a Real Poem and Other Essays,* 1979.

Studies include Cynthia Dubin Edelberg, *Robert Creeley's Poetry,* 1978; and Arthur Ford, *Robert Creeley,* 1978. Carroll F. Terrell edited a collection of essays, *Robert Creeley: The Poet's Workshop,* 1984.

I Know a Man

As I sd to my
friend, because I am
always talking,—John, I

sd, which was not his
name, the darkness sur-
rounds us, what

can we do against
it, or else, shall we &
why not, buy a goddamn big car,

drive, he sd, for
christ's sake, look
out where yr going.

1957

The Rain

All night the sound had
come back again,
and again falls
this quiet, persistent rain.

What am I to myself
that must be remembered,
insisted upon
so often? Is it

that never the ease,
even the hardness,
of rain falling
will have for me

something other than this,
something not so insistent—
am I to be locked in this
final uneasiness.

Love, if you love me,
lie next to me.
Be for me, like rain,
the getting out

of the tiredness, the fatuousness, the semi-
lust of intentional indifference.
Be wet
with a decent happiness.

1962

For Fear

For fear I want
to make myself again
under the thumb
of old love, old time

subservience
and pain, bent
into a nail that will
not come out.

Why, love, does it
make such a difference
not to be heard
in spite of self

or what we may feel,
one for the other,
but as a hammer
to drive again

bent nail
into old hurt?

1962

The Rhythm

It is all a rhythm,
from the shutting
door, to the window
opening,

the seasons, the sun's
light, the moon,
the oceans, the
growing of things,

the mind in men
personal, recurring
in them again,
thinking the end

is not the end, the
time returning,
themselves dead but
someone else coming.

If in death I am dead,
then in life also
dying, dying . . .
And the women cry and die.

The little children
grow only to old men.
The grass dries,
the force goes.

But is met by another
returning, oh not mine,
not mine, and
in turn dies.

The rhythm which projects
from itself continuity

bending all to its force
from window to door,
from ceiling to floor,
light at the opening,
dark at the closing.

1967

"I Keep to Myself Such Measures . . ."

I keep to myself such
measures as I care for,
daily the rocks
accumulate position.

There is nothing
but what thinking makes
it less tangible. The mind,
fast as it goes, loses

pace, puts in place of it
like rocks simple markers,
for a way only to
hopefully come back to

where it cannot. All
forgets. My mind sinks.
I hold in both hands such weight
it is my only description.

1967

One Way

Of the two, one
faces one. In
the air there is

no tremor, no
odor. There is
a house around them,

of wood, of walls.
The mark is silence.
Everything hangs.

As he raises
his hand to
not strike her, as

again his hand
is raised, she has
gone, into another

room. In the room
left by her, he
cannot see himself

as in a mirror, as
a feeling of reflection.
He thinks he thinks,

of something else.
All the locked time,
all the letting go

down into it, as a
locked room, come to.
This time not changed,

but the way of feeling
secured by walls and books,
a picture hanging down,

a center shifted, dust
on all he puts his hand on,
disorder, papers and letters

and accumulations of clothing,
and bedclothes, and under his
feet the rug bunches.

1967

ALLEN GINSBERG
(1926–)

Allen Ginsberg was born in Newark, New Jersey, in 1926. His father, Louis Ginsberg, was a poet and high school English teacher in Paterson, New Jersey. The younger Ginsberg went to high school in Paterson and graduated in 1948 from Columbia University. At Columbia he published in the *Columbia Review;* there and elsewhere in New York in the late 1940's he participated in the activities of the group that came to be known as the Beat Generation. After experiences that included dishwashing, a stint as a welder in the Brooklyn Navy Yard, hospitalization for a nervous breakdown, reviewing for *Newsweek,* and service in the merchant marine, he was catapulted to fame by the obscenity charges leveled against his first book, *Howl and Other Poems* (1956).

It is difficult to dissociate Ginsberg the poet from Ginsberg the public figure. Long before he had secured any widespread reputation for his poems he had already appeared as a fictional character in two Beat novels, Jack Kerouac's *The Town and the City* (1950) and John Clellon Holmes's *Go* (1952), and William Carlos Williams had printed two of his letters in 1951 in *Paterson,* Book IV (another appears in Book V, 1958). His travels in Europe, Asia, and South America, his advocacy of Zen Buddhism, of hallucinatory drugs, and of homosexuality, and his involvement in the civil rights campaign, war resistance, and attacks on the C.I.A. have done as much to keep him in the public eye since the appearance of *Howl* as has his poetry. Of his later works the best known is "Kaddish," a long poem on his mother's illness and death.

Ginsberg defines his poetry as "Beat–Hip–Gnostic–Imagist." After some early experimentation with rhymed, metrical verse in the manner of Thomas Wyatt, he began under the influence of William Carlos Williams to seek a line modeled on speech and breathing patterns. Later familiarity with the incantatory verse of Indian mantras has strengthened his sense of the importance of parallelism and repetition. Influenced also by the Bible, by William Blake, and by Walt Whitman, Ginsberg strives for a prophetic poetry that embraces the sacred and profane.

Ginsberg's *Collected Poems 1947–1980* appeared in 1985. A later volume is *White Shroud: Poems 1980–1985,* 1986. Earlier titles are *Howl and Other Poems,* 1956; *Empty Mirror: Early Poems,* 1961; *Kaddish and Other Poems, 1958–1960,* 1961; *Reality Sandwiches,* 1963; *The Yage Letters* (with William S. Burroughs), 1963; *T.V. Baby Poems,* 1967; *Ankor-Wat,* 1968; *Planet News: 1961–1967,* 1968; *Indian Journals,* 1969; *Airplane Dreams,* 1969; *The Fall of America: Poems of These States, 1965–1971,* 1973; *Mind Breaths: Poems 1972–1977,* 1977; and *Plutonian Ode: Poems 1977–1980,* 1981. Barry Miles edited *Howl: Original Draft Facsimile,* with variants and author's notes, 1986. Gordon Ball edited *Journals: Early Fifties Early Sixties,* 1977. Barry Gifford edited *As Ever: The Collected Correspondence of Allen Ginsberg and Neal Cassady,* 1978. George Dowden compiled *A Bibliography of Works by Allen Ginsberg,* 1971. Studies are Jane Kramer, *Allen Ginsberg in America,* 1969; and T. F. Merrill, *Allen Ginsberg,* 1969; and Lewis Hyde, ed., *On the Poetry of Allen Ginsberg,* 1984.

Howl

For Carl Solomon

I

I saw the best minds of my generation destroyed by madness, starving hysterical naked,
dragging themselves through the negro streets at dawn looking for an angry fix,
angelheaded hipsters burning for the ancient heavenly connection to the starry dynamo
    in the machinery of night;
who poverty and tatters and hollow-eyed and high sat up smoking in the supernatural
    darkness of cold-water flats floating across the tops of cities contemplating jazz,
who bared their brains to Heaven under the El[1] and saw Mohammedan angels staggering
    on tenement roofs illuminated,
who passed through universities with radiant cool eyes hallucinating Arkansas and Blake-
    light tragedy among the scholars of war,
who were expelled from the academies for crazy & publishing obscene odes on the
    windows of the skull,
who cowered in unshaven rooms in underwear, burning their money in wastebaskets and
    listening to the Terror through the wall,
who got busted in their pubic beards returning through Laredo with a belt of marijuana
    for New York,
who ate fire in paint hotels or drank turpentine in Paradise Alley,[2] death, or purgatoried
    their torsos night after night
with dreams, and drugs, with waking nightmares, alcohol and cock and endless balls,
incomparable blind streets of shuddering cloud and lightning in the mind leaping toward
    poles of Canada & Paterson, illuminating all the motionless world of Time between,
Peyote solidities of halls, backyard green tree cemetery dawns, wine drunkenness over
    the rooftops, storefront boroughs of teahead joyride neon blinking traffic light, sun
    and moon and tree vibrations in the roaring winter dusks of Brooklyn, ashcan
    rantings and kind king light of mind,

1. The elevated railway.

2. A slum courtyard N.Y. Lower East Side, site of Kerouac's *Subterraneans,* 1958 [Ginsberg's note].

who chained themselves to subways for the endless ride from Battery to holy Bronx on benzedrine until the noise of wheels and children brought them down shuddering mouth-wracked and battered bleak of brain all drained of brilliance in the drear light of Zoo,[3]
who sank all night in submarine light of Bickford's[4] floated out and sat through the stale beer afternoon in desolate Fugazzi's,[5] listening to the crack of doom on the hydrogen jukebox,
who talked continuously seventy hours from park to pad to bar to Bellevue[6] to museum to the Brooklyn Bridge,
a lost battalion of platonic conversationalists jumping down the stoops off fire escapes off windowsills off Empire State out of the moon,
yacketayakking screaming vomiting whispering facts and memories and anecdotes and eyeball kicks and shocks of hospitals and jails and wars,
whole intellects disgorged in total recall for seven days and nights with brilliant eyes, meat for the Synagogue cast on the pavement,
who vanished into nowhere Zen[7] New Jersey leaving a trail of ambiguous picture postcards of Atlantic City Hall,
suffering Eastern sweats and Tangerian bone-grindings and migraines of China under junk-withdrawal in Newark's bleak furnished room,
who wandered around and around at midnight in the railroad yard wondering where to go, and went, leaving no broken hearts,
who lit cigarettes in boxcars boxcars boxcars racketing through snow toward lonesome farms in grandfather night,
who studied Plotinus Poe St. John of the Cross[8] telepathy and bop kaballa because the cosmos instinctively vibrated at their feet in Kansas,
who loned it through the streets of Idaho seeking visionary indian angels who were visionary indian angels,
who thought they were only mad when Baltimore gleamed in supernatural ecstasy,
who jumped in limousines with the Chinaman of Oklahoma on the impulse of winter midnight streetlight smalltown rain,
who lounged hungry and lonesome through Houston seeking jazz or sex or soup, and followed the brilliant Spaniard to converse about America and Eternity, a hopeless task, and so took ship to Africa,
who disappeared into the volcanoes of Mexico leaving behind nothing but the shadow of dungarees and the lava and ash of poetry scattered in fireplace Chicago,
who reappeared on the West Coast investigating the F.B.I. in beards and shorts with big pacifist eyes sexy in their dark skin passing out incomprehensible leaflets,
who burned cigarette holes in their arms protesting the narcotic tobacco haze of Capitalism,
who distributed Supercommunist pamphlets in Union Square[9] weeping and undressing while the sirens of Los Alamos wailed them down, and wailed down Wall, and the Staten Island ferry also wailed,
who broke down crying in white gymnasiums naked and trembling before the machinery of other skeletons,
who bit detectives in the neck and shrieked with delight in policecars for committing no crime but their own wild cooking pederasty and intoxication,
who howled on their knees in the subway and were dragged off the roof waving genitals and manuscripts,

3. The Bronx Zoo.
4. A cafeteria.
5. Greenwich Village bar.
6. Manhattan hospital; often associated with care of the insane.
7. Zen Buddhism was especially popular in the middle 1950's with members of the Beat Generation.
8. Plotinus (A.D. 205?–270), Roman philosopher; Edgar Allan Poe (1809–1849); St. John of the Cross (1542–1591), Spanish poet.
9. In New York City.

who let themselves be fucked in the ass by saintly motorcyclists, and screamed with joy,
who blew and were blown by those human seraphim, the sailors, caresses of Atlantic and Caribbean love,
who balled in the morning in the evenings in rosegardens and the grass of public parks and cemeteries scattering their semen freely to whomever come who may,
who hiccupped endlessly trying to giggle but wound up with a sob behind a partition in a Turkish Bath when the blonde & naked angel came to pierce them with a sword,
who lost their loveboys to the three old shrews of fate the one eyed shrew of the heterosexual dollar the one eyed shrew that winks out of the womb and the one eyed shrew that does nothing but sit on her ass and snip the intellectual golden threads of the craftsman's loom,
who copulated ecstatic and insatiate with a bottle of beer a sweetheart a package of cigarettes a candle and fell off the bed, and continued along the floor and down the hall and ended fainting on the wall with a vision of ultimate cunt and come eluding the last gyzym of consciousness,
who sweetened the snatches of a million girls trembling in the sunset, and were red eyed in the morning but prepared to sweeten the snatch of the sunrise, flashing buttocks under barns and naked in the lake,
who went out whoring through Colorado in myriad stolen night-cars, N.C.,[1] secret hero of these poems, cocksman and Adonis of Denver—joy to the memory of his innumerable lays of girls in empty lots & diner backyards, moviehouses' rickety rows, on mountaintops in caves or with gaunt waitresses in familiar roadside lonely petticoat upliftings & especially secret gas-station solipsisms of johns, & hometown alleys too,
who faded out in vast sordid movies, were shifted in dreams, woke on a sudden Manhattan, and picked themselves up out of basements hungover with heartless Tokay and horrors of Third Avenue iron dreams & stumbled to unemployment offices,
who walked all night with their shoes full of blood on the snowbank docks waiting for a door in the East River to open to a room full of steamheat and opium,
who created great suicidal dramas on the apartment cliff-banks of the Hudson under the wartime blue floodlight of the moon & their heads shall be crowned with laurel in oblivion,
who ate the lamb stew of the imagination or digested the crab at the muddy bottom of the rivers of Bowery,
who wept at the romance of the streets with their pushcarts full of onions and bad music,
who sat in boxes breathing in the darkness under the bridge, and rose up to build harpsichords in their lofts,
who coughed on the sixth floor of Harlem crowned with flame under the tubercular sky surrounded by orange crates of theology,
who scribbled all night rocking and rolling over lofty incantations which in the yellow morning were stanzas of gibberish,
who cooked rotten animals lung heart feet tail borsht & tortillas dreaming of the pure vegetable kingdom,
who plunged themselves under meat trucks looking for an egg,
who threw their watches off the roof to cast their ballot for Eternity outside of Time, & alarm clocks fell on their heads every day for the next decade,
who cut their wrists three times successively unsuccessfully, gave up and were forced to open antique stores where they thought they were growing old and cried,

1. Neal Cassady, the inspiration for characters in a number of Beat novels, including Kerouac's *On the Road* (1957).

who were burned alive in their innocent flannel suits on Madison Avenue amid blasts of leaden verse & the tanked-up clatter of the iron regiments of fashion & the nitroglycerine shrieks of the fairies of advertising & the mustard gas of sinister intelligent editors, or were run down by the drunken taxicabs of Absolute Reality,
who jumped off the Brooklyn Bridge this actually happened and walked away unknown and forgotten into the ghostly daze of Chinatown soup alleyways & firetrucks, not even one free beer,
who sang out of their windows in despair, fell out of the subway window, jumped in the filthy Passaic, leaped on negroes, cried all over the street, danced on broken wineglasses barefoot smashed phonograph records of nostalgic European 1930's German jazz finished the whiskey and threw up groaning into the bloody toilet, moans in their ears and the blast of colossal steamwhistles,
who barreled down the highways of the past journeying to each other's hotrod-Golgotha[2] jail-solitude watch or Birmingham jazz incarnation,
who drove crosscountry seventytwo hours to find out if I had a vision or you had a vision or he had a vision to find out Eternity,
who journeyed to Denver, who died in Denver, who came back to Denver & waited in vain, who watched over Denver & brooded & loned in Denver and finally went away to find out the Time, & now Denver is lonesome for her heroes,
who fell on their knees in hopeless cathedrals praying for each other's salvation and light and breasts, until the soul illuminated its hair for a second,
who crashed through their minds in jail waiting for impossible criminals with golden heads and the charm of reality in their hearts who sang sweet blues to Alcatraz,
who retired to Mexico to cultivate a habit, or Rocky Mount to tender Buddha or Tangiers to boys or Southern Pacific to the black locomotive or Harvard to Narcissus to Woodlawn[3] to the daisychain or grave,
who demanded sanity trials accusing the radio of hypnotism & were left with their insanity & their hands & a hung jury,
who threw potato salad at CCNY lecturers on Dadaism and subsequently presented themselves on the granite steps of the madhouse with shaven heads and harlequin speech of suicide, demanding instantaneous lobotomy,
and who were given instead the concrete void of insulin metrasol electricity hydrotherapy psychotherapy occupational therapy pingpong & amnesia,
who in humorless protest overturned only one symbolic pingpong table, resting briefly in catatonia,
returning years later truly bald except for a wig of blood, and tears and fingers, to the visible madman doom of the wards of the madtowns of the East,
Pilgrim State's Rockland's and Greystone's[4] foetid halls, bickering with the echoes of the soul, rocking and rolling in the midnight solitude-bench dolmen-realms of love, dream of life a nightmare, bodies turned to stone as heavy as the moon,
with mother finally ******, and the last fantastic book flung out of the tenement window, and the last door closed at 4 AM and the last telephone slammed at the wall in reply and the last furnished room emptied down to the last piece of mental furniture, a yellow paper rose twisted on a wire hanger in the closet, and even that imaginary, nothing but a hopeful little bit of hallucination—
ah, Carl, while you are not safe I am not safe, and now you're really in the total animal soup of time—
and who therefore ran through the icy streets obsessed with a sudden flash of the alchemy of the use of the ellipse the catalog the meter & the vibrating plane,
who dreamt and made incarnate gaps in Time & Space through images juxtaposed, and trapped the archangel of the soul between 2 visual images and joined the elemental verbs and set the noun and dash of consciousness together jumping with sensation of Pater Omnipotens Aeterna Deus[5]

2. Scene of the crucifixion of Jesus.
3. Cemetery in the Bronx.
4. Mental hospitals in New York and New Jersey.
5. "Father omnipotent, eternal God." From a letter of the French painter Paul Cézanne (1839–1906) in which he commented on the nature of art.

to recreate the syntax and measure of poor human prose and stand before you speechless and intelligent and shaking with shame, rejected yet confessing out the soul to conform to the rhythm of thought in his naked and endless head,

the madman bum and angel beat in Time, unknown, yet putting down here what might be left to say in time come after death,

and rose reincarnate in the ghostly clothes of jazz in the goldhorn shadow of the band and blew the suffering of America's naked mind for love into an eli eli lamma lamma sabacthani[6] saxophone cry that shivered the cities down to the last radio

with the absolute heart of the poem of life butchered out of their own bodies good to eat a thousand years.

II

What sphinx of cement and aluminum bashed open their skulls and ate up their brains and imagination?

Moloch![7] Solitude! Filth! Ugliness! Ashcans and unobtainable dollars! Children screaming under the stairways! Boys sobbing in armies! Old men weeping in the parks!

Moloch! Moloch! Nightmare of Moloch! Moloch the loveless! Mental Moloch! Moloch the heavy judger of men!

Moloch the incomprehensible prison! Moloch the crossbone soulless jailhouse and Congress of sorrows! Moloch whose buildings are judgement! Moloch the vast stone of war! Moloch the stunned governments!

Moloch whose mind is pure machinery! Moloch whose blood is running money! Moloch whose fingers are ten armies! Moloch whose breast is a cannibal dynamo! Moloch whose ear is a smoking tomb!

Moloch whose eyes are a thousand blind windows! Moloch whose skyscrapers stand in the long streets like endless Jehovahs! Moloch whose factories dream and croak in the fog! Moloch whose smokestacks and antennae crown the cities!

Moloch whose love is endless oil and stone! Moloch whose soul is electricity and banks! Moloch whose poverty is the specter of genius! Moloch whose fate is a cloud of sexless hydrogen! Moloch whose name is the Mind!

Moloch in whom I sit lonely! Moloch in whom I dream Angels! Crazy in Moloch! Cocksucker in Moloch! Lacklove and manless in Moloch!

Moloch who entered my soul early! Moloch in whom I am a consciousness without a body! Moloch who frightened me out of my natural ecstasy! Moloch whom I abandon! Wake up in Moloch! Light streaming out of the sky!

Moloch! Moloch! Robot apartments! invisible suburbs! skeleton treasuries! blind capitals! demonic industries! spectral nations! invincible madhouses! granite cocks! monstrous bombs!

They broke their backs lifting Moloch to Heaven! Pavements, trees, radios, tons! lifting the city to Heaven which exists and is everywhere about us!

Visions! omens! hallucinations! miracles! ecstasies! gone down the American river!

Dreams! adorations! illuminations! religions! the whole boatload of sensitive bullshit!

Breakthroughs! over the river! flips and crucifixions! gone down the flood! High! Epiphanies! Despairs! Ten years' animal screams and suicides! Minds! New loves! Mad generation! down on the rocks of Time!

Real holy laughter in the river! They saw it all! the wild eyes! the holy yells! They bade farewell! They jumped off the roof! to solitude! waving! carrying flowers! Down to the river! into the street!

6. "My God, my God, why hast thou forsaken me?"—Christ's words at the ninth hour on the Cross (Matthew xxvii: 46 and Mark xv: 34).

7. In the Bible and in Milton's *Paradise Lost* an ancient god worshiped with the sacrifice of children.

III

Carl Solomon! I'm with you in Rockland[8]
where you're madder than I am
I'm with you in Rockland
where you must feel very strange
I'm with you in Rockland
where you imitate the shade of my mother
I'm with you in Rockland
where you've murdered your twelve secretaries
I'm with you in Rockland
where you laugh at this invisible humor
I'm with you in Rockland
where we are great writers on the same dreadful typewriter
I'm with you in Rockland
where your condition has become serious and is reported on the radio
I'm with you in Rockland
where the faculties of the skull no longer admit the worms of the senses
I'm with you in Rockland
where you drink the tea of the breasts of the spinsters of Utica
I'm with you in Rockland
where you pun on the bodies of your nurses the harpies of the Bronx
I'm with you in Rockland
where you scream in a straightjacket that you're losing the game of the actual pingpong of the abyss
I'm with you in Rockland
where you bang on the catatonic piano the soul is innocent and immortal it should never die ungodly in an armed madhouse
I'm with you in Rockland
where fifty more shocks will never return your soul to its body again from its pilgrimage to a cross in the void
I'm with you in Rockland
where you accuse your doctors of insanity and plot the Hebrew socialist revolution against the fascist national Golgotha
I'm with you in Rockland
where you will split the heavens of Long Island and resurrect your living human Jesus from the superhuman tomb
I'm with you in Rockland
where there are twentyfive-thousand mad comrades all together singing the final stanzas of the Internationale[9]
I'm with you in Rockland
where we hug and kiss the United States under our bedsheets the United States that coughs all night and won't let us sleep
I'm with you in Rockland
where we wake up electrified out of the coma by our own souls' airplanes roaring over the roof they've come to drop angelic bombs the hospital illuminates itself imaginary walls collapse O skinny legions run outside O starry-spangled shock of mercy the eternal war is here O victory forget your underwear we're free
I'm with you in Rockland
in my dreams you walk dripping from a sea-journey on the highway across America in tears to the door of my cottage in the Western night

SAN FRANCISCO, 1955–1956 1956

8. New York psychiatric hospital. Ginsberg had met Solomon (born 1928) in 1949 as a fellow patient at Columbia's Psychiatric Institute.
9. Communist anthem.

A Supermarket in California

What thoughts I have of you tonight, Walt Whitman, for I walked down the sidestreets under the trees with a headache self-conscious looking at the full moon.

In my hungry fatigue, and shopping for images, I went into the neon fruit supermarket, dreaming of your enumerations!

What peaches and what penumbras! Whole families shopping at night! Aisles full of husbands! Wives in the avocados, babies in the tomatoes!—and you, García Lorca,[1] what were you doing down by the watermelons?

I saw you, Walt Whitman, childless, lonely old grubber, poking among the meats in the refrigerator and eyeing the grocery boys.

I heard you asking questions of each: Who killed the pork chops? What price bananas? Are you my Angel?

I wandered in and out of the brilliant stacks of cans following you, and followed in my imagination by the store detective.

We strode down the open corridors together in our solitary fancy tasting artichokes, possessing every frozen delicacy, and never passing the cashier.

Where are we going, Walt Whitman? The doors close in an hour. Which way does your beard point tonight?

(I touch your book and dream of our odyssey in the supermarket and feel absurd.)

Will we walk all night through solitary streets? The trees add shade to shade, lights out in the houses, we'll both be lonely.

Will we stroll dreaming of the lost America of love past blue automobiles in driveways, home to our silent cottage?

Ah, dear father, graybeard, lonely old courage-teacher, what America did you have when Charon[2] quit poling his ferry and you got out on a smoking bank and stood watching the boat disappear on the black waters of Lethe?[3]

BERKELEY, 1955 1956

Sunflower Sutra

I walked on the banks of the tincan banana dock and sat down under the huge shade of a Southern Pacific locomotive to look at the sunset over the box house hills and cry.

Jack Kerouac sat beside me on a busted rusty iron pole, companion, we thought the same thoughts of the soul, bleak and blue and sad-eyed, surrounded by the gnarled steel roots of trees of machinery.

The oily water on the river mirrored the red sky, sun sank on top of final Frisco peaks, no fish in that stream, no hermit in those mounts, just ourselves rheumy-eyed and hung-over like old bums on the riverbank, tired and wily.

Look at the Sunflower, he said, there was a dead gray shadow against the sky, big as a man, sitting dry on top of a pile of ancient sawdust—

—I rushed up enchanted—it was my first sunflower, memories of Blake—my visions—Harlem

and Hells of the Eastern rivers, bridges clanking Joes Greasy Sandwiches, dead baby carriages, black treadless tires forgotten and unretreaded, the poem of the riverbank, condoms & pots, steel knives, nothing stainless, only the dank muck and the razor-sharp artifacts passing into the past—

1. Federico García Lorca (1899–1936), Spanish poet, author of "Ode to Walt Whitman."
2. In Greek mythology, the ferryman who transported dead souls across the river Styx in Hades.
3. The river of forgetfulness in Hades.

and the gray Sunflower poised against the sunset, crackly bleak and dusty with the smut and smog and smoke of olden locomotives in its eye—
corolla of bleary spikes pushed down and broken like a battered crown, seeds fallen out of its face, soon-to-be-toothless mouth of sunny air, sunrays obliterated on its hairy head like a dried wire spiderweb,
leaves stuck out like arms out of the stem, gestures from the sawdust root, broke pieces of plaster fallen out of the black twigs, a dead fly in its ear,
Unholy battered old thing you were, my sunflower O my soul, I loved you then!
The grime was no man's grime but death and human locomotives,
all that dress of dust, that veil of darkened railroad skin, that smog of cheek, that eyelid of black mis'ry, that sooty hand or phallus or protuberance of artificial worse-than-dirt—industrial—modern—all that civilization spotting your crazy golden crown—
and those blear thoughts of death and dusty loveless eyes and ends and withered roots below, in the home-pile of sand and sawdust, rubber dollar bills, skin of machinery, the guts and innards of the weeping coughing car, the empty lonely tincans with their rusty tongues alack, what more could I name, the smoked ashes of some cock cigar, the cunts of wheelbarrows and the milky breasts of cars, wornout asses out of chairs & sphincters of dynamos—all these
entangled in your mummied roots—and you there standing before me in the sunset, all your glory in your form!
A perfect beauty of a sunflower! a perfect excellent lovely sunflower existence! a sweet natural eye to the new hip moon, woke up alive and excited grasping in the sunset shadow sunrise golden monthly breeze!
How many flies buzzed round you innocent of your grime, while you cursed the heavens of the railroad and your flower soul?
Poor dead flower? when did you forget you were a flower? when did you look at your skin and decide you were an impotent dirty old locomotive? the ghost of a locomotive? the specter and shade of a once powerful mad American locomotive?
You were never no locomotive, Sunflower, you were a sunflower!
And you Locomotive, you are a locomotive, forget me not!
So I grabbed up the skeleton thick sunflower and stuck it at my side like a scepter,
and deliver my sermon to my soul, and Jack's soul too, and anyone who'll listen,
—We're not our skin of grime, we're not our dread bleak dusty imageless locomotive, we're all golden sunflowers inside, blessed by our own seed & hairy naked accomplishment-bodies growing into mad black formal sunflowers in the sunset, spied on by our eyes under the shadow of the mad locomotive riverbank sunset Frisco hilly tincan evening sitdown vision.

BERKELEY, 1955 — 1956

America

America I've given you all and now I'm nothing.
America two dollars and twentyseven cents January 17, 1956.
I can't stand my own mind.
America when will we end the human war?
Go fuck yourself with your atom bomb.
I don't feel good don't bother me.
I won't write my poem till I'm in my right mind.
America when will you be angelic?
When will you take off your clothes?
When will you look at yourself through the grave?
When will you be worthy of your million Trotskyites?[4]

4. Followers of Leon Trotsky (1879–1940), Russian advocate of world-wide revolution by the proletariat.

America why are your libraries full of tears?
America when will you send your eggs to India?
I'm sick of your insane demands.
When can I go into the supermarket and buy what I need with my good looks?
America after all it is you and I who are perfect not the next world.
Your machinery is too much for me.
You made me want to be a saint.
There must be some other way to settle this argument.
Burroughs[5] is in Tangiers I don't think he'll come back it's sinister.
Are you being sinister or is this some form of practical joke?
I'm trying to come to the point.
I refuse to give up my obsession.
America stop pushing I know what I'm doing.
America the plum blossoms are falling.
I haven't read the newspapers for months, everyday somebody goes on trial for murder.
America I feel sentimental about the Wobblies.[6]
America I used to be a communist when I was a kid I'm not sorry.
I smoke marijuana every chance I get.
I sit in my house for days on end and stare at the roses in the closet.
When I go to Chinatown I get drunk and never get laid.
My mind is made up there's going to be trouble.
You should have seen me reading Marx.
My psychoanalyst thinks I'm perfectly right.
I won't say the Lord's Prayer.
I have mystical visions and cosmic vibrations.
America I still haven't told you what you did to Uncle Max after he came over from Russia.
I'm addressing you.
Are you going to let your emotional life be run by Time Magazine?
I'm obsessed by Time Magazine.
I read it every week.
Its cover stares at me every time I slink past the corner candystore.
I read it in the basement of the Berkeley Public Library.
It's always telling me about responsibility. Businessmen are serious. Movie producers are serious. Everybody's serious but me.
It occurs to me that I am America.
I am talking to myself again.

Asia is rising against me.
I haven't got a chinaman's chance.
I'd better consider my national resources.
My national resources consist of two joints of marijuana millions of genitals an unpublishable private literature that jetplanes 1400 miles an hour and twentyfive-thousand mental institutions.
I say nothing about my prisons nor the millions of underprivileged who live in my flowerpots under the light of five hundred suns.
I have abolished the whorehouses of France, Tangiers is the next to go.
My ambition is to be President despite the fact that I'm a Catholic.

America how can I write a holy litany in your silly mood?
I will continue like Henry Ford my strophes are as individual as his automobiles more so they're all different sexes.
America I will sell you strophes $2500 apiece $500 down on your old strophe

5. William S. Burroughs (1914–), American writer and elder statesman of the Beat Generation.

6. International Workers of the World, an early labor union.

America free Tom Mooney[7]
America save the Spanish Loyalists[8]
America Sacco & Vanzetti[9] must not die
America I am the Scottsboro boys.[1]
America when I was seven momma took me to Communist Cell meetings they sold us garbanzos a handful per ticket a ticket costs a nickel and the speeches were free everybody was angelic and sentimental about the workers it was all so sincere you have no idea what a good thing the party was in 1835 Scott Nearing[2] was a grand old man a real mensch Mother Bloor[3] the Silk-strikers' Ewig-Weibliche[4] made me cry I once saw the Yiddish orator Israel Amter[5] plain. Everybody must have been a spy.
America you don't really want to go to war.
America it's them bad Russians.
Them Russians them Russians and them Chinamen. And them Russians.
The Russia wants to eat us alive. The Russia's power mad. She wants to take our cars from out our garages.
Her wants to grab Chicago. Her needs a Red *Reader's Digest.* Her wants our auto plants in Siberia. Him big bureaucracy running our fillingstations.
That no good. Ugh. Him make Indians learn read. Him need big black niggers. Hah. Her make us all work sixteen hours a day. Help.
America this is quite serious.
America this is the impression I get from looking in the television set.
America is this correct?
I'd better get right down to the job.
It's true I don't want to join the Army or turn lathes in precision parts factories, I'm nearsighted and psychopathic anyway.
America I'm putting my queer shoulder to the wheel.

BERKELEY, JANUARY 17, 1956 — 1956

Fourth Floor, Dawn, Up All Night Writing Letters

Pigeons shake their wings on the copper church roof
out my window across the street, a bird perched on the cross
surveys the city's blue-gray clouds. Larry Rivers
'll come at 10 A.M. and take my picture. I'm taking
your picture, pigeons. I'm writing you down, Dawn.
I'm immortalizing your exhaust, Avenue A bus.
O Thought, now you'll have to think the same thing forever!

NEW YORK, JUNE 7, 1980, 6:48 A.M. — 1982

7. (1882–1942), labor leader imprisoned for alleged bomb-throwing at 1919 rally in San Francisco; later pardoned by Governor Earl Warren.
8. Supporters of the republican government, defeated in the Spanish Civil War (1936–1939).
9. Nicola Sacco (1891–1927) and Bartolomeo Vanzetti (1888–1927), immigrant anarchists convicted and executed for robbery and murder. The case was a cause célèbre among intellectuals of the 1920's and 1930's.
1. Nine young black men accused of the rape of two white women in 1931 in Alabama. All were found guilty, but the national attention drawn to the case, in part when the U.S. Supreme Court twice reversed decisions concerning it, eventually led to the freedom of all. The case became a landmark in the history of civil rights.
2. (1883–1983), sociology professor who opposed World War I. He became an expert on gardening and self-sufficiency and a role model for alternative life styles in the 1960's.
3. Ella Reeve Bloor (1862–1951), union organizer and member of the Communist party.
4. Eternally female figure (German).
5. (1881–1954), a leader of the American Communist party who ran for governor of New York in the 1930's.

American Literature in the 1960's and After

The year 1965 marked the hundredth anniversary of the end of the American Civil War, the twentieth anniversary of the end of World War II. It was also the middle of a decade of important changes in American life. Lyndon Johnson was in his second year as president. U.S. involvement in Vietnam was at its approximate midpoint: four years earlier, the first U.S. support troops had arrived; in 1965, massive U.S. buildups in the South and bombing of the North began; later, in 1968, with the Tet offensive casting serious doubt on U.S. military effectiveness, and amidst growing resistance to the war signaled by burning draft cards and the Peace March on the Pentagon in October, 1967, Johnson decided not to run again for president. Although it was to take five years to arrive at a treaty, in 1968 serious peace talks began in Paris. During the Johnson administration, too, the civil rights movement reached its peak, as Martin Luther King, Jr., brought his dream and 200,000 followers to Washington in the 1963 Peace March, and Congress and President Johnson responded with the Civil Rights Act of 1964. That same year the president called for a war on poverty and outlined a program of economic and social legislation leading to a Great Society. Among the spectacular national traumas of those years were the assassinations—of John F. Kennedy, which elevated Johnson to the presidency; of Martin Luther King and Robert F. Kennedy, in Johnson's last year in office—and the riots that burned black ghettos in Detroit, Los Angeles, and Cleveland in 1967 and 1968.

Less sudden than some of the events above, but perhaps also spectacular in the long view of history, were the growth of the suburbs and the changing nature of the American city. In the years after 1945 the returning soldier's dream of a house and a car was materially realized in the suburbanization of America, as the nation lost its sharp distinctions between town and country, city folk and farmers. The United States became a country with a new identity, massively suburban insofar as its people were financially stable. Shopping centers replaced downtown. Poverty became more and more identified with cities and rural areas, traditional centers of economic vitality before the Great Depression and World War II. Because the move to the suburbs was mostly white, cities became increasingly black, and, as time wore on, increasingly Hispanic and oriental, as large numbers of newer immigrants arrived from countries other than those Western European nations that supplied the bulk of American immigration prior to 1945.

By the mid-1960's, the nation had developed an identity crisis, with the wrenching Vietnam War at its center, squares and hippies at its edges. Flower children placed blossoms in the muzzles of rifles. "Make love, not war" became a popular slogan. At the end of the decade, in 1970, four student anti-war protesters were shot and killed by National Guard soldiers at Kent State University in Ohio. The problem of the cities was apparent, but largely ignored except when the ghettos erupted in riot. In 1963, Bob Dylan wrote an anthem for the period: "The Times They Are A-Changin'."

In literature, too, in the mid-1960's the times were changing. The years 1961 to 1965 saw the passing, in succession, of Ernest Hemingway, William Faulkner, E. E. Cummings, Robert Frost, William Carlos Williams, and T. S. Eliot—writers whose careers, mostly shaped prior to 1945, had shadowed or inspired the careers of younger authors in the period immediately after, helping to define the tradition accepted by critics and taught in colleges and universities. From the 1960's onward, novelists and short story writers who had established reputations in the early post-war years reflected changing conditions with changing emphases in content or technique. Younger writers of fiction embraced the anti-novel and ideas of the absurd, as authors wrote more variously of regions of the country other than the South and Northeast. In 1963, J. D. Salinger, one of the brightest of the literary lights to emerge in fiction after 1945, published his last book and fell silent for the next quarter century as his kind of fiction began to look increasingly old-fashioned. Coincidentally, the same year saw the publication of Thomas Pynchon's *V.*, marking the emergence of a still younger writer, tremendously influential with his version of the newer fiction. The rising consciousness of blacks, women, and other groups produced an increasingly powerful literature of ethnic and cultural diversity. The two streams of poetry merged, as academic poets adopted the methods of the anti-academics and the universities welcomed poets and poems excluded until the 1960's. Confessional poetry and open forms became the watchwords of the day. Drama changed its focus, too, as Broadway weakened in power and influence and serious playwrights moved off-Broadway and into regional theaters.

FICTION: THE CONTINUATION OF THE REALISTIC TRADITION

With the appearance of his second novel, *Rabbit, Run* (1960), John Updike emerged as a paradigmatic realistic writer for his generation. Harry Angstrom, nicknamed Rabbit, reflects the divided nature of the common man of his time, attracted to and running from elements that typify life for many. In subsequent years, Rabbit has evolved into the hero of a trilogy as, confused and beaten in the 1960's by circumstance and his own stupidities, he flirts with the black counterculture in *Rabbit Redux* (1970), and then, in the next decade, largely through luck, becomes a wealthy dealer in foreign cars in *Rabbit Is Rich* (1981). In other novels and numerous short stories, Updike explores other facets of contemporary life, his setting frequently the suburbs outside Boston; in contrast, he has also chronicled America's disappearing past in books derived from his small-town boyhood in Pennsylvania.

In writing so frequently of suburbanites, Updike reflected the social shifts of the times. The older writer John Cheever, like Updike a long-time *New Yorker* contributor, can be seen also as heralding the trends when it is observed that the story with which he made his reputation, "The Enormous Radio," from the late 1940's, is set in Manhattan's Sutton Place, but the two perhaps most read since, both later stories —"The Country Husband" and "The Swimmer"—are set in wealthy suburbs outside New York. Indeed, the city has been in fiction in the 1960's and after more often than not a place dangerous to outsiders and insiders alike, tense with racial, class, and cultural conflicts. A tone established earlier in some Beat novels became more pervasive, more urgent, and more violent in the world of homosexuality and drugs of John Rechy's *City of Night* (1963) and Hubert Selby, Jr.,'s *Last Exit to Brooklyn* (1964).

Prominent among other writers of the Northeast who have emerged in recent decades are Joyce Carol Oates, John Gardner, Gail Godwin, E. L. Doctorow, Toni Morrison, John Irving, William Kennedy, and Ann Beattie. In *them* (1969), tracing a Detroit family from the Depression to the riots of 1967, Oates wrote one of the most celebrated city novels of its time. Much more prolific than most other significant writers of the period, she is especially skilled in her short stories and has ranged into Gothic fantasies in works like *Bellefleur* (1980). John Gardner has also ranged widely, from *Grendel* (1971), telling the Beowulf story from the perspective of the monster, through upstate New York chronicles like *The Sunlight Dialogues* (1972) and *Nickel Mountain* (1973). Writing to assert the high seriousness of the writer's art, Gardner precipitated a critical storm in his attack on trends in contemporary American novels in *On Moral Fiction* (1978). Gail Godwin, raised in the South but long resident in upstate New York, has used both southern and northern locales in psychologically oriented fiction ranging from a highly praised first novel, *The Perfectionists* (1970), through a recent study of growing up, *The Finishing School* (1985). E. L. Doctorow won fame with *Ragtime* (1975), mixing historical and invented characters in a pastiche of the early twentieth century. More recently, he has mimicked his own past in a story of childhood in an earlier New York, *World's Fair* (1985). Toni Morrison's third novel, *Song of Solomon* (1977), established her as a force in contemporary fiction, celebrated also as a woman and a black in a time of increasing public awareness of the contributions of both groups. John Irving, after three earlier novels, attained celebrity with *The World According to Garp* (1978) and sustained his popularity in *The Hotel New Hampshire* (1981) and *The Cider House Rules* (1985). Irving's world is manic, tinged with absurdity and black comedy, but it is also grounded in observed reality as he has attempted to become the Dickens of our time—popular, idiosyncratic, and significant. William Kennedy's Albany trilogy—*Legs* (1975), *Billy Phelan's Greatest Game* (1978), and *Ironweed* (1983)—portrays a city plagued by mobsters and politicians in the years of prohibition and the Depression. Ann Beattie's characters live mostly in New England or the Middle Atlantic states, where, alienated from their surroundings, bewildered by the pace of life around them, they pursue or escape from lost loves. The stories collected in *Distortions* (1976) and subsequent volumes have been especially admired.

Within recent decades, the strong contribution of the South has continued in the work of writers newly emerging. Walker Percy has followed his first novel, *The Moviegoer* (1961), set in New Orleans, with others focused on existential questions of southern identity as his protagonists attempt to cure their severe emotional detachments in order to live effectively in the world in which they find themselves. Reynolds Price, born in North Carolina and a professor at Duke, has written most often of the Upper South, North Carolina and Virginia, from his first novel, *A Long and Happy Life* (1962) through *Kate Vaiden* (1986). George Garrett, poet as well as novelist and short story writer, has written sometimes of his native Florida, as in the title story of his collection *King of the Mountain* (1958) and *The Finished Man* (1959), a novel; highest praise, however, has been reserved for his historical novels of Elizabethan England, *Death of the Fox* (1971) and *The Succession* (1983). Alice Walker, daughter of a Georgia sharecropper, educated at Sarah Lawrence, has brought a powerful new voice, feminine and black, to the poetry and fiction of her region. After *The Color Purple* (1982), a strong narrative of the enduring love of two sisters, was transformed into a major Steven Spielberg film, Alice Walker became a household name. Anne Tyler, writing most often of North Carolina and Maryland, honed her skills through eight earlier novels before the highly praised *Dinner at the Homesick Restaurant* (1982). Bobbie Ann Mason, from rural Kentucky, demonstrated uncanny control in her first book of fiction, *Shiloh and Other Stories* (1982), and followed that with a moving novel, *In Country* (1985), that considered the effects of the Vietnam War on on survivors and relatives. Jayne Anne Phillips writes memorably of several generations in rural West Virginia in her novel *Machine Dreams* (1984), culminating with the effect of the Vietnam War on their lives. In her earlier collection of stories, *Black Tickets* (1979), she ranges from West Virginia to the Southwest, and from the homely and ordinary to shocking stories of drug abuse, promiscuous sex, and murder.

Realistic and naturalistic fiction outside of the Northeast and the South since the 1960's, as in earlier periods, has been scattered. Wright Morris has continued his fine Nebraska work, while in the Pacific Northwest, after a distinguished beginning, Ken Kesey has fallen silent. Among more recent writers, Joan Didion received high praise for her depiction of Southern California life in *Play It As It Lays* (1970); Tim O'Brien, in *Northern Lights* (1974), set in northern Minnesota, portrayed admirably the difficulties met at home by a returning Vietnam War veteran; Robert Pirsig, in *Zen and the Art of Motorcycle Maintenance* (1974), grafted autobiographical and philosophical exploration onto a motorcycle trip of a father and son west from Minnesota; Larry Woiwode followed a North Dakota family through several generations in *Beyond the Bedroom Wall* (1975); Larry McMurtry has depicted Texas in a number of strong novels, culminating in the massive *Lonesome Dove* (1985), the story of an epic cattle drive from Texas to Montana; Raymond Carver, after years of struggle, has emerged as one of the most celebrated short story writers of our time, with fiction set mostly on the West Coast in *Will You Please Be Quiet, Please?* (1976), *What We Talk About When We Talk About Love* (1981), and *Cathedral* (1983); Elizabeth Tallent's home ground is New Mexico, as seen in the stories collected in *In Constant Flight* (1983) and her novel *Museum Pieces* (1985).

Although World War II, like World War I, produced distinguished fiction in the years immediately following, the record of fiction as a result of the Vietnam War is less easy to assess. The two most acclaimed novels to date—Robert Stone's *Dog Soldiers* (1977) and Tim O'Brien's *Going After Cacciato* (1978)—both treat the war in part through indirection. In *Dog Soldiers,* the central incident is a drug deal involving non-combatants. In *Cacciato,* although there are events a reader is meant to accept as real, the bulk of the narrative describes an imaginary journey out of Vietnam to Paris. O'Brien's *Northern Lights* (1974) and Bobbie Ann Mason's *In Country* (1985) are prominent among novels that treat the war by examining its effect on returning soldiers or their friends and relatives; in many other works, like Barry Hannah's *The Tennis Handsome* (1983), the Vietnam War, only briefly examined, serves as backdrop for the actions of veterans in their later lives. Jayne Anne Phillips's *Machine Dreams* (1984), touching on World War II, ends with the anguish of a family whose son is missing in action in Vietnam. Although the war was more fully reported than earlier wars, writers have stressed the great difficulty of arriving at final truths concerning it; this point becomes particularly striking in two of the most interesting books of non-fiction, O'Brien's *If I Die in a Combat Zone* (1973) and Michael Herr's *Dispatches* (1977).

In recent decades, American interest in ethnic and cultural diversity, prodded by human rights movements, has spawned several noteworthy trends in fiction.

Black writers have continued their increasingly active contribution to literature, as novelists emerging in the 1960's and after include John A. Williams, whose *The Man Who Cried I Am* (1967) tells the story of a dying author; William Melvin Kelly, who describes the decision of a black sharecropper to leave his farm in *A Different Drummer* (1962); and Paule Marshall, whose *The Chosen Place, the Timeless People* (1970), depicts an encounter between Caribbean natives and the forces of outside modernization. Two black women especially—Toni Morrison, author of *Song of Solomon* (1977) and other novels and short stories, and Alice Walker, author of *The Color Purple* (1972) and other fiction and poetry—have been among those writers celebrated by the women's movement as in recent years women generally have been more prominent in literature than in earlier periods. More a journalist than a novelist, Alex Haley, ghostwriter of *The Autobiography of Malcolm X* (1965), succeeded in capturing the imagination of the nation in his partly fictional account of his ancestors, traced as far as Africa, in *Roots* (1976).

Literature by American Jews who draw on their Jewish experience has continued strong, much of it in the ongoing work of older writers like Bellow, Singer, and Malamud. Philip Roth, a dominant presence in recent years, has ranged from essentially traditional realism in *Letting Go* (1962) through the ribald humor of *Portnoy's Complaint* (1969) to striking considerations of the profession of literature in *The Ghost Writer* (1979), *Zuckerman Unbound* (1981), and *The Counterlife* (1987). In Jewish literature, too, women have been strong, especially in the arresting short stories of Tillie Olsen, in *Tell Me a Riddle* (1962); Grace Paley, a painstaking writer whose first stories appeared in *The Little Disturbances of Man* (1956) and whose third collection, *Later the Same Day* (1986), was published almost thirty years later; and Cynthia Ozick, author of collections such as *Levitation: Five Fictions* (1982) and the novels *Trust* (1982) and *The Cannibal Galaxy* (1983).

Recent decades have also witnessed an increase in the literary activity of Native Americans, as writers have striven to recreate the legends of their tribes or to report contemporary experience. N. Scott Momaday mingled Kiowa myth and personal memories in *The Way to Rainy Mountain* (1969) and in the same year earned the Pulitzer Prize for *House Made of Dawn,* a novel of a man alienated from both ancestral and white society. In *Winter in the Blood* (1974), James Welch writes of a Blackfeet Indian, now a Montana cattle rancher; his *Fool's Crow* (1986) recreates the lives of nineteenth-century Blackfeet. In *Ceremony* (1977), Leslie Marmon Silko portrays the anguish of a veteran of World War II who sees an analogy between the U.S. treatment of the Japanese and of his own Pueblo people; her *Storyteller* (1981) presents a unique mixture of family stories, verse, and photographs.

Among Asian-Americans, Richard Kim deserves notice for three works of fiction focused on the trials of his native Korea, *The Martyred* (1964), *The Innocent* (1968), and *Lost Names* (1970). Maxine Hong Kingston, second-generation Chinese, blends family stories, legend, and fiction in *The Woman Warrior* (1976) and *China Men* (1980).

CHANGES IN THE TRADITION: INFLUENCES FROM ABROAD

For many writers from the 1960's onward, traditional approaches to literature have seemed less attractive than alternative visions and forms. Disillusioned by the failure to solve the world's problems in the aftermath of World War II, embittered by the Korean War and the Vietnam War, haunted by the possibility of nuclear annihilation, many writers have found realism and naturalism—even as expanded by such early twentieth-century writers as Lawrence, Joyce, Woolf, Faulkner, and Hemingway—inadequate to their ends. Some spoke of the death of the novel, others of anti-fiction (opposed to traditional form and content) or meta-fiction (transcending the traditional mimetic idea of fiction). For many, the result was a new emphasis on parody, undercutting structures or institutions no longer fully accepted as valid. For many others, the result was an emphasis on fiction as play, as the author created self-referential games only remotely connected to life as traditionally observed.

The new movements were assisted at home by the increasing popularity of the Beat writers, but received their primary impetus from abroad in the many European works of existential and absurd literature that became popular in the late 1950's and early 1960's, works by Albert Camus, Jean-Paul Sartre, Samuel Beckett, Jean Genêt, Eugène Ionesco, and others. With *Lolita* (Paris, 1955; New York 1958), the master illusionist Vladimir Nabokov became one of the most influential novelists of his time, and after the publication in English of *Fictions* by the Argentinian Jorge Luis Borges in 1962, that writer's fables became models for many others. The American publication of Henry Miller's *Tropic of Cancer* (Paris, 1934; New York, 1961) and *Tropic of Capricorn* (Paris, 1939; New York, 1962) and William S. Burroughs's *Naked Lunch* (Paris, 1959; New York, 1962) was part of a general movement toward new freedom in sexual content. In the same period, the French *nouveau roman,* or new novel, excited many younger writers with its fresh approach to narratology, as seen especially in works like Alain Robbe-Grillet's *Jealousy* (translated 1959) and *The Erasers* (translated 1964). One sign of the times was the huge success of *The Evergreen Review;* founded in the late 1950's and filled with the works of these writers, that magazine soon attained a widespread popularity far outdistancing that of the earlier little magazines it in some ways resembled.

PARODY AND SATIRE

Since Twain, and even earlier in the humor of the old Southwest, Americans have found much to laugh at in themselves, much to satirize in their institutions. From the 1940's onward, Peter De Vries maintained that tradition in a series of witty, urbane novels: in *The Tents of Wickedness* (1959) he parodied Faulkner, Hemingway, and Fitzgerald; in *Into Your Tent I'll Creep* (1971) he satirized women's liberation; in *I Hear America Swinging* (1976) his target was the new sexual freedom; and so on through many other works. De Vries's humor is less manic, however, and his satire less biting than the work of many of the writers who together have made parodic and satiric visions of the world bulk large in the literature of the United States in recent decades.

For many readers, Kurt Vonnegut has been the chief example. At first primarily of interest to readers of science fiction, he began to attract a more general audience with his unique blend of science fiction, fantasy, and black humor in *Cat's Cradle* (1963) and *God Bless You, Mr. Rosewater* (1965). His colloquial style and breezy pessimism have continued to earn wide readership and the flattery of imitation by other writers from his best work, *Slaughterhouse-Five* (1966), through *Breakfast of Champions* (1973), to the more recent *Galapagos* (1986).

Others have profited as well from a general explosion of interest in science fiction and fantasy in recent decades. Ursula K. Le Guin, for example, is much more serious in her tone than Vonnegut, but equally parodic in the way her fictions reflect off other fictions and make either explicit or implicit their lessons for humanity. Writing frequently for children or adolescents in works like her Earthsea Trilogy (1968–1972) or *The Beginning Place* (1980), she has also attempted to examine serious philosophical issues in space novels like *The Dispossessed* (1974).

For some writers of parody and satire, the world examined is much like that of middle-class America, but seen aslant through the cockeyed perceptions of an improbable narrator or twisted through an exaggerated application of some standard genre, such as a detective story, spy story, or western. Many are variations on the old picaresque novel, following an anti-hero through a series of adventures that display the confusions and contradictions of society. Among the works of Thomas Berger, for example, are a parodic western, *Little Big Man* (1964); an examination of a future society dominated by women, *Regiment of Women* (1973); and the detective novel *Who Is Teddy Villanova?* (1977). Stanley Elkin's *Boswell* (1964) tells of a little man who tries to attach himself to the famous; his *The Dick Gibson Show* (1971) follows the adventures of a radio announcer; his *The Franchiser* (1976) focuses on chain motels and restaurants.

For others, the vision is heavily that of the counterculture that became prominent in the 1960's, with alienation a dominant tone, and sometimes an overlay of idealism in the promise of a different world. Protest may be explicit, but more often it is implicit in the general zaniness of characters who are retreating from families or birthrights, pursuing a "natural" life, seeking spiritual regeneration, heightening their experience through sex or drugs. A frequent result is a mixture of realism and surrealism, shading actuality into dreams and nightmares, merging the present with the past. For some, the picture is not pretty. James Purdy has won a small, passionate following for his bitter and savage comedies portraying subjects like homosexuality and rape. With *Malcolm* (1959), later dramatized by Edward Albee, he obtained general notice, and he has continued his obsessions in later works like *Cabot Wright Begins* (1964). Ishmael Reed has voiced black protest in *Mumbo Jumbo* (1972) and *Flight to Canada* (1976) and other works. Other writers, however, have been generally less angry than Purdy and Reed. Richard Brautigan has impressed many readers with his whimsical fictions celebrating the pastoral values of the counterculture, including *Trout Fishing in America* (1967) and *Watermelon Sugar* (1968). Tom Robbins has been praised for *Even Cowgirls Get the Blues* (1976), with its feminine picaro, and *Still Life with Woodpecker* (1980). In *The Bushwhacked Piano* (1971) and other novels, Thomas McGuane satirizes cowboys, con men, and the world of business in Michigan, Montana, Florida, or on the road between. Barry Hannah's world, rooted in the South, is similarly wide-ranging. Among his several highly praised books, Hannah's *The Tennis Handsome* (1983) is perhaps most evenly successful in displaying his comic genius; short, like many contemporary novels, it nevertheless follows a complex plot over half a century, from Vicksburg and New Orleans to Vietnam, New York, Boston, and Canada. Among writers most recently appearing, Jay McInerney has been especially impressive with the comic vision of his first two novels. In *Bright Lights, Big City* (1984), he follows the adventures of a writer failing at his first job, at a magazine much like *The New Yorker.* In *Ransom* (1985), he depicts an American's attempt to escape from the values of home into the world of martial arts, Zen, and drugs in Japan. In *Less Than Zero* (1985), Bret Easton Ellis communicates a seething anger and despair through a vision of uncontrolled wealth, drugs, and sex among the current lost generation of rootless adolescents in Los Angeles. In *The Broom of the System* (1987), David Foster Wallace writes with an imaginative and satiric exuberance reminiscent of Pynchon as he follows Amherst undergraduates of the 1980's into the future of a crazily envisioned Cleveland of 1990.

Don DeLillo stands somewhat apart from these writers, allied to them by his satiric undertone but intent on pursuing the philosophic or metaphoric implications of his work a bit further than most. His much-admired *Ratner's Star* (1976) has been compared to Pynchon's work in its parade of erudition as it chronicles the adventures of a teenage mathematical genius on another planet. *The Names* (1982), however, is more intriguing, as it unfolds the story of a corporate risk analyst in Greece, an unwitting dupe of the CIA, who discovers a cult that murders arbitrarily, matching the names of its victims to the names of the places where they are killed. In *White Noise* (1985), perhaps his most successful novel to date, DeLillo brings his speculations closer to home, focusing on a professor of Hitler studies at an American college, whose life is disrupted by the threat of large-scale toxic contamination.

SELF-REFLEXIVE AND EXPERIMENTAL FICTIONS

Some of the most impressive writers of recent decades have chosen to express themselves in ways that subvert the mimetic assumptions of traditional realistic or naturalistic fiction, or even of earlier romantic writers like Hawthorne and Melville. Stressing the idea that fiction is an art or a game, they have emphasized its illusionary and playful nature by creating stories supported by a self-sustaining internal logic, but not necessarily by reference to the external world of facts and probabilities. For some, the manner of telling is more important than the tale told or the characters involved, so that the style becomes the story. Among their earlier models are ancient fables and myths, but more important forebears are such twentieth-century destroyers of realistic façades as Kafka and Pirandello in literature, and, in other arts, cubists, Dadaists, and expressionists. Some have been inspired by the linguistic pyrotechnics of James Joyce and others by the montage techniques of the movies. Their immediate impetus has come variously from their personal lives; the general sense of fragmentation of experience that peaked in the 1960's; the European literature of existentialism, the antinovel, and the *nouveau roman;* and the twin examples of Vladimir Nabokov and Jorge Luis Borges.

William Gaddis and John Hawkes began their work before most of the rest. Gaddis's massive *The Recognitions* (1955) stood alone as an experimental novel not much read until after twenty years he published his second, *J R* (1975), also lengthy. *Carpenter's Gothic* (1985) is more recent, much shorter, and more accessible. In each, the subject matter of inheritances, stock markets, religion, and disguises must be teased out of a web of voices, generally unattributed. Scenes and circumstances repeat within novels, and from novel to novel (Gaddis likes cluttered rooms, with books falling off shelves and the piano buried under piles of books, magazines, and potato chip boxes). Hawkes's *The Cannibal* (1949) examined World War II from the German side, surrealistically. Later works, including *Second Skin* (1964), *The Blood Oranges* (1971), and *Virginie* (1982), present Freudian visions of sex and violence.

In the 1960's and after, Thomas Pynchon and John Barth, more widely read than Gaddis and Hawkes, have for many stood as the exemplary self-reflexive writers of their generation. Pynchon, not long out of Cornell, published in *V.* (1963) one of the seminal novels of the period, a rich fabrication of labyrinthine twists and turns that lead mostly back in upon themselves. *The Crying of Lot 49* (1966), though much admired, pales by comparison, but *Gravity's Rainbow* (1973) is again rich and suggestive. Barth, the older of the two, began with novels less experimental than those that followed. With *Giles Goat-Boy* (1966), however, he reached a large audience with a novel at once fantastic, playful, and grounded in myth, an allegory set on the divided campuses of an immense university. His *Lost in the Funhouse* (1968) includes the masterful title story, in part, like many other recent fictions, an allegory on fiction itself.

Like Pynchon and Barth, Donald Barthelme and Robert Coover have had considerable influence on other writers, especially for their deadpan parodic prose that mimics other literature, folk tales, or journalism and the popular press. Barthelme's prowess with zany situations and voices was apparent in his first collection, *Come Back, Dr. Caligari* (1964); the best of that and six other books is collected in *Sixty Stories* (1981). Coover memorably demonstrates the power of illusion to shape lives and sustain fiction in *The Universal Baseball Association, Inc., J. Henry Waugh, Prop.* (1968). His *The Public Burning* (1977) outrageously satirizes Richard Nixon and Uncle Sam, equally real, in an account of the trial and execution of the Rosenbergs.

Among many other writers a few stand out, some truly original, some imitative of others, some not so much experimental as writing in the grand old tradition of parody and satire as overlaid with the spirit of the times. Richard Fariña, one of Pynchon's Cornell friends, wrote a fine novel of undergraduate rebellion in *Been Down So Long It Looks Like Up to Me* (1966). Ronald Sukenick and Steve Katz, two other Cornellians from the same period (undergraduates when Nabokov was teaching there) have been determinedly experimental in novels like Sukenick's *Up* (1968) and *Out* (1973) and Katz's *The Exaggerations of Peter Prince* (1968) and *Saw* (1972). Often in these works the author is himself a character. In Gilbert Sorrentino's *Mulligan Stew* (1979) not only is the author a character writing the novel he appears in, but the other characters are also writers who know they are characters in the novel. Works by William Gass, by profession a philosopher, are informed by his theories as expressed in *Fiction and the Figures of Life* (1971); his most extreme experiment, *Willie Masters' Lonesome Wife* (1968), links text, typography, and graphics in erotic playfulness. Raymond Federman's *Double or Nothing* (1971) goes further than some others in creating visual shapes with typography, on the order of the shaped poems of George Herbert or the Mouse's tale in chapter three of *Alice in Wonderland.* Joseph McElroy's vision is enshrined in metaphors of forgery, kidnapping, and hallucination as the real recedes in confusion behind shifting façades in *A Smuggler's Bible* (1966), *Hind's Kidnap* (1969), and *Lookout Cartridge* (1974). Paul Theroux began his many-volumed career with *Waldo* (1966), treating surrealistically the adventures of a young man who has left a school for delinquent boys; in later books he has earned an almost unique place as a chronicler of life in exotic places around the world. His brother, Alexander Theroux, received considerable praise for *Three Wogs* (1972); Alexander's *Darconville's Cat* (1981) is a sometimes brilliant, sometimes tedious farrago, a love story packed with extraordinary and frequently entertaining invective. Walter Abish forced his first book, *Alphabetical Africa* (1974), into a complicated alphabetical scheme that dictates the beginning of each word in each chapter; in another, *How German Is It* (1980), he derives his form from a coloring book metaphor and the German language. Guy Davenport's *Da Vinci's Bicycle* (1979) collects stories mixing times and places and famous with invented characters, and T. Coraghessan Boyle's *Descent of Man and Other Stories* (1980) makes capital of madcap references to Norse sagas, Idi Amin, astronauts, and Quetzalcoatl.

POETRY

As a result of the new freedom of the 1960's, those anti-academics who had scorned the universities and whose work had been scorned in turn soon found welcome in the classroom. At the same time, traditional poets adopted many of the methods and attitudes of the non-traditionalists, so that it became difficult to talk any longer of two distinct streams of American poetry. With the rise of creative writing as an academic discipline taught in colleges, the division, insofar as there continued to be one, was most often within the university, between those who write poetry and teach others how to write it and those who teach the reading and understanding of poetry and write critical books about it. Poet-scholars, outstanding for both their creative and critical abilities, were much less in evidence than in earlier periods, and the best criticism, written by those who were not poets, seemed curiously removed from practice.

When anti-academics joined the academy and academics took on some of their coloring, the resulting new romanticism displayed most of the traits traditionally associated with older forms of romanticism: a celebration of the individual and of personal—as opposed to group or institutional—worth; a heightened valuation of nature as inspiration and model; an insistence on egalitarian ideals in society and art; a reliance on emotion rather than intellect, intuition rather than learning, the heart rather than the head.

The signs of the shift were everywhere apparent in the 1960's. Confessional poetry dominated the decade. Poets formerly strict in their meters turned to looser lines, among them Robert Lowell, W. S. Merwin, Louis Simpson, and, later, Gwendolyn Brooks. After years of fugitive publication, the Black Mountain poets Charles Olson, Robert Creeley, and Robert Duncan found their first major publishers. In the mid-1960's, A. R. Ammons, Gwendolyn Brooks, James Dickey, and other non-mainstream poets turned from other means of support to become full-time professors. During the 1960's and after, universities increased their emphasis on creative writing as a discipline to be taught; by the 1970's and 1980's, poets qualifying for teaching positions were more likely to pursue the M.F.A. degree, emphasizing practice, than the traditional Ph.D., emphasizing theory.

The confessional poets were mostly grouped around the figure of Robert Lowell. His prominence gave the poetry of personal anguish a special authority when he wrote directly of family problems and madness in *Life Studies* (1959). W. D. Snodgrass, Lowell's student at Iowa (Lowell said generously that the teacher learned much from the student), gave great impetus to this new frankness in *Heart's Needle* (also 1959). Anne Sexton, who had studied with Lowell at Boston University, followed with *To Bedlam and Part Way Back* (1960) and later volumes before her death in 1974. Sylvia Plath, fellow student with Sexton in Lowell's classes, earned almost legendary status with the pain of her posthumous works, beginning with *Ariel* (1965). Closely allied were the poems John Berryman collected as *The Dream Songs* (1969). For many readers, the suicides, first of Plath and then of Berryman and Sexton, endowed their personal poetry with a special power.

Other poets have celebrated their individuality without being as privately personal as the confessional poets. The Deep Image poetry espoused by Robert Bly and James Wright assumes a radically different approach to personality, although individual reactions remain paramount. In this poetry, as seen in Bly's *Silence in the Snowy Fields* (1962) and Wright's *The Branch Will Not Break* (1963), and in later volumes by both, the image examined closely or discovered deep within the writer's psyche is a part of the shared emotional heritage of humankind. Mystically, or transcendentally, the personal becomes universal.

For Deep Image poets, as well as for others who do not identify themselves with the phrase, important inspiration for poetry has commonly been discovered outside the boundaries of the traditional canon of English and American literature. South American poetry and the poetry of Europe in languages other than English has been particularly influential, especially in the work of Juan Ramón Jiménez, Pablo Neruda, Antonio Machado, Georg Trakl, and Cesar Vallejo. Poets who have translated the work of these and other poets, and whose own work testifies to their influence, include Robert Bly, W. S. Merwin, James Wright, Mark Strand, and Clayton Eshleman. Among them, Eshleman, editor of the alternative poetry journal *Sulfur* and author of *The Name Encanyoned River: Selected Poems 1960–1965* (1986), has maintained the strongest sense that the contemporary canon is too much shaped by the expectations of the past and stands now in need of a revitalizing expansion.

Less concerned with questions of expectations or origins is the urban landscape verse of poets sometimes identified together as the New York School—Frank O'Hara, John Ashbery, James Schuyler, and Kenneth Koch. O'Hara, a curator at the Museum of Modern Art who was much influenced by such abstract expressionists as Jackson Pollock, received most of his fame after his death in 1966. His poems, in some ways the antithesis of the Deep Image poems of Bly and Wright, shimmer with the surface of the city. Awash with images, they nevertheless seem to hold personal emotion at arm's length, as words reflect nothing deeper than what they immediately depict. John Ashbery, poet and art critic, displays some of the same qualities, although the title of one of his best-known works, *Self-Portrait in a Convex Mirror* (1975), points alike to the personal and to the distortions of art. In recent years, Ashbery has emerged as one of the most influential poets of his generation. James Schuyler, involved at times with O'Hara and Ashbery in demonstrating a connection between graphic arts and poetry, has so far been less celebrated. Kenneth Koch, less directly connected to the world of modern art than the others, displays an engaging wit and comic disjunctions in poems like *Ko, or A Season on Earth* (1960).

One effect of much New York School poetry is a devaluation of personality, as poems, like many modern novels and stories, become self-reflexive. As artifacts separate from the poet—though idiosyncratic like Dada, Abstract Expressionism, Action Painting, or Minimalism—poems reveal little of the personal life of the maker. Ashbery especially, through the attention given his work in the 1970's and 1980's, has emerged as a focal point for understanding the attraction of poems that tease with possibilities rather than reveal specifics about the world that engendered them. He has become a master at writing poems that almost reach a philosophical conclusion, or almost tell a story, but defeat finality by their extreme abstraction. Similarly, though generally less abstract in their vision, poets like Mark Strand, Norman Dubie, and Louis Simpson have at least at times written narrative poems self-reflexive enough to invite conflicting interpretations—like some of the works of such prose writers as Pynchon, Barth, Hawkes, and Barthelme.

Although most poets since the 1960's have chosen to write generally in open forms, unmetered and unrhymed, others have continued to explore or extend the possibilities of traditional versification. Of these, James Merrill is at present most prominent. A great admirer of W. H. Auden, he has developed a formal skill evident most recently in two compilations from earlier books, *The Changing Light at Sandover* (1982), Ouija board conversations with spirits who talk in meter and rhyme; and *From the First Nine: Poems 1946–1976* (1984). W. D. Snodgrass, although he helped inaugurate the vogue for confessional poetry, did so, unlike the others, in traditional patterns in his *Heart's Needle* (1959). Howard Nemerov and Richard Wilbur have also generally maintained the formal interests with which they began, as have some writers whose first works appeared later, like Isabella Gardner and Carolyn Kizer.

Poets with strong individual voices, but less easy to classify, include William Stafford, A. R. Ammons, Galway Kinnell, and Adrienne Rich. Stafford's brief, conversational poems evoke his youth on the Kansas plains in books like *Traveling through the Dark* (1962). Ammons frequently invests his North Carolina, western, and upstate New York landscapes with an Emersonian transcendentalism, as in *Corsons Inlet* (1965). Kinnell has tried to infuse the personal with the mythical in books like *The Book of Nightmares* (1971) and *Mortal Acts, Mortal Words* (1980). Rich has been prominent among poets expressing the new consciousness of women in works that include *Diving into the Wreck* (1973) and *A Wild Patience Has Taken Me This Far* (1981).

Poets representing themselves and also speaking for ethnic minorities have included especially blacks and Native Americans. Among blacks, LeRoi Jones changed his name to Imamu Amiri Baraka in 1965 in personal tribute to the heightened sensitivity to race that marked that decade; his poetry since that time has been more angry than before. In response to the same currents, Gwendolyn Brooks turned after 1967 to a freer, more political verse. The younger generation has been represented by Don L. Lee, Nikki Giovanni, Lucille Clifton, Michael S. Harper, Alice Walker (better known as a novelist), and Rita Dove, among others. Verse in English by Native Americans has a sparse history, but there has been more activity in recent years by writers such as James Welch, Simon J. Ortiz, Ray A. Youngbear, and Leslie Marmon Silko.

Among many other poets, Philip Levine gained notice with early books like *Not This Pig* (1968); his *Selected Poems* (1986) displays an urban, blue collar sensibility. Poets born since the mid-1930's, besides some mentioned earlier, include Charles Wright and Dave Smith, both of whom write in part of the southern background they share, with Wright's poems more abstract and sometimes tinged with religion, and Smith's concretely nostalgic for people and places; Marge Piercy, poet and novelist frequently concerned with questions of women's identity; Charles Simic, born in Yugoslavia, a poet of archetype and myth; Stanley Plumly, whose strong visual images often reflect personal experience; Robert Pinsky, more comfortable with traditional forms than many recent poets; Louise Glück, whose poetry touches on personal pain and impersonal myth; Norman Dubie, often a narrative poet who submerges his personal voice in those of his characters from the past; Albert Goldbarth, wide-ranging and allusive; and Brad Leithauser, poet of rich visual surfaces.

DRAMA

The major new playwright of the 1960's was Edward Albee. His short plays, including *The Zoo Story* (1960) and *The American Dream* (1961) demonstrated a debt to European theater of the absurd as evident by that time in the work of Samuel Beckett, Eugène Ionesco, and Jean Genêt. His first longer play, *Who's Afraid of Virginia Woolf* (1962), in which the marital tensions of the characters are expressed through sometimes witty and sometimes painful verbal assault, was a huge success, but his later plays were generally not so well received. Coinciding with the rise of Albee and the absurd was the emergence of a vital black theater, first seen in Lorraine Hansberry's *A Raisin in the Sun* (1959), a Chicago drama, which she followed with *The Sign in Sidney Brustein's Window* (1964), exploring relations between ethnic groups in Greenwich Village. LeRoi Jones (later Imamu Amiri Baraka) expressed black anger and frustration in *The Toilet* (1962), *Dutchman* (1964), and other plays. James Baldwin's *Blues for Mister Charlie* (1964) was one of his few excursions into drama. Meanwhile, Tennessee Williams and Arthur Miller continued active.

In the 1960's, as fiction and poetry opened to new forms and techniques, the history of American drama became less and less a matter of what was playing on Broadway. Strong new plays began to appear Off-Broadway, Off-Off-Broadway, and in regional and university theaters, and some playwrights found it possible to earn substantial reputations apart from Broadway production. Jack Gelber, with *The Connection* (1959), was one of the first. Like many prose writers of the period, these dramatists were often critical of mainstream American life. Arthur Kopit's *Oh Dad, Poor Dad, Mama's Hung You in the Closet and I'm Feelin' So Sad* (1960) wickedly satirizes the family; his *Indians* (1968) uses Buffalo Bill to comment on American involvement in Vietnam. And in 1964, the poet Robert Lowell, at the height of his powers, drew from stories by Hawthorne and Melville to create a trilogy on the American myth, *The Old Glory*. On Broadway, the most spectacularly successful playwright in terms of audience has been Neil Simon, author of many comedies and farces, including *Barefoot in the Park* (1963) and *The Odd Couple* (1965).

Among more recent playwrights, Sam Shepard has been greatly admired. A prolific author of mostly short plays, he is especially effective in *The Tooth of Crime* (1972), *Curse of the Starving Class* (1976), *True West* (1979), and *Fool for Love* (1984). David Rabe earned praise with *Sticks and Bones* (1971), its protagonist a blind Vietnam veteran, and *Streamers* (1976), about the army, murder, and homosexuality. David Mamet's *American Buffalo* (1975) comments on American values by portraying a falling out among thieves. Among the works of several successful women playwrights, Marsha Norman's *'night Mother* (1983) is a strong depiction of a suicide.

Fiction

WILLIAM GADDIS

(1922–)

William Gaddis ranks with J. D. Salinger and Thomas Pynchon in the forefront of contemporary American writers celebrated in part for the long silences that have marked their writing careers, and in part for their reticence concerning their personal lives. He was born in New York City and educated on Long Island and in Connecticut before attending Harvard College during the war years. At Harvard, he edited the undergraduate humor magazine, the *Lampoon,* before leaving in 1945 without graduating. Two years in Manhattan as a staff writer for *The New Yorker* were followed by five years traveling—in Mexico and Central America, in Spain, North Africa, and France. By the time he returned to New York in 1951, *The Recognitions* (1955), completed in the next few years, was well under way. Only two more novels have followed to date. For three decades and more he has supported himself as a free-lance writer of speeches, film scripts, and other public relations materials for corporate America, by occasional teaching stints at Bard College and elsewhere, and by grants, including Guggenheim and MacArthur Foundation awards. Of the details of his life, he has said, "I have generally shied from parading personal details, partly from their being just that, partly from the sense that one thing said leaves others equally significant unsaid, and the sense in those lines to the effect that we are never as unlike others as we can be unlike ourselves."

In the twenty years during which it remained Gaddis's only published work, *The Recognitions* attained fame among its relatively few readers as a neglected literary classic. *J R* (1975), his second novel, resurrected an interest in Gaddis without much extending his general readership, although considerations of his work began to accumulate in literary and scholarly journals. Both are mammoth works, difficult to read because of the careful attention required as numerous characters, plots, and thematic materials fold in and out of one another on the printed page like a combination labyrinth and palimpsest, circling, revising, moving forward and then back, but always progressing. Gaddis's third novel, *Carpenter's Gothic* (1985), is much more accessible, in part because there is so much less of it, but it, too, teases almost endlessly with possibilities, leaving few certainties.

Gaddis's admirers have compared him to early-twentieth-century masters, citing most frequently James Joyce, pointing especially to the scale and uncompromising ambition of his efforts, his distinctive voice, his technical experimentation. His work is difficult to summarize, but in subject matter and theme, at least, it circles around a relatively few large poles. At the center is a vision of contemporary American life as slippery with uncertainties, fraudulent, hypocritical, deceitful. Love, politics, religion, business—all are in the hands of counterfeiters and confidence men. Peel off any layer of reality and underneath there is another. Listen twice to any voice and it is saying something else. The eleven-year-old hero of his second novel, *J R,* is a financial wizard who builds a paper empire because brokers and corporate executives cannot tell they are dealing with a voice from a public hallway telephone, or that the voice of the boy is often that of a down and out musician who fronts for him.

Somewhere in all the confusion, Gaddis seems to imply, there may be a stable center. He writes frequently of wills and inheritances. His image for all of this, however, seems to be a closed room with books piled in confusion and a piano and some lost papers somewhere under the mess. If the lost could be found, if the inheritance could be sorted out, there might be some way of organizing the present and preparing for the future. Lacking that final certainty, art itself can do no more than intrude its small presence into the counterfeit and shifting surfaces.

Gaddis's books to date are named above. Studies include Steven Moore, *A Reader's Guide to William Gaddis's "The Recognitions,"* 1982, and John Kuehl and Steven Moore, eds., *In Recognition of William Gaddis,* 1984.

From Carpenter's Gothic

The bird, a pigeon was it? or a dove (she'd found there were doves here) flew through the air, its colour lost in what light remained. It might have been the wad of rag she'd taken it for at first glance, flung at the smallest of the boys out there wiping mud from his cheek where it hit him, catching it up by a wing to fling it back where one of them now with a broken branch for a bat hit it high over a bough caught and flung back and hit again into a swirl of leaves, into a puddle from rain the night before, a kind of battered shuttlecock moulting in a flurry at each blow, hit into the yellow dead end sign on the corner opposite the house where they'd end up that time of day.

When the telephone rang she'd already turned away, catching breath, and going for it in the kitchen she looked up to the clock: not yet five. Had it stopped? The day was gone with the sun dropped behind the mountain, or what passed for one here rising up from the river. —Hello? she said, —who . . . ? Oh yes no, no he's not here he's . . . No I'm not, no. No, I'm . . . Well I'm not his wife no, I just told you. My name is Booth, I don't even know him. We've just . . . Well if you'll just let me finish! We've just rented his house here, I don't know where Mister McCandless is I've never even met him. We got a card from him from Argentina that's all, Rio? Isn't that Argentina? No it was just a card, just something about the furnace here it was just a postcard. I'm sorry I can't help you, there's somebody at the . . . No I have to go goodbye, there's somebody at the door . . .

Somebody hunched down, peering in where she'd stood staring out there a minute before, a line straight through from the kitchen past the newel to the front door fitted with glass, shuddering open. —Wait! she was up, —wait stop, who . . .

—Bibb?

—Oh. You frightened me.

He was inside now, urging the door closed behind him with his weight against it, bearing up her embrace there without returning it. —Sorry, I didn't . . .

—I didn't know who you were out there. Pushing open the door you looked so big I didn't, how did you get here?

—Coming down 9W in a . . .

—No but how did you find it?

—Adolph. Adolph said you'd . . .

—Adolph sent you? Is something wrong?

—No relax Bibb, relax. What's the matter anyhow.

—I'm just, I've just been nervous. I've just been very nervous that's all and when I saw you out there I, when you say Adolph sent you I thought something's wrong. Because something's usually wrong.

—Bibbs I didn't say that. I didn't say Adolph sent me . . . He thrust his legs out from the chair across the hearth from her where she'd come down to the edge of the frayed love seat, knees drawn tight and her hands caught together at her chin, pressed there. —When I saw him last week he told me where you'd moved, I didn't know what you'd . . .

—Well how could you know how could we tell you! How could you know where we'd moved you never, we never know where you are nobody knows. You just show up like this with your, your boots look at your boots they're falling apart look at your, that hole in your knee you don't even have a jacket, you . . .

—Oh Bibb, Bibbs . . .

—And it's cold!

—Well Bibbs Jesus, you think I don't know it's cold? I've been on the road sixteen hours. I'm driving this moving van down from Plattsburgh with no heater, I had to cut it out when the cooling system went. Twice, the whole fucking thing broke down twice and it just broke down again right up here, up on 9W. I saw the sign and remembered this is where Adolph said you moved to so I walked down here. That's all.

—You look tired Billy, she said in a voice near a whisper.—You look so tired . . . and her own hands fell away.

—You kidding? Tired, I mean that fucking truck you wouldn't . . .

—I wish you wouldn't smoke.

He threw them, match and cigarette together, at the cold grate, came forward on a torn knee to pick them up where they'd hit the firescreen. —You got a beer?

—I'll look I don't think so, Paul doesn't . . .

—Where is he? I saw the car I thought he'd be here.

—It's broken, he had to take the bus in this morning. He hates it, Billy . . . ? She was up, calling from the kitchen—Billy? She looked up to the clock, —he'll be here any minute I just don't want . . .

—I know what you don't want! He was up talking loud to walls, to the balustrade mounting from the newel at the door, to furniture —Bibb?

—There's no beer, I'm making tea if you . . .

—You just want me gone before Paul shows up, right? And he was across the room pulling open a door under the stairs on the cellar dark below, jamming it closed and opening another and stepping in without a light, standing over the bowl there. —Bibb? from the opened door. —Can you lend me twenty?

The cup rattled on the saucer, passing. —Oh I should have told you. This one stops up, I should have told you to use the upstairs . . .

—Too late now . . . he came out tugging his zipper, —can you lend me twenty Bibb? I was going to get paid when I got the van down there but . . .

—But what about it, the van. You just left it?

—The hell with it.

—But you can't just leave it there, up there right in the middle of the . . .

—You kidding? The alternator's shot, you think I'm going to sit up there all night with it? Send that heap out on the road they can come haul it in.

—But who? Whose is it, what are you doing driving somebody's moving van down from . . .

—Like what do you think I was doing, Bibb? I was trying to make seventy five bucks, what do you think I was doing.

—But you said you just saw Adolph, I thought you . . .

—Oh come on Bibb, Adolph . . . ? He was down in the chair again, one hand cracking knuckles on the fist of the other.—Adolph wouldn't give me the sweat . . .

—I wish you wouldn't do that.

—What, about Adolph? He . . .

—With your knuckles, you know it makes me nervous. His shrug dropped him deeper into the chair, one hand seized in the other. —Sit there in his paneled office I have to listen to every fucking nickel he's accountable for to the trust, the estate, the lawsuits the nursing home bills his duty to conserve the assets I mean shit, Bibbs. No wonder the old man made Adolph his executor. He sits there guarding the estate with one hand, dealing out this lousy trust with the other him and the bank, Sneddiger down at the bank. Ask one of them for a nickel he says the other one might not approve this expenditure, I mean that's the way the old man set it up. Just to keep us . . .

—Oh I know it, I know . . .

—Just to . . .

—Well it's almost done, isn't it? It's almost done, by next spring you'll . . .

—That's the trust Bibb, that's just the trust that's what I mean. That's how he set it up, just to keep us out of the estate, by the time we get there there won't be one anyhow. Twenty three lawsuits Adolph says, they've got twenty three lawsuits by stockholders against the company and the estate trying to get back what the old man handed out in those payoffs. The estate is using every resource at its disposal in dealing with these cases says Adolph, every resource that's Adolph. That's him and Grimes and all of them do you think they want to settle it? Every resource do you think they give a shit if they win it or lose it they just want to keep things going, adjournments postponements appeals they charge the estate every time they pick up the fucking telephone they're talking to each other, like they're all sitting in each other's laps picking each other's noses two hundred dollars an hour every one of them Bibb, they're talking to each other.

—But what dif . . .

—I mean every time I go in there Adolph has to remind me how they smoothed the way for the old man's retirement when he could have gone to prison instead. I mean why didn't he. He should have gone so should Paul, so should . . .

—Billy please, I don't want to go over it again, just go over it and go over it Paul just did what he was told, it was all going on long before he went there anyway. What was Paul supposed to do, they even said it wasn't against the law didn't they? Even the papers, when the . . .

—Then how come there's all these lawsuits? If it wasn't against the law how come there's twenty three lawsuits, if the old man wasn't as smart as Uncle William he'd be in prison right now but he takes the fast way out like he always did, like he always did Bibb. He crapped on the floor for somebody else to clean up that's all he ever did and there was always somebody there to clean up. There was always Adolph cleaning up that's what he's doing now, that's all he knows how to do. Two hundred dollars an hour he'll keep cleaning up till there's no fucking estate left, you know what he just did? Adolph? He just gave Yale ten thousand dollars did you know that? From the estate, ten thousand dollars for Yale while you're living in this old dump and I'm out driving a broken down . . .

—But it's not! It's a beautiful old house it's what I always . . .

—Come on Bibb it's a heap, look at it. Over there in that alcove, take one look at the ceiling and it's ready to fall down, you know what Adolph just spent on those copper roofs at Longview? He just came back, him and Grimes and Landsteiner all of them, they were all down there. You know why? Reviewing the estate's assets Adolph tells me, you know why? right now? It's duck season. Go down there and blow every duck they can see out of the sky and the estate pays every nickel, Adolph doesn't know a twelve bore Purdey from a Sears, Roebuck but he's down there banging away at anything that moves. Conserving the assets they call it, so they decide to spend thirty seven thousand dollars on the roofs, I mean thirty seven thousand dollars. Those copper roofs they're supposed to turn green to go with all that fucking moss hanging off the trees, Longview they call it Longview you can't see ten feet through the . . .

—Oh I know it I know it . . . ! The saucer rattled the cup and she set it down, —please don't let's keep going over it please!

—All right Bibb, but I mean he could have left it to us couldn't he? Or Bedford, even Bedford, I saw Lilly . . .

—Leave you Bedford? You think he'd have left you Bedford after that last party you had there? That party when he was off in Washington putting cigarettes out on the carpets and all the broken glass and Squeekie passed out right in his own bathtub? and then somebody painting a hat on his portrait in the library with Day-Glo, you thought he'd leave you the house after that?

—He could have left it to you at least.

—I never liked it. Paul would go crazy at Bedford.

—Paul will go crazy right here. Let Lilly go crazy at Bedford, I saw her coming out of Adolph's office. She was in there trying to get some money to heat the place this winter, she's scared all the pipes will break. Not a nickel, not from Adolph. He always hated her.

—He didn't hate her, he just didn't like the idea of a big country house like that going to a secretary who . . .

—Who the old man had been screwing for twenty years? so he leaves her a lousy house without a nickel to run it and Adolph jumps right in and pulls out all the furniture? Where is it anyhow, those two big marquetry chests and those chairs from the . . .

—In New York. It's all in New York, in storage there. We had to rent this furnished, for a while anyhow till they get their things out, or her things, I think it's all hers it's all kind of confused . . .

—But I mean what are you doing here anyway Bibbs, this broken down little town how did you . . .

—We just had to get out of New York that's all, we just found this through an agent and took it. You saw me down there the last time I couldn't even breathe, it's filthy, everything, the air the streets everything, and the noise. They were tearing up the street it sounded like machineguns and then they started blasting right on the corner. They were starting a new building right there on the corner and every time it went off Paul went right up the wall, he still wakes up at night with . . .

—Man like he's already up the wall, he's been up there since he came back whose fault is that.

—Well it's not his! If you'd been old enough to be . . .

—No come off it Bibb, I mean all that southern officer bullshit of his? that dress sabre with his name engraved down the blade from that halfass military school he went to? And I mean what he told you his father said? his fucking own father? That it's a damn good thing he was going in as an officer because . . .

—I've told you! It's not, I never should have told you that it's not your . . .

—I mean how could he tell you! Like how could anybody tell something like that he's already up the wall, he can't get a job he can't even look for one so he pretends he's setting up his own business? I mean he goes in and tells Adolph he's . . .

—Well he is.

—He's what, setting up his own business where, here? Like what's he going to do, open a laundry? buy you a washboard and . . .

—Billy stop it, honestly. It's a consulting, being kind of a consultant, I mean it's what he's done before when he was . . .

—Paul the bagman.

—Please! Don't, start all that . . . She was up, through to the kitchen. —Twenty? is that enough?

—Bibb . . . ? He followed her in, —I mean you know what he . . .

—Please I don't want to talk about it . . . She'd pulled open a drawer, digging under linen napkins, under placemats, —just twenty? You're sure that's enough?

—It's plenty . . . and as she bent tucking the napkins back he ran a hand over her arm bared to the shoulder, over the bruise there. —This some of Paul's work?

—I said I don't want to talk about it! She pulled away, —here! I, I just . . .

—Bumped into a bookcase, great . . . he thrust the bill into a shirt pocket. —I mean you know why he married you, we all . . .

—All right! I, I just . . . she came after him to the front door, —I just wish . . .

—I wish too, Bibb . . . he pulled the door open, grazing the newel there, and he was out, shoulders hunched against the chill. —You any better up here? your asthma?

—I don't know yet I, I think so. Will you be all right Billy?

—You kidding?

—But where do you, where are you staying, we never . . .

—Sheila. Where else.

—I thought that was over. I thought she went to India.

—She came back.

—Will you call? Will you, wait will you hand me the mail? I don't want to come out . . . She reached a bare arm for it, he slapped the mailbox shut and then stopped by the car stalled on the apron there, rocked it with one hand.

—What's wrong with it.

—I don't know, it just doesn't go. Will you, there's the phone, Billy? Please call me . . . ? She came through looking up to the clock, sat down with a shiver. —Yes hello . . . ? No, no but I expect him any minute. Could he call you back when he . . . Yes any time, this evening yes any time this evening, I'll tell him yes . . . She hung it up and left her hands there, resting on it, and her forehead down to rest on the back of a hand drawing breath, drawing breath, till she heard the door.

—Liz . . . ?

—Oh. There was a call for you. Just now, a Mister . . .

—What the hell is he doing out there!

—Is, who . . .

—Billy, your God damn brother Billy he's out there under the car, what the hell is he doing here.

—Well he just, I thought he'd . . .

—The usual? came to borrow money? How did he get here.

—Well he, he just showed up, he . . .

—He always just shows up. Did you lend him any?

—How could I Paul, I've only got nine dollars left from . . .

—Good, don't. Any calls?

—Yes just now, Mister Ude? He said he'd call back.

—That's all?

—Yes. No I mean there was a call for Mister McCandless, it was somebody from the IRS Paul when can we get this phone thing straightened out, all I do is answer these calls for . . .

—Look Liz, I can't help it. I'm trying to get a phone put in here under a company name, as soon as the . . .

—But when they shut it off in New York the bill was over seven hun . . .

—That's why I'm putting it under a company name! Now God damn it Liz stop pushing me like this the minute I walk in the door, you'll just have to put up with it. Hang up on them, now look what about your brother. Will you see what the hell he's doing out there?

—Maybe he's trying to fix it, the car I mean, he . . .

—He couldn't fix a rollerskate. I've got to get that thing fixed, this God damn bus what was I, half an hour late just now? Traffic backed up all the way down 9W to the bridge there.

—On 9W? Was there, was everything all right? I mean . . .

—What do you mean all right, I just told you traffic's backed up for three miles, police cars wreckers the works . . . He'd turned from the kitchen doorway to the one opened under the stairs. He snapped on the light there, —Liz? Look don't let him in the house again, just don't let him in. He doesn't know how to live in a house, he doesn't even know how to flush the toilet when he's . . .

—No wait Paul wait! I told him not to it's stopping up again, don't . . .

—Well Christ . . .

—But I told you not to . . .

—Too late yes, it's all over the God damn floor.

—Paul wait, Billy . . . ? She was up for the door, —Paul? I'll clean it up, Billy what . . .

—Come out here a second Paul? We might get this heap started . . . He let the door go without waiting, was down on his back on the broken stone of the apron. —Starter's jammed. Paul?

—Wait a minute . . .

—Reach in and turn the key when I get under here.

—Wait a minute Billy wait! The whole God damn thing's tipping, this little stick of wood you've got it jacked up on, you can't . . .

—Can't wait or I won't be able to see anything . . . he was already halfway under, bootheels scraping the leaves, the broken stone, —ready?

—Wait . . . The car swayed, he stood back from it reaching in, licked his lips looking down at the dumb angle of the wooden block, the denimed swell of ribs creased under the rocker panel.

—Well turn it!

He stood off as far as his reach allowed, turned the key and stepped back. —My God it started.

—Turn it off!

His hand darted in to the switch, he stumbled back over boots, over knees all coming upright. —Probably torn some teeth off your flywheel, the starter gear hits that dead spot and just spins.

—Well it, anyhow the God damn thing starts.

—Probably sheared your starter gear too, get a new one put in or it can happen again, happen any time . . . Wind from the river caught their collars up, brought down a burst of half yellowed leaves from the maple tree on the corner there. —Thanks, Paul.

—What do you mean thanks.

—Man like I'm thanking you for this good karma you just gave me that's all, I mean you give somebody a chance to do you a favour and that helps out their karma for the next time around, right? So they ought to thank you, right?

—Look Billy don't try to push my, I didn't ask you to do it did I? Crawl under there in the dark this little stick of wood holding it up the whole God damn car could have . . .

—Like this . . . ? and the sudden thrust of a boot sent the wood shivering, the car crashed down splashing broken stone under the rocker panel. —Why didn't you, Paul.

—Billy God damn it don't . . .

—Might have been your last chance when it could still do you some good. Here . . . he'd reached in to pull the keys from the ignition, tossed them over —kids find the keys in it they'll take it for a joyride and leave it in a ditch. An old heap like this Paul, it wouldn't even be grand larceny.

—You would have wouldn't you! Been me under there, wouldn't you! He was down on one knee brushing leaves aside for the keys, —good karma someday Billy God damn it, I'll show you good karma! But the wind threw his words back to him, blowing up from the river, blowing the leaves up in flurries where his fingers raked them aside, smashed wing, muddied mantle barely distinguishable in the protective coloration of death, he straightened up with the keys looking down the hill where the figure hunched smaller against the wind, and then he stooped to pick up the bird by a leg and hold it away as he turned for the door.

—Paul? I thought I heard the car start. Is it fixed?

—Till the next time.

—What's that you've, oh!

He carried it past her to drop in the trash. —Where's the whisky.

—In the refrigerator, you . . .

—What the hell is it doing in the refrigerator.

—You put it there last night.

—Well why didn't you take it out . . . The refrigerator door banged against the counter. —He's crazy Liz. That God damn brother of yours, he's crazy.

—Paul please he, I know sometimes he . . .

—Sometimes! You know what he just did out there?

—I thought he fixed the car, you said . . .

—He ought to be locked up Liz. He's dangerous. Is this glass clean? He ought to be in Payne Whitney with your uncle strutting around in a cutaway, Uncle William strutting around Payne Whitney with no pants on.

—Like the night you folded up all your clothes and put them in the refrig . . .

—Liz that never happened! It never happened, it's something you read someplace.

—I thought it was funny.

—Nothing's funny. When did Ude say he'd call back.

—He just said later. Who's Mister Ude.

—Reverend Ude. He's a client. Did you bring in the mail?

—It's, yes it's somewhere, I think I put it . . .

—Look Liz, we've got to get a system. At least you brought it in, good. Now there's got to be a place for it. If I'm going to get any kind of an operation going here we've got to get a system, I've got to know where the mail is when I walk in, you've got to get a pad there by the phone so I can see who . . .

—No it's there, there behind the bag of onions when I came in I . . .

—See that's what I mean. I mean if I'm going to run any kind of operation from here I can't be looking for the mail under a bag of onions. Did my check come?

—I didn't look, I don't . . .

—God damn bank, somebody in there with a lien they're probably freezing everything I . . . Paper tore, —listen to this. Dear Customer . . .

—Paul?

—Does taking ten percent off any initial purchase at the finest furniture specialty store in America sound attractive to you? If so, you'll be happy to know that the . . .

—Paul what just happened out there. With Billy, you said . . .

—Nothing. Nothing Liz he's crazy, that's all, he ought to be locked up for his own good, what the hell do we need furniture for. This God damn bank look at it, three payments behind on that loan they're threatening to wipe me out now they're trying to sell me furniture. All we've got is furniture!

—I just wish we did. I just wish I could look up and see something of mine sometimes, those two marquetry chests could go right in the . . .

—Look they're not going anywhere without paying the God damn storage bill, get all that stuff in here where the hell would we put it.

—We could, someday if we could take out that wall in the living room onto the porch? just open it all up and put in an arch there right out onto the porch and glass it all in, the whole porch, and that old piano from Longview we could . . .

—Pull out that wall the whole God damn house would fall down Liz what are you talking about, rent somebody's house you want to start knocking walls down? Paper tore.

—I just said, someday . . .

—Gustav Schak MD, two hundred sixty dollars. Who the hell is Gustav Schak.

—The one I saw last week, the one Jack Orsini sent me to and I had that terrible . . .

—One visit? Two hundred sixty dollars for one visit?

—Well they did those tests I told you, how awful his nurse was shouting at me I could hardly breathe, that spirometry test I was right in the middle of a spasm and she was shouting at me about . . .

—Spirometry eighty dollars. CC one hundred dollars, what the hell is CC. Comprehensive consultation, what the . . .

—Well I don't know Paul! It was all so confused, I felt so awful and his nurse was so rude and he was in such a rush he was leaving for a golf vacation in Palm Springs, I hardly saw him for ten minutes. He got me in as a favour to Orsini, because they need to know what these tests say when I see this specialist next week, this Doctor Kissinger I'm seeing next week and Doctor Schak is sending over the . . .

—Yes all right Liz, all right but Christ. Two hundred and six . . .

—I can't help it! I, I don't know what else to . . .

—All right look. Just send him twenty five dollars and write payment in full on the check. Can you call Orsini?

—I did. He's in Geneva. Some big convention of neurologists or something in Geneva.

—So he goes over, reads a paper, gets in a little skiing at Kitzbühel, stops at Deauville to check out his horses, takes the whole God damn thing off his taxes and he's back in town just in time for another giant publishing party, another giant paperback success . . .

—But he's been kind to me Paul, he's always been generous with . . .

—Generous? after the way your father set him up? Look I want to talk to him Liz, the next time you hear from Orsini I want to talk to him.

—I wouldn't Paul I just wouldn't, if he thinks you're interfering with that research thing Daddy set up for him he'll be furious I know he will, he'll be . . .

—I'm not interfering with a God damn thing, that's not what I want to talk to him about now God damn it Liz don't tell me what to do! He brought the bottle tipped over his glass, —what's that one.

—This? She handed it over, —I can't even tell what country it's from.

—Zaire. Who the hell do we know in, wait. Here, it's for McCandless, stick it up in the door there with the rest of his, where the hell is my VA check . . . Paper tore, —from those insurance bastards. In order to complete their records in this case pending trial they would like you to make an appointment for a medical examination relevant to your claims against this God damn airline what the hell are they . . .

—I don't know! I've had seven of them, ten I don't know how many it was four years ago, I don't even remember where I told them it hurt, I can't even . . .

—Well I can . . . the paper crumpled in his hand, —bastards. I can tell them, dizziness, headaches . . . He smoothed it out on the table. —Your failure to complete this appointment may jeopardize your claim for injuries sustained in, I can tell them.

Her head had sunk into her hand where she held it, pulling a deep breath, stood abruptly with a step to the sink for a paper towel blowing her nose there, again with a hollow urgency, looking out. Streetlight brought down another leaf or two on the terrace. —When do you want to eat, she finally said.

—Give me some ice while you're up, will you?

She stood there, looking out. —Paul?

—Who do you know in Eleuthera.

—Nobody she said, the paper towel knotted tight in her hand, turning for the harsh chromo of boats on green water. —Oh it's Edie, a card from Edie.

—She still dragging that Indian around?

—I don't know. I just so long to see her.

—Well I can live without her, I'll tell you that.

—I just wish you wouldn't always have to say that, she's the only, Edie's always been my best friend always, she always . . .

—Look after the way Grimes fixed me up what do you expect me to . . .

—That wasn't Edie! Do you think she tells her father what to do? she even knows what he does? That was you and Mister Grimes and the company after Daddy, did I ever tell Daddy what to do? Did anybody ever blame me for Daddy?

—All right Liz but God damn it, Edie saw what happened didn't she? when your father was out and Grimes moved up as chairman? Grimes got what he wanted didn't he? did he have to push me out too? Couldn't Edie, your best friend Edie couldn't she even put in a word? Right now couldn't she? One word from Grimes to Adolph, one word anyplace one word from Grimes to this God damn airline he sits on their board, he sits on the board of their God damn insurance company too this one, this one right here the one that wrote you this letter, Grimes pulled it off before didn't he? that policy VCR had on your father? Some question how your father met his death and they dig in their heels, Grimes takes off his VCR hat and puts on his insurance company hat, they pay off the twenty million without a whimper, VCR cash flow picks up their stock jumps a few points and there's Grimes back in the driver's seat, whole thing was God damn strange Liz. That twenty million coming right when they needed it did you get me some ice?

She steadied a hand on the chair, sat down and said —no, near a whisper.

—I mean it's yours it's going to be yours, one word to Adolph to release a few thousand we'd be out of the hole, it's just taking part of what's ours out a little ahead of time, part of what's accumulated in the trust we won't even miss it when the whole thing comes through it's nothing, a few thousand, one word to Adolph and we'd be . . .

—Well he won't. Billy just talked to Adolph and he won't even . . .

—Billy that God damn Billy! What the hell does he do with it, he gets as much from the trust every month what does he do with it! You see him just now? he walks into Adolph looking like that what's Adolph going to do, dig into the trust for you and there's Billy with a dirty hand out? What the hell does he do with it! Liz?

—What.

—I said he gets as much as . . .

—Well what do we do with it! The paper towel came apart in her hands —what do we do with it, we get as much as he does Paul what do we do with it!

—No now wait Liz that's, wait. We're trying to do something, trying to do something Liz trying to live like civilized, get out of the God damn hole here live like civilized people Liz I'm trying to build something here, have something to show for it he just wants to show his contempt for it, for everything, worse the use he can find for it the better that's what he does with it. Rock bands, queers, spades out there dealing drugs and all this Buddhist crap you know he just tried to pull that on me again out there? that karma crap he got from those Tibetan creeps he had following him around? Same thing Liz the same God damn thing, that greasy little burr head monk in the red blanket doing him a favour taking his money same God damn thing, giving him a chance to show his contempt for the money, show his contempt for the people he gives it to and the system it came out of like all these God damn kids parading around with their guitars and their hair dyed pink they'll scam, con, deal, the worse fraud they can skim a few dollars off of the better the one God damn thing they won't do is work for it, did he ever earn a nickel? work one God damn day in his life?

—Well he has Paul, he has, that's why he was here just now he'd been driving a . . .

—Borrow some money, that's why he was here just now wasn't it? tried to borrow some money?

—Well but that's not the . . .

—What I'm telling you Liz, what I'm trying to tell you. Work for money means you've got some respect for it, he just wants it to show his contempt for anybody that works for it, anybody trying to do something, trying to put things together, build something like your father did we both know that's what it's about Liz, what the whole God damn thing is about. I came in there your father could see I'd go in and do the job, that I could step in and size things up, see the big picture and take a few risks to bring it off everything your God damn brother will never do, won't even try to that's why he's still getting back at me, getting back at your father, getting back at anybody who's trying to do the job just get out of the hole here. Get that alimony load off my back they've scheduled the hearing, that should be any day now just these bills, all these God damn bills . . . He raised the glass and brought it away, pulling a hand over his mouth—tell me how I always get this glass with the chip in the rim? Liz?

—What.

—I just asked you the, problem I just think you don't really listen to me sometimes, don't really get in there and back me up trying to tell you what I'm trying to do here, trying to put the pieces together your God damn brother in there pulling them apart I'm getting things going Liz, three or four things I've got a spade in here from Guinea says he's in parliament there, polo coat grease spots down the front of it he's got the State Department sending him around to look at prisons and broilers, get their prison system out of the tenth century and set up broiler production may have to take him out to Terre Haute broiler farms and a big federal prison right down the road work it in with this other big client, big drug company's got these animal nutritionists from Europe want to see pigs, Terre Haute's got to be pigs get them out there and show them the pigs and this Ude, this Reverend Ude you said called? Nickel and dime radio station going right into nationwide television global coverage he's already moved in on these African missions, spread the gospel get things moving he's already got this Voice of Salvation radio station right out there Liz, old stamping grounds move in take a few risks and bring it off just get out of the hole here, all these God damn bills here look at them bank loans, storage, travel cards, Diners Club American Express lawyers doctors, ask what we do with the money that's what we do with it, one visit two hundred sixty dollars for one visit that's what you . . .

—I can't help it Paul! If you, do you think I like it going to doctors? Like going to, like you going to restaurants? Plane tickets, car rentals motel bills hotels that's what all this is do you think I . . .

—Look, just once. Let's try to get this straight just once, Liz. I'm trying to get something going. You don't get something going over a ham sandwich and a beer. You don't take the Greyhound bus and stay at the Y when you're digging up new accounts. You don't nickel and dime unless all you're after is nickels and dimes and you won't even get those now look, I've got a couple of . . .

—Put it out, Paul.

—What?

—The cigarette. Put it out.

Instead he swept up his glass and turned abruptly through the doorway, in to stand before the empty fireplace drawing smoke, blowing it out, staring back at the wet rag on the wet floor under the stairs. —Liz . . . ? He threw the cigarette smoking into the grate. —Got to do something about this God damn toilet. Liz?

—What.

—I said we can't live like this. Try to live like civilized people your brother comes in here pisses all over the floor we can't even . . .

—All right! Just leave it, I'll clean it up just leave it.

—Anyplace he goes, somebody cleaning up after him every God damn place he goes. You clean up, Adolph cleans up that's all Adolph's ever done is clean up after him. That car wreck in Encino? and Yale? He's kicked out of every school he gets near so they buy his way into Yale, you know what he told me once? that they'd held him back in eighth grade because he was such a great hockey player? You know God damn well why they . . .

—Paul what's the point! You shout at me, Billy shouts at me as though I could do anything, as though I'm to blame what's the point! It's almost over, a few more months he'll be twenty five what's the point of . . .

—The point Liz, the point is he ought to be locked up, he ought to be locked up till he's twenty five or he'll never be twenty five. The point is this trust brings in about five percent, Adolph says he can't invest for income what about Grimes? He sits on the board of the bank that's co-trustee doesn't he? One word from Grimes, do you think he'd say one word for any of us? with Billy in there? that party they found Squeekie passed out naked in your father's bathtub when she was fifteen do you think her father's going to raise a . . .

—Oh Paul that was a story, that never happened it was just a story that somebody . . .

—That Edie, she's Edie's sister isn't she? Isn't that how we knew, from Edie? after your father called Grimes? You think Grimes would raise a finger for any of us after that? Adolph can't invest it for income he has to invest for long term growth, one word from Grimes to his God damn bank it could be bringing in twelve percent, fifteen, you think he'll say it? With Adolph handing it right out to clean up after Billy, that Indian Mexican whatever she was Adolph paying her off and this Sheila, buying a ticket to get her and her guitar and dope and mantras and the rest of her Buddhist junk on a plane to India, long term growth what long term? Some next generation that's going to look like a God damn zoo? Billy out there sticking it into anything that walks and Adolph right behind them pulling down their skirts and paying them off so they won't put a monkey in the family tree and we can't even do that, we can't even . . .

—Paul it's not my fault! It's, it's not my . . .

—I didn't say that. I didn't say that Liz. I didn't mean . . .

—But you did you do! You always do you, I go to the doctor every time I see a doctor you blame me for the bills even the plane crash, you even blame me for that you . . .

—Liz stop it . . . ! He put down his emptied glass, coming round the table. —How could I blame you for the plane crash.

—Well you do. Every time we go to bed, that lawsuit you started against them with mine every time we . . .

—Liz don't, look. I'm sorry. I didn't mean . . .

—You're always sorry, you always, no don't. Don't, just give me that napkin, don't you're messing my hair . . .

But he came down, closer, his breath stirring it, —Liz? Remember that first time? after that funeral? When I leaned over in the car and told you I was crazy about the back of your neck and . . .

—No please . . . she pulled away, cringed lower, his hand on her bared shoulder —you're hurting my . . .

—Well what the hell are you wearing this thing for! He was back out of reach, a hand out for his glass, —you haven't worn it since summer.

—But what, I just . . .

—Show off your bruise? Sleeveless thing to show off your God damn combat badge to the neighbors and anybody who . . .

—I don't know any neighbors!

—And your brother what about your brother, your . . .

—I said I'd bumped into a bookcase. When do you want supper.

—A bookcase . . . He held the bottle over the glass, held it the way he poured drinks, two handed, one holding the bottle up and away against the other forcing it down, forcing the neck down over the glass, and —a bookcase, he muttered again at the sink for a splash of water, turning past her through the doorway. —Where. What bookcase. Will you show me one God damn bookcase? Everything else here but a bookcase it's like a museum, like living in a museum. Liz . . . ? He'd got as far as the door and he turned on a lamp there, something Japanese under a silk shade that cast the reflection of his unfinished face in the glass-framed sampler hung above it. —Did that agent tell you when they're getting this stuff out of here? Liz?

—They just said his wife's supposed to come for it.

—That means we've got to live with every stick the way she left it? Pictures, mirrors, plants all those God damn plants in the dining room watering all those plants? He raised his glass, brought it down half emptied coming across the room to put it on the mantel his hand's breadth from a china dog there, and no larger. —Looks like she'll be here any minute, whole place looks like she walked out for lunch and expects to be back for dinner . . . He ran a finger over the china dog, brought it up close and it snapped in his hands. —Liz? Got to get somebody in here to clean . . . he fitted the halves together, placed them back and came down blowing on them, pressing them close, blowing again and brushing away with his hand, taking his glass, —that list he left? The plumber, electrician, firewood, some woman on it who comes in and cleans? He'd reached the alcove where he raised his glass and finished it, stood looking down the black crown of the empty road and then ran a finger over the pane and looked at it. —Get her in here to wash the windows, so smoked up you can't see out . . . He turned with the emptied glass, —know where that list is? Get her in here to clean things up, see if she can oww . . . !

—Paul?

—Does this coffee table have to be right in the middle of the God damn room here? Bang my leg every time I walk past it.

—Where else can it go? There's no place to . . .

—Got to get this toilet fixed.

—Well what shall I do! I told you I called the plumber and they have to get in that room to reach some trap in the drain.

—Tell them to break the lock. Just tell them to break the God damn padlock. This McCandless, Argentina Zaire wherever the hell he is, look at these smoked up windows he's probably in a cancer ward someplace what are we supposed to do. He rents us the house with that room locked off and a lease that says he reserves access to his papers in there, what do we do? Sit here waiting for him to show up looking for an old laundry ticket while your brother stands here pissing all over the floor? You know where that list is? Just call and tell them to break that padlock and get in there and fix the God damn drain . . . He was back standing over the bottle, —they can put on a new lock and give the key to the agent, if McCandless ever shows up she can hand it over.

—You'll have to leave me cash.

—Let them send the bill to the agent.

—For the cleaning woman, she . . .

—You sure this is all the mail? He sat down again, sweeping it toward him, —my VA check, where the hell is it . . . Instead he found the newspaper. —What about supper.

—There's that ham, what's left of it.

—See this thing in the paper? these gooks adopting dogs and eating them?

—Please, put it out Paul. I'm having trouble breathing.

—We spend five dollars a week here feeding somebody else's cat while these slopes walk into the ASPCA and go home to a dachshund barbecue. See this gook in there patting a Saint Bernard on the . . .

—Paul, put it out.

—All right! He jammed the cigarette into her teacup, —takes it home to the kiddies whole God damn family eats for a week, can't even . . .

—They can't help it! She was suddenly up, past him into the living room where she simply stood.

—What? What do you mean they can't . . .

—I just wish you didn't have to keep calling them slopes and gooks, it's all such a long time ago and you can't call them that, all of them gooks . . . She bent down for the rag on the wet floor, —the ones who were our friends the ones who . . .

—Liz God damn it I was there! They're all gooks all of them, every God damn one of them I was there Liz . . . ! and his hand, in a sudden tremor reaching for the telephone, knocked over the glass. —It's probably Ude.

She came onto the trash, caught breath dangling the wet rag that moment before she dropped it in where the feathers, mottled? or just mud spattered, still shone in brownish pink at the throat. It was a dove.

1985

CYNTHIA OZICK
(1928–)

"I believe that stories ought to judge and interpret the world," Cynthia Ozick wrote in the preface to her third book, *Bloodshed and Three Novellas* (1976). It is her role especially to judge and interpret the world from the perspective of the American Jew. She has written of the experience of the immigrant, the Holocaust survivor, the Zionist, and the religious Jew for whom secular American life offers constant seduction. In the same preface, she observes that she sometimes feels cramped by the necessity to write in English because "English is a Christian language" and not wholly adequate to communicate her experience. "I have come to it with notions it is too parochial to recognize. A language, like a people, has a history of ideas; but not *all* ideas; only those known to its experience."

Ozick was born and brought up in the Bronx. As a child she sought escape through stories and novels from what she perceived as her lack of social and educational success in the public schools and the long hours her immigrant parents spent in the family pharmacy. She earned degrees in literature from New York University in 1949 and Ohio State University in 1950.

Her master's thesis was on Henry James, whom she has identified as a major and nearly fatal influence on her career. Her first novel *Trust* (1966), begun immediately after she left graduate school, she describes as "a cannibalistically ambitious Jamesian novel." The complicated plot centers on a female narrator, abandoned by her womanizing father and emotionally deprived by the rest of her affluent relatives, who becomes a witness to the aftermath of the Holocaust. Flawed by a disjunction between language and feeling, the book nevertheless contains brilliant passages.

Her first collection of stories, *The Pagan Rabbi and Other Stories* (1971), introduces Ozick's theme of the experiences of Jews transplanted to America. The story "Envy" concerns a Yiddish poet who struggles to have his work translated into English in order to protect it and save the Yiddish language; he envies another writer who has found an audience and become famous in America but who seems unimpressed by the argument that "whoever forgets Yiddish courts amnesia of history." In "Virility" an immigrant poet anglicizes his name and tries to write poetry in English. He has no success until he begins to translate and pass off the work of his Tante Rivka as his own. The poetry is published in five volumes and is especially praised by the critics for its masculinity. When the aunt dies, poor and alone, enough poems are left for one more volume, but he confesses his crime and publishes the rest of the work with Tante Rivka's picture on the dust jacket. Reviewers savage the collection as "girlish" and "domestic."

The title story of Ozick's third book, *Bloodshed,* focuses on one of her major themes: what responsibilities do contemporary American Jews carry in relation to the Holocaust, and how do these responsibilities set Jews apart from others? The five stories of her next collection, *Levitation* (1982), are chiefly about women, though they share concerns with Jewish folklore and the nature of the storyteller's art treated in earlier fictions. In "Puttermesser and Xantippe," for instance, a woman lawyer creates a female *golem* that gets her creator elected mayor. The new mayor transforms New York into an ideal city, but her sexually insatiable *golem* becomes a threat and the mayor must destroy her own creation.

After the success of her shorter fictions,

Ozick turned once again to the novel form in *The Cannibal Galaxy* (1983), where she treats the struggles of spirit endured by a survivor of Nazi-dominated France who becomes headmaster of a school in the Midwest. In *The Messiah of Stockholm* (1987), a novella, she continues her concern with questions of survival, identity, and authorship, imagining what might follow from the discovery of a lost masterpiece by the Polish author Bruno Schulz, killed by the Nazis in 1942.

Ozick's novels and collections of short fiction to date are named above. Essays are collected in *Art and Ardor,* 1983.

Brief studies are included in Catherine Rainwater and William J. Scheick, eds., *Three Contemporary Women Novelists: Hazzard, Ozick and Redmon,* 1983; and in Rainwater and Scheick, eds., *Contemporary American Women Writers: Narrative Strategies,* 1985.

The Shawl[1]

Stella, cold, cold, the coldness of hell. How they walked on the roads together, Rosa with Magda curled up between sore breasts, Magda wound up in the shawl. Sometimes Stella carried Magda. But she was jealous of Magda. A thin girl of fourteen, too small, with thin breasts of her own, Stella wanted to be wrapped in a shawl, hidden away, asleep, rocked by the march, a baby, a round infant in arms. Magda took Rosa's nipple, and Rosa never stopped walking, a walking cradle. There was not enough milk; sometimes Magda sucked air; then she screamed. Stella was ravenous. Her knees were tumors on sticks, her elbows chicken bones.

Rosa did not feel hunger; she felt light, not like someone walking but like someone in a faint, in trance, arrested in a fit, someone who is already a floating angel, alert and seeing everything, but in the air, not there, not touching the road. As if teetering on the tips of her fingernails. She looked into Magda's face through a gap in the shawl: a squirrel in a nest, safe, no one could reach her inside the little house of the shawl's windings. The face, very round, a pocket mirror of a face: but it was not Rosa's bleak complexion, dark like cholera, it was another kind of face altogether, eyes blue as air, smooth feathers of hair nearly as yellow as the Star[2] sewn into Rosa's coat. You could think she was one of *their* babies.

Rosa, floating, dreamed of giving Magda away in one of the villages. She could leave the line for a minute and push Magda into the hands of any woman on the side of the road. But if she moved out of line they might shoot. And even if she fled the line for half a second and pushed the shawl-bundle at a stranger, would the woman take it? She might be surprised, or afraid; she might drop the shawl, and Magda would fall out and strike her head and die. The little round head. Such a good child, she gave up screaming, and sucked now only for the taste of the drying nipple itself. The neat grip of the tiny gums. One mite of a tooth tip sticking up in the bottom gum, how shining, an elfin tombstone of white marble, gleaming there. Without complaining, Magda relinquished Rosa's teats, first the left, then the right; both were cracked, not a sniff of milk. The duct crevice extinct, a dead volcano, blind eye, chill hole, so Magda took the corner of the shawl and milked it instead. She sucked and sucked, flooding the threads with wetness. The shawl's good flavor, milk of linen.

It was a magic shawl, it could nourish an infant for three days and three nights.

1. "The Shawl" was first published in *The New Yorker,* May 26, 1980, the source of the present text. It has not yet been collected in a volume by the author.

2. Star of David, six-pointed, a symbol of Judaism.

Magda did not die, she stayed alive, although very quiet. A peculiar smell, of cinnamon and almonds, lifted out of her mouth. She held her eyes open every moment, forgetting how to blink or nap, and Rosa and sometimes Stella studied their blueness. On the road they raised one burden of a leg after another and studied Magda's face. "Aryan,"[3] Stella said, in a voice grown as thin as a string; and Rosa thought how Stella gazed at Magda like a young cannibal. And the time that Stella said "Aryan," it sounded to Rosa as if Stella had really said "Let us devour her."

But Magda lived to walk. She lived that long, but she did not walk very well, partly because she was only fifteen months old, and partly because the spindles of her legs could not hold up her fat belly. It was fat with air, full and round. Rosa gave almost all her food to Magda, Stella gave nothing; Stella was ravenous, a growing child herself, but not growing much. Stella did not menstruate. Rosa did not menstruate. Rosa was ravenous, but also not; she learned from Magda how to drink the taste of a finger in one's mouth. They were in a place without pity, all pity was annihilated in Rosa, she looked at Stella's bones without pity. She was sure that Stella was waiting for Magda to die so she could put her teeth into the little thighs.

Rosa knew Magda was going to die very soon; she should have been dead already, but she had been buried away deep inside the magic shawl, mistaken there for the shivering mound of Rosa's breasts; Rosa clung to the shawl as if it covered only herself. No one took it away from her. Magda was mute. She never cried. Rosa hid her in the barracks, under the shawl, but she knew that one day someone would inform; or one day someone, not even Stella, would steal Magda to eat her. When Magda began to walk Rosa knew that Magda was going to die very soon, something would happen. She was afraid to fall asleep; she slept with the weight of her thigh on Magda's body; she was afraid she would smother Magda under her thigh. The weight of Rosa was becoming less and less; Rosa and Stella were slowly turning into air.

Magda was quiet, but her eyes were horribly alive, like blue tigers. She watched. Sometimes she laughed—it seemed a laugh, but how could it be? Magda had never seen anyone laugh. Still, Magda laughed at her shawl when the wind blew its corners, the bad wind with pieces of black in it, that made Stella's and Rosa's eyes tear. Magda's eyes were always clear and tearless. She watched like a tiger. She guarded her shawl. No one could touch it; only Rosa could touch it. Stella was not allowed. The shawl was Magda's own baby, her pet, her little sister. She tangled herself up in it and sucked on one of the corners when she wanted to be very still.

Then Stella took the shawl away and made Magda die.

Afterward Stella said: "I was cold."

And afterward she was always cold, always. The cold went into her heart: Rosa saw that Stella's heart was cold. Magda flopped onward with her little pencil legs scribbling this way and that, in search of the shawl; the pencils faltered at the barracks opening, where the light began. Rosa saw and pursued. But already Magda was in the square outside the barracks, in the jolly light. It was the roll-call arena. Every morning Rosa had to conceal Magda under the shawl against a wall of the barracks and go out and stand in the arena with Stella and hundreds of others, sometimes for hours, and Magda, deserted, was quiet under the shawl, sucking on her corner. Every day Magda was silent, and so she did not die. Rosa saw that today

3. A term used in Nazi Germany to designate non-Jewish Caucasians.

Magda was going to die, and at the same time a fearful joy ran in Rosa's two palms, her fingers were on fire, she was astonished, febrile: Magda, in the sunlight, swaying on her pencil legs, was howling. Ever since the drying up of Rosa's nipples, ever since Magda's last scream on the road, Magda had been devoid of any syllable; Magda was a mute. Rosa believed that something had gone wrong with her vocal cords, with her windpipe, with the cave of her larynx; Magda was defective, without a voice; perhaps she was deaf; there might be something amiss with her intelligence; Magda was dumb. Even the laugh that came when the ash-stippled wind made a clown out of Magda's shawl was only the air-blown showing of her teeth. Even when the lice, head lice and body lice, crazed her so that she became as wild as one of the big rats that plundered the barracks at daybreak looking for carrion, she rubbed and scratched and kicked and bit and rolled without a whimper. But now Magda's mouth was spilling a long viscous rope of clamor.

"Maaaa—"

It was the first noise Magda had ever sent out from her throat since the drying up of Rosa's nipples.

"Maaaa . . . aaa!"

Again! Magda was wavering in the perilous sunlight of the arena, scribbling on such pitiful little bent shins. Rosa saw. She saw that Magda was grieving for the loss of her shawl, she saw that Magda was going to die. A tide of commands hammered in Rosa's nipples: Fetch, get, bring! But she did not know which to go after first, Magda or the shawl. If she jumped out into the arena to snatch Magda up, the howling would not stop, because Magda would still not have the shawl; but if she ran back into the barracks to find the shawl, and if she found it, and if she came after Magda holding it and shaking it, then she would get Magda back, Magda would put the shawl in her mouth and turn dumb again.

Rosa entered the dark. It was easy to discover the shawl. Stella was heaped under it, asleep in her thin bones. Rosa tore the shawl free and flew—she could fly, she was only air—into the arena. The sunheat murmured of another life, of butterflies in summer. The light was placid, mellow. On the other side of the steel fence, far away, there were green meadows speckled with dandelions and deep-colored violets; beyond them, even farther, innocent tiger lilies, tall, lifting their orange bonnets. In the barracks they spoke of "flowers," of "rain": excrement, thick turd-braids, and the slow stinking maroon waterfall that slunk down from the upper bunks, the stink mixed with a bitter fatty floating smoke that greased Rosa's skin. She stood for an instant at the margin of the arena. Sometimes the electricity inside the fence would seem to hum; even Stella said it was only an imagining, but Rosa heard real sounds in the wire: grainy sad voices. The farther she was from the fence, the more clearly the voices crowded at her. The lamenting voices strummed so convincingly, so passionately, it was impossible to suspect them of being phantoms. The voices told her to hold up the shawl, high; the voices told her to shake it, to whip with it, to unfurl it like a flag. Rosa lifted, shook, whipped, unfurled. Far off, very far, Magda leaned across her air-fed belly, reaching out with the rods of her arms. She was high up, elevated, riding someone's shoulder. But the shoulder that carried Magda was not coming toward Rosa and the shawl, it was drifting away, the speck of Magda was moving more and more into the smoky distance. Above the shoulder a helmet glinted. The light tapped the helmet and sparkled it into a goblet. Below the helmet a black body like a domino and a pair of black boots hurled themselves in the direction of the electrified fence. The electric voices began to chatter wildly. "Maamaa, maaamaaa," they all hummed together. How far Magda was from Rosa now, across the whole square, past a dozen barracks, all the way on the other side! She was no bigger than a moth.

All at once Magda was swimming through the air. The whole of Magda traveled through loftiness. She looked like a butterfly touching a silver vine. And the moment Magda's feathered round head and her pencil legs and balloonish belly and zigzag arms splashed against the fence, the steel voices went mad in their growling, urging Rosa to run and run to the spot where Magda had fallen from her flight against the electrified fence; but of course Rosa did not obey them. She only stood, because if she ran they would shoot, and if she tried to pick up the sticks of Magda's body they would shoot, and if she let the wolf's screech ascending now through the ladder of her skeleton break out, they would shoot; so she took Magda's shawl and filled her own mouth with it, stuffed it in and stuffed it in, until she was swallowing up the wolf's screech and tasting the cinnamon and almond depth of Magda's saliva; and Rosa drank Magda's shawl until it dried.

1980

URSULA K. LE GUIN

(1929–)

Ursula Kroeber was born into an academic family in Berkeley, California. Her mother, Theodora, was a psychologist, her father, Alfred Kroeber, an anthropologist. From early childhood she was exposed to a variety of cultures. She listened to her father tell Indian tales, and Indian visitors mingled with the academic guests at her parents' house; at the outer limit of the technological culture of the day was Robert Oppenheimer, also a guest at her parents' house and from 1942 to 1945 director of the atomic energy research project at Los Alamos. Summers were spent in pastoral leisure on the family's forty-acre estate in the Napa valley. In the larger world outside the family, Dust Bowl refugees after 1934 sought what for them turned out to be California's largely illusionary pastures of plenty, and after 1941 California braced itself for the feared invasion of the Japanese as the country went to war. In 1941, at age twelve, following a childhood enthusiasm for Indian, Greek, and Norse myths, Ursula discovered fantasy in Lord Dunsany's *A Dreamer's Tales:* "What I hadn't realized," she wrote later, "is that people were still making up myths. One made up stories oneself, of course; but here was a grownup doing it for grownups * * *. I had discovered my native country."

In 1947 she went East to college at Radcliffe. Graduating Phi Beta Kappa in 1951, she earned an M.A. in French from Columbia in 1952 and the following year left for study in France as a Fulbright scholar. On the ship over, she met Charles Le Guin, whom she married in Paris later that year. Turning from Ph.D. work to teaching and, within a few years, motherhood, she also turned more completely to writing. By about 1960, by which time the Le Guins were living in Portland, Oregon, she had written five novels, none published. Then in the 1960's, as her work began to appear in *Fantastic,* she learned to exploit more successfully the mixture of science-fiction and fantasy conventions that underlies her first trilogy, *Rocannon's World* (1966), *Planet of Exile* (1966), and *City of Illusions* (1967); these, however, are still apprentice work.

In the late 1960's and early 1970's, Le Guin's work branched in several directions. The Earthsea Trilogy—*A Wizard of Earthsea* (1968), *The Tombs of Atuan* (1971), and *The Farthest Shore* (1972)—earned her a reputation for mastery of fantastic tales for children and adolescents. Meanwhile, with *The Left Hand of Darkness* (1969), she won both the Hugo and Nebula awards, establishing herself as a major writer of science fiction with a work that explores an androgynous world of alien beings on a frozen planet. In *The Lathe of Heaven* (1971), set in Portland, Oregon, in 1998, and *The Word for World Is Forest* (1972), set on a distant planet some four centuries in the future, her fantasy turns satiric. In the first she imagines a protagonist whose dreaming can change the deteriorating world he inhabits, though not always in the ways he intends; in the second she vents her anger at American actions in Vietnam by inventing a race of Terrans who despoil the forests of the colony they call New Tahiti.

Increasingly, as her career has developed, Le Guin has in her fiction questioned the values of the world she lives in, seeking alternative visions of what life is or might be. Sometimes her vision takes the form of unadulterated fantasy, as in *The Beginning Place* (1980), where two young people leave their troubled adolescence behind by crossing a stream into a land of dreamlike romance, but find that even there they have to grow up, that no world can always be in all ways what we would like. Le Guin's imagined worlds are often utopian in the older tradition that presents a society of ideal possibilities, where humans live in harmony and social and personal fulfillment, but they are also anti-utopian in the more modern tradition that sees the dark underside that frequently destroys human potential. In *The Dispossessed* (1974), a physicist, suggestive in some ways of Oppenheimer, travels between anarchic and capitalistic planets, attempting to end centuries of mistrust but discovering no easy answers. In *Always Coming Home* (1985), a book that seems partly a novel and partly a collection of anthropological materials, she imagines a society that has survived nuclear holocaust with at least some of its computer-age technology intact; the people live, however, in a primitive, tribal way without yet having adopted once again the mechanized ways of the past.

Le Guin's novels, in addition to those named above, include *Very Far from Anywhere Else,* 1976 (for adolescents); and *Malafrena,* 1979. Short fiction is collected in *The Wind's Twelve Quarters,* 1975; *Orsinian Tales,* 1976; and *The Eye of the Heron,* 1980. Volumes of poetry are *Wild Angels,* 1975; and *Hard Words,* 1981. Criticism is collected in *The Language of the Night,* 1979.

Studies include Joe De Bolt, ed., *Ursula K. Le Guin: Voyager to Inner Lands and Outer Spaces,* 1979; Joseph D. Olander and Martin Henry Greenberg, eds., *Ursula K. Le Guin,* 1979; Barbara J. Bucknall, *Ursula K. Le Guin,* 1981; and Charlotte Spivack, *Ursula K. Le Guin,* 1984.

The Ones Who Walk Away from Omelas

With a clamor of bells that set the swallows soaring, the Festival of Summer came to the city Omelas, bright-towered by the sea. The rigging of the boats in harbor sparkled with flags. In the streets between houses with red roofs and painted walls, between old moss-grown gardens and under avenues of trees, past great parks and public buildings, processions moved. Some were decorous: old people in long stiff robes of mauve and grey, grave master workmen, quiet, merry women carrying their babies and chatting as they walked. In other streets the music beat faster, a shimmering of gong and tambourine, and the people went dancing, the procession was a dance. Children dodged in and out, their high calls rising like the swallows' crossing flights over the music and the singing. All the processions wound towards the north side of the city, where on the great water-meadow called the Green Fields boys and girls, naked in the bright air, with mud-stained feet and ankles and long, lithe arms, exercised their restive horses before the race. The horses wore no gear at all but a halter without bit. Their manes were braided with streamers of silver, gold, and green. They flared their nostrils and pranced and boasted to one another; they were vastly excited, the horse being the only animal who has adopted our ceremonies as his own. Far off to the north and west the mountains stood up half encircling Omelas on her bay. The air of morning was so clear that the snow still crowning the Eighteen Peaks burned with white-gold fire across the miles of sunlit air, under the dark blue of the sky. There was just enough wind to make the banners that marked the racecourse snap and flutter now and then. In the silence of the broad green meadows one could hear the music winding through the city streets, farther and nearer and ever approaching, a cheerful faint sweetness of the air that from time to time trembled and gathered together and broke out into the great joyous clanging of the bells.

Joyous! How is one to tell about joy? How describe the citizens of Omelas?

They were not simple folk, you see, though they were happy. But we do not say the words of cheer much any more. All smiles have become archaic. Given a description such as this one tends to make certain assumptions. Given a description such as this one tends to look next for the King, mounted on a splendid stallion and surrounded by his noble knights, or perhaps in a golden litter borne by great-muscled slaves. But there was no king. They did not use swords, or keep slaves. They were not barbarians. I do not know the rules and laws of their society, but I suspect that they were singularly few. As they did without monarchy and slavery, so they also got on without the stock exchange, the advertisement, the secret police, and the bomb. Yet I repeat that these were not simple folk, not dulcet shepherds, noble savages, bland utopians. They were not less complex than us. The trouble is that we have a bad habit, encouraged by pedants and sophisticates, of considering happiness as something rather stupid. Only pain is intellectual, only evil interesting. This is the treason of the artist: a refusal to admit the banality of evil and the terrible boredom of pain. If you can't lick 'em, join 'em. If it hurts, repeat it. But to praise despair is to condemn delight, to embrace violence is to lose hold of everything else. We have almost lost hold; we can no longer describe a happy man, nor make any celebration of joy. How can I tell you about the people of Omelas? They were not naïve and happy children—though their children were, in fact, happy. They were mature, intelligent, passionate adults whose lives were not wretched. O miracle! but I wish I could describe it better. I wish I could convince you. Omelas sounds in my words like a city in a fairy tale, long ago and far away, once upon a time. Perhaps it would be best if you imagined it as your own fancy bids, assuming it will rise to the occasion, for certainly I cannot suit you all. For instance, how about technology? I think that there would be no cars or helicopters in and above the streets; this follows from the fact that the people of Omelas are happy people. Happiness is based on a just discrimination of what is necessary, what is neither necessary nor destructive, and what is destructive. In the middle category, however—that of the unnecessary but undestructive, that of comfort, luxury, exuberance, etc.—they could perfectly well have central heating, subway trains, washing machines, and all kinds of marvelous devices not yet invented here, floating light-sources, fuelless power, a cure for the common cold. Or they could have none of that: it doesn't matter. As you like it. I incline to think that people from towns up and down the coast have been coming in to Omelas during the last days before the Festival on very fast little trains and double-decked trams, and that the train station of Omelas is actually the handsomest building in town, though plainer than the magnificent Farmers' Market. But even granted trains, I fear that Omelas so far strikes some of you as goody-goody. Smiles, bells, parades, horses, bleh. If so, please add an orgy. If an orgy would help, don't hesitate. Let us not, however, have temples from which issue beautiful nude priests and priestesses already half in ecstasy and ready to copulate with any man or woman, lover or stranger, who desires union with the deep godhead of the blood, although that was my first idea. But really it would be better not to have any temples in Omelas—at least, not manned temples. Religion yes, clergy no. Surely the beautiful nudes can just wander about, offering themselves like divine soufflés to the hunger of the needy and the rapture of the flesh. Let them join the processions. Let tambourines be struck above the copulations, and the glory of desire be proclaimed upon the gongs, and (a not unimportant point) let the offspring of these delightful rituals be beloved and looked after by all. One thing I know there is none of in Omelas is guilt. But what else should there be? I thought at first there were no drugs, but that is puritanical. For those who like it, the faint insistent sweetness of *drooz* may perfume the ways of the city, *drooz* which first brings a great lightness and brilliance to the mind and limbs, and then after some hours a dreamy languor, and wonderful visions at last of the very arcana and inmost secrets of the Universe, as well as exciting the pleasure of sex beyond all belief; and it is not habit-forming. For more modest tastes I think there ought to be beer. What else, what else belongs in the joyous city? The sense of victory, surely, the celebration of courage. But as we did without clergy, let us do without soldiers. The joy built upon successful slaughter is not the right kind of joy; it will not do; it is fearful and it is trivial. A boundless and generous contentment, a magnanimous triumph felt not against some outer enemy but in communion with the finest and fairest in the souls of all men everywhere and the splendor of the world's summer: this is what swells the hearts of the people of Omelas, and the victory they celebrate is that of life. I really don't think many of them need to take *drooz*.

Most of the processions have reached the Green Fields by now. A marvelous smell of cooking goes forth from the red and blue tents of the provisioners. The faces of small children are amiably sticky; in the benign grey beard of a man a couple of crumbs of rich pastry are entangled. The youths and girls have mounted their horses and are beginning to group around the starting line of the course. An old woman, small, fat, and laughing, is passing out flowers from a basket, and tall young men wear her flowers in their shining hair. A child of nine or ten sits at the edge of the crowd, alone, playing on a wooden flute. People pause to listen, and they smile, but they do not speak to him, for he never ceases playing and never sees them, his dark eyes wholly rapt in the sweet, thin magic of the tune.

He finishes, and slowly lowers his hands holding the wooden flute.

As if that little private silence were the signal, all at once a trumpet sounds from the pavilion near the starting line: imperious, melancholy, piercing. The horses rear on their slender legs, and some of them neigh in answer. Sober-faced, the young riders stroke the horses' necks and soothe them, whispering, "Quiet, quiet, there my beauty, my hope. . . ." They begin to form in rank along the starting line. The crowds along the racecourse are like a field of grass and flowers in the wind. The Festival of Summer has begun.

Do you believe? Do you accept the festival, the city, the joy? No? Then let me describe one more thing.

In a basement under one of the beautiful public buildings of Omelas, or perhaps in the cellar of one of its spacious private homes, there is a room. It has one locked door, and no window. A little light seeps in dustily between cracks in the boards, secondhand from a cobwebbed window somewhere across the cellar. In one corner of the little room a couple of mops, with stiff, clotted, foul-smelling heads, stand near a rusty bucket. The floor is dirt, a little damp to the touch, as cellar dirt usually is. The room is about three paces long and two wide: a mere broom closet or disused tool room. In the room a child is sitting. It could be a boy or a girl. It looks about six, but actually is nearly ten. It is feeble-minded. Perhaps it was born defective, or perhaps it has become imbecile through fear, malnutrition, and neglect. It picks its nose and occasionally fumbles vaguely with its toes or genitals, as it sits hunched in the corner farthest from the bucket and the two mops. It is afraid of the mops. It finds them horrible. It shuts its eyes, but it knows the mops are still standing there; and the door is locked; and nobody will come. The door is always locked; and nobody ever comes, except that sometimes—the child has no understanding of time or interval—sometimes the door rattles terribly and opens, and a person, or several people, are there. One of them may come in and kick the child to make it stand up. The others never come close, but peer in at it with frightened, disgusted eyes. The food bowl and the water jug are hastily filled, the door is locked, the eyes disappear. The people at the door never say anything, but the child, who has not always lived in the tool room, and can remember sunlight and its mother's voice, sometimes speaks. "I will be good," it says. "Please let me out. I will be good!" They never answer. The child used to scream for help at night, and cry a good deal, but now it only makes a kind of whining, "eh-haa, eh haa," and it speaks less and less often. It is so thin there are no calves to its legs; its belly protrudes; it lives on a half-bowl of corn meal and grease a day. It is naked. Its buttocks and thighs are a mass of festered sores, as it sits in its own excrement continually.

They all know it is there, all the people of Omelas. Some of them have come to see it, others are content merely to know it is there. They all know that it has to be there. Some of them understand why, and some do not, but they all understand that their happiness, the beauty of their city, the tenderness of their friendships, the health of their children, the wisdom of their scholars, the skill of their makers, even the abundance of their harvest and the kindly weathers of their skies, depend wholly on this child's abominable misery.

This is usually explained to children when they are between eight and twelve, whenever they seem capable of understanding; and most of those who come to see the child are young people, though often enough an adult comes, or comes back, to see the child. No matter how well the matter has been explained to them, these young spectators are always shocked and sickened at the sight. They feel disgust, which they had thought themselves superior to. They feel anger, outrage, impotence, despite all the explanations. They would like to do something for the child. But there is nothing they can do. If the child were brought up into the sunlight out of that vile place, if it were cleaned and fed and comforted, that would be a good thing, indeed; but if it were done, in that day and hour all the prosperity and beauty and delight of Omelas would wither and be destroyed. Those are the terms. To exchange all the goodness and grace of every life in Omelas for that single, small improvement: to throw away the happiness of thousands for the chance of the happiness of one: that would be to let guilt within the walls indeed.

The terms are strict and absolute; there may not even be a kind word spoken to the child.

Often the young people go home in tears, or in a tearless rage, when they have seen the child and faced this terrible paradox. They may brood over it for weeks or years. But as time goes on they begin to realize that even if the child could be released, it would not get much good of its freedom: a little vague pleasure of warmth and food, no doubt, but little more. It is too degraded and imbecile to know any real joy. It has been afraid too long ever to be free of fear. Its habits are too uncouth for it to respond to humane treatment. Indeed, after so long it would probably be wretched without walls about it to protect it, and darkness for its eyes, and its own excrement to sit in. Their tears at the bitter injustice dry when they begin to perceive the terrible justice of reality, and to accept it. Yet it is their tears and anger, the trying of their generosity and the acceptance of their helplessness, which are perhaps the true source of the splendor of their lives. Theirs is no vapid, irresponsible happiness. They know that they, like the child, are not free. They know compassion. It is the existence of the child, and their knowledge of its existence, that makes possible the nobility of their architecture, the poignancy of their music, the profundity of their science. It is because of the child that they are so gentle with children. They know that if the wretched one were not there snivelling in the dark, the other one, the flute-player, could make no joyful music as the young riders line up in their beauty for the race in the sunlight of the first morning of summer.

Now do you believe in them? Are they not more credible? But there is one more thing to tell, and this is quite incredible.

At times one of the adolescent girls or boys who go to see the child does not go home to weep or rage, does not, in fact, go home at all. Sometimes also a man or woman much older falls silent for a day or two, and then leaves home. These people go out into the street, and walk down the street alone. They keep walking, and walk straight out of the city of Omelas, through the beautiful gates. They keep walking across the farmlands of Omelas. Each one goes alone, youth or girl, man or woman. Night falls; the traveler must pass down village streets, between the houses with yellow-lit windows, and on out into the darkness of the fields. Each alone, they go west or north, towards the mountains. They go on. They leave Omelas, they walk ahead into the darkness, and they do not come back. The place they go towards is a place even less imaginable to most of us than the city of happiness. I cannot describe it at all. It is possible that it does not exist. But they seem to know where they are going, the ones who walk away from Omelas.

1973, 1975

JOHN BARTH
(1930–)

John Simmons Barth was born in Cambridge, Maryland, attended the Juilliard School of Music in New York, and received his B.A. in 1951 and his M.A. in 1952 from Johns Hopkins University. Briefly a junior instructor in English at Johns Hopkins, he moved in 1953 to Pennsylvania State University and during his twelve years teaching English there published the three novels that earned him his first critical recognition. In 1965 he became professor of English at the State University of New York at Buffalo. He has also held a visiting appointment at Boston University (1972–1973) and has been the recipient of grants from the Rockefeller Foundation and the National Institute of Arts and Letters. Since 1973 he has taught in the creative writing program at Johns Hopkins.

In Barth's first novel, *The Floating Opera* (1956), the narrator reviews his life while contemplating suicide. In his second novel, *The End of the Road* (1958), Barth presents the hero with the multitudinous choices resulting from his involvement in a sexual triangle. In *The Sot-Weed Factor* (1960) he parodies the form and content of an eighteenth-century novel in detailing the life in colonial Maryland of Ebenezer Cook, a poet of whom very little is known. In the immensely complicated *Giles Goat-Boy* (1966) he presents the twentieth-century university as a metaphor for a universe managed with all the irrefutable logic and unpredictability of a computer gone insane. *Letters* (1979), a long and complicated epistolary novel, presents variations on themes and materials of the earlier work.

Enormously inventive, Barth is also continually aware as he writes of the nature of fiction as artifice; his works abound with reminders of their imagined and therefore artificial reality. *Chimera* (1972), with its focus on Scheherazade, Perseus, and Bellerophon, emphasizes his love of myth and allegory and at the same time serves as a reminder that in Barth's eyes it has now become impossible for the novelist to return to the simpler modes of presentation of an earlier age. His comic vision and verbal fecundity, which together push his works at times beyond the edges of farce and tedium, make linear plots and traditionally realistic modes of presentation increasingly irrelevant to him. "I admire writers who can make complicated things simple," he has said, "but my own talent has been to make simple things complicated."

The Floating Opera, 1956, *The End of the Road,* 1958, and *The Sot-Weed Factor,* 1960, were revised in 1967. *Sabbatical: A Romance,* a novel, appeared in 1982. The other novels appeared in the single editions given above. Short stories are collected in *Lost in the Funhouse: Fiction for Print, Tape, Live Voice,* 1968, from which the following selection is taken. Non-fiction is collected in *The Friday Book,* 1984.

Studies include Jac Tharpe, *John Barth: The Comic Sublimity of Paradox,* 1974; David Morrell, *John Barth: An Introduction,* 1976; and Charles B. Harris, *Passionate Virtuosity: The Fiction of John Barth,* 1983.

Lost in the Funhouse

For whom is the funhouse fun? Perhaps for lovers. For Ambrose it is *a place of fear and confusion.* He has come to the seashore with his family for the holiday, *the occasion of their visit is Independence Day, the most important secular holiday of the United States of America.* A single straight underline is the manuscript mark for italic type, *which in turn* is the printed equivalent to oral emphasis of words and phrases as well as the customary type for titles of complete works, not to mention. Italics are also employed, in fiction stories especially, for "outside," intrusive, or artificial voices, such as radio announcements, the texts of telegrams and newspaper articles, et cetera. They should be used *sparingly.* If passages originally in roman type are italicized by someone repeating them, it's customary to acknowledge the fact. *Italics mine.*

Ambrose was "at that awkward age." His voice came out high-pitched as a child's if he let himself get carried away; to be on the safe side, therefore, he moved and spoke with *deliberate calm* and *adult gravity.* Talking soberly of unimportant or irrelevant matters and listening consciously to the sound of your own voice are useful habits for maintaining control in this difficult interval. *En route* to Ocean City he sat in the back seat of the family car with his brother Peter, age fifteen, and Magda

G——, age fourteen, a pretty girl an exquisite young lady, who lived not far from them on B—— Street in the town of D——, Maryland. Initials, blanks, or both were often substituted for proper names in nineteenth-century fiction to enhance the illusion of reality. It is as if the author felt it necessary to delete the names for reasons of tact or legal liability. Interestingly, as with other aspects of realism, it is an *illusion* that is being enhanced, by purely artificial means. Is it likely, does it violate the principle of verisimilitude, that a thirteen-year-old boy could make such a sophisticated observation? A girl of fourteen is *the psychological coeval* of a boy of fifteen or sixteen; a thirteen-year-old boy, therefore, even one precocious in some other respects, might be three years *her emotional junior.*

Thrice a year—on Memorial, Independence, and Labor Days—the family visits Ocean City for the afternoon and evening. When Ambrose and Peter's father was their age, the excursion was made by train, as mentioned in the novel *The 42nd Parallel* by John Dos Passos. Many families from the same neighborhood used to travel together, with dependent relatives and often with Negro servants; schoolfuls of children swarmed through the railway cars; everyone shared everyone else's Maryland fried chicken, Virginia ham, deviled eggs, potato salad, beaten biscuits, iced tea. Nowadays (that is, in 19—, the year of our story) the journey is made by automobile—more comfortably and quickly though without the extra fun though without the *camaraderie* of a general excursion. It's all part of the deterioration of American life, their father declares; Uncle Karl supposes that when the boys take *their* families to Ocean City for the holidays they'll fly in Autogiros. Their mother, sitting in the middle of the front seat like Magda in the second, only with her arms on the seat-back behind the men's shoulders, wouldn't want the good old days back again, the steaming trains and stuffy long dresses; on the other hand she can do without Autogiros, too, if she has to become a grandmother to fly in them.

Description of physical appearance and mannerisms is one of several standard methods of characterization used by writers of fiction. It is also important to "keep the senses operating"; when a detail from one of the five senses, say visual, is "crossed" with a detail from another, say auditory, the reader's imagination is oriented to the scene, perhaps unconsciously. This procedure may be compared to the way surveyors and navigators determine their positions by two or more compass bearings, a process known as triangulation. The brown hair on Ambrose's mother's forearms gleamed in the sun like. Though right-handed, she took her left arm from the seat-back to press the dashboard cigar lighter for Uncle Karl. When the glass bead in its handle glowed red, the lighter was ready for use. The smell of Uncle Karl's cigar smoke reminded one of. The fragrance of the ocean came strong to the picnic ground where they always stopped for lunch, two miles inland from Ocean City. Having to pause for a full hour almost within the sound of the breakers was difficult for Peter and Ambrose when they were younger; even at their present age it was not easy to keep their anticipation, *stimulated by the briny spume,* from turning into short temper. The Irish author James Joyce, in his unusual novel entitled *Ulysses,* now available in this country, uses the adjectives *snot-green* and *scrotum-tightening* to describe the sea. Visual, auditory, tactile, olfactory, gustatory. Peter and Ambrose's father, while steering their black 1936 LaSalle sedan with one hand, could with the other remove the first cigarette from a white pack of Lucky Strikes and, more remarkably, light it with a match forefingered from its book and thumbed against the flint paper without being detached. The matchbook cover merely advertised U.S. War Bonds and Stamps. A fine metaphor, simile, or other figure of speech, in addition to its obvious "first-order" relevance to the thing it describes, will be seen upon reflection to have a second order of significance: it may be drawn from the *milieu* of the action, for example, or be particularly appropriate to the sensibility of the narrator, even hinting to the reader things of which the narrator is unaware; or it may cast further and subtler lights upon the thing it describes, sometimes ironically qualifying the more evident sense of the comparison.

To say that Ambrose's and Peter's mother was *pretty* is to accomplish nothing; the reader may acknowledge the proposition, but his imagination is not engaged. Besides, Magda was also pretty, yet in an altogether different way. Although she lived on B—— Street she had very good manners and did better than average in school. Her figure was very well developed for her age. Her right hand lay casually on the plush upholstery of the seat, very near Ambrose's left leg, on which his own hand rested. The space between their legs, between her right and his left leg, was out of the line of sight of anyone sitting on the other side of Magda, as well as anyone glancing into the rearview mirror. Uncle Karl's face resembled Peter's—rather, vice versa. Both had dark hair and eyes, short husky statures, deep voices. Magda's left hand was probably in a similar position on her left side. The boy's father is difficult to describe; no particular feature of his appearance or manner stood out. He wore glasses and was principal of a T—— County grade school. Uncle Karl was a masonry contractor.

Although Peter must have known as well as Ambrose that the latter, because of his position in the car, would be the first to see the electrical towers of the power plant at V——, the halfway point of their trip, he leaned forward and slightly toward the center of the car and pretended to be looking for them through the flat pinewoods and tuckahoe creeks along the highway. For as long as the boys could remember, "looking for the Towers" had been a feature of the first half of their excursions to Ocean City, "looking for the standpipe" of the second. Though the game was childish, their mother preserved the tradition of rewarding the first to see the Towers with a candybar or piece of fruit. She insisted now that Magda play the game; the prize, she said, was "something hard to get nowadays." Ambrose decided not to join in; he sat far back in his seat. Magda, like Peter, leaned forward. Two sets of straps were discernible through the shoulders of her sun dress; the inside right one, a brassiere-strap, was fastened or shortened with a small safety pin. The right armpit of her dress, presumably the left as well, was damp with perspiration. The simple strategy for being first to espy the Towers, which Ambrose had understood by the age of four, was to sit on the right-hand side of the car. Whoever sat there, however, had also to put up with the worst of the sun, and so Ambrose, without mentioning the matter, chose sometimes the one and sometimes the other. Not impossibly Peter had never caught on to the trick, or thought that his brother hadn't simply because Ambrose on occasion preferred shade to a Baby Ruth or tangerine.

The shade-sun situation didn't apply to the front seat, owing to the windshield; if anything the driver got more sun, since the person on the passenger side not only was shaded below by the door and dashboard but might swing down his sunvisor all the way too.

"Is that them?" Magda asked. Ambrose's mother teased the boys for letting Magda win, insinuating that "somebody [had] a girlfriend." Peter and Ambrose's father reached a long thin arm across their mother to butt his cigarette in the dashboard ashtray, under the lighter. The prize this time for seeing the Towers first was a banana. Their mother bestowed it after chiding their father for wasting a half-smoked cigarette when everything was so scarce. Magda, to take the prize, moved her hand from so near Ambrose's that he could have touched it as though accidentally. She offered to share the prize, things like that were so hard to find; but everyone insisted it was hers alone. Ambrose's mother sang an iambic trimeter couplet from a popular song, femininely rhymed:

> "*What's good is in the Army;*
> *What's left will never harm me.*"

Uncle Karl tapped his cigar ash out the ventilator window; some particles were sucked by the slipstream back into the car through the rear window on the passenger side. Magda demonstrated her ability to hold a banana in one hand and peel it with her teeth. She still sat forward; Ambrose pushed his glasses back onto the bridge of his nose with his left hand, which he then negligently let fall to the seat cushion immediately behind her. He even permitted the single hair, gold, on the second joint of his thumb to brush the fabric of her skirt. Should she have sat back at that instant, his hand would have been caught under her.

Plush upholstery prickles uncomfortably through gabardine slacks in the July sun. The function of the *beginning* of a story is to introduce the principal characters, establish their initial relationships, set the scene for the main action, expose the background of the situation if necessary, plant motifs and foreshadowings where appropriate, and initiate the first complication or whatever of the "rising action." Actually, if one imagines a story called "The Funhouse," or "Lost in the Funhouse," the details of the drive to Ocean City don't seem especially relevant. The *beginning* should recount the events between Ambrose's first sight of the funhouse early in the afternoon and his entering it with Magda and Peter in the evening. The *middle* would narrate all relevant events from the time he goes in to the time he loses his way; middles have the double and contradictory function of delaying the climax while at the same time preparing the reader for it and fetching him to it. Then the *ending* would tell what Ambrose does while he's lost, how he finally finds his way out, and what everybody makes of the experience. So far there's been no real dialogue, very little sensory detail, and nothing in the way of a *theme.* And a long time has gone by already without anything happening; it makes a person wonder. We haven't even reached Ocean City yet: we will never get out of the funhouse.

The more closely an author identifies with the narrator, literally or metaphorically, the less advisable it is, as a rule, to use the first-person narrative viewpoint. Once three years previously the young people *aforementioned* played Niggers and Masters in the backyard; when it was Ambrose's turn to be Master and theirs to be Niggers Peter had to go serve his evening papers; Ambrose was afraid to punish Magda alone, but she led him to the whitewashed Torture Chamber between the woodshed and the privy in the Slaves Quarters; there she knelt sweating among bamboo rakes and dusty Mason jars, pleadingly embraced his knees, and while bees droned in the lattice as if on an ordinary summer afternoon, purchased clemency at a surprising price set by herself. Doubtless she remembered nothing of this event; Ambrose on the other hand seemed unable to forget the least detail of his life. He even recalled how, standing beside himself with awed impersonality in the reeky heat, he'd stared the while at an empty cigar box in which Uncle Karl kept stone-cutting chisels: beneath the words *El Producto,* a laureled, loose-toga'd lady regarded the sea from a marble bench; beside her, forgotten or not yet turned to, was a five-stringed lyre. Her chin reposed on the back of her right hand; her left depended negligently from the bench-arm. The lower half of scene and lady was peeled away; the words EXAMINED BY—— were inked there into the wood. Nowadays cigar boxes are made of pasteboard. Ambrose wondered what Magda would have done, Ambrose wondered what Magda would do when she sat back on his hand as he resolved she should. Be angry. Make a teasing joke of it. Give no sign at all. For a long time she leaned forward, playing cowpoker with Peter against Uncle Karl and Mother and watching for the first sign of Ocean City. At nearly the same instant, picnic ground and Ocean City standpipe hove into view; an Amoco filling station on their side of the road cost Mother and Uncle Karl fifty cows and the game; Magda bounced back, clapping her right hand on Mother's right arm; Ambrose moved clear "in the nick of time."

At this rate our hero, at this rate our protagonist will remain in the funhouse forever. Narrative ordinarily consists of alternating dramatization and summarization. One symptom of nervous tension, paradoxically, is repeated and violent yawning; neither Peter nor Magda nor Uncle Karl nor Mother reacted in this manner. Although they were no longer small children, Peter and Ambrose were each given a dollar to spend on boardwalk amusements in addition to what money of their own they'd brought along. Magda too, though she protested she had ample spending money. The boys' mother made a little scene out of distributing the bills; she pretended that her sons and Magda were small children and cautioned them not to spend the sum too quickly or in one place. Magda promised with a merry laugh and, having both hands free, took the bill with her left. Peter laughed also and pledged in a falsetto to be a good boy. His imitation of a child was not clever. The boys' father was tall and thin, balding, fair-complexioned. Assertions of that sort are not effective; the reader may acknowledge the proposition, but. We should be much farther along than we are; something has gone wrong; not much of this preliminary rambling seems relevant. Yet everyone begins in the same place; how is it that most go along without difficulty but a few lose their way?

"Stay out from under the boardwalk," Uncle Karl growled from the side of his mouth. The boys' mother pushed his shoulder *in mock annoyance.* They were all standing before Fat May the Laughing Lady who advertised the funhouse. Larger than life, Fat May mechanically shook, rocked on her heels, slapped her thighs while recorded laughter—uproarious, female—came amplified from a hidden loudspeaker. It chuckled, wheezed, wept; tried in vain to catch its breath; tittered, groaned, exploded raucous and anew. You couldn't hear it without laughing yourself, no matter how you felt. Father came back from talking to a Coast-Guardsman on duty and reported that the surf was spoiled with crude oil from tankers recently torpedoed offshore. Lumps of it, difficult to remove, made tarry tidelines on the beach and stuck on swimmers. Many bathed in the surf nevertheless and came out speckled; others paid to use a municipal pool and only sunbathed on the beach. We would do the latter. We would do the latter. We would do the latter.

Under the boardwalk, matchbook covers, grainy other things. What is the story's theme? Ambrose is ill. He perspires in the dark passages; candied apples-on-a-stick, delicious-looking, disappointing to eat. Funhouses need men's and ladies' room at intervals. Others perhaps have also vomited in corners and corridors; may even have had bowel movements liable to be stepped in in the dark. The word *fuck* suggests suction and/or and/or flatulence. Mother and Father; grandmothers and grandfathers on both sides; great-grandmothers and great-grandfathers on four sides, et cetera. Count a generation as thirty years: in approximately the year when Lord Baltimore was granted charter to the province of Maryland by Charles I, five hundred twelve women—English, Welsh, Bavarian, Swiss—of every class and character, received into themselves the penises the intromittent organs of five hundred twelve men, ditto, in every circumstance and posture, to conceive the five hundred twelve ancestors of the two hundred fifty-six ancestors of the et cetera et cetera et cetera et cetera et cetera et cetera et cetera et cetera of the author, of the narrator, of this story, *Lost in the Funhouse.* In alleyways, ditches, canopy beds, pinewoods, bridal suites, ship's cabins, coach-and-fours, coaches-and-four, sultry toolsheds; on the cold sand under boardwalks, littered with *El Producto* cigar butts, treasured with Lucky Strike cigarette stubs, Coca-Cola caps, gritty turds, cardboard lollipop sticks, matchbook covers warning that A Slip of the Lip Can Sink a Ship. The shluppish whisper, continuous as seawash round the globe, tidelike falls and rises with the circuit of dawn and dusk.

Magda's teeth. She *was* left-handed. Perspiration. They've gone all the way, through, Magda and Peter, they've been waiting for hours with Mother and Uncle Karl while Father searches for his lost son; they draw french-fried potatoes from a paper cup and shake their heads. They've named the children they'll one day have and bring to Ocean City on holidays. Can spermatozoa properly be thought of as male animalcules when there are no female spermatozoa? They grope through hot, dark windings, past Love's Tunnel's fearsome obstacles. Some perhaps lose their way.

Peter suggested then and there that they do the funhouse; he had been through it before, so had Magda, Ambrose hadn't and suggested, his voice cracking on account of Fat May's laughter, that they swim first. All were chuckling, couldn't help it; Ambrose's father, Ambrose's and Peter's father came up grinning like a lunatic with two boxes of syrup-coated popcorn, one for Mother, one for Magda; the men were to help themselves. Ambrose walked on Magda's right: being by nature left-handed, she carried the box in her left hand. Up front the situation was reversed.

"What are you limping for?" Magda inquired of Ambrose. He supposed in a husky tone that his foot had gone to sleep in the car. Her teeth flashed. "Pins and needles?" It was the honeysuckle on the lattice of the former privy that drew the bees. Imagine being stung there. How long is this going to take?

The adults decided to forgo the pool; but Uncle Karl insisted they change into swimsuits and do the beach. "He wants to watch the pretty girls," Peter teased, and ducked behind Magda from Uncle Karl's pretended wrath. "You've got all the pretty girls you need right here," Magda declared, and Mother said: "Now that's the gospel truth." Magda scolded Peter, who reached over her shoulder to sneak some popcorn. "Your brother and father aren't getting any." Uncle Karl wondered if they were going to have fireworks that night, what with the shortages. It wasn't the shortages, Mr. M—— replied; Ocean City had fireworks from pre-war. But it was too risky on account of the enemy submarines, some people thought.

"Don't seem like Fourth of July without fireworks," said Uncle Karl. The inverted tag in dialogue writing is still considered permissible with proper names or epithets, but sounds old-fashioned with personal pronouns. "We'll have 'em again soon enough," predicted the boys' father. Their mother declared she could do without fireworks: they reminded her too much of the real thing. Their father said all the more reason to shoot off a few now and again. Uncle Karl asked *rhetorically* who needed reminding, just look at people's hair and skin.

"The oil, yes," said Mrs. M——.

Ambrose had a pain in his stomach and so didn't swim but enjoyed watching the others. He and his father burned red easily. Magda's figure was exceedingly well developed for her age. She too declined to swim, and got mad, and became angry when Peter attempted to drag her into the pool. She always swam, he insisted; what did she mean not swim? Why did a person come to Ocean City?

"Maybe I want to lay here with Ambrose," Magda teased.

Nobody likes a pedant.

"Aha," said Mother. Peter grabbed Magda by one ankle and ordered Ambrose to grab the other. She squealed and rolled over on the beach blanket. Ambrose pretended to help hold her back. Her tan was darker than even Mother's and Peter's. "Help out, Uncle Karl!" Peter cried. Uncle Karl went to seize the other ankle. Inside the top of her swimsuit, however, you could see the line where the sunburn ended and, when she hunched her shoulders and squealed again, one nipple's auburn edge. Mother made them behave themselves. "*You* should certainly know," she said to Uncle Karl. Archly. "That when a lady says she doesn't feel like swimming, a gentleman doesn't ask questions." Uncle Karl said excuse *him;* Mother winked at Magda; Ambrose blushed; stupid Peter kept saying "Phooey on *feel like!*" and tugging at Magda's ankle; then even he got the point, and cannonballed with a holler into the pool.

"I swear," Magda said, in mock *in feigned* exasperation.

The diving would make a suitable literary symbol. To go off the high board you had to wait in a line along the poolside and up the ladder. Fellows tickled girls and goosed one another and shouted to the ones at the top to hurry up, or razzed them for bellyfloppers. Once on the springboard some took a great while posing or clowning or deciding on a dive or getting up their nerve; others ran right off. Especially among the younger fellows the idea was to strike the funniest pose or do the craziest stunt as you fell, a thing that got harder to do as you kept on and kept on. But whether you hollered *Geronimo!* or *Sieg heil!*, held your nose or "rode a bicycle," pretended to be shot or did a perfect jackknife or changed your mind halfway down and ended up with nothing, it was over in two seconds, after all that wait. Spring, pose, splash. Spring, neat-o, splash. Spring, aw fooey, splash.

The grown-ups had gone on; Ambrose wanted to converse with Magda; she was remarkably well developed for her age; it was said that that came from rubbing with a turkish towel, and there were other theories. Ambrose could think of nothing to say except how good a diver Peter was, who was showing off for her benefit. You could pretty well tell by looking at their bathing suits and arm muscles how far along the different fellows were. Ambrose was glad he hadn't gone in swimming, the cold water shrank you up so. Magda pretended to be uninterested in the diving; she probably weighed as much as he did. If you knew your way around in the funhouse like your own bedroom, you could wait until a girl came along and then slip away without ever getting caught, even if her boyfriend was right with her. She'd think *he* did it! It would be better to be the boyfriend, and act outraged, and tear the funhouse apart.

Not act; *be.*

"He's a master diver," Ambrose said. In feigned admiration. "You really have to slave away at it to get that good." What would it matter anyhow if he asked her right out whether she remembered, even teased her with it as Peter would have?

There's no point in going farther; this isn't getting anybody anywhere; they haven't even come to the funhouse yet. Ambrose is off the track, in some new or old part of the place that's not supposed to be used; he strayed into it by some one-in-a-million chance, like the time the roller-coaster car left the tracks in the nineteen-teens against all the laws of physics and sailed over the boardwalk in the dark. And they can't locate him because they don't know where to look. Even the designer and operator have forgotten this other part, that winds around on itself like a whelk shell. That winds around the right part like the snakes on Mercury's caduceus. Some people, perhaps, don't "hit their stride" until their twenties, when the growing-up business is over and women appreciate other things besides wisecracks and teasing and strutting. Peter didn't have one-tenth the imagination *he* had, not one-tenth. Peter did this naming-their-children thing as a joke, making up names like Aloysius and Murgatroyd, but Ambrose knew *exactly* how it would feel to be married and have children of your own, and be a loving husband and father, and go comfortably to work in the mornings and to bed with your wife at night, and wake up with her there. With a breeze coming through the sash and birds and mockingbirds singing in the Chinese-cigar trees. His eyes watered, there aren't enough ways to say that. He would be quite famous in his line of work. Whether Magda was his wife or not, one evening when he was wise-lined and gray at the temples he'd smile gravely, at a fashionable dinner party, and remind her of his youthful passion. The time they went with his family to Ocean City; the *erotic fantasies* he used to have about her. How long ago it seemed, and childish! Yet tender, too, *n'est-ce pas?* Would she have imagined that the world-famous whatever remembered how many strings were on the lyre on the bench beside the girl on the label of the cigar box he'd stared at in the toolshed at age ten while she, age eleven. Even then he had felt *wise beyond his years;* he'd stroked her hair and said in his deepest voice and correctest English, as to a dear child: "I shall never forget this moment."

But though he had breathed heavily, groaned as if ecstatic, what he'd really felt throughout was an odd detachment, as though someone else were Master. Strive as he might to be transported, he heard his mind take notes upon the scene: *This is what they call* passion. *I am experiencing it.* Many of the digger machines were out of order in the penny arcades and could not be repaired or replaced for the duration. Moreover the prizes, made now in USA, were less interesting than formerly, pasteboard items for the most part, and some of the machines wouldn't work on white pennies. The gypsy fortune-teller machine might have provided a foreshadowing of the climax of this story if Ambrose had operated it. It was even dilapidateder than most: the silver coating was worn off the brown metal handles, the glass windows around the dummy were cracked and taped, her kerchiefs and silks long-faded. If a man lived by himself, he could take a department-store mannequin with flexible joints and modify her in certain ways. *However:* by the time he was that old he'd have a real woman. There was a machine that stamped your name around a white-metal coin with a star in the middle: A——. His son would be the second, and when the lad reached thirteen or so he would put a strong arm around his shoulder and tell him calmly: "It is perfectly normal. We have all been through it. It will not last forever." Nobody knew how to be what they were right. He'd smoke a pipe, teach his son how to fish and softcrab, assure him he needn't worry about himself. Magda would certainly give, Magda would certainly yield a great deal of milk, although guilty of occasional solecisms. It don't taste so bad. Suppose the lights came on now!

The day wore on. You think you're yourself, but there are other persons in you. Ambrose gets hard when Ambrose doesn't want to, *and obversely.* Ambrose watches them disagree; Ambrose watches him watch. In the funhouse mirror-room you can't see yourself go on forever, because no matter how you stand, your head gets in the way. Even if you had a glass periscope, the image of your eye would cover up the thing you really wanted to see. The police will come; there'll be a story in the papers. That must be where it happened. Unless he can find a surprise exit, an unofficial backdoor or escape hatch opening on an alley, say, and then stroll up to the family in front of the funhouse and ask where everybody's been; *he's* been out of the place for ages. That's just where it happened, in that last lighted room: Peter and Magda found the right exit; he found one that you weren't supposed to find and strayed off into the works somewhere. In a perfect funhouse you'd be able to go only one way, like the divers off the highboard; getting lost would be impossible; the doors and halls would work like minnow traps or the valves in veins.

On account of German U-boats, Ocean City was "browned out": streetlights were shaded on the seaward side; shop-windows and boardwalk amusement places were kept dim, not to silhouette tankers and Liberty-ships for torpedoing. In a short story about Ocean City, Maryland, during World War II, the author could make use of the image of sailors on leave in the penny arcades and shooting galleries, sighting through the crosshairs of toy machine guns at swastika'd subs, while out in the black Atlantic a U-boat skipper squints through his periscope at real ships outlined by the glow of penny arcades. After dinner the family strolled back to the amusement end of the boardwalk. The boys' father had burnt red as always and was masked with Noxzema, a minstrel in reverse. The grownups stood at the end of the boardwalk where the Hurricane of '33 had cut an inlet from the ocean to Assawoman Bay.

"Pronounced with a long *o,*" Uncle Karl reminded Magda with a wink. His short sleeves were rolled up; Mother punched his brown biceps with the arrowed heart on it and said his mind was naughty. Fat May's laugh came suddenly from the funhouse, as if she'd just got the joke; the family laughed too at the coincidence. Ambrose went under the boardwalk to search for out-of-town matchbook covers with the aid of his pocket flashlight; he looked out from the edge of the North American continent and wondered how far their laughter carried over the water. Spies in rubber rafts; survivors in lifeboats. If the joke had been beyond his understanding, he could have said: *"The laughter was over his head."* And let the reader see the serious wordplay on second reading.

He turned the flashlight on and then off at once even before the woman whooped. He sprang away, heart athud, dropping the light. What had the man grunted? Perspiration drenched and chilled him by the time he scrambled up to the family. "See anything?" his father asked. His voice wouldn't come; he shrugged and violently brushed sand from his pants legs.

"Let's ride the old flying horses!" Magda cried. I'll never be an author. It's been forever already, everybody's gone home, Ocean City's deserted, the ghost-crabs are tickling across the beach and down the littered cold streets. And the empty halls of clapboard hotels and abandoned funhouses. A tidal wave; an enemy air raid; a monster-crab swelling like an island from the sea. *The inhabitants fled in terror.* Magda clung to his trouser leg; he alone knew the maze's secret. "He gave his life that we might live," said Uncle Karl with a scowl of pain, as he. The fellow's hands had been tattooed; the woman's legs, the woman's fat white legs had. *An astonishing coincidence.* He yearned to tell Peter. He wanted to throw up for excitement. They hadn't even chased him. He wished he were dead.

One possible ending would be to have Ambrose come across another lost person in the dark. They'd match their wits together against the funhouse, struggle like Ulysses past obstacle after obstacle, help and encourage each other. Or a girl. By the time they found the exit they'd be closest friends, sweethearts if it were a girl; they'd know each other's inmost souls, be bound together *by the cement of shared adventure;* then they'd emerge into the light and it would turn out that his friend was a Negro. A blind girl. President Roosevelt's son. Ambrose's former archenemy.

Shortly after the mirror room he'd groped along a musty corridor, his heart already misgiving him at the absence of phosphorescent arrows and other signs. He'd found a crack of light—not a door, it turned out, but a seam between the plyboard wall panels—and squinting up to it, espied a small old man, *in appearance not unlike* the photographs at home of Ambrose's late grandfather, nodding upon a stool beneath a bare, speckled bulb. A crude panel of toggle- and knife-switches hung beside the open fuse box near his head; elsewhere in the little room were wooden levers and ropes belayed to boat cleats. At the time, Ambrose wasn't lost enough to rap or call; later he couldn't find that crack. Now it seemed to him that he'd possibly dozed off for a few minutes somewhere along the way; certainly he was exhausted from the afternoon's sunshine and the evening's problems; he couldn't be sure he hadn't dreamed part or all of the sight. Had an old black wall fan droned like bees and shimmied two flypaper streamers? Had the funhouse operator—gentle, somewhat sad and tired-appearing, in expression not unlike the photographs at home of Ambrose's late Uncle Konrad—murmured in his sleep? Is there really such a person as Ambrose, or is he a figment of the author's imagination? Was it Assawoman Bay or Sinepuxent? Are there other errors of fact in this fiction? Was there another sound besides the little slap slap of thigh on ham, like water sucking at the chine-boards of a skiff?

When you're lost, the smartest thing to do is stay put till you're found, hollering if necessary. But to holler guarantees humiliation as well as rescue; keeping silent permits some saving of face—you can act surprised at the fuss when your rescuers find you and swear you weren't lost, if they do. What's more you might find your own way yet, *however belatedly.*

"Don't tell me your foot's still asleep!" Magda exclaimed as the three young people walked from the inlet to the area set aside for ferris wheels, carrousels, and other carnival rides, they having decided in favor of the vast and ancient merry-go-round instead of the funhouse. What a sentence, everything was wrong from the outset. People don't know what to make of him, he doesn't know what to make of himself, he's only thirteen, *athletically and socially inept,* not astonishingly bright, but there are antennae; he has . . . some sort of receivers in his head; things speak to him, he understands more than he should, the world winks at him through its objects, grabs grinning at his coat. Everybody else is in on some secret he doesn't know; they've forgotten to tell him. Through simple *procrastination* his mother put off his baptism until this year. Everyone else had it done as a baby; he'd assumed the same of himself, as had his mother, so she claimed, until it was time for him to join Grace Methodist-Protestant and the oversight came out. He was mortified, but pitched sleepless through his private catechizing, intimidated by the ancient mysteries, a thirteen year old would never say that, resolved to experience conversion like St. Augustine. When the water touched his brow and Adam's sin left him, he contrived by a strain like defecation to bring tears into his eyes—but felt nothing. There was some simple, radical difference about him; he hoped it was genius, feared it was madness, devoted himself to amiability and inconspicuousness. Alone on the seawall near his house he was seized by the terrifying transports he'd thought to find in toolshed, in Communion-cup. The grass was alive! The town, the river, himself, were not imaginary; time roared in his ears like wind; the world was *going on!* This part ought to be dramatized. The Irish author James Joyce once wrote. Ambrose M—— is going to scream.

There is no *texture of rendered sensory detail,* for one thing. The faded distorting mirrors beside Fat May; the impossibility of choosing a mount when one had but a single ride on the great carrousel; the *vertigo attendant on his recognition* that Ocean City was worn out, the place of fathers and grandfathers, straw-boatered men and parasoled ladies survived by their amusements. Money spent, the three paused at Peter's insistence beside Fat May to watch the girls get their skirts blown up. The object was to tease Magda, who said: "I swear, Peter M——, you've got a one-track mind! Amby and me aren't *interested* in such things." In the tumbling-barrel, too, just inside the Devil's mouth entrance to the funhouse, the girls were upended and their boyfriends and others could see up their dresses if they cared to. Which was the whole point, Ambrose realized. Of the entire funhouse! If you looked around, you noticed that almost all the people on the boardwalk were paired off into couples except the small children; in a way, that was the whole point of Ocean City! If you had X-ray eyes and could see everything going on at that instant under the boardwalk and in all the hotel rooms and cars and alleyways, you'd realize that all that normally *showed,* like restaurants and dance halls and clothing and test-your-strength machines, was merely preparation and intermission. Fat May screamed.

Because he watched the goings-on from the corner of his eye, it was Ambrose who spied the half-dollar on the boardwalk near the tumbling-barrel. Losers weepers. The first time he'd heard some people moving through a corridor not far away, just after he'd lost sight of the crack of light, he'd decided not to call to them, for fear they'd guess he was scared and poke fun; it sounded like roughnecks; he'd hoped they'd come by and he could follow in the dark without their knowing. Another time he'd heard just one person, unless he imagined it, bumping along as if on the other side of the plywood; perhaps Peter coming back for him, or Father, or Magda lost too. Or the owner and operator of the funhouse. He'd called out once, as though merrily: "Anybody know where the heck we are?" But the query was too stiff, his voice cracked, when the sounds stopped he was terrified: maybe it was a queer who waited for fellows to get lost, or a longhaired filthy monster that lived in some cranny of the funhouse. He stood rigid for hours it seemed like, scarcely respiring. His future was shockingly clear, in outline. He tried holding his breath to the point of unconsciousness. There ought to be a button you could push to end your life absolutely without pain; disappear in a flick, like turning out a light. He would push it instantly! He despised Uncle Karl. But he despised his father too, for not being what he was supposed to be. Perhaps his father hated *his* father, and so on, and his son would hate him, and so on. Instantly!

Naturally he didn't have nerve enough to ask Magda to go through the funhouse with him. With incredible nerve and to everyone's surprise he invited Magda, quietly and politely, to go through the funhouse with him. "I warn you, I've never been through it before," he added, *laughing easily;* "but I reckon we can manage somehow. The important thing to remember, after all, is that it's meant to be a *fun*house; that is, a place of amusement. If people really got lost or injured or too badly frightened in it, the owner'd go out of business. There'd even be lawsuits. No character in a work of fiction can make a speech this long without interruption or acknowledgment from the other characters."

Mother teased Uncle Karl: "Three's a crowd, I always heard." But actually Ambrose was relieved that Peter now had a quarter too. Nothing was what it looked like. Every instant, under the surface of the Atlantic Ocean, millions of living animals devoured one another. Pilots were falling in flames over Europe; women were being forcibly raped in the South Pacific. His father should have taken him aside and said: "There is a simple secret to getting through the funhouse, as simple as being first to see the Towers. Here it is. Peter does not know it; neither does your Uncle Karl. You and I are different. Not surprisingly, you've often wished you weren't. Don't think I haven't noticed how unhappy your childhood has been! But you'll understand, when I tell you, why it had to be kept secret until now. And you won't regret not being like your brother and your uncle. *On the contrary!*" If you knew all the stories behind all the people on the boardwalk, you'd see that *nothing* was what it looked like. Husbands and wives often hated each other; parents didn't necessarily love their children; et cetera. A child took things for granted because he had nothing to compare his life to and everybody acted as if things were as they should be. Therefore each saw himself as the hero of the story, when the truth might turn out to be that he's the villain, or the coward. And there wasn't one thing you could do about it!

Hunchbacks, fat ladies, fools—that no one chose what he was was unbearable. In the movies he'd meet a beautiful young girl in the funhouse; they'd have hairs-breadth escapes from real dangers; he'd do and say the right things; she also; in the end they'd be lovers; their dialogue lines would match up; he'd be perfectly at ease; she'd not only like him well enough, she'd think he was *marvelous;* she'd lie awake thinking about *him,* instead of vice versa—the way *his* face looked in different lights and how he stood and exactly what he'd said—and yet that would be only one small episode in his wonderful life, among many many others. Not a *turning point* at all. What had happened in the toolshed was nothing. He hated, he loathed his parents! One reason for not writing a lost-in-the-funhouse story is that either everybody's felt what Ambrose feels, in which case it goes without saying, or else no normal person feels such things, in which case Ambrose is a freak. "Is anything more tiresome, in fiction, than the problems of sensitive adolescents?" And it's all too long and rambling, as if the author. For all a person knows the first time through, the end could be just around any corner; perhaps, *not impossibly* it's been within reach any number of times. On the other hand he may be scarcely past the start, with everything yet to get through, an intolerable idea.

Fill in: His father's raised eyebrows when he announced his decision to do the funhouse with Magda. Ambrose understands now, but didn't then, that his father was wondering whether he knew what the funhouse was *for*—especially since he didn't object, as he should have, when Peter decided to come along too. The ticket-woman, witchlike, mortifying him when inadvertently he gave her his name-coin instead of the half-dollar, then unkindly calling Magda's attention to the birthmark on his temple: "Watch out for him, girlie, he's a marked man!" She wasn't even cruel, he understood, only vulgar and insensitive. Somewhere in the world there was a young woman with such splendid understanding that she'd see him entire, like a poem or story, and find his words so valuable after all that when he confessed his apprehensions she would explain why they were in fact the very things that made him precious to her . . . and to Western Civilization! There was no such girl, the simple truth being. Violent yawns as they approached the mouth. Whispered advice from an old-timer on a bench near the barrel: "Go crabwise and ye'll get an eyeful without upsetting!" Composure vanished at the first pitch: Peter hollered joyously, Magda tumbled, shrieked, clutched her skirt; Ambrose scrambled crabwise, tight-lipped with terror, was soon out, watched his dropped name-coin slide among the couples. Shame-faced he saw that to get through expeditiously was not the point; Peter feigned assistance in order to trip Magda up, shouted "I see Christmas!" when her legs went flying. The old man, his latest betrayer, cackled approval. A dim hall then of black-thread cobwebs and recorded gibber: he took Magda's elbow to steady her against revolving discs set in the slanted floor to throw your feet out from under, and explained to her in a calm, deep voice his theory that each phase of the funhouse was triggered either automatically, by a series of photo-electric devices, or else manually by operators stationed at peepholes. But he lost his voice thrice as the discs unbalanced him; Magda was anyhow squealing; but at one point she clutched him about the waist to keep from falling, and her right cheek pressed for a moment against his belt-buckle. Heroically he drew her up, it was his chance to clutch her close as if for support and say: "I love you." He even put an arm lightly about the small of her back before a sailor-and-girl pitched into them from behind, sorely treading his left big toe and knocking Magda asprawl with them. The sailor's girl was a string-haired hussy with a loud laugh and light blue drawers; Ambrose realized that he wouldn't have said "I love you" anyhow, and was smitten with self-contempt. How much better it would be to be that common sailor! A wiry little Seaman 3rd, the fellow squeezed a girl to each side and stumbled hilarious into the mirror room, closer to Magda in thirty seconds than Ambrose had got in thirteen years. She giggled at something the fellow said to Peter; she drew her hair from her eyes with a movement so womanly it struck Ambrose's heart; Peter's smacking her backside then seemed particularly coarse. But Magda made a pleased indignant face and cried, "All right for *you,* mister!" and pursued Peter into the maze without a backward glance. The sailor followed after, leisurely, drawing his girl against his hip; Ambrose understood not only that they were all so relieved to be rid of his burdensome company that they didn't even notice his absence, but that he himself shared their relief. Stepping from the treacherous passage at last into the mirror-maze, he saw once again, more clearly than ever, how readily he deceived himself into supposing he was a person. He even foresaw, wincing at his dreadful self-knowledge, that he would repeat the deception, at ever-rarer intervals, all his wretched life, so fearful were the alternatives. Fame, madness, suicide; perhaps all three. It's not believable that so young a boy could articulate that reflection, and in fiction the merely true must always yield to the plausible. Moreover, the symbolism is in places heavy-footed. Yet Ambrose M—— understood, as few adults do, that the famous loneliness of the great was no popular myth but a general truth—furthermore, that it was as much cause as effect.

All the preceding except the last few sentences is exposition that should've been done earlier or interspersed with the present action instead of lumped together. No reader would put up with so much with such *prolixity.* It's interesting that Ambrose's father, though presumably an intelligent man (as indicated by his role as grade-school principal), neither encouraged nor discouraged his sons at all in any way—as if he either didn't care about them or cared all right but didn't know how to act. If this fact should contribute to one of them's becoming a celebrated but wretchedly unhappy scientist, was it a good thing or not? He too might someday face the question; it would be useful to know whether it had tortured his father for years, for example, or never once crossed his mind.

In the maze two important things happened. First, our hero found a name-coin someone else had lost or discarded: AMBROSE, suggestive of the famous lightship and of his late grandfather's favorite dessert, which his mother used to prepare on special occasions out of coconut, oranges, grapes, and what else. Second, as he wondered at the endless replication of his image in the mirrors, second, as he *lost himself in the reflection* that the necessity for an observer makes perfect observation impossible, better make him eighteen at least, yet that would render other things unlikely, he heard Peter and Magda chuckling somewhere together in the maze. "Here!" "No, here!" they shouted to each other; Peter said, "Where's Amby?" Magda murmured. "Amb?" Peter called. In a pleased, friendly voice. He didn't reply. The truth was, his brother was a *happy-go-lucky youngster* who'd've been better off with a regular brother of his own, but who seldom complained of his lot and was generally cordial. Ambrose's throat ached; there aren't enough different ways to say that. He stood quietly while the two young people giggled and thumped through the glittering maze, hurrah'd their discovery of its exit, cried out in joyful alarm at what next beset them. Then he set his mouth and followed after, as he supposed, took a wrong turn, strayed into the pass *wherein he lingers yet.*

The action of conventional dramatic narrative may be represented by a diagram called Freitag's Triangle:[1]

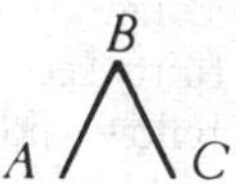

or more accurately by a variant of that diagram:

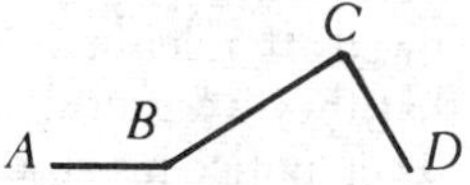

in which *AB* represents the exposition, *B* the introduction of conflict, *BC* the "rising action," complication, or development of the conflict, *C* the climax, or turn of the action, *CD* the dénouement, or resolution of the conflict. While there is no reason to regard this pattern as an absolute necessity, like many other conventions it became conventional because great numbers of people over many years learned

1. After Gustave Freytag (1816–1895), German novelist and critic who analyzed dramatic structure in his *Technique of the Drama.*

by trial and error that it was effective; one ought not to forsake it, therefore, unless one wishes to forsake as well the effect of drama or has clear cause to feel that deliberate violation of the "normal" pattern can better can better effect that effect. This can't go on much longer; it can go on forever. He died telling stories to himself in the dark; years later, when that vast unsuspected area of the funhouse came to light, the first expedition found his skeleton in one of its labyrinthine corridors and mistook it for part of the entertainment. He died of starvation telling himself stories in the dark; but unbeknownst to him, an assistant operator of the funhouse, happening to overhear him, crouched just behind the plyboard partition and wrote down his every word. The operator's daughter, an exquisite young woman with a figure unusually well developed for her age, crouched just behind the partition and transcribed his every word. Though she had never laid eyes on him, she recognized that here was one of Western Culture's truly great imaginations, the eloquence of whose suffering would be an inspiration to unnumbered. And her heart was torn between her love for the misfortunate young man (yes, she loved him, though she had never said though she knew him only—but how well!—through his words, and the deep, calm voice in which he spoke them) between her love et cetera and her womanly intuition that only in suffering and isolation could he give voice et cetera. Lone dark dying. Quietly she kissed the rough plyboard, and a tear fell upon the page. Where she had written in shorthand *Where she had written in shorthand* Where she had written in shorthand *Where she* et cetera. A long time ago we should have passed the apex of Freitag's Triangle and made brief work of the *dénouement;* the plot doesn't rise by meaningful steps but winds upon itself, digresses, retreats, hesitates, sighs, collapses, expires. The climax of the story must be its protagonist's discovery of a way to get through the funhouse. But he has found none, may have ceased to search.

What relevance does the war have to the story? Should there be fireworks outside or not?

Ambrose wandered, languished, dozed. Now and then he fell into his habit of rehearsing to himself the unadventurous story of his life, narrated from the third-person point of view, from his earliest memory parenthesis of maple leaves stirring in the summer breath of tidewater Maryland end of parenthesis to the present moment. Its principal events, on this telling, would appear to have been *A, B, C,* and *D.*

He imagined himself years hence, successful, married, at ease in the world, the trials of his adolescence far behind him. He has come to the seashore with his family for the holiday: how Ocean City has changed! But at one seldom at one ill-frequented end of the boardwalk a few derelict amusements survive from times gone by: the great carrousel from the turn of the century, with its monstrous griffins and mechanical concert band; the roller coaster rumored since 1916 to have been condemned; the mechanical shooting gallery in which only the image of our enemies changed. His own son laughs with Fat May and wants to know what a funhouse is; Ambrose hugs the sturdy lad close and smiles around his pipestem at his wife.

The family's going home. Mother sits between Father and Uncle Karl, who teases him good-naturedly who chuckles over the fact that the comrade with whom he'd fought his way shoulder to shoulder through the funhouse had turned out to be a blind Negro girl—to their mutual discomfort, as they'd opened their souls. But such are the walls of custom, which even. Whose arm is where? How must it feel. He dreams of a funhouse vaster by far than any yet constructed; but by then they may be out of fashion, like steamboats and excursion trains. Already quaint and seedy: the draperied ladies on the frieze of the carrousel are his father's father's moon-cheeked dreams; if he thinks of it more he will vomit his apple-on-a-stick.

He wonders: will he become a regular person? Something has gone wrong; his vaccination didn't take; at the Boy-Scout initiation campfire he only pretended to be deeply moved, as he pretends to this hour that it is not so bad after all in the funhouse, and that he has a little limp. How long will it last? He envisions a truly astonishing funhouse, incredibly complex yet utterly controlled from a great central switchboard like the console of a pipe organ. Nobody had enough imagination. He could design such a place himself, wiring and all, and he's only thirteen years old. He would be its operator: panel lights would show what was up in every cranny of its cunning of its multifarious vastness; a switch-flick would ease this fellow's way, complicate that's, to balance things out; if anyone seemed lost or frightened, all the operator had to do was.

He wishes he had never entered the funhouse. But he has. Then he wishes he were dead. But he's not. Therefore he will construct funhouses for others and be their secret operator—though he would rather be among the lovers for whom funhouses are designed.

1968

DONALD BARTHELME

(1931–)

Donald Barthelme was born in Philadelphia, but raised after age two in Texas, where his father was an architect and later a professor of architecture at the University of Houston. Brought up as a Roman Catholic in an environment in some ways "normal, middle-class," but in other ways bookish and artistic, he read French poets, T. S. Eliot, and James Joyce as a teenager, his tastes shaped in part, he has said, by his father's interest in "artistic modernism." He wrote and edited school publications both in high school and at the University of Houston, which he entered in 1949, and by 1951 he had begun to write also for the *Houston Post.* Drafted in 1953, he served briefly in the army in the last days of the Korean War, before returning to Houston to the *Post* and to work in the public relations office of the University of Houston.

At the university, Barthelme founded and edited a literary magazine, *Forum,* publishing such *avant-garde* writers as Jean-Paul Sartre and Alain Robbe-Grillet. Pursuing a continuing interest in the graphic arts, he served briefly as director of the Contemporary Arts Museum in Houston before moving to New York in 1962 to edit the literary review *Location.* In the following decades, he has been mostly a New York writer, his vision focused on the complexities and confusions of urban life; most of his best work has appeared in *The New Yorker* prior to book publication. He now divides his time between his home in Greenwich Village and the University of Houston, where he teaches writing.

One of the most celebrated of the experimental writers who appeared in America in the 1960's, Barthelme has on at least one occasion suggested that his way of writing has been less a choice than a necessity: "One does not choose to be a 'conventional writer' or 'experimental writer.' One writes as he or she can. It's not a conscious choice." Whatever their sources, the characteristic themes and methods of his fictions were well in place by the time of his first collection, *Come Back, Dr. Caligari* (1964). His is a world of deadpan zaniness, typified in that first volume by "Me and Miss Mandible," where an army veteran, thirty-five years old, sits in a children's classroom: "I am, according to the records, according to the gradebook on her desk, according to the card index in the principal's office, eleven years old. There is a misconception here, one that I haven't quite managed to get cleared up yet." A mordant comedy, sometimes satiric, informs the work and much of the interest stems from the uncanny ability of the shifting narrative voice to mimic the surface concerns of twentieth-century life as witnessed through advertising, popular journalism, television, and movies.

Except for the obvious conclusions that life is absurd, literature a game, and language inadequate to the expression of humankind's deepest thoughts and longings, a reader looks in vain in much of Barthelme's work for evidence of serious concern with history or philosophy, or with contemporary life. Yet he is possessed of a wicked wit and enormous inventiveness, and some of his stories and his most recent novel reach toward the hidden but important truths of dream and myth. *Sixty Stories* (1981) collects many of his best short fictions to that date. In *Snow White* (1967) and *The Dead Father* (1975) he extended the method of his fictions, ordinarily only a few pages long, to book length, with considerable disagreement among critics as to his success. Much more ambitious, however, is *Paradise* (1986). In this comic novel on the life of an aging architect, separated from his wife, who shares his apartment and bed with three unemployed and homeless models, Barthelme touches a number of the nerve ends of contemporary life.

Sixty Stories draws from *Come Back, Dr. Caligari; Unspeakable Practices, Unnatural Acts,* 1968; *City Life,* 1970; *Sadness,* 1972; *Guilty Pleasures,* 1974; *The Dead Father; Amateurs,* 1976; and *Great Days,* 1979; adding nine fictions previously uncollected. *Overnight to Many Distant Cities,* 1983, collects more short fiction. *The Slightly Irregular Fire Engine,* 1971, is a children's book.

Studies include Lois Gordon, *Donald Barthelme,* 1981; Maurice Couturier and Regis Durand, *Donald Barthelme,* 1982; and Charles Molesworth, *Donald Barthelme's Fiction,* 1982.

How I Write My Songs

Some of the methods I use to write my songs will be found in the following examples. Everyone has a song in him or her, Writing songs is a basic human trait. I am not saying that it is easy; like everything else worthwhile in this world it requires concentration and hard work. The methods I will outline are a good way to begin and have worked for me but they are by no means the only methods that can be used. There is no one set way of writing your songs, every way is just as good as the other as Kipling said. (I am talking now about the lyrics; we will talk about the melodies in a little bit.) The important thing is to put true life into your songs, things that people know and can recognize and truly feel. You have to be open to experience, to what is going on around you, the things of daily life. Often little things that you don't even think about at the time can be the basis of a song.

A knowledge of all the different types of songs that are commonly accepted is helpful. To give you an idea of the various types of songs there are I am going to tell you how I wrote various of my own, including "Rudelle," "Last Night," "Sad Dog Blues," and others—how I came to write these songs and where I got the idea and what the circumstances were, more or less, so that you will be able to do the same thing. Just remember, *there is no substitute for sticking to it* and listening to the work of others who have been down this road before you and have mastered their craft over many years.

In the case of "Rudelle" I was sitting at my desk one day with my pencil and yellow legal pad and I had two things that were irritating me. One was a letter from the electric company that said "The check for $75.60 sent us in payment of your bill has been returned to us by the bank unhonored etc. etc." Most of you who have received this type of letter from time to time know how irritating this kind of communication can be as well as embarrassing. The other thing that was irritating me was that I had a piece of white thread tied tight around my middle at navel height as a reminder to keep my stomach pulled in to strengthen the abdominals while sitting—this is the price you pay for slopping down too much beer when your occupation is essentially a sit-down one! Anyhow I had these two things itching me, so I decided to write a lost-my-mind song.

I wrote down on my legal pad the words:

When I lost my baby
I almost lost my mine

This is more or less a traditional opening for this type of song. Maybe it was written by somebody originally way long ago and who wrote it is forgotten. It often helps to begin with a traditional or well-known line or lines to set a pattern for yourself. You can then write the rest of the song and, if you wish, cut off the top part, giving you an original song. *Songs are always composed of both traditional and new elements.* This means that you can rely on the tradition to give your song "legs" while also putting in your own experience or particular way of looking at things for the new.

Incidentally the lines I have quoted may look pretty bare to you but remember you are looking at just one element, the words, and there is also the melody and the special way various artists will have of singing it which gives flavor and freshness. For example, an artist who is primarily a blues singer would probably give the "when" a lot of squeeze, that is to say, draw it out, and he might also sing "baby" as three notes, "bay-ee-bee," although it is only two syllables. Various artists have their own unique ways of doing a song and what may appear to be rather plain or dull on paper becomes quite different when it is a song.

I then wrote:

When I lost my baby
I almost lost my mine
When I lost my baby
I almost lost my mine
When I found my baby
The sun began to shine.

Copyright © 1972 by French Music, Inc.

You will notice I retained the traditional opening because it was so traditional I did not see any need to delete it. With the addition of various material about Rudelle and what kind of woman she was, it became gold in 1976.

Incidentally while we are talking about use of traditional materials here is a little tip: you can often make good use of colorful expressions in common use such as "If the good Lord's willin' and the creek don't rise" (to give you just one example) which I used in "Goin' to Get Together" as follows:

Goin' to get to-geth-er
Goin' to get to-geth-er
If the good Lord's willin' and the creek don't rise.

These common expressions are expressive of the pungent ways in which most people often think—they are the salt of your song, so to say. Try it!

It is also possible to give a song a funny or humorous "twist":

Show'd my soul to the woman at
the bank
She said put that thing away boy,
put that thing away
Show'd my soul to the woman at
the liquor store
She said put that thing away boy,
'fore it turns the wine
Show'd my soul to the woman at
the 7-Eleven
She said: Is that all?

You will notice that the meter here is various and the artist is given great liberties.

Another type of song which is a dear favorite of almost everyone is the song that has a message, some kind of thought that people can carry away with them and think about. Many songs of this type are written and gain great acceptance every day. Here is one of my own that I put to a melody which has a kind of martial flavor:

How do you spell truth? L-o-v-e is
how you spell truth
How do you spell love? T-r-u-t-h
is how you spell love
Where were you last night?
Where were you last night?

When "Last Night" was first recorded, the engineer said "That's a keeper" on the first take and it was subsequently covered by sixteen artists including Walls.

The I-ain't-nothin'-but-a-man song is a good one to write when you are having a dry spell. These occur in songwriting as in any other profession and if you are in one it is often helpful to try your hand at this type of song which is particularly good with a heavy rhythm emphasis in the following pattern

Da da da da *da*
Whomp, whomp

where some of your instruments are playing da da da da *da,* hitting that last note hard, and the others answer whomp, whomp. Here is one of my own:

I'm just an ordinary mane
Da da da da *da*
Whomp, whomp
Just an ordinary mane
Da da da da *da*
Whomp, whomp
Ain't nothin' but a mane
Da da da da *da*
Whomp, whomp
I'm a grizzly mane
Da da da da *da*
Whomp, whomp
I'm a hello-goodbye mane
Da da da da *da*
Whomp, whomp
I'm a ramblin'-gamblin' mane
Da da da da *da*
Whomp, whomp
I'm a *mane's* mane
Da da da da *da*
Whomp, whomp
I'm a woeman's mane
Da da da da *da*
Whomp, whomp
I'm an upstairs-downstairs mane
Da da da da *da*
Whomp, whomp
I'm a today-and-tomorrow mane
Da da da da *da*
Whomp, whomp
I'm a Freeway mane
Da da da da *da*
Whomp, whomp

Well, you see how it is done. It is my hope that these few words will get you started. Remember that although this business may seem closed and standoffish to you, looking at it from the outside, inside it has some very warm people in it, some of the finest people I have run into in the course of a varied life. The main thing is to persevere and to believe in yourself, no matter what the attitude of others may be or appear to be. I could never have written my songs had I failed to believe in Bill B. White, not as a matter of conceit or false pride but as a human being. I will continue to write my songs, for the nation as a whole and for the world.

1981

E. L. DOCTOROW

(1931–)

Born into a Bronx Jewish family and educated in the public schools, E. L. Doctorow attended Kenyon College, where he studied literature with John Crowe Ransom and made friends with James Wright. After graduating from Kenyon in 1952, he studied drama at Columbia. A stint in the army followed and then a variety of jobs before he became a publishing executive at Dial Press. More recently, he has taught creative writing at various universities.

Doctorow has grounded his novels in moments of American history. In his first novel, *Welcome to Hard Times* (1960), he makes use of the traditional themes of civilization versus wilderness and man against nature, presenting them with a political emphasis and in a "false document" form. The book purports to be the journal of the mayor of a dying western town, a believer in the optimism of westward expansion who soon realizes that history is a closed and repeated cycle, not a rising road. In *The Book of Daniel* (1971), he treats the Rosenberg espionage case using fractured time to dramatize the alienation and dislocation of the central figure, Daniel, the surviving son of the executed couple. *Ragtime* (1975) presents American life at the turn of the twentieth century, contrasting the conventional view of the period as one of peace, progress, and innocence with a vision of the social and economic conflicts below the placid surface. Fictional characters like Coalhouse Walker share pages with real people like J. P. Morgan. Imagined events such as Freud and Jung riding through the Tunnel of Love at Coney Island communicate Doctorow's interpretation of the period's intellectual currents. *Loon Lake* (1980) is set during the Depression at a tycoon's hidden mountain estate. In an ironic twist of the Horatio Alger story, the impoverished hero, Joe Korzeniowski of Paterson, New Jersey, becomes Joseph Patterson Bennett, the rich man's adopted son and heir to Loon Lake, but succumbs to the corruption of wealth. In *World's Fair* (1985), seemingly autobiographical, the main character, Edgar, growing up in the Bronx, hears the adults fighting among themselves and musing about Europe's future under Hitler, sees the zeppelin *Hindenburg* as it passes over Manhattan on its way to destruction in New Jersey, and visits the utopian exhibits of the World's Fair of 1939 from which, ironically, visitors exit wearing buttons that say "I HAVE SEEN THE FUTURE."

Lives of the Poets (1984) is in a different form, consisting of six short stories and a novella, all focused on inner tensions between the past and present or memory and reality. The novella has as its main character a novelist whose life is similar in surface detail to Doctorow's life. A major theme is the decline of serious purpose in current literature and the isolation of modern writers from life.

Each book has a different narrative perspective and structure. *The Book of Daniel,* moving freely between the novel's present time during the 1960 student protests and the spy trial in the 1950's, dramatizes the continued tension between the radicals of the two periods. *Ragtime,* adapting cinematic techniques, focuses on different groups of characters to chronicle the transformation of America from small-town ethnic uniformity to urban heterogeneity. *Loon Lake,* with its continual shifts of time and narrative stance, requires active reader participation. The authorial distance of *Lives of the Poets* demands that the reader interpret the connections between its parts.

Doctorow's works, in addition to those named above, include *Big As Life,* 1964, a novel; and *Drinks before Dinner,* 1978, a play. Studies include Richard Tanner, ed., *E. L. Doctorow: Essays and Conversations,* 1983; and Paul Levine, *E. L. Doctorow,* 1985.

The Writer in the Family

In 1955 my father died with his ancient mother still alive in a nursing home. The old lady was ninety and hadn't even known he was ill. Thinking the shock might kill her, my aunts told her that he had moved to Arizona for his bronchitis. To the immigrant generation of my grandmother, Arizona was the American equivalent of the Alps, it was where you went for your health. More accurately, it was where you went if you had the money. Since my father had failed in all the business enterprises of his life, this was the aspect of the news my grandmother dwelled on, that he had finally had some success. And so it came about that as we mourned him at home in our stocking feet, my grandmother was bragging to her cronies about her son's new life in the dry air of the desert.

My aunts had decided on their course of action without consulting us. It meant neither my mother nor my brother nor I could visit Grandma because we were supposed to have moved west too, a family, after all. My brother Harold and I didn't mind—it was always a nightmare at the old people's home, where they all sat around staring at us while we tried to make conversation with Grandma. She looked terrible, had numbers of ailments, and her mind wandered. Not seeing her was no disappointment either for my mother, who had never gotten along with the old woman and did not visit when she could have. But what was disturbing was that my aunts had acted in the manner of that side of the family of making government on everyone's behalf, the true citizens by blood and the lesser citizens by marriage. It was exactly this attitude that had tormented my mother all her married life. She claimed Jack's family had never accepted her. She had battled them for twenty-five years as an outsider.

A few weeks after the end of our ritual mourning my Aunt Frances phoned us from her home in Larchmont. Aunt Frances was the wealthier of my father's sisters. Her husband was a lawyer, and both her sons were at Amherst. She had called to say that Grandma was asking why she didn't hear from Jack. I had answered the phone. "You're the writer in the family," my aunt said. "Your father had so much faith in you. Would you mind making up something? Send it to me and I'll read it to her. She won't know the difference."

That evening, at the kitchen table, I pushed my homework aside and composed a letter. I tried to imagine my father's response to his new life. He had never been west. He had never traveled anywhere. In his generation the great journey was from the working class to the professional class. He hadn't managed that either. But he loved New York, where he had been born and lived his life, and he was always discovering new things about it. He especially loved the old parts of the city below Canal Street, where he would find ships' chandlers or firms that wholesaled in spices and teas. He was a salesman for an appliance jobber with accounts all over the city. He liked to bring home rare cheeses or exotic foreign vegetables that were sold only in certain neighborhoods. Once he brought home a barometer, another time an antique ship's telescope in a wooden case with a brass snap.

"Dear Mama," I wrote. "Arizona is beautiful. The sun shines all day and the air is warm and I feel better than I have in years. The desert is not as barren as you would expect, but filled with wildflowers and cactus plants and peculiar crooked trees that look like men holding their arms out. You can see great distances in whatever direction you turn and to the west is a range of mountains maybe fifty miles from here, but in the morning with the sun on them you can see the snow on their crests."

My aunt called some days later and told me it was when she read this letter aloud to the old lady that the full effect of Jack's death came over her. She had to excuse herself and went out in the parking lot to cry. "I wept so," she said. "I felt such terrible longing for him. You're so right, he loved to go places, he loved life, he loved everything."

We began trying to organize our lives. My father had borrowed money against his insurance and there was very little left. Some commissions were still due but it didn't look as if his firm would honor them. There was a couple of thousand dollars in a savings bank that had to be maintained there until the estate was settled. The lawyer involved was Aunt Frances' husband and he was very proper. "The estate!" my mother muttered, gesturing as if to pull out her hair. "The estate!" She applied for a job part-time in the admissions office of the hospital where my father's terminal illness had been diagnosed, and where he had spent some months until they had sent him home to die. She knew a lot of the doctors and staff and she had learned "from bitter experience," as she told them, about the hospital routine. She was hired.

I hated that hospital, it was dark and grim and full of tortured people. I thought it was masochistic of my mother to seek out a job there, but did not tell her so.

We lived in an apartment on the corner of 175th Street and the Grand Concourse, one flight up. Three rooms. I shared the bedroom with my brother. It was jammed with furniture because when my father had required a hospital bed in the last weeks of his illness we had moved some of the living-room pieces into the bedroom and made over the living room for him. We had to navigate bookcases, beds, a gateleg table, bureaus, a record player and radio console, stacks of 78 albums, my brother's trombone and music stand, and so on. My mother continued to sleep on the convertible sofa in the living room that had been their bed before his illness. The two rooms were connected by a narrow hall made even narrower by bookcases along the wall. Off the hall were a small kitchen and dinette and a bathroom. There were lots of appliances in the kitchen—broiler, toaster, pressure cooker, counter-top dishwasher, blender—that my father had gotten through his job, at cost. A treasured phrase in our house: *at cost.* But most of these fixtures went unused because my mother did not care for them. Chromium devices with timers or gauges that required the reading of elaborate instructions were not for her. They were in part responsible for the awful clutter of our lives and now she wanted to get rid of them. "We're being buried," she said. "Who needs them!"

So we agreed to throw out or sell anything inessential. While I found boxes for the appliances and my brother tied the boxes with twine, my mother opened my father's closet and took out his clothes. He had several suits because as a salesman he needed to look his best. My mother wanted us to try on his suits to see which of them could be altered and used. My brother refused to try them on. I tried on one jacket which was too large for me. The lining inside the sleeves chilled my arms and the vaguest scent of my father's being came to me.

"This is way too big," I said.

"Don't worry," my mother said. "I had it cleaned. Would I let you wear it if I hadn't?"

It was the evening, the end of winter, and snow was coming down on the windowsill and melting as it settled. The ceiling bulb glared on a pile of my father's suits and trousers on hangers flung across the bed in the shape of a dead man. We refused to try on anything more, and my mother began to cry.

"What are you crying for?" my brother shouted. "You wanted to get rid of things, didn't you?"

A few weeks later my aunt phoned again and said she thought it would be necessary to have another letter from Jack. Grandma had fallen out of her chair and bruised herself and was very depressed.

"How long does this go on?" my mother said.

"It's not so terrible," my aunt said, "for the little time left to make things easier for her."

My mother slammed down the phone. "He can't even die when he wants to!" she cried. "Even death comes second to Mama! What are they afraid of, the shock will kill her? Nothing can kill her. She's indestructible! A stake through the heart couldn't kill her!"

When I sat down in the kitchen to write the letter I found it more difficult than the first one. "Don't watch me," I said to my brother. "It's hard enough."

"You don't have to do something just because someone wants you to," Harold said. He was two years older than me and had started at City College; but when my father became ill he had switched to night school and gotten a job in a record store.

"Dear Mama," I wrote. "I hope you're feeling well. We're all fit as a fiddle. The life here is good and the people are very friendly and informal. Nobody wears suits and ties here. Just a pair of slacks and a short-sleeved shirt. Perhaps a sweater in the evening. I have bought into a very successful radio and record business and I'm doing very well. You remember Jack's Electric, my old place on Forty-third Street? Well, now it's Jack's Arizona Electric and we have a line of television sets as well."

I sent that letter off to my Aunt Frances, and as we all knew she would, she phoned soon after. My brother held his hand over the mouthpiece. "It's Frances with her latest review," he said.

"Jonathan? You're a very talented young man. I just wanted to tell you what a blessing your letter was. Her whole face lit up when I read the part about Jack's store. That would be an excellent way to continue."

"Well, I hope I don't have to do this anymore, Aunt Frances. It's not very honest."

Her tone changed. "Is your mother there? Let me talk to her."

"She's not here," I said.

"Tell her not to worry," my aunt said. "A poor old lady who has never wished anything but the best for her will soon die."

I did not repeat this to my mother, for whom it would have been one more in the family anthology of unforgivable remarks. But then I had to suffer it myself for the possible truth it might embody. Each side defended its position with rhetoric, but I, who wanted peace, rationalized the snubs and rebuffs each inflicted on the other, taking no stands, like my father himself.

Years ago his life had fallen into a pattern of business failures and missed opportunities. The great debate between his family on the one side, and my mother Ruth on the other, was this: who was responsible for the fact that he had not lived up to anyone's expectations?

As to the prophecies, when spring came my mother's prevailed. Grandma was still alive.

One balmy Sunday my mother and brother and I took the bus to the Beth El cemetery in New Jersey to visit my father's grave. It was situated on a slight rise. We stood looking over rolling fields embedded with monuments. Here and there processions of black cars wound their way through the lanes, or clusters of people stood at open graves. My father's grave was planted with tiny shoots of evergreen but it lacked a headstone. We had chosen one and paid for it and then the stonecutters had gone on strike. Without a headstone my father did not seem to be honorably dead. He didn't seem to me properly buried.

My mother gazed at the plot beside his, reserved for her coffin. "They were always too fine for other people," she said. "Even in the old days on Stanton Street. They put on airs. Nobody was ever good enough for them. Finally Jack himself was not good enough for them. Except to get them things wholesale. Then he was good enough for them."

"Mom, please," my brother said.

"If I had known. Before I ever met him he was tied to his mama's apron strings. And Essie's apron strings were like chains, let me tell you. We had to live where we could be near them for the Sunday visits. Every Sunday, that was my life, a visit to mamaleh. Whatever she knew I wanted, a better apartment, a stick of furniture, a summer camp for the boys, she spoke against it. You know your father, every decision had to be considered and reconsidered. And nothing changed. Nothing ever changed."

She began to cry. We sat her down on a nearby bench. My brother walked off and read the names on stones. I looked at my mother, who was crying, and I went off after my brother.

"Mom's still crying," I said. "Shouldn't we do something?"

"It's all right," he said. "It's what she came here for."

"Yes," I said, and then a sob escaped from my throat. "But I feel like crying too."

My brother Harold put his arm around me. "Look at this old black stone here," he said. "The way it's carved. You can see the changing fashion in monuments—just like everything else."

Somewhere in this time I began dreaming of my father. Not the robust father of my childhood, the handsome man with healthy pink skin and brown eyes and a mustache and the thinning hair parted in the middle. My dead father. We were taking him home from the hospital. It was understood that he had come back from death. This was amazing and joyous. On the other hand, he was terribly mysteriously damaged, or, more accurately, spoiled and unclean. He was very yellowed and debilitated by his death, and there were no guarantees that he wouldn't soon die again. He seemed aware of this and his entire personality was changed. He was angry and impatient with all of us. We were trying to help him in some way, struggling to get him home, but something prevented us, something we had to fix, a tattered suitcase that had sprung open, some mechanical thing: he had a car but it wouldn't start; or the car was made of wood; or his clothes, which had become too large for him, had caught in the door. In one version he was all bandaged and as we tried to lift him from his wheelchair into a taxi the bandage began to unroll and catch in the spokes of the wheelchair. This seemed to be some unreasonableness on his part. My mother looked on sadly and tried to get him to cooperate.

That was the dream. I shared it with no one. Once when I woke, crying out, my brother turned on the light. He wanted to know what I'd been dreaming but I pretended I didn't remember. The dream made me feel guilty. I felt guilty *in* the dream too because my enraged father knew we didn't want to live with him. The dream represented us taking him home, or trying to, but it was nevertheless understood by all of us that he was to live alone. He was this derelict back from death, but what we were doing was taking him to some place where he would live by himself without help from anyone until he died again.

At one point I became so fearful of this dream that I tried not to go to sleep. I tried to think of good things about my father and to remember him before his illness. He used to call me "matey." "Hello, matey," he would say when he came home from work. He always wanted us to go someplace—to the store, to the park, to a ball game. He loved to walk. When I went walking with him he would say: "Hold your shoulders back, don't slump. Hold your head up and look at the world. Walk as if you meant it!" As he strode down the street his shoulders moved from side to side, as if he was hearing some kind of cakewalk. He moved with a bounce. He was always eager to see what was around the corner.

The next request for a letter coincided with a special occasion in the house: My brother Harold had met a girl he liked and had gone out with her several times. Now she was coming to our house for dinner.

We had prepared for this for days, cleaning everything in sight, giving the house a going-over, washing the dust of disuse from the glasses and good dishes. My mother came home early from work to get the dinner going. We opened the gateleg table in the living room and brought in the kitchen chairs. My mother spread the table with a laundered white cloth and put out her silver. It was the first family occasion since my father's illness.

I liked my brother's girlfriend a lot. She was a thin girl with very straight hair and she had a terrific smile. Her presence seemed to excite the air. It was amazing to have a living breathing girl in our house. She looked around and what she said was: "Oh, I've never seen so many books!" While she and my brother sat at the table my mother was in the kitchen putting the food into serving bowls and I was going from the kitchen to the living room, kidding around like a waiter, with a white cloth over my arm and a high style of service, placing the serving dish of green beans on the table with a flourish. In the kitchen my mother's eyes were sparkling. She looked at me and nodded and mimed the words: "She's adorable!"

My brother suffered himself to be waited on. He was wary of what we might say. He kept glancing at the girl—her name was Susan—to see if we met with her approval. She worked in an insurance office and was taking courses in accounting at City College. Harold was under a terrible strain but he was excited and happy too. He had bought a bottle of Concord-grape wine to go with the roast chicken. He held up his glass and proposed a toast. My mother said: "To good health and happiness," and we all drank, even I. At that moment the phone rang and I went into the bedroom to get it.

"Jonathan? This is your Aunt Frances. How is everyone?"

"Fine, thank you."

"I want to ask one last favor of you. I need a letter from Jack. Your grandma's very ill. Do you think you can?"

"Who is it?" my mother called from the living room.

"OK, Aunt Frances," I said quickly. "I have to go now, we're eating dinner." And I hung up the phone.

"It was my friend Louie," I said, sitting back down. "He didn't know the math pages to review."

The dinner was very fine. Harold and Susan washed the dishes and by the time they were done my mother and I had folded up the gateleg table and put it back against the wall and I had swept the crumbs up with the carpet sweeper. We all sat and talked and listened to records for a while and then my brother took Susan home. The evening had gone very well.

Once when my mother wasn't home my brother had pointed out something: the letters from Jack weren't really necessary. "What is this ritual?" he said, holding his palms up. "Grandma is almost totally blind, she's half deaf and crippled. Does the situation really call for a literary composition? Does it need verisimilitude? Would the old lady know the difference if she was read the phone book?"

"Then why did Aunt Frances ask me?"

"That is the question, Jonathan. Why did she? After all, she could write the letter herself—what difference would it make? And if not Frances, why not Frances' sons, the Amherst students? They should have learned by now to write."

"But they're not Jack's sons," I said.

"That's exactly the point," my brother said. "The idea is *service.* Dad used to bust his balls getting them things wholesale, getting them deals on things. Frances of Westchester really needed things at cost. And Aunt Molly. And Aunt Molly's husband, and Aunt Molly's ex-husband. Grandma, if she needed an errand done. He was always on the hook for something. They never thought his time was important. They never thought every favor he got was one he had to pay back. Appliances, records, watches, china, opera tickets, any goddamn thing. Call Jack."

"It was a matter of pride to him to be able to do things for them," I said. "To have connections."

"Yeah, I wonder why," my brother said. He looked out the window.

Then suddenly it dawned on me that I was being implicated.

"You should use your head more," my brother said.

Yet I had agreed once again to write a letter from the desert and so I did. I mailed it off to Aunt Frances. A few days later, when I came home from school, I thought I saw her sitting in her car in front of our house. She drove a black Buick Roadmaster, a very large clean car with whitewall tires. It was Aunt Frances all right. She blew the horn when she saw me. I went over and leaned in at the window.

"Hello, Jonathan," she said. "I haven't long. Can you get in the car?"

"Mom's not home," I said. "She's working."

"I know that. I came to talk to you."

"Would you like to come upstairs?"

"I can't, I have to get back to Larchmont. Can you get in for a moment, please?"

I got in the car. My Aunt Frances was a very pretty white-haired woman, very elegant, and she wore tasteful clothes. I had always liked her and from the time I was a child she had enjoyed pointing out to everyone that I looked more like her son than Jack's. She wore white gloves and held the steering wheel and looked straight ahead as she talked, as if the car was in traffic and not sitting at the curb.

"Jonathan," she said, "there is your letter on the seat. Needless to say I didn't read it to Grandma. I'm giving it back to you and I won't ever say a word to anyone. This is just between us. I never expected cruelty from you. I never thought you were capable of doing something so deliberately cruel and perverse."

I said nothing.

"Your mother has very bitter feelings and now I see she has poisoned you with them. She has always resented the family. She is a very strong-willed, selfish person."

"No she isn't," I said.

"I wouldn't expect you to agree. She drove poor Jack crazy with her demands. She always had the highest aspirations and he could never fulfill them to her satisfaction. When he still had his store he kept your mother's brother, who drank, on salary. After the war when he began to make a little money he had to buy Ruth a mink jacket because she was so desperate to have one. He had debts to pay but she wanted a mink. He was a very special person, my brother, he should have accomplished something special, but he loved your mother and devoted his life to her. And all she ever thought about was keeping up with the Joneses."

I watched the traffic going up the Grand Concourse. A bunch of kids were waiting at the bus stop at the corner. They had put their books on the ground and were horsing around.

"I'm sorry I have to descend to this," Aunt Frances said. "I don't like talking about people this way. If I have nothing good to say about someone, I'd rather not say anything. How is Harold?"

"Fine."

"Did he help you write this marvelous letter?"

"No."

After a moment she said more softly: "How are you all getting along?"

"Fine."

"I would invite you up for Passover if I thought your mother would accept."

I didn't answer.

She turned on the engine. "I'll say good-bye now, Jonathan. Take your letter. I hope you give some time to thinking about what you've done."

That evening when my mother came home from work I saw that she wasn't as pretty as my Aunt Frances. I usually thought my mother was a good-looking woman, but I saw now that she was too heavy and that her hair was undistinguished.

"Why are you looking at me?" she said.

"I'm not."

"I learned something interesting today," my mother said. "We may be eligible for a V.A. pension because of the time your father spent in the Navy."

That took me by surprise. Nobody had ever told me my father was in the Navy.

"In World War I," she said, "he went to Webb's Naval Academy on the Harlem River. He was training to be an ensign. But the war ended and he never got his commission."

After dinner the three of us went through the closets looking for my father's papers, hoping to find some proof that could be filed with the Veterans Administration. We came up with two things, a Victory medal, which my brother said everyone got for being in the service during the Great War, and an astounding sepia photograph of my father and his shipmates on the deck of a ship. They were dressed in bell-bottoms and T-shirts and armed with mops and pails, brooms and brushes.

"I never knew this," I found myself saying. "I never knew this."

"You just don't remember," my brother said.

I was able to pick out my father. He stood at the end of the row, a thin, handsome boy with a full head of hair, a mustache, and an intelligent smiling countenance.

"He had a joke," my mother said. "They called their training ship the S.S. *Constipation* because it never moved."

Neither the picture nor the medal was proof of anything, but my brother thought a duplicate of my father's service record had to be in Washington somewhere and that it was just a matter of learning how to go about finding it.

"The pension wouldn't amount to much," my mother said. "Twenty or thirty dollars. But it would certainly help."

I took the picture of my father and his shipmates and propped it against the lamp at my bedside. I looked into his youthful face and tried to relate it to the Father I knew. I looked at the picture a long time. Only gradually did my eye connect it to the set of Great Sea Novels in the bottom shelf of the bookcase a few feet away. My father had given that set to me: it was uniformly bound in green with gilt lettering and it included works by Melville, Conrad, Victor Hugo and Captain Marryat. And lying across the top of the books, jammed in under the sagging shelf above, was his old ship's telescope in its wooden case with the brass snap.

I thought how stupid, and imperceptive, and self-centered I had been never to have understood while he was alive what my father's dream for his life had been.

On the other hand, I had written in my last letter from Arizona—the one that had so angered Aunt Frances—something that might allow me, the writer in the family, to soften my judgment of myself. I will conclude by giving the letter here in its entirety.

Dear Mama,

This will be my final letter to you since I have been told by the doctors that I am dying.

I have sold my store at a very fine profit and am sending Frances a check for five thousand dollars to be deposited in your account. My present to you, Mamaleh. Let Frances show you the passbook.

As for the nature of my ailment, the doctors haven't told me what it is, but I know that I am simply dying of the wrong life. I should never have come to the desert. It wasn't the place for me.

I have asked Ruth and the boys to have my body cremated and the ashes scattered in the ocean.

Your loving son,
Jack

1984

TONI MORRISON
(1931–)

Toni Morrison was born Chloe Anthony Wofford in Lorain, Ohio, outside of Cleveland, the town where she also grew up. After graduating from high school, she attended Howard University, earning her B.A. in 1953. Two years later, with an M.A. in English from Cornell University, she began a teaching career that took her to Texas Southern University from 1955 through 1957 and then back to Howard from 1957 to 1964. During these years at Howard, she married Harold Morrison (they were later divorced) and began to write fiction seriously. Accepting an editorial position with Random House, she abandoned teaching as a full-time career and was soon a senior editor in New York. After her novels began to appear, she continued her editorial work, but found time also for part-time lecturing at Yale and at Bard College. She now teaches in the creative writing program at the State University of New York, Albany.

Among her novels to date, *Song of Solomon* (1977) has received the most praise and the widest readership. A complex narrative, rich in myth and symbol, it follows with Faulknerian intensity a northern man's search for the southern sources of his identity, his most significant clue a folksong about a black man who could fly. *The Bluest Eye* (1970) and *Sula* (1973), much shorter, are also mythically and symbolically suggestive, with women as the central characters. Together, these three books explore a world mostly rural and black, centered in a northern town much like Lorain, a kind of later Winesburg, Ohio, full of grotesques. Loneliness and pain are everywhere, and sudden, inexplicable violence, but endurance and great love are also present, expressed in remarkable ways. In *Tar Baby* (1981) Morrison examines a more sophisticated society, bringing blacks and whites together in Paris, on a Caribbean island, and in New York as she continues to develop her considerable talent.

Morrison's books to date are named above. Brief appraisals appear in *Dictionary of Literary Biography, Volume 6: American Novelists Since World War II, Second Series,* 1980; *Dictionary of Literary Biography, Yearbook: 1981,* 1982; and James Vinson, ed., *Contemporary Novelists,* 4th ed., 1986.

From Sula

1922

It was too cool for ice cream. A hill wind was blowing dust and empty Camels wrappers about their ankles. It pushed their dresses into the creases of their behinds, then lifted the hems to peek at their cotton underwear. They were on their way to Edna Finch's Mellow House, an ice-cream parlor catering to nice folks—where even children would feel comfortable, you know, even though it was right next to Reba's Grill and just one block down from the Time and a Half Pool Hall. It sat in the curve of Carpenter's Road, which, in four blocks, made up all the sporting life available in the Bottom. Old men and young ones draped themselves in front of the Elmira Theater, Irene's Palace of Cosmetology, the pool hall, the grill and the other sagging business enterprises that lined the street. On sills, on stoops, on crates and broken chairs they sat tasting their teeth and waiting for something to distract them. Every passerby, every motorcar, every alteration in stance caught their attention and was commented on. Particularly they watched women. When a woman approached, the older men tipped their hats; the younger ones opened and closed their thighs. But all of them, whatever their age, watched her retreating view with interest.

Nel and Sula walked through this valley of eyes chilled by the wind and heated by the embarrassment of appraising stares. The old men looked at their stalklike legs, dwelled on the cords in the backs of their knees and remembered old dance steps they had not done in twenty years. In their lust, which age had turned to kindness, they moved their lips as though to stir up the taste of young sweat on tight skin.

Pig meat. The words were in all their minds. And one of them, one of the young ones, said it aloud. Softly but definitively and there was no mistaking the compliment. His name was Ajax, a twenty-one-year-old pool haunt of sinister beauty. Graceful and economical in every movement, he held a place of envy with men of all ages for his magnificently foul mouth. In fact he seldom cursed, and the epithets he chose were dull, even harmless. His reputation was derived from the way he handled the words. When he said "hell" he hit the *h* with his lungs and the impact was greater than the achievement of the most imaginative foul mouth in the town. He could say "shit" with a nastiness impossible to imitate. So, when he said "pig meat" as Nel and Sula passed, they guarded their eyes lest someone see their delight.

It was not really Edna Finch's ice cream that made them brave the stretch of those panther eyes. Years later their own eyes would glaze as they cupped their chins in remembrance of the inchworm smiles, the squatting haunches, the track-rail legs straddling broken chairs. The cream-colored trousers marking with a mere seam the place where the mystery curled. Those smooth vanilla crotches invited them; those lemon-yellow gabardines beckoned to them.

They moved toward the ice-cream parlor like tightrope walkers, as thrilled by the possibility of a slip as by the maintenance of tension and balance. The least sideways glance, the merest toe stub, could pitch them into those creamy haunches spread wide with welcome. Somewhere beneath all of that daintiness, chambered in all that neatness, lay the thing that clotted their dreams.

Which was only fitting, for it was in dreams that the two girls had first met. Long before Edna Finch's Mellow House opened, even before they marched through the chocolate halls of Garfield Primary School out onto the playground and stood facing each other through the ropes of the one vacant swing ("Go on." "No. You go."), they had already made each other's acquaintance in the delirium of their noon dreams. They were solitary little girls whose loneliness was so profound it intoxicated them and sent them stumbling into Technicolored visions that always included a presence, a someone, who, quite like the dreamer, shared the delight of the dream. When Nel, an only child, sat on the steps of her back porch surrounded by the high silence of her mother's incredibly orderly house, feeling the neatness pointing at her back, she studied the poplars and fell easily into a picture of herself lying on a flowered bed, tangled in her own hair, waiting for some fiery prince. He approached but never quite arrived. But always, watching the dream along with her, were some smiling sympathetic eyes. Someone as interested as she herself in the flow of her imagined hair, the thickness of the mattress of flowers, the voile sleeves that closed below her elbows in gold-threaded cuffs.

Similarly, Sula, also an only child, but wedged into a household of throbbing disorder constantly awry with things, people, voices and the slamming of doors, spent hours in the attic behind a roll of linoleum galloping through her own mind on a gray-and-white horse tasting sugar and smelling roses in full view of a someone who shared both the taste and the speed.

So when they met, first in those chocolate halls and next through the ropes of the swing, they felt the ease and comfort of old friends. Because each had discovered years before that they were neither white nor male, and that all freedom and triumph was forbidden to them, they had set about creating something else to be. Their meeting was fortunate, for it let them use each other to grow on. Daughters of distant mothers and incomprehensible fathers (Sula's because he was dead; Nel's because he wasn't), they found in each other's eyes the intimacy they were looking for.

Nel Wright and Sula Peace were both twelve in 1922, wishbone thin and easy-assed. Nel was the color of wet sandpaper—just dark enough to escape the blows of the pitch-black truebloods and the contempt of old women who worried about such things as bad blood mixtures and knew that the origins of a mule and a mulatto were one and the same. Had she been any lighter-skinned she would have needed either her mother's protection on the way to school or a streak of mean to defend herself. Sula was a heavy brown with large quiet eyes, one of which featured a birthmark that spread from the middle of the lid toward the eyebrow, shaped something like a stemmed rose. It gave her otherwise plain face a broken excitement and blue-blade threat like the keloid[1] scar of the razored man who sometimes played checkers with her grandmother. The birthmark was to grow darker as the years passed, but now it was the same shade as her gold-flecked eyes, which, to the end, were as steady and clean as rain.

Their friendship was as intense as it was sudden. They found relief in each other's personality. Although both were unshaped, formless things, Nel seemed stronger and more consistent than Sula, who could hardly be counted on to sustain any emotion for more than three minutes. Yet there was one time when that was not true, when she held on to a mood for weeks, but even that was in defense of Nel.

Four white boys in their early teens, sons of some newly arrived Irish people, occasionally entertained themselves in the afternoon by harassing black schoolchildren. With shoes that pinched and woolen knickers that made red rings on their calves, they had come to this valley with their parents believing as they did that it was a promised land—green and shimmering with welcome. What they found was a strange accent, a pervasive fear of their religion and firm resistance to their attempts to find work. With one exception the older residents of Medallion scorned them. The one exception was the black community. Although some of the Negroes had been in Medallion before the Civil War (the town didn't even have a name then), if they had any hatred for these newcomers it didn't matter because it didn't show. As a matter of fact, baiting them was the one activity that the white Protestant residents concurred in. In part their place in this world was secured only when they echoed the old residents' attitude toward blacks.

These particular boys caught Nel once, and pushed her from hand to hand until they grew tired of the frightened helpless face. Because of that incident, Nel's route home from school became elaborate. She, and then Sula, managed to duck them for weeks until a chilly day in November when Sula said, "Let's us go on home the shortest way."

Nel blinked, but acquiesced. They walked up the street until they got to the bend of Carpenter's Road where the boys lounged on a disused well. Spotting their prey, the boys sauntered forward as though there were nothing in the world on their minds but the gray sky. Hardly able to control their grins, they stood like a gate blocking

1. An excessive growth of scar tissue.

the path. When the girls were three feet in front of the boys, Sula reached into her coat pocket and pulled out Eva's paring knife. The boys stopped short, exchanged looks and dropped all pretense of innocence. This was going to be better than they thought. They were going to try and fight back, and with a knife. Maybe they could get an arm around one of their waists, or tear . . .

Sula squatted down in the dirt road and put everything down on the ground: her lunchpail, her reader, her mittens, her slate. Holding the knife in her right hand, she pulled the slate toward her and pressed her left forefinger down hard on its edge. Her aim was determined but inaccurate. She slashed off only the tip of her finger. The four boys stared open-mouthed at the wound and the scrap of flesh, like a button mushroom, curling in the cherry blood that ran into the corners of the slate.

Sula raised her eyes to them. Her voice was quiet. "If I can do that to myself, what you suppose I'll do to you?"

The shifting dirt was the only way Nel knew that they were moving away; she was looking at Sula's face, which seemed miles and miles away.

But toughness was not their quality—adventuresomeness was—and a mean determination to explore everything that interested them, from one-eyed chickens high-stepping in their penned yards to Mr. Buckland Reed's gold teeth, from the sound of sheets flapping in the wind to the labels on Tar Baby's wine bottles. And they had no priorities. They could be distracted from watching a fight with mean razors by the glorious smell of hot tar being poured by roadmen two hundred yards away.

In the safe harbor of each other's company they could afford to abandon the ways of other people and concentrate on their own perceptions of things. When Mrs. Wright reminded Nel to pull her nose, she would do it enthusiastically but without the least hope in the world.

"While you sittin' there, honey, go 'head and pull your nose."

"It hurts, Mamma."

"Don't you want a nice nose when you grow up?"

After she met Sula, Nel slid the clothespin under the blanket as soon as she got in the bed. And although there was still the hateful hot comb to suffer through each Saturday evening, its consequences—smooth hair—no longer interested her.

Joined in mutual admiration they watched each day as though it were a movie arranged for their amusement. The new theme they were now discovering was men. So they met regularly, without even planning it, to walk down the road to Edna Finch's Mellow House, even though it was too cool for ice cream.

Then summer came. A summer limp with the weight of blossomed things. Heavy sunflowers weeping over fences; iris curling and browning at the edges far away from their purple hearts; ears of corn letting their auburn hair wind down to their stalks. And the boys. The beautiful, beautiful boys who dotted the landscape like jewels, split the air with their shouts in the field, and thickened the river with their shining wet backs. Even their footsteps left a smell of smoke behind.

It was in that summer, the summer of their twelfth year, the summer of the beautiful black boys, that they became skittish, frightened and bold—all at the same time.

In that mercury mood in July, Sula and Nel wandered about the Bottom barefoot looking for mischief. They decided to go down by the river where the boys sometimes swam. Nel waited on the porch of 7 Carpenter's Road while Sula ran into the house to go to the toilet. On the way up the stairs, she passed the kitchen where Hannah sat with two friends, Patsy and Valentine. The two women were fanning themselves and watching Hannah put down some dough, all talking casually about one thing and another, and had gotten around, when Sula passed by, to the problems of child rearing.

"They a pain."

"Yeh. Wish I'd listened to mamma. She told me not to have 'em too soon."

"Any time atall is too soon for me."

"Oh, I don't know. My Rudy minds his daddy. He just wild with me. Be glad when he growed and gone."

Hannah smiled and said, "Shut your mouth. You love the ground he pee on."

"Sure I do. But he still a pain. Can't help loving your own child. No matter what they do."

"Well, Hester grown now and I can't say love is exactly what I feel."

"Sure you do. You love her, like I love Sula. I just don't like her. That's the difference."

"Guess so. Likin' them is another thing."

"Sure. They different people, you know . . ."

She only heard Hannah's words, and the pronouncement sent her flying up the stairs. In bewilderment, she stood at the window fingering the curtain edge, aware of a sting in her eye. Nel's call floated up and into the window, pulling her away from dark thoughts back into the bright, hot daylight.

They ran most of the way.

Heading toward the wide part of the river where trees grouped themselves in families darkening the earth below. They passed some boys swimming and clowning in the water, shrouding their words in laughter.

They ran in the sunlight, creating their own breeze, which pressed their dresses into their damp skin. Reaching a kind of square of four leaf-locked trees which promised cooling, they flung themselves into the four-cornered shade to taste their lip sweat and contemplate the wildness that had come upon them so suddenly. They lay in the grass, their foreheads almost touching, their bodies stretched away from each other at a 180-degree angle. Sula's head rested on her arm, an undone braid coiled around her wrist. Nel leaned on her elbows and worried long blades of grass with her fingers. Underneath their dresses flesh tightened and shivered in the high coolness, their small breasts just now beginning to create some pleasant discomfort when they were lying on their stomachs.

Sula lifted her head and joined Nel in the grass play. In concert, without ever meeting each other's eyes, they stroked the blades up and down, up and down. Nel found a thick twig and, with her thumbnail, pulled away its bark until it was stripped to a smooth, creamy innocence. Sula looked about and found one too. When both twigs were undressed Nel moved easily to the next stage and began tearing up rooted grass to make a bare spot of earth. When a generous clearing was made, Sula traced intricate patterns in it with her twig. At first Nel was content to do the same. But soon she grew impatient and poked her twig rhythmically and intensely into the earth, making a small neat hole that grew deeper and wider with the least manipulation of her twig. Sula copied her, and soon each had a hole the size of a cup. Nel began a more strenuous digging and, rising to her knee, was careful to scoop out the dirt as she made her hole deeper. Together they worked until the two holes were one and the same. When the depression was the size of a small dishpan, Nel's twig broke. With a gesture of disgust she threw the pieces into the hole they had made. Sula threw hers in too. Nel saw a bottle cap and tossed it in as well. Each then looked around for more debris to throw into the hole: paper, bits of glass, butts of cigarettes, until all of the small defiling things they could find were collected there. Carefully they replaced the soil and covered the entire grave with uprooted grass.

Neither one had spoken a word.

They stood up, stretched, then gazed out over the swift dull water as an unspeakable restlessness and agitation held them. At the same instant each girl heard footsteps in the grass. A little boy in too big knickers was coming up from the lower bank of the river. He stopped when he saw them and picked his nose.

"Your mamma tole you to stop eatin' snot, Chicken," Nel hollered at him through cupped hands.

"Shut up," he said, still picking.

"Come up here and say that."

"Leave him 'lone, Nel. Come here, Chicken. Lemme show you something."

"Naw."

"You scared we gone take your bugger away?"

"Leave him 'lone, I said. Come on, Chicken. Look. I'll help you climb a tree."

Chicken looked at the tree Sula was pointing to—a big double beech with low branches and lots of bends for sitting.

He moved slowly toward her.

"Come on, Chicken, I'll help you up."

Still picking his nose, his eyes wide, he came to where they were standing. Sula took him by the hand and coaxed him along. When they reached the base of the beech, she lifted him to the first branch, saying, "Go on. Go on. I got you." She followed the boy, steadying him, when he needed it, with her hand and her reassuring voice. When they were as high as they could go, Sula pointed to the far side of the river.

"See? Bet you never saw that far before, did you?"

"Uh uh."

"Now look down there." They both leaned a little and peered through the leaves at Nel standing below, squinting up at them. From their height she looked small and foreshortened.

Chicken Little laughed.

"Y'all better come on down before you break your neck," Nel hollered.

"I ain't never coming down," the boy hollered back.

"Yeah. We better. Come on, Chicken."

"Naw. Lemme go."

"Yeah, Chicken. Come on, now."

Sula pulled his leg gently.

"Lemme go."

"OK, I'm leavin' you." She started on.

"Wait!" he screamed.

Sula stopped and together they slowly worked their way down.

Chicken was still elated. "I was way up there, wasn't I? Wasn't I? I'm a tell my brovver."

Sula and Nel began to mimic him: "I'm a tell my brovver; I'm a tell my brovver."

Sula picked him up by his hands and swung him outward then around and around. His knickers ballooned and his shrieks of frightened joy startled the birds and the fat grasshoppers. When he slipped from her hands and sailed away out over the water they could still hear his bubbly laughter.

The water darkened and closed quickly over the place where Chicken Little sank. The pressure of his hard and tight little fingers was still in Sula's palms as she stood looking at the closed place in the water. They expected him to come back up, laughing. Both girls stared at the water.

Nel spoke first. "Somebody saw." A figure appeared briefly on the opposite shore.

The only house over there was Shadrack's. Sula glanced at Nel. Terror widened her nostrils. Had he seen?

The water was so peaceful now. There was nothing but the baking sun and something newly missing. Sula cupped her face for an instant, then turned and ran up to the little plank bridge that crossed the river to Shadrack's house. There was no path. It was as though neither Shadrack nor anyone else ever came this way.

Her running was swift and determined, but when she was close to the three little steps that led to his porch, fear crawled into her stomach and only the something newly missing back there in the river made it possible for her to walk up the three steps and knock at the door.

No one answered. She started back, but thought again of the peace of the river. Shadrack would be inside, just behind the door ready to pounce on her. Still she could not go back. Ever so gently she pushed the door with the tips of her fingers and heard only the hinges weep. More. And then she was inside. Alone. The neatness, the order startled her, but more surprising was the restfulness. Everything was so tiny, so common, so unthreatening. Perhaps this was not the house of the Shad. The terrible Shad who walked about with his penis out, who peed in front of ladies and girl-children, the only black who could curse white people and get away with it, who drank in the road from the mouth of the bottle, who shouted and shook in the streets. This cottage? This sweet old cottage? With its made-up bed? With its rag rug and wooden table? Sula stood in the middle of the little room and in her wonder forgot what she had come for until a sound at the door made her jump. He was there in the doorway looking at her. She had not heard his coming and now he was looking at her.

More in embarrassment than terror she averted her glance. When she called up enough courage to look back at him, she saw his hand resting upon the door frame. His fingers, barely touching the wood, were arranged in a graceful arc. Relieved and encouraged (no one with hands like that, no one with fingers that curved around wood so tenderly could kill her), she walked past him out of the door, feeling his gaze turning, turning with her.

At the edge of the porch, gathering the wisps of courage that were fast leaving her, she turned once more to look at him, to ask him . . . had he . . . ?

He was smiling, a great smile, heavy with lust and time to come. He nodded his head as though answering a question, and said, in a pleasant conversational tone, a tone of cooled butter, "Always."

Sula fled down the steps, and shot through the greenness and the baking sun back to Nel and the dark closed place in the water. There she collapsed in tears.

Nel quieted her. "Sh, sh. Don't, don't. You didn't mean it. It ain't your fault.

Sh. Sh. Come on, le's go, Sula. Come on, now. Was he there? Did he see? Where's the belt to your dress?"

Sula shook her head while she searched her waist for the belt.

Finally she stood up and allowed Nel to lead her away. "He said, 'Always. Always.' "

"What?"

Sula covered her mouth as they walked down the hill. Always. He had answered a question she had not asked, and its promise licked at her feet.

A bargeman, poling away from the shore, found Chicken late that afternoon stuck in some rocks and weeds, his knickers ballooning about his legs. He would have left him there but noticed that it was a child, not an old black man, as it first appeared, and he prodded the body loose, netted it and hauled it aboard. He shook his head in disgust at the kind of parents who would drown their own children. When, he wondered, will those people ever be anything but animals, fit for nothing but substitutes for mules, only mules didn't kill each other the way niggers did. He dumped Chicken Little into a burlap sack and tossed him next to some egg crates and boxes of wool cloth. Later, sitting down to smoke on an empty lard tin, still bemused by God's curse and the terrible burden his own kind had of elevating Ham's sons,[2] he suddenly became alarmed by the thought that the corpse in this heat would have a terrible odor, which might get into the fabric of his woolen cloth. He dragged the sack away and hooked it over the side, so that the Chicken's body was half in and half out of the water.

Wiping the sweat from his neck, he reported his find to the sheriff at Porter's Landing, who said they didn't have no niggers in their county, but that some lived in those hills 'cross the river, up above Medallion. The bargeman said he couldn't go all the way back there, it was every bit of two miles. The sheriff said whyn't he throw it on back into the water. The bargeman said he never shoulda taken it out in the first place. Finally they got the man who ran the ferry twice a day to agree to take it over in the morning.

That was why Chicken Little was missing for three days and didn't get to the embalmer's until the fourth day, by which time he was unrecognizable to almost everybody who once knew him, and even his mother wasn't deep down sure, except that it just had to be him since nobody could find him. When she saw his clothes lying on the table in the basement of the mortuary, her mouth snapped shut, and when she saw his body her mouth flew wide open again and it was seven hours before she was able to close it and make the first sound.

So the coffin was closed.

The Junior Choir, dressed in white, sang "Nearer My God to Thee" and "Precious Memories," their eyes fastened on the songbooks they did not need, for this was the first time their voices had presided at a real-life event.

Nel and Sula did not touch hands or look at each other during the funeral. There was a space, a separateness, between them. Nel's legs had turned to granite and she expected the sheriff or Reverend Deal's pointing finger at any moment. Although she knew she had "done nothing," she felt convicted and hanged right there in the pew—two rows down from her parents in the children's section.

2. Ham, son of Noah and father of Canaan, was traditionally the ancestor of the Negro race (*cf.* Genesis ix: 25–26).

Sula simply cried. Soundlessly and with no heaving and gasping for breath, she let the tears roll into her mouth and slide down her chin to dot the front of her dress.

As Reverend Deal moved into his sermon, the hands of the women unfolded like pairs of raven's wings and flew high above their hats in the air. They did not hear all of what he said; they heard the one word, or phrase, or inflection that was for them the connection between the event and themselves. For some it was the term "Sweet Jesus." And they saw the Lamb's eye and the truly innocent victim: themselves. They acknowledged the innocent child hiding in the corner of their hearts, holding a sugar-and-butter sandwich. That one. The one who lodged deep in their fat, thin, old, young skin, and was the one the world had hurt. Or they thought of their son newly killed and remembered his legs in short pants and wondered where the bullet went in. Or they remembered how dirty the room looked when their father left home and wondered if that is the way the slim, young Jew felt, he who for them was both son and lover and in whose downy face they could see the sugar-and-butter sandwiches and feel the oldest and most devastating pain there is: not the pain of childhood, but the remembrance of it.

Then they left their pews. For with some emotions one has to stand. They spoke, for they were full and needed to say. They swayed, for the rivulets of grief or of ecstasy must be rocked. And when they thought of all that life and death locked into that little closed coffin they danced and screamed, not to protest God's will but to acknowledge it and confirm once more their conviction that the only way to avoid the Hand of God is to get in it.

In the colored part of the cemetery, they sank Chicken Little in between his grandfather and an aunt. Butterflies flew in and out of the bunches of field flowers now loosened from the top of the bier and lying in a small heap at the edge of the grave. The heat had gone, but there was still no breeze to lift the hair of the willows.

Nel and Sula stood some distance away from the grave, the space that had sat between them in the pews had dissolved. They held hands and knew that only the coffin would lie in the earth; the bubbly laughter and the press of fingers in the palm would stay aboveground forever. At first, as they stood there, their hands were clenched together. They relaxed slowly until during the walk back home their fingers were laced in as gentle a clasp as that of any two young girlfriends trotting up the road on a summer day wondering what happened to butterflies in the winter.

1973

JOHN UPDIKE

(1932–)

From his first volume of poetry, *The Carpentered Hen and Other Tame Creatures* (1958), and the novel published the next year, *The Poorhouse Fair,* John Updike has been able to achieve a versatility that ranges from practiced absurdity to irony sharpened and refined by acute observation. His ear for the muted chivalry of youth brought him critical attention remarkably early in his career. A writer who has an accurate eye for the small wonders of the commonplace, Updike can invest an international episode (as in "The Bulgarian Poetess") with vivid poignancy. He has a gift for using banal phrases of domestic joy and discord to give dimension to familial situations, which he seems to absorb from the storms and brief moments of quiet in modern life.

Possessed of sharp insights and a remarkably lucid style, Updike is in some ways reminiscent of his character Henry Bech. Highly praised in his twenties, he attained the age of forty without having satisfied his critics that the quality of his later books had fulfilled the brilliant promise of his earlier ones. The undisputed masterpiece that he seemed to many readers to be capable of producing continued to elude him, while he published book after book that all agreed were finely written but that some of his harshest critics judged to be deficient in significant content. *Rabbit, Run* (1960), one of the best novels of its decade, was published when he was twenty-eight. In *Rabbit Redux* (1971), a decade later, he advanced the central character ten years in age and, without writing a better novel than that brilliant earlier one, nevertheless reminded his readers that Harry Angstrom ("Rabbit") was one of the most interesting fictional characters of his time. That interest is maintained in a third novel, *Rabbit Is Rich* (1981). "Actuality is a running impoverishment of possibility" runs a sentence from Updike's story "The Bulgarian Poetess." It is Rabbit's refusal to learn, or to accept, this fact that gives him the central place that he occupies in Updike's fiction. Time's tyranny, as theme, is the focal point for most of Updike's work.

John Updike was born in 1932 in Shillington, Pennsylvania. He attended Harvard and the Ruskin School of Design and Fine Art in England. For two years, 1955–1957, he was on the staff of *The New Yorker,* where many of his poems and short stories have appeared. Finding New York uncongenial, he became a full-time writer and moved to Massachusetts, where he has lived northeast of Boston since 1957.

Most of Updike's fiction has been carefully wrought from his experience and observation, either as a boy in Pennsylvania or an adult in Massachusetts. *The Centaur* (1963) portrays a high school teacher based upon Updike's father. Harry Angstrom of the "Rabbit" books inhabits a small-town Pennsylvania world not far removed from that of Updike's boyhood and confronts, without benefit of college, an adult life that savors much of might-have-been. *Couples* (1968) explores suburban marital infidelity in Massachusetts. "Separating" is one of the finest of the Maples stories, a sensitive portrayal of a marriage in many details like that of Updike and his first wife. Updike's concentration on self and concern with domesticity, however, are notably diminished in *The Coup* (1978), a highly regarded novel that centers on the career of a black dictator as it examines political and social issues in an emergent African nation. In *The Witches of Eastwick* (1984) he extends his New England scene south to Rhode Island, creating an elegant, sometimes humorous tale of modern witchcraft. In *Roger's Version* (1986) he alludes to *The Scarlet Letter* to relate a story of contemporary marital infidelity from the perspective of the wronged husband.

Novels, besides those named above, are *Of the Farm,* 1966; *A Month of Sundays,* 1975; and *Marry Me: A Romance,* 1976. Short story collections are *The Same Door,* 1959; *Pigeon Feathers and Other Stories,* 1962; *The Music School,* 1966; *Bech: A Book,* 1970; *Museums & Women and Other Stories,* 1972; *Problems and Other Stories,* 1979; *Bech Is Back,* 1982; and *Trust Me,* 1987. The Maples stories were collected in *Too Far to Go,* 1979. *Assorted Prose* was published in 1965. *Hugging the Shore: Essays and Criticism* appeared in 1983. Volumes of poetry are *The Carpentered Hen and Other Tame Creatures,* 1958; *Telephone Poles and Other Poems,* 1963; *Midpoint and Other Poems,* 1969; *Tossing and Turning,* 1977; and *Facing Nature,* 1985.

Critical studies are Alice and Kenneth Hamilton, *The Elements of John Updike,* 1970; Rachael C. Burchard, *John Updike: Yea Sayings,* 1971; Larry E. Taylor, *Pastoral and Anti-Pastoral Patterns in John Updike's Fiction,* 1971; Suzanne Hennings Uphaus, *John Updike,* 1980; Donald J. Greiner, *The Other John Updike,* 1981; Donald J. Greiner, *John Updike's Novels,* 1984; and Robert Detweiler, *John Updike,* rev. ed., 1984.

A & P

In walks these three girls in nothing but bathing suits. I'm in the third checkout slot, with my back to the door, so I don't see them until they're over by the bread. The one that caught my eye first was the one in the plaid green two-piece. She was a chunky kid, with a good tan and a sweet broad soft-looking can with those two crescents of white just under it, where the sun never seems to hit, at the top of the backs of her legs. I stood there with my hand on a box of HiHo crackers trying to remember if I rang it up or not. I ring it up again and the customer starts giving me hell. She's one of these cash-register-watchers, a witch about fifty with rouge on her cheekbones and no eyebrows, and I know it made her day to trip me up. She'd been watching cash registers for fifty years and probably never seen a mistake before.

By the time I got her feathers smoothed and her goodies into a bag—she gives me a little snort in passing, if she'd been born at the right time they would have burned her over in Salem—by the time I get her on her way the girls had circled around the bread and were coming back, without a pushcart, back my way along the counters, in the aisle between the checkouts and the Special bins. They didn't even have shoes on. There was this chunky one, with the two-piece—it was bright green and the seams on the bra were still sharp and her belly was still pretty pale so I guessed she just got it (the suit)—there was this one, with one of those chubby berry-faces, the lips all bunched together under her nose, this one, and a tall one, with black hair that hadn't quite frizzed right, and one of these sunburns right across under the eyes, and a chin that was too long—you know, the kind of girl other girls think is very "striking" and "attractive" but never quite makes it, as they very well know, which is why they like her so much—and then the third one, that wasn't quite so tall. She was the queen. She kind of led them, the other two peeking around and making their shoulders round. She didn't look around, not this queen, she just walked straight on slowly, on these long white prima-donna legs. She came down a little hard on her heels, as if she didn't walk in her bare feet that much, putting down her heels and then letting the weight move along to her toes as if she was testing the floor with every step, putting a little deliberate extra action into it. You never know for sure how girls' minds work (do you really think it's a mind in there or just a little buzz like a bee in a glass jar?) but you got the idea she had talked the other two into coming in here with her, and now she was showing them how to do it, walk slow and hold yourself straight.

She had on a kind of dirty-pink—beige maybe, I don't know—bathing suit with a little nubble all over it and, what got me, the straps were down. They were off her shoulders looped loose around the cool tops of her arms, and I guess as a result the suit had slipped a little on her, so all around the top of the cloth there was this shining rim. If it hadn't been there you wouldn't have known there could have been anything whiter than those shoulders. With the straps pushed off, there was nothing between the top of the suit and the top of her head except just *her,* this clean bare plane of the top of her chest down from the shoulder bones like a dented sheet of metal tilted in the light. I mean, it was more than pretty.

She had sort of oaky hair that the sun and salt had bleached, done up in a bun that was unravelling, and a kind of prim face. Walking into the A & P with your straps down, I suppose it's the only kind of face you *can* have. She held her head so high her neck, coming up out of those white shoulders, looked kind of stretched, but I didn't mind. The longer her neck was, the more of her there was.

She must have felt in the corner of her eye me and over my shoulder Stokesie in the second slot watching, but she didn't tip. Not this queen. She kept her eyes moving across the racks, and stopped, and turned so slow it made my stomach rub the inside of my apron, and buzzed to the other two, who kind of huddled against her for relief, and then they all three of them went up the cat-and-dog-food-breakfast - cereal - macaroni - rice - raisins - seasonings - spreads - spaghetti - soft - drinks - crackers-and-cookies aisle. From the third slot I look straight up this aisle to the meat counter, and I watched them all the way. The fat one with the tan sort of fumbled with the cookies, but on second thought she put the package back. The sheep pushing their carts down the aisle—the girls were walking against the usual traffic (not that we have one-way signs or anything)—were pretty hilarious. You could see them, when Queenie's white shoulders dawned on them, kind of jerk, or hop, or hiccup, but their eyes snapped back to their own baskets and on they pushed. I bet you could set off dynamite in an A & P and the people would by and large keep reaching and checking oatmeal off their lists and muttering "Let me see, there was a third thing, began with A, asparagus, no, ah, yes, applesauce!" or whatever it is they do mutter. But there was no doubt, this jiggled them. A few houseslaves in pin curlers even looked around after pushing their carts past to make sure what they had seen was correct.

You know, it's one thing to have a girl in a bathing suit down on the beach, where what with the glare nobody can look at each other much anyway, and another thing in the cool of the A & P, under the fluorescent lights, against all those stacked packages, with her feet paddling along naked over our checkerboard green-and-cream rubber-tile floor.

"Oh Daddy," Stokesie said beside me. "I feel so faint."

"Darling," I said. "Hold me tight." Stokesie's married, with two babies chalked up on his fuselage already, but as far as I can tell that's the only difference. He's twenty-two, and I was nineteen this April.

"Is it done?" he asks, the responsible married man finding his voice. I forgot to say he thinks he's going to be manager some sunny day, maybe in 1990 when it's called the Great Alexandrov and Petrooshki Tea Company or something.

What he meant was, our town is five miles from a beach, with a big summer colony out on the Point, but we're right in the middle of town, and the women generally put on a shirt or shorts or something before they get out of the car into the street. And anyway these are usually women with six children and varicose veins mapping their legs and nobody, including them, could care less. As I say, we're right in the middle of town, and if you stand at our front doors you can see two banks and the Congregational church and the newspaper store and three real-estate offices and about twenty-seven old freeloaders tearing up Central Street because the sewer broke again. It's not as if we're on the Cape; we're north of Boston and there's people in this town haven't seen the ocean for twenty years.

The girls had reached the meat counter and were asking McMahon something. He pointed, they pointed, and they shuffled out of sight behind a pyramid of Diet Delight peaches. All that was left for us to see was old McMahon patting his mouth and looking after them sizing up their joints. Poor kids, I began to feel sorry for them, they couldn't help it.

Now here comes the sad part of the story, at least my family says it's sad, but I don't think it's so sad myself. The store's pretty empty, it being Thursday afternoon, so there was nothing much to do except lean on the register and wait for the girls to show up again. The whole store was like a pinball machine and I didn't know which tunnel they'd come out of. After a while they come around out of the far aisle, around the light bulbs, records at discount of the Caribbean Six or Tony Martin Sings or some such gunk you wonder they waste the wax on, sixpacks of candy bars, and plastic toys done up in cellophane that fall apart when a kid looks at them anyway. Around they come, Queenie still leading the way, and holding a little gray jar in her hand. Slots Three through Seven are unmanned and I could see her wondering between Stokes and me, but Stokesie with his usual luck draws an old party in baggy gray pants who stumbles up with four giant cans of pineapple juice (what do these bums *do* with all that pineapple juice? I've often asked myself) so the girls come to me. Queenie puts down the jar and I take it into my fingers icy cold. Kingfish Fancy Herring Snacks in Pure Sour Cream: 49¢. Now her hands are empty, not a ring or a bracelet, bare as God made them, and I wonder where the money's coming from. Still with that prim look she lifts a folded dollar bill out of the hollow at the center of her nubbled pink top. The jar went heavy in my hand. Really, I thought that was so cute.

Then everybody's luck begins to run out. Lengel comes in from haggling with a truck full of cabbages on the lot and is about to scuttle into that door marked MANAGER behind which he hides all day when the girls touch his eye. Lengel's pretty dreary, teaches Sunday school and the rest, but he doesn't miss that much. He comes over and says, "Girls, this isn't the beach."

Queenie blushes, though maybe it's just a brush of sunburn I was noticing for the first time, now that she was so close. "My mother asked me to pick up a jar of herring snacks." Her voice kind of startled me, the way voices do when you see the people first, coming out so flat and dumb yet kind of tony, too, the way it ticked over "pick up" and "snacks." All of a sudden I slid right down her voice into her living room. Her father and the other men were standing around in ice-cream coats and bow ties and the women were in sandals picking up herring snacks on toothpicks off a big glass plate and they were all holding drinks the color of water with olives and sprigs of mint in them. When my parents have somebody over they get lemonade and if it's a real racy affair Schlitz in tall glasses with "They'll Do It Every Time" cartoons stencilled on.

"That's all right," Lengel said. "But this isn't the beach." His repeating this struck me as funny, as if it had just occurred to him, and he had been thinking all these years the A & P was a great big dune and he was the head lifeguard. He didn't like my smiling—as I say he doesn't miss much—but he concentrates on giving the girls that sad Sunday-school-superintendent stare.

Queenie's blush is no sunburn now, and the plump one in plaid, that I liked better from the back—a really sweet can—pipes up, "We weren't doing any shopping. We just came in for the one thing."

"That makes no difference," Lengel tells her, and I could see from the way his eyes went that he hadn't noticed she was wearing a two-piece before. "We want you decently dressed when you come in here."

"We *are* decent," Queenie says suddenly, her lower lip pushing, getting sore now that she remembers her place, a place from which the crowd that runs the A & P must look pretty crummy. Fancy Herring Snacks flashed in her very blue eyes.

"Girls, I don't want to argue with you. After this come in here with your shoulders covered. It's our policy." He turns his back. That's policy for you. Policy is what the kingpins want. What the others want is juvenile delinquency.

All this while, the customers had been showing up with their carts but, you know, sheep, seeing a scene, they had all bunched up on Stokesie, who shook open a paper bag as gently as peeling a peach, not wanting to miss a word. I could feel in the silence everybody getting nervous, most of all Lengel, who asks me, "Sammy, have you rung up their purchase?"

I thought and said "No" but it wasn't about that I was thinking. I go through the punches, 4, 9, GROC, TOT—it's more complicated than you think, and after you do it often enough, it begins to make a little song, that you hear words to, in my case "Hello *(bing)* there, you *(gung)* hap-py *pee*-pul *(splat)*!"—the *splat* being the drawer flying out. I uncrease the bill, tenderly as you may imagine, it just having come from between the two smoothest scoops of vanilla I had ever known were there, and pass a half and a penny into her narrow pink palm, and nestle the herrings in a bag and twist its neck and hand it over, all the time thinking.

The girls, and who'd blame them, are in a hurry to get out, so I say "I quit" to Lengel quick enough for them to hear, hoping they'll stop and watch me, their unsuspected hero. They keep right on going, into the electric eye; the door flies open and they flicker across the lot to their car, Queenie and Plaid and Big Tall Goony-Goony (not that as raw material she was so bad), leaving me with Lengel and a kink in his eyebrow.

"Did you say something, Sammy?"

"I said I quit."

"I thought you did."

"You didn't have to embarrass them."

"It was they who were embarrassing us."

I started to say something that came out "Fiddle-de-doo." It's a saying of my grandmother's, and I know she would have been pleased.

"I don't think you know what you're saying," Lengel said.

"I know you don't," I said. "But I do." I pull the bow at the back of my apron and start shrugging it off my shoulders. A couple customers that had been heading for my slot begin to knock against each other, like scared pigs in a chute.

Lengel sighs and begins to look very patient and old and gray. He's been a friend of my parents for years. "Sammy, you don't want to do this to your Mom and Dad," he tells me. It's true, I don't. But it seems to me that once you begin a gesture it's fatal not to go through with it. I fold the apron, "Sammy" stitched in red on the pocket, and put it on the counter, and drop the bow tie on top of it. The bow tie is theirs, if you've ever wondered. "You'll feel this for the rest of your life," Lengel says, and I know that's true, too, but remembering how he made that pretty girl blush makes me so scrunchy inside I punch the No Sale tab and the machine whirs "pee-pul" and the drawer splats out. One advantage to this scene taking place in summer, I can follow this up with a clean exit, there's no fumbling around getting your coat and galoshes, I just saunter into the electric eye in my white shirt that my mother ironed the night before, and the door heaves itself open, and outside the sunshine is skating around on the asphalt.

I look around for my girls, but they're gone, of course. There wasn't anybody but some young married screaming with her children about some candy they didn't get by the door of a powder-blue Falcon station wagon. Looking back in the big windows, over the bags of peat moss and aluminum lawn furniture stacked on the pavement, I could see Lengel in my place in the slot, checking the sheep through. His face was dark gray and his back stiff, as if he'd just had an injection of iron, and my stomach kind of fell as I felt how hard the world was going to be to me hereafter.

1962

Separating

The day was fair. Brilliant. All that June the weather had mocked the Maples' internal misery with solid sunlight—golden shafts and cascades of green in which their conversations had wormed unseeing, their sad murmuring selves the only stain in Nature. Usually by this time of the year they had acquired tans; but when they met their elder daughter's plane on her return from a year in England they were almost as pale as she, though Judith was too dazzled by the sunny opulent jumble of her native land to notice. They did not spoil her homecoming by telling her immediately. Wait a few days, let her recover from jet lag, had been one of their formulations, in that string of gray dialogues—over coffee, over cocktails, over Cointreau—that had shaped the strategy of their dissolution, while the earth performed its annual stunt of renewal unnoticed beyond their closed windows. Richard had thought to leave at Easter; Joan had insisted they wait until the four children were at last assembled, with all exams passed and ceremonies attended, and the bauble of summer to console them. So he had drudged away, in love, in dread, repairing screens, getting the mowers sharpened, rolling and patching their new tennis court.

The court, clay, had come through its first winter pitted and windswept bare of redcoat. Years ago the Maples had observed how often, among their friends, divorce followed a dramatic home improvement, as if the marriage were making one last effort to live; their own worst crisis had come amid the plaster dust and exposed plumbing of a kitchen renovation. Yet, a summer ago, as canary-yellow bulldozers gaily churned a grassy, daisy-dotted knoll into a muddy plateau, and a crew of pigtailed young men raked and tamped clay into a plane, this transformation did not strike them as ominous, but festive in its impudence; their marriage could rend the earth for fun. The next spring, waking each day at dawn to a sliding sensation as if the bed were being tipped, Richard found the barren tennis court—its net and tapes still rolled in the barn—an environment congruous with his mood of purposeful desolation, and the crumbling of handfuls of clay into cracks and holes (dogs had frolicked on the court in a thaw; rivulets had eroded trenches) an activity suitably elemental and interminable. In his sealed heart he hoped the day would never come.

Now it was here. A Friday. Judith was re-acclimated; all four children were assembled, before jobs and camps and visits again scattered them. Joan thought they should be told one by one. Richard was for making an announcement at the table.

She said, "I think just making an announcement is a cop-out. They'll start quarrelling and playing to each other instead of focusing. They're each individuals, you know, not just some corporate obstacle to your freedom."

"O.K., O.K. I agree." Joan's plan was exact. That evening, they were giving Judith a belated welcome-home dinner, of lobster and champagne. Then, the party over, they, the two of them, who nineteen years before would push her in a baby carriage along Fifth Avenue to Washington Square, were to walk her out of the house, to the bridge across the salt creek, and tell her, swearing her to secrecy. Then Richard Jr., who was going directly from work to a rock concert in Boston, would be told, either late when he returned on the train or early Saturday morning before he went off to his job; he was seventeen and employed as one of a golf-course maintenance crew. Then the two younger children, John and Margaret, could, as the morning wore on, be informed.

"Mopped up, as it were," Richard said.

"Do you have any better plan? That leaves you the rest of Saturday to answer any questions, pack, and make your wonderful departure."

"No," he said, meaning he had no better plan, and agreed to hers, though to him it showed an edge of false order, a hidden plea for control, like Joan's long chore lists and financial accountings and, in the days when he first knew her, her too-copious lecture notes. Her plan turned one hurdle for him into four—four knife-sharp walls, each with a sheer blind drop on the other side.

All spring he had moved through a world of insides and outsides, of barriers and partitions. He and Joan stood as a thin barrier between the children and the truth. Each moment was a partition, with the past on one side and the future on the other, a future containing this unthinkable *now.* Beyond four knifelike walls a new life for him waited vaguely. His skull cupped a secret, a white face, a face both frightened and soothing, both strange and known, that he wanted to shield from tears, which he felt all about him, solid as the sunlight. So haunted, he had become obsessed with battening down the house against his absence, replacing screens and sash cords, hinges and latches—a Houdini making things snug before his escape.

The lock. He had still to replace a lock on one of the doors of the screened porch. The task, like most such, proved more difficult than he had imagined. The old lock, aluminum frozen by corrosion, had been deliberately rendered obsolete by manufacturers. Three hardware stores had nothing that even approximately matched the mortised hole its removal (surprisingly easy) left. Another hole had to be gouged, with bits too small and saws too big, and the old hole fitted with a block of wood —the chisels dull, the saw rusty, his fingers thick with lack of sleep. The sun poured down, beyond the porch, on a world of neglect. The bushes already needed pruning, the windward side of the house was shedding flakes of paint, rain would get in when he was gone, insects, rot, death. His family, all those he would lose, filtered through the edges of his awareness as he struggled with screw holes, splinters, opaque instructions, minutiae of metal.

Judith sat on the porch, a princess returned from exile. She regaled them with stories of fuel shortages, of bomb scares in the Underground, of Pakistani workmen loudly lusting after her as she walked past on her way to dance school. Joan came and went, in and out of the house, calmer than she should have been, praising his struggles with the lock as if this were one more and not the last of their long succession of shared chores. The younger of his sons for a few minutes held the rickety screen door while his father clumsily hammered and chiseled, each blow a kind of sob in Richard's ears. His younger daughter, having been at a slumber party, slept on the porch hammock through all the noise—heavy and pink, trusting and forsaken. Time, like the sunlight, continued relentlessly; the sunlight slowly slanted. Today was one of the longest days. The lock clicked, worked. He was through. He had a drink; he drank it on the porch, listening to his daughter. "It was so sweet," she was saying, "during the worst of it, how all the butchers and bakery shops kept open by candlelight. They're all so plucky and cute. From the papers, things sounded so much worse here—people shooting people in gas lines, and everybody freezing."

Richard asked her, "Do you still want to live in England forever?" *Forever:* the concept, now a reality upon him, pressed and scratched at the back of his throat.

"No," Judith confessed, turning her oval face to him, its eyes still childishly far apart, but the lips set as over something succulent and satisfactory. "I was anxious to come home. I'm an American." She was a woman. They had raised her; he and Joan had endured together to raise her, alone of the four. The others had still some raising left in them. Yet it was the thought of telling Judith—the image of her, their first baby, walking between them arm in arm to the bridge—that broke him. The partition between his face and the tears broke. Richard sat down to the celebratory meal with the back of his throat aching; the champagne, the lobster seemed phases of sunshine; he saw them and tasted them through tears. He blinked, swallowed, croakily joked about hay fever. The tears would not stop leaking through; they came not through a hole that could be plugged but through a permeable spot in a membrane, steadily, purely, endlessly, fruitfully. They became, his tears, a shield for himself against these others—their faces, the fact of their assembly, a last time as innocents, at a table where he sat the last time as head. Tears dropped from his nose as he broke the lobster's back; salt flavored his champagne as he sipped it; the raw clench at the back of his throat was delicious. He could not help himself.

His children tried to ignore his tears. Judith, on his right, lit a cigarette, gazed upward in the direction of her too energetic, too sophisticated exhalation; on her other side, John earnestly bent his face to the extraction of the last morsels—legs, tail segments—from the scarlet corpse. Joan, at the opposite end of the table, glanced at him surprised, her reproach displaced by a quick grimace, of forgiveness, or of salute to his superior gift of strategy. Between them, Margaret, no longer called Bean, thirteen and large for her age, gazed from the other side of his pane of tears as if into a shopwindow at something she coveted—at her father, a crystalline heap of splinters and memories. It was not she, however, but John who, in the kitchen, as they cleared the plates and carapaces away, asked Joan the question: "*Why is Daddy crying?*"

Richard heard the question but not the murmured answer. Then he heard Bean cry, "Oh, no-oh!"—the faintly dramatized exclamation of one who had long expected it.

John returned to the table carrying a bowl of salad. He nodded tersely at his father and his lips shaped the conspiratorial words "She told."

"Told what?" Richard asked aloud, insanely.

The boy sat down as if to rebuke his father's distraction with the example of his own good manners. He said quietly, "The separation."

Joan and Margaret returned; the child, in Richard's twisted vision, seemed diminished in size, and relieved, relieved to have had the bogieman at last proved real. He called out to her—the distances at the table had grown immense—"You knew, you always knew," but the clenching at the back of his throat prevented him from making sense of it. From afar he heard Joan talking, levelly, sensibly, reciting what they had prepared: it was a separation for the summer, an experiment. She and Daddy both agreed it would be good for them; they needed space and time to think; they liked each other but did not make each other happy enough, somehow.

Judith, imitating her mother's factual tone, but in her youth off-key, too cool, said, "I think it's silly. You should either live together or get divorced."

Richard's crying, like a wave that has crested and crashed, had become tumultuous; but it was overtopped by another tumult, for John, who had been so reserved, now grew larger and larger at the table. Perhaps his younger sister's being credited with knowing set him off. "Why didn't you *tell* us?" he asked, in a large round voice quite unlike his own. "You should have *told* us you weren't getting along."

Richard was startled into attempting to force words through his tears. "We *do* get along, that's the trouble, so it doesn't show even to us—" *That we do not love each other* was the rest of the sentence; he couldn't finish it.

Joan finished for him, in her style. "And we've always, *especially,* loved our children."

John was not mollified. "What do you care about *us?*" he boomed. "We're just little things you *had.*" His sisters' laughing forced a laugh from him, which he turned hard and parodistic: "Ha ha *ha.*" Richard and Joan realized simultaneously that the child was drunk, on Judith's homecoming champagne. Feeling bound to keep the center of the stage, John took a cigarette from Judith's pack, poked it into his mouth, let it hang from his lower lip, and squinted like a gangster.

"You're not little things we had," Richard called to him. "You're the whole point. But you're grown. Or almost."

The boy was lighting matches. Instead of holding them to his cigarette (for they had never seen him smoke; being "good" had been his way of setting himself apart), he held them to his mother's face, closer and closer, for her to blow out. Then he lit the whole folder—a hiss and then a torch, held against his mother's face. Prismed by tears, the flame filled Richard's vision; he didn't know how it was extinguished. He heard Margaret say, "Oh stop showing off," and saw John, in response, break the cigarette in two and put the halves entirely into his mouth and chew, sticking out his tongue to display the shreds to his sister.

Joan talked to him, reasoning—a fountain of reason, unintelligible. "Talked about it for years . . . our children must help us . . . Daddy and I both want . . ." As the boy listened, he carefully wadded a paper napkin into the leaves of his salad, fashioned a ball of paper and lettuce, and popped it into his mouth, looking around the table for the expected laughter. None came. Judith said, "Be mature," and dismissed a plume of smoke.

Richard got up from this stifling table and led the boy outside. Though the house was in twilight, the outdoors still brimmed with light, the lovely waste light of high summer. Both laughing, he supervised John's spitting out the lettuce and paper and tobacco into the pachysandra. He took him by the hand—a square gritty hand, but for its softness a man's. Yet, it held on. They ran together up into the field, past the tennis court. The raw banking left by the bulldozers was dotted with daisies. Past the court and a flat stretch where they used to play family baseball stood a soft green rise glorious in the sun, each weed and species of grass distinct as illumination on parchment. "I'm sorry, so sorry," Richard cried. "You were the only one who ever tried to help me with all the goddam jobs around this place."

Sobbing, safe within his tears and the champagne, John explained, "It's not just the separation, it's the whole crummy year, I *hate* that school, you can't make any friends, the history teacher's a scud."

They sat on the crest of the rise, shaking and warm from their tears but easier in their voices, and Richard tried to focus on the child's sad year—the weekdays long with homework, the weekends spent in his room with model airplanes, while his parents murmured down below, nursing their separation. How selfish, how blind, Richard thought; his eyes felt scoured. He told his son, "We'll think about getting you transferred. Life's too short to be miserable."

They had said what they could, but did not want the moment to heal, and talked on, about the school, about the tennis court, whether it would ever again be as good as it had been that first summer. They walked to inspect it and pressed a few more tapes more firmly down. A little stiltedly, perhaps trying now to make too much of the moment, Richard led the boy to the spot in the field where the view was best, of the metallic blue river, the emerald marsh, the scattered islands velvety with shadow in the low light, the white bits of beach far away. "See," he said. "It goes on being beautiful. It'll be here tomorrow."

"I know," John answered, impatiently. The moment had closed.

Back in the house, the others had opened some white wine, the champagne being drunk, and still sat at the table, the three females, gossiping. Where Joan sat had become the head. She turned, showing him a tearless face, and asked, "All right?"

"We're fine," he said, resenting it, though relieved, that the party went on without him.

In bed she explained, "I couldn't cry I guess because I cried so much all spring. It really wasn't fair. It's your idea, and you made it look as though I was kicking you out."

"I'm sorry," he said. "I couldn't stop. I wanted to but couldn't."

"You *didn't* want to. You loved it. You were having your way, making a general announcement."

"I love having it over," he admitted. "God, those kids were great. So brave and funny." John, returned to the house, had settled to a model airplane in his room, and kept shouting down to them, "I'm O.K. No sweat." "And the way," Richard went on, cozy in his relief, "they never questioned the reasons we gave. No thought of a third person. Not even Judith."

"That *was* touching," Joan said.

He gave her a hug. "You were great too. Very reassuring to everybody. Thank you." Guiltily, he realized he did not feel separated.

"You still have Dickie to do," she told him. These words set before him a black mountain in the darkness; its cold breath, its near weight affected his chest. Of the four children, his elder son was most nearly his conscience. Joan did not need to add, "That's one piece of your dirty work I won't do for you."

"I know. I'll do it. You go to sleep."

Within minutes, her breathing slowed, became oblivious and deep. It was quarter to midnight. Dickie's train from the concert would come in at one-fourteen. Richard set the alarm for one. He had slept atrociously for weeks. But whenever he closed his lids some glimpse of the last hours scorched them—Judith exhaling toward the ceiling in a kind of aversion, Bean's mute staring, the sunstruck growth in the field where he and John had rested. The mountain before him moved closer, moved within him; he was huge, momentous. The ache at the back of his throat felt stale. His wife slept as if slain beside him. When, exasperated by his hot lids, his crowded heart, he rose from bed and dressed, she awoke enough to turn over. He told her then, "Joan, if I could undo it all, I would."

"Where would you begin?" she asked. There was no place. Giving him courage, she was always giving him courage. He put on shoes without socks in the dark. The children were breathing in their rooms, the downstairs was hollow. In their confusion they had left lights burning. He turned off all but one, the kitchen overhead. The car started. He had hoped it wouldn't. He met only moonlight on the road; it seemed a diaphanous companion, flickering in the leaves along the roadside, haunting his rearview mirror like a pursuer, melting under his headlights. The center of town, not quite deserted, was eerie at this hour. A young cop in uniform kept company with a gang of T-shirted kids on the steps of the bank. Across from the railroad station, several bars kept open. Customers, mostly young, passed in and out of the warm night, savoring summer's novelty. Voices shouted from cars as they passed; an immense conversation seemed in progress. Richard parked and in his weariness put his head on the passenger seat, out of the commotion and wheeling lights. It was as when, in the movies, an assassin grimly carries his mission through the jostle of a carnival—except the movies cannot show the precipitous, palpable slope you cling to within. You cannot climb back down; you can only fall. The synthetic fabric of the car seat, warmed by his cheek, confided to him an ancient, distant scent of vanilla.

A train whistle caused him to lift his head. It was on time; he had hoped it would be late. The slender drawgates descended. The bell of approach tingled happily. The great metal body, horizontally fluted, rocked to a stop, and sleepy teen-agers disembarked, his son among them. Dickie did not show surprise that his father was meeting him at this terrible hour. He sauntered to the car with two friends, both taller than he. He said "Hi" to his father and took the passenger's seat with an exhausted promptness that expressed gratitude. The friends got in the back, and Richard was grateful; a few more minutes' postponement would be won by driving them home.

He asked, "How was the concert?"

"Groovy," one boy said from the back seat.

"It bit," the other said.

"It was O.K.," Dickie said, moderate by nature, so reasonable that in his childhood the unreason of the world had given him headaches, stomach aches, nausea. When the second friend had been dropped off at his dark house, the boy blurted, "Dad, my eyes are killing me with hay fever! I'm out there cutting that mothering grass all day!"

"Do we still have those drops?"

"They didn't do any good last summer."

"They might this." Richard swung a U-turn on the empty street. The drive home took a few minutes. The mountain was here, in his throat. "Richard," he said, and felt the boy, slumped and rubbing his eyes, go tense at his tone, "I didn't come to meet you just to make your life easier. I came because your mother and I have some news for you, and you're a hard man to get ahold of these days. It's sad news."

"That's O.K." The reassurance came out soft, but quick, as if released from the tip of a spring.

Richard had feared that his tears would return and choke him, but the boy's manliness set an example, and his voice issued forth steady and dry. "It's sad news, but it needn't be tragic news, at least for you. It should have no practical effect on your life, though it's bound to have an emotional effect. You'll work at your job, and go back to school in September. Your mother and I are really proud of what you're making of your life; we don't want that to change at all."

"Yeah," the boy said lightly, on the intake of his breath, holding himself up. They turned the corner; the church they went to loomed like a gutted fort. The home of the woman Richard hoped to marry stood across the green. Her bedroom light burned.

"Your mother and I," he said, "have decided to separate. For the summer. Nothing legal, no divorce yet. We want to see how it feels. For some years now, we haven't been doing enough for each other, making each other as happy as we should be. Have you sensed that?"

"No," the boy said. It was an honest, unemotional answer: true or false in a quiz.

Glad for the factual basis, Richard pursued, even garrulously, the details. His apartment across town, his utter accessibility, the split vacation arrangements, the advantages to the children, the added mobility and variety of the summer. Dickie listened, absorbing. "Do the others know?"

"Yes."

"How did they take it?"

"The girls pretty calmly. John flipped out; he shouted and ate a cigarette and made a salad out of his napkin and told us how much he hated school."

His brother chuckled. "He did?"

"Yeah. The school issue was more upsetting for him than Mom and me. He seemed to feel better for having exploded."

"He did?" The repetition was the first sign that he was stunned.

"Yes. Dickie, I want to tell you something. This last hour, waiting for your train to get in, has been about the worst of my life. I hate this. *Hate* it. My father would have died before doing it to me." He felt immensely lighter, saying this. He had dumped the mountain on the boy. They were home. Moving swiftly as a shadow, Dickie was out of the car, through the bright kitchen. Richard called after him, "Want a glass of milk or anything?"

"No thanks."

"Want us to call the course tomorrow and say you're too sick to work?"

"No, that's all right." The answer was faint, delivered at the door to his room; Richard listened for the slam that went with a tantrum. The door closed normally, gently. The sound was sickening.

Joan had sunk into that first deep trough of sleep and was slow to awake. Richard had to repeat, "I told him."

"What did he say?"

"Nothing much. Could you go say goodnight to him? Please."

She left their room, without putting on a bathrobe. He sluggishly changed back into his pajamas and walked down the hall. Dickie was already in bed, Joan was sitting beside him, and the boy's bedside clock radio was murmuring music. When she stood, an inexplicable light—the moon?—outlined her body through the nightie. Richard sat on the warm place she had indented on the child's narrow mattress. He asked him, "Do you want the radio on like that?"

"It always is."

"Doesn't it keep you awake? It would me."

"No."

"Are you sleepy?"

"Yeah."

"Good. Sure you want to get up and go to work? You've had a big night."

"I want to."

Away at school this winter he had learned for the first time that you can go short of sleep and live. As an infant he had slept with an immobile, sweating intensity that had alarmed his babysitters. In adolescence he had often been the first of the four children to go to bed. Even now, he would go slack in the middle of a television show, his sprawled legs hairy and brown. "O.K. Good boy. Dickie, listen. I love you so much, I never knew how much until now. No matter how this works out, I'll always be with you. Really."

Richard bent to kiss an averted face but his son, sinewy, turned and with wet cheeks embraced him and gave him a kiss, on the lips, passionate as a woman's. In his father's ear he moaned one word, the crucial, intelligent word: "*Why?*"

Why. It was a whistle of wind in a crack, a knife thrust, a window thrown open on emptiness. The white face was gone, the darkness was featureless. Richard had forgotten why.

1979

ROBERT COOVER

(1932–)

Robert Coover had a midwestern childhood and education. Born in Charles City, Iowa, he lived there until he was nine. From Charles City his family moved first to Bedford, Indiana, and then to Herrin, Illinois, where his father became managing editor of the Herrin *Daily Journal.* Already writing short stories and poems in high school, he graduated as class president in 1949 and began college near home at Southern Illinois University. Two years later, he transferred to Indiana University, where, in 1953, he received his B.A. in Slavic studies. Immediately upon graduation, he joined the navy, entered Officer Candidate School, emerged as a lieutenant, and spent most of the next three years in Europe.

Back in the United States, Coover turned to writing in earnest in the summer of 1957, beginning the innovative fictions later collected in *Pricksongs and Descants* (1969). Enrolling as a graduate student at the University of Chicago from 1958 to 1961 (he received his M.A. in 1965), he practiced his skills in a national literary atmosphere charged with experimentation as writers challenged the fictional assumptions of the past. In 1958, the publication in the United States of Nabokov's *Lolita* was greeted by bans and court cases. In the same year, the appearance of Samuel Beckett's *The Unnamable* in English completed a trilogy (with *Molloy* and *Malone Dies*) directly influential on Coover. The *Evergreen Review,* which published some of Coover's earliest work, was in the forefront of journals bringing to the attention of Americans the accomplishments of such French *nouveau roman* writers as Alain Robbe-Grillet, whose *Jealousy* appeared in English in 1959. Before long, to the ferment of those years was added an increasing attention to the "anti-novels" or "meta-fictions" of younger Americans like Hawkes, Heller, Pynchon, Barthelme, and Barth.

In an essay on Beckett, Coover has suggested that "the fashion of the world was indeed changing. Not only were we about to leave behind the recent age of expression, of analysis, of words and deeds, for another frantic go at the instable stuff we stood on * * * but in fact a whole cycle of innocence and experience, begun in the Enlightenment, was drawing to an exhausted—even frightened—close." Coover's own fiction presents a violent and absurd world of elusive meaning. His first novel, *The Origin of the Brunists* (1966) traces the growth of a religious cult after a coal mine accident. With his next, *The Universal Baseball Association, Inc., J. Henry Waugh, Prop.* (1968), he reminds the reader that our illusions, including the illusions of fiction, can be more powerful than our realities. In the next, *The Public Burning* (1977), he mixes history, myth, and fiction as Uncle Sam, Richard Nixon, and Ethel and Julius Rosenberg come together in an outrageously impossible plot constructed on the facts of a famous trial and execution. In his most recent novel, *Gerald's Party* (1985), he discovers comic absurdity in the events surrounding a murder.

After the early *Pricksongs & Descants,* Coover has returned frequently to forms shorter than the traditional novel, often constructed of insistent reiterations that serve to emphasize the parodic intent. Among these are *A Political Fable* (1980), in which Dr. Seuss's character the Cat in the Hat is a candidate for president; *Spanking the Maid* (1982), with variations on a pornographic theme; and *A Night at the Movies* (1987), a volume of related short fictions inspired by classic movie genres.

For many years, Coover did much of his work in Europe, where he has lived in England and Spain. In the United States, he has taught at Bard, Iowa, Princeton, and, in recent years, at Brown University.

Coover's fiction to date is named above. Plays are collected in *A Theological Position* (1972).

Studies include Richard Andersen, *Robert Coover,* 1981; Lois Gordon, *Robert Coover: The Universal Fictionmaking Process,* 1983; and Jackson I. Cope, *Robert Coover's Fictions,* 1986.

The Gingerbread House

1

A pine forest in the midafternoon. Two children follow an old man, dropping breadcrumbs, singing nursery tunes. Dense earthy greens seep into the darkening distance, flecked and streaked with filtered sunlight. Spots of red, violet, pale blue, gold, burnt orange. The girl carries a basket for gathering flowers. The boy is occupied with the crumbs. Their song tells of God's care for little ones.

2

Poverty and resignation weigh on the old man. His cloth jacket is patched and threadbare, sunbleached white over the shoulders, worn through on the elbows. His feet do not lift, but shuffle through the dust. White hair. Parched skin. Secret forces of despair and guilt seem to pull him earthward.

3

The girl plucks a flower. The boy watches curiously. The old man stares impatiently into the forest's depths, where night seems already to crouch. The girl's apron is a bright orange, the gay color of freshly picked tangerines, and is stitched happily with blues and reds and greens; but her dress is simple and brown, tattered at the hem, and her feet are bare. Birds accompany the children in their singing and butterflies decorate the forest spaces.

4

The boy's gesture is furtive. His right hand trails behind him, letting a crumb fall. His face is half-turned toward his hand, but his eyes remain watchfully fixed on the old man's feet ahead. The old man wears heavy mud-spattered shoes, high-topped and leather-thonged. Like the old man's own skin, the shoes are dry and cracked and furrowed with wrinkles. The boy's pants are a bluish-brown, ragged at the cuffs, his jacket a faded red. He, like the girl, is barefoot.

5

The children sing nursery songs about May baskets and gingerbread houses and a saint who ate his own fleas. Perhaps they sing to lighten their young hearts, for puce wisps of dusk now coil through the trunks and branches of the thickening forest. Or perhaps they sing to conceal the boy's subterfuge. More likely, they sing for no reason at all, a thoughtless childish habit. To hear themselves. Or to admire their memories. Or to entertain the old man. To fill the silence. Conceal their thoughts. Their expectations.

6

The boy's hand and wrist, thrusting from the outgrown jacket (the faded red cuff is not a cuff at all, but the torn limits merely, the ragged edge of the soft worn sleeve), are tanned, a little soiled, childish. The fingers are short and plump, the palm soft, the wrist small. Three fingers curl under, holding back crumbs, kneading them, coaxing them into position, while the index finger and thumb flick them sparingly, one by one, to the ground, playing with them a moment, balling them, pinching them as if for luck or pleasure, before letting them go.

7

The old man's pale blue eyes float damply in deep dark pouches, half-shrouded by heavy upper lids and beetled over by shaggy white brows. Deep creases fan out from the moist corners, angle down past the nose, score the tanned cheeks and pinch the mouth. The old man's gaze is straight ahead, but at what? Perhaps at nothing. Some invisible destination. Some irrecoverable point of departure. One thing can be said about the eyes: they are tired. Whether they have seen too much or too little, they betray no will to see yet more.

8

The witch is wrapped in a tortured whirl of black rags. Her long face is drawn and livid, and her eyes glow like burning coals. Her angular body twists this way and that, flapping the black rags—flecks of blue and amethyst wink and flash in the black tangle. Her gnarled blue hands snatch greedily at space, shred her clothes, claw cruelly at her face and throat. She cackles silently, then suddenly screeches madly, seizes a passing dove, and tears its heart out.

9

The girl, younger than the boy, skips blithely down the forest path, her blonde curls flowing freely. Her brown dress is coarse and plain, but her apron is gay and white petticoats wink from beneath the tattered hem. Her skin is fresh and pink and soft, her knees and elbows dimpled, her cheeks rosy. Her young gaze flicks airily from flower to flower, bird to bird, tree to tree, from the boy to the old man, from the green grass to the encroaching darkness, and all of it seems to delight her equally. Her basket is full to overflowing. Does she even know the boy is dropping crumbs? or where the old man is leading them? Of course, but it's nothing! a game!

10

There is, in the forest, even now, a sunny place, with mintdrop trees and cotton candy bushes, an air as fresh and heady as lemonade. Rivulets of honey flow over gumdrop pebbles, and lollypops grow wild as daisies. This is the place of the gingerbread house. Children come here, but, they say, none leave.

11

The dove is a soft lustrous white, head high, breast filled, tip of the tail less than a feather's thickness off the ground. From above, it would be seen against the pale path—a mixture of umbers and grays and the sharp brown strokes of pine needles—but from its own level, in profile, its pure whiteness is set off glowingly against the obscure mallows and distant moss greens of the forest. Only its small beak moves. Around a bread crumb.

12

The song is about a great king who won many battles, but the girl sings alone. The old man has turned back, gazes curiously but dispassionately now at the boy. The boy, too, has turned, no longer furtive, hand poised but no crumb dropping from his fingertips. He stares back down the path by which they three have come, his mouth agape, his eyes startled. His left hand is raised, as if arrested a moment before striking out in protest. Doves are eating his bread crumbs. His ruse has failed.

Perhaps the old man, not so ignorant in such matters after all, has known all along it would. The girl sings of pretty things sold in the market.

13

So huddled over her prey is the witch that she seems nothing more than a pile of black rags heaped on a post. Her pale long-nailed hands are curled inward toward her breast, massaging the object, her head lower than her hunched shoulders, wan beaked nose poked in among the restless fingers. She pauses, cackling softly, peers left, then right, then lifts the heart before her eyes. The burnished heart of the dove glitters like a ruby, a polished cherry, a brilliant, heart-shaped bloodstone. It beats still. A soft radiant pulsing. The black bony shoulders of the witch quake with glee, with greed, with lust.

14

A wild blur of fluttering white: the dove's wings flapping! Hands clutch its body, its head, its throat, small hands with short plump fingers. Its wings flail against the dusky forest green, but it is forced down against the umber earth. The boy falls upon it, his hands bloodied by beak and claws.

15

The gingerbread house is approached by flagstones of variegated wafers, through a garden of candied fruits and all-day suckers in neat little rows.

16

No song from the lips of the girl, but a cry of anguish. The basket of flowers is dropped, the kings and saints forgotten. She struggles with the boy for the bird. She kicks him, falls upon him, pulls his hair, tears at his red jacket. He huddles around the bird, trying to elbow free of the girl. Both children are weeping, the boy of anger and frustration, the girl of pain and pity and a bruised heart. Their legs entangle, their fists beat at each other, feathers fly.

17

The pale blue eyes of the old man stare not ahead, but down. The squint, the sorrow, the tedium are vanished; the eyes focus clearly. The deep creases fanning out from the damp corners pinch inward, a brief wince, as though at some inner hurt, some certain anguish, some old wisdom. He sighs.

18

The girl has captured the bird. The boy, small chest heaving, kneels in the path watching her, the anger largely drained out of him. His faded red jacket is torn; his pants are full of dust and pine needles. She has thrust the dove protectively beneath her skirt, and sits, knees apart, leaning over it, weeping softly. The old man stoops down, lifts her bright orange apron, her skirt, her petticoats. The boy turns away. The dove is nested in her small round thighs. It is dead.

19

Shadows have lengthened. Umbers and lavenders and greens have grayed. But the body of the dove glows yet in the gathering dusk. The whiteness of the ruffled breast seems to be fighting back against the threat of night. It is strewn with flowers, now beginning to wilt. The old man, the boy, and the girl have gone.

20

The beams of the gingerbread house are licorice sticks, cemented with taffy, weatherboarded with gingerbread, and coated with caramel. Peppermint-stick chimneys sprout randomly from its chocolate roof and its windows are laced with meringue. Oh, what a house! and the best thing of all is the door.

21

The forest is dense and deep. Branches reach forth like arms. Brown animals scurry. The boy makes no furtive gestures. The girl, carrying her flowerbasket, does not skip or sing. They walk, arms linked, eyes wide open and staring ahead into the forest. The old man plods on, leading the way, his heavy old leather-thonged shoes shuffling in the damp dust and undergrowth.

22

The old man's eyes, pale in the sunlight, now seem to glitter in the late twilight. Perhaps it is their wetness picking up the last flickering light of day. The squint has returned, but it is not the squint of weariness: resistance, rather. His mouth opens as though to speak, to rebuke, but his teeth are clenched. The witch twists and quivers, her black rags whirling, whipping, flapping. From her lean bosom, she withdraws the pulsing red heart of a dove. How it glows, how it rages, how it dances in the dusk! The old man now does not resist. Lust flattens his face and mists his old eyes, where glitter now reflections of the ruby heart. Grimacing, he plummets forward, covering the cackling witch, crashing through brambles that tear at his clothes.

23

A wild screech cleaves the silence of the dusky forest. Birds start up from branches and the undergrowth is alive with frightened animals. The old man stops short, one hand raised protectively in front of him, the other, as though part of the same instinct, reaching back to shield his children. Dropping her basket of flowers, the girl cries out in terror and springs forward into the old man's arms. The boy blanches, shivers as though a cold wind might be wetly wrapping his young body, but manfully holds his ground. Shapes seem to twist and coil, and vapors seep up from the forest floor. The girl whimpers and the old man holds her close.

24

The beds are simple but solid. The old man himself has made them. The sun is setting, the room is in shadows, the children tucked safely in. The old man tells them a story about a good fairy who granted a poor man three wishes. The wishes, he knows, were wasted, but so then is the story. He lengthens the tale with details about the good fairy, how sweet and kind and pretty she is, then lets the children complete the story with their own wishes, their own dreams. Below, a brutal demand is being forced upon him. Why must the goodness of all wishes come to nothing?

25

The flowerbasket lies, overturned, by the forest path, its wilting flowers strewn. Shadows darker than dried blood spread beneath its gaping mouth. The shadows are long, for night is falling.

26

The old man has fallen into the brambles. The children, weeping, help pull him free. He sits on the forest path staring at the boy and girl. It is as though he is unable to recognize them. Their weeping dies away. They huddle more closely together, stare back at the old man. His face is scratched, his clothes torn. He is breathing irregularly.

27

The sun, the songs, the breadcrumbs, the dove, the overturned basket, the long passage toward night: where, the old man wonders, havc all the good fairies gone? He leads the way, pushing back the branches. The children follow, silent and frightened.

28

The boy pales and his heart pounds, but manfully he holds his ground. The witch writhes, her black rags fluttering, licking at the twisted branches. With a soft seductive cackle, she holds before him the burnished cherry-red heart of a dove. The boy licks his lips. She steps back. The glowing heart pulses gently, evenly, excitingly.

29

The good fairy has sparkling blue eyes and golden hair, a soft sweet mouth and gentle hands that caress and soothe. Gossamer wings sprout from her smooth back; from her flawless chest two firm breasts with tips bright as rubies.

30

The witch, holding the flaming pulsing heart out to the boy, steps back into the dark forest. The boy, in hesitation, follows. Back. Back. Swollen eyes aglitter, the witch draws the ruby heart close to her dark lean breast, then past her shoulder and away from the boy. Transfixed, he follows it, brushing by her. The witch's gnarled and bluish fingers claw at his poor garments, his pale red jacket and bluish-brown pants, surprising his soft young flesh.

31

The old man's shoulders are bowed earthward, his face is lined with sorrow, his neck bent forward with resignation, but his eyes glow like burning coals. He clutches his shredded shirt to his throat, stares intensely at the boy. The boy stands alone and trembling on the path, staring into the forest's terrible darkness. Shapes whisper and coil. The boy licks his lips, steps forward. A terrible shriek shreds the forest hush. The old man grimaces, pushes the whimpering girl away, strikes the boy.

32

No more breadcrumbs, no more pebbles, no more songs or flowers. The slap echoes through the terrible forest, doubles back on its own echoes, folding finally into a sound not unlike a whispering cackle.

33

The girl, weeping, kisses the struck boy and presses him close, shielding him from the tormented old man. The old man, taken aback, reaches out uncertainly, gently touches the girl's frail shoulder. She shakes his hand off—nearly a shudder—and shrinks toward the boy. The boy squares his shoulders, color returning to his face. The familiar creases of age and despair crinkle again the old man's face. His pale blue eyes mist over. He looks away. He leaves the children by the last light of day.

34

But the door! The door is shaped like a heart and is as red as a cherry, always half-open, whether lit by sun or moon, is sweeter than a sugarplum, more enchanting than a peppermint stick. It is red as a poppy, red as an apple, red as a strawberry, red as a bloodstone, red as a rose. Oh, what a thing is the door of that house!

35

The children, alone in the strange black forest, huddle wretchedly under a great gnarled tree. Owls hoot and bats flick menacingly through the twisting branches. Strange shapes writhe and rustle before their weary eyes. They hold each other tight and, trembling, sing lullabyes, but they are not reassured.

36

The old man trudges heavily out of the black forest. His way is marked, not by breadcrumbs, but by dead doves, ghostly white in the empty night.

37

The girl prepares a mattress of leaves and flowers and pineneedles. The boy gathers branches to cover them, to hide them, to protect them. They make pillows of their poor garments. Bats screech as they work and owls blink down on their bodies, ghostly white, young, trembling. They creep under the branches, disappearing into the darkness.

38

Gloomily, the old man sits in the dark room and stares at the empty beds. The good fairy, though a mystery of the night, effuses her surroundings with a lustrous radiance. Is it the natural glow of her small nimble body or perhaps the star at the tip of her wand? Who can tell? Her gossamer wings flutter rapidly, and she floats, ruby-tipped breasts downward, legs dangling and dimpled knees bent slightly, glowing buttocks arched up in defiance of the night. How good she is! In the black empty room, the old man sighs and uses up a wish: he wishes his poor children well.

39

The children are nearing the gingerbread house. Passing under mintdrop trees, sticking their fingers in the cotton candy bushes, sampling the air as heady as lemonade, they skip along singing nursery songs. Nonsense songs about dappled horses and the slaying of dragons. Counting songs and idle riddles. They cross over rivulets of honey on gumdrop pebbles, picking the lollypops that grow as wild as daffodils.

40

The witch flicks and flutters through the blackened forest, her livid face twisted with hatred, her inscrutable condition. Her eyes burn like glowing coals and her black rags flap loosely. Her gnarled hands claw greedily at the branches, tangle in the night's webs, dig into tree trunks until the sap flows beneath her nails. Below, the boy and girl sleep an exhausted sleep. One ghostly white leg, with dimpled knee and soft round thigh, thrusts out from under the blanket of branches.

41

But wish again! Flowers and butterflies. Dense earthy greens seeping into the distance, flecked and streaked with midafternoon sunlight. Two children following an old man. They drop breadcrumbs, sing nursery songs. The old man walks leadenly. The boy's gesture is furtive. The girl—but it's no use, the doves will come again, there are no reasonable wishes.

42

The children approach the gingerbread house through a garden of candied fruits and all-day suckers, hopping along on flagstones of variegated wafers. They sample the gingerbread weatherboarding with its caramel coating, lick at the meringue on the windowsills, kiss each other's sweetened lips. The boy climbs up on the chocolate roof to break off a peppermint-stick chimney, comes sliding down into a rainbarrel full of vanilla pudding. The girl, reaching out to catch him in his fall, slips on a sugarplum and tumbles into a sticky rock garden of candied chestnuts. Laughing gaily, they lick each other clean. And how grand is the red-and-white striped chimney the boy holds up for her! how bright! how sweet! But the door: here they pause and catch their breath. It is heart-shaped and blood-stone-red, its burnished surface gleaming in the sunlight. Oh, what a thing is that door! Shining like a ruby, like hard cherry candy, and pulsing softly, radiantly. Yes, marvelous! delicious! insuperable! but beyond: what is that sound of black rags flapping?

1969

JOHN GARDNER
(1933–1982)

John Gardner was born in Batavia, New York, and raised on the family farm there; he attended public schools. After two years at DePauw University, he transferred to Washington University in St. Louis and graduated with a B.A. in 1955. After earning an M.A. in 1956 and a Ph.D. in 1958 from Iowa State University, he became a literary scholar and English professor as well as a prolific writer of fiction. Considering his writing a moral activity related to his teaching, he once said, "If I don't teach and get my point across to younger writers, I will burn in hell for a thousand years." When his career was cut short by a motorcycle accident at the age of forty-nine, he had published more than thirty books and pamphlets, more than one hundred stories, poems, and essays, and more than one hundred interviews. He had taught at nearly a dozen universities, ending up at the State University of New York at Binghamton in the region where he was born.

Gardner's fiction ranges widely in setting and method. His first novel, *Resurrection* (1966), centers on a professor of philosophy who returns to his upstate New York home when he discovers he is dying. *The Wreckage of Agathon* (1970) uses dialogue between the dying Greek philosopher and his disciple to analyze the nature of civilization. *Grendel* (1971) retells the Anglo-Saxon classic *Beowulf* from the monster's point of view. *The Sunlight Dialogues* (1972) and *Nickel Mountain* (1973) are both set in upstate New York. In *October Light* (1976) Gardner uses the device of a novel within the novel to explore the conflict between a Yankee farmer and his sister; the same structural device is also used in *Freddy's Book* (1980).

One of Gardner's pervasive themes is human responsibility. In *October Light, Nickel Mountain,* and many of the short stories, characters battle their own weaknesses and overcome guilt in pursuit of their goals. "Redemption" is a good example of how this theme is presented. It begins with a traumatic episode from Gardner's childhood (the death of his brother in a farm accident), parallels that personal trauma with a larger tragedy (the sufferings of the Russian Revolution), and demonstrates the tenacity of the human spirit in the perseverance of the young music student and his teacher.

Gardner's last years were filled with controversy generated by his literary criticism. His *The Life and Times of Chaucer* (1977) drew charges of plagiarism. More virulent was the reaction to *On Moral Fiction* (1978), an essay that drew a firestorm of criticism from many of his fellow writers.

In it he details the high purpose he postulates for art—to rediscover "what is necessary to humanness." He describes fiction as the great teacher, "presenting valid models for imitation, eternal verities worth keeping in mind, and a benevolent vision of the possible which can inspire and incite human beings toward virtue, toward life affirmation as opposed to destruction or indifference." His measurement of other post-war novelists against this standard found most of them wanting in moral seriousness, love and hope for mankind, consistency or clarity, and he concluded that current fiction was poor because writers were too concerned with form and did not take their role seriously. He harkened back to the altruism of the nineteenth century in asserting that in a democratic society art "ought to be a force bringing people together, breaking down barriers of prejudice and ignorance, and holding up ideals worth pursuing."

Gardner spent most of the rest of his life defending himself against the backlash from *On Moral Fiction.* He engaged in many dialogues and written controversies with other writers and his later novels, *Freddy's Book* and *Mickelsson's Ghosts* (1982), were subjected to stringent criticisms along the lines he had defined himself.

Gardner's novels, in addition to those named above, include *In the Suicide Mountains,* 1977. His short stories are collected in *The King's Indian,* 1974; and *The Art of Living,* 1981. Nicholas Delbanco edited *Stillness and Shadows,* 1986, two unfinished novels, the first autobiographical. Criticism, besides *On Moral Fiction,* includes *The Forms of Fiction,* 1962; and the posthumous *The Art of Fiction: Notes on Craft for Young Writers,* 1984. Scholarly works include *The Complete Works of the Gawain Poet,* 1965. Volumes of verse are *Jason and Medeia,* 1973; and *Poems,* 1978. A volume of opera libretti is *Three Libretti,* 1979. A radio play is *The Temptation Game,* 1980. Children's books include *Dragon, Dragon,* 1975; and *A Child's Bestiary,* 1977.

Studies include Robert A. Morace and Kathryn Van Spanckeren, eds., *John Gardner: Critical Perspectives,* 1982; and Gregory L. Morris, *A World of Order and Light: The Fiction of John Gardner,* 1984.

Redemption

One day in April—a clear, blue day when there were crocuses in bloom—Jack Hawthorne ran over and killed his brother, David. Even at the last moment he could have prevented his brother's death by slamming on the tractor brakes, easily in reach for all the shortness of his legs; but he was unable to think, or, rather, thought unclearly, and so watched it happen, as he would again and again watch it happen in his mind, with nearly undiminished intensity and clarity, all his life. The younger brother was riding, as both of them knew he should not have been, on the cultipacker, a two-ton implement lumbering behind the tractor, crushing new-ploughed ground. Jack was twelve, his brother, David, seven. The scream came not from David, who never got a sound out, but from their five-year-old sister, who was riding on the fender of the tractor, looking back. When Jack turned to look, the huge iron wheels had reached his brother's pelvis. He kept driving, reacting as he would to a half-crushed farm animal, and imagining, in the same stab of thought, that perhaps his brother would survive. Blood poured from David's mouth.

Their father was nearly destroyed by it. Sometimes Jack would find him lying on the cowbarn floor, crying, unable to stand up. Dale Hawthorne, the father, was a sensitive, intelligent man, by nature a dreamer. It showed in old photographs, his smile coded, his eyes on the horizon. He loved all his children and would not consciously have been able to hate his son even if Jack had indeed been, as he thought himself, his brother's murderer. But he could not help sometimes seeming to blame his son, though consciously he blamed only his own unwisdom and—so far as his belief held firm—God. Dale Hawthorne's mind swung violently at this time, reversing itself almost hour by hour, from desperate faith to the most savage, black-hearted atheism. Every sickly calf, every sow that ate her litter, was a new, sure proof that the religion he'd followed all his life was a lie. Yet skeletons were orderly, as were, he thought, the stars. He was unable to decide, one moment full of rage at God's injustice, the next moment wracked by doubt of His existence.

Though he was not ordinarily a man who smoked, he would sometimes sit up all night now, or move restlessly, hurriedly, from room to room, chain-smoking Lucky Strikes. Or he would ride away on his huge, darkly thundering Harley-Davidson 80, trying to forget, morbidly dwelling on what he'd meant to put behind him—how David had once laughed, cake in his fists; how he'd once patched a chair with precocious skill—or Dale Hawthorne would think, for the hundredth time, about suicide, hunting in mixed fear and anger for some reason not to miss the next turn, fly off to the right of the next iron bridge onto the moonlit gray rocks and black water below—discovering, invariably, no reason but the damage his suicide would do to his wife and the children remaining.

Sometimes he would forget for a while by abandoning reason and responsibility for love affairs. Jack's father was at this time still young, still handsome, well-known for the poetry he recited at local churches or for English classes or meetings of the Grange[1]—recited, to loud applause (he had poems of all kinds, both serious and comic), for thrashing crews, old men at the V.A. Hospital, even the tough, flint-eyed orphans at the Children's Home. He was a celebrity, in fact, as much Romantic poet-hero as his time and western New York State could afford—and beyond all that, he was now so full of pain and unassuageable guilt that women's hearts flew to him unbidden. He became, with all his soul and without cynical intent—though fleeing all law, or what he'd once thought law—a hunter of women, trading off his sorrow for the sorrows of wearied, unfulfilled country wives. At times he would be gone from the farm for days, abandoning the work to Jack and whoever was available to help—some neighbor or older cousin or one of Jack's uncles. No one complained, at least not openly. A stranger might have condemned him, but no one in the family did, certainly not Jack, not even Jack's mother, though her sorrow was increased. Dale Hawthorne had always been, before the accident, a faithful man, one of the most fair-minded, genial farmers in the country. No one asked that, changed as he was, he do more, for the moment, than survive.

As for Jack's mother, though she'd been, before the accident, a cheerful woman—one who laughed often and loved telling stories, sometimes sang anthems in bandanna and blackface before her husband recited poems—she cried now, nights, and did only as much as she had strength to do—so sapped by grief that she could barely move her arms. She comforted Jack and his sister, Phoebe—herself as well—by embracing them vehemently whenever new waves of guilt swept in, by constant reassurance and extravagant praise, frequent mention of how proud some relative would be—once, for instance, over a drawing of his sister's, "Oh, Phoebe, if only your great-aunt Lucy could see this!" Great-aunt Lucy had been famous, among the family and friends, for her paintings of families of lions. And Jack's mother forced on his sister and himself comforts more permanent: piano and, for Jack, French-horn lessons, school and church activities, above all an endless, exhausting ritual of chores. Because she had, at thirty-four, considerable strength of charac-

1. A social organization of farmers and their families.

ter—except that, these days, she was always eating—and because, also, she was a woman of strong religious faith, a woman who, in her years of church work and teaching at the high school, had made scores of close, for the most part equally religious, friends, with whom she regularly corresponded, her letters, then theirs, half filling the mailbox at the foot of the hill and cluttering every table, desk, and niche in the large old house—friends who now frequently visited or phoned—she was able to move step by step past disaster and in the end keep her family from wreck. She said very little to her children about her troubles. In fact, except for the crying behind her closed door, she kept her feelings strictly secret.

But for all his mother and her friends could do for him—for all his father's older brothers could do, or, when he was there, his father himself—the damage to young Jack Hawthorne took a long while healing. Working the farm, ploughing, cultipacking, disking, dragging, he had plenty of time to think—plenty of time for the accident to replay, with the solidity of real time repeated, in his mind, his whole body flinching from the image as it came, his voice leaping up independent of him, as if a shout could perhaps drive the memory back into its cave. Maneuvering the tractor over sloping, rocky fields, dust whorling out like smoke behind him or, when he turned into the wind, falling like soot until his skin was black and his hair as thick and stiff as old clothes in an attic—the circles of foothills every day turning greener, the late-spring wind flowing endless and sweet with the smell of coming rain—he had all the time in the world to cry and swear bitterly at himself, standing up to drive, as his father often did, Jack's sore hands clamped tight to the steering wheel, his shoes unsteady on the bucking axlebeam—for stones lay everywhere, yellowed in the sunlight, a field of misshapen skulls. He'd never loved his brother, he raged out loud, never loved anyone as well as he should have. He was incapable of love, he told himself, striking the steering wheel. He was inherently bad, a spiritual defective. He was evil.

So he raged and grew increasingly ashamed of his raging, reminded by the lengthening shadows across the field of the theatricality in all he did, his most terrible sorrow mere sorrow on a stage, the very thunderclaps above—dark blue, rushing sky, birds crazily wheeling—mere opera set, proper lighting for his rant. At once he would hush himself, lower his rear end to the tractor seat, lock every muscle to the stillness of a statue, and drive on, solitary, blinded by tears; yet even now it was theater, not life—mere ghastly posturing, as in that story of his father's, how Lord Byron once tried to get Shelley's skull to make a drinking cup.[2] Tears no longer came, though the storm went on building. Jack rode on, alone with the indifferent, murderous machinery in the widening ten-acre field.

When the storm at last hit, he'd been driven up the lane like a dog in flight, lashed by gusty rain, chased across the tracks to the tractor shed and from there to the kitchen, full of food smells from his mother's work and Phoebe's, sometimes the work of two or three friends who'd stopped by to look in on the family. Jack kept aloof, repelled by their bright, melodious chatter and absentminded humming, indignant at their pretense that all was well. "My, how you've grown!" the old friend or fellow teacher from high school would say, and to his mother, "My, what big *hands* he has, Betty!" He would glare at his little sister, Phoebe, his sole ally, already

2. George Gordon, Lord Byron (1788–1824), Percy Bysshe Shelley (1792–1822): English poets.

half traitor—she would bite her lips, squinting, concentrating harder on the mixing bowl and beaters; she was forever making cakes—and he would retreat as soon as possible to the evening chores.

He had always told himself stories to pass the time when driving the tractor, endlessly looping back and forth, around and around, fitting the land for spring planting. He told them to himself aloud, taking all parts in the dialogue, gesturing, making faces, discarding dignity, here where no one could see or overhear him, half a mile from the nearest house. Once all his stories had been of sexual conquest or of heroic battle with escaped convicts from the Attica Prison or kidnappers who, unbeknownst to anyone, had built a small shack where they kept their captives, female and beautiful, in the lush, swampy woods beside the field. Now, after the accident, his subject matter changed. His fantasies came to be all of self-sacrifice, pitiful stories in which he redeemed his life by throwing it away to save others more worthwhile. To friends and officials of his fantasy, especially to heroines—a girl named Margaret, at school, or his cousin Linda—he would confess his worthlessness at painful length, naming all his faults, granting himself no quarter. For a time this helped, but the lie was too obvious, the manipulation of shame to buy love, and in the end despair bled all color from his fantasies. The foulness of his nature became clearer and clearer in his mind until, like his father, he began to toy—dully but in morbid earnest now—with the idea of suicide. His chest would fill with anguish, as if he were dreaming some nightmare wide awake, or bleeding internally, and his arms and legs would grow shaky with weakness, until he had to stop and get down from the tractor and sit for a few minutes, his eyes fixed on some comforting object, for instance a dark, smooth stone.

Even from his father and his father's brothers, who sometimes helped with the chores, he kept aloof. His father and uncles were not talkative men. Except for his father's comic poems, they never told jokes, though they liked hearing them; and because they had lived there all their lives and knew every soul in the county by name, nothing much surprised them or, if it did, roused them to mention it. Their wives might gossip, filling the big kitchen with their pealing laughter or righteous indignation, but the men for the most part merely smiled or compressed their lips and shook their heads. At the G.L.F. feedstore, occasionally, eating an ice cream while they waited for their grist, they would speak of the weather or the Democrats; but in the barn, except for "Jackie, shift that milker, will you?" or "You can carry this up to the milk house now," they said nothing. They were all tall, square men with deeply cleft chins and creases on their foreheads and muscular jowls; all Presbyterians, sometimes deacons, sometimes elders; and they were all gentle-hearted, decent men who looked lost in thought, especially Jack's father, though on occasion they'd abruptly frown or mutter, or speak a few words to a cow, or a cat, or a swallow. It was natural that Jack, working with such men, should keep to himself, throwing down ensilage from the pitch-dark, sweet-ripe crater of the silo or hay bales from the mow, dumping oats in front of the cows' noses, or—taking the longhandled, blunt wooden scraper from the whitewashed wall—pushing manure into the gutters.

He felt more community with the cows than with his uncles or, when he was there, his father. Stretched out flat between the two rows of stanchions, waiting for the cows to be finished with their silage so he could drive them out to pasture, he would listen to their chewing in the dark, close barn, a sound as soothing, as infinitely restful, as waves along a shore, and would feel their surprisingly warm, scented breath, their bovine quiet, and for a while would find that his anxiety had left him. With the cows, the barn cats, the half-sleeping dog, he could forget and feel at home, feel that life was pleasant. He felt the same when walking up the long, fenced lane at the first light of sunrise—his shoes and pants legs sopping wet with dew, his ears full of birdcalls—going to bring in the herd from the upper pasture. Sometimes on the way he would step off the deep, crooked cow path to pick cherries or red raspberries, brighter than jewels in the morning light. They were sweeter then than at any other time, and as he approached, clouds of sparrows would explode into flight from the branches, whirring off to safety. The whole countryside was sweet, early in the morning—newly cultivated corn to his left; to his right, alfalfa and, beyond that, wheat. He felt at one with it all. It was what life ought to be, what he'd once believed it was.

But he could not make such feelings last. *No,* he thought bitterly on one such morning, throwing stones at the dull, indifferent cows, driving them down the lane. However he might hate himself and all his race, a cow was no better, or a field of wheat. Time and again he'd been driven half crazy, angry enough to kill, by the stupidity of cows when they'd pushed through a fence and—for all his shouting, for all the indignant barking of the dog—they could no longer locate the gap they themselves had made. And no better to be grain, smashed flat by the first rainy wind. So, fists clenched, he raged inside his mind, grinding his teeth to drive out thought, at war with the universe. He remembered his father, erect, eyes flashing, speaking Mark Antony's angry condemnation from the stage at the Grange. His father had seemed to him, that night, a creature set apart. His extended arm, pointing, was the terrible warning of a god. And now, from nowhere, the black memory of his brother's death rushed over him again, mindless and inexorable as a wind or wave, the huge cultipacker lifting—only an inch or so—as it climbed toward the shoulders, then sank on the cheek, flattening the skull—and he heard, more real than the morning, his sister's scream.

One day in August, a year and a half after the accident, they were combining oats —Jack and two neighbors and two of his cousins—when Phoebe came out, as she did every day, to bring lunch to those who worked in the field. Their father had been gone, this time, for nearly three weeks, and since he'd left at the height of the harvest season, no one was sure he would return, though as usual they kept silent about it. Jack sat alone in the shade of an elm, apart from the others. It was a habit they'd come to accept as they accepted, so far as he knew, his father's ways. Phoebe brought the basket from the shade where the others had settled to the shade here on Jack's side, farther from the bright, stubbled field.

"It's chicken," she said, and smiled, kneeling.

The basket was nearly as large as she was—Phoebe was seven—but she seemed to see nothing unreasonable in her having to lug it up the hill from the house. Her face was flushed, and drops of perspiration stood out along her hairline, but her smile was not only uncomplaining but positively cheerful. The trip to the field was an escape from housework, he understood; even so, her happiness offended him.

"Chicken," he said, and looked down glumly at his hard, tanned arms black with oatdust. Phoebe smiled on, her mind far away, as it seemed to him, and like a child playing house she took a dishtowel from the basket, spread it on the grass, then set out wax-paper packages of chicken, rolls, celery, and salt, and finally a small plastic thermos, army green.

She looked up at him now. "I brought you a thermos all for yourself because you always sit alone."

He softened a little without meaning to. "Thanks," he said.

She looked down again, and for all his self-absorption he was touched, noticing that she bowed her head in the way a much older girl might do, troubled by thought, though her not quite clean, dimpled hands were a child's. He saw that there was something she wanted to say and, to forestall it, brushed flying ants from the top of the thermos, unscrewed the cap, and poured himself iced tea. When he drank, the tea was so cold it brought a momentary pain to his forehead and made him aware once more of the grating chaff under his collar, blackening all his exposed skin, gritty around his eyes—aware, too, of the breezeless, insect-filled heat beyond the shade of the elm. Behind him, just at the rim of his hearing, one of the neighbors laughed at some remark from the younger of his cousins. Jack drained the cup, brooding on his aching muscles. Even in the shade his body felt baked dry.

"Jack," his sister said, "did you want to say grace?"

"Not really," he said, and glanced at her.

He saw that she was looking at his face in alarm, her mouth slightly opened, eyes wide, growing wider, and though he didn't know why, his heart gave a jump. "I already said it," he mumbled. "Just not out loud."

"Oh," she said, then smiled.

When everyone had finished eating she put the empty papers, the jug, and the smaller thermos in the basket, grinned at them all and said goodbye—whatever had bothered her was forgotten as soon as that—and, leaning far over, balancing the lightened but still-awkward basket, started across the stubble for the house. As he cranked the tractor she turned around to look back at them and wave. He nodded and, as if embarrassed, touched his straw hat.

Not till he was doing the chores that night did he grasp what her look of alarm had meant. If he wouldn't say grace, then perhaps there was no heaven. Their father would never get well, and David was dead. He squatted, drained of all strength again, staring at the hoof of the cow he'd been stripping, preparing her for the milker, and thought of his absent father. He saw the motorcycle roaring down a twisting mountain road, the clatter of the engine ringing like harsh music against shale. If what he felt was hatred, it was a terrible, desperate envy, too; his father all alone, uncompromised, violent, cut off as if by centuries from the warmth, chatter, and smells of the kitchen, the dimness of stained glass where he, Jack, sat every Sunday between his mother and sister, looking toward the pulpit where in the old days his father had sometimes read the lesson, soft-voiced but aloof from the timid-eyed flock, Christ's sheep.

Something blocked the light coming in through the cowbarn window from the west, and he turned his head, glancing up.

"You all right there, Jackie?" his uncle Walt said, bent forward, near-sightedly peering across the gutter.

He nodded and quickly wiped his wrist across his cheeks. He moved his hands once more to the cow's warm teats.

A few nights later, when he went in from chores, the door between the kitchen and livingroom was closed, and the house was unnaturally quiet. He stood a moment listening, still holding the milk pail, absently fitting the heel of one boot into the bootjack and tugging until the boot slipped off. He pried off the other, then walked to the icebox in his stocking feet, opened the door, carried the pitcher to the table, and filled it from the pail. When he'd slid the pitcher into the icebox again and closed the door, he went without a sound, though not meaning to be stealthy, toward the livingroom. Now, beyond the closed door, he heard voices, his sister and mother, then one of his aunts. He pushed the door open and looked in, about to speak.

Though the room was dim, no light but the small one among the pictures on the piano, he saw his father at once, kneeling by the davenport with his face on his mother's lap. Phoebe was on the davenport beside their mother, hugging her and him, Phoebe's cheeks stained, like her mother's, with tears. Around them, as if reverently drawn back, Uncle Walt, Aunt Ruth, and their two children sat watching, leaning forward with shining eyes. His father's head, bald down the center, glowed, and he had his glasses off.

"Jackie," his aunt called sharply, "come in. It's all over. Your dad's come home."

He would have fled, but his knees had no strength in them and his chest was wild, churning as if with terror. He clung to the doorknob, grotesquely smiling—so he saw himself. His father raised his head. "Jackie," he said, and was unable to say more, all at once sobbing like a baby.

"Hi, Dad," he brought out, and somehow managed to go to him and get down on his knees beside him and put his arm around his back. He felt dizzy now, nauseated, and he was crying like his father. "I hate you," he whispered too softly for any of them to hear.

His father stayed. He worked long days, in control once more, though occasionally he smoked, pacing in his room nights, or rode off on his motorcycle for an hour or two, and seldom smiled. Nevertheless, in a month he was again reciting poetry for schools and churches and the Grange, and sometimes reading Scripture from the pulpit Sunday mornings. Jack, sitting rigid, hands over his face, was bitterly ashamed of those poems and recitations from the Bible. His father's eyes no longer flashed, he no longer had the style of an actor. Even his gestures were submissive, as pliant as the grass. Though tears ran down Jack Hawthorne's face—no one would deny that his father was still effective, reading carefully, lest his voice should break. "Tomorrow's Bridge" and "This Too Will Pass"—Jack scorned the poems' opinions, scorned the way his father spoke directly to each listener, as if each were some new woman, his father some mere suffering sheep among sheep, and scorned the way Phoebe and his mother looked on smiling, furtively weeping, heads lifted. Sometimes his father would recite a poem that Jack himself had written, in the days when he'd tried to write poetry, a comic limerick or some maudlin piece about a boy on a hill. Though it was meant as a compliment, Jack's heart would swell with rage; yet he kept silent, more private than before. At night he'd go out to the cavernous haymow or up into the orchard and practice his French horn. One of these days, he told himself, they'd wake up and find him gone.

He used the horn more and more now to escape their herding warmth. Those around him were conscious enough of what was happening—his parents and Phoebe, his uncles, aunts, and cousins, his mother's many friends. But there was nothing they could do. "That horn's his whole world," his mother often said, smiling but clasping her hands together. Soon he was playing third horn with the Batavia Civic Orchestra, though he refused to play in church or when company came. He began to ride the Bluebus to Rochester, Saturdays, to take lessons from Arcady Yegudkin, "the General," at the Eastman School of Music.

Yegudkin was seventy. He'd played principal horn in the orchestra of Czar Nikolai[3] and at the time of the Revolution had escaped, with his wife, in a dramatic way. At the time of the purge of Kerenskyites,[4] the Bolsheviks had loaded Yegudkin and his wife, along with hundreds more, onto railroad flatcars, reportedly to carry them to Siberia. In a desolate place, machine guns opened fire on the people on the flatcars, then soldiers pushed the bodies into a ravine, and the train moved on. The soldiers were not careful to see that everyone was dead. Perhaps they did not relish their work; in any case, they must have believed that, in a place so remote, a wounded survivor would have no chance against wolves and cold weather. The General and his wife were among the few who lived, he virtually unmarked, she horribly crippled. Local peasants nursed the few survivors back to health, and in time the Yegudkins escaped to Europe. There Yegudkin played horn with all the great orchestras and received such praise—so he claimed, spreading out his clippings—as no other master of French horn had received in all history. He would beam as he said it, his Tartar eyes flashing, and his smile was like a thrown-down gauntlet.

He was a barrel-shaped, solidly muscular man, hard as a boulder for all his age. His hair and moustache were as black as coal except for touches of silver, especially where it grew, with majestic indifference to ordinary taste, from his cavernous nostrils and large, dusty-looking ears. The sides of his moustache were carefully curled, in the fashion once favored by Russian dandies, and he was one of the last men in Rochester, New York, to wear spats. He wore formal black suits, a huge black overcoat, and a black fedora. His wife, who came with him and sat on the long maple bench outside his door, never reading or knitting or doing anything at all except that sometimes she would speak unintelligibly to a student—Yegudkin's wife, shriveled and twisted, watched him as if worshipfully, hanging on his words. She looked at least twice the old man's age. Her hair was snow white and she wore lumpy black shoes and long black shapeless dresses. The two of them would come, every Saturday morning, down the long marble hallway of the second floor of Killburn Hall, the General erect and imperious, like some sharp-eyed old Slavonic king, moving slowly, waiting for the old woman who crept beside him, gray claws on his coat sleeve, and seeing Jack Hawthorne seated on the bench, his books and French horn in its tattered black case on the floor beside him, the General would extend his left arm and boom, "Goot mworning!"

Jack, rising, would say, "Morning, sir."

"You have met my wife?" the old man would say then, bowing and taking the cigar from his mouth. He asked it each Saturday.

"Yes, sir. How do you do?"

The old man was too deaf to play in orchestras anymore. "What's the difference?" he said. "Every symphony in America, they got Yegudkins. I have teach them all. Who teach you this? *The General!*" He would smile, chin lifted, triumphant, and salute the ceiling.

3. Nicholas II (1868–1918), last czar of Russia (1894 to 1917), executed in 1918.

4. Followers of Aleksandr Kerensky (1881–1970), briefly premier of Russia in 1917 before his government was overthrown by the Bolsheviks and he fled to Paris.

He would sit in the chair beside Jack's and would sing, with violent gestures and a great upward leap of the belly to knock out the high B's and C's—*Tee! Tee!*—as Jack read through Kopprasch, Gallay, and Kling, and when it was time to give Jack's lip a rest, the General would speak earnestly, with the same energy he put into his singing, of the United States and his beloved Russia that he would nevermore see. The world was at that time filled with Russophobes. Yegudkin, whenever he read a paper, would be so enraged he could barely contain himself. "In all my age," he often said, furiously gesturing with his black cigar, "if the Russians would come to this country of America, I would take up a rifle and shot at them—*boof!* But the newspapers telling you lies, all lies! You think them dumb fools, these Russians? You think they are big, fat bush-overs?" He spoke of mile-long parades of weaponry, spoke of Russian cunning, spoke with great scorn, a sudden booming laugh, of Napoleon. Jack agreed with a nod to whatever the General said. Nevertheless, the old man roared on, taking great pleasure in his rage, it seemed, sometimes talking like a rabid communist, sometimes like a fascist, sometimes like a citizen helplessly caught between mindless, grinding forces, vast, idiot herds. The truth was, he hated both Russians and Americans about equally, cared only for music, his students and, possibly, his wife. In his pockets, in scorn of the opinions of fools, he carried condoms, dirty pictures, and grimy, wadded-up dollar bills.

One day a new horn he'd ordered from Germany, an Alexander, arrived at his office—a horn he'd gotten for a graduate student. The old man unwrapped and assembled it, the graduate student looking on—a shy young man, blond, in a limp gray sweater—and the glint in the General's eye was like madness or at any rate lust, perhaps gluttony. When the horn was ready he went to the desk where he kept his clippings, his tools for the cleaning and repair of French horns, his cigars, photographs, and medals from the Czar, and pulled open a wide, shallow drawer. It contained perhaps a hundred mouthpieces, of all sizes and materials, from raw brass to lucite, silver, and gold, from the shallowest possible cup to the deepest. He selected one, fitted it into the horn, pressed the rim of the bell into the right side of his large belly—the horn seemed now as much a part of him as his arm or leg—clicked the shining keys to get the feel of them, then played. In that large, cork-lined room, it was as if, suddenly, a creature from some other universe had appeared, some realm where feelings become birds and dark sky, and spirit is more solid than stone. The sound was not so much loud as large, too large for a hundred French horns, it seemed. He began to play now not single notes but, to Jack's astonishment, chords—two notes at a time, then three. He began to play runs. As if charged with life independent of the man, the horn sound fluttered and flew crazily, like an enormous trapped hawk hunting frantically for escape. It flew to the bottom of the lower register, the foundation concert F, and crashed below it, and on down and down, as if the horn in Yegudkin's hands had no bottom, then suddenly changed its mind and flew upward in a split-second run to the horn's top E, dropped back to the middle and then ran once more, more fiercely at the E, and this time burst through it and fluttered, manic, in the trumpet range, then lightly dropped back into its own home range and, abruptly, in the middle of a note, stopped. The room still rang, shimmered like a vision.

"Good horn," said Yegudkin, and held the horn toward the graduate student, who sat, hands clamped on his knees, as if in a daze.

Jack Hawthorne stared at the instrument suspended in space and at his teacher's hairy hands. Before stopping to think, he said, "You think I'll ever play like that?"

Yegudkin laughed loudly, his black eyes widening, and it seemed that he grew larger, beatific and demonic at once, like the music; overwhelming. "Play like *me?*" he exclaimed.

Jack blinked, startled by the bluntness of the thing, the terrible lack of malice, and the truth of it. His face tingled and his legs went weak, as if the life were rushing out of them. He longed to be away from there, far away, safe. Perhaps Yegudkin sensed it. He turned gruff, sending away the graduate student, then finishing up the lesson. He said nothing, today, of the stupidity of mankind. When the lesson was over he saw Jack to the door and bid him goodbye with a brief half-smile that was perhaps not for Jack at all but for the creature on the bench. "Next Saturday?" he said, as if there might be some doubt.

Jack nodded, blushing.

At the door opening on the street he began to breathe more easily, though he was weeping. He set down the horn case to brush away his tears. The sidewalk was crowded—dazed-looking Saturday-morning shoppers herding along irritably, meekly, through painfully bright light. Again he brushed tears away. He'd been late for his bus. Then the crowd opened for him and, with the horn cradled under his right arm, his music under his left, he plunged in, starting home.

1981

PHILIP ROTH

(1933–)

In a 1960 symposium Philip Roth observed, "The American writer in the middle of the twentieth century has his hands full in trying to understand, describe, and then make *credible* much of American reality. It stupefies, it sickens, it infuriates, and finally it is even a kind of embarrassment to one's own meager imagination. The actuality is continually outdoing our talents, and the culture tosses up figures almost daily that are the envy of any novelist." In the lecture, later published as "Writing American Fiction" in *Reading Myself and Others* (1975) he goes on to observe that the difficulties of doing justice to post-war reality led other American writers of his time to turn to fable, mysticism and non-fiction. His own work has changed from early realistic fiction influenced by Henry James and Gustave Flaubert, through purely comic work reminiscent of the borscht belt and American frontier humor and embodying Kafkaesque excursions into surrealism, to more recent explorations of the boundaries between art and reality, and between the creator and his creation.

Roth was born into a middle-class Jewish family during the Depression. He was educated in the Newark, New Jersey, public schools and attended the Newark branch of Rutgers University for one year. He transferred to Bucknell University, where he founded and edited the literary magazine, was inducted into Phi Beta Kappa, and graduated, magna cum laude, with an English major in 1954. He earned an M.A. at the University of Chicago in 1955 and, after a brief stint in the army, he returned to Chicago to begin a Ph.D. program and teach in the English department. From 1958 onward he has supported himself as a writer, with visiting appointments at Iowa, Princeton, the University of Pennsylvania, and elsewhere.

Roth's first book, the short story collection *Goodbye, Columbus* (1959), aroused hostility in some critics, who accused him of portraying Jews in an unflattering way, a charge often repeated with respect to later books. Roth's defense, made to an Israeli audience in 1963 was, "I do not write Jewish books. I am not a Jewish writer, I am a writer who is a Jew. The biggest concern and passion in my life is to write fiction, not to be a Jew." Although his portrayal of Jewish characters may have been unexpected, the narrative methods of the early stories and of the novels *Letting Go* (1962) and *When She was Good* (1967) are traditional, and they introduce the characteristic Roth perspective: whether the point of view is first or third person, the narrator colors the world with the attitudes and prejudices of the main character.

Roth's comic novel *Portnoy's Complaint* (1969) marked a turn in his career that made him wealthy, famous, and still more controversial. In it Roth presents in rambling psychoanalytic monologue Portnoy's frenzied struggle against the restrictions of his Jewish heritage and his family. Strong political satire aimed at the Nixon years is the subject of *Our Gang* (1971); *The Great American Novel* (1973) employs baseball as the background for a work Roth said "exists for the sake of no 'higher' value than the comedy itself." Yet even at his most comic, Roth is never far from one of his major themes, the conflict between seriousness and self-gratification, moral purpose and rebellion. Franz Kafka's influence is obvious in *The Breast* (1972), in which a burlesque premise, the transformation of a professor into a giant breast, is treated in a serious and restrained style. In *The Professor of Desire* (1977), the same man struggles between the attractions of his private lusts and the morality and seriousness manifested in his profession.

Roth's later work has become more and more self-consciously literary. *My Life as a Man* (1974) treats the possibility of dealing with the personal pain of a failed marriage through teaching literature and writing. The hero, a novelist-professor whose biography closely parallels Roth's, creates fiction featuring an alter ego named Nathan Zuckerman, and then analyzes the importance of personal experience to a writer of fiction. Zuckerman reappears in three novels and a novella—*The Ghost Writer* (1979), *Zuckerman Unbound* (1981), *The Anatomy Lesson* (1983), and *The Prague Orgy*—collected in *Zuckerman Bound* in 1985. The tone is tragicomedy as Roth explores the distance between the ideals of rigorous ethnic, familial, and literary traditions and the realities of contemporary life. Most recently, Zuckerman appears once more in *The Counterlife* (1987), an international novel set in the United States, Israel, Switzerland, and Great Britain. Within this book he dies, or seems to, as the narrator plays with complex questions of the relationships between life and fiction, art and morality. Speaking of this latest novel, Roth has said, "If the goal is to be innocent of all innocence, I'm getting there."

Roth's major work to date is named above. *A Philip Roth Reader* was published in 1980.

Studies include John N. McDaniel, *The Fiction of Philip Roth,* 1974; Sanford Pinsker, *The Comedy That "Hoits": An Essay on the Fiction of Philip Roth,* 1975; Bernard F. Rodgers, Jr., *Philip Roth,* 1978; Judith P. Jones and Guinevere Nance, *Philip Roth,* 1981; Sanford Pinsker, ed., *Critical Essays on Philip Roth,* 1982; Hermione Lee, *Philip Roth,* 1982; and Asher Z. Milbauer and Donald G. Watson, eds., *Reading Philip Roth,* 1987.

The Conversion of the Jews

"You're a real one for opening your mouth in the first place," Itzie said. "What do you open your mouth all the time for?"

"I didn't bring it up, Itz, I didn't," Ozzie said.

"What do you care about Jesus Christ for anyway?"

"I didn't bring up Jesus Christ. He did. I didn't even know what he was talking about. Jesus is historical, he kept saying. Jesus is historical." Ozzie mimicked the monumental voice of Rabbi Binder.

"Jesus was a person that lived like you and me," Ozzie continued. "That's what Binder said—"

"Yeah? . . . So what! What do I give two cents whether he lived or not. And what do you gotta open your mouth!" Itzie Lieberman favored closed-mouthedness, especially when it came to Ozzie Freedman's questions. Mrs. Freedman had to see Rabbi Binder twice before about Ozzie's questions and this Wednesday at four-thirty would be the third time. Itzie preferred to keep *his* mother in the kitchen; he settled for behind-the-back subtleties such as gestures, faces, snarls and other less delicate barnyard noises.

"He was a real person, Jesus, but he wasn't like God, and we don't believe he is God." Slowly, Ozzie was explaining Rabbi Binder's position to Itzie, who had been absent from Hebrew School the previous afternoon.

"The Catholics," Itzie said helpfully, "they believe in Jesus Christ, that he's God." Itzie Lieberman used "the Catholics" in its broadest sense—to include the Protestants.

Ozzie received Itzie's remark with a tiny head bob, as though it were a footnote, and went on. "His mother was Mary, and his father probably was Joseph," Ozzie said. "But the New Testament says his real father was God."

"His *real* father?"

"Yeah," Ozzie said, "that's the big thing, his father's supposed to be God."

"Bull."

"That's what Rabbi Binder says, that it's impossible—"

"Sure it's impossible. That stuff's all bull. To have a baby you gotta get laid," Itzie theologized. "Mary hadda get laid."

"That's what Binder says: 'The only way a woman can have a baby is to have intercourse with a man.' "

"He said *that,* Ozz?" For a moment it appeared that Itzie had put the theological question aside. "He said that, intercourse?" A little curled smile shaped itself in the lower half of Itzie's face like a pink mustache. "What you guys do, Ozz, you laugh or something?"

"I raised my hand."

"Yeah? Whatja say?"

"That's when I asked the question."

Itzie's face lit up. "Whatja ask about—intercourse?"

"No, I asked the question about God, how if He could create the heaven and earth in six days, and make all the animals and the fish and the light in six days—the light especially, that's what always gets me, that He could make the light. Making fish and animals, that's pretty good—"

"That's damn good." Itzie's appreciation was honest but unimaginative: it was as though God had just pitched a one-hitter.

"But making light . . . I mean when you think about it, it's really something," Ozzie said. "Anyway, I asked Binder if He could make all that in six days, and He could *pick* the six days he wanted right out of nowhere, why couldn't He let a woman have a baby without having intercourse."

"You said intercourse, Ozz, to Binder?"

"Yeah."

"Right in class?"

"Yeah."

Itzie smacked the side of his head.

"I mean, no kidding around," Ozzie said, "that'd really be nothing. After all that other stuff, that'd practically be nothing."

Itzie considered a moment. "What'd Binder say?"

"He started all over again explaining how Jesus was historical and how he lived like you and me but he wasn't God. So I said I under*stood* that. What I wanted to know was different."

What Ozzie wanted to know was always different. The first time he had wanted to know how Rabbi Binder could call the Jews "The Chosen People" if the Declaration of Independence claimed all men to be created equal. Rabbi Binder tried to distinguish for him between political equality and spiritual legitimacy, but what Ozzie wanted to know, he insisted vehemently, was different. That was the first time his mother had to come.

Then there was the plane crash. Fifty-eight people had been killed in a plane crash at La Guardia. In studying a casualty list in the newspaper his mother had discovered among the list of those dead eight Jewish names (his grandmother had nine but she counted Miller as a Jewish name); because of the eight she said the plane crash was "a tragedy." During free-discussion time on Wednesday Ozzie had brought to Rabbi Binder's attention this matter of "some of his relations" always picking out the Jewish names. Rabbi Binder had begun to explain cultural unity and some other things when Ozzie stood up at his seat and said that what he wanted to know was different. Rabbi Binder insisted that he sit down and it was then that Ozzie shouted that he wished all fifty-eight were Jews. That was the second time his mother came.

"And he kept explaining about Jesus being historical, and so I kept asking him. No kidding, Itz, he was trying to make me look stupid."

"So what he finally do?"

"Finally he starts screaming that I was deliberately simple-minded and a wise guy, and that my mother had to come, and this was the last time. And that I'd never get bar-mitzvahed[1] if he could help it. Then, Itz, then he starts talking in that voice like a statue, real slow and deep, and he says that I better think over what I said about the Lord. He told me to go to his office and think it over." Ozzie leaned his body towards Itzie. "Itz, I thought it over for a solid hour, and now I'm convinced God could do it."

Ozzie had planned to confess his latest transgression to his mother as soon as she came home from work. But it was a Friday night in November and already dark, and when Mrs. Freedman came through the door she tossed off her coat, kissed Ozzie quickly on the face, and went to the kitchen table to light the three yellow candles, two for the Sabbath and one for Ozzie's father.

When his mother lit the candles she would move her two arms slowly towards her, dragging them through the air, as though persuading people whose minds were half made up. And her eyes would get glassy with tears. Even when his father was alive Ozzie remembered that her eyes had gotten glassy, so it didn't have anything to do with his dying. It had something to do with lighting the candles.

1. He would never be allowed the ceremony of Bar Mitzvah, initiating a boy, traditionally at thirteen, into the religious community.

As she touched the flaming match to the unlit wick of a Sabbath candle, the phone rang, and Ozzie, standing only a foot from it, plucked it off the receiver and held it muffled to his chest. When his mother lit candles Ozzie felt there should be no noise; even breathing, if you could manage it, should be softened. Ozzie pressed the phone to his breast and watched his mother dragging whatever she was dragging, and he felt his own eyes get glassy. His mother was a round, tired, gray-haired penguin of a woman whose gray skin had begun to feel the tug of gravity and the weight of her own history. Even when she was dressed up she didn't look like a chosen person. But when she lit candles she looked like something better; like a woman who knew momentarily that God could do anything.

After a few mysterious minutes she was finished. Ozzie hung up the phone and walked to the kitchen table where she was beginning to lay the two places for the four-course Sabbath meal. He told her that she would have to see Rabbi Binder next Wednesday at four-thirty, and then he told her why. For the first time in their life together she hit Ozzie across the face with her hand.

All through the chopped liver and chicken soup part of the dinner Ozzie cried; he didn't have any appetite for the rest.

On Wednesday, in the largest of the three basement classrooms of the synagogue, Rabbi Marvin Binder, a tall, handsome, broad-shouldered man of thirty with thick strong-fibered black hair, removed his watch from his pocket and saw that it was four o'clock. At the rear of the room Yakov Blotnik, the seventy-one-year-old custodian, slowly polished the large window, mumbling to himself, unaware that it was four o'clock or six o'clock, Monday or Wednesday. To most of the students Yakov Blotnik's mumbling, along with his brown curly beard, scythe nose, and two heel-trailing black cats, made of him an object of wonder, a foreigner, a relic, towards whom they were alternately fearful and disrespectful. To Ozzie the mumbling had always seemed a monotonous, curious prayer; what made it curious was that old Blotnik had been mumbling so steadily for so many years, Ozzie suspected he had memorized the prayers and forgotten all about God.

"It is now free-discussion time," Rabbi Binder said. "Feel free to talk about any Jewish matter at all—religion, family, politics, sports—"

There was silence. It was a gusty, clouded November afternoon and it did not seem as though there ever was or could be a thing called baseball. So nobody this week said a word about that hero from the past, Hank Greenberg[2]—which limited free discussion considerably.

And the soul-battering Ozzie Freedman had just received from Rabbi Binder had imposed its limitation. When it was Ozzie's turn to read aloud from the Hebrew book the rabbi had asked him petulantly why he didn't read more rapidly. He was showing no progress. Ozzie said he could read faster but that if he did he was sure not to understand what he was reading. Nevertheless, at the rabbi's repeated suggestion Ozzie tried, and showed a great talent, but in the midst of a long passage he stopped short and said he didn't understand a word he was reading, and started in again at a drag-footed pace. Then came the soul-battering.

Consequently when free-discussion time rolled around none of the students felt

2. (1911–1986), American baseball player for the Detroit Tigers, one of the finest of his time, celebrated also for refusing to play on Jewish holy days.

too free. The rabbi's invitation was answered only by the mumbling of feeble old Blotnik.

"Isn't there anything at all you would like to discuss?" Rabbi Binder asked again, looking at his watch. "No questions or comments?"

There was a small grumble from the third row. The rabbi requested that Ozzie rise and give the rest of the class the advantage of his thought.

Ozzie rose. "I forget it now," he said, and sat down in his place.

Rabbi Binder advanced a seat towards Ozzie and poised himself on the edge of the desk. It was Itzie's desk and the rabbi's frame only a dagger's-length away from his face snapped him to sitting attention.

"Stand up again, Oscar," Rabbi Binder said calmly, "and try to assemble your thoughts."

Ozzie stood up. All his classmates turned in their seats and watched as he gave an unconvincing scratch to his forehead.

"I can't assemble any," he announced, and plunked himself down.

"Stand up!" Rabbi Binder advanced from Itzie's desk to the one directly in front of Ozzie; when the rabbinical back was turned Itzie gave it five-fingers off the tip of his nose, causing a small titter in the room. Rabbi Binder was too absorbed in squelching Ozzie's nonsense once and for all to bother with titters. "Stand up, Oscar. What's your question about?"

Ozzie pulled a word out of the air. It was the handiest word. "Religion."

"Oh, now you remember?"

"Yes."

"What is it?"

Trapped, Ozzie blurted the first thing that came to him. "Why can't He make anything He wants to make!"

As Rabbi Binder prepared an answer, a final answer, Itzie, ten feet behind him, raised one finger on his left hand, gestured it meaningfully towards the rabbi's back, and brought the house down.

Binder twisted quickly to see what had happened and in the midst of the commotion Ozzie shouted into the rabbi's back what he couldn't have shouted to his face. It was a loud, toneless sound that had the timbre of something stored inside for about six days.

"You don't know! You don't know anything about God!"

The rabbi spun back towards Ozzie. "What?"

"You don't know—you don't—"

"Apologize, Oscar, apologize!" It was a threat.

"You don't—"

Rabbi Binder's hand flicked out at Ozzie's cheek. Perhaps it had only been meant to clamp the boy's mouth shut, but Ozzie ducked and the palm caught him squarely on the nose.

The blood came in a short, red spurt on to Ozzie's shirt front.

The next moment was all confusion. Ozzie screamed, "You bastard, you bastard!" and broke for the classroom door. Rabbi Binder lurched a step backwards, as though his own blood had started flowing violently in the opposite direction, then gave a clumsy lurch forward and bolted out the door after Ozzie. The class followed after the rabbi's huge blue-suited back, and before old Blotnik could turn from his window, the room was empty and everyone was headed full speed up the three flights leading to the roof.

If one should compare the light of day to the life of man: sunrise to birth; sunset —the dropping down over the edge—to death; then as Ozzie Freedman wiggled through the trapdoor of the synagogue roof, his feet kicking backwards bronco-style at Rabbi Binder's outstretched arms—at that moment the day was fifty years old. As a rule, fifty or fifty-five reflects accurately the age of late afternoons in November, for it is in that month, during those hours, that one's awareness of light seems no longer a matter of seeing, but of hearing: light begins clicking away. In fact, as Ozzie locked shut the trapdoor in the rabbi's face, the sharp click of the bolt into the lock might momentarily have been mistaken for the sound of the heavier gray that had just throbbed through the sky.

With all his weight Ozzie kneeled on the locked door; any instant he was certain that Rabbi Binder's shoulder would fling it open, splintering the wood into shrapnel and catapulting his body into the sky. But the door did not move and below him he heard only the rumble of feet, first loud then dim, like thunder rolling away.

A question shot through his brain. "Can this be *me?*" For a thirteen-year-old who had just labeled his religious leader a bastard, twice, it was not an improper question. Louder and louder the question came to him—"Is it me? It is me?"—until he discovered himself no longer kneeling, but racing crazily towards the edge of the roof, his eyes crying, his throat screaming, and his arms flying everywhichway as though not his own.

"Is it me? Is it me ME ME ME ME! It has to be me—but is it!"

It is the question a thief must ask himself the night he jimmies open his first window, and it is said to be the question with which bridegrooms quiz themselves before the altar.

In the few wild seconds it took Ozzie's body to propel him to the edge of the roof, his self-examination began to grow fuzzy. Gazing down at the street, he became confused as to the problem beneath the question: was it, is-it-me-who-called-Binder-a-bastard? or, is-it-me-prancing-around-on-the-roof? However, the scene below settled all, for there is an instant in any action when whether it is you or somebody else is academic. The thief crams the money in his pockets and scoots out the window. The bridegroom signs the hotel register for two. And the boy on the roof finds a streetful of people gaping at him, necks stretched backwards, faces up, as though he were the ceiling of the Hayden Planetarium. Suddenly you know it's you.

"Oscar! Oscar Freedman!" A voice rose from the center of the crowd, a voice that, could it have been seen, would have looked like the writing on scroll. "Oscar Freedman, get down from there. Immediately!" Rabbi Binder was pointing one arm stiffly up at him; and at the end of that arm, one finger aimed menacingly. It was the attitude of a dictator, but one—the eyes confessed all—whose personal valet had spit neatly in his face.

Ozzie didn't answer. Only for a blink's length did he look towards Rabbi Binder. Instead his eyes began to fit together the world beneath him, to sort out people from places, friends from enemies, participants from spectators. In little jagged starlike clusters his friends stood around Rabbi Binder, who was still pointing. The topmost point on a star compounded not of angels but of five adolescent boys was Itzie. What a world it was, with those stars below, Rabbi Binder below . . . Ozzie, who a moment earlier hadn't been able to control his own body, started to feel the meaning of the word control: he felt Peace and he felt Power.

"Oscar Freedman, I'll give you three to come down."

Few dictators give their subjects three to do anything; but, as always, Rabbi Binder only looked dictatorial.

"Are you ready, Oscar?"

Ozzie nodded his head yes, although he had no intention in the world—the lower one of the celestial one he'd just entered—of coming down even if Rabbi Binder should give him a million.

"All right then," said Rabbi Binder. He ran a hand through his black Samson hair as though it were the gesture prescribed for uttering the first digit. Then, with his other hand cutting a circle out of the small piece of sky around him, he spoke. "One!"

There was no thunder. On the contrary, at that moment, as though "one" was the cue for which he had been waiting, the world's least thunderous person appeared on the synagogue steps. He did not so much come out the synagogue door as lean out, onto the darkening air. He clutched at the doorknob with one hand and looked up at the roof.

"Oy!"

Yakov Blotnik's old mind hobbled slowly, as if on crutches, and though he couldn't decide precisely what the boy was doing on the roof, he knew it wasn't good—that is, it wasn't-good-for-the-Jews. For Yakov Blotnik life had fractionated itself simply: things were either good-for-the-Jews or no-good-for-the-Jews.

He smacked his free hand to his in-sucked cheek, gently. "Oy, Gut!" And then quickly as he was able, he jacked down his head and surveyed the street. There was Rabbi Binder (like a man at an auction with only three dollars in his pocket, he had just delivered a shaky "Two!"); there were the students, and that was all. So far it-wasn't-so-bad-for-the-Jews. But the boy had to come down immediately, before anybody saw. The problem: how to get the boy off the roof?

Anybody who has ever had a cat on the roof knows how to get him down. You call the fire department. Or first you call the operator and you ask her for the fire department. And the next thing there is great jamming of brakes and clanging of bells and shouting of instructions. And then the cat is off the roof. You do the same thing to get a boy off the roof.

That is, you do the same thing if you are Yakov Blotnik and you once had a cat on the roof.

When the engines, all four of them, arrived, Rabbi Binder had four times given Ozzie the count of three. The big hook-and-ladder swung around the corner and one of the firemen leaped from it, plunging headlong towards the yellow fire hydrant in front of the synagogue. With a huge wrench he began to unscrew the top nozzle. Rabbi Binder raced over to him and pulled at his shoulder.

"There's no fire . . ."

The fireman mumbled back over his shoulder and, heatedly, continued working at the nozzle.

"But there's no fire, there's no fire . . ." Binder shouted. When the fireman mumbled again, the rabbi grasped his face with both his hands and pointed it up at the roof.

To Ozzie it looked as though Rabbi Binder was trying to tug the fireman's head out of his body, like a cork from a bottle. He had to giggle at the picture they made: it was a family portrait—rabbi in black skullcap, fireman in red fire hat, and the little yellow hydrant squatting beside like a kid brother, bareheaded. From the edge of the roof Ozzie waved at the portrait, a one-handed, flapping, mocking wave; in doing it his right foot slipped from under him. Rabbi Binder covered his eyes with his hands.

Firemen work fast. Before Ozzie had even regained his balance, a big, round, yellowed net was being held on the synagogue lawn. The firemen who held it looked up at Ozzie with stern, feelingless faces.

One of the firemen turned his head towards Rabbi Binder. "What, is the kid nuts or something?"

Rabbi Binder unpeeled his hands from his eyes, slowly, painfully, as if they were tape. Then he checked: nothing on the sidewalk, no dents in the net.

"Is he gonna jump, or what?" the fireman shouted.

In a voice not at all like a statue, Rabbi Binder finally answered. "Yes, yes, I think so . . . He's been threatening to . . ."

Threatening to? Why, the reason he was on the roof, Ozzie remembered, was to get away; he hadn't even thought about jumping. He had just run to get away, and the truth was that he hadn't really headed for the roof as much as he'd been chased there.

"What's his name, the kid?"

"Freedman," Rabbi Binder answered. "Oscar Freedman."

The fireman looked up at Ozzie. "What is it with you, Oscar? You gonna jump, or what?"

Ozzie did not answer. Frankly, the question had just arisen.

"Look, Oscar, if you're gonna jump, jump—and if you're not gonna jump, don't jump. But don't waste our time, willya?"

Ozzie looked at the fireman and then at Rabbi Binder. He wanted to see Rabbi Binder cover his eyes one more time.

"I'm going to jump."

And then he scampered around the edge of the roof to the corner, where there was no net below, and he flapped his arms at his sides, swishing the air and smacking his palms to his trousers on the downbeat. He began screaming like some kind of engine, "Wheeeee . . . wheeeeee," and leaning way out over the edge with the upper half of his body. The firemen whipped around to cover the ground with the net. Rabbi Binder mumbled a few words to Somebody and covered his eyes. Everything happened quickly, jerkily, as in a silent movie. The crowd, which had arrived with the fire engines, gave out a long, Fourth-of-July fireworks oooh-aahhh. In the excitement no one had paid the crowd much heed, except, of course, Yakov Blotnik, who swung from the doorknob counting heads. "Fier und tsvantsik . . . finf und tsvantsik[3] . . . Oy, Gut!" It wasn't like this with the cat.

Rabbi Binder peeked through his fingers, checked the sidewalk and net. Empty. But there was Ozzie racing to the other corner. The firemen raced with him but were unable to keep up. Whenever Ozzie wanted to he might jump and splatter

3. Yiddish: "twenty-four . . . twenty-five."

himself upon the sidewalk, and by the time the firemen scooted to the spot all they could do with their net would be to cover the mess.

"Wheeeee . . . wheeeee . . ."

"Hey, Oscar," the winded fireman yelled, "What the hell is this, a game or something?"

"Wheeeee . . . wheeeee . . ."

"Hey, Oscar—"

But he was off now to the other corner, flapping his wings fiercely. Rabbi Binder couldn't take it any longer—the fire engines from nowhere, the screaming suicidal boy, the net. He fell to his knees, exhausted, and with his hands curled together in front of his chest like a little dome, he pleaded, "Oscar, stop it, Oscar. Don't jump, Oscar. Please come down . . . Please don't jump."

And further back in the crowd a single voice, a single young voice, shouted a lone word to the boy on the roof.

"Jump!"

It was Itzie, Ozzie momentarily stopped flapping.

"Go ahead, Ozz—jump!" Itzie broke off his point of the star and courageously, with the inspiration not of a wise-guy but of a disciple, stood alone. "Jump, Ozz, jump!"

Still on his knees, his hands still curled, Rabbi Binder twisted his body back. He looked at Itzie, then, agonizingly, back to Ozzie.

"OSCAR, DON'T JUMP! PLEASE, DON'T JUMP . . . please please . . ."

"Jump!" This time it wasn't Itzie but another point of the star. By the time Mrs. Freedman arrived to keep her four-thirty appointment with Rabbi Binder, the whole little upside down heaven was shouting and pleading for Ozzie to jump, and Rabbi Binder no longer was pleading with him not to jump, but was crying into the dome of his hands.

Understandably Mrs. Freedman couldn't figure out what her son was doing on the roof. So she asked.

"Ozzie, my Ozzie, what are you doing? My Ozzie, what is it?"

Ozzie stopped wheeeeeing and slowed his arms down to a cruising flap, the kind birds use in soft winds, but he did not answer. He stood against the low, clouded, darkening sky—light clicked down swiftly now, as on a small gear—flapping softly and gazing down at the small bundle of a woman who was his mother.

"What are you doing, Ozzie?" She turned towards the kneeling Rabbi Binder and rushed so close that only a paper-thickness of dusk lay between her stomach and his shoulders.

"What is my baby doing?"

Rabbi Binder gaped up at her but he too was mute. All that moved was the dome of his hands; it shook back and forth like a weak pulse.

"Rabbi, get him down! He'll kill himself. Get him down, my only baby . . ."

"I can't," Rabbi Binder said, "I can't . . ." and he turned his handsome head towards the crowd of boys behind him. "It's them. Listen to them."

And for the first time Mrs. Freedman saw the crowd of boys, and she heard what they were yelling.

"He's doing it for them. He won't listen to me. It's them." Rabbi Binder spoke like one in a trance.

"For them?"

"Yes."

"Why for them?"

"They want him to . . ."

Mrs. Freedman raised her two arms upward as though she were conducting the sky. "For them he's doing it!" And then in a gesture older than pyramids, older than prophets and floods, her arms came slapping down to her sides. "A martyr I have. Look!" She tilted her head to the roof. Ozzie was still flapping softly. "My martyr."

"Oscar, come down, *please,*" Rabbi Binder groaned.

In a startlingly even voice Mrs. Freedman called to the boy on the roof. "Ozzie, come down, Ozzie. Don't be a martyr, my baby."

As though it were a litany, Rabbi Binder repeated her words. "Don't be a martyr, my baby. Don't be a martyr."

"Gawhead, Ozz—*be* a Martin!" It was Itzie. "Be a Martin, be a Martin," and all the voices joined in singing for Martindom, whatever *it* was. "Be a Martin, be a Martin . . . ."

Somehow when you're on a roof the darker it gets the less you can hear. All Ozzie knew was that two groups wanted two new things: his friends were spirited and musical about what they wanted; his mother and the rabbi were even-toned, chanting, about what they didn't want. The rabbi's voice was without tears now and so was his mother's.

The big net stared up at Ozzie like a sightless eye. The big, clouded sky pushed down. From beneath it looked like a gray corrugated board. Suddenly, looking up into that unsympathetic sky, Ozzie realized all the strangeness of what these people, his friends, were asking: they wanted him to jump, to kill himself; they were singing about it now—it made them that happy. And there was an even greater strangeness: Rabbi Binder was on his knees, trembling. If there was a question to be asked now it was not "Is it me?" but rather "Is it us? . . . Is it us?"

Being on the roof, it turned out, was a serious thing. If he jumped would the singing become dancing? Would it? What would jumping stop? Yearningly, Ozzie wished he could rip open the sky, plunge his hands through, and pull out the sun; and on the sun, like a coin, would be stamped JUMP or DON'T JUMP.

Ozzie's knees rocked and sagged a little under him as though they were setting him for a dive. His arms tightened, stiffened, froze, from shoulders to fingernails. He felt as if each part of his body were going to vote as to whether he should kill himself or not—and each part as though it were independent of *him.*

The light took an unexpected click down and the new darkness, like a gag, hushed the friends singing for this and the mother and rabbi chanting for that.

Ozzie stopped counting votes, and in a curiously high voice, like one who wasn't prepared for speech, he spoke.

"Mamma?"

"Yes, Oscar."

"Mamma, get down on your knees, like Rabbi Binder."

"Oscar—"

"Get down on your knees," he said, "or I'll jump."

Ozzie heard a whimper, then a quick rustling, and when he looked down where his mother had stood he saw the top of a head and beneath that a circle of dress. She was kneeling beside Rabbi Binder.

He spoke again. "Everybody kneel." There was the sound of everybody kneeling.

Ozzie looked around. With one hand he pointed towards the synagogue entrance. "Make *him* kneel."

There was a noise, not of kneeling, but of body-and-cloth stretching. Ozzie could hear Rabbi Binder saying in a gruff whisper, ". . . or he'll *kill* himself," and when next he looked there was Yakov Blotnik off the doorknob and for the first time in his life upon his knees in the Gentile posture of prayer.

As for the firemen—it is not as difficult as one might imagine to hold a net taut while you are kneeling.

Ozzie looked around again; and then he called to Rabbi Binder.

"Rabbi?"

"Yes, Oscar."

"Rabbi Binder, do you believe in God."

"Yes."

"Do you believe God can do Anything?" Ozzie leaned his head out into the darkness. "Anything?"

"Oscar, I think—"

"Tell me you believe God can do Anything."

There was a second's hesitation. Then: "God can do Anything."

"Tell me you believe God can make a child without intercourse."

"He can."

"Tell me!"

"God," Rabbi Binder admitted, "can make a child without intercourse."

"Mamma, you tell me."

"God can make a child without intercourse," his mother said.

"Make *him* tell me." There was no doubt who *him* was.

In a few moments Ozzie heard an old comical voice say something to the increasing darkness about God.

Next, Ozzie made everybody say it. And then he made them all say they believed in Jesus Christ—first one at a time, then all together.

When the catechizing was through it was the beginning of evening. From the street it sounded as if the boy on the roof might have sighed.

"Ozzie?" A woman's voice dared to speak. "You'll come down now?"

There was no answer, but the woman waited, and when a voice finally did speak it was thin and crying, and exhausted as that of an old man who has just finished pulling the bells.

"Mamma, don't you see—you shouldn't hit me. He shouldn't hit me. You shouldn't hit me about God, Mamma. You should never hit anybody about God—"

"Ozzie, please come down now."

"Promise me, promise me you'll never hit anybody about God."

He had asked only his mother, but for some reason everyone kneeling in the street promised he would never hit anybody about God.

Once again there was silence.

"I can come down now, Mamma," the boy on the roof finally said. He turned his head both ways as though checking the traffic lights. "Now I can come down . . ."

And he did, right into the center of the yellow net that glowed in the evening's edge like an overgrown halo.

1959

GAIL GODWIN
(1937–)

Gail Godwin was born in Birmingham, Alabama, and brought up in Asheville, North Carolina. She spent the first decade of her life in an all-female household and was strongly influenced by her divorced mother, a college literature teacher who wrote romances in her spare time, and her widowed grandmother, a southern traditionalist. Her mother remarried when Godwin was eleven, but she did not meet her biological father until her high school graduation.

She was educated in a convent school, attended a junior college, and graduated from the University of North Carolina in 1959 with a degree in journalism. After an unsuccessful stint as a reporter for the *Miami Herald* and a failed marriage, she worked from 1962 to 1965 at the United States embassy in London. She credits her British second husband as the person who made it possible for her to "start being the writer I knew I could be."

Returning to the United States, she earned an M.A. (1968) and a Ph.D. (1971) at the University of Iowa and spent a year there on the faculty of the Writers Workshop, meanwhile writing and publishing her first two novels. In her first, *The Perfectionists* (1970), an American woman, vacationing with her British husband and his young son, sees the conflict between her need to assert her own identity and her romantic urge to lose herself in union with her cool, rational husband. Her second, *Glass People* (1972), similarly focuses on a conflict between self-realization and surrender as a woman leaves her husband only to find she is untrained to support herself; she returns to her role as a prized possession made more precious because she has been impregnated by a lover during her brief escape.

Since 1973, Godwin has lived in upstate New York, and the locale of her fiction is now the Northeast. Her third novel, *The Odd Woman* (1974), centers on a woman Ph.D. teaching nineteenth-century literature and carrying on an affair with a married art historian from another university. Returning South for the funeral of her grandmother, she realizes the contradictions between her current life and her family's heritage. Carefully unfolding a traditional plot, Godwin presents alternative views of relations between men and women through a series of conversations with female characters, each representing a different possible model. The end of the book finds the scholar still searching for a paradigm in which she can develop personally and be closely paired with a man. In *Violet Clay* (1978), Godwin details the conflicts between a personal and artistic life forced by a series of crises in the life of an illustrator of Gothic romances. *A Mother and Two Daughters* (1982) treats the lives of a woman and her two adult daughters who are able to head off a complete family rupture and learn to care for one another. *The Finishing School* (1985) concerns the relationship between an adolescent and an older woman she admires.

Godwin's novels to date are named above. Short stories are collected in *Dream Children,* 1976; and *Mr. Bedford and the Muses,* 1983. A brief study appears in Anne Z. Mickelson, *Reaching Out: Sensitivity and Order in Recent American Fiction by Women,* 1979.

Dream Children

The worst thing. Such a terrible thing to happen to a young woman. It's a wonder she didn't go mad.

As she went about her errands, a cheerful, neat young woman, a wife, wearing pants with permanent creases and safari jackets and high-necked sweaters that folded chastely just below the line of the small gold hoops she wore in her ears, she imagined people saying this, or thinking it to themselves. But nobody knew. Nobody knew anything, other than that she and her husband had moved here a year ago, as so many couples were moving farther away from the city, the husband commuting, or staying in town during the week—as hers did. There was nobody here, in this quaint, unspoiled village, nestled in the foothills of the mountains, who could have looked at her and guessed that anything out of the ordinary, predictable, auspicious spectrum of things that happen to bright, attractive young women had happened to her. She always returned her books to the local library on time; she bought liquor at the local liquor store only on Friday, before she went to meet her husband's bus from the city. He was something in television, a producer? So many ambitious young couples moving to this Dutch farming village, founded in 1690, to restore ruined fieldstone houses and plant herb gardens and keep their own horses and discover the relief of finding oneself insignificant in Nature for the first time!

A terrible thing. So freakish. If you read it in a story or saw it on TV, you'd say no, this sort of thing could never happen in an American hospital.

DePuy, who owned the old Patroon farm[1] adjacent to her land, frequently glimpsed her racing her horse in the early morning, when the mists still lay on the fields, sometimes just before the sun came up and there was a frost on everything. "One woodchuck hole and she and that stallion will both have to be put out of their misery," he told his wife. "She's too reckless. I'll bet you her old man doesn't know she goes streaking to hell across the fields like that." Mrs. DePuy nodded, silent, and went about her business. She, too, watched that other woman ride, a woman not much younger than herself, but with an aura of romance—of tragedy, perhaps. The way she looked: like those heroines in English novels who ride off their bad tempers and unrequited love affairs, clenching their thighs against the flanks of spirited horses with murderous red eyes. Mrs. DePuy, who had ridden since the age of three, recognized something beyond recklessness in that elegant young woman, in her crisp checked shirts and her dove-gray jodhpurs. *She has nothing to fear anymore,* thought the farmer's wife, with sure feminine instinct; she both envied and pitied her. "What she needs is children," remarked DePuy.

"A Dry Sack, a Remy Martin, and . . . let's see, a half-gallon of the Chablis, and I think I'd better take a Scotch . . . and the Mouton-Cadet . . . and maybe a dry vermouth." Mrs. Frye, another farmer's wife, who runs the liquor store, asks if her

1. A farm on land originally a part of a manorial grant to Dutch settlers of New York. The Patroons (landowners) and their descendants controlled large tracts and founded huge New York fortunes.

husband is bringing company for the weekend. "He sure is; we couldn't drink all that by ourselves," and the young woman laughs, her lovely teeth exposed, her small gold earrings quivering in the light. "You know, I saw his name—on the television the other night," says Mrs. Frye. "It was at the beginning of that new comedy show, the one with the woman who used to be on another show with her husband and little girl, only they divorced, you know the one?" "Of course I do. It's one of my husband's shows. I'll tell him you watched it." Mrs. Frye puts the bottles in an empty box, carefully inserting wedges of cardboard between them. Through the window of her store she sees her customer's pert bottle-green car, some sort of little foreign car with the engine running, filled with groceries and weekend parcels, and that big silver-blue dog sitting up in the front seat just like a human being. "I think that kind of thing is so sad," says Mrs. Frye; "families breaking up, poor little children having to divide their loyalties." "I couldn't agree more," replies the young woman, nodding gravely. Such a personable, polite girl! "Are you sure you can carry that, dear? I can get Earl from the back. . . ." But the girl has it hoisted on her shoulder in a flash, is airily maneuvering between unopened cartons stacked in the aisle, in her pretty boots. Her perfume lingers in Mrs. Frye's store for a half-hour after she has driven away.

After dinner, her husband and his friends drank brandy. She lay in front of the fire, stroking the dog, and listening to Victoria Darrow, the news commentator, in person. A few minutes ago, they had all watched Victoria on TV. "That's right; thirty-nine!" Victoria now whispered to her. "What? That's kind of you. I'm photogenic, thank God, or I'd have been put out to pasture long before. . . . I look five, maybe seven years younger on the screen . . . but the point I'm getting at is, I went to this doctor and he said, 'If you want to do this thing, you'd better go home today and get started.' He told me—did you know this? Did you know that a woman is born with all the eggs she'll ever have, and when she gets to my age, the ones that are left have been rattling around so long they're a little shopworn; then every time you fly you get an extra dose of radioactivity, so those poor eggs. He told me when a woman over forty comes into his office pregnant, his heart sinks; that's why he quit practicing obstetrics, he said; he could still remember the screams of a woman whose baby he delivered . . . she was having natural childbirth and she kept saying, 'Why won't you let me see it, I insist on seeing it,' and so he had to, and he says he can still hear her screaming."

"Oh, what was—what was wrong with it?"

But she never got the answer. Her husband, white around the lips, was standing over Victoria ominously, offering the Remy Martin bottle. "Vicky, let me pour you some more," he said. And to his wife, "I think Blue Boy needs to go out."

"Yes, yes, of course. Please excuse me, Victoria. I'll just be . . ."

Her husband followed her to the kitchen, his hand on the back of her neck. "Are you okay? That stupid yammering bitch. She and her twenty-six-year-old lover! I wish I'd never brought them, but she's been hinting around the studio for weeks."

"But I like them, I like having them. I'm fine. Please go back. I'll take the dog out and come back. Please . . ."

"All right. If you're sure you're okay." He backed away, hands dangling at his sides. A handsome man, wearing a pink shirt with Guatemalan embroidery. Thick black hair and a face rather boyish, but cunning. Last weekend she had sat beside him, alone in this house, just the two of them, and watched him on television: a documentary, in several parts, in which TV "examines itself." There was his double, sitting in an armchair in his executive office, coolly replying to the questions of Victoria Darrow. *"Do you personally watch all the programs you produce, Mr. McNair?"* She watched the man on the screen, how he moved his lips when he spoke, but kept the rest of his face, his body perfectly still. Funny, she had never noticed this before. He managed to say that he did and did not watch all the programs he produced.

Now, in the kitchen, she looked at him backing away, a little like a renegade in one of his own shows—a desperate man, perhaps, who has just killed somebody and is backing away, hands dangling loosely at his sides, Mr. McNair, her husband. That man on the screen. Once a lover above her in bed. That friend who held her hand in the hospital. One hand in hers, the other holding the stopwatch. For a brief instant, all the images coalesce and she feels something again. But once outside, under the galaxies of autumn-sharp stars, the intelligent dog at her heels like some smart gray ghost, she is glad to be free of all that. She walks quickly over the damp grass to the barn, to look in on her horse. She understands something: her husband, Victoria Darrow lead double lives that seem perfectly normal to them. But if she told her husband that she, too, is in two lives, he would become alarmed; he would sell this house and make her move back to the city where he could keep an eye on her welfare.

She is discovering people like herself, down through the centuries, all over the world. She scours books with titles like *The Timeless Moment, The Sleeping Prophet, Between Two Worlds, Silent Union: A Record of Unwilled Communication;* collecting evidence, weaving a sort of underworld net of colleagues around her.

A rainy fall day. Too wet to ride. The silver dog asleep beside her in her special alcove, a padded window seat filled with pillows and books. She is looking down on the fields of dried lithrium, and the fir trees beyond, and the mountains gauzy with fog and rain, thinking, in a kind of terror and ecstasy, about all these connections. A book lies face down on her lap. She has just read the following:

> Theodore Dreiser[2] and his friend John Cowper Powys[3] had been dining at Dreiser's place on West Fifty Seventh Street. As Powys made ready to leave and catch his train to the little town up the Hudson, where he was then living, he told Dreiser, "I'll appear before you here, later in the evening."
>
> Dreiser laughed. "Are you going to turn yourself into a ghost, or have you a spare key?" he asked. Powys said he would return "in some form," he didn't know exactly what kind.
>
> After his friend left, Dreiser sat up and read for two hours. Then he looked up and saw Powys standing in the doorway to the living room. It was Powys' features, his tall stature, even the loose tweed garments which he wore. Dreiser rose at once and strode towards the figure, saying, "Well, John, you kept your word. Come on in and tell me how you did it." But the figure vanished when Dreiser came within three feet of it.
>
> Dreiser then went to the telephone and called Powys' house in the country. Powys answered. Dreiser told him what had happened and Powys said, "I told you I'd be there and you oughtn't to be surprised." But he refused to discuss how he had done it, if, indeed, he knew how.

2. (1871–1945), American naturalistic novelist.

3. (1872–1963), English author whose works frequently emphasize the supernatural and magical.

"But don't you get frightened, up here all by yourself, alone with all these creaky sounds?" asked Victoria the next morning.

"No, I guess I'm used to them," she replied, breaking eggs into a bowl. "I know what each one means. The wood expanding and contracting . . . the wind getting caught between the shutter and the latch . . . Sometimes small animals get lost in the stone walls and scratch around till they find their way out . . . or die."

"Ugh. But don't you imagine things? I would, in a house like this. How old? That's almost three hundred years of lived lives, people suffering and shouting and making love and giving birth, under this roof. . . . You'd think there'd be a few ghosts around."

"I don't know," said her hostess blandly. "I haven't heard any. But of course, I have Blue Boy, so I don't get scared." She whisked the eggs, unable to face Victoria. She and her husband had lain awake last night, embarrassed at the sounds coming from the next room. No ghostly moans, those. "Why can't that bitch control herself, or at least lower her voice," he said angrily. He stroked his wife's arm, both of them pretending not to remember. She had bled for an entire year afterward, until the doctor said they would have to remove everything. "I'm empty," she had said when her husband had tried again, after she was healed. "I'm sorry, I just don't feel anything." Now they lay tenderly together on these weekends, like childhood friends, like effigies on a lovers' tomb, their mutual sorrow like a sword between them. She assumed he had another life, or lives, in town. As she had here. Nobody is just one person, she had learned.

"I'm sure I would imagine things," said Victoria. "I would see things and hear things inside my head much worse than an ordinary murderer or rapist."

The wind caught in the shutter latch . . . a small animal dislodging pieces of fieldstone in its terror, sending them tumbling down the inner walls, from attic to cellar . . . a sound like a child rattling a jar full of marbles, or small stones . . .

"I have so little imagination," she said humbly, warming the butter in the omelet pan. She could feel Victoria Darrow's professional curiosity waning from her dull country life, focusing elsewhere.

Cunning!

As a child of nine, she had gone through a phase of walking in her sleep. One summer night, they found her bed empty, and after an hour's hysterical search they had found her in her nightgown, curled up on the flagstones beside the fishpond. She woke, baffled, in her father's tense clutch, the stars all over the sky, her mother repeating over and over again to the night at large, "Oh, my God, she could have drowned!" They took her to a child psychiatrist, a pretty Austrian woman who spoke to her with the same vocabulary she used on grownups, putting the child instantly at ease. "It is not at all uncommon what you did. I have known so many children who take little night journeys from their beds, and then they awaken and don't know what all the fuss is about! Usually these journeys are quite harmless, because children are surrounded by a magical reality that keeps them safe. Yes, the race of children possesses magically sagacious powers! But the grownups, they tend to forget how it once was for them. They worry, they are afraid of so many things. You do not want your mother and father, who love you so anxiously, to live in fear of you going to live with the fishes." She had giggled at the thought. The woman's steady gray-green eyes were trained on her carefully, suspending her in a kind of bubble. Then she had rejoined her parents, a dutiful "child" again, holding a hand up to each of them. The night journeys had stopped.

A thunderstorm one night last spring. Blue Boy whining in his insulated house below the garage. She had lain there, strangely elated by the nearness of the thunderclaps that tore at the sky, followed by instantaneous flashes of jagged light. Wondering shouldn't she go down and let the dog in; he hated storms. Then dozing off again . . . .

She woke. The storm had stopped. The dark air was quiet. Something had changed, some small thing—what? She had to think hard before she found it: the hall light, which she kept burning during the week-nights when she was there alone, had gone out. She reached over and switched the button on her bedside lamp. Nothing. A tree must have fallen and hit a wire, causing the power to go off. This often happened here. No problem. The dog had stopped crying. She felt herself sinking into a delicious, deep reverie, the kind that sometimes came just before morning, as if her being broke slowly into tiny pieces and spread itself over the world. It was a feeling she had not known until she had lived by herself in this house: this weightless though conscious state in which she lay, as if in a warm bath, and yet was able to send her thoughts anywhere, as if her mind contained the entire world.

And as she floated in this silent world, transparent and buoyed upon the dream layers of the mind, she heard a small rattling sound, like pebbles being shaken in a jar. The sound came distinctly from the guest room, a room so chosen by her husband and herself because it was the farthest room from their bedroom on this floor. It lay above what had been the old side of the house, built seventy-five years before the new side, which was completed in 1753. There was a bed in it, and a chair, and some plants in the window. Sometimes on weekends when she could not sleep, she went and read there, or meditated, to keep from waking her husband. It was the room where Victoria Darrow and her young lover would not sleep the following fall, because she would say quietly to her husband, "No . . . not that room. I—I've made up the bed in the other room." "What?" he would want to know. "The one next to ours? Right under our noses?"

She did not lie long listening to this sound before she understood it was one she had never heard in the house before. It had a peculiar regularity to its rhythm; there was nothing accidental about it, nothing influenced by the wind, or the nerves of some lost animal. *K-chunk, k-chunk, k-chunk,* it went. At intervals of exactly a half-minute apart. She still remembered how to time such things, such intervals. She was as good as any stopwatch when it came to timing certain intervals.

K-chunk, k-chunk, k-chunk. That determined regularity. Something willed, something poignantly repeated, as though the repetition was a means of consoling someone in the dark. Her skin began to prickle. Often, lying in such states of weightless reverie, she had practiced the trick of sending herself abroad, into rooms of the house, out into the night to check on Blue Boy, over to the barn to look in on her horse, who slept standing up. Once she had heard a rather frightening noise, as if someone in the basement had turned on a faucet, and so she forced herself to "go down," floating down two sets of stairs into the darkness, only to discover what she had known all the time: the hookup system between the hot-water tank and the pump, which sounded like someone turning on the water.

Now she went through the palpable, prickly darkness, without lights, down the chilly hall in her sleeveless gown, into the guest room. Although there was no light, not even a moon shining through the window, she could make out the shape of the bed and then the chair, the spider plants on the window, and a small dark shape in one corner, on the floor, which she and her husband had painted a light yellow.

K-chunk, k-chunk, k-chunk. The shape moved with the noise.

Now she knew what they meant, that "someone's hair stood on end." It was true. As she forced herself across the borders of a place she had never been, she felt, distinctly, every single hair on her head raise itself a millimeter or so from her scalp.

She knelt down and discovered him. He was kneeling, a little cold and scared, shaking a small jar filled with some kind of pebbles. (She later found out, in a subsequent visit, that they were small colored shells, of a triangular shape, called coquinas: she found them in a picture in a child's nature book at the library.) He was wearing pajamas a little too big for him, obviously hand-me-downs, and he was exactly two years older than the only time she had ever held him in her arms.

The two of them knelt in the corner of the room, taking each other in. His large eyes were the same as before: dark and unblinking. He held the small jar close to him, watching her. He was not afraid, but she knew better than to move too close.

She knelt, the tears streaming down her cheeks, but she made no sound, her eyes fastened on that small form. And then the hall light came on silently, as well as the lamp beside her bed, and with wet cheeks and pounding heart she could not be sure whether or not she had actually been out of the room.

But what did it matter, on the level where they had met? He traveled so much farther than she to reach that room. *("Yes, the race of children possesses magically sagacious powers!")*

She and her husband sat together on the flowered chintz sofa, watching the last of the series in which TV purportedly examined itself. She said, "Did you ever think that the whole thing is really a miracle? I mean, here we sit, eighty miles away from your studios, and we turn on a little machine and there is Victoria, speaking to us as clearly as she did last weekend when she was in this very room. Why, it's magic, it's time travel and space travel right in front of our eyes, but because it's been 'discovered,' because the world understands that it's only little dots that transmit Victoria electronically to us, it's *all right.* We can bear it. Don't you sometimes wonder about all the miracles that haven't been officially approved yet? I mean, who knows, maybe in a hundred years everybody will take it for granted that they can send an image of themselves around in space by some perfectly natural means available to us now. I mean, when you think about it, what *is* space? What *is* time? Where do the so-called boundaries of each of us begin and end? Can anyone explain it?"

He was drinking Scotch and thinking how they had decided not to renew Victoria Darrow's contract. Somewhere on the edges of his mind hovered an anxious, growing certainty about his wife. At the local grocery store this morning, when he went to pick up a carton of milk and the paper, he had stopped to chat with DePuy. "I don't mean to interfere, but she doesn't know those fields," said the farmer. "Last year we had to shoot a mare, stumbled into one of those holes. . . . It's madness, the way she rides."

And look at her now, her face so pale and shining, speaking of miracles and space travel, almost on the verge of tears. . . .

And last night, his first night up from the city, he had wandered through the house, trying to drink himself into this slower weekend pace, and he had come across a pile of her books, stacked in the alcove where, it was obvious, she lay for hours, escaping into science fiction, and the occult.

Now his own face appeared on the screen. "I want to be fair," he was telling Victoria Darrow. "I want to be objective. . . . Violence has always been part of the human makeup. I don't like it anymore than you do, but there it is. I think it's more a question of whether we want to face things as they are or escape into fantasies of how we would like them to be."

Beside him, his wife uttered a sudden bell-like laugh.

(". . . It's madness, the way she rides.")

He did want to be fair, objective. She had told him again and again that she liked her life here. And he—well, he had to admit he liked his own present setup.

"I am a pragmatist," he was telling Virginia Darrow on the screen. He decided to speak to his wife about her riding and leave her alone about the books. She had the right to some escape, if anyone did. But the titles: *Marvelous Manifestations, The Mind Travellers, A Doctor Looks at Spiritualism, The Other Side* . . . Something revolted in him, he couldn't help it; he felt an actual physical revulsion at this kind of thinking. Still it was better than some other escapes. His friend Barnett, the actor, who said at night he went from room to room, after his wife was asleep, collecting empty glasses. ("Once I found one by the Water Pik, a second on the ledge beside the tub, a third on the back of the john, and a fourth on the floor beside the john. . . .")

He looked sideways at his wife, who was absorbed, it seemed, in watching him on the screen. Her face was tense, alert, animated. She did not look mad. She wore slim gray pants and a loose-knit pullover made of some silvery material, like a knight's chain mail. The lines of her profile were clear and silvery themselves, somehow sexless and pure, like a child's profile. He no longer felt lust when he looked at her, only a sad determination to protect her. He had a mistress in town, whom he loved, but he had explained, right from the beginning, that he considered himself married for the rest of his life. He told this woman the whole story. "And I am implicated in it. I could never leave her." An intelligent, sensitive woman, she had actually wept and said, "Of course not."

He always wore the same pajamas, a shade too big, but always clean. Obviously washed again and again in a machine that went through its cycles frequently. She imagined his "other mother," a harassed woman with several children, short on money, on time, on dreams—all the things she herself had too much of. The family lived, she believed, somewhere in Florida, probably on the west coast. She had worked that out from the little coquina shells: their bright colors, even in moonlight shining through a small window with spider plants in it. His face and arms had been suntanned early in the spring and late into the autumn. They never spoke or touched. She was not sure how much of this he understood. She tried and failed to remember where she herself had gone, in those little night journeys to the fishpond. Perhaps he never remembered afterward, when he woke up, clutching his jar, in a roomful of brothers and sisters. Or with a worried mother or father come to collect him, asleep by the sea. Once she had a very clear dream of the whole family, living in a trailer, with palm trees. But that was a dream; she recognized its difference in quality from those truly magic times when, through his own childish powers, he somehow found a will strong enough, or innocent enough, to project himself upon her still-floating consciousness, as clearly and as believably as her own husband's image on the screen.

There had been six of those times in six months. She dared to look forward to more. So unafraid he was. The last time was the day after Victoria Darrow and her young lover and her own good husband had returned to the city. She had gone farther with the child than ever before. On a starry-clear, cold September Monday, she had coaxed him down the stairs and out of the house with her. He held to the banisters, a child unused to stairs, and yet she knew there was no danger; he floated in his own dream with her. She took him to see Blue Boy. Who disappointed her by whining and backing away in fear. And then to the barn to see the horse. Who perked up his ears and looked interested. There was no touching, of course, no touching or speaking. Later she wondered if horses, then, were more magical than dogs. If dogs were more "realistic." She was glad the family was poor, the mother harassed. They could not afford any expensive child psychiatrist who would hypnotize him out of his night journeys.

He loved her. She knew that. Even if he never remembered her in his other life.

"At last I was beginning to understand what Teilhard de Chardin[4] meant when he said that man's true home is the mind. I understood that when the mystics tell us that the mind is a place, they *don't mean it as a metaphor.* I found these new powers developed with practice. I had to detach myself from my ordinary physical personality. The intelligent part of me had to remain wide awake, and move down into this world of thoughts, dreams and memories. After several such journeyings I understood something else: dream and reality aren't competitors, but reciprocal sources of consciousness." This she read in a "respectable book," by a "respectable man," a scientist, alive and living in England, only a few years older than herself. She looked down at the dog, sleeping on the rug. His lean silvery body actually ran as he slept! Suddenly his muzzle lifted, the savage teeth snapped. Where was he "really" now? Did the dream rabbit in his jaws know it was a dream? There was much to think about, between her trips to the nursery.

Would the boy grow, would she see his body slowly emerging from its child's shape, the arms and legs lengthening, the face thinning out into a man's—like a certain advertisement for bread she had seen on TV where a child grows up, in less than a half-minute of sponsor time, right before the viewer's eyes. Would he grow into a man, grow a beard . . . outgrow the nursery region of his mind where they had been able to meet?

And yet, some daylight part of his mind must have retained an image of her from that single daylight time they had looked into each other's eyes.

The worst thing, such an awful thing to happen to a young woman . . . She was having this natural childbirth, you see, her husband in the delivery room with her, and the pains were coming a half-minute apart, and the doctor had just said, "This

4. Pierre Teilhard de Chardin (1881–1955), French paleontologist, philosopher, and religious mystic.

is going to be a breeze, Mrs. McNair," and they never knew exactly what went wrong, but all of a sudden the pains stopped and they had to go in after the baby without even time to give her a saddle block or any sort of anesthetic. . . . They must have practically had to tear it out of her . . . the husband fainted. The baby was born dead, and they gave her a heavy sedative to put her out all night.

When she woke the next morning, before she had time to remember what had happened, a nurse suddenly entered the room and laid a baby in her arms. "Here's your little boy," she said cheerfully, and the woman thought, with a profound, religious relief, *So that other nightmare was a dream,* and she had the child at her breast feeding him before the nurse realized her mistake and rushed back into the room, but they had to knock the poor woman out with more sedatives before she would let the child go. She was screaming and so was the little baby and they clung to each other till she passed out.

They would have let the nurse go, only it wasn't entirely her fault. The hospital was having a strike at the time; some of the nurses were outside picketing and this nurse had been working straight through for forty-eight hours, and when she was questioned afterward she said she had just mixed up the rooms, and yet, she said, when she had seen the woman and the baby clinging to each other like that, she had undergone a sort of revelation in her almost hallucinatory exhaustion: the nurse said she saw that all children and mothers were interchangeable, that nobody could own anybody or anything, anymore than you could own an idea that happened to be passing through the air and caught on your mind, or anymore than you owned the rosebush that grew in your back yard. There were only mothers and children, she realized, though, afterward, the realization faded.

It was the kind of freakish thing that happens once in a million times, and it's a wonder the poor woman kept her sanity.

In the intervals, longer than those measured by any stopwatch, she waited for him. In what the world accepted as "time," she shopped for groceries, for clothes; she read; she waved from her bottle-green car to Mrs. Frye, trimming the hedge in front of the liquor store, to Mrs. DePuy, hanging out her children's pajamas in the back yard of the old Patroon farm. She rode her horse through the fields of the waning season, letting him have his head; she rode like the wind, a happy, happy woman. She rode faster than fear because she was a woman in a dream, a woman anxiously awaiting her child's sleep. The stallion's hoofs pounded the earth. Oiling his tractor, DePuy resented the foolish woman and almost wished for a woodchuck hole to break that arrogant ride. Wished deep in a violent level of himself he never knew he had. For he was a kind, distracted father and husband, a practical, hard-working man who would never descend deeply into himself. Her body, skimming through time, felt weightless to the horse.

Was she a woman riding a horse and dreaming she was a mother who anxiously awaited her child's sleep; or was she a mother dreaming of herself as a free spirit who could ride her horse like the wind because she had nothing to fear?

I am a happy woman, that's all I know. Who can explain such things?

1976

THOMAS PYNCHON
(1937–)

Born on Long Island, in Glen Cove, Thomas Pynchon graduated at sixteen from nearby Oyster Bay High School in 1953 and entered Cornell University that fall. As a freshman, he enrolled in Cornell's pioneering engineering physics program, with its emphasis on theory rather than practical applications, and maintained an interest in the arts and humanities. In 1955 he left the university for two years of service in the navy, including time at the naval base at Norfolk, Virginia, with leaves in Washington, D.C. Returning to Cornell in the fall of 1957, he graduated as an English major in 1959. Among his classes was Vladimir Nabokov's hugely popular course in Masterpieces in European Fiction. At Cornell, also, he became friends with Richard Fariña, an undergraduate whose academic career was similarly interrupted by semesters elsewhere and whose novel *Been Down So Long It Looks Like Up to Me* (1966) provides a mordantly comic view of life at Cornell in 1958, the year of a memorable student revolt.

With his first fiction appearing in spring, 1959, in two Cornell magazines, the undergraduate *Cornell Writer* and the national literary journal *Epoch,* Pynchon gave up the opportunity to remain as a graduate student of English, leaving instead for New York and the life of a writer. Acceptances from *New World Writing,* the *Kenyon Review,* and *Noble Savage* came early. Working as a technical writer for the Boeing Corporation in Seattle from 1960 to 1962, he prepared for the press his first novel, *V.* (1963), one of the most original fictions of its decade. Since the appearance of that novel, he has managed to keep his life almost entirely unknown. Intensely private, he refuses interviews and has been secretive about his writing and his whereabouts (which have included, apparently, Mexico, California, and Europe). Two other novels have followed, *The Crying of Lot 49* (1966) and *Gravity's Rainbow* (1973). Taken together, the three have earned their author a place among the masters of recent literature.

No writer of his generation has attracted so much critical attention and few have had the broad appeal that makes Pynchon's work attractive both to relatively unsophisticated readers and to scholars dazzled by the range and complexity of his knowledge. His vision, fantastically paranoid as to the mysterious but human forces controlling the world's destiny behind the sham façades of governmental and corporate entities, appears to suit a contemporary vacuum of belief. His fictions, enmeshed within the details of an incredibly precise scientific and historical accuracy, assume the qualities of myth. Enlarged far beyond the bounds of literal belief, they explain things centrally important in our culture. Even his shortest, simplest novel, *The Crying of Lot 49,* defies easy summary. The far more complex *V.* and *Gravity's Rainbow,* still more so, employ multilayered plots involving, together, hundreds of characters, to range far and wide in and around the two world wars of our century, arriving at ambiguous resolutions.

In "Entropy" Pynchon explains and illustrates a concept from thermodynamics, applying it not only to the transfer of heat, but, by analogy, also to the transfer of human energy, including the energy necessary to communicate.

Pynchon's early stories are collected in *Slow Learner,* 1984. His novels to date are named above.

Studies include Joseph W. Slade, *Thomas Pynchon,* 1974; George Levine and David Leverenz, eds., *Mindful Pleasures: Essays on Thomas Pynchon,* 1976; Edward Mendelson, ed., *Pynchon: A Collection of Critical Essays,* 1978; William M. Plater, *The Grim Phoenix: Reconstructing Thomas Pynchon,* 1978; David Cowart, *Thomas Pynchon:*

The Art of Allusion, 1980; John O. Stark, *Thomas Pynchon and the Literature of Information,* 1980; Richard Pearce, ed., *Critical Essays on Thomas Pynchon,* 1981; Thomas H. Schaub, *Pynchon: The Voice of Ambiguity,* 1981; Charles Clerc, ed., *Approaches to Gravity's Rainbow,* 1983; Peter L. Cooper, *Signs and Symptoms: Thomas Pynchon and the Contemporary World,* 1983; and Molly Hite, *Ideas of Order in the Novels of Thomas Pynchon,* 1983.

Entropy[1]

> Boris has just given me a summary of his views. He is a weather prophet. The weather will continue bad, he says. There will be more calamities, more death, more despair. Not the slightest indication of a change anywhere. . . . We must get into step, a lockstep toward the prison of death. There is no escape. The weather will not change.
>
> —*Tropic of Cancer*[2]

Downstairs, Meatball Mulligan's lease-breaking party was moving into its 40th hour. On the kitchen floor, amid a litter of empty champagne fifths, were Sandor Rojas and three friends, playing spit in the ocean and staying awake on Heidseck and benzedrine pills. In the living room Duke, Vincent, Krinkles and Paco sat crouched over a 15-inch speaker which had been bolted into the top of a wastepaper basket, listening to 27 watts' worth of *The Heroes' Gate at Kiev.* They all wore horn rimmed sunglasses and rapt expressions, and smoked funny-looking cigarettes which contained not, as you might expect, tobacco, but an adulterated form of *cannabis sativa.*[3] This group was the Duke di Angelis quartet. They recorded for a local label called Tambú and had to their credit one 10" LP entitled *Songs of Outer Space.*[4] From time to time one of them would flick the ashes from his cigarette into the speaker cone to watch them dance around. Meatball himself was sleeping over by the window, holding an empty magnum to his chest as if it were a teddy bear. Several government girls, who worked for people like the State Department and NSA, had passed out on couches, chairs and in one case the bathroom sink.

This was in early February of '57 and back then there were a lot of American expatriates around Washington, D.C., who would talk, every time they met you, about how someday they were going to go over to Europe for real but right now it seemed they were working for the government. Everyone saw a fine irony in this. They would stage, for instance, polyglot parties where the newcomer was sort of ignored if he couldn't carry on simultaneous conversations in three or four languages. They would haunt Armenian delicatessens for weeks at a stretch and invite you over for bulghour[5] and lamb in tiny kitchens whose walls were covered with bullfight posters. They would have affairs with sultry girls from Andalucía or the Midi who studied economics at Georgetown. Their Dôme[6] was a collegiate Rathskeller out on Wisconsin Avenue called the Old Heidelberg and they had to settle for cherry blossoms instead of lime trees when spring came, but in its lethargic way their life provided, as they said, kicks.

At the moment, Meatball's party seemed to be gathering its second wind. Outside there was rain. Rain splatted against the tar paper on the roof and was fractured into a fine spray off the noses, eyebrows and lips of wooden gargoyles under the eaves, and ran like drool down the windowpanes. The day before, it had snowed and the

1. First published in *Kenyon Review,* Spring, 1960. The source of the present text is *Slow Learner,* 1984.
2. Novel (1934) by Henry Miller (1891–1980).
3. Marijuana.
4. With no air to carry sound waves, songs of outer space would be silent, a point that becomes relevant later in the story.
5. Dried wheat, coarsely ground and cooked, often as a pilaf.
6. Paris café.

day before that there had been winds of gale force and before that the sun had made the city glitter bright as April, though the calendar read early February. It is a curious season in Washington, this false spring. Somewhere in it are Lincoln's Birthday and the Chinese New Year, and a forlornness in the streets because cherry blossoms are weeks away still and, as Sarah Vaughan has put it, spring will be a little late this year. Generally crowds like the one which would gather in the Old Heidelberg on weekday afternoons to drink Würtzburger and to sing Lili Marlene (not to mention The Sweetheart of Sigma Chi) are inevitably and incorrigibly Romantic. And as every good Romantic knows, the soul *(spiritus, ruach, pneuma)* is nothing, substantially, but air; it is only natural that warpings in the atmosphere should be recapitulated in those who breathe it. So that over and above the public components—holidays, tourist attractions—there are private meanderings, linked to the climate as if this spell were a *stretto*[7] passage in the year's fugue: haphazard weather, aimless loves, unpredicted commitments: months one can easily spend *in* fugue, because oddly enough, later on, winds, rains, passions of February and March are never remembered in that city, it is as if they had never been.

The last bass notes of *The Heroes' Gate* boomed up through the floor and woke Callisto[8] from an uneasy sleep. The first thing he became aware of was a small bird he had been holding gently between his hands, against his body. He turned his head sidewise on the pillow to smile down at it, at its blue hunched-down head and sick, lidded eyes, wondering how many more nights he would have to give it warmth before it was well again. He had been holding the bird like that for three days: it was the only way he knew to restore its health. Next to him the girl stirred and whimpered, her arm thrown across her face. Mingled with the sounds of the rain came the first tentative, querulous morning voices of the other birds, hidden in philodendrons and small fan palms: patches of scarlet, yellow and blue laced through this Rousseau-like[9] fantasy, this hothouse jungle it had taken him seven years to weave together. Hermetically sealed, it was a tiny enclave of regularity in the city's chaos, alien to the vagaries of the weather, of national politics, of any civil disorder. Through trial-and-error Callisto had perfected its ecological balance, with the help of the girl its artistic harmony, so that the swayings of its plant life, the stirrings of its birds and human inhabitants were all as integral as the rhythms of a perfectly-executed mobile. He and the girl could no longer, of course, be omitted from that sanctuary; they had become necessary to its unity. What they needed from outside was delivered. They did not go out.

"Is he all right," she whispered. She lay like a tawny question mark facing him, her eyes suddenly huge and dark and blinking slowly. Callisto ran a finger beneath the feathers at the base of the bird's neck; caressed it gently. "He's going to be well, I think. See: he hears his friends beginning to wake up." The girl had heard the rain and the birds even before she was fully awake. Her name was Aubade:[1] she was part French and part Annamese, and she lived on her own curious and lonely planet, where the clouds and the odor of poincianas, the bitterness of wine and the accidental fingers at the small of her back or feathery against her breasts came to her reduced

7. A passage with voices following or overlapping in close succession.
8. His name is the same as that of the Callisto who, in Greek mythology, was the daughter of a king of Arcadia and was changed into a she-bear, hunted, and became the constellation Ursa Major.
9. As in the paintings of Henri Rousseau (1844–1910), French primitive painter.
1. French: morning serenade, a poetic convention of the Middle Ages, ordinarily a love song greeting the dawn, when lovers must part.

inevitably to the terms of sound: of music which emerged at intervals from a howling darkness of discordancy. "Aubade," he said, "go see." Obedient, she arose; padded to the window, pulled aside the drapes and after a moment said: "It is 37. Still 37." Callisto frowned. "Since Tuesday, then," he said. "No change." Henry Adams,[2] three generations before his own, had stared aghast at Power; Callisto found himself now in much the same state over Thermodynamics, the inner life of that power, realizing like his predecessor that the Virgin and the dynamo stand as much for love as for power; that the two are indeed identical; and that love therefore not only makes the world go round but also makes the boccie ball spin, the nebula precess.[3] It was this latter or sidereal[4] element which disturbed him. The cosmologists had predicted an eventual heat-death for the universe (something like Limbo:[5] form and motion abolished, heat-energy identical at every point in it); the meteorologists, day-to-day, staved it off by contradicting with a reassuring array of varied temperatures.

But for three days now, despite the changeful weather, the mercury had stayed at 37 degrees Fahrenheit. Leery at omens of apocalypse, Callisto shifted beneath the covers. His fingers pressed the bird more firmly, as if needing some pulsing or suffering assurance of an early break in the temperature.

It was that last cymbal crash that did it. Meatball was hurled wincing into consciousness as the synchronized wagging of heads over the wastebasket stopped. The final hiss remained for an instant in the room, then melted into the whisper of rain outside. "Aarrgghh," announced Meatball in the silence, looking at the empty magnum. Krinkles, in slow motion, turned, smiled and held out a cigarette. "Tea[6] time, man," he said. "No, no," said Meatball. "How many times I got to tell you guys. Not at my place. You ought to know, Washington is lousy with Feds." Krinkles looked wistful. "Jeez, Meatball," he said, "you don't want to do nothing no more." "Hair of dog," said Meatball. "Only hope. Any juice left?" He began to crawl toward the kitchen. "No champagne, I don't think," Duke said. "Case of tequila behind the icebox." They put on an Earl Bostic side. Meatball paused at the kitchen door, glowering at Sandor Rojas. "Lemons," he said after some thought. He crawled to the refrigerator and got out three lemons and some cubes, found the tequila and set about restoring order to his nervous system. He drew blood once cutting the lemons and had to use two hands squeezing them and his foot to crack the ice tray but after about ten minutes he found himself, through some miracle, beaming down into a monster tequila sour. "That looks yummy," Sandor Rojas said. "How about you make me one." Meatball blinked at him. "*Kitchi lofass a shegitbe,*"[7] he replied automatically, and wandered away into the bathroom. "I say," he called out a moment later to no one in particular. "I say, there seems to be a girl or something sleeping in the sink." He took her by the shoulders and shook. "Wha," she said. "You don't look too comfortable," Meatball said. "Well," she agreed. She stumbled to the shower, turned on the cold water and sat down cross-legged in the spray. "That's better," she smiled.

"Meatball," Sandor Rojas yelled from the kitchen. "Somebody is trying to come in the window. A burglar, I think. A second-story man." "What are you worrying

2. American historian (1838–1918).
3. Move by precession, as a spinning body does when the direction of its rotational axis is changed by an applied torque.
4. Pertaining to the stars.
5. In Milton, and elsewhere, a place of oblivion or neglect for souls that have earned neither heaven nor hell.
6. Slang: marijuana.
7. Hungarian, loosely translated, "Up yours."

about," Meatball said. "We're on the third floor." He loped back into the kitchen. A shaggy woebegone figure stood out on the fire escape, raking his fingernails down the windowpane. Meatball opened the window. "Saul," he said.

"Sort of wet out," Saul said. He climbed in, dripping. "You heard, I guess."

"Miriam left you," Meatball said, "or something, is all I heard."

There was a sudden flurry of knocking at the front door. "Do come in," Sandor Rojas called. The door opened and there were three coeds from George Washington, all of whom were majoring in philosophy. They were each holding a gallon of Chianti. Sandor leaped up and dashed into the living room. "We heard there was a party," one blonde said. "Young blood," Sandor shouted. He was an ex-Hungarian freedom fighter who had easily the worst chronic case of what certain critics of the middle class have called Don Giovannism in the District of Columbia. *Purche porti la gonnella, voi sapete quel che fa.* [8] Like Pavlov's dog: a contralto voice or a whiff of Arpège and Sandor would begin to salivate. Meatball regarded the trio blearily as they filed into the kitchen; he shrugged. "Put the wine in the icebox," he said "and good morning."

Aubade's neck made a golden bow as she bent over the sheets of foolscap, scribbling away in the green murk of the room. "As a young man at Princeton," Callisto was dictating, nestling the bird against the gray hairs of his chest, "Callisto had learned a mnemonic device for remembering the Laws of Thermodynamics: you can't win, things are going to get worse before they get better, who says they're going to get better. At the age of 54, confronted with Gibbs'[9] notion of the universe, he suddenly realized that undergraduate cant had been oracle, after all. That spindly maze of equations became, for him, a vision of ultimate, cosmic heat-death.[1] He had known all along, of course, that nothing but a theoretical engine or system ever runs at 100% efficiency; and about the theorem of Clausius,[2] which states that the entropy[3] of an isolated system always continually increases. It was not, however, until Gibbs and Boltzmann[4] brought to this principle the methods of statistical mechanics that the horrible significance of it all dawned on him: only then did he realize that the isolated system—galaxy, engine, human being, culture, whatever—must evolve spontaneously toward the Condition of the More Probable. He was forced, therefore, in the sad dying fall[5] of middle age, to a radical reëvaluation of everything he had learned up to then; all the cities and seasons and casual passions of his days had now to be looked at in a new and elusive light. He did not know if he was equal to the task. He was aware of the dangers of the reductive fallacy and, he hoped, strong enough not to drift into the graceful decadence of an enervated fatalism. His had always been a vigorous, Italian sort of pessimism: like Machiavelli,[6]

8. Italian: "As long as she wears a skirt, you know what will happen," from Leporello's Catalogue Aria in Mozart's *Don Giovanni,* Act I.

9. Josiah Willard Gibbs (1839–1903), mathematical physicist who was, according to Henry Adams, "the greatest of Americans, judged by his rank in science." His books include *On the Equilibrium of Heterogeneous Substances* (1876) and *Elementary Principles in Statistical Mechanics.*

1. The point when, at maximum entropy (see below), the temperature is everywhere the same and no energy is available for work.

2. Rudolf Julius Emanuel Clausius (1822–1888), German mathematical physicist and pioneer in thermodynamics who introduced the concept of entropy.

3. In physics, the quantity of disorder or randomness in any system containing energy. As the entropy increases, the energy becomes less available for use.

4. Ludwig Boltzmann (1844–1906), Austrian physicist who originated the Boltzmann constant, expressing the ratio of a molecule's energy to its absolute temperature.

5. An echo of the Duke's speech at the beginning of *Twelfth Night:* "If music be the food of love, play on. / Give me excess of it, that, surfeiting, / The appetite may sicken, and so die. / That strain again! It had a dying fall."

6. Niccolò Machiavelli (1469–1527), Florentine author of *The Prince* (1532), a work containing advice to rulers.

he allowed the forces of *virtù* and *fortuna*[7] to be about 50/50; but the equations now introduced a random factor which pushed the odds to some unutterable and indeterminate ratio which he found himself afraid to calculate." Around him loomed vague hothouse shapes; the pitifully small heart fluttered against his own. Counterpointed against his words the girl heard the chatter of birds and fitful car honkings scattered along the wet morning and Earl Bostic's alto rising in occasional wild peaks through the floor. The architectonic purity of her world was constantly threatened by such hints of anarchy: gaps and excrescences and skew lines, and a shifting or tilting of planes to which she had continually to readjust lest the whole structure shiver into a disarray of discrete and meaningless signals. Callisto had described the process once as a kind of "feedback": she crawled into dreams each night with a sense of exhaustion, and a desperate resolve never to relax that vigilance. Even in the brief periods when Callisto made love to her, soaring above the bowing of taut nerves in haphazard double-stops would be the one singing string of her determination.

"Nevertheless," continued Callisto, "he found in entropy or the measure of disorganization for a closed system an adequate metaphor to apply to certain phenomena in his own world. He saw, for example, the younger generation responding to Madison Avenue with the same spleen his own had once reserved for Wall Street: and in American 'consumerism' discovered a similar tendency from the least to the most probable, from differentiation to sameness, from ordered individuality to a kind of chaos. He found himself, in short, restating Gibbs' prediction in social terms, and envisioned a heat-death for his culture in which ideas, like heat-energy, would no longer be transferred, since each point in it would ultimately have the same quantity of energy; and intellectual motion would, accordingly, cease." He glanced up suddenly. "Check it now," he said. Again she rose and peered out at the thermometer. "37," she said. "The rain has stopped." He bent his head quickly and held his lips against a quivering wing. "Then it will change soon," he said, trying to keep his voice firm.

Sitting on the stove Saul was like any big rag doll that a kid has been taking out some incomprehensible rage on. "What happened," Meatball said. "If you feel like talking, I mean."

"Of course I feel like talking," Saul said. "One thing I did, I slugged her."

"Discipline must be maintained."

"Ha, ha. I wish you'd been there. Oh Meatball, it was a lovely fight. She ended up throwing a *Handbook of Chemistry and Physics* at me, only it missed and went through the window, and when the glass broke I reckon something in her broke too. She stormed out of the house crying, out in the rain. No raincoat or anything."

"She'll be back."

"No."

"Well." Soon Meatball said: "It was something earth-shattering, no doubt. Like who is better, Sal Mineo or Ricky Nelson."

"What it was about," Saul said, "was communication theory. Which of course makes it very hilarious."

"I don't know anything about communication theory."

"Neither does my wife. Come right down to it, who does? That's the joke."

When Meatball saw the kind of smile Saul had on his face he said: "Maybe you would like tequila or something."

7. Worth (or power) and fortune (or luck).

"No. I mean, I'm sorry. It's a field you can go off the deep end in, is all. You get where you're watching all the time for security cops: behind bushes, around corners. MUFFET is top secret."

"Wha."

"Multi-unit factorial field electronic tabulator."

"You were fighting about that."

"Miriam has been reading science-fiction again. That and *Scientific American.* It seems she is, as we say, bugged at this idea of computers acting like people. I made the mistake of saying you can just as well turn that around, and talk about human behavior like a program fed into an IBM machine."

"Why not," Meatball said.

"Indeed, why not. In fact it is sort of crucial to communication, not to mention information theory. Only when I said that she hit the roof. Up went the balloon. And I can't figure out *why.* If anybody should know why, I should. I refuse to believe the government is wasting taxpayers' money on me, when it has so many bigger and better things to waste it on."

Meatball made a moue. "Maybe she thought you were acting like a cold, dehumanized amoral scientist type."

"My god," Saul flung up an arm. "Dehumanized. How much more human can I get? I worry, Meatball, I do. There are Europeans wandering around North Africa these days with their tongues torn out of their heads because those tongues have spoken the wrong words. Only the Europeans thought they were the right words."

"Language barrier," Meatball suggested.

Saul jumped down off the stove. "That," he said, angry, "is a good candidate for sick joke of the year. No, ace, it is *not* a barrier. If it is anything it's a kind of leakage. Tell a girl: 'I love you.' No trouble with two-thirds of that, it's a closed circuit. Just you and she. But that nasty four-letter word in the middle, *that's* the one you have to look out for. Ambiguity. Redundance. Irrelevance, even. Leakage. All this is noise. Noise screws up your signal, makes for disorganization in the circuit."

Meatball shuffled around. "Well, now, Saul," he muttered, "you're sort of, I don't know, expecting a lot from people. I mean, you know. What it is is, most of the things we say, I guess, are mostly noise."

"Ha! Half of what you just said, for example."

"Well, you do it too."

"I know." Saul smiled grimly. "It's a bitch, ain't it."

"I bet that's what keeps divorce lawyers in business. Whoops."

"Oh I'm not sensitive. Besides," frowning, "you're right. You find I think that most 'successful' marriages—Miriam and me, up to last night—are sort of founded on compromises. You never run at top efficiency, usually all you have is a minimum basis for a workable thing. I believe the phrase is Togetherness."

"Aarrgghh."

"Exactly. You find that one a bit noisy, don't you. But the noise content is different for each of us because you're a bachelor and I'm not. Or wasn't. The hell with it."

"Well sure," Meatball said, trying to be helpful, "you were using different words. By 'human being' you meant something that you can look at like it was a computer. It helps you think better on the job or something. But Miriam meant something entirely—"

"The hell with it."

Meatball fell silent. "I'll take that drink," Saul said after a while.

The card game had been abandoned and Sandor's friends were slowly getting wasted on tequila. On the living room couch, one of the coeds and Krinkles were engaged in amorous conversation. "No," Krinkles was saying, "no, I can't put Dave *down.* In fact I give Dave a lot of credit, man. Especially considering his accident and all." The girl's smile faded. "How terrible," she said. "What accident?" "Hadn't you heard?" Krinkles said. "When Dave was in the army, just a private E-2, they sent him down to Oak Ridge[8] on special duty. Something to do with the Manhattan Project. He was handling hot stuff one day and got an overdose of radiation. So now he's got to wear lead gloves all the time." She shook her head sympathetically. "What an awful break for a piano-player."

Meatball had abandoned Saul to a bottle of tequila and was about to go to sleep in a closet when the front door flew open and the place was invaded by five enlisted personnel of the U.S. Navy, all in varying stages of abomination. "This is the place," shouted a fat, pimply seaman apprentice who had lost his white hat. "This here is the hoorhouse that chief was telling us about." A stringy-looking 3rd class boatswain's mate pushed him aside and cased the living room. "You're right, Slab," he said. "But it don't look like much, even for Stateside. I seen better tail in Naples, Italy." "How much, hey," boomed a large seaman with adenoids, who was holding a Mason jar full of white lightning.[9] "Oh, my god," said Meatball.

Outside the temperature remained constant at 37 degrees Fahrenheit. In the hothouse Aubade stood absently caressing the branches of a young mimosa, hearing a motif of sap-rising, the rough and unresolved anticipatory theme of those fragile pink blossoms which, it is said, insure fertility. That music rose in a tangled tracery: arabesques of order competing fugally with the improvised discords of the party downstairs, which peaked sometimes in cusps and ogees of noise. That precious signal-to-noise ratio, whose delicate balance required every calorie of her strength, seesawed inside the small tenuous skull as she watched Callisto, sheltering the bird. Callisto was trying to confront any idea of the heat-death now, as he nuzzled the feathery lump in his hands. He sought correspondences. Sade,[1] of course. And Temple Drake,[2] gaunt and hopeless in her little park in Paris, at the end of *Sanctuary.* Final equilibrium. *Nightwood.*[3] And the tango. Any tango, but more than any perhaps the sad sick dance in Stravinsky's *L'Histoire du Soldat.*[4] He thought back: what had tango music been for them after the war, what meanings had he missed in all the stately coupled automatons in the *cafés-dansants,*[5] or in the metronomes which had ticked behind the eyes of his own partners? Not even the clean constant winds of Switzerland could cure the *grippe espagnole:*[6] Stravinsky had had it, they all had had it. And how many musicians were left after Passchendaele,[7] after the Marne?[8] It came down in this case to seven: violin, double-bass. Clarinet, bassoon. Cornet, trombone. Tympani. Almost as if any tiny troupe of saltimbanques[9] had set about conveying the same information as a full pit-orchestra.

8. Oak Ridge, Tennessee, where uranium 235 was first isolated in connection with the Manhattan Project, the World War II effort that culminated in the construction of the atom bomb.
9. "Moonshine," or corn liquor.
1. The marquis de Sade (1740–1814).
2. Heroine of William Faulkner's *Sanctuary* (1931).
3. Novel by Djuna Barnes (1892–1982), American writer.
4. "The Story of a Soldier" (1918).
5. Nightclubs.
6. French: Spanish flu, epidemic in 1918.
7. World War I battlefield in Belgium.
8. World War I battlefield in France.
9. Buffoons.

There was hardly a full complement left in Europe. Yet with violin and tympani Stravinsky had managed to communicate in that tango the same exhaustion, the same airlessness one saw in the slicked-down youths who were trying to imitate Vernon Castle,[1] and in their mistresses, who simply did not care. *Ma maîtresse.*[2] Celeste. Returning to Nice after the second war he had found that café replaced by a perfume shop which catered to American tourists. And no secret vestige of her in the cobblestones or in the old pension next door; no perfume to match her breath heavy with the sweet Spanish wine she always drank. And so instead he had purchased a Henry Miller novel and left for Paris, and read the book on the train so that when he arrived he had been given at least a little forewarning. And saw that Celeste and the others and even Temple Drake were not all that had changed. "Aubade," he said, "my head aches." The sound of his voice generated in the girl an answering scrap of melody. Her movement toward the kitchen, the towel, the cold water, and his eyes following her formed a weird and intricate canon; as she placed the compress on his forehead his sigh of gratitude seemed to signal a new subject, another series of modulations.

"No," Meatball was still saying, "no, I'm afraid not. This is not a house of ill repute. I'm sorry, really I am." Slab was adamant. "But the chief said," he kept repeating. The seaman offered to swap the moonshine for a good piece. Meatball looked around frantically, as if seeking assistance. In the middle of the room, the Duke di Angelis quartet were engaged in a historic moment. Vincent was seated and the others standing: they were going through the motions of a group having a session, only without instruments. "I say," Meatball said. Duke moved his head a few times, smiled faintly, lit a cigarette, and eventually caught sight of Meatball. "Quiet, man," he whispered. Vincent began to fling his arms around, his fists clenched; then, abruptly, was still, then repeated the performance. This went on for a few minutes while Meatball sipped his drink moodily. The navy had withdrawn to the kitchen. Finally at some invisible signal the group stopped tapping their feet and Duke grinned and said, "At least we ended together."

Meatball glared at him. "I say," he said. "I have this new conception, man," Duke said. "You remember your namesake. You remember Gerry."[3]

"No," said Meatball. "I'll remember April, if that's any help."

"As a matter of fact," Duke said, "it was Love for Sale. Which shows how much you know. The point is, it was Mulligan, Chet Baker and that crew, way back then, out yonder. You dig?"

"Baritone sax," Meatball said. "Something about a baritone sax."

"But no piano, man. No guitar. Or accordion. You know what that means."

"Not exactly," Meatball said.

"Well first let me just say, that I am no Mingus, no John Lewis. Theory was never my strong point. I mean things like reading were always difficult for me and all—"

"I know," Meatball said drily. "You got your card taken away because you changed key on Happy Birthday at a Kiwanis Club picnic."

"Rotarian. But it occurred to me, in one of these flashes of insight, that if that first quartet of Mulligan's had no piano, it could only mean one thing."

1. Dancer (1887–1918) popular, with his wife, Irene Castle, in Paris and New York before the war.
2. French: "my mistress."
3. Gerry Mulligan, jazz musician, whose name is echoed by Meatball Mulligan's. Chet Baker, Charlie Mingus, and John Lewis are also jazz musicians.

"No chords," said Paco, the baby-faced bass.

"What he is trying to say," Duke said, "is no root chords. Nothing to listen to while you blow a horizontal line. What one does in such a case is, one *thinks* the roots."

A horrified awareness was dawning on Meatball. "And the next logical extension," he said.

"Is to think everything," Duke announced with simple dignity. "Roots, line, everything."

Meatball looked at Duke, awed. "But," he said.

"Well," Duke said modestly, "there are a few bugs to work out."

"But," Meatball said.

"Just listen," Duke said. "You'll catch on." And off they went again into orbit, presumably somewhere around the asteroid belt. After a while Krinkles made an embouchure and started moving his fingers and Duke clapped his hand to his forehead. "Oaf!" he roared. "The new head we're using, you remember, I wrote last night?" "Sure," Krinkles said, "the new head. I come in on the bridge. All your heads I come in then." "Right," Duke said. "So why—" "Wha," said Krinkles, "16 bars, I wait, I come in—" "16?" Duke said. "No. No, Krinkles. Eight you waited. You want me to sing it? A cigarette that bears a lipstick's traces, an airline ticket to romantic places." Krinkles scratched his head. "These Foolish Things, you mean." "Yes," Duke said, "yes, Krinkles. Bravo." "Not I'll Remember April," Krinkles said. "*Minghe morte,*"[4] said Duke. "I *figured* we were playing it a little slow," Krinkles said. Meatball chuckled. "Back to the old drawing board," he said. "No, man," Duke said, "back to the airless void." And they took off again, only it seemed Paco was playing in G sharp while the rest were in E flat, so they had to start all over.

In the kitchen two of the girls from George Washington and the sailors were singing Let's All Go Down and Piss on the Forrestal.[5] There was a two-handed, bilingual *morra*[6] game on over by the icebox. Saul had filled several paper bags with water and was sitting on the fire escape, dropping them on passersby in the street. A fat government girl in a Bennington sweatshirt, recently engaged to an ensign attached to the Forrestal, came charging into the kitchen, head lowered, and butted Slab in the stomach. Figuring this was as good an excuse for a fight as any, Slab's buddies piled in. The *morra* players were nose-to-nose, screaming *trois, sette* at the tops of their lungs. From the shower the girl Meatball had taken out of the sink announced that she was drowning. She had apparently sat on the drain and the water was now up to her neck. The noise in Meatball's apartment had reached a sustained, ungodly crescendo.

Meatball stood and watched, scratching his stomach lazily. The way he figured, there were only about two ways he could cope: (a) lock himself in the closet and maybe eventually they would all go away, or (b) try to calm everybody down, one by one. (a) was certainly the more attractive alternative. But then he started thinking about that closet. It was dark and stuffy and he would be alone. He did not feature being alone. And then this crew off the good ship Lollipop or whatever it was might take it upon themselves to kick down the closet door, for a lark. And if that happened

4. Italian: "Screw it to death."
5. Naval ship named after James Vincent Forrestal (1892–1949), secretary of the navy during World War II and later first secretary of defense, who committed suicide by jumping from a window.
6. A guessing game involving extended fingers.

he would be, at the very least, embarrassed. The other way was more a pain in the neck, but probably better in the long run.

So he decided to try and keep his lease-breaking party from deteriorating into total chaos: he gave wine to the sailors and separated the *morra* players; he introduced the fat government girl to Sandor Rojas, who would keep her out of trouble; he helped the girl in the shower to dry off and get into bed; he had another talk with Saul; he called a repairman for the refrigerator, which someone had discovered was on the blink. This is what he did until nightfall, when most of the revellers had passed out and the party trembled on the threshold of its third day.

Upstairs Callisto, helpless in the past, did not feel the faint rhythm inside the bird begin to slacken and fail. Aubade was by the window, wandering the ashes of her own lovely world; the temperature held steady, the sky had become a uniform darkening gray. Then something from downstairs—a girl's scream, an overturned chair, a glass dropped on the floor, he would never know what exactly—pierced that private time-warp and he became aware of the faltering, the constriction of muscles, the tiny tossings of the bird's head; and his own pulse began to pound more fiercely, as if trying to compensate. "Aubade," he called weakly, "he's dying." The girl, flowing and rapt, crossed the hothouse to gaze down at Callisto's hands. The two remained like that, poised, for one minute, and two, while the heartbeat ticked a graceful diminuendo down at last into stillness. Callisto raised his head slowly. "I held him," he protested, impotent with the wonder of it, "to give him the warmth of my body. Almost as if I were communicating life to him, or a sense of life. What has happened? Has the transfer of heat ceased to work? Is there no more . . ." He did not finish.

"I was just at the window," she said. He sank back, terrified. She stood a moment more, irresolute; she had sensed his obsession long ago, realized somehow that that constant 37 was now decisive. Suddenly then, as if seeing the single and unavoidable conclusion to all this she moved swiftly to the window before Callisto could speak; tore away the drapes and smashed out the glass with two exquisite hands which came away bleeding and glistening with splinters; and turned to face the man on the bed and wait with him until the moment of equilibrium was reached, when 37 degrees Fahrenheit should prevail both outside and inside, and forever, and the hovering, curious dominant of their separate lives should resolve into a tonic of darkness and the final absence of all motion.

1960, 1984

RAYMOND CARVER

(1938–)

More even than some other writers of his generation, Raymond Carver seems a child of the Great Depression. Born at its tail end in Clatskanie, Oregon, he was the son of a father who had earlier headed northwest from Arkansas seeking a part of the prosperity expected to follow from the federal money flowing into the Columbia Basin Project. When Carver was three, his family moved to Yakima, Washington, where his father found mill work and where he grew up to marry at nineteen and himself father two children by the time he was twenty. A reader of the men's magazines of the 1950's *(Argosy, True, Outdoor Life, Sports Afield),* and of popular fiction by Zane Grey and Edgar Rice Burroughs, he wanted to become a writer, but found the process slow and painful as he struggled to work, to attend school, to write, and to keep a family together.

In 1958, he moved to Paradise, California, took a night job, and enrolled at Chico State College, where the following year he studied writing with John Gardner, whose insistence on close attention to detail and on the moral importance of fiction strongly influenced his work. Transferring to Humboldt State College in 1960, he graduated as an English major in 1963 and began graduate work at the University of Iowa Writers Workshop, but did not complete the year. Back in California, he worked for the next few years at odd jobs, and, after 1967, as an editor of textbooks. Meanwhile he was publishing stories and poems. By the early 1970's, he had sufficient reputation to obtain a series of appointments at universities, including the University of California at Santa Cruz, Stanford, and Iowa. A serious alcoholic, hospitalized at times, he managed a more stable life after quitting drinking in 1977. From 1980 to 1983 he was a professor of English at Syracuse University. Among his awards are a Guggenheim Fellowship and a Strauss Living Award.

Carver's first publication outside of magazines was a collection of poems, *Near Klamath* (1968), issued by the English Club of Sacramento State College. Within the next eight years, two books of poetry and one of fiction were published by small presses before *Will You Please Be Quiet, Please?* (1976) collected the stories of a dozen years to bring him national attention. *What We Talk About When We Talk About Love* (1981) increased his reputation with a group of sparse tales of failed communications, and *Cathedral* (1983) extended it still further with stories in which drained and empty characters manage, sometimes, to reach out to one another. *Where Water Comes Together with Other Water* (1985) is a collection of verse.

Carver's people inhabit the world he passed through on the way to his success. Undereducated working-class inhabitants of California, Oregon, or Washington, they are often unemployed, trapped in depressed small towns, shut away from the glamorous cities and suburbs and from the coastal and mountain beauties of the postcard West. Drinking, they contemplate the failure of their marriages, the losses of their jobs, the futility of their expectations, the emptiness and silences in their lives that suggest few better times to come. As a storyteller, he has an uncanny ability to find the few words that describe best this overall sense of loss. It is a convincing world of alienation, described with a care that suggests that, after all, these are human lives that matter.

Carver's major books to date are named above. *Fires: Essays, Poems, Stories,* 1983, collects works in various genres, and includes, in the English edition only, a memoir, "My Father's Life." *Furious Seasons and Other Stories,* 1977, includes some earlier versions of stories revised in *What We Talk About. Winter Insomnia,* 1970, and *At Night the Salmon Move,* 1976, are early collections of verse.

A brief appraisal appears in *Dictionary of Literary Biography Yearbook: 1984,* 1985.

A Small, Good Thing

Saturday afternoon she drove to the bakery in the shopping center. After looking through a loose-leaf binder with photographs of cakes taped onto the pages, she ordered chocolate, the child's favorite. The cake she chose was decorated with a space ship and launching pad under a sprinkling of white stars, and a planet made of red frosting at the other end. His name, SCOTTY, would be in green letters beneath the planet. The baker, who was an older man with a thick neck, listened without saying anything when she told him the child would be eight years old next Monday. The baker wore a white apron that looked like a smock. Straps cut under his arms, went around in back and then to the front again, where they were secured under his heavy waist. He wiped his hands on his apron as he listened to her. He kept his eyes down on the photographs and let her talk. He let her take her time. He'd just come to work and he'd be there all night, baking, and he was in no real hurry.

She gave the baker her name, Ann Weiss, and her telephone number. The cake would be ready on Monday morning, just out of the oven, in plenty of time for the child's party that afternoon. The baker was not jolly. There were no pleasantries between them, just the minimum exchange of words, the necessary information. He made her feel uncomfortable, and she didn't like that. While he was bent over the counter with the pencil in his hand, she studied his coarse features and wondered if he'd ever done anything else with his life besides be a baker. She was a mother and thirty-three years old, and it seemed to her that everyone, especially someone the baker's age—a man old enough to be her father—must have children who'd gone through this special time of cakes and birthday parties. There must be that between them, she thought. But he was abrupt with her—not rude, just abrupt. She gave up trying to make friends with him. She looked into the back of the bakery and could see a long, heavy wooden table with aluminum pie pans stacked at one end; and beside the table a metal container filled with empty racks. There was an enormous oven. A radio was playing country-Western music.

The baker finished printing the information on the special order card and closed up the binder. He looked at her and said, "Monday morning." She thanked him and drove home.

On Monday morning, the birthday boy was walking to school with another boy. They were passing a bag of potato chips back and forth and the birthday boy was trying to find out what his friend intended to give him for his birthday that afternoon. Without looking, the birthday boy stepped off the curb at an intersection and was immediately knocked down by a car. He fell on his side with his head in the gutter and his legs out in the road. His eyes were closed, but his legs moved back and forth as if he were trying to climb over something. His friend dropped the potato chips and started to cry. The car had gone a hundred feet or so and stopped in the middle of the road. The man in the driver's seat looked back over his shoulder. He waited until the boy got unsteadily to his feet. The boy wobbled a little. He looked dazed, but okay. The driver put the car into gear and drove away.

The birthday boy didn't cry, but he didn't have anything to say about anything either. He wouldn't answer when his friend asked him what it felt like to be hit by a car. He walked home, and his friend went on to school. But after the birthday boy was inside his house and was telling his mother about it—she sitting beside him on the sofa, holding his hands in her lap, saying, "Scotty, honey, are you sure you feel all right, baby?" thinking she would call the doctor anyway—he suddenly lay back on the sofa, closed his eyes, and went limp. When she couldn't wake him up, she hurried to the telephone and called her husband at work. Howard told her to remain calm, remain calm, and then he called an ambulance for the child and left for the hospital himself.

Of course, the birthday party was canceled. The child was in the hospital with a mild concussion and suffering from shock. There'd been vomiting, and his lungs had taken in fluid which needed pumping out that afternoon. Now he simply seemed to be in a very deep sleep—but no coma, Dr. Francis had emphasized, no coma, when he saw the alarm in the parents' eyes. At eleven o'clock that night, when the boy seemed to be resting comfortably enough after the many X-rays and the lab work, and it was just a matter of his waking up and coming around, Howard left the hospital. He and Ann had been at the hospital with the child since that afternoon, and he was going home for a short while to bathe and change clothes. "I'll be back in an hour," he said. She nodded. "It's fine," she said. "I'll be right here." He kissed her on the forehead, and they touched hands. She sat in the chair beside the bed and looked at the child. She was waiting for him to wake up and be all right. Then she could begin to relax.

Howard drove home from the hospital. He took the wet, dark streets very fast, then caught himself and slowed down. Until now, his life had gone smoothly and to his satisfaction—college, marriage, another year of college for the advanced degree in business, a junior partnership in an investment firm. Fatherhood. He was happy and, so far, lucky—he knew that. His parents were still living, his brothers and his sister were established, his friends from college had gone out to take their places in the world. So far, he had kept away from any real harm, from those forces he knew existed and that could cripple or bring down a man if the luck went bad, if things suddenly turned. He pulled into the driveway and parked. His left leg began to tremble. He sat in the car for a minute and tried to deal with the present situation in a rational manner. Scotty had been hit by a car and was in the hospital, but he was going to be all right. Howard closed his eyes and ran his hand over his face. He got out of the car and went up to the front door. The dog was barking inside the house. The telephone rang and rang while he unlocked the door and fumbled for the light switch. He shouldn't have left the hospital, he shouldn't have. "Goddamn it!" he said. He picked up the receiver and said, "I just walked in the door!"

"There's a cake here that wasn't picked up," the voice on the other end of the line said.

"What are you saying?" Howard asked.

"A cake," the voice said. "A sixteen-dollar cake."

Howard held the receiver against his ear, trying to understand. "I don't know anything about a cake," he said. "Jesus, what are you talking about?"

"Don't hand me that," the voice said.

Howard hung up the telephone. He went into the kitchen and poured himself some whiskey. He called the hospital. But the child's condition remained the same; he was still sleeping and nothing had changed there. While water poured into the tub, Howard lathered his face and shaved. He'd just stretched out in the tub and closed his eyes when the telephone rang again. He hauled himself out, grabbed a towel, and hurried through the house, saying, "Stupid, stupid," for having left the hospital. But when he picked up the receiver and shouted, "Hello!" there was no sound at the other end of the line. Then the caller hung up.

He arrived back at the hospital a little after midnight. Ann still sat in the chair beside the bed. She looked up at Howard, and then she looked back at the child. The child's eyes stayed closed, the head was still wrapped in bandages. His breathing was quiet and regular. From an apparatus over the bed hung a bottle of glucose with a tube running from the bottle to the boy's arm.

"How is he?" Howard said. "What's all this?" waving at the glucose and the tube.

"Dr. Francis's orders," she said. "He needs nourishment. He needs to keep up his strength. Why doesn't he wake up, Howard? I don't understand, if he's all right."

Howard put his hand against the back of her head. He ran his fingers through her hair. "He's going to be all right. He'll wake up in a little while. Dr. Francis knows what's what."

After a time, he said, "Maybe you should go home and get some rest. I'll stay here. Just don't put up with this creep who keeps calling. Hang up right away."

"Who's calling?" she asked.

"I don't know who, just somebody with nothing better to do than call up people. You go on now."

She shook her head. "No," she said, "I'm fine."

"Really," he said. "Go home for a while, and then come back and spell me in the morning. It'll be all right. What did Dr. Francis say? He said Scotty's going to be all right. We don't have to worry. He's just sleeping now, that's all."

A nurse pushed the door open. She nodded at them as she went to the bedside. She took the left arm out from under the covers and put her fingers on the wrist, found the pulse, then consulted her watch. In a little while, she put the arm back under the covers and moved to the foot of the bed, where she wrote something on a clipboard attached to the bed.

"How is he?" Ann said. Howard's hand was a weight on her shoulder. She was aware of the pressure from his fingers.

"He's stable," the nurse said. Then she said, "Doctor will be in again shortly. Doctor's back in the hospital. He's making rounds right now."

"I was saying maybe she'd want to go home and get a little rest," Howard said. "After the doctor comes," he said.

"She could do that," the nurse said. "I think you should both feel free to do that, if you wish." The nurse was a big Scandinavian woman with blond hair. There was the trace of an accent in her speech.

"We'll see what the doctor says," Ann said. "I want to talk to the doctor. I don't think he should keep sleeping like this. I don't think that's a good sign." She brought her hand up to her eyes and let her head come forward a little. Howard's grip tightened on her shoulder, and then his hand moved up to her neck, where his fingers began to knead the muscles there.

"Dr. Francis will be here in a few minutes," the nurse said. Then she left the room.

Howard gazed at his son for a time, the small chest quietly rising and falling under the covers. For the first time since the terrible minutes after Ann's telephone call to him at his office, he felt a genuine fear starting in his limbs. He began shaking his head. Scotty was fine, but instead of sleeping at home in his own bed, he was in a hospital bed with bandages around his head and a tube in his arm. But this help was what he needed right now.

Dr. Francis came in and shook hands with Howard, though they'd just seen each other a few hours before. Ann got up from the chair. "Doctor?"

"Ann," he said and nodded. "Let's just first see how he's doing," the doctor said. He moved to the side of the bed and took the boy's pulse. He peeled back one eyelid and then the other. Howard and Ann stood beside the doctor and watched. Then the doctor turned back the covers and listened to the boy's heart and lungs with his stethoscope. He pressed his fingers here and there on the abdomen. When he was finished, he went to the end of the bed and studied the chart. He noted the time, scribbled something on the chart, and then looked at Howard and Ann.

"Doctor, how is he?" Howard said. "What's the matter with him exactly?"

"Why doesn't he wake up?" Ann said.

The doctor was a handsome, big-shouldered man with a tanned face. He wore a three-piece blue suit, a striped tie, and ivory cufflinks. His gray hair was combed along the sides of his head, and he looked as if he had just come from a concert. "He's all right," the doctor said. "Nothing to shout about, he could be better, I think. But he's all right. Still, I wish he'd wake up. He should wake up pretty soon." The doctor looked at the boy again. "We'll know some more in a couple of hours, after the results of a few more tests are in. But he's all right, believe me, except for the hairline fracture of the skull. He does have that."

"Oh, no," Ann said.

"And a bit of a concussion, as I said before. Of course, you know he's in shock," the doctor said. "Sometimes you see this in shock cases. This sleeping."

"But he's out of any real danger?" Howard said. "You said before he's not in a coma. You wouldn't call this a coma, then—would you, doctor?" Howard waited. He looked at the doctor.

"No, I don't want to call it a coma," the doctor said and glanced over at the boy once more. "He's just in a very deep sleep. It's a restorative measure the body is taking on its own. He's out of any real danger, I'd say that for certain, yes. But we'll know more when he wakes up and the other tests are in," the doctor said.

"It's a coma," Ann said. "Of sorts."

"It's not a coma yet, not exactly," the doctor said. "I wouldn't want to call it coma. Not yet, anyway. He's suffered shock. In shock cases, this kind of reaction is common enough; it's a temporary reaction to bodily trauma. Coma. Well, coma is a deep, prolonged unconsciousness, something that could go on for days, or weeks even. Scotty's not in that area, not as far as we can tell. I'm certain his condition will show improvement by morning. I'm betting that it will. We'll know more when he wakes up, which shouldn't be long now. Of course, you may do as you like, stay here or go home for a time. But by all means feel free to leave the hospital for a while if you want. This is not easy, I know." The doctor gazed at the boy again, watching him, and then he turned to Ann and said, "You try not to worry, little mother. Believe me, we're doing all that can be done. It's just a question of a little more time now." He nodded at her, shook hands with Howard again, and then he left the room.

Ann put her hand over the child's forehead. "At least he doesn't have a fever," she said. Then she said, "My God, he feels so cold, though. Howard? Is he supposed to feel like this? Feel his head."

Howard touched the child's temples. His own breathing had slowed. "I think he's supposed to feel this way right now," he said. "He's in shock, remember? That's what the doctor said. The doctor was just in here. He would have said something if Scotty wasn't okay."

Ann stood there a while longer, working her lip with her teeth. Then she moved over to her chair and sat down.

Howard sat in the chair next to her chair. They looked at each other. He wanted to say something else and reassure her, but he was afraid, too. He took her hand

and put it in his lap, and this made him feel better, her hand being there. He picked up her hand and squeezed it. Then he just held her hand. They sat like that for a while, watching the boy and not talking. From time to time, he squeezed her hand. Finally, she took her hand away.

"I've been praying," she said.

He nodded.

She said, "I almost thought I'd forgotten how, but it came back to me. All I had to do was close my eyes and say, 'Please God, help us—help Scotty,' and then the rest was easy. The words were right there. Maybe if you prayed, too," she said to him.

"I've already prayed," he said. "I prayed this afternoon—yesterday afternoon, I mean—after you called, while I was driving to the hospital. I've been praying," he said.

"That's good," she said. For the first time, she felt they were together in it, this trouble. She realized with a start that, until now, it had only been happening to her and to Scotty. She hadn't let Howard into it, though he was there and needed all along. She felt glad to be his wife.

The same nurse came in and took the boy's pulse again and checked the flow from the bottle hanging above the bed.

In an hour, another doctor came in. He said his name was Parsons, from Radiology. He had a bushy mustache. He was wearing loafers, a Western shirt, and a pair of jeans.

"We're going to take him downstairs for more pictures," he told them. "We need to do some more pictures, and we want to do a scan."

"What's that?" Ann said. "A scan?" She stood between this new doctor and the bed. "I thought you'd already taken all your X-rays."

"I'm afraid we need some more," he said. "Nothing to be alarmed about. We just need some more pictures, and we want to do a brain scan on him."

"My God," Ann said.

"It's perfectly normal procedure in cases like this," this new doctor said. "We just need to find out for sure why he isn't back awake yet. It's normal medical procedure, and nothing to be alarmed about. We'll be taking him down in a few minutes," this doctor said.

In a little while, two orderlies came into the room with a gurney. They were black-haired, dark-complexioned men in white uniforms, and they said a few words to each other in a foreign tongue as they unhooked the boy from the tube and moved him from his bed to the gurney. Then they wheeled him from the room. Howard and Ann got on the same elevator. Ann gazed at the child. She closed her eyes as the elevator began its descent. The orderlies stood at either end of the gurney without saying anything, though once one of the men made a comment to the other in their own language, and the other man nodded slowly in response.

Later that morning, just as the sun was beginning to lighten the windows in the waiting room outside the X-ray department, they brought the boy out and moved him back up to his room. Howard and Ann rode up on the elevator with him once more, and once more they took up their places beside the bed.

They waited all day, but still the boy did not wake up. Occasionally, one of them would leave the room to go downstairs to the cafeteria to drink coffee and then, as if suddenly remembering and feeling guilty, get up from the table and hurry back to the room. Dr. Francis came again that afternoon and examined the boy once more and then left after telling them he was coming along and could wake up at any minute now. Nurses, different nurses from the night before, came in from time to time. Then a young woman from the lab knocked and entered the room. She wore white slacks and a white blouse and carried a little tray of things which she put on the stand beside the bed. Without a word to them, she took blood from the boy's arm. Howard closed his eyes as the woman found the right place on the boy's arm and pushed the needle in.

"I don't understand this," Ann said to the woman.

"Doctor's orders," the young woman said. "I do what I'm told. They say draw that one, I draw. What's wrong with him, anyway?" she said. "He's a sweetie."

"He was hit by a car," Howard said. "A hit-and-run."

The young woman shook her head and looked again at the boy. Then she took her tray and left the room.

"Why won't he wake up?" Ann said. "Howard? I want some answers from these people."

Howard didn't say anything. He sat down again in the chair and crossed one leg over the other. He rubbed his face. He looked at his son and then he settled back in the chair, closed his eyes, and went to sleep.

Ann walked to the window and looked out at the parking lot. It was night, and cars were driving into and out of the parking lot with their lights on. She stood at the window with her hands gripping the sill, and knew in her heart that they were into something now, something hard. She was afraid, and her teeth began to chatter until she tightened her jaws. She saw a big car stop in front of the hospital and someone, a woman in a long coat, get into the car. She wished she were that woman and somebody, anybody, was driving her away from here to somewhere else, a place where she would find Scotty waiting for her when she stepped out of the car, ready to say *Mom* and let her gather him in her arms.

In a little while, Howard woke up. He looked at the boy again. Then he got up from the chair, stretched, and went over to stand beside her at the window. They both stared out at the parking lot. They didn't say anything. But they seemed to feel each other's insides now, as though the worry had made them transparent in a perfectly natural way.

The door opened and Dr. Francis came in. He was wearing a different suit and tie this time. His gray hair was combed along the sides of his head, and he looked as if he had just shaved. He went straight to the bed and examined the boy. "He ought to have come around by now. There's just no good reason for this," he said. "But I can tell you we're all convinced he's out of any danger. We'll just feel better when he wakes up. There's no reason, absolutely none, why he shouldn't come around. Very soon. Oh, he'll have himself a dilly of a headache when he does, you can count on that. But all of his signs are fine. They're as normal as can be."

"It is a coma, then?" Ann said.

The doctor rubbed his smooth cheek. "We'll call it that for the time being, until he wakes up. But you must be worn out. This is hard. I know this is hard. Feel free to go out for a bite," he said. "It would do you good. I'll put a nurse in here while you're gone if you'll feel better about going. Go and have yourselves something to eat."

"I couldn't eat anything," Ann said.

"Do what you need to do, of course," the doctor said. "Anyway, I wanted to tell you that all the signs are good, the tests are negative, nothing showed up at all, and just as soon as he wakes up he'll be over the hill."

"Thank you, doctor," Howard said. He shook hands with the doctor again. The doctor patted Howard's shoulder and went out.

"I suppose one of us should go home and check on things," Howard said. "Slug needs to be fed, for one thing."

"Call one of the neighbors," Ann said. "Call the Morgans. Anyone will feed a dog if you ask them to."

"All right," Howard said. After a while, he said, "Honey, why don't *you* do it? Why don't you go home and check on things, and then come back? It'll do you good. I'll be right here with him. Seriously," he said. "We need to keep up our strength on this. We'll want to be here for a while even after he wakes up."

"Why don't *you* go?" she said. "Feed Slug. Feed yourself."

"I already went," he said. "I was gone for exactly an hour and fifteen minutes. You go home for an hour and freshen up. Then come back."

She tried to think about it, but she was too tired. She closed her eyes and tried to think about it again. After a time, she said, "Maybe I *will* go home for a few minutes. Maybe if I'm not just sitting right here watching him every second, he'll wake up and be all right. You know? Maybe he'll wake up if I'm not here. I'll go home and take a bath and put on clean clothes. I'll feed Slug. Then I'll come back."

"I'll be right here," he said. "You go on home, honey. I'll keep an eye on things here." His eyes were bloodshot and small, as if he'd been drinking for a long time. His clothes were rumpled. His beard had come out again. She touched his face, and then she took her hand back. She understood he wanted to be by himself for a while, not have to talk or share his worry for a time. She picked her purse up from the nightstand, and he helped her into her coat.

"I won't be gone long," she said.

"Just sit and rest for a little while when you get home," he said. "Eat something. Take a bath. After you get out of the bath, just sit for a while and rest. It'll do you a world of good, you'll see. Then come back," he said. "Let's try not to worry. You heard what Dr. Francis said."

She stood in her coat for a minute trying to recall the doctor's exact words, looking for any nuances, any hint of something behind his words other than what he had said. She tried to remember if his expression had changed any when he bent over to examine the child. She remembered the way his features had composed themselves as he rolled back the child's eyelids and then listened to his breathing.

She went to the door, where she turned and looked back. She looked at the child, and then she looked at the father. Howard nodded. She stepped out of the room and pulled the door closed behind her.

She went past the nurses' station and down to the end of the corridor, looking for the elevator. At the end of the corridor, she turned to her right and entered a little waiting room where a Negro family sat in wicker chairs. There was a middle-aged man in a khaki shirt and pants, a baseball cap pushed back on his head. A large woman wearing a housedress and slippers was slumped in one of the chairs. A teenaged girl in jeans, hair done in dozens of little braids, lay stretched out in one of the chairs smoking a cigarette, her legs crossed at the ankles. The family swung their eyes to Ann as she entered the room. The little table was littered with hamburger wrappers and Styrofoam cups.

"Franklin," the large woman said as she roused herself. "Is it about Franklin?" Her eyes widened. "Tell me now, lady," the woman said. "Is it about Franklin?" She was trying to rise from her chair, but the man had closed his hand over her arm.

"Here, here," he said. "Evelyn."

"I'm sorry," Ann said. "I'm looking for the elevator. My son is in the hospital, and now I can't find the elevator."

"Elevator is down that way, turn left," the man said as he aimed a finger.

The girl drew on her cigarette and stared at Ann. Her eyes were narrowed to slits, and her broad lips parted slowly as she let the smoke escape. The Negro woman let her head fall on her shoulder and looked away from Ann, no longer interested.

"My son was hit by a car," Ann said to the man. She seemed to need to explain herself. "He has a concussion and a little skull fracture, but he's going to be all right. He's in shock now, but it might be some kind of coma, too. That's what really worries us, the coma part. I'm going out for a little while, but my husband is with him. Maybe he'll wake up while I'm gone."

"That's too bad," the man said and shifted in the chair. He shook his head. He looked down at the table, and then he looked back at Ann. She was still standing there. He said, "Our Franklin, he's on the operating table. Somebody cut him. Tried to kill him. There was a fight where he was at. At this party. They say he was just standing and watching. Not bothering nobody. But that don't mean nothing these days. Now he's on the operating table. We're just hoping and praying, that's all we can do now." He gazed at her steadily.

Ann looked at the girl again, who was still watching her, and at the older woman, who kept her head down, but whose eyes were now closed. Ann saw the lips moving silently, making words. She had an urge to ask what those words were. She wanted to talk more with these people who were in the same kind of waiting she was in. She was afraid, and they were afraid. They had that in common. She would have liked to have said something else about the accident, told them more about Scotty, that it had happened on the day of his birthday, Monday, and that he was still unconscious. Yet she didn't know how to begin. She stood looking at them without saying anything more.

She went down the corridor the man had indicated and found the elevator. She waited a minute in front of the closed doors, still wondering if she was doing the right thing. Then she put out her finger and touched the button.

She pulled into the driveway and cut the engine. She closed her eyes and leaned her head against the wheel for a minute. She listened to the ticking sounds the engine made as it began to cool. Then she got out of the car. She could hear the dog barking inside the house. She went to the front door, which was unlocked. She went inside and turned on lights and put on a kettle of water for tea. She opened some dogfood and fed Slug on the back porch. The dog ate in hungry little smacks. It kept running into the kitchen to see that she was going to stay. As she sat down on the sofa with her tea, the telephone rang.

"Yes!" she said as she answered. "Hello!"

"Mrs. Weiss," a man's voice said. It was five o'clock in the morning, and she thought she could hear machinery or equipment of some kind in the background.

"Yes, yes! What is it?" she said. "This is Mrs. Weiss. This is she. What is it, please?" She listened to whatever it was in the background. "Is it Scotty, for Christ's sake?"

"Scotty," the man's voice said. "It's about Scotty, yes. It has to do with Scotty, that problem. Have you forgotten about Scotty?" the man said. Then he hung up.

She dialed the hospital's number and asked for the third floor. She demanded information about her son from the nurse who answered the telephone. Then she asked to speak to her husband. It was, she said, an emergency.

She waited, turning the telephone cord in her fingers. She closed her eyes and felt sick at her stomach. She would have to make herself eat. Slug came in from the back porch and lay down near her feet. He wagged his tail. She pulled at his ear while he licked her fingers. Howard was on the line.

"Somebody just called here," she said. She twisted the telephone cord. "He said it was about Scotty," she cried.

"Scotty's fine," Howard told her. "I mean, he's still sleeping. There's been no change. The nurse has been in twice since you've been gone. A nurse or else a doctor. He's all right."

"This man called. He said it was about Scotty," she told him.

"Honey, you rest for a little while, you need the rest. It must be that same caller I had. Just forget it. Come back down here after you've rested. Then we'll have breakfast or something."

"Breakfast," she said. "I don't want any breakfast."

"You know what I mean," he said. "Juice, something. I don't know. I don't know anything, Ann. Jesus, I'm not hungry, either. Ann, it's hard to talk now. I'm standing here at the desk. Dr. Francis is coming again at eight o'clock this morning. He's going to have something to tell us then, something more definite. That's what one of the nurses said. She didn't know any more than that. Ann? Honey, maybe we'll know something more then. At eight o'clock. Come back here before eight. Meanwhile, I'm right here and Scotty's all right. He's still the same," he added.

"I was drinking a cup of tea," she said, "when the telephone rang. They said it was about Scotty. There was a noise in the background. Was there a noise in the background on that call you had, Howard?"

"I don't remember," he said. "Maybe the driver of the car, maybe he's a psychopath and found out about Scotty somehow. But I'm here with him. Just rest like you were going to do. Take a bath and come back by seven or so, and we'll talk to the doctor together when he gets here. It's going to be all right, honey. I'm here, and there are doctors and nurses around. They say his condition is stable."

"I'm scared to death," she said.

She ran water, undressed, and got into the tub. She washed and dried quickly, not taking the time to wash her hair. She put on clean underwear, wool slacks, and a sweater. She went into the living room, where the dog looked up at her and let its tail thump once against the floor. It was just starting to get light outside when she went out to the car.

She drove into the parking lot of the hospital and found a space close to the front door. She felt she was in some obscure way responsible for what had happened to the child. She let her thoughts move to the Negro family. She remembered the name Franklin and the table that was covered with hamburger papers, and the teenaged girl staring at her as she drew on her cigarette. "Don't have children," she told the girl's image as she entered the front door of the hospital. "For God's sake, don't."

She took the elevator up to the third floor with two nurses who were just going on duty. It was Wednesday morning, a few minutes before seven. There was a page for a Dr. Madison as the elevator doors slid open on the third floor. She got off behind the nurses, who turned in the other direction and continued the conversation she had interrupted when she'd gotten into the elevator. She walked down the corridor to the little alcove where the Negro family had been waiting. They were gone now, but the chairs were scattered in such a way that it looked as if people had just jumped up from them the minute before. The tabletop was cluttered with the same cups and papers, the ashtray was filled with cigarette butts.

She stopped at the nurses' station. A nurse was standing behind the counter, brushing her hair and yawning.

"There was a Negro boy in surgery last night," Ann said. "Franklin was his name. His family was in the waiting room. I'd like to inquire about his condition."

A nurse who was sitting at a desk behind the counter looked up from a chart in front of her. The telephone buzzed and she picked up the receiver, but she kept her eyes on Ann.

"He passed away," said the nurse at the counter. The nurse held the hairbrush and kept looking at her. "Are you a friend of the family or what?"

"I met the family last night," Ann said. "My own son is in the hospital. I guess he's in shock. We don't know for sure what's wrong. I just wondered about Franklin, that's all. Thank you." She moved down the corridor. Elevator doors the same color as the walls slid open and a gaunt, bald man in white pants and white canvas shoes pulled a heavy cart off the elevator. She hadn't noticed these doors last night. The man wheeled the cart out into the corridor and stopped in front of the room nearest the elevator and consulted a clipboard. Then he reached down and slid a tray out of the cart. He rapped lightly on the door and entered the room. She could smell the unpleasant odors of warm food as she passed the cart. She hurried on without looking at any of the nurses and pushed open the door to the child's room.

Howard was standing at the window with his hands behind his back. He turned around as she came in.

"How is he?" she said. She went over to the bed. She dropped her purse on the floor beside the nightstand. It seemed to her she had been gone a long time. She touched the child's face. "Howard?"

"Dr. Francis was here a little while ago," Howard said. She looked at him closely and thought his shoulders were bunched a little.

"I thought he wasn't coming until eight o'clock this morning," she said quickly.

"There was another doctor with him. A neurologist."

"A neurologist," she said.

Howard nodded. His shoulders were bunching, she could see that. "What'd they say, Howard? For Christ's sake, what'd they say? What is it?"

"They said they're going to take him down and run more tests on him, Ann. They think they're going to operate, honey. Honey, they *are* going to operate. They can't figure out why he won't wake up. It's more than just shock or concussion, they know that much now. It's in his skull, the fracture, it has something, something to do with that, they think. So they're going to operate. I tried to call you, but I guess you'd already left the house."

"Oh, God," she said. "Oh, please, Howard, please," she said, taking his arms.

"Look!" Howard said. "Scotty! Look, Ann!" He turned her toward the bed.

The boy had opened his eyes, then closed them. He opened them again now. The eyes stared straight ahead for a minute, then moved slowly in his head until they rested on Howard and Ann, then traveled away again.

"Scotty," his mother said, moving to the bed.

"Hey, Scott," his father said. "Hey, son."

They leaned over the bed. Howard took the child's hand in his hands and began to pat and squeeze the hand. Ann bent over the boy and kissed his forehead again and again. She put her hands on either side of his face. "Scotty, honey, it's Mommy and Daddy," she said. "Scotty?"

The boy looked at them, but without any sign of recognition. Then his mouth opened, his eyes scrunched closed, and he howled until he had no more air in his lungs. His face seemed to relax and soften then. His lips parted as his last breath was puffed through his throat and exhaled gently through the clenched teeth.

The doctors called it a hidden occlusion and said it was a one-in-a-million circumstance. Maybe if it could have been detected somehow and surgery undertaken immediately, they could have saved him. But more than likely not. In any case, what would they have been looking for? Nothing had shown up in the tests or in the X-rays.

Dr. Francis was shaken. "I can't tell you how badly I feel. I'm so very sorry, I can't tell you," he said as he led them into the doctors' lounge. There was a doctor sitting in a chair with his legs hooked over the back of another chair, watching an early-morning TV show. He was wearing a green delivery-room outfit, loose green pants and green blouse, and a green cap that covered his hair. He looked at Howard and Ann and then looked at Dr. Francis. He got to his feet and turned off the set and went out of the room. Dr. Francis guided Ann to the sofa, sat down beside her, and began to talk in a low, consoling voice. At one point, he leaned over and embraced her. She could feel his chest rising and falling evenly against her shoulder. She kept her eyes open and let him hold her. Howard went into the bathroom, but he left the door open. After a violent fit of weeping, he ran water and washed his face. Then he came out and sat down at the little table that held a telephone. He looked at the telephone as though deciding what to do first. He made some calls. After a time, Dr. Francis used the telephone.

"Is there anything else I can do for the moment?" he asked them.

Howard shook his head. Ann stared at Dr. Francis as if unable to comprehend his words.

The doctor walked them to the hospital's front door. People were entering and leaving the hospital. It was eleven o'clock in the morning. Ann was aware of how slowly, almost reluctantly, she moved her feet. It seemed to her that Dr. Francis was making them leave when she felt they should stay, when it would be more the right thing to do to stay. She gazed out into the parking lot and then turned around and looked back at the front of the hospital. She began shaking her head. "No, no," she said. "I can't leave him here, no." She heard herself say that and thought how unfair it was that the only words that came out were the sort of words used on TV shows where people were stunned by violent or sudden deaths. She wanted her words to be her own. "No," she said, and for some reason the memory of the Negro woman's head lolling on the woman's shoulder came to her. "No," she said again.

"I'll be talking to you later in the day," the doctor was saying to Howard. "There are still some things that have to be done, things that have to be cleared up to our satisfaction. Some things that need explaining."

"An autopsy," Howard said.

Dr. Francis nodded.

"I understand," Howard said. Then he said, "Oh, Jesus. No, I don't understand, doctor. I can't, I can't. I just can't."

Dr. Francis put his arm around Howard's shoulders. "I'm sorry. God, how I'm sorry." He let go of Howard's shoulders and held out his hand. Howard looked at the hand, and then he took it. Dr. Francis put his arms around Ann once more. He seemed full of some goodness she didn't understand. She let her head rest on his shoulder, but her eyes stayed open. She kept looking at the hospital. As they drove out of the parking lot, she looked back at the hospital.

At home, she sat on the sofa with her hands in her coat pockets. Howard closed the door to the child's room. He got the coffee-maker going and then he found an empty box. He had thought to pick up some of the child's things that were scattered around the living room. But instead he sat down beside her on the sofa, pushed the box to one side, and leaned forward, arms between his knees. He began to weep. She pulled his head over into her lap and patted his shoulder. "He's gone," she said. She kept patting his shoulder. Over his sobs, she could hear the coffee-maker hissing in the kitchen. "There, there," she said tenderly. "Howard, he's gone. He's gone and now we'll have to get used to that. To being alone."

In a little while, Howard got up and began moving aimlessly around the room with the box, not putting anything into it, but collecting some things together on the floor at one end of the sofa. She continued to sit with her hands in her coat pockets. Howard put the box down and brought coffee into the living room. Later, Ann made calls to relatives. After each call had been placed and the party had answered, Ann would blurt out a few words and cry for a minute. Then she would quietly explain, in a measured voice, what had happened and tell them about arrangements. Howard took the box out to the garage, where he saw the child's bicycle. He dropped the box and sat down on the pavement beside the bicycle. He took hold of the bicycle awkwardly so that it leaned against his chest. He held it, the rubber pedal sticking into his chest. He gave the wheel a turn.

Ann hung up the telephone after talking to her sister. She was looking up another number when the telephone rang. She picked it up on the first ring.

"Hello," she said, and she heard something in the background, a humming noise. "Hello!" she said. "For God's sake," she said. "Who is this? What is it you want?"

"Your Scotty, I got him ready for you," the man's voice said. "Did you forget him?"

"You evil bastard!" she shouted into the receiver. "How can you do this, you evil son of a bitch?"

"Scotty," the man said. "Have you forgotten about Scotty?" Then the man hung up on her.

Howard heard the shouting and came in to find her with her head on her arms over the table, weeping. He picked up the receiver and listened to the dial tone.

Much later, just before midnight, after they had dealt with many things, the telephone rang again.

"You answer it," she said. "Howard, it's him, I know." They were sitting at the kitchen table with coffee in front of them. Howard had a small glass of whiskey beside his cup. He answered on the third ring.

"Hello," he said. "Who is this? Hello! Hello!" The line went dead. "He hung up," Howard said. "Whoever it was."

"It was him," she said. "That bastard. I'd like to kill him," she said. "I'd like to shoot him and watch him kick," she said.

"Ann, my God," he said.

"Could you hear anything?" she said. "In the background? A noise, machinery, something humming?"

"Nothing, really. Nothing like that," he said. "There wasn't much time. I think there was some radio music. Yes, there was a radio going, that's all I could tell. I don't know what in God's name is going on," he said.

She shook her head. "If I could, could get my hands on him." It came to her then. She knew who it was. Scotty, the cake, the telephone number. She pushed the chair away from the table and got up. "Drive me down to the shopping center," she said. "Howard."

"What are you saying?"

"The shopping center. I know who it is who's calling. I know who it is. It's the baker, the son-of-a-bitching baker, Howard. I had him bake a cake for Scotty's birthday. That's who's calling. That's who has the number and keeps calling us. To harass us about that cake. The baker, that bastard."

They drove down to the shopping center. The sky was clear and stars were out. It was cold, and they ran the heater in the car. They parked in front of the bakery. All of the shops and stores were closed, but there were cars at the far end of the lot in front of the movie theater. The bakery windows were dark, but when they looked through the glass they could see a light in the back room and, now and then, a big man in an apron moving in and out of the white, even light. Through the glass, she could see the display cases and some little tables with chairs. She tried the door. She rapped on the glass. But if the baker heard them, he gave no sign. He didn't look in their direction.

They drove around behind the bakery and parked. They got out of the car. There was a lighted window too high up for them to see inside. A sign near the back door said THE PANTRY BAKERY, SPECIAL ORDERS. She could hear faintly a radio playing inside and something creak—an oven door as it was pulled down? She knocked on the door and waited. Then she knocked again, louder. The radio was turned down and there was a scraping sound now, the distinct sound of something, a drawer, being pulled open and then closed.

Someone unlocked the door and opened it. The baker stood in the light and peered out at them. "I'm closed for business," he said. "What do you want at this hour? It's midnight. Are you drunk or something?"

She stepped into the light that fell through the open door. He blinked his heavy eyelids as he recognized her. "It's you," he said.

"It's me," she said. "Scotty's mother. This is Scotty's father. We'd like to come in."

The baker said, "I'm busy now. I have work to do."

She had stepped inside the doorway anyway. Howard came in behind her. The baker moved back. "It smells like a bakery in here. Doesn't it smell like a bakery in here, Howard?"

"What do you want?" the baker said. "Maybe you want your cake? That's it, you decided you want your cake. You ordered a cake, didn't you?"

"You're pretty smart for a baker," she said. "Howard, this is the man who's been calling us." She clenched her fists. She stared at him fiercely. There was a deep burning inside her, an anger that made her feel larger than herself, larger than either of these men.

"Just a minute here," the baker said. "You want to pick up your three-day-old cake? That it? I don't want to argue with you, lady. There it sits over there, getting stale. I'll give it to you for half of what I quoted you. No. You want it? You can have it. It's no good to me, no good to anyone now. It cost me time and money to make that cake. If you want it, okay, if you don't, that's okay, too. I have to get back to work." He looked at them and rolled his tongue behind his teeth.

"More cakes," she said. She knew she was in control of it, of what was increasing in her. She was calm.

"Lady, I work sixteen hours a day in this place to earn a living," the baker said. He wiped his hands on his apron. "I work night and day in here, trying to make ends meet." A look crossed Ann's face that made the baker move back and say, "No trouble, now." He reached to the counter and picked up a rolling pin with his right hand and began to tap it against the palm of his other hand. "You want the cake or not? I have to get back to work. Bakers work at night," he said again. His eyes were small, mean-looking, she thought, nearly lost in the bristly flesh around his cheeks. His neck was thick with fat.

"I know bakers work at night," Ann said. "They make phone calls at night, too. You bastard," she said.

The baker continued to tap the rolling pin against his hand. He glanced at Howard. "Careful, careful," he said to Howard.

"My son's dead," she said with a cold, even finality. "He was hit by a car Monday morning. We've been waiting with him until he died. But, of course, you couldn't be expected to know that, could you? Bakers can't know everything—can they, Mr. Baker? But he's dead. He's dead, you bastard!" Just as suddenly as it had welled in her, the anger dwindled, gave way to something else, a dizzy feeling of nausea. She leaned against the wooden table that was sprinkled with flour, put her hands over her face, and began to cry, her shoulders rocking back and forth. "It isn't fair," she said. "It isn't, isn't fair."

Howard put his hand at the small of her back and looked at the baker. "Shame on you," Howard said to him. "Shame."

The baker put the rolling pin back on the counter. He undid his apron and threw it on the counter. He looked at them, and then he shook his head slowly. He pulled a chair out from under the card table that held papers and receipts, an adding machine, and a telephone directory. "Please sit down," he said. "Let me get you a chair," he said to Howard. "Sit down now, please." The baker went into the front of the shop and returned with two little wrought-iron chairs. "Please sit down, you people."

Ann wiped her eyes and looked at the baker. "I wanted to kill you," she said. "I wanted you dead."

The baker had cleared a space for them at the table. He shoved the adding machine to one side, along with the stacks of notepaper and receipts. He pushed the telephone directory onto the floor, where it landed with a thud. Howard and Ann sat down and pulled their chairs up to the table. The baker sat down, too.

"Let me say how sorry I am," the baker said, putting his elbows on the table. "God alone knows how sorry. Listen to me. I'm just a baker. I don't claim to be anything else. Maybe once, maybe years ago, I was a different kind of human being. I've forgotten, I don't know for sure. But I'm not any longer, if I ever was. Now I'm just a baker. That don't excuse my doing what I did, I know. But I'm deeply sorry. I'm sorry for your son, and sorry for my part in this," the baker said. He spread his hands out on the table and turned them over to reveal his palms. "I don't have any children myself, so I can only imagine what you must be feeling. All I can say to you now is that I'm sorry. Forgive me, if you can," the baker said. "I'm not an evil man, I don't think. Not evil, like you said on the phone. You got to understand what it comes down to is I don't know how to act anymore, it would seem. Please," the man said, "let me ask you if you can find it in your hearts to forgive me?"

It was warm inside the bakery. Howard stood up from the table and took off his coat. He helped Ann from her coat. The baker looked at them for a minute and then nodded and got up from the table. He went to the oven and turned off some switches. He found cups and poured coffee from an electric coffee-maker. He put a carton of cream on the table, and a bowl of sugar.

"You probably need to eat something," the baker said. "I hope you'll eat some of my hot rolls. You have to eat and keep going. Eating is a small, good thing in a time like this," he said.

He served them warm cinnamon rolls just out of the oven, the icing still runny. He put butter on the table and knives to spread the butter. Then the baker sat down at the table with them. He waited. He waited until they each took a roll from the platter and began to eat. "It's good to eat something," he said, watching them. "There's more. Eat up. Eat all you want. There's all the rolls in the world in here."

They ate rolls and drank coffee. Ann was suddenly hungry, and the rolls were warm and sweet. She ate three of them, which pleased the baker. Then he began to talk. They listened carefully. Although they were tired and in anguish, they listened to what the baker had to say. They nodded when the baker began to speak of loneliness, and of the sense of doubt and limitation that had come to him in his middle years. He told them what it was like to be childless all these years. To repeat the days with the ovens endlessly full and endlessly empty. The party food, the celebrations he'd worked over. Icing knuckle-deep. The tiny wedding couples stuck into cakes. Hundreds of them, no, thousands by now. Birthdays. Just imagine all those candles burning. He had a necessary trade. He was a baker. He was glad he wasn't a florist. It was better to be feeding people. This was a better smell anytime than flowers.

"Smell this," the baker said, breaking open a dark loaf. "It's a heavy bread, but rich." They smelled it, then he had them taste it. It had the taste of molasses and coarse grains. They listened to him. They ate what they could. They swallowed the dark bread. It was like daylight under the fluorescent trays of light. They talked on into the early morning, the high, pale cast of light in the windows, and they did not think of leaving.

1983

Cathedral

This blind man, an old friend of my wife's, he was on his way to spend the night. His wife had died. So he was visiting the dead wife's relatives in Connecticut. He called my wife from his in-laws'. Arrangements were made. He would come by train, a five-hour trip, and my wife would meet him at the station. She hadn't seen him since she worked for him one summer in Seattle ten years ago. But she and the blind man had kept in touch. They made tapes and mailed them back and forth. I wasn't enthusiastic about his visit. He was no one I knew. And his being blind bothered me. My idea of blindness came from the movies. In the movies, the blind moved slowly and never laughed. Sometimes they were led by seeing-eye dogs. A blind man in my house was not something I looked forward to.

That summer in Seattle she had needed a job. She didn't have any money. The man she was going to marry at the end of the summer was in officers' training school. He didn't have any money, either. But she was in love with the guy, and he was in love with her, etc. She'd seen something in the paper: HELP WANTED—*Reading to Blind Man,* and a telephone number. She phoned and went over, was hired on the spot. She'd worked with this blind man all summer. She read stuff to him, case studies, reports, that sort of thing. She helped him organize his little office in the county social-service department. They'd become good friends, my wife and the blind man. How do I know these things? She told me. And she told me something else. On her last day in the office, the blind man asked if he could touch her face. She agreed to this. She told me he touched his fingers to every part of her face, her nose—even her neck! She never forgot it. She even tried to write a poem about it. She was always trying to write a poem. She wrote a poem or two every year, usually after something really important had happened to her.

When we first started going out together, she showed me the poem. In the poem, she recalled his fingers and the way they had moved around over her face. In the poem, she talked about what she had felt at the time, about what went through her mind when the blind man touched her nose and lips. I can remember I didn't think much of the poem. Of course, I didn't tell her that. Maybe I just don't understand poetry. I admit it's not the first thing I reach for when I pick up something to read.

Anyway, this man who'd first enjoyed her favors, the officer-to-be, he'd been her childhood sweetheart. So okay. I'm saying that at the end of the summer she let the blind man run his hands over her face, said goodbye to him, married her childhood etc., who was now a commissioned officer, and she moved away from Seattle. But they'd kept in touch, she and the blind man. She made the first contact after a year or so. She called him up one night from an Air Force base in Alabama. She wanted to talk. They talked. He asked her to send him a tape and tell him about her life.

She did this. She sent the tape. On the tape, she told the blind man about her husband and about their life together in the military. She told the blind man she loved her husband but she didn't like it where they lived and she didn't like it that he was a part of the military-industrial thing. She told the blind man she'd written a poem and he was in it. She told him that she was writing a poem about what it was like to be an Air Force officer's wife. The poem wasn't finished yet. She was still writing it. The blind man made a tape. He sent her the tape. She made a tape. This went on for years. My wife's officer was posted to one base and then another. She sent tapes from Moody AFB, McGuire, McConnell, and finally Travis, near Sacramento, where one night she got to feeling lonely and cut off from people she kept losing in that moving-around life. She got to feeling she couldn't go it another step. She went in and swallowed all the pills and capsules in the medicine chest and washed them down with a bottle of gin. Then she got into a hot bath and passed out.

But instead of dying, she got sick. She threw up. Her officer—why should he have a name? he was the childhood sweetheart, and what more does he want?—came home from somewhere, found her, and called the ambulance. In time, she put it all on a tape and sent the tape to the blind man. Over the years, she put all kinds of stuff on tapes and sent the tapes off lickety-split. Next to writing a poem every year, I think it was her chief means of recreation. On one tape, she told the blind man she'd decided to live away from her officer for a time. On another tape, she told him about her divorce. She and I began going out, and of course she told her blind man about it. She told him everything, or so it seemed to me. Once she asked me if I'd like to hear the latest tape from the blind man. This was a year ago. I was on the tape, she said. So I said okay, I'd listen to it. I got us drinks and we settled down in the living room. We made ready to listen. First she inserted the tape into the player and adjusted a couple of dials. Then she pushed a lever. The tape squeaked and someone began to talk in this loud voice. She lowered the volume. After a few minutes of harmless chitchat, I heard my own name in the mouth of this stranger, this blind man I didn't even know! And then this: "From all you've said about him, I can only conclude—" But we were interrupted, a knock at the door, something, and we didn't ever get back to the tape. Maybe it was just as well. I'd heard all I wanted to.

Now this same blind man was coming to sleep in my house.

"Maybe I could take him bowling," I said to my wife. She was at the draining board doing scalloped potatoes. She put down the knife she was using and turned around.

"If you love me," she said, "you can do this for me. If you don't love me, okay. But if you had a friend, any friend, and the friend came to visit, I'd make him feel comfortable." She wiped her hands with the dish towel.

"I don't have any blind friends," I said.

"You don't have *any* friends," she said. "Period. Besides," she said, "goddamn it, his wife's just died! Don't you understand that? The man's lost his wife!"

I didn't answer. She'd told me a little about the blind man's wife. Her name was Beulah. Beulah! That's a name for a colored woman.

"Was his wife a Negro?" I asked.

"Are you crazy?" my wife said. "Have you just flipped or something?" She picked up a potato. I saw it hit the floor, then roll under the stove. "What's wrong with you?" she said. "Are you drunk?"

"I'm just asking," I said.

Right then my wife filled me in with more detail than I cared to know. I made a drink and sat at the kitchen table to listen. Pieces of the story began to fall into place.

Beulah had gone to work for the blind man the summer after my wife had stopped working for him. Pretty soon Beulah and the blind man had themselves a church wedding. It was a little wedding—who'd want to go to such a wedding in the first place?—just the two of them, plus the minister and the minister's wife. But it was a church wedding just the same. It was what Beulah had wanted, he'd said. But even then Beulah must have been carrying the cancer in her glands. After they had been inseparable for eight years—my wife's word, *inseparable*—Beulah's health went into a rapid decline. She died in a Seattle hospital room, the blind man sitting beside the bed and holding on to her hand. They'd married, lived and worked together, slept together—had sex, sure—and then the blind man had to bury her. All this without his having ever seen what the goddamned woman looked like. It was beyond my understanding. Hearing this, I felt sorry for the blind man for a little bit. And then I found myself thinking what a pitiful life this woman must have led. Imagine a woman who could never see herself as she was seen in the eyes of her loved one. A woman who could go on day after day and never receive the smallest compliment from her beloved. A woman whose husband could never read the expression on her face, be it misery or something better. Someone who could wear makeup or not—what difference to him? She could, if she wanted, wear green eye-shadow around one eye, a straight pin in her nostril, yellow slacks and purple shoes, no matter. And then to slip off into death, the blind man's hand on her hand, his blind eyes streaming tears—I'm imagining now—her last thought maybe this: that he never even knew what she looked like, and she on an express to the grave. Robert was left with a small insurance policy and half of a twenty-peso Mexican coin. The other half of the coin went into the box with her. Pathetic.

So when the time rolled around, my wife went to the depot to pick him up. With nothing to do but wait—sure, I blamed him for that—I was having a drink and watching the TV when I heard the car pull into the drive. I got up from the sofa with my drink and went to the window to have a look.

I saw my wife laughing as she parked the car. I saw her get out of the car and shut the door. She was still wearing a smile. Just amazing. She went around to the other side of the car to where the blind man was already starting to get out. This blind man, feature this, he was wearing a full beard! A beard on a blind man! Too much, I say. The blind man reached into the back seat and dragged out a suitcase. My wife took his arm, shut the car door, and, talking all the way, moved him down the drive and then up the steps to the front porch. I turned off the TV. I finished my drink, rinsed the glass, dried my hands. Then I went to the door.

My wife said, "I want you to meet Robert. Robert, this is my husband. I've told you all about him." She was beaming. She had this blind man by his coat sleeve.

The blind man let go of his suitcase and up came his hand.

I took it. He squeezed hard, held my hand, and then he let it go.

"I feel like we've already met," he boomed.

"Likewise," I said. I didn't know what else to say. Then I said, "Welcome. I've heard a lot about you." We began to move then, a little group, from the porch into the living room, my wife guiding him by the arm. The blind man was carrying his suitcase in his other hand. My wife said things like, "To your left here, Robert. That's right. Now watch it, there's a chair. That's it. Sit down right here. This is the sofa. We just bought this sofa two weeks ago."

I started to say something about the old sofa. I'd liked that old sofa. But I didn't say anything. Then I wanted to say something else, small-talk, about the scenic ride along the Hudson. How going *to* New York, you should sit on the right-hand side of the train, and coming *from* New York, the left-hand side.

"Did you have a good train ride?" I said. "Which side of the train did you sit on, by the way?"

"What a question, which side!" my wife said. "What's it matter which side?" she said.

"I just asked," I said.

"Right side," the blind man said. "I hadn't been on a train in nearly forty years. Not since I was a kid. With my folks. That's been a long time. I'd nearly forgotten the sensation. I have winter in my beard now," he said. "So I've been told, anyway. Do I look distinguished, my dear?" the blind man said to my wife.

"You look distinguished, Robert," she said. "Robert," she said. "Robert, it's just so good to see you."

My wife finally took her eyes off the blind man and looked at me. I had the feeling she didn't like what she saw. I shrugged.

I've never met, or personally known, anyone who was blind. This blind man was late forties, a heavy-set, balding man with stooped shoulders, as if he carried a great weight there. He wore brown slacks, brown shoes, a light-brown shirt, a tie, a sports coat. Spiffy. He also had this full beard. But he didn't use a cane and he didn't wear dark glasses. I'd always thought dark glasses were a must for the blind. Fact was, I wished he had a pair. At first glance, his eyes looked like anyone else's eyes. But if you looked close, there was something different about them. Too much white in the iris, for one thing, and the pupils seemed to move around in the sockets without his knowing it or being able to stop it. Creepy. As I stared at his face, I saw the left pupil turn in toward his nose while the other made an effort to keep in one place. But it was only an effort, for that eye was on the roam without his knowing it or wanting it to be.

I said, "Let me get you a drink. What's your pleasure? We have a little of everything. It's one of our pastimes."

"Bub, I'm a Scotch man myself," he said fast enough in this big voice.

"Right," I said. Bub! "Sure you are. I knew it."

He let his fingers touch his suitcase, which was sitting alongside the sofa. He was taking his bearings. I didn't blame him for that.

"I'll move that up to your room," my wife said.

"No, that's fine," the blind man said loudly. "It can go up when I go up."

"A little water with the Scotch?" I said.

"Very little," he said.

"I knew it," I said.

He said, "Just a tad. The Irish actor, Barry Fitzgerald? I'm like that fellow. When I drink water, Fitzgerald said, I drink water. When I drink whiskey, I drink whiskey." My wife laughed. The blind man brought his hand up under his beard. He lifted his beard slowly and let it drop.

I did the drinks, three big glasses of Scotch with a splash of water in each. Then we made ourselves comfortable and talked about Robert's travels. First the long flight from the West Coast to Connecticut, we covered that. Then from Connecticut up here by train. We had another drink concerning that leg of the trip.

I remembered having read somewhere that the blind didn't smoke because, as speculation had it, they couldn't see the smoke they exhaled. I thought I knew that much and that much only about blind people. But this blind man smoked his cigarette down to the nubbin and then lit another one. This blind man filled his ashtray and my wife emptied it.

When we sat down at the table for dinner, we had another drink. My wife heaped Robert's plate with cube steak, scalloped potatoes, green beans. I buttered him up two slices of bread. I said, "Here's bread and butter for you." I swallowed some of my drink. "Now let us pray," I said, and the blind man lowered his head. My wife looked at me, her mouth agape. "Pray the phone won't ring and the food doesn't get cold," I said.

We dug in. We ate everything there was to eat on the table. We ate like there was no tomorrow. We didn't talk. We ate. We scarfed. We grazed that table. We were into serious eating. The blind man had right away located his foods, he knew just where everything was on his plate. I watched with admiration as he used his knife and fork on the meat. He'd cut two pieces of meat, fork the meat into his mouth, and then go all out for the scalloped potatoes, the beans next, and then he'd tear off a hunk of buttered bread and eat that. He'd follow this up with a big drink of milk. It didn't seem to bother him to use his fingers once in a while, either.

We finished everything, including half a strawberry pie. For a few moments, we sat as if stunned. Sweat beaded on our faces. Finally, we got up from the table and left the dirty plates. We didn't look back. We took ourselves into the living room and sank into our places again. Robert and my wife sat on the sofa. I took the big chair. We had us two or three more drinks while they talked about the major things that had come to pass for them in the past ten years. For the most part, I just listened. Now and then I joined in. I didn't want him to think I'd left the room, and I didn't want her to think I was feeling left out. They talked of things that had happened to them—to them!—these past ten years. I waited in vain to hear my name on my wife's sweet lips: "And then my dear husband came into my life"—something like that. But I heard nothing of the sort. More talk of Robert. Robert had done a little of everything, it seemed, a regular blind jack-of-all-trades. But most recently he and his wife had had an Amway distributorship, from which, I gathered, they'd earned their living, such as it was. The blind man was also a ham radio operator. He talked in his loud voice about conversations he'd had with fellow operators in Guam, in the Philippines, in Alaska, and even in Tahiti. He said he'd have a lot of friends there if he ever wanted to go visit those places. From time to time, he'd turn his blind face toward me, put his hand under his beard, ask me something. How long had I been in my present position? (Three years.) Did I like my work? (I didn't.) Was I going to stay with it? (What were the options?) Finally, when I thought he was beginning to run down, I got up and turned on the TV.

My wife looked at me with irritation. She was heading toward a boil. Then she looked at the blind man and said, "Robert, do you have a TV?"

The blind man said, "My dear, I have two TVs. I have a color set and a black-and-white thing, an old relic. It's funny, but if I turn the TV on, and I'm always turning it on, I turn on the color set. It's funny, don't you think?"

I didn't know what to say to that. I had absolutely nothing to say to that. No opinion. So I watched the news program and tried to listen to what the announcer was saying.

"This is a color TV," the blind man said. "Don't ask me how, but I can tell."

"We traded up a while ago," I said.

The blind man had another taste of his drink. He lifted his beard, sniffed it, and let it fall. He leaned forward on the sofa. He positioned his ashtray on the coffee table, then put the lighter to his cigarette. He leaned back on the sofa and crossed his legs at the ankles.

My wife covered her mouth, and then she yawned. She stretched. She said, "I think I'll go upstairs and put on my robe. I think I'll change into something else. Robert, you make yourself comfortable," she said.

"I'm comfortable," the blind man said.

"I want you to feel comfortable in this house," she said.

"I am comfortable," the blind man said.

After she'd left the room, he and I listened to the weather report and then to the sports roundup. By that time, she'd been gone so long I didn't know if she was going to come back. I thought she might have gone to bed. I wished she'd come back downstairs. I didn't want to be left alone with a blind man. I asked him if he wanted another drink, and he said sure. Then I asked if he wanted to smoke some dope with me. I said I'd just rolled a number. I hadn't, but I planned to do so in about two shakes.

"I'll try some with you," he said.

"Damn right," I said. "That's the stuff."

I got our drinks and sat down on the sofa with him. Then I rolled us two fat numbers. I lit one and passed it. I brought it to his fingers. He took it and inhaled.

"Hold it as long as you can," I said. I could tell he didn't know the first thing.

My wife came back downstairs wearing her pink robe and her pink slippers.

"What do I smell?" she said.

"We thought we'd have us some cannabis," I said.

My wife gave me a savage look. Then she looked at the blind man and said, "Robert, I didn't know you smoked."

He said, "I do now, my dear. There's a first time for everything. But I don't feel anything yet."

"This stuff is pretty mellow," I said. "This stuff is mild. It's dope you can reason with," I said. "It doesn't mess you up."

"Not much it doesn't, bub," he said, and laughed.

My wife sat on the sofa between the blind man and me. I passed her the number. She took it and toked and then passed it back to me. "Which way is this going?" she said. Then she said, "I shouldn't be smoking this. I can hardly keep my eyes open as it is. That dinner did me in. I shouldn't have eaten so much."

"It was the strawberry pie," the blind man said. "That's what did it," he said, and he laughed his big laugh. Then he shook his head.

"There's more strawberry pie," I said.

"Do you want some more, Robert?" my wife said.

"Maybe in a little while," he said.

We gave our attention to the TV. My wife yawned again. She said, "Your bed is made up when you feel like going to bed, Robert. I know you must have had a long day. When you're ready to go to bed, say so." She pulled his arm. "Robert?"

He came to and said, "I've had a real nice time. This beats tapes, doesn't it?"

I said, "Coming at you," and I put the number between his fingers. He inhaled, held the smoke, and then let it go. It was like he'd been doing it since he was nine years old.

"Thanks, bub," he said. "But I think this is all for me. I think I'm beginning to feel it," he said. He held the burning roach out for my wife.

"Same here," she said. "Ditto. Me, too." She took the roach and passed it to me. "I may just sit here for a while between you two guys with my eyes closed. But don't let me bother you, okay? Either one of you. If it bothers you, say so. Otherwise, I may just sit here with my eyes closed until you're ready to go to bed," she said. "Your bed's made up, Robert, when you're ready. It's right next to our room at the top of the stairs. We'll show you up when you're ready. You wake me up now, you guys, if I fall asleep." She said that and then she closed her eyes and went to sleep.

The news program ended. I got up and changed the channel. I sat back down on the sofa. I wished my wife hadn't pooped out. Her head lay across the back of the sofa, her mouth open. She'd turned so that her robe had slipped away from her legs, exposing a juicy thigh. I reached to draw her robe back over her, and it was then that I glanced at the blind man. What the hell! I flipped the robe open again.

"You say when you want some strawberry pie," I said.

"I will," he said.

I said, "Are you tired? Do you want me to take you up to your bed? Are you ready to hit the hay?"

"Not yet," he said. "No, I'll stay up with you, bub. If that's all right. I'll stay up until you're ready to turn in. We haven't had a chance to talk. Know what I mean? I feel like me and her monopolized the evening." He lifted his beard and he let it fall. He picked up his cigarettes and his lighter.

"That's all right," I said. Then I said, "I'm glad for the company."

And I guess I was. Every night I smoked dope and stayed up as long as I could before I fell asleep. My wife and I hardly ever went to bed at the same time. When I did go to sleep, I had these dreams. Sometimes I'd wake up from one of them, my heart going crazy.

Something about the church and the Middle Ages was on the TV. Not your run-of-the-mill TV fare. I wanted to watch something else. I turned to the other channels. But there was nothing on them, either. So I turned back to the first channel and apologized.

"Bub, it's all right," the blind man said. "It's fine with me. Whatever you want to watch is okay. I'm always learning something. Learning never ends. It won't hurt me to learn something tonight. I got ears," he said.

We didn't say anything for a time. He was leaning forward with his head turned at me, his right ear aimed in the direction of the set. Very disconcerting. Now and then his eyelids drooped and then they snapped open again. Now and then he put his fingers into his beard and tugged, like he was thinking about something he was hearing on the television.

On the screen, a group of men wearing cowls was being set upon and tormented by men dressed in skeleton costumes and men dressed as devils. The men dressed as devils wore devil masks, horns, and long tails. This pageant was part of a procession. The Englishman who was narrating the thing said it took place in Spain once a year. I tried to explain to the blind man what was happening.

"Skeletons," he said. "I know about skeletons," he said, and he nodded.

The TV showed this one cathedral. Then there was a long, slow look at another one. Finally, the picture switched to the famous one in Paris, with its flying buttresses and its spires reaching up to the clouds. The camera pulled away to show the whole of the cathedral rising above the skyline.

There were times when the Englishman who was telling the thing would shut up, would simply let the camera move around over the cathedrals. Or else the camera would tour the countryside, men in fields walking behind oxen. I waited as long as I could. Then I felt I had to say something. I said, "They're showing the outside of this cathedral now. Gargoyles. Little statues carved to look like monsters. Now I guess they're in Italy. Yeah, they're in Italy. There's paintings on the walls of this one church."

"Are those fresco paintings, bub?" he asked, and he sipped from his drink.

I reached for my glass. But it was empty. I tried to remember what I could remember. "You're asking me are those frescoes?" I said. "That's a good question. I don't know."

The camera moved to a cathedral outside Lisbon. The differences in the Portuguese cathedral compared with the French and Italian were not that great. But they were there. Mostly the interior stuff. Then something occurred to me, and I said, "Something has occurred to me. Do you have any idea what a cathedral is? What they look like, that is? Do you follow me? If somebody says cathedral to you, do you have any notion what they're talking about? Do you know the difference between that and a Baptist church, say?"

He let the smoke dribble from his mouth. "I know they took hundreds of workers fifty or a hundred years to build," he said. "I just heard the man say that, of course. I know generations of the same families worked on a cathedral. I heard him say that, too. The men who began their life's work on them, they never lived to see the completion of their work. In that wise, bub, they're no different from the rest of us, right?" He laughed. Then his eyelids drooped again. His head nodded. He seemed to be snoozing. Maybe he was imagining himself in Portugal. The TV was showing another cathedral now. This one was in Germany. The Englishman's voice droned on. "Cathedrals," the blind man said. He sat up and rolled his head back and forth. "If you want the truth, bub, that's about all I know. What I just said. What I heard him say. But maybe you could describe one to me? I wish you'd do it. I'd like that. If you want to know, I really don't have a good idea."

I stared hard at the shot of the cathedral on the TV. How could I even begin to describe it? But say my life depended on it. Say my life was being threatened by an insane guy who said I had to do it or else.

I stared some more at the cathedral before the picture flipped off into the countryside. There was no use. I turned to the blind man and said, "To begin with, they're very tall." I was looking around the room for clues. "They reach way up. Up and up. Toward the sky. They're so big, some of them, they have to have these supports. To help hold them up, so to speak. These supports are called buttresses. They remind me of viaducts, for some reason. But maybe you don't know viaducts, either? Sometimes the cathedrals have devils and such carved into the front. Sometimes lords and ladies. Don't ask me why this is," I said.

He was nodding. The whole upper part of his body seemed to be moving back and forth.

"I'm not doing so good, am I?" I said.

He stopped nodding and leaned forward on the edge of the sofa. As he listened to me, he was running his fingers through his beard. I wasn't getting through to him, I could see that. But he waited for me to go on just the same. He nodded, like he was trying to encourage me. I tried to think what else to say. "They're really big," I said. "They're massive. They're built of stone. Marble, too, sometimes. In those olden days, when they built cathedrals, men wanted to be close to God. In those olden days, God was an important part of everyone's life. You could tell from their cathedral-building. I'm sorry," I said, "but it looks like that's the best I can do for you. I'm just no good at it."

"That's all right, bub," the blind man said. "Hey, listen. I hope you don't mind my asking you. Can I ask you something? Let me ask you a simple question, yes or no. I'm just curious and there's no offense. You're my host. But let me ask if you are in any way religious? You don't mind my asking?"

I shook my head. He couldn't see that, though. A wink is the same as a nod to a blind man. "I guess I don't believe in it. In anything. Sometimes it's hard. You know what I'm saying?"

"Sure, I do," he said.

"Right," I said.

The Englishman was still holding forth. My wife sighed in her sleep. She drew a long breath and went on with her sleeping.

"You'll have to forgive me," I said. "But I can't tell you what a cathedral looks like. It just isn't in me to do it. I can't do any more than I've done."

The blind man sat very still, his head down, as he listened to me.

I said, "The truth is, cathedrals don't mean anything special to me. Nothing. Cathedrals. They're something to look at on late-night TV. That's all they are."

It was then the blind man cleared his throat. He brought something up. He took a handkerchief from his back pocket. Then he said, "I get it, bub. It's okay. It happens. Don't worry about it," he said. "Hey, listen to me. Will you do me a favor? I got an idea. Why don't you find us some heavy paper? And a pen. We'll do something. We'll draw one together. Get us a pen and some heavy paper. Go on, bub, get the stuff," he said.

So I went upstairs. My legs felt like they didn't have any strength in them. They felt like they did after I'd done some running. In my wife's room, I looked around. I found some ballpoints in a little basket on her table. And then I tried to think where to look for the kind of paper he was talking about.

Downstairs, in the kitchen, I found a shopping bag with onion skins in the bottom of the bag. I emptied the bag and shook it. I brought it into the living room and sat down with it near his legs. I moved some things, smoothed the wrinkles from the bag, spread it out on the coffee table.

The blind man got down from the sofa and sat next to me on the carpet.

He ran his fingers over the paper. He went up and down the sides of the paper. The edges, even the edges. He fingered the corners.

"All right," he said. "All right, let's do her."

He found my hand, the hand with the pen. He closed his hand over my hand. "Go ahead, bub, draw," he said. "Draw. You'll see. I'll follow along with you. It'll be okay. Just begin now like I'm telling you. You'll see. Draw," the blind man said.

So I began. First I drew a box that looked like a house. It could have been the house I lived in. Then I put a roof on it. At either end of the roof, I drew spires. Crazy.

"Swell," he said. "Terrific. You're doing fine," he said, "Never thought anything like this could happen in your lifetime, did you bub? Well, it's a strange life, we all know that. Go on now. Keep it up."

I put in windows and arches. I drew flying buttresses. I hung great doors. I couldn't stop. The TV station went off the air. I put down the pen and closed and opened my fingers. The blind man felt around over the paper. He moved the tips of his fingers over the paper, all over what I had drawn, and he nodded.

"Doing fine," the blind man said.

I took up the pen again, and he found my hand. I kept at it. I'm no artist. But I kept drawing just the same.

My wife opened up her eyes and gazed at us. She sat up on the sofa, her robe hanging open. She said, "What are you doing? Tell me, I want to know."

I didn't answer her.

The blind man said, "We're drawing a cathedral. Me and him are working on it. Press hard," he said to me. "That's right. That's good," he said. "Sure. You got it, bub. I can tell. You didn't think you could. But you can, can't you? You're cooking with gas now. You know what I'm saying? We're going to really have us something here in a minute. How's the old arm?" he said. "Put some people in there now. What's a cathedral without people?"

My wife said, "What's going on? Robert, what are you doing? What's going on?"

"It's all right," he said to her. "Close your eyes now," the blind man said to me.

I did it. I closed them just like he said.

"Are they closed?" he said. "Don't fudge."

"They're closed," I said.

"Keep them that way," he said. He said, "Don't stop now. Draw."

So we kept on with it. His fingers rode my fingers as my hand went over the paper. It was like nothing else in my life up to now.

Then he said, "I think that's it. I think you got it," he said. "Take a look. What do you think?"

But I had my eyes closed. I thought I'd keep them that way for a little longer. I thought it was something I ought to do.

"Well?" he said. "Are you looking?"

My eyes were still closed. I was in my house. I knew that. But I didn't feel like I was inside anything.

"It's really something," I said.

1983

JOYCE CAROL OATES
(1938–)

Joyce Carol Oates published her first collection of short stories, *By the North Gate* (1963), two years after she had received her M.A. from the University of Wisconsin and become an instructor of English at the University of Detroit. Her productivity since then has been prodigious, accumulating in two and a half decades to about forty titles, including novels, collections of short stories and verse, plays, and literary criticism. In the meantime, she has continued to teach, moving in 1967 from the University of Detroit to the University of Windsor, in Ontario, and, in 1978, to Princeton University. Reviewers have admired her enormous energy, but find a productivity of such magnitude difficult to assess. Clearly her work is uneven, but clearly, also, it is distinguished by passages of brilliance.

She was born in Lockport, New York, and raised in the country nearby, "a part of the world," she has said, "and an economic background where people don't even graduate from high school." A scholarship student at Syracuse University, she wrote voluminously, graduated Phi Beta Kappa in 1960, and then spent a year on a fellowship at the University of Wisconsin.

In a period characterized by the abandonment of so much of the realistic tradition by authors such as John Barth, Donald Barthelme, and Thomas Pynchon, Joyce Carol Oates seemed for years determinedly old-fashioned in her insistence on the essentially mimetic quality of her fiction. Hers is a world of violence, insanity, fractured love, and hopeless loneliness. Although some of it appears to come from her own direct observations, her dreams, her fears, much more is clearly from the experiences of others. Her first novel, *With Shuddering Fall* (1964), dealt with stock car racing, though she had never seen a race. In *them* (1969) she focused on Detroit from the Depression through the riots of 1967, drawing much of her material from the deep impression made on her by the problems of one of her students. Whatever the source and however shocking the events or the motivations, however, her fictive world long remained strikingly akin to that real one reflected in the daily newspapers, the television news and talk shows, the popular magazines of our day. *Wonderland* (1971) opens with a family murder and suicide, from which only the main character escapes. *Do with Me What You Will* (1973) begins with the abduction of a small girl from a school playground. *Unholy Loves* (1979) explores university life. *Bellefleur* (1980), however, is in some ways a striking departure: a mammoth gothic romance covering several generations and centered in the Adirondacks in the nineteenth century. *Angel of Light* (1981) is a strong novel of politics. In *A Bloodsmoor Romance* (1982) and *Mysteries of Winterthurn* (1984) she continues to experiment with form and content. In *Marya: A Life* (1986), however, she constructs a personal and realistic novel, reminiscent in some of its details of the life of its author.

Some of her best work is in her short stories. She early developed a control and an authority that placed her well ahead of most of her contemporaries, and she has maintained her unflagging energy and inventiveness through numerous volumes.

Novels not mentioned above are *A Garden of Earthly Delights,* 1967; *Expensive People,* 1968; *The Assassins,* 1975; *Childwold,* 1976; *Son of the Morning,* 1978; and *Solstice,* 1985. Collections of short stories not mentioned above are *Upon the Sweeping Flood,* 1966; *Marriages and Infidelities,* 1972; *The Goddess and Other Women,* 1974; *The Poisoned Kiss and Other Stories from the Portuguese,* 1975; *The Seduction and Other Stories,* 1975; *Crossing the Border,* 1976; *Night-Side,* 1977; *A Sentimental Education,* 1981; *Last Days,* 1985; and *Raven's Wing,* 1986. *On Boxing,* 1987, is non-fiction. Verse is collected in *Anonymous Sins & Other Poems,* 1969; *Love and Its Derangements,* 1970; *Angel Fire,* 1973; *The Fabulous Beasts,* 1975; *Women Whose Lives Are Food, Men Whose Lives Are Money,* 1979; and *Invisible Woman: New and Selected Poems 1970–1982,* 1982. Criticism is *The Edge of Impossibility: Tragic Forms in Literature,* 1972; *New Heaven, New Earth: The Visionary Experience in Literature,* 1974; and *The Profane Art: Essays and Reviews,* 1983.

Critical studies include Linda Wagner, ed., *Critical Essays on Joyce Carol Oates,* 1979; G. F. Waller, *Dreaming America: Obsession and Transcendence in the Fiction of Joyce Carol Oates,* 1979; Ellen G. Friedman, *Joyce Carol Oates,* 1980; and Eileen Teper Bender, *Joyce Carol Oates: Artist in Residence,* 1987.

The Seasons

Joy, who is now twenty-six years old, is waiting to conceive *as if by accident* a child with the man she loves. This will be irrefutable proof, she reasons, that she loves him and that they must marry. Though she has not believed in God for perhaps thirteen years, she reasons too that conceiving a child in her special circumstances will be a sign of some kind, natural and healthy in effect but supernatural in origin. Her thoughts on the subject are kept secret from her lover, Christopher, but she suspects that he understand and concurs—he has developed such uncanny powers of intuition he sometimes knows what she is going to say before she says it. Frequently he reads her thoughts and announces them playfully, even in the presence of others. (Christopher is a playwright and his head is aswirl, he says, with dialogue. Stray floating dialogue. Aleatory sounds. So perhaps it is altogether natural that he can hear Joy's thoughts even when she doesn't intend to speak them aloud. Also, he loves her very much and certainly would marry her if she had his baby.) Only the accidental is truly significant in Joy's imagination because it is all that remains of grace, and all she remembers of "grace" is that an elderly Catholic novelist, a woman friend of her mother's, told her when she was twelve years old that grace is a direct visitation from God, *unwilled by man.* ("There is nothing we can do to deserve grace," the elderly woman told Joy, who was rather frightened at the time and anxious to escape. "It is a gift from God that not even the most impassioned prayer can guarantee.") Apart from the small circle of friends of Joy's parents in Minneapolis no one ever seemed to have heard of this particular Catholic novelist, so with the passage of years Joy stopped mentioning her. She has never brought up the name to Christopher, for instance, and isn't even certain at the present time that she remembers it correctly.

It is on a blowy and hazardous December evening, the day following the first snowfall of the season, that Christopher and Joy discover the starving kittens on a country road in northern New Jersey and bring them home to the Schankers' place in Millgate. (The Schankers are in Italy and Christopher and Joy are house-sitting for them. This is the third house in which they have lived since they met the previous January.) They are just returning from New York City, from a disappointing workshop production of a play of Christopher's staged in an unheated studio near St. Mark's Place, and Christopher's head is so flooded with thoughts that he doesn't see the kittens by the roadside until Joy cries out excitedly for him to stop. By this time it is nearly one o'clock in the morning and Christopher has been driving nonstop for two hours and he couldn't have said whether he was exhausted by the strain of night driving or by the fresh wound of his play so crudely mangled—so *eerily* mangled it wasn't his any longer—or whether, in fact, he is on the brink of a bout of heart-thumping exhilaration and will be awake the rest of the night while Joy sleeps. (When Joy is exhausted she falls into bed and sleeps at once. This is a talent Christopher associates with his childhood, now long past, and tries not to resent in Joy.)

Christopher has become dazed and near mesmerized by the long drive, and when Joy seizes his arm and tells him to stop the car he hits the brakes at once, without question. Is it an animal? A deer? Has he hit something? For most of his thirty-two years he has lived in cities and he hasn't entirely adapted to life in the country. As soon as dusk falls, in fact, he is besieged by ghostly figures of white-tailed deer running toward the road and preparing to leap into his windshield. ("By the time you see a deer," someone warned him, "it's usually too late to avoid hitting it.") But though Christopher has seen a depressing number of dead deer along the roadsides—some of them so uncannily beautiful even in death it's difficult to believe they have been injured—he hasn't had an accident yet, or even a near accident.

Joy brings the kittens into the car, exclaiming over them—Look at the poor things, the poor starving things, they've been abandoned, someone has dumped them here, someone has left them here to die—and Christopher's heart is won at once. The kittens are no more than a month old, mewing and squeaking, clearly ravenous with hunger, and far too immature to be frightened. White with gray markings, short-haired, with plaintive little faces and watery eyes and stubby tails: How could anyone do such a thing! How could anyone be so cruel! Joy is saying as the livelier of the two climbs up her arm, mewing loudly and evidently looking for milk. How can people be such monsters! Joy is saying passionately.

So they have no choice but to bring the kittens home with them and adopt them. The Schankers had had a cat, an obese Siamese, but the poor creature had died of old age a few weeks after Christopher and Joy moved in. The cat's death had upset Joy but the Schankers had told them they didn't really expect it to be living when they returned from Italy since it was twenty-one years old, a remarkable age for a cat, and quite old enough considering its irascible temper. "What should we do if it dies suddenly?" Christopher asked. He has never owned a pet and knows nothing about cats, only that Siamese are extraordinarily intelligent. "Bury it out somewhere in the woods," Mr. Schanker told him.

In the past ten or twelve years Christopher has been involved with a number of young women but he has never loved anyone as much as he loves Joy. She is nearly his height, slim-hipped, beautiful and melancholy and given to long brooding silences, with wild crimped chestnut-red hair and a very pale complexion. Even when her skin is slightly blemished or when a knife blade of a frown appears between her eyebrows she is remarkably attractive: Christopher thinks of her, with a tinge of resentment, as commandingly attractive. Her voice is soft and vague and sometimes trails off into silence, and her eyes have a queer ghostly-gray quality as if nothing is precisely *there* for her. "Do you love me?" Christopher asked when they first began living together and he'd follow her about the house, into the unfamiliar rooms, anxious that she might disappear. "Do you really love me?" he asked, and Joy would stare at him, baffled, as if she were frightened of giving the wrong answer. Sometimes she drew away from him, saying, "I wish you wouldn't look at me like that. I don't like it when people look at me, like that."

Christopher cannot now clearly remember several of the women with whom he was involved, but he knows that he imagined he was in love at the time, but was deluded. It angers him to realize he was deluded, but there you are. He has a romantic, easily excitable imagination.

When he sees Joy hugging the kittens, exclaiming over them, kneeling on the kitchen floor and feeding them milk in a saucer, tears streaming down her cheeks, he realizes suddenly that he doesn't know her at all. He has often worried that Joy is vague and unfocused and superficial in her emotions, that he is fated to love her more than she loves him—he couldn't have predicted the intensity of her concern for these pathetic little animals. And if they don't survive the night? If in fact they are already dying?

"Why are you crying, Joy?" Christopher asks uneasily. When she doesn't look up he repeats his question in a louder voice; he is standing crouched over her and the kittens, still in his leather jacket and boots, wearing his gloves.

Joy has been susceptible to strange experiences for as long as she can remember. Once, as a child of nine, she was running in her grandmother's house, as she was forbidden to do, through an arched doorway and along a stretch of sun-spangled carpet—it seemed significant, that the carpet was sun-spangled at the time—when something happened, and the next thing she knew, she was being lifted from the floor. Both her parents were frightened that she had fainted but her grandmother said curtly, "Women in our family always faint." So it is that Joy does not mind fainting.

Shortly after Joy moved in with Christopher, in a small stone-and-stucco house overlooking the Raritan River—the Rutgers professor of Asian studies who owned it was traveling at the time—she was breaking eggs in the kitchen when a misshapen yolk streaked with blood slipped out of a shell: and she screamed for Christopher to come. "It's an embryo," she said, shielding her eyes like a child, "it's a living thing—I didn't mean to kill it—" Christopher was amazed that Joy could be so upset but he disposed of the offending egg—in fact, the entire bowl of eggs—and sat with Joy in the darkened living room for nearly an hour, hugging her, and comforting her, and telling her how much he loved her. Joy kept repeating that she hadn't meant to kill the embryo and Christopher kept repeating that she *hadn't* killed it, so far as he knew, so why didn't she simply forget about it? Joy buried her face in his neck and shivered. But she hadn't fainted.

Not long before they brought the kittens home she *had* fainted, at a rowdy informal party given by friends in Newark. Conversation had turned to open-heart surgery and to the implanting of artificial hearts, and Joy had gone dead white, and tried to get to her feet, but succeeded only in crashing heavily against a glass-topped table. Afterward, driving home, Christopher silently reached over to take her hand and squeeze it hard. Joy was a little drunk by this time and feeling unaccountably happy, as if she had narrowly avoided a terrible experience. She said, "You'd never want to marry a woman who breaks tables." Christopher said at once, "You'd never want to marry a man who breaks tables." It struck them both as hilarious at the time; they laughed, fairly snorting with laughter, for much of the drive home. The next morning Joy remembered the laughter but not its cause.

Must laughter have a cause, she wondered, when you are in love, and all the world is perfect?

Joy and Christopher sit in bed, playing with the kittens and thinking up names. It's remarkable how quickly, within a matter of hours, the kittens have been restored to life. Their stomachs are round and tight and full to bursting. Their tawny eyes, black slots at the centers, are bright and guileless. So far as Christopher can determine the smaller of the two is a female, the other a male, emboldened and really quite amazing in his fearlessness. Both are white with odd splotched gunmetal-gray markings on their heads and sides; their tails are gray with neat white tips. There is something clownish about the markings—the kittens have a fey, asymmetrical look—Christopher even wonders if they might be slightly misshapen, their tails so stubby, their heads so large for their bodies. Joy says they are beautiful and not at all misshapen: they are only a few weeks old.

Heloise and Abelard. Yin and Yang. Hamlet and Ophelia. And what was Heathcliff's lover's name? Cathy? Catherine? And there is John Thomas and Lady Jane. When Christopher suggests Peppermint and Red Zinger, Joy is offended, even angered. "You don't take anything seriously," she says in a whisper. Poor Christopher is astounded: hasn't he, of the two of them, always taken things too seriously?

The kittens, taken to a vet in Millgate, are discovered to be both male, so their names become Heathcliff and Rochester. For a long while, until Rochester grows discernibly more husky than Heathcliff, it is difficult to tell one from the other. By then Christopher and Joy have moved from the Schankers' house and are occupying, for a token rent of $100 a month, a studio apartment in a converted carriage house a few miles north of Princeton. Christopher's play, revised for the fifth time, is going to be produced by the Houston Repertory in New York City—or so he seems to have been promised.

Joy is studying macramé and pottery. And then modern dance. And acting. And French conversation: she's a delightful mimic and languages have always been easy for her initially. She begins a ten-week course in computer programming but drops out after a few classes. She begins a six-week course in the techniques of real estate but soon drops out because her nature is violated by the idea of focusing so crudely and deliberately upon *selling,* and *making money,* and *competing with other persons.*

She takes most of her courses at Mercer Community College, where she has a job in the library. Then she gets a better-paying job at Western Electric as a receptionist, where she is much admired for her beauty, her clever clothes, her air of perfectly modulated calm. Even when she is nervous or anxious she gives no sign; her face is a cosmetic mask, her voice is controlled. She has learned to employ a "telephone voice" most of the time.

The years, Joy thinks. The seasons.

Sometimes it seems to her that she has been waiting to conceive a child with the man she loves for a very long time, that they have grown old together yet are still waiting for their lives to begin. Also, certain problems have arisen. Such as: Christopher is often too distracted with worry about his career to make love to her. Such as: she has lost so much weight without quite noticing it, her menstrual periods are erratic and widely spaced; does that mean she might be temporarily infertile?—"infertile" being a blunt neutral term that frequently assaults her when she isn't adequately busy.

Joy has only to close her eyes and (for instance) she is nine years old again running along her grandmother's hall, from the front foyer that smelled of floor wax to the old dining room, and then they are lifting her and staring into her face. But is the child's face really *hers?* And those faces—are they *theirs?* Do they (now) belong to anyone at all?

"Why do you think such disturbing things—can't you help yourself?" Christopher asks one day, watching her closely. Joy smooths the wrinkles from her forehead. She isn't certain she has spoken aloud. "If only you'd trust in me," Christopher says, burying his warm face in her hair, "if only you'd allow me to siphon off those poisonous thoughts."

He is embracing her so tightly she can scarcely breathe. She imagines her ribs are about to crack but of course they don't.

One overcast Saturday Heathcliff and Rochester are driven off to the vet's for their distemper shots and their "neutering" operations, which are evidently so painless (a local anesthetic is administered) they are running and tumbling about the house a few hours later and eating as hungrily as ever.

There is something so refreshingly comic about pets!—good-natured healthy nonpedigreed pets. Both Christopher and Joy speak amusingly of their twin cats to friends, Joy is always retrieving from one pocket or another coupons for cat food she has forgotten to redeem at the A&P, Christopher is always picking white cat hairs off his trousers. Within a year both cats have acquired distinctive habits and mannerisms and ways of calling attention to themselves. Rochester, for instance, is always hungry no matter how often he is fed. Whenever Christopher or Joy goes near the refrigerator Rochester is immediately underfoot, mewing plaintively and nudging with his head. Heathcliff prefers affection. In fact he has become oppressively affectionate—jumping onto Christopher's desk, purring loudly, making frantic kneading movements with his claws against Christopher's sleeves. Sometimes he is so grateful for Christopher's absentminded attention he drools onto Christopher's papers. "For Christ's sake," Christopher shouts, "haven't you been weaned?"

When Joy is sick with a prolonged and debilitating case of the flu it is Rochester who lies with her in bed, sleeping contentedly for hours, and Heathcliff who cuddles up against her in the living room sofa. (At this time Joy and Christopher are renting a small house owned by a professor of American history at Princeton. Joy draws up an ambitious reading program for herself based on the professor's immense library and spends much of the winter dozing over books with titles like *Blacks of the Old South, Union Officer and the Reconstruction, American Slave and American Master.*)

Christopher's play opens to guardedly enthusiastic reviews and most nights the little theater is filled; unfortunately the play is booked for a three-week limited engagement only, and plans to produce it elsewhere never quite materialize. Christopher is gratified, however: he believes he has been baptized, he has proven himself—despite the strain and exhaustion of the past year he hasn't broken down. (The play is even nominated for a Drama Critics Award.)

He begins work immediately on a longer and more ambitious play set in 1950, "the legendary year of his birth." Joy is caught up in his excitement and speaks proudly of him to friends. He *is* a genius, she has known it all along, he isn't like other men. . . . Christopher and Joy are photographed for an admiring article in a local New Jersey paper: Playwright Christopher Flynn and his companion Joy Stephens seated side by side on a sofa, their hands tightly clasped, a white cat sprawled languidly across their laps. Christopher Flynn holds himself rather stiffly for the photograph, his deep-set eyes narrowed as if in suspicion, or simple shyness; his close-cropped beard appears to be a few shades lighter than his hair. He isn't a handsome man but he exudes an unquestioning air of authority. His companion Joy Stephens, however, is a dreamily beautiful young woman with a sad, sweet, rather haunting smile. Her name in the caption beneath the photograph is "Joy Stehpns."

A feverish momentum carries Christopher through the long quiet seemingly interminable workdays at home while Joy is away, at Western Electric or at one of her classes. (She has recently enrolled in a course in silk-screening at the community college.) He writes from seven-thirty in the morning until one o'clock in the afternoon, then from approximately four o'clock until dinner. Often he writes in the evenings as well, locked away in the room designated as his study. Sometimes the day's work has exhilarated or distressed him, or he has consumed too many cups of coffee, or swallowed too many amphetamine tablets (*not* obtained illicitly—but given to him by a friend of his who has a prescription), so that he ends up writing during the night as well. Joy worries about his "pitiless consuming of himself" but she provides most of his meals and keeps herself and the cats out of his way. Perhaps she will sleep with the middle-aged executive at Western Electric who takes her to lunch frequently. Perhaps she will quit her job and see about establishing a permanent household. Or—since she is becoming quite absorbed in silk-screening—perhaps she will become an artist of sorts, after all. Her twenty-eighth birthday is drawing near.

Christopher is invited to have a drink with Mrs. Schanker in New York City, at one of the splendid new midtown hotels. He has not thought of her in a very long time and is mildly surprised to discover how youthful she is, for a woman in her late forties. Her hair is fashionably curly, her makeup is flawless. Why has she invited him for a drink? What is the purpose? So Christopher wonders while Mrs. Schanker talks and smiles and occasionally touches his arm. Evidently Mrs. Schanker is seriously ill: but she is coy about actually naming the disease, or the organs it is ravaging. Christopher is at a loss for words. He says, "I'm sorry to hear that. . . . I'm sorry to hear that." (Lately it has come to Christopher's attention that a number of acquaintances of his and Joy's, and people he has known since college, have been taken seriously ill; or have actually died. But Joy insists that these events are accidental and not related to one another.)

Mrs. Schanker has several martinis and keeps muddling Joy's name. She embarrasses Christopher by asking if they plan to have a family someday, if they plan to get married. She asks about Christopher's new play and nods gravely when Christopher explains that he can't discuss his work—it makes him too tense. Twice, or is it three times, she asks about the kittens—"those darling white foundling kittens of yours"—and Christopher explains laughingly that they are hardly kittens any longer. (Both are solid, husky, muscular cats, fully mature, with insatiable appetites for both food and affection. Rochester is so heavy that Joy staggers when she carries him; he has become a household joke, his nickname "Tank." Poor Heathcliff has developed a "fat pouch," a loose flaccid hunk of flesh that hangs down from his lower abdomen and swings when he trots, making him look pregnant. The vet says it's similar to a hernia in a human being, it isn't a health problem at all, both Heathcliff and Rochester are in superb physical condition. But, perhaps, slightly overweight.)

Mrs. Schanker reminisces about "Domino"—Christopher believes the name is Domino—and gradually it develops that she is speaking of the fat old cranky rheumy-eyed Siamese who died shortly after Christopher and Joy took responsibility for him. Christopher wants to joke that *that* had been a clever trick of the Schankers—to dump a dying cat on him because they hadn't the hardness of heart to have the poor thing put to sleep. But he senses this would be an inappropriate remark.

Some days afterward he realizes that Mrs. Schanker had (perhaps) wanted to initiate a love affair with him. Or the semblance of one. In fact, their meeting itself was a kind of love affair in embryo, a surrogate for the real thing, whatever the "real thing" is. He tells Joy about the meeting and the odd awkward conversation but he doesn't tell her about the miniature love affair. He muddles Mrs. Schanker's first name, which Joy insists is either "Lizzie" or "Bobbie."

Joy has become a vegetarian and has taken up membership in an Animal Rights organization in Philadelphia. For much of an elated week she is certain *though she does not hint of it to Christopher* that she is pregnant: but her condition turns out to be a false alarm. (She is furious with her gynecologist, who keeps insisting that water retention isn't unusual or particularly abnormal: hence Joy's swollen breasts and stomach and the sensitivity of her skin. "But I have never had this condition before!" Joy says angrily. Her voice rises to such a shrill pitch, the doctor's assisting nurse approaches Joy as if to comfort her, or restrain her. "It has never happened to me before, I don't even know what you're talking about!" Joy cries. "I think you're lying!")

One day while Christopher is in the city Joy does a forbidden thing, poking about in his study, scanning drafts and notes for his new play. It frightens her that she is living with a genius. Or with a man who believes himself a genius. It frightens her to discover that the play, though set three decades before, is clearly about Christopher and herself. Despite the fragmentary nature of the scenes and the messy scrawled writing Joy is able to piece together a narrative that relates to her own. She is "Lily," a somnambulist of "uncommon beauty" who has no center to her life, no focus, no identity. But it is said of her, admiringly, by her lover, "Alexander," that she is soulless and therefore cannot be injured. (Alexander defines himself as a "romantic cynic" who can be injured by virtually anyone and anything.) Lily is vague, superficial, charming in a childish manner; she has a habit of allowing her words to drift off into an inconclusive silence. . . .

By the end of the play Lily will have become catatonic, and committed to a mental asylum: and Alexander will spend the rest of his life mourning his loss.

"His loss . . . *his,*" Joy murmurs.

She has been absentmindedly scratching Heathcliff's head and now the burly cat scrambles over Christopher's desk, knocking papers about, nudging and butting against Joy, near frantic with love.

One morning Christopher reappears in the kitchen just as Joy is about to leave for work and tells her, in a hoarse whisper, that he feels very strange. He doesn't feel like himself. He began work at seven-thirty but couldn't concentrate, his heart has been beating erratically, he has been thinking obsessively about. (And here he recites a now-familiar litany of anxieties. Past failures and humiliations; probable failures and humiliations to come. And his fear that his father, who has a serious heart condition, will die. And an old high school friend of his recently killed himself in San Francisco, leaving no note behind. . . .)

"When things speed up their meanings are lost," Christopher says.

The words are so precisely enunciated, Joy knows they are words from his play.

"When things speed up their meanings are lost," Christopher says, staring at her. "But we can't live if meanings are lost. We aren't human . . . if meanings are lost."

"Yes," Joy says carefully.

Across a space of several yards she can feel the trembling in her lover's body. But she must leave for work: it has begun to rain hard and she will have to drive slowly. She is a shy, cautious driver.

As she is about to leave Christopher says abruptly, "You aren't in love with anyone else, are you?" Joy laughs, startled, but doesn't quite turn to him. He says, "Because you've always been happy with me. Before we met—I don't think you were happy, I think you were psychologically troubled. But you've always been happy with me."

"Yes," Joy says.

He kisses her goodbye. She feels him standing in the doorway and watching her until she is out of sight.

One evening after a dress rehearsal of Christopher's new play, an actor shows Joy the remarkably lifelike mask he wears during the final act to make him appear fifty years older than his age. "Feel this," he says, and Joy touches the rubber mask: so light, so delicate, it might be actual human skin. . . . She shivers, touching it.

On stage the actor is altogether convincing as an elderly dying man—haggard, hollow-eyed, ashen-faced. In person, smiling at Joy, he is a striking youngish man, no more than thirty-five. Joy hadn't known the technique of professional mask-making was so complex: the actor shows her not only the mask itself but the plaster mold of his face and a series of charcoal sketches. "Isn't it amazing? I frighten myself when I look in the mirror," the actor says fondly. He holds his elderly face up to his own, smiling at Joy, peering at her through the eye holes.

One April night Christopher makes love to Joy for the first time in many weeks, or has it been months? He is agitated, panting, near sobbing, but finally triumphant. Joy holds him tight and is passive and accommodating in his embrace; she isn't unfaithful to him by thinking of someone else. The years, she thinks. The seasons. Afterward she brushes his damp hair away from his forehead and makes a pretense of smoothing out the wrinkles.

He grips her tight, tight. He is trembling. He murmurs something about starting a baby at last, getting married. . . . When Joy doesn't reply he remains silent, his warm face burrowed against her neck, his ragged breath gradually growing rhythmic.

Shortly after they move to another house, a few miles north of Princeton, Rochester disappears and doesn't return for a full day and a night. But he does return, ravenously hungry. "A false alarm," Christopher says in a fond scolding voice.

Joy has enrolled in a six-week "mandala"[1] course at the YW-YMCA, partly because her lover's wife is also enrolled in the course and she is curious about the woman. (But her curiosity is soon placated. Her lover's wife is in her early forties, slightly washed-out about the eyes but still pretty, wanly attractive, with a Virginia

1. A design representing the cosmos, chiefly composed of concentric geometric shapes, containing abstract or stylized images of a deity.

accent. Her manner is hopeful and zealous but she hasn't much talent for painting mandalas.)

The course is taught by a boisterous woman named Heloise who wears ankle-length gowns of coarse-woven fabric and a good deal of Navaho jewelry. She is an excellent teacher, however, filled with praise and enthusiasm, repeating many times each hour, "Free your innermost impulses, give vent to your *hidden* appetite for beauty and wholeness." She is particularly impressed with Joy's lavish mandalas, which are painted in rainbow colors with no attempt at precision or symmetry. Often she rests her beringed hand on Joy's slender shoulder. "Fantasy is beauty, beauty is fantasy," she says huskily. She carries herself well for a woman of her size though sometimes her breathing is audible. There is a faint downy mustache on her upper lip.

One evening she singles out a mandala of Joy's for especial praise. It is painted on a sheet of stiff construction paper measuring five feet by four but it looks even larger. Flamboyant fiery swaths of paint, peacock tails and cat eyes, heraldic cat figures suggestive of ancient Egyptian art. . . . Joy stands to one side, warm and flushed, her gaze veiled. Gradually she realizes that her lover's wife isn't in class that night and that she hasn't seen the woman for a while.

Christopher imagines that Joy is having a love affair though he has no proof and is too proud to quarry out proof. He has dreams in which he is clean-shaven and his face is a pink round baby's face, his skin so sensitive even the touch of the air irritates it. Dear God, simply to be *looked at* in this condition!—he is filled with chagrin, self-loathing. He has worn a beard since the age of twenty-two and cannot imagine himself without one. In his dreams it is mixed up with his plays, his "career," the woman with whom he lives whose name, in his sleep, he has temporarily forgotten. . . . When he wakes, however, it is to vast heart-pounding relief. He strokes his chin and his beard is still there. He reaches out beside him and Joy is still there, sleeping, or perhaps by now awake. Most nights the cats sleep in the bedroom, one on the bed and one beneath the bed, following an inflexible sort of protocol neither Christopher nor Joy can always predict, though they know it must not be violated.

Christopher reaches out in the dark, toward an inert white shape pressed against his thigh. Rochester?—or Heathcliff?—no matter.

Because it is the only pragmatic thing to do *at the present time* Joy arranges to have an abortion at a clinic in New Brunswick. Christopher drives her there, waits for her, comforts her, weeps quietly with her. For many days he hugs her at odd impulsive moments. It is a queer dreamlike time—the ordinary laws of nature appear suspended—a whisper can be heard throughout the house, a sigh, a stifled sob, a clearing of the throat. Even the cats are anxious and aroused and easily spooked.

A friend of Joy's asks if the procedure is painless and Joy replies at once, "I don't remember."

Christopher's new play opens to warmly enthusiastic notices. It is acclaimed as "powerful," "haunting," "lyric," "poetic"; Christopher himself is acclaimed as a "startling new talent." However, the play is not a commercial success and closes after seven weeks: not a bad run, considering the inhospitable theatrical climate.

Consequently Christopher's plans to move to New York City, to sublet a friend's loft on Vandam Street, are suspended. Consequently he may be forced to accept a playwright-in-residence position—in fact it is quite an attractive position—at the University of Connecticut. Friends congratulate him and go away puzzled by his bitterness.

"It has become so degrading," Christopher tells Joy. "And I meant it to be so ennobling." He speaks with the melancholy precision of the leading man in his play.

One night, slightly high, he angrily corrects Joy's pronunciation of the word "pidgin," which she has mispronounced charmingly in the past. (She pronounces it "pidgin," as it is spelled; or, alternately, "pig-din.")

When Joy does not defend herself he becomes angrier. He accuses her of treachery and "sustained deceit." He knows she is having a love affair with someone in Princeton. He knows the baby wasn't his—if, as he says sarcastically, *there was any baby at all.*

"What do you mean?" Joy says, staring at him.

"You know what I mean," Christopher says. Suddenly he is very drunk. Suddenly, though his thoughts have a razor-sharp precision, his words are incoherent and there is nothing to do but grab Joy and shake her so that her head and shoulders strike the wall. "You want to suck out my soul—I know you!—because you have no soul of your own," he says.

Afterward they cry in each other's arms and eventually fall asleep.

Christopher and Joy have decided to separate, for experimental purposes. So they inform their friends. Perhaps Joy will move out, to live for a while with her married sister in Wilmington. Or Christopher may move out, and rent a small apartment in New York.

Then again, one balmy day in late March, they decide that they will get married after all. And put an end to it.

Christopher rocks Joy in his arms and promises they will have another baby. That is, they will have a baby. He can accept the position in Connecticut and stay there for a few years at least. Perhaps they can buy a farm in the country. An old farmhouse. With a few acres. Aren't the old farms selling very cheaply in New England? Joy sobs, and clutches at him, and grinds herself against him almost convulsively, horribly: Christopher is a little repulsed by her passion. And her physical strength.

In June Christopher makes the decision to move out of their rented house: he has been unable to work for weeks. But he is so obsessed with Joy that he hears her footfall behind him, feels the static electricity of her hair brushing against him, dreams of her constantly. . . . He drinks too much, smokes too much dope with friends who aren't really friends, who don't care about his happiness or whether he and Joy get together again. He listens to bad advice. Cruel rumors. Inflammatory news. One night, driving past his former house, now Joy's house (which is to say, a house he is still renting but in which Joy lives alone), he sees an unfamiliar car in the driveway and knows it is Joy's lover and that *she had been betraying him for a very long time.* Still, he does not wish her dead or even injured. If he had a pistol he wouldn't circle the house to get a good shot through one of the windows, he isn't that kind of man, he is far too civilized. He doesn't even write that kind of play.

That was the night he woke in his car, in a parking lot behind a tavern on Route 1, and had no idea what time it was or where he was or what had happened to him. He couldn't even remember passing out. But in the instant of waking he was suffused with a queer sense of elation because he remembered nothing. Nothing terrible had happened yet.

Or, alternately, everything had happened and he was still alive and why had he ever given a damn?

The telephone rings, rings. Joy picks it up and says carefully, "If you want to talk with me, Christopher, please talk to me. . . . Don't do this, Christopher—" she says, as the line goes dead.

Some days, Heathcliff and Rochester sleep for as many as twenty hours. (Though in different parts of the house. They rarely cuddle together or groom each other as they did as kittens: but Joy can't remember whether their estrangement was gradual or sudden.) Other days, they are skittish and forever underfoot, mewing to be fed.

Joy takes a bus to Wilmington, Delaware, to spend a weekend with her married sister, Irene, whom she decides after all not to confide in—she doesn't want news of the abortion, or the middle-aged lover, or "Lily" to get back to their mother. When she returns to Princeton it seems to her that the house has been broken into but she can't be certain. "Are you here, Christopher?" she calls out. She walks on tiptoe through the rooms, her heart beating oddly. "Christopher? Are you here? Please—" But no one answers.

Every scrap of dry cat food she left out has been devoured, and most of the water lapped up, but Heathcliff and Rochester show no interest in her return and when she tries to take him onto her lap Rochester shrinks away from her. She sits at the kitchen table, still in her raincoat, crying softly.

Christopher and Joy meet for coffee and Christopher tells her he misses her, he misses her and the cats, "and things the way they used to be." His eyes are lightly threaded with blood and his beard is grayer than Joy remembers. When she asks him if he wants to move back, however, he hesitates before saying he does. "You don't have to move back if you don't want to," Joy says, the faintest touch of irony in her voice. But Christopher says yes, yes he does, he *does* want to move back . . . except he's frightened of loving her too much.

Joy begins laughing, showing her perfect white teeth, narrowing her eyes to slits. After a moment or two Christopher lays his hand over hers as if to calm her. "People are looking at you," he whispers.

In the end it is decided that Christopher will move back, since he finds it impossible to work anywhere else; and that Joy will spend the month of September with her sister in Wilmington. (Christopher suspects that she is really going to move in with her lover—if she has a lover—but he's too proud to say anything. He doesn't love her any longer but he is still vulnerable to being wounded by her.)

When he telephones Joy in Wilmington, however, her sister tells him carefully that Joy is out at the moment, or can't come to the phone, and would he like to leave a message?—but he never does, he is sickened at the thought of making a fool of himself, of saying the wrong thing. He is also frightened of breaking down and weeping over the telephone while Joy's sister (whom he has never met) listens on, embarrassed.

One day he decides to give up the house and move to New York City after all. By delaying so long he lost the position at the University of Connecticut but he has been promised a part-time teaching job at New York University starting in January. What the hell, he thinks, excited, he will start a new life, he has begun work on his most ambitious play yet, he's only thirty-five years old. Perhaps, by the time he is thirty-six, he will have been awarded a Pulitzer Prize.

Not that prizes mean anything to him, he thinks, as if making a point to Joy, who is standing silently at the periphery of his vision.

He is ashamed to ask anyone he knows if they will take Heathcliff and Rochester; and he is fearful of turning them over to the county animal shelter—wouldn't they be put to sleep after a few days? The kindest thing to do is drive them out into the country—the deep country, away from busy roads—and give them their freedom. They are such strong healthy alert creatures, they will have no trouble hunting their food.

So he coaxes them into separate cardboard cartons, and carries them out to the car, and drives ten or twelve miles north and west of town, into farming country. The poor things are so piteous in their yowling and panting, such cowards, he doesn't know whether he should be angry with them or stricken to the heart.

In a desolate area in Hunterdon County, on a curve in a narrow unpaved road. Christopher stops the car and releases them. Heathcliff, panting, bounds into the tall grass at once but Rochester is dazed and must be urged to leave the car. (Poor "Tank" so panicked during the jolting ride, he soiled the bottom of his cardboard carton. But no matter: Christopher tosses both cartons into the ditch. He reasons that they can't be traced back to him.)

Driving slowly and cautiously away he sees both cats in his rearview mirror, staring after him. Oversized, clumsy, dumb creatures, with such blank unaccusing faces, simply staring after him. . . . Why don't they protest as any dog would, why don't they run after the car? Can it all end so abruptly? Christopher's heart lurches, he feels sickened and betrayed. He slows the car, brakes to a stop. He tells himself that, if the kittens make the smallest gesture of reconciliation, he will take them back home.

1986

BOBBIE ANN MASON

(1940–   )

Raised on a farm in western Kentucky, Bobbie Ann Mason graduated from the University of Kentucky in 1962 and did magazine work in New York before returning to school to earn an M.A. from the State University of New York at Binghamton in 1966. Marriage followed in 1969 and then a Ph.D. from the University of Connecticut in 1972. Teaching at Mansfield State College in Pennsylvania, she turned her dissertation into her first book, *Nabokov's Garden: A Guide to Ada* (1974). Her second, *The Girl Sleuth: A Feminist Guide* (1975), is a study of the Nancy Drew series and other similar books. She came to fiction later, but her first collection, *Shiloh and Other Stories* (1982), won the Ernest Hemingway Award for the most distinguished first fiction of the year. Her first novel, *In*

Country (1985), describes the lingering effects of the Vietnam War on an American family—a young woman who has never seen her father, who died there; her uncle, a traumatized veteran; and her grandmother—years later as they make a pilgrimage to the Vietnam Veterans Memorial in Washington.

Bobbie Ann Mason's stories invite comparison with Ann Beattie's and Raymond Carver's. All three writers tend to focus on contemporary alienation. Each has a distinctive tone and milieu, however, with Carver's outlook generally the bleakest and Beattie's people the most sophisticated. For Mason, the milieu is a rural Kentucky forever changed by the plastic improvements that have brought every town its McDonald's and Burger King. A retired husband and wife talk of "field peas and country ham" as they sit down to a quick meal in the elaborate camper they have purchased with the proceeds from the sale of their farm. Everywhere the world beyond Kentucky intrudes, from Steve Martin and *Charlie's Angels* on television to the mastectomies of Betty Ford and Happy Rockefeller to the housewife who works part time for H & R Block. Even the man who sells coon hounds at the local flea market is tainted by the present, failing to return one day, "picked up over in Missouri for peddling a hot TV."

Mason's books to date are named above.

Third Monday

Ruby watches Linda exclaiming over a bib, then a terry cloth sleeper. It is an amazing baby shower because Linda is thirty-seven and unmarried. Ruby admires that. Linda even refused to marry the baby's father, a man from out of town who had promised to get Linda a laundromat franchise. It turned out that he didn't own any laundromats; he was only trying to impress her. Linda doesn't know where he is now. Maybe Nashville.

Linda smiles at a large bakery cake with pink decorations and the message, WELCOME, HOLLY. "I'm glad I know it's going to be a girl," she says. "But in a way it's like knowing ahead of time what you're going to get for Christmas."

"The twentieth century's taking all the mysteries out of life," says Ruby breezily.

Ruby is as much a guest of honor here as Linda is. Betty Lewis brings Ruby's cake and ice cream to her and makes sure she has a comfortable chair. Ever since Ruby had a radical mastectomy, Betty and Linda and the other women on her bowling team have been awed by her. They praise her bravery and her sense of humor. Just before she had the operation, they suddenly brimmed over with inspiring tales about women who had had successful mastectomies. They reminded her about Betty Ford and Happy Rockefeller. Happy . . . Every one is happy now. Linda looks happy because Nancy Featherstone has taken all the ribbons from the presents and threaded them through holes in a paper plate to fashion a funny bridal bouquet. Nancy, who is artistic, explains that this is a tradition at showers. Linda is pleased. She twirls the bouquet, and the ends of the ribbons dangle like tentacles on a jellyfish.

After Ruby found the lump in her breast, the doctor recommended a mammogram. In an X-ray room, she hugged a Styrofoam basketball hanging from a metal cone and stared at the two lights overhead. The technician, a frail man in plaid pants and a smock, flipped a switch and left the room. The machine hummed. He took several X-rays, like a photographer shooting various poses of a model, and used his hands to measure distances, as one would to determine the height of a horse. "My guidelight is out," he explained. Ruby lay on her back with her breasts flattened out, and the technician slid an X-ray plate into the drawer beneath the table. He tilted her hip and propped it against a cushion. "I have to repeat that last one," he said. "The angle was wrong." He told her not to breathe. The machine buzzed and shook. After she was dressed, he showed her the X-rays, which were printed on Xerox paper. Ruby looked for the lump in the squiggly lines, which resembled a rainfall map in a geography book. The outline of her breast was lovely—a lilting, soft curve. The technician would not comment on what he saw in the pictures. "Let the radiologist interpret them," he said with a peculiar smile. "He's our chief tea-leaf reader." Ruby told the women in her bowling club that she had had her breasts Xeroxed.

The man she cares about does not know. She has been out of the hospital for a week, and in ten days he will be in town again. She wonders whether he will be disgusted and treat her as though she has been raped, his property violated. According to an article she read, this is what to expect. But Buddy is not that kind of man, and she is not his property. She sees him only once a month. He could have a wife somewhere, or other girlfriends, but she doesn't believe that. He promised to take her home with him the next time he comes to western Kentucky. He lives far away, in East Tennessee, and he travels the flea-market circuit, trading hunting dogs and pocket knives. She met him at the fairgrounds at Third Monday—the flea market held the third Monday of each month. Ruby had first gone there on a day off from work with Janice Leggett to look for some Depression glass to match Janice's sugar bowl. Ruby lingered in the fringe of trees near the highway, the oak grove where hundreds of dogs were whining and barking, while Janice wandered ahead to the tables of figurines and old dishes. Ruby intended to catch up with Janice shortly, but she became absorbed in the dogs. Their mournful eyes and pitiful yelps made her sad. When she was a child, her dog had been accidentally locked in the corncrib and died of heat exhaustion. She was aware of a man watching her watching the dogs. He wore a billed cap that shaded his sharp eyes like an awning. His blue jacket said HEART VALLEY COON CLUB on the back in gold-embroidered stitching. His red shirt had pearl snaps, and his jeans were creased, as though a woman had ironed them. He grabbed Ruby's arm suddenly and said, "What are you staring at, little lady! Have you got something treed?"

He was Buddy Landon, and he tried to sell her a hunting dog. He seemed perfectly serious. Did she want a coonhound or a bird dog? The thing wrong with bird dogs was that they liked to run so much they often strayed, he said. He recommended the Georgia redbone hound for intelligence and patience. "The redbone can jump and tree, but he doesn't bark too much," he said. "He don't cry wolf on you, and he's a good fighter."

"What do I need a coon dog for?" said Ruby, wishing he had a good answer.

"You must be after a bird dog then," he said. "Do you prefer hunting ducks or wild geese? I had some hounds that led me on a wild-goose chase one time after an old wildcat. That thing led us over half of Kentucky. That sucker never *would* climb a tree! He wore my dogs out." He whooped and clapped his hands.

There were eight empty dog crates in the back of his pickup, and he had chained the dogs to a line between two trees. Ruby approached them cautiously, and they all leaped into the air before their chains jerked them back.

"That little beagle there's the best in the field," Buddy said to a man in a blue cap who had sidled up beside them.

"What kind of voice has he got?" the man said.

"It's music to your ears!"

"I don't need a rabbit dog," the man said. "I don't even have any rabbits left in my fields. I need me a good coon dog."

"This black-and-tan's ambitious," said Buddy, patting a black spot on a dog's head. The spot was like a little beanie. "His mama and daddy were both ambitious, and *he's* ambitious. This dog won't run trash."

"What's trash?" Ruby asked.

"Skunk. Possum," Buddy explained.

"I've only knowed two women in my life that I could get out coon hunting," the man in the blue cap said.

"This lady claims she wants a bird dog, but I think I can make a coon hunter out of her," said Buddy, grinning at Ruby.

The man walked away, hunched over a cigarette he was lighting, and Buddy Landon started to sing "You Ain't Nothin' But A Hound Dog." He said to Ruby, "I could have been Elvis Presley. But thank God I wasn't. Look what happened to him. Got fat and died." He sang, " 'Crying all the time. You ain't never caught a rabbit . . .' I love dogs. But I tell you one thing. I'd never let a dog in the house. You know why? It would get too tame and forget its job. Don't forget, a dog is a dog."

Buddy took Ruby by the elbow and steered her through the fairgrounds, guiding her past tables of old plastic toys and kitchen utensils. "Junk," he said. He bought Ruby a Coke in a can, and then he bought some sweet corn from a farmer. "I'm going to have me some roastin' ears tonight," he said.

"I hear your dogs calling for you," said Ruby, listening to the distant bugle voices of the beagles.

"They love me. Stick around and you'll love me too."

"What makes you think you're so cute?" said Ruby. "What makes you think I need a dog?"

He answered her questions with a flirtatious grin. His belt had a large silver buckle, with a floppy-eared dog's head engraved on it. His hands were thick and strong, with margins of dirt under his large, flat nails. Ruby liked his mustache and the way his chin and the bill of his cap seemed to yearn toward each other.

"How much do you want for that speckled hound dog?" she asked him.

He brought the sweet corn and some steaks to her house that evening. By then, the shucks on the corn were wilting. Ruby grilled the steaks and boiled the ears of corn while Buddy unloaded the dogs from his pickup. He tied them to her clothesline and fed and watered them. The pickup truck in Ruby's driveway seemed as startling as the sight of the "Action News" TV van would have been. She hoped her neighbors would notice. She could have a man there if she wanted to.

After supper, Buddy gave the dogs the leftover bones and steak fat. Leaping and snapping, they snatched at the scraps, but Buddy snarled back at them and made them cringe. "You have to let them know who's boss," he called to Ruby, who was looking on admiringly from the back porch. It was like watching a group of people playing "May I?"

Later, Buddy brought his sleeping roll in from the truck and settled in the living room, and Ruby did not resist when he came into her bedroom and said he couldn't sleep. She thought her timing was appropriate; she had recently bought a double bed. They talked until late in the night, and he told her hunting stories, still pretending that she was interested in acquiring a hunting dog. She pretended she was, too, and asked him dozens of questions. He said he traded things—anything he could make a nickel from: retreaded tires, cars, old milk cans and cream separators. He was fond of the dogs he raised and trained, but it did not hurt him to sell them. There were always more dogs.

"Loving a dog is like trying to love the Mississippi River," he said. "It's constantly shifting and changing color and sound and course, but it's just the same old river."

Suddenly he asked Ruby, "Didn't you ever get married?"

"No."

"Don't it bother you?"

"No. What of it?" She wondered if he thought she was a lesbian.

He said, "You're too pretty and nice. I can't believe you never married."

"All the men around here are ignorant," she said. "I never wanted to marry any of them. Were you ever married?"

"Yeah. Once or twice is all. I didn't take to it."

Later, in the hospital, on Sodium Pentothal, Ruby realized that she had about a hundred pictures of Clint Eastwood, her favorite actor, and none of Buddy. His indistinct face wavered in her memory as she rolled down a corridor on a narrow bed. He didn't have a picture of her, either. In a drawer somewhere she had a handful of prints of her high school graduation picture, taken years ago. Ruby Jane MacPherson in a beehive and a Peter Pan collar. She should remember to give him one for his billfold someday. She felt cautious around Buddy, she realized, the way she did in high school, when it had seemed so important to keep so many things hidden from boys. "Don't let your brother find your sanitary things," she could hear her mother saying.

In the recovery room, she slowly awoke at the end of a long dream, to blurred sounds and bright lights—gold and silver flashes moving past like fish—and a pain in her chest that she at first thought was a large bird with a hooked beak suckling her breast. The problem, she kept thinking, was that she was lying down, when in order to nurse the creature properly, she ought to sit up. The mound of bandages mystified her.

"We didn't have to take very much," a nurse said. "The doctor didn't have to go way up under your arm."

Someone was squeezing her hand. She heard her mother telling someone, "They think they got it all."

A strange fat woman with orange hair was holding her hand. "You're just fine, sugar," she said.

When Ruby began meeting Buddy at the fairgrounds on Third Mondays, he always seemed to have a new set of dogs. One morning he traded two pocket knives for a black-and-tan coonhound with limp ears and star-struck eyes. By afternoon, he had made a profit of ten dollars, and the dog had shifted owners again without even getting a meal from Buddy. After a few months, Ruby lost track of all the different dogs. In a way, she realized, their identities did flow together like a river. She thought often of Buddy's remark about the Mississippi River. He was like the river. She didn't even have an address for him, but he always showed up on Third Mondays and spent the night at her house. If he'd had a profitable day, he would take her to the Burger Chef or McDonald's. He never did the usual things, such as carry out her trash or open the truck door for her. If she were a smoker, he probably wouldn't light her cigarette.

Ruby liked his distance. He didn't act possessive. He called her up from Tennessee once to tell her he had bought a dog and named it Ruby. Then he sold the dog before he got back to town. When it was Ruby's birthday, he made nothing of that, but on another day at the fairgrounds he bought her a bracelet of Mexican silver from a wrinkled old black woman in a baseball cap who called everybody "darling." Her name was Gladys. Ruby loved the way Buddy got along with Gladys, teasing her about being his girlfriend.

"Me and Gladys go 'way back," he said, embracing the old woman flamboyantly.

"Don't believe anything this old boy tells you," said Gladys with a grin.

"Don't say I never gave you nothing," Buddy said to Ruby as he paid for the bracelet. He didn't fasten the bracelet on her wrist for her, just as he never opened the truck door for her.

The bracelet cost only three dollars, and Ruby wondered if it was authentic. "What's *Mexican* silver anyway?" she asked.

"It's good," he said. "Gladys wouldn't cheat me."

Later, Ruby kept thinking of the old woman. Her merchandise was set out on the tailgate of her station wagon—odds and ends of carnival glass, some costume jewelry, and six Barbie dolls. On the ground she had several crates of banties and guineas and pigeons. Their intermingled coos and chirps made Ruby wonder if Gladys slept in her station wagon listening to the music of her birds, the way Buddy slept in his truck with his dogs.

The last time he'd come to town—the week before her operation—Ruby traveled with him to a place over in the Ozarks to buy some pit bull terriers. They drove several hours on interstates, and Buddy rambled on excitedly about the new dogs, as though there were something he could discover about the nature of dogs by owning a pit bull terrier. Ruby, who had traveled little, was intensely interested in the scenery, but she said, "If these are mountains, then I'm disappointed."

"You ought to see the Rockies," said Buddy knowingly. "Talk about mountains."

At a little grocery store, they asked for directions, and Buddy swigged on a Dr Pepper. Ruby had a Coke and a bag of pork rinds. Buddy paced around nervously outside, then unexpectedly slammed his drink bottle in the tilted crate of empties with such force that several bottles fell out and broke. At that moment, Ruby knew she probably was irrevocably in love with him, but she was afraid it was only because she needed someone. She wanted to love him for better reasons. She knew about the knot in her breast and had already scheduled the mammogram, but she didn't want to tell him. Her body made her angry, interfering that way, like a nosy neighbor.

They drove up a winding mountain road that changed to gravel, then to dirt. A bearded man without a shirt emerged from a house trailer and showed them a dozen dogs pacing in makeshift kennel runs. Ruby talked to the dogs while Buddy and the man hunkered down together under a persimmon tree. The dogs were squat and broad-shouldered, with squinty eyes. They were the same kind of dog the Little

Rascals had had in the movies. They hurled themselves against the shaky wire, and Ruby told them to hush. They looked at her with cocked heads. When Buddy finally crated up four dogs, the owner looked as though he would cry.

At a motel that night—the first time Ruby had ever stayed in a motel with a man—she felt that the knot in her breast had a presence of its own. Her awareness of it made it seem like a little energy source, like the radium dial of a watch glowing in the dark. Lying close to Buddy, she had the crazy feeling that it would burn a hole through him.

During *The Tonight Show,* she massaged his back with baby oil, rubbing it in thoroughly, as if she were polishing a piece of fine furniture.

"Beat on me," he said. "Just like you were tenderizing steak."

"Like this?" She pounded his hard muscles with the edge of her hand.

"That feels wonderful."

"Why are you so tensed up?"

"Just so I can get you to do this. Don't stop."

Ruby pummeled his shoulder with her fist. Outside, a dog barked. "That man you bought the dogs from looked so funny," she said. "I thought he was going to cry. He must have loved those dogs."

"He was just scared."

"How come?"

"He didn't want to get in trouble." Buddy raised up on an elbow and looked at her. "He was afraid I was going to use those dogs in a dogfight, and he didn't want to be traced."

"I thought they were hunting dogs."

"No. He trained them to fight." He grasped her hand and guided it to a spot on his back. "Right there. Work that place out for me." As Ruby rubbed in a hard circle with her knuckles, he said, "They're good friendly dogs if they're treated right."

Buddy punched off the TV button and smoked a cigarette in the dark, lying with one arm under her shoulders. "You know what I'd like?" he said suddenly. "I'd like to build me a log cabin somewhere—off in the mountains maybe. Just a place for me and some dogs."

"Just you? I'd come with you if you went to the Rocky Mountains."

"How good are you at survival techniques?" he said. "Can you fish? Can you chop wood? Could you live without a purse?"

"I might could." Ruby smiled to herself at the thought.

"Women always have to have a lot of baggage along—placemats and teapots and stuff."

"I wouldn't."

"You're funny."

"Not as funny as you." Ruby shifted her position. His hand under her was hurting her ribs.

"I'll tell you a story. Listen." He sounded suddenly confessional. He sat up and flicked sparks at the ashtray. He said, "My daddy died last year, and this old lady he married was just out to get what he had. He heired her two thousand dollars, and my sister and me were to get the homeplace—the house, the barn, and thirty acres of bottomland. But before he was cold in the ground, she had stripped the place and sold every stick of furniture. Everything that was loose, she took."

"That's terrible."

"My sister sells Tupperware, and she was in somebody's house, and she recognized the bedroom suit. She said, 'Don't I know that?' and this person said, 'Why, yes, I believe that was your daddy's. I bought it at such-and-such auction.' "

"What an awful thing to do to your daddy!" Ruby said.

"He taught me everything I know about training dogs. I learned it from him and he picked it up from his daddy." Buddy jabbed his cigarette in the ashtray. "He knew everything there was to know about field dogs."

"I bet you don't have much to do with your stepmother now."

"She really showed her butt," he said with a bitter laugh. "But really it's my sister who's hurt. She wanted all those keepsakes. There was a lot of Mama's stuff. Listen, I see that kind of sorrow every day in my line of work—all those stupid, homeless dishes people trade. People buy all that stuff and decorate with it and think it means something."

"I don't do that," Ruby said.

"I don't keep anything. I don't want anything to remind me of *any*thing."

Ruby sat up and tried to see him in the dark, but he was a shadowy form, like the strange little mountains she had seen outside at twilight. The new dogs were noisy—bawling and groaning fitfully. Ruby said, "Hey, you're not going to get them dogs to fight, are you?"

"Nope. But I'm not responsible for what anybody else wants to do. I'm just the middleman."

Buddy turned on the light to find his cigarettes. With relief, Ruby saw how familiar he was—his tanned, chunky arms, and the mustache under his nose like the brush on her vacuum cleaner. He was tame and gentle, like his best dogs. "They make good watchdogs," he said. "Listen at 'em!" He laughed like a man watching a funny movie.

"They must see the moon," Ruby said. She turned out the light and tiptoed across the scratchy carpet. Through a crack in the curtains she could see the dark humps of the hills against the pale sky, but it was cloudy and she could not see the moon.

Everything is round and full now, like the moon. Linda's belly. Bowling balls. On TV, Steve Martin does a comedy routine, a parody of the song, "I Believe." He stands before a gigantic American flag and recites his beliefs. He says he doesn't believe a woman's breasts should be referred to derogatorily as jugs, or boobs, or Winnebagos. "I believe they should be referred to as hooters," he says solemnly. Winnebagos? Ruby wonders.

After the operation, she does everything left-handed. She has learned to extend her right arm and raise it slightly. Next, the doctors have told her, she will gradually reach higher and higher—an idea that thrills her, as though there were something tangible above her to reach for. It surprises her, too, to learn what her left hand has been missing. She feels like a newly blind person discovering the subtleties of sound.

Trying to sympathize with her, the women on her bowling team offer their confessions. Nancy has such severe monthly cramps that even the new miracle pills on the market don't work. Linda had a miscarriage when she was in high school. Betty admits her secret, something Ruby suspected anyway: Betty shaves her face every morning with a Lady Sunbeam. Her birth-control pills had stimulated facial hair. She stopped taking the pills years ago but still has the beard.

Ruby's mother calls these problems "female trouble." It is Mom's theory that Ruby injured her breasts by lifting too many heavy boxes in her job with a wholesale grocer. Several of her friends have tipped or fallen wombs caused by lifting heavy objects, Mom says.

"I don't see the connection," says Ruby. It hurts her chest when she laughs, and her mother looks offended. Mom, who has been keeping Ruby company in the afternoons since she came home from the hospital, today is making Ruby some curtains to match the new bedspread on her double bed.

"When you have a weakness, disease can take hold," Mom explains. "When you abuse the body, it shows up in all kinds of ways. And women just weren't built to do man's work. You were always so independent you ended up doing man's work and woman's work both."

"Let's not get into why I never married," says Ruby.

Mom's sewing is meticulous and definite, work that would burn about two calories an hour. She creases a hem with her thumb and folds the curtain neatly. Then she stands up and embraces Ruby carefully, favoring her daughter's right side. She says, "Honey, if there was such of a thing as a transplant, I'd give you one of mine."

"That's O.K., Mom. Your big hooters wouldn't fit me."

At the bowling alley, Ruby watches while her team, Garrison Life Insurance, bowls against Thomas & Sons Plumbing. Her team is getting smacked.

"We're pitiful without you and Linda," Betty tells her. "Linda's got too big to bowl. I told her to come anyway and watch, but she wouldn't listen. I think maybe she *is* embarrassed to be seen in public, despite what she said."

"She doesn't give a damn what people think," says Ruby, as eight pins crash for Thomas & Sons. "Me neither," she adds, tilting her can of Coke.

"Did you hear she's getting a heavy-duty washer? She says a heavy-duty holds forty-five diapers."

Ruby lets a giggle escape. "She's not going to any more laundromats and get knocked up again."

"Are you still going with that guy you met at Third Monday?"

"I'll see him Monday. He's supposed to take me home with him to Tennessee, but the doctor said I can't go yet."

"I heard he didn't know about your operation," says Betty, giving her bowling ball a little hug.

Ruby takes a drink of Coke and belches. "He'll find out soon enough."

"Well, you stand your ground, Ruby Jane. If he can't love you for yourself, then to heck with him."

"But people always love each other for the wrong reasons!" Ruby says. "Don't you know that?"

Betty stands up, ignoring Ruby. It's her turn to bowl. She says, "Just be thankful, Ruby. I like the way you get out and go. Later on, bowling will be just the right thing to build back your strength."

"I can already reach to here," says Ruby, lifting her right hand to touch Betty's arm. Ruby smiles. Betty has five-o'clock shadow.

The familiar crying of the dogs at Third Monday makes Ruby anxious and jumpy. They howl and yelp and jerk their chains—sound effects in a horror movie. As Ruby walks through the oak grove, the dogs lunge toward her, begging recognition. A black Lab in a tiny cage glares at her savagely. She notices dozens of blueticks and beagles, but she doesn't see Buddy's truck. As she hurries past some crates of ducks and rabbits and pullets, a man in overalls stops her. He is holding a pocket knife and, in one hand, an apple cut so precisely that the core is a perfect rectangle.

"I can't 'call your name," he says to her. "But I know I know you."

"I don't know *you,* " says Ruby. Embarrassed, the man backs away.

The day is already growing hot. Ruby buys a Coke from a man with a washtub of ice and holds it with her right hand, testing the tension on her right side. The Coke seems extremely heavy. She lifts it to her lips with her left hand. Buddy's truck is not there.

Out in the sun, she browses through a box of *National Enquirers* and paperback romances, then wanders past tables of picture frames, clocks, quilts, dishes. The dishes are dirty and mismatched—odd plates and cups and gravy boats. There is nothing she would want. She skirts a truckload of shock absorbers. The heat is making her dizzy. She is still weak from her operation. "I wouldn't pay fifteen dollars for a corn sheller," someone says. The remark seems funny to Ruby, like something she might have heard on Sodium Pentothal. Then a man bumps into her with a wire basket containing two young gray cats. A short, dumpy woman shouts to her, "Don't listen to him. He's trying to sell you them cats. Who ever heard of buying cats?"

Gladys has rigged up a canvas canopy extending out from the back of her station wagon. She is sitting in an aluminum folding chair, with her hands crossed in her lap, looking cool. Ruby longs to confide in her. She seems to be a trusty fixture, something stable in the current, like a cypress stump.

"Buy some mushmelons, darling," says Gladys. Gladys is selling banties, Fiestaware, and mushmelons today.

"Mushmelons give me gas."

Gladys picks up a newspaper and fans her face. "Them seeds been in my family over a hundred years. We always saved the seed."

"Is that all the way back to slave times?"

Gladys laughs as though Ruby has told a hilarious joke. "These here's my roots!" she says. "Honey, we's *in* slave times, if you ask me. Slave times ain't never gone out of style, if you know what I mean."

Ruby leans forward to catch the breeze from the woman's newspaper. She says, "Have you seen Buddy, the guy I run around with? He's usually here in a truck with a bunch of dogs?"

"That pretty boy that bought you that bracelet?"

"I was looking for him."

"Well, you better look hard, darling, if you want to find him. He got picked up over in Missouri for peddling a hot TV. They caught him on the spot. They'd been watching him. You don't believe me, but it's true. Oh, honey, I'm sorry, but he'll be back! He'll be back!"

In the waiting room at the clinic, the buzz of a tall floor fan sounds like a June bug on a screen door. The fan waves its head wildly from side to side. Ruby has an appointment for her checkup at three o'clock. She is afraid they will give her radiation treatments, or maybe even chemotherapy. No one is saying exactly what will happen next. But she expects to be baptized in a vat of chemicals, burning her skin and sizzling her hair. Ruby recalls an old comedy sketch, in which one of the Smothers Brothers fell into a vat of chocolate. Buddy Landon used to dunk his dogs in a tub of flea dip. She never saw him do it, but she pictures it in her mind—the stifling smell of Happy Jack mange medicine, the surprised dogs shaking themselves afterward, the rippling black water. It's not hard to imagine Buddy in a jail cell either—thrashing around sleeplessly in a hard bunk, reaching over to squash a cigarette butt on the concrete floor—but the image is so inappropriate it is like something from a bad dream. Ruby keeps imagining different scenes in which he comes back to town and they take off for the Rocky Mountains together. Everyone has always said she had imagination—imagination and a sense of humor.

A pudgy man with fat fists and thick lips sits next to her on the bench at the clinic, humming. With him is a woman in a peach-colored pants suit and with tight white curls. The man grins and points to a child across the room. "That's my baby," he says to Ruby. The little girl, squealing with joy, is riding up and down on her mother's knee. The pudgy man says something unintelligible.

"He loves children," says the white-haired woman.

"My baby," he says, making a cradle with his arms and rocking them.

"He has to have those brain tests once a year," says the woman to Ruby in a confidential whisper.

The man picks up a magazine and says, "This is my baby." He hugs the magazine and rocks it in his arms. His broad smile curves like the crescent phase of the moon.

1982

ANNE TYLER

(1941–)

Born in Minneapolis, Minnesota, but raised in North Carolina, Anne Tyler attended Duke University. Graduating Phi Beta Kappa at nineteen in 1961, she spent the next year in Russian studies at Columbia University before returning to North Carolina as a Russian bibliographer in the Duke University library in 1962–1963. Married in 1963 to Taghi Modarressi, a psychologist, she has lived since then in Montreal, where she worked in the McGill University library in 1964–1965, and in Baltimore, Maryland, where she has devoted herself to her family and her writing.

Her first novel, *If Morning Ever Comes* (1964), was written in the early months of her marriage, when she was briefly unemployed. This and *The Tin Can Tree* (1965) are apprentice works, lacking the power she has since developed. In *A Slipping-Down Life* (1970), however, written under the pressure of new motherhood, the story she tells of a self-mutilated teenager displays an advance she has called "for me, a certain brave stepping forth." Works of increased strength followed. *Celestial Navigation* (1974) tells of an artist's attempt to make contact with others, although he is most comfortable enclosed in his room with his work. *Dinner at the Homesick Restaurant* (1982), her ninth novel and most celebrated to date, portrays a family whose individual members remain continually estranged as they strive again and again to sit down, just once, to complete a family dinner together. In *The Accidental Tourist* (1985), a story of a man who writes travel books for people who prefer to stay home, she develops a metaphor that seems important for all her work, as we all travel paths we didn't choose.

Tyler's world is close to home, North Carolina or Baltimore. Alienation and loneliness haunt her people as they try to connect with a past in another place or a present where they do not fit. They behave sometimes inexplicably, perhaps because, as one of them says in *A Slipping-Down Life,* "Impulse was the clue." They want more from life than ever comes to them within the minor tragedies that the mother summarizes in *Dinner at the Homesick Restaurant:* "Her one mistake: a simple error of judgment. It should not have had such far-reaching effects. You would think that life could be a little more forgiving."

Novels not mentioned above are *The Clock Winder,* 1972; *Searching for Caleb,* 1976; *Earthly Possessions,* 1977; and *Morgan's Passing,* 1980. Tyler's short stories are uncollected. Brief appraisals appear in Catherine Rainwater and William J. Scheick, eds., *Contemporary American Women Writers: Narrative Strategies,* 1985. *Dictionary of Literary Biography, Volume 6: American Novelists Since World War II, Second Series,* 1980; and James Vinson, ed., *Contemporary Novelists,* 4th ed., 1986.

Average Waves in Unprotected Waters[1]

As soon as it got light, Bet woke him and dressed him, and then she walked him over to the table and tried to make him eat a little cereal. He wouldn't, though. He could tell something was up. She pressed the edge of the spoon against his lips till she heard it click on his teeth, but he just looked off at a corner of the ceiling—a knobby child with great glassy eyes and her own fair hair. Like any other nine-year-old, he wore a striped shirt and jeans, but the shirt was too neat and the jeans too blue, unpatched and unfaded, and would stay that way till he outgrew them. And his face was elderly—pinched, strained, tired—though it should have looked as unused as his jeans. He hardly ever changed his expression.

She left him in his chair and went to make the beds. Then she raised the yellowed shade, rinsed a few spoons in the bathroom sink, picked up some bits of magazines he'd torn the night before. This was a rented room in an ancient, crumbling house, and nothing you could do to it would lighten its cluttered look. There was always that feeling of too many lives layered over other lives, like the layers of brownish wallpaper her child had peeled away in the corner by his bed.

She slipped her feet into flat-heeled loafers and absently patted the front of her dress, a worn beige knit she usually saved for Sundays. Maybe she should take it in a little; it hung from her shoulders like a sack. She felt too slight and frail, too wispy for all she had to do today. But she reached for her coat anyhow, and put it on and tied a blue kerchief under her chin. Then she went over to the table and slowly spun, modelling the coat. "See, Arnold?" she said. "We're going out."

Arnold went on looking at the ceiling, but his gaze turned wild and she knew he'd heard.

She fetched his jacket from the closet—brown corduroy, with a hood. It had set her back half a week's salary. But Arnold didn't like it; he always wanted his old one, a little red duffel coat he'd long ago outgrown. When she came toward him, he started moaning and rocking and shaking his head. She had to struggle to stuff his arms in the sleeves. Small though he was, he was strong, wiry; he was getting to be too much for her. He shook free of her hands and ran over to his bed. The jacket

1. Published in *The New Yorker,* February 28, 1977, the source of the present text.

was on, though. It wasn't buttoned, the collar was askew, but never mind; that just made him look more real. She always felt bad at how he stood inside his clothes, separate from them, passive, unaware of all the buttons and snaps she'd fastened as carefully as she would a doll's.

She gave a last look around the room, checked to make sure the hot plate was off, and then picked up her purse and Arnold's suitcase. "Come along, Arnold," she said.

He came, dragging out every step. He looked at the suitcase suspiciously, but only because it was new. It didn't have any meaning for him. "See?" she said. "It's yours. It's Arnold's. It's going on the train with us."

But her voice was all wrong. He would pick it up, for sure. She paused in the middle of locking the door and glanced over at him fearfully. Anything could set him off nowadays. He hadn't noticed, though. He was too busy staring around the hallway, goggling at a freckled, walnut-framed mirror as if he'd never seen it before. She touched his shoulder. "Come, Arnold," she said.

They went down the stairs slowly, both of them clinging to the sticky mahogany railing. The suitcase banged against her shins. In the entrance hall, old Mrs. Puckett stood waiting outside her door—a huge, soft lady in a black crêpe dress and orthopedic shoes. She was holding a plastic bag of peanut-butter cookies, Arnold's favorites. There were tears in her eyes. "Here, Arnold," she said, quavering. Maybe she felt to blame that he was going. But she'd done the best she could: babysat him all these years and only given up when he'd grown too strong and wild to manage. Bet wished Arnold would give the old lady some sign—hug her, make his little crowing noise, just take the cookies, even. But he was too excited. He raced on out the front door, and it was Bet who had to take them. "Well, thank you, Mrs. Puckett," she said. "I know he'll enjoy them later."

"Oh, no . . ." said Mrs. Puckett, and she flapped her large hands and gave up, sobbing.

They were lucky and caught a bus first thing. Arnold sat by the window. He must have thought he was going to work with her; when they passed the red-and-gold Kresge's sign, he jabbered and tried to stand up. "No, honey," she said, and took hold of his arm. He settled down then and let his hand stay curled in hers awhile. He had very small, cool fingers, and nails as smooth as thumbtack heads.

At the train station, she bought the tickets and then a pack of Wrigley's spearmint gum. Arnold stood gaping at the vaulted ceiling, with his head flopped back and his arms hanging limp at his sides. People stared at him. She would have liked to push their faces in. "Over here, honey," she said, and she nudged him toward the gate, straightening his collar as they walked.

He hadn't been on a train before and acted a little nervous, bouncing up and down in his seat and flipping the lid of his ashtray and craning forward to see the man ahead of them. When the train started moving, he crowed and pulled at her sleeve. "That's right, Arnold. Train. We're taking a trip," Bet said. She unwrapped a stick of chewing gum and gave it to him. He loved gum. If she didn't watch him closely, he sometimes swallowed it—which worried her a little because she'd heard it clogged your kidneys; but at least it would keep him busy. She looked down at the top of his head. Through the blond prickles of his hair, cut short for practical reasons, she could see his skull bones moving as he chewed. He was so thin-skinned, almost transparent; sometimes she imagined she could see the blood travelling in his veins.

When the train reached a steady speed, he grew calmer, and after a while he nodded over against her and let his hands sag on his knees. She watched his eyelashes slowly drooping—two colorless, fringed crescents, heavier and heavier, every now and then flying up as he tried to fight off sleep. He had never slept well, not ever, not even as a baby. Even before they'd noticed anything wrong, they'd wondered at his jittery, jerky catnaps, his tiny hands clutching tight and springing open, his strange single wail sailing out while he went right on sleeping. Avery said it gave him the chills. And after the doctor talked to them Avery wouldn't have anything to do with Arnold anymore—just walked in wide circles around the crib, looking stunned and sick. A few weeks later, he left. She wasn't surprised. She even knew how he felt, more or less. Halfway, he blamed her; halfway, he blamed himself. You can't believe a thing like this will just fall on you out of nowhere.

She'd had moments herself of picturing some kind of evil gene in her husband's ordinary, stocky body—a dark little egg like a black jelly bean, she imagined it. All his fault. But other times she was sure the gene was hers. It seemed so natural; she never could do anything as well as most people. And then other times she blamed their marriage. They'd married too young, against her parents' wishes. All she'd wanted was to get away from home. Now she couldn't remember why. What was wrong with home? She thought of her parents' humped green trailer, perched on cinder blocks near a forest of masts in Salt Spray, Maryland. At this distance (parents dead, trailer rusted to bits, even Salt Spray changed past recognition), it seemed to her that her old life had been beautifully free and spacious. She closed her eyes and saw wide gray skies. Everything had been ruled by the sea. Her father (who'd run a fishing boat for tourists) couldn't arrange his day till he'd heard the marine forecast—the wind, the tides, the small-craft warnings, the height of average waves in unprotected waters. He loved to fish, offshore and on, and he swam every chance he could get. He'd tried to teach her to bodysurf, but it hadn't worked out. There was something about the breakers: she just gritted her teeth and stood staunch and let them slam into her. As if standing staunch were a virtue, really. She couldn't explain it. Her father thought she was scared, but it wasn't that at all.

She'd married Avery against their wishes and been sorry ever since—sorry to move so far from home, sorrier when her parents died within a year of each other, sorriest of all when the marriage turned grim and cranky. But she never would have thought of leaving him. It was Avery who left; she would have stayed forever. In fact, she did stay on in their apartment for months after he'd gone, though the rent was far too high. It wasn't that she expected him back. She just took some comfort from enduring.

Arnold's head snapped up. He looked around him and made a gurgling sound. His chewing gum fell onto the front of his jacket. "Here, honey," she told him. She put the gum in her ashtray. "Look out the window. See the cows?"

He wouldn't look. He began bouncing in his seat, rubbing his hands together rapidly.

"Arnold? Want a cookie?"

If only she'd brought a picture book. She'd meant to and then forgot. She wondered if the train people sold magazines. If she let him get too bored, he'd go into one of his tantrums, and then she wouldn't be able to handle him. The doctor had given her pills just in case, but she was always afraid that while he was screaming he would choke on them. She looked around the car. "Arnold," she said, "see the . . . see the hat with feathers on? Isn't it pretty? See the red suitcase? See the, um . . ."

The car door opened with a rush of clattering wheels and the conductor burst in, singing "Girl of my dreams, I love you." He lurched down the aisle, plucking pink tickets from the back of each seat. Just across from Bet and Arnold, he stopped. He was looking down at a tiny black lady in a purple coat, with a fox fur piece biting its own tail around her neck. "You!" he said.

The lady stared straight ahead.

"You, I saw you. You're the one in the washroom."

A little muscle twitched in her cheek.

"You got on this train in Beulah, didn't you. Snuck in the washroom. Darted back like you thought you could put something over on me. I saw that bit of purple! Where's your ticket gone to?"

She started fumbling in a blue cloth purse. The fumbling went on and on. The conductor shifted his weight.

"Why!" she said finally. "I must've left it back in my other seat."

"What other seat?"

"Oh, the one back . . ." She waved a spidery hand.

The conductor sighed. "Lady," he said, "you owe me money."

"I do no such thing!" she said. "Viper! Monger! Hitler!" Her voice screeched up all at once; she sounded like a parrot. Bet winced and felt herself flushing, as if *she* were the one. But then at her shoulder she heard a sudden, rusty clang, and she turned and saw that Arnold was laughing. He had his mouth wide open and his tongue curled, the way he did when he watched "Sesame Street." Even after the scene had worn itself out, and the lady had paid and the conductor had moved on, Arnold went on chortling and la-la-ing, and Bet looked gratefully at the little black lady, who was settling her fur piece fussily and muttering under her breath.

From the Parkinsville Railroad Station, which they seemed to be tearing down or else remodelling—she couldn't tell which—they took a taxicab to Parkins State Hospital. "Oh, I been out there many and many a time," said the driver. "Went out there just the other—"

But she couldn't stop herself; she had to tell him before she forgot. "Listen," she said, "I want you to wait for me right in the driveway. I don't want you to go on away."

"Well, fine," he said.

"Can you do that? I want you to be sitting right by the porch or the steps or whatever, right where I come out of, ready to take me back to the station. Don't just go off and—"

"I *got* you, I got you," he said.

She sank back. She hoped he understood.

Arnold wanted a peanut-butter cookie. He was reaching and whimpering. She didn't know what to do. She wanted to give him anything he asked for, anything; but he'd get it all over his face and arrive not looking his best. She couldn't stand it if they thought he was just ordinary and unattractive. She wanted them to see how small and neat he was, how somebody cherished him. But it would be awful if he went into one of his rages. She broke off a little piece of cookie from the bag. "Here," she told him. "Don't mess, now."

He flung himself back in the corner and ate it, keeping one hand flattened across his mouth while he chewed.

The hospital looked like someone's great, pillared mansion, with square brick buildings all around it. "Here we are," the driver said.

"Thank you," she said. "Now you wait here, please. Just wait till I get—"

"Lady," he said. "I'll wait."

She opened the door and nudged Arnold out ahead of her. Lugging the suitcase, she started toward the steps. "Come on, Arnold," she said.

He hung back.

"Arnold?"

Maybe he wouldn't allow it, and they would go on home and never think of this again.

But he came, finally, climbing the steps in his little hobbled way. His face was clean, but there were a few cookie crumbs on his jacket. She set down the suitcase to brush them off. Then she buttoned all his buttons and smoothed his shirt collar over his jacket collar before she pushed open the door.

In the admitting office, a lady behind a wooden counter showed her what papers to sign. Secretaries were clacketing typewriters all around. Bet thought Arnold might like that, but instead he got lost in the lights—chilly, hanging ice-cube-tray lights with a little flicker to them. He gazed upward, looking astonished. Finally a flat-fronted nurse came in and touched his elbow. "Come along, Arnold. Come, Mommy. We'll show you where Arnold is staying," she said.

They walked back across the entrance hall, then up wide marble steps with hollows worn in them. Arnold clung to the bannister. There was a smell Bet hated, pine-oil disinfectant, but Arnold didn't seem to notice. You never knew; sometimes smells could just put him in a state.

The nurse unlocked a double door that had chicken-wired windows. They walked through a corridor, passing several fat, ugly women in shapeless gray dresses and ankle socks. "Ha!" one of the women said, and fell giggling into the arms of a friend. The nurse said, *"Here* we are." She led them into an enormous hallway lined with little white cots. Nobody else was in it; there wasn't a sign that children lived here except for a tiny cardboard clown picture hanging on one vacant wall. "This one is your bed, Arnold," said the nurse. Bet laid the suitcase on it. It was made up so neatly, the sheets might have been painted on. A steely-gray blanket was folded across the foot. She looked over at Arnold, but he was pivoting back and forth to hear how his new sneakers squeaked on the linoleum.

"Usually," said the nurse, "we like to give new residents six months before the family visits. That way they settle in quicker, don't you see." She turned away and adjusted the clown picture, though as far as Bet could tell it was fine the way it was. Over her shoulder, the nurse said, "You can tell him goodbye now, if you like."

"Oh," Bet said. "All right." She set her hands on Arnold's shoulders. Then she laid her face against his hair, which felt warm and fuzzy. "Honey," she said. But he went on pivoting. She straightened and told the nurse, "I brought his special blanket."

"Oh, fine," said the nurse, turning toward her again. "We'll see that he gets it."

"He always likes to sleep with it; he has ever since he was little."

"All right."

"Don't wash it. He hates if you wash it."

"Yes. Say goodbye to Mommy now, Arnold."

"A lot of times he'll surprise you. I mean there's a whole lot to him. He's not just—"

"We'll take very good care of him, Mrs. Blevins, don't worry."

"Well," she said. "'Bye, Arnold."

She left the ward with the nurse and went down the corridor. As the nurse was unlocking the doors for her, she heard a single, terrible scream, but the nurse only patted her shoulder and pushed her gently on through.

In the taxi, Bet said, "Now, I've just got fifteen minutes to get to the station. I wonder if you could hurry?"

"Sure thing," the driver said.

She folded her hands and looked straight ahead. Tears seemed to be coming down her face in sheets.

Once she'd reached the station, she went to the ticket window. "Am I in time for the twelve-thirty-two?" she asked.

"Easily," said the man. "It's twenty minutes late."

"What?"

"Got held up in Norton somehow."

"But you can't!" she said. The man looked startled. She must be a sight, all swollen-eyed and wet-cheeked. "Look," she said, in a lower voice. "I figured this on purpose. I chose the one train from Beulah that would let me catch another one back without waiting. I do not want to sit and wait in this station."

"Twenty *minutes*, lady. That's all it is."

"What am I going to do?" she asked him.

He turned back to his ledgers.

She went over to a bench and sat down. Ladders and scaffolding towered above her, and only ten or twelve passengers were dotted through the rest of the station. The place looked bombed out—nothing but a shell. "Twenty minutes!" she said aloud. "What am I going to do?"

Through the double glass doors at the far end of the station, a procession of gray-suited men arrived with briefcases. More men came behind them, dressed in work clothes, carrying folding chairs, black trunklike boxes with silver hinges, microphones, a wooden lectern, and an armload of bunting. They set the lectern down in the center of the floor, not six feet from Bet. They draped the bunting across it—an arc of red, white, and blue. Wires were connected, floodlights were lit. A microphone screeched. One of the workmen said, "Try her, Mayor." He held the microphone out to a fat man in a suit, who cleared his throat and said, "Ladies and gentlemen, on the occasion of the expansion of this fine old railway station—"

"Sure do get an echo here," the workman said. "Keep on going."

The Mayor cleared his throat again. "If I may," he said, "I'd like to take about twenty minutes of your time, friends."

He straightened his tie. Bet blew her nose, and then she wiped her eyes and smiled. They had come just for her sake, you might think. They were putting on a sort of private play. From now on, all the world was going to be like that—just something on a stage, for her to sit back and watch.

1977

BARRY HANNAH

(1942–)

Barry Hannah was born in Meridian, Mississippi, and raised in Clinton, where his father was an insurance agent. As an undergraduate at Mississippi College in Clinton, he pursued a premedical program and worked as a research assistant in pharmacology at the University of Mississippi Medical Center in Jackson. He graduated in 1964. Turning to literature, he studied English at the University of Alabama, receiving an M.A. in 1966 and an M.F.A. in 1967. For the next dozen years he taught first at Clemson and then at the University of Alabama. Leaving teaching briefly in 1980 to work on films with Robert Altman in Hollywood, he soon returned and, in addition to visiting appointments at Iowa and Montana, has taught most recently at the University of Mississippi.

Hannah has been acclaimed as the inheritor of the Southern Gothic tradition of Faulkner, Welty, and O'Connor. Close at hand as he grew up were memorials of the defeated South: Jackson had been the headquarters for the Vicksburg campaign of the Civil War, and the Vicksburg National Military Park was not far away. He grew into young manhood amidst the contemporary violence of Vietnam and, much closer to home, the racial unrest and violence of the fifties and sixties, some of it centered in Jackson. Against this background, he wrote his remarkable first novel, *Geronimo Rex* (1972), a *bildungsroman* in which the youthful protagonist moves toward a vocation as a writer but cannot lose his identification with Geronimo, whom he fancies he physically resembles. In graduate school, reading Henry James, he is "just about fainting with boredom." He accentuates his resemblance to Geronimo, however, with his dress and his attitudes, seeing the defeated Indian as "peering out miserably from a cage in the zoo of American history," and asserting that he especially liked him because he "had cheated, lied, stolen, mutinied, usurped, killed, burned, raped, pillaged * * * revenged, prevenged, avenged, and was his own man."

Hannah's work is characterized by physical violence, discontinuous plots, and verbal pyrotechnics. *Nightwatchmen* (1973), which he has called "my most deliberately Gothic book," contains murders, beheadings, and a hurricane. *Airships* (1978) collects stories, some related to incidents in the published novels, some to an ongoing interest in the exploits of Confederate General Jeb Stuart. *Ray* (1981), a very short novel, follows the loves and sexual obsessions of a doctor, formerly a pilot in Vietnam. *The Tennis Handsome* (1983), more self-assured than much of the earlier work, creates a rich and complicated intermingling of the lives of several generations of Vicksburg people, ranging in time from the 1920's onward, and in space from Vicksburg, to New Orleans, to Vietnam, Boston, New York, the West Coast, the Midwest, and Canada. *Captain Maximus* (1985) gathers more short fiction.

Hannah's books to date are named above. A brief appraisal appears in *Dictionary of Literary Biography, Volume 6: American Novelists Since World War II, Second Series,* 1980.

Midnight and I'm Not Famous Yet[1]

I was walking round Gon one night, and this C-man—I saw him open the window, and there was a girl in back of him so I thought it was all right—peeled down on me and shot the heel off my boot. Nearest I came to getting mailed home when I was there. A jeep came by almost instantly with a .30 cal. mounted, couple of Allies in it. I pointed over to the window. They shot out about a box and a half on the apartment, just about burnt out the dark slot up there. As if the dude was hanging around digging the weather after he shot at me. There were shrieks in the night, etc. But then a man opened the bottom door and started running in the street. This ARVN fellow knocked the shit out of his buddy's head turning the gun to zap the running man. Then I saw something as the dude hit a light: he was fat. I never saw a fat Cong. So I screamed out in Vietnamese. He didn't shoot. I took out my machine pistol and ran after the man, who was up the street by now, and I was hobbling without a heel on my left boot.

Some kind of warm nerve sparklers were getting all over me. I believe in ESP, because, millions-to-one odds, it was Ike "Tubby" Wooten, from Redwood, a town just north of Vicksburg. He was leaning on a rail, couldn't run anymore. He was wearing the uniform of our army with a patch on it I didn't even know what was. Old Tubby would remember me. I was the joker at our school. I once pissed in a Dixie cup and eased three drops of it onto the library radiator. But Tubby was serious, reading some photo magazine. He peeped up and saw me do it, then looked down quickly. When the smell came over the place, he asked me, Why? What do you want? What profit is there in that? I would just giggle. Sometimes around midnight I'd wake up and think of his questions, and it disturbed me that there was no answer. I giggled my whole youth away. Then I joined the army. So I thought it was fitting I'd play a Nelda on him now. A Nelda was invented by a corporal when they massacred a patrol up north on a mountain and he was the only one left. The NVA ran all around him and he had this empty rifle hanging on him. They spared him.

"I'm a virgin. Spare me." In Vietnamese.

"You, holding the gun? Did you say you were a virgin?" said poor Tubby, trying to get air.

"I am a virgin," I said, which was true. This was in English.

"And a Southern virgin. A captain. Please to God, don't shoot me. I was cheating on my wife for the first time. The penalty shouldn't be death."

"Why'd you run from the house, Tubby?"

"You know me?"

Up the street they had searchlights moved up all over the apartment house. They shot about fifty rounds into the house. They were shooting tracers now. It must've lit up my face; then a spotlight went by us.

"Bobby Smith," said Tubby. "I thought you were God."

"I'm not. But it seems holy. Here we are looking at each other."

"Aw, Bobby, they were three beautiful girls. I'd never have done the thing with one, but there were three." He was a man with a small pretty face laid around by

1. First published in *Esquire,* "Midnight and I'm Not Famous Yet" was among the stories collected in *Airships* (1978). It was later revised as a chapter in *The Tennis Handsome* (1983), the version here printed.

three layers of jowl and chin. "I heard the machine gun and the guilt struck me. I had to get out. So I just ran."

"Why're you in Nam, anyway?"

"I joined. I wasn't getting anything done but being in love with my wife. That wasn't doing America any good."

"What's that patch on you?"

"Photography." He lifted his hands to hold an imaginary camera. "I'm with the Big Red. I've done a few things out of helicopters."

"You want to see a ground unit? With me. Or does Big Red own you?"

"I have no idea. There hasn't been much to shoot. Some smoking villages. A fire in a bamboo forest. I'd like to see a face."

"You got any pictures of Vicksburg?"

"Oh, well, a few I brought over."

The next day I found out he was doing idlework and Big Red didn't care where he was, so I got him over in my unit. I worried about his weight, etc., and the fact he might get killed. But the boys liked a movie-camerist being along and I wanted to see the pictures from Vicksburg. It was nice to have Tubby alongside. He was my symbol of hometown. Before we flew out north, he showed me what he had. There was always a fine touch in his pictures. There was a cute little Negro on roller skates, an old woman on a porch, a little boy sleeping in a speedboat with the river in the background. It brought back old times. Then there was a blurred picture of his wife naked, just moving through the kitchen, nothing sexy. The last picture was the best. It was French Edward about to crack a tennis ball three inches from his racquet. Tubby had taken it at Forest Hills, the West Side Tennis Club, New York. I used to live about five houses away from the Edwards. French had his mouth open and the forearm muscles were bulked up plain as wires. French was ten years older than me. But I knew about him. He was our only celebrity since the Civil War. In the picture he wore spectacles. It struck me as something deep, brave, mighty, and, well, modern; he had to have the eyeglasses on him to see the mighty thing he was about to do. Maybe I sympathized too much, since I have to wear glasses too, but I thought this picture was worthy of a statue. Tubby had taken it in a striking gray-and-white grain. French seemed to be hitting under a heroic deficiency. You could see the sweat droplets on his neck. His eyes were in an agony. But the thing that got me was that he *cared* so much about what he was doing. It made me love America, to know he was in it, and I hadn't loved anything for maybe three years then. Tubby was talking about all this "our country" eagle and stars mooky and had seen all the war movies coming over on the boat. I never saw a higher case of fresh and crazy in my life. But the picture of French at Forest Hills, it moved me. It was a man at work and play at the same time, doing his damnedest. And French was a beautiful man. They pass that term *beautiful* around like pennies nowadays, but I saw him in the flesh once. It was an autumn in Baton Rouge, around the campus of L.S.U. French Edward was getting out of a car with a gypsyish girl on his hand. I was ten, I guess, and he was twenty. We were down for a ball game, Mississippi vs. Louisiana, a classic that makes you goo-goo-eyed when you're a full-grown man if your heart's in Dixie, etc. At ten, it's Ozville. So in the middle of it, I saw French Edward and his woman.

My dad stopped the car. "Wasn't that French Edward?" he asked my grandfather.

"You mean that little peacock who left football for tennis? He ought to be quarterbacking Ole Miss right now. It wouldn't be no contest," said my grandfather.

I got my whole idea of what a woman should look like that day—and of what a man should be. The way French Edward looked, it sort of rebuked yourself ever hoping to call yourself a man. The girl he was with woke up my clammy dreams about not even sex but the perfect thing if you had to get married and spend your time around a woman—it was something like her. As for French, his face was curled around by that wild hair the color of beer; his chest was deep, just about to bust out of that collar and bowtie.

"That girl he had, she had a drink in her hand. You could hardly see her for her hair," said my grandfather.

"French got him something Cajun," said my father.

Then my grandfather turned around, looking at me like I was a crab who could say a couple of words. "You look like your mother, but you got gray eyes. What's wrong? You have to take a leak?"

Nothing was wrong with me. I'd just seen French Edward and his female, that was all.

Tubby had jumped a half-dozen times at Fort Bragg, but he had that heavy box harnessed on him and I knew he was going down fast and better know how to hit. I explained to him. I went off the plane four behind him, cupping a joint. I didn't want Tubby seeing me smoking grass, but it's just about the only way to get down. If the Cong saw the plane, you'd fall into a barbecue. They'd killed a whole unit before, using shotguns and flame bullets, just like your ducks floating in. You heard a lot of noise going in with a whole unit in the air like this. We start shooting about a hundred feet from the ground.

If you ever hear one bullet pass you, you get sick thinking there might be hundreds of them. All you can do is point your gun down and shoot it out. You can't reload. You never hit anything. There's a sharpshooter, McIntire, who killed a C shooting from his chute. But that's unlikely. They've got you like a gallery of rabbits if they're down there.

I saw Tubby sinking fast over the wrong part of the field. I had two chutes out, so I cut one off and dropped over toward him, pulling on the lift lines so hard I almost didn't have a chute at all for a while. I got level with him and he looked over, pointing down. He was doing his arm up and down. Could have been farmers, or just curious rubbernecks down in the field, but there were about ten of them grouped up together, holding things. They weren't shooting, though. I was carrying an experimental gun, me and about ten of my boys. It was a big light thing—really it was just a launcher. There were five shells in it, bigger than shotgun shells. If you shot one of them, they were supposed to explode on impact and burn out everything in a twenty-five-yard radius. It was a mean little fucker of phosphorous, is what it was.

I saw the boys shooting them down into the other side of the field. This stuff would take down a whole tree and you'd chute into a quiet, smoking, bare area. I don't know. I don't like a group waiting on me when I jump out of a plane. I almost zapped them, but they weren't throwing anything up. Me and Tubby hit the ground about the same time. They were farmers. I talked to them. They said there were three Cong with them until we were about a hundred feet over. The Cong knew we had the phosphorous shotgun and showed ass, loping out to the woods fifty yards to the north when me and Tubby were coming in.

Tubby took some film of the farmers, all of them had thin chin beards and soft hands because their wives did most of the work. They essentially just hung around and were hung with philosophy, and actually were pretty happy. Nothing had happened around here till we jumped in.

These were fresh people.

I told them to get everybody out of the huts because we were going to have a thing in the field. It was a crisis point. A huge army of NVA was coming down and they just couldn't avoid us if they wanted to have any run of the valley five miles south. We were there to harass the front point of the army, whatever it was like.

"We're here to check their advance," Tubby told the farmers.

Then we all collected in the woods, five hundred and fifty souls scared out of mind. What we had going was we knew the NVA general bringing them down was not too bright. He went to the Sorbonne and we had this report from his professor: "Li Dap speaks French very well and had studied Napoleon before he got to me. He knows Robert Lee and the strategy of J.E.B. Stuart, whose daring circles around an immense army captured his mind. Li Dap wants to be J.E.B. Stuart. I cannot imagine him in command of more than five hundred troops."

And what we knew stood up. Li Dap had tried to circle left with twenty thousand and got the hell kicked out of him by idle navy guns sitting outside Saigon. He just wasn't very bright. He had half his army climbing around these bluffs, no artillery or air force with them, and it was New Year's Eve for our side.

"So we're here just to kill the edge of their army," said Tubby.

"That's what I'm here for," I said. "Why I'm elected. We kill more C's than anybody else in the army."

"But what if they take a big run at you, all of them?" said Tubby.

We went out in the edge of the woods and I glassed the field. It was almost night. I saw two tanks come out of the other side and our pickets running back. Pock, pock, pock from the tanks. Then you saw this white glare on one tank where somebody on our team had laid on with one of the phosphorous shotguns. It got white and throbbing, like a star, and the gun wilted off of it. The other tank ran off a gulley into a hell of a cow pond. You would haven't known it was that deep. It went underwater over the gun, and they let off the cannon when they went under, raising the water in a spray. It was the silliest thing damned near I'd ever seen. Some of them got out and a sergeant yelled for me to come up. It was about a quarter mile out there. Tubby got his camera, and we went out with about fifteen troops.

At the edge of the pond, looking into flashlights, two of their tankmen sat, one tiny, the other about my size. They were wet, and the big guy was mad. Lot of the troops were guffawing, etc. It was awfully damned funny, if you didn't happen to be one of the C-men in the tank.

"Of all the fuck-ups. This is truly saddening." The big guy was saying something like that. I took a flashlight and looked him over. Then I didn't believe it. I told Tubby to get a shot of the big cursing one. Then they brought them on back. I told them to tie up the big one and carry him in.

I sat on the ground, talking to Tubby.

"It's so quiet. You'd think they'd be shelling us," he said.

"We're spread out too good. They don't have much ammo now. They really galloped down here. That's the way Li Dap does it. Their side's got big trouble now. And Tubby, me and you're famous."

"Me, what?" Tubby said.

I said, "You took his picture. You can get some more—more arty angles on him tomorrow. Because it's Li Dap himself. He was the one in the tank in the pond."

"Their general?"

"You want me to go prove it?"

We walked over. They had him tied around a tree on a little natural hollow. His hands were above his head and he was sitting down. I smelled some hash in the air. The guy who was blowing it was a boy from Detroit I really liked, and I hated to come down on him, but I really beat him up. He never got a lick in. I kicked his rump when he was crawling away and some friends picked him up. You can't have lighting up that shit at night on the ground. Li Dap was watching the fight, still cursing.

"Asshole of the mountains." He was saying something like that. "Fortune's ninny." Like that, I think.

"Hi, General. My French isn't too good. You speak English. Honor us."

He wouldn't say anything.

I said, "You have a lot of courage, running out front with the tanks." There were some snickers in the bush, but I cut them out quick. We had the real romantic here, and I didn't want him laughed at. He wasn't hearing much, though, because about that time two of their rockets flashed into the woods. They went off in the treetops and scattered.

I said, "It was worthy of Patton. You had some bad luck. But we're glad you made it alive."

"Kiss my ass," Li Dap said.

"You want your hands free? Oliver, get his ropes off the tree." The guy I beat up cut Li Dap off the tree.

I said, "You scared us very deeply. How many tanks do you have over there?"

"Nonsense," he said.

"What do you have except for a few rockets?"

"I had no credence in the phosphorous gun."

"Your men saw us use them when we landed."

"I had no credence."

"So you just came out to see," I said.

"I say to them never to fear the machine when the cause is just. I say to throw oneself past the technology tricks of the monsters and into his soft soul."

"And there you will win, huh?"

"Of course," Li Dap said. "It is our country." He smiled at me. "It's relative to your war in the nineteenth century. The South had slavery. The North must purge it so that it is a healthy zone."

"You were out in the tank as an example to your men."

"Yes!" he said. All this hero needed was a plumed hat.

"Sleep well," I said, and told Oliver to get the general a blanket and feed him, as well as the tiny gunner with him.

When we got back to my dump, I walked away for a while, not wanting to talk with Tubby. I started crying. It came on me with these hard sobs jamming up like rocks in my throat. I started looking out across the field at forever.

They shot up three more rockets from the woods below the hill. I waited for the things to land on us. They fell on top of the trees, nothing near me. But then there was some howling off to the right. Somebody had got some shrapnel.

I'd killed so many gooks. I'd killed them with machine guns, mortars, howitzers, knives, wire—me and my boys. My boys loved me. They were lying all around me, laying this great cloud of trust on me. The picture of French Edward about to hit that ball at Forest Hills was stuck in my head. There was such care in his eyes, and it was only a tennis ball, a goddamned piece of store-bought bounce. But it was wonderful and nobody was being killed. The tears were out on my jaws then. Here we shot each other up. It seemed to me my life had gone straight from teenage giggling to horror. I had never had time to be but two things, a giggler and a killer.

I was crying for myself. I had nothing for the other side, understand that. The South Vietnamese, too. I couldn't believe we had them as our allies. They were such a pretty and uniformly indecent people. I'd seen a little taxi boy, fourteen, walk into a MEDVAC with one arm and a hand blown off by a mine he'd picked up. These housewives were walking behind him in the street, right in the middle of Gon, and they were laughing. Thought it was the most hysterical misadventure they'd ever seen.

That happened early when I got there.

I was a virgin when I got to Nam, and stayed a virgin. There was a girl everywhere, but I did not want to mingle with this race.

An ARVN stole my radio. Somebody saw him. His CO brought six goons into a small room with him. They beat him to death. When I heard what was going on, I got a MEDVAC helicopter in, but I knew he was dead when our corpsmen put him on the stretcher.

In an ARVN hospital tent, you see the headaching officers lined up in front of a private who's holding his runny stuff in with his hands. They'll treat the officer with a festered pimple first, and we're supposed to be shaking hands with these people. Why can't we be fighting for some place like England? When you train yourself to blow gooks away, like I did, something happens to you, and it's all the same, and you don't care who you kill. What I'm saying is what my state of mind was.

I needed away. I was sick. I was crying, and that's the truth.

"Bobby, are you all right?" said Tubby, waddling out to the tree I was hanging on.

"I shouldn't ever've seen that picture of French," I said. "I shouldn't've."

"Do you really think we'll be famous?" Tubby got an enchanted look on him, a sort of a dumb angel look in that small pretty face amid the fat rolls. It was about midnight. There was a fine Southern moon lighting up the field. You could see every piece of straw out there. Tubby had the high daze on him. He'd stepped out here in the boonies and put down his foot in Ozville.

"This'll get me major, anyhow. Sure," I said. "Fame. Both of us."

"I tried to get nice touches in with the light coming over his face. These pictures could turn out awfully interesting. I was thinking about *Time* or *Newsweek*."

"No two ways," I said. "The army'll love it for the prop. It'll change your whole life, Tubby."

Tubby was just about to die for love of fame. He was shivering with his joy.

I started looking at the field again. This time the straws were waving. It was covered with rushing little triangles, these sort of toiling dots. Then our side opened up. All the boys came up to join within a minute, and it was a sheet of lightning rolling back and forth along the outside of the woods. I could see it all while I was walking back to the radio. I mean humping, low. But Tubby must've been walking straight up. He took something big right in the wide of his back. It rolled him up twenty feet in front of me. He was dead and smoking when I made it to him.

"C'mon," he said. "I've got to get the pictures."

He was talking, but I think he was already dead.

I got my phosphorous shotgun. Couldn't think of anything but the radio and getting over how we were being hit so we could get copters with .50 cals. in quick. They're nice. They've got searchlights, and you put two of them over a field like we were looking at, they'd clean it out in half an hour.

So I made it to the radio, but the boys had already called them in. Everything was fine. Only we had to hold them for an hour and plus until the copters got there.

I humped up front. Every now and then you'd see somebody use one of the experimental guns. The bad thing was that it lit up the gunner too much at night, too much shine out of the muzzle. I took note of that to tell them when we got back. But the gun really smacked a good assault. It was good for about seventy-five yards and hit with a huge circle-burn about the way they said it would. Their first force was knocked off. You could see men who were still burning running back through the straw. You could hear them screaming all the way.

I don't remember too well. I was just loitering near the radio, a few fires out in the field, everything mainly quiet. Copters on the way. I decided to go take a look at Li Dap. I thought it was our boys around him, though I didn't know why. They were wearing green and standing up plain as day. There was Oliver, smoking a joint. His rifle was on the ground. You see, the thing was, the NVA were all around him and he hadn't even noticed. There were so many of them—twenty or so—they were clanking rifles against each other. One of them was going up behind Oliver with a bayonet, just about on him. If I'd had a carbine like usual, I could've taken the bayoneteer off and at least five of the others. But there were maybe twenty, as I say.

I couldn't pick and choose. I hardly even thought. The barrel of the shotgun was up and I pulled on the trigger, aiming at the bayoneteer.

Burned them all up. Nobody even made a peep. There was a flare and they were gone. Some of my boys rushed over with guns. But all they were good for was stomping out the little fires on the edges.

When we got back, I handed over Tubby's pictures. The old man was beside himself for my killing a general, a captured general. He couldn't understand what kind of laxity I'd allowed to let twenty gooks come up on us like that. They thought I might have a court martial, and for a fact I was under arrest for a week.

The story got out to UPI and they were saying things like atrocity, with my name spelled all over the column. But it was dropped, and I was pulled out and went home a lieutenant.

That's all right. I've got four hundred and two boys out there—the ones that got back—who love me and know the truth. But it's Tubby's lost fame I dream about.

The army confiscated the roll and all his pictures.

I wrote the Pentagon a letter asking for a print, and waited two years here in Vicksburg without even a statement they received the note.

I see his wife, who's remarried and is fat herself now. I see her at the discount drug every now and then. She has the look of hopeless cheer.

I got a print from the Pentagon when the war was over and it didn't matter. Li Dap looked wonderful—strained, abused, and wild, his hair flying over his eyes while he's making a speech he believes in. It made me start thinking of faces again.

Since I've been home I've got in bed with almost anything that would have me. I've slept with my old high school teachers, with Negroes, and the other night, with my own aunt.

It made her smile. All those years of keeping her body in trim came to something, the big naughty surprise that other women look for in religion, God showing up and killing their neighbors and sparing them. But she knows a lot about books, and I think I'll be in love with her.

We were at the French Edward vs. Whitney Humble match together. It was a piece of wonder. I felt thankful to whoever it was who brought that fine contest into town. When they hit the ball, the sound traveled clean all the way, and when they couldn't hit it, they did it anyway.

My aunt grabbed hold of my fingers when French lost. I liked that part of it too.

Fools! I said, or wanted to say to the people going home. Love it! I wanted to say. Nobody was killed! We saw victory and defeat and they were both wonderful.

Oh, God, thank you for America.

1978, 1983

JOHN IRVING

(1942–)

John Irving was born and raised in Exeter, New Hampshire, where his father taught at Phillips Exeter Academy. A wrestler and indifferent scholar, he was fascinated by Dickens and was telling and writing stories from his middle teens, encouraged and disciplined in his writing by his prep school teachers. After Exeter, he attended the University of Pittsburgh and the University of New Hampshire, dropping out of both to travel to Austria, where he attended the University of Vienna (1963–1964), stored up impressions important to his writing, and married. Back in the United States, he graduated from the University of New Hampshire in 1965 and gained admission to the writing program at the University of Iowa, where his teachers included Vance Bourjaily and Kurt Vonnegut. In 1967, armed with an M.F.A. from Iowa, he began teaching at Mount Holyoke College. Two years later, he published his first novel, *Setting Free the Bears* (1969), a zany picaresque work culminating in the catastrophe created when the narrator sets free the animals in a Vienna zoo.

Irving's second and third novels, *The Water-Method Man* (1972) and *The 158-Pound Marriage* (1974), earned praise but few readers. His fourth, *The World According to Garp* (1978), catapulted him into international celebrity, selling millions of copies but causing some critics to question the enduring literary value of a book so hugely popular. But Irving's model is Dickens. In *Garp,* he imitates the narrative drive, complex plot, digressions, idiosyncratic characters, and lucid prose of the nineteenth-century master, merging these elements with his own gruesome imagination of twentieth-century disasters, as

Garp, a writer, tries to make sense of the gratuitous violence and sexual distortions of his world. *The Hotel New Hampshire* (1981), in some ways more successful, displays many of the same qualities in a family chronicle ranging from teenage rape in New Hampshire through terrorist violence in Vienna to incest in Manhattan. In *The Cider House Rules* (1985) Irving mixes history and sociology, as he examines attitudes and conditions surrounding abortion in Maine during the half century preceding the great social changes of the 1960's.

Vienna, which appears in each of Irving's first five novels, was important to his developing artistry, he has said, because it "gave me great freedom. I didn't have to be responsible to Vienna. Vienna was a place I could *make up*." Günter Grass's *The Tin Drum,* a German masterpiece of the absurd, narrated by a mad dwarf, was on his mind as he wrote *Setting Free the Bears,* narrated by the student Hannes Graff. The lesson of Vienna and *The Tin Drum* was the primacy of invention; reality may be grotesquely distorted to make art. Other modernist and post-modernist works have inspired his work also, as is suggested by the epigraphs from Ford Madox Ford's *The Good Soldier* and John Hawkes's *The Blood Oranges* that set the tone for the sexual infidelities of *The 158-Pound Marriage.*

For all the contemporaneity of his subject matter, and sometimes of his technique, Irving aspires toward the union of artistry and popularity of earlier writers like Dickens. Aiming for clarity, he dismisses the language of some recent literature as self-destructively complicated. "I hate the elitism, the preciousness, the specialness of so much contemporary fiction," he has said. "I hate what is turning the novel—once the most public of forms—into something like contemporary painting and contemporary poetry; namely, largely designed for other painters and poets."

Irving's books to date are named above. A critical book is Carol Harter, *John Irving,* 1986. Brief appraisals appear in *Dictionary of Literary Biography, Volume 6: American Novelists Since World War II, Second Series,* 1980; James Vinson, ed., *Contemporary Novelists,* 4th ed., 1986; and *Dictionary of Literary Biography, Yearbook: 1982,* 1983.

The Bear Called State o' Maine[1]

That first night they saw Freud and his bear, my father and mother did not even kiss. When the band broke up, and the help retired to the male and female dormitories—the slightly less elegant buildings separate from the main hotel—my father and mother went down to the docks and watched the water. If they talked, they never told us children what they said. There must have been a few classy sailboats there, and even the private piers in Maine were sure to have a lobster boat or two moored off them. There was probably a dinghy, and my father suggested borrowing it for a short row; my mother probably refused. Fort Popham was a ruin, then, and not the tourist attraction it is today; but if there were any lights on the Fort Popham shore, they would have been visible from the Arbuthnot-by-the-Sea. Also, the broad mouth of the Kennebec River, at Bay Point, had a bell buoy and a light, and there might have been a lighthouse on Stage Island as long ago as 1939 —my father never remembered.

But generally, in those days, it would have been a dark coast, so that when the white sloop sailed toward them—out of Boston, or New York: out of the southwest and civilization, anyway—my mother and father must have seen it very clearly and watched it undistracted for the time it took to come alongside the dock. My father

1. From chapter one of *The Hotel New Hampshire* (1981).

caught the mooring line; he always told us he was at the point of panic about what to do with the rope—tie it up to something or tug it—when the man in the white dinner jacket, black slacks, and black dress shoes stepped easily off the deck and climbed the ladder up to the dock and took the rope from my father's hands. Effortlessly, the man guided the sloop past the end of the dock before he threw the rope back on board. "You're free!" he called to the boat, then. My mother and father claimed they saw no sailors on board, but the sloop slipped away, back to the sea—its yellow lights leaving like sinking glass—and the man in the dinner jacket turned to my father and said, "Thanks for the hand. Are you new here?"

"Yes, we both are," Father said.

The man's perfect clothes were unaffected by his voyage. For so early in the summer he was very tanned, and he offered my mother and father cigarettes from a handsome flat black box. They didn't smoke. "I'd hoped to catch the last dance," the man said, "but the band has retired?"

"Yes," my mother said. At nineteen, my mother and father had never seen anyone quite like this man. "He had obscene confidence," my mother told us.

"He had money," Father said.

"Have Freud and the bear arrived?" the man asked.

"Yes," Father said. "And the motorcycle."

The man in the white dinner jacket smoked hungrily, but neatly, while he looked at the dark hotel; very few rooms were lit, but the outdoor lights strung to illuminate the paths, the hedgerows, and the docks shone on the man's tanned face and made his eyes narrow and were reflected on the black, moving sea. "Freud's a Jew, you know," the man said. "It's a good thing he got out of Europe when he did, you know. Europe's going to be no place for Jews. My broker told me."

This solemn news must have impressed my father, eager to enter Harvard—and the world—and not yet aware that a war would interrupt his plans for a while. The man in the white dinner jacket caused my father to take my mother's hand into his, for the second time that evening, and again she gave back equal pressure as they politely waited for the man to finish his cigarette, or say good night, or go on.

But all he said was, "And the *world's* going to be no place for *bears!*" His teeth were as white as his dinner jacket when he laughed, and with the wind my father and mother didn't hear the hiss of his cigarette entering the ocean—or the sloop coming alongside again. Suddenly the man stepped to the ladder, and only when he slipped quickly down the rungs did Mary Bates and Win Berry realize that the white sloop was gliding under the ladder and the man was perfectly in time to drop to its deck. No rope passed hands. The sloop, not under sail but chugging slowly under other power, turned southwest (toward Boston, or New York, again)—unafraid of night travel—and what the man in the white dinner jacket last called to them was lost in the sputter of the engine, the slap of the hull on the sea, and the wind that blew the gulls by (like party hats, with feathers, bobbing in the water after drunks had thrown them there). All his life my father wished he'd heard what the man had to say.

It was Freud who told my father that he'd seen the *owner* of the Arbuthnot-by-the-Sea.

"*Ja,* that was him, all right," Freud said. "That's how he comes, just a couple of times a summer. Once he danced with a girl who worked here—the last dance; we never saw her again. A week later, some other guy came for her things."

"What's his name?" Father asked.

"Maybe *he's* Arbuthnot, you know?" Freud said. "Someone said he's Dutch, but I never heard his name. He knows all about *Europe,* though—I can tell you that!"

My father was dying to ask about the Jews; he felt my mother nudge him in his ribs. They were sitting on one of the putting greens, after hours—when the green turned blue in the moonlight and the red golfing flag flapped in the cup. The bear called State o' Maine had his muzzle off and was trying to scratch himself against the thin stem of the flag.

"Come here, stupid!" Freud said to the bear, but the bear paid no attention to him.

"Is your family still in Vienna?" my mother asked Freud.

"My sister is my only family," he said. "And I don't hear nothing from her since a year ago March."

"A year ago March," my father said, "the Nazis took Austria."

"*Ja,* you're telling *me?*" Freud said.

State o' Maine, frustrated by the lack of resistance the flagpole gave him—for scratching—slapped the flagpole out of the cup and sent it spinning across the putting green.

"Jesus God," said Freud. "He's going to start digging holes in the golf course if we don't go somewhere." My father put the silly flag, marked "18," back into the cup. My mother had been given the night off from "serving" and was still in her chambermaid's uniform; she ran ahead of the bear, calling him.

The bear rarely ran. He shambled—and never very far from the motorcycle. He rubbed up against the motorcycle so much that the red fender paint was shined as silvery as the chrome, and the conical point of the sidecar was dented in from his pushing against it. He had often burned himself on the pipes, going to rub against the machine too soon after it had been driven, so that there were ominous patches of charred bear hair stuck to the pipes—as if the motorcycle itself had been (at one time) a furry animal. Correspondingly, State o' Maine had ragged patches in his black coat where his fur was missing, or singed flat and brown—the dull color of dried seaweed.

What exactly the bear was trained to do was a mystery to everyone—even something of a mystery to Freud.

Their "act" together, performed before the lawn parties in the late afternoon, was more of an effort for the motorcycle and Freud than it was an effort for the bear. Around and around Freud would drive, the bear in the sidecar, canopy snapped off—the bear like a pilot in an open cockpit without controls. State o' Maine usually wore his muzzle in public: it was a red leather thing that reminded my father of the face masks occasionally worn in the game of lacrosse. The muzzle made the bear look smaller; it further scrunched up his already wrinkled face and elongated his nose so that, more than ever, he resembled an overweight dog.

Around and around they would drive, and just before the bored guests returned to their conversation and abandoned this oddity, Freud would stop the motorcycle, dismount, with the engine running, and walk to the sidecar, where he would harass the bear in German. This was funny to the crowd, largely because someone speaking German was funny, but Freud would persist until the bear, slowly, would climb out of the sidecar and mount the motorcycle, sitting in the driver's seat, his heavy paws on the handlebars, his short hind legs not able to reach the footposts or the rear-brake controls. Freud would climb into the sidecar and order the bear to drive off.

Nothing would happen. Freud would sit in the sidecar, protesting their lack of motion; the bear would grimly hold the handlebars, jounce in the saddle, paddle his legs back and forth, as if he were treading water.

"State o' Maine!" someone would shout. The bear would nod, with a kind of embarrassed dignity, and stay where he was.

Freud, now raging in a German everyone loved to hear, climbed out of the sidecar and approached the bear at the controls. He attempted to show the animal how to operate the motorcycle.

"Clutch!" Freud would say: he'd hold the bear's big paw over the clutch handle. "Throttle!" he would shout: he'd rev the motorcycle with the bear's other paw. Freud's 1937 Indian had the gearshift mounted alongside the gas tank, so that for a frightening moment the driver needed to take one hand from the handlebars to engage or change gears. "Shift!" Freud cried, and slammed the cycle into gear.

Whereupon the bear on the motorcycle would proceed across the lawn, the throttle held at a steady low growl, neither accelerating nor slowing down but moving resolutely toward the smug and beautifully attired guests—the men, even fresh from their sporting events, wore hats; even the male swimmers at the Arbuthnot-by-the-Sea wore bathing suits with tops, although the thirties saw trunks, on men, prevailing more and more. Not in Maine. The shoulders of the jackets, men's and women's, were padded; the men wore white flannels, wide and baggy; the sportswomen wore saddle shoes with bobby socks; the "dressed" women wore natural waistlines, their sleeves frequently puffed. All of them made quite a colorful stir as the bear bore down on them, pursued by Freud.

"*Nein! Nein!* You dumb bear!"

And State o' Maine, his expression under the muzzle a mystery to the guests, drove forward, turning only slightly, hulking over the handlebars.

"You stupid animal!" Freud cried.

The bear drove away—always through a party tent without striking a support pole or snagging the white linen tablecloths that covered the tables of food and the bar. He was pursued by waiters over the rich expanse of lawn. The tennis players cheered from the courts, but as the bear drew nearer to them, they abandoned their game.

The bear either knew or didn't know what he was doing, but he never hit a hedge, and he never went too fast; he never drove down to the docks and attempted to board a yacht or a lobster boat. And Freud always caught up with him, when it seemed that the guests had seen enough. Freud mounted the cycle behind the bear; hugging himself to the broad back, he guided the beast and the '37 Indian back to the lawn party.

"So, a few *kinks* to work out!" he'd call to the crowd. "A few flies in the ointment, but *nichts* to worry! In no time he will get it right!"

That was the act. It never changed. That was all Freud had taught State o' Maine; he claimed it was all the bear could learn.

"He's not so smart a bear," Freud told Father. "I got him when he was too old. I thought he'd be fine. He was tamed as a cub. But the logging camps taught him nothing. Those people have no manners, anyway. They're just animals, too. They kept the bear as a pet, they fed him enough so he wouldn't get nasty, but they just let him hang around and be lazy. Like them. I think this bear's got a drinking problem because of them loggers. He don't drink now—I don't let him—but he acts like he wants to, you know?"

Father *didn't* know. He thought Freud was wonderful and the 1937 Indian was the most beautiful machine he had ever met. On days off, my father would take my mother driving on the coast roads, the two of them hugged together and cool in the salt air, but they were never alone: the motorcycle could not be driven away from the Arbuthnot without State o' Maine in the sidecar. The bear went berserk if the motorcycle tried to drive away without him; it was the only event that could make the old bear run. A bear can run surprisingly fast.

"Go ahead, you try to get away," Freud told Father. "But better push it down the driveway, all the way out to the road, before you start the engine. And the first time you try it, don't take poor Mary with you. Wear lots of heavy clothes, because if he catches you, he'll paw you all over. He won't be mad—just excited. Go on, try it. But if you look back, after a few miles, and he's still coming, you better stop and bring him back. He'll have a heart attack, or he'll get lost—he's so stupid.

"He don't know how to hunt, or anything. He's helpless if you don't feed him. He's a pet, he's not a real animal no more. And he's only about twice as smart as a German shepherd. And that's not smart enough for the world, you know."

"The world?" Lilly would always ask, her eyes popping.

But the world for my father, in the summer of '39, was new and affectionate with my mother's shy touches, the roar of the '37 Indian and the strong smell of State o' Maine, the cold Maine nights and the wisdom of Freud.

His limp, of course, was from a motorcycle accident; the leg had been set improperly. "Discrimination," Freud claimed.

Freud was small, strong, alert as an animal, a peculiar color (like a green olive cooked slowly until it almost browned). He had glossy black hair, a strange patch of which grew on his cheek, just under one eye: it was a silky-soft spot of hair, bigger than most moles, at least the size of an average coin, more distinctive than any birthmark, and as naturally a part of Freud's face as a limpet attached to a Maine rock.

"It's because my brain is so enormous," Freud told Mother and Father. "My brain don't leave room on my head for hair, so the hair gets jealous and grows a little where it shouldn't."

"Maybe it was bear hair," Frank said once, seriously, and Franny screamed and hugged me around the neck so hard that I bit my tongue.

"Frank is so weird!" she cried. "Show us *your* bear hair, Frank." Poor Frank was approaching puberty at the time; he was ahead of his time, and he was very embarrassed about it. But not even Franny could distract us from the mesmerizing spell of Freud and his bear; we children were as caught up with them as my father and mother must have been that summer of 1939.

Some nights, Father told us, he would walk my mother to her dorm and kiss her good night. If Freud was asleep, Father would unchain State o' Maine from the motorcycle and slip his muzzle off so the bear could eat. Then my father would take him fishing. There was a tarp staked low over the motorcycle, like an open tent, which protected State o' Maine from the rain, and Father would leave his fishing gear wrapped in the flap of that tarp for these occasions.

The two of them would go to the Bay Point dock; it was beyond the row of hotel piers, and choppy with lobster boats and fishermen's dinghies. Father and State o' Maine would sit on the end of the dock while Father cast what he called spooners, for pollack. He would feed the pollack live to State o' Maine. There was only one evening when there was an altercation between them. Father usually caught three or four pollack; that was enough—for both Father and State o' Maine—and then they'd go home. But one evening the pollack weren't running, and after an hour without a nibble Father got up off the dock to take the bear back to his muzzle and chain.

"Come on," he said. "No fish in the ocean tonight."

State o' Maine wouldn't leave.

"Come on!" Father said. But State o' Maine wouldn't let *Father* leave the dock, either.

"Earl!" the bear growled. Father sat down and kept fishing. "Earl!" State o' Maine complained. Father cast and cast, he changed spooners, he tried everything. If he could have dug for clam worms down on the mud flats, he could have bottom-fished for flounder, but State o' Maine became unfriendly whenever Father attempted to leave the dock. Father contemplated jumping in and swimming ashore; he could sneak back to the dorm for Freud, then, and they could come recapture State o' Maine with food from the hotel. But after a while Father got into the spirit of the evening and said, "All right, all right, so you want fish? We'll catch a fish, goddamn it!"

A little before dawn a lobsterman came down to the dock to put out to sea. He was going to pull his traps and he had some new traps with him to drop, and—unfortunately—he had bait with him, too. State o' Maine smelled the bait.

"Better give it to him," Father said.

"Earl!" said State o' Maine, and the lobsterman gave the bear all his baitfish.

"We'll repay you," Father said. "First thing."

"I know what I'd like to do, 'first thing,' " the lobsterman said. "I'd like to put that *bear* in my traps and use *him* for bait. I'd like to see him *et up* by lobsters!"

"Earl!" said State o' Maine.

"Better not tease him," Father told the lobsterman, who agreed.

"*Ja,* he's not so smart, that bear," Freud told Father. "I should have warned you. He can be funny about food. They fed him too much at the logging camps; he ate all the time—lots of junk. And sometimes, now, he just decides he's not eating enough—or he wants a drink, or something. You got to remember: don't ever sit down to eat yourself if you haven't fed him first. He don't like that."

So State o' Maine was always well fed before he performed at the lawn parties—for the white linen tablecloths were everywhere burdened with hors d'oeuvres, fancy raw fish, and grilled meats, and if State o' Maine had been hungry, there might have been trouble. But Freud stuffed State o' Maine before the act, and the bloated bear drove the motorcycle calmly. He was placid, even bored, at the handlebars, as if the greatest physical need soon to seize him would be an awesome belch, or the need to move his great bear's bowels.

"It's a dumb act and I'm losing money," Freud said. "This place is too fancy. There's only snobs who come here. I should be someplace with a little cruder crowd, someplace where there's bingo games—not just dancing. I should be places that are more *democratic*—places where they bet on dog fights, you know?"

My father *didn't* know, but he must have marveled at such places—rougher than the Weirs at Laconia, or even Hampton Beach. Places where there were more drunks, and more careless money for an act with a performing bear. The Arbuthnot was simply too refined a crowd for a man like Freud and a bear like State o' Maine. It was too refined, even, to appreciate that motorcycle: the 1937 Indian.

But my father realized that Freud felt no ambition drawing him away. Freud had an easy summer at the Arbuthnot; the bear simply hadn't turned out to be the gold mine Freud had hoped for. What Freud wanted was a different bear.

"With a bear this dumb," he told my mother and father, "there's no point in trying to better my take. And you got other problems when you hustle them cheap resorts."

My mother took my father's hand and gave it firm, warning pressure—perhaps because she saw him imagining those "other problems," those "cheap resorts." But my father was thinking of his tuition at Harvard; he *liked* the 1937 Indian and the bear called State o' Maine. He hadn't seen Freud put the slightest effort into training the bear, and Win Berry was a boy who believed in himself; Coach Bob's son was a young man who imagined he could do anything he could imagine.

He had earlier planned that, after the summer at the Arbuthnot, he would go to Cambridge, take a room, and find a job—perhaps in Boston. He would get to know the area around Harvard and get employed in the vicinity, so that as soon as there was money for tuition, he could enroll. This way, he imagined, he might even be able to keep a part-time job *and* go to Harvard. My mother, of course, had liked this plan because Boston to Dairy, and back again, was an easy trip on the Boston & Maine—the trains ran regularly then. She was already imagining the visits from my father—long weekends—and perhaps the occasional, though proper, visits she might make to Cambridge or Boston to see him.

"What do you know about bears, anyway?" she asked. "Or motorcycles?"

She didn't like, either, his idea that—*if* Freud was unwilling to part with his Indian or his bear—Father would travel the logging camps with Freud. Win Berry was a strong boy, but not vulgar. And Mother imagined the camps to be vulgar places, from which Father would not emerge the same—or would not emerge at all.

She needn't have worried. That summer and how it would end were obviously planned more hugely and inevitably than any trivial arrangements my father and mother could imagine ahead of them. That summer of '39 was as inevitable as the war in Europe, as it would soon be called, and all of them—Freud, Mary Bates, and Winslow Berry—were as lightly tossed along by the summer as the gulls knocked about in the rough currents at the mouth of the Kennebec.

One night in late August, when Mother had served at the evening meal and had only just had time to change into her saddle shoes and the long skirt she played croquet in, Father was called from his room to assist with an injured man. Father ran past the lawn for croquet where Mother was waiting for him. She held a mallet over her shoulder. The Christmas-like light bulbs strung in the trees lit the lawn for croquet in such a ghostly way that—to my father—my mother "looked like an angel holding a club."

"I'll be right with you," Father said to her. "Someone's been hurt."

She came with him, and some other running men, and they ran down to the hotel piers. Alongside the dock was a throbbing big ship aglow with lights. A band with too much brass was playing on board, and the strong fuel smell and motor exhaust in the salt air mixed with the smell of crushed fruit. It appeared that some enormous bowl of alcoholic fruit punch was being served to the ship's guests, and they were spilling it over themselves or washing the deck down with it. At the end of the dock a man lay on his side, bleeding from a wound in his cheek: he had stumbled coming up the ladder and had torn his face on a mooring cleat.

He was a large man, his face florid in the blue wash of the light from the moon, and he sat up as soon as anybody touched him. *"Scheiss!"* he said.

My father and mother recognized the German word for "shit" from Freud's many performances. With the assistance of several strong young men the German was brought to his feet. He had bled, magnificently, over his white dinner jacket, which seemed large enough to clothe two men; his blue-black cummerbund resembled a curtain, and his matching bow tie stuck up straight at his throat, like a twisted propeller. He was rather jowly and he smelled strongly of the fruit punch served on board ship. He bellowed to someone. From on board came a chorus of German, and a tall, tanned woman in an evening dress with yellow lace, or ruching, came up the dock's ladder like a panther wearing silk. The bleeding man seized her and leaned on her so heavily that the woman, despite her own obvious strength and agility, was pushed into my father, who helped her maintain her balance. She was much younger than the man, my mother noted, and also German—speaking in an easy, clucking manner to him, while he continued to bleat and gesture, nastily, to those members of the German chorus left on board. Up the dock, and up the gravel driveway, the big couple wove.

At the entrance to the Arbuthnot, the woman turned to my father and said, with a controlled accent: "He *vill* need stitches, *ja?* Of course you *haf* a doctor."

The desk manager whispered to Father, "Get Freud."

"Stitches?" Freud said. "The doctor lives all the way in Bath, and he's a drunk. But I know how to stitch anybody."

The desk manager ran out to the dorm and shouted for Freud.

"Get on your Indian and bring old Doc Todd here! We'll sober him up when he arrives," the manager said. "But for God's sake, get going!"

"It will take an hour, *if* I can find him," Freud said. "You know I can handle stitching. Just get me the proper clothes."

"This is different," the desk manager said. "I think it's different, Freud—I mean, the guy. He's a *German,* Freud. And it's his *face* that's cut."

Freud stripped his work clothes off his pitted, olive body; he began to comb his damp hair. "The clothes," he said. "Just bring them. It's too complicated to get old Doc Todd."

"The wound is on his *face,* Freud," Father said.

"So what's a face?" said Freud. "Just skin, *ja?* Like on the hands or foots. I've sewn up lots of foots before. Ax and saw cuts—them stupid loggers."

Outside, the other Germans from the ship were bringing trunks and heavy luggage the shortest distance from the pier to the entranceway—across the eighteenth green. "Look at those swine," Freud said. "Putting dents where the little white ball will get caught."

The headwaiter came into Freud's room. It was the best room in the men's dorm—no one knew how Freud ended up with it. The headwaiter began to undress.

"Everything but your jacket, dummy," Freud said to him. "Doctors don't wear waiters' jackets."

Father had a black tuxedo jacket that more or less agreed with the waiter's black pants, and he brought it to Freud.

"I've told them, a million times," the headwaiter said—although he looked strange saying this with any authority, while he was naked. "There should be a doctor who actually lives at the hotel."

When Freud was all dressed, he said, "There *is.*" The desk manager ran back to the main hotel ahead of him. Father watched the headwaiter looking helplessly at Freud's abandoned clothes; they were not very clean and they smelled strongly of State o' Maine; the waiter, clearly, did not want to put them on. Father ran to catch up with Freud.

The Germans, now in the driveway outside the entrance, were grinding a large trunk across the gravel; someone would have to rake the stones in the morning. "Is der not enough help at dis hotel to help us?" one of the Germans yelled.

On the spotless counter, in the serving room between the main dining hall and the kitchen, the big German with the gashed cheek lay like a corpse, his pale head resting on his folded-up dinner jacket, which would never be white again; his propeller of a dark tie sagged limply at his throat, his cummerbund heaved.

"It'z a *goot* doctor?" he asked the desk manager. The young giantess in the gown with the yellow ruching held the German's hand.

"An excellent doctor," the desk manager said.

"Especially at stitching," my father said. My mother held his hand.

"It'z not too civilized a hotel, I tink," the German said.

"It'z in der *vilderness,*" the tawny, athletic woman said, but she dismissed herself with a laugh. "But it'z *nicht* so bad a cut, I tink," she told Father and Mother, and the desk manager. "We don't need too goot a doctor to fix it up, I tink."

"Just so it'z no *Jew,*" the German said. He coughed. Freud was in the small room, though none of them had seen him; he was having trouble threading a needle.

"It'z no Jew, I'm sure." The tawny princess laughed. "They *haf* no Jews in Maine!" When she saw Freud, she didn't look so sure.

"Guten Abend, meine Dame und Herr," Freud said. *"Was ist los?"*

My father said that Freud, in the black tuxedo, was a figure so runted and distorted by his boil scars that he immediately looked as if he had stolen his clothes; the clothes appeared to have been stolen from at *least* two different people. Even his most visible instrument was black—a black spool of thread, which Freud grasped in the gray-rubber kitchen gloves the dishwashers wore. The best needle to be found in the laundry room of the Arbuthnot looked too large in Freud's small hand, as if he'd grabbed the needle used to sew the sails for the racing boats. Perhaps he *had.*

"Herr *Doktor?*" the German asked, his face whitening. His wound appeared to stop bleeding, instantly.

"Herr Doktor Professor Freud," Freud said, moving in close and leering at the wound.

"Freud?" the woman said.

"Ja," Freud said.

When he poured the first shot glass of whiskey into the German's cut, the whiskey washed into the German's eyes.

"Ooops!" said Freud.

"I'm blind! I'm blind!" the German sang.

"Nein, you're *nicht* so blind," Freud said. "But you should have shut your eyes." He splashed another glass in the wound; then he went to work.

In the morning the manager asked Freud *not* to perform with State o' Maine until after the Germans left—they were leaving as soon as ample provisions could be loaded aboard their large vessel. Freud refused to remain attired as a doctor; he insisted on tinkering with the '37 Indian in his mechanic's costume, so it was in such attire that the German found him, seaward of the tennis courts, not exactly hidden from the main hotel grounds and the lawns of play, but discreetly off to himself. The huge, bandaged face of the German was badly swollen and he approached Freud warily, as if the little motorcycle mechanic might be the alarming twin brother of the "Herr Doktor Professor" of the night before.

"*Nein,* it'z *him,*" said the tanned woman, trailing on the German's arm.

"What's the Jew doctor fixing this morning?" the German asked Freud.

"My hobby," Freud said, not looking up. My father, who was handing Freud his motorcycle tools—like an assistant to a surgeon—took a firmer grip on the three-quarters-inch wrench.

The German couple did not see the bear. State o' Maine was scratching himself against the fence of the tennis courts—making deep, thrusting scratches with his back against the metal mesh, groaning to himself and rocking to a rhythm akin to masturbation. My mother, to make him more comfortable, had removed his muzzle.

"I never heard of such a motorcycle as *dis,*" the German told Freud, critically. "It'z *junk,* I think, *ja?* What's an Indian? I never heard of it."

"You should try riding it yourself," Freud said. "Want to?"

The German woman seemed unsure of the idea—and quite sure that *she* didn't want to—but the idea clearly appealed to the German. He stood close to the motorcycle and touched its gas tank and ran his fingers over its clutch cable and fondled the knob to the gearshift. He seized the throttle at the handlebars and gave it a sharp twist. He felt the soft rubber tube—like an exposed vital organ among so much metal—where the gas ran from the tank into the carburetor. He opened the valve to the carburetor, without asking Freud's permission; he tickled the valve and wet his fingers with gasoline, then wiped his fingers on the seat.

"You don't mind, *Herr Doktor?*" the German asked Freud.

"No, go on," Freud said. "Take it for a spin."

And that was the summer of '39: my father saw how it would end, but he could not move to interfere. "I couldn't have stopped it," Father always said. "It was *coming,* like the war."

Mother, at the tennis court fence, saw the German mount the motorcycle; she thought she'd better put State o' Maine's muzzle back on. But the bear was impatient with her; he shook his head and scratched himself harder.

"Just a standard kick starter, *ja?*" the German asked.

"Just kick it over and she'll start right up," Freud said. Something about the way he and Father stepped away from the motorcycle made the young German woman join them; she stepped back, too.

"Here goes!" the German said, and kicked the starter down.

With the first catch of the engine, before the first rev, the bear called State o' Maine stood erect against the tennis court fence, the coarse fur on his dense chest stiffening; he stared across center court at the 1937 Indian that was trying to go somewhere without him. When the German chunked the machine into gear and began, rather timidly, to advance across the grass to a nearby gravel path, State o' Maine dropped to all fours and charged. He was in full stride when he crossed center court and broke up the doubles game—racquets falling, balls rolling loose. The player who was playing net chose to *hug* the net instead; he shut his eyes as the bear tore by him.

"Earl!" cried State o' Maine, but the German on the throaty '37 Indian couldn't hear anything.

The German woman heard, however, and turned—with Father and Freud—to see the bear. *"Gott!* Vut vilderness!" she cried, and fainted sideways against my father, who wrestled her gently to the lawn.

When the German saw that a bear was after him, he had not yet got his bearings; he was unsure which way the main road was. If he'd found the main road, of course, he could have outdistanced the bear, but confined to the narrow paths and walkways of the hotel grounds, and the soft fields for sports, he lacked the necessary speed.

"Earl!" growled the bear. The German swerved across the croquet lawn and headed for the picnic tents where they were setting up for lunch. The bear was on the motorcycle in less than twenty-five yards, clumsily trying to mount behind the German—as if State o' Maine had finally learned Freud's driving lesson, and was about to insist that the act be performed properly.

The German would not allow Freud to stitch him up *this* time, and even Freud confessed that it was too big a job for him. "What a mess," Freud wondered aloud to my father. "Such a lot of stitches—not for me. I couldn't stand to hear him bawl all the time it would take."

So the German was transported, by the Coast Guard, to the hospital at Bath. State o' Maine was concealed in the laundry room so that the bear's mythical status as "a wild animal" could be confirmed.

"Out of the *voods,* it came," said the revived German woman. "It must haf been *incensed* by der noise from der motorcycle."

"A she-bear with young cubs," Freud explained. *"Sehr* treacherous at this time of year."

But the management of the Arbuthnot-by-the-Sea would not allow the matter to be dismissed so easily; Freud knew that.

"I'm leaving before I have to talk with *him* again," Freud told Father and Mother. They knew that Freud meant the owner of the Arbuthnot, the man in the white dinner jacket who occasionally showed up for the last dance. "I can just hear him, the big shot: 'Now, Freud, you knew the risk—we discussed it. When *I* agreed to have the animal here, *we* agreed he would be *your* responsibility.' And if he tells me I'm a lucky Jew—to be in his fucking America in the first place—I will let State o' Maine *eat* him!" Freud said. "Him and his fancy cigarettes, I don't need. This isn't my kind of hotel, anyway."

The bear, nervous at being confined in the laundry room and worried to see Freud packing his clothes as fast as they came out of the wash—still wet—began to growl to himself. "Earl!" he whispered.

"Oh, shut up!" Freud yelled. "You're not my kind of bear, either."

"It was my fault," my mother said. "I shouldn't have taken his muzzle off."

"Those were just love bites," Freud said. "It was the brute's claws that really carved that fucker up!"

"If he hadn't tried to pull State o' Maine's fur," Father said, "I don't think it would have gotten so bad."

"Of course it wouldn't have!" Freud said. "Who likes to have hair pulled?"

"Earl!" complained State o' Maine.

"That should be your name: 'Earl!' " Freud told the bear. "You're so stupid, that's all you ever say."

"But what will you do?" Father asked Freud. "Where can you go?"

"Back to Europe," Freud said. "They got smart bears there."

"They have Nazis there," Father said.

"Give me a smart bear and fuck the Nazis," Freud said.

"I'll take care of State o' Maine," Father said.

"You can do better than that," Freud said. "You can *buy* him. Two hundred dollars, and what you got for clothes. *These* are all wet!" he shouted, throwing his clothes.

"Earl!" said the bear, distressed.

"Watch your language, Earl," Freud told him.

"Two hundred dollars?" Mother asked.

"That's all they've paid me, so far," Father said.

"I know what they pay you," Freud said. "That's why it's only two hundred dollars. Of course, it's for the motorcycle, too. You've seen why you need to keep the Indian, *ja?* State o' Maine don't get in cars; they make him throw up. And some woodsman chained him in a pickup once—I saw that. The dumb bear tore the tailgate off and beat in the rear window and mauled the guy in the cab. So don't *you* be dumb. Buy the Indian."

"Two hundred dollars," Father repeated.

"Now for your clothes," Freud said. He left his own wet things on the laundry room floor. The bear tried to follow them to my father's room, but Freud told my mother to take State o' Maine outside and chain him to the motorcycle.

"He knows you're leaving and he's nervous, poor thing," Mother said.

"He just misses the motorcycle," Freud said, but he let the bear come upstairs —although the Arbuthnot had asked him not to allow this.

"What do I care now what they allow?" Freud said, trying on my father's clothes. My mother watched up and down the hall; bears *and* women were not allowed in the men's dorm.

"My clothes are all too *big* for you," my father told Freud when Freud had dressed himself.

"I'm still growing," said Freud, who must have been at least forty then. "If I'd had the right clothes, I'd be bigger now." He wore three of my father's suit pants, one pair right over the other; he wore two suit jackets, the pockets stuffed with underwear and socks, and he carried a third jacket over his shoulder. "Why trouble with suitcases?" he asked.

"But how will you *get* to Europe?" Mother whispered into the room.

"By crossing the Atlantic Ocean," Freud said. "Come in here," he said to Mother; he took my mother's and father's hands and joined them together. "You're only teen-agers," he told them, "so listen to me: you are in love. We start from this assumption, *ja?*" And although my mother and father had never admitted any such thing to each other, they both nodded while Freud held their hands. "Okay," Freud said. "Now, three things from this follow. You promise me you will agree to these three things?"

"I promise," said my father.

"So do I," Mother said.

"Okay," said Freud. "Here's number one: you get married, right away, before some clods and whores change your minds. Got it? You get married, even though it will cost you."

"Yes," my parents agreed.

"Here's number two," Freud said, looking only at my father. "You *go* to Harvard—you promise me—even though it will cost you."

"But I'll already be married," my father said.

"I said it will cost you, didn't I?" Freud said. "You promise me: you'll go to Harvard. You take *every* opportunity given you in this world, even if you have too many opportunities. One day the opportunities stop, you know?"

"I want you to go to Harvard, anyway," Mother told Father.

"Even though it will cost me," Father said, but he agreed to go.

"We're up to number three," Freud said. "You ready?" And he turned to my mother; he dropped my father's hand, he even shoved it away from him so that he was holding Mother's hand all alone. "Forgive him," Freud told her, "even though it will cost you."

"Forgive me for what?" Father said.

"Just forgive him," Freud said, looking only at my mother. She shrugged.

"And *you!*" Freud said to the bear, who was sniffing around under Father's bed. Freud startled State o' Maine, who'd found a tennis ball under the bed and put it in his mouth.

"Urp!" the bear said. Out came the tennis ball.

"You," Freud said to the bear. "May you one day be grateful that you were rescued from the disgusting world of *nature!*"

That was all. It was a wedding and a benediction, my mother always said. It was a good old-fashioned Jewish service, my father always said; Jews were a mystery to him—of the order of China, India, and Africa, and all the exotic places he'd never been.

Father chained the bear to the motorcycle. When he and Mother kissed Freud good-bye, the bear tried to butt his head between them.

"Watch out!" Freud cried, and they scattered apart. "He thought we were eating something," Freud told Mother and Father. "Watch out how you kiss around him; he don't understand kissing. He thinks it's *eating.*"

"Earl!" the bear said.

"And please, for me," Freud said, "call him Earl—that's all he ever says, and State o' Maine is such a dumb name."

"Earl?" my mother said.

"Earl!" the bear said.

"Okay," Father said. *"Earl* it is."

"Good-bye, Earl," Freud said. *"Auf Wiedersehen!"*

They watched Freud for a long time, waiting on the Bay Point dock for a boat going to Boothbay, and when a lobsterman finally took him—although my parents knew that in Boothbay Freud would be boarding a larger ship—they thought how it *looked* as if the lobster boat were taking Freud to Europe, all the way across the dark ocean. They watched the boat chug and bob until it seemed smaller than a tern or even a sandpiper on the sea; by then it was out of hearing.

"Did you do it for the first time that night?" Franny always asked.

"Franny!" Mother said.

"Well, you said you *felt* married," Franny said.

"Never mind when we did it," Father said.

"But you *did,* right?" Franny said.

"Never mind that," Father said.

"It doesn't matter *when,*" Lilly said, in her weird way.

And that was true—it didn't really matter *when.* When they left the summer of 1939 and the Arbuthnot-by-the-Sea, my mother and father were in love—and in *their* minds, married. After all, they had promised Freud. They had his 1937 Indian and his bear, now named Earl, and when they arrived home in Dairy, New Hampshire, they drove first to the Bates family house.

"Mary's home!" my mother's mother called.

"What's that *machine* she's on?" said old Latin Emeritus. "Who's that with her?"

"It's a motorcycle and that's Win Berry!" my mother's mother said.

"No, no!" said Latin Emeritus. "Who's the *other* one?" The old man stared at the bundled figure in the sidecar.

"It must be Coach Bob," said my mother's mother.

"That moron!" Latin Emeritus said. "What in hell is he wearing in this weather? Don't they know how to dress in Iowa?"

"I'm going to marry Win Berry!" my mother rushed up and told her parents. "That's his motorcycle. He's going to Harvard. And this . . . is Earl."

1981

ALICE WALKER
(1944–)

Alice Walker was born and raised in Eatonton, Georgia, the youngest child in a sharecropper family. She was blinded in one eye as a child of eight, and the injury and resultant scars had a dramatic effect on her life: first by giving her "the gift of loneliness * * * sometimes a radical vision of society or one's people," later by making her eligible for scholarships to Spelman College in Atlanta, which she attended from 1961 to 1963, and Sarah Lawrence College, where she received her degree in 1965. Muriel Rukeyser, writer in residence at Sarah Lawrence, brought her writing to an editor's attention, and Walker's first book of poetry, *Once,* appeared in 1968.

Active in the civil rights movement of the 1960's, she later remembered herself and friends at that time as "young and bursting with fear and determination to change our world." Her experiences in those years greatly influenced her subsequent work. In her first novel, *The Third Life of Grange Copeland* (1970), she draws on her observations to portray the customs, natural features, and folk heritage of the South. Her admiration for the struggle of black women toward self-realization in a hostile environment, a theme of much of her work, is first expressed in this book and in the short story collection, *In Love and Trouble* (1973). Her poetry collection *Revolutionary Petunias* (1973) and her novel *Meridian* (1976) also use material from that period. In her third volume of poetry, *Good Night Willie Lee, I'll See You in the Morning* (1979), she ranges from personal loss to an understanding of love, sometimes demonstrating a political commitment based on healthier relations between men and women.

Walker's second collection of short stories, *You Can't Keep a Good Woman Down* (1981), seemed to some critics too dogmatically feminist as she focused an impressionistic style and subjective perspective on controversial issues raised by the women's movement of the 1970's: abortion, sadomasochism, pornography, interracial rape, and homosexuality. In her third novel, *The Color Purple* (1982), she effectively used the southern black vernacular of a narrator who preserves the details of her isolated life in letters to God and to her sister. A victim of sexism, racism, ignorance, and poverty, she retains her integrity, is reunited with the people she loves, and learns serenity.

Walker turns frequently in her poetry and fiction to images of gardening or quilting as analogies for the creative struggle of black women. Growing flowers in poor soil or using scraps to create new beauty serve as symbolic activities for characters who must contend against bigotry, poverty, and abuse. In the essay "In Search of Our Mothers' Gardens: The Creativity of Black Women in the South" (1974) she defines three types of black women: the physically or psychologically abused; the woman who represses her past and heritage in order to fulfill her potential; and the "new" black woman who can base her self-realization on the legacy of her maternal ancestors. In the essay "One Child of One's Own" (1980) she discusses women's difficult choice between artistic creativity and motherhood. She recounts her experience of having a daughter born three days after she finished her first novel, and discusses her fears of how being a mother might affect her life. She concludes it is not a child that restricts a woman's freedom, but a social system; Walker has dedicated considerable energy to trying to change that system. She asserts that a change in basic human relationships, especially those between men and women, can alter society for the betterment of women.

Employed early in her career by the Welfare Department of New York City, and by Head Start in Georgia and Mississippi, she has taught at Jackson State University in Mississippi, Tougaloo College, Wellesley, and the University of Massachusetts. Since the mid-1970's she has written and edited for *Ms.* magazine.

Walker's volumes of fiction to date are named above. A recent collection of verse is *Horses Make a Landscape Look More Beautiful,* 1984. Essays are collected in *In Search of Our Mothers' Gardens: Womanist Prose,* 1983. She edited *I Love Myself When I Am Laughing * * *: A Zora Neale Hurston Reader,* 1979. A biography for children is *Langston Hughes,* 1973.

Brief critical assessments appear in *Dictionary of Literary Biography, Volume 6: American Novelists Since World War II, Second Series,* 1980; and *Dictionary of Literary Biography, Volume 33: Afro-American Fiction Writers After 1955,* 1984.

Everyday Use

for your grandmama

I will wait for her in the yard that Maggie and I made so clean and wavy yesterday afternoon. A yard like this is more comfortable than most people know. It is not just a yard. It is like an extended living room. When the hard clay is swept clean as a floor and the fine sand around the edges lined with tiny, irregular grooves, anyone can come and sit and look up into the elm tree and wait for the breezes that never come inside the house.

Maggie will be nervous until after her sister goes: she will stand hopelessly in corners, homely and ashamed of the burn scars down her arms and legs, eying her sister with a mixture of envy and awe. She thinks her sister has held life always in the palm of one hand, that "no" is a word the world never learned to say to her.

You've no doubt seen those TV shows where the child who has "made it" is confronted, as a surprise, by her own mother and father, tottering in weakly from backstage. (A pleasant surprise, of course: What would they do if parent and child came on the show only to curse out and insult each other?) On TV mother and child embrace and smile into each other's faces. Sometimes the mother and father weep, the child wraps them in her arms and leans across the table to tell how she would not have made it without their help. I have seen these programs.

Sometimes I dream a dream in which Dee and I are suddenly brought together on a TV program of this sort. Out of a dark and soft-seated limousine I am ushered into a bright room filled with many people. There I meet a smiling, gray, sporty man like Johnny Carson who shakes my hand and tells me what a fine girl I have. Then we are on the stage and Dee is embracing me with tears in her eyes. She pins on my dress a large orchid, even though she has told me once that she thinks orchids are tacky flowers.

In real life I am a large, big-boned woman with rough, man-working hands. In the winter I wear flannel nightgowns to bed and overalls during the day. I can kill and clean a hog as mercilessly as a man. My fat keeps me hot in zero weather. I can work outside all day, breaking ice to get water for washing; I can eat pork liver cooked over the open fire minutes after it comes steaming from the hog. One winter I knocked a bull calf straight in the brain between the eyes with a sledge hammer and had the meat hung up to chill before nightfall. But of course all this does not show on television. I am the way my daughter would want me to be: a hundred pounds lighter, my skin like an uncooked barley pancake. My hair glistens in the hot bright lights. Johnny Carson has much to do to keep up with my quick and witty tongue.

But that is a mistake. I know even before I wake up. Who ever knew a Johnson with a quick tongue? Who can even imagine me looking a strange white man in the eye? It seems to me I have talked to them always with one foot raised in flight, with my head turned in whichever way is farthest from them. Dee, though. She would always look anyone in the eye. Hesitation was no part of her nature.

"How do I look, Mama?" Maggie says, showing just enough of her thin body enveloped in pink skirt and red blouse for me to know she's there, almost hidden by the door.

"Come out into the yard," I say.

Have you ever seen a lame animal, perhaps a dog run over by some careless person rich enough to own a car, sidle up to someone who is ignorant enough to be kind to him? That is the way my Maggie walks. She has been like this, chin on chest, eyes on ground, feet in shuffle, ever since the fire that burned the other house to the ground.

Dee is lighter than Maggie, with nicer hair and a fuller figure. She's a woman now, though sometimes I forget. How long ago was it that the other house burned? Ten, twelve years? Sometimes I can still hear the flames and feel Maggie's arms sticking to me, her hair smoking and her dress falling off her in little black papery flakes. Her eyes seemed stretched open, blazed open by the flames reflected in them. And Dee. I see her standing off under the sweet gum tree she used to dig gum out of; a look of concentration on her face as she watched the last dingy gray board of the house fall in toward the red-hot brick chimney. Why don't you do a dance around the ashes? I'd wanted to ask her. She had hated the house that much.

I used to think she hated Maggie, too. But that was before we raised the money, the church and me, to send her to Augusta to school. She used to read to us without pity; forcing words, lies, other folks' habits, whole lives upon us two, sitting trapped and ignorant underneath her voice. She washed us in a river of make-believe, burned us with a lot of knowledge we didn't necessarily need to know. Pressed us to her with the serious way she read, to shove us away at just the moment, like dimwits, we seemed about to understand.

Dee wanted nice things. A yellow organdy dress to wear to her graduation from high school; black pumps to match a green suit she'd made from an old suit somebody gave me. She was determined to stare down any disaster in her efforts. Her eyelids would not flicker for minutes at a time. Often I fought off the temptation to shake her. At sixteen she had a style of her own: and knew what style was.

I never had an education myself. After second grade the school was closed down. Don't ask me why: in 1927 colored asked fewer questions than they do now. Sometimes Maggie reads to me. She stumbles along good-naturedly but can't see well. She knows she is not bright. Like good looks and money, quickness passed her by. She will marry John Thomas (who has mossy teeth in an earnest face) and then I'll be free to sit here and I guess just sing church songs to myself. Although I never was a good singer. Never could carry a tune. I was always better at a man's job. I used to love to milk till I was hooked in the side in '49. Cows are soothing and slow and don't bother you, unless you try to milk them the wrong way.

I have deliberately turned my back on the house. It is three rooms, just like the one that burned, except the roof is tin; they don't make shingle roofs any more. There are no real windows, just some holes cut in the sides, like the portholes in a ship, but not round and not square, with rawhide holding the shutters up on the outside. This house is in a pasture, too, like the other one. No doubt when Dee sees it she will want to tear it down. She wrote me once that no matter where we "choose" to live, she will manage to come see us. But she will never bring her friends. Maggie and I thought about this and Maggie asked me, "Mama, when did Dee ever *have* any friends?"

She had a few. Furtive boys in pink shirts hanging about on washday after school. Nervous girls who never laughed. Impressed with her they worshiped the well-turned phrase, the cute shape, the scalding humor that erupted like bubbles in lye. She read to them.

When she was courting Jimmy T she didn't have much time to pay to us, but turned all her faultfinding power on him. He *flew* to marry a cheap city girl from a family of ignorant flashy people. She hardly had time to recompose herself.

When she comes I will meet—but there they are!

Maggie attempts to make a dash for the house, in her shuffling way, but I stay her with my hand. "Come back here," I say. And she stops and tries to dig a well in the sand with her toe.

It is hard to see them clearly through the strong sun. But even the first glimpse of leg out of the car tells me it is Dee. Her feet were always neat-looking, as if God himself had shaped them with a certain style. From the other side of the car comes a short, stocky man. Hair is all over his head a foot long and hanging from his chin like a kinky mule tail. I hear Maggie suck in her breath. "Uhnnnh," is what it sounds like. Like when you see the wriggling end of a snake just in front of your foot on the road. "Uhnnnh."

Dee next. A dress down to the ground, in this hot weather. A dress so loud it hurts my eyes. There are yellows and oranges enough to throw back the light of the sun. I feel my whole face warming from the heat waves it throws out. Earrings gold, too, and hanging down to her shoulders. Bracelets dangling and making noises when she moves her arm up to shake the folds of the dress out of her armpits. The dress is loose and flows, and as she walks closer, I like it. I hear Maggie go "Uhnnnh" again. It is her sister's hair. It stands straight up like the wool on a sheep. It is black as night and around the edges are two long pigtails that rope about like small lizards disappearing behind her ears.

"Wa-su-zo-Tean-o!" she says, coming on in that gliding way the dress makes her move. The short stocky fellow with the hair to his navel is all grinning and he follows up with "Asalamalakim, my mother and sister!" He moves to hug Maggie but she falls back, right up against the back of my chair. I feel her trembling there and when I look up I see the perspiration falling off her chin.

"Don't get up," says Dee. Since I am stout it takes something of a push. You can see me trying to move a second or two before I make it. She turns, showing white heels through her sandals, and goes back to the car. Out she peeks next with a Polaroid. She stoops down quickly and lines up picture after picture of me sitting there in front of the house with Maggie cowering behind me. She never takes a shot without making sure the house is included. When a cow comes nibbling around the edge of the yard she snaps it and me and Maggie *and* the house. Then she puts the Polaroid in the back seat of the car, and comes up and kisses me on the forehead.

Meanwhile Asalamalakim is going through motions with Maggie's hand. Maggie's hand is as limp as a fish, and probably as cold, despite the sweat, and she keeps trying to pull it back. It looks like Asalamalakim wants to shake hands but wants to do it fancy. Or maybe he don't know how people shake hands. Anyhow, he soon gives up on Maggie.

"Well," I say. "Dee."

"No, Mama," she says. "Not 'Dee,' Wangero Leewanika Kemanjo!"

"What happened to 'Dee'?" I wanted to know.

"She's dead," Wangero said. "I couldn't bear it any longer, being named after the people who oppress me."

"You know as well as me you was named after your aunt Dicie," I said. Dicie is my sister. She named Dee. We called her "Big Dee" after Dee was born.

"But who was *she* named after?" asked Wangero.

"I guess after Grandma Dee," I said.

"And who was she named after?" asked Wangero.

"Her mother," I said, and saw Wangero was getting tired. "That's about as far back as I can trace it," I said. Though, in fact, I probably could have carried it back beyond the Civil War through the branches.

"Well," said Asalamalakim, "there you are."

"Uhnnnh," I heard Maggie say.

"There I was not," I said, "before 'Dicie' cropped up in our family, so why should I try to trace it that far back?"

He just stood there grinning, looking down on me like somebody inspecting a Model A car. Every once in a while he and Wangero sent eye signals over my head.

"How do you pronounce this name?" I asked.

"You don't have to call me by it if you don't want to," said Wangero.

"Why shouldn't I?" I asked. "If that's what you want us to call you, we'll call you."

"I know it might sound awkward at first," said Wangero.

"I'll get used to it," I said. "Ream it out again."

Well, soon we got the name out of the way. Asalamalakim had a name twice as long and three times as hard. After I tripped over it two or three times he told me to just call him Hakim-a-barber. I wanted to ask him was he a barber, but I didn't really think he was, so I didn't ask.

"You must belong to those beef-cattle peoples down the road," I said. They said "Asalamalakim" when they met you, too, but they didn't shake hands. Always too busy: feeding the cattle, fixing the fences, putting up salt-lick shelters, throwing down hay. When the white folks poisoned some of the herd the men stayed up all night with rifles in their hands. I walked a mile and a half just to see the sight.

Hakim-a-barber said, "I accept some of their doctrines, but farming and raising cattle is not my style." (They didn't tell me, and I didn't ask, whether Wangero (Dee) had really gone and married him.)

We sat down to eat and right away he said he didn't eat collards and pork was unclean. Wangero, though, went on through the chitlins and corn bread, the greens and everything else. She talked a blue streak over the sweet potatoes. Everything delighted her. Even the fact that we still used the benches her daddy made for the table when we couldn't afford to buy chairs.

"Oh, Mama!" she cried. Then turned to Hakim-a-barber. "I never knew how lovely these benches are. You can feel the rump prints," she said, running her hands underneath her and along the bench. Then she gave a sigh and her hand closed over Grandma Dee's butter dish. "That's it!" she said. "I knew there was something I wanted to ask you if I could have." She jumped up from the table and went over in the corner where the churn stood, the milk in it clabber by now. She looked at the churn and looked at it.

"This churn top is what I need," she said. "Didn't Uncle Buddy whittle it out of a tree you all used to have?"

"Yes," I said.

"Uh huh," she said happily. "And I want the dasher, too."

"Uncle Buddy whittle that, too?" asked the barber.

Dee (Wangero) looked up at me.

"Aunt Dee's first husband whittled the dash," said Maggie so low you almost couldn't hear her. "His name was Henry, but they called him Stash."

"Maggie's brain is like an elephant's," Wangero said, laughing. "I can use the churn top as a centerpiece for the alcove table," she said, sliding a plate over the churn, "and I'll think of something artistic to do with the dasher."

When she finished wrapping the dasher the handle stuck out. I took it for a moment in my hands. You didn't even have to look close to see where hands pushing the dasher up and down to make butter had left a kind of sink in the wood. In fact, there were a lot of small sinks; you could see where thumbs and fingers had sunk into the wood. It was beautiful light yellow wood, from a tree that grew in the yard where Big Dee and Stash had lived.

After dinner Dee (Wangero) went to the trunk at the foot of my bed and started rifling through it. Maggie hung back in the kitchen over the dishpan. Out came Wangero with two quilts. They had been pieced by Grandma Dee and then Big

Dee and me had hung them on the quilt frames on the front porch and quilted them. One was in the Lone Star pattern. The other was Walk Around the Mountain. In both of them were scraps of dresses Grandma Dee had worn fifty and more years ago. Bits and pieces of Grandpa Jarrell's Paisley shirts. And one teeny faded blue piece, about the size of a penny matchbox, that was from Great Grandpa Ezra's uniform that he wore in the Civil War.

"Mama," Wangero said sweet as a bird. "Can I have these old quilts?"

I heard something fall in the kitchen, and a minute later the kitchen door slammed.

"Why don't you take one or two of the others?" I asked. "These old things was just done by me and Big Dee from some tops your grandma pieced before she died."

"No," said Wangero. "I don't want those. They are stitched around the borders by machine."

"That'll make them last better," I said.

"That's not the point," said Wangero. "These are all pieces of dresses Grandma used to wear. She did all this stitching by hand. Imagine!" She held the quilts securely in her arms, stroking them.

"Some of the pieces, like those lavender ones, come from old clothes her mother handed down to her," I said, moving up to touch the quilts. Dee (Wangero) moved back just enough so that I couldn't reach the quilts. They already belonged to her.

"Imagine!" she breathed again, clutching them closely to her bosom.

"The truth is," I said, "I promised to give them quilts to Maggie, for when she marries John Thomas."

She gasped like a bee had stung her.

"Maggie can't appreciate these quilts!" she said. "She'd probably be backward enough to put them to everyday use."

"I reckon she would," I said. "God knows I been saving 'em for long enough with nobody using 'em. I hope she will!" I didn't want to bring up how I had offered Dee (Wangero) a quilt when she went away to college. Then she had told me they were old-fashioned, out of style.

"But they're *priceless!*" she was saying now, furiously; for she has a temper. "Maggie would put them on the bed and in five years they'd be in rags. Less than that!"

"She can always make some more," I said. "Maggie knows how to quilt."

Dee (Wangero) looked at me with hatred. "You just will not understand. The point is these quilts, *these* quilts!"

"Well," I said, stumped. "What would *you* do with them?"

"Hang them," she said. As if that was the only thing you *could* do with quilts.

Maggie by now was standing in the door. I could almost hear the sound her feet made as they scraped over each other.

"She can have them, Mama," she said, like somebody used to never winning anything, or having anything reserved for her. "I can 'member Grandma Dee without the quilts."

I looked at her hard. She had filled her bottom lip with checkerberry snuff and it gave her face a kind of dopey, hangdog look. It was Grandma Dee and Big Dee who taught her how to quilt herself. She stood there with her scarred hands hidden in the folds of her skirt. She looked at her sister with something like fear but she wasn't mad at her. This was Maggie's portion. This was the way she knew God to work.

When I looked at her like that something hit me in the top of my head and ran down to the soles of my feet. Just like when I'm in church and the spirit of God touches me and I get happy and shout. I did something I never had done before: hugged Maggie to me, then dragged her on into the room, snatched the quilts out of Miss Wangero's hands and dumped them into Maggie's lap. Maggie just sat there on my bed with her mouth open.

"Take one or two of the others," I said to Dee.

But she turned without a word and went out to Hakim-a-barber.

"You just don't understand," she said, as Maggie and I came out to the car.

"What don't I understand?" I wanted to know.

"Your heritage," she said. And then she turned to Maggie, kissed her, and said, "You ought to try to make something of yourself, too, Maggie. It's really a new day for us. But from the way you and Mama still live you'd never know it."

She put on some sunglasses that hid everything above the tip of her nose and her chin.

Maggie smiled; maybe at the sunglasses. But a real smile, not scared. After we watched the car dust settle I asked Maggie to bring me a dip of snuff. And then the two of us sat there just enjoying, until it was time to go in the house and go to bed.

1973

TIM O'BRIEN
(1946–)

William Timothy O'Brien was born in Austin, Minnesota, and moved with his family to Worthington when he was ten. At Macalester College he majored in political science, completed a novel, earned election to Phi Beta Kappa, and graduated *summa cum laude* in 1968. Almost immediately upon graduation, he was drafted into the army to serve in the Vietnam War. Although he was opposed to the war, he accepted the induction "by a sort of sleepwalking default," as he wrote later in *If I Die in a Combat Zone* (1973). Serving as a foot soldier, he was mustered out with a Purple Heart earned in action near My Lai. Graduate study in government at Harvard followed, beginning in 1970, with time off for summer internships at the Washington *Post* in 1971 and 1972 and for a year reporting national affairs for the same paper during 1973–1974. Meanwhile, he had begun a serious consideration of the effects of war upon himself and the nation and had published his first book. In 1976 he gave up his graduate study, remaining in Cambridge as a full-time author.

O'Brien's first three books reflect the Vietnam War from different angles. *If I Die in a Combat Zone, Box Me Up and Ship Me Home* is the full title of his first attempt, a memoir in which he tries to assess the experience, knowing that a larger than personal vision will probably escape him: "Can the foot soldier teach anything important about war, merely for having been there? I think not. He can tell war stories." In his next work, the novel *Northern Lights* (1974), he examines the relationship between two brothers after one of them has served in Vietnam and returned to join the other in the northern Minnesota town of their childhood. A strong work, constructed with meticulous care, it achieves its greatest power in long sections in which the brothers, lost on a skiing trip, achieve a new understanding as they struggle to survive in the wilderness. O'Brien's third book, *Going After Cacciato* (1978), has been his most admired. Portions published as stories were selected as O. Henry Award winners in 1976 and 1978 and the complete book won the National Book Award in 1979.

O'Brien's next novel, *The Nuclear Age* (1985), treats the horror of potential nuclear disaster from the perspective of 1995. His hero, obsessed with fear from childhood, has survived forty years of the possibility of world-wide destruction. Now, by a means that looks to others like madness, he wishes to save himself and his family from civilization's apparently headlong thrust toward oblivion. Although its message is urgent, most readers have found this novel less wholly successful than *Cacciato.*

Going After Cacciato is in part a demonstration of Aristotle's idea that poetry (or fiction) is more serious than history because it presents permanent truth more accurately than any mere record of fact. Hence much of the novel reports from memory not so much how it was, but, as one of the chapter headings has it, "The Way It Mostly Was." Hence, also, much that is reported did not happen at all except as a fantasy in the mind of the novel's central character, who imagines pursuing Cacciato (the name is Italian for "the hunted") out of Vietnam and across Asia to Paris. In this, as in O'Brien's other work, the marks of a conscious literary artist are apparent. He writes with conviction and with a skill that is still developing.

O'Brien's books to date are named above. *If I Die in a Combat Zone* was published in a revised edition in 1979. Brief appraisals of O'Brien's work appear in *Contemporary Authors* and *Dictionary of Literary Biography: Yearbook, 1980,* 1981. G. Thomas Couser discusses *Going After Cacciato* in *The Journal of Narrative Technique,* Winter, 1983.

Night March[1]

The platoon of thirty-two soldiers moved slowly in the dark, single file, not talking. One by one, like sheep in a dream, they passed through the hedgerow, crossed quietly over a meadow and came down to the paddy. There they stopped. Lieutenant Sidney Martin knelt down, motioning with his hand, and one by one the others squatted or knelt or sat in the shadows. For a long time they did not move. Except for the sounds of their breathing, and, once, a soft fluid trickle as one of them urinated, the thirty-two men were silent: some of them excited by the adventure, some afraid, some exhausted by the long march, some of them looking forward to reaching the sea where they would be safe. There was no talking now. No more jokes. At the rear of the column, Private First Class Paul Berlin lay quietly with his forehead resting on the black plastic stock of his rifle. His eyes were closed. He was pretending he was not in the war. Pretending he had not watched Billy Boy Watkins die of fright on the field of battle. He was pretending he was a boy again, camping with his father in the midnight summer along the Des Moines River. "Be calm," his father said. "Ignore the bad stuff, look for the good." In the dark, eyes closed, he pretended. He pretended that when he opened his eyes his father would be there by the campfire and, father and son, they would begin to talk softly about whatever came to mind, minor things, trivial things, and then roll into their sleeping bags. And later, he pretended, it would be morning and there would not be a war.

In the morning, when they reached the sea, it would be better. He would bathe in the sea. He would shave. Clean his nails, work out the scum. In the morning he

1. Published first in *Redbook,* May, 1975 as "Where Have You Gone, Charming Billy?" the story was revised for its appearance in *Going After Cacciato* (1978), the source of the present text.

would wash himself and brush his teeth. He would forget the first day, and the second day would not be so bad. He would learn.

There was a sound beside him, a movement, then, "Hey," then louder, "Hey!" He opened his eyes.

"Hey, we're movin'. Get up."

"Okay."

"You sleeping?"

"No, I was resting. Thinking." He could see only part of the soldier's face. It was a plump, round, child's face. The child was smiling.

"No problem," the soldier whispered. "Up an' at 'em."

And he followed the boy's shadow into the paddy, stumbling once, almost dropping his rifle, cutting his knee, but he followed the shadow and did not stop. The night was clear. Before him, strung out across the paddy, he could make out the black forms of the other soldiers, their silhouettes hard against the sky. Already the Southern Cross was out. And other stars he could not yet name. Soon, he thought, he would learn the names. And puffy night clouds. And a peculiar glow to the west. There was not yet a moon.

Wading through the paddy, listening to the lullaby sounds of his boots, and many other boots, he tried hard not to think. Dead of a heart attack, that was what Doc Peret had said. Only he did not know Doc Peret's name. All he knew was what Doc said, dead of a heart attack, but he tried hard not to think of this, and instead he thought about not thinking. The fear wasn't so bad now. Now, as he stepped out of the paddy and onto a narrow dirt path, now the fear was mostly the fear of being so dumbly afraid ever again.

So he tried not to think.

There were tricks to keep from thinking. Counting. He counted his steps along the dirt path, concentrating on the numbers, pretending that the steps were dollar bills and that each step through the night made him richer and richer, so that soon he would become a wealthy man, and he kept counting, considering the ways he might spend the wealth, what he would buy and do and acquire and own. He would look his father in the eye and shrug and say, "It was pretty bad at first, sure, but I learned a lot and I got used to it. I never joined them—not them—but I learned their names and I got along, I got used to it." Then he would tell his father the story of Billy Boy Watkins, only a story, just a story, and he would never let on about the fear. "Not so bad," he would say instead, making his father proud.

And songs, another trick to stop the thinking—*Where have you gone, Billy Boy, Billy Boy, oh, where have you gone, charming Billy?* and other songs, *I got a girl, her name is Jill, she won't do it but her sister will,* and *Sound Off!* and other songs that he sang in his head as he marched toward the sea. And when he reached the sea he would dig a hole in the sand and he would sleep like the high clouds, he would swim and dive into the breakers and hunt crayfish and smell the salt, and he would laugh when the others made jokes about Billy Boy, and he would not be afraid ever again.

He walked, and counted, and later the moon came out. Pale, shrunken to the size of a dime.

The helmet was heavy on his head. In the morning he would adjust the leather binding. In the morning, at the end of the long march, his boots would have lost their shiny black stiffness, turning red and clay-colored like all the other boots, and he would have a start on a beard, his clothes would begin to smell of the country, the mud and algae and cow manure and chlorophyll, decay, mosquitoes like mice, all this: He would begin to smell like the others, even look like them, but, by God, he would not join them. He would adjust. He would play the part. But he would not join them. He would shave, he would clean himself, he would clean his weapon and keep it clean. He would clean the breech and trigger assembly and muzzle and magazines, and later, next time, he would not be afraid to use it. In the morning, when he reached the sea, he would learn the soldiers' names and maybe laugh at their jokes. When they joked about Billy Boy he would laugh, pretending it was funny, and he would not let on.

Walking, counting in his walking, and pretending, he felt better. He watched the moon come higher.

The trick was not to take it personally. Stay aloof. Follow the herd but don't join it. That would be the real trick. The trick would be to keep himself separate. To watch things. "Keep an eye out for the good stuff," his father had said by the river. "Keep your eyes open and your ass low, that's my only advice." And he would do it. A low profile. Look for the beauties: the moon sliding higher now, the feeling of the march, all the ironies and truths, and don't take any of it seriously. That would be the trick.

Once, very late in the night, they skirted a sleeping village. The smells again—straw, cattle, mildew. The men were quiet. On the far side of the village, coming like light from the dark, a dog barked. The barking was fierce. Then, nearby, another dog took up the bark. The column stopped. They waited there until the barking died out, then, fast, they marched away from the village, through a graveyard with conical burial mounds and miniature stone altars. The place had a perfumy smell. His mother's dresser, rows of expensive lotions and colognes, *eau de bain.*[2] She used to hide booze in the larger bottles, but his father found out and carried the whole load out back, started a fire, and, one by one, threw the bottles into the incinerator, where they made sharp exploding sounds like gunfire; a perfumy smell, yes; a nice spot to spend the night, to sleep in the perfumery, the burial mounds making fine strong battlements, the great quiet of the place.

But they went on, passing through a hedgerow and across another paddy and east toward the sea.

He walked carefully. He remembered what he'd been taught. Billy Boy hadn't remembered. And so Billy died of fright, his face going pale and the veins in his arms and neck popping out, the crazy look in his eyes.

He walked carefully.

Stretching ahead of him in the night was the string of shadow-soldiers whose names he did not yet know. He knew some of the faces. And he knew their shapes, their heights and weights and builds, the way they carried themselves on the march. But he could not tell them apart. All alike in the night, a piece, all of them moving with the same sturdy silence and calm and steadiness.

So he walked carefully, counting his steps. And when he had counted to eight thousand and sixty, the column suddenly stopped. One by one the soldiers knelt or squatted down.

The grass along the path was wet. Private First Class Paul Berlin lay back and turned his head so he could lick at the dew with his eyes closed, another trick, closing his eyes. He might have slept. Eyes closed, pretending came easy . . . When he

2. French: "bath oil" (literally, "water").

opened his eyes, the same child-faced soldier was sitting beside him, quietly chewing gum. The smell of Doublemint was clean in the night.

"Sleepin' again?" the boy said.

"No. Hell, no."

The boy laughed a little, very quietly, chewing on his gum. Then he twisted the cap off a canteen and took a swallow and handed it through the dark.

"Take some," he said. He didn't whisper. The voice was high, a child's voice, and there was no fear in it. A big blue baby. A genie's voice.

Paul Berlin drank and handed back the canteen. The boy pressed a stick of gum into his fingers.

"Chew it quiet, okay? Don't blow no bubbles or nothing."

It was impossible to make out the soldier's face. It was a huge face, almost perfectly round.

They sat still. Private First Class Paul Berlin chewed the gum until all the sugars were gone. Then in the dark beside him the boy began to whistle. There was no melody.

"You have to do that?"

"Do what?"

"Whistle like that."

"Geez, was I whistling?"

"Sort of."

The boy laughed. His teeth were big and even and white. "Sometimes I forget. Kinda dumb, isn't it?"

"Forget it."

"Whistling! Sometimes I just forget where I'm at. The guys, they get pissed at me, but I just forget. You're new here, right?"

"I guess I am."

"Weird."

"What's weird?"

"Weird," the boy said, "that's all. The way I forget. Whistling! Was I whistling?"

"If you call it that."

"Geez!"

They were quiet awhile. And the night was quiet, no crickets or birds, and it was hard to imagine it was truly a war. He searched again for the soldier's face, but there was just a soft fullness under the helmet. The white teeth: chewing, smiling. But it did not matter. Even if he saw the kid's face, he would not know the name; and if he knew the name, it would still not matter.

"Haven't got the time?"

"No."

"Rats." The boy popped the gum on his teeth, a sharp smacking sound. "Don't matter."

"How about—"

"Time goes faster when you don't know the time. That's why I never bought no watch. Oscar's got one, an' Billy . . . Billy, he's got *two* of 'em. Two watches, you believe that? I never bought none, though. Goes fast when you don't know the time."

And again they were quiet. They lay side by side in the grass. The moon was very high now, and very bright, and they were waiting for cloud cover. After a time there was the crinkling of tinfoil, then the sound of heavy chewing. A moist, loud sound.

"I hate it when the sugar's gone," the boy said. "You want more?"

"I'm okay."

"Just ask. I got about a zillion packs. Pretty weird, wasn't it?"

"What?"

"Today . . . it was pretty weird what Doc said. About Billy Boy."

"Yes, pretty weird."

The boy smiled his big smile. "You like that gum? I got other kinds if you don't like it. I got—"

"I like it."

"I got Black Jack here. You like Black Jack? Geez, I love it! Juicy Fruit's second, but Black Jack's first. I save it up for rainy days, so to speak. Know what I mean? What you got there is Doublemint."

"I like it."

"Sure," the round soldier said, the child, "except for Black Jack and Juicy Fruit it's my favorite. You like Black Jack gum?"

Paul Berlin said he'd never tried it. It scared him, the way the boy kept talking, too loud. He sat up and looked behind him. Everything was dark.

"Weird," the boy said.

"I guess so. Why don't we be a little quiet?"

"Weird. You never even *tried* it?"

"What?"

"Black Jack. You never even chewed it once?"

Someone up the trail hissed at them to shut up. The boy shook his head, put a finger to his lips, smiled, and lay back. Then a long blank silence. It lasted for perhaps an hour, maybe more, and then the boy was whistling again, softly at first but then louder, and Paul Berlin nudged him.

"Really weird," the soldier whispered. "About Billy Boy. What Doc said, wasn't that the weirdest thing you ever heard? You ever hear of such a thing?"

"What?"

"What Doc said."

"No, I never did."

"Me neither." The boy was chewing again, and the smell now was licorice. The moon was a bit lower. "Me neither. I never heard once of no such thing. But Doc, he's a pretty smart cookie. Pretty darned smart."

"Is he?"

"You bet he is. When he says something, man, you know he's tellin' the truth. You *know* it." The soldier turned, rolling onto his stomach, and began to whistle, drumming with his fingers. Then he caught himself. "Dang it!" He gave his cheek a sharp whack. "Whistling again! I got to stop that dang whistling." He smiled and thumped his mouth. "But, sure enough, Doc's a smart one. He knows stuff. You wouldn't believe the stuff Doc knows. A lot. He knows a lot."

Paul Berlin nodded. The boy was talking too loud again.

"Well, you'll find out yourself. Doc knows his stuff." Sitting up, the boy shook his head. "A heart attack!" He made a funny face, filling his cheeks like balloons, then letting them deflate. "A heart attack! You hear Doc say that? A heart attack on the field of battle, isn't that what Doc said?"

"Yes," Paul Berlin whispered. He couldn't help giggling.

"Can you believe it? Billy Boy getting heart attacked? Scared to death?"

Paul Berlin giggled, he couldn't help it.

"Can you imagine it?"

"Yes," Paul Berlin whispered, and he imagined it clearly. He couldn't stop giggling.

"Geez!"

He giggled. He couldn't stop it, so he giggled, and he imagined it clearly. He imagined the medic's report. He imagined Billy's surprise. He giggled, imagining Billy's father opening the telegram: SORRY TO INFORM YOU THAT YOUR SON BILLY BOY WAS YESTERDAY SCARED TO DEATH IN ACTION IN THE REPUBLIC OF VIETNAM. Yes, he could imagine it clearly.

He giggled. He rolled onto his belly and pressed his face in the wet grass and giggled, he couldn't help it.

"Not so loud," the boy said. But Paul Berlin was shaking with the giggles: scared to death on the field of battle, and he couldn't help it.

"Not so loud."

But he was coughing with the giggles, he couldn't stop. Giggling and remembering the hot afternoon, and poor Billy, how they'd been drinking Coke from bright aluminum cans, and how the men lined the cans up in a row and shot them full of practice holes, how funny it was and how dumb and how hot the day, and how they'd started on the march and how the war hadn't seemed so bad, and how a little while later Billy tripped the mine, and how it made a tinny little sound, unimportant, *poof,* that was all, just *poof,* and how Billy Boy stood there with his mouth open and grinning, sort of embarrassed and dumb-looking, how he just stood and stood there, looking down at where his foot had been, and then how he finally sat down, still grinning, not saying a word, his boot lying there with his foot still in it, just *poof,* nothing big or dramatic, and how hot and fine and clear the day had been.

"Hey," he heard the boy saying in the dark, "not so loud, okay?" But he kept giggling. He put his nose in the wet grass and he giggled, then he bit his arm, trying to stifle it, but remembering—"War's over, Billy," Doc Peret said, "that's a million-dollar wound."

"Hey, not so *loud.*"

But Billy was holding the boot now. Unlacing it, trying to force it back on, except it was already on, and he kept trying to tie the boot and foot on, working with the laces, but it wouldn't go, and how everyone kept saying, "The war's over, man, be cool." And Billy couldn't get the boot on, because it was already on: He kept trying but it wouldn't go. Then he got scared. "Fuckin boot won't go on," he said. And he got scared. His face went pale and the veins in his arms and neck popped out, and he was yanking at the boot to get it on, and then he was crying. "Bullshit," the medic said, Doc Peret, but Billy Boy kept bawling, tightening up, saying he was going to die, but the medic said, "Bullshit, that's a million-dollar wound you got there," but Billy went crazy, pulling at the boot with his foot still in it, crying, saying he was going to die. And even when Doc Peret stuck him with morphine, even then Billy kept crying and working at the boot.

"Shut up!" the soldier hissed, or seemed to, and the smell of licorice was all over him, and the smell made Paul Berlin giggle harder. His eyes stung. Giggling in the wet grass in the dark, he couldn't help it.

"Come on, man, be quiet."

But he couldn't stop. He heard the giggles in his stomach and tried to keep them there, but they were hard and hurting and he couldn't stop them, and he couldn't stop remembering how it was when Billy Boy Watkins died of fright on the field of battle.

Billy tugging away at the boot, rocking, and Doc Peret and two others holding him. "You're okay, man," Doc Peret said, but Billy wasn't hearing it, and he kept getting tighter, making fists, squeezing his eyes shut and teeth scraping, everything tight and squeezing.

Afterward Doc Peret explained that Billy Boy really died of a heart attack, scared to death. "No lie," Doc said, "I seen it before. The wound wasn't what killed him, it was the heart attack. No lie." So they wrapped Billy in a plastic poncho, his eyes still squeezed shut to make wrinkles in his cheeks, and they carried him over the meadow to a dried-up paddy, and they threw out yellow smoke for the chopper, and they put him aboard, and then Doc wrapped the boot in a towel and placed it next to Billy, and that was how it happened. The chopper took Billy away. Later, Eddie Lazzutti, who loved to sing, remembered the song, and the jokes started, and Eddie sang *where have you gone, Billy Boy, Billy Boy, oh, where have you gone, charming Billy?* They sang until dark, marching to the sea.

Giggling, lying now on his back, Paul Berlin saw the moon move. He could not stop. Was it the moon? Or the clouds moving, making the moon seem to move? Or the boy's round face, pressing him, forcing out the giggles. "It wasn't so bad," he would tell his father. "I was a man. I saw it the first day, the very first day at the war, I saw all of it from the start, I learned it, and it wasn't so bad, and later on, later on it got better, later on, once I learned the tricks, later on it wasn't so bad." He couldn't stop.

The soldier was on top of him.

"Okay, man, *okay*."

He saw the face then, clearly, for the first time.

"It's okay."

The face of the moon, and later the moon went under clouds, and the column was moving.

The boy helped him up.

"Okay?"

"Sure, okay."

The boy gave him a stick of gum. It was Black Jack, the precious stuff. "You'll do fine," Cacciato said. "You will. You got a terrific sense of humor."

1975, 1978

ANN BEATTIE

(1947–)

Ann Beattie speaks for her generation, witnesses to the altruism and turmoil of the sixties who came to adulthood in the egocentric seventies. Most Beattie characters are educated and middle class. They live in New England or the Middle Atlantic region. Often they are surrounded by remnants of the past: inherited houses, failing automobiles, past lovers or spouses, and the popular music that is always a part of the background. Their work is tedious, their relatives irritating or mad. Yearning for romance, they often settle for sex. In the face of disillusionment, their habitual stance is inaction. In an interview, Beattie describes the characters of her first novel, *Chilly Scenes of Winter* (1976): "They all feel sort of let down, either by not having involved themselves more in the '60s now that the '70s are so dreadful, or else by having involved themselves very much to no avail," attitudes she admits were common among her own friends.

Beattie was born and raised in Washington, D.C., where her father worked for the Department of Health, Education, and Welfare. She took her undergraduate work at American University (B.A., 1969), earned an M.A. at the University of Connecticut in 1970 and entered the Ph.D. program there, where she met and married David Gates, a musician. She has taught at the University of Virginia and Harvard. With a Guggenheim grant she returned to Connecticut, lived briefly in New York, spent summers writing in Vermont, and then settled in an old house in Charlottesville, Virginia.

Beattie has earned praise for her ability to reproduce the verbal and physical texture of contemporary life. She admits to using incidents gleaned from her acquaintances, insisting that she never uses "a real bitter wound" and that an actual anecdote "comes out very scrambled." Claiming she does not have an ear that retains dialogue, she says that what has impressed her becomes apparent only as she writes, often years later. Part of her effect of immediacy derives from her use of headline events, for instance, the falling of Skylab in *Falling in Place* (1980), or popular entertainment such as soap opera in *Love Always* (1985). In a 1980 interview, she said "I really love the notion of found art. Warhol soup cans—that kind of stuff. When I write something, I like to look out the window the night I'm typing and see what kind of moon it was on July the 15th and put it in."

Often the lyrics of popular songs comment ironically on the lives of her characters. The common experience of popular music weaving a tapestry behind the emotional events of the lives in the foreground is present in all the novels and short stories and made an explicit theme in *Love Always*. "All over America, people were driving around hearing a song and remembering exactly where they were, who they loved, how they thought it would turn out. In traffic jams, women with babies and grocery bags were suddenly eighteen years old, in summer, on the beach in the arms of somebody who hummed that song in their ear. They ironed to songs they had slow-danced to, shot through intersections on yellow lights the way they always had, keeping time with the Doors' drumbeat."

Although she declines to provide an explicitly moral component to her fiction "because I don't think there are answers to give," she succeeds in describing and analyzing contemporary alienation. Her characters know that some crucial ingredient is missing from their lives, but because they cannot identify it, they don't know where to seek it. In spare, elegant prose, Beattie demonstrates their sense of loss.

Beattie's novels to date are named above. Short stories are collected in *Distortions,* 1976; *Secrets and Surprises,* 1978; *The Burning House,* 1982; and *Where You'll Find Me,* 1986.

Brief appraisals appear in *Dictionary of Literary Biography Yearbook: 1982,* 1983; and Catherine Rainwater and William J. Scheick, eds., *Contemporary American Women Writers: Narrative Strategies,* 1985.

Shifting

The woman's name was Natalie, and the man's name was Larry. They had been childhood sweethearts; he had first kissed her at an ice-skating party when they were ten. She had been unlacing her skates and had not expected the kiss. He had not expected to do it, either—he had some notion of getting his face out of the wind that was blowing across the iced-over lake, and he found himself ducking his head toward her. Kissing her seemed the natural thing to do. When they graduated from high school he was named "class clown" in the yearbook, but Natalie didn't think of him as being particularly funny. He spent more time that she thought he needed to studying chemistry, and he never laughed when she joked. She really did not think of him as funny. They went to the same college, in their hometown, but he left after a year to go to a larger, more impressive university. She took the train to be with him on weekends, or he took the train to see her. When he graduated, his parents gave him a car. If they had given it to him when he was still in college, it would have made things much easier. They waited to give it to him until graduation day, forcing him into attending the graduation exercises. He thought his parents were wonderful people, and Natalie liked them in a way, too, but she resented their perfect timing, their careful smiles. They were afraid that he would marry her. Eventually, he did. He had gone on to graduate school after college, and he set a date six months ahead for their wedding so that it would take place after his first-semester final exams. That way he could devote his time to studying for the chemistry exams.

When she married him, he had had the car for eight months. It still smelled like a brand-new car. There was never any clutter in the car. Even the ice scraper was kept in the glove compartment. There was not even a sweater or a lost glove in the back seat. He vacuumed the car every weekend, after washing it at the car wash. On Friday nights, on their way to some cheap restaurant and a dollar movie, he would stop at the car wash, and she would get out so he could vacuum all over the inside of the car. She would lean against the metal wall of the car wash and watch him clean it.

It was expected that she would not become pregnant. She did not. It had also been expected that she would keep their apartment clean, and keep out of the way as much as possible in such close quarters while he was studying. The apartment was messy, though, and when he was studying late at night she would interrupt him and try to talk him into going to sleep. He gave a chemistry-class lecture once a week, and she would often tell him that overpreparing was as bad as underpreparing. She did not know if she believed this, but it was a favorite line of hers. Sometimes he listened to her.

On Tuesdays, when he gave the lecture, she would drop him off at school and then drive to a supermarket to do the week's shopping. Usually she did not make a list before she went shopping, but when she got to the parking lot she would take a tablet out of her purse and write a few items on it, sitting in the car in the cold. Even having a few things written down would stop her from wandering aimlessly in the store and buying things that she would never use. Before this, she had bought several pans and cans of food that she had not used, or that she could have done without. She felt better when she had a list.

She would drop him at school again on Wednesdays, when he had two seminars that together took up all the afternoon. Sometimes she would drive out of town then, to the suburbs, and shop there if any shopping needed to be done. Otherwise, she would go to the art museum, which was not far away but hard to get to by bus. There was one piece of sculpture in there that she wanted very much to touch, but the guard was always nearby. She came so often that in time the guard began to nod hello. She wondered if she could ever persuade the man to turn his head for a few seconds—only that long—so she could stroke the sculpture. Of course she would never dare ask. After wandering through the museum and looking at least twice at the sculpture, she would go to the gift shop and buy a few postcards and then sit on one of the museum benches, padded with black vinyl, with a Calder mobile hanging overhead, and write notes to friends. (She never wrote letters.) She would tuck the postcards in her purse and mail them when she left the museum. But before she left, she often had coffee in the restaurant; she saw mothers and children struggling there, and women dressed in fancy clothes talking with their faces close together, as quietly as lovers.

On Thursdays he took the car. After his class he would drive to visit his parents and his friend Andy, who had been wounded in Vietnam. About once a month she would go with him, but she had to feel up to it. Being with Andy embarrassed her. She had told him not to go to Vietnam—told him that he could prove his patriotism in some other way—and finally, after she and Larry had made a visit together and she had seen Andy in the motorized bed in his parents' house, Larry had agreed that she need not go again. Andy had apologized to her. It embarrassed her that this man, who had been blown sky-high by a land mine and had lost a leg and lost the full use of his arms, would smile up at her ironically and say, "You were right." She also felt as though he wanted to hear what she would say now, and that now he would listen. Now she had nothing to say. Andy would pull himself up, relying on his right arm, which was the stronger, gripping the rails at the side of the bed, and sometimes he would take her hand. His arms were still weak, but the doctors said he would regain complete use of his right arm with time. She had to make an effort not to squeeze his hand when he held hers because she found herself wanting to squeeze energy back into him. She had a morbid curiosity about what it felt like to be blown from the ground—to go up, and to come crashing down. During their visit Larry would put on the class-clown act for Andy, telling funny stories and laughing uproariously.

Once or twice Larry had talked Andy into getting in his wheelchair and had loaded him into the car and taken him to a bar. Larry called her once, late, pretty drunk, to say that he would not be home that night—that he would sleep at his parents' house. "My God," she said. "Are you going to drive Andy home when you're drunk?" "What the hell else can happen to him?" he said.

Larry's parents blamed her for Larry's not being happy. His mother could only be pleasant with her for a short while, and then she would veil her criticisms by putting them as questions. "I know that one thing that helps enormously is good nutrition," his mother said. "He works so hard that he probably needs quite a few vitamins as well, don't you think?" Larry's father was the sort of man who found hobbies in order to avoid his wife. His hobbies were building model boats, repairing clocks, and photography. He took pictures of himself building the boats and fixing the clocks, and gave the pictures, in cardboard frames, to Natalie and Larry for Christmas and birthday presents. Larry's mother was very anxious to stay on close terms with her son, and she knew that Natalie did not like her very much. Once she had visited them during the week, and Natalie, not knowing what to do with her, had taken her to the museum. She had pointed out the sculpture, and his mother had glanced at it and then ignored it. Natalie hated her for her bad taste. She had bad taste in the sweaters she gave Larry, too, but he wore them. They made him look collegiate. That whole world made her sick.

When Natalie's uncle died and left her his 1965 Volvo, they immediately decided to sell it and use the money for a vacation. They put an ad in the paper, and there were several callers. There were some calls on Tuesday, when Larry was in class, and Natalie found herself putting the people off. She told one woman that the car had too much mileage on it, and mentioned body rust, which it did not have; she told another caller, who was very persistent, that the car was already sold. When Larry returned from school she explained that the phone was off the hook because so many people were calling about the car and she had decided not to sell it after all. They could take a little money from their savings account and go on the trip if he wanted. But she did not want to sell the car. "It's not an automatic shift," he said. "You don't know how to drive it." She told him that she could learn. "It will cost money to insure it," he said, "and it's old and probably not even dependable." She wanted to keep the car. "I know," he said, "but it doesn't make sense. When we have more money, you can have a car. You can have a newer, better car."

The next day she went out to the car, which was parked in the driveway of an old lady next door. Her name was Mrs. Larsen and she no longer drove a car, and she told Natalie she could park their second car there. Natalie opened the car door and got behind the wheel and put her hands on it. The wheel was covered with a flaky yellow-and-black plastic cover. She eased it off. A few pieces of foam rubber stuck to the wheel. She picked them off. Underneath the cover, the wheel was a dull red. She ran her fingers around and around the circle of the wheel. Her cousin Burt had delivered the car—a young opportunist, sixteen years old, who said he would drive it the hundred miles from his house to theirs for twenty dollars and a bus ticket home. She had not even invited him to stay for dinner, and Larry had driven him to the bus station. She wondered if it was Burt's cigarette in the ashtray or her dead uncle's. She could not even remember if her uncle smoked. She was surprised that he had left her his car. The car was much more comfortable than Larry's, and it had a nice smell inside. It smelled a little the way a field smells after a spring rain. She rubbed the side of her head back and forth against the window and then got out of the car and went in to see Mrs. Larsen. The night before, she had suddenly thought of the boy who brought the old lady the evening newspaper every night; he looked old enough to drive, and he would probably know how to shift. Mrs. Larsen agreed with her—she was sure that he could teach her. "Of course, everything has its price," the old lady said.

"I know that. I meant to offer him money," Natalie said, and was surprised, listening to her voice, that she sounded old too.

She took an inventory and made a list of things in their apartment. Larry had met an insurance man one evening while playing basketball at the gym who told him that they should have a list of their possessions, in case of theft. "What's worth anything?" she said when he told her. It was their first argument in almost a year—the first time in a year, anyway, that their voices were raised. He told her that several of the pieces of furniture his grandparents gave them when they got married were antiques, and the man at the gym said that if they weren't going to get them appraised every year, at least they should take snapshots of them and keep the pictures in a safe-deposit box. Larry told her to photograph the pie safe (which she used to store linen), the piano with an inlaid mother-of-pearl decoration on the music rack (neither of them knew how to play), and the table with hand-carved wooden handles and a marble top. He bought her an Instamatic camera at the drugstore, with film and flash bulbs. "Why can't you do it?" she said, and an argument began. He said that she had no respect for his profession and no understanding of the amount of study that went into getting a master's degree in chemistry.

That night he went out to meet two friends at the gym, to shoot baskets. She put the little flashcube into the top of the camera, dropped in the film and closed the back. She went first to the piano. She leaned forward so that she was close enough to see the inlay clearly, but she found that when she was that close the whole piano wouldn't fit into the picture. She decided to take two pictures. Then she photographed the pie safe, with one door open, showing the towels and sheets stacked inside. She did not have a reason for opening the door, except that she remembered a *Perry Mason* show in which detectives photographed everything with the doors hanging open. She photographed the table, lifting the lamp off it first. There were still eight pictures left. She went to the mirror in their bedroom and held the camera above her head, pointing down at an angle, and photographed her image in the mirror. She took off her slacks and sat on the floor and leaned back, aiming the camera down at her legs. Then she stood up and took a picture of her feet, leaning over and aiming down. She put on her favorite record: Stevie Wonder singing "For Once in My Life." She found herself wondering what it would be like to be blind, to have to feel things to see them. She thought about the piece of sculpture in the museum—the two elongated mounds, intertwined, the smooth gray stone as shiny as sea pebbles. She photographed the kitchen, bathroom, bedroom and living room. There was one picture left. She put her left hand on her thigh, palm up, and with some difficulty—with the camera nestled into her neck like a violin—snapped a picture of it with her right hand. The next day would be her first driving lesson.

He came to her door at noon, as he had said he would. He had on a long maroon scarf, which made his deep-blue eyes very striking. She had only seen him from her window when he carried the paper in to the old lady. He was a little nervous. She hoped that it was just the anxiety of any teen-ager confronting an adult. She needed to have him like her. She did not learn about mechanical things easily (Larry had told her that he would have invested in a "real" camera, except that he did not have the time to teach her about it), so she wanted him to be patient. He sat on the footstool in her living room, still in coat and scarf, and told her how a stick shift operated. He moved his hand through the air. The motion he made reminded her of the salute spacemen gave to earthlings in a science-fiction picture she had recently watched on late-night television. She nodded. "How much—"she began, but he interrupted and said, "You can decide what it was worth when you've learned." She was surprised and wondered if he meant to charge a great deal. Would it be her fault and would she have to pay him if he named his price when the lessons were over? But he had an honest face. Perhaps he was just embarrassed to talk about money.

He drove for a few blocks, making her watch his hand on the stick shift. "Feel how the car is going?" he said. "Now you shift." He shifted. The car jumped a little, hummed, moved into gear. It was an old car and didn't shift too easily, he said. She had been sitting forward, so that when he shifted she rocked back hard against the seat—harder than she needed to. Almost unconsciously, she wanted to show him what a good teacher he was. When her turn came to drive, the car stalled. "Take it easy," he said. "Ease up on the clutch. Don't just raise your foot off of it like that." She tried it again. "That's it," he said. She looked at him when the car was in third. He sat in the seat, looking out the window. Snow was expected. It was Thursday. Although Larry was going to visit his parents and would not be back until late Friday afternoon, she decided she would wait until Tuesday for her next lesson. If he came home early, he would find out that she was taking lessons, and she didn't want him to know. She asked the boy, whose name was Michael, whether he thought she would forget all he had taught her in the time between lessons. "You'll remember," he said.

When they returned to the old lady's driveway, the car stalled going up the incline. She had trouble shifting. The boy put his hand over hers and kicked the heel of his hand forward. "You'll have to treat this car a little roughly, I'm afraid," he said. That afternoon, after he left, she made spaghetti sauce, chopping little pieces of pepper and onion and mushroom. When the sauce had cooked down, she called Mrs. Larsen and said that she would bring over dinner. She usually ate with the old lady once a week. The old lady often added a pinch of cinnamon to her food, saying that it brought out the flavor better than salt, and that since she was losing her sense of smell, food had to be strongly flavored for her to taste it. Once she had sprinkled cinnamon on a knockwurst. This time, as they ate, Natalie asked the old lady how much she paid the boy to bring the paper.

"I give him a dollar a week," the old lady said.

"Did he set the price, or did you?"

"He set the price. He told me he wouldn't take much because he has to walk this street to get to his apartment anyway."

"He taught me a lot about the car today," Natalie said.

"He's very handsome, isn't he?" the old lady said.

She asked Larry, "How were your parents?"

"Fine," he said. "But I spent almost all the time with Andy. It's almost his birthday, and he's depressed. We went to see Mose Allison."

"I think it stinks that hardly anyone else ever visits Andy," she said.

"He doesn't make it easy. He tells you everything that's on his mind, and there's no way you can pretend that his troubles don't amount to much. You just have to sit there and nod."

She remembered that Andy's room looked like a gymnasium. There were handgrips and weights scattered on the floor. There was even a psychedelic pink hula hoop that he was to put inside his elbow and then move his arm in circles wide enough to make the hoop spin. He couldn't do it. He would lie in bed with the hoop in back of his neck, and holding the sides, lift his neck off the pillow. His arms were barely strong enough to do that, really, but he could raise his neck with no trouble, so he just pretended that his arms pulling the loop were raising it. His parents thought that it was a special exercise that he had mastered.

"What did you do today?" Larry said now.

"I made spaghetti," she said. She had made it the day before, but she thought that since he was mysterious about the time he spent away from her ("in the lab" and "at the gym" became interchangeable), she did not owe him a straight answer. That day she had dropped off the film and then she had sat at the drugstore counter to have a cup of coffee. She bought some cigarettes, though she had not smoked since high school. She smoked one mentholated cigarette and then threw the pack away in a garbage container outside the drugstore. Her mouth still felt cool inside.

He asked if she had planned anything for the weekend.

"No," she said.

"Let's do something you'd like to do. I'm a little ahead of myself in the lab right now."

That night they ate spaghetti and made plans, and the next day they went for a ride in the country, to a factory where wooden toys were made. In the showroom he made a bear marionette shake and twist. She examined a small rocking horse, rhythmically pushing her finger up and down on the back rung of the rocker to make it rock. When they left they took with them a catalogue of toys they could order. She knew that they would never look at the catalogue again. On their way to the museum he stopped to wash the car. Because it was the weekend there were quite a few cars lined up waiting to go in. They were behind a blue Cadillac that seemed to inch forward of its own accord, without a driver. When the Cadillac moved into the washing area, a tiny man hopped out. He stood on tiptoe to reach the coin box to start the washing machine. She doubted if he was five feet tall.

"Look at that poor son of a bitch," he said.

The little man was washing his car.

"If Andy could get out more," Larry said. "If he could get rid of that feeling he has that he's the only freak . . . I wonder if it wouldn't do him good to come spend a week with us."

"Are you going to take him in the wheelchair to the lab with you?" she said. "I'm not taking care of Andy all day."

His face changed. "Just for a week was all I meant," he said.

"I'm not doing it," she said. She was thinking of the boy, and the car. She had almost learned how to drive the car.

"Maybe in the warm weather," she said. "When we could go to the park or something."

He said nothing. The little man was rinsing his car. She sat inside when their turn came. She thought that Larry had no right to ask her to take care of Andy. Water flew out of the hose and battered the car. She thought of Andy, in the woods at night, stepping on the land mine, being blown into the air. She wondered if it threw him in an arc, so he ended up somewhere away from where he had been walking, or if it just blasted him straight up, if he went up the way an umbrella opens. Andy had been a wonderful ice skater. They all envied him his long sweeping turns, with his legs somehow neatly together and his body at the perfect angle. She never saw him have an accident on the ice. Never once. She had known Andy, and they had skated at Parker's pond, for eight years before he was drafted.

The night before, as she and Larry were finishing dinner, he had asked her if she intended to vote for Nixon or McGovern in the election. "McGovern," she said. How could he not have known that? She knew then that they were farther apart than she had thought. She hoped that on Election Day she could drive herself to the polls—not go with him and not walk. She planned not to ask the old lady if she wanted to come along because that would be one vote she could keep Nixon from getting.

At the museum she hesitated by the sculpture but did not point it out to him. He didn't look at it. He gazed to the side, above it, at a Francis Bacon painting.

He could have shifted his eyes just a little and seen the sculpture, and her, standing and staring.

After three more lessons she could drive the car. The last two times, which were later in the afternoon than her first lesson, they stopped at the drugstore to get the old lady's paper, to save him from having to make the same trip back on foot. When he came out of the drugstore with the paper, after the final lesson, she asked him if he'd like to have a beer to celebrate.

"Sure," he said.

They walked down the street to a bar that was filled with college students. She wondered if Larry ever came to this bar. He had never said that he did.

She and Michael talked. She asked why he wasn't in high school. He told her that he had quit. He was living with his brother, and his brother was teaching him carpentry, which he had been interested in all along. On his napkin he drew a picture of the cabinets and bookshelves he and his brother had spent the last week constructing and installing in the house of two wealthy old sisters. He drummed the side of his thumb against the edge of the table in time with the music. They each drank beer, from heavy glass mugs.

"Mrs. Larsen said your husband was in school," the boy said. "What's he studying?"

She looked up, surprised. Michael had never mentioned her husband to her before. "Chemistry," she said.

"I liked chemistry pretty well," he said. "Some of it."

"My husband doesn't know you've been giving me lessons. I'm just going to tell him that I can drive the stick shift, and surprise him."

"Yeah?" the boy said. "What will he think about that?"

"I don't know," she said. "I don't think he'll like it."

"Why?" the boy said.

His question made her remember that he was sixteen. What she had said would never have provoked another question from an adult. The adult would have nodded or said, "I know."

She shrugged. The boy took a long drink of beer. "I thought it was funny that he didn't teach you himself, when Mrs. Larsen told me you were married," he said.

They had discussed her. She wondered why Mrs. Larsen wouldn't have told her that, because the night she ate dinner with her she had talked to Mrs. Larsen about what an extraordinarily patient teacher Michael was. Had Mrs. Larsen told him that Natalie talked about him?

On the way back to the car she remembered the photographs and went back to the drugstore and picked up the prints. As she took money out of her wallet she remembered that today was the day she would have to pay him. She looked around at him, at the front of the store, where he was flipping through magazines. He was tall and he was wearing a very old black jacket. One end of his long thick maroon scarf was hanging down his back.

"What did you take pictures of?" he said when they were back in the car.

"Furniture. My husband wanted pictures of our furniture, in case it was stolen."

"Why?" he said.

"They say if you have proof that you had valuable things, the insurance company won't hassle you about reimbursing you."

"You have a lot of valuable stuff?" he said.

"My husband thinks so," she said.

A block from the driveway she said, "What do I owe you?"

"Four dollars," he said.

"That's nowhere near enough," she said and looked over at him. He had opened the envelope with the pictures in it while she was driving. He was staring at the pictures of her legs. "What's this?" he said.

She turned into the driveway and shut off the engine. She looked at the picture. She could not think what to tell him it was. Her hands and heart felt heavy.

"Wow," the boy said. He laughed. "Never mind. Sorry. I'm not looking at any more of them."

He put the pack of pictures back in the envelope and dropped it on the seat between them.

She tried to think what to say, of some way she could turn the pictures into a joke. She wanted to get out of the car and run. She wanted to stay, not to give him the money, so he would sit there with her. She reached into her purse and took out her wallet and removed four one-dollar bills.

"How many years have you been married?" he asked.

"One," she said. She held the money out to him. He said "Thank you" and leaned across the seat and put his right arm over her shoulder and kissed her. She felt his scarf bunched up against their cheeks. She was amazed at how warm his lips were in the cold car.

He moved his head away and said, "I didn't think you'd mind if I did that." She shook her head no. He unlocked the door and got out.

"I could drive you to your brother's apartment," she said. Her voice sounded hollow. She was extremely embarrassed, but she couldn't let him go.

He got back in the car. "You could drive me and come in for a drink," he said. "My brother's working."

When she got back to the car two hours later she saw a white parking ticket clamped under the windshield wiper, flapping in the wind. When she opened the car door and sank into the seat, she saw that he had left the money, neatly folded, on the floor mat on his side of the car. She did not pick up the money. In a while she started the car. She stalled it twice on the way home. When she had pulled into the driveway she looked at the money for a long time, then left it lying there. She left the car unlocked, hoping the money would be stolen. If it disappeared, she could tell herself that she had paid him. Otherwise she would not know how to deal with the situation.

When she got into the apartment, the phone rang. "I'm at the gym to play basketball," Larry said. "Be home in an hour."

"I was at the drugstore," she said. "See you then."

She examined the pictures. She sat on the sofa and laid them out, the twelve of them, in three rows on the cushion next to her. The picture of the piano was between the picture of her feet and the picture of herself that she had shot by aiming into the mirror. She picked up the four pictures of their furniture and put them on the table. She picked up the others and examined them closely. She began to understand why she had taken them. She had photographed parts of her body, fragments of it, to study the pieces. She had probably done it because she thought so much about Andy's body and the piece that was gone—the leg, below the knee, on his left side. She had had two bourbon-and-waters at the boy's apartment, and drinking always depressed her. She felt very depressed looking at the pictures, so she put them down and went into the bedroom. She undressed. She looked at her body —whole, not a bad figure—in the mirror. It was an automatic reaction with her to close the curtains when she was naked, so she turned quickly and went to the window and did that. She went back to the mirror; the room was darker now and her body looked better. She ran her hands down her sides, wondering if the feel of her skin was anything like the way the sculpture would feel. She was sure that the sculpture would be smoother—her hands would move more quickly down the slopes of it than she wanted—that it would be cool, and that somehow she could feel the grayness of it. Those things seemed preferable to her hands lingering on her body, the imperfection of her skin, the overheated apartment. If she were the piece of sculpture and if she could feel, she would like her sense of isolation.

This was in 1972, in Philadelphia.

1978

LESLIE MARMON SILKO
(1948–)

Leslie Marmon Silko was born in Albuquerque, New Mexico, and brought up on the Laguna Pueblo Reservation, where members of her family had lived for several generations. As a child she was told the traditional myths by her great-aunt, Susan Marmon, and great-grandmother, Marie Anaya Marmon. These women, who had been educated in boarding schools in Pennsylvania, returned to the reservation, where they worked at preserving the traditional lore of their tribe. Silko describes her Aunt Susie, a rancher and schoolteacher, sitting at the kitchen table with notebooks into which she transcribed the old stories, stopping when asked to tell the children the tales.

Silko, already a mother at eighteen, graduated from the University of New Mexico. She has taught English there, and served as writer in residence at the University of Washington and Vassar College. In 1981 she took a leave from her position at the University of Arizona to accept a five-year grant from the MacArthur Foundation.

She lived for a time in the 1970's in Ketchikan, Alaska. While there she stayed for a month in Bethel, a remote village of the Inuit ("the people," as the Eskimo call themselves). She found the setting so congenial she was reluctant to leave. In Bethel she learned some stories of the tribal group who lived there; the title story in her collection *Storyteller* (1981) draws on Inuit tradition. In this story and in many others, Silko combines traditional material with modern experience. Often the characters—steeped in the folklore of their people—equate or confuse the events of their lives with the old stories they know.

Silko's first book was a collection of poetry, *Laguna Woman* (1974). Her first critical notice, however, resulted from the publication of her first novel, *Ceremony* (1977). Tayo, the main character, is a World War II veteran haunted by his wartime experiences, especially the order to kill Japanese soldiers, who had strong facial resemblances to members of his own tribe and family. Tayo, like the author, is a mixed-blood resident of the Laguna Pueblo; he finds the ceremonies that heal his mind through an old Indian of mixed blood whose ancient and more modern wisdom combine in ways that prove stronger than the rituals of the appointed tribal medicine men. The idea that tradition gains strength through change is central to Silko's writing. Her narrative technique is similarly mixed as poetry and traditional chants vie for space with prose history and fiction, especially in *Storyteller,* which combines short fiction, family history, poetry, and family photographs.

Silko's volumes of fiction and poetry are named above. Anne Wright edited *The Delicacy and Strength of Lace,* 1986, letters to and from James Wright.

Yellow Woman

My thigh clung to his with dampness, and I watched the sun rising up through the tamaracks and willows. The small brown water birds came to the river and hopped across the mud, leaving brown scratches in the alkali-white crust. They bathed in the river silently. I could hear the water, almost at our feet where the narrow fast channel bubbled and washed green ragged moss and fern leaves. I looked at him beside me, rolled in the red blanket on the white river sand. I cleaned the sand out of the cracks between my toes, squinting because the sun was above the willow trees. I looked at him for the last time, sleeping on the white river sand.

I felt hungry and followed the river south the way we had come the afternoon before, following our footprints that were already blurred by lizard tracks and bug trails. The horses were still lying down, and the black one whinnied when he saw me but he did not get up—maybe it was because the corral was made out of thick cedar branches and the horses had not yet felt the sun like I had. I tried to look beyond the pale red mesas to the pueblo. I knew it was there, even if I could not see it, on the sandrock hill above the river, the same river that moved past me now and had reflected the moon last night.

The horse felt warm underneath me. He shook his head and pawed the sand. The bay whinnied and leaned against the gate trying to follow, and I remembered him asleep in the red blanket beside the river. I slid off the horse and tied him close to the other horse, I walked north with the river again, and the white stand broke loose in footprints over footprints.

"Wake up."

He moved in the blanket and turned his face to me with his eyes still closed. I knelt down to touch him.

"I'm leaving."

He smiled now, eyes still closed. "You are coming with me, remember?" He sat up now with his bare dark chest and belly in the sun.

"Where?"

"To my place."

"And will I come back?"

He pulled his pants on. I walked away from him, feeling him behind me and smelling the willows.

"Yellow Woman," he said.

I turned to face him. "Who are you?" I asked.

He laughed and knelt on the low, sandy bank, washing his face in the river. "Last night you guessed my name, and you knew why I had come."

I stared past him at the shallow moving water and tried to remember the night, but I could only see the moon in the water and remember his warmth around me.

"But I only said that you were him and that I was Yellow Woman—I'm not really her—I have my own name and I come from the pueblo on the other side of the mesa. Your name is Silva and you are a stranger I met by the river yesterday afternoon."

He laughed softly. "What happened yesterday has nothing to do with what you will do today, Yellow Woman."

"I know—that's what I'm saying—the old stories about the ka'tsina spirit and Yellow Woman can't mean us."

My old grandpa liked to tell those stories best. There is one about Badger and Coyote who went hunting and were gone all day, and when the sun was going down they found a house. There was a girl living there alone, and she had light hair and eyes and she told them that they could sleep with her. Coyote wanted to be with her all night so he sent Badger into a prairie-dog hole, telling him he thought he saw something in it. As soon as Badger crawled in, Coyote blocked up the entrance with rocks and hurried back to Yellow Woman.

"Come here," he said gently.

He touched my neck and I moved close to him to feel his breathing and to hear his heart. I was wondering if Yellow Woman had known who she was—if she knew that she would become part of the stories. Maybe she'd had another name that her husband and relatives called her so that only the ka'tsina from the north and the storytellers would know her as Yellow Woman. But I didn't go on; I felt him all around me, pushing me down into the white river sand.

Yellow Woman went away with the spirit from the north and lived with him and his relatives. She was gone for a long time, but then one day she came back and she brought twin boys.

"Do you know the story?"

"What story?" He smiled and pulled me close to him as he said this. I was afraid lying there on the red blanket. All I could know was the way he felt, warm, damp, his body beside me. This is the way it happens in the stories, I was thinking, with no thought beyond the moment she meets the ka'tsina spirit and they go.

"I don't have to go. What they tell in stories was real only then, back in time immemorial, like they say."

He stood up and pointed at my clothes tangled in the blanket. "Let's go," he said.

I walked beside him, breathing hard because he walked fast, his hand around my wrist. I had stopped trying to pull away from him, because his hand felt cool and the sun was high, drying the river bed into alkali. I will see someone, eventually I will see someone, and then I will be certain that he is only a man—some man from nearby—and I will be sure that I am not Yellow Woman. Because she is from out of time past and I live now and I've been to school and there are highways and pickup trucks that Yellow Woman never saw.

It was an easy ride north on horseback. I watched the change from the cottonwood trees along the river to the junipers that brushed past us in the foothills, and finally there were only piñons, and when I looked up at the rim of the mountain plateau I could see pine trees growing on the edge. Once I stopped to look down, but the pale sandstone had disappeared and the river was gone and the dark lava hills were all around. He touched my hand, not speaking, but always singing softly a mountain song and looking into my eyes.

I felt hungry and wondered what they were doing at home now—my mother, my grandmother, my husband, and the baby. Cooking breakfast, saying, "Where did she go?—maybe kidnapped." And Al going to the tribal police with the details: "She went walking along the river."

The house was made with black lava rock and red mud. It was high above the spreading miles of arroyos and long mesas. I smelled a mountain smell of pitch and buck brush. I stood there beside the black horse, looking down on the small, dim country we had passed, and I shivered.

"Yellow Woman, come inside where it's warm." He lit a fire in the stove. It was an old stove with a round belly and an enamel coffeepot on top. There was only the stove, some faded Navajo blankets, and a bedroll and cardboard box. The floor was made of smooth adobe plaster, and there was one small window facing east. He pointed at the box.

"There's some potatoes and the frying pan." He sat on the floor with his arms around his knees pulling them close to his chest and he watched me fry the potatoes. I didn't mind him watching me because he was always watching me—he had been watching me since I came upon him sitting on the river bank trimming leaves from a willow twig with his knife. We ate from the pan and he wiped the grease from his fingers on his Levi's.

"Have you brought women here before?" He smiled and kept chewing, so I said, "Do you always use the same tricks?"

"What tricks?" He looked at me like he didn't understand.

"The story about being a ka'tsina from the mountains. The story about Yellow Woman."

Silva was silent; his face was calm.

"I don't believe it. Those stories couldn't happen now," I said.

He shook his head and said softly, "But someday they will talk about us, and they will say, 'Those two lived long ago when things like that happened.' "

He stood up and went out. I ate the rest of the potatoes and thought about things—about the noise the stove was making and the sound of the mountain wind outside. I remembered yesterday and the day before, and then I went outside.

I walked past the corral to the edge where the narrow trail cut through the black rim rock. I was standing in the sky with nothing around me but the wind that came down from the blue mountain peak behind me. I could see faint mountain images in the distance miles across the vast spread of mesas and valleys and plains. I wondered who was over there to feel the mountain wind on those sheer blue edges—who walks on the pine needles in those blue mountains.

"Can you see the pueblo?" Silva was standing behind me.

I shook my head. "We're too far away."

"From here I can see the world." He stepped out on the edge. "The Navajo reservation begins over there." He pointed to the east. "The Pueblo boundaries are over here." He looked below us to the south, where the narrow trail seemed to come from. "The Texans have their ranches over there, starting with that valley, the Concho Valley. The Mexicans run some cattle over there too."

"Do you ever work for them?"

"I steal from them," Silva answered. The sun was dropping behind us and the shadows were filling the land below. I turned away from the edge that dropped forever into the valleys below.

"I'm cold," I said, "I'm going inside." I started wondering about this man who could speak the Pueblo language so well but who lived on a mountain and rustled cattle. I decided that this man Silva must be Navajo, because Pueblo men didn't do things like that.

"You must be a Navajo."

Silva shook his head gently. "Little Yellow Woman," he said, "you never give up, do you? I have told you who I am. The Navajo people know me, too." He knelt down and unrolled the bedroll and spread the extra blankets out on a piece of canvas. The sun was down, and the only light in the house came from outside—the dim orange light from sundown.

I stood there and waited for him to crawl under the blankets.

"What are you waiting for?" he said, and I lay down beside him. He undressed me slowly like the night before beside the river—kissing my face gently and running his hands up and down my belly and legs. He took off my pants and then he laughed.

"Why are you laughing?"

"You are breathing so hard."

I pulled away from him and turned my back to him.

He pulled me around and pinned me down with his arms and chest. "You don't understand, do you, little Yellow Woman? You will do what I want."

And again he was all around me with his skin slippery against mine, and I was afraid because I understood that his strength could hurt me. I lay underneath him and I knew that he could destroy me. But later, while he slept beside me, I touched his face and I had a feeling—the kind of feeling for him that overcame me that morning along the river. I kissed him on the forehead and he reached out for me.

When I woke up in the morning he was gone. It gave me a strange feeling because for a long time I sat there on the blankets and looked around the little house for some object of his—some proof that he had been there or maybe that he was coming back. Only the blankets and the cardboard box remained. The .30-30 that had been leaning in the corner was gone, and so was the knife I had used the night before. He was gone, and I had my chance to go now. But first I had to eat, because I knew it would be a long walk home.

I found some dried apricots in the cardboard box, and I sat down on a rock at the edge of the plateau rim. There was no wind and the sun warmed me. I was surrounded by silence. I drowsed with apricots in my mouth, and I didn't believe that there were highways or railroads or cattle to steal.

When I woke up, I stared down at my feet in the black mountain dirt. Little black ants were swarming over the pine needles around my foot. They must have smelled the apricots. I thought about my family far below me. They would be wondering about me, because this had never happened to me before. The tribal police would file a report. But if old Grandpa weren't dead he would tell them what happened—he would laugh and say, "Stolen by a ka'tsina, a mountain spirit. She'll come home—they usually do." There are enough of them to handle things. My mother and grandmother will raise the baby like they raised me. Al will find someone else, and they will go on like before, except that there will be a story about the day I disappeared while I was walking along the river. Silva had come for me; he said he had. I did not decide to go. I just went. Moonflowers blossom in the sand hills before dawn, just as I followed him. That's what I was thinking as I wandered along the trail through the pine trees.

It was noon when I got back. When I saw the stone house I remembered that I had meant to go home. But that didn't seem important any more, maybe because there were little blue flowers growing in the meadow behind the stone house and the gray squirrels were playing in the pines next to the house. The horses were standing in the corral, and there was a beef carcass hanging on the shady side of a big pine in front of the house. Flies buzzed around the clotted blood that hung from the carcass. Silva was washing his hands in a bucket full of water. He must have heard me coming because he spoke to me without turning to face me.

"I've been waiting for you."

"I went walking in the big pine trees."

I looked into the bucket full of bloody water with brown-and-white animal hairs floating in it. Silva stood there letting his hand drip, examining me intently.

"Are you coming with me?"

"Where?" I asked him.

"To sell the meat in Marquez."

"If you're sure it's O.K."

"I wouldn't ask you if it wasn't," he answered.

He sloshed the water around in the bucket before he dumped it out and set the bucket upside down near the door. I followed him to the corral and watched him saddle the horses. Even beside the horses he looked tall, and I asked him again if he wasn't Navajo. He didn't say anything; he just shook his head and kept cinching up the saddle.

"But Navajos are tall."

"Get on the horse," he said, "and let's go."

The last thing he did before we started down the steep trail was to grab the .30-30 from the corner. He slid the rifle into the scabbard that hung from his saddle.

"Do they ever try to catch you?" I asked.

"They don't know who I am."

"Then why did you bring the rifle?"

"Because we are going to Marquez where the Mexicans live."

The trail leveled out on a narrow ridge that was steep on both sides like an animal spine. On one side I could see where the trail went around the rocky gray hills and disappeared into the southeast where the pale sandrock mesas stood in the distance near my home. On the other side was a trail that went west, and as I looked far into the distance I thought I saw the little town. But Silva said no, that I was looking in the wrong place, that I just thought I saw houses. After that I quit looking off into the distance; it was hot and the wildflowers were closing up their deep-yellow petals. Only the waxy cactus flowers bloomed in the bright sun, and I saw every color that a cactus blossom can be; the white ones and the red ones were still buds, but the purple and the yellow were blossoms, open full and the most beautiful of all.

Silva saw him before I did. The white man was riding a big gray horse, coming up the trail towards us. He was traveling fast and the gray horse's feet sent rocks rolling off the trail into the dry tumbleweeds. Silva motioned for me to stop and we watched the white man. He didn't see us right away, but finally his horse whinnied at our horses and he stopped. He looked at us briefly before he lapped the gray horse across the three hundred yards that separated us. He stopped his horse in front of Silva, and his young fat face was shadowed by the brim of his hat. He didn't look mad, but his small, pale eyes moved from the blood-soaked gunny sacks hanging from my saddle to Silva's face and then back to my face.

"Where did you get the fresh meat?" the white man asked.

"I've been hunting," Silva said, and when he shifted his weight in the saddle the leather creaked.

"The hell you have, Indian. You've been rustling cattle. We've been looking for the thief for a long time."

The rancher was fat, and sweat began to soak through his white cowboy shirt and the wet cloth stuck to the thick rolls of belly fat. He almost seemed to be panting from the exertion of talking, and he smelled rancid, maybe because Silva scared him.

Silva turned to me and smiled. "Go back up the mountain, Yellow Woman."

The white man got angry when he heard Silva speak in a language he couldn't understand. "Don't try anything, Indian. Just keep riding to Marquez. We'll call the state police from there."

The rancher must have been unarmed because he was very frightened and if he had a gun he would have pulled it out then. I turned my horse around and the rancher yelled, "Stop!" I looked at Silva for an instant and there was something ancient and dark—something I could feel in my stomach—in his eyes, and when I glanced at his hand I saw his finger on the trigger of the .30-30 that was still in the saddle scabbard. I slapped my horse across the flank and the sacks of raw meat swung against my knees as the horse leaped up the trail. It was hard to keep my balance, and once I thought I felt the saddle slipping backward; it was because of this that I could not look back.

I didn't stop until I reached the ridge where the trail forked. The horse was breathing deep gasps and there was a dark film of sweat on its neck. I looked down in the direction I had come from, but I couldn't see the place. I waited. The wind came up and pushed warm air past me. I looked up at the sky, pale blue and full of thin clouds and fading vapor trails left by jets.

I think four shots were fired—I remember hearing four hollow explosions that reminded me of deer hunting. There could have been more shots after that, but I couldn't have heard them because my horse was running again and the loose rocks were making too much noise as they scattered around his feet.

Horses have a hard time running downhill, but I went that way instead of uphill to the mountain because I thought it was safer. I felt better with the horse running southeast past the round gray hills that were covered with cedar trees and black lava rock. When I got to the plain in the distance I could see the dark green patches of tamaracks that grew along the river; and beyond the river I could see the beginning of the pale sandrock mesas. I stopped the horse and looked back to see if anyone was coming; then I got off the horse and turned the horse around, wondering if it would go back to its corral under the pines on the mountain. It looked back at me for a moment and then plucked a mouthful of green tumbleweeds before it trotted back up the trail with its ears pointed forward, carrying its head daintily to one side to avoid stepping on the dragging reins. When the horse disappeared over the last hill, the gunny sacks full of meat were still swinging and bouncing.

I walked toward the river on a wood-hauler's road that I knew would eventually lead to the paved road. I was thinking about waiting beside the road for someone to drive by, but by the time I got to the pavement I had decided it wasn't very far to walk if I followed the river back the way Silva and I had come.

The river water tasted good, and I sat in the shade under a cluster of silvery willows. I thought about Silva, and I felt sad at leaving him; still, there was something strange about him, and I tried to figure it out all the way back home.

I came back to the place on the river bank where he had been sitting the first time I saw him. The green willow leaves that he had trimmed from the branch were still lying there, wilted in the sand. I saw the leaves and I wanted to go back to him —to kiss him and to touch him—but the mountains were too far away now. And I told myself, because I believe it, he will come back sometimes and be waiting again by the river.

I followed the path up from the river into the village. The sun was getting low, and I could smell supper cooking when I got to the screen door of my house. I could hear their voices inside—my mother was telling my grandmother how to fix the Jell-O and my husband, Al, was playing with the baby. I decided to tell them that some Navajo had kidnapped me, but I was sorry that old Grandpa wasn't alive to hear my story because it was the Yellow Woman stories he liked to tell best.

1981

JAYNE ANNE PHILLIPS

(1952–)

Jayne Anne Phillips was born and raised in Buckhannon, West Virginia, and received a B.A. from West Virginia University in 1974. She had begun writing poetry in high school and soon found herself at the University of Iowa, where she received a master's degree in 1978. Meanwhile, her work in this period, which was already appearing in literary magazines, was collected in *Sweethearts* (1976) and *Counting* (1978), limited editions from small presses. Without a wide readership, she earned several prizes and awards, including a fellowship from the National Endowment for the Arts. *Black Tickets,* her first book from a major publisher, appeared in 1979, was enthusiastically received by reviewers, and earned the Sue Kaufman Award for First Fiction from the American Academy and Institute of Arts and Letters.

Black Tickets is a book of stark contrasts, stories of the seamy underside of American life—prostitution, child abuse, drugs, murder—alternating with stories of more ordinary family tensions, conflicts between parents and children as the parents age and fall ill and the children attempt to establish their separate but still caring lives. Many of the fictions are no more than vignettes, a page or not much more. These are interspersed with the longer, more substantial stories, somewhat in the manner of the interchapters in Hemingway's *In Our Time* (and like Hemingway's interchapters, most of the *Black Tickets* vignettes were published earlier, in *Sweethearts*). The effect is partly one of fragmentation, confusion, and the need to escape. To the extent that she has shocked some readers, it is because of the sense in some stories that the Beat Generation is with us again, but this time its spokesman is a woman. She has listed William S. Burroughs along with earlier masters of the grotesque, including Sherwood Anderson, Faulkner, Katherine Anne Porter, Flannery O'Connor, and Eudora Welty, among those writers who have most influenced her work.

Machine Dreams (1984), Phillips's first novel, derives much of its power from her earlier fictions. Much of the novel is, in fact, an expansion and revision of material central to *Black Tickets. Machine Dreams* is a family saga, a story of second choices, losses, and failed communications. The father's machine dreams are nightmares of burying dead Japanese with a bulldozer on a Pacific island in World War II. Others are similarly haunted by horrors that have happened or are yet to come. The son, missing in action in Vietnam, leaves a legacy of nightmares to his sister, who is left to try to understand them and to survive in her world. Throughout, there is also the struggle of wives, mothers, and daughters to establish meaningful places for themselves within a society radically changing its values.

Phillips has traveled widely within the United States and in India and Nepal, living in recent years on Cape Cod and in Boston. She has been a fellow of the Bunting Institute of Radcliffe College and has taught at Williams College and Boston University.

Jayne Anne Phillips's latest collection of stories is *Fast Lanes,* 1987.

The Heavenly Animal

Jancy's father always wanted to fix her car. Every time she came home for a visit, he called her at her mother's house and asked about the car with a second sentence.

Well, he'd say, How are you?

Fine, I'm fine.

And how's the car? Have any trouble?

He became incensed if Jancy's mother answered. He slammed the receiver down and broke the connection. They always knew who it was by the stutter of silence, then the violent click. He lived alone in a house ten blocks away.

Often, he would drive by and see Jancy's car before she'd even taken her coat off. He stopped his aging black Ford on the sloping street and honked two tentative blasts. He hadn't come inside her mother's house since the divorce five years ago. He wouldn't even step on the grass of the block-shaped lawn. This time Jancy saw his car from the bathroom window. She cursed and pulled her pants up. She walked outside and the heavy car door swung open. Her father wore a wool hat with a turned-up brim and small gray feather. Jancy loved the feather.

Hi, she said.

Well, hi there. When did you get in?

About five minutes ago.

Have any trouble?

She got into the car. The black interior was very clean and the empty litter bag hung from the radio knob. Jancy thought she could smell its new plastic mingling with the odor of his cigar. She leaned over and kissed him.

Thank god, she thought, he looks better.

He pointed to her car. What the hell did you do to the chrome along the side there? he said.

Trying to park, Jancy said. Got in a tight spot.

Her father shook his head and grimaced. He held the butt of the cigar with his thumb and forefinger. Jancy saw the flat chewed softness of the butt where he held it in his mouth, and the stain on his lips where it touched.

Jesus, Honey, he said.

Can't win them all.

But you got to win some of them, he said. That car's got to last you a long time.

It will, Jancy said. It's a good car. Like a tank. I could drive that car through the fiery pits of hell and come out smelling like a rose.

Well. Everything you do to it takes money to fix. And I just don't have it.

Don't want it fixed, Jancy said. Works fine without the chrome.

He never asked her at first how long she was going to stay. For the past few years she'd come home between school terms. Or from far-flung towns up East, out West. Sometimes during her visits she left to see friends. He would rant close to her face, breathing hard.

Why in God's name would you go to Washington, D.C.? Nothing there but niggers. And what the hell do you want in New York? You're going to wear out your car. You've driven that car thirty thousand miles in one year—Why? What the hell for?

The people I care about are far apart. I don't get many chances to see them.

Jesus Christ, you come home and off you go.

I'll be back in four days.

That's not the goddamn point. You'll get yourself crippled up in a car wreck running around like this. Then where will you be?

Jancy would sigh and feel herself harden.

I won't stay in one place all my life out of fear I'll get crippled if I move, she'd say.

Well I understand that, but *Jesus.*

His breathing would grow quiet. He rubbed his fingers and twisted the gold Masonic ring he wore in place of a wedding band.

Honey, he'd say. You got to *think* of these things.

And they would both sit staring.

Down the street Jancy saw red stop signs and the lawns of churches. Today he was in a good mood. Today he was just glad to see her. And he didn't know she was going to see Michael. Or was she?

What do you think? he said. Do you want to go out for lunch tomorrow? I go down to the Catholic church there, they have a senior citizen's meal. Pretty good food.

Jancy smiled. Do you remember when you stopped buying Listerine, she asked, because you found out a Catholic owned the company?

She could tell he didn't remember, but he grinned.

Hell, he said. Damn Catholics own everything.

He was sixty-seven. Tiny blood vessels in his cheeks had burst. There was that redness in his skin, and the blue of shadows, gauntness of the weight loss of a year ago. His skin got softer, his eyelids translucent as crepe. His eyelashes were very short and reddish. The flesh drooped under his heavy brows. As a young man, he'd been almost sloe-eyed. Bedroom eyes, her mother called them. Now his eyes receded in the mysterious colors of his face.

OK, Jancy said. Lunch.

She got out of the car and bent to look in at him through the open window.

Hey, she said. You look pretty snappy in that hat.

Tonight her mother would leave after supper for Ohio. Jancy would be alone in the house and she would stare at the telephone. She tore lettuce while her mother broiled the steaks.

I don't know why you want to drive all the way up there at night, Jancy said. Why don't you leave in the morning?

I can make better time at night, her mother said. And besides, the wedding is in two days. Your aunt wanted me to come last week. It's not every day her only daughter gets married, and since you refuse to go to weddings . . .

She paused. They heard the meat crackle in the oven.

I'm sorry to leave when you've just gotten here. I thought you'd be here two weeks ago, and we'd have some time before I left. But you'll be here when I get back.

Jancy looked intently into the salad bowl.

Jancy? asked her mother. Why are you so late getting here? Why didn't you write?

I was just busy . . . finishing the term, packing, subletting the apartment—

You could have phoned.

I didn't want to. I hate calling long-distance. It makes me feel lost, listening to all that static.

That's ridiculous, her mother said. Let's get this table cleared off. I don't know why you always come in and dump everything on the first available spot.

Because I believe in instant relief, Jancy said.

—books, backpack, maps, your purse—

She reached for the books and Jancy's leather purse fell to the floor. Its contents spilled and rolled. She bent to retrieve the mess before Jancy could stop her, picking up small plastic bottles of pills.

What are these? she said. What are you doing with all these pills?

I cleaned out my medicine cabinet and threw all the bottles in my purse. They're pills I've had for years—

Don't you think you better throw them away? You might forget what you're taking.

They're all labeled, Jancy said.

Her mother glanced down.

Dalmane, she said. What's Dalmane?

A sleeping pill.

Why would you need sleeping pills?

Because I have trouble sleeping. Why do you think?

Since when?

I don't know. A long time. Off and on. Will you cut it out with the third degree?

Why can't you sleep?

Because I dream my mother is relentlessly asking me questions.

It's Michael. Michael's thrown you for a loop.

Jancy threw the bottles in her purse and stood up quickly. No, she said, Or yes. We're both upset right now.

He certainly is. You're lucky to be rid of him.

I don't want to be rid of him.

He'll drive you crazy if you're not careful. He's got a screw loose and you know it.

You liked him, Jancy said. You liked him so much it made me angry.

Yes, I liked him. But not after this whole mess started. Calling you cruel because he couldn't have things his way. If he was so in love it would have lasted. Cruel. There's not a cruel bone in your body.

I should never have told you he said those things.

They were silent. Jancy smelled the meat cooking.

Why shouldn't you tell me? her mother asked quietly. If you can't talk to your mother, who can you talk to?

Oh Christ, Jancy said. Nobody. I'm hungry. Let's eat and change the subject.

They sat down over full plates. There was steak when Jancy or her brothers came home. Their mother saved it for weeks, months, in the freezer. The meat sizzled on Jancy's plate and she tried to eat. She looked up. The lines in her mother's face seemed deeper than before, grown in. And she was so thin, so perfectly groomed. Earrings. Creased pants. Silk scarves. A bath at the same time every morning while the *Today* show played the news. At night she rubbed the calluses off her heels carefully with a pumice stone.

She looked at Jancy. What are you doing tomorrow? she asked.

Having lunch at the Catholic church, Jancy said.

That ought to be good. Canned peaches and weepy mashed potatoes. Your father is something. Of course he doesn't speak to me on the street, but I see him drive by here in that black car. Every day. Watching for one of you to come home.

Jancy said nothing.

He looks terrible, her mother said.

He looks better than he did, said Jancy.

That's not saying much. He looked horrible for months. Thinner and thinner, like a walking death. I'd see him downtown. He went to the pool hall every day, always by himself. He never did have any friends.

He did, Jancy said. He told me. In the war.

I don't know. I didn't meet him till after that, when he was nearly forty. By then he never seemed to belong—

I remember that weekend you went away and he moved out, Jancy said. He never belonged in this house. The house he built had such big rooms.

Did you know that house is for sale again? her mother asked. It's changed hands several times.

I didn't know, Jancy said. Let's not talk about it.

Her mother sighed. All right, she said. Let's talk about washing these dishes. I really have to get started.

Mom, Jancy said, I might call Michael.

What for? He's five states away and that's where he ought to be.

I may go up there.

Oh, Jancy.

I have to. I can't just let it end here.

Her mother was silent. They heard a gentle thunder.

Clouding up, Jancy said. You may have rain. Need help with your bags?

The car's already packed.

Well, Jancy said.

Her mother collected maps, parcels, a large white-ribboned present. Jancy heard her moving around and thought of waking at night in the house her father had built, the house in the country. There would be the cornered light from the bathroom in the hall. Her father would walk slowly past in slippers and robe to adjust the furnace. The motor would kick in and grunt its soft hum several times a night. Half asleep, Jancy knew her father was awake. The furnace. They must have been winter nights.

Can you grab this? her mother asked.

Jancy took the present. I'll walk you out, she said.
No, just give it to me. There, I've got it.
Jancy smiled. Her mother took her hand.
You're gutsy, she said. You'll be OK.
Good, said Jancy. It's always great to be OK.
Give me a hug.
Jancy embraced her. How often did someone hold her? Her hair smelled fragrant and dark.

Jancy left the lights off. She took a sleeping pill and lay down on the living room couch. Rain splattered the windows. She imagined her father standing by the dining room table. When he moved out he had talked to her brothers about guns.
One rifle goes, he'd said. One stays. Which do you want?
Jancy remembered cigarette smoke in the room, how it curled between their faces.
It don't make any difference to me, he said. But this one's the best for rabbit.
He fingered change far down in his trouser pockets. One brother asked the other which he wanted. The other said it didn't matter, didn't matter. Finally the youngest took the gun and climbed the steps to his room. Their father walked into the kitchen, murmuring. It'll kill rabbits and birds. And if you go after deer, just use slugs.
Jancy heard water dripping. How long had it gone on? Rain was coming down the chimney. She got up and closed the flue, mopped up the rain with a towel. The pills didn't work anymore. What would she do all night? She was afraid of this house, afraid of all the houses in this town. After midnight they were silent and blank. They seemed abandoned.
She looked at the telephone. She picked up the receiver.
Michael? she said.
She dialed his number. The receiver clicked and snapped.
What number are you calling please?
He's gone, thought Jancy.
Hello? What number—
Jancy repeated the numerals.
That number has been disconnected. There's a new number. Shall I ring it for you?
The plastic dial of the princess phone was transparent and yellowed with light.
Ma'am? Shall I ring it?
Yes, Jancy said.
No one home.

Jancy took a bottle of whiskey off the shelf. She would drink enough to make her sleep. The rain had stopped and the house was still. Light from streetlamps fell through the windows. Jancy watched the deserted town. Heavy elms loomed over the sidewalks. Limbs of trees rose and fell on a night breeze. Their shadows moved on the lit-up surface of the street.
A black car glided by.
Jancy stepped back from the window. Taillights blinked red as the car turned corners and passed away soundlessly.
She picked up the phone and dialed. She lay in the cramped hallway while the

purr of a connection stopped and started. How did it sound there, ringing in the dark? Loud and empty.

Hello?

His voice, soft. When they lived together, he used to stand looking out the window at the alley late at night. He was naked and perfect. He watched the Midwestern alleys roll across eight city blocks paved in old brick. Telephone poles stood weathered and alone. Their drooping wires glistened, humming one note. He gripped the wooden frame of the window and stood looking, centaur, quiet, his flanks whitened in moonlight.

Jancy, he said now. It's you, isn't it.

Jancy wore a skirt and sat in the living room. Her father would pull up outside. She would see him lean to watch the door of the house, his head inclined toward her. His car shining and just washed. His hat. His cigar. His baggy pants bought at the same store downtown for thirty years.

Jancy walked outside to watch for him. She didn't want to jump when the horn sounded. And it suddenly hurt her that her father was always waiting.

Did he know their old house was being sold again? He had contracted the labor and built it himself. He had designed the heating system, radiant heat piped under the floors so the wooden parquet was always warm. He had raised the ceiling of the living room fifteen inches so that the crown of her mother's inherited antique bookcase would fit into it. He was a road builder, but those last few years, when Jancy was a teen-ager, he'd had a series of bad jobs—selling bulldozers, cars, insurance— After they'd moved he stopped working altogether . . .

The horn sounded suddenly close and shocked her.

Jancy?

Now why did you do that? I'm standing right here, aren't I?

Are you asleep?

No, I just didn't hear you pull up. But you didn't have to blare that horn at me. It's loud enough to wake the dead.

Well, he said, I thought you needed waking, standing there staring into space like a knothead.

Right, said Jancy. She got into the car and he was still smiling. She laughed in spite of herself.

I'm a little early, he said. They don't open at the church till noon. Do you want to go for a drive?

Where to?

We could drive out the falls road, he said.

That would take them past the old house. The hedges and trees would be larger than Jancy could believe, lush with new leaves, and rippling. Her father had planted them all.

I don't think so, said Jancy.

The house is for sale.

I know.

Dumbest thing I ever did was to let your mother talk me into selling that house.

I don't want to hear about my mother.

I'll hate her for the rest of my life for breaking up our family, he said, his breathing grown heavy. He scowled and touched the ridges in the steering wheel.

Jancy leaned back in the seat and watched clouds through the tinted windshield. Remember when you built roads? she asked.

He waited a moment, then looked over at her and pushed his hat back. I built a lot of them around here, he said, but the state don't keep them up anymore. They closed the graveyard road.

He'd taught her how to drive on that road, a narrow unpainted blacktop that wound under train trestles and through the cemetery. He said if she could drive on that road she could drive anywhere. He made her go that way, cutting across a blind curve up the sudden hill of the entrance, past the carved pillars with their lopsided lamps. This way, he'd said, and she'd pulled off onto a gravel path that turned sharply along the crest of a hill. Tombstones were scattered in the lumpy grass. Far below Jancy saw the graveyard road looping west by the river, on through woods to the country towns of Volga and Coalton and Mud Lick.

Stop here, her father directed. He nodded at a patch of ground. There we are, he said, this is where we'll be.

Jancy was sixteen; she'd stared at him and gripped the steering wheel.

All right, he'd said. Back up. Let's see how you do going backward.

Now her father started his black Ford and they passed the clipped lawns of houses. He drove slowly, his cigar in his mouth.

What will they have to eat at the church? Jancy asked.

Oh, he said. They publish a menu in the paper. Meat loaf today. Fifty cents a person over sixty. Not bad food. Cooks used to work up at the junior high. But we don't have to go there. We can go to a restaurant if you want.

No, I'd rather go where you usually go. But are you sure I'm allowed?

Certainly. You're my guest. A dollar for guests.

They pulled into the church parking lot. The doors of the rec center were closed. They sat in the car and waited. Jancy remembered dances held in this building, how she was thirteen and came here to dance with the high school boys. They had danced until they were wet with sweat, then stepped outside into the winter air. Girls stood by the lighted door and shivered while the boys smoked cigarettes, squinting into vaporous trails of smoke rings.

What about your car? asked her father.

What about it?

I'm going to take it up to Smitty's and have him go over it.

No. Doesn't need it. The car is fine. I had it checked—

I've made arrangements with Smitty for today. He's got room and we better—

But the last time he fixed it, one of the sparkplugs flew out while I was driving on the interstate—

Don't you be taking off on Smitty, her father said. He's done us a lot of good work on that car. I'm trying to help you. You don't want my help, why just let me know and I'll bow out anytime.

Jancy sighed. Her father held his hat in his lap and traced the faint lines of the wool plaid with his fingers.

I appreciate your help, she said. But I don't know if Smitty—

He might have made a mistake that one time, her father said. But he usually does real good by us.

Volkswagen buses of old people began to pull up. Drivers opened the double doors of the vans and rolled up a set of mobile steps. Old ladies appeared with their blond canes and black-netted pillbox hats. They stepped out one after another, smiling and peeking about.

Where are the old men? Jancy asked.

I think they die off quicker, her father said. These same old dames have been coming here ever since I have. They just keep moving.

• • •

Inside were long rows of Formica tables. Eight or nine elderly people sat at each. There were rows of empty chairs. Women with a cashbox between them sat beside the door. Jancy's father put his arm around Jancy's waist and patted her.

This is my daughter, he said.

Well, isn't she pretty? said one of the cashiers. The other women nodded and smiled.

Jancy signed the guest book. Under 'address' she wrote 'at large.' Her father was waiting at one of the tables. He had pulled a chair out for her and was standing behind it, waiting to seat her. The women were watching them, like the circling nurses that day at the hospital. Her father lay in bed, his arms so thin that his elbows seemed too large.

This is my daughter, he'd said to the nurses. She came all the way from California to see me.

Isn't that nice, they'd said. Is she married?

Hell no, her father had laughed. She's married to me.

Now Jancy felt the chair press up behind her legs and she sat down. Her father took his hat off and nodded at people across the table. She saw that his eyes were alight.

Aren't you going to have to get yourself a summer hat? she asked.

I reckon so, he said. I just can't find one I like.

Behind the waist-high counter, Jancy saw the fat cooks spooning peaches onto plates from metal cans. They were big women, their hair netted in silver nets, faces round and flushed from the ovens. They passed out cafeteria trays premolded for portions.

I used to eat out of those trays in grade school, Jancy said. Are they going to make us sing 'God is Great?'

No, her father said. But go ahead if it makes you feel better.

He chuckled. The last time they'd eaten together was last December. Michael had come home with Jancy and they'd gone out to lunch with her father at the Elks Club. Afterward he had held Michael's coat for him and eased it onto his shoulders. He'd never done that for anyone but his sons. Later he'd asked her, Are you going to marry this man?

Jancy? Aren't you going to eat? Her father was leaning close to her, pointing at her plate.

What? Oh. I ate a big breakfast. Here, you eat the rest of mine.

You should eat, said her father. Your face looks thin. Have you lost weight?

Maybe a little.

You run around too much. If you'd stay in one place for a while you'd gain a little weight and look better.

Jancy picked up her fork and put it down. Her father had always made her uneasy. He went into rages, especially in the car. If he couldn't pass or the car in front slowed suddenly for a turn, he'd turn red and curse—Goddammit, you son of a bitch, he'd say. That's right, you chucklehead—That word 'chucklehead' was his utmost brand of contempt. He said it stressing the first syllable, fuming like a mad bull.

Jancy? You finished? Ready to go?

Her father pushed his plate away and sat watching her, touching the rim of his empty glass with a finger. She couldn't answer him. She knew that she would leave to see Michael. When she told her father, he would shake his head and stammer as he tried to talk. She got up and started for the door.

Jancy's father burned a coal fire past mid-May. He picked up a poker and stabbed at white embers clinging to the grate. Flakes of ash drifted into the room.

How long will you be up there? he asked.

I don't know, she said.

Christ Almighty. What are you doing? If this thing between you and him is over, just forget it. Why go chasing up there after him? Let him come here, he knows where you are.

I don't have a place for him to stay.

Why couldn't he stay up at the house with you and your mother?

Because we don't want to stay with my mother.

He clenched his fists and glowered into the fire. He shook his head.

I know you're an adult, he said. But goddammit, Jancy, it's not right. I don't care what you say. It's not right and it won't come to no good.

It already *has* come to good, Jancy said. She looked at him until he broke their gaze.

Why don't you give it up? he said. Give it up and marry him.

Give what up?

All this running around you're doing. Jesus, Honey, you can't do this all your life. Aren't you twenty-five this summer? I won't be here forever. What's going to happen to you?

I don't know, Jancy said. How can I know?

He leaned forward, elbows on knees, and clasped his hands. You need a family, he said. No one will ever help you but your family.

Maybe not, said Jancy.

She thought of the drive. Moving up the East Coast to Michael. She would arrive and sit in the car, waiting to stop trembling, waiting for twelve hours of hot road and radio talk to go away. She would want Michael so much and she would be afraid to go into the house.

She looked up at her father.

I have to do this, she said.

What time are you leaving?

Five A.M.

Does your mother know you're going?

I told her I might.

Well. Come down by and we'll hose off the car.

No, you don't need to get up that early.

I'm always awake by then, he said.

Her father was sitting outside on the porch swing as she drove up. He motioned her to pull into the yard under the buckeye tree. The sky had begun to lighten. The stars were gone. The air was chill, misted. He wore a woolen shirt and the hat with the feather nearly hidden in the brim. Before Jancy could get out of the car he picked up the garden hose and twisted the brass nozzle. Water streamed over the windshield. Jancy watched his wavering form as the water broke and runneled. He held the cigar between his teeth and sprayed the bumpers, the headlights, the long sides of the car. He sprayed each tire, walking, revolving, his hand on his hip, the hat pulled low. His face was gentle and gaunt. He would get sicker. Jancy touched her eyes, her mouth. A resignation welled up like tears. He was there and then he was made of moving lines as water flew into the glass. The water stopped slowly.

Jancy got out of the car and they stood looking up at a sky toned the coral of flesh.

It's a long way, he said. You'll get there while it's light?

Yes, Jancy said. Don't worry.

The car sat dripping and poised.

It looks good, Jancy said. I'm taking off in style.

She got in and rolled the window down. Her father came close.

Turn the motor on, he said, then nodded, satisfied at the growl of the engine. Above them the buckeye spread out green and heavy.

When are the buckeyes ripe? Jancy asked.

Not till August.

Can you eat them?

Nope, her father laughed. Buckeyes don't do a thing, don't have a use in the world.

He bent down and kissed her.

Take your time, he said. Go easy.

She drove fast the first few hours. The sun looked like the moon, dim, layered over. Morning fog burned off slowly. Maryland mountains were thick and dipped in pockets of fog. Woods stretched on both sides of the road. Sometimes from an overpass Jancy saw straggled neon lights still burning in a small town. No cars on the highway; she was alone, she ate up the empty ribbon of the road.

She drove up over a rise and suddenly, looming out of the mist, the deer was there. She saw the sexual lines of its head and long neck. It moved into her, lifted like a flying horse. She swerved. The arching body hit the fender with a final thud and bounced again, hard, into the side of the car. Jancy looked through the rearview mirror and saw the splayed form skidding back along the berm of the road, bouncing twice in slow motion, twirling and stopping.

The road seemed to close like a tunnel. The look of the deer's head, the beginning arch of the body, was all around Jancy. She seemed to see through the image into the tunneling road. She heard, close to her ear, the soft whuff of the large head bent over grass, tearing the long grass with its teeth.

She pulled off the road. I should go back and see what I've done, she thought. She turned the motor off. She felt she was still moving, and the road shifted into three levels. Wet grass of the road banks was lush. The road shimmered; one plane of it tilted and moved sideways into the other. Jancy gripped the vinyl seat of the car. She was sinking. The door wouldn't open and she slid across to get out the other side. She stood up in the cool air and there was total silence. Jancy tried to walk. The earth and the asphalt were spongy. She moved around the car and saw first the moonish curve of the dented fender. The door was crumpled where the deer had bounced back and slammed into her. Jancy imagined its flanks, the hard mounds of its rump. The sheen of it. She staggered and stepped back. The sudden cushion of the grass surprised her and she fell. She saw then the sweep of short hairs glistening along the length of the car. The door handle was packed and smeared with golden feces.

There was really nowhere to go.

Once it was Christmas Day. They were driving from home, from the house her father had built in the country. A deer jumped the road in front of them, clearing the snow, the pavement, the fences of the fields, in two bounds. Beyond its arc the hills rumpled in snow. The narrow road wound through white meadows, across the creek, and on. Her father was driving. Her brothers had shining play pistols with leather holsters. Her mother wore clip-on earrings of tiny wreaths. They were all dressed in new clothes, and they moved down the road through the trees.

1979

ELIZABETH TALLENT
(1954–)

Elizabeth Tallent was born in Washington, D.C., the daughter of a father who was a chemist and a mother who was a speech therapist. She attended Illinois State University at Normal, graduating with a B.A. in anthropology in 1975 and marrying the same year. She began to place her fiction in major magazines when she was still in her twenties: "Ice" appeared in *The New Yorker* in 1980 and was included in *Best American Short Stories* for that year. Other stories followed, and in 1983 she received a National Endowment for the Arts Fellowship. She has been a writer in residence at the University of Southern Mississippi Writers Center and a visiting writer at the University of California at Irvine.

In her first book, *Married Men and Magic Tricks: John Updike's Erotic Heroes* (1982), a collection of essays, Tallent demonstrated that in addition to writing fiction she had given much thought to the themes and techniques of one of the best of her older contemporaries. Her stories, like Updike's, focus frequently on the disjunctions of love, as lives lived in counterpoint fail to come together for more than brief satisfactions. Her environment, however, is not Updike's Northeast, but more often the West, where she has lived, first in Colorado and then in New Mexico, in recent years. "Things aren't crowded together here," she has said. "I find that visually and morally attractive."

Tallent's men and women are often privileged in their education, skilled in what they do, though their accomplishment is often at a lower level than their training or ambitions. Skaters, dancers, archeologists, or astronomers, they are frustrated in their careers as in their personal lives. Not sure who they are, they hide behind levels of ironic role-playing, or, in several of the stories of *In Constant Flight* (1983), by literally dressing in costumes: a bear, an iguanodon, Amelia Earhart. In the title story, "In Constant Flight," the couple at the end is left playing in the snow the children's chase game of fox-and-goose, she chasing him. In this game, as not in their adult lives, "He has to run on the lines. Those are the rules."

Museum Pieces (1985), a novel, extends some of the same motifs, the dominant metaphor here the fragments of Indian pottery, shattered for collection, lying in pieces in the museum where the husband, an archeologist, works. "Archeologists look at physical evidence of a life that has permanence, a context, intricacy," Tallent has written. "That's what I'd like in my writing." On the evidence of her work so far, she is a fine observer of the shards of her times.

Elizabeth Tallent's latest collection of stories is *Time with Children,* 1987.

Ice

The Abyssinian cat will not bear kittens; at some point during her pregnancies she aborts them. The veterinarian who sees her refers to these as spontaneous abortions. After the abortions the cat eats roses—yellow roses, tea roses, Seashell roses, white roses on thornless stems. My mother knows she will then find the cat, emptied of her litter, crouched on the highest shelf of the linen closet. My mother always keeps roses in her house. She is adamant about the value of certain things: old Persian rugs, McGredy's Ivory roses, Abyssinian cats. Sometimes I have seen her watch the cat doubtfully, stroking her—not with her fingertips but with her knuckles, her hand curved like a boxer's fist when his manager is lacing the gloves, at once relaxed and expectant—down the nape of the neck to a point between the shoulder blades, where her knuckles rest, having found the cat's center of gravity. The cat stares through the window. Her shoulder blades seem thinner than the bones in my mother's hands. I have seen my mother, when she thinks she is alone, examining her breasts in a mirror.

Whenever I call, she tells me first about the cat, whose nuances of behavior must be studied and reflected upon in the way that Eskimos analyze falling snow.

"Perhaps her pelvis is too narrow," my mother said the last time we talked. "Mine nearly was."

"I didn't know that," I said.

"No?"

"No."

"You don't need to worry," my mother said. "Yours isn't."

My grandmother hated cats. She is supposed to have thrown one of the earlier Abyssinians out of the window of a second-story apartment; the cat landed lightly on the roof of a cream-colored Mercedes-Benz. It was the eve of my mother's wedding when this happened. Her eyes, the next morning, were painfully red behind her veil, which my father forgot to lift before he kissed her. My grandmother was said to have given them an enormous sum of money; she wanted them to buy an island. Islands were the only way you could be sure of what was yours. In the end, she doubted everyone around her—the priest, the neurosurgeons, my mother. I remember her as an old woman who could not sleep. Once, when I went into her room to kiss her good night, she took my hand and held it to her throat, asking me whether I could feel the pulse. Her skin felt like a series of damp veils, like the wet paper you fold over the wires when you are making papier-mâché animals; it was cool against the tips of my fingers. I could smell her Chanel No. 22. "I feel it," I told her, though I wasn't sure. She was angry and thrust my hand away.

I think my mother envisioned oxygen tents and sudden intimacies, but my grandmother broke her neck falling down a flight of icy steps one evening in 1979.

She had rested for a time at the bottom of the steps, one gloved hand below her cheek, the other hand (mysteriously ungloved) outstretched before her in the snow. When they lifted her, one of the ambulance men blew the snow from the deep creases in her knuckles. My mother called the undertaker to inquire about the use of perfume. "She has always, always, worn Chanel No. 22," my mother told them. Worn it, treading delicately down the centers of the icy steps, on the inside of her wrists, above the collarbones that curved like gull's wings against the cloth of her little black dress, and (for all anyone knew) in the blue-veined hollows of her skinny thighs. Before the funeral, my mother daubed Chanel behind my grandmother's ears. Her head was posed oddly on the pillow, her neck craned into a rigid, chin-upward position, the way someone will suddenly stare if you say, "Look, skywriting!" Afterward, immediately before they closed the casket, one of the neurosurgeons who had been attending my grandmother since her first stroke touched my mother lightly on the arm. "You know, she wasn't in any pain," he said. "Your mother probably never even knew what hit her."

My mother made a barely perceptible movement with her left shoulder, upon which the neurosurgeon's hand rested. No one, not even someone who was watching closely, could have called that movement a shrug.

All of this, my mother insists, was probably for the best. "In all seriousness, I don't know whether she could have endured another year," she says. The old woman sometimes forgot the names of the cats, the various species of roses; she confused the names of composers with those of television anchormen. In the last few weeks she is supposed to have taken to hiding food in her bedroom, eating it furtively at night.

And now my grandmother does not have to endure, as my mother does, the spectacle of her grandchild as a figure skater. According to my mother, skating in the Travelling Ice Adventures is only one or two extremely narrow social notches above working in an actual circus. She came to see me once, in a brand-new city amphitheater so luminous and silent that the sounds of our skates hissed back at us from the curving walls. The streets around the amphitheater had been plastered for weeks with posters advertising our coming. I could tell that my mother was shocked by my face on those billboards, two stories high.

When we spoke of the show later, over dinner, she was diplomatic. "Those lights do make your skin look odd, don't they, darling," she said. It is the lights—streaking the ice in gaudy purples, watermelon reds, deep indigo—that most people remember, not the skating. She speared a scallop with the tines of her fork, scrubbing it vigorously in the sauce. "But I did like it when you went into those pirouettes," she said. "If I squinted, I didn't really have to see the ice. I only saw you, and it looked as if you were dancing by yourself instead of with that bear."

"There's nothing wrong with the bear," I said.

"No, darling, I didn't say there was," she said. "He was very amusing."

"Whenever you unsquinted your eyes."

"I dislike glaring lights."

"It is a show. For little kids. Who *like* glaring lights."

"Of course," she said.

The bear's face is painted in an amicable grin. When we waltz, he looks out over my shoulder, grinning and nodding. The photographer used to like to photograph the bear like that, catching the line of my bare back beneath the bear's sloping jaw.

For a while I was sleeping with the photographer, who travelled with us doing publicity stills for local television spots. He was a very good photographer, and he left to work for Japan Air Lines. He called me one evening from Los Angeles, where he has been taking pictures of Japanese stewardesses. They are all beautiful, he says, although he is not used to their eyes; he can't seem to bring out any reflections in them. They arrive at his studio with truckloads of kimonos; they pose with their hands in their sashes, and their skin is powdered to the color of the insides of almonds.

After dinner my mother kissed me good night; I had to catch a taxi to the airport. After the kiss she paused, her hand still cupping my cheek. I could feel her wedding ring, round and cool against the knuckle. "Roses have become my whole life," she told me. "I wish you could find something that would suit you, something you could put your whole heart into." She paused. "Don't think you know everything," she said finally. "It could happen to you. You could end up alone."

"I don't like to see you taking chances," my partner says. He is already half dressed, wearing the bear mask, which rests against his chest. His body always seems incredibly slender before he puts on the rest of his shaggy bear's outfit. Half man, half bear; I rather like him in his hybrid condition. He watches me put on my makeup, blinking at the light in my streaked blond hair. My hair wasn't always blond, but it seems that the promoters of the show cannot envision a dark-haired woman dancing with a bear—only a blond one. He lifts a human hand and strokes his dark bear's cheek softly.

"You could lose your job," he says. "They don't mind canning the women. They can't come by male skaters anymore, so they're careful, but women skaters are a dime a dozen. You've seen those girls following Harry around, trying to catch his eye."

"Harry doesn't *know* skating," I say. I choose my lipstick judiciously. If you take very good care of your lipsticks, you trim the tips with a razor blade so that they give you the cleanest line. My lipsticks are always blunt—I used some of them for years—and sometimes my mouth seems pouting and smeared. I unscrew the lipstick from its gold cylinder, I shape my mouth into a firm oval. The mirror blazes with the reflections of small blue-white bulbs; I can see the bear watching curiously over my shoulder. I am not good with the makeup tonight, and my partner notices.

"It's not whether he knows skating, it's whether you want to keep your job." He is disturbed, because, last week, I fled from him in earnest. I skated fast and hard, eluding his rough bear paws until the last possible moment, when our record was running out. When he caught me I could feel the heat of his breath on my face. The lines we had cut stretched behind us in the glossy ice. My ankles were trembling. He held me softly. No one laughed or applauded. It will not happen again.

"Of course I want to keep my job," I say. "Nobody wants to lose their job. Sometimes I antagonize Harry, sometimes he antagonizes me. That's the way it goes." I fold a Kleenex into an origami swan, which makes me think of the photographer. In L.A. there must be swans. When I was a child I made origami birds, horses, strange fish in many-colored translucent papers. My mother urged me to take up oil painting. "You're so artistic," she would say. "You should make things that will *last.*" It was true—the origami animals did not last. I lost them, or the Abyssinians tore them apart, or they blew out of windows into the street. I blot my lipstick with one of the wings of the origami swan. The bear watches me closely.

"How did you do that with just Kleenex?" he asks.

"Sometime I'll show you."

"I don't want to lose you," he says carefully. "You're a good partner; you really take it seriously. We understand each other."

"You're not going to lose me. You're stuck with me for a long while yet."

"If you could just watch it on the artistic stuff. You know how Harry feels when you get artistic. You raise his blood pressure a couple of points. He likes nice balance, accuracy, definition. You go off into a world of your own, you're lost to the rest of us, you botch the rhythms. That's what Harry sees. We try to cover for you, but he sees."

"It hasn't been that often," I say. "I've been sticking pretty close to the program, and you know you like it when I change things. You know you like it."

"All right, I *like* it," he says. "It gets so damn boring out there—all those little girls in pink birthday dresses, all the mothers in common-sense-care Dacron pant-suits. Sometimes I think they're bringing the same people in to every show—they just haven't told us. I think I recognize some of the faces. I've seen them in Toronto, in Tallahassee, in Sioux Falls. One of these days I'll just start waving at them and I won't be able to stop. The dancing bear always gets a laugh when he does anything human. That's the point. Not that he's a bear but that he's a clumsy, aborted, blotchy human being, puttering around on his ice skates with a blond woman in his arms. I can't skate without music, you know? Even in my head, when I dream about skating I hear this terrible tinny music in the background. I have to hear it before I can face the ice."

The bear's theme is played on trumpets and cymbals. He dances out into the light, he spins into a series of figure eights with his paws arching above his head, he cocks his head at the audience. He told me right away, as soon as we started working together, that he was gay, that he had once wanted to be a welder. Hundreds of little girls wave at him. He is bathed in a pink spotlight that follows him across the ice, veering and pausing skittishly.

"I know," I say. "It can get to you."

"You can't fight it," he says. He shakes his head. "Harry sees you. He's not dumb. He knows you're trying to sabotage the routines, bring the artistic stuff in. You can't go off on your own like that; the spot men don't know what you're doing. You have to stay with me, in my arms."

"I'll stay with you," I tell him. I want the bear to calm down; he seems badly shaken. His huge furry mittens lie side by side on the dressing table, like companionable Scottish terriers. I choose the small jar of plum-colored cheek highlighter. I have always had good cheekbones. The bear pulls on his arms, and then his legs. He has to fight to get his skates on; the massive bear-middle has made him unwieldy. I watch him in the mirror. The bear will court me with wit and elegance while I skate in carefully circumscribed arcs, the light shining in my blond hair. The meaning of this is not lost on the small girls who watch so intently from the bleachers.

He finishes with his skates, and although he is thinking it, he does not say "Come on." I choose an eye pencil and remove its cap. Thoughtfully, taking great pains, I lean forward toward my reflection in the mirror and fill in the colored shadows around my eyes.

Harry watches me from the entrance ramp, keeping his hands in his pockets. Over his shoulder, the no-smoking sign glimmers purple. The narrow-hipped ballerinas sidle meekly past him, emerging one by one from the darkness into the brilliant light of the rink. I have seen Harry interview the ballerinas; he leans forward confidentially across the width of his marble-topped desk, his hands resting palm upward, beseechingly. He wriggles his fingers; it is somehow an extremely intimate gesture. His office is filled with cigarette smoke and old posters of Travelling Ice Adventures. He stares intently into the ballerina's eyes until she looks down, or away. "Are you on the pill?" he asks finally. His fingers tremble.

Now, as the ballerinas move across the ice, the beam falls through the translucent petals of their tutus. Their bare arms, held rigidly above their heads, are goosepimpled in the sudden cold. They hold their heads down shyly, watching one another from the corners of their eyes, and flutter across the ice on their skates.

"*Swan Lake* again," the bear says. "I hope to dance to *Swan Lake* at Harry's funeral."

In the darkness near us, children eat popcorn from oil-stained white paper bags, staring at the rink in a kind of ecstasy, their faces tense. Beside me the bear fidgets with one of his knees, which is loose. I have never really got used to the darkness; you skate from the shadows into the light so fast that there are always a few moments when the nerves in the retina of your eye cannot adjust, when you are skating purely by instinct.

When my mother called me this afternoon, she said that the cat had lost another litter, had vomited the petals of a Kordes' Perfecta all across the Persian rug. "I might as well give up on her," my mother said. "She will never have the temperament for it. The vet has prescribed a series of mild tranquilizers. He says it may be something in the environment that disturbs her, it may be purely psychological. But I really thought she was going to keep them this time. I just had a feeling."

"You couldn't know," I said.

"I shouldn't have forced her," my mother said sadly. "You should see how frightened she is of the toms. She just looks at them with her eyes squeezed almost shut, and then she flattens her whole body against the floor. But her face is so beautifully marked; everyone notices the shadings in the gray around her eyes. I think to myself that if she could only have kittens she would feel tranquil, that she'd adjust to them once they were born. It changes you, you know. I've never seen another like her. Now I have no choice."

"You couldn't have known," I said again. "You've been patient with her, haven't you?"

My mother paused, and I could hear the static in the background rising and falling. It sounded as if someone, not my mother, was breathing, listening impatiently to the awkward silence that had fallen between us. "Did I ever tell you that on the day your grandmother died she was running away from home?" she said softly. "The neurosurgeons had recommended confinement. It wasn't that she was dangerous, but she was badly in need of counselling, absolute quiet and rest. Somehow she overheard a conversation, and she climbed out of the window of her room."

There was a sudden fumbling at her end of the line, and a silence. "Here," she said suddenly. "I'm holding kitty up to the phone so that she can hear you. Whisper something in her ear, just between the two of you, won't you? Whisper something."

"I had a letter from Ben this morning," the bear says suddenly. "Ben is doing fine, isn't he?" Ben is my lover, the photographer.

"If you had a letter from him, then you should know how he is," I say.

"As far as I can tell, he's O.K.," the bear says. "But there is this odd tone to the letter—a disjointedness, as if he can't really make the connections, he just knows where they should be. I'm used to Ben, you know; I've worked with him for months. That's not the way he talks." He pauses, looking away from me into the brilliantly lit rink. The ballerinas skitter and regroup. They cling to one another, glittering, their bodies transparent beads fitted together on the slenderest stems.

"I don't think that anything's really gone wrong," I tell him. "It might just be L.A.—some kind of culture shock."

I can see the profile of the bear, dark and thoughtful. He strokes his cheek, clumsily now that he has his paw on. The paw has no claws—only black rubber hooks that curve down over the broad fur toes. "I don't know," he says. He is thinking hard. "He said he pulled some pictures of you from the developing fluid, and there you were. He said it occurred to him then that he was sorry he'd left."

"Why are you telling me this? Wasn't it supposed to be confidential?"

"I'm not sure about that, either," says the bear. We both hear the cymbals at the same moment, and the bear readies himself. He skates out, gliding alone onto the glaring ice, his head tilted back so that his eyes gaze upward into the crowd. There is an expectant ripple of applause. The bear bows. He moves with a dainty, shaving noise across the ice. Ballerinas file past me in the darkness, on the way back to their dressing rooms. "Damn!" one of them says. "I lost an earring. Everybody look for a small pearl earring." The ice itself is vast, the bear is a solitary misshapen figure gliding in a circle of light. He does his figure eights, and I close my eyes, following his movements on the inside of my mind. I have seen him so many times, and he always uses the same inflections, the same half-humorous, half-mocking gestures. I wait for my cue, then I appear at the entrance to the ramp. The yellow light filters through my hair, it slides in a pale aura across the ice where I am to skate, it falls from a tiny window high in the darkness above us. It brushes the ice soundlessly, colliding playfully with the bear's spot, me in my colored circle, he in his. He stares at me, pretending to be startled. The children laugh. He holds out his arms, he wags his head. My bones will show through my skin, this light is so brilliant. It is very cold. We dance, keeping the slight distance between us, me skating backward, him forward. The blades of our skates cut small curved channels in the mirroring ice, a fine powder clings to the white suede of my skates. The bear rocks forward; he catches me on one of my shy, evasive sprints, and we close and dance together, woman and bear, my blond hair against the massive darkness of his chest. His chin rests lightly on the crown of my head as he stares past me into the crowd. Suddenly, astonishing both of us, I find myself weeping in the circle of his shaggy arms.

The bear tilts his head and whispers, "You know, don't you, that you are not yourself?"

1983

Drama

EDWARD ALBEE

(1928–)

As a two-week-old infant, Edward Albee was adopted by Reed and Frances Albee and brought from his Washington, D.C., birthplace to a mansion in Westchester County, New York. He was named for his adoptive paternal grandfather, Edward Franklin Albee, co-owner of the Keith-Albee vaudeville theaters. As a child he was acquainted with actors such as Ed Wynn, Jimmy Durante, and Walter Pidgeon, friends of his parents, and was driven to Broadway matinees in the family's Rolls Royce. His formal education was constantly interrupted by family travel, and he attended three other prep schools before graduating from the Choate School; he spent a year and a half at Trinity College, leaving without a degree in 1949.

For the next decade he lived in various Greenwich Village apartments and worked at several unskilled jobs to supplement the income from a trust set up by his maternal grandmother, to whom *The Sandbox* is dedicated. *The Zoo Story,* written in 1958, was first produced in Berlin in 1959; the following year it was presented in Greenwich Village's Provincetown Playhouse. For each of the next five years, Albee had at least one play in production, and he has brought out work regularly, though less frequently, since then. Several of his plays are adaptations of fiction by other writers: Herman Melville, Carson McCullers, James Purdy, Giles Cooper, and Vladimir Nabokov.

From the time in 1953 when he was encouraged by Thornton Wilder to try playwriting, Albee had immersed himself in the technical aspects of the theater. He associated himself with Richard Barr and Clinton Wilder, two young producers, and took an active hand in production details of his own plays and the plays of others. Along with his own work, Albee was involved in presentations of plays by Jean Genêt, Eugène Ionesco, and Samuel Beckett, European writers loosely grouped under the rubric "Theater of the Absurd" for the attitudes revealed in their dramatic content and unrealistic techniques, as well as in productions of Harold Pinter, British playwright famous for the menace lurking beneath the surface of his deceptively ordinary domestic settings.

Albee's first Broadway production was *Who's Afraid of Virginia Woolf* in 1962. Critical reaction was intense. Albee was hailed as a major new voice in the theater and excoriated as a writer of dirty plays. The Pulitzer Prize committee fractured over whether to select Albee's controversial work, finally making no award for that year. Later it became a much discussed movie starring Elizabeth Taylor and Richard Burton. *Tiny Alice* (1964) also generated a round of critical exchanges in New York papers; Albee joined in the controversy, enthusiastically defending his work. Later Broadway productions, *A Delicate Balance* (1966) and *Seascape* (1975), were awarded Pulitzers.

Albee has been a popular speaker on college campuses, has lectured abroad representing the State Department, and given many interviews and statements on his views of American life and theater.

The Sandbox was originally commissioned for Gian Carlo Menotti's Festival of Two Worlds in Spoleto, Italy. Albee interrupted his work on *The American Dream* (1961) to complete the brief play, but it was not staged at the Festival. It premiered in New York in April, 1960. The cast of characters is drawn from *The American Dream,* and they are stereotypical: Mommy, Daddy, Grandma, and the Young Man. The scene is stark: a sandbox and three chairs occupied by Mommy, Daddy, and a musician who does not speak. Every effort is made to combat the conventions of realistic theater. The actors prompt each other and the stage crew; they ignore lines being spoken a few feet from their ears, and the acting style used is intentionally unreal. As in the longer *The American Dream,* the theme is the barrenness of the family and the substitution of ritual for real emotion.

Albee's contribution to contemporary theater ranges beyond the immediate legacy of his plays. He has been instrumental in bringing the work of Europeans to attention; he has invested his own money to encourage staging of works by new playwrights; he has experimented with stage technique and adaptation; he has articulated his views in academic and journalistic forums; and in his use of language he has broken old bonds of theatrical speech patterns.

Besides those named above, Albee's plays include *The Death of Bessie Smith* (1960), *Fam and Yam* (1960), *Bartleby* (1961), *The Ballad of the Sad Café* (1963), *Malcolm* (1966), *Everything in the Garden* (1967), *Box* and *Quotations from Chairman Mao Tse-tung* (1968), *All Over* (1971), *Counting the Ways* and *Listening* (1976), *The Lady from Dubuque* (1980), *Lolita* (1981), and *The Man Who Had Three Arms* (1982).

Biographical and critical studies include Gilbert Debusscher, *Edward Albee: Tradition and Renewal,* 1967; C. W. E. Bigsby, *Albee,* 1969; Ruby Cohn, *Edward Albee,* 1969; Ronald Hayman, *Edward Albee,* 1971; Anne Paolucci, *From Tension to Tonic: The Plays of Edward Albee,* 1972; C. W. E. Bigsby, ed., *Edward Albee: A Collection of Critical Essays,* 1975; Richard E. Amacher, *Edward Albee,* Revised Edition, 1982; J. Wasserman, ed., *Edward Albee: An Interview and Essays,* 1983.

The Sandbox

The Players:

THE YOUNG MAN.	25.	A good-looking, well-built boy in a bathing suit.
MOMMY.	55.	A well-dressed, imposing woman.
DADDY.	60.	A small man; gray, thin.
GRANDMA.	86.	A tiny, wizened woman with bright eyes.
THE MUSICIAN.		No particular age, but young would be nice.

Note: When, in the course of the play, MOMMY and DADDY call each other by these names, there should be no suggestion of regionalism. These names are of empty affection and point up the pre-senility and vacuity of their characters.

The Scene: A bare stage, with only the following: Near the footlights, far stage-right, two simple chairs set side by side, facing the audience; near the footlights, far stage-left, a chair facing stage-right with a music stand before it; farther back, and stage-center, slightly elevated and raked, a large child's sandbox with a toy pail and shovel; the background is the sky, which alters from brightest day to deepest night.

At the beginning, it is brightest day; the YOUNG MAN is alone on stage, to the rear of the sandbox, and to one side. He is doing calisthenics; he does calisthenics until quite at the very end of the play. These calisthenics, employing the arms only, should suggest the beating and fluttering of wings. The YOUNG MAN is, after all, the Angel of Death.

MOMMY *and* DADDY *enter from stage-left,* MOMMY *first.*

MOMMY. (*Motioning to Daddy*) Well, here we are; this is the beach.

DADDY. (*Whining*) I'm cold.

MOMMY. (*Dismissing him with a little laugh*) Don't be silly; it's as warm as toast. Look at that nice young man over there: *he* doesn't think it's cold. (*Waves to the* YOUNG MAN) Hello.

YOUNG MAN. (*With an endearing smile*) Hi!

MOMMY. (*Looking about*) This will do perfectly . . . don't you think so, Daddy? There's sand there . . . and the water beyond. What do you think, Daddy?

DADDY. (*Vaguely*) Whatever you say, Mommy.

MOMMY. (*With the same little laugh*) Well, of course . . . whatever I say. Then, it's settled, is it?

DADDY. (*Shrugs*) She's *your* mother, not mine.

MOMMY. *I* know she's my mother. What do you take me for? (*A pause*) All right, now; let's get on with it. (*She shouts into the wings, stage-left*) You! Out there! You can come in now.

(*The* MUSICIAN *enters, seats himself in the chair, stage-left, places music on the music stand, is ready to play.* MOMMY *nods approvingly*)

MOMMY. Very nice; very nice. Are you ready, Daddy? Let's go get Grandma.

DADDY. Whatever you say, Mommy.

MOMMY. (*Leading the way out, stage-left*) Of course, whatever I say. (*To the* MUSICIAN) You can begin now.

(*The* MUSICIAN *begins playing;* MOMMY *and* DADDY *exit; the* MUSICIAN, *all the while playing, nods to the* YOUNG MAN)

YOUNG MAN. (*With the same endearing smile*) Hi!

(*After a moment,* MOMMY *and* DADDY *re-enter, carrying* GRANDMA. *She is borne in by their hands under her armpits; she is quite rigid; her legs are drawn up; her feet do not touch the ground; the expression on her ancient face is that of puzzlement and fear*)

DADDY. Where do we put her?

MOMMY. (*The same little laugh*) Wherever I say, of course. Let me see . . . well . . . all right, over there . . . in the sandbox. (*Pause*) Well, what are you waiting for, Daddy? . . . The sandbox!

(*Together they carry* GRANDMA *over to the sandbox and more or less dump her in*)

GRANDMA. (*Righting herself to a sitting position; her voice a cross between a baby's laugh and cry*) Ahhhhhh! Graaaaa!

DADDY. (*Dusting himself*) What do we do now?

MOMMY. (*To the* MUSICIAN) You can stop now.

(*The* MUSICIAN *stops*)

(*Back to* DADDY) What do you mean, what do we do now? We go over there and sit down, of course. (*To the* YOUNG MAN) Hello there.

YOUNG MAN. (*Again smiling*) Hi!

(MOMMY *and* DADDY *move to the chairs, stage-right, and sit down. A pause*)

GRANDMA. (*Same as before*) Ahhhhhh! Ah-haaaaaa! Graaaaaa!

DADDY. Do you think . . . do you think she's . . . comfortable?

MOMMY. (*Impatiently*) How would I know?

DADDY. (*Pause*) What do we do now?

MOMMY. (*As if remembering*) We . . . wait. We . . . sit here . . . and we wait . . . that's what we do.

DADDY. (*After a pause*) Shall we talk to each other?

MOMMY. (*With that little laugh; picking something off her dress*) Well, *you* can talk, if you want to . . . if you can think of anything to *say* . . . if you can think of anything *new*.

DADDY. (*Thinks*) No . . . I suppose not.

MOMMY. (*With a triumphant laugh*) Of course not!

GRANDMA. (*Banging the toy shovel against the pail*) Haaaaaa! Ah-haaaaaa!

MOMMY. (*Out over the audience*) Be quiet, Grandma . . . just be quiet, and wait.

(GRANDMA *throws a shovelful of sand at* MOMMY)

MOMMY. (*Still out over the audience*) She's throwing sand at me! You stop that, Grandma; you stop throwing sand at Mommy! (*To* DADDY) She's throwing sand at me.

(DADDY *looks around at* GRANDMA, *who screams at him*)

GRANDMA. GRAAAAA!

MOMMY. Don't look at her. Just . . . sit here . . . be very still . . . and wait. (*To the* MUSICIAN) You . . . uh . . . you go ahead and do whatever it is you do.

(*The* MUSICIAN *plays*)

(MOMMY *and* DADDY *are fixed, staring out beyond the audience.* GRANDMA *looks at them, looks at the* MUSICIAN, *looks at the sandbox, throws down the shovel*)

GRANDMA. Ah-haaaaaa! Graaaaaa! (*Looks for reaction; gets none. Now . . . directly to the audience*) Honestly! What a way to treat an old woman! Drag her out of the house . . . stick her in a car . . . bring her out here from the city . . . dump her in a pile of sand . . . and leave her here to set. I'm eighty-six years old! I was married when I was seventeen. To a farmer. He died when I was thirty. (*To the* MUSICIAN) Will you stop that, please?

(*The* MUSICIAN *stops playing*)

I'm a feeble old woman . . . how do you expect anybody to hear me over that peep! peep! peep! (*To herself*) There's no respect around here. (*To the* YOUNG MAN) There's no respect around here!

YOUNG MAN. (*Same smile*) Hi!

GRANDMA. (*After a pause, a mild double-take, continues, to the audience*) My husband died when I was thirty (*indicates* MOMMY), and I had to raise that big cow over there all by my lonesome. You can imagine what *that* was like. Lordy! (*To the* YOUNG MAN) Where'd they get *you?*

YOUNG MAN. Oh . . . I've been around for a while.

GRANDMA. I'll bet you have! Heh, heh, heh. Will you look at you!

YOUNG MAN. (*Flexing his muscles*) Isn't that something? (*Continues his calisthenics*)

GRANDMA. Boy, oh boy; I'll say. Pretty good.

YOUNG MAN. (*Sweetly*) I'll say.

GRANDMA. Where ya from?

YOUNG MAN. Southern California.

GRANDMA. (*Nodding*) Figgers; figgers. What's your name, honey?

YOUNG MAN. I don't know. . . .

GRANDMA. (*To the audience*) Bright, too!

YOUNG MAN. I mean . . . I mean, they haven't given me one yet . . . the studio . . .

GRANDMA. (*Giving him the once-over*) You don't say . . . you don't say. Well . . . uh, I've got to talk some more . . . don't you go 'way.

YOUNG MAN. Oh, no.

GRANDMA. (*Turning her attention back to the audience*) Fine; fine. (*Then, once more, back to the* YOUNG MAN) You're . . . you're an actor, hunh?

YOUNG MAN. (*Beaming*) Yes. I am.

GRANDMA. (*To the audience again; shrugs*) I'm smart that way. *Anyhow,* I had to raise . . . *that* over there all by my lonesome; and what's next to her there . . . that's what she married. Rich? I tell you . . . money, money, money. They took me off the *farm* . . . which was real decent of them . . . and they moved me into the big town house with *them* . . . fixed a nice place for me under the stove . . . gave me an army blanket . . . and my own dish . . . my very own dish! So, what have I got to complain about? Nothing, of course. I'm not complaining. (*She looks up at the sky, shouts to someone off stage*) Shouldn't it be getting dark now, dear?

(*The lights dim; night comes on. The* MUSICIAN *begins to play; it becomes deepest night. There are spots on all the players, including the* YOUNG MAN, *who is, of course, continuing his calisthenics*)

DADDY. (*Stirring*) It's nighttime.

MOMMY. Shhhh. Be still . . . wait.

DADDY. (*Whining*) It's so hot.

MOMMY. Shhhhhh. Be still . . . wait.

GRANDMA. (*To herself*) That's better. Night. (*To the* MUSICIAN) Honey, do you play all through this part?

(*The* MUSICIAN *nods*)

Well, keep it nice and soft; that's a good boy.

(*The* MUSICIAN *nods again; plays softly*)

That's nice.

(*There is an off-stage rumble*)

DADDY. (*Starting*) What was that?

MOMMY. (*Beginning to weep*) It was nothing.

DADDY. It was . . . it was . . . thunder . . . or a wave breaking . . . or something.

MOMMY. (*Whispering, through her tears*) It was an off-stage rumble . . . and you know what *that* means. . . .

DADDY. I forget. . . .

MOMMY. (*Barely able to talk*) It means the time has come for poor Grandma . . . and I can't bear it!

DADDY. (*Vacantly*) I . . . I suppose you've got to be brave.

GRANDMA. (*Mocking*) That's right, kid; be brave. You'll bear up; you'll get over it.

(*Another off-stage rumble . . . louder*)

MOMMY. Ohhhhhhhhhh . . . poor Grandma . . . poor Grandma. . . .

GRANDMA. (*To* MOMMY) I'm fine! I'm all right! It hasn't happened yet!

(*A violent off-stage rumble. All the lights go out, save the spot on the* YOUNG MAN; *the* MUSICIAN *stops playing*)

MOMMY. Ohhhhhhhhhh. . . . Ohhhhhhhhhh. . . .

(*Silence*)

GRANDMA. Don't put the lights up yet . . . I'm not ready; I'm not quite ready. (*Silence*) All right, dear . . . I'm about done.

(*The lights come up again, to brightest day; the* MUSICIAN *begins to play.* GRANDMA *is discovered, still in the sandbox, lying on her side, propped up on an elbow, half covered, busily shoveling sand over herself*)

GRANDMA. (*Muttering*) I don't know how I'm supposed to do anything with this goddam toy shovel. . . .

DADDY. Mommy! It's daylight!

MOMMY. (*Brightly*) So it is! Well! Our long night is over. We must put away our tears, take off our mourning . . . and face the future. It's our duty.

GRANDMA. (*Still shoveling; mimicking*) . . . take off our mourning . . . face the future. . . . Lordy!

(MOMMY *and* DADDY *rise, stretch.* MOMMY *waves to the* YOUNG MAN)

YOUNG MAN. (*With that smile*) Hi!

(GRANDMA *plays dead.* (!) MOMMY *and* DADDY *go over to look at her; she is a little more than half buried in the sand; the toy shovel is in her hands, which are crossed on her breast*)

MOMMY. (*Before the sandbox; shaking her head*) Lovely! It's . . . it's hard to be sad . . . she looks . . . so happy. (*With pride and conviction*) It pays to do things well. (*To the* MUSICIAN) All right, you can stop now, if you want to. I mean, stay around for a swim, or something; it's all right with us. (*She sighs heavily*) Well, Daddy . . . off we go.

DADDY. Brave Mommy!

MOMMY. Brave Daddy!

(*They exit, stage-left*)

GRANDMA. (*After they leave; lying quite still*) It pays to do things well. . . . Boy, oh boy! (*She tries to sit up*) . . . well, kids . . . (*but she finds she can't*) . . . I . . . I can't get up. I . . . I can't move. . . .

(*The* YOUNG MAN *stops his calisthenics, nods to the* MUSICIAN, *walks over to* GRANDMA, *kneels down by the sandbox*)

GRANDMA. I . . . can't move. . . .

YOUNG MAN. Shhhhh . . . be very still. . . .

GRANDMA. I . . . I can't move. . . .

YOUNG MAN. Uh . . . ma'am; I . . . I have a line here.

GRANDMA. Oh, I'm sorry, sweetie; you go right ahead.

YOUNG MAN. I am . . . uh . . .

GRANDMA. Take your time, dear.

YOUNG MAN. (*Prepares; delivers the line like a real amateur*) I am the Angel of Death. I am . . . uh . . . I am come for you.

GRANDMA. What . . . wha . . . (*Then, with resignation*) . . . ohhhh . . . ohhhh, I see.

(*The* YOUNG MAN *bends over, kisses* GRANDMA *gently on the forehead*)

GRANDMA. (*Her eyes closed, her hands folded on her breast again, the shovel between her hands, a sweet smile on her face*) Well . . . that was very nice, dear. . . .

YOUNG MAN. (*Still kneeling*) Shhhhhh . . . be still. . . .

GRANDMA. What I meant was . . . you did that very well, dear. . . .

YOUNG MAN. (*Blushing*) . . . oh . . .

GRANDMA. No; I mean it. You've got that . . . you've got a quality.

YOUNG MAN. (*With his endearing smile*) Oh . . . thank you; thank you very much . . . ma'am.

GRANDMA. (*Slowly; softly—as the* YOUNG MAN *puts his hands on top of* GRANDMA'S) You're . . . you're welcome . . . dear.

(*Tableau. The* MUSICIAN *continues to play as the curtain slowly comes down*)

CURTAIN

1960

DAVID RABE
(1940–)

David Rabe was born and educated in Dubuque, Iowa, where he earned a B.A. at Loras College in 1962. He began work on an M.A. in theater at Villanova University, but was drafted into the army in 1965. He served in the army from 1965 to 1967, the final eleven months in a hospital support unit in Vietnam.

Though he went to Vietnam convinced that he was serving "a cause," the combination of extreme youth and bloody experience that he observed there shocked him. He describes teenage G.I.'s standing around casually discussing the kills their unit suffered in the last battle. He found it impossible to write about his experience while he was there or to keep a journal because he found such concentration "resulted in a kind of double vision that made everything too intense." Close to the sounds of battle, he became "aware acutely, and in a way that makes writing impossible, of the existence of language as mere symbol." The facts were impossible to communicate. "I skimmed over things and hoped they would skim over me."

After returning home, upset by what he perceived as public indifference and lack of understanding, Rabe began to view his Vietnam experience as "decadent, really corrupt." He hoped to educate people about the war as a correspondent, but failed to get a position and returned to his graduate work at Villanova, where he wrote *The Basic Training of Pavlo Hummel* and wrote and first produced *Sticks and Bones.*

In the spring of 1971 *Pavlo Hummel* was produced by Joseph Papp's New York Shakespeare Festival Public Theater. Later the same year, Papp produced *Sticks and Bones,* making Rabe the only playwright except Shakespeare to have two plays run concurrently at the Public. Later moved to an uptown proscenium theater, *Sticks and Bones* was awarded the 1972 Tony for best Broadway play. A third play, *Streamers,* won the 1976 New York Drama Critics' Circle Award for best American play with its dramatization of tensions in an army barracks arising from race and homosexuality.

Sticks and Bones deals with the inability of a stereotypical American family (named after the characters in a 1950's television series) to understand the actions and attitudes of their son David, who has returned from war maimed and sightless. He is tormented by visions of mindless violence and by memories of the love of a Vietnamese woman, who wordlessly haunts the play. The language and staging recalls the Theater of the Absurd that came from abroad to energize American drama in the 1950's, particularly as later adapted to the American scene in the plays of Edward Albee and Arthur Kopit. Rabe's techniques have also been compared to the expressionism of Eugene O'Neill.

Among Rabe's other plays are *The Orphan,* 1973, a play about violence in a modern family with echoes of ancient Greece; *In the Boom Boom Room,* 1974, dramatizing the humiliation and exploitation of a topless dancer; and *Hurlyburly,* 1984, concerned with the Hollywood drug culture.

Sticks and Bones[1]

CHARACTERS

OZZIE
HARRIET
DAVID
RICK
ZUNG (THE GIRL)
FATHER DONALD
SERGEANT MAJOR

Time: Autumn
Place: The family home

Act One

Darkness; silence. Slides appear on both sides of the stage: the first is a black-and-white medium close-up of a young man, mood and clothing of the early 1900s; he is lean, reasonably handsome, black hair parted in the center. Voices speak. They are slow and relaxed, with an improvisational quality.

1ST CHILD'S VOICE. Who zat?
MAN'S VOICE. Grandpa Jacob's father.
New slide: group photo, same era, eight or ten people, all ages.
2ND CHILD'S VOICE. Look at 'em all!
1ST CHILD'S VOICE. How come they're all so serious?
New slide: small boy, black hair, black knickers.
WOMAN'S VOICE. There's Grandpa Oswald as a little boy.
1ST CHILD'S VOICE. Grandpa?
New slide: different boy, same pose.
WOMAN'S VOICE. And that's his brother Thomas. He died real young.
MAN'S VOICE. Scarlet fever.
New slide: young girl, seventeen or eighteen.
And that's his sister Christina.
WOMAN'S VOICE. No, that's Grandma.
MAN'S VOICE. No.
WOMAN'S VOICE. Sure.
New slide: Ozzie and Harriet, young, 1940s era.
There's the two of them.
MAN'S VOICE. Mmmmm, you're right, because that's Grandpa.
New slide: two boys, five and nine years old.
WOMAN'S VOICE. The taller one's David, right?
New slide: color close-up of David from the last moment of the play, a stricken look.
1ST CHILD'S VOICE. What's that one?
MAN'S VOICE. Somebody sick.
1ST CHILD'S VOICE. Boy . . . !

1. *Sticks and Bones* has been revised by the author for this *Contemporary American Literature* edition.

New slide: color photo of Ozzie, Harriet, and Father Donald. Father Donald, wearing a gym suit, his back to the camera, stands holding a basketball in one hand. Ozzie and Harriet face him, one on either side.

2ND CHILD'S VOICE. Oh, look at that one!

MAN'S VOICE. That's a funny one, isn't it.

WOMAN'S VOICE. That's one—I bet somebody took it—they didn't know it was going to be taken.

There is a bright flash and the stage is immediately illuminated. The set is an American home, very modern, with a quality of brightness, green walls, green rug. Stairs lead up to a bedroom—not lighted now—with a hallway leading off to the rest of the upstairs beyond. There is naturalness, yet a sense of space and, oddly, a sense also that this room, these stairs belong in the gloss of an advertisement.

Downstage, a TV on wheels faces upstage, glowing, murmuring. Ozzie, Harriet, and Father Donald—a slightly rotund, serious man—are standing as they were in the slide last seen.

FATHER DONALD. A feel for it is the big thing. A feel for the ball. You know, I mean, bouncing it, dribbling it. You don't even look at it.

Phone rings.

OZZIE. I'll get it.

FATHER DONALD. You can do it, Harriet. Give it a try. (*He bounces the ball to Harriet.*)

OZZIE. Hello? . . .

FATHER DONALD (*as Harriet catches the ball*). That a girl.

HARRIET. Oh, Father . . .

OZZIE, *hanging up.* Nobody there.

FATHER DONALD. That's what I'm telling you. You gotta help kids. Keeps 'em outa trouble. We help. Organized sports activities; it does 'em a world a good. You know that. And they need you.

OZZIE. Well, I was a decent basketball player—I could get around, but my strong suit was track and field. I was quite a miler. Dash man. I told you, Father.

Phone rings.

I could throw the discus.

(*As he runs for the phone.*)

FATHER DONALD. But this is basketball season. (*Moving for Harriet and then the door as Ozzie goes to the phone, says* "Hello," *then listens intently.*) You listen to me, Harriet, you get that husband of yours out there to help us. It'll do him good and he's the kind of man we need. Leaders. We need leaders.

HARRIET. Oh, Father Donald, bless me.

FATHER DONALD. Of course. (*He blesses her, holding the ball under his left arm.*) Bye-bye.

HARRIET (*as Father Donald goes*). Good-bye, Father.

(*And she turns to look for a moment at Ozzie on the phone.*)

Why aren't you talking?

(*Silence: she is looking at him.*)

Ozzie, why aren't you talking?

OZZIE, *slowly lowering the phone.* They're gone. They hung up.

HARRIET. You didn't say a word. You said nothing.

OZZIE. I said my name.

HARRIET. What did they want?

OZZIE. I said hello.

HARRIET. Were they selling something—is that what they wanted?

OZZIE. No, no.

HARRIET. Well . . . who was it?

OZZIE. What?

HARRIET. What are we talking about?

OZZIE. The Government. It was . . . you know. . . .

HARRIET. Ozzie! (*In fear*) No!

OZZIE—*some weariness in him.* No, he's all right, he's coming home!

HARRIET. Why didn't you let me speak? Who was it?

OZZIE. No, no.

HARRIET. It was David.

OZZIE. No, somebody else. Some clerk. I don't know who.

HARRIET. You're lying.

OZZIE. No. There was just all this static—it was hard to hear. But he was coming home was part of it, and they had his records and papers but I couldn't talk to him directly even though he was right there, standing right there.

HARRIET. I don't understand.

OZZIE. That's what they said. . . . And he was fine and everything. And he wanted them to say hello for him. He'd lost some weight. He would be sent by truck. I could hear truck engines in the background—revving. They wanted to know my name. I told them.

HARRIET. No more?

OZZIE. They were very professional. Very brusque . . .

HARRIET. No more . . . at all? . . .

The front door opens and Rick comes in. And the door slams. He is young, seventeen. His hair is long and neat, with sideburns. His clothing is elaborate—very, very up to date. He carries a guitar on his shoulder.

RICK. Hi, Mom. Hi, Dad.

HARRIET. Hi, Rick.

OZZIE. Hi, Rick.

HARRIET. Ohhh, Ricky, Ricky, your brother's on his way home. David's coming home!

OZZIE. We just got a call.

RICK. Ohhh, boy!

HARRIET. Isn't that wonderful? Isn't it? Your father talked to him. Oh, I bet you're starving. Sit, sit.

OZZIE. I talked to *somebody,* Rick.

HARRIET. There's fudge and ice cream in the fridge; would you like that?

RICK. Oh, yeah, and could I have some soda?

(*She is on her way to the kitchen, nodding.*)

Wow, some news. I'm awful hungry.

OZZIE. Never had a doubt. A boy like that—if he leaves, he comes back.

RICK, *as he picks up a comic book.* How about me? What if I left?

OZZIE. Absolutely. Absolutely.

(*Silence. Rick reads the comic.*)

I built jeeps . . . tanks, trucks.

RICK. What?

OZZIE. In the other war, I mean. Number Two. I worked on vehicles. Vehicles were needed and I worked to build them. Sometimes I put on wheels, tightened 'em up. I never . . . served . . . is what I mean. (*Slight pause.*) They got all those people —soldiers, Rick—you see what I mean? They get 'em across the ocean, they don't have any jeeps or tanks or trucks, what are they gonna do, stand around? Wait for a bus on the beachhead? Call a cab?

RICK. No public transportation in a war.

OZZIE. That's right, that's right.

Harriet enters, carrying fudge and ice cream.

HARRIET. Oh, Ozzie, Ozzie, do you remember—I just remembered that time David locked himself in that old icebox. We didn't know where he was. We looked all over. We couldn't find him. And then there was this icebox in this clearing . . . out in the middle. I'll bet you don't even remember.

OZZIE. Of course I remember.

HARRIET. And he leaped to us. So frightened.

OZZIE. He couldn't even speak—he couldn't even speak—just these noises.

HARRIET. Or that time he fell from that tree.

OZZIE. My God, he was somethin'! If he wasn't fallin', he was gettin' hit.

HARRIET. And then there was that day we went out into the woods. It was just all wind and clouds. We sailed a kite!

OZZIE. I'd nearly forgotten! . . .

RICK. Where was I?

HARRIET. You were just a baby, Rick. We had a picnic.

RICK. I'm gonna get some more soda, okay?

Harriet touches him as he passes.

OZZIE. What a day that was. I felt great that day.

HARRIET. And then Hank came along. Hank Grenweller. He came from out of the woods calling that—

OZZIE. That's right.

HARRIET. He was happy.

OZZIE. We were all happy. Except he'd come to tell us he was going away, leaving. And then we had that race. Wasn't that the day?

HARRIET. I don't remember.

OZZIE. Hank and me! Hank Grenweller. A foot race. And I beat him. I did it; got him.

HARRIET. Noooo.

OZZIE. It was only inches, but—

HARRIET. You know that's not true. If it was close—and it was—that race you ran — (*This is not loud: there is intimacy; they are near one another.*) I remember now —it was because he let it be—no other reason. We were all having fun. He didn't want to make you feel badly. He didn't want to ruin all the fun. You know that. You know you do.

RICK, *calling from the kitchen.* You people want some fudge?

HARRIET. No, Rick.

OZZIE. I don't know he didn't try. I don't know that. (*He stares at Harriet.*)

HARRIET. I think I'll be going up to bed; take a little nap.

RICK. Sleepy, Mom?

HARRIET. A little. (*She is crossing toward Ozzie.*)

RICK. That's a good idea then.

HARRIET. Call me.

RICK. Okay.

HARRIET. Do you know, the day he left? It was a winter day. November, Ozzie. (*She moves toward the stairs.*)

OZZIE. I know.

HARRIET. I prayed; did you know that? Now he's home.

OZZIE. It was a winter day.

HARRIET, *at the top of the stairs.* I know.

RICK, *toying with his guitar.* Night, Mom.

(*She doesn't answer but disappears down the hall. He looks up and yells after her.*) Night, Mom!

HARRIET, *from off.* Turn off the TV, somebody.

Rick crosses to the TV. He turns it off and wheels it back under the stairs. Ozzie watches. Silence.

OZZIE. I knew she was praying. She moves her lips.

(*Rick does not look up. He begins, softly, to strum and tune the guitar.*)

And something else—yes, sir, boy, oh, boy, I tell you, huh? What a day, huh? (*Slight pause.*) They got seventeen hundred million men they gotta deal with, how they gonna do that without any trucks and tanks and jeeps? But I'm some kinda jerk because I wasn't out there blastin' away, huh? I was useful. I put my time to use. I been in fights. Fat Kramer. . . . How we used to fight!

(*Rick strums some notes on the guitar. Ozzie stares at him.*)

How come I'm restless? I . . . seen him do some awful, awful things, ole Dave. He was a mean . . . foul-tempered little baby. I'm only glad I was *here* when they sent him off to do his killing. That's right. (*Silence.*) I feel like I swallowed ants, that's how restless I am. Outran a bowlin' ball one time. These guys bet me I couldn't do it and I did, beat it to the pins. Got a runnin' start, then the—

(*A faint, strange rapping sound has stopped him, spun him around.*)

Did you do that?

RICK. Somebody knockin'.

OZZIE. Knockin'?

RICK. The door, Dad.

OZZIE. Oh.

RICK. You want me to get it?

OZZIE. No, no. It's just so late. (*He moves for the door.*)

RICK. That's all right.

OZZIE. Sure.

He opens the door just a crack, as if to stick his head around. But the door is thrust open and a man enters abruptly. He is black or of Spanish descent, and is dressed in the uniform of a sergeant major and wearing many campaign ribbons.

SGT. MAJOR. Excuse me. Listen to me. I'd like to speak to the father here. I'd like to know who . . . is the father? Could . . . you tell me the address?

OZZIE. May I ask who it is who's asking?

SGT. MAJOR. I am. I'm asking. What's the address of this house?

OZZIE. But I mean, who is it that wants to know?

SGT. MAJOR. We called; we spoke. Is this seven-seventeen Dunbar?

OZZIE. Yes.

SGT. MAJOR. What's wrong with you?

OZZIE. Don't you worry about me.

SGT. MAJOR. I have your son.

OZZIE. What?

SGT. MAJOR. Your son.

OZZIE. No.

SGT. MAJOR. But he is. I have papers, pictures, prints. I know your blood and his. This is the right address. Please. Excuse me. (*He pivots, reaches out into the dark.*) I am very busy. I have your father, David.

He draws David in—a tall, thin boy, blond and, in the shadows, wearing sunglasses and a uniform of dress greens. In his right hand is a long, white, red-tipped cane. He moves, probing the air, as the sergeant major moves him past Ozzie toward the couch, where he will sit the boy down like a parcel.

OZZIE. Dave? . . .

SGT. MAJOR. He's blind.

OZZIE. What?

SGT. MAJOR. Blind.

OZZIE. I don't . . . understand.

SGT. MAJOR. We're very sorry.

OZZIE, *realizing.* Ohhhhh. Yes. Ohhhh. I see . . . sure. I mean, we didn't know. Nobody said it. I mean, sure, Dave, sure; it's all right—don't you worry. Rick's here, too, Dave—Rick, your brother, tell him hello.

RICK. Hi, Dave.

DAVID, *worried.* You said . . . "father."

OZZIE. Well . . . there's two of us, Dave; two.

DAVID. Sergeant, you said "home." I don't think so.

OZZIE. Dave, sure.

DAVID. It doesn't feel right.

OZZIE. But it is, Dave—me and Rick—Dad and Rick. Harriet! (*Calling up the stairs*) Harriet!

DAVID. Let me touch their faces. . . . I can't see. (*Rising, his fear increasing*) Let me put my fingers on their faces.

OZZIE, *hurt, startled.* What? Do what?

SGT. MAJOR. Will that be all right if he does that?

OZZIE. Sure. . . . Sure. . . . Fine.

SGT. MAJOR, *helping David to Ozzie.* It will take him time.

OZZIE. That's normal and to be expected. I'm not surprised. Not at all. We figured on this. Sure, we did. Didn't we, Rick?

RICK, *occupied with his camera, an Instamatic.* I wanna take some pictures, okay? How are you, Dave?

DAVID. What room is this?

OZZIE. Middle room, Dave. TV room. TV's in—

HARRIET, *on the stairs.* David! . . . Oh, David! . . . David . . .

And Ozzie, leaving David, hurries toward the stairs and looks up at her as she falters, stops, stares. Rick, moving near, snaps a picture of her.

OZZIE. Harriet . . . don't be upset. . . . They say . . . Harriet, Harriet . . . he can't see! . . . Harriet . . . they say—he—can't . . . see. That man.

HARRIET, *standing very still.* Can't see? What do you mean?

SGT. MAJOR. He's blind.

HARRIET. No. Who says? No, no.

OZZIE. Look at him. He looks so old. But it's nothing, Harriet, I'm sure.

SGT. MAJOR. I hope you people understand.

OZZIE. It's probably just how he's tired from his long trip.

HARRIET, *moving toward him.* Oh, you're home now, David.

SGT. MAJOR, *with a large sheet of paper waving in his hands.* Who's gonna sign this for me, Mister? It's a shipping receipt. I got to have somebody's signature to show you got him. I got to have somebody's name on the paper.

OZZIE. Let me. All right?

SGT. MAJOR. Just here and here, you see? Your name or mark three times.

As they move toward a table and away from Harriet, who is near David.

OZZIE. Fine, listen, would you like some refreshments?

SGT. MAJOR. No.

OZZIE. I mean while I do this. Cake and coffee. Of course, you do.

SGT. MAJOR. No.

OZZIE. Sure.

SGT. MAJOR. No. I haven't time. I've got to get going. I've got trucks out there backed up for blocks. Other boys. I got to get on to Chicago, and some of them to Denver and Cleveland, Reno, New Orleans, Boston, Trenton, Watts, Atlanta. And when I get back they'll be layin' all over the grass; layin' there in pieces all over the grass, their backs been broken, their brains jellied, their insides turned into garbage. One-legged boys and no-legged boys. I'm due in Harlem; I got to get to the Bronx and Queens, Cincinnati, Saint Louis, Reading. I don't have time for coffee. I got deliveries to make all across this country.

DAVID, *with Harriet, his hands on her face, a kind of realization.* Noooooo. . . . Sergeant . . . nooo; there's something wrong; it all feels wrong. Where are you? Are you here? I don't know these people!

SGT. MAJOR. That's natural, Soldier; it's natural you feel that way.

DAVID. Nooooo.

HARRIET, *attempting to guide him back to a chair.* David, just sit, be still.

DAVID. Don't you hear me?

OZZIE. Harriet, calm him.

DAVID. The air is wrong; the smells and sounds, the wind.

HARRIET. David, please, please. What is it? Be still. Please . . .

DAVID. GODDAMN YOU, SERGEANT, I AM LONELY HERE! I AM LONELY!

SGT. MAJOR. I got to go. (*And he pivots to leave.*)

DAVID, *following the sound of the sergeant major's voice.* Sergeant!

SGT. MAJOR, *whirling, bellowing.* You shut up. You piss-ass soldier, you shut the fuck up!

OZZIE, *walking to the sergeant major, putting his hand on the man's shoulder.* Listen, let me walk you to the door. All right? I'd like to take a look at that truck of yours. All right?

SGT. MAJOR. There's more than one.

OZZIE. Fine.

SGT. MAJOR. It's a convoy.

OZZIE. Good.

They exit, slamming the door, and Rick, running close behind them, pops it open, leaps out. He calls from off.

RICK. Sure are lots a trucks, Mom!

HARRIET, *as he re-enters.* Are there?

RICK. Oh, yeah. Gonna rain some more too. (*And turning, he runs up the stairs.*) See you in the morning. Night, Dave.

HARRIET. It's so good to have you here again; so good to see you. You look . . . just . . .

(*Ozzie has slipped back into the room behind her, he stands, looking.*)

fine. You look—

(*She senses Ozzie's presence, turns, immediately, speaking.*)

He bewilders you, doesn't he.

(*And Ozzie, jauntily, heads for the stairs.*)

Where are you going?

(*He stops; he doesn't know. And she is happily sad now as she speaks—sad for poor Ozzie and David, they are so whimsical, so childlike.*)

You thought you knew what was right, all those years, teaching him sports and fighting. Do you understand what I'm trying to say? A mother knows *things* . . . a father cannot ever know them. The measles, smallpox, cuts and bruises. Never have you come upon him in the night as he lay awake and staring . . . praying.

OZZIE. I saw him put a knife through the skin of a cat. I saw him cut the belly open.

DAVID. Noooo. . . .

HARRIET, *moving toward him in response.* David, David. . . .

DAVID. Ricky!

(*There is a kind of accusation in this as if he were saying Ricky did the killing of the cat. He says it loudly and directly into her face.*)

HARRIET. He's gone to bed.

DAVID. I want to leave.

There is furniture around him; he is caged. He pokes with his cane.

HARRIET. What is it?

DAVID. Help me. (*He crashes.*)

OZZIE. Settle down! Relax.

DAVID. I want to leave! I want to leave! I want to leave. I . . .

(*And he smashes into the stairs, goes down, flails, pounding his cane.*)

want to leave.

OZZIE AND HARRIET. Dave! David! Davey!

DAVID. . . . to leave! Please.

He is on the floor, breathing. Long, long silence in which they look at him sadly, until Harriet announces the problem's solution.

HARRIET. Ozzie, get him some medicine. Get him some Ezy Sleep.

OZZIE. Good idea.

HARRIET. It's in the medicine cabinet; a little blue bottle, little pink pills.

(*And when Ozzie is gone up the stairs, there is quiet. She stands over David.*)

It'll give you the sleep you need, Dave—the sleep you remember. You're our child and you're home. Our good . . . beautiful boy.

And front door bursts open. There is a small girl in the doorway, an Asian girl. She wears the Vietnamese ao dai, *black slacks and white tunic slit up the sides.*

Slowly, she enters, carrying before her a small straw hat. Harriet is looking at the open door.

HARRIET. What an awful . . . wind. (*She shuts the door.*)

Blackout. Guitar music.

A match flickers as Harriet lights a candle in the night. And the girl silently moves from before the door across the floor to the stairs, where she sits, as Harriet moves toward the stairs and Ozzie, asleep sitting up in a chair, stirs.

HARRIET. Oh! I didn't mean to wake you. I lit a candle so I wouldn't wake you. (*He stares at her.*)

I'm sorry.

OZZIE. I wasn't sleeping.

(*He turns on a flashlight.*)

HARRIET. I thought you were.

(*Heading up the stairs.*)

OZZIE. Couldn't. Tried. Couldn't. Thinking. Thoughts running very fast. Trying to remember the night David . . . was made. Do you understand me? I don't know why. But the feeling in me that I had to figure something out and if only I could remember that night . . . the mood . . . I would be able. You're . . . shaking your head.

HARRIET. I don't understand.

OZZIE. No.

HARRIET. Good night.

(*As Ozzie, with his flashlight, goes out the front door, Harriet, arriving at David's door, raps softly and then opens the door. David is lying unmoving on the bed. She speaks to him.*)

I heard you call.

DAVID. What?

HARRIET. I heard you call.

DAVID. I didn't.

HARRIET. Would you like a glass of warm milk?

DAVID. I was sleeping.

HARRIET, *after a slight pause.* How about that milk? Would you like some milk?

DAVID. I didn't call. I was sleeping.

HARRIET. I'll bet you're glad you didn't bring her back. Their skins are yellow, aren't they?

DAVID. What?

HARRIET. You're troubled, warm milk would help. Do you pray at all any more? If I were to pray now, would you pray with me?

DAVID. What . . . do you want?

HARRIET. They eat the flesh of dogs.

DAVID. I know. I've seen them.

HARRIET. Pray with me; pray.

DAVID. What . . . do . . . you want?

HARRIET. Just to talk, that's all. Just to know that you're home and safe again. Nothing else; only that we're all together, a family. You must be exhausted. Don't worry; sleep. (*She is backing into the hallway. In a whisper*) Good night.

(*She blows out the candle and is gone, moving down the hall. Meanwhile the girl is stirring, rising, climbing from the living room up toward David's room, which she enters, moving through a wall, and David sits up.*)

DAVID. Who's there?

(*As she drifts by, he waves the cane at the air.*)

Zung? (*He stands.*) Chào, Cô Zung.

(*He moves for the door, which he opens, and steps into the hall, leaving her behind him in the room.*)

Zung. Chào, Cô Zung.

(*And he moves off up the hallway. She follows*)

Zung! . . .

Blackout. Music.

Lights up. It is a bright afternoon, and Ozzie is under the stairs with a screwdriver in his hand, poking about at the TV set.

OZZIE. C'mon, c'mon. Ohhhh, c'mon, this one more game and ole State's Bowl-bound. C'mon, what is it? Ohhh, hey . . . ohhhhh. . . .

HARRIET, *entering from the kitchen carrying a tray with a bowl of soup and a glass of juice.* Ozzie, take this up to David; make him eat it.

OZZIE. Harriet, the TV is broke.

HARRIET. What?

OZZIE. There's a picture but no sound. I don't—

Grabbing her by the arm, he pulls her toward a place before the set.

HARRIET. Stoppit, you're spilling the soup. (*She pulls free.*)

OZZIE. It's Sunday. I want to watch it. I turned it on, picture came on just like normal. I got the volume up full blast.

(*Having set the tray down, Harriet now shoves the TV set deeper under the stairs, deeper into the place where it is kept when not in use.*)

Hey! I want to watch it!

HARRIET. I want to talk about David.

OZZIE. David's all right.

(*He turns, crosses toward the phone, picks up the phone book.*)

I'm gonna call the repairman.

HARRIET, *following him.* Ozzie, he won't eat. He just lays there. I offer him food, he won't eat it. No, no. The TV repairman won't help, you silly. (*She takes the phone book from him.*) He doesn't matter. There's something wrong with David. He's been home days and days and still he speaks only when spoken to; there's no light in his eye, no smile; he's not happy to be here and not once has he touched me or held me, nor has he even shaken your hand.

Ozzie flops down in a chair.

OZZIE. Oh, I don't mind that. Why should I mind—

HARRIET. And now he's talking to himself! What about that? Do you mind that? He mutters in his sleep.

OZZIE, *exasperated.* Ohhhhhh.

HARRIET. Yes. And it's not a regular kind of talking at all. It's very strange—very spooky.

OZZIE. Spooky?

HARRIET. That's right.

OZZIE. I never heard him.

HARRIET. You sleep too deeply. I took a candle and followed. I was in his room. He lay there, speaking.

OZZIE. Speaking what?

HARRIET. I don't know. I couldn't understand.

OZZIE. Was it words?

HARRIET. All kind of funny and fast.

OZZIE. Maybe prayer; praying.

HARRIET. No. No, it was secret. Oh, Ozzie, I know praying when I hear it and it wasn't praying he was doing. We meant our son to be so different—I don't understand—good and strong. And yet . . . perhaps he is. But there are moments when I see him . . . hiding . . . in that bed behind those awful glasses, and I see the chalkiness that's come into—

OZZIE, *headed for the kitchen, looking for juice to drink.* Those glasses are simply to ease his discomfort.

HARRIET. I hate them.

OZZIE. They're tinted glass and plastic. Don't be so damn suspicious.

HARRIET. I'm not, I'm not. It's seeing I'm doing, not suspicion. Suspicion hasn't any reasons. It's you—now accusing me for no reason when I'm only worried.

OZZIE, *returning from the kitchen, angered.* Where's my juice?

HARRIET. I want to talk.

OZZIE. The hell with David for a minute—I want some juice.

HARRIET. Shut up. You're selfish. You're so selfish.

OZZIE, *walking to the tray and juice, attempting to threaten her.* I'll pour it on the floor. I'll break the glass.

She turns to move to get the juice.

HARRIET. A few years ago you might have done that kind of thing.

OZZIE. I woke up this morning, I could see so clearly the lovely way you looked when you were young. Beside me this morning, you were having trouble breathing. You kept . . . trying . . . to breathe.

(*She approaches him to hand him the juice.*)

What do you give me when you give me this?

HARRIET. I always looked pretty much as I do now. I never looked so different at all.

David appears from off upstairs, dressed in a red robe, and descends toward them.

DAVID, *sounding happy, yet moving with urgency.* Good morning.

OZZIE. Oh, David! Ohhh, good morning. Hello. How do you feel this fine bright morning; how do you feel?

DAVID. He was a big man, wasn't he?

OZZIE. What?

DAVID. Hank. You were talking about Hank Grenweller. I thought you were.

OZZIE. Oh, yes. Hank. Very big. Big. A good fine friend, ole Hank.

DAVID. You felt when he was with you he filled the room.

OZZIE. It was the way he talked that did that. He boomed. His voice just boomed.

DAVID. He was here once and you wanted me to sit on his lap, isn't that right? It was after dinner. He was in a chair in the corner.

HARRIET. That's right.

DAVID. His hand was gone—the bone showed in the skin.

OZZIE. My God, what a memory—did you hear that, Harriet? You were only four or five. He'd just had this terrible, awful auto accident. His hand was hurt, not gone.

DAVID. No. It was congenital.

OZZIE. What?

DAVID. That hand. The sickness in it.

OZZIE. Congenital?

DAVID. I'd like some coffee.

He is seated now, but not without tension.

HARRIET. Of course. And what else with it?

DAVID. Nothing.

HARRIET. Oh, no, no, you've got to eat. To get back your strength. You must. Pancakes? How do pancakes sound? Or wheat cakes? Or there's eggs? And juice? Orange or prune: or waffles. I bet it's eggs you want. Over, David? Over easy? Scrambled?

DAVID. I'm only thirsty.

HARRIET. Well, all right then, coffee is what you'll have and I'll just put some eggs on the side; you used to love them so; remember?

And, picking up the tray, she is off toward the kitchen. There is a pause.

OZZIE. I mean, I hate to harp on a thing, but I just think you're way off base on Hank, Dave.

DAVID. He told me.

OZZIE. Who?

DAVID. Hank.

OZZIE. You . . . talked to Hank?

DAVID. In California. The day before they shipped me overseas.

OZZIE. No, no. He went to Georgia when he left here. We have all his letters postmarked Georgia.

DAVID, *with great urgency.* It was California. I was in the barracks. The C.Q. came to tell me there was someone to see me. It was Hank asking did I remember him? He'd seen my name on a list and wondered if I was Ozzie's boy. He was dying, he said. The sickness was congenital. We had a long, long talk.

OZZIE. But his parents were good fine people, David.

DAVID. Don't you understand? We spoke.

OZZIE. Did he wanna know about me? Did he mention me?

DAVID, *after thinking a moment.* He asked . . . how you were.

OZZIE. Well, I'm fine. Sure. You told him.

HARRIET, *entering with a cup of coffee.* It must be so wonderful for you to be home. It must just be so wonderful. A little strange, maybe . . . just a little, but time will take care of all that. It always does. You get sick and you don't know how you're going to get better and then you do. You just do. You must have terrible, awful, ugly dreams, though.

Slight pause.

OZZIE. She said you probably have terrible, awful, ugly dreams . . . though.

DAVID. What?

HARRIET. Don't you remember when we spoke last night?

DAVID. Who?

HARRIET. You called to me and then you claimed you hadn't.

DAVID. I didn't.

HARRIET. Ohhh, we had a lovely conversation, David. Of course you called. You called; we talked. We talked and laughed and it was very pleasant. Could I see behind your glasses?

DAVID. What? (*Moving away, crossing in flight from them*) Do . . . what?

HARRIET. See behind your glasses; see your eyes.

OZZIE. Me too, Dave; could we?

DAVID. My eyes . . . are ugly.

OZZIE. We don't mind.

HARRIET. We're your parents, David.

DAVID. I think it better if you don't.

OZZIE. And something else I've been meaning to ask you—why did you cry out against us that first night—to that stranger, I mean, that sergeant?

HARRIET. And you do dream. You do.

OZZIE. Sure. You needn't be ashamed.

HARRIET. We all do it. All of us.

OZZIE. We have things that haunt us.

HARRIET. And it would mean nothing at all—it would be of no consequence at all—if only you didn't speak.

DAVID. I don't understand.

OZZIE. She says she heard you, Dave.

HARRIET. I stood outside your door.

DAVID. No.

OZZIE. A terrible experience for her, Dave; you can see that.

HARRIET. Whatever it is, David, tell us.

OZZIE. What's wrong?

DAVID. No.

HARRIET. We'll work it out.

OZZIE. You can't know how you hurt us.

DAVID. I wasn't asleep.

OZZIE. Not until you have children of your own.

HARRIET. What?

(*Silence.*)

Not . . . asleep? . . .

DAVID. I was awake; lying awake and speaking.

OZZIE. Now wait a minute.

DAVID. Someone was with me—there in the dark—I don't know what's wrong with me.

HARRIET. It was me. I was with you. There's nothing wrong with you.

DAVID. No. In my room. I could feel it.

HARRIET. I was there.

And they have him cornered in another chair.

DAVID. No.

OZZIE. Harriet, wait!

HARRIET. What are you saying, "Wait"? I was there.

OZZIE. Oh, my God. Oh, Christ, of course. Oh, Dave, forgive us.

HARRIET. What?

OZZIE. Dave, I understand. It's buddies left behind.

DAVID. No.

OZZIE. But I do. Maybe your mother can't but I can. Men serving together in war, it's a powerful thing—and I don't mean to sound like I think I know it—all of it, I mean—I don't, I couldn't—but I respect you having had it—I almost envy you having had it, Dave. I mean . . . true comradeship.

DAVID. Dad . . .

OZZIE. I had just a taste—not that those trucks and factory were any battlefield, but there was a taste of it there—in the jokes we told and the way we saw each other first in the morning. We told dirty, filthy jokes, Dave. We shot pool, played cards, drank beer late every night, singing all these crazy songs.

DAVID. That's not right, Dad.

OZZIE. But all that's nothing, I'm sure, to what it must be in war. The things you must touch and see. Honor. You must touch honor. And then one of you is hurt, wounded . . . made blind . . .

DAVID. No. I had fear of all the kinds of dying that there are when I went from here. And then there was this girl with hands and hair like wings. (*The poetry is like a thing possessing him, a frenzy in which he does not know where he is.*) There were candles above the net of gauze under which we lay. Lizards. Cannon could be heard. A girl to weigh no more than dust.

HARRIET. A nurse, right . . . David?

OZZIE. No, no, one of them foreign correspondents, English maybe or French.

Silence.

HARRIET. Oh, how lovely! A Wac or Red Cross girl? . . .

DAVID. No.

OZZIE. Redhead or blonde, Dave?

DAVID. No.

Harriet is shaken.

OZZIE. I mean, what you mean is you whored around a lot. Sure. You whored around. That's what you're saying. You banged some whores . . . had some intercourse. Sure, I mean, that's my point.

(*David, turning away, seems about to rise.*)

Now Dave, take it easy. What I mean is, okay, sure, you shacked up with. I mean, hit on. Hit on, Dave. Dicked. Look at me. I mean, you pronged it, right? Right? Sure, attaboy. (*Patting David on the shoulder*) Look, Dave, what are you doing?

(*A rage is building in David, tension forcing him to stand, his cane pressing the floor.*)

We can talk this over. We can talk this over.

(*David, heading for the stairs, crashes into Ozzie.*)

Don't—goddamnit, don't walk away from me. (*He pushes David backward.*) What the hell do you think you're doing? It's what you did. Who the hell you think you are? You screwed it. A yellow whore. Some yellow ass. You put in your prick and humped your ass. You screwed some yellow fucking whore!

(*He has chased David backward, Harriet joining in with him.*)

HARRIET. That's right, that's right. You were lonely and young and away from home for the very first time in your life, no white girls around—

DAVID. They are the color of the earth, and what is white but winter and the earth under it like a suicide?

(*Harriet's voice is a high humming in her throat.*)

Why didn't you tell me what I was?

(*And Harriet vomits, her hands at her mouth, her back turning. There is a silence. They stand. Ozzie starts toward her, falters, starts, reaches, stops.*)

OZZIE. Why . . . don't . . . you ask her to cook something for you, David, will you? Make her feel better . . . okay.

DAVID. I think . . . some eggs might be good, Mom.

OZZIE, *wanting to help her.* Hear that, Harriet? David wants some eggs.

HARRIET. I'm *all right.*

OZZIE. Of course you are. (*Patting her tenderly, he offers his clean white handkerchief.*) Here, here: wipe your mouth; you've got a little something—on the corner, left side. That's it. Whattayou say, David?

HARRIET. What's your pleasure, David?

DAVID. Scrambled.

OZZIE. There you go. Your specialty, his pleasure.

(*Ozzie, between them, claps his hands; off she goes for the kitchen. Ozzie, looking about the room like a man in deep water looking for something to keep him afloat, sees a pack of cigarettes.*)

How about a cigarette? (*Running to grab them, show them*) Filter, see, I switched. Just a little after you left, and I just find them a lot smoother, actually. I wondered if you'd notice. (*And speaking now, his voice and manner take on a confidence; he demonstrates; he is self-assured.*) The filter's granulated. It's an off-product of corn husks. I light up—I feel like I'm on a ship at sea. Isn't that one hell of a good tasting cigarette? Isn't that one beautiful goddamn cigarette?

Harriet enters with two bowls. One has a grapefruit cut in half; the second has eggs and a spoon sticking out.

HARRIET. Here's a little grapefruit to tide you over till I get the eggs.

(*And now she stirs the eggs in preparation for scrambling them.*)

Won't be long, I promise—but I was just wondering, wouldn't it be nice if we could all go to church tonight. All together and we could make a little visit in thanksgiving of your coming home.

(*David is putting his cigarette out in his grapefruit. They see.*)

I wouldn't ask that it be long—just—

(*He is rising now, dropping the grapefruit on the chair.*)

I mean, we could go to whatever saint you wanted, it wouldn't . . . matter . . .

(*He has turned his back, is walking toward the stairs.*)

Just in . . . just out . . .

(*He is climbing the stairs.*)

David.

OZZIE. Tired . . . Dave?

(*They watch him plodding unfalteringly toward his room.*)

Where you going . . . bathroom?

DAVID. No.

OZZIE. Oh.

(*David disappears into his room and Harriet whirls and heads for the telephone. Ozzie, startled, turns to look at her.*)

Harriet, what's up?

HARRIET. I'm calling Father Donald.

OZZIE. Father Donald?

HARRIET, *dialing.* We need help, I'm calling for help.

OZZIE. Now wait a minute. No; oh, no, we—

HARRIET. Do you still refuse to see it? He was involved with one of them. You know what the Bible says about those people. You heard him.

OZZIE. Just not Father Donald; please, please. That's all I ask—just—

(*She is obstinate, he sees. She turns her back waiting for someone to answer.*)

Why must everything be personal vengeance?

The front door pops open and in comes bounding Rick, guitar upon his back.

RICK, *happy.* Hi, Mom. Hi, Dad.

HARRIET, *waiting, telephone in hand—overjoyed.* Hi, Rick!

RICK, *happy.* Hi, Mom.

OZZIE, *feeling fine.* Hi, Rick.

RICK. Hi, Dad.

OZZIE. How you doin', Rick? (*He is happy to see good ole regular Rick.*)

RICK. Fine, Dad. You?

OZZIE. Fine.

RICK. Good.

HARRIET. I'll get you some fudge in just a minute, Rick!

RICK. Okay. How's Dave doin', Dad?

He is fiddling with his camera.

OZZIE. Dave's doin' fine, Rick.

RICK. Boy, I'm glad to hear that. I'm really glad to hear that, because, boy, I'll sure be glad when everything's back to the regular way. Dave's too serious, Dad; don't you think so? That's what I think. Whattayou think, Dad?

He snaps a picture of Ozzie, who is posing, smiling, while Harriet waves angrily at them.

HARRIET. SHHHHHHH! *Everybody!* (*And then, more pleasantly she returns to the phone.*) Yes, yes. Oh, Father, I didn't recognize your voice. No, I don't know who. Well, yes, it's about my son, Father, David. Yes. Well, I don't know if you know it or not, but he just got back from the war and he's troubled. Deeply. Yes.

(*As she listens silently for a moment, Rick, crouching, snaps a picture of her. She tries to wave him away.*)

Deeply.

(*He moves to another position, another angle, and snaps another picture.*)

Deeply, yes. Oh. So do you think you might be able to stop over some time soon to talk to him or not? Father, any time that would be convenient for you. Yes. Oh, that would be wonderful. Yes. Oh, thank you. And may God reward *you*, Father.

(*Hanging up the phone, she stands a moment, dreaming, as Ozzie is pacing, talking to her.*)

OZZIE. I say to myself, what does it mean that he is my son? How the hell is it that . . . he . . . is my son? I mean, they say something of you joined to something of me and became . . . him . . . but what kinda goddamn thing is that? One mystery replacing another? Mystery doesn't explain mystery!

RICK, *scarcely looking up from his comic.* Mom, hey, c'mon, how about that fudge, will ya?

HARRIET. Ricky, oh, I'm sorry. I forgot.

OZZIE. They've got . . . diseases! . . .

HARRIET, *having been stopped by his voice.* What? . . .

OZZIE. Dirty, filthy diseases. They got 'em. Those girls. Infections. From the blood of their parents into the very fluids of their bodies. Malaria, TB. An actual rot alive in them . . . gonorrhea, syphilis. There are some who have the plague. He touched them. It's disgusting. It's—

RICK. Mom, I'm starving, honest to God; and I'm thirsty too.

HARRIET, *as she scurries off, clapping, for the kitchen.* Yes, of course. Oh, oh.

RICK. And bring a piece for Dad, too; Dad looks hungry.

OZZIE. No.

RICK. Sure, a big sweet chocolate piece of fudge.

OZZIE. No. Please. I don't feel well.

RICK. It'll do you good.

HARRIET, *entering with fudge and milk in each hand.* Ricky, here, come here.

RICK, *hurrying toward her.* What?

HARRIET—*hands him fudge and milk.* Look good? (*And she moves toward Ozzie.*)

OZZIE. And something else—maybe it could just be that he's growing away from us, like we did ourselves, only we thought it would happen in some other way, some lesser way.

HARRIET, *putting the fudge and milk into Ozzie's hands.* What are you talking about, "going away"? He's right upstairs.

OZZIE. I don't want that.

HARRIET. You said you did.

OZZIE. He said I did.

RICK, *having gobbled the fudge and milk.* You want me to drive you, Mom?

HARRIET. Would you, Ricky, please?

RICK, *running.* I'll go around and get the car.

HARRIET, *scolding, as Ozzie has put the fudge and milk down on a coffee table.* It's all cut and poured, Ozzie; it'll just be a waste.

OZZIE. I don't care.

HARRIET. You're so childish.

She marches off toward the front door, where she takes a light jacket from a hook, starts to slip it on.

OZZIE. Don't you know I could throw you down onto this floor and make another child live inside you . . . now! . . .

HARRIET. I . . . doubt that . . . Ozzie.

OZZIE. You want me to do it?

HARRIET, *going out the door.* Ohhh, Ozzie, Ozzie.

OZZIE. (*The door slams.*) They think they know me and they know nothing. They don't know how I feel. . . . How I'd like to beat Ricky with my fists till his face is ugly! How I'd like to banish David to the streets. . . . How I'd like to cut her tongue from her mouth.

(*David moves around upstairs.*)

I was myself.

(*And now he is clearly speaking to the audience, making them see his value. They are his friends and buddies, and he talks directly to them.*)

I lived in a time beyond anything they can ever know—a time beyond and separate, and I was nobody's goddamn father and nobody's goddamn husband! I was myself! And I could run. I got a scrapbook of victories, a bag of medals and ribbons. In the town in which I lived my name was spoken in the factories and in the fields all around because I was the best there was. I'd beaten the finest anybody had to offer. Summer . . . I would sit out on this old wood porch on the front of our house and my strength was in me, quiet and mine. Round the corner would come some old Model T Ford and scampering up the walk this ancient, bone-stiff, buck-toothed farmer, raw as winter and cawing at me like a crow: they had one for me. Out at the edge of town. A runner from another county. My shoes are in a brown-paper bag at my feet. I snatch 'em up. I set out into the dusk, easy as breathing. There's an old white fence and we run for the sun. . . . For a hundred yards or a thousand yards or a thousand thousand. It doesn't matter. Whatever they want. We run the race they think their specialty and I beat them. They sweat and struggle; I simply glide on, one step beyond, no matter what their effort, and the sun bleeds before me. . . . We cross rivers and deserts; we clamber over mountains. I run the races the farmers arrange and win the bets they make. And then a few days after the race, money comes to me anonymously in the mail; but it's not for the money that I run. In the fields and factories they speak my name when they sit down to their lunches. If there's a prize to be run for, it's me they send for. It's to be the-one-sent-for that I run.

David, entering from his room, has listened to the latter part of this.

DAVID. And . . . then . . . you left.

OZZIE, *whirling to look at him.* What?

DAVID. I said . . . "And . . . then you left." That town.

OZZIE. Left?

DAVID. Yes. Went away; traveled.

OZZIE. No. What do you mean?

DAVID. I mean, you're no longer there; you're here . . . now.

OZZIE. But I didn't really *leave* it. I mean, not *leave.* Not really.

DAVID. Of course you did. Where are you?

OZZIE. That's not the point, Dave. Where I am isn't the point at all.

DAVID. But it is. It's everything; all that other is gone. Where are you going?

OZZIE. Groceries. Gotta go get groceries. You want anything at the grocery store? (*He looks at his watch.*) It's late. I gotta get busy.

DAVID, *as Ozzie exits.* That's all right, Dad. That's fine.

Blackout.

The lights rise to brightness, and Rick enters from the kitchen, carrying his guitar, plinking a note or two as Harriet emerges also from the kitchen, carrying a bowl of chips and a tray of drinks, and Ozzie appears upstairs, coming down the hall carrying an 8-mm movie projector already loaded with film.

HARRIET. Tune her up now, Rick.

OZZIE. What's the movie about anyway?

HARRIET. It's probably scenery, don't you think?—trees and fields and those little ponds. Everything over there's so green and lovely. Enough chips, Ricky?

All during this, they scurry about with their many preparations.

RICK. We gonna have pretzels too? 'Cause if there's both pretzels and chips then there's enough chips.

OZZIE, *at the projector.* David shoot it or somebody else? . . . Anybody know? I tried to peek—put a couple feet up to the light . . .

HARRIET. What did you see?

OZZIE. Nothing. Couldn't.

HARRIET. Well, I'll just bet there's one of those lovely little ponds in it somewhere.

OZZIE. Harriet . . . you know when David was talking about that trouble in Hank's hand being congenital, what did you think? You think it's possible? I don't myself.

I mean, we knew Hank well. I think it's just something David got mixed up about and nobody corrected him. What do you think? Is that what you think? Whatsamatter? Oh.

He stops, startled, as he sees she is waving at him. Looking up the stairs, which are behind him, he sees David is there, preparing to descend. David wears his robe and a bright-colored tie.

HARRIET. Hello!

OZZIE. Oh. Hey, oh, let me give you a hand. Yes. Yes. You look good. Good to see you.

(*And he is on the move to David to help him down the stairs.*)

Yes, sir. I think, all things considered, I think we can figure we're over the hump now and it's all downhill and good from here on in. I mean, we've talked things over, Dave, what do you say? The air's been cleared, that's what I mean—the wounds acknowledged, the healing begun. It's the ones that aren't acknowledged—the ones that aren't talked over—they're the ones that do the deep damage. That's always what happens.

HARRIET, *moving to David.* I've baked a cake, David. Happy, happy being home.

David, on his own, finds his way to a chair and sits.

OZZIE. And we've got pop and ice and chips, and Rick is going to sing some songs.

HARRIET. Maybe we can all sing along if we want.

RICK. Anything special you'd like to hear, Dave?

OZZIE. You just sing what you know, Rick; sing what you care for and you'll do it best.

And he and Harriet settle down upon the couch to listen, all smiles.

RICK. How about "Baby, When I Find You"?

HARRIET. Ohhh, that's such a good one.

RICK. Dave, you just listen to me go! I'm gonna build! (*He plays an excited lead into the song.*) I'm gonna build, build, build.

(*And he sings.*)

Baby, when I find you,
never gonna stand behind you,
gonna, gonna lead
softly at the start,
gently by the heart,
Sweet . . . Love! . . .

Slipping softly to the sea
you and me both mine
wondrous as a green
growing forest vine. . . .

Baby, when I find you,
never gonna stand behind you,
gonna, gonna lead you
softly at the start,
gently by the heart,
Sweet . . . Love! . . .
Baby, when I find you.

OZZIE, *as both he and Harriet clap and laugh.* Ohhh, great, Rick, great. You burn me up with envy, honest to God.

HARRIET. It was just so wonderful. Oh, thank you so much.

RICK. I just love to do it so much, you know?

OZZIE. Has he got something goin' for him, Dave? Huh? Hey! You don't even have a drink. Take this one; take mine!

Now they hurry back and forth from David to the table.

HARRIET. And here's some cake.

OZZIE. How 'bout some pretzels, Dave?

RICK. Tell me what you'd like to hear.

DAVID. I'd like to sing.

This stops them. They stare at David for a beat of silence.

RICK. What?

OZZIE. What's that?

DAVID. I have something I'd like to sing.

RICK. Dave, you don't sing.

DAVID, *reaching at the air.* I'd like to use the guitar, if I could.

HARRIET. What are you saying?

OZZIE. C'mon, you couldn't carry a tune in a bucket and you know it. Rick's the singer, Rick and your mom.

(*Not really listening, thinking that his father has gotten everything back to normal, Rick strums and strums the guitar, drifting nearer to David.*)

C'mon, let's go, that all we're gonna hear?

DAVID. You're so selfish, Rick. Your hair is black; it glistens. You smile. You sing. People think you are the songs you sing. They never see you. Give me the guitar.

And he clamps his hand closed on the guitar, stopping the music.

RICK. Mom, what's wrong with Dave?

DAVID. Give me.

RICK. Listen, you eat your cake and drink your drink, and if you still wanna, I'll let you.

David stands, straining to take the guitar.

DAVID. Now!

HARRIET. Ozzie, make David behave.

OZZIE. Don't you play too roughly. . . .

DAVID. Ricky! . . .

RICK. I don't think he's playing, Dad.

OZZIE (*as David, following Rick, bumps into a chair*). You watch out what you're doing . . .

David drops his glass on the floor, grabs the guitar.

You got cake all over your fingers, you'll get it all sticky, the strings all sticky—(*Struggling desperately to keep his guitar*) Just tell me what you want to hear, I'll do it for you!

HARRIET. What is it? What's wrong?

DAVID. GIVE ME! (*With great anger*) GIVE ME!

OZZIE. David! . . .

And David wrenches the guitar from Rick's hands, sends Rick sprawling, and loops the strap of the guitar over his shoulder, smiling, smiling.

HARRIET. Ohhhh, no, no, you're ruining everything. What's wrong with you?

OZZIE. I thought we were gonna have a nice party—

DAVID. I'm singing! We are!

OZZIE. No, no, I mean a *nice* party—one where everybody's happy!

DAVID. I'm happy. I'm singing. Don't you see them? Don't you see them?

OZZIE. Pardon, Dave?

HARRIET. What . . . are you saying?

DAVID, *changing, turning.* I have some movies. I thought you . . . knew.

HARRIET. Well . . . we . . . do.

OZZIE. Movies?

DAVID. Yes, I took them.

RICK. I thought you wanted to sing.

OZZIE. I mean, they're what's planned, Dave. That's what's up. The projector's all wound and ready. I don't know what you had to get so angry for.

HARRIET. Let's get everything ready.

OZZIE. Sure, sure. No need for all that yelling.

He moves to set up the projector.

DAVID. I'll narrate.

OZZIE. Fine, sure. What's it about anyway?

HARRIET. Are you in it?

OZZIE. Ricky, plug it in. C'mon, c'mon.

DAVID. It's a kind of story.

RICK. What about my guitar?

DAVID. No.

OZZIE. We oughta have some popcorn, though.

HARRIET. Oh, yes, what a dumb movie house, no popcorn, huh, Rick!

Rick switches off the lights.

OZZIE. Let her rip, Dave.

(*Dave turns on the projector; Ozzie is hurrying to a seat.*)

Ready when you are, C.B.

HARRIET. Shhhhhhh!

OZZIE, *a little child playing.* Let her rip, C.B. I want a new contract, C.B.

The projector runs for a moment. (*Note: In proscenium, a screen should be used if possible, or the film may be allowed to seem projected on the fourth wall; in three-quarter or round the screen may be necessary. If the screen is used, nothing must show upon it but a flickering of green.*)

HARRIET. Ohhh, what's the matter? It didn't come out, there's nothing there.

DAVID. Of course there is.

HARRIET. Noooo. . . . It's all funny.

DAVID. Look.

OZZIE. It's underexposed, Dave.

DAVID, *moving nearer.* No. Look.

HARRIET. What?

DAVID. They hang in the trees. They hang by their wrists half-severed by the wire.

OZZIE. Pardon me, Dave?

HARRIET. I'm going to put on the lights.

DAVID. NOOOOOO! LOOK! (*He uses his cane to point to the flickering screen with great specificity as if the events were there.*) They hang in the greenish haze afflicted by insects; a woman and a man, middle aged. They do not shout or cry. He is too small. Look—he seems all bone, shame in his eyes; his wife even here comes with him, skinny also as a broom and her hair is straight and black, hanging to mask her eyes.

The girl, Zung, drifts into the room.

OZZIE. I don't know what you're doing, David; there's nothing there.

DAVID. LOOK! (*And he points.*) They are all bone and pain, uncontoured and ugly but for the peculiar melon-swelling in her middle which is her pregnancy, which they do not see—look! these soldiers who have found her—as they do not see that she is not dead but only dying until saliva and blood bubble at her lips. Look. . . . Yet . . . she dies. Though a doctor is called in to remove the bullet-shot baby she would have preferred . . . to keep since she was dying and it was dead.

(*And Zung silently, drifting, departs.*)

In fact, as it turned out they would have all been better off left to hang as they had been strung on the wire—he with the back of his head blown off and she, the rifle jammed exactly and deeply up into her, with a bullet fired directly into the child living there. For they ended each buried in a separate place; the husband by chance alone was returned to their village, while the wife was dumped into an alien nearby plot of dirt, while the child, too small a piece of meat, was burned. (*He strums the guitar.*) Put into fire, as the shattered legs and arms cut off of men are burned. There's an oven. It is no ceremony. It is the disposal of garbage! . . .

Harriet gets to her feet, marches to the projector, pulls the plug, begins a little lecture.

HARRIET. It's so awful the things those yellow people do to one another. Yellow people hanging yellow people. Isn't that right? Ozzie, I told you—animals—Christ, burn them. David, don't let it hurt you. All the things you saw. People aren't themselves in war. I mean like that sticking that gun into that poor woman and then shooting that poor little baby, that's not human. That's inhuman. It's inhuman, barbaric and uncivilized and inhuman.

DAVID. I'm thirsty.

HARRIET. For what? Tell me. Water? Or would you like some milk? How about some milk?

DAVID, *shaking his head.* No.

HARRIET. Or would you like some orange juice? All golden and little bits of ice.

OZZIE. Just all those words and that film with no picture and these poor people hanging somewhere—so you can bring them home like this house is a meat house—

HARRIET. Oh, Ozzie, no, it's not that—no—he's just young, a young boy . . . and he's been through terrible, terrible things and now he's home, with his family he loves, just trying to speak to those he loves—just—

DAVID. Yes! That's right. Yes. What I mean is, yes, of course, that's what I am —a young . . . blind man in a room . . . in a house in the dark, raising nothing in a gesture of no meaning toward two voices who are not speaking . . . of a certain . . . incredible . . . *connection!*

All stare. Rick leaps up, running for the stairs.

RICK. Listen, everybody, I hate to rush off like this, but I gotta. Night.

HARRIET. Good night, Rick.

OZZIE, *simultaneously.* Good night.

David moves toward the stairs, looking upward.

DAVID. Because I talk of certain things . . . don't think I did them. Murderers don't even know that murder happens.

HARRIET. What are you saying? No, no. We're a family, that's all—we've had a little trouble—David, you've got to stop—please—no more yelling. Just be happy and home like all the others—why can't you?

DAVID. (*Strumming the guitar, he sings dissonantly.*) You mean take some old man to a ditch of water, shove his head under, talk of cars and money till his feeble pawing stops, and then head on home to go in and out of doors and drive cars and sing sometimes. (*He stops singing.*) I left her like you wanted . . . where people are thin and small all their lives. (*The beginning of realization*) Or did . . . you . . . think it was a . . . place . . . like this? Sinks and kitchens all the world over? Is that what you believe? Water from faucets, light from wires? Trucks, telephones, TV. Ricky sings and sings, but if I were to cut his throat, he would no longer and you would miss him—you would miss his singing. We are hoboes! (*And it is the first time in his life he has ever thought these things.*) We make signs in the dark. You know yours. I understand my own. We share . . . coffee!

(*There is nearly joy in this discovery: a hint of new freedom that might be liberation. And somewhere in the thrill of it he has whirled, his cane has come near to Ozzie, frightening him, though Harriet does not notice. Now David turns, moving for the stairs, thinking.*)

I'm going up to bed . . . now. . . . I'm very . . . tired.

OZZIE. Well . . . you have a good sleep, Son. . . .

DAVID. Yes, I think I'll sleep in.

OZZIE. You do as you please. . . .

DAVID. Good night.

HARRIET. Good night.

OZZIE. Good night.

HARRIET. Good night. (*Slight pause.*) You get a good rest. (*Silence.*) Try . . .

(*Silence. David has gone into his room. Ozzie and Harriet stand.*)

I'm . . . hungry . . . Ozzie. . . . Are you hungry?

OZZIE. Hungry? . . .

HARRIET. Yes.

OZZIE. No. Oh, no.

HARRIET. How do you feel? You look a little peaked. Do you feel all right?

OZZIE. I'm fine; I'm fine.

HARRIET. You look funny.

OZZIE. Really. No. How about yourself?

HARRIET. I'm never sick; you know that. Just a little sleepy.

OZZIE. Well . . . that's no wonder. It's been a long day.

HARRIET. Yes, it has.

OZZIE. No wonder.

HARRIET. Good night.

(*She is climbing the stairs toward bed.*)

OZZIE. Good night.

HARRIET. Don't stay up too late now.

OZZIE. Do you know when he pointed that cane at me, I couldn't breathe. I felt . . . for an instant I . . . might never breathe. . . .

HARRIET. Ohhh . . . I'm so sleepy. So . . . sooooo sleepy. Aren't you sleepy?

OZZIE, *to make her answer.* Harriet! I couldn't breathe.

HARRIET. WHAT DO YOU WANT? TEACHING HIM SPORTS AND FIGHTING.

(*This moment—one of almost a primal rage—should be the very first shattering of her motherly self-sacrificing image.*)

WHAT . . . OZZIE . . . DO YOU WANT?

OZZIE. Well . . . I was . . . wondering, do we have any aspirin down here . . . or are they all upstairs?

HARRIET. I thought you said you felt well.

OZZIE. Well, I do, I do. It's just a tiny headache. Hardly worth mentioning.

HARRIET. There's aspirin in the desk.

OZZIE, *crossing.* Fine. Big drawer?

HARRIET. Second drawer, right-hand side.

OZZIE. Get me a glass of water, would you, please?

HARRIET. Of course.

She gets a glass from a nearby table, a drink left over from the party, and hands it to him.

OZZIE. Thank you. It's not much of a headache, actually. Actually it's just a tiny headache.

He pops the tablets into his mouth and drinks to wash them down.

HARRIET. Aspirin makes your stomach bleed.

(*He tries to keep from swallowing the aspirin, but it is too late.*)

Did you know that? Nobody knows why. It's part of how it works. It just does it, makes you bleed. This extremely tiny series of hemorrhages in those delicate inner tissues.

(*He is staring at her: there is vengeance in what she is doing.*)

It's like those thin membranes begin, in a very minor way, to sweat blood and you bleed; inside yourself you bleed.

She crosses away.

OZZIE. That's not true. None of that. You made all that up. . . . Where are you going?

(*With a raincoat on, she is moving out the front door.*)

I mean . . . are you going out? Where . . . are you off to?

(*She is gone.*)

Goddamnit, there's something going on around here, don't you want to know what it is? (*Yelling at the shut door*) I want to know what it is. (*Turning, marching to the phone, dialing*) I want to know what's going on around here. I want to; I do. Want to—got to. Police. That's right, goddamnit—I want one of you people to get on out to seven-seventeen Dunbar and do some checking, some checking at seven-seventeen— What? Ohhh— (*Hissing*) Christ! . . . (*And he is pulling a handkerchief from his pocket, and covering the mouthpiece.*) I mean, they got a kid living there who just got back from the war and something's going on and I want to know what it. . . . No, I don't wanna give my name—it's them, not me— Hey! Hey!

RICK, *popping in at the hallway at the top of the stairs.* Hey, Dad! How you doin'?

Ozzie slams down the phone.

OZZIE. Oh, Rick! Hi!

RICK. Hi! How you doin'?

He is heading down the stairs and toward the front door.

OZZIE. Fine. Just fine.

RICK. Good.

OZZIE. How you doin', Rick?

RICK. Well, I'll see you later.

OZZIE, *running with the guitar David left.* I WANT YOU TO TEACH ME GUITAR!

RICK, *faltering.* What?

OZZIE. I want you to teach me . . . guitar! . . . To play it.

RICK. Sure. Okay.

OZZIE. I want to learn to play it. They've always been a kind of mystery to me, pianos, guitars.

RICK. Mystery?

And Ozzie is trying, awkwardly, desperately, to play.

OZZIE. I mean, what do you think? Do you ever have to think what your fingers should be doing? What I mean is do you ever have to say—I don't know what—"This finger goes there and this other one does—" I mean, "It's on *this* ridge; now I chord all the strings and then switch it all." See? And do you have to tell yourself, "Now switch it all—first finger this ridge—second finger, down—third—somewhere." I mean, does that kind of thing ever happen? I mean, *How do you play it?* I keep having this notion of wanting some . . . thing . . . some material thing, and I've built it. And then there's this feeling I'm of value, that I'm on my way—I mean, moving—and I'm going to come to something eventually, some kind of achievement. All these feelings of a child . . . in me. . . . They shoot through me and then they're gone and they're not anything . . . anymore. But it's . . . a . . . wall . . . that I want . . . I think. I see myself doing it sometimes . . . all brick and stone . . . coils of steel. And then I finish . . . and the success of it is monumental and people come from far . . . to see . . . to look. They applaud. Ricky . . . teach me . . .

RICK. Ahhh . . . what, Dad?

OZZIE. Guitar, guitar.

RICK. Oh, sure. First you start with the basic C chord. You put the first finger on the second string—

OZZIE. But that's what I'm talking about. You don't do that. I know you don't.

RICK, *not understanding.* Oh.

OZZIE. You just pick it up and play it. I don't have time for all that you're saying. That's what I've been telling you.

RICK, *on his way for the door.* Well, maybe some other day then. Maybe Mom'll wanna learn, too.

All this dialogue is rapid, overlapping.

OZZIE. No, no.

RICK. Just me and you then.

OZZIE. Right. Me and you.

RICK. I'll see you later.

OZZIE. What?

RICK. Maybe tomorrow.

OZZIE. No.

RICK. Well, maybe the next day then.

And he is gone out the door.

OZZIE. NOW! Now!

(*And the door slams shut.*)

I grew too old too quick. It was just a town, I thought, and no one remained to test me. I didn't even know it was leaving I was doing. I thought I'd go away and come back. Not leave. (*And he looks up at David's room.*) YOU SONOFABITCH

(*And he is running up to David's room*), NOT LEAVE! (*And he bursts into David's room. Silence.*) Restless, Dave; restless. Got a lot on my mind. Some of us can't just lay around, you know. You said I left that town like I was wrong, but I was right. A man proved himself out there, tested himself. So I went and then I ended up in the goddamn depression, what about that? I stood in goddamn lines of people begging bread and soup. You're not the only one who's had troubles. All of us, by God, David; think about that a little. (*Stepping out the door, slamming it*) Just give somebody besides yourself some goddamn thought for a change.

(*He now talks to the audience; they are his friends.*)

Lived in goddamn dirty fields, made tents of our coats. Again and again . . . the whole of the length of this country, soot in our fingers, riding the rails . . . , a bum, hobo but young. And then one day . . . the brakeman, sees me hunched down in that railroad car and he orders me off. He stands distant, ordering that I jump . . . ! I don't understand and then he stops speaking . . . and . . . when he speaks again, pain is in his eyes and voice—"You're a runner," he says, "Christ, I didn't know you were a runner." And he moves to embrace me and with both hands lifts me high above his head—holds me there trembling, then flings me far out and I fall, I roll. All in the air, then slam down breathless, raw from the cinders . . . bruised and dizzy at the outskirts of this town, and I'm here, gone from that other town. I'm here. I make friends. We have good times even though things are rough. We point young girls out on the street. How good it feels to touch them. I start thinking of their bodies, having dreams of horses, breasts and crotches. And then one day the feeling is in me that I must see a train go by and I'll get on it or I won't, something will happen, but halfway down to where I was thrown off, I see how the grass in among the ties is tall, the rails rusted . . . Grass grows in abundance. No trains any longer come that way; they all go some other way . . . and far behind me, I turn to see Harriet young and lovely weaving among the weeds. I feel the wonder of her body moving toward me. She's the thing I think I'll enter to find my future . . . "Yes," I yell, "Sonofabitch! Bring her here. C'mon!" Swollen with pride, screaming and yelling, I stand there: "I'm ready. I'm ready . . . I'm ready."

He has come down the stairs. He stands, arms spread, yelling. Blackout. Music.

Lights slowly up. Ozzie sleeps on the couch. Rick sits in a chair, looking at his guitar. Zung is in David's room, sitting on the bed behind David, who is slouched in a chair. Harriet, dressed in a blue robe, enters from the upstairs hallway and comes down the stairs.

HARRIET. Have you seen my crossword-puzzle book?

RICK. In the bathroom, Mom.

HARRIET. Bathroom? . . . Did I leave it there?

Turning, she heads back up the stairs.

RICK. Guess so, Mom.

DAVID, *sitting abruptly up in his chair as if at a sudden, frightening sound.* Who's there? There's someone there?

(*Rick looks up; David is standing, poking the air with his cane.*)

Who's there?

He opens the door to his room and steps into the hallway.

RICK. Whatsamatter? It's just me and Dad, and Dad's sleeping.

DAVID. Sleeping? Is he?

RICK. On the davenport. . . . You want me to wake him?

DAVID. Nooo . . . nooo.

He moves swiftly to descend to the living room.

RICK. Hey . . . could I get some pictures, Dave? Would you mind?

DAVID. Of course not. No.

RICK, *dashing off up the stairs, while David gropes to find the couch.* Let me just go get some film and some flashes, okay.

DAVID, *standing behind the couch on which Ozzie sleeps and looking after Rick.* Sure . . .

OZZIE. Pardon? Par . . . don?

DAVID, *whispering into his father's ear.* I think you should know I've begun to hate you and I don't think you can tell me any more. If I had been an orphan with no one to count on me, I would have stayed there. Now . . . she is everywhere I look. (*Ozzie stirs.*)

You think us good, we steal all you have.

OZZIE. Good . . . ole. . . .

DAVID. No, no.

OZZIE. Noooo . . . nooooooo. . . .

DAVID. She would tell me you would not like her. She would touch her fingers to her eyes, and she knew how I must feel sometimes as you do.

OZZIE. Ohhh, noooo . . . sleeping. . . .

DAVID. You must hear me. It is only fraud that keeps us sane, I swear it.

OZZIE. David, sleeping! . . . Oh, oh . . .

DAVID. It is not innocence I have lost. What is it I have lost?

OZZIE. Oh . . . oh . . .

Rick has appeared high in the hallway and hesitates there.

DAVID. Don't you know? Do you see her in your sleep?

RICK, *hurrying down.* I meant to get some good shots at the party, but I never got a chance the way things turned out. You can stay right there.

DAVID, *moving toward the chair on which Rick's guitar rests.* I'll sit, all right?

Rick rushes to save the guitar.

RICK. Sure. How you feelin' anyway, Dave? I mean, honest ta God, I'm hopin' you get better. Everybody is. I mean . . . (*He takes a picture.*) . . . you're not gonna go talkin' anymore crazy like about that guitar and all that, are you? You know what I mean. Not to Mom and Dad anyway. It scares 'em and then I get scared and I don't like it, okay?

(*He moves on, taking more pictures.*)

DAVID. Sure. That guitar business wasn't serious anyway, Rick. None of that. It was all just a little joke I felt like playing, a kind of little game. I was only trying to show you how I hate you.

RICK. Huh? (*Stunned, he stares.*)

DAVID. To see you die is why I live, Rick.

RICK. Oh.

HARRIET, *appearing from off upstairs, the crossword-puzzle book in her hands.* Goodness gracious, Ricky, it was just where you said it would be, though I'm sure I don't know how it got there because I didn't put it there. Hello, David.

DAVID. Hello.

OZZIE. OHHHHHHHHHHHHHHHH! (*Screaming, he comes awake, falling off the couch.*) Oh, boy, what a dream! Oh. . . . (*Trying to get to his feet, but collapsing*) Ohhhhhhh! God, leg's asleep. Jesus! (*And he flops about, sits there rubbing his leg*) Ohhhh, everybody. Scared hell out of me, that dream. I hollered. Did you hear me? And my leg's asleep, too.

(*He hits the leg, stomps the floor. Harriet sits on the couch, working her crossword-puzzle book. Rick, slumped in a chair, reads a comic. David, though, leans forward in his chair. He wants to know the effect of his whispering on his father.*)

Did anybody hear me holler?

HARRIET. Not me.

RICK. What did you dream about, Dad?

OZZIE. I don't remember, but it was awful. (*Stomping the foot*) Ohhhh, wake up, wake up. Hank was in it, though. And Dave. They stood over me, whispering—I could feel how they hated me.

RICK. That really happened; he really did that, Dad.

OZZIE. Who did?

RICK. What you said.

OZZIE. No. No, I was sleeping. It scared me awful in my sleep. I'm still scared, honest ta God, it was so awful.

DAVID. It's that sleeping in funny positions, Dad. It's that sleeping in some place that's not a bed.

OZZIE. Pardon?

DAVID. Makes you dream funny. What did Hank look like?

HARRIET. Ozzie, how do you spell "Apollo"?

OZZIE. What?

RICK. Jesus, Dad, Schroeder got three home runs, you hear about that? Two in the second of the first and one in the third of the second. Goddamn, if he don't make MVP in the National, I'll eat my socks. You hear about that, Dad?

OZZIE. Yes, I did. Yes.

RICK. He's somethin'.

OZZIE. A pro.

HARRIET. Ozzie, can you think of a four letter word that starts with G and ends with B?

RICK. Glub.

HARRIET. Glub?

OZZIE (*almost simultaneously*). Glub?

RICK. It's a cartoon word. Cartoon people say it when they're drowning. G-L-U-B.

OZZIE, *on his feet now.* Ricky. Ricky, I was wondering . . . when I was sleeping, were my eyes open? Was I seeing?

RICK. I didn't notice, Dad.

HARRIET. *Glub* doesn't work, Rick.

RICK. Try *grub.* That's what sourdoughs call their food. It's G-R—

OZZIE. WAIT A MINUTE!

RICK. G-R—

OZZIE. ALL OF YOU WAIT A MINUTE! LISTEN! Listen. I mean, I look for explanations. I look inside myself. For an explanation. I mean, I look inside *my* self. As I would look into water . . . or the sky . . . the ocean. They're silver. Answers . . . silver and elusive . . . like fish. But if you can catch them in the sea . . . hook them as they flash by, snatch them . . . drag them down like birds from the sky . . . against all their struggle . . . when you're adrift . . . and starving . . . they . . . can help you live.

He falters; he stands among them, straining to go further, searching some sign of comprehension in their faces.

RICK. Mom . . . Dad's hungry . . . I think. He wants some fish, I—

OZZIE. SHUT UP!

RICK, *hurt deeply.* Dad?

OZZIE. PIECE OF SHIT! SHUT UP! SHUT UP!

HARRIET. Ozzie! . . .

OZZIE, *roaring down at David.* I don't want to hear about her. I'm not interested in her. You did what you did and I was no part of it. You understand me? I don't want to hear any more about her! Look at him. Sitting there. Listening. I'm tired of hearing you, Dave. You understand that? I'm tired of hearing you and your crybaby voice and your crybaby stories. And your crybaby slobbering and your . . . (*And his voice is possessed with astonished loathing.*) LOOK . . . AT . . . HIM! YOU MAKE ME WANT TO VOMIT! HARRIET! YOU— (*He whirls on Harriet.*) YOU! Your internal organs—your internal female organs—they've got some kind of poison in them. They're backing up some kind of rot into the world. I think you ought to have them cut out of you. I MEAN, I JUST CAN'T STOP THINKING ABOUT IT. I JUST CAN'T STOP THINKING ABOUT IT. LITTLE BITTY CHINKY KIDS HE WANTED TO HAVE! LITTLE BITTY CHINKY YELLOW KIDS! DIDN'T YOU! FOR OUR GRANDCHILDREN! (*And he slaps David with one hand.*) LITTLE BITTY YELLOW PUFFY—(*He breaks, groping for the word.*) . . . creatures! . . . FOR OUR GRANDCHILDREN! (*He slaps David again, again.*) THAT'S ALL YOU CARED!

David, a howl in his throat, has stood up.

HARRIET. Ohhh, Ozzie, God forgive you the cruelty of your words. All children are God's children.

David is standing rigid. The front door blows open, and in a fierce and sudden light Zung steps forward to the edge of David's room, as he looks up at her.

DAVID. I didn't know you were here. I didn't know. I will buy you clothing. I have lived with them all my life. I will make them not hate you. I will buy you boots.

(*And he is moving toward her, climbing the stairs.*)

They will see you. The seasons will amaze you. Texas is enormous. Ohio is sometimes green. There will be time. We will learn to speak. And it will be as it was in that moment when we looked in the dark and our eyes were tongues that could speak and the hurting . . . all of it . . . stopped, and there was total understanding in you of me and in me of you . . . and . . .

(*Near her now, stepping into his room through the wall, he reaches in a tentative way toward her.*)

such delight in your eyes that I felt it;

(*And she has begun to move away from him.*)

yet . . . I

(*She is moving away and down the stairs.*)

discarded you. I discarded you. Forgive me. You moved to leave as if you were struggling not to move, not to leave. "She's the thing most possibly of value in my life," I said. "She is garbage and filth and I must get her back if I wish to live.

Sickness. I must cherish her." Zung, there were old voices inside me I had trusted all my life as if they were my own. I didn't know I shouldn't hear them. So reasonable and calm they seemed a source of wisdom. "She's all of everything impossible made possible, cast her down," they said. "Go home." And I did as they told; and now I know that I am not awake but asleep, and in my sleep . . . there is nothing. . . .

(*Zung is now standing before the open door, facing it, about to leave.*)

Nothing! . . . What do you want from me to make you stay? I'll do it. I'll do what you want!

RICK, *in the dark before his father, camera in hand.* Lookee here, Dad. Cheer up! Cheer up!

DAVID (*as Zung turns to look up at him*). Nooooooo. . . .

(*And there is a flash as Rick takes the picture.*)

NOOOOOOOOOOOOOO! STAAAAAAAY!

And the door slams shut, leaving Zung still inside. A slide of Ozzie appears on the screen, a close-up of his pained and puzzled face. Music, a falling of notes. The lights are going to black. Perhaps "Intermission" is on the bottom of the slide. The slide blinks out.

Act Two

Blackness. Slide: color close-up of a man's ruddy, smiling, round face.

1ST CHILD'S VOICE. Who zat?

WOMAN'S VOICE. I don't know.

MAN'S VOICE. Looks like a neighbor.

WOMAN'S VOICE. How can you say it's a neighbor? You don't know.

New slide appears: scenery, in color.

2ND CHILD'S VOICE. Oh, that's a pretty one.

New slide: Father Donald in a boxing pose, color.

1ST CHILD'S VOICE. Oh, lookee that.

MAN'S VOICE. Father What's-his-name. You know.

Another slide: Father Donald, slightly different boxing pose.

WOMAN'S VOICE. There he is again.

2ND CHILD'S VOICE. Wow.

Lights up on the downstairs. David is up in his room on his bed. Downstairs, Harriet sits on the couch, Father Donald is on a chair; Ozzie is in the chair beside him. We have the feeling they have been there a long, long time.

FATHER DONALD. I deal with people and their uneasiness on a regular basis all the time, you see. Everybody I talk to is nervous . . . one way or another . . . so . . . I anticipate no real trouble in dealing with Dave. You have no idea the things people do and then tell me once that confessional door is shut. I'm looking forward actually, to speaking with him. Religion has been sloughed off a lot lately, but I think there's a relevancy much larger than the credit most give. We're growing—and our insights, when we have them, are twofold. I for one have come recently to understand how very often what seems a spiritual problem is in fact a problem of the mind rather than the spirit—not that the two can in fact be separated, though, in theory, they very often are. So what we must do is apply these theories to fact. At which point we would find that mind and spirit are one and I, a priest, am a psychiatrist, and psychiatrists are priests. I mean—I feel like I'm rambling. Am I rambling?

HARRIET. Oh, no, Father.

OZZIE. Nooo . . . noo.

HARRIET. Father, this is hard for me to say, but I . . . feel . . . his problem is he sinned against the sixth commandment with whores.

FATHER DONALD. That's very likely over there.

HARRIET. And then the threat of death each day made it so much worse.

FATHER DONALD. I got the impression from our earlier talk that he'd had a relationship of some duration.

HARRIET. A day or two, wouldn't you say, Ozzie?

OZZIE, *distracted, oddly preoccupied with his chair.* A three-day pass I'd say . . . though I don't know, of course.

FATHER DONALD. They're doing a lot of psychiatric studies on that phenomenon right now, did you know that?

The front door pops open, and in bounds Rick.

HARRIET. Oh, Rick! . . .

RICK. Hi, Mom. Hi, Dad.

OZZIE. Hi, Rick.

FATHER DONALD, *rising.* Rick, hello!

RICK. Oh, Father Donald . . . hi.

No time for Father Donald, Rick is speeding for the kitchen.

OZZIE. Look at him heading for the fudge.

FATHER DONALD. Well, he's a good big strong sturdy boy.

RICK, *as he goes out.* Hungry and thirsty.

FATHER DONALD. And don't you ever feel bad about it, either!

(*He stands for an instant, a little uncertain what to do.*)

Dave's up in his room, I imagine, so maybe I'll just head on up and have my little chat. He is why I'm here, after all.

HARRIET. Fine.

OZZIE, *standing, still distracted, he stares at the chair in which Father Donald was sitting.* First door top of the stairs.

FATHER DONALD. And could I use the bathroom, please, before I see ole Dave? Got to see a man about a horse.

HARRIET. Oh, Father, certainly: it's just down the hall. Fifth door.

OZZIE, *stepping nearer to the chair.* What's wrong with that chair? . . .

HARRIET. It's the blue door, Father! . . .

OZZIE. I . . . don't like that chair. I think it's stupid . . . looking. . . .

(*As Rick enters from the kitchen, eating fudge*)

Ricky, sit. Sit in that chair.

RICK. What? . . .

OZZIE. Go on, sit, sit.

Rick hurries to the chair, sits, eats. Ozzie is fixated on the chair.

HARRIET. Oh, Ricky, take your father's picture, he looks so silly.

OZZIE. I just don't think that chair is any good. I just don't think it's comfortable. Father Donald looked ill at ease all the while he was sitting there.

HARRIET. Well, he had to go to the bathroom, Ozzie, what do you expect?

OZZIE, *to Ricky.* Get up. It's just not right.

(*Rick gets up and Ozzie flops into the chair, sits, fidgets. Rick goes back out to the kitchen.*)

Noooooo. It's just not a comfortable chair at all, I don't know why.

(*He rises and moves toward the couch.*)

I don't like it. How much did we pay?

HARRIET. What do you think you're doing?

OZZIE. And this couch isn't comfortable either.

HARRIET. It's a lovely couch.

OZZIE—*tests it.* But it isn't comfortable. Noooo. And I'm not really sure it's lovely, either. Did we pay two hundred dollars?

HARRIET. What? Oh, more.

OZZIE. How much?

HARRIET. I don't know, I told you.

OZZIE. You don't. I don't. It's gone anyway, isn't it?

HARRIET. Ozzie, what does it matter?

OZZIE, *already on the move for the stairs.* I'm going upstairs. I'll be upstairs.

HARRIET. Wait a minute.

(*As he keeps moving, up the stairs*)

I want to talk to you. *I think we ought to talk!*

(*Emotion well beneath her voice stops him, turns him.*)

I mean, it's nothing to worry about or anything, but you don't know about it and it's your house, you're involved—so it's just something I mention. You're the man of the house, you ought to know. The police were here . . . earlier today.

OZZIE. What? Oh, my God.

HARRIET. The police. Two of them. Two. A big and a small . . . they—

(*He is dazed; he doesn't know whether to go up or down, listen or leave. He nods.*)

It was just a little bit ago; not long at all.

OZZIE. Jesus Christ. (*He descends.*)

HARRIET. Oh, I know, I know. Just out of the blue like that—it's how I felt, too. I did, I did.

OZZIE. *What—police?*

HARRIET. It was when you were gone for groceries. I mean, they thought they were supposed to be here. We wanted it, they thought.

OZZIE. No, no.

HARRIET. Somebody called them to come here. They thought it had been us. They were supposed to look through David's luggage, they thought.

OZZIE. They . . . were . . . what?

HARRIET. That's what I mean. That's exactly what I—

OZZIE. *Look through his luggage? There's nothing wrong with his luggage!*

HARRIET. Isn't it incredible? Somebody called them—they didn't know who—no name was given and it sounded muffled through a handkerchief, they said. I said, "Well, it wasn't us." Told them, "Don't you worry; we're all all right here." It must have been a little joke by somebody.

OZZIE. What about Dave?

HARRIET. No, no.

OZZIE. Or Ricky? Did you ask Ricky?

HARRIET. Ricky?

OZZIE. RICKY! RICKY!

RICK, *popping in from the kitchen, thinking he was called.* What's up, Dad?

OZZIE. I DON'T KNOW.

RICK. I thought you called.

He pops back out into the kitchen.

OZZIE, *to Harriet.* You ask him; you ask him. I think the whole thing's preposterous—absolutely—

HARRIET, *as Rick re-emerges to look and listen.* Ricky, do you know anything about anybody calling the police to come here?

OZZIE, *turning and moving for the stairs.* I'm going upstairs. I'll be upstairs.

RICK. The police?

(*As Harriet turns to look and half step after Ozzie*)

Oh, no, Mom, not me. Okay if I use the car?

HARRIET. What?

FATHER DONALD, *encountering Ozzie in the upstairs hallway.* Gonna take care of old Dave right now.

OZZIE. I'm going upstairs. I'll be upstairs.

He exits, as Harriet stands looking up at them.

RICK. Bye, Mom.

HARRIET. What? Oh. (*Looking back as Rick goes out the door*) BE CAREFUL!

FATHER DONALD, *after a slight hesitation.* Ozzie said to tell you he was going upstairs.

HARRIET. What?

FATHER DONALD. Ozzie said to tell you he was going upstairs.

HARRIET—*stares at him a moment.* Oh, Father, I'm so glad you're here.

And she exits into the kitchen, leaving Father Donald. He nods, knocks on David's door.

FATHER DONALD. Dave?

(*He opens the door, eases into the semidark of the room.*)

Dave? It's me . . . Dave. . . .

(*Finding a light, he flicks it on.*)

Ohh, Dave, golly, you look just fine. Here I expected to see you all worn out and there you are looking so good. It's me, Dave, Father Donald. Let me shake your hand.

(*David's rising hand comes up far off from Father Donald. The priest, his own hand extended, has to move nearly around the bed before he can shake David's hand.*)

No, no, David. Here. Over here. Can't see me, can you? There you go. Yes, sir, let me tell you, I'm proud. A lot of people might tell you that, I know, but I mean it, and I'll stand behind it if there's anything I can do for you—anything at all.

DAVID. No. I'm all right.

FATHER DONALD. And that's the amazing part of it, Dave, you are. You truly are. It's plain as day. Golleee, I just don't know how to tell you how glad I am to see you in such high fine spirits. Would you like my blessing? (*He gets to his feet.*) Let me just give you my blessing and then we'll talk things over a little and—

David slashes with his cane and strikes the hand moving into the position to bless.)

Ohhhhhhhhhhhhhh! (*Wincing, teeth gritted*) Oh, Dave; oh, watch out what you're doing!

DAVID. I know.

FATHER DONALD. No, no, I mean, you swung it in the air, you—hit me.

DAVID. Yes.

FATHER DONALD. No, no, you don't understand, you—

DAVID. I was trying to hit you, Father.

Father Donald stares, taking this in.

FATHER DONALD. What?

DAVID. I didn't send for you.

FATHER DONALD. I know, I know, your poor mother—your poor mother—

DAVID. I don't want you here, Father; get out!

FATHER DONALD. David!

DAVID. Get out, I'm sick of you. You've been in one goddamn corner or another of this room all my life making signs at me, whispering, wanting to splash me with water or mark me with oil—some goddamn hocus-pocus. I feel reverence for the air and the air is empty, Father. Now get the fuck out of here.

FATHER DONALD. No, no, no, no, David. No, no. I can't give that to you. You'll have to get that from somewhere else.

DAVID. I don't want anything from you!

FATHER DONALD. I'm supposed to react now in some foolish way—I see—some foolish, foolish way that will discredit me—isn't that right? Oh, of course it is. It's an excuse to dismiss my voice that you're seeking, an excuse for the self-destruction your anger has made you think you want, and I'm supposed to give it. I'm supposed to find all this you're doing obscene and sacrilegious instead of seeing it as the gesture of true despair that it is. You're trying to make me disappear, but it's not going to happen. No, no. No such luck, David. I understand you, you see. Everything about you.

DAVID. Do you?

FATHER DONALD. The way you're troubled.

DAVID. I didn't know that, Father.

FATHER DONALD. You say that sarcastically—"Do you? I didn't know that." As if to imply you're so complicated I couldn't ever understand you when I already have. You see, I've been looking into a few things, David, giving some things some thought. (*Producing a magazine with a colorful cover*) I have in my hand a magazine —you can't see it, I know—but it's there. A psychiatric journal in which there is an article of some interest and it deals with soldiers and some of them carried on as you did and then there's some others who didn't. It's not all just a matter of hocus-pocus any longer.

DAVID. Carried . . . on . . . Father?

FATHER DONALD. That whore. That yellow whore. You understand. You knew I was bringing the truth when I came which is why you hit me.

DAVID. I thought you didn't even know the problem. You came in here all bubbly and jolly asking how did I feel.

FATHER DONALD. That was only a little ruse, David; a little maneuver to put you off your guard. I only did that to mislead you. That's right. Your mother gave me all the basics some weeks ago and I filled in the rest from what I know. You see, if it's a fight you want, it's what you'll get. Your soul is worth some time and sweat from me. You're valued by others, David, even if you don't value yourself. (*Waving the magazine in the air*) It's all here—right here—in these pages. It was demonstrated beyond any possible doubt that people—soldiers—who are compelled for some reason not even they themselves understand to establish personal sexual relationships with whores are inferior to those who don't; they're maladjusted, embittered, non-goal-oriented misfits. The sexual acceptance of another person, David, is intimate and extreme; this kind of acceptance of an alien race is in fact the rejection of one's own race—it is in fact the rejection of one's own self—it is sickness, David. Now I'm a religious man, a man of the spirit, but knowledge is knowledge and I must accept what is proven fact whether that fact come from science or philosophy or whatever. What kind of man are you that you think you can deny it? You're in despair, David, whether you think of it that way or not. It's only into a valley of ruin that you are trying to lock yourself. You can only die there, David. Accept me. Let God open your eyes; let Him. He will redeem you. Not I nor anyone, but only Him—yet if you reject me, you reject Him. My hand is His. His blessing.

(*The hand is rising as if the very words elevate it.*)

My blessing. Let me give you my blessing.

(*And David's cane hits like a snake. Father Donald cries out in surprise and pain. He recovers and begs*)

Let me bless you. (*His hand is again rising in blessing.*) Please!

(*David, striking again, stands. He hits again and again.*)

David! David! (*Terrified*) Stop it. Let me bless you.

David hits Father Donald's arm, hits his leg.

DAVID. I don't want you here!

FATHER DONALD. You don't know what you're saying.

(*But now the blow seems about to come straight down on his head. He yells and covers his head with his arms. The blow hits. He picks up a chair, holds it up for protection.*)

Stop it. Stop it. Goddamnit, stop hitting me. Stop it. You are in despair.

(*He slams the chair down.*)

A man who hits a priest is in despair!

(*Whistling, the cane slams into his arm.*)

Ohhhhh, this pain—this terrible pain in my arm—I offer it to earn you your salvation.

DAVID. Get out!

FATHER DONALD. Death! Do you understand that. Death. Death is your choice. You are in despair.

He turns to leave.

DAVID. And may God reward *you,* Father.

FATHER DONALD, *turning back, as David flops down on the bed.* Oh yes; yes of course, you're so confident now, young and strong. Look at you—full of spunk, smiling. But all that'll change. Your tune'll change in time. What about pain, Dave? Physical pain. What do you do when it comes? Now you send me away, but in a little while you'll call me back, run down by time, lying with death on your bed . . . in an empty house . . . gagging on your own spit you cannot swallow; you'll call me then, nothing left to you but fear and Christ's black judging eyes about to find and damn you; you'll call.

Slight pause.

DAVID. That's not impossible, Father.

FATHER DONALD. I don't even like you; do you know that? I DON'T EVEN LIKE YOU!

DAVID. Tell them I hit you when you go down.

FATHER DONALD, *near the door, thinking about trying to bless from there.* No. No, they've pain enough already.

DAVID. Have they? You get the fuck out of here before I kill you.

As if he has read Father Donald's mind and knows what the man is thinking, David's cane is rising ready to strike.

FATHER DONALD, *moving not a muscle.* THOUGH I DO NOT MOVE MY HAND, I BLESS YOU! YOU ARE BLESSED!

And he exits hurriedly, heading straight down the hall toward the bathroom. Lights up downstairs: it seems a lovely afternoon as Rick and Harriet enter from the kitchen, chatting.

HARRIET. So the thing I want to do—I just think it would be so nice if we could get Dave a date with some nice girl.

RICK. Oh, sure.

HARRIET. Do you think that would be a good idea?

Ozzie, descending from the attic, pauses to peek into David's room; he finds David asleep, and, after a moment, continues on down.

RICK. Sure.

HARRIET. Do you know any girls you think might get along with David?

RICK. No, but I still think it's really a good idea and I'll keep it in mind for all the girls I meet and maybe I'll meet one. Here comes Dad. Hi, Dad. Bye, Mom.

HARRIET. Oh, Ozzie, did you see what they were doing?

OZZIE. Dave's sleeping, Harriet; Father Donald's gone.

HARRIET. What? He can't be gone.

OZZIE. I thought maybe he was down here. How about the kitchen?

HARRIET. No, no, I just came out of the kitchen. Where were you upstairs? Are you sure he wasn't in David's room?

OZZIE. I was in the attic.

HARRIET. Well, maybe he saw the light and came up to join you and you missed each other on the way up and down. Why don't you go check?

OZZIE. I turned off all the lights, Harriet. The attic's dark now.

HARRIET. Well, yell up anyway—

OZZIE. But the attic's dark now, Harriet.

HARRIET. Just in case.

OZZIE. What are you trying to say? Father Donald's up in the attic in the dark? I mean, if he was up there and I turned off the lights, he'd have said something—"Hey, I'm here," or something. It's stupid to think he wouldn't.

And he sits down.

HARRIET. No more stupid to think that than to think he'd leave without telling us what happened with David.

OZZIE. All right, all right. (*Storming to the foot of the stairs*) HEEEEEEYYYYYYYYYYYY! HEEEEYYYYYYYY! UP THEEEEERRE! ANYBODY UP THERE?

There is a brief silence. He turns toward Harriet.

DAVID, *on his bed in his room.* WHAT'S THAT, DAD?

OZZIE—*falters, looks about.* What?

DAVID. WHAT'S UP, DAD?

OZZIE. OH, DAVE, NO, NOT YOU.

DAVID. WHY ARE YOU YELLING?

OZZIE. NO, NO, WE JUST THOUGHT FATHER DONALD WAS UP THERE IN THE ATTIC, DAVE. DON'T YOU WORRY ABOUT IT.

DAVID. I'M THE ONLY ONE UP HERE, DAD!

OZZIE. BUT . . . YOU'RE NOT IN THE ATTIC, SEE?

DAVID. I'M IN MY ROOM.

OZZIE. I KNOW YOU'RE IN YOUR ROOM.

DAVID. YOU WANT ME TO GO UP IN THE ATTIC?

OZZIE. NO! GODDAMNIT, JUST—

DAVID. I DON'T KNOW WHAT YOU WANT.

OZZIE. I WANT YOU TO SHUT UP, DAVE, THAT'S WHAT I WANT, JUST—

FATHER DONALD, *appearing from off upstairs.* What's the matter? What's all the yelling?

HARRIET. Oh, Father!

OZZIE. Father, hello, hello.

HARRIET. How did it go? Did it go all right?

FATHER DONALD, *coming down the steps, seeming as if nothing out of the ordinary has happened.* Fine, just fine.

HARRIET. Oh, you're perspiring so though—look at you.

FATHER DONALD, *maneuvering for the door.* Well, I've got a lot on my mind. It happens. Nerves. I've other appointments. Many, many.

HARRIET. You mean you're leaving? What are you saying?

FATHER DONALD. I must.

HARRIET. But we've got to talk.

FATHER DONALD. Call me.

HARRIET. Father . . . bless me! . . .

FATHER DONALD. What? . . .

HARRIET. Bless me. . . .

FATHER DONALD. Of course.

She bows her head, and the priest blesses her, murmuring the Latin.

HARRIET. Ohhh, Father, thank you so much. (*Touching his hand*) Shall I walk you to your car?

FATHER DONALD, *backing for the door.* Fine, fine. That's all right. Sure.

OZZIE, *nodding.* DAVE, SAY GOOD-BYE TO FATHER DONALD, HE'S LEAVING NOW.

FATHER DONALD. GOOD-BYE, DAVE!

DAVID. GOOD-BYE, FATHER!

Blackout as Harriet and Father Donald are going out the door. Music.

Ozzie is discovered in late night light, climbing the stairs to David's door, where, after hesitating an instant, he gently knocks.

OZZIE. Dave, I'd like to come in . . . if I could. (*Easing in*) Awful dark; can I put on a light?

(*Silence.*)

I mean, we don't need one—not really. I just thought we might . . . I mean, first of all, I want to apologize for the way I hit you the other day. I don't know why I did it. I'm . . . gonna sit down here on the edge of the bed. Are you awake enough to understand? I am your father, you know, and I could command . . . if I wanted. I don't; but I could. I'm going to sit.

(*Slight pause.*)

I mean, it's so sad the way you just go on and on . . . and I'd like to have time for you, but you want so much; I have important things, too. I have plans; I'm older, you know; if I fail to fulfill them, who will do it: Not you, though you could. And Rick's too busy. Do you understand? There's no evidence in the world of me, no sign or trace, as if everything I've ever done were no more than smoke. My life has closed behind me like water. But I must not care about it. I must not. Though I have inside me a kind of grandeur I can't realize, many things and memories of a darker time when we were very different—harder—nearer to the air and we thought of nothing as a gift. But I can't make you see that. There's no way. It's what I am, but it's not what you are. Even if I had the guitar, I would only stand here telling my fingers what to do, but they would do nothing. You would not see. . . . I can't get beyond these hands. I jam in the fingers. I break on the bone. I am . . . lonely. I mean, oh, no, not exactly lonely, not really. That's a little strong, actually. . . .

(*Silence.*)

I mean . . . Dave . . . (*He pulls from his back pocket David's overseas cap.*) What's this?

DAVID. What?

OZZIE. This cap. What is it? I cut myself on it. I was rummaging in your stuff upstairs, your bags and stuff, and I grabbed it. It cut me.

DAVID, *reaching for the cap.* Oh . . . yes.

OZZIE. There are razors sewn into it. Why is that?

DAVID. To cut people.

Slowly he puts the cap on his head.

OZZIE. Oh.

DAVID. Here . . . I'll show you . . . (*Getting slowly to his feet*) You're on the street, see. You walk . . . and see someone who's after you. . . . You wait. . . .

(*He tenses. His hand rises to the tip of the cap.*)

As they get near . . . slowly you remove the hat—they think you're going to toss it aside, see? You . . . *snap it! You snap it!*

(*Seizing the front edge of the cap between thumb and finger, he snaps it down. It whistles past Ozzie, who jumps.*)

It cuts them. They hold their face. However you want them, they're yours. You can stomp them, kick them. This is on the street. I'd like to do that to somebody, wouldn't you?

OZZIE. Huh?

DAVID. It'd be fun.

OZZIE. Oh, sure. I . . .

DAVID. Who told you to buy this house?

OZZIE. It's a good house. Solid. Not one of those prefabs, those—

DAVID. It's a coffin. You made it big so you wouldn't know, but that's what it is, and not all the curtains and pictures and lamps in the world can change it. He threw you off a fast free train, Ozzie.

OZZIE. I don't care, I—

Zung appears.

DAVID. Do you know, Dad, it seemed sometimes I would rise and slam with my fists into the walls of a city. Pointing at buildings, I turned them into fire. I took the fleeing people into my fingers and bent them to touch their heads to their heels, each screaming at the sight of their brain turning black. And now sometimes I miss them, all those screaming people. I wish they were here with us, you and Mom and Rick and Zung and me.

Pause.

OZZIE. Mom and Rick and who and you, Dave?

DAVID. Zung.

Zung is moving nearer to them now.

OZZIE. Zung, Dave?

DAVID. She's here. They were all just hunks of meat that had no mind to know of me until I cared for her. It was simple. We lived in a house. She didn't want to come back here, Dad; she wanted me to stay there. And in all the time I knew her, she cost me six dollars that I had to sneak into her purse. Surprised? In time I'll show you some things. You'll see them. I will be your father.

He tosses the cap at Ozzie.

OZZIE, *shaken, struggling to catch the cap.* Pardon, Dave?

DAVID. What's wrong? You sound like something's terribly wrong?

OZZIE. No. No, no. I'm fine. Your poor mother—she's why I'm here. Your poor mother, sick with grief. She's mine to care for, you know. It's me you're after, yet you torment her. No more. No more. That's what I came up here to tell you.

DAVID, *getting to his feet.* Good.

OZZIE. You're phony, David—phony—trying to make up for the thousands you butchered, when if you were capable of love at all you would love us, your mother and me—not that we matter—instead of some poor little whore who isn't even here.

DAVID, *exiting the room.* I know.

OZZIE. I want her happy.

DAVID (*as Ozzie follows a little into the hall*). I know.

And David is gone. Harriet enters slowly from the kitchen, sees Ozzie, then the room's open door.

HARRIET. Did you have a nice talk?

OZZIE, *heading toward her.* Harriet, what would you say if I said I wanted some checking done?

HARRIET. I don't know what you mean. In what way do you mean?

OZZIE. Take a look at that. But just be careful.

HARRIET. What is it?

OZZIE. His cap. There are razor blades sewn in it; all along the edge.

HARRIET. Ozzie . . . ohhh! Goodness.

OZZIE. That's what I mean. And I was reading just yesterday—some of them bring back guns and knives. Bombs. We've got somebody living in this house who's killed people, Harriet, and that's a fact we've got to face. I mean, I think we ought to do some checking. You know that test where they check teeth against old X-rays. I think—

HARRIET. Ohhh . . . my God! . . .

OZZIE. I know, I know, it scares me, too, but what are we talking about? We're talking about bombs and guns and knives, and sometimes I don't even think it's David up there. I feel funny . . . sometimes . . . I mean, and I want his fingerprints taken. I think we should have his blood type—

HARRIET. Oh, Ozzie, Ozzie, it was you.

OZZIE. Huh?

HARRIET. You did it. You got this out of his luggage, all his baggage upstairs. You broke in and searched and called the police.

OZZIE. No. What?

HARRIET. You told them to come here, and then you lied and said you didn't.

OZZIE. What?

HARRIET. You did, and then you lied and now you're lying again.

OZZIE. Oh, no. No.

HARRIET. What's wrong with you? What's happening to you?

OZZIE. But I didn't do that. I didn't.

(*David appears in the upstairs hallway, moving to return to his room.*)

I didn't. No, no. And even if I did, what would it mean but I changed my mind, that's all. Sure. (*Looking up at David moving in the hall toward his room*) I called and then changed my mind and said I didn't when I did, and since when is there anything wrong in that? It would mean only that I have a little problem of ambivalence. I got a minor problem of ambiguity goin' for me here, is all, and you're exaggerating everything all out of proportion. You're distorting everything! All of you! (*And he whirls to leave.*) If I have to lie to live, I will! (*He runs.*)

HARRIET. Where are you going? Come back here, Ozzie. Where are you going?

OZZIE. Kitchen. Kitchen.

He gallops out the front door. Blackout. Music.

Lights up. Bright afternoon. Harriet is alone, dusting. Rick, carrying books, enters from the kitchen and heads for the stairs to go to his room.

HARRIET. One day, Ricky . . . there were these two kittens and a puppy all in our back yard fighting. The kittens were little fur balls, so angry, and the little puppy, yapping and yapping. I was just a girl, but I picked them up in my arms. I held them all in my arms and they got very, very quiet.

RICK. I'm going up to my bedroom and study my history and English and trigonometry, Mom.

HARRIET. Do you know, I've called Father Donald seven times now—seven times, and haven't got an answer. Isn't that funny? He's starting to act like Jesus. You never hear from him. Isn't that funny?

RICK. I'm going up to my bedroom and study my history and English and trigonometry, Mom, okay?

HARRIET. Fine, Ricky. Look in on David, would you?

RICK. Sure.

HARRIET. Good night.

RICK, *calling as he passes David's door.* Hi, Dave.

DAVID. Hi, Rick.

RICK. DAVE'S OKAY, MOM.

She is at the foot of the stairs. Rick goes from view. She turns back to her work, and the front door opens and Ozzie enters.

OZZIE, *excited, upset.* Harriet! Can you guess what happened? You'll never guess what happened.

(*She continues cleaning.*)

Harriet, wait. Stop.

HARRIET. Ozzie, I've got work to do.

OZZIE. But I want to tell you something.

HARRIET. All right, tell me; I can clean and listen; I can do both.

As she moves away, he rushes toward her, stretching out the lapel of his jacket to show her a large stain on it. She must see.

OZZIE. Lookit; look at that. What do you think that is? That spot on my coat, do you see it? That yellow?

HARRIET, *distressed, touching the spot.* Ohhhh, Ozzie! . . .

OZZIE. And the red mark on my neck.

HARRIET, *wincing.* Ohh, Ozzie, what happened? A bee sting! You got stung by a bee!

OZZIE. No, no; I was walking—thinking—trying to solve our problems. Somebody hit me with an egg. They threw it at me. I got hit with an egg.

(*She stares, incredulous.*)

That's right. I was just walking down the street and—bang—I was hit. I almost blacked out; I almost fell down.

HARRIET. Ozzie, my God, who would do such a thing?

OZZIE. I don't know. That's the whole point. I've racked my brain to understand and I can't. I was just walking along. That's all I was doing.

HARRIET. You mean you didn't even see them?

OZZIE, *pacing, his excitement growing.* They were in a car. I saw the car. And I saw the hand, too. Somebody's hand. A very large hand. Incredibly large.

HARRIET. What kind of car?

OZZIE. I don't know. An old one—black—big high fenders.

HARRIET. A Buick.

OZZIE. I think so; yes. Cruising up and down, up and down.

HARRIET. Was it near here? Why don't you sit down? (*Trying to help him sit, to calm and comfort him*) Sit down. Relax.

He obeys, hardly aware of what he is doing, sort of squatting on the couch, his body rigid with tension, as the story obsesses him.

OZZIE. And I heard them, too. They were hollering.

HARRIET. What did they say?

OZZIE. I don't know. It was just all noise. I couldn't understand.

HARRIET, *as if the realization doubles the horror.* It was more than one? My God!

OZZIE. I don't know. Two at least, at the very least. One to drive and one to throw. Maybe even three. A lookout sort of, peering up and down, and then he sees me. "There," he says; he points me out. I'm strolling along like a stupid ass, I don't even see them. The driver picks up speed.

(*And now he is rising from the couch, reliving the story, cocking his arm.*)

The thrower cocks his arm . . .

HARRIET. Ozzie, please, can't you relax? You look awful.

OZZIE. Nooo, I can't relax, goddamnit!

Off he goes, pacing again.

HARRIET. You look all flushed and sweating; please.

OZZIE. It just makes me so goddamn mad the more I think about it. It really does. GODDAMNIT! GODDAMNIT!

HARRIET. Oh, you poor thing.

OZZIE. Because it was calculated; it was calculated, Harriet, because that egg had been boiled to just the right point so it was hard enough to hurt but not so hard it wouldn't splatter. The filthy sonsabitches, but I'm gonna find 'em, I swear that to God, I'm gonna find 'em. I'm gonna kill 'em. I'm gonna cut out their hearts!

Rick appears at the top of the stairs.

RICK. Hey! What's all the racket? What's—

OZZIE. Ricky, come down here! . . . Goddamn 'em. . . .

HARRIET. Ricky, somebody hit your father with an egg!

RICK. Hit him? (*Descending hurriedly, worried*) Hit Dad?

OZZIE. They just threw it! Where's Dave? Dave here?
(*He is suddenly looking around, moving for the stairs.*)
I wanna tell Dave. DAVE!

HARRIET. Ozzie, give me your jacket!

She follows him part way up the stairs, tugging at the jacket.

OZZIE. I wanna tell Dave!

He and Harriet struggle to get the jacket off.

HARRIET. I'll take the spot off.

OZZIE. I gotta tell ole Dave!
(*And the jacket is in her arms. He races on up the stairs.*)
DAVE? DAVE! HEY, DAVE?

But David is not in his room. While Harriet descends and goes to a wall counter with drawers, Ozzie hurries off down the hallway. From a drawer Harriet takes a spray container and begins to clean the jacket.

RICK, *wandering near to her.* Boy, that's something, huh. What you got there, Mom?

HARRIET (*as Rick watches*). Meyer Spot Remover, do you know it? It gives just a sprinkling . . . like snow, which brushed away, leaves the fabric clean and fresh like spring.

Ozzie and David rush out from the hallway and down the stairs. Rick moves toward them to take a picture.

OZZIE. But it happened—and then there's this car tearin' off up the street. "Christ Jesus," I said, "I just been hit with an egg. Jesus Christ, that's impossible." And the way I felt—the way I feel—Harriet, let's have some beer; let's have some good beer for the boys and me.
(*With a sigh, she moves to obey. As Ozzie continues, she brings beer, she brings peanuts. Ozzie now is pleased with his high energy, with his being the center of attention.*)
It took me back to when I was a kid. Ole Fat Kramer. He lived on my street and we used to fight every day. For fun. Monday he'd win, and Tuesday, I'd beat him silly, my knees on his shoulders, blam, blam, blam. Later on, he grew up, became a merchant marine, sailed all over the world, and then he used to race sailboats up and down both coasts—he had one he lived on—anything that floated, he wanted to sail. And he wasn't fat either. We just called him that . . . and boy, oh boy, if he was around now—ohhhh, would we go get those punks threw that egg at me. We'd run 'em into the ground. We'd kill 'em like dogs . . . poor little stupid ugly dogs, we'd cut out their hearts.

RICK, *suddenly coughing and coughing—having gulped down beer—and getting to his feet.* Excuse me, Dad; excuse me. Listen, I've got to get going. You don't mind, do you? Got places to go; you're just talking nonsense anyway. (*He moves for the front door.*)

HARRIET. Have a good time, Rick.

RICK. I'm too pretty not to, Mom! (*And he is gone.*)

OZZIE. Where is . . . he . . . going? Where does he always go? Why does he always go and have some place to go? Always! . . .

HARRIET. Just you never mind, Ozzie. He's young and you're not. I'm going to do the dishes, but you just go right ahead with your little story and I'll listen from the kitchen.

Gathering the beer and glasses, she goes.

OZZIE, *following a little after her, not knowing quite what to do.* I . . . outran a bowling ball. . . . They bet I couldn't.

(*And he starts as if at a sound. He turns toward David.*)

What are you . . . looking . . . at? What do you think you're seeing?

DAVID. I'm not looking.

OZZIE. I feel watched; looked at.

DAVID. No.

OZZIE. Observed.

DAVID. I'm blind.

OZZIE. Did you do it? Had you anything to do with it?

DAVID. What?

OZZIE. That egg.

DAVID. I can't see.

OZZIE. I think you did. I feel like you did it.

DAVID. I don't have a car. I can't drive. How could I?

HARRIET, *hurrying in to clean up more of the party leftovers.* Ohh, it's so good to hear men's voices in the house again, my two favorite men in all the world—it's what I live for really. Would you like some coffee? Oh, of course you would. Let me put some on. Your humble servant at your command; I do your bidding, bid me be gone.

And she is gone without a pause, leaving Ozzie staring after her.

OZZIE. I could run again if I wanted. I'd . . . like . . . to want to. Christ, Fat Kramer is probably dead . . . now . . . not bouncing about in the ocean in some rattletrap, tin-can joke of a ship . . . but dust . . . locked in a box . . . held in old . . . cold hands. . . . And I just stand here, don't I? and let you talk any way you want. And Ricky gets up in the middle of some sentence I'm saying and walks right out and I let him. Because I fear him as I fear her . . . and you. Because I know the time is close when I will be of no use to any of you any longer . . . and I am so frightened that if I do not seem inoffensive . . . and pleasant . . . if I am not careful to never disturb any of you unnecessarily, you will all abandon me. I can no longer compel recognition. I can no longer impose myself, make myself seen.

HARRIET, *entering now happily with a tray of coffee.* Here you go. One for each and tea for me. Cream for David . . . (*Setting a cup for David, moving toward Ozzie*) and cream and sugar for—

OZZIE. Christ how you must have beguiled me!

HARRIET. Pardon?

OZZIE. Beguiled and deceived!

HARRIET. Pardon . . . Ozzie? . . .

OZZIE. And I don't even remember. I say "must" because I don't remember, I was so innocent, so childish in my strength, never seeing that it was surrendering I was doing, innocently and easily giving to you the love that was to return in time as flesh to imprison, detain, disarm and begin . . . to kill.

HARRIET, *examining him, scolding him.* Ozzie, how many beers have you had? You've had too many beers!

OZZIE. Get away!

(*He whirls to point at David who sits on the floor facing upstage.*)

Shut up! You've said enough! Detain and kill! Take and give nothing. It's what you meant, isn't it. You said it, a warning, nearly exactly this. This is your meaning!

DAVID. You're doing so well, Dad.

OZZIE, *not understanding.* What?

DAVID. You're doing so well.

OZZIE. No.

DAVID. You are.

OZZIE. Nooo, I'm doing awful. I'm doing terrible.

DAVID. This is the way you start, Dad. We'll be runners. Dad and Dave!

OZZIE. What's he saying?

HARRIET. My God, you're shaking; you're shaking.

OZZIE. I don't know what he's talking about. What's he talking about? (*To Harriet*) Just let me alone. Just please let me be. I don't really mean these things I'm saying. They're not really important. They'll go away and I don't mean them; they're just coming out of me; I'm just saying them, but I don't mean them. Oh, please, please, go away.

And David, behind them, pivots to go up the stairs. She whirls, drawn by his sudden movement.

HARRIET, *dismayed.* David? . . .

DAVID. I'm going upstairs.

HARRIET. Oh, yes. Of course, of course.

DAVID. Just for a while.

HARRIET. Fine. Good. Of course.

DAVID. I'll see you all later.

And he quietly enters his room, lies down.

OZZIE. (*Coiled on the couch, constricted with pain.*) I remember . . . there was a day . . . when I wanted to leave you, all of you, and I wanted desperately to leave, and I thought, "No. No," I couldn't. "Think of the children," I said. I meant something by that. I meant something and I understood it. But now . . . I don't. I no longer have it—that understanding. It's left me. What did I mean?

HARRIET, *approaching, a little fearful.* You're trembling again. Look at you.

OZZIE. For a while . . . just a while, stay away. That's all I ask.

HARRIET, *reaching to touch him.* What?

OZZIE. Stay the hell away from me!

HARRIET. Stay away? How far away? Ozzie, how far away? I'll move over . . . (*And she scurries, frightened.*) . . . here. Is this far enough away? Ozzie . . .

OZZIE. It's my hands, my feet. There's tiredness in me. I wake up each morning, it's in my fingers . . . sleep. . . .

HARRIET. Ohhh, it's such a hateful thing in you the way you have no love for people different than yourself . . . even when your son has come home to tell you of them. You have no right to carry on this way. He didn't bring her back—didn't marry her—we have those two things to thank God for. You've got to stop thinking only of yourself. We don't matter, only the children. When are you going to straighten out your thinking? Promise. You've got to straighten out your thinking.

OZZIE. I do. I know.

HARRIET. We don't matter; we're nothing. You're nothing, Ozzie. Only the children.

OZZIE. I know. I promise.

HARRIET, *moving toward the stairs.* All right . . . just . . . rest . . . for a little; I'll be back. . . .

OZZIE. I promise, Harriet.

HARRIET, *more to herself than to him.* I'll go see how he is.

OZZIE, *coiled on the couch.* It's my hands; they hurt . . . I want to wrap them; my feet . . .

HARRIET. I'll tell him for you. I'll explain—how you didn't mean those terrible things you said. I'll explain.

OZZIE. It's going to be so cold; and I hurt . . . already. . . . So cold; my ankles! . . .

HARRIET, *hesitating on the stairway.* Oh, Ozzie, Ozzie, we're all so worried, but I just think we must hope for the fine bright day coming when we'll be a family again, as long as we try for what is good, truly for one another, please.

And she goes upstairs. The front door pops open.

RICK. Hi, Mom. Hi, Dad.

OZZIE. Hi, Rick. Your mom's upstairs. You have a nice time? I bet you did.

RICK. Fine; sure. How about you?

OZZIE. Fine; sure.

RICK. Whata you doin', restin'?

OZZIE. Workin'. Measurin'. Not everybody can play the guitar, *you know.* I'm going to build a wall . . . I think—a wall. Pretty soon . . . or . . . six walls. Thinkin' through the blueprints, lookin' over the plans.

RICK, *moving for the kitchen.* I'm gonna get some fudge, Dad; you want some?

OZZIE. No. Too busy.

RICK. I had the greatest piece a tail tonight, Dad; I really did. What a beautiful piece of ass.

OZZIE. Did you, Rick?

RICK. She was beee-uuuuu-ti-ful.

OZZIE. Who was it?

RICK. Nobody you'd know, Dad.

OZZIE. Oh. Where'd you do it—I mean, get it.

RICK. In her car.

OZZIE. You were careful, I hope.

RICK, *laughing a little.* C'mon, Dad.

OZZIE. I mean, it wasn't any decent girl.

RICK. Hell, no. . . .

He is still laughing, as Ozzie gets to his feet.

OZZIE, *starting for the door.* Had a dream of the guitar last night, Rick. It was huge as a building—all flecked with ice. You swung it in the air and I exploded.

RICK. I did?

OZZIE. Yes. I was gone.

RICK. Fantastic.

OZZIE, *exaggeratedly happy, almost singing.* Good night.

Ozzie is gone out the door. Blackout. Music.

Late night. Harriet comes down the hall toward David's room. She is wearing a bathrobe and carries a towel, soap, a basin of water. Giving just the lightest tap on the door, she enters, smiling.

HARRIET. A little bath . . . David? A little sponge bath, all right? You must be all hot and sticky always in that bed. And we can talk. Why don't you take your shirt off? We've an awful lot to talk about. Take your shirt off, David. Your poor father . . . he has no patience, no strength. Something has to be done. . . . A little sponge bath would be so nice. Have you talked to him lately? I think he thinks you're angry, for instance, with . . . us . . . for some reason . . . I don't know. (*Tugging at his shirt a little*) Take your shirt off, David. You'll feel cool. That's all we've ever wanted, your father and me—good sweet things for you and Rick—ease and lovely children, a car, a wife, a good job. Time to relax and go to church on Sundays . . . and on holidays all the children and grandchildren come together, mingling. It would be so wonderful—everyone so happy—turkey. Twinkling lights! (*She is puzzled, a little worried.*) David, are you going to take your shirt off for me?

DAVID. They hit their children, did you know that? They hit them with sticks.

HARRIET. What?

DAVID. The yellow people. They punish the disobedience of their children with sticks. And then they sleep together, one family in a bed, limbs all entwined like puppies. They work. I've seen them . . . laugh. They go on picnics. They murder —out of petty jealousy. Young girls wet their cunts with spit when they are dry from wear and yet another GI stands in line. They spit on their hands and rub themselves, smiling, opening their arms.

HARRIET. That's not true.

DAVID. I saw—

HARRIET, *smilingly scolding him.* None of what you say. No. No. All you did was something normal and regular, can't you see? And hundreds of boys have done it before you. Thousands and thousands. Even now. Now. Now. Why do you have to be so sick and morbid about something so ordinary?

DAVID. She wasn't always a whore. Not always. Not—

HARRIET. If she is now, she was then, only you didn't know. You didn't know. (*She is reaching for him. He eludes her, stands above her, as she is left sitting on the bed, looking up.*)

Oh, David, David, I'm sure she was a lovely little girl, but I would be insane if I didn't want you to marry someone of your own with whom you could be happy, if I didn't want grandchildren who could be free and welcome in their world. I couldn't want anything else and still think I loved you. David, think of their faces, their poor funny little faces. . . .

And the cane is moving, slowly moving along the floor; it grazes her ankle.

DAVID. I know . . . I know. . . .

The cane moves now along her inner calf, rising under the hem of her robe, lifting. She tries to ignore it.

HARRIET. The human face was not meant to be that way. A nose is a thinness—you know that. And lips that are not thin are ugly, and it is we who disappear, David. They don't change, and we are gone. It is our triumph, our whiteness. We disappear. What are you doing?

(*The cane has driven her back along the bed; no longer can it be ignored. It has pressed against her.*)

They take us back and down if our children are theirs—it is not a mingling of blood, it is theft.

(*And she hits the cane away. In revulsion she stands, wanting only to flee.*)

Oh, you don't mean these awful things you do. Your room stinks—odors come from under the door. You don't clean yourself. David, David, you've lost someone you love and it's pain for you, don't you see? I know, I know. But we will be the same, lost from you—you from us—and what will that gain for anyone? What?

Now the cane begins to scrape along the floor. It begins to lift toward her, and, shuddering, she flees down the hall. David opens the door, listens. Stepping into the hall, he carefully shuts the door before moving down the stairs. In the living room, he moves to plant himself before the front door. Harriet, wearing a raincoat over her robe and a scarf on her head, comes down the stairs, when she turns toward the door and she sees David, she stops, nods hello, and stands as he begins to advance upon her.

DAVID. Do you remember? It was a Sunday when we had all gone to church and there was a young man there with his yellow wife and child. You spoke to us . . . Dad and Rick and me, as if we were conspirators. "I feel so sorry for that poor man—the baby looks like *her,*" you said, and your mouth twisted as if you had been forced to swallow someone else's spit.

HARRIET. No, no. You want only to hurt us, don't you? Isn't that right? That's all you want. Only to give us unhappiness. You cheat her, David. That lovely, lovely little girl you spoke of. She merits more to be done in her memory than cruelty.

She has seated herself on the couch, clinging to some kind of normalcy, an odd and eerie calmness on both of them now.

DAVID. And I felt that I must go to her if I was to ever live, and I felt that to touch truly her secret stranger's tongue and mind would kill me. Now she will not forgive the way I was.

HARRIET, *standing up.* No. No, no. No, you don't know how badly I feel. I've got a fever, the start of a cold or flu. Let me be. I can't hardly . . . (*And she is moving away from him, back toward the stairs*) move . . . or stand up. I just want to flop somewhere and not have to move. I'm so weak . . . don't hurt me anymore. Don't hurt me—no more—I've got fever; please, fever; don't hurt me. (*She is on the stairs.*)

DAVID. But I have so much to show you.

HARRIET—*stops to stare helplessly down at him.* Who are you? I don't know who you are.

DAVID. David.

HARRIET. Noooooo.

DAVID. But I am.

HARRIET. No, no. Oh, no.

Moving now as in a trance, she walks up the stairs and down the hallway, all slowly, while Zung comes forward in David's room, and David, in the living room, calls after his mother.

DAVID. But it's what you want, don't you see? You can see it. Her wrists are bound in coils of flowers. Flowers are strung in her hair. She hangs from the wind and men strike and kick her. They are blind so that they may not see her, yet they howl, wanting not to hurt her but only as I do, to touch and hold her . . . and they howl. I'm home. Little David. . . . Home.

(*And he is turning now to take possession of the house. As he speaks, he moves to take the space. A conquerer, he parades in the streets he has taken; among the chairs, around the lamp.*)

Little Davey . . . of all the toys and tops and sailor suits, the plastic cars and Tinkertoys. Drum-player, bed-wetter, home-run-hitter, I'm home . . . now . . . and I want to drink from the toilet, wash there.

(*As he climbs the stairs, he passes by Zung, who stands in his room looking out at him. He walks on down the hall in the direction Harriet fled.*)

And you will join me. You . . . will . . . join me!

When he was gone, Zung sits to gaze down upon the living room, as the front door opens. Ozzie, dressed in a suit or perhaps even a tuxedo, enters from the outside. Under his arm he carries a packet of several hundred sheets of paper. He moves now with an absolute confidence, almost smugness, as he carefully sets down the papers and proceeds to arrange three items of furniture—perhaps two chairs and a footstool—in such a way that they face him. He is cocky. Now he addresses them.

OZZIE, *to the large chair.* Harriet. . . . (*Nodding to the second chair*) David. . . . (*Patting the footstool*) Ricky.

(*He looks them over, the three empty chairs, and then speaks in the manner of a chairman of the board addressing the members of his board, explaining his position and plan of action for total solution. This is a kind of commercial on the value of Ozzie.*)

I'm glad we've gotten finally together here, because the thing I've decided to do —and you all, hopefully, will understand my reasoning—is to *combat* the weariness beginning in me. It's like stepping into a hole, the way I feel each morning when I awaken, I see the day and the sun and I'm looking upward into the sky with a sense of looking down. A sense of hovering over a great pit into which I am about to fall. The sky. Foolishness and deceit, you say, and I know you're right—a trick of feeling inside me being played against me, seeking to diminish me and increase itself until it is larger than me filling me and who will I be then? It. That feeling of being nothing. At first . . . at first . . . I thought the thing to do would be to learn the guitar. . . . But *that* I realized in just the nick of time was a folly that would have taken me into the very agony of frustration I was seeking to avoid. The skill to play like Ricky does is a great gift and only Ricky has it. He has no acids rotting his heart. He is all lies and music, his brain small and scaly, the brain of a snake forever innocent of the fact that it crawls. Lucky Ricky. But there are other things that people can do. And I've come at last to see the one that I must try if I am to become strong again in my opinion of myself. (*Holding up, with great confidence, one of the many packets of paper*) What I have here is an inventory of everything I own. Everything. Every stick of furniture, pot and pan, every sock, T-shirt, pen or pencil. And opposite is its price. For instance—here—that davenport—five hundred an' twelve dollars an' ninety-eight cents. That chair—a hundred twenty ninety-nine. That table . . . (*He hurries to the table.*) . . . this table—thirty-two twenty-nine. Et cetera. Et cetera. Now the idea is that you each carry a number of these at all times.

(*He is distributing more papers to the chairs, his control, however, diminishing, so that the papers are thrown about.*)

Two or three copies at all times, and you are to pass them out at the slightest provocation. Let people know who I am, what I've done. Someone says to you, "Who are you?" You say, "I'm Ozzie's son." "I'm Ozzie's wife." "Who?" they'll say. "Take a look at that!" you tell 'em. Spit it out, give 'em a copy, turn on your heel and walk right out. That's the way I want it; from all of you from here on out, that's the WAY I WANT IT!

(*And the room goes suddenly into eerie light. Zung, high behind him in David's room, is hit with a sudden light that makes Ozzie go rigid, as if some current from her has entered into him, and he turns slowly to look up at her.*)

Let him alone. Let David alone.

Harriet is in the hallway.

HARRIET. Is there any aspirin down there? I don't feel well . . . Ozzie. I don't feel well at all. David poked me with his cane and I don't like . . . what's . . . going on.

(*Ozzie is only staring at Zung.*)

I don't want what's happening to happen.

(*She has halted on the stairway.*)

It must be some awful flu, I'm so weak, or some awful cold. There's an odor . . .

OZZIE. I'll go to the drugstore. My eyes hurt; funny . . .

HARRIET. Oh, Ozzie . . . oh my God. It was awful. I can't help it. He's crazy—he—

OZZIE. I don't want to hear about him. I don't want to hear. Oh, no, oh, no. I can't. No more, no more. Let him do what he wants. No more of him, no more. Just you—you're all that I can see. All that I care for or want.

He has moved to her as she moved down, and they embrace.

HARRIET. David's crazy! . . .

OZZIE. You're everything.

HARRIET. Please . . .

OZZIE. Listen; we must hide; please.

HARRIET, *moving to kneel and he, while helping her, kneels also.* Pray with me.

OZZIE. We won't move. We'll hide by not moving.

HARRIET. We must beg God to not turn against him; convince him. Ozzie, pray. . . .

OZZIE. Yes! . . .

HARRIET. Now! . . .

They pray: kneeling, murmuring, and it goes on and on. The front door opens.

RICK. Hi, Mom. Hi, Dad.

(*They continue. He stops.*)

Hi . . . Mom. Hi, Dad. . . . (*very puzzled*) Hi . . . Mom. . . . Hi . . . Dad. . . .

(*He thinks and thinks.*)

DAVID!

(*He screams at David. He goes running up to look in David's room, but the room is empty. David, in ragged combat fatigues, appears on the top of the stairs. Rick, frightened, backs away.*)

Dave . . . what have you got to say for yourself? What can you? Honest ta God, I've had it. I really have. I can't help it, even if you are sick, and I hate to complain, but you're getting them so mixed up they're not themselves anymore. Just a minute ago—one minute—they were on their knees, do you know that? Just a minute ago—right here on the living-room floor. Now what's the point of that? They're my mom and dad, too.

DAVID. He doesn't know, does he, Dad? Did you hear him?

RICK (*as Ozzie and Harriet are getting from their knees and struggling to sit on the couch*). Let Dad alone.

DAVID, *on the landing, looking down on them.* He doesn't know how when you finally see yourself, there's nothing really there to see . . . isn't that right? Mom?

RICK. Dave, honest to God, I'm warning you, let them alone.

David descends with Zung behind him. Calmly he speaks, growing slowly happy.

DAVID. Do you know how north of here, on farms, gentle loving dogs are raised, while in the forests, other dogs run wild? And upon occasion, one of those that's wild is captured and put in among the others that are tame, bringing with it the memory of when they had all been wild—the dark and terror—that had made them wolves. Don't you hear them?

And there is a rumbling.

RICK. What? Hear what?

It is windlike, the rumbling of many trucks.

DAVID. Don't you hear the trucks? They're all over town, lined up from the center of town into the country. Don't you hear? They've stopped bringing back the blind. They're bringing back the dead now. The convoy's broken up. There's no control . . . they're walking from house to house, through the shrubbery, under the trees, carrying one of the dead in a bright blue rubber bag for which they have no papers, no name or number. No one knows whose it is. They're at the Jensens' now. Now Al Jensen's at the door, all his kids behind him trying to peek. Al looks for a long, long time into the open bag before he shakes his head. They zipper shut the bag and turn away. They've been to the Mayers', the Kellys', the Irwins' and Kresses'. They'll be here soon.

OZZIE. Nooo.

DAVID. And Dad's going to let them in. We're going to let them in

HARRIET. What's he saying?

DAVID. He's going to knock.

OZZIE. I DON'T KNOW.

DAVID. Yes. Yes.

A knocking sound. Is it David knocking with his fist against the door or table?

OZZIE. Nooooo.

RICK. Mom, he's driving Dad crazy.

Knocking loud: it seems to be at the front door.

OZZIE. David, will I die?

He moves toward the door.

HARRIET. Who do you suppose it could be so late?

RICK, *intercepting Ozzie, blocking the way to the door.* I don't think you should just go opening the door to anybody this time of the night, there's no telling who it might be.

DAVID. We know who it is.

OZZIE. Oh, David, why can't you wait? Why can't you rest?

But David is the father now, and he will explain. He loves them all.

DAVID. Look at her. See her, Dad. Tell her to go to the door. Tell her yes, it's your house, you want her to open the door and let them in. Tell her yes, the one with no name is ours. We'll put it in that chair. We can bring them all here. I want them all here, all the trucks and bodies. There's room. (*Handing Rick the guitar*) Ricky can sing. We'll stack them along the walls . . .

OZZIE. Nooo . . .

DAVID. Pile them over the floor . . .

OZZIE. No, no . . .

DAVID. They will become the floor and they will become the walls, the chairs. We'll sit in them; sleep. We will call them "home." We will give them as gifts—call them "ring" and "pot" and "cup." No, no; it's not a thing to fear. . . . We will notice them no more than all the others.

He is gentle, happy, consoling to them.

OZZIE. What others? There are no others.

(*And he scurries to the TV where it sits beneath the stairs.*)

I'll get it fixed. I'll fix it. Who needs to hear it? We'll watch it. (*Wildly turning TV channels.*) I flick my rotten life. Oh, there's a good one. Look at that one. Ohhh, isn't that a good one? That's the best one. That's the best one.

DAVID. They will call it madness. We will call it seeing.

Calmly he lifts Ozzie.

OZZIE. I don't want to disappear.

DAVID. Let her take you to the door. We will be runners. You will have eyes.

OZZIE. I will be blind. I will disappear.

Knocking is heard again. Again.

DAVID. You stand and she stands. "Let her go," you say; "she is garbage and filth and you must get her back if you wish to live. She is sickness, I must cherish her." Old voices you have trusted all your life as if they were your own, speaking always friendly. "She's all of everything impossible made possible!"

OZZIE. Ricky . . . nooo! . . .

DAVID. Don't call to Ricky. You love her. You will embrace her, see her and—

OZZIE. He has no right to do this to me.

DAVID. Don't call to Ricky!

OZZIE, *suddenly raging, rushing at David, pushing him.* You have no right to do this.

RICK. Noooooo!

(*Savagely he smashes his guitar down upon David, who crumples.*)

Let Dad alone. Let him alone. He's sick of you. What the hell's the matter with you? He doesn't wanna talk anymore about all the stupid stuff you talk. He wants to talk about cake and cookies and cars and coffee. He's sick a you and he wants you to shut up. We hate you, goddamn you.

Silence: David lies still.

ZUNG. Chào ông!

(*Ozzie pivots, looks at her.*)

Chào ông! Hôm nay ông manh không?

OZZIE. Oh, what is it that you want? I'm tired. I mean it. Forgive me. I'm sick of the sight of you, squatting all the time. In filth like animals, talking gibberish, your breath sick with rot. . . . And yet you look at me with those sad pleading eyes as if there is some real thing that can come between us when you're not even here. You are deceit.

(*His hands, rising, have driven to her throat. The fingers close.*)

I'm not David. I'm not silly and soft . . . little David. The sight of you sickens me. YOU HEAR ME, DAVID? Believe me. I am speaking my honest true feelings. I spit on you, the both of you; I piss on you and your eyes and pain. Flesh is lies. You are garbage and filth. You are darkness. I cast you down. Deceit. Animal. Dirty animal.

And he is over her. They are sprawled on the ground. Silence as no one moves. She lies like a rag beneath him.

RICK. I saw this really funny movie last night. This really . . . funny, funny movie about this young couple and they were going to get a divorce but they didn't. It was really funny.

Ozzie is hiding the girl. In a proscenium production, he can drag her behind the couch; in three-quarter, he puts her in a green garbage bag brought to him by Harriet.

HARRIET. What's that? What's that?

RICK. This movie I saw.

HARRIET. Anybody want to go for groceries? We need Kleenex, sugar, milk.

RICK. What a really funny movie.

OZZIE. I'll go; I'll go.

HARRIET. Good. Good.

OZZIE. I think I saw it on TV.

They are cleaning up the house now, putting the chairs back in order, dumping all of Ozzie's leaflets in the waste can.

HARRIET. Did you enjoy it, Rick?

RICK. Oh, yeh. I loved it.

OZZIE. I laughed so much I almost got sick. It was really good. I laughed.

RICK. I bet it was; I bet you did.

OZZIE. Oh, I did.

Even David helps with the cleaning: he gets himself off the floor and seated in a chair.

HARRIET. How are you feeling, Ricky?

RICK. Fine.

HARRIET. Good.

RICK. How do you feel?

HARRIET. Oh, I'm all right. I feel fine.

OZZIE. Me, too. I feel fine, too. What day is it anyway? Monday?

HARRIET. Wednesday.

RICK. Tuesday, Mom.

Now all three are seated on the couch.

OZZIE. I thought it was Monday.

RICK. Oh, no.

HARRIET. No, no. You're home now, David. . . .

RICK, *moving to David, who sits alone in a chair.* Hey, Dave, listen, will you. I mean I know it's not my place to speak out and give advice and everything because I'm the youngest, but I just gotta say my honest true feelings and I'd kill myself if I were you, Dave. You're in too much misery. I'd cut my wrists. Honestly speaking, brother to brother, you should have done it long ago.

(*David is looking about.*)

You looking for her, Dave? You looking for her? She's not here.

DAVID. What?

RICK. Nooo. She's never been here. You just thought so. You decided not to bring her, Dave, remember? You decided, all things considered that you preferred to come back without her. Too much risk and inconvenience . . . you decided. Isn't that right? Sure. You know it is. You've always known.

(*Silence. Harriet moves to look out the front door.*)

Do you want to use my razor, Dave? (*Pulling a straight razor from his pocket*) I have one right here and you can use it if you want.

(*David seems to be looking at the razor.*)

Just take it if you want it, Dave.

HARRIET. Go ahead, David. The front yard's empty. You don't have to be afraid. The streets, too . . . still and empty.

RICK. It doesn't hurt like you think it will. Go ahead; just take it, Dave.

OZZIE. You might as well.

RICK. That's right.

OZZIE. You'll feel better.

RICK. I'll help you now, Dave, okay?

HARRIET. I'll go get some pans and towels.

RICK, *moving about David, patting him, buddying him.* Oh, you're so confused, you don't know what to do. It's just a good thing I got this razor, Boy, that's all I gotta say. You're so confused. You see, Dave, where you're wrong is your point of view, it's silly. It's just really comical because you think people are valuable or something and, given a chance like you were to mess with 'em, to take a young girl like that and turn her into a whore, you shouldn't, when of course you should or at least might . . . on whim . . . you see? I mean, you're all backwards, Dave—you're upside down. You don't know how to go easy and play—I bet you didn't have any fun the whole time you were over there—no fun at all—and it was there. I got this buddy Gerry, he was there, and he used to throw bags of cement at 'em from off the back a his truck. They'd go whizzin' through those villages, throwin' off these bags a cement. You could kill people, he says, you hit 'em right. Especially the kids. There was this once they knocked this ole man off his bicycle—fifty pounds a dry cement—and then the back a the truck got his legs. It was hysterical—can't you just see that, Dave? Him layin' there howlin', all the guys in the truck bowin' and wavin' and tippin' their hats. What a goddamn funny story, huh?

Harriet has brought silver pans and towels with roosters on them. The towels cover the arms of the chair and David's lap. The pans will catch the blood. All has been neatly placed. David, with Ricky's help, cuts one wrist, then the other, as they talk.

DAVID. I wanted . . . to kill you . . . all of you.

RICK. I know, I know; but you're hurt; too weak.

DAVID. I wanted for you to need what I had and I wouldn't give it.

HARRIET. That's not possible.

OZZIE. Nooooo.

DAVID. I wanted to get you. Like poor bug-eyed fish flung up from the brief water to the lasting dirt, I would gut you.

HARRIET. David, no, no, you didn't want that.

OZZIE. No, no.

RICK. I don't even know why you'd think you did.

OZZIE. We kill you is what happens.

RICK. That's right.

OZZIE. And then, of course, we die, too. . . . Later on, I mean. And nothing stops it. Not words . . . or walls . . . or even guitars.

RICK. Sure.

OZZIE. That's what happens.

HARRIET. It isn't too bad, is it?

RICK. How bad is it?

OZZIE. He's getting weaker.

HARRIET. And in a little, it'll all be over. You'll feel so grand. No more funny talk.

RICK. You can shower; put on clean clothes. I've got deodorant you can borrow. After Roses, Dave. The scent of a thousand roses.

He is preparing to take a picture—crouching, aiming.

HARRIET. Take off your glasses, David.

OZZIE. Do as you're told.

RICK (*as David's hands are rising toward the glasses to remove them*). I bet when you were away there was only plain water to wash in, huh? You prob'ly hadda wash in the rain.

(*He takes the picture; there is a flash. A slide appears on the screen: a close-up of David, nothing visible but his face. It is the slide that, appearing at the start of the play, was referred to as "somebody sick." Now it hovers, stricken, sightless, revealed.*)

Mom, I like David like this.

HARRIET. He's happier.

OZZIE. We're all happier.

RICK. Too bad he's gonna die.

OZZIE. No, no, he's not gonna die, Rick. He's only gonna nearly die. Only nearly.

RICK. Ohhhhhhhhhhh.

HARRIET. Mmmmmmmmmmmm

And Rick, sitting, begins to play his guitar for David. The music is alive and fast. It has a rhythm, a drive of happiness that is contagious. The lights slowly fade.

1971

SAM SHEPARD
(1943–)

Sam Shepard was born Samuel Shepard Rogers, Jr., in 1943 at Fort Sheridan, Illinois, an army base near Chicago. His father was a bomber pilot stationed in Europe. After the war the family moved from army base to army base and Sam Jr. was much alone with his mother. In 1955, Sam Rogers left the army, and the family eventually settled on a ranch in Duarte, California, outside Los Angeles. Sam Jr. helped with the animals on the ranch, attended public high school, and sought excitement in the movies. Exposed to jazz through his father, a drummer in an amateur Dixieland band, he too became a drummer, later playing in a rock music group; that background has remained important to his plays, as he considers music a vital part of theater that "brings the audience to terms with an emotional reality." During his high school years, Shepard read the Beat writers and Samuel Beckett's *Waiting for Godot.* He began writing himself, and after graduation from high school toured with a traveling repertory company, calling himself Sam Shepard, a name change that caused resentment in his family.

Shepard arrived in New York in 1963 to work at the Village Gate, a jazz club, and share an apartment with Charlie Mingus, Jr., a high school friend and son of the famous jazz musician. Soon he was writing for the Off-Off-Broadway theater, an anti-establishment movement presenting plays in church basements, small cafés, storefronts, and lofts on the Lower East Side of Manhattan. His first two plays, *Cowboys* and *The Rock Garden,* premiered at Theatre Genesis on October 10, 1964. Panned in the establishment press, the production was favorably reviewed in the *Village Voice.*

After this start, Shepard continued to have two or three plays a year produced in small New York theaters, won several Obie awards, received Rockefeller and Guggenheim grants and wrote screenplays, including, with Michelangelo Antonioni, the script for *Zabriskie Point* in 1970. In 1971 he and his wife and son moved to London; during their three-year stay several of his plays, including *The Tooth of Crime* (1972), were successfully produced. The Shepard family settled in northern California in 1974. More recently he has left his wife to live with the actress Jessica Lange in New Mexico.

Shepard's greatest success to date has come with three related plays, united by the theme of family discord, written in the late seventies: *Curse of the Starving Class* (1977), *Buried Child* (1978), and *True West* (1980). These plays confirmed his reputation as the most gifted dramatic writer of his generation. His *Fool for Love* (1983) won four Obie awards during its Off-Broadway run. Themes of guilt, love, and violence dominate this play and also *A Lie of the Mind,* produced in 1985. In twenty years, Shepard has written over forty plays and screenplays as well as acting in and directing his own and other writers' work. He has appeared in several films and, in 1984, was nominated for an Oscar for his portrayal of test pilot Chuck Yeager in *The Right Stuff.*

Taken together, Shepard's plays present a picture of America torn between its idealistic values and the painful realities of a frontier paved over for a parking lot and cowboys enclosed in movie and television screens. Like Eugene O'Neill, Tennessee Williams, and Arthur Miller, Shepard stretches the potential of the stage and tries to exert authorial control over all aspects of the production. His stage directions specify music and background sound effects, lighting, acting technique, stage furniture and costume details. Learning his trade by doing it, Shepard has absorbed influences from related popular arts and from travel and observation. His colloquial American speech draws its rhythms in part from popular music. His long monologues and heavy physical action make demands upon an actor that sometimes seem more appropriate to the special-effect techniques, varying camera angles, and multiple takes of the movies.

Shepard's characters struggle to define and assert their identities. The resulting tension, especially between brothers and between fathers and sons, is a major theme. Often the personalities of characters are merged, or they switch places as Austin and Lee do in *True West.* His characters are unpredictable and incoherent; in the notes to *Angel City* (1976) the actors are advised that in place of playing "whole" characters with logical motivation they should "consider instead a fractured whole with bits and pieces of characters flying off the central theme. Collage construction, jazz improvisation. Music or painting in space."

Shepard describes his creative process as beginning with a visualization in which the character begins to speak; in writing he follows the picture with his mind as it moves. "If I find myself pushing the character in a certain direction, it's almost always a sure sign that I've fallen back on technique and lost the real thread of the thing." He predicates an "open-ended structure where anything could happen," and says he began writing plays to "extend the sensation of *play* (as in 'kid') on into adult life." He describes the storing of images from life as "some kind of an inner library" that can be drawn on, sometimes producing "whole scenes from our past

* * * in living technicolor," a process he equates with the method-acting technique of "recall."

Writing in 1977 about his career, Shepard said, "It seems that the more you write, the harder it gets, because you're not so easily fooled by yourself anymore. I can still sit down and whip off a play like I used to, but it doesn't have the same meaning now as it did when I was nineteen. Even so, writing becomes more and more interesting as you go along, and it starts to open up some on its secrets. One thing I'm sure of, though. That I'll never get to the bottom of it." Since then, he has written some of his best work. More is almost certain to follow.

Many of Shepard's plays have been collected in *Five Plays,* 1967; *Action and the Unseen Hand: Two Plays,* 1975; *Buried Child and Other Plays,* 1979; *Four Two-Act Plays,* 1980; *Seven Plays,* 1981 (including *Buried Child, Curse of the Starving Class, The Tooth of Crime,* and *True West*); *Fool for Love and Other Plays,* 1984; and *A Lie of the Mind,* 1986. Stories are collected in *Hawk Moon,* 1972. Shepard's account of the 1975 Bob Dylan tour is *Rolling Thunder Logbook,* 1977.

Critical and biographical studies include Bonnie Marranca, ed., *American Dreams: The Imagination of Sam Shepard,* 1981; Ron Mottram, *Inner Landscapes: The Theater of Sam Shepard,* 1984; and Ellen Oumano, *Sam Shepard: The Life and Work of an American Dreamer,* 1986.

True West

Characters

AUSTIN. *early thirties, light blue sports shirt, light tan cardigan sweater, clean blue jeans, white tennis shoes*

LEE. *his older brother, early forties, filthy white t-shirt, tattered brown overcoat covered with dust, dark blue baggy suit pants from the Salvation Army, pink suede belt, pointed black forties dress shoes scuffed up, holes in the soles, no socks, no hat, long pronounced sideburns, "Gene Vincent" hairdo, two days' growth of beard, bad teeth*

SAUL KIMMER. *late forties, Hollywood producer, pink and white flower print sports shirt, white sports coat with matching polyester slacks, black and white loafers*

MOM. *early sixties, mother of the brothers, small woman, conservative white skirt and matching jacket, red shoulder bag, two pieces of matching red luggage*

SCENE: *All nine scenes take place on the same set; a kitchen and adjoining alcove of an older home in a Southern California suburb, about 40 miles east of Los Angeles. The kitchen takes up most of the playing area to stage left. The kitchen consists of a sink, upstage center, surrounded by counter space, a wall telephone, cupboards, and a small window just above it bordered by neat yellow curtains. Stage left of sink is a stove. Stage right, a refrigerator. The alcove adjoins the kitchen to stage right. There is no wall division or door to the alcove. It is open and easily accessible from the kitchen and defined only by the objects in it: a small round glass breakfast table mounted on white iron legs, two matching white iron chairs set across from each other. The two exterior walls of the alcove which prescribe a corner in the upstage right are composed of many small windows, beginning from a solid wall about three feet high and extending to the ceiling. The windows look out to bushes and citrus trees. The alcove is filled with all sorts of house plants in various pots, mostly Boston ferns hanging in planters at different levels. The floor of the alcove is composed of green synthetic grass.*

All entrances and exits are made stage left from the kitchen. There is no door. The actors simply go off and come onto the playing area.

NOTE ON SET AND COSTUME: *The set should be constructed realistically with no attempt to distort its dimensions, shapes, objects, or colors. No objects should be introduced which might draw special attention to themselves other than the props demanded by the script. If a stylistic "concept" is grafted onto the set design it will only serve to confuse the evolution of the characters' situation, which is the most important focus of the play.*

Likewise, the costumes should be exactly representative of who the characters are and not added onto for the sake of making a point to the audience.

NOTE ON SOUND: *The Coyote of Southern California has a distinct yapping, dog-like bark, similar to a Hyena. This yapping grows more intense and maniacal as the pack grows in numbers, which is usually the case when they lure and kill pets from suburban yards. The sense of growing frenzy in the pack should be felt in the background, particularly in Scenes 7 and 8. In any case, these Coyotes never make the long, mournful, solitary howl of the Hollywood stereotype.*

The sound of Crickets can speak for itself.

These sounds should also be treated realistically even though they sometimes grow in volume and numbers.

Act One

Scene I

Night. Sound of crickets in dark. Candlelight appears in alcove, illuminating AUSTIN, *seated at glass table hunched over a writing notebook, pen in hand, cigarette burning in ashtray, cup of coffee, typewriter on table, stacks of paper, candle burning on table.*

Soft moonlight fills kitchen illuminating LEE, *beer in hand, six-pack on counter behind him. He's leaning against the sink, mildly drunk; takes a slug of beer.*

LEE: So, Mom took off for Alaska, huh?

AUSTIN: Yeah.

LEE: Sorta' left you in charge.

AUSTIN: Well, she knew I was coming down here so she offered me the place.

LEE: You keepin' the plants watered?

AUSTIN: Yeah.

LEE: Keepin' the sink clean? She don't like even a single tea leaf in the sink ya' know.

AUSTIN: (*trying to concentrate on writing*) Yeah, I know.

(*pause*)

LEE: She gonna' be up there a long time?

AUSTIN: I don't know.

LEE: Kinda' nice for you, huh? Whole place to yourself.

AUSTIN: Yeah, it's great.

LEE: Ya' got crickets anyway. Tons a' crickets out there. (*looks around kitchen*) Ya' got groceries? Coffee?

AUSTIN: (*looking up from writing*) What?

LEE: You got coffee?

AUSTIN: Yeah.

LEE: At's good. (*short pause*) Real coffee? From the bean?

AUSTIN: Yeah. You want some?

LEE: Naw. I brought some uh— (*motions to beer*)

AUSTIN: Help yourself to whatever's—(*motions to refrigerator*)

LEE: I will. Don't worry about me. I'm not the one to worry about. I mean I can uh— (*pause*) You always work by candlelight?

AUSTIN: No—uh—Not always.

LEE: Just sometimes?

AUSTIN: (*puts pen down, rubs his eyes*) Yeah. Sometimes it's soothing.

LEE: Isn't that what the old guys did?

AUSTIN: What old guys?

LEE: The Forefathers. You know.

AUSTIN: Forefathers?

LEE: Isn't that what they did? Candlelight burning into the night? Cabins in the wilderness.

AUSTIN: (*rubs hand through his hair*) I suppose.

LEE: I'm not botherin' you am I? I mean I don't wanna break into yer uh—concentration or nothin'.

AUSTIN: No, it's all right.

LEE: That's good. I mean I realize that yer line a' work demands a lota' concentration.

AUSTIN: It's okay.

LEE: You probably think that I'm not fully able to comprehend somethin' like that, huh?

AUSTIN: Like what?

LEE: That stuff yer doin'. That art. You know. Whatever you call it.

AUSTIN: It's just a little research.

LEE: You may not know it but I did a little art myself once.

AUSTIN: You did?

LEE: Yeah! I did some a' that. I fooled around with it. No future in it.

AUSTIN: What'd you do?

LEE: Never mind what I did! Just never mind about that. (*pause*) It was ahead of its time.

(*pause*)

AUSTIN: So, you went out to see the old man, huh?

LEE: Yeah, I seen him.

AUSTIN: How's he doing?

LEE: Same. He's doin' just about the same.

AUSTIN: I was down there too, you know.

LEE: What d'ya' want, an award? You want some kinda' medal? You were down there. He told me all about you.

AUSTIN: What'd he say?

LEE: He told me. Don't worry.

(*pause*)

AUSTIN: Well—

LEE: You don't have to say nothin'.

AUSTIN: I wasn't.

LEE: Yeah, you were gonna' make somethin' up. Somethin' brilliant.

(*pause*)

AUSTIN: You going to be down here very long, Lee?

LEE: Might be. Depends on a few things.

AUSTIN: You got some friends down here?

LEE: (*laughs*) I know a few people. Yeah.

AUSTIN: Well, you can stay here as long as I'm here.

LEE: I don't need your permission do I?

AUSTIN: No.

LEE: I mean she's my mother too, right?

AUSTIN: Right.

LEE: She might've just as easily asked me to take care of her place as you.

AUSTIN: That's right.

LEE: I mean I know how to water plants.

(*long pause*)

AUSTIN: So you don't know how long you'll be staying then?

LEE: Depends mostly on houses, ya' know.

AUSTIN: Houses?

LEE: Yeah. Houses. Electric devices. Stuff like that. I gotta' make a little tour first.

(*short pause*)

AUSTIN: Lee, why don't you just try another neighborhood, all right?

LEE: (*laughs*) What'sa' matter with this neighborhood? This is a great neighborhood. Lush. Good class a' people. Not many dogs.

AUSTIN: Well, our uh— Our mother just happens to live here. That's all.

LEE: Nobody's gonna' know. All they know is somethin's missing. That's all. She'll never even hear about it. Nobody's gonna' know.

AUSTIN: You're going to get picked up if you start walking around here at night.

LEE: Me? I'm gonna' git picked up? What about you? You stick out like a sore thumb. Look at you. You think yer regular lookin'?

AUSTIN: I've got too much to deal with here to be worrying about—

LEE: Yer not gonna' have to worry about me! I've been doin' all right without you. I haven't been anywhere near you for five years! Now isn't that true?

AUSTIN: Yeah.

LEE: So you don't have to worry about me. I'm a free agent.

AUSTIN: All right.

LEE: Now all I wanna' do is borrow yer car.

AUSTIN: No!

LEE: Just fer a day. One day.

AUSTIN: No!

LEE: I won't take it outside a twenty mile radius. I promise ya'. You can check the speedometer.

AUSTIN: You're not borrowing my car! That's all there is to it.

(*pause*)

LEE: Then I'll just take the damn thing.

AUSTIN: Lee, look— I don't want any trouble, all right?

LEE: That's a dumb line. That is a dumb fuckin' line. You git paid fer dreamin' up a line like that?

AUSTIN: Look, I can give you some money if you need money.

(LEE *suddenly lunges at* AUSTIN, *grabs him violently by the shirt and shakes him with tremendous power*)

LEE: Don't you say that to me! Don't you ever say that to me! (*just as suddenly he turns him loose, pushes him away and backs off*) You may be able to git away with that with the Old Man. Git him tanked up for a week! Buy him off with yer Hollywood blood money, but not me! I can git my own money my own way. Big money!

AUSTIN: I was just making an offer.

LEE: Yeah, well keep it to yourself!

(*long pause*)

Those are the most monotonous fuckin' crickets I ever heard in my life.

AUSTIN: I kinda' like the sound.

LEE: Yeah. Supposed to be able to tell the temperature by the number a' pulses. You believe that?

AUSTIN: The temperature?

LEE: Yeah. The air. How hot it is.

AUSTIN: How do you do that?

LEE: I don't know. Some woman told me that. She was a Botanist. So I believed her.

AUSTIN: Where'd you meet her?

LEE: What?

AUSTIN: The woman Botanist?

LEE: I met her on the desert. I been spendin' a lota' time on the desert.

AUSTIN: What were you doing out there?

LEE: (*pause, stares in space*) I forgit. Had me a Pit Bull there for a while but I lost him.

AUSTIN: Pit Bull?

LEE: Fightin' dog. Damn I made some good money off that little dog. Real good money.

(*pause*)

AUSTIN: You could come up north with me, you know.

LEE: What's up there?

AUSTIN: My family.

LEE: Oh, that's right, you got the wife and kiddies now don't ya'. The house, the car, the whole slam. That's right.

AUSTIN: You could spend a couple days. See how you like it. I've got an extra room.

LEE: Too cold up there.

(*pause*)

AUSTIN: You want to sleep for a while?

LEE: (*pause, stares at* AUSTIN) I don't sleep.

(*lights to black*)

Scene 2

Morning. AUSTIN *is watering plants with a vaporizer,* LEE *sits at glass table in alcove drinking beer.*

LEE: I never realized the old lady was so security-minded.

AUSTIN: How do you mean?

LEE: Made a little tour this morning. She's got locks on everything. Locks and double-locks and chain locks and—What's she got that's so valuable?

AUSTIN: Antiques I guess. I don't know.

LEE: Antiques? Brought everything with her from the old place, huh. Just the same crap we always had around. Plates and spoons.

AUSTIN: I guess they have personal value to her.

LEE: Personal value. Yeah. Just a lota' junk. Most of it's phony anyway. Idaho decals. Now who in the hell wants to eat offa' plate with the State of Idaho starin' ya' in the face. Every time ya' take a bite ya' get to see a little bit more.

AUSTIN: Well it must mean something to her or she wouldn't save it.

LEE: Yeah, well personally I don't wann' be invaded by Idaho when I'm eatin'. When I'm eatin' I'm home. Ya' know what I'm sayin'? I'm not driftin', I'm home. I don't need my thoughts swept off to Idaho. I don't need that!

(*pause*)

AUSTIN: Did you go out last night?

LEE: Why?

AUSTIN: I thought I heard you go out.

LEE: Yeah, I went out. What about it?

AUSTIN: Just wondered.

LEE: Damn coyotes kept me awake.

AUSTIN: Oh yeah, I heard them. They must've killed somebody's dog or something.

LEE: Yappin' their fool heads off. They don't yap like that on the desert. They howl. These are city coyotes here.

AUSTIN: Well, you don't sleep anyway do you?

(*pause,* LEE *stares at him*)

LEE: You're pretty smart aren't ya?

AUSTIN: How do you mean?

LEE: I mean you never had any more on the ball than I did. But here you are gettin' invited into prominent people's houses. Sittin' around talkin' like you know somethin'.

AUSTIN: They're not so prominent.

LEE: They're a helluva' lot more prominent than the houses I get invited into.

AUSTIN: Well you invite yourself.

LEE: That's right. I do. In fact I probably got a wider range a' choices than you do, come to think of it.

AUSTIN: I wouldn't doubt it.

LEE: In fact I been inside some pretty classy places in my time. And I never even went to an Ivy League school either.

AUSTIN: You want some breakfast or something?

LEE: Breakfast?

AUSTIN: Yeah. Don't you eat breakfast?

LEE: Look, don't worry about me pal. I can take care a' myself. You just go ahead as though I wasn't even here, all right?

(AUSTIN *goes into kitchen, makes coffee*)

AUSTIN: Where'd you walk to last night?

(*pause*)

LEE: I went up in the foothills there. Up in the San Gabriels. Heat was drivin' me crazy.

AUSTIN: Well, wasn't it hot out on the desert?

LEE: Different kinda' heat. Out there it's clean. Cools off at night. There's a nice little breeze.

AUSTIN: Where were you, the Mojave?

LEE: Yeah. The Mojave. That's right.

AUSTIN: I haven't been out there in years.

LEE: Out past Needles there.

AUSTIN: Oh yeah.

LEE: Up here it's different. This country's real different.

AUSTIN: Well, it's been built up.

LEE: Built up? Wiped out is more like it. I don't even hardly recognize it.

AUSTIN: Yeah. Foothills are the same though, aren't they?

LEE: Pretty much. It's funny goin' up in there. The smells and everything. Used to catch snakes up there, remember?

AUSTIN: You caught snakes.

LEE: Yeah. And you'd pretend you were Geronimo or some damn thing. You used to go right out to lunch.

AUSTIN: I enjoyed my imagination.

LEE: That what you call it? Looks like yer still enjoyin' it.

AUSTIN: So you just wandered around up there, huh?

LEE: Yeah. With a purpose.

AUSTIN: See any houses?

(*pause*)

LEE: Couple. Couple a' real nice ones. One of 'em didn't even have a dog. Walked right up and stuck my head in the window. Not a peep. Just a sweet kinda' surburban silence.

AUSTIN: What kind of a place was it?

LEE: Like a paradise. Kinda' place that sorta' kills ya' inside. Warm yellow lights. Mexican tile all around. Copper pots hangin' over the stove. Ya' know like they got in the magazines. Blonde people movin' in and outa' the rooms, talkin' to each other. (*pause*) Kinda' place you wish you sorta' grew up in, ya' know.

AUSTIN: That's the kind of place you wish you'd grown up in?

LEE: Yeah, why not?

AUSTIN: I thought you hated that kind of stuff.

LEE: Yeah, well you never knew too much about me did ya'?

(*pause*)

AUSTIN: Why'd you go out to the desert in the first place?

LEE: I was on my way to see the old man.

AUSTIN: You mean you just passed through there?

LEE: Yeah. That's right. Three months of passin' through.

AUSTIN: Three months?

LEE: Somethin' like that. Maybe more. Why?

AUSTIN: You lived on the Mojave for three months?

LEE: Yeah. What'sa' matter with that?

AUSTIN: By yourself?

LEE: Mostly. Had a couple a' visitors. Had that dog for a while.

AUSTIN: Didn't you miss people?

LEE: (*laughs*) People?

AUSTIN: Yeah. I mean I go crazy if I have to spend three nights in a motel by myself.

LEE: Yer not in a motel now.

AUSTIN: No, I know. But sometimes I have to stay in motels.

LEE: Well, they got people in motels don't they?

AUSTIN: Strangers.

LEE: Yer friendly aren't ya'? Aren't you the friendly type?

(*pause*)

AUSTIN: I'm going to have somebody coming by here later, Lee.

LEE: Ah! Lady friend?

AUSTIN: No, a producer.

LEE: Aha! What's he produce?

AUSTIN: Film. Movies. You know.

LEE: Oh, movies. Motion Pictures! A Big Wig huh?

AUSTIN: Yeah.

LEE: What's he comin' by here for?

AUSTIN: We have to talk about a project.

LEE: Whadya' mean, "a project"? What's "a project"?

AUSTIN: A script.

LEE: Oh. That's what yer doin' with all these papers?

AUSTIN: Yeah.

LEE: Well, what's the project about?

AUSTIN: We're uh—it's a period piece.

LEE: What's "a period piece"?

AUSTIN: Look, it doesn't matter. The main thing is we need to discuss this alone. I mean—

LEE: Oh, I get it. You want me outa' the picture.

AUSTIN: Not exactly. I just need to be alone with him for a couple of hours. So we can talk.

LEE: Yer afraid I'll embarrass ya' huh?

AUSTIN: I'm not afraid you'll embarrass me!

LEE: Well, I tell ya' what— Why don't you just gimme the keys to yer car and I'll be back here around six o'clock or so. That give ya' enough time?

AUSTIN: I'm not loaning you my car, Lee.

LEE: You want me to just git lost huh? Take a hike? Is that it? Pound the pavement for a few hours while you bullshit yer way into a million bucks.

AUSTIN: Look, it's going to be hard enough for me to face this character on my own without—

LEE: You don't know this guy?

AUSTIN: No I don't know—He's a producer. I mean I've been meeting with him for months but you never get to know a producer.

LEE: Yer tryin' to hustle him? Is that it?

AUSTIN: I'm not trying to hustle him! I'm trying to work out a deal! It's not easy.

LEE: What kinda' deal?

AUSTIN: Convince him it's a worthwhile story.

LEE: He's not convinced? How come he's comin' over here if he's not convinced? I'll convince him for ya'.

AUSTIN: You don't understand the way things work down here.

LEE: How do things work down here?
(*pause*)
AUSTIN: Look, if I loan you my car will you have it back here by six?
LEE: On the button. With a full tank a' gas.
AUSTIN: (*digging in his pocket for keys*) Forget about the gas.
LEE: Hey, these days gas is gold, old buddy.
(AUSTIN *hands the keys to* LEE)
You remember that car I used to loan you?
AUSTIN: Yeah.
LEE: Forty Ford. Flathead.
AUSTIN: Yeah.
LEE: Sucker hauled ass didn't it?
AUSTIN: Lee, it's not that I don't want to loan you my car—
LEE: You are loanin' me yer car.
(LEE *gives* AUSTIN *a pat on the shoulder, pause*)
AUSTIN: I know. I just wish—
LEE: What? You wish what?
AUSTIN: I don't know. I wish I wasn't—I wish I didn't have to be doing business down here. I'd like to just spend some time with you.
LEE: I thought it was "Art" you were doin'.
(LEE *moves across kitchen toward exit, tosses keys in his hand*)
AUSTIN: Try to get it back here by six, okay?
LEE: No sweat. Hey, ya' know, if that uh—story of yours doesn't go over with the guy—tell him I got a couple a' "projects" he might be interested in. Real commercial. Full a' suspense. True-to-life stuff.
(LEE *exits,* AUSTIN *stares after* LEE *then turns, goes to papers at table, leafs through pages, lights fade to black*)

Scene 3

Afternoon. Alcove, SAUL KIMMER and AUSTIN *seated across from each other at table.*

SAUL: Well, to tell you the truth Austin, I have never felt so confident about a project in quite a long time.
AUSTIN: Well, that's good to hear, Saul.
SAUL: I am absolutely convinced we can get this thing off the ground. I mean we'll have to make a sale to television and that means getting a major star. Somebody bankable. But I think we can do it. I really do.
AUSTIN: Don't you think we need a first draft before we approach a star?
SAUL: No, no, not at all. I don't think it's necessary. Maybe a brief synopsis. I don't want you to touch the typewriter until we have some seed money.
AUSTIN: That's fine with me.
SAUL: I mean it's a great story. Just the story alone. You've really managed to capture something this time.
AUSTIN: I'm glad you like it, Saul.
(LEE *enters abruptly into kitchen carrying a stolen television set, short pause*)
LEE: Aw shit, I'm sorry about that. I am really sorry Austin.
AUSTIN: (*standing*) That's all right.

LEE: (*moving toward them*) I mean I thought it was way past six already. You said to have it back here by six.

AUSTIN: We were just finishing up. (*to Saul*) This is my, uh—brother, Lee.

SAUL: (*standing*) Oh, I'm very happy to meet you.

(LEE *sets T.V. on sink counter, shakes hands with* SAUL)

LEE: I can't tell ya' how happy I am to meet you sir.

SAUL: Saul Kimmer.

LEE: Mr. Kipper.

SAUL: Kimmer.

AUSTIN: Lee's been living out on the desert and he just uh—

SAUL: Oh, that's terrific! (*to* LEE) Palm Springs?

LEE: Yeah. Yeah, right. Right around in that area. Near uh—Bob Hope Drive there.

SAUL: Oh I love it out there. I just love it. The air is wonderful.

LEE: Yeah. Sure is. Healthy.

SAUL: And the golf. I don't know if you play golf, but the golf is just about the best.

LEE: I play a lota' golf.

SAUL: Is that right?

LEE: Yeah. In fact I was hoping I'd run into somebody out here who played a little golf. I've been lookin' for a partner.

SAUL: Well, I uh—

AUSTIN: Lee's just down for a visit while our mother's in Alaska.

SAUL: Oh, your mother's in Alaska?

AUSTIN: Yes. She went up there on a little vacation. This is her place.

SAUL: I see. Well isn't that something. Alaska.

LEE: What kinda' handicap do ya' have, Mr. Kimmer?

SAUL: Oh I'm just a Sunday duffer really. You know.

LEE: That's good 'cause I haven't swung a club in months.

SAUL: Well we ought to get together sometime and have a little game. Austin, do you play?

(SAUL *mimes a Johnny Carson golf swing for* AUSTIN)

AUSTIN: No. I don't uh—I've watched it on T.V.

LEE: (*to* SAUL) How 'bout tomorrow morning? Bright and early. We could get out there and put in eighteen holes before breakfast.

SAUL: Well, I've got uh—I have several appointments—

LEE: No, I mean real early. Crack a'dawn. While the dew's still thick on the fairway.

SAUL: Sounds really great.

LEE: Austin could be our caddie.

SAUL: Now that's an idea. (*laughs*)

AUSTIN: I don't know the first thing about golf.

LEE: There's nothin' to it. Isn't that right, Saul? He'd pick it up in fifteen minutes.

SAUL: Sure. Doesn't take long. 'Course you have to play for years to find your true form. (*chuckles*)

LEE: (*to* AUSTIN) We'll give ya' a quick run-down on the club faces. The irons, the woods. Show ya' a couple pointers on the basis swing. Might even let ya' hit the ball a couple times. Whadya' think, Saul?

SAUL: Why not. I think it'd be great. I haven't had any exercise in weeks.

LEE: 'At's the spirit! We'll have a little orange juice right afterwards.

(*pause*)

SAUL: Orange juice?

LEE: Yeah! Vitamin C! Nothin' like a shot a' orange juice after a round a' golf. Hot shower. Snappin' towels at each others' privates. Real sense a' fraternity.

SAUL: (*smiles at* AUSTIN) Well, you make it sound very inviting, I must say. It really does sound great.

LEE: Then it's a date.

SAUL: Well, I'll call the country club and see if I can arrange something.

LEE: Great! Boy, I sure am sorry that I busted in on ya' all in the middle of yer meeting.

SAUL: Oh that's quite all right. We were just about finished anyway.

LEE: I can wait out in the other room if you want.

SAUL: No really—

LEE: Just got Austin's color T.V. back from the shop. I can watch a little amateur boxing now.

(LEE *and* AUSTIN *exchange looks*)

SAUL: Oh—Yes.

LEE: You don't fool around in Television, do you Saul?

SAUL: Uh—I have in the past. Produced some T.V. Specials. Network stuff. But it's mainly features now.

LEE: That's where the big money is, huh?

SAUL: Yes. That's right.

AUSTIN: Why don't I call you tomorrow, Saul, and we'll get together. We can have lunch or something.

SAUL: That'd be terrific.

LEE: Right after the golf.

(*pause*)

SAUL: What?

LEE: You can have lunch right after the golf.

SAUL: Oh, right.

LEE: Austin was tellin' me that yer interested in stories.

SAUL: Well, we develop certain projects that we feel have commercial potential.

LEE: What kinda' stuff do ya' go in for?

SAUL: Oh, the usual. You know. Good love interest. Lots of action. (*chuckles at* AUSTIN)

LEE: Westerns?

SAUL: Sometimes.

AUSTIN: I'll give you a ring, Saul.

(AUSTIN *tries to move* SAUL *across the kitchen but* LEE *blocks their way*)

LEE: I got a Western that'd knock yer lights out.

SAUL: Oh really?

LEE: Yeah. Contemporary Western. Based on a true story. 'Course I'm not a writer like my brother here. I'm not a man of the pen.

SAUL: Well—

LEE: I mean I can tell ya' a story off the tongue but I can't put it down on paper. That don't make any difference though does it?

SAUL: No, not really.

LEE: I mean plenty a' guys have stories don't they? True-life stories. Musta' been a lota' movies made from real life.

SAUL: Yes. I suppose so.

LEE: I haven't seen a good Western since "Lonely Are the Brave." You remember that movie?

SAUL: No, I'm afraid I—

LEE: Kirk Douglas. Helluva' movie. You remember that movie, Austin?

AUSTIN: Yes.

LEE: (*to* SAUL) The man dies for the love of a horse.

SAUL: Is that right.

LEE: Yeah. Ya' hear the horse screamin' at the end of it. Rain's comin' down. Horse is screamin'. Then there's a shot. BLAM! Just a single shot like that. Then nothin' but the sound of rain. And Kirk Douglas is ridin' in the ambulance. Ridin' away from the scene of the accident. And when he hears that shot he knows that his horse has died. He knows. And you see his eyes. And his eyes die. Right inside his face. And then his eyes close. And you know that he's died too. You know that Kirk Douglas has died from the death of his horse.

SAUL: (*eyes* AUSTIN *nervously*) Well, it sounds like a great movie. I'm sorry I missed it.

LEE: Yeah, you shouldn't a' missed that one.

SAUL: I'll have to try to catch it some time. Arrange a screening or something. Well, Austin, I'll have to hit the freeway before rush hour.

AUSTIN: (*ushers him toward exit*) It's good seeing you, Saul.

(AUSTIN *and* SAUL *shake hands*)

LEE: So ya' think there's room for a real Western these days? A true-to-life Western?

SAUL: Well, I don't see why not. Why don't you uh—tell the story to Austin and have him write a little outline.

LEE: You'd take a look at it then?

SAUL: Yes. Sure. I'll give it a read-through. Always eager for new material. (*smiles at* AUSTIN)

LEE: That's great! You'd really read it then huh?

SAUL: It would just be my opinion of course.

LEE: That's all I want. Just an opinion. I happen to think it has a lota' possibilities.

SAUL: Well, it was great meeting you and I'll—

(SAUL *and* LEE *shake*)

LEE: I'll call you tomorrow about the golf.

SAUL: Oh. Yes, right.

LEE: Austin's got your number, right?

SAUL: Yes.

LEE: So long Saul. (*gives* SAUL *a pat on the back*)

(SAUL *exits,* AUSTIN *turns to* LEE, *looks at T.V. then back to* LEE)

AUSTIN: Give me the keys.

(AUSTIN *extends his hand toward* LEE, LEE *doesn't move, just stares at* AUSTIN, *smiles, lights to black*)

Scene 4

Night. Coyotes in distance, fade, sound of typewriter in dark, crickets, candlelight in alcove, dim light in kitchen, lights reveal AUSTIN *at glass table typing,* LEE *sits across from him, foot on table, drinking beer and whiskey, the T.V. is still on sink counter,* AUSTIN *types for a while, then stops.*

LEE: All right, now read it back to me.

AUSTIN: I'm not reading it back to you, Lee. You can read it when we're finished. I can't spend all night on this.

LEE: You got better things to do?

AUSTIN: Let's just go ahead. Now what happens when he leaves Texas?

LEE: Is he ready to leave Texas yet? I didn't know we were that far along. He's not ready to leave Texas.

AUSTIN: He's right at the border.

LEE: (*sitting up*) No, see this is one a' the crucial parts. Right here. (*taps paper with beer can*) We can't rush through this. He's not right at the border. He's a good fifty miles from the border. A lot can happen in fifty miles.

AUSTIN: It's only an outline. We're not writing an entire script now.

LEE: Well ya' can't leave things out even if it is an outline. It's one a' the most important parts. Ya' can't go leavin' it out.

AUSTIN: Okay, okay. Let's just—get it done.

LEE: All right. Now. He's in the truck and he's got his horse trailer and his horse.

AUSTIN: We've already established that.

LEE: And he sees this other guy comin' up behind him in another truck. And that truck is pullin' a gooseneck.

AUSTIN: What's a gooseneck?

LEE: Cattle trailer. You know the kind with a gooseneck, goes right down in the bed a' the pick-up.

AUSTIN: Oh. All right. (*types*)

LEE: It's important.

AUSTIN: Okay. I got it.

LEE: All these details are important.

(AUSTIN *types as they talk*)

AUSTIN: I've got it.

LEE: And this other guy's got his horse all saddled up in the back a' the gooseneck.

AUSTIN: Right.

LEE: So both these guys have got their horses right along with 'em, see.

AUSTIN: I understand.

LEE: Then this first guy suddenly realizes two things.

AUSTIN: The guy in front?

LEE: Right. The guy in front realizes two things almost at the same time. Simultaneous.

AUSTIN: What were the two things?

LEE: Number one, he realizes that the guy behind him is the husband of the woman he's been—

(LEE *makes gesture of screwing by pumping his arm*)

AUSTIN: (*sees* LEE'*s gesture*) Oh. Yeah.

LEE: And number two, he realizes he's in the middle of Tornado Country.

AUSTIN: What's "Tornado Country"?

LEE: Panhandle.

AUSTIN: Panhandle?

LEE: Sweetwater. Around in that area. Nothin'. Nowhere. And number three—

AUSTIN: I thought there was only two.

LEE: There's three. There's a third unforeseen realization.

AUSTIN: And what's that?

LEE: That he's runnin' outa' gas.

AUSTIN: (*stops typing*) Come on, Lee.

(AUSTIN *gets up, moves to kitchen, gets a glass of water*)

LEE: Whadya' mean, "come on"? That's what it is. Write it down! He's runnin' outa' gas.

AUSTIN: It's too—

LEE: What? It's too what? It's too real! That's what ya' mean isn't it? It's too much like real life!

AUSTIN: It's not like real life! It's not enough like real life. Things don't happen like that.

LEE: What! Men don't fuck other men's women?

AUSTIN: Yes. But they don't end up chasing each other across the Panhandle. Through "Tornado Country."

LEE: They do in this movie!

AUSTIN: And they don't have horses conveniently along with them when they run out of gas! And they don't run out of gas either!

LEE: These guys run outa' gas! This is my story and one a' these guys runs outa' gas!

AUSTIN: It's just a dumb excuse to get them into a chase scene. It's contrived.

LEE: It is a chase scene! It's already a chase scene. They been chasin' each other fer days.

AUSTIN: So now they're supposed to abandon their trucks, climb on their horses and chase each other into the mountains?

LEE: (*standing suddenly*) There aren't any mountains in the Panhandle! It's flat!

(LEE *turns violently toward windows in alcove and throws beer can at them*)

LEE: Goddamn these crickets! (*yells at crickets*) Shut up out there! (*pause, turns back toward table*) This place is like a fuckin' rest home here. How're you supposed to think!

AUSTIN: You wanna' take a break?

LEE: No, I don't wanna' take a break! I wanna' get this done! This is my last chance to get this done.

AUSTIN: (*moves back into alcove*) All right. Take it easy.

LEE: I'm gonna' be leavin' this area. I don't have time to mess around here.

AUSTIN: Where are you going?

LEE: Never mind where I'm goin'! That's got nothin' to do with you. I just gotta' get this done. I'm not like you. Hangin' around bein' a parasite offa' other fools. I gotta' do this thing and get out.

(*pause*)

AUSTIN: A parasite? Me?

LEE: Yeah, you!

AUSTIN: After you break into people's houses and take their televisions?

LEE: They don't need their televisions! I'm doin' them a service.

AUSTIN: Give me back my keys, Lee.

LEE: Not until you write this thing! You're gonna' write this outline thing for me or that car's gonna' wind up in Arizona with a different paint job.

AUSTIN: You think you can force me to write this? I was doing you a favor.

LEE: Git off yer high horse will ya'! Favor! Big favor. Handin' down favors from the mountain top.

AUSTIN: Let's just write it, okay? Let's sit down and not get upset and see if we can just get through this.

(AUSTIN *sits at typewriter*)

(*long pause*)

LEE: Yer not gonna' even show it to him, are ya'?

AUSTIN: What?

LEE: This outline. You got no intention of showin' it to him. Yer just doin' this 'cause yer afraid a' me.

AUSTIN: You can show it to him yourself.

LEE: I will, boy! I'm gonna' read it to him on the golf course.

AUSTIN: And I'm not afraid of you either.

LEE: Then how come yer doin' it?

AUSTIN: (*pause*) So I can get my keys back.

(*pause as* LEE *takes keys out of his pocket slowly and throws them on table, long pause,* AUSTIN *stares at keys*)

LEE: There. Now you got yer keys back.

(AUSTIN *looks up at* LEE *but doesn't take keys*)

LEE: Go ahead. There's yer keys.

(AUSTIN *slowly takes keys off table and puts them back in his own pocket*)

Now what're you gonna' do? Kick me out?

AUSTIN: I'm not going to kick you out, Lee.

LEE: You couldn't kick me out, boy.

AUSTIN: I know.

LEE: So you can't even consider that one. (*pause*) You could call the police. That'd be the obvious thing.

AUSTIN: You're my brother.

LEE: That don't mean a thing. You go down to the L.A. Police Department there and ask them what kinda' people kill each other the most. What do you think they'd say?

AUSTIN: Who said anything about killing?

LEE: Family people. Brothers. Brothers-in-law. Cousins. Real American-type people. They kill each other in the heart mostly. In the Smog-Alerts. In the Brush Fire Season. Right about this time a' year.

AUSTIN: This isn't the same.

LEE: Oh no? What makes it different?

AUSTIN: We're not insane. We're not driven to acts of violence like that. Not over a dumb movie script. Now sit down.

(*long pause,* LEE *considers which way to go with it*)

LEE: Maybe not. (*he sits back down at table across from* AUSTIN) Maybe you're right. Maybe we're too intelligent, huh? (*pause*) We got our heads on our shoulders. One of us has even got a Ivy League diploma. Now that means somethin' don't it? Doesn't that mean somethin'?

AUSTIN: Look, I'll write this thing for you, Lee. I don't mind writing it. I just don't want to get all worked up about it. It's not worth it. Now, come on. Let's just get through it, okay?

LEE: Nah. I think there's easier money. Lotsa' places I could pick up thousands. Maybe millions. I don't need this shit. I could go up to Sacramento Valley and steal me a diesel. Ten thousand a week dismantling one a' those suckers. Ten thousand a week!

(LEE *opens another beer, puts his foot back up on table*)

AUSTIN: No, really, look, I'll write it out for you. I think it's a great idea.

LEE: Nah, you got yer own work to do. I don't wanna' interfere with yer life.

AUSTIN: I mean it'd be really fantastic if you could sell this. Turn it into a movie. I mean it.

(*pause*)

LEE: Ya' think so huh?

AUSTIN: Absolutely. You could really turn your life around, you know. Change things.

LEE: I could get me a house maybe.

AUSTIN: Sure you could get a house. You could get a whole ranch if you wanted to.

LEE: (*laughs*) A ranch? I could get a ranch?

AUSTIN: 'Course you could. You know what a screenplay sells for these days?

LEE: No. What's it sell for?

AUSTIN: A lot. A whole lot of money.

LEE: Thousands?

AUSTIN: Yeah. Thousands.

LEE: Millions?

AUSTIN: Well—

LEE: We could get the old man outa' hock then.

AUSTIN: Maybe.

LEE: Maybe? Whadya' mean, maybe?

AUSTIN: I mean it might take more than money.

LEE: You were just tellin' me it'd change my whole life around. Why wouldn't it change his?

AUSTIN: He's different.

LEE: Oh, he's of a different ilk huh?

AUSTIN: He's not gonna' change. Let's leave the old man out of it.

LEE: That's right. He's not gonna' change but I will. I'll just turn myself right inside out. I could be just like you then, huh? Sittin' around dreamin' stuff up. Gettin' paid to dream. Ridin' back and forth on the freeway just dreamin' my fool head off.

AUSTIN: It's not all that easy.

LEE: It's not, huh?

AUSTIN: No. There's a lot of work involved.

LEE: What's the toughest part? Deciding whether to jog or play tennis?

(*long pause*)

AUSTIN: Well, look. You can stay here—do whatever you want to. Borrow the car. Come in and out. Doesn't matter to me. It's not my house. I'll help you write this thing or—not. Just let me know what you want. You tell me.

LEE: Oh. So now suddenly you're at my service. Is that it?

AUSTIN: What do you want to do Lee?

(*long pause,* LEE *stares at him then turns and dreams at windows*)

LEE: I tell ya' what I'd do if I still had that dog. Ya' wanna' know what I'd do?

AUSTIN: What?

LEE: Head out to Ventura. Cook up a little match. God that little dog could bear down. Lota' money in dog fightin'. Big money.

(*pause*)

AUSTIN: Why don't we try to see this through, Lee. Just for the hell of it. Maybe you've really got something here. What do you think?

(*pause,* LEE *considers*)

LEE: Maybe so. No harm in tryin' I guess. You think it's such a hot idea. Besides, I always wondered what'd be like to be you.

AUSTIN: You did?

LEE: Yeah, sure. I used to picture you walkin' around some campus with yer arms fulla' books. Blondes chasin' after ya'.

AUSTIN: Blondes? That's funny.

LEE: What's funny about it?

AUSTIN: Because I always used to picture you somewhere.

LEE: Where'd you picture me?

AUSTIN: Oh, I don't know. Different places. Adventures. You were always on some adventure.

LEE: Yeah.

AUSTIN: And I used to say to myself, "Lee's got the right idea. He's out there in the world and here I am. What am I doing?"

LEE: Well you were settin' yourself up for somethin'.

AUSTIN: I guess.

LEE: We better get started on this thing then.

AUSTIN: Okay.

(AUSTIN *sits up at typewriter, puts new paper in*)

LEE: Oh. Can I get the keys back before I forget?

(AUSTIN *hesitates*)

You said I could borrow the car if I wanted, right? Isn't that what you said?

AUSTIN: Yeah. Right.

(AUSTIN *takes keys out of his pocket, sets them on table,* LEE *takes keys slowly, plays with them in his hand*)

LEE: I could get a ranch, huh?

AUSTIN: Yeah. We have to write it first though.

LEE: Okay. Let's write it.

(*lights start dimming slowly to end of scene as* AUSTIN *types,* LEE *speaks*)

So they take off after each other straight into an endless black prairie. The sun is just comin' down and they can feel the night on their backs. What they don't know is that each one of 'em is afraid, see. Each one separately thinks that he's the only one that's afraid. And they keep ridin' like that straight into the night. Not knowing. And the one who's chasin' doesn't know where the other one is taking him. And the one who's being chased doesn't know where he's going.

(*lights to black, typing stops in the dark, crickets fade*)

Act Two

Scene 5

Morning. LEE *at the table in alcove with a set of golf clubs in a fancy leather bag,* AUSTIN *at sink washing a few dishes.*

AUSTIN: He really liked it, huh?

LEE: He wouldn't a' gave me these clubs if he didn't like it.

AUSTIN: He gave you the clubs?

LEE: Yeah. I told ya' he gave me the clubs. The bag too.

AUSTIN: I thought he just loaned them to you.

LEE: He said it was part a' the advance. A little gift like. Gesture of his good faith.

AUSTIN: He's giving you an advance?

LEE: Now what's so amazing about that? I told ya' it was a good story. You even said it was a good story.

AUSTIN: Well that is really incredible Lee. You know how many guys spend their whole lives down here trying to break into this business? Just trying to get in the door?

LEE: (*pulling clubs out of bag, testing them*) I got no idea. How many?

(*pause*)

AUSTIN: How much of an advance is he giving you?

LEE: Plenty. We were talkin' big money out there. Ninth hole is where I sealed the deal.

AUSTIN: He made a firm commitment?

LEE: Absolutely.

AUSTIN: Well, I know Saul and he doesn't fool around when he says he likes something.

LEE: I thought you said you didn't know him.

AUSTIN: Well, I'm familiar with his tastes.

LEE: I let him get two up on me goin' into the back nine. He was sure he had me cold. You shoulda' seen his face when I pulled out the old pitching wedge and plopped it pin-high, two feet from the cup. He 'bout shit his pants. "Where'd a guy like you ever learn how to play golf like that?" he says.

(LEE *laughs,* AUSTIN *stares at him*)

AUSTIN: 'Course there's no contract yet. Nothing's final until it's on paper.

LEE: It's final, all right. There's no way he's gonna' back out of it now. We gambled for it.

AUSTIN: Saul, gambled?

LEE: Yeah, sure. I mean he liked the outline already so he wasn't risking that much. I just guaranteed it with my short game.

(*pause*)

AUSTIN: Well, we should celebrate or something. I think Mom left a bottle of champagne in the refrigerator. We should have a little toast.

(AUSTIN *gets glasses from cupboard, goes to refrigerator, pulls out bottle of champagne*)

LEE: You shouldn't oughta' take her champagne, Austin. She's gonna' miss that.

AUSTIN: Oh, she's not going to mind. She'd be glad we put it to good use. I'll get her another bottle. Besides, it's perfect for the occasion.

(*pause*)

LEE: Yer gonna' get a nice fee fer writin' the script a' course. Straight fee.

(AUSTIN *stops, stares at* LEE, *puts glasses and bottle on table, pause*)

AUSTIN: I'm writing the script?

LEE: That's what he said. Said we couldn't hire a better screenwriter in the whole town.

AUSTIN: But I'm already working on a script. I've got my own project. I don't have time to write two scripts.

LEE: No, he said he was gonna' drop that other one.

(*pause*)

AUSTIN: What? You mean mine? He's going to drop mine and do yours instead?

LEE: (*smiles*) Now look, Austin, it's jest beginner's luck ya' know. I mean I sank a fifty foot putt for this deal. No hard feelings.

(AUSTIN *goes to phone on wall, grabs it, starts dialing*)

He's not gonna' be in, Austin. Told me he wouldn't be in 'till late this afternoon.

AUSTIN: (*stays on phone, dialing, listens*) I can't believe this. I just can't believe it. Are you sure he said that? Why would he drop mine?

LEE: That's what he told me.

AUSTIN: He can't do that without telling me first. Without talking to me at least. He wouldn't just make a decision like that without talking to me!

LEE: Well I was kinda' surprised myself. But he was real enthusiastic about my story.

(AUSTIN *hangs up phone violently, paces*)

AUSTIN: What'd he say! Tell me everything he said!

LEE: I been tellin' ya'! He said he liked the story a whole lot. It was the first authentic Western to come along in a decade.

AUSTIN: He liked that story! Your story?

LEE: Yeah! What's so surprisin' about that?

AUSTIN: It's stupid! It's the dumbest story I ever heard in my life.

LEE: Hey, hold on! That's my story yer talkin' about!

AUSTIN: It's a bullshit story! It's idiotic. Two lamebrains chasing each other across Texas! Are you kidding? Who do you think's going to go see a film like that?

LEE: It's not a film! It's a movie. There's a big difference. That's somethin' Saul told me.

AUSTIN: Oh he did, huh?

LEE: Yeah, he said, "In this business we make movies, American movies. Leave the films to the French."

AUSTIN: So you got real intimate with old Saul huh? He started pouring forth his vast knowledge of Cinema.

LEE: I think he liked me a lot, to tell ya' the truth. I think he felt I was somebody he could confide in.

AUSTIN: What'd you do, beat him up or something?

LEE: (*stands fast*) Hey, I've about had it with the insults buddy! You think yer the only one in the brain department here? Yer the only one that can sit around and cook things up? There's other people got ideas too, ya' know!

AUSTIN: You must've done something. Threatened him or something. Now what'd you do Lee?

LEE: I convinced him!

(LEE *makes sudden menacing lunge toward* AUSTIN, *wielding golf club above his head, stops himself, frozen moment, long pause,* LEE *lowers club*)

AUSTIN: Oh, Jesus. You didn't hurt him did you?

(*long silence,* LEE *sits back down at table*)

Lee! Did you hurt him?

LEE: I didn't do nothin' to him! He liked my story. Pure and simple. He said it was the best story he's come across in a long, long time.

AUSTIN: That's what he told me about my story! That's the same thing he said to me.

LEE: Well, he musta' been lyin'. He musta' been lyin' to one of us anyway.

AUSTIN: You can't come into this town and start pushing people around. They're gonna' put you away!

LEE: I never pushed anybody around! I beat him fair and square. (*pause*) They can't touch me anyway. They can't put a finger on me. I'm gone. I can come in through the window and go out through the door. They never knew what hit 'em. You, yer stuck. Yer the one that's stuck. Not me. So don't be warnin' me what to do in this town.

(*pause,* AUSTIN *crosses to table, sits at typewriter, rests*)

AUSTIN: Lee, come on, level with me will you? It doesn't make any sense that suddenly he'd throw my idea out the window. I've been talking to him for months. I've got too much at stake. Everything's riding on this project.

LEE: What's yer idea?

AUSTIN: It's just a simple love story.

LEE: What kinda' love story?

AUSTIN: (*stands, crosses into kitchen*) I'm not telling you!

LEE: Ha! 'Fraid I'll steal it huh? Competition's gettin' kinda' close to home isn't it?

AUSTIN: Where did Saul say he was going?

LEE: He was gonna' take my story to a couple studios.

AUSTIN: That's *my* outline you know! I wrote that outline! You've got no right to be peddling it around.

LEE: You weren't ready to take credit for it last night.

AUSTIN: Give me my keys!

LEE: What?

AUSTIN: The keys! I want my keys back!

LEE: Where you goin'?

AUSTIN: Just give me my keys! I gotta' take a drive. I gotta' get out of here for a while.

LEE: Where you gonna' go, Austin?

AUSTIN: (*pause*) I might just drive out to the desert for a while. I gotta' think.

LEE: You can think here just as good. This is the perfect setup for thinkin'. We got some writin' to do here, boy. Now let's just have us a little toast. Relax. We're partners now.

(LEE *pops the cork of the champagne bottle, pours two drinks as the lights fade to black*)

Scene 6

Afternoon. LEE *and* SAUL *in kitchen,* AUSTIN *in alcove.*

LEE: Now you tell him. You tell him, Mr. Kipper.

SAUL: Kimmer.

LEE: Kimmer. You tell him what you told me. He don't believe me.

AUSTIN: I don't want to hear it.

SAUL: It's really not a big issue, Austin. I was simply amazed by your brother's story and—

AUSTIN: Amazed? You lost a bet! You gambled with my material!

SAUL: That's really beside the point, Austin. I'm ready to go all the way with your brother's story. I think it has a great deal of merit.

AUSTIN: I don't want to hear about it, okay? Go tell it to the executives! Tell it to somebody who's going to turn it into a package deal or something. A T.V. series. Don't tell it to me.

SAUL: But I want to continue with your project too, Austin. It's not as though we can't do both. We're big enough for that aren't we?

AUSTIN: "We"? *I* can't do both! I don't know about "we."

LEE: (*to* SAUL) See, what'd I tell ya'. He's totally unsympathetic.

SAUL: Austin, there's no point in our going to another screenwriter for this. It just doesn't make sense. You're brothers. You know each other. There's a familiarity with the material that just wouldn't be possible otherwise.

AUSTIN: There's no familiarity with the material! None! I don't know what "Tornado Country" is. I don't know what a "gooseneck" is. And I don't want to know! (*pointing to* LEE) He's a hustler! He's a bigger hustler than you are! If you can't see that, then—

LEE: (*to* AUSTIN) Hey, now hold on. I didn't have to bring this bone back to you, boy. I persuaded Saul here that you were the right man for the job. You don't have to go throwin' up favors in my face.

AUSTIN: Favors! I'm the one who wrote the fuckin' outline! You can't even spell.

SAUL: (*to* AUSTIN) Your brother told me about the situation with your father. (*pause*)

AUSTIN: What? (*looks at* LEE)

SAUL: That's right. Now we have a clear-cut deal here, Austin. We have big studio money standing behind this thing. Just on the basis of your outline.

AUSTIN: (*to* SAUL) What'd he tell you about my father?

SAUL: Well—that he's destitute. He needs money.

LEE: That's right. He does.

(AUSTIN *shakes his head, stares at them both*)

AUSTIN: (*to* LEE) And this little assignment is supposed to go toward the old man? A charity project? Is that what this is? Did you cook this up on the ninth green too?

SAUL: It's a big slice, Austin.

AUSTIN: (*to* LEE) I gave him money! I already gave him money. You know that. He drank it all up!

LEE: This is a different deal here.

SAUL: We can set up a trust for your father. A large sum of money. It can be doled out to him in parcels so he can't misuse it.

AUSTIN: Yeah, and who's doing the doling?

SAUL: Your brother volunteered.

(AUSTIN *laughs*)

LEE: That's right. I'll make sure he uses it for groceries.

AUSTIN: (*to* SAUL) I'm not doing this script! I'm not writing this crap for you or anybody else. You can't blackmail me into it. You can't threaten me into it. There's no way I'm doing it. So just give it up. Both of you.

(*long pause*)

SAUL: Well, that's it then. I mean this is an easy three hundred grand. Just for a first draft. It's incredible, Austin. We've got three different studios all trying to cut each other's throats to get this material. In one morning. That's how hot it is.

AUSTIN: Yeah, well you can afford to give me a percentage on the outline then. And you better get the genius here an agent before he gets burned.

LEE: Saul's gonna' be my agent. Isn't that right, Saul?

SAUL: That's right. (*to* AUSTIN) Your brother has really got something, Austin. I've been around too long not to recognize it. Raw talent.

AUSTIN: He's got a lota' balls is what he's got. He's taking you right down the river.

SAUL: Three hundred thousand, Austin. Just for a first draft. Now you've never been offered that kind of money before.

AUSTIN: I'm not writing it.

(*pause*)

SAUL: I see. Well—

LEE: We'll just go to another writer then. Right, Saul? Just hire us somebody with some enthusiasm. Somebody who can recognize the value of a good story.

SAUL: I'm sorry about this, Austin.

AUSTIN: Yeah.

SAUL: I mean I was hoping we could continue both things but now I don't see how it's possible.

AUSTIN: So you're dropping my idea altogether. Is that it? Just trade horses in midstream? After all these months of meetings.

SAUL: I wish there was another way.

AUSTIN: I've got everything riding on this, Saul. You know that. It's my only shot. If this falls through—

SAUL: I have to go with what my instincts tell me—

AUSTIN: Your instincts!

SAUL: My gut reaction.

AUSTIN: You lost! That's your gut reaction. You lost a gamble. Now you're trying to tell me you like his story? How could you possibly fall for that story? It's as phony as Hopalong Cassidy.[1] What do you see in it? I'm curious.

SAUL: It has the ring of truth, Austin.

AUSTIN: (*laughs*) Truth?

LEE: It is true.

SAUL: Something about the real West.

AUSTIN: Why? Because it's got horses? Because it's got grown men acting like little boys?

1. Cowboy hero of novels by Clarence E. Mulford (1883–1956), including *Hopalong Cassidy* (1910) and *Hopalong Cassidy Returns* (1924), later a character in the movies and on television, where he was more romanticized than in the books.

SAUL: Something about the land. Your brother is speaking from experience.

AUSTIN: So am I!

SAUL: But nobody's interested in love these days, Austin. Let's face it.

LEE: That's right.

AUSTIN: (*to* SAUL) He's been camped out on the desert for three months. Talking to cactus. What's he know about what people wanna' see on the screen! I drive on the freeway every day. I swallow the smog. I watch the news in color. I shop in the Safeway. I'm the one who's in touch! Not him!

SAUL: I have to go now, Austin.

(SAUL *starts to leave*)

AUSTIN: There's no such thing as the West anymore! It's a dead issue! It's dried up, Saul, and so are you.

(SAUL *stops and turns to* AUSTIN)

SAUL: Maybe you're right. But I have to take the gamble, don't I?

AUSTIN: You're a fool to do this, Saul.

SAUL: I've always gone on my hunches. Always. And I've never been wrong. (*to* LEE) I'll talk to you tomorrow, Lee.

LEE: All right, Mr. Kimmer.

SAUL: Maybe we could have some lunch.

LEE: Fine with me. (*smiles at* AUSTIN)

SAUL: I'll give you a ring.

(SAUL *exits, lights to black as brothers look at each other from a distance*)

Scene 7

Night. Coyotes, crickets, sound of typewriter in dark, candlelight up on LEE *at typewriter struggling to type with one finger system,* AUSTIN *sits sprawled out on kitchen floor with whiskey bottle, drunk.*

AUSTIN: (*singing, from floor*)
"Red sails in the sunset
Way out on the blue
Please carry my loved one
Home safely to me

Red sails in the sunset—"

LEE: (*slams fist on table*) Hey! Knock it off will ya'! I'm tryin' to concentrate here.

AUSTIN: (*laughs*) You're tryin' to concentrate?

LEE: Yeah. That's right.

AUSTIN: Now you're tryin' to concentrate.

LEE: Between you, the coyotes and the crickets a thought don't have much of a chance.

AUSTIN: "Between me, the coyotes and the crickets." What a great title.

LEE: I don't need a title! I need a thought.

AUSTIN: (*laughs*) A thought! Here's a thought for ya'—

LEE: I'm not askin' fer yer thoughts! I got my own. I can do this thing on my own.

AUSTIN: You're going to write an entire script on your own?

LEE: That's right.

(*pause*)

AUSTIN: Here's a thought. Saul Kimmer—

LEE: Shut up will ya'!

AUSTIN: He thinks we're the same person.

LEE: Don't get cute.

AUSTIN: He does! He's lost his mind. Poor old Saul. (*giggles*) Thinks we're one and the same.

LEE: Why don't you ease up on that champagne.

AUSTIN: (*holding up bottle*) This isn't champagne anymore. We went through the champagne a long time ago. This is serious stuff. The days of champagne are long gone.

LEE: Well, go outside and drink it.

AUSTIN: I'm enjoying your company, Lee. For the first time since your arrival I am finally enjoying your company. And now you want me to go outside and drink alone?

LEE: That's right.

(LEE *reads through paper in typewriter, makes an erasure*)

AUSTIN: You think you'll make more progress if you're alone? You might drive yourself crazy.

LEE: I could have this thing done in a night if I had a little silence.

AUSTIN: Well you'd still have the crickets to contend with. The coyotes. The sounds of the Police Helicopters prowling above the neighborhood. Slashing their searchlights down through the streets. Hunting for the likes of you.

LEE: I'm a screenwriter now! I'm legitimate.

AUSTIN: (*laughing*) A screenwriter!

LEE: That's right. I'm on salary. That's more'n I can say for you. I got an advance coming.

AUSTIN: This is true. This is very true. An advance. (*pause*) Well, maybe I oughta' go out and try my hand at your trade. Since you're doing so good at mine.

LEE: Ha!

(LEE *attempts to type some more but gets the ribbon tangled up, starts trying to re-thread it as they continue talking*)

AUSTIN: Well why not? You don't think I've got what it takes to sneak into people's houses and steal their T.V.s?

LEE: You couldn't steal a toaster without losin' yer lunch.

(AUSTIN *stands with a struggle, supports himself by the sink*)

AUSTIN: You don't think I could sneak into somebody's house and steal a toaster?

LEE: Go take a shower or somethin' will ya!

(LEE *gets more tangled up with the typewriter ribbon, pulling it out of the machine as though it was fishing line*)

AUSTIN: You really don't think I could steal a crumby toaster? How much you wanna' bet I can't steal a toaster! How much? Go ahead! You're a gambler aren't you? Tell me how much yer willing to put on the line. Some part of your big advance? Oh, you haven't got that yet have you. I forgot.

LEE: All right. I'll bet you your car that you can't steal a toaster without gettin' busted.

AUSTIN: You already got my car!

LEE: Okay, your house then.

AUSTIN: What're you gonna' give me! I'm not talkin' about my house and my car, I'm talkin' about what are you gonna' give me. You don't have nothin' to give me.

LEE: I'll give you—shared screen credit. How 'bout that? I'll have it put in the contract that this was written by the both of us.

AUSTIN: I don't want my name on that piece of shit! I want something of value. You got anything of value? You got any tidbits from the desert? Any Rattlesnake bones? I'm not a greedy man. Any little personal treasure will suffice.

LEE: I'm gonna' just kick yer ass out in a minute.

AUSTIN: Oh, so now you're gonna' kick me out! Now I'm the intruder. I'm the one who's invading your precious privacy.

LEE: I'm trying to do some screenwriting here!

(LEE *stands, picks up typewriter, slams it down hard on table, pause, silence except for crickets*)

AUSTIN: Well, you got everything you need. You got plenty a' coffee? Groceries. You got a car. A contract. (*pause*) Might need a new typewriter ribbon but other than that you're pretty well fixed. I'll just leave ya' alone for a while.

(AUSTIN *tries to steady himself to leave,* LEE *makes a move toward him*)

LEE: Where you goin'?

AUSTIN: Don't worry about me. I'm not the one to worry about.

(AUSTIN *weaves toward exit, stops*)

LEE: What're you gonna' do? Just go wander out into the night?

AUSTIN: I'm gonna' make a little tour.

LEE: Why don't ya' just go to bed for Christ's sake. Yer makin' me sick.

AUSTIN: I can take care a' myself. Don't worry about me.

(AUSTIN *weaves badly in another attempt to exit, he crashes to the floor,* LEE *goes to him but remains standing*)

LEE: You want me to call your wife for ya' or something?

AUSTIN: (*from floor*) My wife?

LEE: Yeah. I mean maybe she can help ya' out. Talk to ya' or somethin'.

AUSTIN: (*struggles to stand again*) She's five hundred miles away. North. North of here. Up in the North country where things are calm. I don't need any help. I'm gonna' go outside and I'm gonna' steal a toaster. I'm gonna' steal some other stuff too. I might even commit bigger crimes. Bigger than you ever dreamed of. Crimes beyond the imagination!

(AUSTIN *manages to get himself vertical, tries to head for exit again*)

LEE: Just hang on a minute, Austin.

AUSTIN: Why? What for? You don't need my help, right? You got a handle on the project. Besides, I'm lookin' forward to the smell of the night. The bushes. Orange blossoms. Dust in the driveways. Rain bird sprinklers. Lights in people's houses. You're right about the lights, Lee. Everybody else is livin' the life. Indoors. Safe. This is a Paradise down here. You know that? We're livin' in a Paradise. We've forgotten about that.

LEE: You sound just like the old man now.

AUSTIN: Yeah, well we all sound alike when we're sloshed. We just sorta' echo each other.

LEE: Maybe if we could work on this together we could bring him back out here. Get him settled down some place.

(AUSTIN *turns violently toward* LEE, *takes a swing at him, misses and crashes to the floor again,* LEE *stays standing*)

AUSTIN: I don't want him out here! I've had it with him! I went all the way out there! I went out of my way. I gave him money and all he did was play Al Jolson records and spit at me! I gave him money!

(*pause*)

LEE: Just help me a little with the characters, all right? You know how to do it, Austin.

AUSTIN: (*on floor, laughs*) The characters!

LEE: Yeah. You know. The way they talk and stuff. I can hear it in my head but I can't get it down on paper.

AUSTIN: What characters?

LEE: The guys. The guys in the story.

AUSTIN: Those aren't characters.

LEE: Whatever you call 'em then. I need to write somethin' out.

AUSTIN: Those are illusions of characters.

LEE: I don't give a damn what ya' call 'em! You know what I'm talkin' about!

AUSTIN: Those are fantasies of a long lost boyhood.

LEE: I gotta' write somethin' out on paper!!

(*pause*)

AUSTIN: What for? Saul's gonna' get you a fancy screenwriter isn't he?

LEE: I wanna' do it myself!

AUSTIN: Then do it! Yer on your own now, old buddy. You bulldogged yer way into contention. Now you gotta' carry it through.

LEE: I will but I need some advice. Just a couple a' things. Come on, Austin. Just help me get 'em talkin' right. It won't take much.

AUSTIN: Oh, now you're having a little doubt huh? What happened? The pressure's on, boy. This is it. You gotta' come up with it now. You don't come up with a winner on your first time out they just cut your head off. They don't give you a second chance ya' know.

LEE: I got a good story! I know it's a good story. I just need a little help is all.

AUSTIN: Not from me. Not from yer little old brother. I'm retired.

LEE: You could save this thing for me, Austin. I'd give ya' half the money. I would. I only need half anyway. With this kinda' money I could be a long time down the road. I'd never bother ya' again. I promise. You'd never even see me again.

AUSTIN: (*still on floor*) You'd disappear?

LEE: I would for sure.

AUSTIN: Where would you disappear to?

LEE: That don't matter. I got plenty a' places.

AUSTIN: Nobody can disappear. The old man tried that. Look where it got him. He lost his teeth.

LEE: He never had any money.

AUSTIN: I don't mean that. I mean his teeth! His real teeth. First he lost his real teeth, then he lost his false teeth. You never knew that did ya'? He never confided in you.

LEE: Nah, I never knew that.

AUSTIN: You wanna' drink?

(AUSTIN *offers bottle to* LEE, LEE *takes it, sits down on kitchen floor with* AUSTIN, *they share the bottle*)

Yeah, he lost his real teeth one at a time. Woke up every morning with another tooth lying on the mattress. Finally, he decides he's gotta' get 'em all pulled out but he doesn't have any money. Middle of Arizona with no money and no insurance and every morning another tooth is lying on the mattress. (*takes a drink*) So what does he do?

LEE: I dunno'. I never knew about that.

AUSTIN: He begs the government. G.I. Bill or some damn thing. Some pension plan he remembers in the back of his head. And they send him out the money.

LEE: They did?

(*they keep trading the bottle between them, taking drinks*)

AUSTIN: Yeah. They send him the money but it's not enough money. Costs a lot to have all yer teeth yanked. They charge by the individual tooth, ya' know. I mean one tooth isn't equal to another tooth. Some are more expensive. Like the big ones in the back—

LEE: So what happened?

AUSTIN: So he locates a Mexican dentist in Juarez who'll do the whole thing for a song. And he takes off hitchhiking to the border.

LEE: Hitchhiking?

AUSTIN: Yeah. So how long you think it takes him to get to the border? A man his age.

LEE: I dunno.

AUSTIN: Eight days it takes him. Eight days in the rain and the sun and every day he's droppin' teeth on the blacktop and nobody'll pick him up 'cause his mouth's full a' blood.

(*pause, they drink*)

So finally he stumbles into the dentist. Dentist takes all his money and all his teeth. And there he is, in Mexico, with his gums sewed up and his pockets empty.

(*long silence,* AUSTIN *drinks*)

LEE: That's it?

AUSTIN: Then I go out to see him, see. I go out there and I take him out for a nice Chinese dinner. But he doesn't eat. All he wants to do is drink Martinis outa' plastic cups. And he takes his teeth out and lays 'em on the table 'cause he can't stand the feel of 'em. And we ask the waitress for one a' those doggie bags to take the Chop Suey home in. So he drops his teeth in the doggie bag along with the Chop Suey. And then we go out to hit all the bars up and down the highway. Says he wants to introduce me to all his buddies. And in one a' those bars, in one a' those bars up and down the highway, he left that doggie bag with his teeth laying in the Chop Suey.

LEE: You never found it?

AUSTIN: We went back but we never did find it. (*pause*) Now that's a true story. True to life.

(*they drink as lights fade to black*)

Scene 8

Very early morning, between night and day. No crickets, coyotes yapping feverishly in distance before light comes up, a small fire blazes up in the dark from alcove area, sound of LEE *smashing typewriter with a golf club, lights coming up,* LEE *seen smashing typewriter methodically then dropping pages of his script into a burning bowl set on the floor of alcove, flames leap up,* AUSTIN *has a whole bunch of stolen toasters lined up on the sink counter along with* LEE'S *stolen T.V., the toasters are of a wide variety of models, mostly chrome,* AUSTIN *goes up and down the line of toasters, breathing on them and polishing them with a dish towel, both men are drunk, empty whiskey bottles and beer cans litter floor of kitchen, they share a half empty bottle on one of the chairs in the alcove,* LEE *keeps periodically taking deliberate ax-chops at the typewriter using a nine-iron as* AUSTIN *speaks, all of their mother's house plants are dead and drooping.*

AUSTIN: (*polishing toasters*) There's gonna' be a general lack of toast in the neighborhood this morning. Many, many unhappy, bewildered breakfast faces. I guess it's best not to even think of the victims. Not to even entertain it. Is that the right psychology?

LEE: (*pauses*) What?

AUSTIN: Is that the correct criminal psychology? Not to think of the victims?

LEE: What victims?

(LEE *takes another swipe at typewriter with nine-iron, adds pages to the fire*)

AUSTIN: The victims of crime. Of breaking and entering. I mean is it a prerequisite for a criminal not to have a conscience?

LEE: Ask a criminal.

(*pause,* LEE *stares at* AUSTIN)

What're you gonna' do with all those toasters? That's the dumbest thing I ever saw in my life.

AUSTIN: I've got hundreds of dollars worth of household appliances here. You may not realize that.

LEE: Yeah, and how many hundreds of dollars did you walk right past?

AUSTIN: It was toasters you challenged me to. Only toasters. I ignored every other temptation.

LEE: I never challenged you! That's no challenge. Anybody can steal a toaster.

(LEE *smashes typewriter again*)

AUSTIN: You don't have to take it out on my typewriter ya' know. It's not the machine's fault that you can't write. It's a sin to do that to a good machine.

LEE: A sin?

AUSTIN: When you consider all the writers who never even had a machine. Who would have given an eyeball for a good typewriter. Any typewriter.

(LEE *smashes typewriter again*)

AUSTIN: (*polishing toasters*) All the ones who wrote on matchbook covers. Paper bags. Toilet paper. Who had their writing destroyed by their jailers. Who persisted beyond all odds. Those writers would find it hard to understand your actions.

(LEE *comes down on typewriter with one final crushing blow of the nine-iron then collapses in one of the chairs, takes a drink from bottle, pause*)

AUSTIN: (*after pause*) Not to mention demolishing a perfectly good golf club. What about all the struggling golfers? What about Lee Trevino? What do you think he would've said when he was batting balls around with broomsticks at the age of nine. Impoverished.

(*pause*)

LEE: What time is it anyway?

AUSTIN: No idea. Time stands still when you're havin' fun.

LEE: Is it too late to call a woman? You know any women?

AUSTIN: I'm a married man.

LEE: I mean a local woman.

(AUSTIN *looks out at light through window above sink*)

AUSTIN: It's either too late or too early. You're the nature enthusiast. Can't you tell the time by the light in the sky? Orient yourself around the North Star or something?

LEE: I can't tell anything.

AUSTIN: Maybe you need a little breakfast. Some toast! How 'bout some toast?

(AUSTIN *goes to cupboard, pulls out loaf of bread and starts dropping slices into every toaster,* LEE *stays sitting, drinks, watches* AUSTIN)

LEE: I don't need toast. I need a woman.

AUSTIN: A woman isn't the answer. Never was.

LEE: I'm not talkin' about permanent. I'm talkin' about temporary.

AUSTIN: (*putting toast in toasters*) We'll just test the merits of these little demons. See which brands have a tendency to burn. See which one can produce a perfectly golden piece of fluffy toast.

LEE: How much gas you got in yer car?

AUSTIN: I haven't driven my car for days now. So I haven't had an opportunity to look at the gas gauge.

LEE: Take a guess. You think there's enough to get me to Bakersfield?

AUSTIN: Bakersfield? What's in Bakersfield?

LEE: Just never mind what's in Bakersfield! You think there's enough goddamn gas in the car!

AUSTIN: Sure.

LEE: Sure. You could care less, right. Let me run outa' gas on the Grapevine. You could give a shit.

AUSTIN: I'd say there was enough gas to get you just about anywhere, Lee. With your determination and guts.

LEE: What the hell time is it anyway?

(LEE *pulls out his wallet, starts going through dozens of small pieces of paper with phone numbers written on them, drops some on the floor, drops others in the fire*)

AUSTIN: Very early. This is the time of morning when the coyotes kill people's cocker spaniels. Did you hear them? That's what they were doing out there. Luring innocent pets away from their homes.

LEE: (*searching through his papers*) What's the area code for Bakersfield? You know?

AUSTIN: You could always call the operator.

LEE: I can't stand that voice they give ya'.

AUSTIN: What voice?

LEE: That voice that warns you that if you'd only tried harder to find the number in the phone book you wouldn't have to be calling the operator to begin with.

(LEE *gets up, holding a slip of paper from his wallet, stumbles toward phone on wall, yanks receiver, starts dialing*)

AUSTIN: Well I don't understand why you'd want to talk to anybody else anyway. I mean you can talk to me. I'm your brother.

LEE: (*dialing*) I wanna' talk to a woman. I haven't heard a woman's voice in a long time.

AUSTIN: Not since the Botanist?
LEE: What?
AUSTIN: Nothing. (*starts singing as he tends toast*)
"Red sails in the sunset
Way out on the blue
Please carry my loved one
Home safely to me"
LEE: Hey, knock it off will ya'! This is long distance here.
AUSTIN: Bakersfield?
LEE: Yeah, Bakersfield. It's Kern County.
AUSTIN: Well, what County are *we* in?
LEE: You better get yourself a 7-Up, boy.
AUSTIN: One County's as good as another.
(AUSTIN *hums "Red Sails" softly as* LEE *talks on phone*)

LEE: (*to phone*) Yeah, operator look—first off I wanna' know the area code for Bakersfield. Right. Bakersfield! Okay. Good. Now I wanna' know if you can help me track somebody down. (*pause*) No, no I mean a phone number. Just a phone number. Okay. (*holds a piece of paper up and reads it*) Okay, the name is Melly Ferguson. Melly. (*pause*) I dunno'. Melly. Maybe. Yeah. Maybe Melanie. Yeah. Melanie Ferguson. Okay. (*pause*) What? I can't hear ya' so good. Sounds like yer under the ocean. (*pause*) You got ten Melanie Fergusons? How could that be? Ten Melanie Fergusons in Bakersfield? Well gimme all of 'em then. (*pause*) What d'ya' mean? Gimmie all ten Melanie Fergusons! That's right. Just a second. (*to* AUSTIN) Gimme a pen.

AUSTIN: I don't have a pen.
LEE: Gimme a pencil then!
AUSTIN: I don't have a pencil.

LEE: (*to phone*) Just a second, operator. (*to* AUSTIN) Yer a writer and ya' don't have a pen or a pencil!

AUSTIN: I'm not a writer. You're a writer.
LEE: I'm on the phone here! Get me a pen or a pencil.
AUSTIN: I gotta' watch the toast.
LEE: (*to phone*) Hang on a second, operator.

(LEE *lets the phone drop then starts pulling all the drawers in the kitchen out on the floor and dumping the contents, searching for a pencil,* AUSTIN *watches him casually*)

LEE: (*crashing through drawers, throwing contents around kitchen*) This is the last time I try to live with people, boy! I can't believe it. Here I am! Here I am again in a desperate situation! This would never happen out on the desert. I would never be in this kinda' situation out on the desert. Isn't there a pen or a pencil in this house! Who lives in this house anyway!

AUSTIN: Our mother.

LEE: How come she don't have a pen or a pencil! She's a social person isn't she? Doesn't she have to make shopping lists? She's gotta' have a pencil. (*finds a pencil*) Aaha! (*he rushes back to phone, picks up receiver*) All right operator. Operator? Hey! Operator! Goddamnit!

(LEE *rips the phone off the wall and throws it down, goes back to chair and falls into it, drinks, long pause*)

AUSTIN: She hung up?

LEE: Yeah, she hung up. I knew she was gonna' hang up. I could hear it in her voice.

(LEE *starts going through his slips of paper again*)

AUSTIN: Well, you're probably better off staying here with me anyway. I'll take care of you.

LEE: I don't need takin' care of! Not by you anyway.

AUSTIN: Toast is almost ready.

(AUSTIN *starts buttering all the toast as it pops up*)

LEE: I don't want any toast!

(*long pause*)

AUSTIN: You gotta' eat something. Can't just drink. How long have we been drinking, anyway?

LEE: (*looking through slips of paper*) Maybe it was Fresno. What's the area code for Fresno? How could I have lost that number! She was beautiful.

(*pause*)

AUSTIN: Why don't you just forget about that, Lee. Forget about the woman.

LEE: She had green eyes. You know what green eyes do to me?

AUSTIN: I know but you're not gonna' get it on with her now anyway. It's dawn already. She's in Bakersfield for Christ's sake.

(*long pause,* LEE *considers the situation*)

LEE: Yeah. (*looks at windows*) It's dawn?

AUSTIN: Let's just have some toast and—

LEE: What is this bullshit with the toast anyway! You make it sound like salvation or something. I don't want any goddamn toast! How many times I gotta' tell ya'! (LEE *gets up, crosses upstage to windows in alcove, looks out,* AUSTIN *butters toast*)

AUSTIN: Well it is like salvation sort of. I mean the smell. I love the smell of toast. And the sun's coming up. It makes me feel like anything's possible. Ya' know?

LEE: (*back to* AUSTIN, *facing windows upstage*) So go to church why don't ya'.

AUSTIN: Like a beginning. I love beginnings.

LEE: Oh yeah. I've always been kinda' partial to endings myself.

AUSTIN: What if I come with you, Lee?

LEE: (*pause as* LEE *turns toward* AUSTIN) What?

AUSTIN: What if I come with you out to the desert?

LEE: Are you kiddin'?

AUSTIN: No. I'd just like to see what it's like.

LEE: You wouldn't last a day out there pal.

AUSTIN: That's what you said about the toasters. You said I couldn't steal a toaster either.

LEE: A toaster's got nothin' to do with the desert.

AUSTIN: I could make it, Lee. I'm not that helpless. I can cook.

LEE: Cook?

AUSTIN: I can.

LEE: So what! You can cook. Toast.

AUSTIN: I can make fires. I know how to get fresh water from condensation.

(AUSTIN *stacks buttered toast up in a tall stack on plate*)

(LEE *slams table*)

LEE: It's not somethin' you learn out of a Boy Scout handbook!

AUSTIN: Well how do you learn it then! How're you supposed to learn it! (*pause*)

LEE: Ya' just learn it, that's all. Ya' learn it 'cause ya' have to learn it. You don't *have* to learn it.

AUSTIN: You could teach me.

LEE: (*stands*) What're you, crazy or somethin'? You went to college. Here, you are down here, rollin' in bucks. Floatin' up and down in elevators. And you wanna' learn how to live on the desert!

AUSTIN: I do, Lee. I really do. There's nothin' down here for me. There never was. When we were kids here it was different. There was a life here then. But now— I keep comin' down here thinkin' it's the fifties or somethin'. I keep finding myself getting off the freeway at familiar landmarks that turn out to be unfamiliar. On the way to appointments. Wandering down streets I thought I recognized that turn out to be replicas of streets I remember. Streets I misremember. Streets I can't tell if I lived on or saw in a postcard. Fields that don't even exist anymore.

LEE: There's no point cryin' about that now.

AUSTIN: There's nothin' real down here, Lee! Least of all me!

LEE: Well I can't save you from that!

AUSTIN: You can let me come with you.

LEE: No dice, pal.

AUSTIN: You could let me come with you, Lee!

LEE: Hey, do you actually think I chose to live out in the middle a' nowhere? Do ya'? Ya' think it's some kinda' philosophical decision I took or somethin'? I'm livin' out there 'cause I can't make it here! And yer bitchin' to me about all yer success!

AUSTIN: I'd cash it all in in a second. That's the truth.

LEE: (*pause, shakes his head*) I can't believe this.

AUSTIN: Let me go with you.

LEE: Stop sayin' that will ya'! Yer worse than a dog.

(AUSTIN *offers out the plate of neatly stacked toast to* LEE)

AUSTIN: You want some toast?

(LEE *suddenly explodes and knocks the plate out of* AUSTIN'S *hand, toast goes flying, long frozen moment where it appears* LEE *might go all the way this time when* AUSTIN *breaks it by slowly lowering himself to his knees and begins gathering the scattered toast from the floor and stacking it back on the plate,* LEE *begins to circle* AUSTIN *in a slow, predatory way, crushing pieces of toast in his wake, no words for a while,* AUSTIN *keeps gathering toast, even the crushed pieces*)

LEE: Tell ya' what I'll do, little brother. I might just consider makin' you a deal. Little trade. (AUSTIN *continues gathering toast as* LEE *circles him through this*) You write me up this screenplay thing just like I tell ya'. I mean you can use all yer usual tricks and stuff. Yer fancy language. Yer artistic hocus pocus. But ya' gotta' write everything like I say. Every move. Every time they run outa' gas, they run outa' gas. Every time they wanna' jump on a horse, they do just that. If they wanna' stay in Texas, by God they'll stay in Texas! (*Keeps circling*) And you finish the whole thing up for me. Top to bottom. And you put my name on it. And I own all the rights. And every dime goes in my pocket. You do that and I'll sure enough take ya' with me to the desert. (LEE *stops, pause, looks down at* AUSTIN) How's that sound?

(*pause as* AUSTIN *stands slowly holding plate of demolished toast, their faces are very close, pause*)

AUSTIN: It's a deal.

(LEE *stares straight into* AUSTIN'S *eyes, then he slowly takes a piece of toast off the plate, raises it to his mouth and takes a huge crushing bite never taking his eyes off* AUSTIN'S, *as* LEE *crunches into the toast the lights black out*)

Scene 9

Mid-day. No sound, blazing heat, the stage is ravaged; bottles, toasters, smashed typewriter, ripped out telephone, etc. All the debris from previous scene is now starkly visible in intense yellow light, the effect should be like a desert junkyard at high noon, the coolness of the preceding scenes is totally obliterated. AUSTIN *is seated at table in alcove, shirt open, pouring with sweat, hunched over a writing notebook, scribbling notes desperately with a ballpoint pen.* LEE *with no shirt, beer in hand, sweat pouring down his chest, is walking a slow circle around the table, picking his way through the objects, sometimes kicking them aside.*

LEE: (*as he walks*) All right, read it back to me. Read it back to me!

AUSTIN: (*scribbling at top speed*) Just a second.

LEE: Come on, come on! Just read what ya' got.

AUSTIN: I can't keep up! It's not the same as if I had a typewriter.

LEE: Just read what we got so far. Forget about the rest.

AUSTIN: All right. Let's see—okay—(*wipes sweat from his face, reads as* LEE *circles*) Luke says uh—

LEE: Luke?

AUSTIN: Yeah.

LEE: His name's Luke? All right, all right—we can change the names later. What's he say? Come on, come on.

AUSTIN: He says uh—(*reading*) "I told ya' you were a fool to follow me in here. I know this prairie like the back a' my hand."

LEE: No, no, no! That's not what I said. I never said that.

AUSTIN: That's what I wrote.

LEE: It's not what I said. I never said "like the back a' my hand." That's stupid. That's one a' those—whadya' call it? Whadya' call that?

AUSTIN: What?

LEE: Whadya' call it when somethin's been said a thousand times before. Whadya' call that?

AUSTIN: Um—a cliché?

LEE: Yeah. That's right. Cliché. That's what that is. A cliché. "The back a' my hand." That's stupid.

AUSTIN: That's what you said.

LEE: I never said that! And even if I did, that's where yer supposed to come in. That's where yer supposed to change it to somethin' better.

AUSTIN: Well how am I supposed to do that and write down what you say at the same time?

LEE: Ya' just do, that's all! You hear a stupid line you change it. That's yer job.

AUSTIN: All right. (*makes more notes*)

LEE: What're you changin' it to?

AUSTIN: I'm not changing it. I'm just trying to catch up.

LEE: Well change it! We gotta' change that, we can't leave that in there like that. ". . . the back a' my hand." That's dumb.

AUSTIN: (*stops writing, sits back*) All right.

LEE: (*pacing*) So what'll we change it to?

AUSTIN: Um—How 'bout—"I'm on intimate terms with this prairie."

LEE: (*to himself considering line as he walks*) "I'm on intimate terms with this prairie." Intimate terms, intimate terms. Intimate—that means like uh—sexual right?

AUSTIN: Well—yeah—or—

LEE: He's on sexual terms with the prairie? How dya' figure that?

AUSTIN: Well it doesn't necessarily have to mean sexual.

LEE: What's it mean then?

AUSTIN: It means uh—close—personal—

LEE: All right. How's it sound? Put it into the uh—the line there. Read it back. Let's see how it sounds. (*to himself*) "Intimate terms."

AUSTIN: (*scribbles in notebook*) Okay. It'd go something like this: (*reads*) "I told ya' you were a fool to follow me in here. I'm on intimate terms with this prairie."

LEE: That's good. I like that. That's real good.

AUSTIN: You do?

LEE: Yeah. Don't you?

AUSTIN: Sure.

LEE: Sounds original now. "Intimate terms." That's good. Okay. Now we're cookin! That has a real ring to it.

(AUSTIN *makes more notes,* LEE *walks around, pours beer on his arms and rubs it over his chest feeling good about the new progress, as he does this* MOM *enters unobtrusively down left with her luggage, she stops and stares at the scene still holding luggage as the two men continue, unaware of her presence,* AUSTIN *absorbed in his writing,* LEE *cooling himself off with beer*)

LEE: (*continues*) "He's on intimate terms with this prairie." Sounds real mysterious and kinda' threatening at the same time.

AUSTIN: (*writing rapidly*) Good.

LEE: Now—(LEE *turns and suddenly sees* MOM, *he stares at her for a while, she stares back,* AUSTIN *keeps writing feverishly, not noticing,* LEE *walks slowly over to* MOM *and takes a closer look, long pause*)

LEE: Mom?

(AUSTIN *looks up suddenly from his writing, sees* MOM, *stands quickly, long pause,* MOM *surveys the damage*)

AUSTIN: Mom. What're you doing back?

MOM: I'm back.

LEE: Here, lemme take those for ya.

(LEE *sets beer on counter then takes both her bags but doesn't know where to set them down in the sea of junk so he just keeps holding them*)

AUSTIN: I wasn't expecting you back so soon. I thought uh—How was Alaska?

MOM: Fine.

LEE: See any igloos?

MOM: No. Just glaciers.

AUSTIN: Cold huh?

MOM: What?

AUSTIN: It must've been cold up there?

MOM: Not really.

LEE: Musta' been colder than this here. I mean we're havin' a real scorcher here.

MOM: Oh? (*she looks at damage*)

LEE: Yeah. Must be in the hundreds.

AUSTIN: You wanna' take your coat off, Mom?

MOM: No. (*pause, she surveys space*) What happened in here?

AUSTIN: Oh um—Me and Lee were just sort of celebrating and uh—

MOM: Celebrating?

AUSTIN: Yeah. Uh—Lee sold a screenplay. A story, I mean.

MOM: Lee did?

AUSTIN: Yeah.

MOM: Not you?

AUSTIN: No. Him.

MOM: (*to* LEE) You sold a screenplay?

LEE: Yeah. That's right. We're just sorta' finishing it up right now. That's what we're doing here.

AUSTIN: Me and Lee are going out to the desert to live.

MOM: You and Lee?

AUSTIN: Yeah. I'm taking off with Lee.

MOM: (*she looks back and forth at each of them, pause*) You gonna go live with your father?

AUSTIN: No. We're going to a different desert Mom.

MOM: I see. Well, you'll probably wind up on the same desert sooner or later. What're all these toasters doing here?

AUSTIN: Well—wc had kind of a contest.

MOM: Contest?

LEE: Yeah.

AUSTIN: Lee won.

MOM: Did you win a lot of money, Lee?

LEE: Well not yet. It's comin' in any day now.

MOM: (*to* LEE) What happened to your shirt?

LEE: Oh. I was sweatin' like a pig and I took it off.

(AUSTIN *grabs* LEE'*s shirt off the table and tosses it to him,* LEE *sets down suitcases and puts his shirt on*)

MOM: Well it's one hell of a mess in here isn't it?

AUSTIN: Yeah, I'll clean it up for you, Mom. I just didn't know you were coming back so soon.

MOM: I didn't either.

AUSTIN: What happened?

MOM: Nothing. I just started missing all my plants.

(*she notices dead plants*)

AUSTIN: Oh.

MOM: Oh, they're all dead aren't they. (*she crosses toward them, examines them closely*) You didn't get a chance to water I guess.

AUSTIN: I was doing it and then Lee came and—

LEE: Yeah I just distracted him a whole lot here, Mom. It's not his fault.

(*pause, as* MOM *stares at plants*)

MOM: Oh well, one less thing to take care of I guess. (*turns toward brothers*) Oh, that reminds me—You boys will probably never guess who's in town. Try and guess.

(*long pause, brothers stare at her*)

AUSTIN: Whadya' mean, Mom?

MOM: Take a guess. Somebody very important has come to town. I read it, coming down on the Greyhound.

LEE: Somebody very important?

MOM: See if you can guess. You'll never guess.

AUSTIN: Mom—we're trying to uh—(*points to writing pad*)

MOM: Picasso. (*pause*) Picasso's in town. Isn't that incredible? Right now. (*pause*)

AUSTIN: Picasso's dead, Mom.

MOM: No, he's not dead. He's visiting the museum. I read it on the bus. We have to go down there and see him.

AUSTIN: Mom—

MOM: This is the chance of a lifetime. Can you imagine? We could all go down and meet him. All three of us.

LEE: Uh—I don't think I'm really up fer meetin' anybody right now. I'm uh—What's his name?

MOM: Picasso! Picasso! You've never heard of Picasso? Austin, you've heard of Picasso.

AUSTIN: Mom, we're not going to have time.

MOM: It won't take long. We'll just hop in the car and go down there. An opportunity like this doesn't come along every day.

AUSTIN: We're gonna' be leavin' here, Mom!

(*pause*)

MOM: Oh.

LEE: Yeah.

(*pause*)

MOM: You're both leaving?

LEE: (*looks at* AUSTIN) Well we were thinkin' about that before but now I—

AUSTIN: No, we are! We're both leaving. We've got it all planned.

MOM: (*to* AUSTIN) Well you can't leave. You have a family.

AUSTIN: I'm leaving. I'm getting out of here.

LEE: (*to* MOM) I don't really think Austin's cut out for the desert do you?

MOM: No. He's not.

AUSTIN: I'm going with you, Lee!

MOM: He's too thin.

LEE: Yeah, he'd just burn up out there.

AUSTIN: (*to* LEE) We just gotta' finish this screenplay and then we're gonna' take off. That's the plan. That's what you said. Come on, let's get back to work, Lee.

LEE: I can't work under these conditions here. It's too hot.

AUSTIN: Then we'll do it on the desert.

LEE: Don't be tellin' me what we're gonna do!

MOM: Don't shout in the house.

LEE: We're just gonna' have to postpone the whole deal.

AUSTIN: I can't postpone it! It's gone past postponing! I'm doing everything you said. I'm writing down exactly what you tell me.

LEE: Yeah, but you were right all along see. It is a dumb story. "Two lamebrains chasin' each other across Texas." That's what you said, right?

AUSTIN: I never said that.

(LEE *sneers in* AUSTIN'S *face then turns to* MOM)

LEE: I'm gonna' just borrow some a' your antiques, Mom. You don't mind do ya'? Just a few plates and things. Silverware.

(LEE *starts going through all the cupboards in kitchen pulling out plates and stacking them on counter as* MOM *and* AUSTIN *watch*)

MOM: You don't have any utensils on the desert?

LEE: Nah, I'm fresh out.

AUSTIN: (*to* LEE) What're you doing?

MOM: Well some of those are very old. Bone China.

LEE: I'm tired of eatin' outa' my bare hands, ya' know. It's not civilized.

AUSTIN: (*to* LEE) What're you doing? We made a deal!

MOM: Couldn't you borrow the plastic ones instead? I have plenty of plastic ones.

LEE: (*as he stacks plates*) It's not the same. Plastic's not the same at all. What I need is somethin' authentic. Somethin' to keep me in touch. It's easy to get outa' touch out there. Don't worry I'll get em' back to ya'.

(AUSTIN *rushes up to* LEE, *grabs him by shoulders*)

AUSTIN: You can't just drop the whole thing, Lee!

(LEE *turns, pushes* AUSTIN *in the chest knocking him backwards into the alcove,* MOM *watches numbly,* LEE *returns to collecting the plates, silverware, etc.*)

MOM: You boys shouldn't fight in the house. Go outside and fight.

LEE: I'm not fightin'. I'm leavin'.

MOM: There's been enough damage done already.

LEE. (*his back to* AUSTIN *and* MOM, *stacking dishes on counter*) I'm clearin' outa' here once and for all. All this town does is drive a man insane. Look what it's done to Austin there. I'm not lettin' that happen to me. Sell myself down the river. No sir. I'd rather be a hundred miles from nowhere than let that happen to me.

(*during this* AUSTIN *has picked up the ripped-out phone from the floor and wrapped the cord tightly around both his hands, he lunges at* LEE *whose back is still to him, wraps the cord around* LEE'S *neck, plants a foot in* LEE'S *back and pulls back on the cord, tightening it,* LEE *chokes desperately, can't speak and can't reach* AUSTIN *with his arms,* AUSTIN *keeps applying pressure on* LEE'S *back with his foot, bending him into the sink,* MOM *watches*)

AUSTIN: (*tightening cord*) You're not goin' anywhere! You're not takin' anything with you. You're not takin' my car! You're not takin' the dishes! You're not takin' anything! You're stayin' right here!

MOM: You'll have to stop fighting in the house. There's plenty of room outside to fight. You've got the whole outdoors to fight in.

(LEE *tries to tear himself away, he crashes across the stage like an enraged bull dragging* AUSTIN *with him, he snorts and bellows but* AUSTIN *hangs on and manages to keep clear of* LEE'S *attempts to grab him, they crash into the table, to the floor,* LEE *is face down thrashing wildly and choking,* AUSTIN *pulls cord tighter, stands with one foot planted on* LEE'S *back and the cord stretched taut*)

AUSTIN: (*holding cord*) Gimme back my keys, Lee! Take the keys out! Take 'em out!

(LEE *desperately tries to dig in his pockets, searching for the car keys,* MOM *moves closer*)

MOM: (*calmly to* AUSTIN) You're not killing him are you?

AUSTIN: I don't know. I don't know if I'm killing him. I'm stopping him. That's all. I'm just stopping him.

(LEE *thrashes but* AUSTIN *is relentless*)

MOM: You oughta' let him breathe a little bit.

AUSTIN: Throw the keys out, Lee!

(LEE *finally gets keys out and throws them on floor but out of* AUSTIN'S *reach,* AUSTIN *keeps pressure on cord, pulling* LEE'S *neck back,* LEE *gets one hand to the cord but can't relieve the pressure*)

Reach me those keys would ya', Mom.

MOM: (*not moving*) Why are you doing this to him?

AUSTIN: Reach me the keys!

MOM: Not until you stop choking him.

AUSTIN: I can't stop choking him! He'll kill me if I stop choking him!

MOM: He won't kill you. He's your brother.

AUSTIN: Just get me the keys would ya'!

(*pause.* MOM *picks keys up off floor, hands them to* AUSTIN)

AUSTIN: (*to* MOM) Thanks.

MOM: Will you let him go now?

AUSTIN: I don't know. He's not gonna' let me get outa' here.

MOM: Well you can't kill him.

AUSTIN: I can kill him! I can easily kill him. Right now. Right here. All I gotta' do is just tighten up. See? (*he tightens cord,* LEE *thrashes wildly,* AUSTIN *releases pressure a little, maintaining control*) Ya' see that?

MOM: That's a savage thing to do.

AUSTIN: Yeah well don't tell me I can't kill him because I can. I can just twist. I can just keep twisting. (AUSTIN *twists the cord tighter,* LEE *weakens, his breathing changes to a short rasp*)

MOM: Austin!

(AUSTIN *relieves pressure,* LEE *breathes easier but* AUSTIN *keeps him under control*)

AUSTIN: (*eyes on* LEE, *holding cord*) I'm goin' to the desert. There's nothing stopping me. I'm going by myself to the desert.

(MOM *moving toward her luggage*)

MOM: Well, I'm going to go check into a motel. I can't stand this anymore.

AUSTIN: Don't go yet!

(MOM *pauses*)

MOM: I can't stay here. This is worse than being homeless.

AUSTIN: I'll get everything fixed up for you, Mom. I promise. Just stay for a while.

MOM: (*picking up luggage*) You're going to the desert.

AUSTIN: Just wait!

(LEE *thrashes,* AUSTIN *subdues him,* MOM *watches holding luggage, pause*)

MOM: It was the worst feeling being up there. In Alaska. Staring out a window. I never felt so desperate before. That's why when I saw that article on Picasso I thought—

AUSTIN: Stay here, Mom. This is where you live.

(*she looks around the stage*)

MOM: I don't recognize it at all.

(*she exits with luggage,* AUSTIN *makes a move toward her but* LEE *starts to struggle and* AUSTIN *subdues him again with cord, pause*)

AUSTIN: (*holding cord*) Lee? I'll make ya' a deal. You let me get outa' here. Just let me get to my car. All right, Lee? Gimme a little headstart and I'll turn you loose. Just gimme a little headstart. All right?

(LEE *makes no response,* AUSTIN *slowly releases tension cord, still nothing from* LEE)

AUSTIN: Lee?

(LEE *is motionless,* AUSTIN *very slowly begins to stand, still keeping a tenuous hold on the cord and his eyes riveted to* LEE *for any sign of movement,* AUSTIN *slowly drops the cord and stands, he stares down at* LEE *who appears to be dead*)

AUSTIN: (*whispers*) Lee?

(*pause,* AUSTIN *considers, looks toward exit, back to* LEE, *then makes a small movement as if to leave. Instantly* LEE *is on his feet and moves toward exit, blocking* AUSTIN'S *escape. They square off to each other, keeping a distance between them. Pause, a single coyote heard in distance, lights fade softly into moonlight, the figures of the brothers now appear to be caught in a vast desert-like landscape, they are very still but watchful for the next move, lights go slowly to black as the after-image of the brothers pulses in the dark, coyote fades*)

1980

Poetry

A. R. AMMONS
(1926–)

A. R. Ammons was born and raised on a farm near Whiteville, North Carolina. He attended local schools, graduating from Whiteville High School in 1943. After brief employment in a Wilmington, North Carolina, shipyard, he served in the navy in the South Pacific. The G.I. Bill brought him to Wake Forest College, where his chief interest was science. Married in 1949, the year of his graduation, he served briefly as principal of an elementary school on Cape Hatteras, North Carolina, but before long enrolled in graduate school at the University of California, Berkeley, where he came under the influence of the poet Josephine Miles. He left Berkeley without taking a degree, and for the next dozen years worked for a manufacturer of laboratory glass in southern New Jersey. His first book, *Ommateum* (1955), appeared during this period, attracting little notice. A reading at Cornell University in 1963 led to a teaching appointment the next year. He has taught there since, in 1973 becoming Goldwin Smith Professor of English.

Ammons bases his poetry in careful observation. *Ommateum,* a title derived from the term for the compound eye of an insect, suggests both scientific precision and fragmented vision, qualities appearing frequently in his work. His science, however, is not that of the laboratory, but of the gifted amateur in the field, like Thoreau a walker, a sitter, and a recorder. Natural landscapes are prominent even among the titles of his books, as in *Expressions of Sea Level* (1964), *Corsons Inlet* (1965), *Northfield Poems* (1966), *Uplands* (1970), *The Snow Poems* (1977), *A Coast of Trees* (1981), and *Lake Effect Country* (1983), and the individual poems turn frequently to fields, seashores, plains, mountains, and forests, and to the sun and wind everywhere experienced. From farm to windswept dunes, to tidewater marshes, to mountain summits and rocky gorges, the "I" that speaks the poems gives witness to the places Ammons has lived and thoughtfully explored.

In form, his poems are open, rooted in common speech, experimental in rhythm and line length. Some are short, precise, imagistic. Others are small fables of a man who talks to the wind, the sea, or a tree, and sometimes receives, and sometimes does not receive, an answer. The long poem *Tape for the Turn of the Year* (1965) was an experiment in short lines forced by the mechanical restriction of typing on a roll of adding machine tape. A more recent long poem, *Sphere: The Form of a Motion* (1974), expresses a weariness with "good poems, all those little rondures / splendidly brought off, painted gourds on a shelf."

Emersonian in his search for the all in the particular, Ammons is also reminiscent of Williams, with his "No ideas / but in things," and Stevens, with his concern for harmony and order. Focusing upon moment-by-moment perceptions, he implies and sometimes states a concern with eternal oneness. In a poem with the transcendental title "One: Many," he has written of our inadequacy as humans to understand and control experience: "only the book of laws * * * , / founded on freedom of each event to occur as itself, / lasts into the inevitable balances events will take."

The Selected Poems: 1951–1977, 1977, supplements *Collected Poems: 1951–1971,* 1972. *Selected Longer Poems* appeared in 1980. Individual titles in addition to those given above are *Briefings: Poems Small and Easy,* 1971; *Diversifications,* 1975; and *Worldly Hopes,* 1982.

Studies include Alan Holder, *A. R. Ammons,* 1978; and Harold Bloom, ed., *A. R. Ammons,* 1986.

Apologia pro Vita Sua[1]

I started picking up the stones
throwing them into one place
and by sunrise I was going far away
for the large ones
always turning to see never lost
the cairn's height
lengthening my radial reach:

the sun watched with deep concentration
and the heap through the hours grew
and became by nightfall
distinguishable from all the miles around
of slate and sand:

during the night the wind falling
turned earthward its lofty freedom and speed
and the sharp blistering sound muffled
toward dawn and the blanket was
drawn up over a breathless face:

even so you can see in full dawn
the ground there lifts
a foreign thing desertless in origin.

1955

Hardweed Path Going

Every evening, down into the hardweed
going,
the slop bucket heavy, held-out, wire handle
freezing in the hand, put it down a minute, the jerky
smooth unspilling levelness of the knees,
meditation of a bucket rim,
lest the wheat meal,
floating on clear greasewater, spill,
down the grown-up path:

don't forget to slop the hogs,
feed the chickens,
water the mule,

1. A defense of one's way of life, alluding to the great spiritual autobiography *Apologia pro Vita Sua* (1864) by John Henry Cardinal Newman (1801–1890), Newman's response to the charge that he was insufficiently interested in truth.

cut the kindling,
build the fire,
call up the cow:

supper is over, it's starting to get
dark early,
better get the scraps together, mix a little meal in,
nothing but swill.

The dead-purple woods hover on the west.
I know those woods.
Under the tall, ceiling-solid pines, beyond the edge of
field and brush, where the wild myrtle grows,
I let my jo-reet loose.
A jo-reet is a bird. Nine weeks of summer he
sat on the well bench in a screened box,
a stick inside to walk on,
"jo-reet," he said, "jo-reet."
and I
would come up to the well and draw the bucket down
deep into the cold place where red and white marbled
clay oozed the purest water, water celebrated
throughout the county:
"Grits all gone?"
"jo-reet."
Throw a dipper of cold water on him. Reddish-black
flutter.
"reet, reet, reet!"

Better turn him loose before
cold weather comes on.
Doom caving in
inside
any pleasure, pure
attachment
of love.

Beyond the wild myrtle away from cats I turned him loose
and his eye asked me what to do, where to go;
he hopped around, scratched a little, but looked up at me.
Don't look at me. Winter is coming.
Disappear in the bushes. I'm tired of you and will
be alone hereafter. I will go dry in my well.
I will turn still.
Go south. Grits is not available in any natural form.
Look under leaves, try mushy logs, the floors of pinywoods.
South into the dominion of bugs.

They're good woods.
But lay me out if a mourning dove far off in the dusky pines
starts.

Down the hardweed path going,
leaning, balancing, away from the bucket, to

Sparkle, my favorite hog, sparse, fine black hair,
grunted while feeding if rubbed,
scratched against the hair, or if talked to gently:
got the bottom of the slop bucket:
"Sparkle . . .
You hungry?
Hungry, girly?"
blowing, bubbling in the trough.

Waiting for the first freeze:
"Think it's going to freeze tonight?" say the neighbors,
the neighbors, going by.

Hog-killing.

Oh, Sparkle, when the axe tomorrow morning falls
and the rush is made to open your throat,
I will sing, watching dry-eyed as a man, sing my
love for you in the tender feedings.

She's nothing but a hog, boy.

Bleed out, Sparkle, the moon-chilled bleaches
of your body hanging upside-down
hardening through the mind and night of the first freeze.

1964

The Wide Land

Having split up the chaparral
blasting my sight
the wind said
You know I'm
the result of
forces beyond my control
I don't hold it against you
I said
It's all right I understand

Those pressure bowls and cones
the wind said
are giants in their continental gaits
I know I said I know
they're blind giants
Actually the wind said I'm
if anything beneficial
resolving extremes
filling up lows with highs
No I said you don't have
to explain
It's just the way things are
Blind in the wide land I

turned and risked my feet
to loose stones and sudden

alterations of height

1965

Corsons Inlet[2]

I went for a walk over the dunes again this morning
to the sea,
then turned right along
the surf
rounded a naked headland
and returned

along the inlet shore:

it was muggy sunny, the wind from the sea steady and high,
crisp in the running sand,
some breakthroughs of sun
but after a bit

continuous overcast:

the walk liberating, I was released from forms,
from the perpendiculars,
straight lines, blocks, boxes, binds
of thought
into the hues, shadings, rises, flowing bends and blends
of sight:

I allow myself eddies of meaning:
yield to a direction of significance
running
like a stream through the geography of my work:
you can find
in my sayings
swerves of action
like the inlet's cutting edge:
there are dunes of motion,
organizations of grass, white sandy paths of remembrance
in the overall wandering of mirroring mind:
but Overall is beyond me: is the sum of these events
I cannot draw, the ledger I cannot keep, the accounting
beyond the account:

in nature there are few sharp lines: there are areas of
primrose
more or less dispersed;
disorderly orders of bayberry; between the rows
of dunes,
irregular swamps of reeds,

2. In southern New Jersey.

though not reeds alone, but grass, bayberry, yarrow, all . . .
predominantly reeds:

I have reached no conclusions, have erected no boundaries,
shutting out and shutting in, separating inside
        from outside: I have
        drawn no lines:
        as

manifold events of sand
change the dune's shape that will not be the same shape
tomorrow,

so I am willing to go along, to accept
the becoming
thought, to stake off no beginnings or ends, establish
        no walls:

by transitions the land falls from grassy dunes to creek
to undercreek: but there are no lines, though
      change in that transition is clear
      as any sharpness: but "sharpness" spread out,
allowed to occur over a wider range
than mental lines can keep:

the moon was full last night: today, low tide was low:
black shoals of mussels exposed to the risk
of air
and, earlier, of sun,
waved in and out with the waterline, waterline inexact,
caught always in the event of change:
      a young mottled gull stood free on the shoals
      and ate
to vomiting: another gull, squawking possession, cracked a crab,
picked out the entrails, swallowed the soft-shelled legs, a ruddy
turnstone running in to snatch leftover bits:

risk is full: every living thing in
siege: the demand is life, to keep life: the small
white blacklegged egret, how beautiful, quietly stalks and spears
          the shallows, darts to shore
                      to stab—what? I couldn't
      see against the black mudflats—a frightened
      fiddler crab?

          the news to my left over the dunes and
reeds and bayberry clumps was
          fall: thousands of tree swallows
          gathering for flight:
          an order held
          in constant change: a congregation
rich with entropy: nevertheless, separable, noticeable
        as one event,
                not chaos: preparations for
flight from winter,

cheet, cheet, cheet, cheet, wings rifling the green clumps,
beaks
at the bayberries
   a perception full of wind, flight, curve,
   sound:
   the possibility of rule as the sum of rulelessness:
the "field" of action
with moving, incalculable center:

in the smaller view, order tight with shape:
blue tiny flowers on a leafless weed: carapace of crab:
snail shell:
      pulsations of order
      in the bellies of minnows: orders swallowed,
broken down, transferred through membranes
to strengthen larger orders: but in the large view, no
lines or changeless shapes: the working in and out, together
      and against, of millions of events: this,
            so that I make
            no form of
            formlessness:

orders as summaries, as outcomes of actions override
or in some way result, not predictably (seeing me gain
the top of a dune,
the swallows
could take flight—some other fields of bayberry
      could enter fall
      berryless) and there is serenity:

      no arranged terror: no forcing of image, plan,
or thought:
no propaganda, no humbling of reality to precept:

terror pervades but is not arranged, all possibilities
of escape open: no route shut, except in
   the sudden loss of all routes:

      I see narrow orders, limited tightness, but will
not run to that easy victory:
      still around the looser, wider forces work:
      I will try
    to fasten into order enlarging grasps of disorder, widening
scope, but enjoying the freedom that
Scope eludes my grasp, that there is no finality of vision,
that I have perceived nothing completely,
      that tomorrow a new walk is a new walk.

1965

Reflective

I found a
weed
that had a

mirror in it
and that
mirror

looked in at
a mirror
in

me that
had a
weed in it

1966

Cascadilla Falls[3]

I went down by Cascadilla
Falls this
evening, the
stream below the falls,
and picked up a
handsized stone
kidney-shaped, testicular, and

thought all its motions into it,
the 800 mph earth spin,
the 190-million-mile yearly
displacement around the sun,
the overriding
grand
haul

of the galaxy with the 30,000
mph of where
the sun's going:
thought all the interweaving
motions
into myself: dropped

the stone to dead rest:
the stream from other motions
broke
rushing over it:
shelterless,
I turned

to the sky and stood still:
oh
I do
not know where I am going
that I can live my life
by this single creek.

1970

3. At the edge of the Cornell University campus.

Poetics

I look for the way
things will turn
out spiralling from a center,
the shape
things will take to come forth in

so that the birch tree white
touched black at branches
will stand out
wind-glittering
totally its apparent self:

I look for the forms
things want to come as

from what black wells of possibility,
how a thing will
unfold:

not the shape on paper—though
that, too—but the
uninterfering means on paper:

not so much looking for the shape
as being available
to any shape that may be
summoning itself
through me
from the self not mine but ours.

1971

Bonus

The hemlocks slumped
already as if bewailing
the branch-loading

shales of ice, the rain
changes and a snow
sifty as fog

begins to fall, brightening
the ice's bruise-glimmer
with white holdings:

the hemlocks, muffled,
deepen to the grim
taking of a further beauty on.

1975

Easter Morning

I have a life that did not become,
that turned aside and stopped,
astonished:
I hold it in me like a pregnancy or
as on my lap a child
not to grow or grow old but dwell on

it is to his grave I most
frequently return and return
to ask what is wrong, what was
wrong, to see it all by
the light of a different necessity
but the grave will not heal
and the child,
stirring, must share my grave
with me, an old man having
gotten by on what was left

when I go back to my home country in these
fresh far-away days, it's convenient to visit
everybody, aunts and uncles, those who used to say,
look how he's shooting up, and the
trinket aunts who always had a little
something in their pocketbooks, cinnamon bark
or a penny or nickel, and uncles who
were the rumored fathers of cousins
who whispered of them as of great, if
troubled, presences, and school
teachers, just about everybody older
(and some younger) collected in one place
waiting, particularly, but not for
me, mother and father there, too, and others
close, close as burrowing
under skin, all in the graveyard
assembled, done for, the world they
used to wield, have trouble and joy
in, gone

the child in me that could not become
was not ready for others to go,
to go on into change, blessings and
horrors, but stands there by the road
where the mishap occurred, crying out for
help, come and fix this or we
can't get by, but the great ones who
were to return, they could not or did
not hear and went on in a flurry and
now, I say in the graveyard, here
lies the flurry, now it can't come
back with help or helpful asides, now
we all buy the bitter
incompletions, pick up the knots of

horror, silently raving, and go on
crashing into empty ends not
completions, not rondures[4] the fullness
has come into and spent itself from

I stand on the stump
of a child, whether myself
or my little brother who died, and
yell as far as I can, I cannot leave this place, for
for me it is the dearest and the worst,
it is life nearest to life which is
life lost: it is my place where
I must stand and fail,
calling attention with tears
to the branches not lofting
boughs into space, to the barren
air that holds the world that was my world

though the incompletions
(& completions) burn out
standing in the flash high-burn
momentary structure of ash, still it
is a picture-book, letter-perfect
Easter morning: I have been for a
walk: the wind is tranquil: the brook
works without flashing in an abundant
tranquility: the birds are lively with
voice: I saw something I had
never seen before: two great birds,
maybe eagles, blackwinged, whitenecked
and -headed, came from the south oaring
the great wings steadily; they went
directly over me, high up, and kept on
due north: but then one bird,
the one behind, veered a little to the
left and the other bird kept on seeming
not to notice for a minute: the first
began to circle as if looking for
something, coasting, resting its wings
on the down side of some of the circles:
the other bird came back and they both
circled, looking perhaps for a draft;
they turned a few more times, possibly
rising—at least, clearly resting—
then flew on falling into distance till
they broke across the local bush and
trees: it was a sight of bountiful
majesty and integrity: the having
patterns and routes, breaking
from them to explore other patterns or
better ways to routes, and then the
return: a dance sacred as the sap in

4. Circles or spheres.

the trees, permanent in its descriptions
as the ripples round the brook's
ripplestone: fresh as this particular
flood of burn breaking across us now
from the sun.

1981

Neighbors

How little I have really cared about nature: I always
thought the woods idyllic and let it go at that: but,
look, one tree, the near pine, cracked off in high wind,

dry rot at the ground, and coming down sheared every
branch off one side of the sweetgum: one tree, trying
to come up under another, has only one bough in light:

an ice storm some years ago broke the tops off several
trees that now splinter into sprouts: one sweetgum,
bent over bow-like to the ground, has given up its

top and let an arrow of itself rise midway: ivy has
made Ann Pollard's pine an ivy tree: I can't regain
the lost idyllic at all, but the woods are here with us.

1981

Extrication

I tangled with
the world to
let it go
but couldn't free

it: so I made
words
to wrestle in my
stead and went

off silent to
the quick flow
of brooks, the
slow flow of stone

1982

I Could Not Be Here At All

Momentous and trivial, I
walk along the lake cliff
and look north where the lake
curls to a wisp through the hills

and say as if to the lake,
I'm here, too,
and to the winter storm centered
gnarl-black over the west bank,

I nearly call out, it's me, I'm here:
the wind-fined
snow nicks
my face, mists my lashes

and the sun, not dwindling me, goes
on down behind the storm and the reed
withes' wind doesn't whistle, brother! brother!
and no person comes.

1983

ROBERT BLY
(1926–)

Robert Bly was born in Madison, Minnesota, a town of fewer than 3,000 people located near the South Dakota border almost 150 miles from Minneapolis. After 1958 he edited a journal and managed a press there, both titled after the appropriate decade as *The Fifties, The Sixties,* and so on. He came back to Madison after spending two years in the navy in World War II and earning degrees from Harvard (A.B., 1950) and the University of Iowa (M.A., 1956). A recipient of many awards, he has lived recently in another small town in Minnesota, Moose Lake.

Unlike many poets of his time, he has earned his living not by teaching, but through translations and poetry readings, supplemented by stipends from fellowships and writing grants. Particularly interested in such South American and European poets as Juan Ramón Jiménez, Pablo Neruda, Antonio Machado, and Georg Trakl, he has made his magazine a showcase for their talents and has been much influenced by them in his own writing. Poetry in English, he is convinced, has for the most part gone the wrong way in modern times. Blake he admires, and Whitman, but too many other poets he sees as hampered by a respect for technique that prevents them from breaking through to the "corridors to the unconscious" where the vital symbolic roots of poetry are to be found. His poems are often composed of freely associated and elemental images; starkly simple evocations of earth, air, fire, and water tumble rapidly upon one another in the "leaping about the psyche" he admires in the ancients and perceives in too few moderns. Not only a dedicated poet, but a long-time political activist, he writes poems that range from the lyrical to the apocalyptic.

Selected Poems appeared in 1986. Other volumes of verse are *Silence in the Snowy Fields,* 1962; *The Light Around the Body,* 1967; *The Morning Glory,* 1969; *Shadow Mothers: Poetry,* 1970; *The Teeth-Mother Naked at Last,* 1971; *Sleepers Joining Hands,* 1972; *Point Reyes Poems,* 1974; *This Body Is Made of Camphor and Gopherwood,* 1977; *This Tree Will Be Here for a Thousand Years,* 1979; *The Man in the Black Coat Turns,* 1981; and *Loving a Woman in Two Worlds,* 1985. Among works edited is *The Winged Life: The Poetic Voice of Henry David Thoreau* (1987). Bly's many translations include *Twenty Poems of Pablo Neruda* (with James Wright), 1968; *Juan Ramón Jiménez,* 1969; *Basho,* 1974; and *The Kabir Book,* 1977.

A study is Richard P. Sugg, *Robert Bly,* 1986.

Driving Toward the Lac Qui Parle River

I

I am driving; it is dusk; Minnesota.
The stubble field catches the last growth of sun.
The soybeans are breathing on all sides.
Old men are sitting before their houses on carseats
In the small towns. I am happy,
The moon rising above the turkey sheds.

II

The small world of the car
Plunges through the deep fields of the night,
On the road from Willmar to Milan.
This solitude covered with iron
Moves through the fields of night
Penetrated by the noise of crickets.

III

Nearly to Milan, suddenly a small bridge,
And water kneeling in the moonlight.
In small towns the houses are built right on the ground;
The lamplight falls on all fours in the grass.
When I reach the river, the full moon covers it;
A few people are talking low in a boat.

1962

Driving to Town Late to Mail a Letter

It is a cold and snowy night. The main street is deserted.
The only things moving are swirls of snow.
As I lift the mailbox door, I feel its cold iron.
There is a privacy I love in this snowy night.
Driving around, I will waste more time.

1962

Watering the Horse

How strange to think of giving up all ambition!
Suddenly I see with such clear eyes
The white flake of snow
That has just fallen in the horse's mane!

1962

In a Train

There has been a light snow.
Dark car tracks move in out of the darkness.
I stare at the train window marked with soft dust.
I have awakened at Missoula, Montana, utterly happy.

1962

The Executive's Death

Merchants have multiplied more than the stars of heaven.
Half the population are like the long grasshoppers
That sleep in the bushes in the cool of the day:
The sound of their wings is heard at noon, muffled, near the earth.
The crane handler dies, the taxi driver dies, slumped over
In his taxi. Meanwhile, high in the air, executives
Walk on cool floors, and suddenly fall:
Dying, they dream they are lost in a snowstorm in mountains,
On which they crashed, carried at night by great machines.
As he lies on the wintry slope, cut off and dying,
A pine stump talks to him of Goethe and Jesus.
Commuters arrive in Hartford at dusk like moles
Or hares flying from a fire behind them,
And the dusk in Hartford is full of their sighs;
Their trains come through the air like a dark music,
Like the sound of horns, the sound of thousands of small wings.

1967

Looking at New-Fallen Snow from a Train

Snow has covered the next line of tracks,
And filled the empty cupboards in the milkweed pods;
It has stretched out on the branches of weeds,
And softened the frost-hills, and the barbed-wire rolls
Left leaning against a fencepost—
It has drifted onto the window ledges high in the peaks of barns.

A man throws back his head, gasps
And dies. His ankles twitch, his hands open and close,
And the fragment of time that he has eaten is exhaled from his pale mouth to nourish the snow.
A salesman falls, striking his head on the edge of the counter.

Snow has filled out the peaks on the tops of rotted fence posts.
It has walked down to meet the slough water,
And fills all the steps of the ladder leaning against the eaves.
It rests on the doorsills of collapsing children's houses,
And on transformer boxes held from the ground forever in the center of cornfields.

A man lies down to sleep.
Hawks and crows gather around his bed.
Grass shoots up between the hawks' toes.
Each blade of grass is a voice.
The sword by his side breaks into flame.

1967

Fishing on a Lake at Night

Someone has left a light on at the boathouse
to guide the fishermen back after dark.
The light makes no sound as it comes.
It flies over the waves like a bird with one wing.
Its path is a boatful of the dead, trying to return to life
over the broken waters.

And the light
simply comes, bearing no gifts,
as if the camels had arrived without the Wise Men.
It is steady, holding us to our old mountain home.
Now as we watch the moon rises over the popple forest.
It too arrives without fuss,
it goes between the boards around the pulp-cutter's house—
the same fence we pass through by opening the gate.

1979

Snowbanks North of the House

Those great sweeps of snow that stop suddenly six feet from the house . . .
Thoughts that go so far.
The boy gets out of high school and reads no more books;
the son stops calling home.
The mother puts down her rolling pin and makes no more bread.
And the wife looks at her husband one night at a party, and loves him no more.
The energy leaves the wine, and the minister falls leaving the church.
It will not come closer—
the one inside moves back, and the hands touch nothing, and are safe.

The father grieves for his son, and will not leave the room where the coffin stands.
He turns away from his wife, and she sleeps alone.

And the sea lifts and falls all night, the moon goes on through the unattached heavens
alone.
The toe of the shoe pivots
in the dust . . .
And the man in the black coat turns, and goes back down the hill.
No one knows why he came, or why he turned away, and did not climb the hill.

1981

JAMES MERRILL
(1926–   )

James Merrill was born in New York City, the son of Charles Edward Merrill, a founder of the investment firm now known as Merrill Lynch, Pierce, Fenner & Smith. Frequently in his poems he turns to the world of his childhood, attempting to understand it in the light of adult experience. His father, he tells us in "The Broken Home," had descended from his role as aviator in World War I "in cloud banks well above Wall Street and wife" to an earthbound existence where "time was money" and "the point was to win." Married "each thirteenth year," Charles Merrill was even at seventy "warming up for a green bride." In another poem, "Lost in Translation," Merrill describes a boy's loneliness in a "summer without parents," filling in his time and feeding his imagination completing an exotic, expensive jigsaw puzzle with the aid of his French governess. When he was sixteen, Merrill's first musings were privately published in *Jim's Book: A Collection of Poems and Short Stories* (1942). After preparatory education at Lawrenceville School, he attended Amherst College, left briefly for service in the army in 1944–1945, and graduated in 1947. Meanwhile, he had published in Athens a book of verse, *The Black Swan* (1946). Recognition began with the publication in New York of *First Poems* (1951) and his reputation has grown slowly through a number of succeeding volumes. For years he has resided in Stonington, Connecticut, but has traveled frequently, spending much time in a second home in Greece.

Merrill is technically proficient, fond of iambic pentameters and of balanced phrases and formal restrictions. His content is often narrative in movement, lyric in intensity, and rooted deeply in autobiography. A concern with the relationship of past and present draws him frequently to images of mirrors and reflections in water and to discussions of the occult transcendence of time. Learned, allusive, and densely evocative, he is sometimes reminiscent of Pound or Eliot, or of Robert Lowell among poets more nearly his contemporaries. He has also much of the wit of Auden, with whom he obviously feels a deep kinship. Recently he has undertaken to bring all these qualities together in long poems constructed around conversations with spirits reached through a Ouija board. "The Book of Ephraim" in *Divine Comedies* (1976) is composed of twenty-six segments organized alphabetically by the letters that begin them. *Mirabell: Books of Number* (1978) is a lengthy sequel, a tour of a spirit world inhabited by Auden, Einstein, the poet's mother, and other characters angelic and demonic, who discourse on God, the creation, poetry, and the ancient peoples of legend and fantasy fiction who inhabited earth before mankind. In *Scripts for the Pageant* (1980), Merrill explores at still greater length the same materials and methods. These Ouija board books are brought together, with a coda, "The Higher Keys," in *The Changing Light at Sandover* (1982).

Merrill's play *The Immortal Husband* (1956) and two novels, *The Seraglio* (1957) and *The (Diblos) Notebook* (1965), express interests similar to those of his verse. Earlier books of verse display the fruits of his travel, urbanity, and wit in the polished forms of a poet who has always been concerned with shaping and recording his experiences in order to understand them. "The point," he has said, "is to feel and keep the eyes open. Then what you feel is expressed, is mimed back at you by the scene * * *. We don't *know* what we feel until we see it distanced by this kind of transformation."

From the First Nine: Poems 1946–1976, 1983, is a selection from the books of the years listed. Individual titles, besides those named above, include *Short Stories,* 1954; *The Country of a Thousand Years of Peace and Other Poems,* 1959, revised 1970; *Selected Poems,* 1961; *Water Street,* 1962; *The Thousand and Second Night,* 1963; *Violent Pastoral,* privately printed, 1965; *Nights and Days: Poems,* 1966; *The Fire Screen: Poems,* 1969; *Two Poems,* 1972; *Braving the Elements,* 1972; *The Yellow Pages,* 1974; and *Late Settings,* 1985. *Recitative: Prose by James Merrill* (1986) was edited by J. D. McClatchy.

Critical assessments include an essay by David Kalstone in *Five Temperaments,* 1977; David Lehman and Charles Berger, eds., *James Merrill: Essays in Criticism,* 1983; and Judith Moffett, *James Merrill: An Introduction to the Poetry,* 1983.

The Octopus

There are many monsters that a glassen surface
Restrains. And none more sinister
Than vision asleep in the eye's tight translucence.
Rarely it seeks now to unloose
Its diamonds. Having divined how drab a prison
The purest mortal tissue is,
Rarely it wakes. Unless, coaxed out by lusters
Extraordinary, like the octopus
From the gloom of its tank half-swimming half-drifting
Toward anything fair, a handkerchief
Or child's face dreaming near the glass, the writher
Advances in a godlike wreath
Of its own wrath. Chilled by such fragile reeling
A hundred blows of a boot-heel
Shall not quell, the dreamer wakes and hungers.
Percussive pulses, drum or gong,
Build in his skull their loud entrancement,
Volutions of a Hindu dance.
His hands move clumsily in the first conventional
Gestures of assent.
He is willing to undergo the volition and fervor
Of many fleshlike arms, observe
These in their holiness of indirection
Destroy, adore, evolve, reject—
Till on glass rigid with his own seizure
At length the sucking jewels freeze.

1959

A Timepiece

Of a pendulum's mildness, with her feet up
My sister lay expecting her third child.
Over the hammock's crescent spilled
Her flushed face, grazing clover and buttercup.

Her legs were troubling her, a vein had burst.
Even so, among partial fullnesses she lay
Of pecked damson,[1] of daughters at play
Who in the shadow of the house rehearsed

1. A small, dark purple plum.

Her gait, her gesture, unnatural to them,
But they would master it soon enough, grown tall
Trusting that out of themselves came all
That full grace, while she out of whom these came

Shall have thrust fullness from her, like a death.
Already, seeing the little girls listless
She righted herself in a new awkwardness.
It was not *her* life she was heavy with.

Let us each have some milk, my sister smiled
Meaning to muffle with the taste
Of unbuilt bone a striking in her breast,
For soon by what it tells the clock is stilled.

1959

Charles on Fire

Another evening we sprawled about discussing
Appearances. And it was the consensus
That while uncommon physical good looks
Continued to launch one, as before, in life
(Among its vaporous eddies and false calms),
Still, as one of us said into his beard,
"Without your intellectual and spiritual
Values, man, you are sunk." No one but squared
The shoulders of his own unloveliness.
Long-suffering Charles, having cooked and served the meal,
Now brought out little tumblers finely etched
He filled with amber liquor and then passed.
"Say," said the same young man, "in Paris, France,
They do it this way"—bounding to his feet
And touching a lit match to our host's full glass.
A blue flame, gentle, beautiful, came, went
Above the surface. In a hush that fell
We heard the vessel crack. The contents drained
As who should step down from a crystal coach.
Steward of spirits, Charles's glistening hand
All at once gloved itself in eeriness.
The moment passed. He made two quick sweeps and
Was flesh again. "It couldn't matter less,"
He said, but with a shocked, unconscious glance
Into the mirror. Finding nothing changed,
He filled a fresh glass and sank down among us.

1966

The Broken Home

Crossing the street,
I saw the parents and the child
At their window, gleaming like fruit
With evening's mild gold leaf.

In a room on the floor below,
Sunless, cooler—a brimming
Saucer of wax, marbly and dim—
I have lit what's left of my life.

I have thrown out yesterday's milk
And opened a book of maxims.
The flame quickens. The word stirs.

Tell me, tongue of fire,
That you and I are as real
At least as the people upstairs.

My father, who had flown in World War I,
Might have continued to invest his life
In cloud banks well above Wall Street and wife.
But the race was run below, and the point was to win.

Too late now, I make out in his blue gaze
(Through the smoked glass of being thirty-six)
The soul eclipsed by twin black pupils, sex
And business; time was money in those days.

Each thirteenth year he married. When he died
There were already several chilled wives
In sable orbit—rings, cars, permanent waves.
We'd felt him warming up for a green bride.

He could afford it. He was "in his prime"
At three score ten. But money was not time.

When my parents were younger this was a popular act:
A veiled woman would leap from an electric, wine-dark car
To the steps of no matter what—the Senate or the Ritz Bar—
And bodily, at newsreel speed, attack

No matter whom—Al Smith or José Maria Sert
Or Clemenceau[2]—veins standing out on her throat
As she yelled *War mongerer! Pig! Give us the vote!*,
And would have to be hauled away in her hobble skirt.

What had the man done? Oh, made history.
Her business (he had implied) was giving birth,
Tending the house, mending the socks.

Always that same old story—
Father Time and Mother Earth,
A marriage on the rocks.

One afternoon, red, satyr-thighed
Michael, the Irish setter, head

2. Alfred E. Smith (1873–1944), governor of New York and candidate for president in 1928; José María Sert (1876–1945), Spanish mural painter who decorated the lobby of the Waldorf-Astoria Hotel in 1930; Georges Clemenceau (1841–1929), twice premier of France and opponent of Woodrow Wilson at the Paris Peace Conference.

Passionately lowered, led
The child I was to a shut door. Inside,

Blinds beat sun from the bed.
The green-gold room throbbed like a bruise.
Under a sheet, clad in taboos
Lay whom we sought, her hair undone, outspread,

And of a blackness found, if ever now, in old
Engravings where the acid bit.
I must have needed to touch it
Or the whiteness—was she dead?
Her eyes flew open, startled strange and cold.
The dog slumped to the floor. She reached for me. I fled.

Tonight they have stepped out onto the gravel.
The party is over. It's the fall
Of 1931. They love each other still.

She: Charlie, I can't stand the pace.
He: Come on, honey—why, you'll bury us all!

A lead soldier guards my windowsill:
Khaki rifle, uniform, and face.
Something in me grows heavy, silvery, pliable.

How intensely people used to feel!
Like metal poured at the close of a proletarian novel,
Refined and glowing from the crucible,
I see those two hearts, I'm afraid,
Still. Cool here in the graveyard of good and evil,
They are even so to be honored and obeyed.

. . . Obeyed, at least, inversely. Thus
I rarely buy a newspaper, or vote.
To do so, I have learned, is to invite
The tread of a stone guest[3] within my house.

Shooting this rusted bolt, though, against him,
I trust I am no less time's child than some
Who on the heath impersonate Poor Tom[4]
Or on the barricades risk life and limb.

Nor do I try to keep a garden, only
An avocado in a glass of water—
Roots pallid, gemmed with air. And later,

When the small gilt leaves have grown
Fleshy and green, I let them die, yes, yes,
And start another. I am earth's no less.

A child, a red dog roam the corridors,
Still, of the broken home. No sound. The brilliant

3. A stone statue wreaks revenge upon Don Juan in versions of the old story by Molière and Mozart.

4. Edgar, in Shakespeare's *King Lear,* disowned by his father, pretends madness and calls himself "Poor Tom."

Rag runners halt before wide-open doors.
My old room! Its wallpaper—cream, medallioned
With pink and brown—brings back the first nightmares,
Long summer colds, and Emma, sepia-faced,
Perspiring over broth carried upstairs
Aswim with golden fats I could not taste.

The real house became a boarding-school.
Under the ballroom ceiling's allegory
Someone at last may actually be allowed
To learn something; or, from my window, cool
With the unstiflement of the entire story,
Watch a red setter stretch and sink in cloud.

1966

Days of 1964

Houses, an embassy, the hospital,
Our neighborhood sun-cured if trembling still
In pools of the night's rain . . .
Across the street that led to the center of town
A steep hill kept one company part way
Or could be climbed in twenty minutes
For some literally breathtaking views,
Framed by umbrella pines, of city and sea.
Underfoot, cyclamen, autumn crocus grew
Spangled as with fine sweat among the relics
Of good times had by all. If not Olympus,
An out-of-earshot, year-round hillside revel.

I brought home flowers from my climbs.
Kyria Kleo who cleaned for us
Put them in water, sighing *Virgin, Virgin.*
Her legs hurt. She wore brown, was fat, past fifty,
And looked like a Palmyra matron
Copied in lard and horsehair. How she loved
You, me, loved us all, the bird, the cat!
I think now she *was* love. She sighed and glistened
All day with it, or pain, or both.
(We did not notably communicate.)
She lived nearby with her pious mother
And wastrel son. She called me her real son.

I paid her generously, I dare say.
Love makes one generous. Look at us. We'd known
Each other so briefly that instead of sleeping
We lay whole nights, open, in the lamplight,
And gazed, or traded stories.

One hour comes back—you gasping in my arms
With love, or laughter, or both,
I having just remembered and told you
What I'd looked up to see on my way downtown at noon:
Poor old Kleo, her aching legs,
Trudging into the pines. I called,

Called three times before she turned.
Above a tight, skyblue sweater, her face
Was painted. Yes. Her face was painted
Clown-white, white of the moon by daylight,
Lidded with pearl, mouth a poinsettia leaf,
Eat me, pay me—the erotic mask
Worn the world over by illusion
To weddings of itself and simple need.

Startled mute, we had stared—was love illusion?—
And gone our ways. Next, I was crossing a square
In which a moveable outdoor market's
Vegetables, chickens, pottery kept materializing
Through a dream-press of hagglers each at heart
Leery lest he be taken, plucked,
The bird, the flower of that November mildness,
Self lost up soft clay paths, or found, foothold,
Where the bud throbs awake
The better to be nipped, self on its knees in mud—
Here I stopped cold, for both our sakes;

And calmer on my way home bought us fruit.

Forgive me if you read this. (And may Kyria Kleo,
Should someone ever put it into Greek
And read it aloud to her, forgive me, too.)
I had gone so long without loving,
I hardly knew what I was thinking.

Where I hid my face, your touch, quick, merciful,
Blindfolded me. A god breathed from my lips.
If that was illusion, I wanted it to last long;
To dwell, for its daily pittance, with us there,
Cleaning and watering, sighing with love or pain.
I hoped it would climb when it needed to the heights

Even of degradation, as I for one
Seemed, those days, to be always climbing
Into a world of wild
Flowers, feasting, tears—or was I falling, legs
Buckling, heights, depths,
Into a pool of each night's rain?
But you were everywhere beside me, masked,
As who was not, in laughter, pain, and love.

1966

Matinees

For David Kalstone

A gray maidservant lets me in
To Mrs Livingston's box. It's already begun!
The box is full of grownups. She sits me down
Beside her. Meanwhile a ravishing din

Swells from below—Scene One
Of *Das Rheingold.* The entire proscenium
Is covered with a rippling azure scrim.
The three sopranos dart hither and yon

On invisible strings. Cold lights
Cling to bare arms, fair tresses. Flat
And natural aglitter like paillettes
Upon the great green sonorous depths float

Until with pulsing wealth the house is filled,
No one believing, everybody thrilled.

Lives of the Great Composers make it sound
Too much like cooking: "Sore beset,
He put his heart's blood into that quintet . . ."
So let us try the figure turned around

As in some Lives of Obscure Listeners:
"The strains of Cimarosa and Mozart
Flowed through his veins, and fed his solitary heart.
Long beyond adolescence [One infers

Your elimination, sweet Champagne
Drunk between acts!] the aria's remote
Control surviving his worst interval,

Tissue of sound and tissue of the brain
Would coalesce, and what the Masters wrote
Itself compose his features sharp and small."

Hilariously Dr Scherer took the guise
Of a bland smoothshaven Alberich whose ageold
Plan had been to fill my tooth with gold.
Another whiff of laughing gas,

And the understanding was implicit
That we must guard each other, this gold and I,
Against amalgamation by
The elemental pit.

Vague as to what dentist and tooth "stood for,"
One patient dreamer gathered something more.
A voice said in the speech of birds,

"My father having tampered with your mouth,
From now on, metal, music, myth
Will seem to taint its words."

We love the good, said Plato? He was wrong.
We love as well the wicked and the weak.
Flesh hugs its shaved plush. Twenty-four-hour-long
Galas fill the hulk of the Comique.

Flesh knows by now what dishes to avoid,
Tries not to brood on bomb or heart attack.
Anatomy is destiny, said Freud.
Soul is the brilliant hypochondriac.

Soul will cough blood and sing, and softer sing,[5]
Drink poison, breathe her joyous last, a waltz
Rubato from his arms who sobs and stays

Behind, death after death, who fairly melts
Watching her turn from him, restored, to fling
Kisses into the furnace roaring praise.

The fallen cake, the risen price of meat,
Staircase run ten times up and down like scales
(Greek proverb: He who has no brain has feet)—
One's household opera never palls or fails.

The pipes' aubade. Recitatives.—Come back!
—I'm out of pills!—We'd love to!—What?—*Nothing,*
Let me be!—No, no, I'll drink it black . . .
The neighbors' chorus. The quick darkening

In which a prostrate figure must inquire
With every earmark of its being meant
Why God in Heaven harries him/her so.

The love scene (often cut). The potion. The tableau:
Sleepers folded in a magic fire,
Tongues flickering up from humdrum incident.

When Jan Kiepura sang His Handsomeness
Of Mantua those high airs light as lust
Attuned one's bare throat to the dagger-thrust.
Living for them would have been death no less.

Or Lehmann's Marschallin!—heartbreak so shrewd,
So ostrich-plumed, one ached to disengage
Oneself from a last love, at center stage,
To the beloved's dazzled gratitude.

What havoc certain Saturday afternoons
Wrought upon a bright young person's morals
I now leave to the public to condemn.

The point thereafter was to arrange for one's
Own chills and fever, passions and betrayals,
Chiefly in order to make song of them.

You and I, caro, seldom
Risk the real thing any more.
It's all too silly or too solemn.
Enough to know the score

5. An echo of Yeats's "Sailing to Byzantium," 1. 11: "Soul clap its hands and sing, and louder sing."

From records or transcription
For our four hands. Old beauties, some
In advanced stages of decomposition,

Float up through the sustaining
Pedal's black and fluid medium.
Days like today

Even recur (wind whistling themes
From *Lulu,* and sun shining
On the rough Sound) when it seems
Kinder to remember than to play.

Dear Mrs Livingston,
I want to say that I am still in a daze
From yesterday afternoon.
I will treasure the experience always—

My very first Grand Opera! It was very
Thoughtful of you to invite
Me and am so sorry
That I was late, and for my coughing fit.

I play my record of the Overture
Over and over. I pretend
I am still sitting in the theatre.

I also wrote a poem which my Mother
Says I should copy out and send.
Ever gratefully, Your little friend . . .

1969

Yánnina[6]

For Stephen Yenser

There lay the peninsula stretching far into the dark gray water, with its mosque, its cypress tufts and fortress walls; there was the city stretching far and wide along the water's edge; there was the fatal island, the closing scene of the history of the once all-powerful Ali.

—EDWARD LEAR[7]

Somnambulists along the promenade
Have set up booths, their dreams:
Carpets, jewelry, kitchenware, halvah,[8] shoes.
From a loudspeaker passionate lament
Mingles with the penny Jungle's roars and screams.
Tonight in the magician's tent
Next door a woman will be sawed in two,
But right now she's asleep, as who is not, as who . . .

6. Yánnina, also spelled Ioánnina or Jannina, is a city in northwestern Greece, located on a lake of the same name.
7. Edward Lear (1812–1888), English humorist and artist, visited Yánnina in 1848. He recorded his visit in *Journals of a Landscape Painter in Greece and Albania* (1851).
8. A Turkish confection of honey mixed with a paste of ground sesame seeds and nuts.

An old Turk at the water's edge has laid
His weapons and himself down, sleeps
Undisturbed since, oh, 1913.[9]
Nothing will surprise him should he wake,
Only how tall, how green the grass has grown
There by the dusty carpet of the lake
Sun beats, then sleepwalks down a vine-festooned arcade,
Giving himself away in golden heaps.

And in the dark gray water sleeps
One who said no to Ali.[1] Kiosks all over town
Sell that postcard, "Kyra Frossíni's Drown,"[2]
Showing her, eyeballs white as mothballs, trussed
Beneath the bulging moon of Ali's lust.
A devil (turban and moustache and sword)
Chucks the pious matron overboard—
Wait—Heaven help us—SPLASH!

The torch smokes on the prow. Too late.
(A picture deeply felt, if in technique slapdash.)
Wherefore the Lion of Epirus,[3] feared
By Greek and Turk alike, tore his black beard
When to barred casements rose the song
Broken from bubbles rising all night long:
"A ton of sugar pour, oh pour into the lake
To sweeten it for poor, for poor Frossíni's sake."[4]

Awake? Her story's aftertaste
Varies according to the listener.
Friend, it's bitter coffee you prefer?
Brandy for me, and with a fine
White sandy bottom. Not among those braced
By action taken without comment, neat,
Here's how! Grounds of our footnote infiltrate the treat,
Mud-vile to your lips, crystal-sweet to mine.

Twilight at last. Enter the populace.
One little public garden must retrace
Long after school its childish X,
Two paths that cross and cross. The hollyhock, the rose,
Zinnia and marigold hear themselves named
And blush for form's sake, unashamed
Chorus out of *Ignoramus Rex:*[5]
"What shall the heart learn, that already knows

9. In 1913 Yánnina became part of Greece, after centuries of Turkish domination.

1. Ali Pasha (1744?–1822), military governor of Yánnina, who at the height of his power controlled with his sons southern Albania, western Macedonia, and most of Greece. He was famous for the violence, sensuality, and luxury of his court.

2. "The Drowning of Lady Frossíni." The Christian wife of a Greek merchant, she was arrested by Ali and a few days later drowned in the lake by his men.

3. Ali Pasha. Epirus, an ancient Greek state, was in Ali's time a large province.

4. " 'Time was kind to the reputation of this woman who had been unfaithful to her husband, vain, and grasping. She came to be regarded as a Christian martyr and even as an early heroine in the struggle for Greek independence. She has been celebrated in legend, in poetry, in popular songs and historical fiction, and surrounded with the glamour which so often attaches to women whose love affairs have been of an intense nature and have involved men of political or historical importance.' William Plomer, *The Diamond of Jannina*" [Merrill's note].

5. With a nod toward *Oedipus Rex,* "Ignoramus the King."

Its place by water, and its time by sun?"
Mother wit fills the stately whispering sails
Of girls someone will board and marry. Who?
Look at those radiant young males.
Their morning-glory nature neon blue
Wilts here on the provincial vine. Where did it lead,
The race, the radiance? To oblivion
Dissembled by a sac of sparse black seed.

Now under trees men with rush baskets sell
Crayfish tiny and scarlet as the sins
In any fin-de-siècle[6] villanelle.[7]
Tables fill up. A shadow play begins.
Painted, translucent cut-outs fill the screen.
It glows. His children by a jumping bean
Karaghiozi[8] clobbers, baits the Turk,
Then all of them sing, dance, tell stories, go berzerk.

Tomorrow we shall cross the lake to see
The cottage tumbling down, where soldiers killed
Ali. Two rugless rooms. Cushions. Vitrines[9]
In which, to this day, silks and bracelets swim.
Above, a painting hangs. It's him,
Ali. The end is near, he's sleeping between scenes
In a dark lady's lap. Vassilikí.[1]
The mood is calm, the brushwork skilled

By contrast with Frossíni's mass-produced
Unsophisticated piece of goods.
The candle trembles in the watching god's
Hand—almost a love-death, höchste Lust![2]
Her drained, compliant features haunt
The waters there was never cause to drown her in.
Your grimiest ragamuffin comes to want
Two loves, two versions of the Feminine:

One virginal and tense, brief as a bubble,
One flesh and bone—gone up no less in smoke
Where giant spits revolving try their rusty treble,
Sheep's eyes pop, and death-wish ravens croak.
Remember, the Romantic's in full feather.
Byron has visited. He likes
The luxe, and overlooks the heads on pikes;
Finds Ali "Very kind . . . indeed, a father . . ."[3]

6. End of the century; generally, as here, the nineteenth century.
7. A complicated verse form in six stanzas, repeating whole lines in a precisely prescribed pattern throughout.
8. A stock character, similar to Punch.
9. Glass showcases.
1. Taken into Ali's harem at twelve, and later married to him, Vassilikí was a great favorite and was allowed to remain a Christian.
2. German, "the highest pleasure," the last words of Isolde's "Liebestod" in Wagner's *Tristan und Isolde.*
3. "Letter to his mother, November 12, 1809. Plomer observes: '. . . even allowing for Oriental effusiveness, it seems doubtful whether [Ali's] interest in Byron was exactly as paternal as he pretended, for a father does not give his son sweets twenty times a day and beg him to visit him at night. It is worth remarking that Ali was a judge of character and a connoisseur of beauty, whether male or female, and that the like of Byron, and Byron at twenty one, is not often seen' " [Merrill's note]. Byron recorded his visit not only in his letters, but in his enormously popular *Childe Harold's Pilgrimage* (1812).

Funny, that is how I think of Ali.
On the one hand, the power and the gory
Details, pigeon-blood rages and retali-
ations, gouts of fate that crust his story;
And on the other, charm, the whimsically
Meek brow, its motives all ab ulteriori,[4]
The flower-blue gaze twining to choke proportion,
Having made one more pretty face's fortune.

A dove with Parkinson's disease[5]
Selects *our* fortunes: TRAVEL AND GROW WISE
And A LOYAL FRIEND IS MORE THAN GOLD.
But, at the island monastery, eyes
Gouged long since to the gesso sockets will outstare
This or that old timer on his knees
Asking the candlelight for skill to hold
The figures flush against the screen's mild glare.

Ali, my father—both are dead.
In so many words, so many rhymes,
The brave old world sleeps. Are we what it dreams
And is a rude awakening overdue?
Not in Yánnina. To bed, to bed.
The Lion sets. The lights wink out along the lake.
Weeks later, in this study gone opaque,
They are relit. See through me. See me through.

For partings hurt although we dip the pain
Into a glowing well—the pen I mean.
Living alone won't make some inmost face to shine
Maned with light, ember and anodyne,
Deep in a desktop burnished to its grain.
That the last hour be learned again
By riper selves, couldn't you doff this green
Incorruptible, the might-have-been,

And arm in arm with me dare the magician's tent?
It's hung with asterisks. A glittering death
Is hefted, swung. The victim smiles consent.
To a sharp intake of breath she comes apart
(Done by mirrors? Just one woman? Two?
A fight starts—in the provinces, one feels,
There's never that much else to do)
Then to a general exhalation heals

Like anybody's life, bubble and smoke
In afterthought, whose elements converge,
Glory of windless mornings that the barge
(Two barges, one reflected, a quicksilver joke)
Kept scissoring and mending as it steered
The old man outward and away,

4. Remote or future, not immediately apparent.

5. A degenerative brain disorder, causing shaking and paralysis.

Amber mouthpiece of a narghilé[6]
Buried in his by then snow white beard.[7]

1976

Lost in Translation

For Richard Howard

> Diese Tage, die leer dir scheinen
> und wertlos für das All,
> haben Wurzeln zwischen den Steinen
> und trinken dort überall.[8]

A card table in the library stands ready
To receive the puzzle which keeps never coming.
Daylight shines in or lamplight down
Upon the tense oasis of green felt.
Full of unfulfillment, life goes on,
Mirage arisen from time's trickling sands
Or fallen piecemeal into place:
German lesson, picnic, see-saw, walk
With the collie who "did everything but talk"—
Sour windfalls of the orchard back of us.
A summer without parents in the puzzle,
Or should be. But the boy, day after day,
Writes in his Line-a-Day *No puzzle.*

He's in love, at least. His French Mademoiselle,
In real life a widow since Verdun,[9]
Is stout, plain, carrot-haired, devout.
She prays for him, as does a curé[1] in Alsace,
Sews costumes for his marionettes,
Helps him to keep behind the scene
Whose sidelit goosegirl, speaking with his voice,
Plays Guinevere as well as Gunmoll Jean.
Or else at bedtime in his tight embrace
Tells him her own French hopes, her German fears,
Her—but what more is there to tell?
Having known grief and hardship, Mademoiselle
Knows little more. Her languages. Her place.
Noon coffee. Mail. The watch that also waited
Pinned to her heart, poor gold, throws up its hands—
No puzzle! Steaming bitterness
Her sugars draw pops back into his mouth, translated:
"Patience, chéri. Geduld, mein Schatz."[2]
(Thus, reading Valéry the other evening
And seeming to recall a Rilke version of "Palme,"
That sunlit paradigm whereby the tree

6. A pipe constructed with a long tube to draw its smoke through a water chamber.
7. Ali Pasha is depicted in this pose in illustrations facing pages 64 and 81 in William Plomer, *The Diamond of Jannina,* New York, 1970.
8. Lines from a translation by Rainer Maria Rilke (1875–1926), Austrian poet, of *Palme,* by Paul Valéry (1871–1945), French poet. See ll. 32–33 below. "These days that seem totally empty and worthless have roots between the stones, and drinks found everywhere."
9. City in France, scene of a World War I battle in 1916.
1. French priest.
2. In French and then German: "Patience, my dear."

Taps a sweet wellspring of authority,
The hour came back. Patience dans l'azur.
Geduld im . . . Himmelblau?[3] Mademoiselle.)

Out of the blue, as promised, of a New York
Puzzle-rental shop the puzzle comes—
A superior one, containing a thousand hand-sawn,
Sandal-scented pieces. Many take
Shapes known already—the craftsman's repertoire
Nice in its limitation—from other puzzles:
Witch on broomstick, ostrich, hourglass,
Even (surely not just in retrospect)
An inchling, innocently branching palm.
These can be put aside, made stories of
While Mademoiselle spreads out the rest face-up,
Herself excited as a child; or questioned
Like incoherent faces in a crowd,
Each with its scrap of highly colored
Evidence the Law must piece together.
Sky-blue ostrich? Likely story.
Mauve of the witch's cloak white, severed fingers
Pluck? Detain her. The plot thickens
As all at once two pieces interlock.

Mademoiselle does borders—(Not so fast.
A London dusk, December last.
Chatter silenced in the library
This grown man reenters, wearing grey.
A medium. All except him have seen
Panel slid back, recess explored,
An object at once unique and common
Displayed, planted in a plain tole
Casket the subject now considers
Through shut eyes, saying in effect:
"Even as voices reach me vaguely
A dry saw-shriek drowns them out,
Some loud machinery—a lumber mill?
Far uphill in the fir forest
Trees tower, tense with shock,
Groaning and cracking as they crash groundward.
But hidden here is a freak fragment
Of a pattern complex in appearance only.
What it seems to show is superficial
Next to that long-term lamination
Of hazard and craft, the karma that has
Made it matter in the first place.
Plywood, Piece of a puzzle." Applause
Acknowledged by an opening of lids
Upon the thing itself. A sudden dread—
But to go back. All this lay years ahead.)

Mademoiselle does borders. Straight-edge pieces
Align themselves with earth or sky

3. Again, in French and German: "Patience in the blue sky."

In twos and threes, naive cosmogonists
Whose views clash. Nomad inlanders meanwhile
Begin to cluster where the totem
Of a certain vibrant egg-yolk yellow
Or pelt of what emerging animal
Acts on the straggler like a trumpet call
To form a more sophisticated unit.
By suppertime two ragged wooden clouds
Have formed. In one, a Sheik with beard
And flashing sword hilt (he is all but finished)
Steps forward on a tiger skin. A piece
Snaps shut, and fangs gnash out at us!
In the second cloud—they gaze from cloud to cloud
With marked if undecipherable feeling—
Most of a dark-eyed woman veiled in mauve
Is being helped down from her camel (kneeling)
By a small backward-looking slave or page-boy
(Her son, thinks Mademoiselle mistakenly)
Whose feet have not been found. But lucky finds
In the last minutes before bed
Anchor both factions to the scene's limits
And, by so doing, orient
Them eye to eye across the green abyss.
The yellow promises, oh bliss,
To be in time a sumptuous tent.

Puzzle begun I write in the day's space,
Then, while she bathes, peek at Mademoiselle's
Page to the curé: ". . . cette innocente mère,
Ce pauvre enfant, que deviendront-ils?"[4]
Her azure script is curlicued like pieces
Of the puzzle she will be telling him about.
(Fearful incuriosity of childhood!
"Tu as l'accent allemand,"[5] said Dominique.
Indeed. Mademoiselle was only French by marriage.
Child of an English mother, a remote
Descendant of the great explorer Speke,[6]
And Prussian father. No one knew. I heard it
Long afterwards from her nephew, a UN
Interpreter. His matter-of-fact account
Touched old strings. My poor Mademoiselle,
With 1939 about to shake
This world where "each was the enemy, each the friend"
To its foundations, kept, though signed in blood,
Her peace a shameful secret to the end.)
"Schlaf wohl, chéri."[7] Her kiss. Her thumb
Crossing my brow against the dreams to come.

This World that shifts like sand, its unforeseen
Consolidations and elate routine,
Whose Potentate had lacked a retinue?
Lo! it assembles on the shrinking Green.

4. This innocent mother, this poor child, what will become of them?
5. You have a German accent.
6. John Hanning Speke (1827–1864), English explorer of Africa.
7. Sleep well, dear.

Gunmetal-skinned or pale, all plumes and scars,
Of Vassalage the noblest avatars—
The very coffee-bearer in his vair[8]
Vest is a swart Highness, next to ours.

Kef[9] easing Boredom, and iced syrups, thirst,
In guessed-at glooms old wives who know the worst
Outsweat that virile fiction of the New:
"Insh'Allah, he will tire—" "—or kill her first!"

(Hardly a proper subject for the Home,
Work of—dear Richard, I shall let *you* comb
Archives and learned journals for his name—
A minor lion attending on Gérôme.[1])

While, thick as Thebes[2] whose presently complete
Gates close behind them, Houri and Afreet[3]
Both claim the Page. He wonders whom to serve,
And what his duties are, and where his feet,

And if we'll find, as some before us did,
That piece of Distance deep in which lies hid
Your tiny apex sugary with sun,
Eternal Triangle, Great Pyramid!

Then Sky alone is left, a hundred blue
Fragments in revolution, with no clue
To where a Niche will open. Quite a task,
Putting together Heaven, yet we do.

It's done. Here under the table all along
Were those missing feet. It's done.

The dog's tail thumping. Mademoiselle sketching
Costumes for a coming harem drama
To star the goosegirl. All too soon the swift
Dismantling. Lifted by two corners,
The puzzle hung together—and did not.
Irresistibly a populace
Unstitched of its attachments, rattled down.
Power went to pieces as the witch
Slithered easily from Virtue's gown.
The blue held out for time, but crumbled, too.
The city had long fallen, and the tent,
A separating sauce mousseline,
Been swept away. Remained the green
On which the grown-ups gambled. A green dusk.
First lightning bugs. Last glow of west
Green in the false eyes of (coincidence)
Our mangy tiger safe on his bared hearth.

8. Fur.
9. A narcotic made from hemp leaves.
1. Jean Léon Gérôme (1824–1904), French historical and genre painter.
2. City in ancient Egypt.
3. Figures in Muslim mythology, the first a virgin awarded those who attain paradise, the second an evil spirit.

Before the puzzle was boxed and readdressed
To the puzzle shop in the mid-Sixties,
Something tells me that one piece contrived
To stay in the boy's pocket. How do I know?
I know because so many later puzzles
Had missing pieces—Maggie Teyte's[4] high notes
Gone at the war's end, end of the vogue for collies,
A house torn down; and hadn't Mademoiselle
Kept back her pitiful bit of truth as well?
I've spent the last days, furthermore,
Ransacking Athens for that translation of "Palme."
Neither the Goethehaus nor the National Library
Seems able to unearth it. Yet I can't
Just be imagining. I've seen it. Know
How much of the sun-ripe original
Felicity Rilke made himself forego
(Who loved French words—verger, mûr, parfumer[5])
In order to render its underlying sense.
Know already in that tongue of his
What Pains, what monolithic Truths
Shadow stanza to stanza's symmetrical
Rhyme-rutted pavement. Know that ground plan left
Sublime and barren, where the warm Romance
Stone by stone faded, cooled; the fluted nouns
Made taller, lonelier than life
By leaf-carved capitals in the afterglow.
The owlet umlaut peeps and hoots
Above the open vowel. And after rain
A deep reverberation fills with stars.

Lost, is it, buried? One more missing piece?

But nothing's lost. Or else: all is translation
And every bit of us is lost in it
(Or found—I wander through the ruin of S
Now and then, wondering at the peacefulness)
And in that loss a self-effacing tree,
Color of context, imperceptibly
Rustling with its angel, turns the waste
To shade and fiber, milk and memory.

1976

Samos[6]

And still, at sea all night, we had a sense
Of sunrise, golden oil poured upon water,
Soothing its heave, letting the sleeper sense
What inborn, amniotic homing sense[7]

4. English soprano (1888–1976).
5. "Orchard, ripe, to perfume."
6. Samos is a Greek island in the Aegean Sea, east of Athens, near the coast of Turkey. Reprinted here is the first part of a three-part poem introducing the middle section, "&," in *Scripts for the Pageant* (1980). The text is from *The Changing Light at Sandover* (1982).
7. A sense engendered before birth, in the amnion, the membrane containing the amniotic fluid and embryo.

Was ferrying him—now through the dream-fire
In which (it has been felt) each human sense
Burns, now through ship's radar's cool sixth sense,
Or mere unerring starlight—to an island.
Here we were. The twins of Sea and Land,
Up and about for hours—hues, cries, scents—
Had placed at eye level a single light
Croissant: the harbor glazed with warm pink light.

Fire-wisps were weaving a string bag of light
For sea stones. Their astounding color sense!
Porphyry, alabaster, chrysolite
Translucences that go dead in daylight
Asked only the quick dip in holy water
For the saint of cell on cell to come alight—
Illuminated crystals thinking light,
Refracting it, the gray prismatic fire
Or yellow-gray of sea's dilute sapphire . . .
Wavelengths daily deeply score the leit-
Motifs[8] of Loom and Wheel upon this land.
To those who listen, it's the Promised Land.[9]

A little spin today? Dirt roads inland
Jounce and revolve in a nerve-jangling light,
Doing the ancient dances of the land
Where, gnarled as olive trees that shag the land
With silver, old men—their two-bladed sense
Of spendthrift poverty, the very land
Being, if not loaf, tomb—superbly land
Upright on the downbeat. We who water
The local wine, which "drinks itself" like water,
Clap for more, cry out to *be* this island
Licked all over by a white, salt fire,
Be noon's pulsing ember raked by fire,

Know nothing, now, but Earth, Air, Water, Fire![1]
For once out of the frying pan to land
Within their timeless, everlasting fire![2]
Blood's least red monocle, O magnifier
Of the great Eye that sees by its own light
More pictures in "the world's enchanted fire"
Than come and go in any shrewd crossfire
Upon the page, of syllable and sense,
We want unwilled excursions and ascents,
Crave the upward-rippling rungs of fire,
The outward-rippling rings (enough!) of water . . .
(Now some details—how else will this hold water?)

8. A leitmotif is a dominant theme or pattern in a musical or literary composition, here the pattern "of Loom and Wheel" (weaving and spinning) in a land-based economy.

9. Canaan, "the land wherein thou art a stranger," promised by God to Abraham and his descendants (Genesis xvii: 8).

1. The four elements of the ancients.

2. An allusion to the Pythagorean doctrine of transmigration of souls, holding that the soul must be born and reborn again in earthly shapes, continually striving toward the purification that results in union with the infinite.

Our room's three flights above the whitewashed water-
front where Pythagoras[3] was born. A fire
Escape of sky-blue iron leads down to water.
Yachts creak on mirror berths, and over water
Voices from Sweden or Somaliland
Tell how this or that one crossed the water
To Ephesus,[4] came back with toilet water
And a two kilo[5] box of Turkish delight
—Trifles. Yet they shine with such pure light
In memory, even they, that the eyes water.
As with the setting sun, or innocence,
Do things that fade especially make sense?

Samos. We keep trying to make sense
Of what we can. Not souls of the first water—
Although we've put on airs, and taken fire—
We shall be dust of quite another land
Before the seeds here planted come to light.

1980

FRANK O'HARA
(1926–1966)

Placed by his friend John Ashbery among artists of the 1950's and early 1960's who were "too hip for the squares and too square for the hips," Frank O'Hara occupied a place apart from the major movements of those years. The Black Mountain and Beat poets traveled from Majorca to North Carolina to California, publishing journals and manifestos and seeking to establish a new kind of verse in an environment they saw as dominated by an outmoded academic tradition. O'Hara settled in New York, pursued a successful career as an art critic and museum curator, and wrote original poems much admired after his death.

Born in Baltimore, Maryland, O'Hara was raised from infancy in Grafton, Massachusetts, where his father farmed and sold farm machinery. After graduation from St. John's High School in Worcester in 1944, he enlisted in the navy and served in the South Pacific before entering Harvard with other returning servicemen in 1946. In college, he soon forsook his earlier ambition to be a great pianist and became an English major. Graduating from Harvard in 1950, he earned an M.A. at the University of Michigan in 1951 before settling in New York, where he worked in a bookstore, wrote for *Art News,* and after a long association with the Museum of Modern Art became an associate curator in 1965. O'Hara's years in New York were also the years in which the city emerged as the art capital of the world, and he met, wrote

3. Founder (*c.* 582–*c.* 507 B.C.) of the Pythagorean school of philosophy, noted for teaching the transmigration of souls and also the theory that the true nature of things is found in numbers.
Observe the heavy use of numbers underlying the structure of this poem, as in the various forms of *canzoni* by Dante, whom Merrill much admires. Here, the sound of each of five key words (sense, water, fire, land, light) is repeated thirteen times at line ends in five stanzas and an envoy. Merrill's pattern, a more complicated form of the interweaving of words found in a sestina, was used by Dante in his *canzone* beginning *"Amor, tu vedi ben che questa donna"* ("Love, you see well that this lady"). Merrill's envoy (or *tornata*), however, differs slightly from Dante's.

4. Ancient Greek city, now part of Turkey.

5. Two kilograms, approximately four and a half pounds.

about, and learned from such painters as Jackson Pollock, Jasper Johns, Claes Oldenburg, and Larry Rivers, absorbing into his poetry such concepts as Action Painting and Minimalism. In 1966 he was struck and killed by a beach buggy on Fire Island.

O'Hara's poetry celebrates the city, its flashing surfaces, its sudden surprises, its sidewalks, newspaper headlines, billboards, and movie marquees. Highly personal, it records the friendships, observations, and emotions of a life lived day to day, with each moment another instance of survival. As a junior in college, O'Hara confessed to his journal "I often wish I had the strength to commit suicide, but on the other hand, if I had, I probably wouldn't feel the need." So in his poetry he stands often balanced on the edge of the present, looking neither to the past nor the future, grasping at what he can before it passes from him, thankful to be there to perceive it. Seldom a theorist, he seems in his practice to have aspired to the non-referential condition of abstract art, making the poem "*be* the subject, not just about it," as he placed the words on the page for their surface meanings only and eliminated most possibilities for metaphoric or symbolic interpretation. Although he was friendly with John Ashbery, Kenneth Koch, James Schuyler, and other poets identified with New York in the period, he generally avoided poetic movements and did little to promote his poetry beyond his immediate circle, leaving much of his work to be collected after his death.

Donald Allen edited *The Collected Poems of Frank O'Hara,* 1971; *The Selected Poems of Frank O'Hara,* 1972; *Poems Retrieved, 1951–1966,* 1975; and *Early Poems, 1946–1951,* 1976. Earlier titles include *A City Winter,* 1952; *Oranges,* 1953; *Meditations in an Emergency,* 1956; *Second Avenue,* 1960; *Odes,* 1960; *Lunch Poems,* 1964; and *Love Poems (Tentative Title),* 1965. Bill Berkson edited *In Memory of My Feelings, A Selection of Poems by Frank O'Hara,* 1967, with illustrations by thirty artists, including Willem de Kooning and Jasper Johns. Art criticism and other prose is collected in *Art Chronicles 1954–1966,* 1974; and *Standing Still and Walking in New York,* ed. Donald Allen, 1975. *Selected Plays* was published in 1978.

Studies include Marjorie Perloff, *Frank O'Hara: Poet Among Painters,* 1977; Bill Berkson and Joe LeSueur, eds., *Homage to Frank O'Hara,* volumes 11 and 12 of *Big Sky,* 1978; and Alan Feldman, *Frank O'Hara,* 1979.

To My Dead Father

Don't call to me father
wherever you are I'm
still your little son
running through the dark

I couldn't do what you
say even if I could hear
your roses no longer grow
my heart's black as their

bed their dainty thorns
have become my face's
troublesome stubble you
must not think of flowers

And do not frighten my
blue eyes with hazel flecks
or thicken my lips when
I face my mirror don't ask

that I be other than your
strange son understanding
minor miracles not death
father I am alive! father

forgive the roses and me

1953? 1971

To the Film Industry in Crisis

Not you, lean quarterlies and swarthy periodicals
with your studious incursions toward the pomposity of ants,
nor you, experimental theatre in which Emotive Fruition
is wedding Poetic Insight perpetually, nor you,
promenading Grand Opera, obvious as an ear (though you
are close to my heart), but you, Motion Picture Industry,
it's you I love!

In times of crisis, we must all decide again and again whom we love.
And give credit where it's due: not to my starched nurse, who taught me
how to be bad and not bad rather than good (and has lately availed
herself of this information), not to the Catholic Church
which is at best an oversolemn introduction to cosmic entertainment,
not to the American Legion, which hates everybody, but to you,
glorious Silver Screen, tragic Technicolor, amorous Cinemascope,
stretching Vistavision and startling Stereophonic Sound, with all
your heavenly dimensions and reverberations and iconoclasms! To
Richard Barthelmess as the "tol'able" boy barefoot and in pants,
Jeanette MacDonald of the flaming hair and lips and long, long neck,
Sue Carroll as she sits for eternity on the damaged fender of a car
and smiles, Ginger Rogers with her pageboy bob like a sausage
on her shuffling shoulders, peach-melba-voiced Fred Astaire of the feet,
Eric von Stroheim, the seducer of mountain-climbers' gasping spouses,
the Tarzans, each and every one of you (I cannot bring myself to prefer
Johnny Weissmuller to Lex Barker, I cannot!), Mae West in a furry sled,
her bordello radiance and bland remarks, Rudolph Valentino of the moon,
its crushing passions, and moonlike, too, the gentle Norma Shearer,
Miriam Hopkins dropping her champagne glass off Joel McCrea's yacht
and crying into the dappled sea, Clark Gable rescuing Gene Tierney
from Russia and Allan Jones rescuing Kitty Carlisle from Harpo Marx,
Cornel Wilde coughing blood on the piano keys while Merle Oberon berates,
Marilyn Monroe in her little spike heels reeling through Niagara Falls,
Joseph Cotten puzzling and Orson Welles puzzled and Dolores del Rio
eating orchids for lunch and breaking mirrors, Gloria Swanson reclining,
and Jean Harlow reclining and wiggling, and Alice Faye reclining
and wiggling and singing, Myrna Loy being calm and wise, William Powell
in his stunning urbanity, Elizabeth Taylor blossoming, yes, to you

and to all you others, the great, the near-great, the featured, the extras
who pass quickly and return in dreams saying your one or two lines,
my love!
Long may you illumine space with your marvellous appearances, delays
and enunciations, and may the money of the world glitteringly cover you

as you rest after a long day under the kleig lights with your faces
in packs for our edification, the way the clouds come often at night
but the heavens operate on the star system. It is a divine precedent
you perpetuate! Roll on, reels of celluloid, as the great earth rolls on!

1955 1957

A Step Away from Them

It's my lunch hour, so I go
for a walk among the hum-colored
cabs. First, down the sidewalk
where laborers feed their dirty
glistening torsos sandwiches
and Coca-Cola, with yellow helmets
on. They protect them from falling
bricks, I guess. Then onto the
avenue where skirts are flipping
above heels and blow up over
grates. The sun is hot, but the
cabs stir up the air. I look
at bargains in wristwatches. There
are cats playing in sawdust.
On
to Times Square, where the sign
blows smoke over my head, and higher
the waterfall pours lightly. A
Negro stands in a doorway with a
toothpick, languorously agitating.
A blonde chorus girl clicks: he
smiles and rubs his chin. Everything
suddenly honks: it is 12:40 of
a Thursday.
Neon in daylight is a
great pleasure, as Edwin Denby[1] would
write, as are light bulbs in daylight.
I stop for a cheeseburger at JULIET'S
CORNER. Giulietta Masina, wife of
Federico Fellini, *è bell' attrice.*[2]
And chocolate malted. A lady in
foxes on such a day puts her poodle
in a cab.
There are several Puerto
Ricans on the avenue today, which
makes it beautiful and warm. First
Bunny died, then John Latouche,
then Jackson Pollock.[3] But is the
earth as full as life was full, of them?
And one has eaten and one walks,
past the magazines with nudes

1. (1923–), poet and ballet critic.
2. "Beautiful actress" in many of Fellini's films, including *La Strada* (1954) and *Nights of Cabiria* (1956).
3. Friends of the poet who died the year the poem was written. "Bunny" was V. R. Lang (1924–1956), director of the Poet's Theater in Cambridge, Massachusetts, and producer of some of O'Hara's plays. John Latouche (1917–1956) was a lyricist of New York musicals. Jackson Pollock (1912–1956) was the abstract expressionist painter.

and the posters for BULLFIGHT and
the Manhattan Storage Warehouse,
which they'll soon tear down. I
used to think they had the Armory
Show[4] there.
A glass of papaya juice
and back to work. My heart is in my
pocket, it is Poems by Pierre Reverdy.[5]

1956 1957, 1964

Why I Am Not a Painter

I am not a painter, I am a poet.
Why? I think I would rather be
a painter, but I am not. Well,

for instance, Mike Goldberg
is starting a painting. I drop in.
"Sit down and have a drink" he
says. I drink; we drink. I look
up. "You have SARDINES in it."
"Yes, it needed something there."
"Oh." I go and the days go by
and I drop in again. The painting
is going on, and I go, and the days
go by. I drop in. The painting is
finished. "Where's SARDINES?"
All that's left is just
letters, "It was too much," Mike says.

But me? One day I am thinking of
a color: orange. I write a line
about orange. Pretty soon it is a
whole page of words, not lines.
Then another page. There should be
so much more, not of orange, of
words, of how terrible orange is
and life. Days go by. It is even in
prose, I am a real poet. My poem
is finished and I haven't mentioned
orange yet. It's twelve poems, I call
it ORANGES. And one day in a gallery
I see Mike's painting, called SARDINES.

1956 1957, 1971

A True Account of Talking to the Sun at Fire Island

The Sun woke me this morning loud
and clear, saying "Hey! I've been
trying to wake you up for fifteen

4. International exhibition of modern art, held in 1913 at the 69th regiment armory in New York City, famed for its impact on American art.
5. (1899–1960), French poet.

minutes. Don't be so rude, you are
only the second poet I've ever chosen
to speak to personally
so why
aren't you more attentive? If I could
burn you through the window I would
to wake you up. I can't hang around
here all day."
"Sorry, Sun, I stayed
up late last night talking to Hal."

"When I woke up Mayakovsky[6] he was
a lot more prompt" the Sun said
petulantly. "Most people are up
already waiting to see if I'm going
to put in an appearance."
I tried
to apologize "I missed you yesterday."
"That's better" he said. "I didn't
know you'd come out." "You may be
wondering why I've come so close?"
"Yes" I said beginning to feel hot
wondering if maybe he wasn't burning me
anyway.
"Frankly I wanted to tell you
I like your poetry. I see a lot
on my rounds and you're okay. You may
not be the greatest thing on earth, but
you're different. Now, I've heard some
say you're crazy, they being excessively
calm themselves to my mind, and other
crazy poets think that you're a boring
reactionary. Not me.
Just keep on
like I do and pay no attention. You'll
find that people always will complain
about the atmosphere, either too hot
or too cold too bright or too dark, days
too short or too long.
If you don't appear
at all one day they think you're lazy
or dead. Just keep right on, I like it.

And don't worry about your lineage
poetic or natural. The Sun shines on
the jungle, you know, on the tundra
the sea, the ghetto. Wherever you were
I knew it and saw you moving. I was waiting
for you to get to work.

And now that you
are making your own days, so to speak,
even if no one reads you but me

6. Vladimir Vladimirovich Mayakovsky (1893–1930), Russian poet and dramatist.

you won't be depressed. Not
everyone can look up, even at me. It
hurts their eyes."
"Oh Sun, I'm so grateful to you!"

"Thanks and remember I'm watching. It's
easier for me to speak to you out
here. I don't have to slide down
between buildings to get your ear.
I know you love Manhattan, but
you ought to look up more often.
And
always embrace things, people earth
sky stars, as I do, freely and with
the appropriate sense of space. That
is your inclination, known in the heavens
and you should follow it to hell, if
necessary, which I doubt.
Maybe we'll
speak again in Africa, of which I too
am specially fond. Go back to sleep now
Frank, and I may leave a tiny poem
in that brain of yours as my farewell."

"Sun, don't go!" I was awake
at last. "No, go I must, they're calling
me."
"Who are they?"
Rising he said "Some
day you'll know. They're calling to you
too." Darkly he rose, and then I slept.

1958 1968, 1971

The Day Lady[7] Died

It is 12:20 in New York a Friday
three days after Bastille day,[8] yes
it is 1959 and I go get a shoeshine
because I will get off the 4:19 in Easthampton[9]
at 7:15 and then go straight to dinner
and I don't know the people who will feed me

I walk up the muggy street beginning to sun
and have a hamburger and a malted and buy
an ugly NEW WORLD WRITING to see what the poets
in Ghana are doing these days
I go on to the bank
and Miss Stillwagon (first name Linda I once heard)
doesn't even look up my balance for once in her life
and in the GOLDEN GRIFFIN[1] I get a little Verlaine

7. Billie Holiday, "Lady Day" (1915–1959), the great blues singer.
8. July 14, the French national day.
9. A village and summer resort on the southeastern shore of Long Island.
1. Bookstore near the Museum of Modern Art.

for Patsy[2] with drawings by Bonnard although I do
think of Hesiod, trans. Richmond Lattimore or
Brendan Behan's new play or *Le Balcon* or *Les Nègres*
of Genet, but I don't, I stick with Verlaine
after practically going to sleep with quandariness

and for Mike I just stroll into the PARK LANE
Liquor Store and ask for a bottle of Strega and
then I go back where I came from to 6th Avenue
and the tobacconist in the Ziegfeld Theatre and
casually ask for a carton of Gauloises and a carton
of Picayunes, and a NEW YORK POST with her face on it

and I am sweating a lot by now and thinking of
leaning on the john door in the 5 SPOT
while she whispered a song along the keyboard
to Mal Waldron[3] and everyone and I stopped breathing

1959 1964

Steps

How funny you are today New York
like Ginger Rogers in *Swingtime*
and St. Bridget's steeple leaning a little to the left

here I have just jumped out of a bed full of V-days
(I got tired of D-days) and blue you there still
accepts me foolish and free
all I want is a room up there
and you in it
and even the traffic halt so thick is a way
for people to rub up against each other
and when their surgical appliances lock
they stay together
for the rest of the day (what a day)
I go by to check a slide and I say
that painting's not so blue

where's Lana Turner
she's out eating
and Garbo's backstage at the Met
everyone's taking their coat off
so they can show a rib-cage to the rib-watchers
and the park's full of dancers with their tights and shoes
in little bags
who are often mistaken for worker-outers at the West Side Y
why not
the Pittsburgh Pirates shout because they won
and in a sense we're all winning
we're alive

2. For Patsy Southgate, his hostess, he buys a book by the French poet Paul Verlaine (1844–1896), illustrated by the French artist Pierre Bonnard (1867–1947); he considers Richmond Lattimore's translation of Hesiod and plays then current by the Irish Brendan Behan (1923–1964) and the French Jean Genêt (1910–).

3. Billie Holiday's accompanist (1925–).

the apartment was vacated by a gay couple
who moved to the country for fun
they moved a day too soon
even the stabbings are helping the population explosion
though in the wrong country
and all those liars have left the U N
the Seagram Building's no longer rivalled in interest
not that we need liquor (we just like it)

and the little box is out on the sidewalk
next to the delicatessen
so the old man can sit on it and drink beer
and get knocked off it by his wife later in the day
while the sun is still shining

oh god it's wonderful
to get out of bed
and drink too much coffee
and smoke too many cigarettes
and love you so much

1960 1964

Ave Maria[4]

Mothers of America
let your kids go to the movies!
get them out of the house so they won't know what you're up to
it's true that fresh air is good for the body
but what about the soul
that grows in darkness, embossed by silvery images
and when you grow old as grow old you must
they won't hate you
they won't criticize you they won't know
they'll be in some glamorous country
they first saw on a Saturday afternoon or playing hookey

they may even be grateful to you
for their first sexual experience
which only cost you a quarter
and didn't upset the peaceful home
they will know where candy bars come from
and gratuitous bags of popcorn
as gratuitous as leaving the movie before it's over
with a pleasant stranger whose apartment is in the Heaven on Earth Bldg
near the Williamsburg Bridge
oh mothers you will have made the little tykes
so happy because if nobody does pick them up in the movies
they won't know the difference
and if somebody does it'll be sheer gravy
and they'll have been truly entertained either way

4. "Hail Mary," an allusion to the Roman Catholic prayer to the Virgin.

instead of hanging around the yard
                                        or up in their room
                                                                hating you
prematurely since you won't have done anything horribly mean yet
except keeping them from the darker joys
                                            it's unforgivable the latter
so don't blame me if you won't take this advice
                                                    and the family breaks up
and your children grow old and blind in front of a TV set
                                                            seeing
movies you wouldn't let them see when they were young

1960   1961, 1964

W. D. SNODGRASS

(1926–   )

Born in Wilkinsburg, Pennsylvania, W. D. Snodgrass studied at Geneva College, entered the navy for three years, was graduated from the State University of Iowa (1949), and continued to the degree of M.F.A. He has taught at Cornell University, the University of Rochester, Wayne State University, Syracuse University, and the University of Delaware. Snodgrass won the Pulitzer Prize for Poetry in 1960 with his first volume of poems, *Heart's Needle* (1959).

Snodgrass's verse reveals a concern for totality—a need to reveal the entirety of a given subject on a level deeper than the conscious mind. Expertise with form and rhythm plays an important part. Neither the style nor the subject of his poem is likely to be complex. On the contrary, the musical fluidity of his verse is pleasing, and his themes, even when lyrical, suggest an attractive undertone of matured experience.

Snodgrass's verse is collected in *Heart's Needle,* 1959; *After Experience: Poems and Translations,* 1968; *The Führer Bunker: A Cycle of Poems in Progress,* 1977; and *The Death of Cock Robin* (1987).

April Inventory

The green catalpa tree has turned
All white; the cherry blooms once more.
In one whole year I haven't learned
A blessed thing they pay you for.
The blossoms snow down in my hair;
The trees and I will soon be bare.

The trees have more than I to spare.
The sleek, expensive girls I teach,
Younger and pinker every year,
Bloom gradually out of reach.
The pear tree lets its petals drop
Like dandruff on a tabletop.

The girls have grown so young by now
I have to nudge myself to stare.

This year they smile and mind me how
My teeth are falling with my hair.
In thirty years I may not get
Younger, shrewder, or out of debt.

The tenth time, just a year ago,
I made myself a little list
Of all the things I'd ought to know;
Then told my parents, analyst,
And everyone who's trusted me
I'd be substantial, presently.

I haven't read one book about
A book or memorized one plot.
Or found a mind I didn't doubt.
I learned one date. And then forgot.
And one by one the solid scholars
Get the degrees, the jobs, the dollars.

And smile above their starchy collars.
I taught my classes Whitehead's notions;
One lovely girl, a song of Mahler's.
Lacking a source-book or promotions,
I showed one child the colors of
A luna moth and how to love.

I taught myself to name my name,
To bark back, loosen love and crying;
To ease my woman so she came,
To ease an old man who was dying.
I have not learned how often I
Can win, can love, but choose to die.

I have not learned there is a lie
Love shall be blonder, slimmer, younger;
That my equivocating eye
Loves only by my body's hunger;
That I have poems, true to feel,
Or that the lovely world is real.

While scholars speak authority
And wear their ulcers on their sleeves,
My eyes in spectacles shall see
These trees procure and spend their leaves.
There is a value underneath
The gold and silver in my teeth.

Though trees turn bare and girls turn wives,
We shall afford our costly seasons;
There is a gentleness survives
That will outspeak and has its reasons.
There is a loveliness exists,
Preserves us. Not for specialists.

1959

From Heart's Needle[1]

6

Easter has come around
again; the river is rising
over the thawed ground
and the banksides. When you come you bring
an egg dyed lavender.
We shout along our bank to hear
our voices returning from the hills to meet us.
We need the landscape to repeat us.

You lived on this bank first.
While nine months filled your term, we knew
how your lungs, immersed
in the womb, miraculously grew
their useless folds till
the fierce, cold air rushed in to fill
them out like bushes thick with leaves. You took your hour,
caught breath, and cried with your full lung power.

Over the stagnant bight[2]
we see the hungry bank swallow
flaunting his free flight
still; we sink in mud to follow
the killdeer from the grass
that hides her nest. That March there was
rain; the rivers rose; you could hear killdeers flying
all night over the mudflats crying.

You bring back how the red-
winged blackbird shrieked, slapping frail wings,
diving at my head—
I saw where her tough nest, cradled, swings
in tall reeds that must sway
with the winds blowing every way.
If you recall much, you recall this place. You still
live nearby—on the opposite hill.

After the sharp windstorm
of July Fourth, all that summer
through the gentle, warm
afternoons, we heard great chain saws chirr
like iron locusts. Crews
of roughneck boys swarmed to cut loose
branches wrenched in the shattering wind, to hack free
all the torn limbs that could sap the tree.

In the debris lay
starlings, dead. Near the park's birdrun
we surprised one day

1. "Heart's Needle," a sequence of ten poems addressed to the poet's daughter after his divorce and remarriage, provided the title for his *Heart's Needle* (1959), the book that with Robert Lowell's *Life Studies* (1959) pointed the way to the so-called "confessional" poetry fashionable in the 1960's.

2. A curve, here along a river.

a proud, tan-spatted, buff-brown pigeon.
In my hands she flapped so
fearfully that I let her go.
Her keeper came. And we helped snarl her in a net.
You bring things I'd as soon forget.

You raise into my head
a Fall night that I came once more
to sit on your bed;
sweat beads stood out on your arms and forehead and you wheezed for breath,
for help, like some child caught beneath
its comfortable woolly blankets, drowning there.
Your lungs caught and would not take the air.

Of all things, only we
have power to choose that we should die;
nothing else is free
in this world to refuse it. Yet I,
who say this, could not raise
myself from bed how many days
to the thieving world. Child, I have another wife,
another child. We try to choose our life.

1959

The Examination

Under the thick beams of that swirly smoking light,
The black robes are clustering, huddled in together.
Hunching their shoulders, they spread short, broad sleeves like night-
Black grackles' wings; then they reach bone-yellow leather-

y fingers, each to each. And are prepared. Each turns
His single eye—or since one can't discern their eyes,
That reflective, single, moon-pale disc which burns
Over each brow—to watch this uncouth shape that lies

Strapped to their table. One probes with his ragged nails
The slate-sharp calf, explores the thigh and the lean thews
Of the groin. Others raise, red as piratic sails,
His wing, stretching, trying the pectoral sinews.

One runs his finger down the whet of that cruel
Golden beak, lifts back the horny lids from the eyes,
Peers down in one bright eye malign as a jewel,
And steps back suddenly. "He is anaesthetized?"

"He is. He is. Yes. Yes." The tallest of them, bent
Down by the head, rises: "This drug possesses powers
Sufficient to still all gods in this firmament.
This is Garuda who was fierce. He's yours for hours.

"We shall continue, please." Now, once again, he bends
To the skull, and its clamped tissues. Into the cran-
ial cavity, he plunges both of his hands
Like obstetric forceps and lifts out the great brain,

Holds it aloft, then gives it to the next who stands
    Beside him. Each, in turn, accepts it, although loath,
Turns it this way, that way, feels it between his hands
    Like a wasp's nest or some sickening outsized growth.

They must decide what thoughts each part of it must think;
    They tap at, then listen beside, each suspect lobe;
Next, with a crow's quill dipped into India ink,
    Mark on its surface, as if on a map or globe,

Those dangerous areas which need to be excised.
    They rinse it, then apply antiseptics to it;
Now silver saws appear which, inch by inch, slice
    Through its ancient folds and ridges, like thick suet.

It's rinsed, dried, and daubed with thick salves. The smoky saws
    Are scrubbed, resterilized, and polished till they gleam.
The brain is repacked in its case. Pinched in their claws,
    Glimmering needles stitch it up, that leave no seam.

Meantime, one of them has set blinders to the eyes,
    Inserted light packing beneath each of the ears
And calked the nostrils in. One, with thin twine, ties
    The genitals off. With long wooden-handled shears,

Another chops pinions out of the scarlet wings.
    It's hoped that with disuse he will forget the sky
Or, at least, in time, learn, among other things,
    To fly no higher than his superiors fly.

Well; that's a beginning. The next time, they can split
    His tongue and teach him to talk correctly, can give
Him opinions on fine books and choose clothing fit
    For the integrated area where he'll live.

Their candidate may live to give them thanks one day.
    He will recover and may hope for such success
He might return to join their ranks. Bowing away,
    They nod, whispering, "One of ours; one of ours. Yes. Yes."

1968

JOHN ASHBERY

(1927–)

John Ashbery was born in Rochester, New York, and grew up east of there on his father's farm in Sodus. After attending Deerfield Academy in western Massachusetts, he majored in English at Harvard, served on the editorial board of *The Harvard Advocate,* and graduated in 1949. He received an M.A. in English from Columbia University, worked four years in publishing in New York, and then went to France as a Fulbright student of French literature from 1955 to 1957. After ten months at New York University, he returned to France for another seven years, writing art criticism for the European edition of the New York *Herald Tribune* and for *Art International* and editing *Art and Literature.* In 1965 he came back to New York to serve seven years as executive editor of *Art News.* In 1974 he began teaching English at Brooklyn College. In 1976 he became poetry editor of *Partisan Review.* Since 1980 he has been an art critic and editor at *Newsweek.*

Ashbery painted as a teenager and later was associated with the "New York School" of poets of the 1950's, most of whom were influenced by the anti-representational work and ideas of such painters as Jackson Pollock, Willem de Kooning, and Robert Motherwell. The air was alive with abstract expressionism and action painting and with a renewed attention to earlier twentieth-century movements such as Dada and surrealism. Like Ashbery, the poets Frank O'Hara and James Schuyler wrote regularly for *Art News,* and O'Hara was a curator at the Museum of Modern Art.

Ashbery's first book, *Turandot and Other Poems* (1953), was published by the Tibor de Nagy art gallery, also a publisher of O'Hara. His second, *Some Trees* (1956), received much wider dissemination as part of the Yale Series of Younger Poets and contained some of his most widely anthologized pieces. Like "The Painter," a sestina, some of these early poems are carefully structured, but Ashbery's work over the years is more characteristically unconventional than traditional in form, with content fragmented and elliptical. Of his work in general, he has written that "there are no themes or subjects in the usual sense, except the very broad one of an individual consciousness confronting or confronted by a world of external phenomena. The work is a very complex but, I hope, clear and concrete transcript of the impressions left by these phenomena on that consciousness." From *Rivers and Mountains* (1966) onward, he has turned at times to longer, rambling meditations, philosophical and introspective. Of the poems in this manner, the title piece of *Self-Portrait in a Convex Mirror* (1975) is a good example. A more recent long experiment with shifting tones and perspectives is the poem "Litany," a pair of "simultaneous but independent monologues" printed side by side and occupying over half of *As We Know* (1979). Other experiments in brevity are represented by the four one-line poems in *As We Know* that consist of partial sentences completing a statement begun in the title. Between these extremes lie the short poems, constructed with careful attention to words and phrases, that have continued to absorb much of Ashbery's attention and are preponderant in *Houseboat Days* (1977) and in *Shadow Train* (1981), fifty poetic meditations, each of sixteen lines, organized in quatrains of varying line length. *A Wave* (1985) is more varied in method, ranging from loose prose to the long, carefully crafted title poem, as Ashbery's concern with passing phenomena focuses with increasing insistence on the theme of mutability.

Selected Poems appeared in 1985. Other volumes of verse, besides those named above, include *The Poems,* 1960; *The Tennis Court Oath,* 1962; *Selected Poems,* 1967; *Sunrise in Suburbia,* 1968; *Three Madrigals,* 1968; *Fragment,* 1969; *The Double Dream of Spring,* 1970; *The New Spirit,* 1970; *Three Poems,* 1972; and *Fragment, Clepsydre, Poèmes Français,* 1975. With James Schuyler, Ashbery has written a novel, *A Nest of Ninnies,* 1969. Critical assessments include David Shapiro, *John Ashbery: An Introduction to the Poetry,* 1980; and David Lehman, ed., *Beyond Amazement: New Essays on John Ashbery,* 1980.

Some Trees

These are amazing: each
Joining a neighbor, as though speech
Were a still performance.
Arranging by chance

To meet as far this morning
From the world as agreeing
With it, you and I
Are suddenly what the trees try

To tell us we are:
That their merely being there
Means something; that soon
We may touch, love, explain.

And glad not to have invented
Such comeliness, we are surrounded:
A silence already filled with noises,
A canvas on which emerges

A chorus of smiles, a winter morning.
Placed in a puzzling light, and moving,
Our days put on such reticence
These accents seem their own defense.

1956

The Painter

Sitting between the sea and the buildings
He enjoyed painting the sea's portrait.
But just as children imagine a prayer
Is merely silence, he expected his subject
To rush up the sand, and, seizing a brush,
Plaster its own portrait on the canvas.

So there was never any paint on his canvas
Until the people who lived in the buildings
Put him to work: "Try using the brush
As a means to an end. Select, for a portrait,
Something less angry and large, and more subject
To a painter's moods, or, perhaps, to a prayer."

How could he explain to them his prayer
That nature, not art, might usurp the canvas?
He chose his wife for a new subject,
Making her vast, like ruined buildings,
As if, forgetting itself, the portrait
Had expressed itself without a brush.

Slightly encouraged, he dipped his brush
In the sea, murmuring a heartfelt prayer:
"My soul, when I paint this next portrait
Let it be you who wrecks the canvas."
The news spread like wildfire through the buildings:
He had gone back to the sea for his subject.

Imagine a painter crucified by his subject!
Too exhausted even to lift his brush,

He provoked some artists leaning from the buildings
To malicious mirth: "We haven't a prayer
Now, of putting ourselves on canvas,
Or getting the sea to sit for a portrait!"

Others declared it a self-portrait.
Finally all indications of a subject
Began to fade, leaving the canvas
Perfectly white. He put down the brush.
At once a howl, that was also a prayer,
Arose from the overcrowded buildings.

They tossed him, the portrait, from the tallest of the buildings;
And the sea devoured the canvas and the brush
As though his subject had decided to remain a prayer.

1956

Self-Portrait in a Convex Mirror

As Parmigianino[1] did it, the right hand
Bigger than the head, thrust at the viewer
And swerving easily away, as though to protect
What it advertises. A few leaded panes, old beams,
Fur, pleated muslin, a coral ring run together
In a movement supporting the face, which swims
Toward and away like the hand
Except that it is in repose. It is what is
Sequestered. Vasari[2] says, "Francesco one day set himself
To take his own portrait, looking at himself for that purpose
In a convex mirror, such as is used by barbers . . .
He accordingly caused a ball of wood to be made
By a turner, and having divided it in half and
Brought it to the size of the mirror, he set himself
With great art to copy all that he saw in the glass,"
Chiefly his reflection, of which the portrait
Is the reflection once removed.
The glass chose to reflect only what he saw
Which was enough for his purpose: his image
Glazed, embalmed, projected at a 180-degree angle.
The time of day or the density of the light
Adhering to the face keeps it
Lively and intact in a recurring wave
Of arrival. The soul establishes itself.
But how far can it swim out through the eyes
And still return safely to its nest? The surface
Of the mirror being convex, the distance increases
Significantly; that is, enough to make the point
That the soul is a captive, treated humanely, kept
In suspension, unable to advance much farther
Than your look as it intercepts the picture.

1. Francesco Mazzola (1503–1540), called Parmigianino after Parma, the city of his birth, was an Italian Mannerist painter. His self-portrait, painted on a convex piece of wood, as described in the following lines, provided the title and the central metaphor for Ashbery's poem.
2. Giorgio Vasari (1511–1574), Italian art historian.

Pope Clement[3] and his court were "stupefied"
By it, according to Vasari, and promised a commission
That never materialized. The soul has to stay where it is,
Even though restless, hearing raindrops at the pane,
The sighing of autumn leaves thrashed by the wind,
Longing to be free, outside, but it must stay
Posing in this place. It must move
As little as possible. This is what the portrait says.
But there is in that gaze a combination
Of tenderness, amusement and regret, so powerful
In its restraint that one cannot look for long.
The secret is too plain. The pity of it smarts,
Makes hot tears spurt: that the soul is not a soul,
Has no secret, is small, and it fits
Its hollow perfectly: its room, our moment of attention.
That is the tune but there are no words.
The words are only speculation
(From the Latin *speculum,* mirror):
They seek and cannot find the meaning of the music.
We see only postures of the dream,
Riders of the motion that swings the face
Into view under evening skies, with no
False disarray as proof of authenticity.
But it is life englobed.
One would like to stick one's hand
Out of the globe, but its dimension,
What carries it, will not allow it.
No doubt it is this, not the reflex
To hide something, which makes the hand loom large
As it retreats slightly. There is no way
To build it flat like a section of wall:
It must join the segment of a circle,
Roving back to the body of which it seems
So unlikely a part, to fence in and shore up the face
On which the effort of this condition reads
Like a pinpoint of a smile, a spark
Or star one is not sure of having seen
As darkness resumes. A perverse light whose
Imperative of subtlety dooms in advance its
Conceit to light up: unimportant but meant.
Francesco, your hand is big enough
To wreck the sphere, and too big,
One would think, to weave delicate meshes
That only argue its further detention.
(Big, but not coarse, merely on another scale,
Like a dozing whale on the sea bottom
In relation to the tiny, self-important ship
On the surface.) But your eyes proclaim
That everything is surface. The surface is what's there
And nothing can exist except what's there.
There are no recesses in the room, only alcoves,
And the window doesn't matter much, or that
Sliver of window or mirror on the right, even

3. Clement VII, pope from 1523 to 1534.

As a gauge of the weather, which in French is
Le temps, the word for time, and which
Follows a course wherein changes are merely
Features of the whole. The whole is stable within
Instability, a globe like ours, resting
On a pedestal of vacuum, a ping-pong ball
Secure on its jet of water.
And just as there are no words for the surface, that is,
No words to say what it really is, that it is not
Superficial but a visible core, then there is
No way out of the problem of pathos vs. experience.
You will stay on, restive, serene in
Your gesture which is neither embrace nor warning
But which holds something of both in pure
Affirmation that doesn't affirm anything.

The balloon pops, the attention
Turns dully away. Clouds
In the puddle stir up into sawtoothed fragments.
I think of the friends
Who came to see me, of what yesterday
Was like. A peculiar slant
Of memory that intrudes on the dreaming model
In the silence of the studio as he considers
Lifting the pencil to the self-portrait.
How many people came and stayed a certain time,
Uttered light or dark speech that became part of you
Like light behind windblown fog and sand,
Filtered and influenced by it, until no part
Remains that is surely you. Those voices in the dusk
Have told you all and still the tale goes on
In the form of memories deposited in irregular
Clumps of crystals. Whose curved hand controls,
Francesco, the turning seasons and the thoughts
That peel off and fly away at breathless speeds
Like the last stubborn leaves ripped
From wet branches? I see in this only the chaos
Of your round mirror which organizes everything
Around the polestar of your eyes which are empty,
Know nothing, dream but reveal nothing.
I feel the carousel starting slowly
And going faster and faster: desk, papers, books,
Photographs of friends, the window and the trees
Merging in one neutral band that surrounds
Me on all sides, everywhere I look.
And I cannot explain the action of leveling,
Why it should all boil down to one
Uniform substance, a magma of interiors.
My guide in these matters is your self,
Firm, oblique, accepting everything with the same
Wraith of a smile, and as time speeds up so that it is soon
Much later, I can know only the straight way out,
The distance between us. Long ago
The strewn evidence meant something,
The small accidents and pleasures

Of the day as it moved gracelessly on,
A housewife doing chores. Impossible now
To restore those properties in the silver blur that is
The record of what you accomplished by sitting down
"With great art to copy all that you saw in the glass"
So as to perfect and rule out the extraneous
Forever. In the circle of your intentions certain spars
Remain that perpetuate the enchantment of self with self:
Eyebeams, muslin, coral. It doesn't matter
Because these are things as they are today
Before one's shadow ever grew
Out of the field into thoughts of tomorrow.

Tomorrow is easy, but today is uncharted,
Desolate, reluctant as any landscape
To yield what are laws of perspective
After all only to the painter's deep
Mistrust, a weak instrument though
Necessary. Of course some things
Are possible, it knows, but it doesn't know
Which ones. Some day we will try
To do as many things as are possible
And perhaps we shall succeed at a handful
Of them, but this will not have anything
To do with what is promised today, our
Landscape sweeping out from us to disappear
On the horizon. Today enough of a cover burnishes
To keep the supposition of promises together
In one piece of surface, letting one ramble
Back home from them so that these
Even stronger possibilities can remain
Whole without being tested. Actually
The skin of the bubble-chamber's as tough as
Reptile eggs; everything gets "programmed" there
In due course: more keeps getting included
Without adding to the sum, and just as one
Gets accustomed to a noise that
Kept one awake but now no longer does,
So the room contains this flow like an hourglass
Without varying in climate or quality
(Except perhaps to brighten bleakly and almost
Invisibly, in a focus sharpening toward death—more
Of this later). What should be the vacuum of a dream
Becomes continually replete as the source of dreams
Is being tapped so that this one dream
May wax, flourish like a cabbage rose,
Defying sumptuary laws, leaving us
To awake and try to begin living in what
Has now become a slum. Sydney Freedberg in his
Parmigianino[4] says of it: "Realism in this portrait
No longer produces an objective truth, but a *bizarria.*[5] . . .
However its distortion does not create
A feeling of disharmony. . . . The forms retain

4. A study of Mazzola's work published in 1950. 5. Distortion.

A strong measure of ideal beauty," because
Fed by our dreams, so inconsequential until one day
We notice the hole they left. Now their importance
If not their meaning is plain. They were to nourish
A dream which includes them all, as they are
Finally reversed in the accumulating mirror.
They seemed strange because we couldn't actually see them.
And we realize this only at a point where they lapse
Like a wave breaking on a rock, giving up
Its shape in a gesture which expresses that shape.
The forms retain a strong measure of ideal beauty
As they forage in secret on our idea of distortion.
Why be unhappy with this arrangement, since
Dreams prolong us as they are absorbed?
Something like living occurs, a movement
Out of the dream into its codification.

As I start to forget it
It presents its stereotype again
But it is an unfamiliar stereotype, the face
Riding at anchor, issued from hazards, soon
To accost others, "rather angel than man" (Vasari).
Perhaps an angel looks like everything
We have forgotten, I mean forgotten
Things that don't seem familiar when
We meet them again, lost beyond telling,
Which were ours once. This would be the point
Of invading the privacy of this man who
"Dabbled in alchemy, but whose wish
Here was not to examine the subtleties of art
In a detached, scientific spirit: he wished through them
To impart the sense of novelty and amazement to the spectator"
(Freedberg). Later portraits such as the Uffizi[6]
"Gentleman," the Borghese "Young Prelate" and
The Naples "Antea" issue from Mannerist
Tensions, but here, as Freedberg points out,
The surprise, the tension are in the concept
Rather than its realization.
The consonance of the High Renaissance
Is present, though distorted by the mirror.
What is novel is the extreme care in rendering
The velleities of the rounded reflecting surface
(It is the first mirror portrait),
So that you could be fooled for a moment
Before you realize the reflection
Isn't yours. You feel then like one of those
Hoffmann characters who have been deprived
Of a reflection, except that the whole of me
Is seen to be supplanted by the strict
Otherness of the painter in his
Other room. We have surprised him
At work, but no, he has surprised us
As he works. The picture is almost finished,

6. Uffizi and (in the next line) Borghese: museums in Florence and Rome.

The surprise almost over, as when one looks out,
Startled by a snowfall which even now is
Ending in specks and sparkles of snow.
It happened while you were inside, asleep,
And there is no reason why you should have
Been awake for it, except that the day
Is ending and it will be hard for you
To get to sleep tonight, at least until late.

The shadow of the city injects its own
Urgency: Rome where Francesco
Was at work during the Sack:[7] his inventions
Amazed the soldiers who burst in on him;
They decided to spare his life, but he left soon after;
Vienna where the painting is today, where
I saw it with Pierre in the summer of 1959; New York
Where I am now, which is a logarithm
Of other cities. Our landscape
Is alive with filiations, shuttlings;
Business is carried on by look, gesture,
Hearsay. It is another life to the city,
The backing of the looking glass of the
Unidentified but precisely sketched studio. It wants
To siphon off the life of the studio, deflate
Its mapped space to enactments, island it.
That operation has been temporarily stalled
But something new is on the way, a new preciosity
In the wind. Can you stand it,
Francesco? Are you strong enough for it?
This wind brings what it knows not, is
Self-propelled, blind, has no notion
Of itself. It is inertia that once
Acknowledged saps all activity, secret or public:
Whispers of the word that can't be understood
But can be felt, a chill, a blight
Moving outward along the capes and peninsulas
Of your nervures and so to the archipelagoes
And to the bathed, aired secrecy of the open sea.
This is its negative side. Its positive side is
Making you notice life and the stresses
That only seemed to go away, but now,
As this new mode questions, are seen to be
Hastening out of style. If they are to become classics
They must decide which side they are on.
Their reticence has undermined
The urban scenery, made its ambiguities
Look willful and tired, the games of an old man.
What we need now is this unlikely
Challenger pounding on the gates of an amazed
Castle. Your argument, Francesco,
Had begun to grow stale as no answer
Or answers were forthcoming. If it dissolves now

7. An army of Charles V (1500–1558), Holy Roman Emperor (1519–1558) sacked Rome and besieged Pope Clement VII in 1527.

Into dust, that only means its time had come
Some time ago, but look now, and listen:
It may be that another life is stocked there
In recesses no one knew of; that it,
Not we, are the change; that we are in fact it
If we could get back to it, relive some of the way
It looked, turn our faces to the globe as it sets
And still be coming out all right:
Nerves normal, breath normal. Since it is a metaphor
Made to include us, we are a part of it and
Can live in it as in fact we have done,
Only leaving our minds bare for questioning
We now see will not take place at random
But in an orderly way that means to menace
Nobody—the normal way things are done,
Like the concentric growing up of days
Around a life: correctly, if you think about it.

A breeze like the turning of a page
Brings back your face: the moment
Takes such a big bite out of the haze
Of pleasant intuition it comes after.
The locking into place is "death itself,"
As Berg[8] said of a phrase in Mahler's[9] Ninth;
Or, to quote Imogen in *Cymbeline*,[1] "There cannot
Be a pinch in death more sharp than this," for,
Though only exercise or tactic, it carries
The momentum of a conviction that had been building.
Mere forgetfulness cannot remove it
Nor wishing bring it back, as long as it remains
The white precipitate of its dream
In the climate of sighs flung across our world,
A cloth over a birdcage. But it is certain that
What is beautiful seems so only in relation to a specific
Life, experienced or not, channeled into some form
Steeped in the nostalgia of a collective past.
The light sinks today with an enthusiasm
I have known elsewhere, and known why
It seemed meaningful, that others felt this way
Years ago. I go on consulting
This mirror that is no longer mine
For as much brisk vacancy as is to be
My portion this time. And the vase is always full
Because there is only just so much room
And it accommodates everything. The sample
One sees is not to be taken as
Merely that, but as everything as it
May be imagined outside time—not as a gesture
But as all, in the refined, assimilable state.
But what is this universe the porch of
As it veers in and out, back and forth,
Refusing to surround us and still the only

8. Alban Berg (1885–1935), Austrian composer.
9. Gustav Mahler (1860–1911), Austrian composer.
1. Shakespeare, *Cymbeline*, I, ii, 61–62.

Thing we can see? Love once
Tipped the scales but now is shadowed, invisible,
Though mysteriously present, around somewhere.
But we know it cannot be sandwiched
Between two adjacent moments, that its windings
Lead nowhere except to further tributaries
And that these empty themselves into a vague
Sense of something that can never be known
Even though it seems likely that each of us
Knows what it is and is capable of
Communicating it to the other. But the look
Some wear as a sign makes one want to
Push forward ignoring the apparent
Naïveté of the attempt, not caring
That no one is listening, since the light
Has been lit once and for all in their eyes
And is present, unimpaired, a permanent anomaly,
Awake and silent. On the surface of it
There seems no special reason why that light
Should be focused by love, or why
The city falling with its beautiful suburbs
Into space always less clear, less defined,
Should read as the support of its progress,
The easel upon which the drama unfolded
To its own satisfaction and to the end
Of our dreaming, as we had never imagined
It would end, in worn daylight with the painted
Promise showing through as a gage, a bond.
This nondescript, never-to-be defined daytime is
The secret of where it takes place
And we can no longer return to the various
Conflicting statements gathered, lapses of memory
Of the principal witnesses. All we know
Is that we are a little early, that
Today has that special, lapidary
Todayness that the sunlight reproduces
Faithfully in casting twig-shadows on blithe
Sidewalks. No previous day would have been like this.
I used to think they were all alike,
That the present always looked the same to everybody
But this confusion drains away as one
Is always cresting into one's present.
Yet the "poetic," straw-colored space
Of the long corridor that leads back to the painting,
Its darkening opposite—is this
Some figment of "art," not to be imagined
As real, let alone special? Hasn't it too its lair
In the present we are always escaping from
And falling back into, as the waterwheel of days
Pursues its uneventful, even serene course?
I think it is trying to say it is today
And we must get out of it even as the public
Is pushing through the museum now so as to
Be out by closing time. You can't live there.
The gray glaze of the past attacks all know-how:

Secrets of wash and finish that took a lifetime
To learn and are reduced to the status of
Black-and-white illustrations in a book where colorplates
Are rare. That is, all time
Reduces to no special time. No one
Alludes to the change; to do so might
Involve calling attention to oneself
Which would augment the dread of not getting out
Before having seen the whole collection
(Except for the sculptures in the basement:
They are where they belong).
Our time gets to be veiled, compromised
By the portrait's will to endure. It hints at
Our own, which we were hoping to keep hidden.
We don't need paintings or
Doggerel written by mature poets when
The explosion is so precise, so fine.
Is there any point even in acknowledging
The existence of all that? Does it
Exist? Certainly the leisure to
Indulge stately pastimes doesn't,
Any more. Today has no margins, the event arrives
Flush with its edges, is of the same substance,
Indistinguishable. "Play" is something else;
It exists, in a society specifically
Organized as a demonstration of itself.
There is no other way, and those assholes
Who would confuse everything with their mirror games
Which seem to multiply stakes and possibilities, or
At least confuse issues by means of an investing
Aura that would corrode the architecture
Of the whole in a haze of suppressed mockery,
Are beside the point. They are out of the game,
Which doesn't exist until they are out of it.
It seems like a very hostile universe
But as the principle of each individual thing is
Hostile to, exists at the expense of all the others
As philosophers have often pointed out, at least
This thing, the mute, undivided present,
Has the justification of logic, which
In this instance isn't a bad thing
Or wouldn't be, if the way of telling
Didn't somehow intrude, twisting the end result
Into a caricature of itself. This always
Happens, as in the game where
A whispered phrase passed around the room
Ends up as something completely different.
It is the principle that makes works of art so unlike
What the artist intended. Often he finds
He has omitted the thing he started out to say
In the first place. Seduced by flowers,
Explicit pleasures, he blames himself (though
Secretly satisfied with the result), imagining
He had a say in the matter and exercised
An option of which he was hardly conscious,

Unaware that necessity circumvents such resolutions.
So as to create something new
For itself, that there is no other way,
That the history of creation proceeds according to
Stringent laws, and that things
Do get done in this way, but never the things
We set out to accomplish and wanted so desperately
To see come into being. Parmigianino
Must have realized this as he worked at his
Life-obstructing task. One is forced to read
The perfectly plausible accomplishment of a purpose
Into the smooth, perhaps even bland (but so
Enigmatic) finish. Is there anything
To be serious about beyond this otherness
That gets included in the most ordinary
Forms of daily activity, changing everything
Slightly and profoundly, and tearing the matter
Of creation, any creation, not just artistic creation
Out of our hands, to install it on some monstrous, near
Peak, too close to ignore, too far
For one to intervene? This otherness, this
"Not-being-us" is all there is to look at
In the mirror, though no one can say
How it came to be this way. A ship
Flying unknown colors has entered the harbor.
You are allowing extraneous matters
To break up your day, cloud the focus
Of the crystal ball. Its scene drifts away
Like vapor scattered on the wind. The fertile
Thought-associations that until now came
So easily, appear no more, or rarely. Their
Colorings are less intense, washed out
By autumn rains and winds, spoiled, muddied,
Given back to you because they are worthless.
Yet we are such creatures of habit that their
Implications are still around *en permanence,* confusing
Issues. To be serious only about sex
Is perhaps one way, but the sands are hissing
As they approach the beginning of the big slide
Into what happened. This past
Is now here: the painter's
Reflected face, in which we linger, receiving
Dreams and inspirations on an unassigned
Frequency, but the hues have turned metallic,
The curves and edges are not so rich. Each person
Has one big theory to explain the universe
But it doesn't tell the whole story
And in the end it is what is outside him
That matters, to him and especially to us
Who have been given no help whatever
In decoding our own man-size quotient and must rely
On second-hand knowledge. Yet I know
That no one else's taste is going to be
Any help, and might as well be ignored.
Once it seemed so perfect—gloss on the fine
Freckled skin, lips moistened as though about to part

Releasing speech, and the familiar look
Of clothes and furniture that one forgets.
This could have been our paradise: exotic
Refuge within an exhausted world, but that wasn't
In the cards, because it couldn't have been
The point. Aping naturalness may be the first step
Toward achieving an inner calm
But it is the first step only, and often
Remains a frozen gesture of welcome etched
On the air materializing behind it,
A convention. And we have really
No time for these, except to use them
For kindling. The sooner they are burnt up
The better for the roles we have to play.
Therefore I beseech you, withdraw that hand,
Offer it no longer as shield or greeting,
The shield of a greeting, Francesco:
There is room for one bullet in the chamber:
Our looking through the wrong end
Of the telescope as you fall back at a speed
Faster than that of light to flatten ultimately
Among the features of the room, an invitation
Never mailed, the "it was all a dream"
Syndrome, though the "all" tells tersely
Enough how it wasn't. Its existence
Was real, though troubled, and the ache
Of this waking dream can never drown out
The diagram still sketched on the wind,
Chosen, meant for me and materialized
In the disguising radiance of my room.
We have seen the city; it is the gibbous[2]
Mirrored eye of an insect. All things happen
On its balcony and are resumed within,
But the action is the cold, syrupy flow
Of a pageant. One feels too confined,
Sifting the April sunlight for clues,
In the mere stillness of the ease of its
Parameter. The hand holds no chalk
And each part of the whole falls off
And cannot know it knew, except
Here and there, in cold pockets
Of remembrance, whispers out of time.

1975

Crazy Weather

It's this crazy weather we've been having:
Falling forward one minute, lying down the next
Among the loose grasses and soft, white, nameless flowers.
People have been making a garment out of it,
Stitching the white of lilacs together with lightning
At some anonymous crossroads. The sky calls
To the deaf earth. The proverbial disarray

2. Convex at both edges.

Of morning corrects itself as you stand up.
You are wearing a text. The lines
Droop to your shoelaces and I shall never want or need
Any other literature than this poetry of mud
And ambitious reminiscences of times when it came easily
Through the then woods and ploughed fields and had
A simple unconscious dignity we can never hope to
Approximate now except in narrow ravines nobody
Will inspect where some late sample of the rare,
Uninteresting specimen might still be putting out shoots, for all we know.

1977

As We Know

All that we see is penetrated by it—
The distant treetops with their steeple (so
Innocent), the stair, the windows' fixed flashing—
Pierced full of holes by the evil that is not evil,
The romance that is not mysterious, the life that is not life,
A present that is elsewhere.

And further in the small capitulations
Of the dance, you rub elbows with it,
Finger it. That day you did it
Was the day you had to stop, because the doing
Involved the whole fabric, there was no other way to appear.
You slid down on your knees
For those precious jewels of spring water
Planted on the moss, before they got soaked up
And you teetered on the edge of this
Calm street with its sidewalks, its traffic,
As though they are coming to get you.
But there was no one in the noon glare,
Only birds like secrets to find out about
And a home to get to, one of these days.

The light that was shadowed then
Was seen to be our lives,
Everything about us that love might wish to examine,
Then put away for a certain length of time, until
The whole is to be reviewed, and we turned
Toward each other, to each other.
The way we had come was all we could see
And it crept up on us, embarrassed
That there is so much to tell now, really now.

1979

Paradoxes and Oxymorons

This poem is concerned with language on a very plain level.
Look at it talking to you. You look out a window
Or pretend to fidget. You have it but you don't have it.
You miss it, it misses you. You miss each other.

The poem is sad because it wants to be yours, and cannot.
What's a plain level? It is that and other things,
Bringing a system of them into play. Play?
Well, actually, yes, but I consider play to be

A deeper outside thing, a dreamed role-pattern,
As in the division of grace these long August days
Without proof. Open-ended. And before you know
It gets lost in the steam and chatter of typewriters.

It has been played once more. I think you exist only
To tease me into doing it, on your level, and then you aren't there
Or have adopted a different attitude. And the poem
Has set me softly down beside you. The poem is you.

1981

A Prison All the Same

Spoken over a yellow kitchen table (just the ticket
For these recycling-minded times): *You've got to show them who you are.*
Just being a person doesn't work anymore. Many of them drink beer.
A crisis or catastrophe goes off in their lives

Every few hours. They don't get used to it, having no memory.
Nor do they think it's better that way. What happens for them
Is part of them, an appendage. There's no room to step back
To get a perspective. The old one shops and thinks. The fragrant bulbs

In the cellar are no use either. Last week a man was here.
But just try sorting it out when you're on top
Of your destiny, like angels elbowing each other on the head of a pin.
Not until someone falls, or hesitates, does the renewal occur,

And then it's only for a second, like a breath of air
On a hot, muggy afternoon with no air conditioning. I was scared
Then. Now it's over. It can be removed like a sock
And mended, a little. One for the books.

1981

The Desperado[3]

What kind of life is this that we are leading
That so much strong vagary can slip by unnoticed?
Is there a future? It seems that all we'd planned
To find in it is rolling around now, spending itself.

You step aside, and the rock invasion from the fifties
Dissipates in afternoon smoke. And disco
Retreats a little, wiping large brown eyes.
They come along here. Now, all will be gone.

3. The title echoes the title of Gérard de Nerval's sonnet "El Desdichado" (Spanish: "The Unhappy One"), the first line of which ("Je suis le ténébreux,—le veuf,—l'inconsolé,") Ashbery translates in l. 9 of his poem.

I am the shadowed, widower, the unconsoled.
But if it weren't for me I should also be the schoolmaster
Coaching, pruning young spring thoughts
Surprised to be here, in this air.

But their barely restrained look suits the gray
Importance of what we expect to be confronted with
Any day. Send the odious one a rebuke. Can one deny
Any longer that it is, and going to be?

1981

At North Farm

Somewhere someone is traveling furiously toward you,
At incredible speed, traveling day and night,
Through blizzards and desert heat, across torrents, through narrow passes.
But will he know where to find you,
Recognize you when he sees you,
Give you the thing he has for you?

Hardly anything grows here,
Yet the granaries are bursting with meal,
The sacks of meal piled to the rafters.
The streams run with sweetness, fattening fish;
Birds darken the sky. Is it enough
That the dish of milk is set out at night,
That we think of him sometimes,
Sometimes and always, with mixed feelings?

1985

The Ongoing Story

I could say it's the happiest period of my life.
It hasn't got much competition! Yesterday
It seemed a flatness, hotness. As though it barely stood out
From the rocks of all the years before. Today it sheds
That old name, without assuming any new one. I think it's still there.

It was as though I'd been left with the empty street
A few seconds after the bus pulled out. A dollop of afternoon wind.
Others tell you to take your attention off it
For awhile, refocus the picture. Plan to entertain,
To get out. (Do people really talk that way?)

We could pretend that all that isn't there never existed anyway.
The great ideas? What good are they if they're misplaced,
In the wrong order, if you can't remember one
At the moment you're so to speak mounting the guillotine
Like Sydney Carton,[4] and can't think of anything to say?
Or is this precisely material covered in a course
Called Background of the Great Ideas, and therefore it isn't necessary

4. In Charles Dickens's *A Tale of Two Cities* (1859). Carton's thoughts as he mounts the guillotine conclude the book and end with the famous "It is a far, far better thing that I do, than I have ever done; it is a far, far better rest that I go to than I have ever known."

To say anything or even know anything? The breath of the moment
Is breathed, we fall and still feel better. The phone rings,

It's a wrong number, and your heart is lighter,
Not having to be faced with the same boring choices again
Which doesn't undermine a feeling for people in general and
Especially in particular: you,
In your deliberate distinctness, whom I love and gladly
Agree to walk blindly into the night with,
Your realness is real to me though I would never take any of it
Just to see how it grows. A knowledge that people live close by is,
I think, enough. And even if only first names are ever exchanged
The people who own them seem rock-true and marvelously self-sufficient.

1985

Down by the Station, Early in the Morning

It all wears out. I keep telling myself this, but
I can never believe me, though others do. Even things do.
And the things they do. Like the rasp of silk, or a certain
Glottal stop in your voice as you are telling me how you
Didn't have time to brush your teeth but gargled with Listerine
Instead. Each is a base one might wish to touch once more

Before dying. There's the moment years ago in the station in Venice.
The dark rainy afternoon in fourth grade, and the shoes then,
Made of a dull crinkled brown leather that no longer exists.
And nothing does, until you name it, remembering, and even then
It may not have existed, or existed only as a result
Of the perceptual dysfunction you've been carrying around for years.
The result is magic, then terror, then pity at the emptiness,
Then air gradually bathing and filling the emptiness as it leaks.
Emoting all over something that is probably mere reportage
But nevertheless likes being emoted on. And so each day
Culminates in merriment as well as a deep shock like an electric one.

As the wrecking ball bursts through the wall with the bookshelves
Scattering the works of famous authors as well as those
Of more obscure ones, and books with no author, letting in
Space, and an extraneous babble from the street
Confirming the new value the hollow core has again, the light
From the lighthouse that protects as it pushes us away.

1985

GALWAY KINNELL

(1927–)

Galway Kinnell was born in Providence, Rhode Island, and raised in Pawtucket. After an education interrupted by a year in the navy, he graduated from Princeton in 1948 and earned an M.A. from the University of Rochester the next year. In the early 1950's he taught at the Downtown Center of the University of Chicago. Two years in France, teaching at the University of Grenoble, were followed by two in New

York, and then a year at the University of Teheran in Iran. The serious interest in poetry shown as an undergraduate at Princeton had matured over the years and was now displayed in a first book of verse, *What a Kingdom It Was* (1960). With this volume well received, his career blossomed with the aid of a Guggenheim Fellowship and a National Institute of Arts and Letters Award. *Flower Herding on Mount Monadnock* (1964) and *Body Rags* (1968) extended his range and subject matter. Assisted by other awards and by brief teaching engagements at several universities, he has spent much time writing at his home in Sheffield, Vermont, and has lived recently in New York City and in Hawaii. He has been among those poets deeply engaged in the social movements of his time, serving with the Congress of Racial Equality in the 1960's and active in Poets Against the Vietnam War.

Kinnell's subjects are nature, personal exploration, and social commentary. Some of his early work is reminiscent of Yeats, whom he first read in the company of W. S. Merwin at Princeton. His early iambic pentameters, however, tended to be ragged, and he soon turned to the free verse characteristic of his mature voice. He has expressed strong admiration for John Clare, Christopher Smart, and D. H. Lawrence among English poets, and for Pablo Neruda, whose work he first read with his Spanish wife. His long poem *The Book of Nightmares* (1971) owes something to Rilke's *Duino Elegies,* though it is clearly personal in content and dedicated to Kinnell's children. The personal note also dominates in the poems of *Mortal Acts, Mortal Words* (1980) and *The Past* (1985). His most obvious American kinships are to Whitman, Hart Crane, and Williams, with whom he has shared both an impatience with formal structures and an ambition to record an American complexity observed clearly in the particulars of experience and heightened at times to the level of myth.

Selected Poems, 1982, gathers poems from six earlier books. *The Avenue Bearing the Initial of Christ into the New World: Poems 1946–1964,* 1974, is an earlier collection. Other major titles to date are named above. *The Hen Flower,* 1970, and *The Shoes of Wandering,* 1971, are separately published sections of *The Book of Nightmares,* 1971. *First Poems, 1946–1954* was published in 1970. *Black Light,* 1967, is a novel. *The Poems of François Villon,* 1965, is one of several translations. Some of Kinnell's commentary on poetry is gathered in his *Walking Down the Stairs: Selections from Interviews,* 1978. James Guimond wrote *Seeing and Healing: A Study of the Poetry of Galway Kinnell,* 1985. Brief critical assessments are by Richard Howard in *Alone with America,* 1969; and Daniel Hoffman in his *Harvard Guide to Contemporary American Writing,* 1979.

To Christ Our Lord

The legs of the elk punctured the snow's crust
And wolves floated lightfooted on the land
Hunting Christmas elk living and frozen;
Inside snow melted in a basin, and a woman basted
A bird spread over coals by its wings and head.

Snow had sealed the windows; candles lit
The Christmas meal. The Christmas grace chilled
The cooked bird, being long-winded and the room cold.
During the words a boy thought, is it fitting
To eat this creature killed on the wing?

He had killed it himself, climbing out
Alone on snowshoes in the Christmas dawn,
The fallen snow swirling and the snowfall gone,
Heard its throat scream as the gunshot scattered,
Watched it drop, and fished from the snow the dead.

He had not wanted to shoot. The sound
Of wings beating into the hushed air
Had stirred his love, and his fingers
Froze in his gloves, and he wondered,
Famishing, could he fire? Then he fired.

Now the grace praised his wicked act. At its end
The bird on the plate
Stared at his stricken appetite.
There had been nothing to do but surrender,
To kill and to eat; he ate as he had killed, with wonder.

At night on snowshoes on the drifting field
He wondered again, for whom had love stirred?
The stars glittered on the snow and nothing answered.
Then the Swan spread her wings, cross of the cold north,
The pattern and mirror of the acts of earth.

1960

Freedom, New Hampshire

1

We came to visit the cow
Dying of fever,
Towle said it was already
Shoveled under, in a secret
Burial-place in the woods.
We prowled through the woods
Weeks, we never

Found where. Other
Children other summers
Must have found the place
And asked, Why is it
Green here? The rich
Guess a grave, maybe,
The poor think a pit

For dung, like the one
We shoveled in in the fall
That came up green
The next year, and that,
For all that shows, may as well
Have been the grave
Of a cow or something.

2

We found a cowskull once; we thought it was
From one of the asses in the Bible, for the sun
Shone into the holes through which it had seen
Earth as an endless belt carrying gravel, had heard
Its truculence cursed, had learned how sweat

Stinks, and had brayed—shone into the holes
With solemn and majestic light, as if some
Skull somewhere could be Baalbek or the Parthenon.

That night passing Towle's Barn
We saw lights. Towle had lassoed a calf
By its hind legs, and he tugged against the grip
Of the darkness. The cow stood by chewing millet.
Derry and I took hold, too, and hauled.
It was sopping with darkness when it came free.
It was a bullcalf. The cow mopped it awhile,
And we walked around it with a lantern,

And it was sunburned, somehow, and beautiful.
It took a dug as the first business
And sneezed and drank at the milk of light.
When we got it balanced on its legs, it went wobbling
Toward the night. Walking home in darkness
We saw the July moon looking on Freedom, New Hampshire,
We smelled the fall in the air, it was the summer,
We thought, Oh this is but the summer!

3

Once I saw the moon
Drift into the sky like a bright
Pregnancy pared
From a goddess doomed
To keep slender to be beautiful—
Cut loose, and drifting up there
To happen by itself—
And waning, in lost labor;

As we lost our labor
Too—afternoons
When we sat on the gate
By the pasture, under the Ledge,
Buzzing and skirling on toilet-
papered combs tunes
To the rumble-seated cars
Taking the Ossipee Road

On Sundays; for
Though dusk would come upon us
Where we sat, and though we had
Skirled out our hearts in the music,
Yet the dandruffed
Harps we skirled it on
Had done not much better than
Flies, which buzzed, when quick

We trapped them in our hands,
Which went silent when we
Crushed them, which we bore
Downhill to the meadowlark's
Nest full of throats

Which Derry charmed and combed
With an Arabian air, while I
Chucked crushed flies into

Innards I could not see,
For the night had fallen
And the crickets shrilled on all sides
In waves, as if the grassleaves
Shrieked by hillsides
As they grew, and the stars
Made small flashes in the sky,
Like mica flashing in rocks

On the chokecherried Ledge
Where bees I stepped on once
Hit us from behind like a shotgun,
And where we could see
Windowpanes in Freedom flash
And Loon Lake and Winnipesaukee
Flash in the sun
And the blue world flashing.

4

The fingerprints of our eyeballs would zigzag
On the sky; the clouds that came drifting up
Our fingernails would drift into the thin air;
In bed at night there was music if you listened,
Of an old surf breaking far away in the blood.

Children who come by chance on grass green for a man
Can guess cow, dung, man, anything they want,
To them it is the same. To us who knew him as he was
After the beginning and before the end, it is green
For a name called out of the confusions of the earth—

Winnipesaukee coined like a moon, a bullcalf
Dragged from the darkness where it breaks up again,
Larks which long since have crashed for good in the grass
To which we fed the flies, buzzing ourselves like flies,
While the crickets shrilled beyond us, in July . . .

The mind may sort it out and give it names—
When a man dies he dies trying to say without slurring
The abruptly decaying sounds. It is true
That only flesh dies, and spirit flowers without stop
For men, cows, dung, for all dead things; and it is good, yes—

But an incarnation is in particular flesh
And the dust that is swirled into a shape
And crumbles and is swirled again had but one shape
That was this man. When he is dead the grass
Heals what he suffered, but he remains dead,
And the few who loved him know this until they die.

For my brother, 1925–1957

1960

The Bear

1

In late winter
I sometimes glimpse bits of steam
coming up from
some fault in the old snow
and bend close and see it is lung-colored
and put down my nose
and know
the chilly, enduring odor of bear.

2

I take a wolf's rib and whittle
it sharp at both ends
and coil it up
and freeze it in blubber and place it out
on the fairway of the bears.

And when it has vanished
I move out on the bear tracks,
roaming in circles
until I come to the first, tentative, dark
splash on the earth.

And I set out
running, following the splashes
of blood wandering over the world.
At the cut, gashed resting places
I stop and rest,
at the crawl-marks
where he lay out on his belly
to overpass some stretch of bauchy ice
I lie out
dragging myself forward with bear-knives in my fists.

3

On the third day I begin to starve,
at nightfall I bend down as I knew I would
at a turd sopped in blood,
and hesitate, and pick it up,
and thrust it in my mouth, and gnash it down,
and rise
and go on running.

4

On the seventh day,
living by now on bear blood alone,
I can see his upturned carcass far out ahead, a scraggled,
steamy hulk,
the heavy fur riffling in the wind.

I come up to him
and stare at the narrow-spaced, petty eyes,
the dismayed
face laid back on the shoulder, the nostrils
flared, catching
perhaps the first taint of me as he
died.

I hack
a ravine in his thigh, and eat and drink,
and tear him down his whole length
and open him and climb in
and close him up after me, against the wind,
and sleep.

5

And dream
of lumbering flatfooted
over the tundra,
stabbed twice from within,
splattering a trail behind me,
splattering it out no matter which way I lurch,
no matter which parabola of bear-transcendence,
which dance of solitude I attempt,
which gravity-clutched leap,
which trudge, which groan.

6

Until one day I totter and fall—
fall on this
stomach that has tried so hard to keep up,
to digest the blood as it leaked in,
to break up
and digest the bone itself: and now the breeze
blows over me, blows off
the hideous belches of ill-digested bear blood
and rotted stomach
and the ordinary, wretched odor of bear,

blows across
my sore, lolled tongue a song
or screech, until I think I must rise up
and dance. And I lie still.

7

I awaken I think. Marshlights
reappear, geese
come trailing again up the flyway.
In her ravine under old snow the dam-bear
lies, licking
lumps of smeared fur
and drizzly eyes into shapes

with her tongue. And one
hairy-soled trudge stuck out before me,
the next groaned out,
the next,
the next,
the rest of my days I spend
wandering: wondering
what, anyway,
was that sticky infusion, that rank flavor of blood, that poetry, by which I lived?

1968

Under the Maud Moon

1

On the path,
by this wet site
of old fires—
black ashes, black stones, where tramps
must have squatted down,
gnawing on stream water,
unhouseling themselves on cursed bread,
failing to get warm at a twigfire—

I stop,
gather wet wood,
cut dry shavings, and for her,
whose face
I held in my hands
a few hours, whom I gave back
only to keep holding the space where she was,

I light
a small fire in the rain.

The black
wood reddens, the deathwatches inside
begin running out of time, I can see
the dead, crossed limbs
longing again for the universe, I can hear
in the wet wood the snap
and re-snap of the same embrace being torn.

The raindrops trying
to put the fire out
fall into it and are
changed: the oath broken,
the oath sworn between earth and water, flesh and spirit, broken,
to be sworn again,
over and over, in the clouds, and to be broken again,
over and over, on earth.

2

I sit a moment
by the fire, in the rain, speak
a few words into its warmth—
stone saint smooth stone—and sing
one of the songs I used to croak
for my daughter, in her nightmares.

Somewhere out ahead of me
a black bear sits alone
on his hillside, nodding from side
to side. He sniffs
the blossom-smells, the rained earth,
finally he gets up,
eats a few flowers, trudges away,
his fur glistening
in the rain.

The singed grease streams
out of the words, the one
held note
remains—a love-note
twisting under my tongue, like the coyote's bark,
curving off, into a
howl.

3

A round-
cheeked girlchild comes awake
in her crib. The green
swaddlings tear open,
a filament or vestment
tears, the blue
flower opens.

And she who is born,
she who sings and cries,
she who begins the passage, her hair
sprouting out,
her gums budding for her first spring on earth,
the mist still clinging about
her face, puts
her hand
into her father's mouth, to take hold of
his song.

4

It is all over,
little one, the flipping
and overleaping, the watery
somersaulting alone in the oneness

under the hill, under
the old, lonely bellybutton
pushing forth again
in remembrance,
the drifting there furled in the dark,
pressing a knee or elbow
along a slippery wall, sculpting
the world with each thrash—the stream
of omphalos blood humming all about you.

5

Her head
enters the headhold
that starts sucking her forth: being itself
closes down all over her, gives her
into the shuddering
grip of departure, the slow,
agonized clenches making
the last molds of her life in the dark.

6

The black eye
opens, the pupil
droozed with black hairs
stops, the chakra
on top of the brain throbs a long moment in world light,

and she skids out on her face into light,
this peck
of stunned flesh
clotted with celestial cheesiness, glowing
with the astral violet
of the underlife. And as they cut

her tie to the darkness
she dies
a moment, turns blue as a coal,
the limbs shaking
as the memories rush out of them. When

they hang her up
by the feet, she sucks
air, screams
her first song—and turns rose,
the slow,
beating, featherless arms
already clutching at the emptiness.

7

When it was cold
on our hillside, and you cried

in the crib rocking
through the darkness, on wood
knifed down to the curve of the smile, a sadness
stranger than ours, all of it
flowing from the other world,

I used to come to you
and sit by you
and sing to you. You did not know,
and yet you will remember,
in the silent zones
of the brain, a specter, descendant
of the ghostly forefathers, singing
to you in the nighttime—
not the songs
of light said to wave
through the bright hair of angels,
but a blacker
rasping flowering on that tongue.

For when the Maud moon
glimmered in those first nights,
and the Archer lay
sucking the icy biestings[1] of the cosmos,
in his crib of stars,

I had crept down
to riverbanks, their long rustle
of being and perishing, down to marshes
where the earth oozes up
in cold streaks, touching the world
with the underglimmer
of the beginning,
and there learned my only song.

And in the days
when you find yourself orphaned,
emptied
of all wind-singing, of light,
the pieces of cursed bread on your tongue,

may there come back to you
a voice,
spectral, calling you
sister!
from everything that dies.

And then
you shall open
this book, even if it is the book of nightmares.

1971

1. The first milk given by a cow after calving.

Fergus Falling

He climbed to the top
of one of those million white pines
set out across the emptying pastures
of the fifties—some program to enrich the rich
and rebuke the forefathers
who cleared it all once with ox and axe—
climbed to the top, probably to get out
of the shadow
not of those forefathers but of this father,
and saw for the first time,
down in its valley, Bruce Pond, giving off
its little steam in the afternoon,

pond where Clarence Akley came on Sunday mornings to cut down the cedars around the shore, I'd sometimes hear the slow spondees[2] of his work, he's gone,
where Milton Norway came up behind me while I was fishing and stood awhile before I knew he was there, he's the one who put the cedar shingles on the house, some have curled or split, a few have blown off, he's gone,
where Gus Newland logged in the cold snap of '58, the only man willing to go into those woods that never got warmer than ten below, he's gone,
pond where two wards of the state wandered on Halloween, the National Guard searched for them in November, in vain, the next fall a hunter found their skeletons huddled together, in vain, they're gone,
pond where an old fisherman in a rowboat sits, drowning hooked worms, when he goes he's replaced and is never gone,

and when Fergus
saw the pond for the first time
in the clear evening, saw its oldness down there
in its old place in the valley, he became heavier suddenly
in his bones
the way fledglings do just before they fly,
and the soft pine cracked . . .

I would not have heard his cry
if my electric saw had been working,
its carbide teeth speeding through the bland spruce of our time, or burning
black arcs into some scavenged hemlock plank,
like dark circles under eyes
when the brain thinks too close to the skin,
but I was sawing by hand and I heard that cry
as though he were attacked; we ran out,
when we bent over him he said, "Galway, Inés,[3] I saw a pond!"
His face went gray, his eyes fluttered closed a frightening moment . . .

Yes—a pond
that lets off its mist
on clear afternoons of August, in that valley
to which many have come, for their reasons,

2. Metrical feet, each consisting, in English, of two stressed syllables: whāck, whāck.

3. The poet's wife.

from which many have gone, a few for their reasons, most not,
where even now an old fisherman only the pinetops can see
sits in the dry gray wood of his rowboat, waiting for pickerel.

1980

W. S. MERWIN
(1927–)

Born in Pennsylvania in 1927, W. S. Merwin has been able to attain the difficult goal of making his way as professional writer and man of letters. After graduation from Princeton in 1947, he studied French at McGill and Romance languages at Princeton. His appointment as private tutor to the son of Robert Graves on Majorca enabled him to travel to various parts of Spain, Portugal, and France. He found in England and Europe a market for his translations into contemporary English prose or poetry of works originally in Provençal or Catalan, modern French, Spanish, or Portuguese. He also wrote original plays of an experimental character. Meanwhile he has collected his poems in a number of volumes, beginning with *A Mask for Janus* (1952) in the Yale Series of Younger Poets.

Although many of Merwin's subjects are traditional, his rendering and his style are completely modern, even in the longer poems in which fantastic or grotesque sources are employed. Many of his poems are short, of course, and in general these deal with contemporary experience. His basic concept is that art, and particularly a created poem, is in itself an experience; it is not enough for the poem simply to "evoke" experience. Consistent with his "realization" of experience is his emphasis upon sensory response, in which poignant and even painful detail are frequently employed.

In the sixties, his poems began to display a definite strain of surrealism. *The Lice* (1967), the source of "The Last One," is a much admired collection. He has also written short prose fables, somewhat in the manner of the Argentine writer Jorge Luis Borges, collected in *The Miner's Pale Children* (1970) and *Houses and Travellers* (1977).

Merwin's poems to date are collected in *A Mask for Janus,* 1952; *The Dancing Bears,* 1954; *Green with Beasts,* 1956; *The Drunk in the Furnace,* 1960; *The Moving Target,* 1963; *The Lice,* 1967; *The Carrier of Ladders,* 1970; *Writings to an Unfinished Accompaniment,* 1973; *The Compass Flower,* 1977; and *Opening the Hand,* 1983. *The First Four Books of Poems,* 1975, collects the first four titles. *Selected Translations: 1948–69* was published in 1969. *Unframed Originals: Recollections,* 1982, consists of six essays by Merwin on his family. Critical assessments may be found in Cary Nelson and Ed Folsom, eds., *W. S. Merwin: Essays on the Poetry,* 1987.

Grandmother and Grandson

As I hear it, now when there is company
Always the spindly granddam, stuck standing
In her corner like a lady clock long
Silent, out of some hole in the talk
Is apt to clack cup, clatter teeth, and with
Saucer gesturing to no one special,
Shake out her paper voice concerning
That pimply boy her last grandson: "Now who,
Who does he remind you of?"

(Who stuffs there
With cake his puffed face complected half
Of yellow crumbs, his tongue loving over
His damp hands to lick the sticky
From bitten fingers; chinless; all boneless but
His neck and nose; and who now rolls his knowing
Eyes to their attention.)

In vain, in vain,
One after the other, their lusterless
Suggestions of faint likenesses; she
Nods at none, her gaze absent and more
Absent, as though watching for someone through
A frosted window, until they are aware
She has forgotten her own question.

When he is alone, though, with only her
And her hazy eyes in the whole house
To mind him, his way is to take himself
Just out of her small sight and there stay
Till she starts calling; let her call till she
Sounds in pain; and as though in pain, at last,
His answers, each farther, leading her
Down passages, up stairs, with her worry
Hard to swallow as a scarf-end, her pace
A spun child's in a blindfold, to the piled
Dust-coop, trunk- and junk-room at the top
Of all the stairs, where he hides till she sways
Clutching her breath in the very room, then
Behind her slips out, locking the door. His
Laughter down stair after stair she hears
Being forgotten. In the unwashed light,
Lost, she turns among the sheeted mounds
Fingering hems and murmuring, "Where, where
Does it remind me of?" Till someone comes.

1960

The Drunk in the Furnace

For a good decade
The furnace stood in the naked gully, fireless
And vacant as any hat. Then when it was
No more to them than a hulking black fossil
To erode unnoticed with the rest of the junk-hill
By the poisonous creek, and rapidly to be added
To their ignorance,

They were afterwards astonished
To confirm, one morning, a twist of smoke like a pale
Resurrection, staggering out of its chewed hole,
And to remark then other tokens that someone,
Cosily bolted behind the eye-holed iron
Door of the drafty burner, had there established
His bad castle.

Where he gets his spirits
It's a mystery. But the stuff keeps him musical:
Hammer-and-anvilling with poker and bottle
To his jugged bellowings, till the last groaning clang
As he collapses onto the rioting
Springs of a litter of car-seats ranged on the grates,
To sleep like an iron pig.

In their tar-paper church
On a text about stoke-holes that are sated never
Their Reverend lingers. They nod and hate trespassers.
When the furnace wakes, though, all afternoon
Their witless offspring flock like piped rats to its siren
Crescendo, and agape on the crumbling ridge
Stand in a row and learn.

1960

The Last One

Well they'd made up their minds to be everywhere because why not.
Everywhere was theirs because they thought so.
They with two leaves they whom the birds despise.
In the middle of stones they made up their minds.
They started to cut.

Well they cut everything because why not.
Everything was theirs because they thought so.
It fell into its shadows and they took both away.
Some to have some for burning.

Well cutting everything they came to the water.
They came to the end of the day there was one left standing.
They would cut it tomorrow they went away.
The night gathered in the last branches.
The shadow of the night gathered in the shadow on the water.
The night and the shadow put on the same head.
And it said Now.

Well in the morning they cut the last one.
Like the others the last one fell into its shadow.
It fell into its shadow on the water.
They took it away its shadow stayed on the water.

Well they shrugged they started trying to get the shadow away.
They cut right to the ground the shadow stayed whole.
They laid boards on it the shadow came out on top.
They shone lights on it the shadow got blacker and clearer.
They exploded the water the shadow rocked.
They built a huge fire on the roots.
They sent up black smoke between the shadow and the sun.
The new shadow flowed without changing the old one.
They shrugged they went away to get stones.

They came back the shadow was growing.
They started setting up stones it was growing.
They looked the other way it went on growing.
They decided they would make a stone out of it.
They took stones to the water they poured them into the shadow.
They poured them in they poured them in the stones vanished.
The shadow was not filled it went on growing.
That was one day.

The next day was just the same it went on growing.
They did all the same things it was just the same.
They decided to take its water from under it.
They took away water they took it away the water went down.
The shadow stayed where it was before.
It went on growing it grew onto the land.
They started to scrape the shadow with machines.
When it touched the machines it stayed on them.
They started to beat the shadow with sticks.
Where it touched the sticks it stayed on them.
They started to beat the shadow with hands.
Where it touched the hands it stayed on them.
That was another day.

Well the next day started about the same it went on growing.
They pushed lights into the shadow.
Where the shadow got onto them they went out.
They began to stomp on the edge it got their feet.
And when it got their feet they fell down.
It got into eyes the eyes went blind.

The ones that fell down it grew over and they vanished.
The ones that went blind and walked into it vanished.
The ones that could see and stood still
It swallowed their shadows.
Then it swallowed them too and they vanished.
Well the others ran.

The ones that were left went away to live if it would let them.
They went as far as they could.
The lucky ones with their shadows.

1967

For the Anniversary of My Death

Every year without knowing it I have passed the day
When the last fires will wave to me
And the silence will set out
Tireless traveller
Like the beam of a lightless star

Then I will no longer
Find myself in life as in a strange garment

Surprised at the earth
And the love of one woman
And then shamelessness of men
As today writing after three days of rain
Hearing the wren sing and the falling cease
And bowing not knowing to what

1967

A Door

This is a place where a door might be
here where I am standing
in the light outside all the walls

there would be a shadow here
all day long
and a door into it
where now there is me

and somebody would come and knock
on this air
long after I have gone
and there in front of me a life
would open

1973

Vision

What is unseen
flows to what is unseen
passing in part
through what we partly see
we stood up from all fours
far back in the light
to look
as long as there is day
and part of the night

1977

Trees

I am looking at trees
they may be one of the things I will miss
most from the earth
though many of the ones that I have seen
already I cannot remember
and though I seldom embrace the ones I see
and have never been able to speak
with one
I listen to them tenderly

their names have never touched them
they have stood round my sleep
and when it was forbidden to climb them
they have carried me in their branches

1977

The Fields

Saturday on Seventh Street
full-waisted gray-haired women in Sunday sweaters
moving through the tan shades of their booths
bend over cakes they baked at home
they gaze down onto the sleep of stuffed cabbages
they stir with huge spoons sauerkraut and potato dumplings
cooked as those dishes were cooked on deep
misty plains among the sounds of horses
beside fields of black earth on the other side of the globe
that only the oldest think they remember
looking down from their windows into the world
where everybody is now

none of the young has yet wept at the smell
of cabbages
those leaves all face
none of the young after long journeys
weeks in vessels
and staring at strange coasts through fog in first light
has been recognized by the steam of sauerkraut
that is older than anyone living
so on the street they play the music
of what they do not remember
they sing of places they have not known
they dance in new costumes under the windows
in the smell of cabbages from fields
nobody has seen

1983

JAMES WRIGHT

(1927–1980)

A native of Martins Ferry, Ohio, James Wright was graduated from Kenyon College, took an M.A. at Vienna and his Ph.D. from the University of Washington. He taught at the University of Minnesota, Macalester College, and Hunter College in New York City. He described himself as "a bookish man." Wright received many honors, including a Fulbright Fellowship, a Guggenheim Fellowship, and the *Kenyon Review* Poetry Fellowship, 1958–1959.

Communication of ideas and emotions was vitally important to Wright, and the intensity that must be a part of this communication results in great awareness and understanding on the part of the reader. In his lyric and powerful voice, he wrote, as he once expressed it, "about the things I am deeply concerned with—crickets outside my window, cold and hungry old men, * * * a red-haired child in her mother's arms, a feeling of desolation in fall, some cities I've known."

Collected Poems was published in 1971. Individual volumes are *The Green Wall,* 1957; *Saint Judas,* 1959; *The Branch Will Not Break,* 1963; *Shall We Gather at the River,* 1968; *Two Citizens,* 1973; *To a Blossoming Pear Tree,* 1977; and *This Journey,* 1982. His translations include *Twenty Poems of Cesar Vallejo* (with Robert Bly and John Knoepfle), 1963; *The Rider on the White Horse: Selected Short Fiction of Theodor Storm,* 1964; and *Twenty Poems of Pablo Neruda* (with Robert Bly), 1966. Anne Smith edited his letters to and from Leslie Marmon Silko in *The Delicacy and Strength of Lace,* 1986. Dave Smith edited *The Pure Clear Word: Essays on the Poetry of James Wright,* 1982.

Morning Hymn to a Dark Girl

Summoned to desolation by the dawn,
I climb the bridge over the water, see
The Negro mount the driver's cabin and wave
Goodbye to the glum cop across the canal,
Goodbye to the flat face and empty eyes
Made human one more time. That uniform
Shivers and dulls against the pier, is stone.

Now in the upper world, the buses drift
Over the bridge, the gulls collect and fly,
Blown by the rush of rose; aseptic girls
Powder their lank deliberate faces, mount
The fog under the billboards. Over the lake
The windows of the rich waken and yawn.
Light blows across the city, dune on dune.

Caught by the scruff of the neck, and thrown out here
To the pale town, to the stone, to burial,
I celebrate you, Betty, flank and breast
Rich to the yellow silk of bed and floors;
Now half awake, your body blossoming trees;
One arm beneath your neck, your legs uprisen,
You blow dark thighs back, back into the dark.

Your shivering ankles skate the scented air;
Betty, burgeoning your golden skin, you poise
Tracing gazelles and tigers on your breasts,
Deep in the jungle of your bed you drowse;
Fine muscles of the rippling panthers move
And snuggle at your calves; under your arms
Mangoes and melons yearn; and glittering slowly,
Quick parakeets trill in your heavy trees,
O everywhere, Betty, between your boughs.

Pity the rising dead who fear the dark.
Soft Betty, locked from snickers in a dark
Brothel, dream on; scatter the yellow corn
Into the wilderness, and sleep all day.
For the leopards leap into the open grass,
Bananas, lemons fling air, fling odor, fall.
And, gracing darkly the dark light, you flow
Out of the grove to laugh at dreamy boys,

You greet the river with a song so low
No lover on a boat can hear, you slide
Silkily to the water; where you rinse
Your fluted body, fearless; though alive
Orangutans sway from the leaves and gaze,
Crocodiles doze along the oozy shore.

1957

A Note Left in Jimmy Leonard's Shack

Near the dry river's water-mark we found
    Your brother Minnegan,
Flopped like a fish against the muddy ground.
Beany, the kid whose yellow hair turns green,
Told me to find you, even in the rain,
    And tell you he was drowned.

I hid behind the chassis on the bank,
    The wreck of someone's Ford:
I was afraid to come and wake you drunk:
You told me once the waking up was hard,
The daylight beating at you like a board.
    Blood in my stomach sank.

Beside, you told him never to go out
    Along the river-side
Drinking and singing, clattering about.
You might have thrown a rock at me and cried
I was to blame, I let him fall in the road
    And pitch down on his side.

Well, I'll get hell enough when I get home
    For coming up this far,
Leaving the note, and running as I came.
I'll go and tell my father where you are.
You'd better go find Minnegan before
    Policemen hear and come.

Beany went home, and I got sick and ran,
    You old son of a bitch.
You better hurry down to Minnegan;
He's drunk or dying now, I don't know which,
Rolled in the roots and garbage like a fish,
    The poor old man.

1959

Autumn Begins in Martins Ferry, Ohio

In the Shreve High football stadium,
I think of Polacks nursing long beers in Tiltonsville,
And gray faces of Negroes in the blast furnace at Benwood,
And the ruptured night watchman of Wheeling Steel,
Dreaming of heroes.

All the proud fathers are ashamed to go home.
Their women cluck like starved pullets,
Dying for love.

Therefore,
Their sons grow suicidally beautiful
At the beginning of October,
And gallop terribly against each other's bodies.

1963

Lying in a Hammock at William Duffy's Farm in Pine Island, Minnesota

Over my head, I see the bronze butterfly,
Asleep on the black trunk,
Blowing like a leaf in green shadow.
Down the ravine behind the empty house,
The cowbells follow one another
Into the distances of the afternoon.
To my right,
In a field of sunlight between two pines,
The droppings of last year's horses
Blaze up into golden stones.
I lean back, as the evening darkens and comes on.
A chicken hawk floats over, looking for home.
I have wasted my life.

1963

Having Lost My Sons, I Confront the Wreckage of the Moon: Christmas, 1960

After dark
Near the South Dakota border,
The moon is out hunting, everywhere,
Delivering fire,
And walking down hallways
Of a diamond.

Behind a tree,
It lights on the ruins
Of a white city:
Frost, frost.

Where are they gone,
Who lived there?

Bundled away under wings
And dark faces.

I am sick
Of it, and I go on,
Living, alone, alone,
Past the charred silos, past the hidden graves
Of Chippewas and Norwegians.

This cold winter
Moon spills the inhuman fire
Of jewels
Into my hands.

Dead riches, dead hands, the moon
Darkens,
And I am lost in the beautiful white ruins
Of America.

1963

In Terror of Hospital Bills

I still have some money
To eat with, alone
And frightened, knowing how soon
I will waken a poor man.

It snows freely and freely hardens
On the lawns of my hope, my secret
Hounded and flayed. I wonder
What words to beg money with.

Pardon me, sir, could you?
Which way is St. Paul?
I thirst.
I am a full-blooded Sioux Indian.
Soon I am sure to become so hungry
I will have to leap barefoot through gas-fire veils of shame,
I will have to stalk timid strangers
On the whorsehouse corners.

Oh moon, sow leaves on my hands,
On my seared face, oh I love you.
My throat is open, insane,
Tempting pneumonia.

But my life was never so precious
To me as now.
I will have to beg coins
After dark.

I will learn to scent the police,
And sit or go blind, stay mute, be taken for dead
For your sake, oh my secret,
My life.

1968

Two Postures Beside a Fire

1

Tonight I watch my father's hair,
As he sits dreaming near his stove.
Knowing my feather of despair,
He sent me an owl's plume for love,
Lest I not know, so I've come home.
Tonight Ohio, where I once
Hounded and cursed my loneliness,
Shows me my father, who broke stones,
Wrestled and mastered great machines,
And rests, shadowing his lovely face.

2

Nobly his hands fold together in his repose.
He is proud of me, believing
I have done strong things among men and become a man
Of place among men of place in the large cities.
I will not waken him.
I have come home alone, without wife or child
To delight him. Awake, solitary and welcome,
I too sit near his stove, the lines
Of an ugly age scarring my face, and my hands
Twitch nervously about.

1968

Small Frogs Killed on the Highway

Still,
I would leap too
Into the light,
If I had the chance.
It is everything, the wet green stalk of the field
On the other side of the road.
They crouch there, too, faltering in terror
And take strange wing. Many
Of the dead never moved, but many
Of the dead are alive forever in the split second
Auto headlights more sudden
Than their drivers know.
The drivers burrow backward into dank pools
Where nothing begets
Nothing.

Across the road, tadpoles are dancing
On the quarter thumbnail
Of the moon. They can't see,
Not yet.

1971

The Vestal in the Forum

This morning I do not despair
For the impersonal hatred that the cold
Wind seems to feel
When it slips fingers into the flaws
Of lovely things men made,
The shoulders of a stone girl[1]
Pitted by winter.
Not a spring passes but the roses
Grow stronger in their support of the wind,
And now they are conquerors,
Not garlands any more,
Of this one face:
Dimming,
Clearer to me than most living faces.
The slow wind and the slow roses
Are ruining an eyebrow here, a mole there.
But in this little while
Before she is gone, her very haggardness
Amazes me. A dissolving
Stone, she seems to change from stone to something
Frail, to someone I can know, someone
I can almost name.

1982

PHILIP LEVINE

(1928–)

Born in Detroit, Michigan, into a family of Russian Jewish immigrants, Philip Levine was educated there in public schools during the years of the Depression and World War II. After graduation from Wayne University in 1950, he held a succession of unsatisfying jobs, discovering a major part of his subject matter in his experience as "an industrial worker and bum in America." Those he worked with, he has said, have been his inspiration: "I try to pay homage to the people who taught me my life was a holy thing, who convinced me that my formal education was a lie." Mainly rural southerners who had come to find work in Detroit, they taught him "we were meant to come into this world and live as best we could with the beasts and the trees and plants and to leave the place with our love and respect for it intact * * *." Already writing poems as an undergraduate, he continued in the next few years trying to "find a voice for the voiceless," those people around him who "weren't being heard." Enrolling later than some other students at the University of Iowa, he earned an M.F.A there in 1957, accepted a fellowship at Stanford, and then in 1958 a teaching position at California State University at Fresno. In recent years he has taught at Tufts University.

Levine's early poetry was traditional in form. Later he experimented with syllabic verse before turning to free forms. Like others who matured as poets in the 1950's, he cites especially the influence of William Carlos Williams in providing him with an

1. *I.e.,* a statue of a vestal virgin standing, as the title makes clear, in the ruins of the Roman Forum.

alternative to a poetic practice modeled on the work of Yeats, Eliot, Auden, and Dylan Thomas—the stars of the poetic firmament immediately after World War II. His subjects have continued to be the scenes and concerns of his youth—city streets, family, the Jewish heritage, menial labor. Sometimes bleak and almost always described in a flat, colloquial voice, without ornamentation, his landscapes, and the stories that evolve within them, evade hopelessness by driving toward the condition summarized in the last words of his *Selected Poems:* "American, beautiful, and true."

Selected Poems, 1984, is drawn from ten earlier books: *On the Edge,* 1963; *Not This Pig,* 1968; *Red Dust,* 1971; *Pili's Wall,* 1971; *They Feed They Lion,* 1972; *1933,* 1974; *The Names of the Lost,* 1976; *Ashes,* 1979; *7 Years from Somewhere,* 1979; and *One for the Rose,* 1981. More recent is *Sweet Will,* 1985. Other poetry titles are *Silent in America: Vivas for Those Who Failed,* 1965; and *Five Detroits,* 1970. Interviews are collected in *Don't Ask,* 1981. A brief assessment appears in *Dictionary of Literary Biography, Volume 5: American Poets Since World War II,* 1980.

Heaven

If you were twenty-seven
and had done time for beating
your ex-wife and had
no dreams you remembered
in the morning, you might
lie on your bed and listen
to a mad canary sing
and think it all right to be
there every Saturday
ignoring your neighbors, the streets,
the signs that said join,
and the need to be helping.
You might build, as he did,
a network of golden ladders
so that the bird could roam
on all levels of the room;
you might paint the ceiling blue,
the floor green, and shade
the place you called the sun
so that things came softly to order
when the light came on.
He and the bird lived
in the fine weather of heaven;
they never aged, they
never tired or wanted
all through that war,
but when it was over
and the nation had been saved,
he knew they'd be hunted.
He knew, as you would too,
that he'd be laid off
for not being braver,
and it would do no good
to show how he had taken
clothespins and cardboard
and made each step safe.
It would do no good
to have been one of the few

that climbed higher and higher
even in time of war,
for now there would be the poor
asking for their share,
and hurt men in uniforms,
and no one to believe
that heaven was really here.

1968

They Feed They Lion

Out of burlap sacks, out of bearing butter,
Out of black bean and wet slate bread,
Out of the acids of rage, the candor of tar,
Out of creosote, gasoline, drive shafts, wooden dollies,
They Lion grow.
Out of the gray hills
Of industrial barns, out of rain, out of bus ride,
West Virginia to Kiss My Ass, out of buried aunties,
Mothers hardening like pounded stumps, out of stumps,
Out of the bones' need to sharpen and the muscles' to stretch,
They Lion grow.
Earth is eating trees, fence posts,
Gutted cars, earth is calling in her little ones,
"Come home, Come home!" From pig balls,
From the ferocity of pig driven to holiness,
From the furred ear and the full jowl come
The repose of the hung belly, from the purpose
They Lion grow.
From the sweet glues of the trotters
Come the sweet kinks of the fist, from the full flower
Of the hams the thorax of caves,
From "Bow Down" come "Rise Up,"
Come they Lion from the reeds of shovels,
The grained arm that pulls the hands,
They Lion grow.
From my five arms and all my hands,
From all my white sins forgiven, they feed,
From my car passing under the stars,
They Lion, from my children inherit,
From the oak turned to a wall, they Lion,
From they sack and they belly opened
And all that was hidden burning on the oil-stained earth
They feed they Lion and he comes.

1972

You Can Have It

My brother comes home from work
and climbs the stairs to our room.
I can hear the bed groan and his shoes drop
one by one. You can have it, he says.

The moonlight streams in the window
and his unshaven face is whitened
like the face of the moon. He will sleep
long after noon and waken to find me gone.

Thirty years will pass before I remember
that moment when suddenly I knew each man
has one brother who dies when he sleeps
and sleeps when he rises to face this life,

and that together they are only one man
sharing a heart that always labors, hands
yellowed and cracked, a mouth that gasps
for breath and asks, Am I gonna make it?

All night at the ice plant he had fed
the chute its silvery blocks, and then I
stacked cases of orange soda for the children
of Kentucky, one gray boxcar at a time

with always two more waiting. We were twenty
for such a short time and always in
the wrong clothes, crusted with dirt
and sweat. I think now we were never twenty.

In 1948 in the city of Detroit, founded
by de la Mothe Cadillac[1] for the distant purposes
of Henry Ford, no one wakened or died,
no one walked the streets or stoked a furnace,

for there was no such year, and now
that year has fallen off all the old newspapers,
calendars, doctors' appointments, bonds,
wedding certificates, drivers licenses.

The city slept. The snow turned to ice.
The ice to standing pools or rivers
racing in the gutters. Then bright grass rose
between the thousands of cracked squares,

and that grass died. I give you back 1948.
I give you all the years from then
to the coming one. Give me back the moon
with its frail light falling across a face.

Give me back my young brother, hard
and furious, with wide shoulders and a curse
for God and burning eyes that look upon
all creation and say, You can have it.

1979

1. Antoine de la Mothe Cadillac (1657?–1730), French colonial governor in North America, who founded Detroit in 1701.

One for the Rose

Three weeks ago I went back
to the same street corner where
27 years before I took a bus for Akron,
Ohio, but now there was only a blank space
with a few concrete building blocks
scattered among the beer cans
and broken bottles and a view of
the blank backside of an abandoned hotel.
I wondered if Akron was still down there
hidden hundreds of miles south among
the small, shoddy trees of Ohio,
a town so ripe with the smell
of defeat that its citizens lied
about their age, their height, sex,
income, and previous condition
of anything. I spent all of a Saturday
there, disguised in a cashmere suit
stolen from a man twenty pounds
heavier than I, and I never unbuttoned
the jacket. I remember someone
married someone, but only the bride's
father and mother went out
on the linoleum dance floor and leaned
into each other like whipped school kids.
I drank whatever I could find and made
my solitary way back to the terminal
and dozed among the drunks and widows
toward dawn and the first thing north.
What was I doing in Akron, Ohio
waiting for a bus that groaned slowly
between the sickened farms of 1951
and finally entered the smeared air
of hell on US 24 where the Rouge plant[2]
destroys the horizon? I could have been
in Paris at the foot of Gertrude Stein,[3]
I could have been drifting among
the reeds of a clear stream
like the little Moses,[4] to be found
by a princess and named after a conglomerate
or a Jewish hero. Instead I was born
in the wrong year and in the wrong place,
and I made my way so slowly and badly
that I remember every single turn,
and each one smells like an overblown rose,
yellow, American, beautiful, and true.

1981

2. Ford Motor Company plant at River Rouge, just outside Detroit.
3. (1874–1946), American expatriate writer who befriended Hemingway and other younger writers.
4. The story of Moses, discovered in the bulrushes by Pharaoh's daughter, is told in Exodus ii: 1–10.

ANNE SEXTON

(1928–1974)

Anne Sexton was born in Newton, Massachusetts, and grew up in Wellesley, where she attended local schools. She attended Garland Junior College and married in 1948. In addition to her life as a wife and mother and her writing, she taught at Wayland High School in Massachusetts, and at Colgate and Boston University. From her youth she was determined to learn the art she had practiced, and she early gained acceptance in a wide circle of magazines. She wrote as an intensely subjective woman with the searching imagination necessary to identify with the experience of others: and she wrote with the utmost subjectivity without seeming in most cases to be writing of herself. Her interests were primarily in the domestic scene or crisis, in the cycle of life and human companionship, and in nature—primarily that of the Massachusetts coast and Maine. She studied poetry with Robert Lowell as professor and Sylvia Plath as a fellow student at Boston University and was awarded numerous fellowships. She committed suicide in 1974.

The Complete Poems was published in 1981. Earlier titles are *To Bedlam and Part Way Back,* 1960; *All My Pretty Ones,* 1962; *Selected Poems,* 1964; *Live or Die,* 1966; *Love Poems,* 1969; *Transformations,* 1971; *The Book of Folly,* 1972; *The Death Notebooks,* 1974; and *The Awful Rowing Toward God,* 1975. Linda Gray Sexton edited two posthumous collections, *45 Mercy Street,* 1976; and *Words for Dr. Y.: Uncollected Poems with Three Stories,* 1978. Linda Gray Sexton and Lois Ames edited *Anne Sexton: A Self-Portrait in Letters,* 1977. Steven E. Colburn edited *No Evil Star: Selected Essays, Interviews, and Prose,* 1985. J. D. McClatchy edited *Anne Sexton: The Artist and Her Critics,* 1978.

A study is Diana Hume George, *Oedipus Anne: The Poetry of Anne Sexton,* 1987.

Her Kind

I have gone out, a possessed witch,
haunting the black air, braver at night;
dreaming evil, I have done my hitch
over the plain houses, light by light:
lonely thing, twelve-fingered, out of mind.
A woman like that is not a woman, quite.
I have been her kind.

I have found the warm caves in the woods,
filled them with skillets, carvings, shelves,
closets, silks, innumerable goods;
fixed the suppers for the worms and the elves:
whining, rearranging the disaligned.
A woman like that is misunderstood.
I have been her kind.

I have ridden in your cart, driver,
waved my nude arms at villages going by,
learning the last bright routes, survivor
where your flames still bite my thigh
and my ribs crack where your wheels wind.
A woman like that is not ashamed to die.
I have been her kind.

1960

The Farmer's Wife

From the hodge porridge
of their country lust,
their local life in Illinois,
where all their acres look
like a sprouting broom factory,
they name just ten years now
that she has been his habit;
as again tonight he'll say
honey bunch let's go
and she will not say how there
must be more to living
than this brief bright bridge
of the raucous bed or even
the slow braille touch of him
like a heavy god grown light,
that old pantomime of love
that she wants although
it leaves her still alone,
built back again at last,
mind's apart from him, living
her own self in her own words
and hating the sweat of the house
they keep when they finally lie
each in separate dreams
and then how she watches him,
still strong in the blowzy bag
of his usual sleep while
her young years bungle past
their same marriage bed
and she wishes him cripple, or poet,
or even lonely, or sometimes,
better, my lover, dead.

1959 1960

The Truth the Dead Know

For my mother, born March 1902, died March 1959
and my father, born February 1900, died June 1959

Gone, I say, and walk from church,
refusing the stiff procession to the grave,
letting the dead ride alone in the hearse.
It is June. I am tired of being brave.

We drive to The Cape. I cultivate
myself where the sun gutters from the sky,
where the sea swings in like an iron gate
and we touch. In another country people die.

My darling, the wind falls in like stones
from the whitehearted water and when we touch
we enter touch entirely. No one's alone.
Men kill for this, or for as much.

And what of the dead? They lie without shoes
in their stone boats. They are more like stone
than the sea would be if it stopped. They refuse
to be blessed, throat, eye, and knucklebone.

1962

All My Pretty Ones[1]

Father, this year's jinx rides us apart
where you followed our mother to her cold slumber;
a second shock boiling its stone to your heart,
leaving me here to shuffle and disencumber
you from the residence you could not afford:
a gold key, your half of a woolen mill,
twenty suits from Dunne's, an English Ford,
the love and legal verbiage of another will,
boxes of pictures of people I do not know.
I touch their cardboard faces. They must go.

But the eyes, as thick as wood in this album,
hold me. I stop here, where a small boy
waits in a ruffled dress for someone to come . . .
for this soldier who holds his bugle like a toy
or for this velvet lady who cannot smile.
Is this your father's father, this commodore
in a mailman suit? My father, time meanwhile
has made it unimportant who you are looking for.
I'll never know what these faces are all about.
I lock them into their book and throw them out.

This is the yellow scrapbook that you began
the year I was born; as crackling now and wrinkly
as tobacco leaves: clippings where Hoover[2] outran
the Democrats, wiggling his dry finger at me
and Prohibition; news where the *Hindenburg*[3] went
down and recent years where you went flush
on war. This year, solvent but sick, you meant
to marry that pretty widow in a one-month rush.
But before you had that second chance, I cried
on your fat shoulder. Three days later you died.

These are the snapshots of marriage, stopped in places.
Side by side at the rail toward Nassau[4] now;
here, with the winner's cup at the speedboat races,
here, in tails, at the Cotillion,[5] you take a bow,
here, by our kennel of dogs with their pink eyes,
running like show-bred pigs in their chain-link pen;
here, at the horseshow where my sister wins a prize;
and here, standing like a duke among groups of men.

1. A quotation from Macduff's reaction to the news that Macbeth has had his wife and children killed, *Macbeth,* IV, iii, 216.
2. Herbert Hoover (1874–1964) was elected president in 1928, during the period when the sale of alcoholic beverages was prohibited in the United States (1920–1933).
3. A German airship, or zeppelin, that exploded and burned at Lakehurst, New Jersey, in 1937.
4. Capital of the Bahama Islands.
5. Usually a ball to introduce debutantes to society.

Now I fold you down, my drunkard, my navigator,
my first lost keeper, to love or look at later.

I hold a five-year diary that my mother kept
for three years, telling all she does not say
of your alcoholic tendency. You overslept,
she writes. My God, father, each Christmas Day
with your blood, will I drink down your glass
of wine? The diary of your hurly-burly years
goes to my shelf to wait for my age to pass.
Only in this hoarded span will love persevere.
Whether you are pretty or not, I outlive you,
bend down my strange face to yours and forgive you.

1962

With Mercy for the Greedy

For my friend, Ruth, who urges me to make an appointment for the Sacrament of Confession

Concerning your letter in which you ask
me to call a priest and in which you ask
me to wear The Cross that you enclose;
your own cross,
your dog-bitten cross,
no larger than a thumb,
small and wooden, no thorns, this rose—

I pray to its shadow,
that gray place
where it lies on your letter . . . deep, deep.
I detest my sins and I try to believe
in The Cross. I touch its tender hips, its dark jawed face,
its solid neck, its brown sleep.

True. There is
a beautiful Jesus.
He is frozen to his bones like a chunk of beef.
How desperately he wanted to pull his arms in!
How desperately I touch his vertical and horizontal axes!
But I can't. Need is not quite belief.

All morning long
I have worn
your cross, hung with package string around my throat.
It tapped me lightly as a child's heart might,
tapping secondhand, softly waiting to be born.
Ruth, I cherish the letter you wrote.

My friend, my friend, I was born
doing reference work in sin, and born
confessing it. This is what poems are:
with mercy
for the greedy,

they are the tongue's wrangle,
the world's pottage, the rat's star.

1962

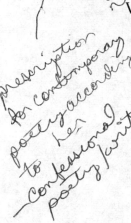

Letter Written on a Ferry While Crossing Long Island Sound

I am surprised to see
that the ocean is still going on.
Now I am going back
and I have ripped my hand
from your hand as I said I would
and I have made it this far
as I said I would
and I am on the top deck now
holding my wallet, my cigarettes
and my car keys
at 2 o'clock on a Tuesday
in August of 1960.

Dearest,
although everything has happened,
nothing has happened.
The sea is very old.
The sea is the face of Mary,
without miracles or rage
or unusual hope,
grown rough and wrinkled
with incurable age.

Still,
I have eyes.
These are my eyes:
the orange letters that spell
ORIENT on the life preserver
that hangs by my knees;
the cement lifeboat that wears
its dirty canvas coat;
the faded sign that sits on its shelf
saying KEEP OFF.
Oh, all right, I say,
I'll save myself.

Over my right shoulder
I see four nuns
who sit like a bridge club,
their faces poked out
from under their habits,
as good as good babies who
have sunk into their carriages.
Without discrimination
the wind pulls the skirts
of their arms.
Almost undressed,

I see what remains:
that holy wrist,
that ankle,
that chain.

Oh God,
although I am very sad,
could you please
let these four nuns
loosen from their leather boots
and their wooden chairs
to rise out
over this greasy deck,
out over this iron rail,
nodding their pink heads to one side,
flying four abreast
in the old-fashioned side stroke;
each mouth open and round,
breathing together
as fish do,
singing without sound.

Dearest,
see how my dark girls sally forth,
over the passing lighthouse of Plum Gut,
its shell as rusty
as a camp dish,
as fragile as a pagoda
on a stone;
out over the little lighthouse
that warns me of drowning winds
that rub over its blind bottom
and its blue cover;
winds that will take the toes
and the ears of the rider
or the lover.

There go my dark girls,
their dresses puff
in the leeward air.
Oh, they are lighter than flying dogs
or the breath of dolphins;
each mouth opens gratefully,
wider than a milk cup.
My dark girls sing for this.
They are going up.
See them rise
on black wings, drinking
the sky, without smiles
or hands
or shoes.
They call back to us
from the gauzy edge of paradise,
good news, good news.

1962

January 1st

Today is favorable for joint financial affairs but do not take any chances with speculation.

My daddy played the market.
My mother cut her coupons.
The children ran in circles.
The maid announced, the soup's on.

The guns were cleaned on Sunday.
The family went out to shoot.
We sat in the blind for hours.
The ducks fell down like fruit.

The big fat war was going on.
So profitable for daddy.
She drove a pea green Ford.
He drove a pearl gray Caddy.

In the end they used it up.
All that pale green dough.
The rest I spent on doctors
who took it like gigolos.

My financial affairs are small.
Indeed they seem to shrink.
My heart is on a budget.
It keeps me on the brink.

I tell it stories now and then
and feed it images like honey.
I will not speculate today
with poems that think they're money.

August 26, 1971 1981

ADRIENNE RICH

(1929–)

Born in Baltimore in 1929, Adrienne Rich was graduated from Radcliffe College (1951). In her senior year at college she had her first volume of poetry, *A Change of World* (1951), accepted by Auden for the Yale Series of Younger Poets. Two years after graduation, she married Alfred Conrad, who died in 1970; they had three sons.

As with many American poets, her creative sensibilities have found excitement in contact with the current impulse abroad, in older civilizations. She has discovered an affinity with contemporary Dutch poets, having lived in the Netherlands in 1961–1962, and published a number of translations of these in *Necessities of Life* (1966). Primarily considered, however, the inspiration of her own work has been the great tradition of American poetry from Frost and Williams to Roethke, discovering, like the latter, an individual style and technique for communicating her complex inner consciousness of the "Necessities of Life." Robert Lowell, for example, saw her verse as "a poised and intact completion," deeply reminiscent of "old poets, mostly American ones, and still more * * * of our old prose writers—Hawthorne above all, with his dark and musical sense, the gaiety of his almost breathless resignation."

In the late 1950's, she found herself "able to write, for the first time, directly about experiencing myself as a woman." Her poems and prose writings since that time have been an important part of the women's movement in America.

The Fact of a Doorframe: Poems Selected and New 1950–1984, 1984, selects from nine earlier books and includes some new poems. Other poetry titles are *A Change of World,* 1951; *The Diamond Cutters,* 1955; *Snapshots of a Daughter-in-Law,* 1963; *Necessities of Life,* 1966; *Selected Poems,* 1967; *Leaflets: Poems 1965–1968,* 1969; *Will to Change: Poems,* 1971; *Diving into the Wreck: Poems 1971–1972,* 1973; *Poems: Selected and New, 1950–1974,* 1975; *The Dream of a Common Language: Poems 1974–1977,* 1978; *A Wild Patience Has Taken Me This Far: Poems 1978–1981,* 1981; and *Your Native Land, Your Life,* 1987. Prose works are *Of Woman Born: Motherhood as Experience and Institution,* 1976; *On Lies, Secrets, and Silence: Selected Prose 1966–1978,* 1979; and *Blood, Bread, and Poetry: Selected Prose 1979–1985,* 1987. Selections from Rich's poetry and prose, as well as essays about her work, are in *Adrienne Rich's Poetry,* ed. Barbara Charlesworth Gelpi and Albert Gelpi, 1975.

Critical assessments include Jane Roberta Cooper, ed., *Reading Adrienne Rich,* 1984; Wendy Martin, *An American Triptych: Anne Bradstreet, Emily Dickinson, Adrienne Rich,* 1984; and Claire Keyes, *The Aesthetics of Power: The Poetry of Adrienne Rich,* 1986.

Aunt Jennifer's Tigers

Aunt Jennifer's tigers prance across a screen,
Bright topaz denizens of a world of green.
They do not fear the men beneath the tree;
They pace in sleek chivalric certainty.

Aunt Jennifer's fingers fluttering through her wool
Find even the ivory needle hard to pull.
The massive weight of Uncle's wedding band
Sits heavily upon Aunt Jennifer's hand.

When Aunt is dead, her terrified hands will lie
Still ringed with ordeals she was mastered by.
The tigers in the panel that she made
Will go on prancing, proud and unafraid.

1951

The Middle-aged

Their faces, safe as an interior
Of Holland tiles and Oriental carpet,
Where the fruit-bowl, always filled, stood in a light
Of placid afternoon—their voices' measure,
Their figures moving in the Sunday garden
To lay the tea outdoors or trim the borders,
Afflicted, haunted us. For to be young
Was always to live in other peoples' houses
Whose peace, if we sought it, had been made by others,
Was ours at second-hand and not for long.
The custom of the house, not ours, the sun
Fading the silver-blue Fortuny curtains,
The reminiscence of a Christmas party
Of fourteen years ago—all memory,

Signs of possession and of being possessed,
We tasted, tense with envy. They were so kind,
Would have given us anything; the bowl of fruit
Was filled for us, there was a room upstairs
We must call ours: but twenty years of living
They could not give. Nor did they ever speak
Of the coarse stain on that polished balustrade,
The crack in the study window, or the letters
Locked in a drawer and the key destroyed.
All to be understood by us, returning
Late, in our own time—how that peace was made,
Upon what terms, with how much left unsaid.

1955

The Diamond Cutters

However legendary,
The stone is still a stone,
Though it had once resisted
The weight of Africa,
The hammer-blows of time
That wear to bits of powder
The mountain and the pebble—
But not this coldest one.

Now, you intelligence
So late dredged up from dark
Upon whose smoky walls
Bison took fumbling form
Or flint was edged on flint—
Now, careful arriviste,
Delineate at will
Incisions in the ice.

Be serious, because
The stone may have contempt
For too-familiar hands,
And because all you do
Loses or gains by this:
Respect the adversary,
Meet it with tools refined,
And thereby set your price.

Be hard of heart, because
The stone must leave your hand.
Although you liberate
Pure and expensive fires
Fit to enamour Shebas,
And because all you do
For too-familiar hands,
Keep your desire apart.
Love only what you do,
And not what you have done.

Be proud, when you have set
The final spoke of flame
In that prismatic wheel,
And nothing's left this day
Except to see the sun
Shine on the false and the true,
And know that Africa
Will yield you more to do.

1955

Necessities of Life

Piece by piece I seem
to re-enter the world: I first began

a small, fixed dot, still see
that old myself, dark-blue thumbtack

pushed into the scene,
a hard little head protruding

from the pointillist's buzz and bloom.
After a time the dot

begins to ooze. Certain heats
melt it.
Now I was hurriedly

blurring into ranges
of burnt red, burning green,

whole biographies swam up and
swallowed me like Jonah.

Jonah! I was Wittgenstein,
Mary Wollstonecraft, the soul

of Louis Jouvet,[1] dead
in a blown-up photograph.

Till, wolfed almost to shreds,
I learned to make myself

unappetizing. Scaly as a dry bulb
thrown into a cellar

I used myself, let nothing use me.
Like being on a private dole,

sometimes more like kneading bricks in Egypt.
What life was there, was mine,

1. Ludwig Wittgenstein (1889–1951), Austrian philosopher; Mary Wollstonecraft (1759–1797), English author and feminist; Louis Jouvet (1887–1951), French actor and director.

now and again to lay
one hand on a warm brick

and touch the sun's ghost
with economical joy,

now and again to name
over the bare necessities.

So much for those days. Soon
practice may make me middling-perfect, I'll

dare inhabit the world
trenchant in motion as an eel, solid

as a cabbage-head. I have invitations:
a curl of mist steams upward

from a field, visible as my breath,
houses along a road stand waiting

like old women knitting, breathless
to tell their tales.

1962 1966

The Trees

The trees inside are moving out into the forest,
the forest that was empty all these days
where no bird could sit
no insect hide
no sun bury its feet in shadow
the forest that was empty all these nights
will be full of trees by morning.

All night the roots work
to disengage themselves from the cracks
in the veranda floor.
The leaves strain toward the glass
small twigs stiff with exertion
long-cramped boughs shuffling under the roof
like newly discharged patients
half-dazed, moving
to the clinic doors.

I sit inside, doors open to the veranda
writing long letters
in which I scarcely mention the departure
of the forest from the house.
The night is fresh, the whole moon shines
in a sky still open
the smell of leaves and lichen
still reaches like a voice into the rooms.

My head is full of whispers
which tomorrow will be silent.

Listen. The glass is breaking.
The trees are stumbling forward
into the night. Winds rush to meet them.
The moon is broken like a mirror,
its pieces flash now in the crown
of the tallest oak.

1963 1966

Face to Face

Never to be lonely like that—
the Early American figure on the beach
in black coat and knee-breeches
scanning the didactic storm in privacy,

never to hear the prairie wolves
in their lunar hilarity
circling one's little all, one's claim
to be Law and Prophets

for all that lawlessness,
never to whet the appetite
weeks early, for a face, a hand
longed-for and dreaded—

How people used to meet!
starved, intense, the old
Christmas gifts saved up till spring,
and the old plain words,

and each with his God-given secret,
spelled out through months of snow and silence,
burning under the bleached scalp; behind dry lips
a loaded gun.

1965 1966

Diving into the Wreck

First having read the book of myths,
and loaded the camera,
and checked the edge of the knife-blade,
I put on
the body-armor of black rubber
the absurd flippers
the grave and awkward mask.
I am having to do this
not like Cousteau[2] with his

2. Jacques Yves Cousteau (1910–), French underwater explorer and author, co-inventor of the aqualung.

assiduous team
aboard the sun-flooded schooner
but here alone.

There is a ladder.
The ladder is always there
hanging innocently
close to the side of the schooner.
We know what it is for,
we who have used it.
Otherwise
it's a piece of maritime floss
some sundry equipment.

I go down.
Rung after rung and still
the oxygen immerses me
the blue light
the clear atoms
of our human air.
I go down.
My flippers cripple me,
I crawl like an insect down the ladder
and there is no one
to tell me when the ocean
will begin.

First the air is blue and then
it is bluer and then green and then
black I am blacking out and yet
my mask is powerful
it pumps my blood with power
the sea is another story
the sea is not a question of power
I have to learn alone
to turn my body without force
in the deep element.

And now: it is easy to forget
what I came for
among so many who have always
lived here
swaying their crenellated[3] fans
between the reefs
and besides
you breathe differently down here.

I came to explore the wreck.
The words are purposes.
The words are maps.
I came to see the damage that was done
and the treasures that prevail.
I stroke the beam of my lamp

3. Notched with indentations or scallops.

slowly along the flank
of something more permanent
than fish or weed

the thing I came for:
the wreck and not the story of the wreck
the thing itself and not the myth

the drowned face[4] always staring
toward the sun
the evidence of damage
worn by salt and sway into this threadbare beauty
the ribs of the disaster
curving their assertion
among the tentative haunters.

This is the place.
And I am here, the mermaid whose dark hair
streams black, the merman in his armored body
We circle silently
about the wreck
we dive into the hold.
I am she: I am he

whose drowned face sleeps with open eyes
whose breasts still bear the stress
whose silver, copper, vermeil[5] cargo lies
obscurely inside barrels
half-wedged and left to rot
we are the half-destroyed instruments
that once held to a course
the water-eaten log
the fouled compass

We are, I am, you are
by cowardice or courage
the one who find our way
back to this scene
carrying a knife, a camera
a book of myths
in which
our names do not appear.

1972 1973

For the Dead

I dreamed I called you on the telephone
to say: *Be kinder to yourself*
but you were sick and would not answer

The waste of my love goes on this way
trying to save you from yourself

4. A reference to the figurehead, a carved figure at the bow of a ship, usually female.

5. Gilded copper, bronze, or silver.

I have always wondered about the leftover
energy, water rushing down a hill
long after the rains have stopped

or the fire you want to go to bed from
but cannot leave, burning-down but not burnt-down
the red coals more extreme, more curious
in their flashing and dying
than you wish they were
sitting there long after midnight

1972 1973

Upper Broadway

The leafbud straggles forth
toward the frigid light of the airshaft   this is faith
this pale extension of a day
when looking up   you know   something is changing
winter has turned   though the wind is colder
Three streets away   a roof collapses   onto people
who thought they still had time   Time out of mind

I have written so many words
wanting to live inside you
to be of use to you

Now I must write for myself   for this blind
woman scratching the pavement   with her wand of thought
this slippered crone   inching on icy streets
reaching into wire trashbaskets   pulling out
what was thrown away   and infinitely precious

I look at hands and see   they are still unfinished
I look at the vine and see the leafbud
inching towards life

I look at my face in the glass   and see
a halfborn woman

1975 1978

Integrity

the quality or state of being complete; unbroken condition; entirety
—Webster

A wild patience has taken me this far

as if I had to bring to shore
a boat with a spasmodic outboard motor
old sweaters, nets, spray-mottled books
tossed in the prow
some kind of sun burning my shoulder-blades.
Splashing the oarlocks. Burning through.
Your fore-arms can get scalded, licked with pain

in a sun blotted like unspoken anger
behind a casual mist.

The length of daylight
this far north, in this
forty-ninth year of my life
is critical.

The light is critical: of me, of this
long-dreamed, involuntary landing
on the arm of an inland sea.
The glitter of the shoal
depleting into shadow
I recognize: the stand of pines
violet-black really, green in the old postcard
but really I have nothing but myself
to go by; nothing
stands in the realm of pure necessity
except what my hands can hold.

Nothing but myself? . . . My selves.
After so long, this answer.
As if I had always known
I steer the boat in, simply.
The motor dying on the pebbles
cicadas taking up the hum
dropped in the silence.

Anger and tenderness: my selves.
And now I can believe they breathe in me
as angels, not polarities.
Anger and tenderness: the spider's genius
to spin and weave in the same action
from her own body, anywhere—
even from a broken web.

The cabin in the stand of pines
is still for sale. I know this. Know the print
of the last foot, the hand that slammed and locked that door,
then stopped to wreathe the rain-smashed clematis
back on the trellis
for no one's sake except its own.
I know the chart nailed to the wallboards
the icy kettle squatting on the burner.
The hands that hammered in those nails
emptied that kettle one last time
are these two hands
and they have caught the baby leaping
from between trembling legs
and they have worked the vacuum aspirator
and stroked the sweated temples
and steered the boat here through this hot
misblotted sunlight, critical light
imperceptibly scalding
the skin these hands will also salve.

1978 1981

For the Record

The clouds and the stars didn't wage this war
the brooks gave no information
if the mountain spewed stones of fire into the river
it was not taking sides
the raindrop faintly swaying under the leaf
had no political opinions

and if here or there a house
filled with backed-up raw sewage
or poisoned those who lived there
with slow fumes, over years
the houses were not at war
nor did the tinned-up buildings

intend to refuse shelter
to homeless old women and roaming children
they had no policy to keep them roaming
or dying, no, the cities were not the problem
the bridges were non-partisan
the freeways burned, but not with hatred

Even the miles of barbed-wire
stretched around crouching temporary huts
designed to keep the unwanted
at a safe distance, out of sight
even the boards that had to absorb
year upon year, so many human sounds

so many depths of vomit, tears
slow-soaking blood
had not offered themselves for this
The trees didn't volunteer to be cut into boards
nor the thorns for tearing flesh
Look around at all of it

and ask whose signature
is stamped on the orders, traced
in the corner of the building plans
Ask where the illiterate, big-bellied
women were, the drunks and crazies,
the ones you fear most of all: ask where you were.

1983 1984

GARY SNYDER

(1930–)

Gary Sherman Snyder was born in San Francisco and "raised up on a feeble sort of farm just north of Seattle." He graduated from Reed College in 1951 with a B.A. in anthropology and studied linguistics for a term at Indiana University before enrolling at the University of California, Berkeley (1953–1956), as a student of Japanese and Chinese culture. Recipient of a Zen Institute of America Award and a Bollingen Grant for Buddhist Studies, he spent much of his time after the mid-1950's living and writing in Japan.

One of the most successful of the poets of the Pacific Northwest, Snyder was influential in the West Coast Beat movement in the 1950's. His interest in Buddhism, in oriental poetry and the culture of the American Indians, and in the rocks, trees, and rivers of man's physical environment helped to strengthen the beatific (as opposed to beaten-down) element in the work of such East Coast Beats as Jack Kerouac and Allen Ginsberg. In his life, as in his work, there has been implied a rejection of many of the values of western civilization. Although he was briefly a lecturer in English at Berkeley (1964–1965), he has not pursued an academic career. His poems reflect his experiences as a logger, forest ranger, merchant seaman, and student of Zen, and are influenced as much by non-western poetic traditions as they are by the verse traditions of English. An advocate of open forms, he believes that "each poem grows from an energy-mind-field-dance, and has its own inner grain. To let it grow, to let it speak for itself, is a large part of the work of the poet."

Volumes of verse include *Riprap,* 1959; *Myths & Texts,* 1960; *Riprap and Cold Mountain Poems,* 1965; *Six Sections from Mountains and Rivers Without End,* 1965, rev. ed. 1970; *A Range of Poems,* 1966; *The Back Country,* 1967; *Regarding Wave,* 1970; and *Axe Handles,* 1983. *Turtle Island,* 1974, contains verse and prose. A collection of prose is *Earth House Hold,* 1969. A critical assessment is Charles Molesworth, *Gary Snyder's Vision: Poetry and the Real Work,* 1983.

The Late Snow & Lumber Strike of the Summer of Fifty-four

Whole towns shut down
        hitching the Coast road, only gypos
Running their beat trucks, no logs on
Gave me rides. Loggers all gone fishing
Chainsaws in a pool of cold oil
On back porches of ten thousand
Split-shake houses, quiet in summer rain.
Hitched north all of Washington
Crossing and re-crossing the passes
Blown like dust, no place to work.

Climbing the steep ridge below Shuksan
        clumps of pine
        float out the fog
No place to think or work
        drifting.

On Mt. Baker, alone
In a gully of blazing snow:
Cities down the long valleys west
Thinking of work, but here,
Burning in sun-glare
Below a wet cliff, above a frozen lake,
The whole Northwest on strike
Black burners cold,
The green-chain still,
I must turn and go back:

caught on a snowpeak
between heaven and earth
And stand in lines in Seattle.
Looking for work.

1959

Hay for the Horses

He had driven half the night
From far down San Joaquin
Through Mariposa, up the
Dangerous mountain roads,
And pulled in at eight a.m.
With his big truckload of hay
behind the barn.
With winch and ropes and hooks
We stacked the bales up clean
To splintery redwood rafters
High in the dark, flecks of alfalfa
Whirling through shingle-cracks of light,
Itch of haydust in the
sweaty shirt and shoes.
At lunchtime under Black oak
Out in the hot corral,
—The old mare nosing lunchpails,
Grasshoppers crackling in the weeds—
"I'm sixty-eight" he said,
"I first bucked hay when I was seventeen.
I thought, that day I started,
I sure would hate to do this all my life.
And dammit, that's just what
I've gone and done."

1959

Riprap[1]

Lay down these words
Before your mind like rocks.
placed solid, by hands
In choice of place, set
Before the body of the mind
in space and time:
Solidity of bark, leaf, or wall
riprap of things:
Cobble of milky way,
straying planets,
These poems, people,
lost ponies with
Dragging saddles—
and rocky sure-foot trails.

1. "Riprap: a cobble of stone laid on steep slick rock to make a trail for horses in the mountains" [Snyder's note].

The worlds like an endless
        four-dimensional
Game of *Go*.[2]
        ants and pebbles
In the thin loam, each rock a word
        a creek-washed stone
Granite: ingrained
        with torment of fire and weight
Crystal and sediment linked hot
        all change, in thoughts,
As well as things.

1959

this poem is for bear

"As for me I am a child of the god of the mountains."

A bear down under the cliff.
She is eating huckleberries.
They are ripe now
Soon it will snow, and she
Or maybe he, will crawl into a hole
And sleep. You can see
Huckleberries in bearshit if you
Look, this time of year
If I sneak up on the bear
It will grunt and run

The others had all gone down
From the blackberry brambles, but one girl
Spilled her basket, and was picking up her
Berries in the dark.
A tall man stood in the shadow, took her arm,
Led her to his home. He was a bear.
In a house under the mountain
She gave birth to slick dark children
With sharp teeth, and lived in the hollow
Mountain many years.
        snare a bear: call him out:
honey-eater
forest apple
light-foot
Old man in the fur coat, Bear! come out!
Die of your own choice!
Grandfather black-food!
        this girl married a bear
Who rules in the mountains, Bear!
        you have eaten many berries
        you have caught many fish
        you have frightened many people

Twelve species north of Mexico
Sucking their paws in the long winter

2. Japanese game played on a board with small stones.

Tearing the high-strung caches down
Whining, crying, jacking off
(Odysseus was a bear)

Bear-cubs gnawing the soft tits
Teeth gritted, eyes screwed tight
but she let them.

Til her brothers found the place
Chased her husband up the gorge
Cornered him in the rocks.
Song of the snared bear:
"Give me my belt.
"I am near death.
"I came from the mountain caves
"At the headwaters,
"The small streams there
"Are all dried up.

—I think I'll go hunt bears.
"hunt bears?
Why shit Snyder,
You couldn't hit a bear in the ass
with a handful of rice!"

1960

Vapor Trails

Twin streaks twice higher than cumulus,
Precise plane icetracks in the vertical blue
Cloud-flaked light-shot shadow-arcing
Field of all future war, edging off to space.

Young expert U.S. pilots waiting
The day of criss-cross rockets
And white blossoming smoke of bomb,
The air world torn and staggered for these
Specks of brushy land and ant-hill towns—

I stumble on the cobble rockpath,
Passing through temples,
Watching for two-leaf pine
—spotting that design.

1966

Not Leaving the House

When Kai is born
I quit going out

Hang around the kitchen—make cornbread
Let nobody in.
Mail is flat.

Masa lies on her side, Kai sighs,
Non washes and sweeps
We sit and watch
Masa nurse, and drink green tea.

Navajo turquoise beads over the bed
A peacock tail feather at the head
A badger pelt from Nagano-ken
For a mattress; under the sheet;
A pot of yogurt setting
Under the blankets, at his feet.

Masa, Kai,
And Non, our friend
In the green garden light reflected in
Not leaving the house.
From dawn til late at night
making a new world of ourselves
around this life.

1970

Axe Handles

One afternoon the last week in April
Showing Kai how to throw a hatchet
One-half turn and it sticks in a stump.
He recalls the hatchet-head
Without a handle, in the shop
And go gets it, and wants it for his own.
A broken-off axe handle behind the door
Is long enough for a hatchet,
We cut it to length and take it
With the hatchet head
And working hatchet, to the wood block.
There I begin to shape the old handle
With the hatchet, and the phrase
First learned from Ezra Pound
Rings in my ears!
"When making an axe handle
the pattern is not far off."
And I say this to Kai
"Look: We'll shape the handle
By checking the handle
Of the axe we cut with—"
And he sees. And I hear it again:
It's in Lu Ji's *Wên Fu,* fourth century
A.D. "Essay on Literature"—in the
Preface: "In making the handle
Of an axe
By cutting wood with an axe
The model is indeed near at hand."
My teacher Shih-hsiang Chen
Translated that and taught it years ago

And I see: Pound was an axe,
Chen was an axe, I am an axe
And my son a handle, soon
To be shaping again, model
And tool, craft of culture,
How we go on.

1983

SYLVIA PLATH
(1932–1963)

Born in Boston, Sylvia Plath was the precocious child of parents who were both teachers. Her father's German background and his death when she was eight were to become obsessive in her poetry. At Smith College she performed brilliantly, graduating *summa cum laude* in 1955. A Fulbright Fellowship took her to Newnham College, Cambridge, where she received her M.A. in 1957. In England she married the British poet Ted Hughes and had a daughter and a son. They came to this country, where she taught for a year at Smith College before the family went back to England to live. Before her death, the marriage had gone sour. Plath was living in Devon, apart from her husband, and seeking a legal separation.

Plath's books of poetry are *The Colossus* (1960) and, posthumously, *Ariel* (1965), *Crossing the Water* (1971), and *Winter Trees* (1971). She began as a poet of great stylistic skill and somberness, but in *Ariel* she reached what Robert Lowell called "appalling and triumphant fulfillment." These are poems of intensity so great as to be painful. She committed suicide in 1963.

The Collected Poems, edited by Ted Hughes, was published in 1981. Earlier volumes of poetry are named above. *The Bell Jar,* 1963, is a partially autobiographical novel. Plath's mother, Aurelia Schober Plath, edited *Letters Home: Correspondence 1950–1963,* 1975. Prose is collected in *Johnny Panic and the Bible of Dreams: Short Stories, Prose and Diary Excerpts,* 1979. *The Journals of Sylvia Plath* was edited by Ted Hughes and Frances McCullough, 1982.

Biographical and critical studies include Charles Newman, ed., *The Art of Sylvia Plath,* 1970; Eileen Aird, *Sylvia Plath: Her Life and Work,* 1975; David Holbrook, *Sylvia Plath: Poetry and Existence,* 1976; Judith Kroll, *Chapters in a Mythology,* 1976; Edward Butscher, ed., *Sylvia Plath: The Woman and the Work,* 1978; Gary Lane, ed., *Sylvia Plath: New Views on the Poetry,* 1979; Margaret Dickie Uroff, *Sylvia Plath and Ted Hughes,* 1979; Jon Rosenblatt, *Sylvia Plath: The Poetry of Initiation,* 1979; Mary Lynn Broe, *Protean Poetic: The Poetry of Sylvia Plath,* 1980; Lynda K. Bundtzen, *Plath's Incarnations: Woman and the Creative Process,* 1985; and Susan Bassnet, *Sylvia Plath,* 1987.

Black Rook in Rainy Weather

On the stiff twig up there
Hunches a wet black rook
Arranging and rearranging its feathers in the rain.
I do not expect a miracle
Or an accident

To set the sight on fire
In my eye, nor seek
Any more in the desultory weather some design,
But let spotted leaves fall as they fall,
Without ceremony, or portent.

Although, I admit, I desire,
Occasionally, some backtalk
From the mute sky, I can't honestly complain:
A certain minor light may still
Lean incandescent

Out of kitchen table or chair
As if a celestial burning took
Possession of the most obtuse objects now and then—
Thus hallowing an interval
Otherwise inconsequent

By bestowing largesse, honor,
One might say love. At any rate, I now walk
Wary (for it could happen
Even in this dull, ruinous landscape); skeptical,
Yet politic; ignorant

Of whatever angel may choose to flare
Suddenly at my elbow. I only know that a rook
Ordering its black feathers can so shine
As to seize my senses, haul
My eyelids up, and grant

A brief respite from fear
Of total neutrality. With luck,
Trekking stubborn through this season
Of fatigue, I shall
Patch together a content

Of sorts. Miracles occur,
If you care to call those spasmodic
Tricks of radiance miracles. The wait's begun again,
The long wait for the angel,
For that rare, random descent.

1956 1960

The Colossus

I shall never get you put together entirely,
Pieced, glued, and properly jointed.
Mule-bray, pig-grunt and bawdy cackles
Proceed from your great lips.
It's worse than a barnyard.

Perhaps you consider yourself an oracle,
Mouthpiece of the dead, or of some god or other.
Thirty years now I have labored
To dredge the silt from your throat.
I am none the wiser.

Scaling little ladders with gluepots and pails of Lysol
I crawl like an ant in mourning
Over the weedy acres of your brow

To mend the immense skull-plates and clear
The bald, white tumuli of your eyes.

A blue sky out of the Oresteia[1]
Arches above us. O father, all by yourself
You are pithy and historical as the Roman Forum.

1959 1960

Morning Song

Love set you going like a fat gold watch.
The midwife slapped your footsoles, and your bald cry
Took its place among the elements.

Our voices echo, magnifying your arrival. New statue.
In a drafty museum, your nakedness
Shadows our safety. We stand round blankly as walls.

I'm no more your mother
Than the cloud that distills a mirror to reflect its own slow
Effacement at the wind's hand.

All night your moth-breath
Flickers among the flat pink roses. I wake to listen:
A far sea moves in my ear.

One cry, and I stumble from bed, cow-heavy and floral
In my Victorian nightgown.
Your mouth opens clean as a cat's. The window square

Whitens and swallows its dull stars. And now you try
Your handful of notes;
The clear vowels rise like balloons.

1961 1965

The Rival

If the moon smiled, she would resemble you.
You leave the same impression
Of something beautiful, but annihilating.
Both of you are great light borrowers.
Her O-mouth grieves at the world; yours is unaffected,

And your first gift is making stone out of everything.
I wake to a mausoleum; you are here,
Ticking your fingers on the marble table, looking for cigarettes,
Spiteful as a woman, but not so nervous,
And dying to say something unanswerable.

The moon, too, abases her subjects,
But in the daytime she is ridiculous.

1. A trilogy, among the greatest of Greek tragedies, by Aeschylus (525–456 B.C.).

Your dissatisfactions, on the other hand,
Arrive through the mailslot with loving regularity,
White and blank, expansive as carbon monoxide.

No day is safe from news of you,
Walking about in Africa maybe, but thinking of me.

1961 1965

Blackberrying

Nobody in the lane, and nothing, nothing but blackberries,
Blackberries on either side, though on the right mainly,
A blackberry alley, going down in hooks, and a sea
Somewhere at the end of it, heaving. Blackberries
Big as the ball of my thumb, and dumb as eyes
Ebon in the hedges, fat
With blue-red juices. These they squander on my fingers.
I had not asked for such a blood sisterhood; they must love me.
They accommodate themselves to my milkbottle, flattening their sides.

Overhead go the choughs in black, cacophonous flocks—
Bits of burnt paper wheeling in a blown sky.
Theirs is the only voice, protesting, protesting.
I do not think the sea will appear at all.
The high, green meadows are glowing, as if lit from within.
I come to one bush of berries so ripe it is a bush of flies,
Hanging their bluegreen bellies and their wing panes in a Chinese screen.
The honey-feast of the berries has stunned them; they believe in heaven.
One more hook, and the berries and bushes end.

The only thing to come now is the sea.
From between two hills a sudden wind funnels at me,
Slapping its phantom laundry in my face.
These hills are too green and sweet to have tasted salt.
I follow the sheep path between them. A last hook brings me
To the hills' northern face, and the face is orange rock
That looks out on nothing, nothing but a great space
Of white and pewter lights, and a din like silversmiths
Beating and beating at an intractable metal.

1961 1971

The Arrival of the Bee Box

I ordered this, this clean wood box
Square as a chair and almost too heavy to lift.
I would say it was the coffin of a midget
Or a square baby
Were there not such a din in it.

The box is locked, it is dangerous.
I have to live with it overnight
And I can't keep away from it.

There are no windows, so I can't see what is in there.
There is only a little grid, no exit.

I put my eye to the grid.
It is dark, dark,
With the swarmy feeling of African hands
Minute and shrunk for export,
Black on black, angrily clambering.

How can I let them out?
It is the noise that appalls me most of all,
The unintelligible syllables.
It is like a Roman mob,
Small, taken one by one, but my god, together!

I lay my ear to furious Latin.
I am not a Caesar.
I have simply ordered a box of maniacs.
They can be sent back.
They can die, I need feed them nothing, I am the owner.

I wonder how hungry they are.
I wonder if they would forget me
If I just undid the locks and stood back and turned into a tree.
There is the laburnum, its blond colonnades,
And the petticoats of the cherry.

They might ignore me immediately
In my moon suit and funeral veil.
I am no source of honey
So why should they turn on me?
Tomorrow I will be sweet God, I will set them free.

The box is only temporary.

1962 1965

The Applicant

First, are you our sort of a person?
Do you wear
A glass eye, false teeth or a crutch,
A brace or a hook,
Rubber breasts or a rubber crotch,

Stitches to show something's missing? No, no? Then
How can we give you a thing?
Stop crying.
Open your hand.
Empty? Empty. Here is a hand

To fill it and willing
To bring teacups and roll away headaches
And do whatever you tell it.

Will you marry it?
It is guaranteed

To thumb shut your eyes at the end
And dissolve of sorrow.
We make new stock from the salt.
I notice you are stark naked.
How about this suit—

Black and stiff, but not a bad fit.
Will you marry it?
It is waterproof, shatterproof, proof
Against fire and bombs through the roof.
Believe me, they'll bury you in it.

Now your head, excuse me, is empty.
I have the ticket for that.
Come here, sweetie, out of the closet.
Well, what do you think of *that?*
Naked as paper to start

But in twenty-five years she'll be silver,
In fifty, gold.
A living doll, everywhere you look.
It can sew, it can cook,
It can talk, talk, talk.

It works, there is nothing wrong with it.
You have a hole, it's a poultice.
You have an eye, it's an image.
My boy, it's your last resort.
Will you marry it, marry it, marry it.

1962 1965

Daddy

You do not do, you do not do
Any more, black shoe
In which I have lived like a foot
For thirty years, poor and white,
Barely daring to breathe or Achoo.

Daddy, I have had to kill you.
You died before I had time——
Marble-heavy, a bag full of God,
Ghastly statue with one grey toe[2]
Big as a Frisco seal

And a head in the freakish Atlantic
Where it pours bean green over blue
In the waters off beautiful Nauset.[3]

2. The result of diabetes.

3. A beach at the outermost edge of Cape Cod, in Massachusetts.

I used to pray to recover you.
Ach, du.[4]

In the German tongue, in the Polish town[5]
Scraped flat by the roller
Of wars, wars, wars.
But the name of the town is common.
My Polack friend

Says there are a dozen or two.
So I never could tell where you
Put your foot, your root,
I never could talk to you.
The tongue stuck in my jaw.

It stuck in a barb wire snare.
Ich,[6] ich, ich, ich,
I could hardly speak.
I thought every German was you.
And the language obscene

An engine, an engine
Chuffing me off like a Jew.
A Jew to Dachau, Auschwitz, Belsen.[7]
I began to talk like a Jew.
I think I may well be a Jew.

The snows of the Tyrol, the clear beer of Vienna
Are not very pure or true.
With my gypsy ancestress and my weird luck
And my Taroc[8] pack and my Taroc pack
I may be a bit of a Jew.

I have always been scared of *you*,
With your Luftwaffe,[9] your gobbledygoo.
And your neat mustache
And your Aryan eye, bright blue.
Panzer man,[1] panzer-man, O You——

Not God but a swastika
So black no sky could squeak through.
Every woman adores a Fascist,
The boot in the face, the brute
Brute heart of a brute like you.

You stand at the blackboard, daddy,
In the picture I have of you,
A cleft in your chin instead of your foot
But no less a devil for that, no not
Any less the black man who

4. "Ah, you," a reference to her father's German background.
5. Grabow, her father's birthplace.
6. I.
7. World War II death camps.
8. Frequently "Tarot," fortune-telling cards.
9. German air force.
1. Soldier in an armored division.

Bit my pretty red heart in two.
I was ten when they buried you.
At twenty I tried to die
And get back, back, back to you.
I thought even the bones would do.

But they pulled me out of the sack,
And they stuck me together with glue.
And then I knew what to do.
I made a model of you,
A man in black with a Meinkampf[2] look

And a love of the rack and the screw.
And I said I do, I do.
So daddy, I'm finally through.
The black telephone's off at the root,
The voices just can't worm through.

If I've killed one man, I've killed two——
The vampire who said he was you
And drank my blood for a year,
Seven years, if you want to know.
Daddy, you can lie back now.

There's a stake in your fat black heart
And the villagers never liked you.
They are dancing and stamping on you.
They always *knew* it was you.
Daddy, daddy, you bastard, I'm through.

1962 1965

Lady Lazarus[3]

I have done it again.
One year in every ten
I manage it——

A sort of walking miracle, my skin
Bright as a Nazi lampshade,[4]
My right foot

A paperweight,
My face a featureless, fine
Jew linen.

Peel off the napkin
O my enemy.
Do I terrify?——

The nose, the eye pits, the full set of teeth?
The sour breath
Will vanish in a day.

2. *Mein Kampf* ("My Struggle") is the title of Hitler's autobiography.

3. Jesus raised Lazarus from the dead (John xi: 39–44).

4. Made, sometimes, of human skin.

Soon, soon the flesh
The grave cave ate will be
At home on me

And I a smiling woman.
I am only thirty.
And like the cat I have nine times to die.

This is Number Three.
What a trash
To annihilate each decade.

What a million filaments.
The peanut-crunching crowd
Shoves in to see

Them unwrap me hand and foot——
The big strip tease.
Gentlemen, ladies

These are my hands
My knees.
I may be skin and bone,

Nevertheless, I am the same, identical woman.
The first time it happened I was ten.
It was an accident.

The second time I meant
To last it out and not come back at all.
I rocked shut

As a seashell.
They had to call and call
And pick the worms off me like sticky pearls.

Dying
Is an art, like everything else.
I do it exceptionally well.

I do it so it feels like hell.
I do it so it feels real.
I guess you could say I've a call.

It's easy enough to do it in a cell.
It's easy enough to do it and stay put.
It's the theatrical

Comeback in broad day
To the same place, the same face, the same brute
Amused shout:

"A miracle!"
That knocks me out.
There is a charge

For the eyeing of my scars, there is a charge
For the hearing of my heart——
It really goes.

And there is a charge, a very large charge
For a word or a touch
Or a bit of blood

Or a piece of my hair or my clothes.
So, so, Herr Doktor.
So, Herr Enemy.

I am your opus,
I am your valuable,
The pure gold baby

That melts to a shriek.
I turn and burn.
Do not think I underestimate your great concern.

Ash, ash—
You poke and stir.
Flesh, bone, there is nothing there——

A cake of soap,
A wedding ring,
A gold filling.

Herr God, Herr Lucifer
Beware
Beware.

Out of the ash[5]
I rise with my red hair
And I eat men like air.

1962 1965

Death & Co.

Two, of course there are two.[6]
It seems perfectly natural now——
The one who never looks up, whose eyes are lidded
And balled, like Blake's,[7]
Who exhibits

The birthmarks that are his trademark——
The scald scar of water,
The nude
Verdigris[8] of the condor.
I am red meat. His beak

5. Like the phoenix, rising from its own ashes.
6. Plath said these were "two aspects of death" imagined as "two business friends, who have come to call."
7. Like the eyes in the death mask of William Blake (1757–1827), English poet and artist.
8. The greenish blue color of the condor's head and neck.

Claps sidewise: I am not his yet.
He tells me how badly I photograph.
He tells me how sweet
The babies look in their hospital
Icebox, a simple

Frill at the neck,
Then the flutings of their Ionian[9]
Death-gowns,
Then two little feet.
He does not smile or smoke.

The other does that,
His hair long and plausive.
Bastard
Masturbating a glitter,
He wants to be loved.

I do not stir.
The frost makes a flower,
The dew makes a star,
The dead bell,
The dead bell.

Somebody's done for.

1962 1965

Sheep in Fog

The hills step off into whiteness.
People or stars
Regard me sadly, I disappoint them.

The train leaves a line of breath.
O slow
Horse the color of rust,

Hooves, dolorous bells—
All morning the
Morning has been blackening,

A flower left out.
My bones hold a stillness, the far
Fields melt my heart.

They threaten
To let me through to a heaven
Starless and fatherless, a dark water.

1962, 1963 1965

9. Having the appearance of Ionian columns.

Mystic

The air is a mill of hooks—
Questions without answer,
Glittering and drunk as flies
Whose kiss stings unbearably
In the fetid wombs of black air under pines in summer.

I remember
The dead smell of sun on wood cabins,
The stiffness of sails, the long salt winding sheets.
Once one has seen God, what is the remedy?
Once one has been seized up

Without a part left over,
Not a toe, not a finger, and used,
Used utterly, in the sun's conflagrations, the stains
That lengthen from ancient cathedrals
What is the remedy?

The pill of the Communion tablet,
The walking beside still water? Memory?
Or picking up the bright pieces
Of Christ in the faces of rodents,
The tame flower-nibblers, the ones

Whose hopes are so low they are comfortable—
The humpback in her small, washed cottage
Under the spokes of the clematis.
Is there no great love, only tenderness?
Does the sea

Remember the walker upon it?
Meaning leaks from the molecules.
The chimneys of the city breathe, the window sweats,
The children leap in their cots.
The sun blooms, it is a geranium.

The heart has not stopped.

1963 1971

MARK STRAND

(1934–)

Born in Summerside, Prince Edward Island, Mark Strand traveled as a child, attending many schools, but always returning with his parents to Canada's maritime provinces. He has included among his poems a significant number that evoke the bays, fields, boats, and pines of that childhood. Nostalgia is sometimes the tone, but there is a tension, too, as the sea rubs against the shore, time passes, and people look outward to other places, travel to other countries, grow old and die. Sperm whales feeding in a bay are an event watched from a nearby hill, but their feeding disrupts the fishing industry and in the end the men and children go out in boats to shoot them.

As a student at Antioch College, Strand wrote poetry, then turned his attention to painting. Receiving his B.A. in 1957, he entered Yale School of Art, studied painting under Josef Albers, and left with a B.F.A. in 1959. By this time already turning again to poetry, he spent a year as a Fulbright scholar at the University of Florence and returned to the United States to earn an M.A. at the University of Iowa in 1962. Three years as an English instructor at Iowa were followed by a year as a Fulbright lecturer in Brazil (1965–1966) and then by appointments at many colleges and universities, including Mount Holyoke, Yale, Princeton, the University of Virginia, and Harvard. In 1981 he became professor of English at the University of Utah.

Placing himself among his contemporaries, Strand said in a 1971 interview, "I feel very much a part of a new international style that has a lot to do with plainness of diction, a certain reliance on surrealist techniques, a certain reliance on journalistic techniques, a strong narrative element, etc." In some of this, particularly at his more surreal, he resembles Robert Bly among slightly older poets, though he has attributed his sense of the surreal especially to an admiration for the collages of Max Ernst and the paintings of Georgio de Chirico and René Magritte. Writing he has admired includes the stories of Jorge Luis Borges and Franz Kafka and the poetry of Wallace Stevens and Elizabeth Bishop. He has edited and translated South American, Mexican, and European authors.

Writing is for Strand a way of defamiliarizing the familiar. Hence his poems are often plain and concrete, generally without meter or rhyme, in everyday language, but perched on the edge of emptiness and estrangement. The central irony in the thought that "Keeping Things Whole" requires withdrawal of self turns in the much later poem "Always" to a vision of tragic menace as "the great forgetters" work toward their goal of total obliteration, "the cold zero of perfection." We are left then with the ache of nostalgia for "everything known."

Selected Poems, 1980, gathers work from earlier books. Other poetry titles include *Sleeping with One Eye Open,* 1964; *Reasons for Moving,* 1968; *Darker,* 1970; *The Story of Our Lives,* 1973; and *The Late Hour,* 1978. Miscellaneous prose is collected in *The Monument,* 1978; short fiction in *Mr. and Mrs. Baby,* 1985. Translations include *18 Poems from the Quechua,* 1971; *The Owl's Insomnia: Selected Poems of Rafael Alberti,* 1973; and *Selected Poems of Carlos Drummond de Andrade,* 1976, 1983.

Brief appraisals appear in Richard Howard, *Alone with America,* 1969; and *Dictionary of Literary Biography, Volume 5: American Poets Since World War II,* 1980.

Keeping Things Whole

In a field
I am the absence
of field.
This is
always the case.
Wherever I am
I am what is missing.

When I walk
I part the air
and always
the air moves in
to fill the spaces
where my body's been.

We all have reasons
for moving.
I move
to keep things whole.

1964

The Prediction

That night the moon drifted over the pond,
turning the water to milk, and under
the boughs of the trees, the blue trees,
a young woman walked, and for an instant

the future came to her:
rain falling on her husband's grave, rain falling
on the lawns of her children, her own mouth
filling with cold air, strangers moving into her house,

a man in her room writing a poem, the moon drifting into it,
a woman strolling under its trees, thinking of death,
thinking of him thinking of her, and the wind rising
and taking the moon and leaving the paper dark.

1970

The Coming of Light

Even this late it happens:
the coming of love, the coming of light.
You wake and the candles are lit as if by themselves,
stars gather, dreams pour into your pillows,
sending up warm bouquets of air.
Even this late the bones of the body shine
and tomorrow's dust flares into breath.

1978

Where Are the Waters of Childhood?

See where the windows are boarded up,
where the gray siding shines in the sun and salt air
and the asphalt shingles on the roof have peeled or fallen off,
where tiers of oxeye daisies float on a sea of grass?
That's the place to begin.

Enter the kingdom of rot,
smell the damp plaster, step over the shattered glass,
the pockets of dust, the rags, the soiled remains of a mattress,
look at the rusted stove and sink, at the rectangular stain
on the wall where Winslow Homer's[1] *Gulf Stream* hung.

1. Winslow Homer (1836–1910), American painter.

Go to the room where your father and mother
would let themselves go in the drift and pitch of love,
and hear, if you can, the creak of their bed,
then go to the place where you hid.

Go to your room, to all the rooms whose cold, damp air you breathed,
to all the unwanted places where summer, fall, winter, spring,
seem the same unwanted season, where the trees you knew have died
and other trees have risen. Visit that other place
you barely recall, that other house half hidden.

See the two dogs burst into sight. When you leave,
they will cease, snuffed out in the glare of an earlier light.
Visit the neighbors down the block; he waters his lawn,
she sits on her porch, but not for long.
When you look again they are gone.

Keep going back, back to the field, flat and sealed in mist.
On the other side, a man and a woman are waiting;
they have come back, your mother before she was gray,
your father before he was white.

Now look at the North West Arm, how it glows a deep cerulean blue.
See the light on the grass, the one leaf burning, the cloud
that flares. You're almost there, in a moment your parents
will disappear, leaving you under the light of a vanished star,
under the dark of a star newly born. Now is the time.

Now you invent the boat of your flesh and set it upon the waters
and drift in the gradual swell, in the laboring salt.
Now you look down. The waters of childhood are there.

1978

Shooting Whales

for Judith and Leon Major

When the shoals of plankton
swarmed into St. Margaret's Bay,
turning the beaches pink,
we saw from our place on the hill
the sperm whales feeding,
fouling the nets
in their play,
and breaching clean
so the humps of their backs
rose over the wide sea meadows.

Day after day
we waited inside
for the rotting plankton to disappear.
The smell stilled even the wind,
and the oxen looked stunned,
pulling hay on the slope

of our hill.
But the plankton kept coming in
and the whales would not go.

That's when the shooting began.
The fishermen got in their boats
and went after the whales,
and my father and uncle
and we children went, too.
The froth of our wake sank fast
in the wind-shaken water.

The whales surfaced close by.
Their foreheads were huge,
the doors of their faces were closed.
Before sounding, they lifted
their flukes into the air
and brought them down hard.
They beat the sea into foam,
and the path that they made
shone after them.

Though I did not see their eyes,
I imagined they were
like the eyes of mourning,
glazed with rheum,
watching us, sweeping along
under the darkening sheets of salt.

When we cut our engine and waited
for the whales to surface again,
the sun was setting,
turning the rock-strewn barrens a gaudy salmon.
A cold wind flailed at our skin.
When finally the sun went down
and it seemed like the whales had gone,
my uncle, no longer afraid,
shot aimlessly into the sky.

Three miles out
in the rolling dark
under the moon's astonished eyes,
our engine would not start
and we headed home in the dinghy.
And my father, hunched over the oars,
brought us in. I watched him,
rapt in his effort, rowing against the tide,
his blond hair glistening with salt.
I saw the slick spillage of moonlight
being blown over his shoulders,
and the sea and spindrift
suddenly silver.

He did not speak the entire way.
At midnight

when I went to bed,
I imagined the whales
moving beneath me,
sliding over the weed-covered hills of the deep;
they knew where I was;
they were luring me
downward and downward
into the murmurous
waters of sleep.

1980

Nights in Hackett's Cove

Those nights lit by the moon and the moon's nimbus,
the bones of the wrecked pier rose crooked in air
and the sea wore a tarnished coat of silver.
The black pines waited. The cold air smelled
of fishheads rotting under the pier at low tide.
The moon kept shedding its silver clothes
over the bogs and pockets of bracken.
Those nights I would gaze at the bay road,
at the cottages clustered under the moon's immaculate stare,
nothing hinted that I would suffer so late
this turning away, this longing to be there.

1980

A Morning

I have carried it with me each day: that morning I took
my uncle's boat from the brown water cove
and headed for Mosher Island.
Small waves splashed against the hull
and the hollow creek of oarlock and oar
rose into the woods of black pine crusted with lichen.
I moved like a dark star, drifting over the drowned
other half of the world until, by a distant prompting,
I looked over the gunwale and saw beneath the surface
a luminous room, a light-filled grave, saw for the first time
the one clear place given to us when we are alone.

1980

My Mother on an Evening in Late Summer

1

When the moon appears
and a few wind-stricken barns stand out
in the low-domed hills
and shine with a light
that is veiled and dust-filled

and that floats upon the fields,
my mother, with her hair in a bun,
her face in shadow, and the smoke
from her cigarette coiling close
to the faint yellow sheen of her dress,
stands near the house
and watches the seepage of late light
down through the sedges,
the last gray islands of cloud
taken from view, and the wind
ruffling the moon's ash-colored coat
on the black bay.

2

Soon the house, with its shades drawn closed, will send
small carpets of lampglow
into the haze and the bay
will begin its loud heaving
and the pines, frayed finials
climbing the hill, will seem to graze
the dim cinders of heaven.
And my mother will stare into the starlanes,
the endless tunnels of nothing,
and as she gazes,
under the hour's spell,
she will think how we yield each night
to the soundless storms of decay
that tear at the folding flesh,
and she will not know
why she is here
or what she is prisoner of
if not the conditions of love that brought her to this.

3

My mother will go indoors
and the fields, the bare stones
will drift in peace, small creatures—
the mouse and the swift—will sleep
at opposite ends of the house.
Only the cricket will be up,
repeating its one shrill note
to the rotten boards of the porch,
to the rusted screens, to the air, to the rimless dark,
to the sea that keeps to itself.
Why should my mother awake?
The earth is not yet a garden
about to be turned. The stars
are not yet bells that ring
at night for the lost.
It is much too late.

1980

Always

for Charles Simic

Always so late in the day
in their rumpled clothes, sitting
around a table lit by a single bulb,
the great forgetters were hard at work.
They tilted their heads to one side, closing their eyes.
Then a house disappeared and a man in his yard
with all his flowers in a row.
The moon was next to go.
The great forgetters wrinkled their brows.
Then Florida went and San Francisco
where tugs and barges leave
small gleaming scars across the Bay.
One of the great forgetters struck a match.
Gone were the harps of beaded lights
that vault the rivers of New York.
Another filled his glass
and that was it for crowds at evening
under sulphur yellow streetlamps coming on.
And afterwards Bulgaria was gone, and then Japan.
'Where will it end?' one of them said.
'Such difficult work, pursuing the fate
of everything known,' said another.
'Yes,' said a third, 'down to the last stone,
and only the cold zero of perfection
left for the imagination.'
The great forgetters slouched in their chairs.
Suddenly Asia was gone, and the evening star
and the common sorrows of the sun.
One of them yawned. Another coughed.
The last one gazed at the window:
not a cloud, not a tree,
the blaze of promise everywhere.

1983

CHARLES WRIGHT

(1935–)

Born in Pickwick Dam, Tennessee, near the borders of Mississippi and Alabama, Charles Wright grew up steeped in the landscapes of the rural South. His father was an engineer for the Tennessee Valley Authority, his mother a woman who encouraged her son to be a writer. After a tenth grade in a school with only eight students, he was sent for his last two years of high school to an Episcopal boarding school in Arden, North Carolina. From there he went to Davidson College, also in North Carolina—"four years of amnesia, as much my fault as theirs,"—graduating in 1957. Four years in the Army Intelligence Corps followed, three of them spent in Italy and establishing his permanent affection for that country, its language, and its literature. After the army, he spent two years in the writing program at the

University of Iowa, receiving his M.F.A. in 1963. During the next two years, 1963–1965, he studied as a Fulbright Fellow at the University of Rome. A long teaching career at the University of California at Irvine, begun in 1966, ended when he moved in 1983 to the University of Virginia. Meanwhile, he has received a Guggenheim award, has returned to Italy as a Fulbright lecturer at the University of Padua, and has held visiting appointments at other universities, including Iowa, Princeton, and Columbia.

Influenced especially by Dante, Pound, and Eugenio Montale, Wright has developed a verse style that avoids narrative and conventional meter as it strives to strike through the core of personality to touch on eternal truths. His is a concrete poetry of names and places, sights and sounds, sometimes difficult to follow in its juxtapositions of the real and the surreal, the observed and the dreamlike. As David Kalstone has expressed it, he "has been assembling an arresting verse autobiography out of radiant fragments." It might be added that, like some other autobiographies, Wright's seems at times almost religious in its intensity. Handmaiden to this intent, his free verse is tightly controlled: "Architecture, structure," he has said, "I don't care what you call it, there is a great overall form."

The best of Wright's earlier verse is collected in *Country Music: Selected Early Poems,* 1982, which draws from *The Grave of the Right Hand,* 1970; *Hard Freight,* 1973; *Bloodlines,* 1975; and *China Trace,* 1977. More recent poems have appeared in *The Southern Cross* (1981) and *The Other Side of the River* (1984). His translations include Eugenio Montale, *The Storm and Other Poems,* 1978.

A brief critical assessment appears in James Vinson, ed., *Contemporary Poets,* 4th ed., 1985.

Dog Creek Mainline

Dog Creek: cat track and bird splay,
Spindrift and windfall; woodrot;
Odor of muscadine, the blue creep
Of kingsnake and copperhead;
Nightweed; frog spit and floating heart,
Backwash and snag pool: Dog Creek

Starts in the leaf reach and shoal run of the blood;
Starts in the falling light just back
Of the fingertips; starts
Forever in the black throat
You ask redemption of, in wants
You waken to, the odd door:

Its sky, old empty valise,
Stands open, departure in mind; its three streets,
Y-shaped and brown,
Go up the hills like a fever;
Its houses link and deploy
—This ointment, false flesh in another color.

*

Five cutouts, five silhouettes
Against the American twilight; the year
Is 1941; remembered names
—Rosendale, Perry and Smith—
Rise like dust in the deaf air;
The tops spin, the poison swells in the arm:

The trees in their jade death-suits,
the birds with their opal feet,
Shimmer and weave on the shoreline;
The moths, like forget-me-nots, blow
Up from the earth, their wet teeth
Breaking the dark, the raw grain;

The lake in its cradle hums
The old songs: out of its ooze, their heads
Like tomahawks, the turtles ascend
And settle back, leaving their chill breath
In blisters along the bank;
Locked in their wide drawer, the pike lie still as knives.

*

Hard freight. It's hard freight
From Ducktown to Copper Hill, from Six
To Piled High: Dog Creek is on this line,
Indigent spur; cross-tie by cross-tie it takes
You back, the red wind
Caught at your neck like a prize:

(The heart is a hieroglyph;
The fingers, like praying mantises, poise
Over what they have once loved;
The ear, cold cave, is an absence,
Tapping its own thin wires;
The eye turns in on itself.

The tongue is a white water.
In its slick ceremonies the light
Gathers, and is refracted, and moves
Outward, over the lips,
Over the dry skin of the world.
The tongue is a white water.).

1973

Blackwater Mountain

That time of evening, weightless and disparate,
When the loon cries, when the small bass
Jostle the lake's reflections, when
The green of the oak begins
To open its robes to the dark, the green
Of water to offer itself to the flames,
When lily and lily pad
Husband the last light
Which flares like a white disease, then disappears:
This is what I remember. And this:

The slap of the jacklight on the cove;
The freeze-frame of ducks
Below us; your shots; the wounded flop
And skid of one bird to the thick brush;

The moon of your face in the fire's glow;
The cold; the darkness. Young,
Wanting approval, what else could I do?
And did, for two hours, waist-deep in the lake,
The thicket as black as death,
Without success or reprieve, try.

The stars over Blackwater Mountain
Still dangle and flash like hooks, and ducks
Coast on the evening water;
The foliage is like applause.
I stand where we stood before and aim
My flashlight down to the lake. A black duck
Explodes to my right, hangs, and is gone.
He shows me the way to you;
He shows me the way to a different fire
Where you, black moon, warm your hands.

1973

Self-Portrait in 2035

The root becomes him, the road ruts
That are sift and grain in the powderlight
Recast him, sink bone in him,
Blanket and creep up, fine, fine:

Worm-waste and pillow tick; hair
Prickly and dust-dangled, his arms and black shoes
Unlinked and laceless, his face false
In the wood-rot, and past pause . . .

Darkness, erase these lines, forget these words.
Spider recite his one sin.

1977

Stone Canyon Nocturne

Ancient of Days,[1] old friend, no one believes you'll come back.
No one believes in his own life anymore.

The moon, like a dead heart, cold and unstartable, hangs by a thread
At the earth's edge,
Unfaithful at last, splotching the ferns and the pink shrubs.

In the other world, children undo the knots in their tally strings.
They sing songs, and their fingers blear.

And here, where the swan hums in his socket, where bloodroot
And belladonna insist on our comforting,
Where the fox in the canyon wall empties our hands, ecstatic for more,

1. God. See Daniel vii: 9.

Like a bead of clear oil the Healer revolves through the night wind,
Part eye, part tear, unwilling to recognize us.

1977

Spider Crystal Ascension

The spider, juiced crystal and Milky Way, drifts on his web through the night sky
And looks down, waiting for us to ascend . . .

At dawn he is still there, invisible, short of breath, mending his net.

All morning we look for the white face to rise from the lake like a tiny star.
And when it does, we lie back in our watery hair and rock.

1977

Clear Night

Clear night, thumb-top of a moon, a back-lit sky.
Moon-fingers lay down their same routine
On the side deck and the threshold, the white keys and the black keys.
Bird hush and bird song. A cassia flower falls.

I want to be bruised by God.
I want to be strung up in a strong light and singled out.
I want to be stretched, like music wrung from a dropped seed.
I want to be entered and picked clean.

And the wind says "What?" to me.
And the castor beans, with their little earrings of death, say "What?" to me.
And the stars start out on their cold slide through the dark.
And the gears notch and the engines wheel.

1977

Sitting at Night on the Front Porch

I'm here, on the dark porch, restyled in my mother's chair.
10:45 and no moon.
Below the house, car lights
Swing down, on the canyon floor, to the sea.

In this they resemble us,
Dropping like match flames through the great void
Under our feet.
In this they resemble her, burning and disappearing.

Everyone's gone
And I'm here, sizing the dark, saving my mother's seat.

1977

Laguna Blues

It's Saturday afternoon at the edge of the world.
White pages lift in the wind and fall.
Dust threads, cut loose from the heart, float up and fall.
Something's off-key in my mind.
Whatever it is, it bothers me all the time.

It's hot, and the wind blows on what I have had to say.
I'm dancing a little dance.
The crows pick up a thermal that angles away from the sea.
I'm singing a little song.
Whatever it is, it bothers me all the time.

It's Saturday afternoon and the crows glide down,
Black pages that lift and fall.
The castor beans and the pepper plant trundle their weary heads.
Something's off-key and unkind.
Whatever it is, it bothers me all the time.

1981

Dead Color

I lie for a long time on my left side and my right side
And eat nothing,
                        but no voice comes on the wind
And no voice drops from the cloud.
Between the grey spiders and the orange spiders,
                                    no voice comes on the wind . . .

Later, I sit for a long time by the waters of Har,[2]
And no face appears on the face of the deep.

Meanwhile, the heavens assemble their dark map.
The traffic begins to thin.
Aphids munch on the sweet meat of the lemon trees.
The lawn sprinklers rise and fall . . .

And here's a line of brown ants cleaning a possum's skull.
And here's another, come from the opposite side.

Over my head, star-pieces dip in their yellow scarves toward their black desire.

Windows, rapturous windows!

1981

2. A place name in *The Book of Thel* and *Tiriel* by English poet William Blake (1757–1827).

MICHAEL S. HARPER
(1938–)

Born in Brooklyn, New York, Michael Harper has attributed an important part of his early education to his parents' forbidden record collection (when they were out of the house, he listened to the jazz of Bessie Smith and Billie Holiday) and to stolen subway rides to Manhattan to hear Charlie Parker play. In 1951, his family moved to Los Angeles, where he attended high school and entered college. Turning from a potential career in medicine to one in writing, he graduated from California State University, Los Angeles, in 1961 and entered the University of Iowa Writers Workshop. With time off for student teaching at Pasadena City College in California, he graduated from Iowa with an M.A. in 1963. For the next several years he taught, first at Contra Costa College, San Pablo, California, then at Reed College, Lewis and Clark College, and California State University, Hayward. Taking occasional leaves for travel and visiting appointments elsewhere, he has taught at Brown University since 1971.

Harper's first book, *Dear John, Dear Coltrane* (1970) earned him widespread respect and established his debt to jazz for both material and method. His poems, he has said, are rhythmic rather than metrical, meant to be read aloud or sung. The titles and contents of the next three books, *History Is Your Own Heartbeat* (1971), *Photographs: Negatives: History as Apple Tree* (1972), and *Song: I Want a Witness* (1972) stress the connections with the past and with other people that Harper considers important for poetry and life. *Nightmare Begins Responsibility* (1975) contained some of his most admired poetry to that date, and *Images of Kin: New and Selected Poems* (1977) brought together some of his best work from the earlier books.

Harper's verse varies from the immediately personal to observations about the wider present and historical context we all inhabit. He has been interested, for example, in the fact that his forebears include not only his black ancestors who "walked north and west during the Civil War," but his American Indian great-great-grandmother. The title *Nightmare Begins Responsibility,* with its echo of Delmore Schwartz's *In Dreams Begin Responsibilities* (itself an echo of a Yeats epigraph) points toward the fusion that underlies his work. Recognizing the duality of the world, he struggles toward a unification of opposites. As a writer, he has learned from recent poets as diverse in aim and method as Gwendolyn Brooks, Countee Cullen, T. S. Eliot, Robert Hayden, Robert Lowell, Theodore Roethke, and William Carlos Williams. "I don't believe in either/or," he has written. "I believe in both/and."

Besides those named above, Harper's books of verse include ***Debridement,*** 1973; ***Rhode Island: Eight Poems,*** 1981; and ***Healing Song for the Inner Ear,*** 1984. With Robert B. Stepto, he edited ***Chant of Saints: A Gathering of Afro-American Literature, Art, and Scholarship,*** 1979. A brief appraisal appears in ***Dictionary of Literary Biography, Volume 41: Afro-American Poets Since 1955,*** 1985.

We Assume: On the Death of Our Son, Reuben Masai Harper

We assume
that in 28 hours,
lived in a collapsible isolette,
you learned to accept pure oxygen

as the natural sky;
the scant shallow breaths
that filled those hours
cannot, did not make you fly—
but dreams were there
like crooked palmprints on
the twin-thick windows of the nursery—
in the glands of your mother.

We assume
the sterile hands
drank chemicals in and out
from lungs opaque with mucus,
pumped your stomach,
eeked the bicarbonate in
crooked, green-winged veins,
out in a plastic mask;

A woman who'd lost her first son
consoled us with an angel gone ahead
to pray for our family—
gone into that sky
seeking oxygen,
gone into autopsy,
a fine brown powdered sugar,
a disposable cremation:

We assume
you did not know we loved you.

1970

Last Affair: Bessie's[1] Blues Song

Disarticulated
arm torn out,
large veins cross
her shoulder intact,
her tourniquet
her blood in all-white big bands:

Can't you see
what love and heartache's done to me
I'm not the same as I used to be
this is my last affair

Mail truck or parked car
in the fast lane,
afloat at forty-three
on a Mississippi road,
Two-hundred-pound muscle on her ham bone,
'nother nigger dead 'fore noon:

1. Bessie Smith (1898?–1937), American blues singer, died after an automobile accident. Many felt that immediate treatment, denied because she was black, might have saved her life.

Can't you see
what love and heartache's done to me
I'm not the same as I used to be
this is my last affair

Fifty-dollar record
cut the vein in her neck,
fool about her money
toll her black train wreck,
white press missed her fun'ral
in the same stacked deck:

Can't you see
what love and heartache's done to me
I'm not the same as I used to be
this is my last affair

Loved a little blackbird
heard she could sing,
Martha in her vineyard
pestle in her spring,
Bessie had a bad mouth
made my chimes ring:

Can't you see
what love and heartache's done to me
I'm not the same as I used to be
this is my last affair

1972

Grandfather

In 1915 my grandfather's
neighbors surrounded his house
near the dayline he ran
on the Hudson
in Catskill, NY
and thought they'd burn
his family out
and be rid of his kind:
in a movie they'd just seen
the death of a lone black
family is *the Birth*
of a Nation,[2]
or so they thought.
His 5′4″ waiter gait
quenched the white jacket smile
he'd brought back from watered
polish of my father
on the turning seats,

2. D. W. Griffith's *The Birth of a Nation* (1915), powerful and innovative, was a landmark in the history of film but shocking in its racism.

and he asked his neighbors
up on his thatched porch
for the first blossom of fire
that would burn him down.

They went away, his nation,
spittooning their torched necks
in the shadows of the riverboat
they'd seen, posse decomposing;
and I see him on Sutter
with white bag from your
restaurant, challenged by his first
grandson to a foot-race
he will win in white clothes.

I see him as he buys galoshes
for his railed yard near Mineo's
metal shop, where roses jump
as the el circles his house
toward Brooklyn, where his rain fell;
and I see cigar smoke in his eyes,
chocolate Madison Square Garden chews
he breaks on his set teeth,
stitched up after cancer,
the great white nation immovable
as his weight wilts
and he is on a porch
that won't hold my arms,
or the legs of the race run
forwards, or the film
played backwards on his grandson's eyes.

1975

Nightmare Begins Responsibility

I place these numbed wrists to the pane
watching white uniforms whisk over
him in the tube-kept
prison
fear what they will do in experiment
watch my gloved stickshifting gasolined hands
breathe *boxcar-information-please* infirmary tubes
distrusting white-pink mending paperthin
silkened end hairs, distrusting tubes
shrunk in his *trunk-skincapped*
shaven head, in thighs
distrusting-white-hands-picking-baboon-light
on this son who will not make his second night
of this wardstrewn intensive airpocket
where his father's asthmatic
hymns of *night-train,* train done gone
his mother can only know that he has flown
up into essential calm unseen corridor

going boxscarred home, *mamaborn, sweetsonchild*
gonedowntown into *researchtestingwarehousebatteryacid*
mama-son-done-gone/ me telling her 'nother
train tonight, no music, no breathstroked
heartbeat in my infinite distrust of them:

and of my distrusting self
white-doctor-who-breathed-for-him-all-night
say it for two sons gone,
say nightmare, say it loud
panebreaking heartmadness:
nightmare begins responsibility.

1975

CHARLES SIMIC

(1938–)

Born in Belgrade, Yugoslavia, Charles Simic survived the bombings of that city that began when he was three, the chaos with which the war wound down in 1944–1945, and some years of poverty and hunger afterwards, to settle with his reunited family in Chicago in 1954. "I'm the product of chance," he has said, "the baby of ideologies, the orphan of history. Hitler and Stalin conspired to make me homeless." In time, his native Serbian was no longer the language of his thoughts or his writing. In high school, he began writing poetry in English, influenced by midwestern poets—Edgar Lee Masters, Carl Sandburg, Vachel Lindsay, and Hart Crane. He also fell under the spell of jazz and blues, both influential to his work: "Jazz made me both an American and a poet."

After Oak Park High School in suburban Chicago, he studied at the University of Chicago before moving to New York. There he worked days at odd jobs, attended New York University at night, saw his education interrupted by two years in the army (from 1961 to 1963), married, continued writing poetry, and finally received an N.Y.U. degree in 1967. That same year he published his first collection of verse, *What the Grass Says.* For several years he served as an editorial assistant on *Aperture,* a photography magazine, before accepting a teaching position at California State University, Hayward, in 1970. Since 1973 he has taught at the University of New Hampshire. Meanwhile, his verse has brought him increasing recognition, including both a Guggenheim and a MacArthur Fellowship.

As a serious young poet in the 1950's and 1960's, Simic read avidly in the folklore collection of the New York Public Library and fell under the influence of poets like Robert Bly who were suggesting models in the work of South American and European poets. Frequently himself a translator of the poems of others, he has sought in his own work to lower himself, as he has expressed it, "one notch below language," finding the hidden origins of humanity's common experience. Hence his poetry discovers surprising, sometimes surrealistic conjunctions, reaching back to myth while simultaneously reflecting the frightening distortions of our time. "My subject," he has said, "is really poetry in times of madness." His aim is "to remind people of their imagination and their humanity."

Selected Poems 1963–1983 appeared in 1985. Earlier books of verse are *What the Grass Says,*

1967; *Somewhere among Us a Stone Is Taking Notes,* 1969; *Dismantling the Silence,* 1971; *White,* 1972; *Return to a Place Lit by a Glass of Milk,* 1974; *Biography and a Lament,* 1976; *Charon's Cosmology,* 1977; *Classic Ballroom Dances,* 1980; *Austerities,* 1982; and *Weather Forecast for Utopia and Vicinity,* 1983. A more recent collection is *Unending Blues,* 1986. *The Uncertain Certainty,* 1985, collects interviews, essays, and notes. Among Simic's translations are poems of the Yugoslav poet Vasco Popa in *The Little Box,* 1970, and *Homage to the Lame Wolf,* 1979; and *Four Modern Yugoslav Poets,* 1970. With Mark Strand, he edited a collection of European and South American poetry, *Another Republic,* 1976.

Fear

Fear passes from man to man
Unknowing,
As one leaf passes its shudder
To another.

All at once the whole tree is trembling
And there is no sign of the wind.

1971

Bestiary for the Fingers of My Right Hand

1

Thumb, loose tooth of a horse.
Rooster to his hens.
Horn of a devil. Fat worm
They have attached to my flesh
At the time of my birth.
It takes four to hold him down,
Bend him in half, until the bone
Begins to whimper.

Cut him off. He can take care
Of himself. Take root in the earth,
Or go hunting with wolves.

2

The second points the way.
True way. The path crosses the earth,
The moon and some stars.
Watch, he points further.
He points to himself.

3

The middle one has backache.
Stiff, still unaccustomed to this life;
An old man at birth. It's about something
That he had and lost,
That he looks for within my hand,
The way a dog looks
For fleas
With a sharp tooth.

4

The fourth is mystery.
Sometimes as my hand
Rests on the table
He jumps by himself
As though someone called his name.

After each bone, finger,
I come to him, troubled.

5

Something stirs in the fifth
Something perpetually at the point
Of birth. Weak and submissive,
His touch is gentle.
It weighs a tear.
It takes the mote out of the eye.

1971

Fork

This strange thing must have crept
Right out of hell.
It resembles a bird's foot
Worn around the cannibal's neck.

As you hold it in your hand,
As you stab with it into a piece of meat,
It is possible to imagine the rest of the bird:
Its head which like your fist
Is large, bald, beakless and blind.

1971

Charon's[1] Cosmology

With only his dim lantern
To tell him where he is
And every time a mountain
Of fresh corpses to load up

Take them to the other side
Where there are plenty more
I'd say by now he must be confused
As to which side is which

I'd say it doesn't matter
No one complains he's got

1. In Greek mythology Charon ferries the dead across the river Styx to Hades.

Their pockets to go through
In one a crust of bread in another a sausage

Once in a long while a mirror
Or a book which he throws
Overboard into the dark river
Swift and cold and deep

1977

A Wall

That's the only image
That turns up.

A wall all by itself,
Poorly lit, beckoning,
But no sense of the room,
Not even a hint
Of why it is I remember
So little and so clearly:

The fly I was watching,
The details of its wings
Glowing like turquoise.
Its feet, to my amusement
Following a minute crack—
An eternity
Around that simple event.

And nothing else; and nowhere
To go back to;
And no one else
As far as I know to verify.

1977

Euclid Avenue

All my dark thoughts
laid out
in a straight line.

An abstract street
on which an equally abstract intelligence
forever advances, doubting
the sound of its own footsteps.

*

Interminable cortege.
Language
as old as rain.
Fortune-teller's spiel

from where it has its beginning,
its kennel and bone,
the scent of a stick
I used to retrieve.

*

A sort of darkness without the woods,
crow-light but without the crow,
Hotel Splendide
all locked up for the night.

And out there,
in sight of some ultimate bakery
the street-light
of my insomnia.

A place
known as infinity
toward which that old self
advances.

The poor son of poor parents
who aspires to please
at such a late hour.

The magical coins
in his pocket
occupying all his thoughts.

A place known
as infinity,
its screendoor screeching,
endlessly screeching.

1977

Prodigy

I grew up bent over
a chessboard.

I loved the word *endgame.*

All my cousins looked worried.

It was a small house
near a Roman graveyard.
Planes and tanks
shook its windowpanes.

A retired professor of astronomy
taught me how to play.

That must have been in 1944.

In the set we were using,
the paint had almost chipped off
the black pieces.

The white King was missing
and had to be substituted for.

I'm told but do not believe
that that summer I witnessed
men hung from telephone poles.

I remember my mother
blindfolding me a lot.
She had a way of tucking my head
suddenly under her overcoat.

In chess, too, the professor told me,
the masters play blindfolded,
the great ones on several boards
at the same time.

1980

My Weariness of Epic Proportions

I like it when
Achilles
Gets killed
And even his buddy Patroclus—
And that hothead Hector—
And the whole Greek and Trojan
Jeunesse doree[2]
Is more or less
Expertly slaughtered
So there's finally
Peace and quiet
(The gods having momentarily
Shut up)
One can hear
A bird sing
And a daughter ask her mother
Whether she can go to the well
And of course she can
By that lovely little path
That winds through
The olive orchard

1982

2. "Gilded youth," a French phrase applied originally to a group prominent in 1794, during the French Revolution, and later to any of the young and idle rich. Simic applies it to the heroes killed in the Trojan War, as told in Homer's *Iliad.*

STANLEY PLUMLY

(1939–   )

Born in Barnesville, Ohio, Stanley Plumly has constructed his best poems on images from childhood and nature. In Winchester, Virginia, children watch as German prisoners of war are marched through town on their way to plant apple trees for their captors. In Troy, Ohio, a boy frightens his mother by playing on a railroad bridge over the Great Miami River "forty feet below." Harry and Bess Truman wave from the platform of a train making a whistle stop. Birds rise from water. Light shines on trees.

Plumly grew up in Virginia and Ohio, in a family where he remembers the father as alcoholic, the mother framed in symbolic doorways. At Wilmington College in Ohio he studied sculpture and painting, and after graduation in 1961 he exercised his visual imagination for a while by teaching painting in a private school. Turning to images in words, however, he enrolled in graduate school at Ohio University, earning an M.A. in English in 1968. A teaching position at Louisiana State University led to his first book, *In the Outer Dark* (1970), and that in turn to the Guggenheim Fellowship that encouraged his second major volume, *Out-of-the-Body Travel* (1977). Since 1970 he has taught at a number of universities, including Ohio University, Princeton, Columbia, Houston, and Maryland.

A pictorial poet, Plumly has said that "art must represent as it transforms." Among writers he admires and whose influence he has felt, he has listed Thomas Hardy and D. H. Lawrence (for their fiction more than for their poetry), fellow Ohio poet James Wright, and W. B. Yeats, "the greatest poet in English ever, if you count Shakespeare as a dramatist rather than a poet."

Poetry titles, besides those named above, include *How the Plains Indians Got Horses,* 1973; *Giraffe,* 1973; and *Summer Celestial,* 1983.

A brief assessment appears in *Dictionary of Literary Biography, Volume 5, American Poets Since World War II,* 1980.

For Esther

1

From the back it looks like a porch,
portable, the filigree railing French.

And Truman, Bess and the girl[1] each come out
waving, in short sleeves, because the heat
is worse than Washington.

The day is twelve hours old, Truman is talking.
You tell me to pay attention,

so I have my ball-
cap in my hands when he gets to the part that the sun

is suicidal, his dry voice barely audible above the train.

1. Harry S. Truman (1884–1972), thirty-third president of the United States (1945–1953), and his wife and daughter.

It makes a noise like steam.
He says, he says, he says.

His glasses silver in the sun. He says
there is never enough, and leans down to us.

2

Shultz and I put pennies on the track to make
the train jump. It jumps.

Afternoons you nap—one long pull of the body
through the heat.

I go down to the depot
against orders; it's practically abandoned
except for the guy who hangs out

the mail and looks for pennies. He's president

of this place, he says. We pepper his B & O[2]
brick building with tar balls when he's gone.

You hate the heat and sleep and let
your full voice go when I get caught.

You can't stand my noise or silence.
And I can hear a train in each bent coin.

You're thirty. I still seem to burden that young body.

3

Light bar, dark bar, all the way down. The trick is
if a train comes there is room for only the river.

I look down between the crossties at the Great Miami.
Three miles back, near home,

Kessler has already climbed to his station.
The trick is waiting for the whistle.

I remember
your dream about bridges: how, as a child, they shook
you off, something the wind compelled.

You woke up holding on. And now this August morning

I don't know enough to be afraid or care.
I do my thinking here,

looking down at the long ladder on the water,
forty feet below.

2. Initials of the Baltimore and Ohio Railroad.

4

The engine at idle, coasting in the yard, the call bell
back and forth, back and forth above the lull . . .

I hang on like the mail as the cars lock in
to one another, couple, and make a train.

The time I break my arm you swear
me to the ground—no more rivers,
no more side-car rides—

and stay up half
the night to rub my legs to sleep.

Sometimes you talk as if Roosevelt[3]

were still alive. Recovery is memory.
I never broke my arm.

Back and forth. The names
of the states pass every day in front of us, single-file.

5

If a house were straw there'd be a wind,
if a house were wood there'd be a fire,

if a house were brick there'd be a track
and a train to tell the time.

I wish each passage
well—wind, fire, time, people on a train.
From here to there, three minutes, whistle-stop.

And the speech each night, the seconds clicking off.

The whole house shakes—or seems to. At intervals,
the ghost smoke fills

all the windows on the close-in side.
It's our weather. It's what we hear all night,
between Troy[4] and anywhere, what you meant

to tell me, out of the body, out of the body travel.

1977

Out-of-the-Body Travel

1

And then he would lift this finest
of furniture to his big left shoulder

3. Franklin Delano Roosevelt (1882–1945), thirty-second president of the United States (1933–1945).

4. Troy, Ohio, scene of the memories in this poem.

and tuck it in and draw the bow
so carefully as to make the music

almost visible on the air. And play
and play until a whole roomful of the sad
relatives mourned. They knew this was
drawing of blood, threading and rethreading

the needle. They saw even in my father's
face how well he understood the pain
he put them to—his raw, red cheek
pressed against the cheek of the wood . . .

2

And in one stroke he brings the hammer
down, like mercy, so that the young bull's
legs suddenly fly out from under it . . .
While in the dream he is the good angel

in Chagall,[5] the great ghost of his body
like light over the town. The violin
sustains him. It is pain remembered.
Either way, I know if I wake up cold,

and go out into the clear spring night,
still dark and precise with stars,
I will feel the wind coming down hard
like his hand, in fever, on my forehead.

1977

My Mother's Feet

How no shoe fit them,
and how she used to prop them,
having dressed for bed,
letting the fire in the coal-stove blue

and blink out, falling asleep in her chair.
How she bathed and dried them, night after night,
and rubbed their soreness like an intimacy.
How she let the fire pull her soft body through them.

She was the girl who grew just standing,
the one the picture cut at the knees.
She was the girl who seemed to be dancing
out on the lawn, after supper, alone.

I have watched her climb the militant stairs
and down again, watched the ground go out from under her.
I have seen her on the edge of chances—
she fell, when she fell, like a girl.

5. Marc Chagall (1887–1985), Russian-born French surrealist painter.

Someone who loved her said she walked on water.
Where there is no path nor wake. As a child
I would rise in the half-dark of the house,
from a bad dream or a noisy window,

something, almost, like snow in the air,
and wander until I could find those feet, propped
and warm as a bricklayer's hands,
every step of the way shining out of them.

1983

Waders and Swimmers

The first morning it flew out of the fog
I thought it lived there.
It floated into shore all shoulders,
all water and air. It was cold that summer.
In the white dark the sun coming up was the moon.
And then this beautiful bird,
its wings as large as a man, drawing the line
of itself out of the light behind it.
A month or more it flew out of the fog,
fished, fed, gone in a moment.

There are no blue herons in Ohio.
But one October in a park I saw a swan
lift itself from the water in singular, vertical strokes.
It got high enough to come back down wild.
It ate bread from the hand
and swallowed in long, irregular gestures.
It seemed, to a child, almost angry.
I remember what I hated
when someone tied it wing-wide to a tree.
The note nailed to its neck said this is nothing.

The air is nothing, though it rise
and fall. Another year
a bird the size of a whooping crane
flew up the Hocking—
people had never seen a bird that close
so large and white at once.
They called it their ghost and went back to their Bibles.
It stood on houses for days, lost,
smoke from the river.
In the wing-light of the dawn it must have passed

its shadow coming and going. I wish I knew.
I still worry a swan alive
through an early Ohio winter, still worry
its stuttering, clipped wings.
It rises in snow, white on white, the way
in memory one thing is confused with another.
From here to a bird that flies

with its neck folded back to its shoulders
is nothing but air, nothing but first light and summer
and water rising in a smoke of waters.

Merriman's Cove, Maine 1983

Snowing, Sometimes

You couldn't keep it out.
You could see it drifting
from one side of the road
to the other—you could watch
the wind work it back and forth
across the hard white surfaces.
You could see the maple, with
its ten dead leaves, winded,
wanting it. But sometimes
you couldn't keep it out.

It was like dust, an elegance,
like frost. All you had to
do was stand at the window
and it passed, like the light,
over your face—softer than light
at the edges, the seams,
the separations in the glass.
All you had to do was stand
still in the dark and the room
seemed alive with it, crystalline,
a bright breath on the air.

If you fell asleep you knew
it could cover you, cover you
the way cold closes on water.
It would shine, like ice,
inside you. If you woke up
early, the cup on the bureau
cracked, you were sure that
even the pockets of your pants,
hung on the back of the chair,
would be filled. Nothing could
stop it, could keep it out.

Not the room in sunlight, nor
smoky with the rain. Not
the mother sweeping, nor
building the woodfire each
morning. Not the wind blowing
backwards, without sound.
Not the boy at the window
who loves the look of it
dusting the ground, whiter
than flour, piled in the

small, far corners.

1983

ROBERT PINSKY
(1940–)

Born in Long Branch, New Jersey, Robert Pinsky graduated from Rutgers in 1962 and earned a Ph.D. in English at Stanford in 1966, studying under the poet and critic Yvor Winters. His first book, *Landor's Poetry,* an examination of the nineteenth-century English poet, was published in 1968 by the University of Chicago, where he also held his first teaching position. That year he moved to Wellesley College, where he taught for a number of years before becoming a professor at the University of California at Berkeley. Meanwhile, after publishing a critique of some of the tendencies of poetry in our time in *The Situation of Poetry: Contemporary Poetry and Its Tradition* (1976), he had in 1978 become poetry editor of the *New Republic,* a position he held for several years. A versatile writer, he has also experimented with computer interactive fiction, publishing on disks for reader participation his "quest romance" *Mindwheel* in 1987.

In his verse to date, Pinsky has shown himself a poet of subtle intellectuality, discursive and even philosophical. Although in some other recent poets a focus on the particulars of existence suggests a mystic or surreal fascination with things in and of themselves, Pinsky almost always connects his particulars to suggestions of an overarching meaning as the concrete drives toward the abstract. A careful metrical craftsman, he characteristically shapes his verse to emphasize poetry as a thing made, not found; at the same time he possesses the wit to remind readers of the roots of meter in everyday language: " 'All politics is local politics' / Said Mayor Daly (in pentameters)."

Pinsky's third book of verse, *History of My Heart* (1984), displays a developing talent, here focused often on childhood memories of a small-town boyhood near the New Jersey shore. Never far from home and woods and boardwalk, however, is the sense of life as change and luck. The pull backward to family and friends, some now dead, suggests a still more backward pull to ancestors and Indians, and as the poems move outward from the breakers they sometimes probe the symbolic ocean depths far offshore. In the title poem, the poet becomes a high school musician, his saxophone fighting against the anguish of the lost past, crying for all children to all mothers, and all poets to all readers, "Listen to *me* * * * "

Pinsky's verse is collected in *Sadness and Happiness,* 1975; *An Explanation of America,* 1979; and *History of My Heart,* 1984. He is co-translator of *The Separate Notebooks: Poems by Czeslaw Milosz,* 1984.

Local Politics[1]

And so the things the country wants to see
Are like a nest made out of circumstance;
And when, as in the great old sermon "The Eagle
Stirreth Her Nest," God like a nesting eagle
Pulls out a little of the plush around us
And lets the thorns of trial, and the bramble,
Stick through and scrape and threaten the fledgling soul,
We see that that construction of thorn and bramble
Is like a cage: the tight and sheltering cage
Of Law and circumstance, scraping through the plush

1. From "An Explanation of America," a poem addressed to the poet's daughter.

Like death—whenever the eagle stirreth her nest;
The body with its bony cage of law
And politics, the thorn of death and taxes.

You, rich in rhetoric and indignation,
The jailbird-lawyer of the Hunnewell School,
Come home from some small, wicked parliament
To elaborate a new theme: forceful topics
Touching the sheeplike, piggish ways of that tyrant
And sycophantic lout, the Majority.
The two lame cheers for democracy that I
Borrow and try to pass to you ("It is
The worst of all the forms of government,
Except for all the others"—Winston Churchill[2])
You brush aside: Political Science bores you,
You prefer the truth, and with a Jesuit firmness
Return to your slogan: "Voting *is not* fair."

I have another saw that I can scrape
For you, out of the hoard of antique hardware,
Cliches and Great Ideas, quaintly-toothed
Black ironwork that we heap about our young:
Voting is one of the *"necessary evils."*
Avoid all groups and institutions, they
Are necessary evils: necessary
Unto the general Happiness and Safety,
And evil because they are deficient in being.
Such is the hardware; and somewhere in between
The avoidance and the evil necessity
We each conclude a contract with the Beast.

America is, as Malcolm X[3] once said,
A prison. And that the world and all its parts
Are also prisons (Chile, the Hunnewell School,
One's own deficient being, each prison after
Its own degree and kind), does not diminish
Anything that he meant about his country:
When the Dan Ryan Expressway in Chicago
Was flooded, "Black youths" who the paper said
Pillaged the stranded motorists like beached whales
Were rioting prisoners . . . a weight of lead
Sealed in their hearts was lighter for some minutes
Amid the riot.
                    Living inside a prison,
Within its many other prisons, what
Should one aspire to be? a kind of chaplain?
But chaplains, I have heard, are often powers,
Political, within their prisons, patrons
And mediators between the frightened groups:
Blue People, Gray People, and their constricting fears,
The mutual circumstance of ward and warder.

2. (1874–1965), British statesman, prime minister 1940–1945 and 1951–1955.

3. (1925–1965), black leader, born Malcolm Little, whose story was told by Alex Haley in *The Autobiography of Malcolm X,* 1964.

No kind of chaplain ever will mediate
Among the conquering, crazed immigrants
Of El Camino and the Bergen Mall,
The Jews who dream up the cowboy films, the Blacks
Who dream the music, the people who dream the cars
And ways of voting, the Japanese and Basques
Each claiming a special sense of humor, as do
Armenian photo-engravers, and the people
Who dream the saws: "*You cannot let men live
Like pigs, and make them freemen, it is not safe,*"
The people who dream up the new diseases
For use in warfare, the people who design
New shapes of pants, and sandwiches sumptuous
Beyond the dreams of innocent Europe: crazed
As carpet-bombing or the Berlin Airlift—
Crazed immigrants and prisoners, rioting
Or else, alone as in the secrecy
Of a narrow bunk or cell, whittling or painting
Some desperate weapon or crude work of art:
A spoon honed to a dagger or a bauble,
A pistol molded from a cake of soap,
A fumbling poem or a lurid picture
Urgent and sentimental as a tattoo. . . .
The Dorians,[4] too, were conquering immigrants,
And hemmed in by their own anarchic spirits
And new peninsula, they too resorted
To invented institutions, and the vote,
With a spirit nearly comic, and in fear.

The plural-headed Empire, manifold
Beyond my outrage or my admiration,
Is like a prison which I leave to you
(And like a shelter)—where the people vote,
And where the threats of riot and oppression
Inspire the inmates as they whittle, scribble,
Jockey for places in the choir, or smile
Passing out books on weekdays.
On the radio,
The FM station that plays "All Country and Western"
Startled me, when I hit its button one day,
With a voice—inexplicable and earnest—
In Vietnamese or Chinese, lecturing
Or selling, or something someone wanted broadcast,
A paid political announcement, perhaps. . . .
"All politics is local politics"
Said Mayor Daley[5] (in pentameter):
And this then is the locus where we vote,
Prisonyard fulcrum of knowledge, fear and work—
Nest where an Eagle balances and screams,
The wild bird with its hardware in its claws.

1979

4. Ancient people who migrated into Greece, displacing the earlier Achaeans in the Peloponnesian peninsula between about 1100 and 950 B.C., and greatly influenced subsequent art and architecture.
5. Long-time mayor of Chicago.

Memorial

(J.E. and N.M.S.)

Here lies a man. And here, a girl. They live
In the kind of artificial life we give

To birds or statues: imagining what they feel,
Or that like birds the dead each had one call,

Repeated, or a gesture that suspends
Their being in a forehead or the hands.

A man comes whistling from a house. The screen
Snaps shut behind him. Though there is no man

And no house, memory sends him to get tools
From a familiar shed, and so he strolls

Through summer shade to work on the family car.
He is my uncle, and fresh home from the war,

With little for me to remember him doing yet.
The clock of the cancer ticks in his body, or not,

Depending if it is there, or waits. The search
Of memory gains and fails like surf: the porch

And trim are painted cream, the shakes are stained.
The shadows could be painted (so little wind

Is blowing there) or stains on the crazy-paving
Of the front walk. . . . Or now, the shadows are moving:

Another house, unrelated; a woman says,
Is this your special boy, and the girl says, yes,

Moving her hand in mine. The clock in her, too—
As someone told me a month or two ago,

Months after it finally took her. A public building
Is where the house was: though a surf, unyielding

And sickly, seethes and eddies at the stones
Of the foundation. The dead are made of bronze,

But dying they were like birds with clocklike hearts—
Unthinkable, how much pain the tiny parts

Of even the smallest bird might yet contain.
We become larger than life in how much pain

Our bodies may encompass . . . all Titans[6] in that,
Or heroic statues. Although there is no heat

6. In Greek mythology, twelve primeval deities and, sometimes, their descendants; hence, any heroic, godlike figure.

Brimming in the fixed, memorial summer, the brows
Of lucid metal sweat a faint warm haze

As I try to think the pain I never saw.
Though there is no pain there, the small birds draw

Together in crowds above the houses—and cry
Over the surf: as if there were a day,

Memorial, marked on the calendar for dread
And pain and loss—although among the dead

Are no hurts, but only emblematic things;
No hospital beds, but a lifting of metal wings.

1979

The Figured Wheel

The figured wheel rolls through shopping malls and prisons,
Over farms, small and immense, and the rotten little downtowns.
Covered with symbols, it mills everything alive and grinds
The remains of the dead in the cemeteries, in unmarked graves and oceans.

Sluiced by salt water and fresh, by pure and contaminated rivers,
By snow and sand, it separates and recombines all droplets and grains,
Even the infinite sub atomic particles crushed under the illustrated,
Varying treads of its wide circumferential track.

Spraying flecks of tar and molten rock it rumbles
Through the Antarctic station of American sailors and technicians,
And shakes the floors and windows of whorehouses for diggers and smelters
From Bethany, Pennsylvania to a practically nameless, semi-penal New Town

In the mineral-rich tundra of the Soviet northernmost settlements.
Artists illuminate it with pictures and incised mottoes
Taken from the Ten-Thousand Stories and the Register of True Dramas.
They hang it with colored ribbons and with bells of many pitches.

With paints and chisels and moving lights they record
On its rotating surface the elegant and terrifying doings
Of the inhabitants of the Hundred Pantheons of major Gods
Disposed in iconographic stations at hub, spoke and concentric bands,

And also the grotesque demi-Gods, Hopi gargoyles and Ibo dryads.
They cover it with wind-chimes and electronic instruments
That vibrate as it rolls to make an all-but-unthinkable music,
So that the wheel hums and rings as it turns through the births of stars

And through the dead-world of bomb, fireblast and fallout
Where only a few doomed races of insects fumble in the smoking grasses.
It is Jesus oblivious to hurt turning to give words to the unrighteous,
And is also Gogol's[7] feeding pig that without knowing it eats a baby chick

7. Nikolai Vasilyevich Gogol (1809–1852), Russian novelist, short story writer, and dramatist.

And goes on feeding. It is the empty armor of My Cid,[8] clattering
Into the arrows of the credulous unbelievers, a metal suit
Like the lost astronaut revolving with his useless umbilicus
Through the cold streams, neither energy nor matter, that agitate

The cold, cyclical dark, turning and returning.
Even in the scorched and frozen world of the dead after the holocaust
The wheel as it turns goes on accreting ornaments.
Scientists and artists festoon it from the grave with brilliant

Toys and messages, jokes and zodiacs, tragedies conceived
From among the dreams of the unemployed and the pampered,
The listless and the tortured. It is hung with devices
By dead masters who have survived by reducing themselves magically

To tiny organisms, to wisps of matter, crumbs of soil,
Bits of dry skin, microscopic flakes, which is why they are called "great,"
In their humility that goes on celebrating the turning
Of the wheel as it rolls unrelentingly over

A cow plodding through car-traffic on a street in Iasi,[9]
And over the haunts of Robert Pinsky's mother and father
And wife and children and his sweet self
Which he hereby unwillingly and inexpertly gives up, because it is

There, figured and pre-figured in the nothing-transfiguring wheel.

1984

Dying

Nothing to be said about it, and everything—
The change of changes, closer or further away:
The Golden Retriever next door, Gussie, is dead,

Like Sandy, the Cocker Spaniel from three doors down
Who died when I was small; and every day
Things that were in my memory fade and die.

Phrases die out: first, everyone forgets
What doornails are; then after certain decades
As a dead metaphor, "*dead as a doornail*" flickers

And fades away. But someone I know is dying—
And though one might say glibly, "everyone is,"
The different pace makes the difference absolute.

The tiny invisible spores in the air we breathe,
That settle harmlessly on our drinking water
And on our skin, happen to come together

With certain conditions on the forest floor,
Or even a shady corner of the lawn—
And overnight the fleshy, pale stalks gather,

8. Spanish hero of the eleventh century, celebrated in the anonymous twelfth-century poem *The Song of the Cid* and in many later works.
9. City in Rumania.

The colorless growth without a leaf or flower;
And around the stalks, the summer grass keeps growing
With steady pressure, like the insistent whiskers

That grow between shaves on a face, the nails
Growing and dying from the toes and fingers
At their own humble pace, oblivious

As the nerveless moths, that live their night or two—
Though like a moth a bright soul keeps on beating,
Bored and impatient in the monster's mouth.

1984

DAVE SMITH

(1942–   )

Born in Portsmouth, Virginia, a suburb of Norfolk, David Jeddie Smith grew up there and in nearby Poquoson, spending time also among relatives in Cumberland, Maryland, and Green Springs, West Virginia. In these places he absorbed the emotional and geographical background for much of his poetry. Poquoson is a fishing village extending between the Poquoson River and the Back River toward Chesapeake Bay, a country of marshes, clamdiggers, and oystermen. In Cumberland and Green Springs, a few miles apart on opposite sides of the Potomac, he saw a depressed area on a decaying railroad line, surrounded by beautiful countryside, not far from the mountains. Between these poles of his early experience lay large stretches of land bloodily fought over in the Civil War. In Norfolk, a navy town, prostitutes and thriving bars provided continuing testimony to the world's tensions as they vied for the custom of sailors on shore leave and served as magnets for cruising teenagers from the local high schools.

After receiving his B.A. from the University of Virginia, Charlottesville, in 1965, Smith taught English and French and coached football for two years at Poquoson High School before enrolling in graduate school at Southern Illinois University and receiving an M.A. in 1969. From 1969 to 1972 he served in the air force, finding time to establish and edit a poetry journal, *Back Door,* and to publish his first small book of poetry, *Bull Island* (1970) from his own Back Door Press in Poquoson. After his military service, he taught briefly at Western Michigan University and at Cottey College in Missouri, meanwhile publishing two more collections of verse, *Mean Rufus Throw Down* (1973) and *The Fisherman's Whore* (1974), before returning to graduate school. Armed with a Ph.D. from Ohio University (1976), he has since then taught at the University of Utah and, more recently, at Virginia Commonwealth University in Richmond.

The Roundhouse Voices: Selected and New Poems (1985), the source of the texts below, presents much of the best of Smith's work to date, culled and sometimes revised from seven previous books. Like James Dickey, whom he has much admired, he has rooted his poems in the southern soil. They are strong in a sense of landscape and history, sometimes violent or grotesque in narrative content. Frequently seeming autobiographical, many tell of people who are, he has said, "my family, but I'm not confessing"—his is not the voice, in other words, of the "confessional poets" of the late 1950's and early 1960's. He writes of people and places close to him to record and celebrate. Nostalgia for what we have lost tells us we must risk much to grasp and keep what we still have. As the speaker of "The Roundhouse Voices" expresses it, "All I ever wanted / to steal was life * * * "

In addition to those named above, Smith's books of poetry include *Cumberland Station,* 1976; *Goshawk, Antelope,* 1979; *Dream Flights,* 1981; *Homage to Edgar Allan Poe,* 1981; *In the House of the Judge,* 1983; and *Gray Soldiers,* 1983. *Onliness,* 1981, is a novel, and *Southern Delights,* 1984, a collection of stories. Essays are collected in *Local Assays in Our Contemporary American Poetry,* 1984. Smith edited *The Pure Clear Word: Essays on the Poetry of James Wright,* 1982.

Brief assessments may be found in Helen Vendler, *Part of Nature, Part of Us: Modern American Poets,* 1980; and *Dictionary of Literary Biography, Volume 5: American Poets Since World War II,* 1980.

On a Field Trip at Fredericksburg[1]

The big steel tourist shield says maybe
fifteen thousand got it here. No word
of either Whitman[2] or one uncle
I barely remember in the smoke
that filled his tiny mountain house.

If each finger were a thousand of them
I could clap my hands and be dead
up to my wrists. It was quick
though not so fast as we can do it
now, one bomb, atomic or worse,
the tiny pod slung on wingtip,
high up, an egg cradled
by some rapacious mockingbird.

Hiroshima canned nine times their number
in a flash. Few had the time
to moan or feel the feeling
ooze back in the groin.

In a ditch I stand
above Marye's Heights,[3] the book-
bred faces of Brady's[4] fifteen-year-old
drummers, before battle, rigid
as August's dandelions
all the way to the Potomac
rolling in my skull.

If Audubon[5] came here, the names
of birds would gush, the marvel
single feathers make
evoke a cloud, a nation,
a gray blur preserved
on a blue horizon, but

1. Fredericksburg, Virginia, site of a Civil War battle, a Confederate victory, December 13, 1862.
2. Walt Whitman (1819–1892), American poet who served as a volunteer nurse and described his experiences with the dead and wounded from Fredericksburg in his prose memoir *Specimen Days* (1882).
3. Site of the deaths of many Union soldiers as the troops tried unsuccessfully to storm the position taken by General James Longstreet's men.
4. Mathew B. Brady (*c.* 1823–1896), pioneer photographer, recorded many Civil War scenes.
5. John James Audubon (1785–1851), naturalist famed for his paintings and descriptions of American birds.

there is only a wandering child,
one dark stalk snapped off
in her hand. Hopeless teacher,
I take it, try to help her
hold its obscure syllables
one instant in her mouth,
like a drift of wind
at the forehead, the front door,
the black, numb fingernails.

1976

Cumberland Station

Gray brick, ash, hand-bent railings, steps so big
it takes hours to mount them, polished oak
pews holding the slim hafts of sun, and one
splash of the *Pittsburgh Post-Gazette.* The man
who left Cumberland gone, come back, no job
anywhere. I come here alone, shaken
the way I came years ago to ride down
mountains in Big Daddy's cab.[6] He was
the first set cold in the black meadow.

Six rows of track gleam, thinned, rippling
like water on walls where famous engines steam, half
submerged in frothing crowds with something
to celebrate and plenty to eat. One engineer takes
children for a free ride, a frolic
like an earthquake. Ash cakes their hair.
I am one of those who walked uphill
through flowers of soot to zing
scared to death into the world.

Now whole families afoot cruise South Cumberland
for something to do, no jobs, no money for bars,
the old stories cracked like wallets.
This time there's no fun in coming back. The second
death. My roundhouse[7] uncle coughed his youth
into a gutter. His son, the third, slid on the ice,
losing his need to drink himself
stupidly dead. In this vaulted hall
I think of all the dirt poured down
from shovels and trains and empty pockets.
I stare into the huge malignant headlamps
circling the gray walls and catch a stuttered
glimpse of faces stunned like deer on a track,
children getting drunk, shiny as Depression apples.

Churning through the inner space of this godforsaken
wayside, I feel the ground try to upchuck and I dig
my fingers in my temples to bury a child

6. The cab of his locomotive.

7. A building housing a rotating platform for turning a train locomotive around.

diced on a cowcatcher, a woman smelling
alkaline from washing out the soot.
Where I stood in that hopeless, hateful room
will not leave me. The scarf of smoke I saw
over a man's shoulder runs through me
like the sored Potomac River.

Grandfather, you ask why I don't visit you
now you have escaped the ticket-seller's cage
to fumble hooks and clean the Shakespeare reels.[8]
What could we catch? I've been sitting in the pews
thinking about us a long time, long enough to see
a man can't live in jobless, friendless Cumberland
anymore. The soot owns even the fish.

I keep promising I'll come back, we'll get out,
you and me, like brothers, and I mean it.
A while ago a man with the look of a demented cousin
shuffled across this skittery floor and snatched up
the *Post-Gazette* and stuffed it in his coat
and nobody gave a damn because nobody cares
who comes or goes here or even who steals
what nobody wants: old news, photographs
of dead diesels behind chipped glass.

I'm the man who stole it and I wish you were here
to beat the hell out of me for it because
what you said a long time ago welts my face
and won't go away. I admit
it isn't mine even if it's nobody else's.
Anyway, that's all I catch this trip—bad
news. I can't catch my nephew's life, my uncle's,
Big Daddy's, yours, or the ash-haired kids'
who fell down to sleep here after the war.

Outside new families pick their way along tracks
you and I have walked home on many nights.
Every face on the walls goes on smiling,
and, Grandfather, I wish I had the guts
to tell you this is a place I hope
I never have to go through again.

1976

Night Fishing for Blues

At Fortress Monroe, Virginia,
the big-jawed Bluefish, ravenous, sleek muscle slamming
at rock, at pier legs, drives into Chesapeake
shallows, convoys rank after rank,
        wheeling through flume and flute of blood,
        something like hunger's throb hooking

8. Fishing equipment.

until you hear it and know them there,
                                                  the family.
        Tonight, not far from where Jefferson Davis[9]

hunched in a harrowing cell, gray eyes quick
as crabs' nubs, I come back over planks
deep drummed under boots years ago, tufts of hair

floating at my eyes, thinking it is right now
        to pitch through tideturn and mudslur
        for fish with teeth like snapped sabers.
        In blue crescents of base lights, I cast hooks

baited with Smithfield ham: they reel, zing,
plummet, coil in corrosive swirls, bump on
scum-skinned rocks. No skin divers prowl here,

        visibility an arm's length, my visions

hand-to-hand in the line's warp. A meat-
baited lure limps through limbs nippling the muck,
silhouettes, shoots forward, catches a cruising Blue

        sentry's eye, snags and sets

case-hardened barbs. Suddenly, I am not alone:
    three Negroes plump down in lawn chairs, shudder-
    casting into the black pod plodding under us. One

        ripples with age, a grandmotherly obelisk,

her breath puffing like a coal stove. She swivels
heavily, chewing her dark nut, spits thick juice
like a careful churn.

                When I yank the first Blue
    she mumbles, her eyes roll far out on the black-
    blue billowing sea-screen. I hear her canting

        to Africa, a cluck in her throat, a chain

song from the fisherman's house. I cannot
understand. Bluefish are pouring at me in squads.
I haul two, three at a time, torpedoes, moon-shiners,
jamming my feet into the splintered floor, battling
whatever comes. I know I have waited
a whole life for this minute. Like dreams

        graven on cold cell walls, Blues walk over

our heads, ground on back-wings, grind their teeth.
They splash rings of blue and silver around us, tiaras

9. (1808–1889), president of the Confederacy, confined for two years after the Civil War in Fortress Monroe.

of lost battalions. I can smell the salt of ocean
runners as she hollers *I ain't doing so bad*
for an old queen. No time to answer. Two

car-hoods down her descendants swing sinewy arms

in Superfly shirts, exotic butterflies: I hear them
pop beer cans, the whoosh released like stale breath
through a noose no one remembers. We hang

fast flat casts, artless, no teasing fishermen,

beyond the book-bred lures of the pristine streams,
speeded-up, centrifugal, machines wound
too far, belts slipped, gears gone, momentum

hauling us back, slinging lines, winging wildly

as howitzers. Incredibly it happens: I feel
the hook hammer and shake and throw my entire weight
to dragging, as if I have caught the goddamndest

Blue in the Atlantic. She screams: *Oh my God!*

Four of us fumbling in beamed headlight and blue
arc light cut the hook from her face. Gnats butterfly,
nag us: I put it deep and it must be gouged out
like a cyst. When it is free, I hear Blues not yet

dead flopping softly. I tell her it is a lucky
thing she can see. She mops blood blued over
gold-lined teeth and opens her arms so her dress

billows like a caftan. She wants

nothing but to fish. I hand her her pole, then cast
as far as I can. She pumps, wings a sinker and hooks
into flashing slop and reels hard. In one instant both

our lines leap rigid as daguerreotypes; we have

caught each other but we go on for the blue blood of
ghosts that thrash in the brain's empty room.
We pull at shadows until we see there is nothing, then
sit on the shaky pier like prisoners. Coil after coil
we trace the path of Bluefish-knots backward,

unlooping, feeling for holes, giving, testing,

slapping the gnats from our skins. Harried, unbound,
we leap to be fishers. But now a gray glow
shreds with the cloud curtain, an old belly-fire

guts the night. Already the tide humps around

on itself. Lights flicker like campfires in duty windows
at Fort Monroe. She hooks up, saying *Sons they done*
let us go. I cast once more but nothing bites. Everywhere

a circle of Blues bleaches, stiffens

in flecks of blood. We kneel, stuff styrofoam
boxes with blankets of ice, break their backs
to keep them cold and sweet, the woman gravely
showing us what to do. By dawn the stink has passed

out of our noses. We drink beer like family.

All the way home thousands of Blues fall from my head,
falling with the gray Atlantic, and a pale veiny light
fills the road with sea-shadows that drift in figure

eights, knot and snarl and draw me forward.

1976

The Roundhouse Voices

In full glare of sunlight I came here, man-tall but thin
as a pinstripe, and stood outside the rusted fence
with its crown of iron thorns while
the soot cut into our lungs with tiny diamonds.
I walked through houses with my grain-lovely slugger
from Louisville that my uncle bought and stood
in the sun that made its glove soft on my hand
until I saw my chance to crawl under and get past
anyone who would demand a badge and a name.

The guard hollered that I could get the hell from there quick
when I popped in his face like a thief. All I ever wanted
to steal was life and you can't get that easy
in the grind of a railyard. *You can't catch me,*
lardass, I can go left or right good as the Mick,[1]
I hummed to him, holding my slugger by the neck
for a bunt laid smooth where the coal cars
jerked and let me pass between tracks
until, in a slide on ash, I fell safe and heard
the wheeze of his words: *Who the hell are you, kid?*

I hear them again tonight, Uncle, hard as big brakeshoes,
when I lean over your face in the box of silk. The years
you spent hobbling from room to room alone crawl
up my legs and turn this house to another
house, round and black as defeat, where slugging
comes easy when you whip the gray softball over
the glass diesel globe. Footsteps thump on the stairs
like that fat ball against bricks and when I miss
I hear you warn me to watch the timing, to keep
my eyes on your hand and forget the fence,

1. Mickey Mantle (1931–), switch-hitting baseball player for the New York Yankees.

hearing also that other voice that keeps me out and away
from you on a day worth playing good ball. Hearing
Who the hell . . . I see myself like a burning speck
of cinder come down the hill and through a tunnel
of porches like stands, running on deep ash,
and I give him the finger, whose face still gleams
clear as a B&O[2] headlight, just to make him get up
and chase me into a dream of scoring at your feet.
At Christmas that guard staggered home sobbing,
the thing in his chest tight as a torque wrench.
In the summer I did not have to run and now

who is the one who dreams of a drink as he leans over
tools you kept bright as a first-girl's promise? I
have no one to run from or to, nobody to give
my finger to as I steal his peace. Uncle, the light
bleeds on your gray face like the high barbed-wire
shadows I had to get through and maybe you don't remember
you said to come back, to wait and you'd show me
the right way to take a hard pitch
in the sun that shudders on the ready man. I'm here

though this is a day I did not want to see. In the roundhouse
the rasp and heel-click of compressors is still,
soot lies deep in every greasy fingerprint.
I called you from the pits and you did not come up
and I felt the fear when I stood on the tracks
that are like stars which never lead us
into any kind of light and I don't know who'll
tell me now when the guard sticks his blind snoot
between us: take off and beat the bastard out.
Can you hear him over the yard, grabbing his chest,
cry out, *Who the goddamn hell are you, kid?*

I gave him every name in the book, Uncle, but he caught us
and what good did all those hours of coaching do?
You lie on your back, eyeless forever, and I think
how once I climbed to the top of a diesel and stared
into that gray roundhouse glass where, in anger,
you threw up the ball and made a star
to swear at greater than the Mick ever dreamed.
It has been years but now I know what followed there
every morning the sun came up, not light
but the puffing bad-bellied light of words.

All day I have held your hand, trying to say back that life,
to get under that fence with words I lined
and linked up and steamed into a cold room
where the illusion of hope means skin torn in boxes
of tools. The footsteps come pounding into words
and even the finger I give death is words
that won't let us be what we wanted, each one
chasing and being chased by dreams in the dark.

2. Baltimore and Ohio Railroad.

Words are all we ever were and they did us
no damn good. Do you hear that?

Do you hear the words that, in oiled gravel, you gave me
when you set my feet in the right stance to swing?
They are coal-hard and they come in wings
and loops like despair not even the Mick
could knock out of this room, words softer
than the centers of hearts in guards or uncles,
words skinned and numbed by too many bricks.
I have had enough of them and bring them back here
where the tick and creak of everything dies
in your tiny starlight and I stand down
on my knees to cry, *Who the hell are you, kid?*

1979

Elegy in an Abandoned Boatyard

. . . mindful of the unhonored dead
—THOMAS GRAY[3]

Here they stood, whom the Kecoughtan first believed
gods from another world, one pair of longjohns
each, bad-yellow, knotted with lice,
the godless bandy-legged runts
with ear bit off, or eye gouged,
who killed and prayed
over whatever flew, squatted, or swam.

In huts hacked from mulberry, pine, and swamp cypress,
they huddled ripe as hounds.
At cockcrow scratched, shuffled paths,
took skiffs and ferried to dead-rise scows,
twenty-footers of local design and right draft
for oysters, crabs, and croakers.
They were seaworthy.

According to diaries hand-scrawled, and terse court records,
our ancestors: barbarous, habitual, Virginians.

Some would not sail, came ashore, walked on the land,
kept faces clenched, lay seed and family,
moved often, and are gone. Of them
this harbor says nothing.
Of the sea's workmen, not much,
no brass plate of honor, no monument in the square,
no square, merely the wreckage of a place.
But they stood,
proud, surly in mist at the hovel of the boatwright,
the arm pointed: *Build me one like that yonder!*
Meaning the hull I see bottom up in ashen water—

3. (1716–1771), English poet. The quoted phrase is from his "Elegy Written in a Country Churchyard."

nameless now as themselves, except to the squat one
known to crush clams in his palms, our kin,
the boatwright. He gave credit to each son,
barring feud, and took stick in hand
to dig from earth the grave first line of a keel,

who often would lift his brow seaward, but nothing said,
while a shape buried in air hove up
and he made it become what they wanted,
Like that one yonder!

And this was all the image for tomorrow he would give,
each reimagined, the best guess changing
to meet the sea's habitual story
of rot and stink and silence.
To make the hulls he knew
would riddle to nothing, he came
into this world as I have now entered his place
and sit at his charred and flood-finished log.

Only when I begin to hear the lies
he allowed each to invent
can I feel the hugeness of his belief, when I take up
a cap left as worthless, hung on a cypress stump, or feel
the plain cast of a stick pulse down my arm like the current
of conception—
then I see it,
an immense shadow
on water.
My eyes harden,
and there it is,
the wind cradle
of the Eagle's wings. As it might be for men,
even the least, riding the rising funnel
of air, dreaming change,
until I think of chicks screeching,
and the unborn who need us
to honor the places and the names of their passage
as we sit and try to dream back
the first wreckage, the last hope. I see
the one brother
become many floating and sinking,
lovely shadows all over the earth, and put my back
against the trunk they left me here, and pull
the stick to shape the dirt.
The line grows
quick with hunger, not perfect
but man-shaped and flight-worthy, a kind
of speech I take
for the unfinished country
the boatwright must have
dreamed, looking for his image
to rise and loom clearer
out of the water that beats in,
out of the water that bore us all here.

1981

In the House of the Judge

All of them asleep, the suspiring everywhere is audible weight
in the winter-shadowed house where I have dreamed
night after night and stand now trying
to believe it is only dust, no more than vent-spew
risen from the idiotically huffing
grandfather of a furnace in the coal room's heart of darkness.

Haven't I touched the flesh-gray sift on bookshelves, on framed
dim photographs of ancestors, on the clotted arms
of the banjo clock that tolls past
all resemblance to time and clicks like a musket's
steel hammer? And every day I wipe my glasses but still it comes,
as now, at the top of the whining stairs, I am

come to wait with my hand laid light on the moon-slicked railing.
I hear the house-heave of sleepers, and go jittery
with no fear I can name. I feel myself
shaped by the mica-fine motes that once were one
body in earth until gouged, cracked,
left tumbled apart and scarcely glowing in a draft-fanned pit.

Pipes clank and gargle like years in the ashen veins of the Judge
when they came to his house, the dung-heeled, some
drunk, all with stuttered pleas to free
their young, who could make it given a chance, just
one more good chance, so they said. Impassive, in skin-folds thick
as a lizard, he stared at the great one for a sign,

the dog across the room, who kept a wary eye and was a one-man dog.
Overhead do the same unbearable stars yet wheel
in bright, ubiquitous malice, and what
am I, wiping my glasses, certain this house walks
in nail-clicking threat, going to plead?
I look out through warped Civil War glass buffed by men now ash

where the small park he gave in civic pride lies snow-blistered.
Subzero then, as now, sent fire in the opening
throat, but they came: tethered horses,
striding shadows, and women who shrieked nightlong
until even gone they continued in his head. He heard them
breathing. He painted his house perfectly white.

I stare at that snow as at a scaffold. Whose lightening footprints
could soften my fear or say why I sniff like a
dog, seem to taste a skim of black air
upsweeping the maple stairwell, and feel my hair
go slowly white? How many hours must
a man watch snow shift the world before he sees it is only a dream

of useless hope stamped and restamped by the ash-steps of those we
can do no justice to except in loving them? But
what could he do before the raw facts
of men cleaving flesh like boys hacking ice?

I think how he must have thought of his barking teacher of law:
   There is only truth and law! He had learned the law.

But what was the truth to leave him trembling like a child in prayer?
   In late years he kept the monster by his side, two shades
      walking alone in the ice, the nail-raker, one
   who howled without reason and clawed at the heart
      of door after door. In the end he was known
inseparable from his beast who, it was said, kept the Judge alive.

Until he was not. Until his house emptied. Until we came who I hear
   breathing, those heads warm as banked ash under my hand
      laid light as I have laid it on this railing.
   But are we only this upfloating and self-clinging ash
that loops freely through dark houses? Those enigmatic fissures
   I see circling the snow—are those only the tracks

of the dog I locked out, those black steps no more than a gleaming
   ice, or the face of some brother in the dirt betrayed,
      pleading, accusing? The moon, far off and dim,
   plays tricks with my eyes and the snow path turns dark as
a line of men marched into the earth. Whitely, my breath floats
   back at me, crying *I did not do this,* when the shuddering

courthouse clock across the square booms me back to myself. Dream's
   aftershock, the heirloom banjo starts to thud and drum
      so I turn and hustle downstairs to halt it.
   Even with my hands laid on its hands it wants to thump
      its malicious heart out, but I can do this
at least: I can hold on to help them sleep through another night.

I can sit for a while with love's ice-flickering darkness where ash
   is heavily filling my house. I can sit with my own
      nailed walker in the snow, one whistled
   under my hand without question or answer. If I sleep
he will pad the floors above the fire-pit. He will claw me awake
   to hear breathing in the still house of the Judge

where I live.

1983

The Chesapeake and Ohio Canal

Thick now with sludge from the years of suburbs, with toys,
fenders, wine bottles, tampons, skeletons of possums,
edged by blankets of leaves, jellied wrappers unshakably
stuck to the scrub pines that somehow lift themselves
from the mossed wall of blockstone headlined a hundred
years back, this water is bruised as a shoe at Goodwill.[4]
Its brown goes nowhere, neither does it remain, and elms
bend over its heavy back like patient fans, dreamlessly.
This is the death of hope's commerce, the death of cities

4. A charitable organization offering used clothing and furniture for sale in many American cities.

blank as winter light, the death of people who are gone
erratic and passive as summer's glittering water-skimmers.
Yet those two climbing that path like a single draft horse
saw the heart of the water break open only minutes ago,
and the rainbow trout walked its tail as if the evening
was only an offering in an unimaginable room where plans
inch ahead for the people, as if the trout always meant
to hang from their chain, to be borne through last shades
like a lure drawn carefully, deviously in the blue ache
of air that thickens still streets between brown walls.

1985

AMY CLAMPITT

(1920–)

Amy Clampitt belongs by age to the generation of poets that includes Gwendolyn Brooks, Robert Lowell, Howard Nemerov, Richard Wilbur, James Dickey, Denise Levertov, and Louis Simpson, all of whom had earned some measure of celebrity by the mid-1960's. Her success came much later, however. After a collection privately published in 1973, she began publishing accomplished poetry in *The New Yorker* in 1978, and by the time of her first full collection, *The Kingfisher* (1983), she had clearly mastered her poetic gifts. Second and third volumes, *What the Light Was Like* (1985) and *Archaic Figure* (1987), have confirmed her skill.

Born and raised in New Providence, Iowa, Clampitt graduated from Grinnell College and attended Columbia University. In 1943 she took a position with Oxford University Press in New York City. Eight years later she left Oxford to become a reference librarian for the National Audubon Society, also in New York. In the 1960's and most of the 1970's, she supported herself as a free-lance editor and researcher, and then from 1977 to 1982 as an editor for E. P. Dutton. She has been a writer in residence at the University of Wisconsin-Milwaukee, the College of William and Mary, and Amherst College.

Clampitt's verse is meticulously constructed, brilliant in imagery, and sharply focused on places and things observed at first hand in Iowa, England, Greece, New York, New Jersey, Maine. She observes with the eye of a naturalist. She is also in her verse a reader, a devourer of reference books, so that her lines echo the lines of other poets, or allude to them directly, and are layered with references to biography, history, philosophy, natural science, and folklore. Turning frequently to images of change and more than once reminding the reader of Heraclitus' observation that you cannot step into the same river twice, she writes a poetry frequently elegiac as it celebrates time past or passing.

Clampitt's major collections to date are named above.

The Kingfisher

In a year the nightingales were said to be so loud
they drowned out slumber, and peafowl strolled screaming
beside the ruined nunnery, through the long evening
of a dazzled pub crawl, the halcyon color, portholed

by those eye-spots' stunning tapestry, unsettled
the pastoral nightfall with amazements opening.

Months later, intermission in a pub on Fifty-fifth Street
found one of them still breathless, the other quizzical,
acting the philistine, puncturing Stravinsky[1]—"Tell
me, what *was* that racket in the orchestra about?"—
hauling down the Firebird, harum-scarum, like a kite,
a burnished, breathing wreck that didn't hurt at all.

Among the Bronx Zoo's exiled jungle fowl, they heard
through headphones of a separating panic, the bellbird
reiterate its single *chong*, a scream nobody answered.
When he mourned, "The poetry is gone," she quailed,
seeing how his hands shook, sobered into feeling old.
By midnight, yet another fifth would have been killed.

A Sunday morning, the November of their cataclysm
(Dylan Thomas[2] brought in *in extremis*[3] to St. Vincent's,
that same week, a symptomatic datum) found them
wandering a downtown churchyard. Among its headstones,
while from unruined choirs the noise of Christendom
poured over Wall Street, a benison in vestments,

a late thrush paused, in transit from some grizzled
spruce bog to the humid equatorial fireside: berry-
eyed, bark-brown above, with dark hints of trauma
in the stigmata of its underparts—or so, too bruised
just then to have invented anything so fancy,
later, re-embroidering a retrospect, she had supposed.

In gray England, years of muted recrimination (then
dead silence) later, she could not have said how many
spoiled takeoffs, how many entanglements gone sodden,
how many gaudy evenings made frantic by just one
insomniac nightingale, how many liaisons gone down
screaming in a stroll beside the ruined nunnery;

a kingfisher's burnished plunge, the color
of felicity afire, came glancing like an arrow
through landscapes of untended memory: ardor
illuminating with its terrifying currency
now no mere glimpse, no porthole vista
but, down on down, the uninhabitable sorrow.

1983

The Woodlot

Clumped murmuring above a sump of loam—
grass-rich, wood-poor—that first the plow,
then the inventor (his name plowed under

1. Igor Stravinsky (1882–1971), Russian composer, whose many ballets include *The Firebird* (1910), mentioned below.
2. (1914–1953), English poet.
3. Latin: "dying."

somewhere in the Patent Office) of barbed wire,
taught, if not fine manners, how at least to follow
the surveyor's rule, the woodlot nodes of willow,
evergreen or silver maple gave the prairie grid
what little personality it had.
Who could
have learned fine manners where the air,
that rude nomad, still domineered,
without a shape it chose to keep,
oblivious of section lines, in winter
whisking its wolfish spittle to a froth
that turned whole townships into
one white wallow? Barbed wire
kept in the cattle but would not abrade
the hide or draw the blood
of gales hurled gnashing like seawater over fences'
laddered apertures, rigging the landscape
with the perspective of a shipwreck. Land-chained,
the blizzard paused to caterwaul
at every windbreak, a rage the worse
because it was in no way personal.
Against
the involuted tantrums of spring and summer—
sackfuls of ire, the frightful udder
of the dropped mammocumulus
become all mouth, a lamprey
swigging up whole farmsteads, suction
dislodging treetrunks like a rotten tooth—
luck and a cellarhole were all
a prairie dweller had to count on.
Whether
the inventor of barbed wire was lucky
finally in what he found himself
remembering, who knows? Did he
ever, even once, envision
the spread of what he'd done
across a continent: whale-song's
taut dulcimer still thrumming as it strung together
orchard, barnyard, bullpen, feedlot,
windbreak: wire to be clambered over,
crawled through or slid under, shepherded—
the heifers staring—to an enclosure
whose ceiling's silver-maple tops
stir overhead, uneasy, in the interminably
murmuring air? Deep in it, under
appletrees like figures in a ritual, violets
are thick, a blue cellarhole
of pure astonishment.
It is
the earliest memory. Before it,
I/you, whatever that conundrum may yet
prove to be, amounts to nothing.

1983

The Reedbeds of the Hackensack[4]

Scummed maunderings that nothing loves but reeds,
Phragmites, neighbors of the greeny asphodel[5]
that thrive among the windings of the Hackensack,
collaborating to subvert the altogether ugly
though too down-to-earth to be quite fraudulent:
what's landfill but the backside of civility?

Dreckpot,[6] the Styx[7] and Malebolge[8] of civility,
brushed by the fingering plumes of beds of reeds:
Manhattan's moat of stinks, the rancid asphodel
aspiring from the gradually choking Hackensack,
ring-ditch inferior to the vulgar, the snugly ugly,
knows-no-better, fake but not quite fraudulent:

what's scandal but the candor of the fraudulent?
Miming the burnish of a manicured civility,
the fluent purplings of uncultivated reeds,
ex post cliché survivors like the asphodel,
drink, as they did the Mincius,[9] the Hackensack
in absent-minded benediction on the merely ugly.

Is there a poetry of the incorrigibly ugly,
free of all furbishings that mark it fraudulent?
When toxins of an up-against-the-wall civility
have leached away the last patina of these reeds,
and promised landfill, with its lethal asphodel
of fumes, blooms the slow dying of the Hackensack,

shall I compare thee, Mincius, to the Hackensack?
Now Italy knows how to make its rivers ugly,
must, ergo, all such linkages be fraudulent,
gilding the laureate hearse of a defunct civility?
Smooth-sliding Mincius, crowned with vocal reeds,[1]
coevals of that greeny local weed the asphodel,

that actual, unlettered entity the asphodel,
may I, among the channels of the Hackensack—
those Edens-in-the-works of the irrevocably ugly,

4. For this densely textured poem, the poet supplies notes in *What the Light Was Like* (1985). She begins by quoting the *Webster's New Universal Unabridged Dictionary* definition of "reed," giving *Phragmites communis* as the taxonomic name for the common reed, and ending with its "use as the symbol of pastoral poetry." She then quotes from Gavin Young's *Return to the Marshes: Life with the Marsh Arabs of Iraq* (1977), drawing attention to the links between reeds, music, and civilization. Finally, she writes "Allusions to and/or borrowings from the poems of William Carlos Williams, Dante, Milton, Keats, and Shakespeare will be noted in this poem, which may be regarded as a last-ditch effort to associate the landscape familiarly known as the Jersey Meadows with the tradition of elegiac poetry."

5. Calling to mind the fine late poem "Asphodel, that Greeny Flower," by William Carlos Williams (1883–1963), who lived in Rutherford, on a hill above the Jersey Meadows.

6. Pot of filth.

7. In classical mythology, a river in Hell.

8. In Dante's *Inferno,* the region of Hell containing those who committed malicious frauds on humankind.

9. Italian river, associated with the poet Virgil and described in the *Inferno,* Canto XX, in images echoed in this poem.

1. The entire line is quoted from Milton's "Lycidas," l. 86.

where any mourning would of course be fraudulent—
invoke the scrannel[2] ruth of a forsooth civility,
the rathe,[3] the deathbed generations of these reeds?

1985

Time

It may be we are in the last days.
Seven hundred years ago to the week,
on the eleventh of December, the kingdom of Wales went under.
Today, the sixth day of the twelfth month of the nineteen hundred eighty-second year,
according to the current reckoning,
there are roses the size of an obsolete threepenny bit—
one fingernail-pink, the other minute, extravagant crimson—
flanked by masses of sweet alyssum
and one time-exempt purple pansy
on the site of what was formerly the Women's House of Detention
at the triangular intersection of Tenth Street with Greenwich and Sixth Avenues,
just back of the old Jefferson Market courthouse
whose tower clock, revived, goes on keeping time.
And I think again of October violets,
of their hardy refusal to adhere to conventional expectation—
so hardy that I've finally ceased to think of it as startling,
this phenomenon which, in fact, I devoted myself in October to looking for—
a tame revenant of the blue fire-alarm of the original encounter with the evidence,
among the dropped leaves and superannuated grass of the season of hickory nuts,
that neither time nor place could be counted on to remain self-sufficient,
that you might find yourself slipping back toward the past at any moment,
or watch it well up in artesian springs of anachronism,
with the prospect of being drowned in that aperture's abrupt blue,
in that twinkling of an eye, at any moment.
It was November, or near then, I found violets massed at the foot of the foundations
of the castle of Chepstow,
at the edge of Wales—not any longer, as once, covert, fecklessly undermining
that sense of fitness, so fragile that at any moment of one's childhood
whatever sense of continuity has not ebbed or been marked for demolition
may break like an eggshell, and be overrun from within by the albumen of ruin—
their out-of-season purple not any longer hinting at something, but announcing it with
a flourish:
the entire gorgeous, intractable realm of the forgotten,
the hieratic, the heraldic, the royal, sprung open
at the gouty foot of that anachronism
on the fringes of a kingdom that went under
at or near the downward slope of the thirteenth century. I have seen
the artesian spring of the past foam up at the foot of the castle of Chepstow
on a day in November, or thereabouts. I have seen a rose the size of a perfectly manicured
crimson fingernail
alive in a winter that does not arrive, though we plunge again toward the solstice.

1985

2. Lean or shriveled; calling to mind especially the poets in Milton's "Lycidas" whose "lean and flashy songs / Grate on their scrannel pipes of wretched straw."

3. Early; again with a nod to Milton's "Lycidas": "the rathe primrose that forsaken dies."

LOUISE GLÜCK
(1943–)

Born in New York City and raised on Long Island, Louise Glück turned early to poetry, writing by age fifteen lines that became later part of her published work, although by that time significantly changed in context. A student in 1962 at Sarah Lawrence College, she also attended Columbia from 1963 to 1965. By her early twenties she had poems accepted in major magazines such as *The Atlantic, The New Yorker,* and *Poetry.* In the 1970's she taught poetry in various places, including the Fine Arts Workshop in Provincetown, Massachusetts, Goddard College, the University of North Carolina at Greensboro, the University of Iowa, and the University of Cincinnati. More recently, she has lived in Vermont and taught at Williams College.

In her initial collection, *Firstborn* (1968), she displayed a strongly personal talent, with echoes of the confessional poetry of Robert Lowell and Sylvia Plath, and by 1985 she seemed to one reviewer to have established herself in her first three books as "our foremost poet speaking for adolescent angst." Clearly evident in her work is her struggle with anorexia and her obsession with sisters, especially with the sister who died before she was born and for whom, as she expressed it, "I took on the guilty responsibility of the survivor." Far from the immediate anguish of some poems, however, is the broader reference of many that speak only obscurely of particulars, supporting their themes with references to myth or through the creation of broadly allusive symbols. "My work," she has written, "has always been strongly marked by a disregard for the circumstantial, except insofar as it could be transformed into paradigm."

Between the poles of personality and abstraction, Glück creates a tension that springs in part from a method she describes as "a search for context," wherein "some word or phrase will detach itself from the language, taking on a kind of radiance" that the poet must justify in the rest of the poem, discovering subject and meaning as she writes. Always she seems haunted by the danger of separation, of divorce from an existence validated by feeling. In the insight of the narrator of "The Garden," when we contemplate "stone animals," we must "Admit that it is terrible to be like them, / beyond harm."

Glück's verse is collected in *Firstborn* (1968), *The House on Marshland* (1975), *Descending Figure* (1980), and *The Triumph of Achilles* (1985). A brief appraisal appears in *Dictionary of Literary Biography, Volume 5, American Poets Since World War II,* 1980.

Poem

In the early evening, as now, a man is bending
over his writing table.
Slowly he lifts his head; a woman
appears, carrying roses.
Her face floats to the surface of the mirror,
marked with the green spokes of rose stems.

It is a form
of suffering: then always the transparent page
raised to the window until its veins emerge
as words finally filled with ink.

And I am meant to understand
what binds them together
or to the gray house held firmly in place by dusk

because I must enter their lives:
it is spring, the pear tree
filming with weak, white blossoms.

1975

The School Children

The children go forward with their little satchels.
And all morning the mothers have labored
to gather the late apples, red and gold,
like words of another language.

And on the other shore
are those who wait behind great desks
to receive these offerings.

How orderly they are—the nails
on which the children hang
their overcoats of blue or yellow wool.

And the teachers shall instruct them in silence
and the mothers shall scour the orchards for a way out,
drawing to themselves the gray limbs of the fruit trees
bearing so little ammunition.

1975

The Garden

1. The Fear of Birth

One sound. Then the hiss and whir
of houses gliding into their places.

And the wind
leafs through the bodies of animals—

But my body that could not content itself
with health—why should it be sprung back
into the chord of sunlight?

It will be the same again.
This fear, this inwardness,
until I am forced into a field
without immunity
even to the least shrub that walks
stiffly out of the dirt, trailing
the twisted signature of its root,
even to a tulip, a red claw.

And then the losses,
one after another,
all supportable.

2. The Garden

The garden admires you.
For your sake it smears itself with green pigment,
the ecstatic reds of the roses,
so that you will come to it with your lovers.

And the willows—
see how it has shaped these green
tents of silence. Yet
there is still something you need,
your body so soft, so alive, among the stone animals.

Admit that it is terrible to be like them,
beyond harm.

3. The Fear of Love

That body lying beside me like obedient stone—
once its eyes seemed to be opening,
we could have spoken.

At that time it was winter already.
By day the sun rose in its helmet of fire
and at night also, mirrored in the moon.

Its light passed over us freely,
as though we had lain down
in order to leave no shadows,
only these two shallow dents in the snow.
And the past, as always, stretched before us,
still, complex, impenetrable.

How long did we lie there
as, arm in arm in their cloaks of feathers,
the gods walked down
from the mountain we built for them?

4. Origins

As though a voice were saying
You should be asleep by now—
But there was no one. Nor
had the air darkened,
though the moon was there,
already filled in with marble.

As though, in a garden crowded with flowers,
a voice had said
How dull they are, these golds,
so sonorous, so repetitious

until you closed your eyes,
lying among them, all
stammering flame:

And yet you could not sleep,
poor body, the earth
still clinging to you—

5. *The Fear of Burial*

In the empty field, in the morning,
the body waits to be claimed.
The spirit sits beside it, on a small rock—
nothing comes to give it form again.

Think of the body's loneliness.
At night pacing the sheared field,
its shadow buckled tightly around.
Such a long journey.

And already the remote, trembling lights of the village
not pausing for it as they scan the rows.
How far away they seem,
the wooden doors, the bread and milk
laid like weights on the table.

1980

Lamentations

1. *The Logos*[1]

They were both still,
the woman mournful, the man
branching into her body.

But god was watching.
They felt his gold eye
projecting flowers on the landscape.

Who knew what he wanted?
He was god, and a monster.
So they waited. And the world
filled with his radiance,
as though he wanted to be understood.

Far away, in the void that he had shaped,
he turned to his angels.

2. *Nocturne*

A forest rose from the earth.
O pitiful, so needing
God's furious love—

1. Greek: "the word," here a reference to the Gospel according to St. John, i: 1: "In the beginning was the Word, and the Word was with God, and the Word was God."

Together they were beasts.
They lay in the fixed
dusk of his negligence;
from the hills, wolves came, mechanically
drawn to their human warmth,
their panic.

Then the angels saw
how He divided them:
the man, the woman, and the woman's body.

Above the churned reeds, the leaves let go
a slow moan of silver.

3. The Covenant

Out of fear, they built a dwelling place.
But a child grew between them
as they slept, as they tried
to feed themselves.

They set it on a pile of leaves,
the small discarded body
wrapped in the clean skin
of an animal. Against the black sky
they saw the massive argument of light.

Sometimes it woke. As it reached its hands
they understood they were the mother and father,
there was no authority above them.

4. The Clearing

Gradually, over many years,
the fur disappeared from their bodies
until they stood in the bright light
strange to one another.
Nothing was as before.
Their hands trembled, seeking
the familiar.

Nor could they keep their eyes
from the white flesh
on which wounds would show clearly
like words on a page.

And from the meaningless browns and greens
at last God arose, His great shadow
darkening the sleeping bodies of His children,
and leapt into heaven.

How beautiful it must have been,
the earth, that first time
seen from the air.

1980

Palais des Arts

Love long dormant showing itself:
the large expected gods
caged really, the columns
sitting on the lawn, as though perfection
were not timeless but stationary—that
is the comedy, she thinks,
that they are paralyzed. Or like the matching swans,
insular, circling the pond: restraint so passionate
implies possession. They hardly speak.
On the other bank, a small boy throws bits of bread
into the water. The reflected monument
is stirred, briefly, stricken with light—
She can't touch his arm in innocence again.
They have to give that up and begin
as male and female, thrust and ache.

1980

Brooding Likeness

I was born in the month of the bull,[2]
the month of heaviness,
or of the lowered, the destructive head,
or of purposeful blindness. So I know, beyond the shadowed
patch of grass, the stubborn one, the one who doesn't look up,
still senses the rejected world. It is
a stadium, a well of dust. And you who watch him
looking down in the face of death, what do you know
of commitment? If the bull lives
one controlled act of revenge, be satisfied
that in the sky, like you, he is always moving,
not of his own accord but through the black field
like grit caught on a wheel, like shining freight.

1985

NORMAN DUBIE
(1945–)

Norman Dubie was born in Barre, Vermont, and spent his childhood, as he has observed, "in another culture and in another time" near Bath, Maine, where many homes were still without electricity and modern ways had not yet changed the essentials of life. When he left at twelve, he has said, he realized he "would never again find the nineteenth century." His was a religious family, his father having abandoned an insurance career to become a minister. Strong on traditional values, they exposed the son early to such masters of narration as Dickens, Conrad, Mann,

2. Taurus, one of the signs of the zodiac, April 20–May 20.

Dostoevski, Turgenev, and Chekhov, writers who have influenced the narrative element in his work. By eleven he had written his first poem.

As a student at Goddard College in Vermont, he continued writing, publishing a first collection of verse, *The Horsehair Sofa* (1968). After graduation from Goddard in 1969, two years at the Writers Workshop at the University of Iowa brought him an M.F.A., publication of a second book, *Alehouse Sonnets,* and an appointment as lecturer in creative writing at Iowa, all in 1971. After three more years at Iowa, he taught briefly at Ohio University before moving to Arizona State University, where he has taught since 1975.

More often than many of his contemporaries, Dubie adopts a persona from another time and place, writing in the voice of an imagined or historical character. Of one of these, he once wrote, "I honestly believe I wrote this poem just for Nora; she was a reality for me living outside my poem." His ability to imagine realities other than his own is one of his strengths. Increasingly in his later work, however, his voices speak of things in or near his personal experience, as, most recently, in a few of the most striking poems of *The Springhouse* (1986).

Selected and New Poems, 1983, draws from four earlier collections: *In the Dead of Night,* 1975; *The Illustrations,* 1977; *The City of Olesha Fruit,* 1979; and *The Everlastings,* 1980. Besides those mentioned above, other verse titles are *Prayers of the North American Martyrs,* 1974; *Popham of the New Song,* 1974; *A Thousand Little Things,* 1978; *Odalisque in White,* 1979; and *The Window in the Field,* 1982.

Norway

For Elizabeth Paūs

The raw slopes of meat are stabbed with pikes
And the flesh of the whale is torn away
With the use of hands and feet. Here and there
A gull cries. This fish turned to oil, the oil turning
To a carbon band around the chimney of a crystal lamp,

And, at midnight, a man closes his book. He sighs,
Closes his eyes,
And, then, it is there in the purple haze of his mind
That the whale leaps
For a last time; dancing a little, just an element
Of white oval light in a lamp.
It had spread past the seated man,
Past the table at his right hand to a sleeping dog,
But it failed at touching the far corner
Of the room—its tiny vase of blue and black pansies stands

With the smudged faces of exhausted whalers,
Their red arms stirring the big iron pots while
Above them on the deck a cabin boy leans on a broom,
Stopped at his work, his mouth open: he just gazes
At a brain of a whale
That is steaming like a newborn calf outside
In the early spring rain that has turned to hail.

1979

Elizabeth's War with the Christmas Bear: 1601

For Paul Zimmer

The bears are kept by hundreds within fences, are fed cracked
Eggs; the weakest are
Slaughtered and fed to the others after being scented
With the blood of deer brought to the pastures by Elizabeth's
Men—the blood spills from deep pails with bottoms of slate.

The balding Queen had bear-gardens in London and in the country.
The bear is baited: the nostrils
Are blown full with pepper, the Irish wolf dogs
Are starved, then, emptied, made crazy with fermented barley;

And the bear's hind leg is chained to a stake, the bear
Is blinded and whipped, kneeling in his own blood and slaver, he is
Almost instantly worried by the dogs. At the very moment that
Elizabeth took Essex's[1] head, a giant brown bear
Stood in the gardens with dogs hanging from his fur . . .
He took away the sun, took
A wolfhound in his mouth and tossed it into
The white lap of Elizabeth I—arrows and staves rained

On his chest, and standing, he, then, stood even taller, seeing
Into the Queen's private boxes—he grinned into her battered eggshell face.
Another volley of arrows and poles, and opening his mouth he showered
Blood all over Elizabeth and her Privy Council.

The very next evening, a cool evening, the Queen demanded
13 bears and the justice of 113 dogs: She slept
All that Sunday night and much of the next morning.
Some said she was guilty of *this* and *that.*
The Protestant Queen gave the defeated bear
A grave in a Catholic cemetery. The marker said:
Peter, a Solstice[2] Bear, a gift of the Tsarevitch[3] to Elizabeth.

After a long winter she had the grave opened. The bear's skeleton
Was cleared with lye, she placed it at her bedside,
Put a candle inside behind the sockets of the eyes, and, then
She spoke to it:

You were a Christmas bear—behind your eyes
I see the walls of a snow cave where you are a cub still smelling
Of your mother's blood which has dried in your hair; you have
Troubled a Queen who was afraid when seated in *shade* which, standing,

You had created! A Queen who often wakes with a dream of you at night—
Now, you'll stand by my bed in your long white bones; alone, you
Will frighten away at night all visions of bear, and all day
You will be in this cold room—your constant grin,

1. Robert Devereux (1567–1601), second earl of Essex, long-time favorite of Queen Elizabeth I, fell out of favor and was executed by beheading.

2. A gift for the winter solstice, December 22, Christmas season.

3. The eldest son of the czar.

You'll stand in the long, white prodigy of your bones, and you are,
Every inch of you, a terrible vision, not bear, but virgin!

1979

The Fox Who Watched for the Midnight Sun

Across the snowy pastures of the estate
Open snares drift like pawprints under rain, everywhere
There is the conjured rabbit being dragged
Up into blowing snow: it struggles
Upside down by a leg, its belly
Is the slaked white of cottages along the North Sea.

Inside the parlor Ibsen[4] writes of a summer garden, of a
Butterfly sunken inside the blossoming tulip.
He describes the snapdragon with its little sconce of dew.
He moves from the desk to a window. Remembers his studies
In medicine, picturing the sticky
Overlapping eyelids of drowned children. On the corner
Of the sofa wrapped in Empress-silks there's a box
Of fresh chocolates. He mimics the deceptively distant,
Chittering birdsong within the cat's throat.
How it attracts finches to her open window.
He turns toward the fire, now thinking of late sessions in Storting.
Ibsen had written earlier of an emotional girl
With sunburnt shoulders,

Her surprise when the heavy dipper came up
From the well with frogs' eggs bobbing in her water.
He smiles.
Crosses the room like the fox walking away
From the woodpile.
He picks up his lamp and takes it
To the soft chair beneath the window. Brandy is poured.
Weary, he closes his eyes and dreams
Of his mother at a loom, how she would dip, dressing
The warp with a handful of coarse wool.

Henrik reaches for tobacco— tomorrow, he'll write
Of summer some more, he'll begin with a fragrance . . .
Now, though, he wonders about the long
Devotion of his muscles to his bones. He's worried by
The wind which hurries the pages in this drafty room.
He looks out
Into the March storm for an illustration: under a tree
A large frozen hare swings at the end of a snare-string.
The fox sits beneath it, his upturned head swinging with it,
The jaws are locked in concentration,

As if the dead hare were soon to awaken!

1980

4. Henrik Ibsen (1828–1906), Norwegian dramatist.

Danse Macabre[5]

The broken oarshaft was stuck in the hill
In the middle of chicory,
Puke-flowers, the farmers called them, sturdy
Little evangels that the white deer drift through . . .

Nobody on the hill before
Had heard of a horse
Breaking its leg in a rowboat. But the mare
Leapt the fence, passed
The tar-paper henhouse,
And then crumpled at the shore.

It was April and bees were floating
In the cold evening barn; from the loft
We heard them shoot the poor horse.
We tasted gunpowder and looked
While your cousin, the sick
Little bastard, giggled and got
So excited he started to dance
Like the slow sweeping passes
Of a drawing compass—

Its cruel nail to its true pencil.

1986

Lamentations

The scrub woman for the old bank and jailhouse,
Her face reddening

Over supper on a steamy night
Is thinking of the village spillway being

Answered by a dry clucking over mud, *she is*
Touching the burrs on the tongue of the azalea . . .

Exhaustion puts knotted rags in the neck
And shoulders:

As a girl, in Poland, she watched her husband
Be dragged through the shade of five pines

To the execution wall. A year earlier
She had watched him bathe

In the bronze tub the landlord had put
Out in the field as a trough for horses.

5. Dance of death, in the art of the Middle Ages an allegorical depiction of Death leading people to the grave.

She picked him from among the men
Smoking pipes after haying, *she rolled*

Over on her stomach
To study the blue cornflower; she shyly
Rained on the wildflowers, a hot urine . . .
They laughed, and never knew her brother

Was taken by train to Hamburg, was infected
With tuberculosis, was
In the last days of the war
Stripped along with six other children

And hanged in the boiler room of a post office.
What she has understood

Is there are only
Two speeches the naked make well,

One is of welcome, the other farewell.

1986

ALBERT GOLDBARTH
(1948–)

Albert Goldbarth has written poetry concerned with prehistory, evolution, the heritage of western civilization, and stellar spaces—matter encapsulated in the title of his recent collection, *Arts and Sciences* (1986). He is wide-ranging and prolific, pushing often at the boundaries of poetry to compose prose poems, without line breaks, or poems with poetic line breaks that read like prose. Sometimes within a poem his subject turns from the matter at hand to the poet writing; as Dave Smith observed in reviewing his long poem *Opticks* (1974), "he is everywhere stepping forward as a poet * * * . He poses and prances." In ways that suggest especially the practice of Robert Pinsky among his close contemporaries, he seems to search for connections pointing toward meanings in widely separated phenomena. Of his poems, he has written, "They ask to be small worlds of details in an interesting clutter—tactile objects, eldritch facts, textured language, jazzy and unforeseen actions large and small—that are finally functional subcomponents of what was, all along and overall, a directed shapeliness."

Goldbarth was born in Chicago; his father was an insurance man, his mother a secretary. After receiving a B.A. from the University of Illinois at Chicago Circle (1969), and an M.F.A. from the University of Iowa (1971), he taught at various schools, including the University of Texas in Austin from 1977 to 1987. In 1987 he accepted a position as Distinguished Professor of the Humanities of Wichita State University. He has received Guggenheim and National Endowment for the Arts fellowships.

In addition to those named above, Goldbarth's most important verse collections include *Jan. 31,* 1974; *Comings Back,* 1976; *Different Fleshes,* 1979; *Faith,* 1981; and *Original Light: New and Selected Poems 1973–1983,* 1983.

A History of Civilization

In the dating bar, the potted ferns lean down
conspiratorially, little spore-studded
elopement ladders. The two top buttons
of every silk blouse have already half-undone all
introduction. Slices of smile, slices of sweet brie,
dark and its many white wedges. In back

of the bar, the last one-family grocer's is necklaced
over and over: strings of leeks, greek olives, sardines.
The scoops stand at attention in the millet barrel,
the cordovan sheen of the coffee barrel, the kidney beans.
And a woman whose pride is a clean linen apron polishes
a register as intricate as a Sicilian shrine. In back

of the grocery, dozing and waking in fitful starts
by the guttering hearth, a ring of somber-gabardined grandpas
plays dominoes. Their stubble picks up the flicker like filaments
still waiting for the bulb or the phone to be invented. Even their
coughs, their phlegms, are in an older language. They move the simple
pieces of matching numbers. In back

of the back room, in the unlit lengths of storage, it's
that season: a cat eyes a cat. The sacks and baskets
are sprayed with the sign of a cat's having eyed a cat, and
everything to do with rut and estrus comes down to a few
sure moves. The dust motes drift, the continents.
In the fern bar a hand tries a knee, as if unplanned.

1983

The Form and Function of the Novel

My parents have come to town for my wedding.
Because of some way a shadow falls, or a hand
in conversation cuts air as if laboring, my father
reminds me increasingly of a man in a small
Canadian village, who manufactures racks
for drying lace curtains, who catches shadow in
that same way, and who moves his hands as if against
a current, in a book

I've been reading but leave, to shop
for cheese, bouquets and the wedding trousseau.
While we pick over veils and daffodils, life
according to narrative forces set in motion
continues: the backlands
moon slips up like a washed dish, and a rig
clops heavily toward the main street's tethering-rail.
His son's come home, for that sturdy Canadian

spring with the flowers like nailheads everywhere,
home from study in Europe, his son the biologist

talking Darwin and opera these last two years
over cognac in snifters like goldfish bowls.
They argue. The father is oafish, gruff, a
squared-off man whose lips move reading.
The son knows quiche and genetics. He's
embarrassed. Their words are ugly weather. I

see, although the son ironically can't despite
his interests, how the distance between them is
nothing, you hear me?, nothing, compared to the first
irrepressible land plants over 400 million
years ago stretching familially to the flax
in the lace that's hung in the front display case
under the sign with the father's name but *and*
Son freshly painted out. I think he's special

in his plainness and hurt. In this chapter he's
alone. It's night, he paces in the store he loves, and
so the moon through the fine white nets of his trade
makes him a complicated figure at last,
doilied over by dark and silver, eloquent, pensive, oblique . . .
"Do you think she'll like this one?" I turn.
He's holding a lace dress up to the late deep light
and it's all I can do to stop crying.

1983

The Elements

The cool, dusk-blue of the shadows of these Dutch plums
is mixed with a quarter-thimble of gray that matches
glints in the skins of the pears, the berries, the liver-paste.
If the dull swell of a herring on a plate picks up
red chevrons meaning a candle (out of sight) is lit,
the crystal of burgundy weighting another corner is given
a small red heart of light at its center so
everything, in shape and weight, is balanced, and
the keen lines angled like stylized rain around
the base of the creamer say the same green as the stems
that have been set like accent-marks for the scansion of cherries.
In the back, in the middle, a hot loaf is broken
for steam to rise in a perfect column of nearly
corinthian detail, at the edges of which it thins
in equilibrium with the night, as a breath might
leave a body and settle, composed and ubiquitous.
I wonder if this still-life exists in the universe

*

of a wormy handfull of rice. I wonder what the sense of time
in which it was painted has to do with a year
in the dog cages. When a prisoner's released
from one of those, he "walks" by sitting, moving his legs
ahead of him by hand, like huge quaint compasses.
This group was abducted out of their homes and now will be kept

at an "interim camp." They face the camera with something
in their eyes beyond despair. Before the film goes
to a New York-based reporter summing it up, we see
a newly-uncaged woman catch a doll
a soldier tosses her, then start to comb its patchy hair, and only
hours later will we come to understand this
is her infant daughter dead of cold water and lye.
I wonder, in all of science-fiction, if there have been
two universes this discordant, or what it means
that there can be a suffering so intense its balance only
exists somewhere in the next life. And

*

I wonder if I should hate that painting, I wonder
if out of faith kept with the brutalized, I should revile
the easy leisure with which another world applied its dedication
to a study of shadow lengthening under tangerines, I
wonder if now we must love that painting more than ever,
its calm, its idea of order and abidingness, I wonder
isn't this exactly the freedom for which we risk the cage
and dream of in the cage to keep us living, this
aloof, light space in which the heft of a peach against
washed linen can grow important and exact,
I wonder if I should burn a painting like that
and turn to the knife and the placard, I wonder if
I should give my days to the completion of its housing
under temperature control, I wonder what we give
our nights to, and how much our days define our nights, I
wonder until I sleep, and I sleep like a fresh bread
cooling, reaching an agreement with the elements.

1986

Poem Whose Last Sentence Is 17 Syllables After a Suggestion

The little we need. Thoreau[1] demoted flour in favor of lowlier
Indian meal *which the farmer will offer his hogs,* but he
baked savorily enough in a pit-fire, yeastless and
utter, this final plank of bread his food reduced to.
So: another night with woodsmoke and *The Odyssey*[2] being
sufficience along his pond's sweet weed-hipped shore. The

little we need, we *need.* And for me it's down, these days,
to a soapstone rabbit, so slick even light slips off
its globous haunches' skin; a quiet Steinberg[3] print
(the still-life items held in a consensus of pastels); and
the carton for **DR. STRONG'S BLOOD PURIFIER** "heals
Man or Beast," its bottle (I'm sorry) long gone. —Far cry

1. Henry David Thoreau (1817–1862), American author, whose *Walden* (1854) reports his experiment in living with reduced needs at Walden Pond, in Concord, Massachusetts.

2. Epic poem attributed to Homer, eighth century B.C.

3. Saul Steinberg (1914–), American cartoonist and illustrator.

from the minimal whisper at Walden, I know; but
what can I say? Some deepening afternoons, the shadows
of lamp posts falling across the streets make a gauntlet;
each next one is a heavier blow in a day of heaviness,
yes, and I cringe home to where these objects say,
however they do and whatever the reason, some version of

serenity. So: friends most opposed to ownership still
own talismanic knickknacks. At her handlopped-beam and adobe
home in the sand stone steerskull gully land of New Mexico,
that she bought for ten dollars, O'Keeffe[4] shows her bedroom:
the bed, one plain straight chair, a wedge of fireplace.
"This is my corner," she says. "I haven't anything

you can't get along without." And so the one
adornment startles: the hand of a Buddha statue, straightup
in "The *mudra*[5] That Banishes Fear." Dark hand fixed high
on a dull buff wall, it seems the Buddha is parting
the veil between our world and his plane of
fire tigers and Absolute Composure—in a moment he'll

step full-bodied in. O'Keeffe is 94; maybe she *can't*
"get along without" his Banishing Fear. Night's indigo
mysteries seep through, and the hand is a great calm, and
an easiness. Here, in my room, I look at 3 objects,
I'm the curator for 3 objects. They make something
of the way the center of wood accepts pressure. Sometimes

reading filler on the whizz!bang! megabuck microchip
dreck-stuffs smugly cached in cornerstones for the future's
drooling of oohs, I think a solid block of mahogany more
the ideal time capsule. They mean that to me.
3 objects. It works like this: by night, some nights,
the lamp posts' shadows sink compacted in my body,

deeply: striated muscle. The world's worked
worry, busyness and its hooplah gratuitous feedbacks,
finally, that far into my fibers. There's much
too much. Even my own residue-accumulating
daydreams. Even these detailed superexempletive stanzas
you're reading. —When something . . . . the hand of the Buddha

breaks into the poem /right here/ and a voice says
Simplify, and cherish. One haiku. Three objects.
Outside, the ribs of one bananatree leaf
individuate late spring breeze. At the end of an arm
of moonlight, DR. STRONG will heal me, "guaranteed."
It's my Indian meal—one cupworth. It's "a restorative,"

it says—yes, it says it's a restorative.

1986

4. Georgia O'Keeffe (1887–1986), American painter.

5. Symbolic gesture.

Reading In

. . . a foisting of our sentiments onto an inert and indifferent scenery.
—HELEN VENDLER

1.

And then I said the bus's wheels in fresh
Chicago snow left long
albino alligators. I said it was
happy snow. I know, I was reading
into things again. You were with me,
you kissed me under a lamp post growing
a skullcap of snow as white as the Pope's, so
I wasn't surprised that it blessed us.
It winked. It had a light and it winked.
The snow against the sky was white and then
against the cone of wattage was black. That's
true, that's photographically exact. And
the post, I know, was a post: pure,
and with a globe of glass on top that was pure and
beyond interpretation. I know that.
Snow is water knitted a little tighter,
that's all, and I know that too. It's water
doilies, that's all. It's a statement of physics.
But look: it gave itself up
to the night, to something
larger, with an easy resignation anybody
would have to call happy. It shone,
it was happy snow, some landed on your tongue
and that was happy, happy snow.

2.

Then why do we cringe at the world of willows
bent in bereavement, mercury rising slim and
passionately up thermometers, the abnegation
of bone-white Japanese tea cups? There were
cultures where the wind in the bough was your future.
The leaves on the stream were your future.
The gut of a sheep.
The cracks burnt into a tortoise shell.
The gut of a bull. The gut of a peacock.
Even now, a man is thinking his own mood
into the wind, then thinking the wind is a forecast.
How many leaves in a tree, how many
small green hands, are scrubbing up like surgeons
in wind? And he'll call it a feeling, a hunch,
"in my gut." Now the shadows of Japanese tea cups
are a portrait of ripening plums, precisely. Now
they're the loose gray fannings in silt
a fishtail clears for the spawning.
Now they're dragged back into their cups,
black slips drawn up below white uniforms.

The nothing-gut of a slug.
The gut of a whale hung up like a tabernacle.

3.

Up the road from the whaleworks, maybe an hour
by horse then ferry, is the woolen-mill and
up the shale walkway is its miller. For him,
the blades are an enormous, steady
timepiece; wool is his weather, the time is always
simply life o'clock. He loves his hands
in the sorting-bin. They lose direction in wool as a hundred
years later, astronauts will float
in space—no "up" or "down." He loves his wife
lost just that way, a woman in the odor
and money and buffer-against-December
of wool, of angeltufts of wool to grade in their baskets.
These are the days of their lives:
some wool, more wool, bad wool, good.

*

In a different place, and time, a different man
will put an end to that. Out of his own and only
life, with its consistent rat-jawed gnawings of failure,
its lover with the blue tattoo and the little tube of gel,
its precision, its decade in the lab, its deliberate turnings,
he'll invent a blend of synthetic fibers,
newer, better. And so these two are nexus-points
defining a narrative line, though they
don't know it, though neither sees right now
the worm-holes through the newel of the abandoned mill,
its frost-cracked shelf of baskets. But
these two are points—of my plot and yours. It's
what we do to the stars—read in

*

the catscradle interconnection of story
up there, as an earthworm reads,
by total braille,
its wants and horrors into its sky
our planet. We read in: monstrousness
and grace. A throne. A weapon. A wedding. Yes and
at last we read our needings so
emphatically and crosshatched
into the sky, we call it heaven, and
our reading ends in
translating ourselves. / Listen:

*

weeping. Simply, he's weeping
the morning away in his hands. Simply,
she's died—the miller's wife. And now

the black-toothed tortoise chignon-comb on the bureau
is an eloquent mouth with an eloquent history
issuing, it could drive a man to tears.
And now he walks with a special acuity
to his vision: all of February
ice and shadow is edged as if it's stropped
past fineness. It snows. It
snows. He witnesses the absolute spider
spinning at the center of those absolute webs.
And he sees where she's gone to: the wings,
the harp, the headware like an o of honey,
her face in a cloud.

*

Heaven, in some Turkish illustration, is a garden
flowered bottom to top like a silk gown: raw pink
blooms the unvarying size of lettuces, divvying up blue background.
The perspective is shaky: an angel
opening orange wings as rigid as the side-leaves of a table
snapped open when guests arrive, is either walking
lightly through the middle distance or flying
by taking standard child-sized steps through the air.
A camel kneels. Three other camels talk
by touching noses while their riders exchange bouquets.
And somebody's riding a deer
with the face of a beautiful woman
through a cloud of fire, or into a pool of chased gold.
It's more recognizable over Medieval Europe:
here's St. Peter holding his familiar key as heavy
and ornate as a Flash Gordon ray-gun, here's
the heavenly choir around His throne in rows
of schoolroom order, and here's the bordering
glow of gauzy ochers shot with amber licks
that means The Glory. This

*

is the other world, as it once must have been
above the world of plowing, riding, swimming
in a real place, in a real time: "August," say,
from *Les Très Riches Heures du Duc de Berry,*[6]
15th century, France. The land is complicated
yellows leading to deep green tufts that mean
the beginnings of trees, then hills. It isn't easy
walking once the slopes go steep, and especially
by November, when the leaves are a lovely layer
covering dips and twists. By now our breath
is grayish shapes in the air, like a glassblower's.
Night comes on. You shiver—I've read us
into this world—and so we walk half-hugging.
It snows. It muffles everything—cows,
Toyotas, who knows? You lean on a lamp post.

6. A lavishly illustrated devotional manual. This line, misprinted in *Arts and Sciences,* is here corrected.

The stars are a scintillant pollen,
burning but austere! Or that's the zodiac
of fresh Chicago snow
in the black expanse of your hair.

1986

RITA DOVE
(1952–)

Rita Dove was born and raised in Akron, Ohio, where her father was a chemist. She attended Miami University in Ohio, graduating *summa cum laude* in 1973. As a Fulbright scholar, she studied modern European literature at the University of Tübingen in 1974–1975 before returning to the United States to earn an M.F.A. at Iowa in 1977. Grants from the National Endowment for the Arts and the Ohio Arts Council helped to support her early work, and in 1980, after two chapbooks, she published her first full collection, *The Yellow House on the Corner.* A second collection, *Museum,* appeared in 1983. Her third, *Thomas and Beulah* (1986), which won a Pulitzer Prize, collects lyrics to tell "two sides of a story," following the title characters from their turn-of-the-century births in Tennessee and Georgia through their move north to Akron and their lives there into the 1960's. Since 1981, Dove has been teaching at Arizona State University. She has also served as a writer in residence at Tuskegee Institute (1982) and has been honored as a Guggenheim Fellow (1983).

Dove's is a verse of plain statement, often in the present tense, a direct and immediate representation of the world. It reflects her personal experience growing up in Ohio and traveling in Europe, the experience of her family, and the more general experience of blacks in the United States and elsewhere.

Dove's major volumes of verse to date are named above. *Fifth Sunday,* 1985, collects short stories.

Champagne

The natives here have given up their backyards
and are happy living where we cannot see them,
No shade! The sky insists upon its blueness,
the baskets their roped ovals.
Gravel blinds us, blurring the road's shoulders.
Figures moving against the corduroyed hills
are not an industry to speak of, just
an alchemy whose yield is pleasure.

Come quickly—a whiff of yeast
means bubbles are forming, trapped
by sugar and air. The specialist who turns
30,000 bottles a day 10° to the right
lines up in a vaulted cellar
for an Italian red at the end of the day.
On either side for as far as we can see,
racks of unmarked bottles lying in cool fever.

Three centuries before in this dim corridor
a monk paused to sip, said it pricked
the tongue like stars. When we emerge
it is as difficult to remember the monk
as it is to see things as they are:
houses waver in the heat, stone walls
blaze. The hurt we feel is delicate—
all for ourselves and all for nothing.

1980

Ö

Shape the lips to an *o*, say *a*.
That's *island*.

One word of Swedish has changed the whole neighborhood.
When I look up, the yellow house on the corner
is a galleon stranded in flowers. Around it

the wind. Even the high roar of a leaf-mulcher
could be the horn-blast from a ship
as it skirts the misted shoals.

We don't need much more to keep things going.
Families complete themselves
and refuse to budge from the present,
the present extends its glass forehead to sea
(backyard breezes, scattered cardinals)

and if, one evening, the house on the corner
took off over the marshland,
neither I nor my neighbor
would be amazed. Sometimes

a word is found so right it trembles
at the slightest explanation.
You start out with one thing, end
up with another, and nothing's
like it used to be, not even the future.

1980

Dusting

Every day a wilderness—no
shade in sight. Beulah
patient among knicknacks,
the solarium a rage
of light, a grainstorm
as her gray cloth brings
dark wood to life.

Under her hand scrolls
and crests gleam
darker still. What
was his name, that
silly boy at the fair with
the rifle booth? And his kiss and
the clear bowl with one bright
fish, rippling
wound!

Not Michael—
something finer. Each dust
stroke a deep breath and
the canary in bloom.
Wavery memory: home
from a dance, the front door
blown open and the parlor
in snow, she rushed
the bowl to the stove, watched
as the locket of ice
dissolved and he
swam free.

That was years before
Father gave her up
with her name, years before
her name grew to mean
Promise, then
Desert-in-Peace.
Long before the shadow and
sun's accomplice, the tree.

Maurice.

1983

Roast Possum

The possum's a greasy critter
that lives on persimmons and what
the Bible calls carrion.
So much from the 1909 Werner
Encyclopedia, three rows of deep green
along the wall. A granddaughter
propped on each knee,
Thomas went on with his tale—

but it was for Malcolm, little
Red Delicious, that he invented
embellishments: *We shined that possum*
with a torch and I shinnied up,
being the smallest,
to shake him down. He glared at me,
teeth bared like a shark's

in that torpedo snout.
Man he was tough but no match
for old-time know-how.

Malcolm hung back, studying them
with his gold hawk eyes. When the girls
got restless, Thomas talked horses:
Strolling Jim, who could balance
a glass of water on his back
and trot the village square
without spilling a drop. Who put
Wartrace[1] on the map and was buried
under a stone, like a man.

They liked that part.
He could have gone on to tell them
that the Werner admitted Negro children
to be intelligent, though briskness
clouded over at puberty, bringing
indirection and laziness. Instead,
he added: *You got to be careful*
with a possum when he's on the ground;
he'll turn on his back and play dead
till you give up looking. That's
what you'd call sullin'.

Malcolm interrupted to ask
who owned Strolling Jim,
and who paid for the tombstone.
They stared each other down
man to man, before Thomas,
as a grandfather, replied:
Yessir,
we enjoyed that possum. We ate him
real slow, with sweet potatoes.

1986

BRAD LEITHAUSER
(1953–)

Born in Detroit, Brad Leithauser grew up in Michigan in a professional family, where his father was an attorney, his mother a professor and author. After winning prizes for poetry as an undergraduate, he graduated from Harvard College with a B.A. in 1975 and entered Harvard Law School. In 1980, the year he received his J.D., he married the poet Mary Jo Salter and accepted a post as research fellow at the Kyoto Comparative Law Center in Japan, where he remained, with time off for travel, for the next few years. A growing reputation as a poet earned him numerous awards, including Guggenheim and MacArthur fellowships. In 1984–1985 he served as visiting writer at Amherst College. More recently, he has lived in Italy.

1. Town in Tennessee, where the character Thomas was born in 1900.

Leithauser's first collection of verse, *Hundreds of Fireflies* (1982) earned him widespread praise. A novel, *Equal Distance* (1985), showed him adapting to prose some of the verbal skills and brilliant imagery of his poetry. A second volume of verse, *Cats of the Temple* (1986), though criticized by one reviewer for "the slightness and impersonality of the material," confirmed his technical mastery.

Leithauser has learned much from those twentieth-century poets who have most successfully resisted the temptations of free verse. Some of his poems echo Robert Frost's easy and witty combinations of colloquial speech and formal meters. Others, in their careful attention to syllable count and to visual specifics, are reminiscent of Marianne Moore. Among poets of larger reputation still writing, he seems most akin to James Merrill, though he has thus far probed less deeply beneath his flashing surfaces than Merrill.

Leithauser's books to date are named above.

An Expanded Want Ad

Rent—cttge Pig Riv
3 bdrm stove fridge
20 acr—lovely view

Although it's true
a few screens are torn and various
uninvited types may flutter through,
some of them to bite you,

and true the floors
buckle and sag like a garden plowed
by moles, which makes the shaky chairs
seem shakier, and the bedroom doors

refuse to close
(you'll have three bright bedrooms—and a fine
kitchen, a living room with fireplace,
and bath with shower hose),

there's a good view
of the Pigeon, a river that carries
more than its share of sunny jewelry,
for days here are mostly blue,

and nights so clear
and deep that in a roadside puddle
you can spot the wobbly flashlight flare
of even a minuscule star.

The jolting road,
two muddy ruts, flanks a weedy fan
that slithers against the underside
of a car, then rises unbowed,

but better still,
go on foot—though this means mosquitoes—

and stop at the overgrown sawmill,
    with its fragrant wood-chip pile,

    and, stooping, enter
that shack the length of a compact car
where two loggers outbraved the bitter
    sting of a Michigan winter.

    The room is dim,
spider-strung; you'll sense the whittled lives
they led—how plain, pure, and coldly grim
    the long months were to them . . .

    Just a short ways
up the road you'll come to a birch clump
which on all overcast mornings glows
    with a cumulus whiteness

    and in the brief
light after sunset holds a comely
allusive blush—a mix that's one half
    modesty, the other mischief.

    While if you hike
to where the road feeds a wider road
you'll find a mailbox above a choke
    of weeds, leaning on its stake;

    it looks disowned,
worthless, but will keep your letters dry
though its broken door trails to the ground
    like the tongue of a panting hound.

    Venture across
this wider road to reach a pasture,
whose three horses confirm that "the grass
    is always greener" applies

    to them as well:
offered shoots from your side of the fence,
they'll joggle forward to inhale
    a verdant airy handful,

    and will emit
low shivering snorts of joy, and will—
while you feed them—show no appetite
    for the grass growing at their feet.

    Now, it may happen
the first nights you'll feel an odd unease,
not lessened by the moths' crazed tapping
    at the glass; and later, sleeping

    unsteadily,
as bullfrogs hurl harsh gravelly notes

from slingshot throats, you may wonder why
  you ever left the city.

  Should this occur,
think of the creatures you've not yet glimpsed,
the owl and woodchuck and tense-necked deer
  you'll meet if you remain here;

  remember, too,
morning's flashy gift—for when day breaks
it mends all wrongs by offering you
  drenched fields, nearly drowned in dew.

1982

Between Leaps

  Binoculars I'd meant for birds
catch instead, and place an arm's length away,
    a frog
compactly perched on a log that lies
  half in, half out of the river.

  He may be preying, tongue wound to strike,
but to judge from his look of grave languor
    he seems
to be sunning merely. His skin gleams with light
  coming, rebuffed, off the water; his back's

  tawny-spotted, like an elderly hand,
but flank's the crisp, projecting green
    of new
leafage, as if what ran through his veins
  was chlorophyll and he'd

  tapped that vegetal sorcery
which, making light of physical bounds,
    makes food
of light. Given the amplitude of his
  special greenness, it requires no large hop

  of imagination to see him as
the downed trunk's surviving outlet, from which,
    perhaps,
dragged-out years of collapsing roots
  may prove reversible. With a reflection-

  shattering *plop*, a momentary
outbreak of topical, enlarging rings
    that chase
one another frenziedly, the place's spell
  is lifted: the trunk bare, the frog elsewhere.

1982

A Quilled Quilt, a Needle Bed

Under the longleaf pines
The curved, foot-long needles have
Woven a thatchwork quilt—threads,
Not patches, windfall millions
Looped and overlapped to make
The softest of needle beds.

The day's turned hot, the air
Coiling around the always
Cool scent of pine. As if lit
From below, a radiance
Milder yet more clement than
The sun's, the forest-carpet

Glows. It's a kind of pelt:
Thick as a bear's, tawny like
A bobcat's, more wonderful
Than both—a maize labyrinth
Spiraling down through tiny
Chinks to a caked, vegetal

Ferment where the needles
Crumble and blacken. And still
The mazing continues . . . whorls
Within whorls, the downscaling
Yet-perfect intricacies
Of lichens, seeds and crystals.

1982

The Ghost of a Ghost

I

The pleasures I took from life
were simple things—to play catch
in the evenings with my son,
or tease my daughter (whom I addressed
as Princess Pea), or to watch
television, curled on the floor.
Sometimes I liked to drink too much,
but not too often. Perhaps best
of all was the delight I found
waking to a drowse at one
or two at night and my wife
huffing (soft, not quite a snore)
beside me, a comforting sound.

We had our problems of course,
Emily and I, occasions when
things got out of hand.—Once she threw

a juice glass at me that broke
on the wall (that night I drew
a face there, a clownish man
catching it square on the nose,
and Emily laughed till she cried).
It's true I threatened divorce
a few times (she did too), but those
were ploys, harmless because love ran
through every word we spoke—
and then, an accident, I died.

II

Afterwards, my kids began
having nightmares—when they slept
at all; Emily moved in a haze,
looking older, ruined now, and wept
often and without warning.
The rooms had changed, become mere
photographs in which my face
was oddly missing . . . That first year
without me: summer twilight, and those
long leaf-raking Saturdays
without me, and Christmas morning—
the following August a new man,
a stranger, moved in and took my place.

You could scarcely start to comprehend
how queer it is, to have your touch
go unfelt, your cries unheard
by your family. Princess!—I called—
Don't let that stranger take your hand!
And—*Em, dear, love, he has no right*
to you.
Where did they think I'd gone?
who walked the house all day, all night,
all night. It was far too much
for anyone to endure, and,
hammered by grief one ugly dawn,
I broke. I am still here!—I bawled
from the den—Still here! And no one stirred.
But in time I learned a vicious trick,
a way of gently positing
a breath upon a person's neck
to send an icy run of fear
scampering up the spine—anything,
anything to show them who was near!
. . . Anything, but only to retrieve
some sense that nothing is more
lasting than the love built week by week
for years; I had to believe
again that these were people I'd
give everything, even a life, for.
Then—a second time, and slow—I died.

III

Now I am a shadow of my
former shadow. Seepage of a kind
sets in. Settled concentrations thin.
Amenably—like the smile become
a pond, the pond a mud-lined
bed, from which stems push, pry
and hoist aloft seed-pods that
crack into a sort of grin—
things come almost but not quite
full circle; within the slow
tide of years, water dilutes to light,
light to a distant, eddying hum . . .
In another time, long ago,

I longed for a time when I'd
still felt near enough to recall
the downy scrape of a peach skin
on my tongue, the smell of the sea,
the pull of something resinous.
By turns, I have grown other-wise.
I move with a drift, a drowse that roams
not toward sleep but a clarity
of broadened linkages; it's in
a state wholly too gratified
and patient to be called eagerness
that I submit to a course which homes
outward, and misses nothing at all.

1982

The Tigers of Nanzen-Ji

These light-footed, celebrated
cats, created
on gold-leaf screens by a man
who'd never seen a tiger
(there were none in Japan),
who worked, as he'd been taught,
from pelts, and from paintings brought
from distant, brilliant China,

wander an extraordinary
maze whose very
air's alive, alit with breeze-
borne inebriants. It's a place
of tumbled boundaries
and whetted penchants, in which
big-chested brutes whose eyes are rich
outsize eggs of burnished gold,

whose coats are cloudy, glowing
masses flowing

behind an emerald palisade
   of bamboo and the row
      of darker palings made
by their own sable bands, glide
fatefully in the failing light, wide
   mouths agape and bared teeth flashing.

   It's an hour of satisfying
      runs and flying
ambitions, as gravity's
   traction relaxes a little
      and hunting tigers freeze
into a fine, deepening
tensity, muscles marshaling
   toward that signal opportune instant

   when the commanding soul emerges:
      Now—
                  Now, it urges,
and the breaking body slides
   upon the air's broad back
      and hangs there, rides and rides
with limbs outstretched—but claws
bedded in their velvet-napped paws,
   for there will be no killings tonight.

   All bloodshed is forbidden
      here. . . .
                        That's the hidden
message of these grounds, which threads
   like a stream around the pines
      and rocks and iris-beds.
The danger's all a bluff, an
artful dumb show staged by a clan-
   destine family of tigers

   with Chinese dragon faces,
      whose grimaces
and slashing, cross-eyed glances serve
   to conceal the grins that beckon
      you into the preserve
of a rare, ferociously
playful mind. Enter. You are free
   from harm here. There's nothing to fear.

1986

Bibliography

For the authors represented in this work, fundamental bibliographies appear in the headnotes. Following are more general sources of information.

REFERENCE WORKS

American Literary Scholarship, 1963–. James Woodress and others, eds. Annual, 1965–.

American Literature, Periodical.

Bakerman, Jane. *Adolescent Female Portraits in the American Novel, 1961–1981: An Annotated Bibliography.* 1985.

Biblowitz, Iris, ed. *Women and Literature: An Annotated Bibliography of Women Writers.* 3rd ed. 1976.

Carruth, Gorton, and others. *The Encyclopedia of American Facts and Dates.* 7th ed. 1979.

Colonnese, Tom, and Owens, Louis D. *American Indian Novelists: An Annotated Critical Bibliography.* 1983.

Contemporary Authors. (A Series, with various editors.)

Contemporary Authors: Bibliographical Series. 1986–.

Dictionary of Literary Biography. (A series, each volume arranged by topic, with various editors.)

Frye, Northrop; Baker, Sheridan; and Perkins, George. *The Harper Handbook to Literature.* 1985.

Gohdes, Clarence, and Marovitz, Sanford E. *Bibliographical Guide to the Study of the Literature of the U.S.A.* 5th ed. 1984.

Hoffman, Daniel, ed. *Harvard Guide to Contemporary American Writing.* 1979.

Koster, Donald N. *American Literature and Language: A Guide to Information Sources.* 1982. (Mostly on individual authors.)

Leary, Lewis. *American Literature: A Study and Research Guide.* 1976.

———. *Articles on American Literature, 1950–1967.* 1970. (The best guide to scholarly articles on authors and literary subjects.)

———. *Articles on American Literature, 1968–1975.* 1979.

Miller, Wayne C., ed. *A Comprehensive Bibliography for the Study of American Minorities.* 2 vols. 1976. (Surveys the field through 1975.)

———. *Minorities in America: The Annual Bibliography.* (For years subsequent to 1975.)

Mitterling, Philip I. *United States Cultural History: A Guide to Information Sources.* 1980.

Morris, Mary. *Southwestern Fiction, 1960–1980: A Classified Bibliography.* 1986.

Morris, R. B., ed. *Encyclopedia of American History.* 6th ed. 1982.

Nadel, Ira Bruce. *Jewish Writers of North America: A Guide to Information Sources.* 1981.

Readers' Guide to Periodical Literature. Annual, 1900–. (Useful for locating articles and literature in general interest magazines.)

Rubin, Louis D., Jr., ed. *A Bibliographical Guide to the Study of Southern Literature.* 1969. (See Williams, below.)

———. *The History of Southern Literature.* 1985.

Rush, Teresa Gunnels, and others, eds. *Black American Writers Past and Present: A Biographical and Bibliographical Dictionary.* 1975.

Salzman, Jack, ed. *American Studies: An Annotated Bibliography.* 1986.

———. *The Cambridge Handbook of American Literature.* 1986.

Schweik, Robert C., and Reisner, Dieter. *Reference Sources in English and American Literature: An Annotated Bibliography.* 1977.

Stineman, Esther. *Women's Studies: A Recommended Core Bibliography.* 1979.

Vinson, James, ed. *Contemporary Dramatists.* 3rd ed. 1982.

———. *Contemporary Novelists.* 4th ed. 1986.

———. *Contemporary Poets.* 4th ed. 1985.

———. *Great Writers of the English Language.* 3 vols. 1979.

White, Barbara Anne, ed. *American Women Writers: An Annotated Bibliography of Criticism.* 1977.

Who's Who in America. Biennial, 1899–.

Who Was Who in America. Vol. II, *1943–1950,* 1950; Vol. III, *1951–1960,* 1960; Vol. IV, *1961–1968,* 1968.

Williams, Jerry T., ed. *Southern Literature, 1968–1975: A Checklist of Scholarship.* 1978. (Supplements Rubin, above.)

Wyld, Lionel D., ed. *American Civilization: An Introduction to Research and Bibliography.* 1975.

LITERARY HISTORY AND CRITICISM

Aldridge, John W. *After the Lost Generation: A Critical Study of the Writers of Two Wars.* 1951.

———. *The American Novel and the Way We Live Now.* 1983.

Baker, Houston A., Jr. *Blues, Ideology and Afro-American Literature: A Vernacular Theory.* 1985.

Baumbach, Jonathan. *Landscape of Nightmare: Studies in the Contemporary American Novel.* 1965.

Beidler, Philip D. *American Literature and the Experience of Vietnam.* 1982.

Bellamy, Joe D., ed. *American Poetry Observed: Poets on Their Work.* 1985.

Berger, Alan L. *Crisis and Covenant: The Holocaust in American Jewish Fiction.* 1985.

Berthoff, Warner. *A Literature without Qualities: American Writing Since 1945.* 1979.

Bone, Robert A. *The Negro Novel in America.* Rev. ed. 1965.

Boyers, Robert. *Atrocity and Amnesia: The Political Novel Since 1945.* 1985.

Breslin, James E. B. *From Modern to Contemporary American Poetry, 1945–1965.* 1984.

Bridgman, Richard. *The Colloquial Style in America.* 1966.

Cooke, Michael G. *Afro-American Literature in the Twentieth Century.* 1985.

Cowley, Malcolm. *The Flower and the Leaf: A Contemporary Record of American Writing Since 1941.* 1985.

Du Plessis, Rachel. *Writing Beyond the Ending: Narrative Strategies of Twentieth-Century Women Writers.* 1985.

Evans, Mari, ed. *Black Women Writers (1950–1980): A Critical Evaluation.* 1984.

Frye, Joanne S. *Living Stories, Telling Lives: Women and the Novel in Contemporary Experience.* 1986.

Hassan, Ihab. *Radical Innocence: The Contemporary American Novel.* 1961.

Holden, Jonathan. *Style and Authenticity in Postmodern Poetry.* 1986.

Howard, Richard. *Alone with America: Essays on the Art of Poetry in the United States Since 1950.* 1969.

Kalstone, David. *Five Temperaments: Elizabeth Bishop, Robert Lowell, James Merrill, Adrienne Rich, John Ashbery.* 1977.

Karl, Frederick R. *American Fictions: 1940–1980.* 1984.

Klinkowitz, Jerome. *The New American Novel of Manners.* 1986. (Richard Yates, Dan Wakefield, Thomas McGuane.)

———. *The Self-Apparent Word: Fiction as Language, Language as Fiction.* 1984.

LeClair, Thomas, and McCaffrey, Larry, eds. *Anything Can Happen: Interviews with Contemporary American Novelists.* 1983.

Margolies, Edward. *Native Sons: A Critical Study of Twentieth-Century Negro American Authors.* 1968.

Miller, R. Baxter, ed. *Black American Poets between Worlds, 1940–1960.* 1986.

Miller, Wayne Charles. *An Armed America, Its Face in Fiction: A History of the American Military Novel.* 1970.

O'Donnell, Patrick. *Passionate Doubts: Designs of Interpretation in Contemporary American Fiction.* 1986.

Ostriker, Alicia. *Stealing the Language: The Emergence of Women's Poetry in America.* 1986.

———. *Writing Like a Woman.* 1986. (Anne Sexton, Adrienne Rich, May Swenson, Sylvia Plath, H. D.)

Perkins, David. *A History of Modern Poetry: Modernism and After.* 1987.

Perloff, Marjorie. *The Dance of the Intellect: Studies in the Poetry of the Pound Tradition.* 1986.

Pope, Deborah. *A Separate Vision: Isolation in Contemporary Women's Poetry.* 1984.

Prenshaw, Peggy Whitman, ed. *Women Writers of the Contemporary South.* 1986.

Pryse, Marjorie, and Spillers, Hortense J. *Conjuring: Black Women, Fiction, and Literary Tradition.* 1985.

Rainwater, Catherine, and Scheick, William J., eds. *Contemporary American Women Writers: Narrative Strategies.* 1985.

Revels History of Drama in English, The. Vol. 8. *American Drama.* By Travis Bogard and others. 1978.

Rosenthal, M. L., and Gall, Sally M. *Modern Poetic Sequence: The Genius of Modern Poetry.* 1986.

Ruas, Charles. *Conversations with American Writers.* 1985.

Shaw, Robert B., ed. *American Poetry Since 1960: Some Critical Perspectives.* 1973.

Shechner, Mark. *After the Revolution: Studies in the Contemporary Jewish Imagination.* 1987.

Tanner, Tony. *City of Words: American Fiction, 1935–1970.* 1971.

Taylor, Gordon. O. *Chapters of Experience: Studies in Modern American Autobiography.* 1983.

Vendler, Helen. *Part of Nature, Part of Us: Modern American Poets.* 1980.

Von Hallberg, Robert. *American Poetry and Culture: 1945–1980.* 1985.

Voss, Arthur. *The American Short Story: A Critical Survey.* 1973.

Weales, Gerald. *American Drama Since World War Two.* 1962.

Wiget, Andrew. *Native American Literature.* 1985.

Williamson, Alan. *Introspection and Contemporary Poetry.* 1984.

Ziegler, Heide, and Bigsby, Christopher, eds. *The Radical Imagination and the Liberal Tradition.* 1986. (Interviews with English and American novelists.)

Index

The following index is primarily to those authors (their names printed in **boldface**) whose work is represented in this volume. It includes the titles of selections reprinted here and the first lines of poetry. As an aid to study, the index also includes the names of writers mentioned in the author headnotes and in the general introductions, whether or not their work appears in this volume.

About the Editors

George Perkins is Professor of English at Eastern Michigan University and General Editor of *The Journal of Narrative Technique.* He received his Ph.D. from Cornell University and has taught at Washington University, Baldwin-Wallace College, Fairleigh Dickinson University, and the University of Edinburgh, where he has also held a Fellowship at the Institute for Advanced Studies in the Humanities. His books include *The Theory of the American Novel, Realistic American Short Fiction, American Poetic Theory, The American Tradition in Literature* (sixth edition), *The Harper Handbook to Literature* (with Northrop Frye and Sheridan Baker), and *The Practical Imagination* (compact edition, with Frye, Baker, and Barbara Perkins).

Barbara Perkins is Managing Editor of *The Journal of Narrative Technique* and Secretary-Treasurer of the Society for the Study of Narrative Literature. She received her Ph.D. from the University of Pennsylvania and has taught at Baldwin-Wallace College, the University of Pennsylvania, Fairleigh Dickinson University, and Eastern Michigan University. She has contributed to a number of books, including *Contemporary Novelists, Great Writers of the English Language, The Harper Handbook to Literature,* and *The World Book Encyclopedia.* She is co-author of *The Practical Imagination* (compact edition).